Marketing Decision Making
A Model-Building Approach

Gary L. Lilien
The Pennsylvania State University
AND
Philip Kotler
J. L. Kellogg School of Management
Northwestern University

1817

HARPER & ROW, PUBLISHERS, New York
Cambridge, Philadelphia, San Francisco,
London, Mexico City, São Paulo, Sydney

To our four daughters
Amy Jo Lilien
and
Amy, Melissa, and Jessica Kotler
with love

Sponsoring Editor: Art Sotak
Project Editor: Eleanor Castellano
Designer: Off-Broadway Graphics
Production Manager: Jeanie Berke
Compositor: Science Press
Printer and Binder: R. R. Donnelley & Sons Company
Art Studio   Vantage Art, Inc.

Marketing Decision Making: A Model-Building Approach

Library of Congress Cataloging in Publication Data

Lilien, Gary L., 1946–
   Marketing decision making.

   Rev. ed. of: Marketing decision making / Philip
Kotler. [1971]
   Bibliography: p.
   Includes indexes.
   1. Marketing—Decision making—Mathematical models.
I. Kotler, Philip.   II. Kotler, Philip. Marketing
decision making.   III. Title.
HF5415.135.L54   1983   658.8'02   83-12699
   ISBN 0-06-044076-7

Contents

Preface   XV

PART **1**   **Introduction**   1

   1 **Marketing Decision Making**   3

   The Trend Toward Marketing   3

   The Complexity of Marketing Decision Making   5
     Sales Response to a Single Marketing Instrument   6
     Marketing-Mix Interaction   6
     Competitive Effects   6
     Delayed Response   6
     Multiple Territories   7
     Multiple Products   7
     Functional Interactions   7
     Multiple Goals   7

   Managerial Response: A Model-Building Approach   7
     Modes of Response   8
     Models   10
     Feelings About Models   14

   Plan of the Book   16
     Model-Building Disciplines   16
     Part 2: Marketing, Management Decisions, and Models   17
     Part 3: The Working of Markets   18
     Part 4: Micromarketing Decision Models   18
     Part 5: Marketing-Planning Models   18
     Part 6: Making It Happen   19

   A View Ahead and a Caveat   19

   Summary   20

PART **2**   **Marketing, Management Decisions, and Models**   23

    2   **The Model-Building Approach: Identifying and Structuring
Marketing Problems**   25

        Scientific Inquiry in Marketing   25

        The Research Process   29
           Stages of the Process   31
           Finding and Formulating Problems   32
           Classifying Problems and Solutions   34
           The Best Solution   38

        Summary   40

    3   **Marketing Model Building: Determining Objectives**   42

        Decision Makers and Objectives   43

        Single-Goal/Single-Decision-Maker Formulations   44
           Absolute Profits (Short Run)   44
           Rate of Return on Investment (Short Run)   46
           Internal Rate of Return on Investment (Long Run)   47
           Present Value: Discounted Cash Flow (Long Run)   49
           Incorporating Risk: Assessing Utility Functions   49

        Multiple-Goal Formulations: Single Decision Maker   54
           Utility Assessments for Two Objectives   55
           More Than Two Objectives   60

        Multiple Decision Makers   60

        Summary   62

    4   **Modeling Marketing Phenomena**   66

        Mathematical Forms   67
           Linear Models   68
           Models with Linear Parameters and Nonlinear Variables   69
           Models Nonlinear in Parameters but Linearizable   73
           Intrinsically Nonlinear Models   75

        Dynamic Effects   80
           Discrete-Time Models   80
           Continuous-Time Models   84
           Continuous-Time Example: The Vidale-Wolfe Model   84

        Handling Uncertainty: Deterministic Versus Stochastic Models   86

        Individual Versus Aggregate Models   88

        Level of Demand Modeled   91
           Product-Class-Sales Models   92
           Brand-Sales Models   93
           Market-Share Models   94

Contents

Choosing and Evaluating a Mathematical Form 96
Summary 97

5 Model Calibration 102

Model Calibration and Data 102
Objective Parameter Estimation 104
    Simple Linear-Regression Model 104
    Multiple Linear Regression 108
    Relaxing the Assumptions: Generalized Least Squares 109
    Parameter Estimation for Nonlinear Models 116
    Parameter Estimation for Binary Dependent Variables 119
    Multiple-Equation Problems and Solutions 121
    Causal Models and Unobserved Variables 125

Subjective Parameter Estimation 128
    Justification and Background 128
    Single-Assessor Model Calibration 129
    Combining Subjective Estimates 138

Blending Judgmental and Empirical Data: Bayesian Estimation 139
    The Idea and an Example 140
    Formal Analysis for the Multivariate Bayesian-Regression
        Model 142

Summary 143

6 Marketing-Policy-Evaluation Procedures 147

Policy Generation in a Certain Environment 148
    Classical Optimization Procedures 148
    Linear Programming 158
    Integer and Mixed-Integer Programming 163
    Nonlinear-Programming Problems 165
    Multiple-Objective Optimization 170
    Optimal-Control Problems 171

Decisions Under Uncertainty 173
    Decision Analysis 173
    Dynamic Programming 179
    Linear Programming Under Uncertainty 181
    Stochastic Control Theory 183

Deterministic-Policy-Analysis Tools 183
    Marginal-Change Analysis (Sensitivity Analysis) 183
    Deterministic Simulation 184
    Econometric-Model Analysis 185

Stochastic-Policy-Analysis Tools 185
    Monte Carlo Simulation 185
    Stochastic Processes 188

Forlorn Foods Revisited   189
Summary   191

PART **3**   **The Working of Markets**   195

7 Consumer Behavior Models   197

The Dimensions of Consumer Behavior   197
   Phases of the Process   198
   An Alternative View   201
A Range of Models   204
Large-System Models   205
   Bettman's Model   206
   The Howard-Sheth Model   208
Perceptual-Evaluation Models   211
   Nonmetric Multidimensional Scaling (NMS)   211
   Factor Analysis   213
Models of Attitude and Preference Formation   219
   Compensatory Models   220
   Noncompensatory Models   222
   Incorporating Uncertainty   223
Choice Models   225
   High-Involvement Choice Models   225
   Low-Involvement (Stochastic) Choice Models   229
   Brand-Choice Models   232
   Purchase-Incidence Models   246
   Future of Stochastic Choice Modeling   250
Summary   251

8 Organizational-Buying Models   258

The Structure of Organizational Buying   259
   Group Influence   259
   Buying Situations   262
   Individual Forces   262
Models of Elements of Organizational Buying   263
   Supplier Selection   263
   Source Loyalty   264
Large-System Models of Organizational Buying   268
   The Sheth Model   268
   Webster-Wind Model   271
   The Choffray-Lilien Model   273

Organizational-Buying Models: Current Status and Research Needs 285

Summary 287

9 Market Segmentation 289

Segmentation: Problem Definition and Model Development 290
Geographic and Demographic Variables 291
Psychographic Variables 293
Brand-Use/Consumption Variables 293
Behavioristic Variables 294

The Normative Theory of Segmentation 295

Market Segmentation in Practice 298
Cross-Classification Analysis 298
Automatic Interaction Detection (AID) 299
Regression Analysis 301
Cluster Analysis 305
Discriminant Analysis 307

An Approach for Industrial-Market Segmentation 309

Segmentation Theory, Practice and Future 313
Behavioral School 313
Decision-Oriented School 314

Summary 315

10 Demand Assessment and Forecasting 318

Concepts in Demand Assessment and Forecasting 318

Assessing Current Demand 319
Total Market Potential 319
Territorial or Sectoral Potential 320

Forecasting Demand 326
Judgmental Methods 329
Market and Product Analysis 330
Time-Series Methods 332
Causal Methods 341

Accuracy of Forecasting Methods 348

Summary 350

PART **4** **Micromarketing Decision Models** 353

11 Product Design and Development Models 355

Product Design in Perspective 356

Idea Sources and Generation 359

Product-Design Techniques   363
    Perceptual Mapping   363
    Preference/Choice Models   363

Model-based Procedures for Product Design   370
    PERCEPTOR   371
    Shocker and Srinivasan's LINMAP Procedure   374
    Other Product-Design Models   377

Organizing for Product Design and Development   383
    By Product Type   383
    Organizational Structure   385

Summary   386

12   **Pricing Models**   389

The Classical Economic Model: Consumer Behavior, Elasticity,
and the Law of Demand   390
    Rational Consumer Behavior   390
    Elasticity   390
    Two Demand Models   392

Limitations of the Classical Model   395
    The Problem of Objectives   395
    The Problem of Multiple Parties   397
    The Problem of Marketing-Mix Interaction   398
    The Problem of Estimating Demand and Cost Functions   398
    The Problem of Price Discretion   398
    The Problem of Varying Buyer Reactions to Price Changes:
        Information and Expectations   399

Extensions of the Classical Model   399
    Price Consciousness and Price Image   400
    The Relationship Between Price and Quality   401
    Variations and Extensions of the Concept of Elasticity   404

Setting Price in Practice   405
    Cost-Oriented Pricing   405
    Demand-Oriented Pricing   407
    Competition-Oriented Pricing   407

Recent Contributions to the Pricing Literature   408
    Simon's Model   409
    The Rao-Shakun Model   414
    The Dolan-Jeuland Model   418

Other Pricing Models   422
    Market-Pricing Models   422

Contents

Competitive-Bidding Models   424
Product-Line-Pricing Models   428

Summary   430

13   Distribution Decision Models   433

Distribution Strategy   438

Distribution Location   445
   Market-Selection Decision   445
   Number-of-Outlets Decision   449
   Site-Selection Decision   454
   Store-Size and -Characteristic Decisions   462

Distribution Logistics   463
   Geoffrion-Graves Model   466
   Application and Assessment   467

Distribution Management   469

Summary   471

14   Advertising Decision Models   475

The Effects of Advertising   477
   Response Phenomena   477
   Copy Research   482
   Frequency Phenomena   483

Objective Setting and Budgeting: Practice and Models   485
   Objectives   485
   Setting Advertising Goals   487
   Setting the Advertising Budget   490
   Model-based Approaches   492

Message and Copy Decisions   501
   Copy Testing and Measures of Copy Effectiveness   502
   Estimating the Creative Quality of Ads   503
   How Many Advertisements Should Be Created and Pretested?   505

Media Selection and Scheduling   511
   The Choice of an Objective Function   514
   Modeling Approaches   515

Summary   524

15   Sales-Promotion Models   529

Sales Promotion: Types and Effects   529
   Objectives of Promotions   530
   Characteristics of Promotions   531

Evidence of Promotional Effects   532
Sales-Promotion Decisions   534
Evaluating the Effects of Promotions   535

Promotional Models   537
The Kuehn-Rohloff Model   537
Rao-Lilien Model   543
Little's BRANDAID Promotional Model   549
Other Promotional Models   552

Summary   554

16   Salesforce Models   558

Personal Selling: Tasks, Importance, and Models   559
The Role of the Salesforce   559
Salesforce Decision Problems   559
The Importance of Salesforce Planning   561
Modeling Salesforce Problems   562

Salesforce Sizing   562
Breakdown and Work-Load Methods   563
Industry-Guidelines Methods   564
Market-Response Methods   564

Allocation of Selling Effort   567
Time Allocation: Salesperson Call Planning (CALLPLAN)   568
Allocation of Selling Resources Across Products (DETAILER)   571
Allocation-Model Extensions and Related Work   575

Sales Territory Design   577
GEOLINE Model   584
Related Work   587

Setting Commissions and Quotas: Indirect Control of the
Salesforce   588
Davis and Farley   589
Assessment and Related Work   593

Integrative Models for Salesforce Decisions   594
Beswick-Cravens Model   594
Other Multiple-Resource Models   598

Summary   598

PART 5   Market-Planning Models   603

17   Market Planning and Strategy   605

Marketing-Planning and Strategy Decisions   605
The Product Life Cycle   608

Cost Dynamics: Scale and Experience Effects 613
   Economies of Scale 613
   Experience-Curve Effects 614

Market Definition and Market Structure 620
   Methods for Market Definition 620
   Market Structure 623

Analytic Approaches to Market-Strategy Development 626
   The Shared-Experience Approach: PIMS 626
   Product-Portfolio Classification and Analysis Models 634
   Normative Models 649

Summary 654

18 Modeling the Marketing Mix and Competitive Response 657

The Marketing Mix: Definition and Theoretical Approaches 657

Marketing-Mix Interactions 660
   Elements of the Marketing-Mix Interact 660
   Advertising Reduces Price Sensitivity 661
   Promotional Interactions Vary 662
   Response Varies by Market Segment and over Time 662
   Advertising and Selling Interact 662

Competitive Response: Evidence and Models 663
   Microeconomic Approaches 663
   Empirical Evidence 664
   Marketing-Model Approaches 665
   Assessment 667

Descriptive Models of the Industrial-Marketing Communications
Mix 668
   The ADVISOR Models 669
   The PIMS/Buzzell-Farris Models 672
   Evaluation and Use 672

Normative-Marketing-Mix Models 675
   An Industrial-Marketing Approach 675
   A Consumer Approach: BRANDAID 682
   Other Marketing-Mix Models 691

Summary 693

19 Sales Models for New Products 699

Types of New-Product Situations 700
   Product Newness 700
   Product Repurchasability 700

The Consumer-Adoption Process for New Products 703

Diffusion Models: Models of First Purchase 706

A Pure Innovative Model   706
Pure Imitative Diffusion Models   708
Bass' Model   711
Horsky-Simon Model   715
Dodson-Muller Model   716
Other Diffusion Models   718

Repeat-Purchase Models for New Products   720
Parfitt-Collins Model   723
The Tracker Model   726
ASSESSOR   728
Other Models   734

Summary   739

PART **6**   **Making It Happen**   745

20   The Marketing Decision-Support System   747

Information Needs   748

The Evolution of Business Systems: From TBS to DSS   748
Transaction-based Systems   749
Management-Information Systems   749
Decision-Support Systems   749

The Marketing Decision-Support System   753
Data   753
Models   758
Statistics   758
Optimization   759
Q/A   759

MDSSs in Practice: Three Cases   760

MDSS Design: Some Guidelines   766
Predesign Stage   766
Design Stage   766
Postdesign Stage   768

MDSS: A Bridge to Implementation for Marketing Models   768

A View Ahead for MDSSs   769
Hardware Trends   769
Software Trends   769
Hardware-Software Trade-offs   769
Communications-Technology Trends   769
Data-Collection Trends   770
Human-Development Trends   770

Summary   770

21 Implementation   772

The Meaning of Implementation   773

What Is Being Used?   774

The Dimensions of Implementation Success   776
  Model-related Dimensions   776
  Organizational Dimensions of Implementation Success   784

Implementation Strategy   789
  Effective Management Scientists in Marketing   789
  Organizational Placement of the Marketing Management
    Scientist   790
  Educational Programs for Line Management   791
  Choice of Problems   791
  Degree of Management Participation in Model Building   793

Summary   795

22 Marketing Models Today and Tomorrow   797

Marketing Models Today   797

The Inevitability of Implementation   800

A Look Ahead   801
  Data and Data Analysis   804
  Interactions and Competitive Response   804
  Dynamics   804
  Consumer Behavior   804
  Bargaining Theory   805
  Market Planning   805
  Other Marketing Applications   805
  Implementation   805

Summary and Commencement   806

Bibliography   809

Name Index   859

Subject Index   867

Preface

The battle for markets will increase in intensity in the coming years. Sales in many markets have been flat or declining. Competitors have been growing in number and in desperation. Products and brands are exhibiting shorter life cycles. These developments underscore the need for more-sophisticated marketing decision making.

At the same time many company executives despair of putting marketing on a more scientific basis. They see marketing processes as lacking the neat quantitative properties found in production and finance. In marketing, human factors play a large role, marketing expenditures affect demand and cost simultaneously, and information is rarely adequate. Furthermore, the effects of marketing decisions are typically lagged, nonlinear, stochastic, and downright interactive.

Yet the truth is that the tools and models now exist for improving marketing-decision effectiveness. Recent scientific and data-base developments have already enabled some leading companies to increase their marketing productivity, to get "more marketing bang for the buck." This book will examine the more promising scientific and data-base developments that assist managers in arriving at cost-effective marketing strategies and budgets.

Companies are increasingly applying the modeling approach to marketing decision making. Several trends are driving the process:

1. Marketing decision-support systems are being developed. The amount of data is exploding, the reporting of data is becoming more timely, and the quality of marketing data is improving. Marketing models provide tools to summarize, interpret, and make normative use of these data.
2. Quantitative MBAs are becoming managers. The new generation of marketing managers is trained in and receptive to decision support.
3. Marketing theory is improving. More experiences are being shared

through the marketing literature, leading to improved theories and better models.

4. The value of marketing models is being reported. Throughout this book there are situations where not only was implementation reported but the *value* of implementation was reported as well. As such reports continue, the use of marketing models will accelerate.

5. Marketing budgets continue to rise, therefore raising management's need to find ways to increase marketing productivity.

Underlying Disciplines for Marketing Model Building

Four major disciplines provide a foundation for the model-building approach to marketing decision making.

Consumer Behavior. Psychologists and behavioral scientists have produced a vast literature on buying behavior and buying motives. This behavior must be understood before it can be used for marketing plans. Consumer behavior theory provides a theoretical base upon which to build models of market size, growth, and behavior.

Economics. The economic theory of the firm provides a starting point for developing models that can be used to understand markets and guide optimal marketing decision making. It provides useful building blocks in forming models of marketing systems.

Management Science/Operations Research (MS/OR). Management science is the application of mathematics and scientific methods to problems of organizational systems with a view toward improving such systems. The MS/OR field provides an approach, the mathematical tools for analysis, and an explicit specification of (often) multiple organizational objectives.

Statistics/Econometrics. Research into marketing problems often generates a large amount of data. The fields of statistics and econometrics provide methodology for parameter estimation, hypothesis testing, and forecasting.

These four disciplines—consumer behavior/behavioral science, economics, management science/operations research, and statistics/econometrics—provide the pieces of structure and the tools that are needed to develop and implement a model-building approach in marketing.

Organization of the Book

The book is divided into six parts.

Part 1: Introduction (Chapter 1)

This part is an appetizer, introducing the role of models in analyzing and solving marketing problems.

Part 2: Marketing, Management Decisions, and Models (Chapters 2–6)

This part describes the major tools for building, estimating, and using quantitative models in marketing. The five chapters deal with the following issues:

Chapter 2: how creative marketers recognize and characterize problems

Chapter 3: how they structure those conceptions in model form

Chapter 4: how they characterize their organizational goals in terms of quantitative objectives

Chapter 5: how data can be integrated into the model structure in the form of parameter estimates

Chapter 6: how the model can be tested on the data and how it can be manipulated (solved) to develop marketing decisions

Part 3: The Working of Markets (Chapters 7–10)

Every marketing decision model must incorporate a submodel describing how the particular market behaves and responds to marketing stimuli. The chapters in this part of the book provide tools for modeling the structure and functioning of markets, as follows:

Chapter 7: various ways to model the behavior and size of consumer markets

Chapter 8: various ways to model the behavior and size of organizational markets

Chapter 9: ways to segment markets effectively

Chapter 10: models for forecasting demand

Part 4: Micromarketing Decision Models (Chapters 11–16)

Here, the elements of the marketing mix—product design, advertising, distribution, price, promotion, salesforce issues—are studied separately. This technique has two advantages: (1) single elements in the marketing mix are more easily understood than are interactions in the mix, and (2) the individual elements of the mix have to be understood separately before they can be integrated in marketing-planning models.

Part 5: Marketing-planning Models (Chapters 17–19)

Part 5 addresses broader marketing decisions: marketing-strategy questions (product-line planning and portfolio analysis, market-structure analysis), marketing-mix decisions for established products, and analysis of new products. The building blocks of the previous sections are now integrated in larger-scale, marketing-planning models.

Part 6: Making It Happen (Chapters 20–22)

Here, the concept and application of a marketing decision-support system (MDSS) is developed. Marketing knowledge, better models, better data, and better statistical tools evolve together to provide improved decision support.

How can we plan for successful implementation of marketing models so that they are used by managers? The discussion centers around what is needed for improving marketing decision making, independent of the tools used. The revision of marketing models in response to new developments is discussed as well.

Finally, what are the trends in models, measurements, and computer-related, decision-support tools that the marketing manager and the marketing model builder should be looking toward in the 1980s and 1990s? Trends suggest that some future shock may be in store for the traditional marketing manager, making the 1980s a very exciting time in which to be in the profession.

Approach Within Each Chapter

Most chapters start with a review of the theory in the area, followed by in-depth analyses of a small number of models. The complete details of a few models will suggest how to approach problems. Any model must be customized for a particular situation, and we prefer to develop a few models in depth; each model will give insight into the problem-solving process. Following the in-depth analysis is a short review of model-based work in the area.

Each chapter ends with a set of discussion questions and problems. The best way to learn about models is to push some numbers through existing models and to build some new models. Both types of problems are provided at the end of each chapter. The problems range from those requiring average mathematical ability to those requiring stronger mathematical training.

Uses of the Book

The book is designed to be a general reference for practitioners and a text for students.

The student should have some knowledge of calculus, probability and statistics, and matrix algebra in order to follow the complete exposition in the book. Not many marketing or business students have such a background. The text therefore provides, in Part 2, a review of the mathematical tools needed to carry on marketing model building.

The book can be used over a one-term or a two-term sequence. A one-term course is appropriate for students who are motivated and have the necessary quantitative and marketing background. A two-term sequence is appropriate where the students' mathematical skills need building. In this case Chapters 1–6 or 1–10 might constitute the first term, supplemented by several computerized or model-based cases to provide flavor of application.

The book can also be used as a background reader in a case-based course in analytic marketing. A sufficient number of analytical cases are available to provide substance for an advanced case course in marketing: this book is well suited to provide preparatory/supplementary material and background readings.

Acknowledgments

Many colleagues and students contributed to the development of this book. The Bibliography at the end of the book is testimony to the many influences in the field, all of whom cannot be cited here individually.

Our colleagues at Penn State (Pete Bennett, Gene Kelly, Heikki Rinne, and Dave Wilson), at MIT (John Little, John Hauser, Rick Bagozzi, Manu Kalwani, Al Silk, and Glen Urban), and at Northwestern (Jehoshua Eliashberg, Api Ruzdic, and Andris A. Zoltners) helped provide the environment needed to prepare this book. Additional thoughtful reviews by Jean-Marie Choffray, Jean-Claude Larréché, Claes Fornell, Ron Turner, Kent Monroe, and Len Lodish and comments by Dave Stewart, Berend Wierenga, Dale Wilson, Franco Nicosia, Paul Green, René Darmon, and Fred Zufryden were influential and helpful.

Research support was provided by Eunsang Yoon, Shlomo Kalish, S. Kumar, Peter Cooperstein, Bill Mills, Winthrop Smith, Ed Weisberg, Mark Palmer, David Golden, Susan Podger, Jason Cohen, Shaheen Husain, and Michael Horn.

Excellent typing and editorial support were provided by Elaine Moore, Dianne Smith, Norma Pappas, Linda Fryer, and Barbara Bush.

Chapter problems came from several sources; many were developed as part of the marketing-models course at MIT by Giles Laurent, John Little, and Manu Kalwani, whose individual contributions have, like the passenger pigeon, been lost to time.

The College of Business Administration at Penn State provided important support during the writing and final development of this book.

Finally, the contributions of Ethel L., while of singular import, are known to few.

Thanks to all!

Gary L. Lilien
Philip Kotler

1

Introduction

Marketing Decision Making

If the first half of the twentieth century will be remembered as the age of production, the second half will be remembered as the age of marketing. Marketing is a cornerstone of policy and practice in such giant organizations as General Electric, Procter and Gamble, Sears, and IBM. Organizations large and small are beginning to appreciate the differences between selling and marketing and are organizing to do the latter. In 1974 the Marketing Sciences Department at AT&T Long Lines contained a single individual; by 1980 that department had grown to include a staff of over three hundred.

Marketing thinking is also making inroads into nonprofit organizations—museums, universities, hospitals, and government agencies—that wish to satisfy the needs of their various publics. Furthermore, developing nations are looking to marketing principles for ways to compete more effectively in world markets. Even socialist nations are beginning to study the use of marketing principles for increasing effectiveness in planning and distributing their goods.

The Trend Toward Marketing

At first glance this increased interest in marketing appears paradoxical: while marketing may be new as a scientific discipline, it is also one of the world's oldest professions. Exchanges, the essence of marketing, have been taking place since the time of simple barter. But marketing as a science—the study of exchange processes and relationships—made its formal appearance only in the early part of the twentieth century.

Some companies quickly saw the potential of marketing. General Electric, General Motors, Sears, and Procter and Gamble (P&G) were among the earliest to seize marketing opportunities. Marketing spread most rapidly through consumer-packaged-goods companies, consumer-durable companies, and then to industrial-equipment companies. Industrial-commodity companies—steel, chemical, paper producers—have been slower to embrace marketing thinking and still have a long way to go. However, service companies, such as airlines, banks, and hotels, are increasingly adopting marketing concepts. The most recent organizations to embrace marketing are those in the nonprofit sector of the economy, such as colleges, museums, and social-service organizations.

Interest in marketing is frequently triggered by one of the following circumstances:

Sales decline.   This factor is the most common cause. AT&T, seeing inroads being made by independents into several segments of their long-distance market, responded with the development of a major department and a complete analysis of their markets.

Slow growth.   Companies often reach the limits of their growth in given industries and search about for new markets. Dow Chemical, wanting new sources of profits, decided to enter consumer markets and invested heavily in marketing expertise to carry out the job.

Changing buying patterns.   Consumer wants and needs are changing rapidly. The automobile industry is facing a crisis brought about by an unprecedented demand for small cars. This crisis is shifting more responsibility for product design to marketing departments.

Increasing competition.   A complacent company may suddenly be attacked by a master marketer and may be forced to learn marketing to meet the challenge. Consider the following:

In the late 1950's when P&G moved into paper products, Scott Paper didn't pay much attention. From a standing start, P&G has built a $1.3 billion business in toilet and facial tissues and diapers. Along the way it reduced Scott . . . to an also-ran, last earning a paltry 4.3% on total assets versus P&G's 10.3% (Gibson, 1978, p. 34).

More recently, P&G has begun test marketing disposable gowns and uniforms for use by nurses and surgeons in hospitals. American Hospital Supply, the prime target of this potential entry, has awakened and is hastily performing marketing analyses in preparation for a counter offensive.

Increasing sales expenditures.   When expenditures for advertising, sales, promotion, marketing research, or customer service increase without apparent cause, management may investigate and attempt to improve its organization and control of these functions.

The indicators above signal needs to expand marketing thinking; trends in the demographic, economic, and natural environments will increase those needs. The age distribution, the concept of the family, and the population centers in the United States have been changing dramatically, providing key inputs into the strategic marketing-planning process for alert firms. The economic environment, which is presently showing drops in real per capita income, makes markets for many goods highly vulnerable and more competitive. Increasingly, we are being faced with raw-materials shortages, which impact market demand in a poorly understood way and provide challenges for marketers in diverse industries.

Technologically, changes are taking place faster than ever; it is not inconceivable that ". . . the changes in the final quarter of this century will be of equal magnitude to those that have occurred between 1925 and 1975" (Baker, 1975, p. 1). Components in industries such as electronics often go through their entire life cycles in 2–3 yr, providing new challenges for dynamic marketing decision making.

In summary, we are moving into an era of constraints, with lower growth in sales, shifting populations, and scarce resources, as well as a faster-moving technological environment. Consequently, the marketing manager is facing a dramatic new frontier in decision making.

> In order to understand the revolution which is occurring in the practice of management, it is first necessary to accept the fact that the severe discontinuities in the environment of business—abrupt changes from what has happened in the past—have made obsolete the experience-based intuitive style of management that was very effective through the 1950's and even into the 1960's.
>
> Experience-based management means the utilization of skills that are learned from experience on the job. Business has historically been managed by executives who have learned how to manage from the lessons of work-based experience. Today, *research-based* staff work, systematically researching the business environment, gathering and summarizing information and making analytical studies, is necessary to support the experience-based, seat-of-the-pants manager (Gruber and Niles, 1976, p. 1).

The new marketing constraints suggest that the 1980s will be an era of market share, with competitors vying for the same market, more than an era of market size. This more constrained, fast-moving environment will make marketing a more important discipline than ever before.

The Complexity of Marketing Decision Making

Several problematic aspects of the marketing system make it difficult to predict the market's response to variations in marketing effort. The major problematic aspects are described below.

Sales Response to a Single Marketing Instrument

The first problem is that the relationship between the market's response and the level of marketing input is typically unknown. The market is made up of buyers at various stages of awareness, interest, preference, and intention. Consequently, there is much variation in their propensity to respond to marketing offerings and efforts. Summarizing their individual behaviors into a measure of total sales response is a challenging task.

Marketing-mix Interaction

Marketing effort, far from being a homogeneous input, is a composite of many different types of activities undertaken by the firm to improve its sales. Marketing effort includes (1) pricing; (2) promotional activities, such as advertising, personal selling, sales promotion, and public relations; (3) distribution activities related to the availability of goods and servicing of orders; and (4) product-development and product-improvement activities. The firm's marketing problem is to develop a sound mix of these activities under great uncertainty about their separate and joint effects. The market's response to variations in the level of any one marketing input is conditional on the level of the other activities. Furthermore, the variation of two or more marketing activities at the same time can have effects that are greater or less than the sum of the separate effects, leading to difficult measurement and evaluation problems.

Competitive Effects

The market's response is related to the competitors' efforts, as well as to the firm's efforts, and the firm rarely has good knowledge of or control over competitors' actions. However, the firm can try to forecast competitive behavior and to make the best decision in light of those forecasts.

Delayed Response

The market's response to current marketing outlays is not immediate but in many instances stretches out over several time periods beyond the occurrence of the outlays. The buying cycle for many industrial capital expenditures lasts for several years; advertising and selling efforts expended now may be translated into sales only after a significant delay. The carry-over effects of many marketing expenditures create a problem in the timing and distribution of marketing expenditures over a planning horizon of several years, rather than in the current year alone.

Multiple Territories

The firm typically sells in several territories with different rates of response to additional marketing expenditures. Should the company's marketing funds be concentrated in areas where the firm is doing well or in the areas where it is doing poorly? In one form or another the question of spatial allocation of marketing funds plagues most firms.

Multiple Products

Most companies market more than one product and need to allocate limited marketing funds among them. Marketing strategies cannot be evolved for each product separately because of the strong demand and cost interactions that generally prevail among the different products in a company's line. For example, price on a particular company product cannot be raised without considering the effect on other products, and a new product often cannot be added to the product line on its own merits because it might severely reduce the revenues of existing company products.

Functional Interactions

Marketing decisions cannot be optimized without joint decision making in the production and financial areas. Whether or not a new advertising campaign will be profitable depends not only on the sales it produces but also on its effect on company employment, inventories, and cash flows. Marketing, production, and financial decisions must be coordinated to achieve corporate goals, a tall order both politically and operationally in most corporations.

Multiple Goals

A company tends to pursue multiple and often contradictory goals. Company presidents are often heard to say that they seek maximum sales at minimum cost. The firm must clearly state its objectives to guide the choice of a marketing strategy from a potentially large number of alternatives.

In addition to the above complexities, we add the uncertainties of operating in a volatile legislative, technological, and economic environment, making marketing decision making a particularly challenging task.

Managerial Response: A Model-building Approach

In the face of this formidable set of challenges, marketing decisions must be made. One tack is described by a well-known marketing writer as follows:

A good many marketing executives, in the deepest recesses of their psyches, are artists, not analysts. For them, marketing is an art form, and, in my opinion, they really do not want it to be any other way. Their temperament is antipathetic to system, order, knowledge. They enjoy flying by the seats of their pants—though you will never get them to admit it. They revel in chaos, abhor facts, and fear research. They hate to be trammeled by written plans. And they love to spend, but are loath to assess the results of their spending (Adler, 1967, p. 166).

Historically, this position has been acceptable and understandable. While production managers can turn to a body of engineering theory and financial managers can turn to a body of financial theory, marketing managers cannot turn to a comparable body of marketing knowledge.

It is easy to evaluate relationships in production and finance because those relationships are clear and the data are reliable. For example, the production manager can usually estimate the units of output per period that would result from different combinations of workers, material, and machines. Similarly, the financial manager can usually estimate the cash flow implications of different plans for raising, disbursing, and collecting money. But the marketing manager is rarely in a good position to estimate the sales rate resulting from different combinations of prices, advertising messages, ad media, sales call strategies, and product-styling and packaging investments. The problem is that marketing effort works through a maze of highly unpredictable behavioral relationships, rather than through a fairly stable set of technological relationships.

Modes of Response

There are four major modes of response by marketing executives to decision-making challenges.

Experience   Marketing people often say that marketing experience is the best teacher, that planning and performing a diversity of marketing activities—selling, pricing, advertising, servicing—create sound judgment about what will work and what will backfire. For instance, through experience the marketing practitioner learns that inspired marketing ideas are not enough, that salespeople are unevenly endowed and motivated, that customers vary immensely in their perceptions of product and company attributes, and that production and financial managers greatly influence marketing outcomes.

Experience is extraordinarily valuable but has several limitations. It is unique in every person, and there is no objective way of choosing between the experience-based recommendation of individual A and that of individual B. It is often fraught with personal bias: it is not a coincidence that sales managers ascribe proportionally more power to personal selling while advertising managers ascribe more power to advertising. And since it is not transferable, experience-based decision making may leave a company vulnerable in a fast-moving environment characterized by rapid turnover.

Practice Standards Companies tend to evolve standard policies and procedures to guide decision makers. Instead of allowing individual experience to govern each decision, companies develop guidelines that codify the best management judgment and experience: product managers are given advertising budgets that reflect historical ratios of advertising budgets to sales; salesmen are advised on how many calls to make to different-sized customers; pricing executives abide by certain traditional markups on cost. These and many other marketing activities become rule-bound over time. Such rules and practices often start off with the most successful situations acting as prototypes. Over time, however, they linger on past the point where they are still relevant. In a particular year a large increase in the advertising budget might be highly profitable, but practices, such as those listed above, lobby against variation from historical policy. Thus they produce guidelines for decisions that are often good on average but that act counter to the increasing need for flexibility in marketing action.

Data or facts There is a strong reliance on basic market research for primary-source data collection. A marketing manager who can say that "72 percent of consumers preferred package A to package B" appears to have a compelling argument in favor of package A. Yet data are deceptively seductive. The manager is saying that he is letting the facts speak for themselves, but underlying his statement, is at least the following set of assumptions:

> Higher preference measures lead to higher purchase rates.
>
> His sample of consumers represents the target market.
>
> The package is a tangible factor in the purchase decision.
>
> Choice context (existence/nonexistence of competing brands) will not affect preference.
>
> The sample is large enough so that preference is not due to chance.
>
> The package will not affect brand image adversely.
>
> The package will not affect usage adversely.

In other words, managers have a framework of assumptions and theory that they use when viewing data. Solutions to problems are as sensitive to the assumptions for analysis as are the base facts themselves. Facts are important, but they must be interpreted in a framework.

Model Building The model-building approach, which is increasingly being adopted by practitioners, has the following characteristics:

> explicit and coherent specification of objectives, variables, and relationships
>
> reliance on theory and management judgment for the development of relationships
>
> a framework for evaluating facts or data

Because the modeling approach requires explicit specification of relation-ships, it incorporates experience but does not rely on it. Furthermore, as a vehicle for interpreting data, a model specifies the data that should be collected and allows for informed decisions with less data than would otherwise be possible. Finally, the model permits an explicit evaluation of the costs and benefits of breaking with standard business practices.

The benefits described above require modifications in decision-making style:

The approach calls for systematic thinking—specifying objectives, variables, and relationships.

The approach makes all assumptions explicit instead of burying them in a category called "manager's experience."

The approach requires changes in modes of thinking and decision making.

In total, the modeling approach poses several threats to the nonanalyti-cal marketing manager. These threats are understandable and must be addressed at the outset. But before addressing these issues, we must define the model-building approach more carefully.

Models

Because marketing systems are too complex to manage in all their detail, people deal with models of them. A *model* is the specification of a set of variables and their interrelationships, designed to represent some real system or process in whole or in part. Models can be understood according to their *purpose* and their *structure*.

Model Purpose   Most structured thinking can be considered model build-ing. We relate things to one another when we think about them, and those relationships are models. The purpose of many models is to describe the workings of a system. For example, we might observe that (1) the last brand an individual bought helps us explain what the individual is most likely to buy next and (2) a constant percentage of the people who bought brand A last period (say 70 percent) buy that brand again this period. We then might use this information, given knowledge of what people bought last period, to predict what people will buy in the future.

This purpose has several components. The model that is being used to *describe* behavior here is that "a certain (constant) proportion of people who buy a brand in one period buy it again in the next period." This descriptive model suggests that past purchase behavior is an important indicator of future behavior. But the model was also used to *predict* behavior (what sales would be next period). So a model that describes behavior (a descriptive model) can often predict behavior (a predictive model).

A most important model purpose is to help the manager decide what to do. If the model of repeat-purchase behavior is taken as a base, a manager might legitimately ask, "Given my knowledge of consumer behavior (my descriptive/predictive model), what if I change the system by offering a price-off promotion or deal? Would that action be cost-beneficial?" A *normative*, or *decision*, model generally combines an understanding of the process with management goals and objectives to get an answer.

Exhibit 1.1 illustrates the operations we are describing. On the left side the actions of the marketer, his competitors, and the environment are integrated into the workings of the marketplace, producing a response (sales, profits, awareness, intent to purchase, etc.). Models of these operations are descriptive or predictive models. On the right side the effects of marketer actions are compared with company goals and are evaluated to determine directions for improving future marketer actions. Models that help perform these tasks are normative models. Note that this exhibit is asymmetrical; the marketer and his actions are controllable, and competitive actions are

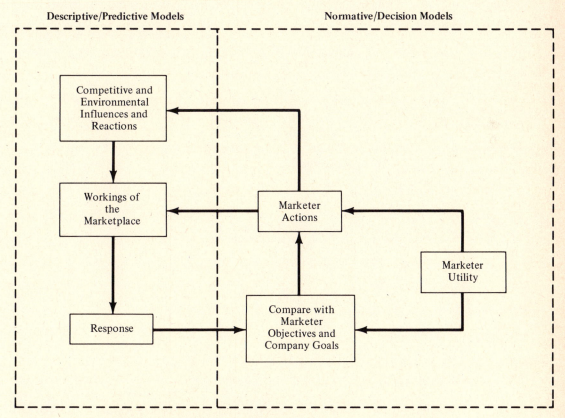

EXHIBIT 1-1 **A marketing system, showing the domains of descriptive/ predictive and normative models.**

included in the environment. Thus this view presents a split from a specific marketer's perspective.

Model Structure   Models, whether of the descriptive or normative type, can have many different kinds of structure. The most common are verbal, graphical, and mathematical structures.

In verbal models the variables and their relationships are cast in prose form. Many of the great theories of individual, social, and societal behavior, such as those of Freud, Darwin, and Marx, are set in verbal terms. Many models of consumer behavior are verbal models. Lavidge and Steiner (1961) state that ". . . advertising should move people from awareness . . . to knowledge . . . to liking . . . to preference . . . to conviction . . . to purchase."

Graphical or conceptual models are usually more specific than verbal models. They are a useful bridge in the process of symbolizing a verbal model. Most graphical or conceptual models are used to isolate variables and suggest directions of relationships, but few are designed to provide specific numerical results. Graphical models have the virtues found in pictures. The phenomenon is stripped of nonessentials, allowing the viewer to grasp the whole and select relationships to examine. For marketing analysis, graphic and conceptual models improve exposition, facilitate discussion, and guide analysis. They are logical preliminary steps to developing mathematical models.

Mathematical models specify the relationships among variables, usually in equation form. All relationships and assumptions must be clearly stated. Furthermore, objectives, variables, and unknowns are included explicitly. Thus these models can be used as guides for collecting other data and have the advantage of *manipulability*. For example, by making slight changes to an input variable, such as advertising expenditures, the analyst will be able to see the movements of an output variable, such as sales revenues.

Exhibit 1.2 illustrates some simple concepts of new-product growth with verbal, graphical, and mathematical models.

So we have several different kinds of models. But what about marketing decision makers? Which of these models is both available to and useful for them? Little (1970) notes the following:

Good models are hard to find.

Good parameterization is even harder.

Managers do not understand models.

Most models are incomplete.

Given these barriers, Naert and Leeflang (1978) argue that the cost/benefit ratio should be sufficiently low to overcome them. Another suggestion, given by Urban (1974), is to build models in an evolutionary manner; the user starts with a simple structure at a low cost and adds detail as required. This technique makes each step either cost-beneficial or low enough in absolute

Verbal Model

New-product growth often starts slowly, until some people (early triers) become aware of the product. These early triers interact with nontriers to lead to acceleration of sales growth. Finally, as market potential is approached, growth slows down.

(a)

Graphical/Conceptual Model

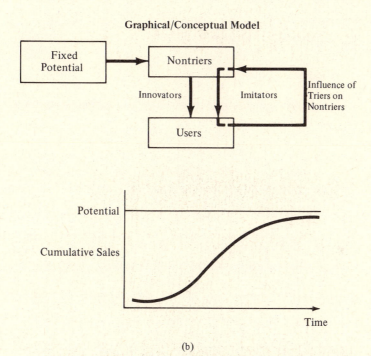

(b)

Mathematical Model

$$\frac{dx}{dt} = (a + bx)(N - x)$$

where

x = number of purchases by t
N = market potential
a, b = constants

(c)

EXHIBIT 1-2   An illustration of three model structures.

cost to be worth the investment as an expected benefit. Taking this position further, Little (1975) argues that the evolutionary nature of model building should extend to calibration, with parameters estimated judgmentally at first and then statistically as the proper data are collected.

Feelings About Models

Many managers feel threatened by models. Models require (1) systematic thinking, (2) specification of assumptions, (3) data (judgmental or otherwise), and (4) exposure to new and often difficult-to-understand concepts.

In a decision-making situation a marketing manager often wants support for his positions

in black-and-white terms
in simple, concrete language
as soon as possible
at no cost

The modeling approach seems to buy him support for positions he often may not wish to take, that is,

with uncertain results
in complex, conceptual language
after significant delays
with a possible budget headache

So why do we see a trend toward increasing use of model-based decision making? The answer is simple: managers can't afford *not* to take a model-building approach in their fast-moving, competitive environment! Little (1979*a*, p. 25) predicts that within the next 5–10 yr there will be

an order-of-magnitude increase in the amount of marketing data used; a similar tenfold increase in computer power available for marketing analysis; a shift from market-status reporting to market-response reporting; and a new methodology for supporting strategy development

Little's first two points suggest that the amount of information a manager can obtain will be growing exponentially and that his ability to handle it (through a computer) will rise comparably. Therefore if he is to proceed and comprehend this information, he needs a model to relate the data to his decision-making needs.

The third point is critical. While manager A (without models) gets reports on what things are—data points for sales, shares, prices, advertising expenditures—manager B, using models to interpret his data, gets reports on how things react—price elasticities, advertising responses, promotional-effectiveness indicators. Manager B is clearly in a better position to make informed decisions.

The last point calls for a look ahead, with new models and methodology leading to better decision making. In a darwinian sense the fittest organizations tend to survive. The development and proven value of model-based aids to marketing-strategy development will provide more profitable, healthier environments for those organizations using the tools correctly.

An Example of Value   During the course of this book, we will present a number of examples showing the value of models, such as the following, given by Shapiro (1976). H. J. Heinz, in promoting one of its products, began an analysis of promotional effectiveness in 1972. A preliminary study indicated that promotional effectiveness, in terms of effect on market share, was different for different package sizes within a district and varied across districts. A model, based on the results of the initial study, showed wide variation in promotional effectiveness across markets. That model, a simple regression model, linked share of features and promotions by size to market share. An overall analysis indicated that a budget reallocation might be in order. Specifically:

> For the first fiscal year 1973–1974, the total number of promotions was reduced by 40% from what it had been the previous year. At the same time, by concentrating mostly on those promotions which proved themselves to be effective, market share was increased by more than three share points (Shapiro, 1976, p. 86).

This example of marketing modeling and analysis has several important points:

> Standard business practice (the prior promotional policy) may be less than cost-effective.
>
> Marketing models do not have to be complex to be valuable.
>
> Models may help isolate situations where profitability can be increased by reallocation of resources or by *cutting* spending.
>
> Models help focus on the key variable of interest (the market-varying, promotional-response parameter) and help serve as vehicles for analyzing its impact.

Model results were implemented here because it was clearly cost-effective to do so. As our marketing systems respond more quickly and become increasingly complex, more marketing managers will use model-based analyses because it will be too costly to ignore them.

Postscript on the Heinz Story   The analysis detailed above did not lead to a regular, model-based, monitoring-and-control procedure (e.g., redoing the analysis on an annual basis). Heinz management was convinced that new, market-specific spending norms had been developed and that further analysis was not needed. This view is a manifestation of what we will call modeling myopia—the feeling that once model-based analysis is done, it does not need to be done again, ever. The causes and cures for this syndrome are discussed in Chapter 21.

Plan of the Book

So far in this chapter, we have suggested the following:

Marketing decision making is a complex and difficult task.

That task is becoming *more* difficult.

A model-building approach can provide timely and valuable support for marketing decision making.

Model-building Disciplines

Several disciplines provide a basis for the approach developed here.

Consumer Behavior Psychologists and behavioral scientists have produced a vast literature on buying behavior and buying motives. This behavior needs to be understood before it can be used in developing marketing plans. Who is in the market? When do they buy? What do they buy? Why do they buy? What is the purchasing process? The buyer goes through a process consisting of need arousal, information search, product evaluation, purchase decision, and postpurchase feelings. At each stage, characteristics of the buyer, product, seller, and selling situation interact to influence the buying outcome. Consumer behavior theory, dealing with the issues above, provides a theoretical base upon which to build models of market operation.

Economics The economic theory of the firm provides a starting point for developing models that can be used to understand markets and develop optimum market behavior. But because much of economic theory deals with optimum behavior when a firm is selling a single product in a single territory with only one or two marketing instruments, it is not sufficiently developed to handle the full complexities of marketing decision making. However, many economic developments are useful as building blocks in forming models of marketing systems and as bases for modeling consumer behavior.

Management Science/Operations Research (MS/OR) As used here, the essential elements of operations research are the applications of mathematics and scientific methods to problems of organizational systems with a view toward improving such systems. The MS/OR field provides an approach, the mathematical tools for analysis, and an explicit specification of (often) multiple organizational objectives. Unfortunately, the field is most often associated with its techniques (linear programming, Markov processes, queueing theory, etc.) rather than its approach, which includes the following features:

1. defining the problem

2. developing the model
3. solving the model (parameter estimation and policy analysis)
4. testing the model and evaluating the solution
5. implementing, maintaining, and controlling the solution

In professional MS/OR work the problem suggests the model and the analysis approach rather than vice versa.

Statistics/Econometrics Marketing problems often generate a large amount of data. The fields of statistics and econometrics provide methodology for the following:

estimating the parameters (the unknowns) in the models

providing tests to determine which models are most consistent with observation

generating forecasts of future demand and of other quantities of interest to the marketing manager

These four disciplines—consumer behavior, economics, management science/operations research, and statistics/econometrics—provide the structure and the tools that are necessary to develop and implement a model-building approach in marketing.

The book is a view of marketing decision making using a model-building approach. The remainder is structured as described below.

Part 2: Marketing, Management Decisions, and Models

The most difficult step in model building is problem recognition. Whether you are a quantitative analyst or a marketing manager, the single most important (and most creative!) act you face in the decision-making process is *recognizing the problem*. All situations are specific; this book will not provide an exhaustive encyclopedia of solutions to fit every problem. Rather, we will try to outline the following:

how creative marketers recognize and characterize problems

how they structure those concepts in model form

how they characterize their organizational goals in terms of quantitative objectives

how data can be integrated into the model structure in the form of parameter estimates

how the model can be tested on the data and how it can be manipulated (solved) to develop marketing decisions

Next, we need the pieces of marketing theory and methodology that can be used to characterize and understand markets. These we present in Part 3.

Part 3: The Working of Markets

The theory and models of consumer and organizational buying behavior are the focus of the first section of Part 3. The field of consumer behavior, which provides a basis for all marketing analyses, is fairly well developed, while that of organizational buying behavior—involving multiple decision makers and varying personal versus organizational objectives—is more complex and therefore in an early stage of development. The progress that has been made and promising new developments are discussed.

The second section of Part 3 presents the theory of market segmentation and tools for understanding market structure. Market segmentation is the division of a market into distinct subsets of customers, where each subset reacts to media or product offerings differently. The implementation of market-segmentation theory, perhaps the most important development in marketing in the past 15 yr, has been accompanied by the application of a number of multivariate techniques, which are described.

Part 3 concludes with the presentation of tools for assessing and forecasting market demand. These tasks are integral parts of key management functions. The analysis of what would be expected to happen in a market, *ceteris paribus*, provides the basis against which the results of marketer actions need to be compared.

The next two parts of the book deal with marketing decision making.

Part 4: Micromarketing Decision Models

In Part 4 the elements of the marketing mix—product design, pricing, distribution, advertising, promotion, and salesforce issues—are discussed. Although decisions relating to these elements should be made in concert with broader marketing decisions, in practice, a problem with one element of the marketing mix is frequently identified and studied separately. Nevertheless, this approach is not without advantages: (1) single elements in the marketing mix are more easily understood than are interactions in the mix, and (2) the individual elements of the mix may have to be understood separately before they can be integrated in market-planning models.

Part 5: Marketing-planning Models

In Part 5 the building blocks of the previous sections are integrated in larger-scale, market-planning models. Broader marketing decisions are addressed: marketing-strategy questions (product-line planning and portfolio analysis, market-structure analysis) and marketing-mix decisions for established products and analysis of new products.

Part 6: Making It Happen

The concept and application of a marketing decision-support system (MDSS) is developed in Part 6. The approach stresses the evolution of marketing knowledge, better models, better data, and better statistical tools, together with a powerful but friendly computer, to provide improved decision support.

How can the process be implemented and controlled? How can we plan for implementation, making certain that the best use of the modeling approach is made? The discussion centers around what is needed for improving marketing decision making, independent of the tools used. The control of marketing solutions (When has the environment changed enough so that a new look, new analysis, or new model is needed?) is discussed as well.

We finish with a look forward. What are the trends in models, measurements, and computer-related, decision-support tools that the marketing manager should be looking for in the 1980s? Trends suggest that some future shock may be in store for the traditional marketing manager, making the 1980s a very exciting time in which to be practicing.

A View Ahead and a Caveat

This book is an advanced view of marketing management, providing a systematic approach (and some important tools) that can be used in analyzing many marketing decisions. Each chapter begins with a review of existing theory, followed by in-depth analyses of a small number of models and a short review of model-based work in the area. Because any model must be customized for a particular situation, we prefer to develop a few models in depth, showing how the development is done, and we hope that these examples will give important insight into the problem-solving process. Then the short reviews can be used to locate related work for the reader's particular problem.

Each chapter ends with a selection of problems. Because the best way to learn about models is first to push some numbers through existing models and then to build some models, both types of problems are provided. The book is appropriate for individuals with varying levels of mathematical skill, although it will clearly be easier for individuals with strong skills. Where possible, models are presented verbally and graphically, as well as mathematically. This redundancy of exposition will help the less mathematically oriented individual through the more technical parts of the book.

As a motivating thought, remember that all situations are specific; models must be customized to the particular situation. Model building is hard (even for model builders), but implementation is just as hard and just as creative. The required input—systematic and careful thought—results in better preparation for informed and systematic decision making in marketing. The outcome is worth the effort.

Not all marketing problems can be modeled, however. Case teaching is the norm in many marketing programs. The modeling approach of this book will not replace in-depth case analysis. Many marketing situations are unique, do not repeat themselves, generate little or no data, and need an immediate resolution or decision. For such situations the informed commonsense approach, supported mainly by qualitative argument, may be best. For other situations, where the problem has occurred before (in the same firm or elsewhere) and where data and theory exist, the model-building approach is applicable.

The well-armed marketing decision maker, facing both sets of problems in these fast-moving times, needs to have *both* approaches at his or her disposal, since neither is sufficient for all marketing problems.

Summary

Marketing is an exciting, interdisciplinary, and fast-evolving field. It is becoming more complex: decisions have to be made more quickly (and accurately) in more-constrained environments after processing more and better information. In the face of these challenges the model-building approach provides support for the decision maker. Consumer behavior theory, economics, management science/operations research, and statistics/econometrics provide the theory and methodology upon which to build better procedures for marketing decision making. The result of studying this approach to problem solving is better preparation for the practice of marketing management in the 1980s.

Problems

1.1 Does there appear to be any ordering by importance of the complexities of the marketing process listed? Are these complexities independent of each other, or are they interrelated?

1.2 What is the value of theory in marketing?

1.3 While standard operating procedures have decided disadvantages in some instances, they do have a definite value in others. As stated in the chapter, many of these procedures are sound at the time of their inception but become obsolete as time passes. In what types of situations are standard operating procedures most useful and feasible?

1.4 Give examples of descriptive, predictive, and normative models that are applicable to marketing, providing a brief statement of their content and purpose.

1.5 The Tempus Company is a small producer of a laundry bleach that has successfully competed against its larger competitors selling laundry detergents that claim to have bleaching power. Tempus management has just learned that its competitors are considering the introduction in the near future of a detergent with soaking characteristics. Management at Tempus must decide whether or not they should also develop and market such a soak product. Carry out a brief analysis of the problem faced by Tempus management in this situation, following the list of steps through which the operations researcher should go in analyzing a problem.

1.6 Differentiate between experience-based response and the response specified through a descriptive/predictive model. Give an example of each.

1.7 The ABC Company has been making standard-grade paper towels and bathroom tissue and selling them at prices slightly below those of its competitors. Sales have been stagnant over the last 2 yr. ABC Company wants to increase growth and is considering the following options:
a. introduce some new products (napkins, disposable cloth kitchen wipes, etc.)
b. introduce higher-grade items of the products they are already producing, advertise them heavily, and sell them at premium prices
c. invest heavily in an advertising campaign that shows "equal quality at discount prices" for their existing products
Develop a verbal model and an associated graphical/conceptual model that can aid in deciding among the three options above and a fourth, do-nothing option.

1.8 "Many managers feel threatened by models." What steps can an analyst take to help make models less threatening?

1.9 What steps can be taken to reduce the likelihood of the modeling-myopia problem associated with the Heinz story?

2

Marketing, Management Decisions, and Models

The Model-Building Approach: Identifying and Structuring Marketing Problems

CHAPTER 2

Scientific Inquiry in Marketing

Is marketing a science? Ultimately, we hope your answer to this question will be yes. The advanced view of marketing we develop here deals with the marketing-modeling process as a form of operational science. This relationship with science is useful because scientists have developed methods of inquiry that we can adapt to marketing problems. The process of problem finding and solving, common to most sciences, is adapted for marketing situations in this chapter.

Science is a process of inquiry. It is a procedure for answering questions and solving problems and for developing more effective methods for answering questions and solving problems. Too often, we mistake science for the body of knowledge it has produced. In our development of an understanding of science in marketing, we will concentrate on the process that generates that knowledge—the modeling-and-inquiry process—rather than on the knowledge itself.

EXAMPLE: Consider the PIMS (profit impact of marketing strategy) project, discussed in detail in Chapter 17. This study is aimed at collecting product, market, and company financial data on a large number of businesses and deriving efficient operating rules from a careful study of what has been tried and what has worked. The project has produced regression models that provide strategy norms. Is this marketing-modeling effort scientific? The knowledge base produced by the project has been questioned by some (Does high market share *cause* high profitability?). But as an inquiry process, the PIMS project is clearly scientific, producing better models and better analysis procedures as the base of observations and the analysis of past results have grown.

EXAMPLE: The recognition that sales of new, frequently purchased products can be modeled by a trial-repeat process was a scientific discovery. That discovery provided an explanation of the typical sales curve for new consumer products—with an overshoot prior to steady state—illustrated in Exhibit 2.1. This separation of curve (c) into its factor curves, (a) and (b), provides both an explanation for the shape of curve (c) and a means for diagnosing new-product problems and forecasting results. (See Chapter 19 for details.)

Then what of the intuitive manager, who takes his gut feeling, his experience, and flies by the seat of his pants in making decisions? Is he scientific? Or, alternatively, is he using common sense? The distinction between common sense and scientific inquiry is not one of quality but one of degree.

> Science is, I believe, nothing but trained and organized common sense, dif-fering from the latter only as a veteran may differ from a raw recruit: and its methods differ from those of common sense only so far as the guardsman's cut and thrust differ from the manner in which a savage wields his club (Huxley, in Wiener, 1953, p. 130).

Or again:

> Scientific statements, no less than those of common experience, are opin-ions—only, enlightened (grounded and testable) opinions rather than arbitrary dicta or unchecked gossip. What can be proved beyond reasonable doubt are either theorems of logic and mathematics or trivial (particular and observa-tional) statements of fact, such as "This volume is heavy" (Bunge, 1967, p. 5).

It is generally recognized that as a process of inquiry becomes more scientific, we are more likely to obtain correct answers to questions and better solutions to problems. This is not to assert that better results always occur when scientific approaches are used but that we are *more likely* to achieve superior results with a scientific approach.

In fact, even a systematization of managers' actions seems to provide superior results. Bowman's (1963) managerial coefficients theory is based on the interesting and challenging assertion that a model calibrated on a manager's past actions will perform better than that manager in future, similar decision situations. Bowman's argument is that the calibration procedure separates the signal from decision-making noise, leading to a more consistent decision-making process. He and others (see Kunreuther, 1969, for example) have shown that this systemization of past actions has wide applicability.

The scientific process of inquiry is superior because it is controlled. "A process is controlled to the extent that it is efficiently directed toward the

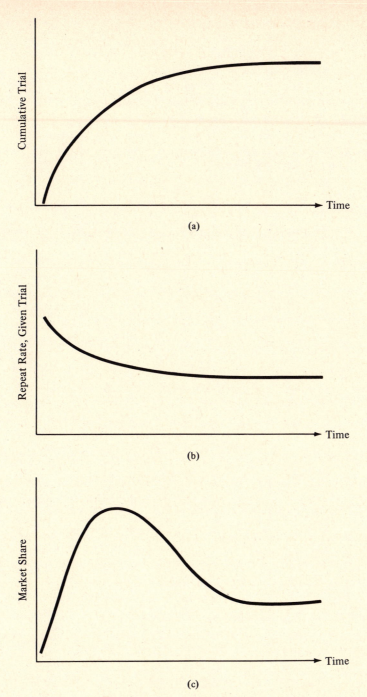

Exhibit 2-1   **Market share (c), modeled as the product of trial (a) and repeat (b): a scientific discovery.**

attainment of certain objectives" (Ackoff, 1962, p. 3). Every inquiry process in marketing and elsewhere has some controlled, as well as some uncontrolled, aspects. Scientific inquiry (when it occurs in marketing) is more controlled than intuition and is characterized by the goals of self-improvement and self-perpetuation. Marketing is scientific when the research effort has, along with the objective of solving a particular problem, the objective of improving the procedures employed.

Two things should be noted here. First, by our discussion above, there are clearly many degrees of inquiry, not just scientific and nonscientific. So our objective will generally be to see how we move along this continuum in the scientific direction. Second, even where a scientific approach leads to better results than those of common sense, it is not always preferred. In many small, fragmented markets the cost of an advertising experiment may be many times the potential profit from discovering the optimal advertising policy. Many small businesses cannot justify the fixed cost entailed in a model-building effort and must rely on common sense and rules of thumb. Furthermore, marketing emergencies often arise where a suboptimum but timely answer is preferred to one that is better but too late to be of use.

Let us take this issue of control to an extreme. Experimentation is often taken to be synonymous with scientific research, and physical manipulation is taken to be identical with control: "In scientific experimentation, we control everything that happens" (Giddings, 1924, p. 55). But controlled inquiry may clearly occur without physical manipulation. The astronomer does not manipulate the objects of the study. The astronomer's control is the *conceptual* manipulation, with models and mathematics, of the phenomena under study.

Developments in science as a whole and in marketing in particular have proceeded in two directions. First, a body of knowledge—the results of scientific inquiries—has been developed to enable us to better understand and control our environment. Second, a body of procedures has been developed that enables us to add to this body of knowledge. We identify the model-building process with this latter direction of development.

As a science, marketing is applied. It addresses two types of problem situations: evaluative and developmental. *Evaluative* problems deal with choosing the best of a set of alternative courses of action, each of which is specified in advance. For example, a new product may be (1) marketed nationally now, (2) sent back for more test marketing, or (3) discarded. On the other hand, *developmental* problems involve the search for (and sometimes the construction of) techniques that yield a course of action that is better than any other available at the time. Recent work in developing pretest-market evaluation procedures for packaged goods aimed at improved measurement and modeling methods is an example. (See Chapter 19.)

Approaches toward both types of problems will be presented in this book. But as applied researchers, we will most often be concerned with evaluative research, choosing courses of action and the tools to support them.

In addition, because the aims of the research processes we develop here are mainly normative—suggesting, evaluating, and prescribing courses of action—we will stress *operational* science over *descriptive* science. Descriptive science in marketing deals with those measurement and analysis procedures used to understand the behavior of individuals and firms in market situations. Such inquiries, which are covered in detail in marketing research texts (Green and Tull, 1975, for example) and in newer treatises on marketing theory development (Bagozzi, 1979b), provide bases for and interact with normative developments and therefore complement the treatment here.

The Research Process

D'Abro (1951, p. 3) lists the three stages of the scientific method as the following:

1. the observational stage
2. the experimental stage
3. the theoretical and mathematical stage.

Furthermore, he states:

> The order in which these stages have been listed is the order in which they arise in the study of any group of physical phenomena. It is also the chronological order in which they were discovered (p. 3).

This characterization, especially in terms of chronology and order, is too restricted to apply to marketing and other operational sciences. Theory, in terms of prior mathematical relationships, often precedes observation and is, in turn, modified by it.

A broader view of a research process better suited for marketing is provided by Bunge (1967, p. 9) and is reproduced here in Exhibit 2.2. He summarizes this process as follows:

1. Ask well-formulated and likely fruitful questions.
2. Devise well-grounded and testable hypotheses to answer the questions.
3. Derive the logical consequences of the assumptions.
4. Design techniques to test the assumptions.
5. Test the techniques for relevance and reliability.
6. Execute the tests and interpret their results.
7. Evaluate the truth claims of the assumptions and the fidelity of the techniques.

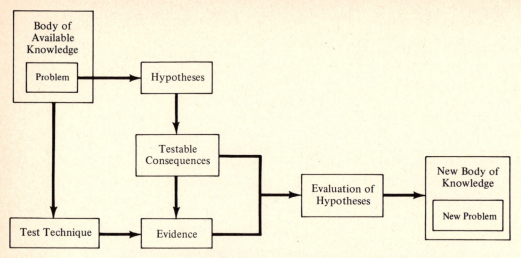

Exhibit 2-2   An outline of the research process. (Source: Bunge, 1967, p. 9. Reprinted with permission of Springer Verlag.)

8. Determine the domains in which the assumptions and the techniques hold and state the new problems raised by the research.

Bunge (1967) also gives some general rules for the adequate execution of the above operations, which can be summarized as follows:

Rule 1: State the problem precisely and as specifically as possible, especially in the beginning.

If you want to know how spot TV advertising affects sales of Cocoa Critters in Missouri, ask that question. "How does advertising affect sales?" is too general (and, as we will see later, not well formulated).

Rule 2: Develop definite conjectures, not trivial (or wild) hunches.

"Selling effort increases sales" is trivial.
"Selling effort is optimal if it is 7 percent of sales" is too specific to be accepted.
"Selling effort is related to sales by a function $f(X; a, b)$, where a and b are parameters that are product/market-specific" is probably most reasonable.

Rule 3: Subject assumptions to tough tests. Don't throw out outliers without careful analysis.

Just because the sales response in Milwaukee is different from the one assumed in the model doesn't mean it is bad data. Milwaukee may provide new phenomena to include in the model.

Rule 4: Be aware that you are not likely to prove that all hypotheses are true. At best, a result will be "probably" true.

Newton's law of gravitation was long thought to be true. In retrospect, it was probably true but actually false.

Rule 5: Ask why the answer should be so and not otherwise.

Much of what masquerades as model building in marketing is data summarization: finding generalizations that fit data. Because of model misspecification, bad data, and multicollinearity, such data-generalizing exercises often do not lead to sensible models. Try to explain the results in terms of stronger laws: "A positive advertising-selling interaction follows from. . . ."

Stages of the Process

These and other rules about scientific inquiry are far from infallible, but like any checklist, they can help keep us on track. We cannot expect the rules of scientific inquiry to replace insight, intelligence, and astute observation. If that were possible, research would be programmable, and computers would become the next generation of scientists.

To apply this thinking to an area like marketing, consider these five stages of inquiry and problem solving (Ackoff and Sasieni, 1968):

1. *Formulating the problem.* To be tractable, a problem must be identified and formulated in a way that makes it susceptible to research. Marketing analysts, like physicians, are usually presented with symptoms, rather than a diagnosis, and must probe for enough additional symptoms to complete the picture (identify the disease—the cause).

2. *Constructing the model.* Few marketing systems are amenable to traditional physical manipulation of decision variables. Although experimentation may be possible on subsystems, more often than not the total system under study cannot be subjected to controlled experimentation. Therefore, like the astronomer, the scientific marketer must rely on models—representations—of systems for study.

3. *Deriving a solution.* Once a model is constructed, it can be used to find optimal values of the decision variables, that is, those values that produce the best performance of the system for given values of the exogenous variables. These solutions may be derived by conducting experiments on the model (simulation) or by mathematical analysis. For some types of problems classical mathematics provides explicit results, that is, without regard to specific numerical values of the variables. In other cases the values of the variables must be known and the solutions derived numerically (through algorithms). Finally, in certain situations where the role of the decision maker is important but poorly understood, people, in role-playing capacities, may be involved in solution procedures called operational gaming.

4. *Testing the model and evaluating the solution.* Model results are only useful if the model represents an adequate picture of what was being

modeled. Thus the performance of the model must be tested against the policy or procedures it is meant to replace.

5. *Implementing and maintaining the solution.*   The objective of this approach is to improve the performance of systems; therefore the results must be implemented. It is in this phase that the ultimate test and evaluation of the research is made.

These phases, though often initiated in the order above, are rarely completed in that order. In particular, each phase continues through to the end of the project, and a successful project most often ends in the identification of a new problem for analysis.

Finding and Formulating Problems

Perhaps the most creative and critical aspect of marketing model building and problem solving is finding and formulating problems. Exhibit 2.3 reproduces Urban's (1974) suggestions for building models for decision makers. We focus here on the first three steps: formulation of priors, entry, and problem finding.

In the first step the model builder starts with a certain abstract understanding of or way of thinking about a problem and with certain biases toward favored techniques and approaches. This attitude is not undesirable, because the process of problem solving requires organizational entry and self-confidence on the part of the problem solver, who will have to sell himself and establish credibility in an organizational environment. But it is critical that these priors or biases be weak and adaptable; there is no worse problem solver than the one who sees all problems as math-programming problems, for example.

Specific priors can be developed by a study of the decision environment, by discussion with people in the field, by a review of the literature, and by interaction with a problem-solving team. This background work should be undertaken before confirmation with the real-world situation.

EXAMPLE: A firm is about to introduce a new brand of coffee and is unsure about its potential. Prior to analysis a model builder might consider a pretest-market evaluation procedure with a trial-repeat framework, a copy-testing procedure, and so on.

In many situations the second step, entry, means management education. A model-building approach to solving marketing problems requires that managers (1) understand modeling vocabulary, (2) review modeling applications, and (3) have some hands-on experience with models. This entry step is where commitment from the management team and the appropriate level of resources are gathered. In addition to the manager, Urban (1974) suggests a team of one or two staff people and a change agent—an individual who can work from a neutral position within the

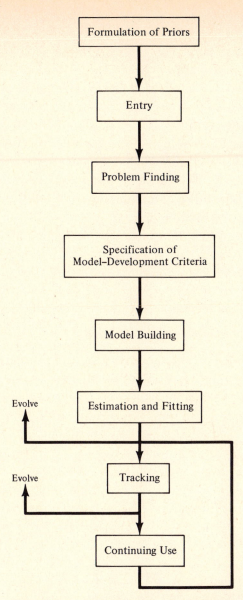

Exhibit 2-3 **The process of building models for decision makers.** (Source: Urban, 1974, p. 3. Reprinted by permission of The Institute of Management Sciences, *Interfaces,* Vol. 4, No. 3, May 1974.)

organization to effect change. Thus even prior to the key step of problem finding, a commitment of time, personnel, and resources is crucial if the effort is to have credibility and support.

EXAMPLE: During the process of entry the firm's management might attend presentations about trial-repeat models and pretest-market evaluation procedures.

They also might manipulate the models with an interactive computer system.

As noted earlier, we are most often presented with problem symptoms; finding the problem is as much an art in the marketing area as is posing the right questions in physical sciences research. Urban suggests that 2–3 wk is sometimes necessary to identify and define a problem correctly. Overlooking this step, which might occur in an hurried effort, could result in solving a problem that didn't exist. Studies should be carried out to determine the following, among other things:

existing procedures and rules of thumb

characteristics of the decision process

existing flows and uses of information

goals and objectives of the organization

relationships among managers, the organization, and real and perceived problems

the basic issues that led to the recognition of the current crisis

Churchman, Ackoff, and Arnoff (1957) present a more elaborate checklist based on three basic steps: (1) analyze the operations and the communications system, (2) formulate management's problem, and (3) formulate the research problem. This process is presented in Exhibit 2.4. The critical thing to note is that analysis of operations precedes formulation of management's problem, which, in turn, precedes actual problem definition.

This final step, formulating the research problem, is essentially separating chaff from wheat—editing and condensing the model, the objectives, and the potential courses of action.

EXAMPLE: Even if a pretest-market procedure is finally selected to answer the question, the procedure and the model analysis are customized to the problem situation of the firm. Model customization is as creative as, and often more difficult than, the original model building.

The process outlined here and in the many works on problem identification and problem solving (see Churchman and Schainblatt, 1965; Huysmans, 1970; Mitroff et al., 1974; and others) does not pretend to be a formula. It is the distilled wisdom of practitioners who have been successful in the science of problem solving. But its use as a guide and checklist will make the problem-solving process simpler.

Classifying Problems and Solutions

For a problem to exist, according to Ackoff (1962), there are several necessary (and sufficient) conditions:

Someone (a decision maker) has to have the problem.

A desired outcome and at least one alternative must exist.

Exhibit 2-4   **Churchman, Ackoff, and Arnoff's procedure
for identifying and formulating a problem.**

A. Analyze the relevant operations and the communication system by which they are controlled.
   1. Identify and trace each communication related to operations under study.
   2. Identify each transformation of information and decision process.
   3. Identify each step in the relevant operations.
   4. Drop from consideration each communication or transformation which has no effect on operations (e.g., billing in production operations).
   5. Group operations between control points.
   6. Prepare a flowchart showing
      a. control points and decisions made
      b. flow of pertinent information between control points and time consumed
      c. flow of materials and time of grouped operations
B. Formulate management's problem.
   1. Identify decision-makers and the decision-making procedure.
   2. Determine the decision-makers' relevant objectives.
   3. Identify other participants and the channels of their influence on a solution.
   4. Determine objectives of the other participants.
   5. Determine alternative courses of action available to decision-makers.
   6. Determine counteractions available to other participants.
C. Formulate the research problem.
   1. Edit and condense the relevant objectives.
   2. Edit and condense the relevant courses of action.
   3. Define the measure of effectiveness to be used.
      a. Define the measure of efficiency to be used relative to each objective.
      b. Weight objectives (if qualitative) or units of objectives (if quantitative).
      c. Define the criterion of best decision as some function of the sum of weighted efficiencies (e.g., maximum expected return, minimum expected loss).

SOURCE: Churchman, Ackoff, and Arnoff, 1957, p. 132.

There must be at least two courses of action that are not equally efficient in bringing about the desired outcome.

Some state of doubt must exist about which action is best.

A problem context must be identified, that is, those environmental factors not under the control of the decision maker that can affect the outcome.

Then there are several factors that can complicate the decision problem, such as the following:

Multiple decision makers.   We will see this problem having considerable importance in the industrial-marketing area.

Competitive reactions to the decision.   This factor leads to models that must incorporate game-theoretic concepts. We will develop some approaches to this problem in Chapters 12, 17, and 18.

Multiple, conflicting objectives.   Multiple and conflicting objectives, such as maximization of profits, market share, and distribution penetration, make specification of a single measure of effectiveness a challenge. These objectives may also change over time. Chapter 3 deals with the issue of objective function evaluation.

Too many alternatives.   The number of alternatives may be unmanageably large or infinite.

To solve a problem, we must make the best choice among the available courses of action. Clearly, we must understand what "best" means. The fields of decision analysis and decision theory provide concepts and methodology (see Keeney and Raiffa, 1976; Raiffa, 1968). The methodology for choosing the best outcomes depends on whether the conditions are those of

Certainty.   When every action is known to lead invariably to a specific outcome.

Risk.   Where each action leads to one of a set of possible actions with probabilities of results known to the decision maker.

Uncertainty.   Where the set of possible outcomes is known, but the likelihood of those outcomes occurring is either unknown or not well defined.

Note that the problem-solving strategy is profoundly dependent on the amount of information known about the problem. In situations of *certainty* it is clear that if the decision maker can determine the value of each outcome, he should simply select that course of action with the maximum outcome.

EXAMPLE: Suppose sales for a particular product is related to advertising, A, as $k \log A$. If the margin for the product is m, then the profit from the advertising spending is

$$\Pi = \underset{\text{gross profit}}{km \log A} - \underset{\text{advertising investment}}{A}$$

Differentiating Π with respect to A, setting the result equal to zero, and solving for A, we get

$$A^* = km$$

which is the optimal level of advertising spending.

In problems arising under *risk* conditions, an optimal decision is one that maximizes the mathematical expectation of value or utility.

Exhibit 2-5 Outcome likelihoods and associated profitabilities for different ad campaigns.

Action	Result Likelihood		
	High Sales	Medium Sales	Low Sales
Campaign C_1	0.3	0.2	0.5
Campaign C_2	0.4	0.0	0.6
Profit	$10 million	$6 million	−$5 million (loss)

EXAMPLE: Suppose that we are considering two advertising campaigns, C_1 and C_2, and our pretest results show that these campaigns can yield high, medium, or low sales with different probabilities, as given in Exhibit 2.5. The last line in the exhibit gives the profitability of the three outcomes. If the decision maker is risk-neutral, the expected monetary value of the results may be an appropriate measure of effectiveness (Raiffa, 1968). Under campaign C_1,

$$E(\Pi \mid C_1) = 0.3(10) + 0.2(6) + 0.5(-5) = \$1.7 \text{ million}$$

where E means expected value. Similarly, under campaign C_2,

$$E(\Pi \mid C_2) = 0.4(10) + 0(5) + 0.6(-5) = \$1.5 \text{ million}$$

Thus the expected profit, or utility condition, suggests the choice of campaign C_1.

In conditions of *uncertainty*, where probabilities are unknown and cannot be estimated, game-theoretic approaches can be used to select strategies.

EXAMPLE: Assume we have a market with two brands, A and B, both of which are developing pricing strategies and can charge either high or low prices. Assume that brand A estimates its profit as shown in Exhibit 2.6. Clearly, if A knows that B will set a high price, A should charge a low price. If A knows that B will set a low price, A should set a high price. Brand A may reason as follows: brand B observes that if it charges a high price, the most A can gain (and B can lose, if this is a zero-sum market) is $2 million; but if B sets a low price, A can gain (and B can lose) as much as $4 million. Therefore A reasons that B will set a high price, so it sets a low price. Repeating this argument

Exhibit 2-6 Brand A's profit matrix (brand B's loss matrix).

A's Pricing Actions	B's Pricing Actions	
	High	Low
High	$1 million	$4 million
Low	$2 million	$3 million

from B's perspective leads to the same conclusion—a saddle point or solution to the game.

This last situation, where outcome likelihoods are not fixed, is the most difficult to deal with even in a game-theoretic manner. Many games do not have saddle points. In addition, this analysis assumes perfect information about the options available, the relative utilities, and the outcomes that will occur following the actions of decision makers. For these reasons game theory has seen limited operational use in marketing. Nevertheless, its concepts are useful in understanding competitive environments. In most practical marketing situations, problems of uncertainty are translated into problems of risk with sample information, subjective-probability judgments from the decision makers, or both.

The Best Solution

How do we know when a solution to a marketing problem is best? This concept is critical in developing a viewpoint of modeling as a way of scientifically approaching and solving applied marketing problems.

Our view is that there is no single best theory or model for a given problem. Rather, several or many models can be employed to describe a situation, depending on both the user (technically skeptical manager versus sophisticated analyst) and the use (long-range planning versus short-range scheduling). What this view means is that the best theory of consumer behavior currently available should not be proposed for a situation where the marketing manager or decision maker cannot understand it and, therefore, will not use it. The best representation of consumer behavior that the manager can understand, accept, and feel comfortable with supports the best model. [See Lilien (1975) for a fuller discussion of this concept.]

EXAMPLE: Consider a salesforce-sizing problem during the introductory stage of a product's life cycle. It might be formulated as an optimal-control or a dynamic-programming problem: How many salespeople should I deploy to support this product in each of n periods in order to maximize profitability? Such a problem can be modeled and solved. But the (likely) period-to-period fluctuations in required salesforce efforts, suggested by the solutions, are likely to antagonize the salesforce manager, and he will find excuses not to use the results.

A better solution is one that is acceptable in the organizational context: perhaps sales effort should be in the form of a guideline for the first 6 mo (during introduction), tapering off to a lower level as the product matures.

This concept has important implications. If no approach, theory, or model is best in an absolute sense, then no model can be transferred from one context (firm) to another without adaptation or customization. Thus the models we review in this book cannot be directly applied to a given outside situation without careful evaluation and (generally) some customization. The understanding of this concept is critical: *models should be as situation-specific as the problems they try to help solve.*

This concept will guide our model-building efforts and will be developed in more detail when we speak of implementation in Chapter 21. It is a principle that is used by good marketing model builders, though in many organizations it seems only to be learned the hard way.

EXAMPLE: To illustrate another dimension of best answers to problems, we assume that we are running an experiment to estimate the profit-maximizing level of advertising spending for Club Cola, and that we model the results and find the optimum. As an extreme example, suppose the model says that for every dollar we underspend from this optimum, we lose $1000 in profit; while for every dollar we overspend, we lose $2. It seems clear that in this situation we should deliberately spend something above the best amount to reduce the expected loss from errors in our data and our estimation procedure. In a pure scientific sense this tack seems to be a compromise; in the sense of applied science it is clearly logical. In other situations the penalties for misestimation may be reversed so that we would bias our response in the other direction.

Thus the solutions that we seek for our marketing problems—and models—are relative, not absolute. They are relative to the problem, the problem solver, the time available for solution, and the organizational and environmental situation. This view suggests that the ultimate measure of the quality of our results comes in the real world that generated the problems and not in the abstract world of pure questions: marketing is an applied discipline.

One last thought on solutions: for a solution to be an improvement, the firm must believe it is feasible. A good exercise is to relax a constraint. While some constraints are real, others simply justify past practices.

EXAMPLE: In a firm we know, advertising was set sometime in the distant past at 2% of sales. Increases or decreases in that budget were thought to lead to competitive reactions that would be harmful to the company. Most analysts took this constraint as given, until one checked to see if anyone had ever tested the assumption. No one ever had, and relatively major changes in the ad-spending level were found to lead to no undesirable competitive response. This folklore about competitive response grew up as support for an otherwise difficult-to-justify, ad-spending rule. After a while, even the managers began to believe the historical justification.

Thus constraint relaxation may lead to feasible solutions that are superior to current operations.

Summary

In this text we see marketing as a form of scientific inquiry, with the model-building process a part of that approach. As such, we have a rich history of thought in solving problems scientifically that is directly applicable to marketing problems.

Science is a process of inquiry rather than a body of knowledge. Marketing is scientific insofar as the problem-solving effort has, along with the objective of solving a particular problem, the goal of improving the procedures employed.

The approaches we are concerned with are of two types: evaluative and developmental. Evaluative approaches choose the best of a given set of courses of action, while developmental approaches involve the search for techniques that yield courses of action better than those otherwise available.

The research process in marketing has five main stages: (1) formulating the problem, (2) constructing the model, (3) deriving a solution, (4) testing the model and evaluating the solution, and (5) implementing and maintaining the solution. These phases, although they may start in the above order, continue throughout the problem-solving process.

Finding and formulating marketing problems is as difficult and creative as modeling and solving those problems. A number of approaches and checklists are provided here, including an evaluation of existing procedures, current characteristics of the decision process, existing flows and uses of information, and so on. Problems manifest themselves as symptoms; a careful diagnosis is required to determine the identity of the disease and the appropriate cure.

Problems in marketing involve (1) a decision maker with (2) a desired outcome, (3) two or more alternative courses of action, (4) doubt about which alternative is best, and (5) an environmental context in which the problem is set. The model-building approach to marketing decision making addresses all these aspects of the problem and attempts to deal with them in concrete terms. The methods for dealing with problems depend on whether the problem is one of certainty, risk, or uncertainty. We argue that most problems in marketing are (or can be transformed into) problems of risk.

To solve problems, we need a concept of a best solution. This concept must be related to the model builder, the decision maker, the time available for problem solution, the information available, and the problem context, as well as other factors. As such, models in marketing should be as situation-specific as the problems they try to help solve.

Most important, problem finding (as well as problem solving) is an art, as well as a skill, and like any art, it entails creativity. Not all approaches will end in success:

Creative solutions are often not accepted. This is not surprising in view of the widespread resistance to change, particularly to something new and unconventional. Because of such resistance, the creative problem solver is not likely to be successful unless he is also competent, communicative, concerned and, most of all, courageous (Ackoff, 1978, pp. 17–18).

We believe the model-building approach will help maximize the likelihood of successfully solving marketing problems.

Problems

2.1 Many marketers consider themselves artists, not analysts. Compare this view with the view of marketing as scientific inquiry. Are these views compatible? Why?

2.2 Give an example of an evaluative problem and a developmental problem in marketing. Discuss the differences.

2.3 A new product manager for the XYZ Company performs a model-based analysis of the market potential for a new laundry detergent. The analysis shows that the product is unlikely to achieve the firm's cutoff of return. He decides to introduce the product anyway. Has the model been implemented? Is it being used?

2.4 Discuss the importance of the first three stages of Urban's process of building models.

2.5 "The process of model implementation is more creative than that of model building." Comment.

2.6 "A model is situation-specific and must be customized to any individual situation." Is this statement true? If so, why should we study models in other situations? Give examples.

2.7 Assume that regional sales for an instant breakfast food have been related to advertising as follows:

$$S = 27 + 2.1A - 0.025A^2$$
where A = advertising dollars, 1000s
        S = sales dollars, 1000s

What is the optimal advertising level? Assuming that current advertising is $15,000, what is the marginal value of increasing advertising spending by $1000? What is the interpretation of the 27 in the above formula?

2.8 An individual has an opportunity to participate in a game for which there is a $10 entry fee each time he plays. In this game he stands to win $50, $20, or $8, with the respective probabilities of 0.3, 0.1, and 0.4, and has a probability of 0.2 of losing $45. If there is no limit to the number of times he can play, should he play the game?

2.9 Is management science a science, a discipline, a profession, a field of study, a methodology, a set of techniques, a philosophy, or a new name for an old thing?

2.10 Models $f(X)$, $g(X)$, and $h(X)$ all fit historical data equally well. What criteria should be used to determine which model is best? Give a specific example.

2.11 What is a model? What is a law? What is a theory? What is a hypothesis? How are these concepts related?

Marketing Model Building: Determining Objectives

As outlined earlier, a marketing problem is characterized by:

one or more decision makers

certain aspects of the problem that the decision maker can control (decision variables)

other aspects of the problem that the decision maker cannot control (exogenous variables)

constraints, imposed from within or without, on the possible values of these variables

possible outcomes of varying value produced by the decision makers' actions and the exogenous variables

For example, suppose a manager of a firm (the decision maker) wishes to allocate an advertising budget (the decision variable) for a given product within certain regional and national restrictions (constraints). He is working in a competitive environment, so the level of competitive response is not under his control. Neither are product prices, new product entries, nor other effects, such as copy wear-out. The outcome he seeks is a profitable level of sales (the objective), produced jointly by his advertising spending, competitive spending, and other environmental effects.

The purpose of this chapter and the following chapters is to operationalize some of these concepts. First, we discuss decision makers and their objectives. Then we develop models, and we describe the relationships between models and data—parameter estimation or model calibration—and finally the derivation of solutions from models.

EXAMPLE: As an illustration of some of the points we will be developing, consider the problem of Forlorn Foods. This company has been manufacturing a single

Exhibit 3-1   **Sales and advertising spending for Forlorn Foods in its four marketing areas.**

Market Area	Last Year's Sales	Proposed Ad Budget
Market A	$ 9.0 million	$450,000
Market B	1.0 million	50,000
Market C	4.0 million	200,000
Market D	4.0 million	200,000
Total	$18.0 million	$900,000

product, Crunchy Crackers (CC), and distributing it in four northeastern United States cities for over 20 yr. Given the nature of the organization, the firm sets advertising spending centrally, allowing regional managers to set promotion, distribution, and selling-effort levels.

Historical Situation: During the past several years, the firm had evolved a two-part spending rule for advertising: (1) spend 5% of last year's sales on advertising, and (2) allocate advertising spending to the four market areas in proportion to sales. Sales for CC were $18 million last year, divided as shown in Exhibit 3.1.

Managerial Problem: Management wanted to examine the historic advertising rule above. In particular:

Was *total* spending too high? Too low? About right?

Was the allocation correct?

Approach: The problem was structured in four steps:

1. setting objectives—finding a measure of effectiveness for the program
2. developing response models—determining a representation of how advertising affects sales
3. calibrating the models—relating those response models to the data and situation of Forlorn Foods
4. evaluating alternatives—determining the cost and effectiveness of various alternative actions

We will return to this problem throughout the next three chapters, showing how a formal approach helps answer the questions Forlorn's company management was raising.

Decision Makers and Objectives

We often assume that the company's objective is to maximize profit. However, not only is this statement vague, but there is no consensus that even if it were properly defined, it would be true. Companies are groups of individuals who may have personal objectives as well as corporate ones. Certainly, their value systems may differ. Furthermore, companies may wish to pursue single or multiple goals. Current profit is an appealing and frequently stated goal and has the additional advantage of providing an easily quantified objective function to guide policy determination. Yet the use of this criterion has been criticized for years (Berle and Means, 1932; Kaplan, Dirlam, and Lanzellotti, 1958; Simon, 1952). Criticisms have centered on its neglect of long-term effects, alternative goals, multiple decision makers, and risk. These criticisms will be addressed below.

We now explore a variety of formal ways in which goals can be stated to provide a clear guide for policy analysis.

Single-goal/Single-decision-maker Formulations

Here, we assume that the company (or, equivalently, the decision maker) is motivated by a single goal. The company accepts no other goals or constraints in governing its conduct, except the observance of legal and ethical rules. The goal it seeks is the maximization of profits, which it applies to all of its decisions.

But "profits" is an ambiguous term. A company can pursue profits in one of four forms: they can be either absolute or relative, and either current or long run. The four distinctions are illustrated in Exhibit 3.2.

Absolute Profits (Short Run)

Current absolute profits (Z) are defined as the difference between the company's sales revenue (R) and the cost (C) of producing and selling the goods and services that constitute these sales; that is,

$$Z = R - C \tag{3.1}$$

The revenue and cost components can be broken down further: sales revenue is the product of price (P) times quantity (Q), or PQ, and costs can be classified into fixed (F), variable [$C(Q)$], and discretionary (X) costs:

$$Z = PQ - F - C(Q) - X \tag{3.2}$$

Operationalizing this equation leads to a number of difficult problems.

First, consider price P. This term should refer to the most likely average price at which the merchandise will be sold in the market and therefore must reflect any discounts to the list price that customers are expected to take. These factors include discounts for early payment, volume discounts, regional pricing variation, and so on. [Webster (1979, chap. 7) discusses such pricing conventions in industrial markets.]

Exhibit 3-2　**Four types of profit objectives.**

	Current	Long run
Absolute	Current absolute profits	Present value
Relative	Current rate of return on investment	Internal rate of return on investment

Next, consider the quantity Q of goods sold. When do sales take place? At the time of order arrival, or at the time of shipment? Orders for large industrial equipment can precede shipment by 6 mo to a year or more. Sales recorded on the basis of orders received may be overstated to the extent that some backlogged orders may be canceled. However, recording sales at time of shipment may also lead to overstatement because of returned merchandise.

Third, fixed costs F raise a key question that has been at the heart of accounting debates for as long as anyone can remember: any product produced by a multiproduct firm can look good or bad depending on the proportion of overhead charged to the production and sale of the product. Theoretically, the product should be charged with its fair share of overhead. In practice, this fair share is hard to determine. Any part of present overhead that would eventually disappear if the product were dropped is properly charged to the product. For example, personnel who spend full time managing the product are clearly chargeable to that product. But how does one deal with the president's salary?

The estimate of fixed costs will affect the absolute level of profit but not necessarily the profit-maximizing course of action. Assume that the firm is considering the price to charge for a product. Price will affect sales, revenues, variable costs, and profit. But we usually assume that, by definition, fixed costs are "fixed" so that a change in a decision variable, such as price, will have no effect on them, that is, $dF/dP = 0$. Therefore these costs do not affect the determination of the profit-maximizing course of action. However, if fixed costs are high enough, absolute profitability may be negative, leading to a decision by the firm to drop the product or to not enter the market (i.e., they serve as a barrier to entry).

Finally, the company must be sure that fixed costs are really fixed throughout the range of policy investigation. A tripling of the advertising budget may be assumed to increase sales of the product by 50 percent. But this increase may be more than can be produced with given facilities, leading to capacity-expansion requirements. More normally, fixed costs are locally fixed—that is, fixed within ranges of demand—and shift to different levels beyond certain thresholds. Exhibit 3.3 illustrates this phenomenon.

The estimation of variable costs $C(Q)$ is the next problem. For accounting purposes most companies establish standard costs for different production operations. These are the costs that enter the books. But these book costs

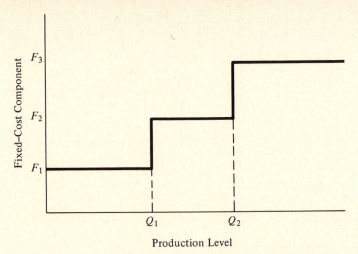

EXHIBIT 3-3   **An illustration of fixed-cost thresholds: production of more than quantity Q_1 requires plant expansion from F_1 to F_2; a second expansion is required past Q_2.**

may not be affected by the scale of operation, although that scale may make a difference in true costs. Unit variable costs are affected not only by the current scale of operations but by cumulative output over time. Experience-curve and learning-curve effects, discussed in Chapter 17, are increasingly becoming critical elements in business strategy, especially for new products and processes.

Finally, even the estimate of discretionary marketing costs X is not without some problems. In principle, each alternative marketing program implies a level of marketing cost. The estimate of marketing cost is subject to some uncertainty: many costs arise that are hard to anticipate, such as the need to change packaging, meet a competitive attack, or support a weakening price structure. Marketing costs must be estimated as accurately as possible, not only because of the effect they will have on total costs but also because of the difference they will make on sales through the level of output, that is, $Q = f(X)$.

Many analysts prefer to estimate the net cash value of each policy alternative rather than current profits, where net cash value is defined as profits after taxes plus accounting depreciation charges. A company is usually concerned about its cash position in the short run and therefore wants to consider the cash flow consequences of different policies. But in the long run, earnings are what matter.

Rate of Return on Investment (Short Run)

Most companies recognize the importance of relating current absolute profits (or cash flow) to the relevant investment base to determine how efficiently they are investing their funds. Obviously, top management cannot learn much from information on the absolute profit in the different divisions because each division has a different amount of resources committed to its operation. The logical basis is to consider the return on investment (popularly called ROI) for each division.

ROI can be looked at usefully as the product of three ratios:

$$\frac{\text{net sales}}{\text{total assets}} \times \frac{\text{net profits}}{\text{net sales}} \times \frac{\text{total assets}}{\text{net worth}} = \frac{\text{net profits}}{\text{net worth}} \qquad (3.3)$$

These ratios suggest three profit paths available to an enterprise: a firm seeking to improve its return on net worth can seek to increase its rate of sales turnover (capital management), its profit margin (margin management), or its financial leverage (financial management). This model dramatizes the need for the firm to interrelate its capital, margin, and financial plans effectively.

Internal Rate of Return on Investment (Long Run)

In most cases in which marketing-policy alternatives are compared, their financial consequences extend into the indefinite future. This result is certainly true for the evaluation of alternative new-product strategies, channel strategies, advertising strategies, and logistics strategies. In these cases management should estimate the earnings (or cash flows) for each year in the future to determine the best course of action. In practice, management only makes the estimate for a 5- or 10-yr period, called the planning horizon. Management is willing to ignore the years beyond the planning horizon because of uncertainty and the low current value of earnings in the future.

But because of the timing of cash flows, estimated earnings streams by themselves are often insufficient to indicate the best alternatives. An appropriate summary measure to use in evaluating alternatives, which accounts for different levels of required investment as well as for the time value of money, is the *internal rate of return* on investment, r.

Consider a marketing opportunity that requires an investment of I dollars today and that is expected to yield a sequence of annual earnings over the next n years of $Z_1, Z_2, \ldots, Z_n$. The internal rate of return on this investment is found by solving for r in the following formula:

$$I = \frac{Z_1}{1 + r} + \frac{Z_2}{(1 + r)^2} + \cdots + \frac{Z_n}{(1 + r)^n} \qquad (3.4)$$

The logic of this formula is as follows: Z_1 earnings will be received at the end of the first year (this condition is assumed for simplicity). Since the firm will not receive this amount for a year, its *present value*, V_0, is less than its dollar value Z_1. In fact, if the firm is able to earn r percent on its investments, then it would be indifferent between receiving a sum V_0 now and Z_1 a year from now; that is,

$$V_0(1 + r) = Z_1 \qquad (3.5)$$

or

$$V_0 = \frac{Z_1}{(1 + r)} \qquad (3.6)$$

Similarly, the firm would be indifferent between a sum V_0, which will earn r for 2 yr, and a sum Z_2, which it will receive 2 yr from now; that is,

$$V_0(1 + r)(1 + r) = Z_2 \qquad (3.7)$$

or

$$V_0 = \frac{Z_2}{(1 + r)^2} \qquad (3.8)$$

Continuing the same logic, we see that the rate-of-return formula (3.4) simply converts future sums into their present value equivalent by discounting them at the rate at which the firm is able to invest its money.

In fact, careful examination of eq. (3.4) and the substitution of x for $1/(1 + r)$ yields a real algebraic equation:

$$Z_n x^n + \cdots + Z_2 x^2 + Z_1 x - I = 0 \qquad (3.9)$$

By Descartes' rule of signs the number of real roots of eq. (3.9) is either equal to the number of sign changes in the coefficients $(I, Z_1, \ldots, Z_n)$ or is less than this number by a positive even integer. Thus if all Z's are positive, x (and hence r) can be determined uniquely. This determination is usually done by a numerical search procedure that can easily be performed by computer. If some of the Z's are negative (e.g., if a further investment in production equipment is required in year 2, making Z_2 negative), then more than one value of r may solve eq. (3.9)! (For further discussion of how to interpret and handle such a situation, see any advanced text on financial management.)

Let us assume that all policies we wish to evaluate have unique values of r. Then these policies can be ranked. The policy alternative ranking highest is presumably the most desirable course of action, provided that its internal rate of return exceeds the company's target rate of return. If the company's target rate of return is 20 percent, and the best policy alternative promises only a 15 percent rate of return, the company will presumably want to search for better alternatives.

The internal-rate-of-return criterion is not without some conceptual difficulties. For example, the best policy alternative might be estimated to yield 35 percent but involves only a small investment, whereas the next policy alternative might yield 25 percent on a much larger investment. Before choosing the first alternative, management has to consider what it can earn on the next-best opportunity with the remaining investment money. Another complication arises when different policy alternatives involve earning streams of different longevities. In a comparison of their merits some assumption must be made about the likely rate at which money can be reinvested at the time the shorter projects expire.

Present Value: Discounted Cash Flow (Long Run)

Difficulties with the internal-rate-of-return formula have led many to prefer a *present value* measure for appraising alternative courses of action. This criterion does not involve any change in the estimation of future annual earnings. The only difference is that the company assumes a discount rate d and solves for present value PV in the following formula:

$$PV = \frac{Z_1}{1 + d} + \frac{Z_2}{(1 + d)^2} + \cdots + \frac{Z_n}{(1 + d)^n} \tag{3.10}$$

Thus present value is the present worth of an annuity of n future annual payments, where future dollars are discounted at rate d.

In evaluating a particular opportunity, the company estimates its future earnings stream, discounts it at rate d, and compares the resulting present value (PV) with the present dollar investment (I) required to take advantage of the opportunity. If $PV > I$, the estimated earnings stream will more than return the rate of return assumed in d. The theory is that the firm should invest in all opportunities that have a positive excess present value, assuming that it can borrow all the funds it needs at a cost of no more than d percent.

Current thinking is mixed about the selection of an appropriate discount rate d. One school holds that d should represent the firm's cost of capital. Another school feels that the company should discount the future earnings stream at the rate of return it seeks to earn as a company.

Thus the present value approach has its problems. However, this method and the rate-of-return approach are often quite consistent in the ranking they suggest for policy alternatives.

Incorporating Risk: Assessing Utility Functions

The approaches detailed above assume that the resulting profit streams are known with certainty. But this is seldom the case. A firm may have a choice of investing in a project that will lose $50,000 if it fails and make $70,000 if it succeeds, with equal likelihood, and of investing in an alternative that is almost certain to return $10,000 on the same investment. These alternatives both return $10,000 on average (i.e., have an expected return of $10,000), but the first is riskier (has higher variance) than the other. The development of methodology to assess utility functions, allowing decision alternatives with

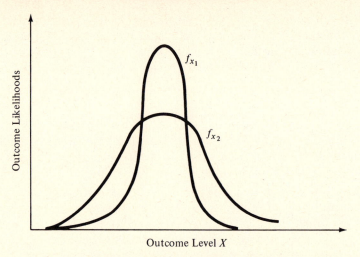

EXHIBIT 3-4   **Action 1 leads to a distribution of outcome f_{x_1} that is less risky (has lower variance) than action 2 with a distribution of outcome f_{x_2}.**

varying risk to be compared, has been one of the most important operational advances of the last decade.

The literature has not yet agreed on consistent terminology. Nevertheless, it is useful to distinguish between a value (ordinal utility) function and a utility (cardinal utility) function. A value function is a real-valued function $V(\cdot)$ such that, when the outcomes of two alternative actions X_1 and X_2 are known with certainty, $V(X_1) > V(X_2)$ if consequence X_1 is preferred to X_2. Adding a constant to a value function or multiplying it by a positive constant, b, will not affect the relationship. That is, if

$$V(X_1) > V(X_2) \tag{3.11}$$

then

$$a + bV(X_1) > a + bV(X_2) \tag{3.12}$$

Suppose now that X_1 and X_2 are not known with certainty but, rather, have some probability distributions $f_{x_1}(X_1)$ and $f_{x_2}(X_2)$, as shown in Exhibit 3.4. Then X_1 is preferred to X_2 if and only if $E_1[u(X_1)] > E_2[u(X_2)]$, where E_1 and E_2 are the expected values of the utility functions $u(X_1)$ and $u(X_2)$, respectively. For example, if f_{x_1} is characterized by discrete possible outcomes $X_{11}, \ldots, X_{1n}$ with probabilities $p_{11}, \ldots, p_{1n}$, and f_{x_2} is characterized similarly by $X_{21}, \ldots, X_{2m}$ with probabilities $p_{21}, \ldots, p_{2m}$, then f_{x_1} is preferred to f_{x_2} if

$$\sum_{i=1}^{n} u(x_{1i})p_{1i} > \sum_{j=1}^{m} u(x_{2j})p_{2j} \tag{3.13}$$

As with the value function (which is a special type of utility function), adding a constant or multiplying by a positive constant will still yield a utility function. That is, if

$$u(X_1) > u(X_2) \qquad (3.14)$$

then

$$a + bu(X_1) > a + bu(X_2) \qquad (3.15)$$

Now let us assess a decision maker's utility function for profits from an investment, which has two possible outcomes, $0 and $1,000,000. By the statement above [i.e., a and b are arbitrary in eq. (3.15)], we can set $u(1,000,000) = 100$ and $u(0) = 0$. To aid in determining the function u, we introduce the concept of a lottery, denoted by

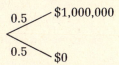

which represents a 0.5 chance of receiving $1,000,000 and a 0.5 chance of receiving nothing. Then the first question to the decision maker is how much he would be willing to sell this lottery for. This amount is called the *certainty monetary equivalent* (CME) of the lottery. Suppose he said $400,000. That means he is indifferent between $400,000 and a 50–50 chance of getting $1,000,000. Mathematically,

$$u(400,000) = 0.5u(0) + 0.5u(1,000,000) = 50 \qquad (3.16)$$

which represents one point in his utility function. To assess other points, we ask the decision maker what his CME is for

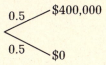

Suppose it is $180,000. Then

$$u(180,000) = 0.5u(0) + 0.5u(400,000) = 25 \qquad (3.17)$$

Similarly, we ask him what his CME is for

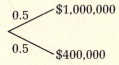

If the answer is 650,000, then

$$u(650,000) = 0.5u(1,000,000) + 0.5u(400,000) = 75 \qquad (3.18)$$

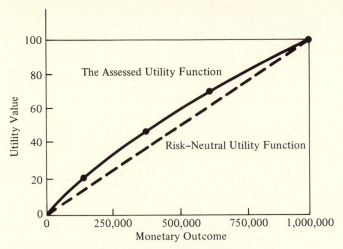

EXHIBIT 3-5   The assessed utility function.

Our initial conditions plus eqs. (3.16)–(3.18) give us the utility function plotted in Exhibit 3.5.

One can always proceed with the above steps. However, it is useful to get an idea of the shape of the utility curve. A simple characteristic that many utility curves have is monotonicity: that is, $u(X_i) > u(X_j)$ if $X_i > X_j$. This condition should hold for most profit-related measures. (But what if profit beyond a certain level would be likely to trigger FTC action? How might that affect the firm's utility function?)

A second prevalent characteristic of utility functions is risk aversion. If the decision maker always prefers taking the monetary equivalent of the average payoff of a lottery to the lottery, he is said to be *risk-averse*. That is, he prefers a certain payment of $(X_1 + X_2)/2$ to any lottery of the form

$$
\begin{array}{c}
0.5 \diagup X_1 \\
\diagdown \\
0.5 \diagdown X_2
\end{array}
$$

Much of financial theory—and, indeed, the capital-asset pricing model—is based on the concept of empirically observed risk aversion. [See Brigham (1980, chap. 5) or any comparable text on financial management.]

Knowing that someone is risk-averse and that the utility function is monotonic restricts its shape considerably. If a person is risk-averse, his utility function must be concave: a line segment connecting any two points on the utility curve lies below the curve, or $u[(X_1 + X_2)/2] > \frac{1}{2}u(X_1) + \frac{1}{2}u(X_2)$. He is *risk-neutral* if $u[(X_1 + X_2)/2] = \frac{1}{2}u(X_1) + \frac{1}{2}u(X_2)$ for all X_1 and X_2, and he is *risk-prone* if $u[(X_1 + X_2)/2] < \frac{1}{2}u(X_1) + \frac{1}{2}u(X_2)$.

Finally, suppose that the decision maker were *constantly risk-averse*. This concept is defined as follows. Consider a 50–50 lottery with a $100 difference:

$$
\begin{array}{l}
0.5 \quad \$200 \\
0.5 \quad \$100
\end{array}
$$

Suppose our decision maker's CME for this lottery is $140. Then because the average payout of this lottery is $150, the decision maker's *risk premium* is $10. If he has a risk premium of $10 for every 50–50 lottery where there is $100 difference in potential outcomes, then he is *constantly risk-averse*. Under these circumstances Pratt (1964) has shown that the form of the utility function is restricted to

$$u(X) = k_1 + k_2 e^{-cx} \tag{3.19}$$

Since k_1 and k_2 are arbitrary, knowledge of the risk premium is sufficient to establish an equation that can be solved for c in eq. (3.19); specifically,

$$u(\$40) = \tfrac{1}{2}u(\$0) + \tfrac{1}{2}u(\$100) \tag{3.20}$$

Note that the risk or uncertainty associated with certain courses of action has been explicitly included in the assessment of these utility functions.

EXAMPLE: Suppose advertising program A_1 produces $100,000 profits with certainty, while program A_2 produces a 50% chance of $150,000 profits and a 50% chance of $75,000 profits. Which should the decision maker choose? He should choose the one with the highest expected utility.

$$u(A_1) = u(\$100,000) \tag{3.21}$$

$$E[u(A_2)] = 0.5u(\$150,000) + 0.5u(\$75,000) \tag{3.22}$$

Choose A_1 if $u(A_1) > E[u(A_2)]$. (The utilities for these outcomes can be calculated through the lottery method described above.)

EXAMPLE: This concept easily extends to a continuous set of outcomes. Suppose that A_3 yielded an estimated mean profit return of $100(000), with a standard deviation of 30. Assume that the distribution of the return can be approximated with a normal distribution.

$$E[u(A_3)] = \int_{-\infty}^{\infty} \frac{u(x)e^{(x-100)^2/1800}}{30\sqrt{2\pi}} \, dx \tag{3.23}$$

In this way the risky nature of outcomes is explicitly included in the utility assessment.

In practice, questions can be restated and asked again of decision makers to help catch any errors in assessing their utility functions. A commonly used check involves asking the decision maker his preference between any lottery and any consequence or between any pair of lotteries. For consistency the expected utility of the preferred solution must be greater than that of the other. Keeney and Raiffa (1976) discuss consistency checking in more detail, both for single-attribute and for multiple-attribute utility functions.

Multiple-goal Formulations: Single Decision Maker

Although profit is an overriding goal of some firms, it is not the only factor that an organization considers when trying to decide among alternative plans of action. An organization is a complex hierarchical social system pursuing a variety of organizational and personal goals.

Generally, the announced or published objectives of the company are of little operational help in choosing among alternative plans. Firms frequently state their objectives in such broad terms that it is difficult to know what they have in mind, other than to sound virtuous. Even if specific objectives are mentioned, there is often no indication of their relative importance. Furthermore, there is typically no recognition that the stated objectives are in competition—that one can be pursued only at the expense of another.

Consider the following sample of statements that businessmen make:

"We want to maximize our sales and our profits."

"We want to achieve the greatest sales at the least cost."

"We want to keep down inventory costs and maximize sales."

"We want to design the best possible product in the shortest time."

All of these statements involve attractive rhetoric but faulty logic. Consider the first objective, joint maximization of sales and profits. To show the difficulty of developing a marketing strategy that will simultaneously maximize both objectives, we let eqs. (3.24)–(3.26) be demand, cost, and profit equations, respectively.

$$Q = 1000 - 4P \tag{3.24}$$

$$C = 6000 + 50Q \tag{3.25}$$

$$Z = PQ - C \tag{3.26}$$

Then to find the profit-maximizing price, we substitute eqs. (3.24) and (3.25) into (3.26):

$$Z = -56,000 + 1200P - 4P^2 \tag{3.27}$$

Elementary calculus shows the profit-maximizing price to be $150. Now suppose that the company also wants to maximize sales revenue PQ. The sales revenue equation is

$$PQ = 1000P - 4P^2 \qquad (3.28)$$

Differentiating the sales revenue function with respect to price, we find that the sales-revenue-maximizing price is $125. Thus the same price does not simultaneously maximize profits and sales revenue.

This development leads us to formally state the problem of multiple goals. If we have a set of n objectives, $Z_1, Z_2, \ldots, Z_n$, all of which cannot be simultaneously maximized by any one conceivable plan, how can the goals be operationalized in such a way as to provide an unambiguous ranking of alternative plans?

There are several approaches to this problem. One is to assign all but one of the objectives to constraints, so that management *optimizes* one criterion (a profit measure) while *satisficing* on others (e.g., a market-share restriction might be that share must not drop below 12 percent). Another approach is the goal-programming approach, where targets for each objective are set and a loss function (the differences between the target and actual performance, summed over objectives) is minimized.

We sketch below a consistent approach to the multicriteria problem relying on multiattribute utility theory. As with the single-attribute development, the approach incorporates risk naturally. [See Fishburn (1977) or Keeney and Raiffa (1976) for more thorough developments.]

Utility Assessments for Two Objectives

A logical first step in evaluating a multiple-objective function with a utility-based approach is to assess utility functions for each of the individual objectives. The procedure developed earlier is useful for this step. In this subsection we deal with two objectives only and sketch extensions to more than two.

To proceed (in fact, to determine if assessing a single-attribute utility function is a well-defined operation), we need the concept of utility independence. Assume we have two objectives: (1) to maximize Y, a market-share measure, and (2) to maximize Z, a measure of profitability. Let us further assume that we wish to explore Y and Z at values (y, z) in the following ranges:

$$10\% \le y \le 40\% \qquad \text{and} \qquad \$1 \text{ million} \le z \le \$5 \text{ million} \qquad (3.29)$$

Thus there are upper and lower bounds on the values of the utility function $u(y, z)$ that we wish to assess.

Now we can begin asking lottery questions of the following sort. "If your profit is fixed at $25 million throughout, what is your certainty equivalent for a 50–50 gamble yielding market shares of 20 percent and 30 percent?" Suppose the answer is 24 percent, so that the decision maker is indifferent between

$$
(24\%, \$25 \text{ million}) \quad \text{and} \quad
\begin{cases}
0.5 \longrightarrow 30\%, \$25 \text{ million} \\
0.5 \longrightarrow 20\%, \$25 \text{ million}
\end{cases}
$$

Next we ask the same question with profit fixed at, say, $30 million. Would the certainty equivalent value for market share shift from 24 percent? According to Keeney and Raiffa (1976, p. 226), "in a surprisingly large number of contexts, it does not shift." We formalize this statement in the following definition:

DEFINITION: Y is utility-independent of Z when conditional preferences for lotteries on Y, given any value of Z, do not depend on the particular level of Z.

This definition implies that

$$u(y, z) = g(z) + h(z)u(y) \tag{3.30}$$

Note that Y can be utility-independent of Z and *not vice versa*. All cases are possible: neither holds, one holds without the other, or both hold.

Two conditions that simplify our search for utility-function forms are utility independence and additive independence.

Utility Independence   If Y and Z are mutually utility independent, then $u(y, z)$ can be represented by the multilinear form

$$u(y, z) = k_1 u_Y(y) + k_2 u_Z(z) + k_3 u_Y(y)u_Z(z) \tag{3.31}$$

The coefficient k_3 in eq. (3.31) measures the interrelationship between the objectives. For $k_3 > 0$ the objectives complement each other; for $k_3 < 0$ the objectives are substitutes. When $k_3 = 0$, we have the special case of an additive utility function.

Additive Independence   If Y and Z are mutually utility-independent and if there are some values of Y and Z such that the decision maker is indifferent to the two lotteries

$$
\begin{cases}
0.5 \longrightarrow (y_1, z_1) \\
0.5 \longrightarrow (y_2, z_2)
\end{cases}
\quad \text{and} \quad
\begin{cases}
0.5 \longrightarrow (y_1, z_2) \\
0.5 \longrightarrow (y_2, z_1)
\end{cases}
$$

and where $u(y_1, z_1)$ is not equal to either $u(y_1, z_2)$ or $u(y_2, z_1)$, then

$$u(y, z) = k_1 u_Y(y) + k_2 u_Z(z) \tag{3.32}$$

The conditions and procedures for more than two objectives are generalizations of what is presented above. The process of checking for types of independence, specifying the form, and assessing utility functions is a relatively straightforward process after some practice. If utility independence does not hold, Keeney and Raiffa (1976) suggest some transformations and approximations that can be used. Alternatively, the joint utility function can be assessed over a sample of points in the space of alternatives and a curve-fitting technique can be used to approximate it.

As an illustration of the procedure, we offer the following example.

EXAMPLE: The first step in addressing the advertising-budget problem faced by Forlorn Foods, introduced earlier, is the assessment of its objectives. As a first pass, John Stubbs, Forlorn's CEO, has said that he would consider only short-run results and that he wanted to maximize both market share and profits. The regions of most interest for his objectives, share (y) and profit (z), are

$$10\% \leq y \leq 40\% \qquad \text{and} \qquad \$1 \text{ million} \leq z \leq \$5 \text{ million}$$

Step 1: Checking for additive independence. Y and Z are additive-independent if and only if all lotteries of the form

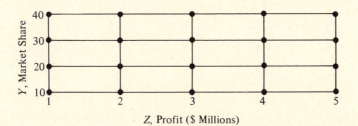

are of equal value (utility) to Stubbs. To determine this condition, we divide both Y and Z into four equal subsegments and check all pairs in the grid shown in Exhibit 3.6, starting with (10%, $1 million) and (10%, $2 million), then going to (10%, $1 million) and (10%, $3 million), and so on. In practice, a small sampling of these pairs of points will usually suffice to suggest (or reject) the existence of additive independence. Suppose Stubbs' preferences are *not* additive-independent; then we proceed to step 2. If they are additive-independent, we go directly to step 4.

Step 2: Check for utility independence. We choose a value of market share, say 25%, and find out what value of certain profit makes Stubbs

EXHIBIT 3-6 **A graphical aid for assessing additive-independence conditions—finding *Y-Z* pairs.**

indifferent between this share and

$$
\begin{array}{c}
0.5 \quad (25\%, \$5 \text{ million}) \\
\diagdown \\
0.5 \quad (25\%, \$1 \text{ million})
\end{array}
$$

Let us assume it is $2.4 million. We repeat the above operation for three or four values of market share. If Stubbs stays with his certainty equivalent of $2.4 million at each step, we conclude that profit is utility-independent of market share. We then reverse the operation to see if market share is utility-independent of profit. If it is (we assume here that it is), we conclude that the multilinear form of the utility function is the proper form and proceed to step 4. Otherwise, we must go to step 3.

Step 3:   Investigate alternative procedures. The simple additive and multilinear forms have failed. The analyst realistically has two options at this point:

1. Proceed with more-general utility functions and more-complex assessment procedures.
2. Use a simpler model, recognizing the limitations.

Keeney and Raiffa (1976) develop procedures for option 1 in detail. However, they conclude, "For many problems, the simpler models are likely good enough approximations even if they are not precisely valid" (p. 261).

Step 4:   Assess the utility function. If we had reached step 4 via step 1, we would have had an additive utility function. However, we reached this step via step 3, and therefore Stubbs has a utility function with a multilinear form:

$$u(y, z) = k_1 u_Y(y) + k_2 u_Z(z) + k_3 u_Y(y)u_Z(z) \tag{3.33}$$

To fully specify u, we must know u_Y, u_Z, k_1, k_2, and k_3. By utility independence, we can assess u_Y without regard to u_Z and vice versa. Thus we can assess u_Y and u_Z with the lottery methods given in the previous section.

Assuming u_Y and u_Z are known, we now must assess k_1, k_2, and k_3. Without loss of generality we can scale the utility functions between zero and one:

$$u(10\%, \$1 \text{ million}) = 0 \quad u_Y(10\%) = 0 \quad u_Z(\$1 \text{ million}) = 0$$

and $\hspace{10cm}$ (3.34)

$$u(40\%, \$5 \text{ million}) = 1 \quad u_Y(40\%) = 1 \quad u_Z(\$5 \text{ million}) = 1$$

With eqs. (3.33) and (3.34), we now have one equation among the k's.

$$u(40\%, \$5 \text{ million}) = k_1 u_Y(40\%) + k_2 u_Z(\$5 \text{ million})$$
$$+ k_3 u_Y(40\%)u_Z(\$5 \text{ million}) \tag{3.35}$$

or

$$1 = k_1 + k_2 + k_3 \qquad (3.36)$$

Now if we evaluate eq. (3.35) at (10%, $5 million), with eq. (3.34) we obtain

$$u(10\%, \$5 \text{ million}) = k_2 \qquad (3.37)$$

Similarly, we get

$$u(40\%, \$1 \text{ million}) = k_1 \qquad (3.38)$$

Now we ask Stubbs which he prefers, (10%, $5 million) or (40%, $1 million). He chooses the former, so $k_2 > k_1$.

Next, we ask what level of profit z* will make him indifferent between (10%, z*) and (40%, $1 million). If that level is $3.8 million, we have established that

$$u(10\%, \$3.8 \text{ million}) = u(40\%, \$1 \text{ million}) \qquad (3.39)$$

or by eqs. (3.33) and (3.38) that

$$k_1 = k_2 u_Z(\$3.8 \text{ million}) \qquad (3.40)$$

We now have two equations for k_1, k_2, and k_3, eqs. (3.36) and (3.40). To obtain one more, we now ask what level of profit z′ will make Stubbs indifferent between (10%, $5 million) and (40%, z′).

Let us suppose that that value is $1.8 million. Then we know that

$$u(10\%, \$5 \text{ million}) = u(40\%, \$1.8 \text{ million}) \qquad (3.41)$$

or

$$k_2 = k_1 + k_2 u_Z(\$1.8 \text{ million}) + k_3 u_Z(\$1.8 \text{ million}) \qquad (3.42)$$

Finally, in the range of values considered here, we have found that Forlorn Foods is approximately risk-neutral. Thus $u_Z = \frac{1}{4}(z - 1)$ and $u_y = \frac{1}{30}(y - 10)$. These conditions imply that $u_Z(1.8) = 0.2$ and $u_Z(3.8) = 0.7$. Thus we have the following set of three equations with three unknowns:

$$k_1 + k_2 + k_3 = 1$$
$$k_1 = 0.7k_2$$
$$k_2 = k_1 + 0.2k_2 + 0.2k_3 \qquad (3.43)$$

which can be solved to yield

$$k_1 = 0.318 \qquad k_2 = 0.455 \qquad k_3 = 0.227$$

And, finally, we get

$$u(y, z) = \frac{0.318}{4}(z - 1) + \frac{0.455}{30}(y - 10) + \frac{0.227}{4 \cdot 30}(z - 1)(y - 10) \qquad (3.44)$$

$$= 0.0606z + 0.0133y + 0.00189yz - 0.2125$$

Step 5:   Check results. As a fifth step we checked a number of other values for consistency. For example, plugging in any two pairs of market-share and profit numbers in eq. (3.44) will give different utility values. We could then ask the decision maker which he prefers and compare it with the results we have obtained from eq. (3.44) directly. For examples of utility assessment procedures, see Keeney and Raiffa (1976) and Keeney (1981). Hauser and Urban (1979) and Eliashberg (1980) discuss and illustrate the application of utility theory to consumer-preference measurement.

More Than Two Objectives

The direct assessment of utility functions, even for two attributes, begins to get tricky. For three or more objectives the tasks involved in verifying utility independence, evaluating scaling constants, and scaling conditional utility functions are somewhat burdensome. However, we are beginning to see the emergence of computer packages to aid in empirical assessment of multiattribute utility functions. One of these, called MUFCAP [see Sicherman (1975) for details], helps by producing a series of computer-generated commands that structure the utility function, specify the single-attribute utility function, and specify scaling constants. The program also allows users to evaluate alternatives at the terminal and to perform sensitivity analysis simply. Utility assessment is a matter of skill and experience and will become more widely used with superior training. Schoemaker and Waid (1982) review the strengths and limitations of alternative methods for calibrating utility functions.

Multiple Decision Makers

Rarely is a single indivdual solely responsible for specifying the objectives of an organization. Rather, the setting of organizational goals and objectives is a group decision, involving several individuals.

Theoretically, a group should be considered an entity with its own utility function. Hence, in a manner similar to the above procedures, the group should select a course of action that maximizes its expected utility function. In other words, it should choose alternative a_j from set $\{a_1, \ldots a_n\}$ that maximizes

$$E_j[u_G(c)] = \sum_{i=1}^{m} u_G(c_i)p_j(c_i) \qquad (3.45)$$

where $c = (c_1, \ldots, c_m) = $ possible consequences

$p_j(c) = $ likelihood of consequence c occurring following action (alternative) a_j

$u_G = $ group utility function

This issue—that of assessing social-welfare functions—has been investigated by numerous researchers. Most of the work has concerned ordinal social-welfare (value) functions. Arrow (1963) proved that, in general, there is no procedure for obtaining a group ordering of alternatives consistent with five reasonable assumptions. This result has been used to conclude that knowledge about group structures (hierarchy, dictatorship, power levels, communication patterns, etc.) is required for a group-welfare function.

For cardinal utilities the group's decision problem is concerned with both the existence and the specification of $u_G = u_G(u_1, \ldots, u_n)$ where $u_1, \ldots, u_n$ represent the individual utility functions of the group members.

Harsanyi (1955) developed conditions for a group utility function to be a weighted average of individual group members' utility functions:

$$u_G = \sum_i \lambda_i u_i \qquad (3.46)$$

The key condition is that if each individual within a group is indifferent to two alternatives (with associated probability distributions), the group as a whole must also be indifferent to them.

Keeney and Kirkwood (1975) develop a more general form, which follows from relaxing Harsanyi's conditions somewhat. They present two conditions which say, in essence, that if only one or two people in the group care about what happens (are not indifferent between alternatives), then they should decide what to do. These conditions imply a group utility function of the form

$$u_G = \sum_{i=1}^{n} \lambda_i u_i + \sum_{\substack{i=1 \\ j>i}}^{n} \lambda_{ij} u_i u_j + \cdots + \lambda_{12\ldots n} u_1 \cdots u_n \qquad (3.47)$$

Note that for two individuals eq. (3.47) reduces to

$$u_G = \lambda_1 u_1 + \lambda_2 u_2 + \lambda_3 u_1 u_2 \qquad (3.48)$$

This form is the multilinear form introduced in eq. (3.31); Keeney and Kirkwood (1975) replace "attributes" with "decision-participants" and specify conditions that are equivalent to utility independence.

Their assumptions seem quite reasonable. However, the estimation of the parameters $\{\lambda_i\}$ requires a group decision that may not easily be resolved. In addition, there may be disagreement among group members about the likelihood of varying consequences occurring (the subjective probabilities).

Thus under certain sets of assumptions, objectives can be developed for groups of decision makers as well. Computer programs for aiding in the group-utility-assessment problem are available (e.g., Leal et al., 1978). However, there are clearly more practical (as well as theoretical) difficulties in dealing with groups than with individuals: ". . . there is no such thing as the group decision problem. We should talk in the plural about group decision problems" (Keeney and Raiffa, 1976, p. 515). This area is an exciting one that will be of increasing practical importance in marketing in the years to come.

Summary

When we look closely at company goals, we see that enterprises define their objectives in a variety of ways that defy simple formulation. The central issue is whether the analysis of optimal marketing policy should be based on maximizing a single goal or some function of several goals. If a single-goal formulation is to be used, there are at least four choices. One is to treat current profits as the objective function. As a variant of this, current cash value rather than current profit might be used; the current cash value includes depreciation and excludes taxes. A second choice is to maximize ROI, the ratio of current profit to investment or net worth. A third choice is to measure the internal rate of return of the proposed marketing plan, where the internal rate of return is the interest rate that reconciles the anticipated earnings stream and the current required investment. This choice is closely related to the fourth choice, present value, which is found by discounting the anticipated earnings stream by either the company's cost of capital or its desired rate of return.

For the incorporation of risk and multiple goals, the most promising operational approach involves the direct assessment of single-objective and multiple-objective utility functions. Theory and operational procedures have been developed in the past few years to specify a functional form for utility and to estimate its parameters. Utility-function assessment is being made easier by the development of interactive computer programs.

Finally, extensions of the operational utility-theory concept to a group of decision makers is an important current topic of study. Use of single-individual and multiple-individual utility-theory procedures should see much more use in the next few years.

It is important to note that the determination of objectives, frequently overlooked in the model-building process, is an important and vital step, and that methodology is available to make evaluation of objectives explicit.

Problems

3.1 "Making profits is not the prime purpose of this company," the chairman of the Board of Directors of Maicel Company stated at a party. Does that mean that his objectives are counter to the objectives of the shareholders?

3.2 You are chairman of a new-product committee facing a decision with respect to a new product that has just been test marketed by your company. Each of the 10 company executives who has been closely involved in the product's development is asked to make an independent forecast of the product's most likely rate of return. The results, in percents, are 10, 12, 12, 12, 15, 15, 15, 18, 18, 20. The company generally invests in products where the estimated rate of return exceeds 14 percent. Considering the estimates above, determine the character of the distribution of the estimates, and indicate whether you would invest in the product.

3.3 "Government policymakers are satisficers, not optimizers."
  a. Explain the terms "satisficer" and "optimizer" in this context.
  b. Do you agree? Why or why not?

3.4 Suppose a decision maker has the choice between lottery 1 and lottery 2:

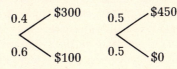

He has utilities for dollars given as follows:

Dollars	0	100	180	225	300	450
Utility	10	18	23	25	26	30

  a. Which lottery should he choose? Why?
  b. Is he risk-prone? Risk-averse? Risk-neutral?
  c. He has a chance to exchange $100 for a 60% chance of $180 (40% chance of losing all money). Should he do it? Why or why not?

3.5 Suppose the XYZ Company's utility function for dollars, denoted by x, is

$$u_0(x) = -e^{-0.002x}$$

  a. Should the company accept an investment with the following risk profile?

  b. For $0 \le x \le 1000$, consider lotteries of the form

where $g(x)$ is then the maximum, one would be willing to risk a $\frac{1}{2}$ chance of losing in order to have a $\frac{1}{2}$ chance to win x. Plot $g(x)$ for the company in the range of $0 \le x \le 1000$.

3.6 A company executive is asked, "If you have a 50–50 chance of making either $400,000 or nothing, what is the least amount of money for which you would sell this chance?" The executive's answer is $200,000. He is then asked, "If you have a 50–50 chance of making $200,000 or nothing, how much money would you accept for this chance?" He answers $100,000. Finally, he is asked, "If you have a 50–50 chance of losing $100,000 or nothing, how much would you pay to be rid of the gamble?" His answer is $50,000. Suppose the utility of the upper dollar-reference amount $u(Z)$ is set at 160, and the utility of the lower dollar-reference amount $u(Z_L)$ is set at -40. It is assumed that $u(0) = 0$.

a.   Determine the executive's utility for $200,000, $100,000, and $-$50,000.

b.   Determine the equation that represents the executive's utility curve for money.

c.   Using the equation from part b, determine the executive's utility for $150,000, $-$75,000, and $50,000.

d.   How reliable do you think this interviewing method is in obtaining an accurate utility curve?

3.7   Mr. Jones, president of a small business, is considering various marketing opportunities that may result in anything from a $5000 loss to a $5000 profit. To assist with a decision analysis of these opportunities, we want to obtain Mr. Jones' utility function for changes in profits, over the range specified. In questioning Mr. Jones about his basic preferences, he stated that "obviously, more money is preferred to less" and "I would always prefer to sell a lottery involving uncertainties for its expected payoff than to hold the lottery until the actual payoff occurs." Furthermore, Mr. Jones says he is indifferent between losing $800 and owning the lottery shown in Figure 1.

a.   Is Mr. Jones risk-averse?

b.   Illustrate how this information restricts Mr. Jones' utility function.

c.   What is the possible range of probability p that Mr. Jones is indifferent between $0 and the lottery shown in Figure 2?

d.   What is the possible range for the certainty equivalent of the lottery shown in Figure 3?

e.   Suppose that originally Mr. Jones could not be precise about the certainty equivalent of the lottery shown in Figure 1. But he was sure that it was between $-$1000 and $-$500, meaning a $500 loss is preferred to the lottery, which, in turn, is preferred to a $1000 loss. Illustrate how this information restricts Mr. Jones' utility function.

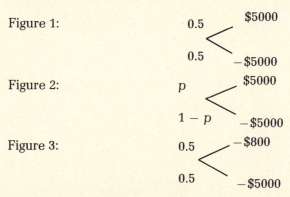

Figure 1:

0.5 $5000

0.5 $-$5000

Figure 2:

p $5000

$1 - p$ $-$5000

Figure 3:

0.5 $-$800

0.5 $-$5000

3.8   Assess a friend's utility function for salary and job satisfaction. Assume a job-satisfaction scale of 1 to 10, where

10 = ideal job

7 = good, acceptable, interesting job

5 = average job, of modest interest

3 = boring job

1 = unbearable job

Specify a range of possible salary levels, say $20,000 to $75,000 (which should cover possibilities for most of you).

a. Test to determine if these objectives are additive-independent.

b. Test for utility independence.

c. Assume utility independence. Assess the marginal utility function for salary and for job satisfaction, as well as the joint utility function. Include the following:

a fully labeled graph of the marginal utility functions

a list of the qualitative aspects, such as risk aversion, that this utility function possesses

the qualitative information (CMEs, certainty satisfaction equivalent) you used in the assessment process

the consistency checks you included

your appraisal of the assessment process

d. Interpret the utility function. Does your assessor value job satisfaction or salary more? How would your assessor rank the following job offers?

Offer	Salary	Satisfaction
1	$75,000	1
2	$50,000	3
3	$35,000	7
4	$30,000	9
5	$25,000	10

3.9 In many new-product screening procedures, individuals must do the following:

a. evaluate a product on a set of scales (x_{ij} = rating of product i on scale j).

b. weight the ratings by the importance of the scale (w_j) to yield

$$\text{Score } i = \sum_j x_{ij} w_j$$

What does this procedure assume about the evaluators' utility function for the scales (attributes)?

CHAPTER

Modeling Marketing Phenomena

The modeling approach requires a mathematical understanding of the marketplace. In this section we introduce some simple mathematical approaches that have been developed and applied in the marketing area. In all cases we deal with mathematical models. We will characterize models here along several critical dimensions:

Mathematical form.   Is the model linear? Nonlinear but linearizable? Inherently nonlinear?

Static/dynamic.   Does the model try to capture the flow of actions over time or is it merely a static look at the world?

Deterministic/probabilistic.   Nothing is known with certainty. Whether a deterministic model is used as an approximation or a stochastic model is used explicitly is a matter of model-building style.

Aggregate versus individual.   Individual response can be modeled and aggregated. Or total market response can be modeled directly.

Level of demand.   Product-class, brand-sales, or market-share demand can be the focus of the modeling effort.

The major elements of these dimensions are outlined with examples in Exhibit 4.1.

In this chapter we develop a framework for model building and begin an inventory of simple models that characterize various phenomena. Throughout the rest of the book we will expand on these developments as the modeling situation demands.

EXHIBIT 4-1 **Dimensions of model development.**

Dimension	Examples
1. Mathematical Form	
Linear in parameters and variables	$Q = a_0 + a_1 X$
Nonlinear in variables, linear in parameters	$Q = a_0 + a_1 X + a_2 X^2$
Nonlinear in parameters, linearizable	$Q = a_0 X_1^{a_1} X_2^{a_2}$
Inherently nonlinear	$Q = a_0(1 - e^{-a_1 x})$
2. Dynamic Effects	
Discrete time	$Q_t = a_0 + a_1 X_t + \lambda Q_{t-1}$
Continuous time	$\dfrac{dQ}{dt} = \dfrac{rX(V - Q)}{V} - \lambda Q$
3. Uncertainty	
Deterministic	$Q = a_0 + a_1 X$
Deterministic with stochastic error	$Q = a_0 + a_1 X + \epsilon$
Inherently stochastic	$p = f(\text{past purchase behavior})$
4. Level of Aggregation	
Individual	$p = f(\text{past behavior, marketing variables})$
Segment or market	$Q_i = a_0 + a_i Q$
5. Level of Demand	
Product class	$Y = f(\text{demographic trends, total marketing spending})$
Brand sales	$Q = SV$
Market share	$S = \dfrac{\text{us}}{\text{us} + \text{them}}$

Mathematical Forms

Following Naert and Leeflang (1978), we employ four classes of mathematical forms, structured around the issue of linearity:

1. linear in parameters and variables
2. nonlinear in variables but linear in parameters
3. nonlinear in parameters but linearizable
4. inherently nonlinear

In this section we will be modeling quantity sold Q as a function of some marketing variables $(X_1, \ldots, X_n)$, where X_1 may be advertising, X_2 price, and so on. We will present static models first, treating temporal effects in the next section. Finally, for simplicity we assume one product, one territory, and no competition.

Linear Models

Also known as linear additive models, linear models are represented mathematically in eq. (4.1) and graphically in Exhibit 4.2:

$$Q = a_0 + a_1 X_1 + \cdots + a_n X_n \tag{4.1}$$

where $a_0, a_1, \ldots, a_n$ are the model parameters.

Linear models have several characteristics that make them appealing:

Classical econometric methods are applicable for parameter estimation.

They are easy to visualize and understand.

Locally, at least, they can approximate many more-complicated functions fairly well.

However, linear models do have several problems.

First, they assume constant returns to scale for each of the marketing instruments. (This fact can be seen by the fact that $\partial Q / \partial X_i = a_i$, assumed constant.) While this assumption may be true locally, most marketing instruments, such as advertising, are assumed to have threshold and

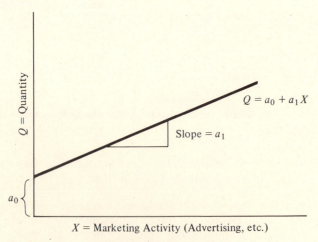

EXHIBIT 4-2   Additive, linear response model.

saturation effects. Thus this assumption may be reasonable only within a relatively narrow range.

Second, the model assumes no interactions between variables. Once again, because $\partial Q/\partial X_i = a_i$, changes in demand are assumed to be unrelated to the levels of the other marketing variables. Clearly, advertising will be more effective if distribution is higher (i.e., the product is more generally available).

Third, linear models have poor normative implications. If there is a constant margin m per unit sold, and if $\partial Q/\partial X_i = a_i$, the marginal revenue associated with incremental spending on marketing activity i is $a_i m$. If $a_i m$ is greater than one, then a unit of spending in activity i returns more than a unit of profit. The normative implication of this result is to allow spending on activity i to expand without limit. Conversely, if $a_i m$ is less than one, the rational decision maker should not spend anything on this marketing activity. Clearly, a model that has these kinds of normative implications is of limited value for decision making.

On the plus side, though, if $a_i m$ is greater than one, the linear model suggests that, at least locally, a spending increase in activity i should be considered. Similarly, if $a_i m$ is less than one, a decrease should be considered. But the linear model gives no clue as to how much.

Models with Linear Parameters and Nonlinear Variables

A much larger and more flexible class of models is nonlinear in variables but linear in the parameters. These are called nonlinear additive models and have the following general form:

$$Q = a_0 + a_1 g_1 (X_1) + a_2 g_2 (X_2) + \cdots + a_n g_n (X_n) \tag{4.2}$$

where $g_1, \ldots, g_n$ are some simple, well-defined functions of the marketing variables. Note that eq. (4.1) is a special case of eq. (4.2), with $g_i (X_i) = X_i$ for all marketing variables.

This model is nonlinear and additive because if we replace the original variables $(X_1, \ldots, X_n)$ with a new set of variables $(Y_1, \ldots, Y_n)$, where $Y_1 = g_1 (X_1)$, $Y_2 = g_2(X_2)$, and so on, an equation similar to (4.1) emerges with one important difference: $\partial Q/\partial X_i$ is no longer simply equal to a_i but is equal to $a_i (dg_i/dX_i)$. Thus we no longer have constant returns to scale everywhere, but we do have considerable flexibility in choosing the form for g_i.

Let us consider some commonly used g's.

Power-series Model.   Suppose we are interested in how sales are affected by advertising X but we are not certain what that relationship should look like. One alternative is to let $g_1 = X$, $g_2 = X^2$, and so on. By a fundamental principle of calculus, any smooth function can be approximated with a function of the form $f(X) = a_0 + a_1 X + a_2 X^2 +$ and so on. Depending on our knowledge of f and how closely we wish to approximate it, we may be

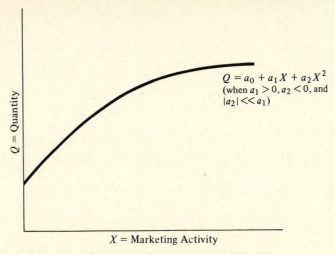

$$Q = a_0 + a_1 X + a_2 X^2$$
(when $a_1 > 0$, $a_2 < 0$, and $|a_2| \ll a_1$)

Q = Quantity

X = Marketing Activity

EXHIBIT 4-3   Power-series model, quadratic.

satisfied with two terms:

$$Q = a_0 + a_1X + a_2X^2 \tag{4.3}$$

Now when a_2 is negative and small relative to a_1, eq. (4.3) represents decreasing returns to scale. (See Exhibit 4.3.)

To see the implications of this model, we form a simple profit function:

$$Z = Qm - X \tag{4.4}$$

or

$$\text{Profit} = \text{volume} \times \text{margin} - \text{marketing expense}$$

(where X is measured in the same dollar units as m, the contribution margin). Substituting eq. (4.3) in eq. (4.4), we get

$$Z = (a_0 + a_1X + a_2X^2)\, m - X \tag{4.5}$$

Taking the derivative of Z and setting it equal to zero yields

$$0 = a_1m - 1 + 2a_2Xm$$

or

$$X = \frac{1 - a_1m}{2a_2m} \tag{4.6}$$

For eq. (4.6) to represent a maximum, d^2Z/dX^2 must be less than zero or $a_2 < 0$. If this condition is true, a profit-maximizing spending level can be found as long as $a_1m > 1$.

This type of model has some problems. First, sales are maximized at

$X = a_1/2a_2$. Beyond this point sales decline with further increases in spending for X. This result may run counter to intuition. However, the model does have the advantage of allowing, at least within a range, varying returns to scale, leading to clearer suggestions for policymaking.

There are a number of other ways of representing decreasing returns to scale; all have various problems.

Fractional-root Model. The fractional-root model is

$$Q = a_0 + a_1 X^\beta \qquad 0 < \beta < 1 \tag{4.7}$$

A special case of this model is the square root model in which $\beta = \frac{1}{2}$.

Semilog Model. Another frequently used form is the semilog model, which is portrayed mathematically in eq. (4.8) and graphically in Exhibit 4.4:

$$Q = a_0 + a_1 \ln X \tag{4.8}$$

This model has the problem that for some values of X, Q will be less than zero (assuming a_0 and a_1 are greater than zero). This result is evident from the fact that

$$Q < 0 \qquad \text{when } a_0 + a_1 \ln X < 0$$

or when

$$X < e^{-a_0/a_1} \tag{4.9}$$

Thus the model will not be reasonable for low values of X. However, it can be used roughly to describe situations where there is a threshold effect. In

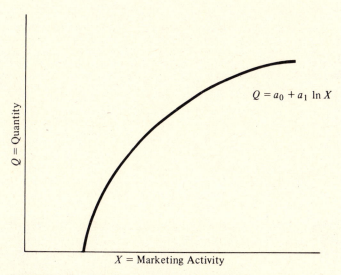

$$Q = a_0 + a_1 \ln X$$

Q = Quantity

X = Marketing Activity

EXHIBIT 4-4 Semilog response model.

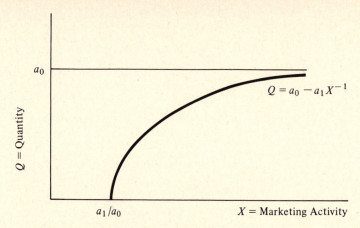

$$Q = a_0 - a_1 X^{-1}$$

Q = Quantity

a_0

a_1/a_0

X = Marketing Activity

EXHIBIT 4-5   Reciprocal response model.

eq. (4.8) no response to marketing activity X is seen until X is greater than e^{-a_0/a_1}. This model can be thought of as a "poor man's S curve."

None of the models represented thus far handle large values of X properly. The quadratic model has sales declining, while the semilog and the fractional-root models have Q approaching infinity. One way to handle large values of X is with a saturation model.

Saturation Model with Decreasing Returns.

$$Q = a_0 - a_1 X^{-\beta} \qquad \text{for } \beta > 0 \tag{4.10}$$

In eq. (4.10) a_0 represents the market potential—the value that Q tends toward as the level of marketing effort grows large. Thus the larger the value of β, the faster the market will saturate. The threshold is $(a_1/a_0)^{1/\beta}$. A special case of this form is the reciprocal model in which $\beta = 1$, and the threshold is a_1/a_0. Exhibit 4.5 shows what the model looks like.

S-Shaped Model.   To model first increasing returns to scale followed by decreasing returns, Leeflang (1975) suggests the use of the following model:

$$\ln Q = a_0 - \frac{a_1}{X} \tag{4.11}$$

This model, illustrated in Exhibit 4.6, has increasing returns to scale for $X < a_1/2$ and decreasing returns to scale for $X > a_1/2$. An equivalent form for eq. (4.11) is

$$Q = e^{a_0 - a_1/X} \tag{4.12}$$

Adding Interactions.   As we have stated, an objection to the use of the simple additive model is that it does not allow interactions. One way to overcome this objection is to incorporate interactions explicitly:

$$Q = a_0 + a_1 X_1 + a_2 X_2 + a_3 X_1 X_2 \tag{4.13}$$

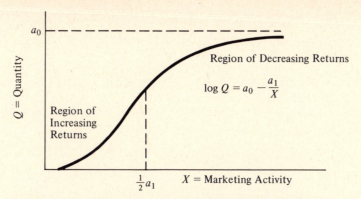

EXHIBIT 4-6   The log-reciprocal response model.

In this case the effect of a marginal change in X_1 depends on the level of X_2:

$$\frac{\partial Q}{\partial X_1} = a_1 + a_3 X_2 \qquad (4.14)$$

If a_3 is positive, this equation says that the marginal effect of X_1 is greater with more X_2; the activities are synergistic (as we might expect with, say, advertising and distribution). If a_3 is negative, the activities are substitutes. This result was found to be the case in a study of several different gasoline promotions—gasoline games and unsolicited credit card mailouts—used in the late 1960s. (See Chapter 15.)

A major problem with interaction models is that without knowledge about which interactions to include, the number of model terms grows rapidly. Consider a full interaction model with three variables:

$$Q = a_0 + a_1 X_1 + a_2 X_2 + a_3 X_3 + a_4 X_1 X_2 + a_5 X_1 X_3 + a_6 X_2 X_3$$
$$+ a_7 X_1 X_2 X_3 \quad (4.15)$$

In general, with n explanatory variables a full interaction model will have 2^n terms—clearly an intractable number if n is large.

Models Nonlinear in Parameters but Linearizable

Perhaps the most pervasive response model found in marketing and economics is the multiplicative model:

$$Q = a_0 X_1^{a_1} X_2^{a_2} \ldots X_n^{a_n} \qquad (4.16)$$

This model allows interactions of all levels between marketing variables:

$$\frac{\partial Q}{\partial X_i} = a_0 a_i X_1^{a_1} \ldots X_i^{a_i - 1} \ldots X_n^{a_n} \qquad (4.17)$$

Note that eq. (4.17) can also be written as

$$\frac{\partial Q}{\partial X_i} = \frac{a_i Q}{X_i} \tag{4.18}$$

Thus the impact of a change in X_i is a function of Q, which, in turn, is a function of all other variables.

The exponents $\{a_i\}$ have an important interpretation in this model. Note that from eq. (4.18) we get

$$a_i = \frac{\partial Q}{\partial X_i} \cdot \frac{X_i}{Q} \tag{4.19}$$

The right-hand side of eq. (4.19) is the definitional form of an elasticity: $a_i = \eta_i$, where η_i is the elasticity of Q with respect to marketing variable i. Thus the multiplicative model is a constant-elasticity model.

The model is linearized by taking logarithms of eq. (4.17):

$$\ln Q = \ln a_0 + a_1 \ln X_1 + \cdots + a_n \ln X_n \tag{4.20}$$

Equation (4.20) is linear with $Q^* = \ln Q$, $X_i^* = \ln X_i^*$, and $a_0^* = \ln a_0$. We will deal with models in multiplicative form in several later chapters.

One reason this function is used frequently is that it is extremely flexible. With a single marketing activity X, it becomes $Q = a_0 X^{a_1}$, called the simple power function (not to be confused with the power series). The possible shapes of this function are shown in Exhibit 4.7. If a_1 is equal to zero, then the power function becomes a horizontal line at a_0 and says that marketing effort does not influence the level of demand. If $a_1 < 0$, then demand and marketing effort are inversely related, as is the case when the

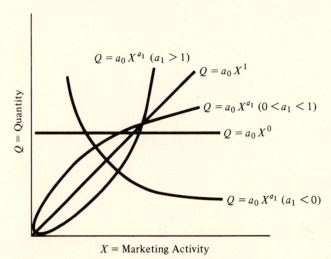

EXHIBIT 4-7   **The simple power function.**

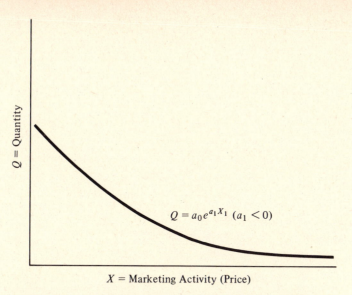

X = Marketing Activity (Price)

EXHIBIT 4-8   A single-variable exponential model.

marketing effort is price. If $0 < a_1 < 1$, this function produces the concave relationship mentioned above. If $a_1 = 1$, then the function produces a straight line with the origin at zero and a slope of a_0. Finally, if $a_1 > 1$, the function produces a relationship that is increasing at an increasing rate.

One of the nice properties of this functional form is that it spells out a linear relationship on double-logarithm paper, that is $Q = a_0 X_1^{a_1}$ is the same as $\log Q = \log a_0 + a_1 \log X$.

Another easily linearizable model is the exponential model:

$$Q = a_0 e^{a_1 X_1 + \cdots + a_n X_n} \tag{4.21}$$

where $\ln Q = \ln a_0 + a_1 X_1 + \cdots + a_n X_n \tag{4.22}$

Although not quite as flexible or as widely used as eq. (4.17), this model characterizes increasing-returns-to-scale situations well. It is particularly useful when one of the marketing variables is price, which is expected to force sales to zero as it becomes large. This case is illustrated in Exhibit 4.8 with $a_i < 0$.

Intrinsically Nonlinear Models

The models described above were all either in linear form or easily transformed to a linear form. Our focus on linearity is prompted mostly for ease of estimation; most classical estimation procedures have required that the models at least be linearizable. However, computer routines for nonlinear estimation problems are increasingly becoming available. [See Bard

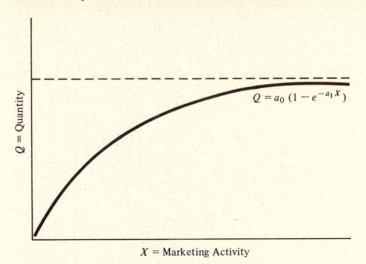

EXHIBIT 4-9   **Modified exponential model.**

(1974) for a comprehensive discussion of nonlinear-parameter-estimation theory and practice.] But the statistical properties of the estimates from these methods, especially in small samples, are still not particularly well understood.

Modified Exponential. A simple example of an intrinsically nonlinear model is the modified exponential model, represented mathematically in eq. (4.23) and graphically in Exhibit 4.9:

$$Q = a_0(1 - e^{-a_1 X}) \tag{4.23}$$

This model is useful when demand approaches an upper limit (a_0) as marketing effort (X) becomes large. The model has two important parameters, a_0 and a_1, where a_0 is the market potential and a_1 is the rate at which sales approach the limit as marketing effort becomes large. A nice feature of this model is that it implies that the marginal sales response will be proportional to the level of untapped potential, $a_0 - Q$.

The parameters are most often estimated separately. Analysts often assume that a_0, the market potential, is known. If it is, in fact, known, then the model reduces to

$$Q^* = \frac{a_0 - Q}{a_0} = e^{-a_1 X} \tag{4.24}$$

or

$$\ln Q^* = -a_1 X \tag{4.25}$$

Next we consider some S-shaped models. There are a number of compelling reasons for the use of S-shaped models in marketing. First, they have regions of increasing, decreasing, and constant returns to scale. Furthermore, they capture the threshold and the saturation effects that many theorists believe exist in a range of marketing situations.

Logistic Equation. Several S-shaped models are widely used in marketing. One of the most common is the logistic equation:

$$Q = \frac{\overline{Q}}{1 + e^{-(a_0 + a_1 X_1 + \cdots + a_n X_n)}} \tag{4.26}$$

With a single marketing variable X, this equation will produce an S-shaped curve, starting from a value of $\overline{Q}/(1 + e^{-a_0})$ when $X = 0$ and rising to a higher asymptote of $\overline{Q}$ when X gets large. Exhibit 4.10 illustrates the logistic function for the case of one marketing variable.

As with the modified exponential, if market potential ($\overline{Q}$) is known, it becomes possible to linearize the logistic function. We first define Q^* as

$$Q^* = \frac{Q}{\overline{Q}} = \frac{1}{1 + e^{-(a_0 + a_1 X_1 + \cdots + a_n X_n)}} \tag{4.27}$$

Then we take the so-called logit transformation of Q^*, $\ln [Q^*/(1 - Q^*)]$, which yields

$$\ln \frac{Q^*}{1 - Q^*} = a_0 + a_1 X_1 + \cdots + a_n X_n \tag{4.28}$$

This model is an important one, and interpreted in a slightly different way (with $\overline{Q} = 1$ and Q as a probability), it is frequently used to model choice behavior: "... [the logistic model] is the most useful analogue for binary response data of the linear model for normally distributed data" (Cox, 1970, p. 19).

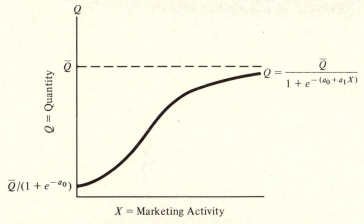

EXHIBIT 4-10   **Logistic response function.**

Various forms of the logistic function have been proposed in the marketing literature. In particular, if

$$\ln \frac{Q^*}{1 - Q^*} = \ln a_0 + a_1 \ln X_1 + \cdots + a_n \ln X_n \tag{4.29}$$

then

$$\frac{Q^*}{1 - Q^*} = a_0 X_1^{a_1} X_2^{a_2} \ldots X_n^{a_n} \tag{4.30}$$

This equation is roughly the analogy of eq. (4.16) in which the dependent variable, instead of sales, is sales relative to unsaturated potential $(1 - Q^*)$.
Gompertz Model.   Another frequently used model is the Gompertz model:

$$Q = a_0 a_1^{a_2^X} \tag{4.31}$$

with $a_0 > 0$, $1 > a_1 > 0$, and $a_2 < 1$. Exhibit 4.11 illustrates this function: when X gets large, Q approaches a_0; when X is zero, Q equals $a_0 a_1$.

Taking logarithms in eq. (4.31) yields

$$\ln Q = \ln a_0 + a_2^X \ln a_1 \tag{4.32}$$

As with the logistic curve, one parameter here, a_0, can be interpreted as market potential. If this parameter can be estimated separately, then we have

$$Q^* = \ln a_0 - \ln Q = -a_2^X \ln a_1 \tag{4.33}$$

or taking logs again,

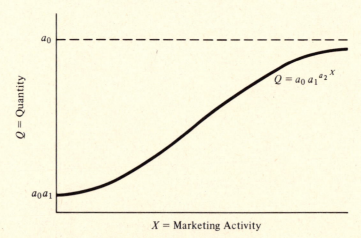

EXHIBIT 4-11   **Gompertz response function.**

$$\ln Q^* = \ln(\ln a_0 - \ln Q) = X \ln a_2 + \ln(-\ln a_1) \qquad (4.34)$$

The Gompertz model represents a situation in which the growth increments of the logarithms are declining by a constant proportion, a_2. The curve can be fitted to the relationship between demand and the level of marketing effort, although it is more often used to explain a law of population or product-demand growth over time.

Both the Gompertz and the logistic curves operate between a lower bound and an upper asymptote and describe a curve that increases at a decreasing rate of growth. The Gompertz curve involves a constant ratio of successive first differences of log Q values, while the logistic curve involves a constant ratio of successive first differences of the values of $1/Q$. In practice, the function used is the one that seems more reasonable on theoretical grounds or the one that gives a better fit to the data.

ADBUDG curve. Another S-shaped function used in the marketing literature is the one proposed by Little (1970) in his ADBUDG model. It has an upper asymptote (a_0), a lower asymptote (a_1), and two shape parameters $(a_2$ and $a_3)$:

$$Q = a_1 + (a_0 - a_1) \frac{X^{a_2}}{a_3{}^{a_2} + X^{a_2}} \qquad (4.35)$$

Exhibit 4.12 illustrates this function when $a_2 > 1$ and $a_2 < 1$, respectively. The parameters of this model are usually calibrated judgmentally.

A variety of other functions, S-shaped and otherwise, have been proposed in the literature; those presented here provide a good basic vocabulary for understanding most model forms.

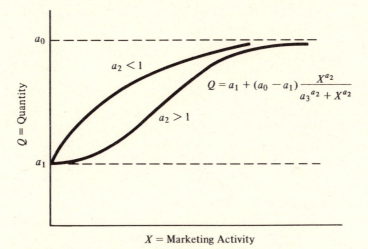

EXHIBIT 4-12   **Little's ADBUDG function.**

Dynamic Effects

Response to marketing variables does not always take place immediately. The effect of an ad campaign does not end when that campaign is over; the effect, or part of it, will remain perceptible for some future time. Many customers purchase more than they can consume of a product during a short-term price promotion. This action leads to inventory buildup and a lowering of sales in subsequent periods. Furthermore, the effect of that sales promotion will clearly depend on how much inventory buildup occurred in past periods (i.e., how much potential buildup is left). If customers stocked up on brand A cola last week, a new promotion this week is likely to be less productive than one in which a long period existed since the last such promotion.

"Carry-over effects" is the general term used to describe the influence of a current marketing expenditure on sales in future periods. Two types of carry-over effects can be distinguished. One type, the *delayed-response effect*, arises from delays that occur between the time marketing dollars are spent and the time induced purchases occur. This response is especially evident in industrial markets, where the delay, especially for capital equipment, can be a year or more. The other type of effect, the *customer-holdover effect*, arises from new customers created by the marketing expenditures, who remain customers for many subsequent periods. Their later purchases should be credited to some extent to the earlier expenditures. Some percentage of the new customers will be retained each period; this situation gives rise to the notion of the *customer retention rate* and its converse, the *customer decay rate* (also called attrition or erosion rate).

In this section we will illustrate how some of the effects have been modeled in equation form. In subsequent chapters we will explore these relationships in more detail.

Discrete-Time Models

To simplify the discussion in this section, we will focus on linear lag structures with only one marketing activity. The activity X and the response variable Q will be subscripted by the discrete time interval t. Conceptually, the problem we face is the following: Q_t will be affected not only by X_t but by X_{t-1}, X_{t-2}, and so on. The equation for Q_t can thus be written as

$$Q_t = a_0 + a_1 X_t + a_2 X_{t-1} + a_3 X_{t-2} + \ldots \qquad (4.36)$$

Attempts to estimate the coefficients in eq. (4.36) are hampered by several problems. The first deals with how far back it is reasonable to go and still see effects (i.e., how long does advertising last?) Second, because of data problems, ordinary estimation procedures may lead to patterns in the a_i's that are not reasonable. Suppose that $\hat{a}_1 > \hat{a}_2$ but that $\hat{a}_3 < 0$ and $\hat{a}_4 > \hat{a}_2$ (where $\hat{a}$ means estimated value of a). This condition may not be consistent with a commonsense understanding of the marketplace. Finally, spending levels of X may be rather consistent from period to period. As a simple example, let us assume $X_t = X$ for all t and truncate eq. (4.36) at $t - 3$:

$$Q_t = a_0 + a_1 X_t + a_2 X_{t-1} + a_3 X_{t-2} + a_4 X_{t-3} \qquad (4.37)$$

The substitution of $X_t = X$ in eq. (4.37) yields

$$Q_t = a_0 + (a_1 + a_2 + a_3 + a_4)X \qquad (4.38)$$

Clearly, this (constant) historical spending pattern will not allow us to distinguish separate values of a_1, a_2, a_3, and a_4 but merely permit us to estimate their sum. In general, X_t will vary somewhat, but this problem, called multicollinearity, is a further reason to limit the number of independently estimated coefficients.

Many alternative specifications of the relationships between the $\{a_i\}$ have been proposed in the marketing literature. The most common one develops as follows: assume that the effects of X on Q decays with time in a consistent way—that is, it loses a constant proportion of its influence each time period. This assumption is equivalent to

$$\frac{a_{i+1}}{a_i} = \lambda \qquad \text{for all } i \qquad (4.39)$$

Using eq. (4.39), we get

$$\frac{a_2}{a_1} = \lambda \qquad \frac{a_3}{a_1} = \frac{a_2}{a_1}\frac{a_3}{a_2} = \lambda \cdot \lambda = \lambda^2$$

and, in general,

$$\frac{a_i}{a_1} = \lambda^{i-1} \qquad \text{or} \qquad a_i = a_1 \lambda^{i-1} \qquad (4.40)$$

Now we can rewrite eqs. (4.36) as

$$Q_t = a_0 + a_1 X_t + a_1 \lambda X_{t-1} + a_1 \lambda^2 X_{t-2} + \dots \qquad (4.41)$$

which has only three unknowns, a_0, a_1, and λ. (Exhibit 4.13 displays this type of geometrically decaying lag structure.)

But eq. (4.41) still depends on the whole history, X_t, X_{t-1}, $\dots$; so our truncation problem still is with us. This problem can be solved by lagging eq. (4.41) one period and multiplying it by λ:

$$\lambda Q_{t-1} = \lambda a_0 + \lambda a_1 X_{t-1} + \lambda^2 a_1 X_{t-2} + \dots \qquad (4.42)$$

Subtracting eq. (4.42) from eq. (4.41) yields

$$Q_t - \lambda Q_{t-1} = a_0(1 - \lambda) + a_1 X_t$$

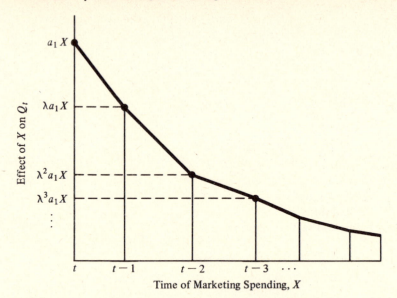

EXHIBIT 4-13   A geometrically declining lag structure.

or

$$Q_t = a^* + \lambda Q_{t-1} + a_1 X_t \tag{4.43}$$

where $a^* = a_0 (1 - \lambda)$. This procedure, attributed to Koyck (1954), is often referred to as the Koyck transformation. Estimation problems are now greatly reduced, with but three parameters and two variables.

Note that the parameters λ and a_1 give measures of the short- and long-term effects of marketing instrument X. Clearly, a_1 measures the short-term effect of X from eq. (4.43). Now suppose $X_t = X$ for a long time and that $Q_t = Q_{t-1} = Q$, that is, that sales stabilize. Then eq. (4.43) becomes

$$Q = a^* + \lambda Q + a_1 X$$

$$Q - \lambda Q = a^* + a_1 X$$

or

$$Q = \frac{a^*}{1 - \lambda} + \frac{a_1}{1 - \lambda} X \tag{4.44}$$

Thus $a_1/(1 - \lambda)$ measures the long-term effect of marketing instrument X.

However, there are several problems with this model. First, there are estimation problems, because the model in the reduced form (4.44) will not usually satisfy the assumptions of classical linear-regression models. [See Parsons and Schultz (1976) for fuller discussion of problems and solutions here.]

Second, this simple geometric-decay structure may not be realistic for the problem at hand. With frequently collected data (biweekly or monthly), sales effects may increase for a few periods and then decay.

There are many other alternatives, most of which can be reduced by a Koyck-type transformation to a form similar to eq. (4.43). For example, suppose we wish to include two direct lags, the geometric decline taking effect after two periods. We would then have

$$Q_t = a_0 + a_1 X_t + a_2 X_{t-1} + a_2\lambda X_{t-2} + a_2\lambda^2 X_{t-3} + \cdots \qquad (4.45)$$

Applying the Koyck transformation [subtracting Q_{t-1} from eq. (4.45)] yields

$$Q_t - \lambda Q_{t-1} = a_0(1 - \lambda) + a_1 X_t + (a_2 - \lambda a_1)X_{t-1}$$

or

$$Q_t = a_0^* + a_1 X_t + a_2^* X_{t-1} + \lambda Q_{t-1} \qquad (4.46)$$

where $a_0^* = a_0(1 - \lambda)$

$a_2^* = a_2 - \lambda a_1$

This procedure can easily be extended to account for more lags.

More-general lag structures can be developed, leading to models with several different decays. For example, Bass and Clarke (1972) use a model that reduces to

$$Q_t = a_0 + a_1 X_t + \lambda_1 Q_{t-1} + \lambda_2 Q_{t-2} \qquad (4.47)$$

In this equation a combination of two geometric-lag decay rates is used. [Parsons and Schultz (1976) provide several examples of how to construct and evaluate lag structures.]

To illustrate more-general lags, we postulate two different geometric-decay functions and obtain

$$Q_t = a_0 + a_1 X_t + a_1\lambda_x X_{t-1} + a_1\lambda_x^2 X_{t-2} + \cdots$$
$$+ b_1 Y_t + b_1\lambda_y Y_{t-1} + b_1\lambda_y^2 Y_{t-2} + \cdots \qquad (4.48)$$

Here, we need two applications of the Koyck transformation. First, we lag eq. (4.48) one period, multiply both sides of the equation by λ_x, and subtract it from eq. (4.48). This manipulation yields

$$Q_t = a_0^* + \lambda_x Q_{t-1} + a_1 X_t + b_1 Y_t$$
$$+ (\lambda_y - \lambda_x)(b_1 Y_{t-1} + \lambda_y b_1 Y_{t-2} + \cdots) \qquad (4.49)$$

Next, we lag eq. (4.49) one period, multiply both sides of the equation by λ_y, and subtract it from eq. (4.49) to get

$$Q_t = a_0' + (\lambda_x + \lambda_y)Q_{t-1} + a_1(X_t - \lambda_y X_{t-1}) + b_1(Y_t - \lambda_x Y_{t-1}) \qquad (4.50)$$

where $a_0' = (1 - \lambda_x)(1 - \lambda_y)a_0$ (4.51)

Note that eq. (4.50) is more complex than eq. (4.43) and is nonlinear in the parameters as well, calling for special estimation procedures.

To conclude this section, we return to eq. (4.43):

$$Q_t = a_0^* + a_1 X_t + \lambda Q_{t-1} \qquad (4.43)$$

Recall that a_1 is the short-term effect of marketing expenditure X, while $a_1/(1 - \lambda)$ is the long-run effect. The term $1/(1 - \lambda)$ is often called the *long-run, marketing-expenditure multiplier*.

We can also look at elasticities:

$$\eta_{QX} = \frac{dQ}{dX} \cdot \frac{X}{Q} \qquad (4.52)$$

Note that from our discussion above, $dQ_t/dX_t = a_1$, which yields

$$\eta_{QX} = a_1 \frac{X}{Q} \qquad (4.53)$$

Finally, another useful concept is that of long-run elasticity (at a level of marketing spending X):

$$\eta_{Q_\infty X} = \frac{a_1 X}{Q_\infty (1 - \lambda)} \qquad (4.54)$$

This equation follows by differentiating eq. (4.48) with respect to X for dQ/dX.

Continuous–Time Models

The models reviewed above are discrete-time models. In other words, observations are assumed to take place at discrete points in time (months, quarters, etc.). However, much marketing modeling is done in continuous time with "sales volume per unit time" as the dependent variable. Since observations of sales and marketing spending are usually collected over certain units of time, such as months or quarters, what is the value of continuous-time modeling? Because of superior methods of analysis (primarily differential-equation methods), the analyst can often derive more policy implications in a continuous-time model than in a discrete-time model, even though discrete-time models appear to be more useful operationally. As an example, we will briefly analyze one continuous-time model.

Continuous-Time Example: The Vidale-Wolfe Model

Vidale and Wolfe (1957) proposed a continuous-time model in which they sought to explain the rate of change of sales with lagged effects of advertising handled through a sales-decay term:

$$\frac{dQ}{dt} = \frac{rX(V-Q)}{V} - \lambda Q \qquad (4.55)$$

where Q = sales volume

$\frac{dQ}{dt}$ = change in sales at time t

X = marketing instrument (advertising spending rate)

V = market volume

r = sales-response constant (sales generated per dollar of X when $Q = 0$)

λ = sales-decay constant (proportion of sales lost per unit of time when $X = 0$)

The right-hand side of eq. (4.55) shows that the change in the rate of sales, dQ/dt, depends on several factors: it will be greater for higher levels of r, X, and $(V - Q)/V$ (untapped potential) and it will be lower for higher values of λ and Q. Thus dQ/dt is equal to the response r of sales per dollar of marketing spending times the number X of marketing dollars spent reduced by the percentage of unsaturated sales, $(V - Q)/V$, less sales λQ lost through decay.

Equation (4.55) can be solved [see Bass et al. (1961, pp. 375–377)] for $Q(t)$ when $X(t) = X$, a constant:

$$Q(t) = \frac{V}{1 + (\lambda V/rX)} (1 - e^{-[(rX/V)+\lambda]t}) + Q(0)e^{-[(rX/V)+\lambda]t} \qquad (4.56)$$

Suppose we are interested in how a marketing program carries over. Consider a program of the form

$$X(t) = X \qquad \text{for } t \le T$$

and $\qquad X(t) = 0 \qquad \text{for } t > T \qquad (4.57)$

Here, the program we are considering spends at the level X up until time T and then cuts off. After the program has stopped, sales decrease exponentially:

$$Q(t) = Q(T)e^{-\lambda(t-T)} \qquad \text{for } t > T \qquad (4.58)$$

This sales pattern is shown in Exhibit 4.14. For this model sales increase most rapidly at $t = 0$ and taper off as saturation is approached; after T, sales decline exponentially.

The exponential decay here is very similar to the carry-over effects modeled in eq. (4.43). For $t > T$ in eq. (4.43), assume $X_t = 0$ (and, for simplicity, assume $a^* = 0$). Then we get

$$Q_t = \lambda^{t-T}Q_T \qquad t > T \qquad (4.59)$$

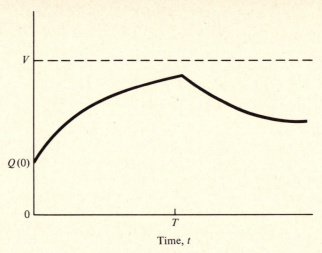

EXHIBIT 4-14   Sales response to an advertising campaign of duration *T*: Vidale-Wolfe model.

If we compare eq. (4.59) with eq. (4.58), we see that if we let λ in eq. (4.59) be equal to $e^{-\lambda}$ (with different values of λ, of course) in eq. (4.58), the expressions look identical. Thus this form of decay is a continuous-time analog of some of the simple discrete-time models described above.

The Vidale-Wolfe model will be reviewed and critiqued in the context of advertising models in Chapter 14. One point to note about the analysis above is that, in practice, almost any marketing program can be approximated by $X(t) = X$ (constant) for some (perhaps short) time. Thus a model's behavior can usually be characterized accurately by understanding (1) how it responds to an upward change in the level of marketing effort from $X(t) = X_1$ to $X_1 + \Delta X_1$ and (2) how it responds to a drop from $X(t) = X_2$ to $X_2 - \Delta X_2$. In practice, as shown above, a model is often analyzed by studying its response to changes in the level of X from zero to a saturation level and then its decay as X returns to zero.

Handling Uncertainty: Deterministic Versus Stochastic Models

The models we have introduced thus far have been primarily deterministic in nature. However, models of behavioral phenomena may be probabilistic (stochastic) in nature. Thus the marketing modeler may set up a system of equations that either does or does not include probabilistic elements.

Models may be classified as follows:

deterministic

deterministic with stochastic error

inherently stochastic

The choice of model type depends more on the user and the application than on any philosophical understanding of the workings of markets. Whether behavior is really stochastic ["there is a stochastic element in the brain" (Bass, 1974a, p. 2)] or whether it is indeed predictable in exact terms is irrelevant from an operational standpoint. Any model capable of making exact predictions would be hopelessly complex, and the data requirements would be enormous: a complete history of all past actions by all individuals involved, all choices available, and a complete picture of the environment would be required. Therefore deterministic models are used as approximations, with the stochastic elements omitted for simplicity.

The use of probabilistic components in a model of market behavior can serve to summarize and formalize assumptions about the net effect of all elements not included in the model. Whether because of errors of measurement or sampling, a lack of complete understanding of the process, or inherently random behavior, a model will rarely match behavior exactly. Therefore probabilistic elements are often added to a model even if the original theoretical formulation included no such elements.

For example, our simple linear model,

$$Q = a_0 + a_1 X \qquad (4.60)$$

can be made stochastic by adding a random-disturbance term ϵ to it to form

$$Q = a_0 + a_1 X + \epsilon \qquad (4.61)$$

In this equation quantity purchased Q is linearly related to marketing effort X. But effort X is not sufficient to explain Q; other elements in the marketplace, whose effects presumably are small, random, or nonmeasurable, affect Q also. Those effects are captured in the disturbance term ϵ. This approach—adding a disturbance term to an inherently deterministic relationship—is the traditional approach taken in building econometric models. The addition of the random term is an important element, both for parameter estimation and for model testing.

Suppose model (4.60) is specified as

$$Q = 10 + 15X \qquad (4.62)$$

If we set $X = 5$, eq. (4.62) predicts that Q will be 85. But, in practice, a model rarely fits exactly; so suppose the actual level of Q is 90. Is the model good? Bad?

Suppose that we use model (4.61) and that ϵ is found to have a normal distribution with a mean of zero and a standard deviation of 10. In this case we use model (4.61) and find

$$\hat{\epsilon} = Q - 10 - 15X \qquad (4.63)$$

Our data imply that $\hat{\epsilon}$, the observed value of ϵ, is $90 - 85$, or 5. Is this result consistent with a normally distributed ϵ with mean zero and standard deviation 10? Reference to a table of normal random variables shows that under these assumptions we can expect a deviation of at least five units 61.7 percent of the time. Thus we conclude that a deviation of this size is consistent with eq. (4.63).

An inherently stochastic model is one in which the probability elements are built in at the outset, rather than added on after the fact, to account for discrepancies between predicted and observed results.

As an example, consider a two-brand market where an individual's likelihood of buying brand 1 on his next purchase occasion is

$$p(\text{next purchase} = 1) = \begin{cases} p_{11} & \text{if brand 1 was purchased last} \\ p_{21} & \text{if brand 2 was purchased last} \end{cases} \qquad (4.64)$$

Now p (next purchase = 2) = $1 - p$ (next purchase = 1) in this two-brand market. Inherently stochastic models such as this one have been developed primarily to describe behavior at the individual-consumer level. (See Chapter 7.)

To summarize, models can be built that are either deterministic or probabilistic. Probabilistic models generally fall into two categories: deterministic with stochastic error or inherently stochastic. The choice of model type will be influenced by the type of data available, the use to which the model is to be put, and the preferences of the model builder.

Individual Versus Aggregate Models

Market-response models can be classified by whether they model market behavior directly or indirectly through individual behavior, which is then aggregated to determine market response. In physics these classifications are analogous to macroscopic and microscopic perspectives: in "processes involving heat phenomena, the macroscopic point of view is given by thermodynamics and the microscopic one by the atomic theory of heat" (Resnick and Halliday, 1960, p. 448).

Few deterministic models of individual behavior have been proposed; individual behavior is sufficiently variable to require at least some stochastic component. Therefore we will discuss only stochastic models in this section.

Stochastic models may deal with either individual or aggregate behavior. In models of individual behavior, probability distributions are usually constructed for choices over the set of all possible responses. In eq. (4.64) the likelihood of purchasing one of two brands was modeled; the probability depended on the brand bought last. Inherent in this view of modeling is the concept that the outcome of any observation, or purchase occasion, cannot be predicted exactly. (We might guess that about half the tosses of a fair coin will turn up heads, but on any particular toss, if we guess heads, we will be wrong half the time.) Thus there is a lower limit of response uncertainty that cannot be eliminated by using known theories and practical model-building techniques.

As an example, consider the results of an experiment reported by Bass, Pessemier, and Lehmann (1972), predicting brand choice for soft drinks. They used three bases for prediction: (1) stated brand preferred by the respondent, (2) brand last chosen by the respondent, and (3) inferred attitude toward the brand, measured through the respondent's beliefs about and stated importance of the soft-drink attributes of the different brands. The results are summarized in Exhibit 4.15. These results suggest that respondents chose the brand they preferred only 55 percent of the time. The brand last chosen by the respondent provided correct predictions only 45 percent of the time, suggesting that respondents were switching 55 percent of the time. Thus either consumer behavior is inherently stochastic or it is at least difficult to understand and measure deterministically.

Models of aggregate response can be constructed in one of two ways. First, models of individual-consumer behavior can be added together to form a model of aggregate (either market or market-segment) response. The probabilistic properties of the aggregate models are then derived from the properties of the individual-component models. Second, a model of aggregate behavior can be postulated directly, having its own component of response uncertainty, and applied to aggregate data. The characteristics of the aggregate model are obtained directly in this case.

EXHIBIT 4-15   Predicted versus actual behavior: soft-drink choice.

Basis for Prediction	Percentage of Correct Predictions of Brand Choice
Stated brand preferred by respondent	55%
Brand last chosen by respondent	45%
Brand toward which respondent had most favorable attitude	41%

SOURCE: Bass, Pessemier, and Lehmann, 1972, p. 537. Reprinted with permission from "An Experimental Study of Relationships between Attitudes Brand Preference and Choice," *Behavioral Science*, vol. 17, November 1972.

The most widely used models in the marketing area are econometric models of aggregate behavior. The many developments of this type are a good match with the time-series and cross-sectional data most often available to market researchers. Fewer applications of individual stochastic models have been reported, although there has been a resurgence of interest in the field in the last few years.

Stochastic models of individual choice have not been as widely used as aggregate models because of lack of data and because of

mathematical complexity

newness of the field

oversimplicity of model assumptions

model-analysis and estimation problems (Massy, Montgomery, and Morrison, 1970, pp. 5–6)

However, as the field has matured, many of these problems have been overcome. In particular, data have become increasingly available. Stochastic models of individual choice require observations at the level of the individual purchaser; market-level figures are not sufficient. But with wider use of automatic checkout systems in supermarkets and direct computer data entry at the customer level in other retail establishments, such data are becoming more readily available. We believe the 1980s will see a growth in the development and application of individual-choice models as the relevant data become available.

To illustrate, we consider three simple models of individual brand choice in a two-brand market.

EXAMPLE: *A Simple Homogeneous Bernoulli Model.* This model has p, the probability of buying brand 1, constant for all consumers. Suppose that market share for brand 1 is 22%. Then for this model to be consistent with observation, $p = 0.22$ for all individuals. Note that p for this model is (1) constant across individuals, (2) constant over time, and (3) unaffected by marketing variables.

EXAMPLE: *A Heterogeneous Bernoulli Model.* This model differs from the one above in that p varies across the population. So instead of p, we have p_i, $i = 1, \ldots, I$, where I is the number of individuals in the market. For this model to be consistent with observation, on average, 22% of the individuals should buy brand 1, which is equivalent to saying

$$\frac{1}{I}(p_1 + \cdots + p_I) = 0.22 \tag{4.65}$$

That is, $p = 22\%$ *on average*, not for every individual.

This model allows individuals to differ but is still (1) constant over time and (2) unaffected by marketing variables.

EXAMPLE: *A Markov Model.*   As a final example, consider the following Markov model:

$$p_t = \begin{cases} p_{11} & \text{if brand 1 were bought last} \\ p_{21} & \text{if brand 2 were bought last} \end{cases} \qquad (4.66)$$

Equation (4.66) says that purchase behavior is controlled by what the individual did last. Suppose that we observe no change in market share at time t and $t + 1$. This observation says that market share at $t + 1 = S =$ market share at t. But eq. (4.66) gives us the following switching equation:

$$S_{t+1} = p_{11}S_t + p_{21}(1 - S_t) \qquad (4.67)$$

This equation says that the fraction p_{11} of individuals who bought brand 1 last period (S_t) will buy again, while the fraction p_{21} of those who bought brand 2 last period $(1 - S_t)$ will buy brand 1 this period. To be consistent with the observation that $S_t = S_{t+1} = 0.22$, we need the condition that

$$0.22 = 0.22p_{11} + 0.78p_{21}$$

or

$$p_{11} = 1 - 3.55p_{21} \qquad (4.68)$$

Note that this model allows purchase probabilities to shift (depending on brand last bought), but it assumes (1) constant behavior across individuals and (2) no effect of marketing variables.

These are three simple models of brand choice. Stochastic models of individual-buyer behavior are usually divided into two groups:

1. brand-choice models, focusing on what brand will be purchased on a particular purchase occasion given that a purchase event will, in fact, occur
2. purchase-timing models, focusing on when purchase events will take place or, equivalently, how many events will occur in a specified period of time

These models are discussed in detail in Chapter 7.

Level of Demand Modeled

Naert and Leeflang (1978, chap. 8) distinguish among three classes of models by the level of aggregate market demand they handle: (1) product-class sales, (2) brand sales, and (3) market share. This distinction is useful because the data available and the mathematical forms used for these model types are quite different.

Note that the three model types are definitionally related by

$$Q = SV \qquad \text{or} \qquad S = \frac{Q}{V} \tag{4.69}$$

where Q = brand quantity
 V = product-class sales
 S = market share

Thus if we model two of the three quantities (V and S, for example), the third element will be determined by the relationship in eq. (4.69).

Product-Class-Sales Models

Consumer-demand theory, as developed in economics, has produced a large number of product-class-sales models. The usual approach is to hypothesize a form for a utility function and to look for the utility-maximizing allocation of consumer budgets over a number of products. However, these product classes are often too broadly defined for marketing use. [See Barten (1977), Brown and Deaton (1972), and Theil (1975, 1976).]

In marketing, most models for product-class demand use time-series data and explain demand by environmental variables and aggregate values of marketing variables. Environmental variables include population size, income, weather, and prices and availability of complementary products and/or substitutes. Aggregation of marketing variables usually means product-class (total) advertising expenditures, total number of retail outlets, average market price, and so on.

As an example of this type of modeling, consider the study by Lambin (1970) in which he estimated the demand function for per capita consumption of a food product:

$$\frac{V_t}{N_t} = a_0 \left(\frac{Y_t}{N_t}\right)^{a_1} t^{a_2} R_t^{-a_3} K_t^{-a_4} \tag{4.70}$$

where V_t = product–class sales
 N_t = population size
 Y_t = private disposable income
 t = time
 R = rainfall
 K_t = general price index at time t

Equation (4.70) shows per capita market demand going up with disposable income and down with rainfall and increases in the general price trend. The results also show a positive trend in product-class sales.

Brand-Sales Models

Brand sales can be modeled directly (through brand effects, competitive effects, and environmental factors) or indirectly as the product of product-class sales and brand market share.

Naert and Leeflang (1978, pp. 149–150) argue that modeling brand sales indirectly is preferable for the following reasons:

1. It explicitly accounts for the distinction between brand-sales variation through variation in product-class sales and through market-share fluctuation.
2. When one is studying key variables affecting the brand, the use of market share allows the omission of environmental and seasonal factors affecting the whole market (product class) so that attention can be focused on interactions among brands in the product class.

The Vidale-Wolfe (1957) model is an example of a *direct* brand-sales model. Another example is Zentler and Ryde's (1956) model of the optimal geographic distribution of advertising expenditure:

$$Q = \frac{\overline{Q}(X/X^*)^2}{1 + (X/X^*) + (X/X^*)^2} \tag{4.71}$$

where Q = brand-sales level
X = advertising spending
X^* = value of X for which Q/X (sales per dollar of advertising) is greatest
$\overline{Q}$ = upper bound for Q (i.e., when X gets very large)

Note that eq. (4.71) has a saturation effect (i.e., Q cannot exceed $\overline{Q}$) but no threshold effect and is static (i.e., does not consider the effects of advertising over time).

Because indirect brand-sales models can be derived from eq. (4.69), we will not pursue them here. However, it is useful to observe the following:

$$Q = SV$$

so

$$\frac{\partial Q}{\partial X} = S \frac{\partial V}{\partial X} + V \frac{\partial S}{\partial X} \tag{4.72}$$

With a single marketing instrument X, multiplying both sides of eq. (4.72) by X/Q gives

$$\frac{\partial Q}{\partial X} \frac{X}{Q} = \frac{XS}{Q} \frac{\partial V}{\partial X} + \frac{XV}{Q} \frac{\partial S}{\partial X} \tag{4.73}$$

Substituting SV for Q in the two terms on the right-hand side of eq. (4.73) yields

$$\frac{\partial Q}{\partial X}\frac{X}{Q} = \frac{X}{V}\frac{\partial V}{\partial X} + \frac{X}{S}\frac{\partial S}{\partial X} \tag{4.74}$$

which is simply

$$\eta_Q = \eta_V + \eta_S \tag{4.75}$$

where η is the elasticity with respect to X. Equation (4.75) says that the elasticity of brand sales with respect to some marketing instrument X is the sum of total product-class elasticity and market-share elasticity with respect to the same instrument. Although this relationship does not incorporate competitive response (Chapter 18 extends these results), it captures the essence of the argument for modeling brand sales indirectly through product-class and market-share effects.

Market-Share Models

By definition, market share for brands in a product must sum to one. This constraint is not satisfied by many simple functional forms. For example, consider a two-brand market with brands 1 and 2 and a single marketing instrument X. At first glance the following model looks reasonable:

$$S_{1t} = \lambda_1 S_{1t-1} + \gamma_1 \frac{X_{1t}}{X_{1t} + X_{2t}} \tag{4.76}$$

and

$$S_{2t} = \lambda_2 S_{2t-1} + \gamma_2 \frac{X_{2t}}{X_{1t} + X_{2t}}$$

where S_{1t} = market share of brand 1 at time t
         X_{1t} = advertising spending of brand 1 at time t

Model (4.76) says that market share for brand 1 is some fraction of last period's share (λ_1) and is affected by the current share of marketing effort $[X_{1t}/(X_{1t} + X_{2t})]$. For shares to sum to one with this model structure, the following conditions are required (Naert and Bultez, 1973):

$$\lambda_1 = \lambda_2 = \lambda$$
$$\gamma_1 = \gamma_2 = \gamma \tag{4.77}$$
$$\lambda + \gamma = 1$$

But these conditions are not desirable because they imply that different brands respond in exactly the same way to changes in the marketing instrument. Furthermore, the multiplicative analogy of eq. (4.76), $S_t =$

$S_{t-1}^{\lambda} X_t^{\gamma}$, leads to even more problems because there are no restrictions on the parameters that can ensure that market shares sum to one.

Thus multiplicative- and additive-form market-share functions are not robust (i.e., they will not, in general, add to one). Yet in a variety of empirical studies (Beckwith, 1972; Lambin, Naert, and Bultez, 1975), they are used and provide a good fit to the observed data. Therefore these models, while simple and understandable, do not satisfy the conditions of model consistency (market share can be greater than one, less than zero, and, across brands, can sum to something other than one) and must be treated cautiously in practice.

A class of models that does satisfy both range (falling in the zero-to-one region) and sum constraints and that deals with competing brands in a disaggregate form is known as attraction models, where the attraction of a brand depends on its marketing mix. Essentially, these models say our share = us/(us + them).

If we allow S_i to represent market share of brand i and A_i the attraction of brand i, the general attraction model can be defined as

$$S_i = \frac{A_i}{\displaystyle\sum_{j-1}^{I} A_j} \qquad i = 1, \ldots, I, \text{ the number of brands in the market} \quad (4.78)$$

From eq. (4.78) it is clear that as long as the $\{A_i\}$ are nonnegative, all S_i are greater than zero and less than one and that $\Sigma_{i-1}^{I} S_i = 1$. Bell, Keeney, and Little (1975) and Barnett (1976) develop the conditions under which a function, such as that in eq. (4.78), can be expected to be observed; the conditions are intuitively plausible and are an extension of the range-and-sum-constraint arguments. It must be noted that, in general, each A_i is made up of the components of that brand's marketing mix and could have differential effects for different brands. In addition, brand i's advertising could be included in brand j's attractiveness (most likely, but not always, in a negative way, especially with an "our brand versus their brand" advertising campaign); this type of specification is not ruled out with an attraction model.

Several forms of attraction functions have been proposed, including

$$A_i = a_{0i} X_{1i}^{a_1} X_{2i}^{a_2} \ldots X_{ni}^{a_n} \qquad (4.79)$$

where X_{ji} is the value of marketing instrument j for brand i, and a_{0i} is brand-specific. In this case eq. (4.78) becomes

$$S_i = \frac{a_{0i} X_{1i}^{a_1} \ldots X_{ni}^{a_n}}{\displaystyle\sum_{j-1}^{I} a_{0j} X_{1j}^{a_1} \ldots X_{nj}^{a_n}} \qquad (4.80)$$

This and similar forms have been suggested by Nakanishi (1972) and Kuehn, McGuire, and Weiss (1966).

A logical extension is to have the attractiveness functions differ by brand (i.e., allow a_1 to differ as a_{11}, a_{21}, etc., depending on brand). For two components of the attractiveness function, this extended attraction model for brand 1 becomes

$$S_1 = \frac{a_{01}X_{11}{}^{a_{11}}X_{12}{}^{a_{12}}}{a_{01}X_{11}{}^{a_{11}}X_{12}{}^{a_{12}} + a_{02}X_{21}{}^{a_{21}}X_{22}{}^{a_{22}}} \tag{4.81}$$

Note that although eq. (4.81) looks inherently nonlinear, the following transformation simplifies matters:

$$\frac{S_1}{S_2} = \frac{a_{01}}{a_{02}} X_{11}{}^{a_{11}}X_{12}{}^{a_{12}}X_{21}{}^{-a_{21}}X_{22}{}^{-a_{22}} \tag{4.82}$$

A log transformation linearizes eq. (4.82). For n brands, $n - 1$ relationships like eq. (4.82) or, after taking logs, like eq. (4.83) can be developed:

$$\ln \frac{S_1}{S_2} = \ln \frac{a_{01}}{a_{02}} + a_{11} \ln X_{11} + a_{12} \ln X_{12} - a_{21} \ln X_{21} - a_{22} \ln X_{22} \tag{4.83}$$

The analyst then is free to choose any $n - 1$ out of the n possible equations for evaluation or estimation.

Other forms of attraction functions, such as $e^{\Sigma a_i X_i}$, can be linearized as well. All in all, attraction functions provide intuitively plausible and flexible mechanisms for estimating market share consistently. However, as the next chapter will show, their estimation requires care because of the logical interrelationships among market shares. Such models have seen less use than they should because of their apparent estimation difficulties, but these estimation problems are often easily surmounted.

Choosing and Evaluating a Mathematical Form

The model forms reviewed in this chapter present a number of trade-offs. In line with the development in Chapter 2, one model form is not better than another. Rather, the situation and the model's use need to be considered. Although there are a number of useful criteria for model selection, there are three that can be generally used:

1. **Theoretical soundness.** Is there an empirical or theoretical reason to believe a model should have certain characteristics? Is an S shape appropriate? Is there an upper bound on sales? If the answers to these questions are yes, a linear model is inappropriate, and the set of possible functional forms is restricted.
2. **Descriptive soundness.** Does the model fit the data well (better than competing models)? In essence, this criterion addresses the question of goodness of fit to historical or judgmental data.

3. **Normative soundness.** Two models may fit equally well, but one may produce normative suggestions that are unreasonable. Therefore a third criterion for model-form selection deals with finding a model that produces decision-making guidelines that are believable.

In addition, models need to be adapted to the use and user and should incorporate a level of detail that is consistent with the availability of data. For example, an individual-response model will require data at the individual level for calibration.

When one is selecting a model, the three criteria above can be summarized as one question: "Does this model make sense for this situation?" That is, does the model have the right form, theoretically, empirically, and normatively? If the answer is yes, then the model is appropriate.

EXAMPLE: Forlorn Foods, having chosen an objective function in the previous chapter, needs to characterize advertising response in its markets. As a first pass, it is interested in a static, short-term-response model at the aggregate level. Because of the inelasticity of product-class sales, it chooses a brand-sales model. In addition, for historical and theoretical reasons management believes that (1) brand sales are relevant only in certain regions (between upper and lower bounds) in each market and (2) advertising response has either an S-shaped or a concave form. Finally, for this initial analysis competitive factors are being ignored. Therefore the functional form that was chosen is the ADBUDG model, shown in eq. (4.35):

$$Q = a_1 + (a_0 - a_1) \frac{X^{a_2}}{a_3{}^{a_2} + X^{a_2}} \qquad (4.35)$$

Summary

In this chapter we developed some simple, basic models of response to marketing activities. Five dimensions of model development were introduced: mathematical form, dynamics, uncertainty, level of aggregation, and level of demand modeled.

First, four classes of mathematical forms were introduced and reviewed: linear models, models linear in their parameters but with nonlinear variables, models nonlinear in parameters but linearizable, and intrinsically nonlinear models. These models were shown to characterize different marketing phenomena, trading off ease of analysis and extention with complexity and realism.

Next, it was recognized that marketing effects take place over time, and therefore the models must incorporate carry-over effects. A geometric lag structure is most frequently used to model these effects. Continuous-time models that are rough analogs of discrete-time models are often useful for developing insight into the time-dependent structure of carry-over effects, although their discrete analogs are more frequently used for estimation and policy analysis.

In addition, we saw that models can be deterministic or probabilistic. Probabilistic models generally fall into two categories: deterministic with stochastic error or inherently stochastic. The choice of model type will be influenced by the type of data available, the application, and the preferences of the model builder.

Furthermore, market modeling can be done at the individual or aggregate level. Aggregate modeling specifies total market response directly, while individual modeling characterizes individual behavior, which can be aggregated to yield models of total market response. Methodological and data-collection improvements are leading to wider use of individual models.

Finally, when one is dealing with models of demand, the modeling can be performed at the product-class, the individual-product, or the market-share level. When interest is focused on brand sales, there are compelling reasons to model those sales as the product of product-class sales and market share. The models developed and variables chosen frequently separate neatly when one is modeling demand in the two-step approach. When one is modeling market share, a form of model called an attraction model seems to incorporate most of the desirable properties.

Throughout this chapter trade-offs are implied in the model-development process, balancing increased complexity and realism with analytical and potential estimation problems. An understanding of objectives and modeling approaches allows the marketing analyst to make informed decisions and to choose the right model for the right situation.

Problems

4.1 In 1967 Booth Appliances, Inc., sold the following numbers of units in relation to its marketing effort:

	Jan.	Feb.	Mar.	Apr.	May	June	July	Aug.	Sept.	Oct.	Nov.	Dec.
Sales in 1000s	105	100	145	117	155	138	177	136	157	167	168	123
Marketing in 1000s Effort	30	20	60	35	70	57	100	50	80	85	95	40

a. Suggest some forms of demand functions that could be used to represent the data.

b. Effort in November was $10,000 more than in October, yet sales were almost the same. To what can this be attributed?

c. Suppose the demand function $Q = \overline{Q}(1 - e^{-a_0 x})$ gives a good fit to the data. Assume the company has a linear cost function, $C = a_1 + bQ$. Derive a rule for determining the optimal level of marketing effort.

d. What would be the effect on demand of an increase in the *quality* of marketing effort per dollar?

4.2 Determine the shape of each of the following functions, and indicate whether it would constitute a plausible representation of the relationship between marketing effort and demand.

a. $Q = \overline{Q}X/(a + X)$, where $\overline{Q}$ is demand potential and X is marketing effort

b. $Q = \overline{Q} - a/X^b$; $X > 1$, $a/X^b < Q$

c. $Q = \overline{Q}e^{-x}$

d. $Q = \overline{Q}X^2/(1 + X + X^2)$

4.3 A manufacturer sells its product in two distinct markets, A and B. The demand equation associated with each market, respectively, is

$$Q_A = 400 - 2P_A$$
$$Q_B = 150 - 0.5P_B$$

The firm's total cost equation is

$$C = 10{,}000 + 20(Q_A + Q_B)$$

The current selling price is \$120 in both markets. Assuming that the conditions necessary for the successful practice of price discrimination hold true, could the company benefit by charging different prices in markets A and B? If so, what prices should be set in each market?

4.4 A television manufacturer wishes to determine the price for a new portable model that will maximize the company's current profits on the model. The marketing research department's estimate of demand for the new product is represented by the function $Q = 15{,}000 - 80P$, where Q is the quantity demanded and P is the price. In manufacturing the product, the company will incur fixed costs of \$300,000 and variable costs of \$20 per unit.

a. Find the optimum price and determine the level of demand, costs, and profit at this price.

b. The demand equation shown above is a familiar one. What assumptions are implicit in such a demand equation that may greatly limit its usefulness?

4.5 The market research group for Oligopoly Fidgets has established that each fidget buyer (*i*) acts on each purchase occasion as if he had a constant probability (p_i) of buying from Oligopoly, independent of his past behavior. It has also been established that these probabilities have a distribution across the market of $f_p(p)$. Thus the chance that a randomly selected fidget buyer has less than a probability of 0.7 (say) of purchasing from Oligopoly is

$$\int_0^{0.7} f_p(p)dp$$

The research group also determined that $f_p(p)$ could be approximated as

$$f_p(p) = \begin{cases} -a + bp & 0 \le p \le 1, 0 < a < 2 \\ 0 & \text{elsewhere} \end{cases}$$

and that the parameter a is related to the level of advertising (in millions of dollars) as

$$a = \begin{cases} 2 - x^{1/2} & 4 \geq x \geq 0 \\ 0 & x > 4 \end{cases}$$

Suppose total industry sales are $100,000,000 and are inelastic with respect to advertising expenditures, and that incremental company profit is 6% of retail sales. The fixed-cost rate for fidgets is $500,000/yr. Also assume that individuals always purchase the same amount at the same frequency.
a. What are the maximum and minimum values of Oligopoly's expected market share?
b. Find the level of advertising that maximizes Oligopoly's expected profit.
c. What is the expected market share at this advertising level?

4.6 In a given company, let

s = sales rate, $/yr

x = advertising rate, $/yr

p = profit rate, $/yr

c_0 = fixed-cost rate, $/yr

g = incremental profit (before advertising costs) as fraction of sales (assume g is constant)

For each of the following sales-response functions:
a. Make a rough sketch of the function.
b. Find the advertising rate for maximum profit rate.
c. Find the sales rate at maximum profit rate.

(1) $s = \alpha \ln \beta x$ **(4)** $s = \alpha + \beta(1 - e^{-\gamma x})$

(2) $s = \alpha + \beta \dfrac{(\gamma x)^\epsilon}{1 + (\gamma x)^\epsilon}$ **(5)** $s = \alpha + \beta \left(\dfrac{x}{\beta}\right)^\gamma, \gamma < 1$

(3) $s = \alpha + \beta x$

4.7 In Problem 4.6 we expressed advertising in terms of dollar-spending rates, whereas exposure rate is more fundamental. Let

v = advertising-exposure rates, exp/yr
k = media efficiency, exp/$
x = advertising-spending rates, $/yr

Thus

$v = kx$

Consider the sales-response curves (1), (2), and (4) in Problem 4.6 but with x replaced by v (e.g., $s = \alpha \ln \beta v$).
a. By inspection of Problem 4.6, write down the spending rates for maximum profit.
b. Suppose the advertising agency could make a more efficient media buy, thereby increasing k. Would this company's budget increase or decrease? (Discuss each curve.)

4.8 A model of advertising effects on sales is of the form

$$\frac{dQ}{dt} = \frac{rx(V - Q)}{V} - \lambda Q$$

where Q = sales volume

x = advertising spending

V = market volume

r = sales-response rate

λ = sales-decay rate

   a. Interpret the meaning of the terms in this model, $(V - Q)$, r, and λ, in particular.
   b. Suppose that $Q(0) = Q_0$ and $x = 0$ for all future time. Solve for $Q(t)$.
   c. Suppose that $Q(0) = 0$ and $x(t) = x$ (constant) for all future t. Solve for $Q(t)$.

4.9 Growth models in biology usually take on a form characterized by several assumptions. Assume that a population has size N at time zero and the growth of that population is a constant fraction of its current size.
   a. Formulate this problem as a differential equation.
   b. Solve the equation.
   Assume that the total growth rate in the population is a sum of two factors: the natural growth rate (above) plus modification due to the environment. Assume that an incoming member must compete with existing members of the population for resources. If A represents the number of individuals in the population at time t, there are $A(A - 1)/2$ possible pairs in conflict. Assume that this competition restricts the growth by an amount proportional to $A(A - 1)/2$.
   c. Incorporate this information in a differential equation.
   d. Solve the equation.
   e. Can you think of any uses for such a model in marketing?

Model Calibration

For a model to be concrete, it must be calibrated: values must be assigned to the model's parameters (the unknowns). In this chapter we cover this key step in the model-building process. At one extreme, calibration encompasses a classical statistical-estimation procedure. At the other extreme, a parameter or set of parameters may be selected judgmentally. We discuss the appropriateness of the calibration procedure, as well as its relation to the model's structure.

Knowledge of calculus is assumed here, and although some matrix notation is introduced, it is not essential for comprehension of the basic concepts. The reader with a good understanding of statistical, judgmental, and bayesian methods may wish to skip the chapter.

Model Calibration and Data

A model's value cannot exceed the value of what is put into it; we cannot expect to derive significant policy statements from our models if the parameters of those models are based on shaky data. Model calibration can be either data-based (objective) or subjective. With objective model calibration, the type, quantity, quality, availability, variability, and timing of the data all bear significantly on the model-building task.

Data come in various types. There are sales data, measured at several points along the distributor's chain—company sales, distributor sales, retail sales, and shipments. There are data on elements of the marketing mix—advertising, promotion, price—available on company and competitive levels. There are other internal company data, such as personal-selling effort, retailer and wholesaler margins. And there are attitudinal data from consumer surveys on such things as product quality. Each type of data has its limitations.

As an example, take consumer-purchase-panel data, such as that collected by MRCA, the Market Research Corporation of America. For these data a sample of consumers records all purchases in certain product classes, including price, purchase quantity, promotion, and sometimes media-consumption habits. These data suffer from (1) lack of control over the retail establishment, (2) potential respondent errors, (3) selection bias among respondents (high-socioeconomic-status and minority-group members are difficult to recruit for panel use), and (4) multiple consumers and multiple purposes for product consumption—other members of the household may buy and consume products, products may be bought for a variety of occasions and uses, and the purchaser may be an agent for the actual consumer of the product. In spite of these limitations, purchase panels have provided the data for some of the most sophisticated and challenging model-based efforts in the marketing area, especially for frequently purchased packaged goods.

Another source of data is retail-store audit firms, such as A. C. Nielsen, which provide information on sales, market share, availability, and inventory of many different brands. The data are collected by auditing shelf movements and in-store inventory of goods. Although the data are not collected at the individual level, careful control over data-collection procedures make this source of data a highly reliable one for many uses. But because the audit takes place continuously and all stores are not monitored at the same time, such data smooth responses, making it difficult to read short, intense market effects. Therefore Nielsen data are less valuable than they could be to the marketing modeler, who is interested in reading the precise variability that Nielsen's smoothing masks.

Many service bureaus collect data (such as advertising expenditures) that are relevant to a specific market. Because the quality of the message, the market coverage, and the media mix may vary from brand to brand, care must be taken when one is using these data in marketing models. Furthermore, advertising may be paid for in a different period than that in which it is seen, making it difficult to relate expenditures to effects.

Thus all the above data sources have associated problems, whether they be reporting or sampling errors, the lack of variability, or response biases.

Finally, a large amount of data is generally desirable. Aside from the fact that the reliability of parameter estimates tends to improve with the (square root of the) number of observations, large data sets are useful for model validation, where two nonoverlapping data sets—one for estimation and the second for prediction—are required. An ideal model that can neither be calibrated nor be validated may be of much less use than a far cruder model that blends well with available data and estimation procedures.

In the sections that follow we present three basic approaches to the calibration process: (1) objective procedures, (2) subjective procedures, and (3) bayesian procedures, which blend objective and subjective procedures.

Objective Parameter Estimation

We do not develop a complete treatment of objective model-calibration procedures here. Such a subject is several semesters' worth of work in statistics and econometrics. Rather, we develop the basic concepts of parameter estimation for the most frequently encountered type of marketing models and provide further references and examples for the interested reader.

First, we sketch simple linear-regression procedures and extend them to multiple regression. We then show how generalized least squares can be used to handle problems of heteroscedasticity and autocorrelation. These procedures are appropriate for estimating parameters of linear or linearizable models. Estimation procedures for nonlinear models are handled next. We then deal with models in which the dependent variable is a probability value (an unobserved value). Finally, we discuss issues in multiple-equation modeling and estimation, including causal- or structural-equation modeling.

Simple Linear-Regression Model

Suppose we observe sales levels $\{Q_i\}$ and advertising intensities $\{X_i\}$ in a number of markets, where i refers to market area. Let us assume a linear model is appropriate here. (The benefits and limitations of these models were reviewed in Chapter 4.) In addition, we are unlikely to model sales so simply with 100 percent accuracy, so a disturbance or error term is used to account for the deviation of the observed level of Q_i from its expected value. This discussion leads to the following model structure:

$$Q_i = a_0 + a_1 X_i + \epsilon_i \tag{5.1}$$

where Q_i = sales in region i
X_i = advertising intensity in i
a_0, a_1 = unknown parameters
ϵ_i = random disturbance

Let us assume the following:

1. The X_i are measured without error.
2. For a given value of X_i the variation in Q_i can be explained by a probability distribution, $f(Q_i | X_i)$, with the same variance σ^2 for all X_i.

$f(Q|X)$

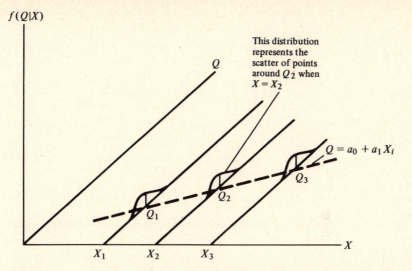

This distribution
represents the
scatter of points
around Q_2 when
$X = X_2$

Q

$Q = a_0 + a_1 X_i$

Q_3

Q_2

Q_1

X

X_1 X_2 X_3

EXHIBIT 5-1   The assumptions of the simple linear-regression model.

3. The values of Q_i are statistically independent (i.e., large sales in one region do not tend to affect sales in other regions).
4. The mean values of our observations, $E(Q_i)$, lie on the straight line

$$E(Q_i) = q_i = a_0 + a_1 X_i \qquad (5.2)$$

Exhibit 5.1 illustrates these relationships.

Then the problem we face is the estimation of a_0 and a_1. A frequently used approach is the least-squares solution. In this approach the values of a_0 and a_1 ($\hat{a}_0$ and $\hat{a}_1$) that minimize the sum of squared (observed) deviations of the Q_i from their mean values, $a_0 + a_1 X_i$, are estimated: find a_0 and a_1 to minimize

$$\Sigma(Q_i - a_0 - a_1 X_i)^2 \qquad (5.3)$$

The simplest minimizing technique for eq. (5.3) is calculus and results in

$$\hat{a}_0 = \sum_{i=1}^{I} \frac{Q_i}{I} \qquad (5.4)$$

and

$$\hat{a}_1 = \frac{\sum_{i=1}^{I} (X_i - \overline{X})Q_i}{\sum_{i=1}^{I} (X_i - \overline{X})^2}$$

where $\overline{X} = \dfrac{\Sigma X_i}{I} \qquad (5.5)$

A major justification for using the least-squares estimates in eqs. (5.4) and (5.5) is the *Gauss-Markov theorem*: within the class of linear, unbiased estimators, the least-squares estimators have minimum variance (are most efficient). This theorem is important because it follows from assumptions 1–4 above and does not require any assumption about the shape of the distribution of the error term.

There are several properties desirable in estimators: they should be unbiased, efficient, consistent, and best normal. These properties are defined below.

Unbiased.   An unbiased estimator is one that, on the average, is equal to its true value. Formally, $\hat{a}_1$ is unbiased if

$$E(\hat{a}_1) = a_1 \tag{5.6}$$

Efficiency.   We might wish to compare several estimators, some more biased perhaps and others spread out around their median. Analysts are concerned about how an estimator $\hat{a}_1$ is spread out around its true value a_1, or about its efficiency. The most common measure of this property is the mean squared error (MSE):

$$\text{MSE} = E(\hat{a}_i - a_i)^2 \tag{5.7}$$

It can be shown that MSE is a measure of both variance and bias:

$$\text{MSE} = \sigma^2 + \text{bias}^2 \tag{5.8}$$

Then for any two estimators $\hat{a}_1$ and $\hat{\hat{a}}_1$, the relative efficiency of $\hat{a}_1$ compared with $\hat{\hat{a}}_1$ is defined as

$$\frac{\text{MSE}(\hat{\hat{a}}_1)}{\text{MSE}(\hat{a}_1)} \tag{5.9}$$

Consistency.   A consistent estimator is one that is concentrated in a narrower and narrower range around its target as the sample size gets larger. Formally, this definition is stated as follows: $\hat{a}_1$ is consistent if, for any $\delta > 0$

$$p(|\hat{a}_1 - a_1| < \delta) \rightarrow 1 \text{ as the sample size} \rightarrow \infty \tag{5.10}$$

It can be shown that an estimator whose MSE $\rightarrow$ 0 as the sample size increases is consistent (although the converse does not hold).

Best Asymptotically Normal (BAN).   An estimator is best asymptotically normal if the following conditions hold:

1. Its distribution is approximately normal when its sample size gets large.
2. It is a consistent estimator.
3. No other consistent, normal estimator is more efficient (has a lower MSE).

To make use of these characteristics of estimators, we must make assumptions about the distribution of the error term ϵ. Assume that the characteristics of the product and the marketplace that affect Q (other than advertising) are large in number and essentially independent of one another and that no single excluded effect is dominant. In this case the central-limit theorem (see Mood and Graybill, 1963) suggests that the distribution of the error term is likely to be approximately normal with mean zero (by construction) and variance σ^2:

$$p_\epsilon(\epsilon) = \frac{1}{\sqrt{2\pi}\,\sigma}\,e^{-1/2(\epsilon/\sigma)^2} \tag{5.11}$$

or, equivalently,

$$p_Q(Q_i) = \frac{1}{\sqrt{2\pi}\,\sigma}\,e^{-1/2[(Q_i - a_0 - a_1 X_i)/\sigma]^2}$$

We introduce here another estimation concept, that of maximum-likelihood estimation.

Likelihood Function. The likelihood function of n random variables, $Q_1, \ldots, Q_n$, is the joint-probability density function of those variables, $p(Q_1, \ldots, Q_n; a_0, a_1)$, considered to be some function of the parameters a_0 and a_1. In particular, if the $\{Q_i\}$ are independent and identically distributed, then the likelihood function is

$$p(Q_1, \ldots, Q_n; a_0, a_1) = p_Q(Q_1; a_0, a_1) \ldots p_Q(Q_n; a_0, a_1) \tag{5.12}$$

That is, the likelihood function is the product of the individual probability densities.

This function gives the relative likelihood that a particular sample $(Q_1, \ldots, Q_n)$ could have been generated by a probability distribution with parameters a_0 and a_1. The principle of maximum-likelihood estimation is to choose parameter values that maximize this likelihood.

Maximum-likelihood Estimator. If the likelihood function is

$$L(a_0, a_1) = p(Q_1, \ldots, Q_n; a_0, a_1) \tag{5.13}$$

then the $\hat{a}_0$ and $\hat{a}_1$ that maximize the value of the likelihood function are the maximum-likelihood estimates of a_0 and a_1.

Much use is made of maximum-likelihood estimators for model parameters for two reasons. First, under fairly general conditions, maximum-likelihood estimators are the most efficient estimators in large samples, consistent, and best asymptotically normal. What these conditions mean is that, in general, if we have fairly large samples, not only can we do no better than the maximum-likelihood estimators in terms of estimator variance and bias, but we even know the distribution of the parameter estimators (normal) and can make probability statements about their statistical significance. Second, in a *normal* regression model (errors being normal), the maximum-likelihood estimates of the parameters are identical to the least-squares estimates. This condition establishes a key theoretical justification for the least-squares method: it follows from applying maximum-likelihood techniques to a model with normally distributed errors. Note that the results of this section and the next apply to any model that can be transformed into a linear model and that satisfies the assumptions.

Multiple Linear Regression*

In modeling situations there will be two or more independent variables that influence the variable of interest, Q in our case. The multiple linear equation analogous to eq. (5.1) is

$$Q = a_0 + a_1 X_1 + a_2 X_2 + \cdots + a_K X_K + \epsilon \tag{5.14}$$

where
$$X_1 = \text{advertising}$$
$$X_2 = \text{price (etc.)}$$
$$a_0, a_1, a_2, \ldots, a_K = \text{parameters to be estimated}$$
$$\epsilon = \text{stochastic-error term, with mean zero}$$
$$\text{and standard deviation } \sigma$$

We will assume for the moment that assumptions 1–4 from the previous section hold here as well.

In general, it is easier to describe and present the multiple-regression model in matrix form:

$$Q_j = \begin{bmatrix} 1 & X_{j1} & X_{j2} \ldots X_{jK} \end{bmatrix} \begin{bmatrix} a_0 \\ a_1 \\ \vdots \\ a_K \end{bmatrix} + \epsilon_j \tag{5.15}$$

If we stack all Q observations into a column vector, we get

$$\mathbf{Q} = \mathbf{X}\,\mathbf{a} + \epsilon \tag{5.16}$$

or

$$\begin{bmatrix} Q_1 \\ \vdots \\ \vdots \\ Q_J \end{bmatrix} = \begin{bmatrix} 11 & X_{11} & \ldots & X_{1K} \\ \cdots & \cdots & \cdots & \cdots \\ \cdots & \cdots & \cdots & \cdots \\ \cdots & \cdots & \cdots & \cdots \\ 1 & X_{J1} & \ldots & X_{JK} \end{bmatrix} \begin{bmatrix} a_0 \\ \vdots \\ a_K \end{bmatrix} + \begin{bmatrix} \epsilon_1 \\ \vdots \\ \epsilon_J \end{bmatrix}$$

*This section uses matrix algebra extensively.

Again we assume that $\{\epsilon_i\}$ are independent errors with mean zero and variance σ^2, so

$$E(\epsilon) = \mathbf{0} \tag{5.17}$$

and the covariance matrix of ϵ is

$$\text{Cov}(\epsilon) = E(\epsilon \, \epsilon') = \sigma^2 \mathbf{I} \tag{5.18}$$

or

$$\text{Cov}(\epsilon) = \begin{vmatrix} E(\epsilon_1\epsilon_1) \dots E(\epsilon_1\epsilon_j) \\ \cdots\cdots\cdots\cdots \\ E(\epsilon_j\epsilon_1) \dots E(\epsilon_j\epsilon_j) \end{vmatrix} = \begin{vmatrix} \sigma^2 & 0 & \dots & 0 \\ 0 & \sigma^2 & \dots & 0 \\ & \cdots\cdots\cdots & \\ 0 & \dots & 0 & \sigma^2 \end{vmatrix}$$

Note that the ϵ distribution is, in fact, the $\mathbf{Q}$ distribution translated onto a mean of zero—the only difference between the ϵ and $\mathbf{Q}$ distributions is their mean values:

$$E(\mathbf{Q}) = \mathbf{Xa} \tag{5.19}$$
$$\text{Cov}(\mathbf{Q}) = \sigma^2 \mathbf{I} \tag{5.20}$$

Now in the multiple-variable case (as in the single-variable case), we consider minimizing the sum of squared deviations. In matrix form this condition becomes

$$\text{Minimize}(\mathbf{Q} - \mathbf{Xa})'(\mathbf{Q} - \mathbf{Xa}) \tag{5.21}$$

Using principles of matrix multiplication and differentiation (analogous to scalar multiplication and differentiation), we obtain

$$\hat{\mathbf{a}} = (\mathbf{X'X})^{-1} \mathbf{X'Q} \tag{5.22}$$

By the Gauss-Markov theorem, $\hat{\mathbf{a}}$ is the best linear unbiased estimator of $\mathbf{a}$. Under the additional assumption that the $\{\epsilon_i\}$ are normally distributed, eq. (5.22) represents the maximum-likelihood estimator of $\mathbf{a}$, with the properties described above.

Key properties of the distribution of $\hat{\mathbf{a}}$ used in testing hypotheses about model parameters are

$$E(\hat{\mathbf{a}}) = \mathbf{a} \tag{5.23}$$

(i.e., the estimators are unbiased) and

$$\text{Cov}(\hat{\mathbf{a}}) = \sigma^2 (\mathbf{X'X})^{-1} \tag{5.24}$$

Relaxing the Assumptions: Generalized Least Squares

Marketing data and the associated marketing models often do not satisfy the neat assumptions needed for optimality of the ordinary-least-squares (OLS) approach. The most common problems seen in building multiple-variable marketing models are (1) heteroscedasticity, where the disturbance terms do not have the same variance; (2) autocorrelation, where the disturbance terms are not independent; and (3) multicollinearity, where two or more of the independent variables are related. The first two can be handled by a single procedure known as *generalized least squares* (GLS).

If eq. (5.18) does not hold, then, in general,

$$\text{Cov}(\epsilon) = \begin{vmatrix} \sigma_{11} & \sigma_{12} & \sigma_{1J} \\ \cdot & \cdot \cdot \cdot \cdot \cdot \cdot & \cdot \\ \sigma_{J1} & \cdots & \sigma_{JJ} \end{vmatrix} = \sigma^2 \Omega^* = \Omega \tag{5.25}$$

where Ω is a positive, definite, symmetric, $J \times J$ matrix of full rank. Now we introduce the matrix, $\mathbf{V}$:

$$\mathbf{V'V} = \Omega^{*-1} \quad \text{or} \quad (\mathbf{V'V})^{-1} = \Omega^* \tag{5.26}$$

If we go back to eq. (5.16) and premultiply by $\mathbf{V}$, we get

$$\mathbf{VQ} = \mathbf{VXa} + \mathbf{V\epsilon} \tag{5.27}$$

After substitution and some matrix manipulations, we obtain

$$E[(\mathbf{V\epsilon})(\mathbf{V\epsilon})'] = \sigma^2 \mathbf{I} \tag{5.28}$$

This equation means that the disturbance term in the transformed model, eq. (5.27), satisfies the standard least-squares regression conditions. Then applying the least-squares procedure to eq. (5.27) yields

$$\hat{\mathbf{a}} = (\mathbf{X'}\Omega^{-1}\mathbf{X})^{-1}\mathbf{X'}\Omega^{-1}\mathbf{Q} \tag{5.29}$$

which is known as the generalized-least-squares (GLS) estimator of $\hat{\mathbf{a}}$. Note that in the special case where $\Omega = \sigma^2 \mathbf{I}$, eq. (5.29) reduces to eq. (5.22), the ordinary-least-squares estimator.

Two special cases frequently arise in marketing analysis. The first is common in analyses of cross-sectional data where the assumption of homoscedasticity (all disturbance terms having the same variance) is often violated. In the model $Q = a_0 + a_1 X$, it might be reasonable for $\sigma^2 = f(X)$; that is, the amount of error around the sales figure might increase with larger levels of advertising (and hence sales). In this case,

$$\Omega = \begin{vmatrix} \sigma_1^2 \cdots & 0 \\ \cdot & \cdot \cdot \cdot \cdot \cdot \\ 0 & \cdots \ \sigma_J^2 \end{vmatrix} \tag{5.30}$$

Because the Ω matrix is diagonal,

$$\Omega^{-1} = \begin{vmatrix} \dfrac{1}{\sigma_1{}^2} & \cdots & 0 \\ \cdot\cdot\cdot & \cdot\cdot & \cdot\cdot\cdot \\ 0 & \cdots & \dfrac{1}{\sigma_J{}^2} \end{vmatrix} \tag{5.31}$$

and the least-squares solultion to eq. (5.27) turns out to be

$$\text{Minimize} \quad \sum_{j=1}^{J} \left(\frac{Q_j - \mathbf{X}_j \mathbf{a}}{\sigma_j}\right)^2 \tag{5.32}$$

where $\mathbf{X}_j$ is the jth row of matrix $\mathbf{X}$. Equation (5.32) is identical to the least-squares criterion, except for the $\{\sigma_j^2\}$ in the denominator. These weights give rise to the term "weighted least squares" (WLS), a special case of generalized least squares.

A second problem that frequently arises in analysis of time-series data is serially correlated error. For example, relatively high sales in period t may be associated with relatively high sales (due to some common cause) or relatively low sales (due to inventory buildup) in $t - 1$. In this situation let us index the observations on Q by t to suggest temporal effects. Each row of our equation looks like

$$Q_t = \mathbf{X}_t \mathbf{a} + \epsilon_t \qquad t = 1, \ldots, T \tag{5.33}$$

or

$$\mathbf{Q} = \mathbf{X}\mathbf{a} + \boldsymbol{\epsilon}$$

For purposes of illustration we assume that the $\{\epsilon_t\}$ are no longer independent of one another but are related in a simple autoregressive scheme:

$$\epsilon_t = \rho\epsilon_{t-1} + \nu_t \qquad t = \ldots, -2, -1, 0, 1, 2, \ldots \tag{5.34}$$

where $|\rho| < 1$. Here the disturbances $\{\nu_t\}$ are assumed to have the usual characteristics:

$$E(\nu) = \mathbf{0} \tag{5.35}$$

$$\text{Cov}(\nu) = \sigma^2 \mathbf{I} \tag{5.36}$$

In this case $E(\epsilon) = 0$, but $E(\epsilon\epsilon')$ is

$$\text{Cov}(\epsilon) = \Omega = \frac{\sigma^2}{1 - \rho^2} \begin{bmatrix} 1 & \rho & \rho^2 & \cdots & \cdot \\ \rho & 1 & \rho & \cdots & \cdot \\ \rho^2 & \rho & 1 & \cdots & \cdot \\ \rho^3 & \rho^2 & \rho & \cdots & \cdot \\ \cdot & \cdot & \cdot & \cdot & \cdot \\ \cdot & \cdot & \cdot & \cdot & \cdot \\ \cdot & \cdot & \cdot & & \cdot \\ \cdot & \cdot & \cdot & & 1 \cdot \end{bmatrix} \tag{5.37}$$

Note that

$$\Omega^{-1} = \frac{1}{\sigma^2} \begin{bmatrix} 1 & -\rho & \cdots & \cdots & \cdots & \cdots & 0 \\ -\rho & 1 + \rho^2 & & & & & \vdots \\ \vdots & & \ddots & & & & \vdots \\ \vdots & & & 1 + \rho^2 & & & \vdots \\ \vdots & & & & \ddots & & \vdots \\ \vdots & & & & & 1 + \rho^2 & -\rho \\ 0 & \cdots & \cdots & \cdots & \cdots & -\rho & 1 \end{bmatrix} \tag{5.38}$$

and substitution of eq. (5.38) into eq. (5.29) yields the GLS solution.

In the preceding discussion we have assumed that Ω is known. This is rarely the case, and we usually must rely on sample information to estimate Ω. For the case of heteroscedasticity the data must be segregated into m groups that are more or less homogeneous, with n_j observations in each group, such that $\sum_{j=1}^m n_j = J$.

A useful procedure is to use ordinary least squares to estimate $\hat{a}_0, \ldots, \hat{a}_K$ and to use the residuals from this regression to estimate $\hat{\sigma}_j, j = 1, \ldots, m$:

$$\sigma_{n_j} = \sum \frac{\left(Q_i - \sum_{\ell=1}^K \hat{a}_\ell X_{\ell i}\right)}{n_j} \qquad \text{for } j = 1, \ldots, m \tag{5.39}$$

where the summation is over those observations (i) in group n_j.

The estimates from eq. (5.39) can then be substituted into eq. (5.32) to obtain the generalized- (or weighted-) least-squares solution.

For the case of the first-order autoregressive scheme, an estimation approach is often required to estimate ρ. One direct approach is to estimate ρ as

$$\hat{\rho} = \frac{\sum_{t=2}^{T} \hat{\epsilon}_t \hat{\epsilon}_{t-1}}{\sum_{t=2}^{T} \hat{\epsilon}_t^2} \tag{5.40}$$

where $\{\hat{\epsilon}_t\}$ are estimated from ordinary least squares in the original equation. Note that eq. (5.40) produces the least-squares estimate of $\hat{\rho}$ from eq. (5.34). The value of $\hat{\rho}$ can be included in eq. (5.38), which, in turn, is substituted into eq. (5.29) to estimate **a**. Other procedures for estimating $\hat{\rho}$ are given by Cochrane and Orcutt (1949) and by Goldberger (1964).

Marketing models often face data that are gathered across geographic areas (or products) and over time. In these cases the disturbance terms may be cross-sectionally heteroscedastic and timewise autoregressive. For approaches to this problem, see Moriarty (1975), Moriarty and Salamon (1980), and Bass and Wittink (1975).

EXAMPLE: Just how much better are GLS estimators than OLS estimators? First, we note that GLS estimators are (1) unbiased, (2) maximum-likelihood estimators if normality of errors is assumed, and (3) BLUE (best linear unbiased estimators). Thus although OLS estimators are unbiased, the GLS estimators have smaller variance. But how much is the smaller variance worth? It can be shown that if Ω is a general matrix, then

$$\text{Cov}(\hat{\mathbf{a}}_{\text{OLS}}) = (\mathbf{X}'\mathbf{X})^{-1}\mathbf{X}'\Omega\mathbf{X}(\mathbf{X}'\mathbf{X})^{-1} \tag{5.41}$$

and

$$\text{Cov}(\hat{\mathbf{a}}_{\text{GLS}}) = (\mathbf{X}'\Omega^{-1}\mathbf{X})^{-1} \tag{5.42}$$

As an example of heteroscedasticity, assume that we have five values for advertising, $\{X_i\}$, that are (1, 2, 3, 4, 5) with $\{\epsilon_i\}$ = (1, 2, 3, 4, 5)—that is, proportional to $\{X_i\}$. Then by eqs. (5.41) and (5.42),

$$\text{Cov}(\hat{\mathbf{a}}_{\text{GLS}}) = \begin{bmatrix} 2.4 & -1.1 \\ -1.1 & 0.7 \end{bmatrix} \tag{5.43}$$

and

$$\text{Cov}(\hat{\mathbf{a}}_{\text{OLS}}) = \begin{bmatrix} 6.2 & -2.5 \\ -2.5 & 1.2 \end{bmatrix} \tag{5.44}$$

Here we see that the GLS estimations have considerably reduced the variance of the estimators.

Next, for serial correlation, assume that the values of $\{X_i\}$ are $(-2, -1, 0, 1, 2)$ and that the errors in Q follow eq. (5.34) with $\sigma_\nu^2 = 1$ and $\rho = \frac{1}{2}$. Then

$$\text{Cov}(\hat{\mathbf{a}}_{\text{GLS}}) = \begin{bmatrix} 0.57 & 0 \\ 0 & 0.154 \end{bmatrix} \tag{5.45}$$

and

$$\text{Cov}(\hat{\mathbf{a}}_{\text{OLS}}) = \begin{bmatrix} 0.59 & 0 \\ 0 & 0.160 \end{bmatrix} \tag{5.46}$$

Here we see that the OLS estimators are quite efficient.

Therefore with $\{X_i\}$ increasing regularly and ρ positive, OLS is quite efficient. For heteroscedasticity, this result is not the case, nor are OLS estimators efficient when ρ is very high and/or negative or when the $\{X_i\}$ series varies considerably.

A third problem that is common in multiple-regression models is *multicollinearity*. This situation occurs if two or more variables are significantly related to one another. For example, a firm might always split their marketing budget 10 percent for advertising and 90 percent for selling, in which case knowledge of advertising (or selling expenses) gives all available information about the effect of marketing-spending levels. Therefore if X_1 is advertising and X_2 is selling, multicollinearity occurs, as shown in the **X** matrix below:

$$\mathbf{X} = \begin{bmatrix} 1 & X_{11} & 9X_{11} & X_{31} \cdots \\ 1 & & & \\ 1 & & & \\ \vdots & \vdots & \vdots & \vdots \\ 1 & X_{1J} & 9X_{1J} & X_{3J} \cdots \end{bmatrix} \tag{5.47}$$

Multicollinearity is reflected in the X_2 column, which is a multiple of the X_1 column (i.e., the columns are linearly dependent).

The result of multicollinearity is some very large values in the inverse matrix $(\mathbf{X'X})^{-1}$. Because $\sigma^2(\mathbf{X'X})^{-1}$ is the covariance matrix of $\hat{\mathbf{a}}$, large variances and wide confidence intervals for the values of **a** result. In these circumstances it is difficult to establish that Q is influenced by any particular independent variable. When two (or more) variables are so related, the influence of one is easily attributable to another.

EXAMPLE: Consider the following example, where advertising spending X_1 is about half of personal-selling spending X_2: $X_1 = (1, 2, 3, 4, 5)$ and $X_2 = (2, 4, 6, 8, 11)$. Then

$$\mathbf{X'X} = \begin{pmatrix} 55 & 115 \\ 115 & 241 \end{pmatrix} \tag{5.48}$$

and

$$(\mathbf{X'X})^{-1} = \begin{pmatrix} 8.03 & 3.83 \\ 3.83 & 1.83 \end{pmatrix} \tag{5.49}$$

If the error in Q is σ_q, then the estimated standard error of a_1 (the coefficient of X_1) is $\sqrt{8.03}\ \sigma_q = 2.8\sigma_q$. In general, the errors associated with coefficient estimates should be much smaller than σ_q.

Multicollinearity is most often handled in one of three ways:

1. eliminating some independent variables
2. reducing the independent variables to a smaller number of principal components
3. using RIDGE regression

These methods are discussed in turn below.

Eliminating Variables. If two variables are meant to measure the same thing, or, computationally, turn out to be linearly related, then the model loses nothing by eliminating one of the variables. When appropriate variables to eliminate are not apparent, a common procedure is principal components.

Principal Components. Principal components is a technique for reexpressing the X's with a smaller number of Y variables that are linear combinations of the X's. These new Y variables are orthogonal (and therefore have no multicollinearity problems) and capture as much of the variation in the X's as possible, with the first Y capturing the most variation, the second Y capturing the maximum remaining, and so on.

In essence, the use of principal components is equivalent to multiple regression under constraints, where the constraints are on the relationships between the coefficients in the original variables. It is often preferred to discarding a variable, since the principal components capture the essence of the most important variables without eliminating any.

The main difficulty with this approach is that the effects of truly important independent variables can be lost in among the principal components, which are selected for their ability to explain the X's and therefore may not be the best set for explaining Q. A good alternative approach is to have important explanatory variables retained in their original form, with variables of lesser importance grouped as principal components. [See

Harman (1976) for a complete discussion of principal-component analysis and its relationship to various factor-analysis models.]

RIDGE Regression.   To retain all the independent variables in their original form, we can adjust the data matrix to stabilize the model coefficients. Multicollinearity exists when $\mathbf{X'X}$ has large off-diagonal elements and relatively small diagonal elements. RIDGE regression deals with this problem directly by augmenting the main diagonal of $\mathbf{X'X}$ with the addition of a matrix $\mathbf{D}$, which has positive diagonal elements and zeros elsewhere. The RIDGE regression estimate then becomes

$$\hat{\mathbf{a}} = (\mathbf{X'X} + \mathbf{D})^{-1}\mathbf{X'Q} \qquad (5.50)$$

When multicollinearity is present, these estimators are much more stable than the OLS estimators. But the procedure introduces bias. Therefore for the RIDGE estimators to be superior to the OLS estimators, the elements of $\mathbf{D}$ must be chosen to minimize the bias. [See Hoerl and Kennard (1970) for details and Erickson (1981), for a marketing application.]

Thus the general linear-regression model is a widely used estimation procedure in marketing. Under fairly general conditions GLS estimators provide estimators that have minimum variance among unbiased linear estimators. They are also maximum-likelihood estimators if the error terms are normally distributed.

The procedures presented here apply to any of the models in the last chapter that are either *linear, linear in the parameters,* or *linearizable.* However, they rely on a fairly large number of observations for estimation precision because standard errors contract with the square root of sample size. Furthermore, the least-squares criterion is sensitive to extreme points. If a few unusual or outlying points exist, they may greatly affect the parameter estimates, and more-robust regression procedures—bounded-loss functions and others—may be more appropriate (Hampel, 1974). The interested reader is referred to Draper and Smith (1966) for a more thorough discussion of the workings of the linear-regression model and to Theil (1971) or Goldberger (1964) for a more detailed presentation of econometrics in general.

Finally, these procedures do not apply to models that are inherently nonlinear or to models with binary dependent variables. These models are treated next.

Parameter Estimation for Nonlinear Models[*]

When a least-squares approach is applied to the estimation of parameters for nonlinear models, the resulting equations may be difficult to solve for unique values. Two approaches can be used: numerical solution or iterative

---

*This section contains technical material.

application of least squares with a Taylor series approximation to the original series. The problems and alternatives are illustrated through the following example.

EXAMPLE: Suppose we assume that sales go up with advertising, although nonlinearly, and that there is a base level of sales the firm would see even if advertising were zero. In this case we might model sales as

$$Q = a_0 + a_1 X^{a_2} + \epsilon \tag{5.51}$$

It can easily be seen that eq. (5.51) cannot be directly transformed to a linear form. However, least-squares estimates can still be justified with the maximum-likelihood argument, and a normally distributed error term ϵ in eq. (5.51) might be a reasonable assumption. Then the problem is to find a_0, a_1, and a_2 to

$$\text{Minimize } W = \Sigma(Q_i - a_0 - a_1 X_i^{a_2})^2 \tag{5.52}$$

The procedure here is the same as that of a linear model. We take derivatives of eq. (5.52) with respect to the parameters and set those derivatives equal to zero. (We must check second derivatives more carefully now because nonlinear models may lead us to local optima.)

$$\frac{\partial W}{\partial a_0} = \sum 2(-1)(Q_i - a_0 - a_1 X_i^{a_2}) = 0 \tag{5.53a}$$

$$\frac{\partial W}{\partial a_1} = \sum 2(-X_i^{a_2})(Q_i - a_0 - a_1 X_i^{a_2}) = 0 \tag{5.53b}$$

$$\frac{\partial W}{\partial a_2} = \sum 2(a_1 X_i^{a_2} \ln a_2)(Q_i - a_0 - a_1 X_i^{a_2}) = 0 \tag{5.53c}$$

Given values of $\{Q_i\}$ and $\{X_i\}$, eq. (5.53) must be solved for a_0, a_1, and a_2. The difficulty is that they are nonlinear, and even a single nonlinear equation may be difficult to solve. Moreover, there may no longer be a unique solution to the equations; therefore each set of values would have to be plugged into eq. (5.52) to see which minimizes W. Because of these analytical difficulties, an iterative, numerical computer routine is usually used to solve such problems.

Let us outline a solution procedure that is of general value. Redefine eq. (5.52) as

$$Q = f(X_1, \ldots, X_K; a_0, \ldots, a_p) + \epsilon \tag{5.54a}$$

$$= f(a_0, \ldots, a_p) + \epsilon \tag{5.54b}$$

where eq. (5.54b) suppresses the X's to simplify the notation.

We now use a Taylor series expansion of $f(\cdot)$, truncated after the linear term. The Taylor series must be expanded around a particular set of parameter values. Call these values $\{a_{ji}\}$, where i refers to the iteration number. We start with $\{a_{j0}\}$:

$$f(a_0, \ldots, a_p) = f(a_{00}, \ldots, a_{p0}) + \frac{\partial f}{\partial a_0}(a_0 - a_{00})$$

$$+ \cdots + \frac{\partial f}{\partial a_p}(a_p - a_{p0}) + \text{Taylor error} \qquad (5.55)$$

where the partial derivations $(\partial f/\partial a_k)$ on the right-hand side of eq. (5.55) are evaluated at $\{a_{00}, \ldots, a_{p0}\}$. In the example we have

$$\frac{\partial f}{\partial a_0} = 1 \qquad (5.56a)$$

$$\frac{\partial f}{\partial a_1} = X_1^{a_{20}} \qquad (5.56b)$$

and
$$\frac{\partial f}{\partial a_2} = a_{10}X_1^{a_{20}} \ln a_{20} \qquad (5.56c)$$

Then the *only unknowns* in eq. (5.55) are $a_0, \ldots, a_p$ because $\{\partial f/\partial a_i\}$ are determined by eq. (5.56) for each value of Q_i and X_i.

Rearranging terms in eq. (5.55) and collecting both Taylor error and stochastic error into one term ϵ', we get

$$Q - f(a_{00}, \ldots, a_{p0}) + \frac{\partial f}{\partial a_0}a_{00} + \cdots + \frac{\partial f}{\partial a_p}a_{p0}$$

$$= a_0\frac{\partial f}{\partial a_0} + \cdots + a_p\frac{\partial f}{\partial a_p} + \epsilon' \qquad (5.57)$$

or

$$Q^* = a_0X_0^* + \cdots + a_pX_p^* + \epsilon' \qquad (5.58)$$

In this linearized form we can solve for $\hat{a}_0, \ldots, \hat{a}_p$, which are likely to be better than $a_{00}, \ldots, a_{p0}$. Call these values $a_{01}, \ldots, a_{p1}$, return to eq. (5.55), and repeat the process. The process is repeated, obtaining new and better estimates at each step, until it converges, that is, $(a_{0i}, \ldots, a_{pi}) \approx (a_{0i+1}, \ldots, a_{pi+1})$.

The procedure, however, may not converge, or it may converge to a local minimum. To alleviate the latter problem, one should use several different starting values. However, if the model is reasonable, the procedure will often converge in a short period of time, and the least-squares routine will produce standard errors of the estimates of $a_0, \ldots, a_p$.

A number of more powerful computer-based methods have been developed, some using second-order series expansions, some providing numerical estimates of the derivatives, and others permitting constraints on the parameters. Many are readily available on standard computer packages. [See Bard (1974, app. G) for a partial list of available packages.] Naert and Leeflang (1978, pp. 238–241) allude to the use of such estimation procedures in marketing models.

Parameter Estimation for Binary Dependent Variables

Throughout this section we have assumed that the dependent variable of interest was a single, observable marketing variable, such as sales. But a class of very useful marketing models, individual-choice models, presented in Chapter 4, have a 0–1 type of dependent variable. For example, we often observe consumer purchasing response as a 0–1 variable (bought the brand or not); an underlying probability model may be generating this (observed) 0–1 response.

Suppose we feel that individual probability of purchase p would increase with advertising exposure. To model this relationship, we might use the logit model, with

$$Y = \begin{cases} 1 & \text{if purchase is made} \\ 0 & \text{otherwise} \end{cases} \tag{5.59}$$

$$p = \text{probability that } Y = 1 \tag{5.60}$$

$$x = \text{advertising level}$$

and

$$p = \frac{1}{1 + e^{-(a_0 + a_1 x)}} \tag{5.61}$$

or

$$\log \frac{p}{1 - p} = a_0 + a_1 x \tag{5.62}$$

It appears that eq. (5.62) can be used to estimate a_0 and a_1 by ordinary least squares. But if we use the original buy/not-buy data (0–1 responses) to replace p in eq. (5.62), $\log [p/(1 - p)]$ is undefined. Therefore we must partition the X axis into cells with enough observations to construct observed proportions $\hat{p}$. However, even with five or ten observations per cell, the number of purchases may still be zero or n, making the observed proportion $\hat{p}$ still zero or one. In addition, in grouping, we introduce an error in X that causes bias (an errors-in-variables bias that is described in the next section). Finally, if we had, say, four independent variables and wanted to break the regions up into five parts along each variable, we would have $5^4 =$ 625 cells. To have ten or more observations per cell would require over 6000 observations as a minimum.

A more commonly applied approach is that of maximum likelihood. We develop this approach as follows: Assume we had only one observation Y_1 associated with X_1. The probability that $Y_1 = 1$, called p_1, is given by eq. (5.61); the probability of $Y_1 = 0$ is simply $1 - p_1$. We can combine these two cases in a (Bernoulli) distribution function:

$$p(Y_1) = p_1^{Y_1}(1 - p_1)^{1 - Y_1} \tag{5.63}$$

Note that p_1 is a function of a_0 and a_1 from eq. (5.62). In like manner, we can get

$$p(Y_1, \ldots, Y_n) = p(Y_1) \ldots p(Y_n) \tag{5.64}$$

$$= \prod_{i=1}^{n} p_i^{Y_i}(1 - p_i)^{1 - Y_i} \tag{5.65}$$

Although eq. (5.65) looks like a complicated expression, in fact, it is only a function of two parameters, a_0 and a_1. Equation (5.65) is the *likelihood function* for this sample of n observations, and because it is a function of a_0 and a_1, we denote it as $L(a_0, a_1)$.

As in the previous section on nonlinear optimization, the values of a_0 and a_1 that maximize $L(\cdot)$ must be developed numerically. Many standard computer packages include numerical routines for the linear logit model, usually employing some modification of the Newton-Raphson method. McFadden (1970) shows that under quite general conditions the maximum of eq. (5.65) exists and is unique. As indicated earlier, these maximum-likelihood estimates are best asymptotically normal, and, as such, most computer routines automatically provide standard errors of the estimates. [See Gensch and Recker (1979) and Punj and Staelin (1978) for some marketing applications and Urban and Hauser (1980) for the development of statistical theory to test such models against one another.]

Although this section has been framed in terms of the logit model, as long as the purchase events are independent of one another, eq. (5.65) holds for any assumed equation for p_i.

EXAMPLE: Suppose $p_i = p$ for all individuals in the population. This model is the so-called homogeneous Bernoulli model (and is one of few that allows for an analytical solution of the likelihood function).

Here, eq. (5.65) becomes

$$L(p) = \prod_{i=1}^{n} p^{Y_i}(1 - p)^{1 - Y_i} = p^{\Sigma Y_i}(1 - p)^{n - \Sigma Y_i} \tag{5.66}$$

Note that since the log transformation is monotonic, we can maximize $\ln[L(p)]$ to determine p:

$$L^*(p) = \ln[L(p)] = \Sigma Y_i \ln p + (n - \Sigma Y_i)\ln(1 - p) \tag{5.67}$$

$$\frac{dL^*}{dp} = \frac{\Sigma\,Y_i}{p} - \frac{n - \Sigma\,Y_i}{1 - p} \qquad (5.68)$$

Then setting eq. (5.68) equal to zero yields

$$p(n - \Sigma\,Y_i) = (1 - p)\Sigma\,Y_i \qquad (5.69)$$

or

$$\hat{p} = \frac{\Sigma\,Y_i}{n}$$

In this case the maximum-likelihood estimator for the single parameter p equals the proportion of the population who bought the product.

Two other approaches to parameter estimation for individual-brand-choice models are notable. The first approach is a form of the least-squares approach noted above. The main problems with the ordinary- or generalized-least-squares approach for probabililty-of-purchase models are that (1) they don't force probabilities of purchase across brands to sum to one (an individual buys one and only one brand per purchase occasion), and (2) they don't force each separate probability to fall in the 0–1 range. However, the advent of more powerful, generalized nonlinear-programming routines [such as SUMT, see Fiacco and McCormick (1968)] have allowed such problems to be solved more readily than before. In fact, with linear constraints and the least-squares criterion as an objective, this type of problem reduces to what is called a quadratic-programming problem—one that is solved in much the same way as a linear-programming problem. [See Bradley, Hax, and Magnanti (1977) for a discussion.]

Finally, the concept of entropy has recently been employed for determining parameters of probability systems. Entropy is a measure of the degree of randomness or disorder in a probabilistic system. The concept assumes that at equilibrium a probabilistic system will be at maximum entropy, subject to system constraints (which are usually taken to be empirical market shares). Switching probabilities between brands are taken as those that maximize entropy, subject to the constraints. Maximizing the mathematical expression for system entropy leads to estimates of system parameters. This concept replaces assumptions about the distribution of the error term, needed for other estimation procedures. We develop the entropy concept further in Chapter 7 in the discussion of the Hendry system.

Multiple-Equation Problems and Solutions*

In the preceding sections we assumed that the requirements of a single-equation model held at least roughly, that is, that the direction of causality

*This section deals with technical issues.

between Q and X is clear and that X is not measured with error. If either X is measured with error or our single equation is an integral part of a larger equation system, then OLS coefficient estimates will be biased and inconsistent.

To get an idea of what is going on here, assume that both sales and advertising are measured with some error:

$$Q = Q^T + \epsilon \tag{5.70}$$

$$X = X^T + \mu \tag{5.71}$$

where Q^T and X^T represent true values of Q and X, respectively. For simplicity suppose further that

$$Q^T = a_0 + a_1 X^T \tag{5.72}$$

that is, true sales and true advertising are related to one another in a perfect linear manner. Substituting eqs. (5.70) and (5.71) into eq. (5.72) yields

$$Q = a_0 + a_1 X + \omega \tag{5.73}$$

where $\omega = \epsilon - a_1\mu$ \hfill (5.74)

Even if errors ϵ and μ are mutually independent and serially independent with constant variances, the assumptions for least squares do not apply because ω is not independent of X. It can be shown (Johnston, 1963, p. 150) that the least-squares estimator of a_1 $(\hat{a}_1)$ is biased:

$$E(\hat{a}_1) = a_1 \left[\frac{1}{1 + (\sigma_\mu^2/\sigma_X^2)} \right] \tag{5.75}$$

What eq. (5.75) says is that if the variance of the error in measuring X (advertising, say) is 10 percent of the variation observed in the analysis, then straightforward least squares would underestimate a_1 by about 10 percent even in very large samples. Intuitively, the reason for this underestimation (inconsistency) is clear. As illustrated in Exhibit 5.2, with a positive relationship between X and ϵ, the true line should be below the least-squares line for X large and above it for X small (or negative). In single-equation situations this problem is often handled through the introduction of *instrumental variables*, variables that are related to the X's but that are uncorrelated with the error term ϵ. Other approaches include grouping observations to get estimates of the level of error and the so-called classical approach, relying on strong assumptions about the error terms (Johnston, 1963).

We bring up the problem of correlation between error and independent variables here because it occurs when an equation to be estimated is part of a whole system of simultaneous equations. Such equation systems occur in marketing models when the direction of causality is unclear or when a series of (brand-specific) market-share equations must be consistent. As an example, consider the dilemma faced by the marketing analyst who believes that advertising (X) and level of distribution (D) affect sales (Q), but advertising

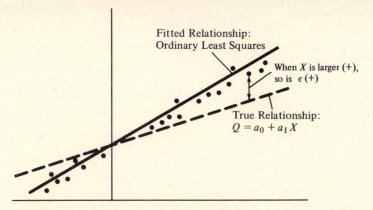

EXHIBIT 5-2 **Positive correlation between ϵ and X makes $\hat{a}_1$ biased and inconsistent (too small).**

in his firm is set at a fixed percentage of sales. These two relationships can be described as

$$Q = a_0 + a_1 X + a_2 D + \epsilon_1 \tag{5.76}$$

$$X = b_0 + b_1 Q + \epsilon_2 \tag{5.77}$$

If we substitute eq. (5.77) into eq. (5.76), we get

$$Q = \frac{a_0 + a_1 b_0}{1 - a_1 b_1} + \frac{a_2}{1 - a_1 b_1} D + \frac{\epsilon_1 + a_1 \epsilon_2}{1 - a_1 b_1} \tag{5.78}$$

Equation (5.78) clearly shows that Q and ϵ_2 are correlated, as in the errors-in-variables case described above. Similarly, it can be shown that ϵ_1 and X are correlated. Thus if we apply OLS to either eq. (5.76) or (5.77), our estimates will be biased and inconsistent. A variety of methods have been suggested for handling these problems, of which the simplest to apply is two-stage least squares (2SLS).

The idea behind 2SLS is to purge Q of its dependency on ϵ_2. This feat is done by replacing Q by $\hat{Q}$, which resembles Q but is independent of ϵ_2 (i.e., an instrumental variable). To find $\hat{Q}$, regress Q on D:

$$\hat{Q} = c_0 + c_1 D \tag{5.79}$$

Because, by assumption, D is independent of ϵ_2, this linear function will be independent of ϵ_2 as well. This step is the first stage of 2SLS: regress each endogenous (dependent) variable against all related exogenous (independent) variables.

The second stage of 2SLS simply substitutes eq. (5.79) into eq. (5.78) to get

$$X = b_0 + b_1 \hat{Q} + \epsilon_3 \tag{5.80}$$

We can now apply OLS to eq. (5.78), which leads to consistent estimators because $\hat{Q}$ is uncorrelated with the (adjusted) error term ϵ_3.

An additional problem in multiple equation estimation concerns *identification*. In terms of our original objectives, which were to estimate a_0, a_1, a_2, b_0, and b_1, we have produced consistent estimates of b_0 and b_1. But what of a_0, a_1, and a_2? Comparing eqs. (5.78) and (5.79), we find we have established the following relationships:

$$\hat{c}_0 = \frac{a_0 + a_1 b_0}{1 - a_1 b_1} \tag{5.81}$$

$$\hat{c}_1 = \frac{a_2}{1 - a_1 b_1} \tag{5.82}$$

In eqs. (5.81) and (5.82) we have two equations but three unknowns. In such circumstances we say that the equation is underidentified. This is a critical point for multiple-equation systems: an equation can be underidentified [as is eq. (5.76)], just-identified [as is eq. (5.77)], or overidentified. A condition that must be satisfied for an equation to be identified is called the order condition. This condition relates the number of excluded exogenous (independent) variables (m_0) to the number of included endogenous (dependent) variables (q). There are three cases:

1. If $m_0 < q - 1$, the equation is *underidentified*, or unidentified, and the coefficients of the original equation cannot be estimated.
2. If $m_0 = q - 1$, the equation is *exactly identified*, and the coefficients can be estimated exactly.
3. If $m_0 > q - 1$, the equation is *overidentified* because more equations are available than are necessary to estimate the coefficients.

In eq. (5.76) $q = 3$ (including the constant), and in eq. (5.77) $q = 2$. In both cases $m_0 = 1$. Then by the above rule, eq. (5.76) is unidentified, while eq. (5.77) is just-identified. This simple order condition is usually a good indicator of the identifiability of each equation in a multiple-equation system. [See Fisher (1966) for treatment of this issue.]

There are many other methods for estimating coefficients in multiple-equation systems. These methods usually fall into two categories: (1) limited-information methods and (2) full-information methods. Limited-information methods address one equation in the system at a time and include 2SLS and limited-information maximum likelihood. Full-information methods estimate all system coefficients simultaneously and include three-stage least squares and full-information maximum likelihood. Although full-information methods may, on the surface, appear superior, they are much more sensitive to model misspecification (including or excluding incorrect variables or functional relationships) than limited-information methods are. The limited-information methods insulate estimation of any equation from specification errors committed in other equations:

". . . in an economic world where [the dependent variables] depend on a large number of other variables in the economy, the more one reduces the model size in order to provide theoretical and mathematical simplicity . . . the greater may be the risk of mis-specification; accordingly, the more one might prefer 2SLS" (Wonnacott and Wonnacott, 1979, p. 520). See any econometrics text for development of these estimation approaches in detail.

Finally, 2SLS has been applied to a large number of marketing studies reported in the literature, including Cowling and Cubbin (1971), Farley and Leavitt (1968), Bass and Parsons (1969), Lambin, Naert, and Bultez (1975), and Lambin (1976).

Causal Models and Unobserved Variables*

Before leaving the realm of estimation and multiple-equation modeling, we introduce an approach in the social and behavioral sciences called causal modeling. In the model systems we have reviewed, the associations between variables can be either empirical or causal. When the relationships are causal, the model is called a *structural-equation model*. All the variables in these models are assumed to represent a single, theoretical construct and are usually assumed to be measured without error. From a marketing standpoint such an assumption is very limiting; in many contexts, especially where perceptual or psychological variables are included, single indicators are unlikely to capture all the richness of the theoretical construct and may well be measured with error.

Within the context of linear systems of equations and subject to restrictions imposed by the necessities of identification, hypothetical constructs, called unobserved variables, can be included and estimated in structural-equation models. For example, an unobserved variable may be preference for a brand, where the measurement of preference is a scale of 1–10 or a paired comparison with another brand. Another example is individual and job-related attitudes of salespeople, which may be unobserved variables related to objective performance and stated job satisfaction.

Ideally, one would like to employ a modeling-and-estimation procedure that directly measures the degree of correspondence between unobservable constructs and measurements, the level of error in those measurements, the level of error in equations, and the relationship between the observable constructs themselves. These measurements and diagnostics can all be achieved in a linear causal-modeling framework, provided that the system is linear and identified, that there are multiple measurements of at least some of the unobservable variables in the model, and that errors are approximately normal.

*This section deals with technical material.

Structural-equation models are popularly represented in causal diagrams with the following conventions (Bagozzi, 1979b):

$$y = \beta x \Longleftrightarrow x \xrightarrow{\beta} Y$$

$$y = \beta x + \mu \Longleftrightarrow x \xrightarrow{\beta} Y \leftarrow \mu$$

$$y = \beta_1 x_1 + \beta_2 x_2 + \beta_3 x_3 + \mu \Longleftrightarrow$$

$\square$ = observed variable

$\bigcirc$ = theoretical construct

EXAMPLE: Consider a model in which one theoretical construct B causes another, A. Both A and B are operationalized by two variables—each, measured with error.

Exhibit 5.3 shows the associated causal diagram, which yields the following *structural equation*:

$$A = \gamma B + \phi \tag{5.83}$$

and the following four equations relating observables to unobservables:

$$Y_1 = \lambda_1 A + \epsilon_1 \tag{5.84a}$$

$$Y_2 = \lambda_2 A + \epsilon_2 \tag{5.84b}$$

$$X_1 = \lambda_1' B + \delta_1 \tag{5.84c}$$

$$X_2 = \lambda_2' B + \delta_2 \tag{5.84d}$$

In terms of available information, the variables Y_1, Y_2, X_1, and X_2

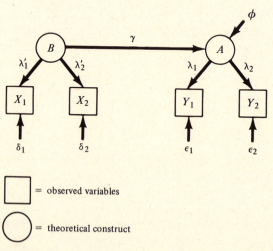

= observed variables

= theoretical construct

EXHIBIT 5-3   **Example of a causal model where one theoretical variable causes a second, each operationalized by two indicators.**

provide four variances and six covariances. Assuming the variances of A and B are standardized, there are nine parameters to be estimated: λ_1, λ_1', λ_2, λ_2', γ, $\sigma_{\delta_1}^2$, $\sigma_{\delta_2}^2$, $\sigma_{\epsilon_1}^2$, and $\sigma_{\epsilon_2}^2$. These parameters can be related to the observed variances and covariances as follows:

$$\mathrm{Cov}(X_1 X_2) = \lambda_1' \lambda_2 \tag{5.85a}$$

$$\mathrm{Cov}(X_2 Y_2) = \lambda_2' \gamma \lambda_2 \tag{5.85b}$$

and so on.

With ten relations among nine unknowns, the system is overidentified. Bagozzi (1979b, pp. 109–110) describes a study using a model such as the above where attitudes (affect) toward the church (B) affect behavioral intentions (A). B is operationalized by two scale measurements, as is A.

Jöreskog's development (1969, 1970, 1973, 1974) of a maximum-likelihood approach to estimate and test causal models addresses the issue of measurement errors and unobservables directly. In general, a causal model may be represented as a set of recursive or simultaneous linear structural equations:

$$\mathbf{aN} = \mathbf{bM} + \Theta \tag{5.86}$$

where $\mathbf{N} = m \times 1$ vector of true, unobservable dependent variables
$\mathbf{M} = n \times 1$ vector of true, unobservable independent variables
$\mathbf{a} = m \times m$ matrix of parameters
$\mathbf{b} = m \times n$ matrix of parameters
$\Theta = $ vector of random residuals

Equation (5.86) represents the relationship among the variables $\mathbf{N}$ through the parameters in $\mathbf{a}$ and their relationship to the true independent variables $\mathbf{M}$ through the parameters in $\mathbf{b}$. The unobserved theoretical constructs, $\mathbf{M}$ and $\mathbf{N}$, are related to the observations as follows:

$$\mathbf{Y} = \boldsymbol{\mu}_Y + \Lambda_Y \mathbf{N} + \epsilon \tag{5.87a}$$

$$\mathbf{X} = \boldsymbol{\mu}_X + \Lambda_X \mathbf{M} + \delta \tag{5.87b}$$

where $\mathbf{Y} = $ vector of observed dependent variables
$\mathbf{X} = $ vector of observed independent variables
$\boldsymbol{\mu}_X, \boldsymbol{\mu}_Y = $ mean vectors for $\mathbf{X}$ and $\mathbf{Y}$
$\Lambda_X, \Lambda_Y = $ matrices of regression or factor coefficients
$\epsilon, \delta = $ errors in measurement (also known as unique factors in $\mathbf{X}$ and $\mathbf{Y}$)

In Jöreskog's development the errors in these relationships are assumed to have a multivariate normal distribution. Under this assumption a maximum-likelihood procedure, LISREL (Jöreskog and Sörbom, 1981), is available to perform the estimation. However, although it is the most popular estimation procedure, LISREL suffers from the problems of full-information methods—sensitivity of the whole system to misspecification. Fornell and Bookstein (1981), in a marketing context, compare the LISREL approach to a partial-least-squares (PLS) approach, which is not sensitive to the multinormality assumption. [See Jöreskog and Wald (1981) for further development and comparison of these approaches.] Bagozzi (1979b) provides a thorough description of the causal-modeling approach, describing numerous applications in marketing.

Causal modeling has seen wide applicability in the social sciences, and its use in marketing research is beginning to emerge. Bagozzi (1979b) and Bagozzi, Fornell, and Larchen (1981) show that factor analysis, regression, and canonical correlation are special cases of the mathematical implementation of causal modeling. Indeed, the November 1982 issue of the *Journal of Marketing Research* is devoted to causal modeling. The approach appears extremely useful for testing a linear theory and for describing the relationships in a behavioral system. However, the linearity and multinormality restrictions limit the use of the approach for calibrating response models.

Subjective Parameter Estimation

Justification and Background

Data for many marketing situations are either not available at all or not available soon enough for decision making. The econometric approach, characterized by some as "looking forward through a rear-view mirror" (a remark attributed to Robert Shlaiffer of Harvard), implicitly assumes that historical data will be a good indication of responses in the future. In many demand situations this assumption may be a reasonable one; in others, it corresponds to a risky leap of faith. [See Stobaugh and Yergin (1979) for a critique of this assumption in the area of energy demand.] Econometric, data-based models are best suited for interpolative tasks, estimating responses within the range and the time period of the collected data; extensions beyond the data base, either in time or in space (such as assuming that an advertising-response parameter is valid at double the highest observed level of spending), may be difficult to justify. Thus econometric models are limited by their data and by the fact that parameters and model structure are usually assumed fixed throughout the period of calibration.

But all is not lost. Decision makers have been making decisions based on their experience for a long time and will continue to do so in the future. These decisions make implicit assumptions about response parameters. The purpose of subjective estimation then is to elicit judgments from decision makers and quantify them (turn them into model parameters). This method of subjective estimation is not necessarily inferior to objective estimation and may be clearly superior in many cases, especially when objective data are subject to significant biases or errors. Surely a market manager working closely with a product amasses a great amount of valuable information about it.

The quantification of judgments for use in marketing models has several important benefits:

Executives and experts who are asked to put their judgments in the forms of numbers tend to give harder thought to the problem, especially if the numbers are a matter of record.

Quantification helps pinpoint the extent and importance of differences among executives with respect to the decision problem. Numbers permit the analyst to perform a sensitivity analysis to determine how dependent a decision is on particular differences in judgment.

Judgmental data allow the use of many interesting decision models that could not otherwise be used because of a lack of objective data. Clearly, the analyst collecting judgmental data must exercise care in how he asks the experts for their estimates. He must form his questions with the same care he uses in interviewing customers, dealers, and others. The manner in which the questions are asked will affect the answer.

There are two fundamental problems in gathering and using data. The first concerns methods of obtaining useful estimates for the decision model from a single expert (consultant, company executive, etc.). The second concerns the problem of pooling the estimates of two or more experts when there may be some divergence of opinion (the consensus problem).

Single-Assessor Model Calibration

Little (1970) introduced the concept of decision calculus for formally incorporating managerial judgment in the calibration task for marketing models. A large number of models based on decision calculus have been proposed and implemented [see Chakravarti, Mitchell, and Staelin (1979) for a review], suggesting the impact the approach has had on the field.

Decision-calculus model calibration structures a manager's experience into a formal model that is then used in subsequent decision making. Support for this mode of thinking comes from several sources. The research of Bowman (1963), Kunreuther (1969), and others has shown that a quantitative procedure formulated from an individual's previous decisions may outperform his future decisions. Theoretically, this result occurs through the analytical systemization of past experiences in the model. A second source of support comes from the work of Armstrong (1978) and of Brown (1969), who discuss the principle of decomposition. They report that predictions can be improved by first decomposing a complex problem into a series of simpler prediction problems that are more relevant to the respondent and then recombining these estimates to predict desired outcomes.

There are at least four major categories of judgmental information obtainable from a single assessor that might be important to a marketing analyst. First, he might need a *point estimate* of the value of some independent variable or coefficient, such as a size-of-market estimate or a unit-cost figure. Second, he might need a *sales-response function*—that is, an indication of how the expert feels sales would vary with variations in the level of one or more marketing factors. Third, he might need estimates of the *uncertainty* surrounding parameter estimates, function estimates, or key events. Finally, he might need a set of *ratings and/or weights* to assign to certain variables in his model.

Point Estimates.   Gathering point estimates often must be performed by a homing-in principle; most marketing managers have more quantitative information at their disposal than they readily admit. For example, the following dialogue is not atypical:

ANALYST: What do you think your annual sales will be in the new territory?

EXECUTIVE: I don't have the foggiest idea. I just think it will be a good territory.

ANALYST: Do you think sales will go over $10 million a year?

EXECUTIVE: No, that's very unlikely.

ANALYST: Do you think sales will go over $8 million a year?

EXECUTIVE: That's possible.

ANALYST: Could sales be as low as $4 million a year?

EXECUTIVE: Absolutely not. We wouldn't open the territory if we thought sales would be that low.

ANALYST: Is it more likely that sales will be around $6 million?

EXECUTIVE: That's quite possible. In fact, I would say that's a little on the low side.

ANALYST: Where would you place sales?

EXECUTIVE: Around $7 million.

The interesting thing about this dialogue is how the executive went from a statement that he had no idea of the expected level of sales to a definite estimate from a questioning procedure that confronted him with extreme possibilities.

For the point-estimation task the analyst should consider the wording of questions (mean? median? mode?), the conditions of the environment (what is happening to the economy? the competitors?), and what level of certainty the estimator feels about his judgment.

Response-function Estimates.   A series of point-estimate questions, combined with an analytical form, can lead to the calibration of a marketing-response model. Consider the calibration task associated with an awareness-response function (the ADBUDG model, Little, 1970). During a given time period of unit length, the model assumes the following:

1. If there is no advertising, the fraction of the population evoking the product will decrease to a value W_0, where "evoking" refers to unaided product awareness.
2. No matter how much is spent, the fraction evoking the product cannot exceed an amount $W*$.
3. There is some rate of advertising $A*$ that will maintain initial evoking share $W = W(A*)$.
4. An estimate is available of evoking $W^1 = W(A^1)$ by the end of the period with a 50 percent increase in advertising ($A^1 = 1.5A*$) over maintenance.

Exhibit 5.4 gives a representation of this information.

The ADBUDG model can now be specified as

$$W = W_0 + (W* - W_0)\frac{A^\delta}{\gamma + A^\delta} \qquad (5.88)$$

where the constants W_0, $W*$, γ, and δ are to be determined from the input data.

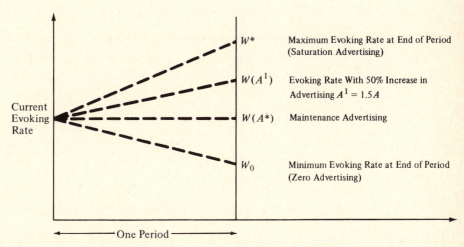

EXHIBIT 5-4   **Subjective input data for fitting an awareness-response function.**

We now ask the following questions:

What value (W_{00}) would awareness decay to if there were no advertising for a long time?

What fraction (ρ) of the current level would awareness decay to with zero advertising in a single period?

The model further assumes that the decay rate ρ is constant over time, as is the affectable range $(W^* - W_0)$, and can now be written as

$$W(t) = W_{00} + \rho[W(t-1) - W_{00}] + \Psi \frac{A(t)^\delta}{\gamma + A(t)^\delta} \tag{5.89}$$

where $A(t)$ = advertising at t
$\quad\quad\quad W(t)$ = evoking rate at t

W_{00} is given by the input data and ρ, Ψ, γ, and δ are calculated as

$$\rho = \frac{W_0 - W_{00}}{W - W_{00}} \tag{5.90}$$

$$\Psi = W^* - W_0 \tag{5.91}$$

$$\delta = \frac{1}{\ln(1.5)} \ln\left(\frac{W^* - W}{W - W_0} \frac{W^1 - W_0}{W^* - W^1}\right) \tag{5.92}$$

$$\gamma = A^\delta \frac{W^* - W}{W - W_0} \tag{5.93}$$

EXAMPLE: Suppose that the product under consideration is a new industrial cooling system, and the product manager provided the following information concerning awareness among target users of air-conditioning systems:

current awareness level, $W = 0.41$

short-run awareness level in the absence of expenditures, $W_0 = 0.39$

short-run awareness level if communication expenditures were pushed to saturation level, $W^* = 0.51$

long-run awareness level if communication expenditures were set to zero for a long period of time, $W_{00} = 0.32$

maintenance-advertising expenditures, $A^* = \$0.68$ per target air-conditioning buyer

awareness rate induced by a 50% increase in advertising expenditures $W^1 = W(1.5 \times \$0.68) = W(\$1.02) = 0.47$

Hence,

$$\rho = \frac{0.39 - 0.32}{0.41 - 0.32} = 0.778 \tag{5.94}$$

$$\Psi = 0.51 - 0.39 = 0.12 \tag{5.95}$$

$$\delta = \frac{1}{\ln(1.5)} \ln \left(\frac{0.51 - 0.41}{0.41 - 0.39} \frac{0.47 - 0.39}{0.51 - 0.47} \right) = 5.68 \tag{5.96}$$

and

$$\gamma = \frac{0.51 - 0.41}{0.41 - 0.39} 0.68^{5.68} = 0.56 \tag{5.97}$$

The awareness function for air conditioning is therefore given by

$$W(t) = 0.32 + 0.778 [W(t-1) - 0.32] + 0.12 \frac{[A(t)]^{5.68}}{0.56 + [A(t)]^{5.68}} \tag{5.98}$$

EXAMPLE: Management of Forlorn Foods has also chosen the ADBUDG model to evaluate the (short-run) effect of its advertising program. Due to the risk-neutral utility function, only expected returns are required, and the uncertainty of the several strategies is not evaluated. Similar to the above, Exhibit 5.5 gives the parameter estimates and the resulting response models. These response models will be used to help evaluate Forlorn's advertising-allocation policy in the next chapter.

Although this procedure has resulted in the calibration of a rather flexible response curve, we could argue for more observations and then fit the curve with (nonlinear) econometric methods to check internal consistency. However, the disadvantage of this further collection of information is the increased burden it places on the respondent: "it is doubtful that . . . we

EXHIBIT 5-5 Parameter estimates and response model for Forlorn Foods.
(a) Parameter Estimates

Parameter	Market A	Market B	Market C	Market D
$W_0 = W(A = 0)$	7.5	0.5	3.25	2.5
$W^* = W(A = \infty)$	10	3.0	5.0	7.0
$W = W(A^*)$	9	1.0	4.0	4.0
$W^1 = W(1.5A^*)$	9.5	2.0	4.2	5.5
$A^* =$ current advertising	0.45	0.05	0.20	0.20

(b) Response Model

$$Q_A = 7.5 + 2.5 \frac{A^{2.42}}{0.10 + A^{2.42}}$$

$$Q_B = 0.5 + 2.5 \frac{A^{4.42}}{7.1 \times 10^{-6} + A^{4.42}}$$

$$Q_C = 3.25 + 1.75 \frac{A^{1.13}}{0.215 + A^{1.13}}$$

$$Q_D = 2.5 + 4.5 \frac{A^{3.42}}{0.008 + A^{3.42}}$$

could specify a sales response curve in any greater detail than represented by a smooth curve through four appropriately chosen points" (Little, 1970, p. B-472).

Lodish (1971b) suggests a similar calibration procedure, and in one of few field experiments of such models, Fudge and Lodish (1977) report significant, profitable improvements in salesmen's call-planning activities with a subjectively calibrated response model.

However, the use of judgmental assessment of response is not without controversy. In their laboratory work Chakravarti, Mitchell, and Staelin (1979, 1980, 1981) found that subjects using the ADBUDG model made *worse* decisions than those who did not. In a response Little and Lodish (1981) conclude that the ADBUDG model is not robust, especially in its ability to deal with dynamic effects, and recommend the BRANDAID model (Chapter 18) as more robust and easier to control. In addition, Little and Lodish argue that subjects in a laboratory experiment rarely have access to certain kinds of information, such as supplemental background knowledge of the dynamics of the particular market. They conclude:

> A main thrust of the decision calculus concept is to capture useful information from the manager's rich knowledge of the marketing environment and blend it into decision making. [Chakravarti, Mitchell and Staelin, 1981], coming from experiments that show the manager to be a mediocre data processor, tend to display a desire to replace him or her with a competent econometric package. We are happy to support formal statistical methods whenever valid inferences can be made from the data, but we are oriented toward the overall management process and see judgmental calibration as plugging an important gap in problem solving (Little and Lodish, 1981, p. 28).

McIntyre (1982) and McIntyre and Currim (1982) provide evaluation and support for the decision calculus approach, but we have not heard the last word on this important subject.

Probability Assessments. It is often important to obtain a probability distribution of the outcome of a particular event or of the result of some marketer's actions. A simple, straightforward way to extract such information is the fractile method, which is closely related to the method for assessing utility functions presented in Chapter 3.

In the fractile method the analyst solicits a few franctile values in the cumulative probabililty distribution of interest and then fits an appropriate curve to these points. The procedure often makes use of reference lotteries.

EXAMPLE: Assume we wish to assess the uncertainty around the added sales a firm would see with an additional $2000 in advertising.

The first piece of information we would try to obtain is what is referred to as the 0.5 fractile; the probability that sales is less than this fractile (denoted as $Q_{0.5}$) is 0.5. We ask, "Considering all possible levels of sales response accruing from this $2000 in additional advertising, at what amount is it equally likely that sales would be more or less than this value?" The use of reference lottery helps here; the above question can be rephrased as "For what value of $Q_{0.5}$ are you indifferent between the two lotteries below?"

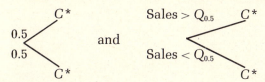

If the response is $8000, then $Q_{0.5} = 8000$.

Now we look for the 0.25 and 0.75 fractiles by asking, "Given that sales are, in fact, less than $8000, what amount of sales would you think divides the interval from $0 to $8000 into equally likely parts?" This value is the 0.25 fractile, denoted as $Q_{0.25}$. Suppose $Q_{0.25} = \$6,000$.

Similarly, the response to the question "How would you divide the interval of sales over $8000 into equally likely parts?" gives us the 0.75 fractile. Suppose $Q_{0.75} = \$11,000$. These values are placed on a Q scale in Exhibit 5.6.

Other fractiles can be obtained in like manner for $Q_{0.125}$, $Q_{0.0625}$, $Q_{0.875}$, and so on. We can also try to obtain $Q_{0.01}$ (and $Q_{0.99}$) by asking, "What value of sales would you select so that the chance of sales being greater (less) than this value is only one in 100?"

Values have been selected, by definition, so that $p(Q < Q_k) = k$ for all values of k between zero and one. Thus we can construct a smooth curve for the probability distribution of sales simply by plotting the (Q_k, k) values and fitting a smooth curve (or an analytical form of a probability function) to the data. Exhibit 5.7 illustrates this curve.

With no a priori knowledge about the shape of the subjective distribution, the results of inquiries, such as those described above, must be investigated prior to selecting a functional form. (An alternative is to use a smoothed, or piecewise, linear representation of the raw data.)

In an attempt to calibrate a probability curve, a simplification of the above procedure might read as follows:

"Give me a low estimate of sales such that there is a 97.5 percent chance in your mind that we will do better" (Q_L).

"Give me an estimate of the most likely level of sales" (Q_M).

"Give me a high estimate of sales such that there is a 97.5 percent chance in your mind that we won't do this well" (Q_H).

	$Q_{0.25}$	$Q_{0.5}$	$Q_{0.75}$			
0	5	10		15	20	Sales in $1000

EXHIBIT 5-6   **Placing fractiles on the sales scale for judgmental-probability assessment.**

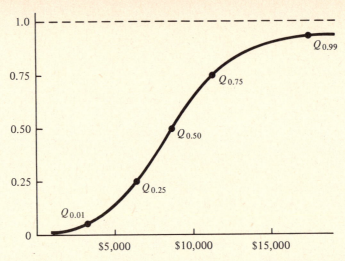

EXHIBIT 5-7   The cumulative subjective-probability distribution for sales.

If the low and high estimates average close to the model estimate, the analyst may assume a normal distribution. Then the mean and standard deviation are given by the following relationships:

$$\overline{Q} = \frac{Q_L + Q_H}{2} \tag{5.99}$$

$$\sigma = \frac{Q_H - Q_L}{4} \tag{5.100}$$

Thus the mean is found by averaging the low and high estimates, and the standard deviation is found by taking one-fourth of the distance between them (because approximately four standard deviations span a 95 percent confidence interval, which is the likelihood that sales are greater than Q_L and less than Q_H).

A similar procedure for asymmetric low-high estimates uses a shifted beta distribution. (The actual beta distribution applies to a continuous variate whose admissible values lie between zero and one.) The distribution is widely used for estimating activity completion times in PERT (Program Evaluation and Review Technique) projects. In our context the analyst asks the following questions:

"What is the most pessimistic estimate of sales?" (Q_L).
"What is the most likely estimate of sales?" (Q_M).
"What is the most optimistic estimate of sales?" (Q_H).

The mean of the beta distribution is assumed to be one-third of the way between the mode Q_M and the average of the extremes; this value is given by the formula

$$\overline{Q} = \frac{Q_L + 4Q_M + Q_H}{6} \tag{5.101}$$

The standard deviation is (arbitrarily) established as one-sixth of the range; that is,

$$\sigma = \frac{Q_H - Q_L}{6} \tag{5.102}$$

The whole distribution is given by

$$p_\beta(Q) = \begin{cases} 0 & Q < Q_L \\ k(Q - Q_L)^\alpha (Q_H - Q)^\beta & Q_L \leqslant Q \leqslant Q_H \\ 0 & Q > Q_H \end{cases} \tag{5.103}$$

where the parameters k, α, and β are calculated from the estimates of Q_L, Q_M, and Q_H and the required characteristics of the distribution.

Other distributions, such as the log-normal and Weibull distributions, have few parameters, are flexible, and can also be used to approximate subjective distributions.

In several interesting experiments and studies, Winkler (1967a, 1967b, 1967c, 1968) reports that the quality of subjective-probability assessments depends on the assessment technique and the assessor. Winkler argues that "honest reward functions" are required to promote honesty. (What of the marketing manager who gets a bonus if he exceeds his sales forecast and gets nothing if he falls short of it? Is he motivated to give you an honest assessment?) Another problem is that managers (experts) say they know little but assess their judgment as if they knew a lot. In some informal classroom experiments with MBA students, one of the authors found that for general knowledge questions (populations of United States cities), over 25 percent of the true answers fell outside the experts' range from the 0.01 fractile to the 0.99 fractile; that is, the true values were either greater than the 0.99 fractile or less than the 0.01 fractile over 25 percent of the time. For good assessments you would expect this result to occur only about 2 percent of the time. This problem continued to occur (although to a lesser degree) even after the problem was explained to the assessors!

In terms of the assessor's impact Winkler showed that people with previous training in quantitative methods are able to translate their judgments into probabilities better than those without previous training. Most people, with some practice, can be taught to provide these kinds of data. But Dalkey (1969) reports that people's self-rating of their "perceived" accuracy in probability assessments does not, in fact, relate to their actual accuracy in completing these tasks.

Ratings and Weights.   Many marketing decision models call for ratings or weights to assess certain variables. For example, a weighted-scoring model for evaluating new-product ideas calls for each manager to rate how well the company fares on each of several dimensions (management skills, production capabilities, marketing capabilities, etc.), to weight these dimensions in new-product success, and then to weight the knowledge (or importance) of the assessor. Also, in the description of the decision matrix in Chapter 9, managers are asked to rate the relative importance of different participants in the purchasing-decision process.

Much work, reported both in the psychological and the market research literature, has been done on the design and application of scales. They are used to measure quantitative attributes, trade-offs between characteristics, relative importances (utilities), and so on. The construction of scales, their reliability and validity, and their application in developing marketing information is a large, specialized field. See Green and Tull (1975) or any other good marketing research text.

Combining Subjective Estimates

Frequently, we want to combine the judgment of several individuals—a brand manager, a group manager, an advertising manager, staff people, and so forth. Different experts will normally provide different subjective estimates, which must be combined into a single response. There are two methods for combining subjective judgments: analyst-selected and group-selected.

Analyst-selected Pooling Methods.   A frequently used method for combining individual estimates is to have the analyst do it with some justifiable procedure. For example, if the separate estimates are substantially alike, they must simply be averaged. A substantial similarity of independent estimates has the effect of heightening the decision maker's confidence in the estimation. On the other hand, when there is substantial divergence in the estimates of two or more experts, the decision maker has two options. The first is to use the estimate of a favored expert, dismissing the others from consideration. The second option is to use some set of weights for combining the estimates. Winkler (1968) distinguishes four logical bases for the weights:

1. Assign equal weights to the estimates if there is no further indicator of the relative expertness of each expert.
2. Assign weights that are proportional to someone's subjective ranking or rating of the experts' relative competence.
3. Assign weights that are proportional to the experts' self-ratings of their competence.
4. Assign weights that are proportional to the past predictive accuracy of the various experts.

There is no one best method of determining weights; the analyst must rely on his or her experience in using different procedures. [See Winkler (1968) for further discussion and critique and Bordley (1982) for conditions under which a multiplicative rule is appropriate.]

Group-selected Pooling Methods.   If the group itself is asked to resolve its differences, there are two common ways to do this: cooperatively or by the Delphi method.

In a cooperative group, questions or differences are discussed openly, and the group continues discussion until a single collective answer is reached. Although very common, this method is viewed with some misgivings because an actual confrontation of experts is likely to create certain psychological effects that may spoil the independence of the experts' estimation processes. In particular, one might be concerned with bandwagon effects, hierarchical managerial effects, and issues of power politics. [See Dalkey and Helmer (1963) for elaboration.]

It was partially in response to these problems that the Delphi method was developed by a group at the RAND Corporation. The method has three key features: (1) *anonymous response*, in which opinions and assessments are obtained formally but anonymously; (2) *interaction and controlled feedback*, in which interaction is brought about by a systematic exercise conducted in several interactions with controlled feedback between rounds; and (3) *statistical group response*, where group opinion is an aggregate of individual opinions in the final round. These procedures are designed to mitigate the impact of dominant individuals, irrelevant comments, and group pressure toward conformity.

The general procedure is to ask each expert for his best estimate, process and feed back some of the information obtained, and then repeat the process. On the last set of responses the median is usually chosen as the best estimate for the group.

Several experiments have shown that the Delphi method does, in fact, produce good results. In a controlled experiment Jolson and Rossow (1971) showed that a group of individuals was able to produce a median response near the (known) true value, and that the dispersion was narrower for those questions on which the individuals were truly experts. Another interesting application of the Delphi method, performed by well-known model builders and aimed at evaluating the likelihood of managers accepting a number of marketing models, is found in Larréché and Montgomery (1977).

Blending Judgmental and Empirical Data: Bayesian Estimation

The procedures for estimation presented above were either purely data-based (objective) or subjective. However, these are extreme cases. In many situations some field data and some judgmental data are available. These two types of information can be combined and logically incorporated into an estimation procedure. Such types of analyses are usually called bayesian analyses.

The Idea and an Example

We introduced earlier the idea of a likelihood function: the relative probability of observing a sample given (or as a function of) specific parameter values. To this idea we add the distinction of prior and posterior distributions. A *prior distribution* is a probability distribution of the parameter(s) *before* observing any data. This distribution is our judgmental assessment about the value of the system's parameters. A *posterior distribution* is an update of the prior distribution *after* observing the data, combining objective and subjective information.

EXAMPLE: After a quick look at a coin, you may conclude it is a fair coin. Your prior estimate about the probability of heads on any one toss may be a mean of 0.5 and a standard deviation of 0.10. If you toss the coin 100 times and 95 come up heads, you might want to revise your mean (prior) estimate of 0.5 to something closer to 0.95.

Suppose we go back to our sales and advertising model,

$$Q = a_0 + a_1 X \tag{5.104}$$

where we are most interested in the advertising-response parameter a_1. Furthermore, suppose that either through past experience with this product or through judgment, management provides a prior distribution on the response parameter a_1 that is normal with mean a_{10} and variance σ_{10}^2. Therefore the prior distribution of a_1 is $N(a_{10}, \sigma_{10}^2)$.

Assume further that our sample provides an estimator of a_1 (perhaps by least squares), call it a_1, with mean a_1 and variance $\sigma^2/\Sigma(X_i - \overline{X})^2$ (where a_1 is the population mean and σ^2 is the error variance). If we use the notation

$$V^2 = \frac{1}{n} \Sigma (X_i - \overline{X})^2 \tag{5.105}$$

we can denote the variance of $\hat{a}_1$ as $\sigma^2/V^2/n$, where n is the sample size. So assuming normality again, we have

$$\hat{a}_1 \sim N\left(a_1, \frac{\sigma^2/V^2}{n}\right) \tag{5.106}$$

To derive a posterior distribution, we apply Bayes' rule, which states that

(Posterior distribution) $\propto$ (prior distribution) $\times$ (likelihood function)   (5.107)

where $\propto$ means "is proportional to." [(See Raiffa and Schlaifer (1961).] In addition, the normal distributions of the prior and the likelihood functions provide what is referred to as a natural conjugate process, producing a normal posterior distribution. This natural conjugate process allows a closed-form result for the posterior distribution that is also normal:

$$\text{Posterior distribution of } a_1 \sim N\left(\frac{n_0 a_0 + n\hat{a}_1}{n_0 + n}, \; \frac{\sigma^2/V^2}{n_0 + n}\right) \qquad (5.108)$$

where

$$n_0 = \frac{\sigma^2/V^2}{\sigma_{10}^2} \qquad (5.109)$$

The term n_0 is known as the pseudo–sample size because the effect of bayesian regression on our parameter estimates is to add a pseudosample of size n_0 to our actual sample.

In general, bayesian estimates have smaller variance than classical estimates and yield mean values that are compromises between the classical-regression estimates and the means of the prior distributions. We compare bayesian and classical 95 percent confidence intervals in Exhibit 5.8.

EXAMPLE: Suppose the prior distribution for a_1 is distributed normally around 5 with a variance of 0.25. Eight observations in different sales regions provide the following statistics: $\Sigma(X_i - \overline{X})(Q_i - \overline{Q}) = 2400$, $\Sigma(X_i - \overline{X})^2 = 400$, and squared residuals $s^2 = \frac{1}{8}\Sigma(Q_i - \hat{Q}_i)^2$. Using s^2 to approximate σ^2, we find that

$$a_{10} = 5 \qquad \sigma_{10}^2 = 25 \qquad \hat{a}_1 = \frac{\Sigma(X_i - \overline{X})(Q_i - \overline{Q})}{\Sigma(X_i - \overline{X})^2} = 6.0$$

and

$$V^2 = \frac{1}{8}\Sigma(X_i - \overline{X})^2 = \frac{400}{8} = 5$$

So

$$n_0 = \frac{\sigma^2/V^2}{\sigma_{10}^2} = \frac{25/50}{0.25} = 2$$

the pseudo–sample size.

EXHIBIT 5-8 **A classical and a bayesian confidence interval around the regression coefficient a_1.**

95% Bayesian Confidence Interval	95% Classical Confidence Interval
$a_1 = \dfrac{n_0 a_{10} + n\hat{a}_1}{n_0 + n} \pm 1.96 \sqrt{\dfrac{\sigma^2/V^2}{n_0 + n}}$	$a_1 = \hat{a}_1 \pm 1.96 \sqrt{\dfrac{\sigma^2/V^2}{n}}$

Now with the results in Exhibit 5.8, we get

$$a_1(\text{bayesian}) = 5.80 \pm 0.44$$

$$a_1(\text{classical}) = 6.0 \pm 0.49$$

This result illustrates the narrower confidence interval of the bayesian estimator, as well as the compromise in the value of the mean. (Note that, strictly speaking, t values rather than the normal value 1.96 should be used here, which widens the confidence interval somewhat.)

Formal Analysis for the Multivariate Bayesian-Regression Model[*]

Repeating eq. (5.16), we get

$$\mathbf{Q} = \mathbf{X}\mathbf{a} + \epsilon \tag{5.110}$$

Assume we now have a set of prior estimates of $\mathbf{a}$, say $\hat{\mathbf{a}}_0$. These estimates will have mean $\mathbf{a}$ if they are unbiased:

$$E(\hat{\mathbf{a}}_0) = \mathbf{a} \tag{5.111}$$

With uncertainty in the prior,

$$\hat{a}_{j0} = a_{j0} + \epsilon_0 \tag{5.112}$$

where ϵ_0 is the error term for the jth estimate. Then the prior covariance matrix is

$$E(\epsilon_0 \epsilon_0') = \mathbf{\Phi} \tag{5.113}$$

In matrix form we can write eq. (5.112) as

$$\mathbf{a}_0 = \mathbf{I}\mathbf{a}_0 + \epsilon_0 \tag{5.114}$$

Combining eq. (5.110) with eq. (5.14) yields

$$\left[\begin{array}{c} \mathbf{Q} \\ \hline \mathbf{a}_0 \end{array}\right] = \left[\begin{array}{c} \mathbf{X} \\ \hline \mathbf{I} \end{array}\right] \mathbf{a} + \left[\begin{array}{c} \epsilon \\ \epsilon_0 \end{array}\right] \tag{5.115}$$

or

$$\mathbf{Q}^* = \mathbf{Y}\mathbf{A} + \epsilon^* $$

with

$$E(\epsilon^* \epsilon^{*\prime}) = \left[\begin{array}{cc} \sigma^2 \mathbf{I} & 0 \\ 0 & \mathbf{\Phi} \end{array}\right] \tag{5.116}$$

Thus the bayesian estimate of $\mathbf{a}$ can be calculated from eq. (5.115) by generalized least squares (GLS). In particular, when there is no assumed

[*]This section uses matrix algebra.

covariation between the prior estimates of **a**, formulas (5.31) and (5.32) hold, giving weighted least-squares estimators for the parameters. The weights reflect the compromise between the prior and the likelihood functions. A look at eq. (5.115) shows that bayesian regression is equivalent to adding observations to the data matrix from the prior distribution, the number of such observations being determined by the precision (level of confidence) of the prior distribution.

Summary

Following objective setting and model specification, the next logical step in marketing model building is model calibration. Models are linear or nonlinear, have observable or unobservable variables, and come in single- or multiple-equation varieties. The field of econometrics has provided powerful methods of calibration of such models (along with associated statistical-evaluation procedures) when sample data are available.

Methods for calibrating single-equation models include ordinary and generalized least squares in linear and linearizable models, iterative procedures for nonlinear models, and maximum-likelihood methods for binary dependent variables. Errors in measurement and two-way causation require multiple-equation systems to be developed and estimated. Causal models, correcting for measurement error in systems with unobservable variables, incorporate powerful procedures for handling linear models, especially those with normally distributed errors.

In many cases little or no data are available for calibration. In such situations subjective model-calibration procedures are used. Methods for developing point estimates, response-function estimates, and probability assessments were reviewed and illustrated. Subjective estimation is an area of current research, with a controversial field record.

When several assessors are available for subjective estimation, their estimates need to be combined. Two approaches are available, one with an analyst selecting a pooling method and the other with a group selecting the method. The best-known, group-selected pooling method is the Delphi approach.

Finally, many model situations combine some data and some managerial experience. Under these circumstances the field of bayesian estimation provides a convenient and logically sound structure to combine the two sources of information.

Problems

5.1 The Carmine Company has been keeping detailed records on new salespeople under the premise that sales will increase with salesforce experience. A sample of eight people produced the data shown below:

Months on Job	Monthly Sales in $1000s
2	2.4
5	7.2
9	12.3
12	14.7
1	0.8
6	3.9
10	13.2
4	6.7

a. Fit a least-squares line to the data and calculate its parameters.
b. Predict the sales that could be expected from persons who have been on the job for 3 mo, 7 mo, and 9 mo.
c. Is this a reasonable model? Why? (Why not?)

5.2 A leading pharmaceutical company wants to model the revenue generated by a new hypertension pill. The company researchers believe that the revenue depends on the price per pill, the percentage of the population that is susceptible to hypertension, and the amount of research money spent. Data are available for 1972–1979 and are given below (dollar figures have been adjusted for inflation):

Year	Revenue ($ in Millions)	Research (in $1000s)	Price per Pill	Percentage Hypertension
1972	5.0	10	0.50	0.25
1973	5.1	30	0.48	0.25
1974	5.5	40	0.40	0.26
1975	5.6	50	0.50	0.26
1976	5.8	80	0.55	0.26
1977	6.5	90	0.55	0.27
1978	7.5	100	0.65	0.27
1979	8.2	110	0.60	0.28

At first, the model $y = a_0 + a_1 x_1 + a_2 x_2 + a_3 x_3 + \epsilon$ was proposed. A company statistician warned that the assumption of homoscedasticity might be violated if that model was used. He proposed that the model

$$\ln y = a_0 + a_1 x_1 + a_2 x_2 + a_3 x_3 + \epsilon$$

be used instead.

a. Fit both models to the data given and determine which is best. (Define "best.")
b. Is heteroscedasticity present in the simple linear model? How do you know?

5.3 What are the drawbacks of the ordinary-least-squares method when applied to multiple-equation problems? How does the two-stage, least-squares (2SLS) method take care of these drawbacks?

5.4 Delta Corporation has been studying the market for its industrial turbines and the impact of selling effort (A). The marketing department, after doing market research and questioning the concerned managers, decided that the model given by eq. (5.88) would be a good one for it to use. The department presents the following figures:

$$W_0 = 0.42 \qquad W^* = 0.50 \qquad W = 0.45 \qquad W' = W(1.5A) = 0.47$$

where the units are $100 millions. Fit the model for the above data. You are also given that $W_{00} = 0.31$ and current selling effort is $10 million/yr. Fit the model of eq. (5.89) to the data. Plot the results.

5.5 Suppose the top manager of a firm is asked to give an educated guess about the most probable level of sales (Q_e) for a given period (assuming a specific state of marketing environment and a specific marketing strategy). Suppose that he indicated that his average expectation (Q_e) is $500. Further, assume that his pessimistic estimate is $Q_p = $450 such that the probability of a sales level lower than Q_p would be 0.20; and that his optimistic estimate is $Q_o = $550 such that the probability distribution of demand is normally distributed. Determine the mean and the standard deviation of the distribution.

5.6 Can the following expressions be transformed to a form suitable for multiple regression? How?
   a. $y = b_0 x_1^{b_1} x_2^{b_2} x_3^{b_3 x_4}$
   b. $y = b_0 + b_1 e^{-b_2 x}$
   c. $y = (1 + e^{b_0 + b_1 x_1 + b_2 x_2})^{-1}$

5.7 The annual sales for widgets from 1963 to 1979 are given below, along with associated advertising spending. Company management had a major price decrease during the years 1970–1975 that was believed to shift sales upward.
   a. Run a simple linear regression of advertising on sales.
   b. Add a dummy variable for the years 1970–1975. Are the results significantly different?
   c. Interpret the coefficients in your model.

Year	Advertising (in $10 millions)	Sales (in $100 millions)
1963	2.4	2.6
1964	2.8	3.0
1965	3.1	3.6
1966	3.4	3.7
1967	3.9	3.8
1968	4.0	4.1
1969	4.2	4.4
1970*	5.1	7.1
1971*	6.3	8.0
1972*	8.1	8.9
1973*	8.8	9.7
1974*	9.6	10.2
1975*	9.7	10.1
1976	9.6	7.9
1977	10.4	8.7
1978	12.0	9.1
1979	12.9	10.1

*Different pricing program.

5.8 A hydraulic-value manufacturer saw the following sales levels and personal-selling expenditures in four territories (in thousands of dollars):

Sales Level (S)	Personal-Selling Expenditures (P)
500	40
600	40
400	30
500	50

a. Fit a regression line of P on S.
b. Graph the data and the fitted line.
c. Does this regression line show how personal selling affects sales?

5.9 Why is it useful to combine several subjective estimates? What about combining subjective and objective estimates?

5.10 A marketing analyst was given a prior distribution, based on managerial judgment, for the advertising-effectiveness parameter in a regression analysis (β). It was assumed to be distributed normally about a mean of 2.0 with a standard deviation of 80. Calculate bayesian 95% confidence intervals for β as more data are collected.

a. $n = 5$, $\Sigma xy = 50$, $\Sigma x^2 = 25$, $s^2 = 12.8$
b. $n = 10$, $\Sigma xy = 80$, $\Sigma x^2 = 50$, $s^2 = 8.0$
c. $n = 20$, $\Sigma xy = 150$, $\Sigma x^2 = 100$, $s^2 = 9.6$

Note: **(a)** x and y are deviations from the mean.
      (b) $\beta = \Sigma xy / \Sigma x^2$.
      (c) s^2 should be used to approximate σ^2.

5.11 Assume a simple linear-regression model with a normal error term:

$$Y = a + bx + \epsilon$$

and

$$f(Y_i) = \frac{1}{\sqrt{2\pi\sigma^2}}\, e^{-(Y_i - a - bx_i)^2 / 2\sigma^2}$$

a. Assuming N independent observations, write the likelihood function for $f(Y_1 \ldots Y_n)$.
b. Find the maximum-likelihood estimators for a and b. Are they biased?
c. Find the maximum-likelihood estimator for σ^2. Is it biased? Is it consistent?

Marketing-Policy-Evaluation Procedures

The last three chapters dealt with formulating and calibrating marketing models. In this chapter we deal with the derivation of policy implications from those models, or policy evaluation. Other treatments use the term "optimization," but a mathematical model-based optimization may well produce a suggestion that cannot be implemented or is outside the range of data on which the model was calibrated. For example, if we have

$$Q = \hat{a}_1 X + \hat{a}_2 X^2 \qquad (6.1)$$

where X is advertising spending and Q is sales, we might very well be able to find a profit-maximizing value of X. But if the model's parameters were estimated from historical data in the range $\$0.25 \leq X \leq \$2$ per capita, and our optimal X suggests $\$8$ per capita, it may be unwise to take the model's output and implement it. Equation (6.1) was estimated on (and may only be valid for) levels of spending in the range of $\$0.25$ to $\$2$ per capita. It would be risky to assume the same basic relationship holds (with no competitive reaction expected) at a level of $\$8$. It might be considerably less risky to assert "the model suggests spending levels in the range of $\$2+$ would be cost effective" and then gradually move spending rates in that direction while carefully monitoring the results.

Some of the more important types of mathematical policy-evaluation approaches, including classical optimization procedures, are listed in Exhibit 6.1, classified by the nature of the analytical support sought, as well as by the assumptions about risk in the model environment. Clearly, the real environment is uncertain, but in the model environment the decision of whether or not to incorporate uncertainty balances added reality against the increased difficulty of formulating and solving such problems.

EXHIBIT 6-1   **Classification of key policy-evaluation techniques used in marketing.**

Nature of Environment	Nature of Support Required	
	Policy Generation	**Policy Analysis**
Certain	I. Classical optimization procedures	III. Marginal analysis
	Linear programming	Deterministic simulation
	Network-type problems	Econometric-model analysis
	Integer and mixed-integer programming	
	Nonlinear programming	
	Control theory	
Uncertain	II. Decision analysis	IV. Monte Carlo simulation
	Dynamic programming	
	Linear programming under uncertainty	
	Stochastic-control theory	

In this chapter we introduce and illustrate the use of the policy-evaluation techniques noted in Exhibit 6.1. References to more complete treatments are given in each section, and an evaluation of the procedure's use in model-based marketing analyses is given.

Policy Generation in a Certain Environment

Classical Optimization Procedures

In this section we briefly review classical methods of calculus for maximizing or minimizing (1) a function of a single variable (marketing instrument), (2) a function of several variables, and (3) a function of several variables subject to constraints on the variables. We assume throughout that all functions of interest possess continuous first and second derivatives and partial derivatives.

Consider a (rather strange) sales-response function Q, illustrated in Exhibit 6.2. A necessary condition for a particular value of X, say X^*, to be

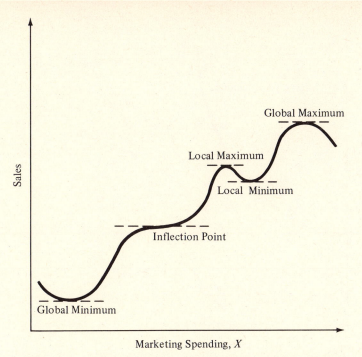

EXHIBIT 6-2   A sales-response function with several maxima and minima.

either a maximum or a minimum is that

$$\frac{dQ(X)}{dX} = 0 \qquad \text{at } X = X^* \tag{6.2}$$

Note that in Exhibit 6.2 there are *five* solutions satisfying this condition. These solutions are called critical points, and we must evaluate the second derivative at each point to obtain further information about it. In particular, if eq. (6.3) holds,

$$\frac{d^2Q(X)}{dX^2} > 0 \qquad \text{at } X = X^* \tag{6.3}$$

then X^* must be a *local* minimum [$Q(X^*) \leq Q(X)$ for X near X^*].

To further explain, we introduce the properties of concavity and convexity. If any line segment connecting two points of a function lies entirely on or below the function, that function is *concave*. Conversely, if it lies on or above the function, the function is *convex*. This idea is illustrated in Exhibit 6.3. Then X^* is a *local minimum* if the function is locally convex at X^* ($d^2Q/dX^2 > 0$) and a *global minimum* if the function is *strictly convex* (everywhere convex). Similarly, for X^* to be a *local maximum*, it must

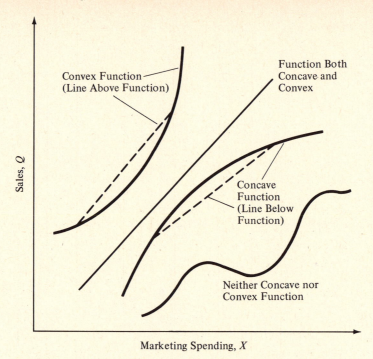

EXHIBIT 6-3 **Concave and convex response functions.**

satisfy eq. (6.2), and the function must be locally concave at X^* ($d^2Q/dX^2 < 0$). And if the function is *strictly concave*, X^* is the *global maximum* as well. If Q is not strictly convex, then to find a global minimum, we must compare the values of Q at all the local minima as well as at the endpoints of the function, assuming it is defined only in a finite interval. The key point is that $dQ/dX = 0$ at $X = X^*$ defines a unique global maximum if Q is concave and a unique global minimum if Q is convex.

The analysis of a function of several decision variables, $Q(X_1, \ldots, X_n)$, is similar. A necessary condition for a solution $(X_1, \ldots, X_n) = (X_1^*, \ldots, X_n^*)$ to be either a maximum or a minimum is for

$$\frac{\partial Q}{\partial X_j} = 0 \qquad \text{at } (X_1, \ldots, X_n) = (X_1^*, \ldots, X_n^*) \qquad \text{for } j = 1, \ldots, n \quad (6.4)$$

After identifying critical points that satisfy eq. (6.4), we would classify each point as a local maximum or a local minimum, depending on whether Q is concave or convex, respectively, within a neighborhood of each critical point. (More detailed analysis is required if the function is neither.)

Formally, a function is concave if its hessian matrix, the matrix of second-order partial derivatives,

$$H = \begin{pmatrix} \dfrac{\partial^2 Q}{\partial X_1^{\,2}} & \dfrac{\partial^2 Q}{\partial X_1 \, \partial X_2} & \cdots & \dfrac{\partial^2 Q}{\partial X_1 \, \partial X_n} \\ \cdots\cdots\cdots\cdots\cdots\cdots\cdots\cdots\cdots\cdots \\ \dfrac{\partial^2 Q}{\partial X_n \, \partial X_1} & & \cdots & \dfrac{\partial^2 Q}{\partial X_n^{\,2}} \end{pmatrix} \qquad (6.5)$$

is negative semidefinite. [A matrix is negative semidefinite if its determinant and all its principal minors are negative or zero. See Noble (1969, p. 395).] Similarly, a function is convex if its hessian matrix is positive definite or semidefinite. These conditions on the hessian are known as the second-order conditions. The global maximum or minimum then is found by comparing all the local maxima or minima as well as the endpoints of the region.

However, if the function is known to be convex or concave, then a critical point must be a global maximum or minimum, respectively. Note that the least-squares criterion for parameter estimation requires a minimization of a quadratic function. This quadratic function is convex as long as the estimation problem is linear in the parameters. Thus we know that least-squares estimates are unique and, in fact, minimize the sum of squares.

EXAMPLE: Suppose a manufacturer is concerned with establishing an optimal weekly promotional budget X and assumes that there is no interaction effect between price and promotion. On the basis of some early test-market results, the sales response to promotion is estimated as

$$Q = 0.8 \sqrt{X} \qquad (6.6)$$

Assume a simple total-cost function with the company planning to charge $150 per unit. Also, assume that marginal cost of production is $50 per unit, and the fixed cost is $6000. To solve for the best weekly promotional budget, we form a profit function:

$$Z = PQ - C - X \qquad (6.7)$$

Substituting the information above, we get

$$Z = 150Q - 6000 - 50Q - X \qquad (6.8)$$

$$Z = 100(0.8 \sqrt{X}) - 6000 - X \qquad (6.9)$$

$$Z = 80 \sqrt{X} - X - 6000 \qquad (6.10)$$

The next step is to take this profit function and set the first derivative equal to zero:

$$\frac{dZ}{dX} = 40X^{-1/2} - 1 = 0 \tag{6.11}$$

$$\frac{40}{\sqrt{X}} = 1$$

$$\sqrt{X} = 40$$

and therefore,

$$X = 1600 \tag{6.12}$$

(Note that $d^2Z/dX^2 = -20X^{-3/2}$, so for $X > 0$, the function is concave, and the solution $X = 1600$ is a unique maximum.)

This solution says that the company should spend \$1600 a week for promotion to produce extra sales (compared with the case of no promotion) equal to

$$Q = 0.8 \sqrt{1600} = 0.8(40) = 32 \text{ units per week} \tag{6.13}$$

and extra profits of

$$Z = 80 \sqrt{1600} - 1600 = \$1600/\text{wk} \tag{6.14}$$

and an average promotional cost per sales dollar of

$$\frac{X}{PQ} = \frac{1600}{(150)(32)} = 33\tfrac{1}{3}\% \tag{6.15}$$

The problem of finding the best promotional outlay is illustrated graphically in Exhibit 6.4. The top curve describes sales revenue as growing with promotion at a diminishing rate. From this sales revenue curve we subtract the cost of production to get the curve showing gross profit before promotional cost. Then to find net profit after promotion, we look for the promotional budget X at which the vertical distance is greatest between the gross profit curve and the 45° line, representing promotional costs. This budget is X^*. At X^* the slope of the tangent to the gross profit curve is parallel to the 45° line. This point is the geometric equivalent of the fact that marginal promotional cost and marginal gross profit are equal where net profit is a maximum.

EXAMPLE: In this example, we derive the *Dorfman-Steiner theorem on marketing-mix optimization* (Dorfman and Steiner, 1954).

Assume a company faces the general marketing-mix demand and cost functions

$$Q = q(P, A, D, R) \tag{6.16}$$

$$C = c(Q, R)Q + A + D + F \tag{6.17}$$

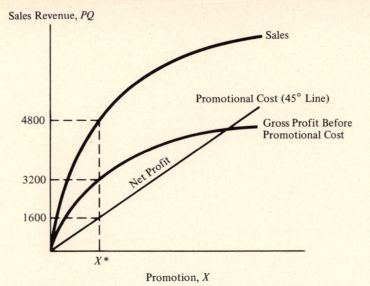

EXHIBIT 6-4   Finding the best promotional outlay.

The unit cost c is a function of the quantity produced (Q) and the product quality (R). Thus the unit variable cost may vary with output and/or with the level of product quality. Advertising (A) and distribution (D) are treated as discretionary fixed costs, and F represents the sum of nondiscretionary fixed costs.

The short-run profit function is

$$Z = PQ - C \tag{6.18}$$

$$Z = Pq(P, A, D, R) - c(Q, R)Q - A - D - F \tag{6.19}$$

$$Z = Pq(P, A, D, R) - c\{q(P, A, D, R), R\}q(P, A, D, R) - A - D - F \tag{6.20}$$

Thus sales and costs and therefore profit depend on the levels and mix of marketing effort chosen by the firm.

Given eq. (6.20), marketing-mix optimization occurs (assuming second-order conditions are satisfied) when

$$\frac{\partial Z}{\partial P} = \frac{\partial Z}{\partial A} = \frac{\partial Z}{\partial D} = \frac{\partial Z}{\partial R} \tag{6.21}$$

Price optimization implies

$$\frac{\partial Z}{\partial P} = Pq_P + q - cq_P - c_q q_P q = 0 \tag{6.22}$$

where $\quad q_P = \dfrac{\partial q}{\partial P} \qquad c_q = \dfrac{\partial c}{\partial q} \qquad q = Q$

Therefore,

$$P = [q_P(c + c_q q) - q]\, q_P$$

$$= c + c_q q - \frac{q}{q_P} \tag{6.23}$$

For optimum advertising expenditure,

$$\frac{\partial Z}{\partial A} = Pq_A - cq_A - c_q q_A q - 1 = 0 \tag{6.24}$$

Therefore

$$Pq_A = q_A(c + c_q q) + 1$$

$$P = c + c_q q + \frac{1}{q_A} \tag{6.25}$$

For optimum distribution expenditure,

$$\frac{\partial Z}{\partial D} = Pq_D - cq_D - c_q q_D q - 1 = 0 \tag{6.26}$$

Therefore,

$$Pq_D = q_D(c + c_q q) + 1$$

$$P = c + c_q q + \frac{1}{q_D} \tag{6.27}$$

Finally, for optimum quality,

$$\frac{\partial Z}{\partial R} = Pq_R - cq_R - c_q q_R q - c_R q = 0 \tag{6.28}$$

Therefore,

$$Pq_R = q_R(c + c_q q) + c_R q \tag{6.29}$$

$$P = c + c_q q + \frac{c_R q}{q_R}$$

Hence from eqs. (6.22)–(6.29) and the condition that all partial derivatives be set to zero,

$$-\frac{q}{q_P} = \frac{1}{q_A} = \frac{1}{q_D} = \frac{c_R q}{q_R} \tag{6.30}$$

Taking the reciprocals, we get

$$-\frac{q_P}{q} = q_A = q_D = \frac{q_R}{c_R q} \tag{6.31}$$

Multiplying by P, we find

$$-q_P \frac{P}{q} = Pq_A = Pq_D = \frac{q_R}{c_R} \frac{P}{q}$$

or

$$e_P \frac{P}{q} = MRP_A = MRP_D = e_R \frac{P}{c} \qquad (6.32)$$

where $\quad e_P = -\dfrac{\partial q}{\partial P} \dfrac{P}{q}$ = price elasticity of demand

Pq_A = marginal revenue product of advertising
expenditure (MRP_A)

Pq_D = marginal revenue product of distribution
expenditure (MRP_D)

$e_R \dfrac{P}{c} = \left[\dfrac{\partial q}{\partial R} \dfrac{\partial R}{\partial c} \dfrac{c}{q}\right] \dfrac{P}{c} = \dfrac{q_R}{c_R} \dfrac{P}{q}$ = product-quality-rating:
elasticity times ratio of price to unit cost

Thus eq. (6.32) states that for profit maximization the values of price, advertising, distribution, and product quality must be set so that the price elasticity, the marginal revenue products of advertising and distribution, and the quality elasticity times price over unit costs are equal.

Note that this theorem does not directly give the optimal values of the marketing-policy variables but rather the conditions that will be satisfied when the optimal values are found.

Some analysts prefer to work completely with measures of elasticity, in which case it is possible to recast the Dorfman-Steiner theorem in the following form:

$$e_P = \frac{PQ}{A} e_A = \frac{PQ}{D} e_D = \frac{P}{c} e_R \qquad (6.33)$$

which follows from the observation

$$MRP_A = P\frac{\partial Q}{\partial A} = P\frac{\partial Q}{\partial A} \frac{AQ}{QA} = Pe_A \frac{Q}{A} = \frac{PQ}{A} e_A \qquad (6.34)$$

This form enables a direct comparison of the elasticities of the different policy instruments (modified by the other terms) to determine whether the marketing mix is optimum. If the equality is not satisfied at the present levels of the policy instruments, then the instruments should be adjusted in the appropriate direction.

Now consider the problem of finding the maximum or minimum of the function $Q(X_1, \ldots, X_n)$, subject to certain restrictions on the values of $X_1, \ldots, X_n$:

$$\text{max (min) } Q(X_1, \ldots, X_n) \tag{6.35}$$

subject to

$$g_1(X_1, \cdots, X_n) = b_1$$
$$\vdots$$
$$g_n(X_1, \cdots, X_n) = b_m$$

where $m < n$.

The classical approach to handling this problem is with Lagrange multipliers. The procedure starts by formulating the composite function, the *lagrangian*:

$$L(X_1, \ldots, X_n, \lambda_1, \ldots, \lambda_m) = Q(X_1, \ldots, X_n)$$
$$+ \Sigma \lambda_i [g_i(X_1, \ldots, X_n) - b_i] \tag{6.36}$$

where the new variables $\lambda_1, \ldots, \lambda_m$ are called *Lagrange multipliers*. The key thing to observe from eq. (6.36) is that for all permissible values of $X_1, \ldots, X_n$, $g_i(X_1, \ldots, X_n) - b_i = 0$ for all i. Thus $L(X_1, \ldots, X_n, \lambda_1, \ldots, \lambda_m) = Q(X_1, \ldots, X_n)$, and if $(X_1^*, \ldots, X_n^*, \lambda_1^*, \ldots, \lambda_m^*)$ is a critical point (local or global optimum) of eq. (6.36), then $X_1^*, \ldots, X_n^*$ is a corresponding critical point of the original problem.

Thus the Lagrange-multiplier method reduces to analyzing (6.36) by the procedure suggested above for unconstrained functions. The $m + n$ partial derivatives are set equal to zero:

$$\frac{\partial L}{\partial X_i} = \frac{\partial Q}{\partial X_i} - \sum_{i=1}^{m} \lambda_i \frac{\partial g_i}{\partial X_j} = 0 \quad j = 1, 2, \ldots, n \tag{6.37}$$

$$\frac{\partial L}{\partial \lambda_i} = g_i(X_1, \ldots, X_n) - b_i = 0 \quad i = 1, \ldots, m \tag{6.38}$$

and the critical points are derived by solving eqs. (6.37) and (6.38) for $X_1, \ldots, X_n$ and $\lambda_1, \ldots, \lambda_m$. Note that eq. (6.38) gives the constraints in the original equations, so only permissible solutions are considered.

Although the Lagrange-multiplier method is a neat procedure conceptually, it suffers from computational difficulties. It is often difficult or impossible to solve eq. (6.37) and (6.38), and the solutions, when found, are often large in number, or infinite, making evaluation of the results difficult. Nevertheless, for certain types of small problems, the approach can sometimes be used successfully. For example, if the constraint is a budget constraint:

$$X_1 + X_2 = B \tag{6.39}$$

then λ from eq. (6.37) can be interpreted as the amount that would be added to profit if the budget B were increased by \$1, to $B + 1$.

EXAMPLE: Assume that a company sells in two territories, and the estimated demand functions are, respectively,

$$Q_1 = 6X_1^{1/2} \qquad (6.40)$$

$$Q_2 = 3X_2^{1/2} \qquad (6.41)$$

Territory 1 shows twice the response to promotional-marketing expenditures (X_1) as territory 2, although in both cases there are diminishing marginal returns. The total costs of selling in the two territories are assumed to be

$$C_1 = 60 + 4Q_1 + X_1 \qquad (6.42)$$

$$C_2 = 28 + 5Q_2 + X_2 \qquad (6.43)$$

Territory 1 is the company's home territory, and territory 2 is a distant territory. The fixed cost is substantially higher in territory 1 because of the presence of the main plant and headquarters, but the unit variable cost is lower because of lower shipment costs to customers. Now assume that average prices in the two territories are $P_1 = \$7$ and $P_2 = \$9$; the average price is lower in the home territory because it is a larger market and has attracted more competition.

The company's sales in the last period were \$407 (in thousands). Management typically sets the promotional-marketing budget (i.e., advertising and personal selling) at 16% of sales. Thus the promotional budget for the coming year is \$65 (in thousands). The company is seeking to divide funds optimally between the two territories. How much of the budget should be spent in the home territory, considering that it responds better to promotion and shows lower unit variable costs but, on the other hand, shows higher fixed costs and brings in a lower price per unit?

The solution is found with the lagrangian approach. First, we form the lagrangian profit function:

$$L = (7 - 4)6X_1^{1/2} - 60 - X_1 + (9 - 5)3X_2^{1/2} - 28 - X_2$$
$$+ \lambda(65 - X_1 - X_2) \quad (6.44)$$
$$= 18X_1^{1/2} - 60 - X_1 + 12X_2^{1/2} - 28 - X_2 + \lambda(65 - X_1 - X_2) \qquad (6.45)$$

Then we find the partial derivatives of L in eq. (6.45) with respect to X_1, X_2, and λ and set each of them equal to zero:

$$\frac{\partial L}{\partial X_1} = 9X_1^{-1/2} - 1 - \lambda = 0 \qquad (6.46)$$

$$\frac{\partial L}{\partial X_2} = 6X_2^{-1/2} - 1 - \lambda = 0 \qquad (6.47)$$

$$\frac{\partial L}{\partial \lambda} = 65 - X_1 - X_2 = 0 \tag{6.48}$$

Setting eqs. (6.46) and (6.47) equal to each other, we have

$$9X_1^{-1/2} = 6X_2^{-1/2} \tag{6.49}$$

Solving eq. (6.48) for X_2 and substituting it into eq. (6.49), we find that it becomes

$$9X_1^{-1/2} = 6(65 - X_1)^{-1/2} \tag{6.50}$$

Solving eqs. (6.50) for X_1^*, we find $X_1^* = \$45$ (this figure and the following dollar figures are in thousands of dollars). Thus territory 1 receives $45 and territory 2 receives the remaining $20. According to eq. (6.45), this allocation of the $65 will generate total profits of $21.40. Total sales will be $402.50, and the company's profits-to-sales ratio will be 5.3%.

Linear Programming

The general mathematical-programming problem is essentially equivalent to eq. (6.35) above. But as previously noted, the Lagrange-multiplier method is not a panacea, and some other solution methods must be used for special forms of the objective function and the constraints. The most widely used and discussed alternative to the classical approach is linear programming.

A linear program is a problem with a linear objective function subject to linear constraints. The linearity of the problem prevents a solution by classical methods because the objective function is neither strictly concave nor strictly convex and therefore has an optimum at an extreme point of the feasible region. It is precisely this extreme-point property that leads to the solution procedure. A usual form of the linear-programming problem is

$$\text{Maximize} \sum_{i=1}^{n} a_i X_i \tag{6.51}$$

subject to

$$\sum_{i=1}^{n} b_i X_i \le c_j \qquad j = 1, \dots, m$$

$$X_i \ge 0$$

The approach to solving linear-programming problems is perhaps best understood by way of an example.

EXAMPLE: The Oxite Company produces a portable oxygen unit and sells it to two types of distributors, fire-equipment distributors and surgical supply houses.

Oxite's profit margin varies between the two types of distributors because of differences in selling costs, typical order sizes, and different credit policies. On the basis of a distribution-cost analysis, the company estimates that the current profit margins are $15 and $10, respectively.

The company's sales are generated by a combination of personal salesforce calls and selective media advertising. The company has four trained salespeople on its payroll, representing 4000 hours of available customer-contact time during the next 6 mo. Furthermore, the company has allotted $14,000 toward advertising during this period.

An examination of past data indicates that a unit sale to a fire-equipment distributor requires about a half-hour sales call and $1 of advertising, while a unit sale to a surgical house requires a quarter-hour sales call and $2 of advertising.

The company would like to achieve sales of at least 3000 units in each customer segment and will accept any allocation of its marketing resources that will maximize profits, provided that these minimum sales levels are achieved.

Therefore the company must determine how much sales it should seek to develop in each customer segment to maximize its total profits. The actual amount of sales in each territory will depend on the mix of advertising and selling resources it applies in each segment, both of which are limited. Offhand, it would seem that the company should seek more sales to fire-equipment distributors because of the higher profit margin. But selling to fire-equipment distributors consumes relatively more salesforce time per unit sold, and the limited call time may be a bottleneck.

We now formulate the mathematical objective function and constraints. The objective is to maximize total profits by establishing optimal sales-target volumes and marketing mixes for the two customer segments. Let Q_1 = sales-target volume (in units) for fire-equipment distributors and Q_2 = sales-target volume (in units) for surgical supply houses. Since every unit sold to a fire-equipment distributor and a surgical supply house will yield $15 and $10 net profit, respectively, total profit is shown by the objective function:

$$\text{Profits} = 15Q_1 + 10Q_2 \qquad (6.52)$$

Each possible target sales volume requires a different amount of personal selling and advertising effort. The marketing-input requirements and constraints for different sales levels can be expressed mathematically. The salesforce, for example, has 4000 h of selling time available during the next 6 mo. The estimated amount of selling time consumed will be $\frac{1}{2}$ h (on the average) for every unit sold to fire-equipment distributors and $\frac{1}{4}$ h for every unit sold to surgical supply houses. (The numbers $\frac{1}{2}$ and $\frac{1}{4}$ are called the marketing-input coefficients.) The expected amount of selling time cannot exceed the available amount, which is 4000 h. Therefore the salesforce constraint is

$$\tfrac{1}{2}Q_1 + \tfrac{1}{4}Q_2 \leq 4000 \tag{6.53}$$

Similarly, unit sales to fire-equipment distributors and surgical supply houses require $1 and $2 of advertising, respectively, and cannot exceed $14,000. Therefore the advertising budget constraint is

$$Q_1 + 2Q_2 \leq 14,000 \tag{6.54}$$

In addition to these constraints, the company has decided that it must strive to sell at least 3000 units in each segment. The minimum-sales-quota constraints are

$$Q_1 \geq 3000$$
$$Q_2 \geq 3000 \tag{6.55}$$

Normally, an iterative-solution technique called the simplex method is used to find the values of Q_1 and Q_2 that maximize the profit function while satisfying the constraints. Because of the small size of the problem here, we can illustrate the idea behind the solution procedure graphically.

The necessary graphs are shown in Exhibit 6.5. First, we prepare a two-dimensional graph, where the Q_1 and Q_2 axes represent possible target sales volumes for fire-equipment distributors and surgical supply houses, respectively [Exhibit 6.5(a)]. Any point in this space represents a conceivable solution before the constraints are specified. In Exhibit 6.5(b) the salesforce constraint is added. All the points in the shaded region represent the (now smaller) feasible region. In Exhibit 6.5(c) the advertising constraint has been added. The shaded region shows the points that satisfy both the advertising and personal-selling constraints and is called the feasible polygon. Exhibit 6.5(d) shows further modifications in the feasible polygon, resulting from the introduction of the last two constraints regarding minimum-sales-volume targets.

The problem is to find the one best point in the feasible polygon. To measure the desirability of the different points, we insert each point into the objective function. For example, for the point (3000, 3000), which is at one corner of the feasible region, profit will be

$$\text{Profit} = 15(3000) + 10(3000) = \$75,000 \tag{6.56}$$

There is an axiom in linear programming that says that the optimal solution will be at one (or more) of the corner points of the feasible polygon. Graphically, the profit function $Z = 15Q_1 + 10Q_2$ is drawn for different assumed values of Z. Higher values of Z shift the line to the right, parallel to itself. This shifting continues until the line touches the last corner of the feasible polygon before leaving it. This point is the optimal corner point.

The coordinates of all the corner points are shown in Exhibit 6.5(d). It is an easy matter in this simple case to test each. We find that the corner point

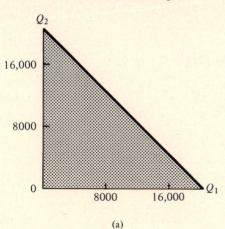

Initial Feasible Region

(a)

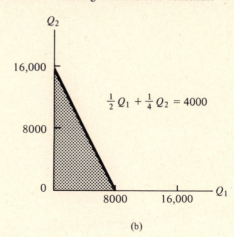

Adding the Salesforce Constraint

$$\tfrac{1}{2} Q_1 + \tfrac{1}{4} Q_2 = 4000$$

(b)

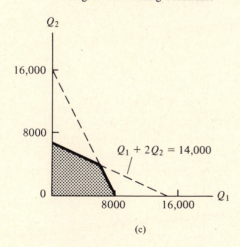

Adding the Advertising Constraint

$$Q_1 + 2Q_2 = 14,000$$

(c)

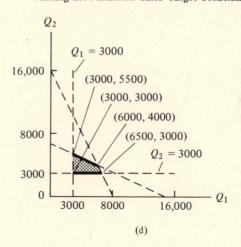

Adding the Minimum–Sales–Target Constraints

$Q_1 = 3000$

(3000, 5500)

(3000, 3000)

(6000, 4000)

(6500, 3000)

$Q_2 = 3000$

(d)

▓ Feasible Region

EXHIBIT 6-5 **Steps in the graphic solution of a simple linear-programming problem.**

(6000, 4000) gives the largest value of profits. Specifically,

$$\text{Profit} = 15(6000) + 10(4000) = \$130{,}000 \qquad (6.57)$$

Thus the Oxite Company should divide its total marketing effort between the two segments so as to try to sell 6000 units to the fire-equipment distributors and 4000 units to surgical supply houses. This effort will result in $130,000 profit. To attain sales of 6000 units to fire-equipment distributors will require 300 sales calls (because a half-hour call is required for each call), that is, (3000, $6000). To attain sales of 4000 units to surgical supply houses wil require 1000 sales calls and $8000 of advertising, that is, (1000, $8000). These allocations just exhaust the total of the company's marketing resources. No other allocation of marketing resources can produce more profit.

Solving a linear-programming problem provides more information about the optimal solution than simply the values of the decision variables: associated with an optimal solution are *shadow prices* (also known as *dual variables, marginal values,* or *pi values*) for the constraints. The shadow price of a particular constraint represents the change in the value of the objective function per unit increase in the value of the constant.

EXAMPLE: Suppose we could relax the salesforce constraint. How much would it be worth to us to get a salesman to work overtime? This condition is equivalent to adding an hour of time to the salesman's time restriction. The optimal solution is now the intersection of

$$Q_1 + 2Q_2 = 14{,}000$$
$$\tfrac{1}{2}Q_1 + \tfrac{1}{4}Q_2 = 4001 \tag{6.58}$$

and

The new solution is $(Q_1, Q_2) = (3998 - \tfrac{2}{3}, 6002 - \tfrac{2}{3})$, with associated profit $15(6002 - \tfrac{2}{3}) + 10(3998 - \tfrac{2}{3}) = 130{,}026 - \tfrac{2}{3}$. Thus the shadow price for this constraint is $(130{,}026 - \tfrac{2}{3}) - 130{,}000 = 26 - \tfrac{2}{3}$. It would thus be worth $26.67 in expected added profit to increase the amount of salesman's time. If the incremental cost of such an activity is less than this amount, then it should be considered.

Although this example considered only two market segments, two marketing instruments, and four constraints, larger problems can be handled analogously by computer. [See Bradley, Hax, and Magnanti (1977) or any text on mathematical programming for details.] The chief limitation to the use of linear programming in marketing is that most interesting problems have inherent nonlinearities, as discussed in Chapters 3 and 4. Objectives are rarely linear and may be multiple in nature. Furthermore, even the restrictions on the variables (the constraints) are often nonlinear. Nevertheless, linear-programming applications have been reported in marketing literature, especially in the areas of media decisions (Bass and Lonsdale, 1966; Day, 1963; Engel and Warshaw, 1964), distribution models (Kuehn and Hamburger, 1963), and consumer-preference measurement (Braun and

Srinivasan, 1975; Hauser and Shugan, 1980; Pekelman and Sen, 1979; Shocker and Srinivasan, 1979; Srinivasan and Shocker, 1973).

A broad subclass of problems with special structures called network models can be formulated as linear-programming problems. Among these specialized problems are the *assignment problem,* used as a decision aid to assign salespeople to territories [see King (1967) or Stern (1966)]; the *transportation and transhipment problems,* used to analyze distribution networks and to perform warehouse- and plant-location studies; and *critical-path analysis* [including the program-evaluation-and-review technique (PERT) and the critical-path method (CPM)] used in planning, scheduling, monitoring, and controlling progress of new-product launches (Urban and Hauser, 1980).

Integer and Mixed-Integer Programming

In linear programming the decision space is assumed to be continuous. In integer or mixed-integer programming, only integer values are allowed for some or all variables. A simple approach to solving integer programs is to round off the linear-programming solution. But this approach has several problems: the optimal integer solution may not be near the optimal continuous solution, and even if it is, it may not be clear whether to round up or to round down.

Basically, the integer-programming problem is inherently difficult to solve and falls in the domain of combinatorial analysis rather than simple linear programming. Special algorithms have been developed to find optimal integer solutions; however, the size of the problem that can be solved successfully by these algorithms is an order of magnitude smaller than the size of linear programs that can easily be solved. However, where the numbers are fairly large, rounding to feasible integer solution usually results in a good approximation.

Four problems, best handled with an integer program, are described below.

Either-or Constraints. Frequently, one of two restrictions must hold, but not necessarily both. For example, one of two warehouses (each with holding-cost schedules) will be used for storing product in transit: warehouse A charges $3 per unit of product 1 and $2 per unit of product 2, while in warehouse B the charges are reversed. Furthermore, we have an inventory-cost spending limit of $2000. These two constraints can be formulated separately:

$$3X_1 + 2X_2 \le 2000 \tag{6.59}$$

$$2X_1 + 3X_2 \le 2000 \tag{6.60}$$

For only one of these constraints to hold at a time, we introduce the 0–1 variable y and the very large positive number M and append them to eqs. (6.59) and (6.60) to form

$$3X_1 + 2X_1 \leq 2000 + yM \tag{6.61}$$

$$2X_1 + 3X_2 \leq 2000 + (1 - y)M \tag{6.62}$$

Here if $y = 1$, constraint (6.62) holds; and if $y = 0$, constraint (6.61) holds.

k out of K constraints. This idea is extended to the situation in which k out of K constraints hold:

$$g_1(X_1, \ldots, X_n) \leq b_1 + My_1$$
$$\vdots \tag{6.63}$$
$$g_k(X_1, \ldots, X_n) \leq b_K + My_K$$

$$\sum_{i=1}^{K} y_i = K - k \tag{6.64}$$

$$y_i = 0 \text{ or } 1 \qquad \text{for all } i \tag{6.65}$$

Constraints (6.64) and (6.65) force k out of the K constraints in eq. (6.63) to hold while the others are ineffective.

Functions with K Possible Values. Suppose a given function (perhaps representing production capacity) is required to take on any one of K discrete values:

$$g(X_1, \ldots, X_n) = b_1 \text{ or } b_2 \text{ or } \ldots \text{ or } b_k. \tag{6.66}$$

This equation can be written as an integer-programming constraint:

$$g(X_1, \ldots, X_n) = \sum_{i=1}^{K} b_i y_i$$

$$\sum_{i=1}^{K} y_i = 1$$

$$y_i = 0 \text{ or } 1 \tag{6.67}$$

Fixed-charge Problem. A situation that comes up frequently in marketing, especially in distribution planning, is the fixed-charge problem, in which there is a fixed charge for a production facility (as well as a variable charge) if it is used and no charge otherwise. If we let X_j denote the amount of production or use of the jth facility, we might have a cost function that looks like

$$C_j(X_j) = \begin{cases} b_j + d_j X_j & \text{if } X_j > 0 \\ 0 & \text{otherwise} \end{cases} \tag{6.68}$$

Then if our original objective function was to

$$\text{Minimize } C(X_1, \ldots, X_n) = \sum_{j=1}^{n} C_j(X_j) \tag{6.69}$$

(Subject to constraint (6.68), it can be replaced by

$$\text{Minimize } C(X_1, \ldots, X_n) = \sum_{j=1}^{n} b_j y_j + d_j X_j \tag{6.70}$$

subject to

$$X_j - M y_j \leq 0 \qquad j = 1, \ldots, n \tag{6.71}$$
$$y_j = 0 \text{ or } 1 \qquad j = 1, \ldots, n \tag{6.72}$$

Constraint (6.71) is needed to ensure that $y_j = 1$ rather than zero whenever facility j is used $(X_j > 0)$.

Many different algorithms have been developed to solve integer-programming and mixed-integer-programming problems. [See, for example, Garfinkel and Nemhauser (1972), Geoffrion and Marsten (1972), or Taha, (1975).] The most popular solution strategies employ the divide-and-conquer approach. The idea is that if, in the unrestricted linear program, y_j does not equal zero or one, define two new problems, one with $y_j = 0$ and another with $y_j = 1$ and then solve each of these problems separately. Much of the theory of solving integer-programming problems is based on clever solutions to such problems.

For example, consider a salesforce-determination problem where the number of salespeople in each territory j, X_j, must be integral. Suppose a linear-programming solution is tried and $X_4 = 7.2$. The divide-and-conquer approach might have you try two new linear-programming problems, one with constraint $X_4 \leq 7$ and the other with $X_4 \geq 8$. This approach would be repeated until an optimal integer solution is found. The theory of solving integer programs is a technical issue beyond the scope of this book. The approach has been applied in marketing primarily in two areas: salesforce problems [see Zoltners and Sinha (1980) for a review] and distribution-system planning and facility location [see Geoffrion and Graves (1974) and Meyer (1973) for examples].

Nonlinear-programming Problems

As noted earlier, many key decision problems in marketing have a relatively complicated, nonlinear structure. However, as with linear programming, there are classes of nonlinear-programming problems that often arise in marketing analyses that are inherently simpler to solve than others. The general, nonlinear-programming problem is

$$
\begin{aligned}
\text{Maximize} \quad & f(X_1, \ldots, X_n) \\
\text{Subject to} \quad & g_1(X_1, \ldots, X_n) \le b_1 \\
& \quad \vdots \qquad\qquad\qquad \vdots \\
& g_m(X_1, \ldots, X_n) \le b_m
\end{aligned}
$$

(6.73)

EXAMPLE: A marketing manager has \$10 million in promotional spending to allocate between two of his (related) products. Let X_j, $j = 1, 2$, denote his promotional spending for product j, in thousands of dollars. Past data indicate that within ranges of historical spending levels, products 1 and 2 have expected annual returns of 20% and 16%, respectively. Also, the total risk associated with promotional spending for these products—measured by the variance of total return— is $2X_1^2 + X_2^2 + (X_1 + X_2)^2$. Therefore that risk increases with total promotional spending, as well as with the amount of each separate promotional disbursement.

The marketing manager would like to maximize return and at the same time minimize risk. One way of combining these objectives is in a single objective function:

$$
\text{Maximize } f(X_1, X_2) = 20X_1 + 16X_2 - \theta \,[2X_1^2 + X_2^2 + (X_1 + X_2)^2]
$$

(6.74)

subject to

$$
\begin{aligned}
X_1 + X_2 &\le 10{,}000 \\
X_1 &\ge 0 \\
X_2 &\ge 0
\end{aligned}
$$

The nonnegative constant θ reflects the trade-off between risk and return. Problem (6.74) is a nonlinear program that often arises in making marketing-allocation decisions.

Two special mathematical-programming problems that often arise in marketing are separable- and quadratic-programming problems.
Separable Programming. An objective function is separable when it can be written as a sum of separate terms, each of which involves only a single variable:

$$
f(X_1, \ldots, X_n) = f_1(X_1) + \cdots + f_n(X_n)
$$

(6.75)

For an approximate solution to such a problem, it can be reduced to a linear-programming problem by approximating each $f_i(X_i)$ with a piecewise linear function. The procedure guarantees a unique optimal solution if each $f_i(X_i)$ is concave (for a maximization problem) or convex (for a minimization problem). The following example illustrates the approach.

EXAMPLE: Assume that XYZ Company sells two products and uses two marketing instruments to stimulate demand, advertising (A) and selling (D). In each planning period the company must decide on the amount of advertising and selling resources to devote to the two products (A_1, A_2, D_1, D_2). The total advertising and selling resources of the company for the planning period are $A = \$22,600$ and $D = 6000$ person-hours. On the basis of historical records and experienced judgment, management has arrived at productivity coefficients for its advertising and selling efforts for each product. A dollar of advertising is estimated to yield $6 of profit when spent for product 1 and $10 of profit when spent for product 2. Assume that this result holds over the whole range of the advertising budget—that is, there are no increasing or diminishing returns to advertising. In the case of selling effort, however, assume the situation is more complicated and characterized by diminishing returns (a concave function). If the company devotes up to 2000 of the 6000 available person-hours in selling product 1, the profit margin per person-hour is $24; if it devotes between 2000 and 6000 person-hours to selling product 1, the profit margin per selling hour is $18. To describe this decline in productivity, let the auxiliary variables D_{11} and D_{12} represent the amounts of selling effort against product 1 at the higher and lower levels of productivity, respectively. Then the range of the auxiliary variables are constrained as follows:

$$0 \le D_{11} \le 2000$$
$$0 \le D_{12} \le 4000$$
(6.76)

Note that, even if all the selling time is devoted to product 1, the amount $(D_{11} + D_{12})$ will not exceed the available selling time of 6000 person-hours. This condition amounts to defining a piecewise linear approximation to a concave function, as shown in Exhibit 6.6.

Similarly, if the company devotes up to 1500 hr in selling product 2, the profit margin per selling hour is $40; if it devotes between 1500 and 6000 to selling product 2, the profit margin per selling hour falls to $20. Then we obtain

$$0 \le D_{21} \le 1500$$
$$0 \le D_{22} \le 4500$$
(6.77)

Finally, because it wants to ensure the continuation of both products in the product line due to their complementarity, management imposes some policy constraints on the minimum and maximum amounts of advertising and personal selling devoted to each product. Specifically, management insists that at least 2200 persons-hours and $5000 of advertising and no more than 4500 person-hours and $18,000 of advertising be devoted to each product. Then the whole problem can be stated as a separable linear program as shown in Exhibit 6.7.

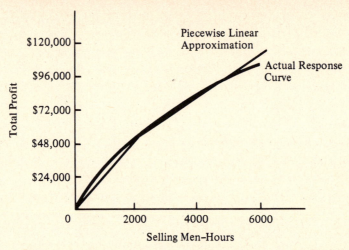

EXHIBIT 6-6   Approximating a concave function with two linear segments.

EXHIBIT 6-7   Separable-linear-programming statement of a marketing-resource-allocation problem.

Find the allocation of marketing effort $(A_1, A_2, D_{11}, D_{12}, D_{21}, D_{22})$ that maximizes the profit function

$$Z = 6A_1 + 10A_2 + 24D_{11} + 18D_{12} + 40D_{21} + 20D_{22}$$

subject to the following conditions

$$\left.\begin{array}{r}A_1 + A_2 \le 22{,}600 \\ D_{11} + D_{12} + D_{21} + D_{22} \le 6{,}000\end{array}\right\} \begin{array}{l}\text{marketing-resource} \\ \text{constraints}\end{array}$$

$$\left.\begin{array}{r}D_{11} \le 2{,}000 \\ D_{12} \le 4{,}000 \\ D_{21} \le 1{,}500 \\ D_{22} \le 4{,}500\end{array}\right\} \begin{array}{l}\text{auxiliary-variable} \\ \text{constraints (for} \\ \text{productivity} \\ \text{changeovers)}\end{array}$$

$$\left.\begin{array}{r}D_{11} + D_{12} \ge 2{,}200 \\ D_{21} + D_{22} \ge 2{,}200 \\ D_{11} + D_{12} \le 4{,}500 \\ D_{21} + D_{22} \le 4{,}500 \\ A_1 \ge 5{,}000 \\ A_2 \ge 5{,}000 \\ A_1 \le 18{,}000 \\ A_2 \le 18{,}000\end{array}\right\} \begin{array}{l}\text{policy constraints} \\ \text{(minimum- and} \\ \text{maximum-usage} \\ \text{levels)}\end{array}$$

$$A_1, A_2, D_{11}, D_{12}, D_{21}, D_{22}, \text{ all } \ge \quad 0 \left.\right\} \begin{array}{l}\text{nonnegativity} \\ \text{constraints}\end{array}$$

The problem has been stated in a form appropriate for solution by the simplex method. The optimal program turns out to be

$$
\begin{aligned}
A_1 &= \$5000 \\
A_2 &= \$17{,}600 \\
D_{11} &= 2000 \\
D_{12} &= 200 \\
D_{21} &= 1500 \\
D_{22} &= 2300
\end{aligned}
$$

(6.78)

This solution will produce total profits of \$363,600.

The separable-programming approach outlined above can be extended to multiple products and any number of marketing variables. All that are required are an estimate of the shape of the sales-response function, its approximation by linear segments, and a test of the curve's concavity. Note that concavity in a range for a marketing-response function is a reasonable assumption whenever there is a well-defined upper bound on market demand. The analyst need only be concerned that all marketing variables are beyond the range of threshold effects and that a concave response function is a reasonable approximation.

Quadratic Programming.   Quadratic programming refers to the maximization of a quadratic objective function subject to linear constraints:

$$
\text{Maximize } f(X_1, \ldots, X_n) = \Sigma \, c_j X_j + \tfrac{1}{2} \Sigma \Sigma \, q_{jk} X_j X_k \tag{6.79}
$$

subject to

$$
\sum_{j=1}^{n} a_{ij} X_j \le b_i \qquad i = 1, 2, \ldots, m
$$

$$
X_j \ge 0
$$

Powerful solution procedures similar to the simplex method have been developed for the special quadratic-programming case where the objective function in eq. (6.79) is concave. For f to be concave,

$$
\Sigma \Sigma \, q_{jk} X_j X_k \ge 0 \tag{6.80}
$$

for all feasible values of $X_1, \ldots, X_n$. This condition is equivalent to the condition that the q_{jk} be elements of a positive semidefinite matrix.

A problem that often arises in marketing is that of constrained regression. The linear least-squares regression with linear constraints on the coefficients is a concave-quadratic-programming problem, as is the promotional-budget-allocation problem introduced at the beginning of this section. [See Boot (1964) for development of quadratic-programming algorithms.]

Quadratic programming is often employed when a quadratic objective function is used to approximate a more complex functional form.

More-general, Nonlinear-programming Methods.   As with general integer-programming methods, the general nonlinear-programming problem is inherently a difficult problem. General solution procedures are not always successful; special insight into the structure of the problem is often required in order to choose a solution strategy. [See Simmons (1975) or Zangwill (1969) for detailed reviews of the field.]

We conclude this section with a brief note on what appear to be the most successful approaches to general nonlinear-programming problems: penalty and barrier methods. Because penalty functions and barrier methods do not consider constraints separately, they are computationally efficient, especially for nonlinear-programming problems with nonlinear constraints. Briefly, the nonlinear-programming (NLP) problem is

$$\text{Maximize } f(X_1, \ldots, X_n) \qquad (6.81)$$

subject to

$$g_i(X_1, \ldots, X_n) \leq 0 \qquad i = 1, \ldots, m$$

An associated problem is to consider the function

$$P(X_1, \ldots, X_n) = \begin{cases} 0 & \text{if } X_1, \ldots, X_n \text{ is feasible} \\ & \text{(satisfies the constraints)} \\ -\infty & \text{otherwise} \end{cases} \qquad (6.82)$$

Penalty-function methods transform eq. (6.81) into

$$\text{Maximize } C(X_1, \ldots, X_n) = f(X_1, \ldots, X_n) + P(X_1, \ldots, X_n) \qquad (6.83)$$

Intuitively, $P(X_1, \ldots, X_n)$ produces an infinite penalty for leaving the feasible region defined by the constraints in eq. (6.81). Clearly, $X_1^*, \ldots, X_n^*$ is optimal for eq. (6.81) if and only if it also solves the unconstrained problem (6.83). Penalty-function methods approximate eq. (6.83) by defining a sequence of functions, $P_1, P_2, \ldots$, that impose larger and larger penalties for leaving the feasible region. The astute selection of penalty-function sequences (that are continuous and differentiable) allows numerical methods based on classical optimization procedures to be used for solving the NLP. [See Fiacco and McCormick (1968) for a definitive treatment of this subject.]

Multiple-Objective Optimization

As noted in Chapter 3, a decision maker often has more than one objective. The different objectives may be of equal importance, or, at least, it may be difficult for the decision maker to compare the importance of one objective with another. The utility-theory-based approach has been applied in this area. An alternative approach is known as the Pareto optimality approach. In certain cases if the decision variables are subject to linear constraints, the alternatives can be evaluated as described below.

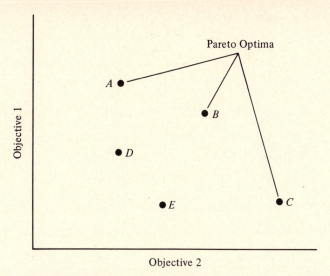

EXHIBIT 6-8   The Pareto optimum approach to multiple-criterion problems.

We seek a feasible point X^* that dominates all other feasible points in the sense that there is no other feasible Y^* at which all objectives are at least as good as X^* and at which at least one objective value is better. Such a point X^* is termed a Pareto optimum, and the set of points $\{X\}$ that satisfy this condition are called the efficient frontier. Exhibit 6.8 illustrates this concept: points A, B, and C correspond to Pareto optima for the problem. The problem of finding Pareto optima can be put into a linear-programming framework. For discussion and some recent extensions of this approach, see Kornbluth and Stever (1981).

Optimal-Control Problems*

Most of the problems presented in this chapter focused on allocating resources (financial and otherwise) among competing alternatives at a single point in time. These problems, choosing *values of variables* to maximize an *objective function* subject to restrictions (*constraints*), are mathematical-programming problems.

The optimal-control problem occurs when the problem is to choose time paths for certain variables, called control variables [advertising rate, $X = X(t)$], from a given feasible *control set*. The choice of time paths for the control variables leads, through a set of differential equations called the *equations of motion,* to time paths for various variables describing the system called *state variables* (sales rates, for example). Time paths of the control variables are chosen to maximize an *objective functional* (e.g.,

*This section contains technical material.

profit). (A *function* is defined over variables; a *functional* is defined over other functions.)

EXAMPLE:

Tapiero and Farley (1975) considered the problem of controlling sales effort over time. Their dynamic model has each salesperson i selling $q_{ij}(t)$ units of product j at time t and price $p_j(t)$ and receiving a commission rate of $r_j(t)$. Each salesperson realizes commission income in the period from $t = 0$ to T:

$$\text{Salesperson's commission} = \int_0^T \left\{ \sum_{j=1}^{n} r_j(t)p_j(t)q_{ij}(t) \right\} dt \qquad i = 1, \ldots, m \quad (6.84)$$
$$[Z_i(t)]$$

The firm sees total sales of product j of

$$\text{Sales} = Q_j(t) = \sum_{j=1}^{m} q_{i_j}(t) \tag{6.85}$$

and total profits of

$$
\begin{aligned}
\text{Total firm profits} &= \int_0^T \left\{ \sum_{j=1}^{n} [1 - r_j(t)][p_j(t)Q_j(t)] - C_j[Q_j(t)] \right\} dt \\
[Z_0(t)] \qquad\qquad &= \int_0^T \text{(net revenue rate after selling costs} \\
&\qquad - \text{cost rate of production)}
\end{aligned}
\tag{6.86}
$$

Market demand is modeled as sales-response functions:

$$q_{ij}(t) = f_{ij}\left(Z_{ij}(t) \right) \tag{6.87}$$

which relate sales of each product to the time t expended by each salesperson on it.

Under a reasonable set of assumptions about effort allocation, the shape of the response functions in eq. (6.87), and constraints on amount of selling time available, control theory allows (from the company's standpoint) evaluation of the relative optimal commission rates [$r_{ij}(t)$ the control variables] to apply across products to maximize $Z_0(T)$, company profit. This model is a continuous analog of the simple static model in Davis and Farley (1971).

Optimal-control theory was developed to control the time paths of dynamic systems. Most early developments (and published applications) are reported in the engineering literature. The use of control theory in marketing has been reported primarily in the area of advertising. [See Bensoussan, Bultez, and Naert (1978), Sasieni (1971), Schmalensee (1972), and Sethi (1973) for example.] Furthermore, it has been used in marketing primarily to derive the theoretical structure (time path) of optimal policies rather than to empirically estimate the policies [Turner and Wiginton (1976) is an exception]. The interested reader is referred to Intriligator (1971) or Sethi and Thompson (1981) for an introduction to control theory.

Decisions Under Uncertainty

One of the factors that makes modern marketing so frustrating and at the same time so intriguing is the presence of uncertainty. Up to now, we have assumed that the decision maker knows exactly the nature of the demand and cost functions facing the firm. His problem was to find the marketing program that would maximize some utility function representing the company's set of goals. Because of the presence of carry-over effects, product interactions, nonlinear responses, and other complications, finding the solution was not always easy, even under the assumption of certainty. Now that the additional possibility of uncertainty is introduced, finding the optimum marketing program is even more complex.

Uncertainty faces every business executive, but few cope with it in any formal way. They absorb the uncertainty through a variety of organizational and individual devices, ranging from committee decision making to substantial investments in marketing research to the use of risk-reducing criteria.

The models considered in this chapter so far are appropriate for executives who wish to make decisions under assumed certainty. They make their best single estimate of every relevant factor in the situation and compute the value of the outcome. They consider whether the outcome is attractive, and if it is, they adopt the course of action.

Conservative executives often choose to imagine the worst-possible case in which demand is lower than expected and costs are higher than expected. If the investment still appears attractive, they may go ahead. Other executives tend to be optimistic about the future of a project and prefer to take a risk. Many executives make three estimates of the relevant variables: an expected, an optimistic, and a pessimistic estimate. But, few executives proceed to process these estimates in a formal way to obtain the best decision.

Several types of methodologies have been developed for precisely those situations where the executive wishes to consider and handle uncertainty explicitly.

Decision Analysis

Decision analysis is an approach for solving problems with the following characteristics:

A choice or sequence of choices must be made among various courses of action.

The choice or sequence of choices will ultimately lead to some consequence, but the decision maker cannot be sure in advance what the consequence will be because it depends not only on his decisions but on an unpredictable event or sequence of events.

The choice of action should depend on the likelihood that the decision maker's action will result in various possible consequences, as well as the desirability (utility) of the various consequences.

The decision-analysis approach usually includes four steps:

1. **Structuring the problem.**   This step involves defining general objectives, specifiying measures of effectiveness, identifying restrictions on actions, and characterizing the problem chronologically. It also includes identification of alternative courses of action.
2. **Assigning probabilities to possible outcomes.**   The likelihood of various outcomes occurring, depending on managerial actions, needs to be assessed. This assessment can be purely subjective or can include analysis of past system behavior (objective assessment).
3. **Assigning utilities to consequences.**   Decision-maker preferences need to be assessed with the utility-based procedure developed in Chapter 3.
4. **Analyzing the problem.**   The best course of action is identified by a method called averaging out and folding back. In order to illustrate the basic procedure, we present the following example.

EXAMPLE: This is example is based on Keeney (undated notes).

The QRS Company must decide whether or not to introduce a new product. If it chooses to introduce it, sales will either be high or low. For simplicity, we assume that firm objectives are to maximize expected profits (the firm is risk-neutral).

The firm is considering a market survey to collect information on expected sales. The market research firm contacted will report one of three results: great, good, or poor, where "great" means that high sales are likely (and does not refer to the quality of the survey).

Marketing management feels that the probability that the product will have high sales is 0.4. The company has had past experience with this market research firm and knows that for high-sales products in the past, 60% had great survey results, 30% had good survey results, and 10% had poor survey results. Similarly, for their low-sales products, 10% had great survey results, 30% had good survey results, and 60% had poor survey results.

If sales are high, net profits (excluding the cost of the survey) are expected to be $100,000; if sales are low, there will be a net loss of $50,000, exclusive of market-survey costs.

Exhibit 6.9 illustrates the structure of this problem in a form known as a decision tree. The chronology of events begins on the left and flows to the right. The first thing that happens is that marketing management must decide whether or not to take a survey. Then management learns the results of the survey and decides whether or not to produce the product. Finally, sales results are learned.

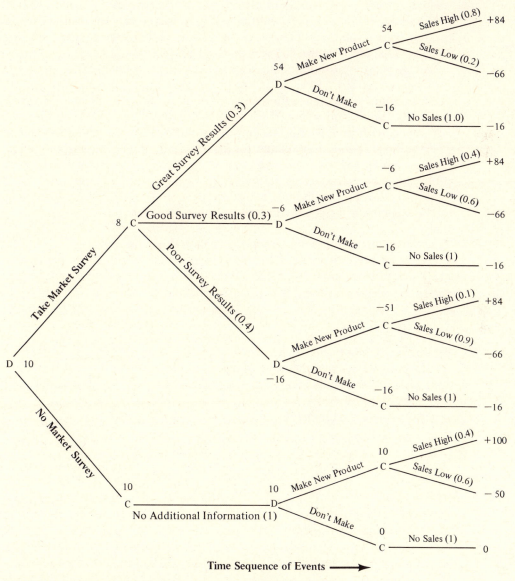

Consequences ($1000s)

EXHIBIT 6-9   **Structure of decision tree for QRS Company.**

Two types of nodes are included in the exhibit: those marked D are decision nodes, meaning management has control over the course of action while those marked C are chance nodes, where the decision maker has no control.

Consequences of the several courses of action are indicated at the end of the path. For instance, if a market survey is taken with great results, the product is manufactured and sales are high; the result is a net gain of $84,000: $100,000 less the $16,000 survey cost. All consequences are measured against the do-nothing strategy of no survey, no manufacturing, and no sales.

The numbers in parentheses beside those segments of the tree beginning at chance nodes are the conditional probabilities that the event associated with that segment occurs, given that everything else up to that point in the tree *does* occur. Thus, for instance, the probability that the suvey is *great*, given that we make the survey, is 0.3, or 30%. The conditional probability that sales are high, given that survey results are great and we decide to manufacture, is 0.8, or 80%.

To calculate these probabilities, we use Bayes' theorem, which states that if events $\{B_i\}$, $i = 1, \ldots, n$, are mutually exclusive and collectively exhaustive, and if A is some other event, then the conditional probability of B_i occurring, given A occurs, is

$$p(B_i \mid A) = \frac{p(A \mid B_i)p(B_i)}{\sum\limits_{j=1}^{n} p(A \mid B_j)p(B_j)} \qquad (6.88)$$

Therefore to assess the probabilities in the tree, we need to find unconditional probabilities that the market survey will be great, good, and poor and conditional probabilities for sales being high and low for each of the survey outcomes.

To summarize the given information, we know

$$
\begin{aligned}
p(\text{great survey} \mid \text{high sales}) &= 0.6 \\
p(\text{good} \mid \text{high}) &= 0.3 \\
p(\text{poor} \mid \text{high}) &= 0.1 \\
p(\text{great} \mid \text{low}) &= 0.1 \\
p(\text{good} \mid \text{low}) &= 0.3 \\
p(\text{poor} \mid \text{low}) &= 0.6 \\
p(\text{high}) &= 0.4 \\
p(\text{low}) &= 0.6
\end{aligned}
\qquad (6.89)
$$

To get the probability that the survey would be great, we use

$$p(\text{great}) = p(\text{great} \mid \text{high})p(\text{high}) + p(\text{great} \mid \text{low})p(\text{low})$$
$$= 0.6 \times 0.4 + 0.1 \times 0.6 = 0.3 \qquad (6.90)$$

Similarly,

$$p \text{ (good)} = 0.3$$

$$p \text{ (poor)} = 0.4$$

To get p (high | great), we use Bayes' theorem:

$$p(\text{high} | \text{great}) = \frac{p(\text{great} | \text{high})p(\text{high})}{p(\text{great})}$$

$$= \frac{0.6 \times 0.4}{0.3} = 0.8 \tag{6.91}$$

Similarly, we get

$$p(\text{high} | \text{good}) = 0.4$$
$$p(\text{high} | \text{poor}) = 0.1$$
$$p(\text{low} | \text{great}) = 0.2$$
$$p(\text{low} | \text{good}) = 0.6$$
$$p(\text{low} | \text{poor}) = 0.9$$

We now use these probabilities to average out and fold back. The numbers beside each node represent the expected profit associated with being there. If we make a market survey, have great results, and manufacture the product, then there is an 80% chance of high sales, implying a net profit of $84,000, and a 20% chance of low sales, with a net loss of $66,000. Thus the expected profit (averaging out) of being at that chance node is

$$0.8 (\$84,000) + 0.2 (\$66,000), = \$54,000 \tag{6.92}$$

At the node immediately below, if we have the same great results of the survey and then choose not to manufacture, we will lose $16,000.

Now backing up (folding back) to the decision node before these chance nodes, the decision maker can either make the product with expected profit of $54,000 or not make the product with an expected loss of $16,000. The best choice is to make the product; therefore the expected profit of that decision node is $54,000.

Proceeding in like manner to complete the analysis of the tree, we conclude that the best course of action is not to take a market survey. Therefore we introduce the expected value of sample information.

Expected Value of Sample Information. From our analysis we learned that the survey information we obtained was not worth $16,000. Just how much is it worth? If we label the survey cost as S and average out and fold back, we find that the value of being at the first chance node is $24,000 − S. If S is $14,000, one is indifferent between making a survey and not making it, since the decision "no market survey" is worth an expected $10,000. This amount is the maximum one should pay for the survey.

Expected Value of Perfect Information.   An important question is how much one should pay for perfect information. This idea is important because no survey can give us perfect information, and thus the value of perfect information is the most one should ever pay for sample information.

By "perfect information" we mean a forecast such that

$$p(\text{high forecast} \mid \text{high sales}) = 1$$
$$p(\text{low forecast} \mid \text{low sales}) = 1$$

(6.93)

and other outcomes have probability zero of occurring.

If sales are forecast as high, the best strategy is to introduce the product. This forecast will occur with probability 0.4:

$$p(\text{high forecast}) - p\,(\text{high sales}) = 0.4$$

(6.94)

The net profit of this consequence is $\$100,000 - R$, where R is the cost of the perfect information. Similarly, the probability of the forecast being low is 0.6, and in that case the best strategy is not to make the product. This strategy has a net profit associated with it of $-R$.

Therefore, the expected profit with perfect information is

$$0.4\,(\$100,000 - R) + 0.6\,(-R) = \$40,000 - R$$

(6.95)

When $R = \$30,000$, the marketing manager should be indifferent between obtaining the perfect information and not making a market survey. Both strategies would have an expected net profit of $\$10,000$. Thus the expected value of perfect information is $\$30,000$.

Continuous Consequences.   In a more realistic situation, profits may be better expressed by a variable Z that can take on any value between $-\$50,000$ and $\$100,000$. Moreover, it might be felt that any of the possible values are equally likely. In this case the two consequences on the original tree are replaced by a continuum of consequences, described by a probability density function

$$f_Z(z) = \begin{cases} \dfrac{1}{150,000} & -50,000 \le z \le 100,000 \\ 0 & \text{otherwise} \end{cases}$$

(6.96)

Expected profit—that is, the expected value of Z associated with the chance node—is

$$E(Z) = \int_{\text{all } z} z f_Z(z)\,dz = \int_{-50,000}^{100,000} \frac{z\,dz}{150,000} = 25,000$$

(6.97)

This net expected profit of $\$25,000$ would then be used to work back through the tree as before.

In Chapter 3 we developed the concept of utility assessment for quantifying preferences. All the analyses presented here follow, with the term "profit" replaced by "utility." In particular, in eq. (6.97) the only change would be that we would be considering

$$E(\mu(Z)) = \int_{\text{all } z} \mu(z) \, f_Z(z) dz \qquad (6.98)$$

The rest of the decision-analysis procedure (constructing the tree, averaging out, and folding back) holds as before.

Decision analysis is a model-based analytical procedure that has important uses in structuring and analyzing marketing situations, such as the one described above. Urban and Hauser (1980) describe the use of decision analysis in new-product-planning decisions, drawing on earlier work by Bass (1963), Green and Frank (1966), and Allaire (1975). For a good basic treatment of the concepts of decision analysis, see Raiffa (1968), while Raiffa and Schlaifer (1961) and Schlaifer (1969) provide a more formal development of the procedures and theoretical underpinnings.

Dynamic Programming

Dynamic programming is an optimization approach that transforms a complex problem into a sequence of simple problems. The basic features of dynamic programming problems are (Zoltners, 1981) as follows:

1. The marketing problem can be divided into stages, with each stage having a set of states associated with it.
2. For each state, say j_k, there is a set of decisions, $D(j_k)$, for the decision maker.
3. The system will enter one state at each stage.
4. Only one decision from the set $D(j_k)$ can be chosen.
5. When a decision d_{jk} is taken at stage k, a system utility is incurred.
6. The state entered at stage $k - 1$ is a function of the state the system found itself in at k plus the adopted decision.
7. The stages are independent: an optimal policy for the remaining stages is independent of the policy adopted in previous stages.

The structure of a simple dynamic-programming problem is illustrated in Exhibit 6.10.

In contrast to linear programming, dynamic programming has no standard mathematical formulation. Rather, dynamic programming is a general type of approach to problem solving, and the particular equations used must be developed to fit each individual solution.

Dynamic programming can be used to solve multistage problems in both continuous- and discrete-state space, under certainty as well as under uncertainty. The averaging-out-and-folding-back approach used in the

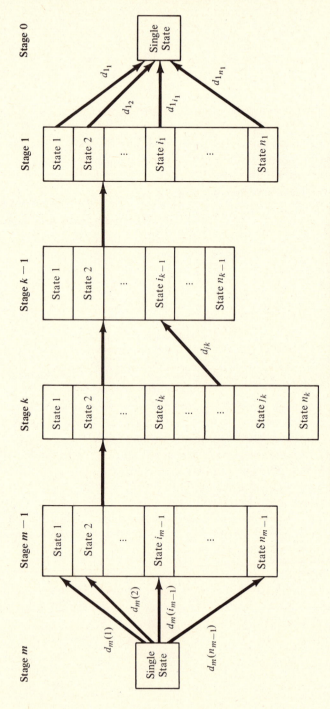

EXHIBIT 6-10 Overview of dynamic programming.

previous sections is a dynamic-programming procedure. The essential characteristic of dynamic-programming problem is the lack of memory, called separability; in general, if a sequence of decisions is required over time or over space (sales regions), a dynamic-programming approach is viable, given that the current state of the system conveys all the information required about previous system behavior for determining the optimal policy henceforth.

Some key references are Bellman and Dreyfus (1962) and (especially for stochastic dynamic programming) Howard (1960). There have been a number of reported applications of dynamic programming in marketing, including Little and Lodish (1969) for media scheduling, Lodish (1980a) for broadcast spot pricing, Robinson and Lakhani (1975) for optimal new-product pricing under experience-curve price declines and diffusion, and Blattberg and colleagues (1979), who proposed a household-and-inventory model for identifying a deal-prone consumer and solved it by using dynamic programming.

Linear Programming Under Uncertainty

A common problem in the practical application of linear programming is the difficulty of assessing the model parameters exactly. True values of costs, constraints, and activity parameters may be known only after a solution has been chosen and implemented; therefore some or all of the model parameters may be random variables.

There are several ways of formulating linear-programming problems under uncertainty. In the first, called *stochastic programming*, the constraints are required to hold with a probability of one. In the second, called *chance-constrained programming*, feasible solutions are allowed to have a small probability of violating each constraint. The general approach to both types reduces the problems to ordinary linear-programming problems that can be solved by the simplex method.

Stochastic Linear Programming.   Consider the linear program formulated in eq. (6.51). Let us assume that some of the parameters (the a's, b's, and c's) are random variables rather than constants. This situation requires a reformulation of the objective function. Since the objective $Z = \Sigma a_j X_j$ becomes a random variable if any of the a_j are random variables (and it is meaningless to maximize a random variable), Z must be replaced by a deterministic function, the most usual of which is the expected value of Z, $E(Z)$.

For the constraints most practical applications of stochastic programming assume that each parameter can take on only a finite number of values. Then all these possible values are enumerated and added to the constraint set. As an example, suppose that our problem had a single constraint:

$$b_1 X_1 + b_2 X_2 \le C_1 \qquad (6.99)$$

and each b could take on two values, b' and b''. Then eq. (6.99) would be replaced by

$$
\begin{aligned}
b_1' \, X_1 + b_2' \, X_2 &\le C_1 \\
b_1'' X_1 + b_2' \, X_2 &\le C_1 \\
b_1' \, X_1 + b_2'' X_2 &\le C_1 \\
b_1'' X_1 + b_2'' X_2 &\le C_1
\end{aligned}
\tag{6.100}
$$

Clearly, as eq. (6.100) shows, if there is uncertainty in a large number of constraint coefficients, the size of the problem is greatly increased, potentially beyond acceptable limits. See Tinter and Sengupta (1972) for a more complete development of approaches toward solving stochastic programs.

Chance-constrained Programming. Charnes and Cooper (1959) developed an approach for situations where it is highly desirable but not absolutely essential that all of the constraints hold for all possible combinations of the constraint values. The chance-constrained formulation replaces each of the original constraints,

$$
\Sigma \, b_{ij} X_j \le a_i \qquad i = 1, \ldots, m
\tag{6.101}
$$

with

$$
p \left(\Sigma \, b_{ij} x_j \le c_i \right) \ge \alpha_i \qquad i = 1, \ldots, m
$$

where $\{\alpha_i\}$ are the probabilities that the associated constraint holds, and therefore $\{1 - \alpha_i\}$ represent the risk of the respective constraints being violated.

The most common form of the chance-constraint linear program is the situation where (1) all the b_{ij} are known constants, so that only $\{c_i\}$ and the $\{a_i\}$ are random variables, (2) the probability distribution of the $\{c_i\}$ is a known multivariate normal distribution, and (3) the $\{a_i\}$ are statistically independent of the $\{b_{ij}\}$. If the expected-value criterion is used, these assumptions are sufficient to specify all but the constraints of a linear program.

Under the assumptions,

$$
p \left(\sum_{j=1}^{n} b_{ij} X_j \le c_i \right) = p \left[\frac{\Sigma b_{ij} X_j - E(c_i)}{\sigma_{c_i}} \le \frac{c_i - E(c_i)}{\sigma_{c_i}} \right]
\tag{6.102}
$$

Now $[c_i - E(c_i)]/\sigma_{c_i}$ has a normal distribution with a mean of zero and a variance of one. If we let K_β be a constant such that $P(Z \ge K_\beta) = \beta$, where $Z \sim N(0,1)$, then

$$
p \left[\frac{\Sigma \, b_{ij} X_j - E(c_i)}{\sigma_{c_i}} \le \frac{c_i - E(c_i)}{\sigma_{c_i}} \right] \ge \alpha_i
\tag{6.103}
$$

holds if and only if

$$
\frac{\Sigma \, b_{ij} X_j - E(c_i)}{\sigma_{c_i}} \le K_{\alpha_i}
\tag{6.104}
$$

or if

$$\sum_{j=1}^{n} b_{ij}X_j \le E(c_i) + K_{\alpha_i}\sigma_{c_i} \qquad i = 1, \ldots, m \tag{6.105}$$

Thus the chance-constrained-programming problem reduces to a linear-programming problem with constraints (6.105).

The DEMON model (Charnes et al. 1968) presents perhaps the best-known marketing application of chance-constrained programming.

Stochastic Control Theory

Stochastic control theory—the extension of control theory to situations where the equations of motion are not known with certainty—has not been applied to any significant marketing problem. Most continuous stochastic-control formulations have been put in discrete terms and solved with a dynamic-programming approach.

Deterministic-Policy-Analysis Tools

In many cases our objective is simply to determine the impact of a particular policy or to study the evolution of a marketing model or a system that we have specified and calibrated. There are a number of ways to accomplish this objective, the simplest and most direct of which may be marginal-change analysis (sensitivity analysis).

Marginal-Change Analysis (Sensitivity Analysis)

All the optimization-based procedures rely on a single underlying principle: the equations are assumed valid over a range of decision alternatives that include the model-derived optimum. If our model relating profit (Z) to marketing spending (X) is

$$Z = f(X) \tag{6.106}$$

and X^* is four times the current level of spending X_C, then changing X_C to X^* may either cause competitive response or move us outside the region where eq. (6.106) is valid or both. In any case an alternative is to calibrate eq. (6.106) and then evaluate dZ/dX at $X = X_C$, the marginal impact on profit of additional marketing spending. This information may be the most valuable and reliable data that can be achieved from the model for two reasons. First, because model uncertainty increases with the distance from the middle of the data, the model will be most reliable and have minimum predictive error here. Second, small changes are unlikely to affect the operation of current marketing systems.

For a fuller discussion of the use and application of this approach, see Chapter 17.

Deterministic Simulation

In practice, simulation is nothing more than performing experiments on models of marketing systems. Therefore the principles of experimental design apply. Furthermore, most simulation models have incorporated probabilistic components and have utilized Monte Carlo procedures for analysis. However, the evaluation of simulations and simulation models is usually beyond the capability of existing analytical procedures. Finally, simulations are usually performed on a digital computer, but only because of the large amount of computing usually required and not because of any inherent problem with manual computing.

A viable use of simulation (both deterministic and stochastic) is the assessment of competitive-marketing situations where the nature of competitive interaction and behavior is difficult to specify.

EXAMPLE: Kotler (1965a) sets up the following general marketing model:

$$Q_{jt} = G_t V_t M_t m_{jt} \qquad (6.107)$$

where G_t = market-growth term, specified by a Gompertz function
V_t = seasonal index, specified by a sinusoid
M_t = marketing-effort index, specified by eq. $\qquad$ (6.108)

and

$$M_t = \left\{ \frac{\sum_{i-1}^{n} P_{it}{}^e A_{it}{}^w D_{it}{}^v}{n \overline{P}^e \overline{A}^w \overline{D}^v} \right\} cd^{-t} \qquad c, d > 1, \ w, v > 0, \ e < 0 \qquad (6.108)$$

where P = price
A = advertising
D = distribution

and the overbar refers to a reference marketing program. Market share m_{jt} is determined by its marketing-effort share relative to competitors:

$$m_{jt} = \frac{P_{jt}{}^e A_{jt}{}^w D_{jt}{}^v}{\sum_{i-1}^{n} P_{it}{}^e A_{it}{}^w D_{it}{}^v} \qquad (6.109)$$

Kotler then uses these equations to look at competitive-marketing strategies, where a strategy is defined as a decision rule that adjusts P_t, A_t, and D_t from period t to period $t + 1$. Some of the competitive scenarios he considers are nonadaptive (constant marketing mix), time-dependent (providing automatic adjustments dependent on time only), competitive-adaptive (relying on signaling or responding to competitive actions), sales-responsive (responding to how the company's own past sales have been), and profit-responsive, collusive (joint profit maximizing). This set of conditions was specified mathematically (with arbitrary but reasonable coefficients) and scenarios simulated in a duopolistic market over a 60-mo period. Cumulative profit and terminal market share were considered as objectives. The analysis provided suggestive answers to questions like the following:

> Which long-run strategy is best to adopt if the firm wants to guarantee a minimum return regardless of what the competitor does?
>
> Which long-run strategies are the riskiest?
>
> Which long-run strategies give the greatest profit potential?
>
> If a rival's strategy is known, which policy is best?

Although many model modifications and improvements could be suggested [see Simon (1978) for an explicit critique of this model], deterministic simulation clearly serves as a tool for policy evaluation here, especially when the nature of competitive response is not known.

Econometric-Model Analysis

The econometric models developed in Chapter 5 also serve as predictive instruments and hence policy-evaluation tools. In a deterministic form an econometric model often provides an answer to the question, "If I spend X on advertising, what will sales (Q) be?" Plugging X into the econometric equation will give an estimate of Q.

In like manner, the treatment of error in these models also gives a stochastic answer to the above question in the form of a prediction interval for Q, which answers the question, "If $X = X^*$, what is the probability that Q will lie between Q_L and Q_U?"

Stochastic-Policy-Analysis Tools

For policy analysis in a stochastic framework, the two main tools are Monte Carlo simulation and stochastic-process models. When the equations are too complex for analytical solution, simulation is used.

Monte Carlo Simulation

Both macroanalytic and microanalytic problems under uncertainty can be addressed with Monte Carlo simulation, a procedure where, at each chance node in a model-based network (usually indexed by time), some random event takes place whose probability distribution is assumed known. When the system reaches such a node, further progress is made by sampling from the probability distribution (the computer usually performing this task). Multiple passes through the model generate distributions of selected variables.

When the problem under consideration is an investment or managerial decision, the Monte Carlo simulation approach is often called *risk analysis* (Hertz, 1964). In typical applications, such as new-product introduction and site selection, there are a number of uncertain variables, such as market price, unit variable cost, and total investment, as well as quantity sold over time. Management is often asked to formalize uncertainty in these quantities in a probability distribution (often from three perspectives: optimistic, pessimistic, and best guess). Thus the risk analysis is the combination of various inputs into a final probability distribution of return on investment. This problem is dramatized in Exhibit 6.11.

EXAMPLE: Pessemier (1966) has used this technique for a new-product decision problem. His approach calls for the decision maker to assume some marketing environment (the state of the economy, technology, distribution channels, etc.) and some marketing strategy for each of the years in the planning horizon. The decision maker estimates expected values and the 0.1 and 0.9 decile values for unit sales, price, unit cost, and investment for each year in the planning horizon. The computer then draws a sample value for each uncertain variable for the coming year. These values are drawn from random probability numbers that are translated into a value for each variable. The sample values for the coming year permit the determination of first-year profits. Sample values are then drawn for the second, third, . . . , and nth years, and profit is determined for each year. The profit stream is then solved for the internal rate of return that brings it into equality with the company's investment.

The computer repeats the same process many times, producing many internal rates of return for this marketing strategy and environment. These rates are summarized in a frequency distribution, which becomes the probability distribution of the return expected with the particular marketing strategy in the particular environment.

Monte Carlo simulation models can be useful tools for analyzing the performance of complex, stochastic marketing systems. Their main limitation is that they are, by nature, difficult to verify (establish the appropriateness of the model's logical structure) and to validate (establish a relationship between the model and the system). The latter problem deals with testing if the real world is an apparent sample from the simulation model or an extreme point. The validation problem is particularly severe in simulation

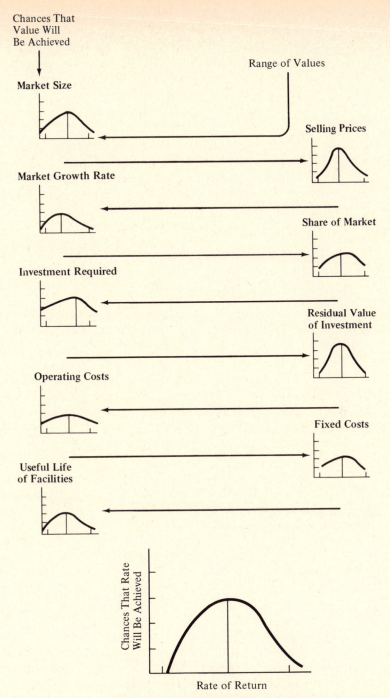

EXHIBIT 6-11 **Deriving a probability distribution of rate of return from a set of input probability distributions.** (Source: Reprinted by permission of the Harvard Business Review. An exhibit from "Risk Analysis in Capital Investment" by David B. Hertz (January/February 1964, p. 102). Copyright © 1964 by the President and Fellows of Harvard College; all rights reserved.)

models for which the real-world data are sparse. [For a complete discussion of the statistical and methodological aspects of simulation, see Mihram (1972).]

Stochastic Processes*

When insight into the structure of a system governed by fairly simple laws of motion is desired, stochastic processes can often be used. A stochastic process is a collection of random variables $\{Y_1\}$ whose behavior is governed by a known set of probability laws. Some stochastic-process analyses will be developed in more depth in the next chapter; we introduce one example here.

EXAMPLE: Ehrenberg (1959, 1972) and Chatfield, Ehrenberg, and Goodhardt (1966) have developed and applied a set of stochastic models based on the following two assumptions:

1. Each individual k purchases a number of units Y_k of the product during a certain time period according to a Poisson distribution with parameter λ_k, $k = 1, \ldots, K$, the number of consumers.

$$p(Y_{kt} = y) = f_Y(y \mid \lambda_k, t) = \frac{e^{-\lambda_k t}(\lambda_k t)^y}{y!} \qquad k = 1, \ldots, K, t = 1, \ldots, T \quad (6.110)$$

2. The purchasing rate λ_k is distributed across the population of consumers according to a gamma distribution:

$$f_\lambda(\lambda \mid \tau, \nu) = \frac{e^{\lambda \tau}(\lambda \tau)^{\nu - 1}\tau}{(\nu - 1)!} \qquad 0 \le \lambda < \infty, \nu > 0, \tau > 0 \qquad (6.111)$$

From eqs. (6.110) and (6.111), it can be shown, by integrating out λ, that the distribution of the consumer purchases of a product during a unit time period will be negative binomial (NBD):

$$f_Y(y \mid k, m) = \int_0^\infty f_\lambda(\lambda \mid \tau, \nu) \, f_Y(y \mid \lambda, t) d\lambda \qquad (6.112)$$

$$= \frac{(y + \nu - 1)!}{y!(\nu - 1)!} \left(\frac{\nu}{\nu + m} \right)^\nu \left(\frac{m}{\nu + m} \right)^y \qquad (6.113)$$

where $E(\lambda) = m$.

This model, once fit to data, gives two key measures of market response to a brand: penetration and purchase frequency. Penetration is the fraction of customers who buy the brand at least once in a given time period; purchase frequency is the average number of times these buyers purchase the brand in the specified time period.

*This section includes technical material.

$$\text{Penetration} = 1 - \left(1 + \frac{m}{\nu}\right)^{-\nu} \tag{6.114}$$

$$\text{Frequency} = \frac{m}{1 - [1 + (m/\nu)]^{-\nu}} \tag{6.115}$$

The NBD model is most often used to study repeat buying behavior, where a repeat buyer is one who buys at least once in two consecutive time periods. It shows that

Proportion of new buyers in a period

$$= \left(1 + \frac{m}{\nu}\right)^{-\nu} - \left(1 + \frac{2m}{\nu}\right)^{-\nu} \tag{6.116}$$

and

$$\text{Proportion of repeat buyers} = 1 - 2\left(1 + \frac{m}{\nu}\right)^{-\nu} + \left(1 + \frac{2m}{\nu}\right)^{-\nu} \tag{6.117}$$

The fractions of total product-class sales purchased by each class of buyer can be easily calculated as well. Furthermore, the model can be used before and after a marketing promotion to evaluate the impact of that promotion on key behavioral quantities of interest. We will return to this model in the next chapter when we discuss consumer behavior models in more detail.

Forlorn Foods Revisited

When we last left Forlorn Foods, they had (1) set an objective function based on market share and profit, (2) selected a response-function form, and (3) calibrated the response function in each of four market areas. We now turn to this model to assess the allocation of advertising dollars. In the evaluation of profit, it is important to note that the contribution margins in each market differ:

Margin in market A = $0.21 per unit
Margin in market B = $0.25 per unit
Margin in market C = $0.16 per unit
Margin in market D = $0.18 per unit

In addition, the market is believed to be relatively inelastic, with total market sales equal to $80 million.

The budget-allocation problem can be expressed as a constrained, nonlinear mathematical-programming problem:

$$\text{Maximize } U = 0.0949Z + 0.00871Y + 0.00189YZ - 0.2009 \qquad (6.118)$$

subject to

$$A_A + A_B + A_C + A_D \leq 0.900$$

where $\text{Profit} = Z = 0.17S_A + 0.20S_B + 0.13S_C + 0.16S_D - \sum_{\substack{i-A,B \\ C,D}} A_i$

$$\text{Market share} = Y = \tfrac{1}{80}(S_A + S_B + S_C + S_D) \times 100$$

and where $S_A, \ldots, S_D$ are as defined in Exhibit 5.5(b).

A heuristic procedure, similar to the procedure used for the CALL-PLAN model (Chapter 16), is used here. Exhibit 6.12 shows the results under three sets of constraints: (1) the current spending level ($900,000), (2) the spending level reduced to $800,000, and (3) the spending level raised to $1 million.

Several pieces of information are revealed in this exhibit. First, the current spending level is clearly inefficient. An advertising budget of $800,000 can, according to the model, achieve almost four share points more (26.2 percent compared with 22.5 percent) and $720,000 more profit ($3.32 million compared with $2.60 million) than the current spending level.

Note also that the utility of optimal allocation goes *up* with an increasing budget (from 0.506 to 0.516); however, profit goes *down* (from $3.32 million to $3.28 million). The increase in market share compensates for this loss of profitability in the objective function.

EXHIBIT 6-12   **Solution summary of Forlorn Foods model.**

| | Fixed-Ratio Rule | | Optimal Allocation | | | | | |
| | Budget Size $900,000 | | Budget Size $800,000 | | Budget Size $900,000 | | Budget Size $1,000,000 | |
Market	A_i	Sales	A_i	Sales	A_i	Sales	A_i	Sales
A	0.45	9.0	0	7.5	0.350	8.62	0.405	8.84
B	0.05	1.0	0.155	2.94	0.135	2.88	0.140	2.90
C	0.20	4.0	0.160	3.90	0	3.25	0.035	3.42
D	0.20	4.0	0.485	6.60	0.45	6.36	0.42	6.39
Total	0.900	18.0	0.800	20.9	0.900	21.1	1.00	21.5
Y (Share)	22.5		26.2		26.4		26.9	
Z (Profit)	2.6		3.32		3.29		3.28	
U (Utility)	0.35		0.506		0.506		0.516	

Note: All economic figures, except budget size, are in millions of dollars.

The gain in profit and share (due to improved spending efficiency) is gained primarily by reallocating funds from markets A and C (large but low-response markets) to markets B and D (small, higher-response markets). In all cases market D sees a major increase of advertising-budget allocations.

This example, developed over the last several chapters, was designed to illustrate the stages of model development and solution. It did not include the dynamics of time or competitive response. However, it does illustrate how to structure objectives, to select and calibrate a response function, and to use a model to evaluate firm behavior. In this case the modeling task cast doubt on the current budget-allocation rule (percent of sales), and other, more efficient allocations were suggested.

The next critical step for Forlorn Foods is implementation, a topic discussed in detail in Chapter 21.

Summary

This chapter surveyed a number of procedures for evaluating marketing policies in a model-based manner. Such procedures can be classified by whether the environment is viewed as deterministic or stochastic and whether one's aim is to generate policies or to evaluate them.

Deterministic-policy-generation tools include classical optimization methods with and without constraints, linear-programming problems, integer-programming problems, and several special nonlinear-programming approaches, all of which have been widely applied to marketing problems. We also showed that the problem of multiple-criteria optimization corresponds to a situation where an efficient frontier of Pareto optimal solutions can be determined. Finally, optimal-control theory, a continuous-time procedure, was developed as well.

There have been some important applications of decision analysis in stochastic environments. The sequential, uncertain nature of many marketing problems corresponds well to the decision-analysis paradigm. These techniques were discussed, as were dynamic programming—an approach to solving sequential, separable problems under certainty or uncertainty—and stochastic extensions of linear programming, including stochastic programming and chance-constrained programming, both of which have been applied in marketing.

When the problem is to evaluate rather than generate policies, marginal analysis is quite variable. It is used to determine the most reasonable direction of change from the status quo. Deterministic simulation can be a powerful tool for exploring a large number of policies in a deterministic setting. Econometric models can be used to evaluate policy alternatives as well.

In an uncertain environment Monte Carlo simulation is frequently used to study the implications of proposed policies. When the system is amenable to functional analysis, stochastic-process models can be used to study the effects of alternative policies on the operation of a marketing system.

This chapter concludes the coverage of some various tools needed to build and use marketing models. Laws governing the behavior in marketing-decision environments are covered next.

Problems

6.1 Contrast policy evaluation with optimization in a marketing-modeling environment. What are some of the pitfalls to look for after reaching a solution?

6.2 **a.** What is the difference between a concave function and a convex function?
b. What is the difference between a local minimum (maximum) and a global minimum (maximum)?
c. Which of the following functions are convex, which are concave, and which are neither convex nor concave?

   i. $f(x) = |x|$
   ii. $f(x) = 1/x \ (x > 0)$
   iii. $f(x) = \log x \ (x > 0)$
   iv. $f(x) = e^{x^2}$
   v. $f(x_1, x_2) = x_1 x_2$
   vi. $f(x_1, x_2) = x_1^2 + x_2^2$

6.3 Given the following sales-response and profit functions, determine the rules for selecting price and advertising levels, and show that the Dorfman-Steiner conditions hold at these levels.

$$Q = K - pP + aA$$

$$Z = (P - c)Q - A - F$$

6.4 The manufacturer of a line of inexpensive watches determines that the demand for one of its products is represented by the following equation:

$$Q = 30{,}000P^{-2}A^{1/6}D^{1/3}$$

Unit cost for the product is estimated at $8. What are the firm's optimal price, distribution, and advertising levels for this product?

6.5 A seller of inexpensive men's suits is currently selling one of the products in his line for $70 while spending $10,000 in advertising for this particular product. The sales and cost functions for this product can be expressed as

$$Q = 10{,}000 - 100P + 5A^{0.5}$$

$$C = 180{,}000 + 10Q + A$$

a. What are the seller's current sales and profits?

b. Are the current price and advertising-expenditure levels optimum? If not, what are the optimum levels?

6.6 A manufacturer produces two products that yield profits of $3 and $2 per unit, respectively. Each product goes through three processes. Each unit of product 1 requires 8 h in process 1, 2 h in process 2, and 4 h in process 3. Each unit of product 2 requires 4, 2, and 2 h in the respective processes. The amount of time available each day in processes 1, 2, and 3 are 320, 120, and 160 h, respectively. State the above as a linear-programming problem, and determine the solution graphically. Calculate the shadow prices of the constraints and interpret them.

6.7 The selling prices of a number of houses in a particular section of the city, overlooking the bay, are available along with the size of the lot and its elevation. A real estate agent wishes to construct a model to forecast the selling prices of other houses in this section of the city from their lot sizes and elevations. The agent feels that a linear model of the form

$$P = b_0 + b_1 L + b_2 E$$

would be reasonably accurate and easy to use. Here b_1 and b_2 indicate how the price varies with lot size and elevation, respectively, while b_0 reflects a base price for this section of the city.

    The agent would like to select the best linear model in some sense, but he is unsure how to proceed. If he knew the three parameters b_0, b_1, and b_2, the six observations in the table would each provide a forecast of the selling price as follows:

$$\hat{P}_i = b_0 + b_1 L_i + b_2 E_i \qquad i = 1, 2, \dots, 6$$

However, since b_0, b_1, and b_2 cannot, in general, be chosen so that the actual prices P_i are exactly equal to the forecast prices $\hat{P}_i$ for all observations, the agent would like to minimize the absolute value of the residuals $R_i = P_i - \hat{P}_i$. Formulate mathematical programs to find the best values of b_0, b_1, and b_2 by minimizing each of the following criteria (*Hint:* Parts b and c can be formulated as linear programs. How should part a be solved?):

a. $\sum_{i=1}^{n} (P_i - \hat{P}_i)^2$, least squares

b. $\sum_{i=1}^{n} |P_i - \hat{P}_i|$, linear absolute residual

c. $\max_{1 \le i \le n} |P_i - \hat{P}_i|$, maximum absolute residual

6.8 The Chemco Corporation currently sells a commercial lubricant product at $1.00/qt and enjoys a current market share of approximately 30%. The company's major competitor sells a similar product of somewhat lower quality for $0.90/qt and holds a market share of approximately 65%. Chemco management is considering reducing the price of its product to $0.90 in order to increase its market share. Without such a price change the company's market share is expected to remain unchanged in the coming period. If the price reduction is implemented, the competitor is expected to react in one of two ways: (1) it will maintain its price at $0.90 with probability of 0.4, or (2) it will lower its price to $0.81 with probability 0.6. If the competitor maintains its price at $0.90, Chemco's market share will either increase to 40% with probability of 0.7 or to 50% with probability of 0.3. If the competitor reduces its price to $0.81, Chemco's market share is expected to remain unchanged with probability of 0.8 or to decrease to 25% with probability of 0.2. Use decision-tree analysis to determine if Chemco management should implement the price reduction.

6.9 A wholesale dealer is considering the introduction of a new product throughout the eastern region of the United States. We will assume the following:

1. If the product is introduced, it will cost $150,000 to introduce it.
2. The result of introducing the product would be great success, mild success, or failure.
3. It is possible to conduct a test-marketing project to be able to predict the degree of success of the new product. This test will cost $20,000 and will indicate the results as being RI (good chances of success), RII (less favorable), and RIII (unfavorable). The following probabilities have been assigned by the company specialist:

P (great success $|$ RI) $= 0.4$ P (mild success $|$ RI) $= 0.3$

P (great success $|$ RII) $= 0.1$ P (mild success $|$ RII) $= 0.4$

P (great success $|$ RIII) $= 0.0$ P (mild success $|$ RIII) $= 0.3$

$P(\text{RI}) = 0.2$ $\text{Pr}(\text{RII}) = 0.3$ $P(\text{RIII}) = 0.5$

4. If the product turns out to be a great success, the dealer will get a $900,000 bonus from the manufacturing company; he will receive only $300,000 if it is a mild success.

Assume that the decision maker wants to maximize his expected profit for answering the following questions:

a. Draw the decision tree for the problem and show all the possibilities and outcomes.
b. What is the probability of the product being a success (either great or mild)?
c. The manager would like to know the best-possible strategy to use. What is it?
d. What is the expected value of the test-marketing project?
e. What should the manager be willing to pay to get perfect information about the success of the product?
f. Calculate P(RII|mild success) and P(RI|great success).

6.10 Refer to the QRS Company example.

a. Should the decision maker pay a seer $35,000 to tell him for certain if sales will be high or low? What if the seer's rate of success were 0.95?
b. If the manager had to choose between making no survey, making a survey for $10,000, and paying $26,000 for perfect information, what should he do?
c. How would the solution to the problem change (if at all) if the firm's utility function were as follows?

$$u(x) = 14.4 - 9.20e^{-0.0052x}$$

3

The Working of Markets

Consumer Behavior Models

This chapter represents the first building block of our model-building approach to decision making. At the heart of marketing's equations of motion are models of consumer behavior. The understanding of consumer (and, in the next chapter, industrial) markets is the starting point for all marketing planning and action.

    The literature on consumer behavior and related models is vast. Our objective in this chapter is to review some of the basic theories (and complexities) and discuss the type of models that have been developed. In the following sections we review *behavioral-science models* (drawn from the behavioral sciences) and *individual-choice models* of consumer behavior and discuss the uses and limitations of each.

The Dimensions of Consumer Behavior

Models of consumer behavior differ drastically in their objectives and forms. The area of consumer behavior deals with the definition of a market, the identification of potential participants in the market, and questions, such as what is purchased (brand choice), when it is bought (purchase timing), who participates in the decision, what benefits are sought, and how (through what channels) consumers buy. We define a market as the set of all individuals and organizations who are actual or potential buyers of a product or service, thus limiting the term to the buyer side. The seller side we call "industry" or "competition." (We return to the operational or economic definition of the market in Chapter 17.)

Phases of the Process

A useful map of the consumer decision process, which helps categorize the focus of many consumer behavior models, is presented in Exhibit 7.1. It emphasizes that the consumer behavior or choice process starts long before the actual purchase, and that in each phase marketers can do certain things to facilitate or influence the process. We identify these phases in turn.

Need Arousal.   The buying process starts with need arousal. A need can be activated through internal or external stimuli. In the first case one of the person's normal drives—hunger, thirst, sex—rises to a threshold level and becomes a drive. In the second case need is caused by an external stimulus or *triggering cue* (an advertisement, sight of an acquaintance's product, etc.).

Information Search.   If an aroused need is intense (e.g., hunger) and a well-defined gratification object is at hand (a candy bar), the person is likely

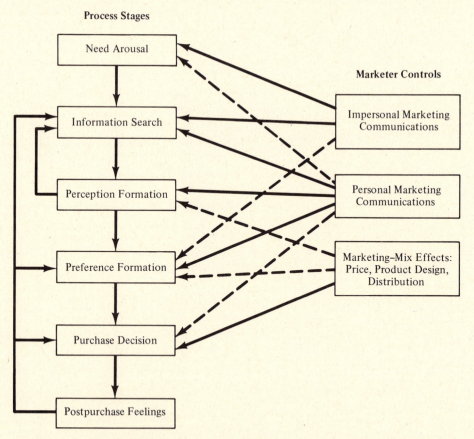

EXHIBIT 7-1   An outline of a consumer's purchasing process and the impacts of marketing variables.

to gratify the need right then. In most cases, however, an aroused need is not immediately gratified. The need enters the memory's register as an item for future gratification.

Depending on the intensity of the stored need, one of two states is produced in the individual. The first state is called *heightened attention,* where the individual becomes alert to information bearing upon the need and its gratification. Under conditions of more intense need, the individual enters a state of active *information search,* where information is sought from personal, commercial, and public sources.

Perceptual Formation.   Incoming information helps the consumer clarify and evaluate alternatives and therefore form attitudes and perceptions about product alternatives. Unfortunately, there is no simple, single evaluation process used by all consumers—or even by one consumer—in all buying situations; there appear to be alternative processes. Most current models of the consumer evaluation process are *cognitively oriented*—that is, they see the consumer as forming product judgments largely on a conscious and rational basis.

Certain basic concepts help in understanding consumer evaluation processes and are used in the models developed later in this chapter. The first is that of *product attributes.* The consumer sees a product as having several attributes. A particular product is perceived in terms of where it stands on a set of attributes relevant to its product class. For example, in the aspirin category important attributes might be speed of relief, reliability, side effects, and price. While these attributes are of general interest, individual consumers will vary as to which they consider relevant. The market for a product is often segmented by the attributes that are of primary interest to a group of buyers.

Second, the relevant attributes are likely to have different levels of importance to the consumer. A distinction can be drawn between *attribute importance* and *attribute salience* (Myers and Alpert, 1976). Salient attributes are those that come to the consumer's mind when asked about a product's attributes, but the marketer must not conclude that these are necessarily the most important attributes. Some of them may be salient because the consumer has just been exposed to a commercial message mentioning them or has had a problem involving them; hence these attributes are "top of the mind." Furthermore, in the class of nonsalient attributes may be some that the consumer has forgotten but whose importance would be recognized when they are mentioned.

Third, the consumer is likely to develop opinions about where each brand stands on each attribute. The set of beliefs held about a particular brand is known as the *brand image.* The consumer's beliefs or perceptions may be at variance with the true attributes because of the consumer's particular experience and the effect of selective perception, selective distortion, and selective retention.

Preference Formation.   The individual must now structure these perceptions into brand preferences. The consumer is assumed to have a *utility function* for attributes, which describes how he expects product satisfaction to vary with alternative levels and combinations of attributes.

The consumer arrives at an attitude (judgment, preference) toward the brand alternative through some *evaluation procedure*. Starting with an evoked set, he compares products by using some procedure and ends up with an order of preferences. Consumers have been found to apply a variety of evaluation procedures, many of which are reviewed in subsequent sections.

Purchase Decision.   In the evaluation stage the consumer forms a ranked set of preferences among the alternative objects in his evoked set and an intent to purchase the object he likes best. But a number of additional factors often intervene before the purchase is made (Sheth, 1974).

The first factor is the *attitude of others*. The extent to which negative attitudes of others will reduce a favorable attitude depends on two things: the intensity of others' negative attitudes, and the consumer's motivation to comply with the others' wishes (Fishbein, 1967).

Purchase intention is also influenced by *anticipated situational factors*. The consumer forms a purchase intention on the basis of such factors as expected family income, the expected total cost of the product, and the expected benefits of the product. Furthermore, when the consumer is about to act, *unanticipated situational factors* may intervene to prevent him from doing so.

Finally, the decision of an individual to modify, postpone, or avoid a purchase decision is also influenced by perceived risk. [See Bauer (1967) and Taylor (1974), for example.] Consumers cannot be certain about the performance of the product or the psychosocial consequences of their purchase decision. This uncertainty produces anxiety. The amount of perceived risk varies with the amount of money at stake, the amount of attribute uncertainty, and the amount of consumer self-confidence.

Thus preferences and purchase intentions are not completely reliable predictors of actual buying behavior. They give direction to purchase behavior but fail to include a number of additional factors that may intervene.

Postpurchase Feelings.   After buying and trying the product, the consumer will experience some level of satisfaction or dissatisfaction. If asked, he may report being satisfied or dissatisfied. What determines the level of postpurchase satisfaction? A major theory (Swan and Combs, 1976) holds that a consumer's satisfaction S is a function of *expectations* (E) and the product's *perceived performance* (P), that is, $S = f(E, P)$. If the product matches up to expectations, the consumer is satisfied; if it exceeds them, the consumer is highly satisfied, but if it falls short, the consumer is dissatisfied.

Consumers form their expectations on the basis of messages and claims sent out by the seller and other communication sources. If the seller makes exaggerated claims for the product, the consumer experiences *disconfirmed expectations*, which lead to dissatisfaction. The amount of dissatisfaction depends on the size of the difference between expectations and performance. Different psychological theories have been advanced suggesting that consumers may either magnify or diminish the importance of the differences between expectations and performance (Anderson, 1973). For example, *contrast theory* says that the amount of dissatisfaction will be larger than the performance gap, while *cognitive-dissonance theory* says that the amount of dissatisfaction will be less because the consumer will try to reduce the dissonance by imputing higher performance.

An Alternative View

Most of the models we review here have been devoted to situations in which the purchasing process is assumed to require complex decision making or brand loyalty. But as pointed by Kassarjian and Kassarjian (1979), many purchase decisions are better described by low-involvement conditions:

> Subjects do not care much about products; they are unimportant to them . . . the emerging conclusion must be that true attitudes about these items most likely do not exist for many subjects. Bicycles, colas and toothpaste generally do not have attitudes associated with them (p. 8).

While a typical high-involvement purchase is assumed to follow the process illustrated in Exhibit 7.1, this process does a poor job of describing low-involvement decisions. For a product like flour, for example, the consumer may receive information through a TV commercial, where the ad may not even really be perceived in the sense that it is comprehensible. If the ad was for, say, Gold Star Flour, the consumer may buy the brand when the need arises because of familiarity, where repetitive advertising produces the familiarity.

Under these conditions an attitude toward the brand is not believed to be formed; the consumer regards the brand as relatively neutral because it is not associated with any important benefits. But relatively weak attitudes toward the brand may develop, for example, if a new feature (nonstick granulation) is introduced or if the product performs poorly. But such attitudes form *after* purchase, not before. Therefore the hierarchy of effects for low-involvement products might best be described as follows:

1. Brand beliefs are formed by passive learning.
2. Then a purchase decision is made.
3. Afterward, the brand may or may not be evaluated.

Exhibit 7.2 summarizes four types of consumer behavior, depending on level of involvement and brand differences in the market. The upper

Type of Good

	High Involvement	Low Involvement

Market Structure

	High Involvement	Low Involvement
Significant Brand Differences	Purchase Process Beliefs Evaluation Behavior Theory Cognitive Learning Decision Process Complex Decision Making or True Loyalty	Purchase Process Beliefs Behavior Evaluation Theory Low-Involvement Decision Making Decision Process ┌─Variety Seeking─┐ Random Choice Experimentation
No Significant Brand Differences	Purchase Process Behavior Beliefs Evaluation Theory Dissonance or Attribution Theory Decision Process Dissonance Reduction or Attribution	Purchase Process Beliefs Behavior Theory Low-Involvement Decision Making Decision Process ┌──Inertia──┐ Random Choice Spurious Loyalty

EXHIBIT 7-2   **Classification of types of consumer behavior.** Source: Adapted from Henry Assael, *Consumer Behavior and Marketing Action* (Boston: Kent Publishing Company, 1981), p. 80. © 1981 by Wadsworth, Inc. Reprinted by permission of Kent Publishing, a division of Wadsworth, Inc.)

left-hand box—high involvement and significant brand differences—represents the more traditional view of consumer decision making represented earlier. The lower right-hand box is the case discussed above: low involvement and few differences among brands. Under these conditions consumers will either choose a brand at random (pick the first brand they see, so that probability of purchase may be proportional to market share) or develop *spurious loyalty* (repeatedly buy a brand because it is familiar and thereby avoid a decision process). In both of these cases the governing principle is inertia—a passive process of information processing, a passive process of brand choice, and little or no brand evaluation.

The upper right-hand box—low involvement but significant brand differences (breakfast cereals, for many consumers)—yields a decision process called *variety seeking*. Here the motivation to switch brands is a desire for change, a search for novelty rather than any serious dissatisfaction with a brand. Such dissatisfaction is unlikely given the low level of purchase involvement. Venkatesan (1973) suggests that variety-seeking behavior is the result of routinized choice and boredom with the familiar.

The fourth box, the lower left, has high consumer involvement with few perceived differences among brands. This situation can result from one of two types of behavior. The first is dissonance theory. Consider the selection of a money-market fund, clearly a high-involvement purchase. Yet the differences among the funds range from subtle to nonexistent, depending on who is asked for an opinion. In such a situation the first contradictory piece of information received (e.g., the chosen fund this week yields $\frac{1}{4}$ percent less than one of the alternatives considered) is likely to produce postpurchase dissonance—a feeling that the alternative should have been bought. To reduce dissonance, the consumer will seek out positive information and ignore negative information about the chosen alternative. Such information-and-brand evaluation occurs after behavior:

1. Behavior occurs first.
2. Beliefs are found to support the chosen brand.
3. The brand is favorably evaluated.

An alternative explanation for the behavior/beliefs/evaluation hierarchy is provided by *self-perception theory*, which states that consumers attribute certain motives to their actions after the fact.

This view of the structure of different consumer decision-making paradigms has a number of implications for model building and decision making. First, if this classification is relevant, then different mathematical models are needed to describe the choice process for the same individual facing different products; and because of differences in the degree of involvement in a product class and in the perceived degree of brand differences, different models of choice are required to describe the workings of a single market. Second, the role of several elements in the marketing mix will differ depending on which of these decision processes is predominant. In the low-involvement case the role of advertising is to create awareness and familiarity through repetition (Rothchild, 1979). A small number of points should be emphasized in the ads; repetition creates a relationship between advertising symbols and brand use. In the high-involvement case advertising seeks to go beyond awareness but seeks to influence the consumer through a persuasive message. The content of the message, rather than repetition, is the key. Messages are likely to be more complex, more varied, dealing more directly with desired product benefits. There are implications for price and promotional strategies here, too. With low-involvement products little prepurchase evaluation is done. Therefore brand choice is frequently made in the store. Thus in-store conditions become much more important for low-involvement products.

The field of consumer behavior is evolving quickly and is far from reaching a theoretical synthesis or a unified theory of behavior. A number of useful books on the theory and marketing implications of consumer behavior studies have been published in the last decade or so, including the works of Bettman (1979), Howard and Sheth (1969), Kassarjian and Robinson (1973), Nicosia (1966), Walters (1978), and Zaltman and Wallendorf (1979).

A Range of Models

Along with the diversity of purchase situations and theories, we find a diverse range of models of consumer behavior. These models can be classified in a number of ways. Several important dimensions are the following:

The breadth of phenomena incorporated. This dimension refers to the degree to which a model unifies theories in mapping the whole or a part of a decision-making process.

The level of aggregation. A dichotomy in consumer behavior models exists depending on whether the unit of analysis is the individual or the market-group of individuals.

The ambitiousness of the model in dealing with issues of causation. Ideally, a model would behave as follows:

1. identify and measure all major variables making up a behavioral system
2. specify fundamental relationships between the variables
3. specify exact sequences and cause-and-effect relationships
4. permit sensitivity analysis in order to explore the impact of changes in the major variables

One way of classifying the work in consumer behavior is along a continuum representing degree of behavioral detail and specificity. At one end we have what we call large-system models; at the other extreme we have macromarket models; and in between we have individual attitude-formation, evaluation, and choice models.

Exhibit 7.3 presents a taxonomy for understanding and evaluating consumer behavior models. It shows the stages of the consumer behavior

Stages of Consumer Behavior

Process Modeled

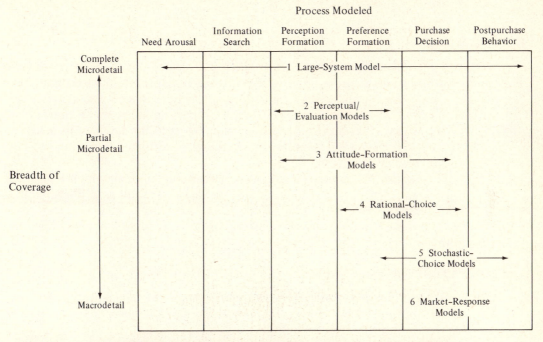

| | Information Search | Perception Formation | Preference Formation | Purchase Decision | Postpurchase Behavior |

EXHIBIT 7-3   **A taxonomy of consumer behavior models: level of detail versus the consumer processes modeled.**

process modeled and relates those stages to the breadth of coverage. In this chapter we will deal with model classes 1–5. Class 6, macromarket models, relates market changes (sales, share) to market activities (advertising, price) without resorting to intermediate behavioral mechanisms and relying solely on aggregate or market-level data. A current research topic is the relationship between individual-response models and these aggregate-market models. [See Bass and Pilon (1979), Blattberg and Jeuland (1981), Givon and Horsky (1978), and Jones (1979).] Many macromarket models are reviewed in Section 4.

Large-System Models

Large-system models are large in scope, accounting for and unifying more variables than other types of models. Their strength is in describing complex decision-making processes, while their weakness is in estimation, measurement, and policy analysis.

We will review here two influential large-system models, those of Bettman and of Howard and Sheth.

Bettman's Model

Bettman (1979) introduced an integrated theory of consumer behavior from an information-processing point of view. His work provides an analytical framework for understanding consumer behavior in a choice environment, where choice is viewed as a selection process among a set of alternatives. The information-processing perspective refers to the types of information used by consumers, how the information is evaluated, and, finally, how decisions are made.

Exhibit 7.4 shows the structure of Bettman's model, which is usefully broken down into two submodules: the basic hierarchy and intermediate/modulating processes. Bettman points out that there is no logical starting or ending point for the process. For expositional clarity, then, we will start at the top.

The Basic Hierarchy

Motivation and goal hierarchy.   These are the mechanisms serving to control the movement of an individual from some critical state toward some desired state (goal).

Attention.   This stage can be broken down into voluntary attention—the consumer's allocation of the information-processing effort—and involuntary attention, treated below.

Information acquisition and evaluation.   The goals being pursued influence attention and, hence, information acquisition. Evaluation determines when information is sufficient for decision.

Decision process.   Decision processes go on all the time in this model, focusing on the comparison of alternatives. A variety of (unspecified) choice heuristics are viewed as the vehicles for these comparisons.

Consumption and learning.   The purchase and consumption of the product opens a new source of information to the consumer, affecting the structure of future choices.

Intermediate/Modulating Processes.   Several processes affect and constrain the basic hierarchy:

Perceptual encoding.   This process is the interpretation process an individual goes through after being exposed to a stimulus. Bettman believes that this process is affected both by memory (the way things were) and by the stimulus itself (the way things are).

Processing capacity.   The entire information-processing stream is limited by capacity, which is positively related to effort and motivation.

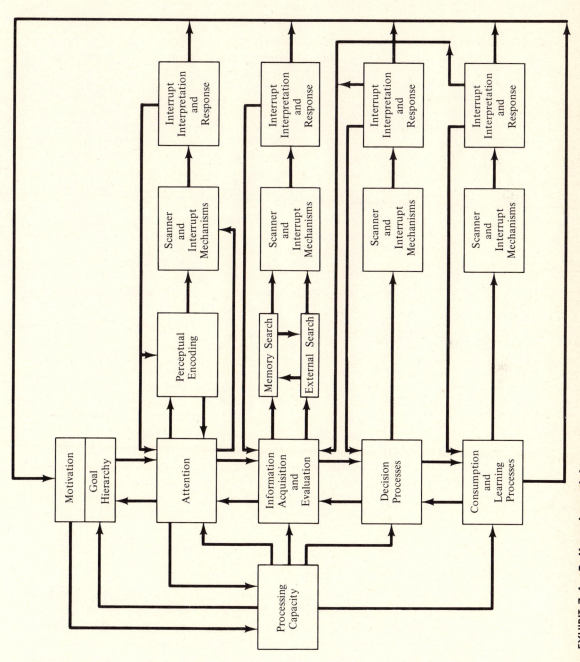

EXHIBIT 7-4 Bettman's model.

The implications of processing capacity are that capacity must be allocated to a decision task and that choice tasks are so complex that simplifying heuristics may be used.

Memory and external search. In a choice situation, information acquisition may occur through internal search (memory) and external search (redirecting attention and perceptual encoding). The level of information search is affected by the costs versus the benefits of the information, the availability of the information, the difficulty of the choice task, and time pressure.

Scanner and interrupt mechanisms. Adopting ideas from Simon, Bettman notes that consumers are interruptible and not single-minded in their pursuit of goals. The scanner is postulated as a mechanism for monitoring the environment for the purpose of noting conditions that require changes in current actions or beliefs. When a theoretical *scanner threshold* is reached, an *interrupt mechanism* is triggered and new responses are generated. Scanner and interrupt mechanisms affect virtually the entire decision-process hierarchy.

Assessment. This model represents an attempt at developing a rather complete theory of the consumer-choice process. It provides insight into the kind of information sought by the consumer, how the consumer acquires such information, and how the information is likely to be processed. Such knowledge is useful in guiding the development, presentation, and timing of marketing communications.

The theory also positions decision rules or choice heuristics within the broader concept of consumer decision making. The structure takes a broad view of purchase decisions, which are choices among product classes as well as among competing alternatives in a product class.

As with all large-scale-system models of individual choice, the main drawback is that it is not directly operational: it does not provide quantitative support for marketing decisions. But it does provide insight into the structure of the process and guidance on the types of issues that can be expected to affect and influence consumer choice, and, as Ratchford (1982) shows, does have the potential to be linked to economic theory and resource allocation decisions.

The Howard-Sheth Model

The Howard-Sheth (1969) model, funded under a commission from the Ford Foundation, is an attempt to identify and unify the main variables that affect consumer behavior. The model assumes a *rational*-choice decision—that is, that the consumer is rational within the limits of his cognitive, learning, and information-processing capabilities—and consists of four sets of constructs or variables: input variables, output variables, hypothetical constructs, and exogenous variables.

These constructs and their relationships are illustrated in Exhibit 7.5. The *input* variables are essentially the stimuli from the buyer's social and commercial environment (communications from marketing firms). The *output* variables are (1) attention, (2) brand comprehension, (3) attitude, (4) intention, and (5) purchase. These variables have the same names as some of the hypothetical constructs discussed below, but the hypothetical constructs are more abstract and less well defined, operationally, than either the input or output variables; their structure and interrelationships are based on research findings from the behavioral sciences. The hypothetical constructs are of two types: those dealing with *perception* and those dealing with *learning*. The perceptual constructs are concerned with obtaining and processing information from the three input channels relevant to the purchase decision—attention, stimulus ambiguity, and search—while the learning constructs are concerned with concept formation and include motive, brand comprehension, choice criteria, attitude, intention, confidence, and satisfaction.

The Howard-Sheth model deals essentially with adaptive behavior that results from a learning process (Hull, 1952): motives are drives; brand comprehension and attitude are cues; confidence and satisfaction are reinforcements; and the entire range of output variables encompasses response. In addition, Howard and Sheth focus on the role of repetitive brand-choice decisions and are concerned with how individuals store information and routinize their purchase processes. In the model it is assumed that the consumer is endowed with a set of motives, a set of alternative brands, and choice criteria with which these motives are matched with the various alternatives. The consumer does not consider all brands but only an evoked set—those brands perceived to possess the necessary characteristics to be satisfactory alternatives. The consumer actively seeks information from his commercial and social environment and generalizes his experiences from past purchase activities to current purchasing processes.

Assessment.   This model ties together a large number of variables that have been found to operate on purchase behavior. Its major contribution has been to unify a large set of previously unrelated research findings. Although not structured to explain consumer choice between product classes as satisfactorily as Bettman's model, it provides a broader range of exogenous and explanatory variables.

The most glaring deficiency of the model is the deficiency of all such complex models of human behavior: the inability to specify how the variables interact with one another and what the specific nature of these interaction processes is. Thus the model represents more of a conceptual framework, an aid to thought, rather than an operational model that can provide specific decision-making support.

Efforts by Farley and Ring (1970, 1974) to develop empirical representations and tests of the model structure have provided results that are

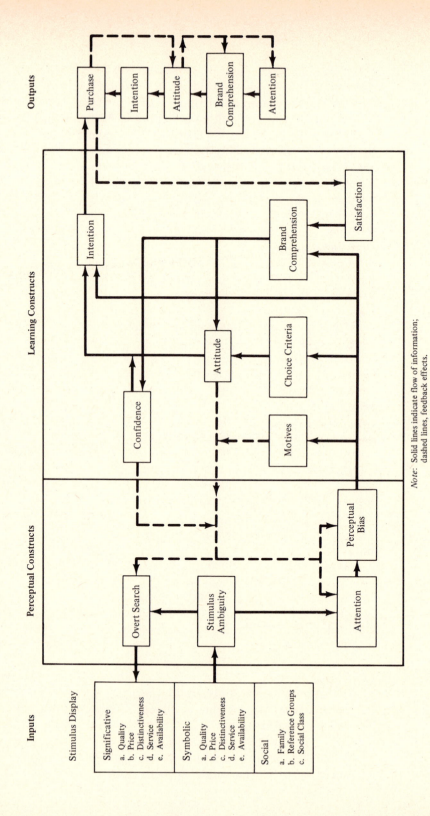

EXHIBIT 7-5 Howard-Sheth model of consumer behavior. (Source: Howard and Sheth, 1969, p. 31.)

Note: Solid lines indicate flow of information; dashed lines, feedback effects.

generally consistent with the proposed relationships. Howard (1977) clarifies and applies many of the Howard-Sheth concepts, stating that the psychological, economic, and marketing views of consumer behavior must be reconciled. Finally Howard's (1977) typology of problem-solving behavior is investigated by Lehmann, Moore, and Elrod (1982) and two problem-solving segments are identified.

In conclusion, then, large-system models have made two major contributions. First, they provide an integrating framework to understand the complexities of consumer behavior. Second, they point to specific, simple (but *operational*) models that may realistically be able to characterize attitudes, behavior, and choice in specific decision situations.

Perceptual-Evaluation Models

A set of useful consumer behavior models has been developed to handle consumer attitudes toward various brands in a marketplace. Hauser and Urban (1977), in a new-product setting, describe the processing of attributes as compression into a smaller number of aggregate dimensions called "evaluation criteria." The central idea is that the brands in a market can be represented as a set of points in a multidimensional space. The axes of this space represent the perceived attributes that characterize the stimuli. Two main analytical approaches most frequently used to derive evaluation criteria and build perceptual maps are decompositional methods, based on nonmetric multidimensional scaling, and compositional methods, based on factor analysis. It is beyond the scope of this book to present these procedures in detail, but we sketch the main ideas below.

Nonmetric Multidimensional Scaling (NMS)

Nonmetric multidimensional scaling (NMS) is a set of procedures in which a reduced space of product alternatives reflects perceived similarities and dissimilarities between products by the interproduct distances. Exhibit 7.6 gives an example of the input and output of an NMS study of four graduate schools of business. The idea behind it is to have the distances in (b) have the same rank order as the direct similarity judgments in (a).

Let δ_{ij} denote the perceived dissimilarity between product alternatives i and j. This variable is a measure of how alternative a_i is viewed differently from a_j, which can be either obtained directly or derived from distances on the original attribute scales. Then with NMS we find a configuration of points (the product alternatives) in a space of lowest dimensionality such that the ranking of interpoint distances d_{ij} is as close as possible to the ranking of the original dissimilarities δ_{ij}. This result is called a monotonic

Multidimensional–Scaling Input

	MIT	Harvard	Stanford	Columbia
MIT				
Harvard	6			
Stanford	5	1		
Columbia	4	3	2	

Similarity-measure rank: 1 = most similarity; 6 = most dissimilarity.

(a)

Resulting Perceptual Map

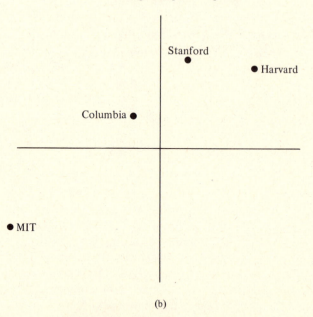

(b)

EXHIBIT 7-6 **The input and output of a nonmetric multidimensional scaling of four graduate schools of business.**

relationship between the d_{ij}'s and the δ_{ij}'s. Green and Rao (1972) provide an excellent presentation of NMS theory along with examples.

To reach their objective, NMS algorithms minimize a quantity called stress:

$$\text{Stress} = \left[\frac{\sum_{i<j} (\hat{d}_{ij} - d_{ij})^2}{\sum_{i<j} d_{ij}^2} \right]^{1/2} \qquad (7.1)$$

where $\hat{d}_{ij}$ is a distance as close as possible to the d_{ij} but is monotonic with the original dissimilarities δ_{ij}.

For a given dimensionality the configuration retained is the one that minimizes the stress function. Several issues need to be considered here:

Number of products needed.   Klabir (1969) shows that at least eight products are needed for a good two-dimensional map. Green and Wind (1973) suggest that the number of dimensions should be less than one-third of the number of products.

Naming the dimensions.   One can name the dimensions judgmentally. However, if attribute scales are available, a technique called PROFIT (Carroll and Chang, 1964) can be used to name the dimensions by estimating the association between the map coordinates and the attribute ratings.

Determining the number of dimensions.   As in factor analysis, discussed below, there is little theory to guide the selection of the number of dimensions. However, the stress measure [eq. (7.1)] can be plotted against k (the number of dimensions) to determine when marginal changes in stress are becoming small.

New approaches to NMS using structural-modeling ideas [see Fornell and Denison (1981), for example] may lead to a revival of this approach.

Factor Analysis

Factor analysis was originally developed in connection with efforts to identify the major factors making up human intelligence. Educational and psychological researchers did not believe that every test in an educational battery measured a different facet of intelligence. In fact, test scores for certain pairs of tests were highly intercorrelated, indicating that a more basic mental ability underlies test performance. Factor analysis was developed to explain these intercorrelations in the test results of a few basic intelligence factors, subsequently identified as verbal ability, quantitative ability, and spatial ability. Since that time, factor analysis has been applied to many other problems and is a frequently used technique in performing product-evaluation analyses in marketing.

The basic factor-analysis model assumes that original perceptual ratings about a product are generated by a small number of *latent variables*, or *factors*, and that the variance observed in each original perceptual variable is accounted for partly by a set of *common factors* and partly by a factor specific to that variable. The common factors account for the correlations observed among the original variables.

This model can be written as

$$x_{ki} = a_{k1}F_{i1} + \cdots + a_{kR}F_{iR} + d_k y_{ki} \qquad (7.2)$$

where
- R = number of common factors
- x_{ki} = person i's rating of product on attribute k
- a_{k1} = effect of common factor 1 on attribute k (called a *loading*)
- F_{i1} = person i's score on common factor 1
- d_k = weight of unique factor y
- y_{ki} = unique factor associated with item k

Thus in common-factor analysis, the perceptual model has each observed variable being described in terms of a set of R $(R < k)$ common factors plus a factor unique to the original observed variable. Generally, the original items are standardized [if x_i^* is an original score, then $x_i = (x_i^* - \bar{x})/\sigma_x$ is used], so that certain relationships hold:

The loadings $\{a_{kr}\}$ represent the correlation between (hypothetical) factor r and the variable k, and a_{kr}^2 represents the fraction of variance in variable k accounted for by factor r.

The communality h_k^2 expresses the percentage of the variance in variable k accounted for by the R common factors:

$$h_k^2 = \sum_{r=1}^{R} a_{kr}^2 \qquad (7.3)$$

The eigenvalue λ_r represents the contribution of each factor in the total variance in the original variables:

$$\lambda_r = \sum_{k=1}^{K} a_{kr}^2 \qquad (7.4)$$

In a specific application it is not uncommon to extract a small number of factors that account for the major part of the total variance (80–90 percent). In these cases factor analysis is deemed successful in having identified a small number of composite dimensions that underlie the set of given variables (or item ratings).

Another useful aspect of factor analysis is the construction of a perceptual map—the matrix of *factor-score coefficients*—that describes the factor scores as a linear function of the original ratings:

$$F_{ir} = b_{r1}x_{i1} + \cdots + b_{rK}x_{iK} + \text{error}$$

$$r = 1, \ldots, R \text{ for each individual } i \quad (7.5)$$

An average product position is usually constructed by averaging the F_{ir} over i:

$$F_1^*, \ldots, F_r^* = \frac{1}{I}\sum_i F_{i1}, \ldots, \frac{1}{I}\sum_i F_{iR} \quad (7.6)$$

By inputting the original items (x's) into eqs. (7.5) and (7.7), the average positions of a product (or set of products, if multiple products are being evaluated) in a reduced factor space can be constructed. Alternatively, individual factor positions could be retained and segmented into groups with similar perceptions.

EXAMPLE: Hauser and Shugan (1980) structured the views of scientists and managers at Los Alamos Scientific Laboratory on telephone and personal visits and three new-product concepts in communications. A total of 25 items was generated, using focus-group-type procedures; a summary of the resulting evaluations is reproduced as Exhibit 7.7.

A common-factor analysis was run with the ratings of each of five products by 41 managers on the 25 scales. Exhibit 7.8(a) gives the factor loadings relating the resulting two factors to the 25 attributes following a varimax rotation. By underlining the heavy loadings (those with correlations of 0.40 or larger) and examining the relationships among the heavy loadings, these factors were named "effectiveness" and "ease of use."

The product map is produced by using the matrix of factor-score coefficients shown in Exhibit 7.8(b). Suppose that, when standardized, individual 1's ratings for the telephone are $x_{1,1} = 1.5$, $x_{1,2} = 0.8$, $\ldots$, $x_{1,25} = -1.3$. The estimate of the effectiveness factor for the telephone becomes

$$F_{1,\text{effectiveness}} = (-0.10)(1.5) + (-0.03)(0.8) \cdots (0.07)(-1.3) = 0.3$$

where the b_{j1}'s come from the first column of Exhibit 7.8(b).

When averaged across individuals, a perceptual map is produced, as shown in Exhibit 7.9. The map has a reduced number of dimensions characterizing the way individuals perceive products in the space. As indicated in Exhibit 7.9, the space provides room for a new-product opportunity, a point we will return to in Chapter 11.

A series of analytical issues that must be addressed in factor analysis include the following:

Communality. How are these values to be estimated? Many researchers regress each variable against all the others and use the multiple correlation coefficient, although other approaches are viable.

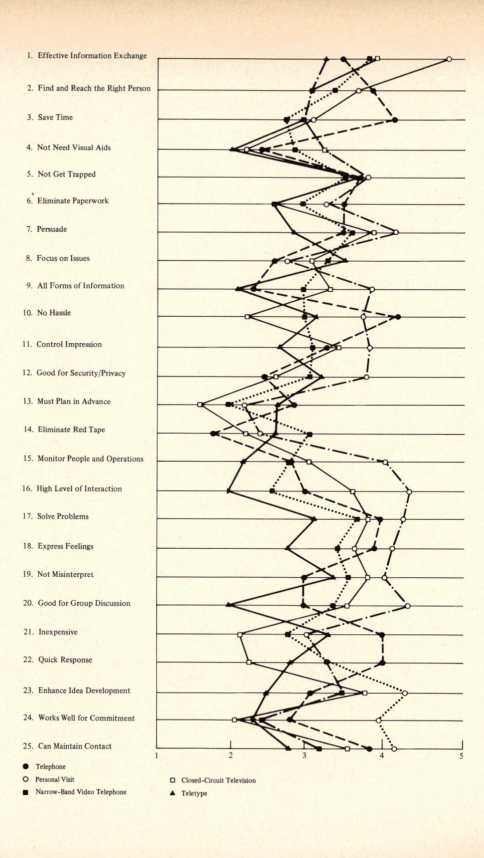

1. Effective Information Exchange
2. Find and Reach the Right Person
3. Save Time
4. Not Need Visual Aids
5. Not Get Trapped
6. Eliminate Paperwork
7. Persuade
8. Focus on Issues
9. All Forms of Information
10. No Hassle
11. Control Impression
12. Good for Security/Privacy
13. Must Plan in Advance
14. Eliminate Red Tape
15. Monitor People and Operations
16. High Level of Interaction
17. Solve Problems
18. Express Feelings
19. Not Misinterpret
20. Good for Group Discussion
21. Inexpensive
22. Quick Response
23. Enhance Idea Development
24. Works Well for Commitment
25. Can Maintain Contact

● Telephone
○ Personal Visit
■ Narrow-Band Video Telephone
□ Closed-Circuit Television
▲ Teletype

The number of factors. There is no well-developed theory here; judgment and intuition are most frequently used with one of the following criteria:

1. Stop extracting factors when the eigenvalue drops below 1 (such a factor explains less variance than an average item).

2. Stop extracting factors when the plot of explained variance versus the number of factors levels off.

3. Stop factoring when you see a similar result with a random data set in a Monte Carlo simulation.

Factor naming. A combination of intuition plus examination of the factor matrices will generally allow meaningful interpretations.

Rotation. In most studies the factor loadings are rotated to a smaller factor matrix in which each variable has loadings on only a few factors. A number of analytical definitions of simple structure exist, with the varimax criterion possibly being most widely used in marketing applications.

Furthermore, there are several other difficulties associated with factor analysis. Note that in the Hauser-Shugan study, regression *estimates* of factors are used in place of actual factors (factor scores that one cannot determine since they are elements of theoretical constructs). These factors are interpreted, post hoc here, by reference to their loadings. The differences between the estimated factors and the true theoretical constructs are usually overlooked, although these differences may compromise the interpretability of the results. In addition, since there are an infinite number of other factor structures than can fit the observed data equally well, many of which will be quite different, one must be cautious in interpretation. Group-level effects may be significant as well (Dillon, Frederick and Tangpanichdee, 1982).

Finally, it should be noted that the causal-modeling approach to factor analysis provides a unique maximum-likelihood estimate of the structure and also provides a chi-square statistic to test the number of factors necessary to account for the correlation matrix. However, this approach assumes multinormality of errors (Jöreskog and Sörbom, 1979). The interested reader should also see Harman (1976) for a thorough discussion of classical factor analysis.

In comparing factor analysis with nonmetric multidimensional scaling,

---

EXHIBIT 7-7 (on facing page) **Snake plot of scientists' and managers' perceptions of new communications options.** (Source: Glen L. Urban and John R. Hauser, *Design and Marketing of New Products*, © 1980, p. 191. Adapted by permission of Prentice-Hall, Inc., Englewood Cliffs, N.J.)

EXHIBIT 7-8 Factor loadings and factor-score coefficients from communications-options study.

Attributes[a]	(a) Loadings Used to Name the Dimension of the Perceptual Map for Factor Analysis		(b) Factor-Score Coefficients Used to Estimate Product Positions in Perceptual Map	
	Effectiveness	Ease of Use	Effectiveness	Ease of Use
1. Effective Information Exchange (−)	−0.77	−0.17	−0.10	−0.04
2. Find and Reach Right Person	0.25	0.43	−0.08	0.11
3. Save Time	0.17	0.47	−0.05	0.26
4. Not Need Visual Aids	0.39	−0.16	0.06	0.04
5. Get Trapped (−)	−0.33	−0.20	0.07	0.06
6. Eliminate Paperwork	0.31	0.43	0.02	0.18
7. Persuade (−)	−0.70	−0.20	0.13	0.01
8. Focus on Issues	−0.04	−0.07	0.01	−0.00
9. All Forms of Information	0.65	−0.18	−0.02	−0.05
10. Real Hassle (−)	−0.11	−0.83	0.07	−0.29
11. Control Impression	0.56	0.07	0.03	−0.04
12. Security	0.18	0.11	−0.00	−0.02
13. Plan in Advance (−)	0.23	−0.44	0.04	0.00
14. Eliminate Red Tape	−0.00	−0.21	0.00	0.01
15. Monitor People, Operations, Experiments	0.65	0.15	0.05	0.01
16. Interaction	0.78	0.05	0.25	−0.07
17. Solve Problems (−)	−0.55	−0.27	−0.02	−0.09
18. Express Feelings	0.66	0.17	0.13	−0.05
19. Misinterpret (−)	−0.49	0.00	0.00	0.05
20. Group Discussion	0.75	0.05	0.20	−0.08
21. Inexpensive	−0.27	0.52	−0.04	0.09
22. Quick Response	0.07	0.71	−0.04	0.20
23. Enhance Idea Development	0.77	0.09	0.22	−0.05
24. Commitment	0.44	0.32	0.06	0.05
25. Maintain Contact	0.50	0.52	0.07	0.18

[a](−) indicates question was worded so that a high attribute rating would mean a poor evaluation.

SOURCE: Glen L. Urban, John R. Hauser, *Design and Marketing of New Products*, © 1980, pp. 200, 205. Adapted by permission of Prentice-Hall, Inc., Englewood Cliffs, N.J.

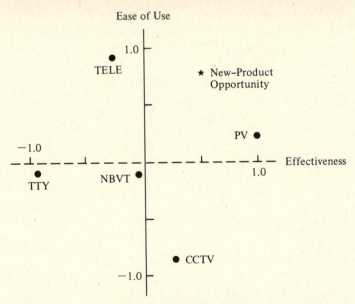

EXHIBIT 7-9   **Perceptual map for communications options.** (Source: Hauser and Shugan, 1980, p. 303.)

Hauser and Koppelman (1979) conclude that factor analysis is superior from the standpoint of predictive ability, interpretability, and ease of use. However, in the absence of a well-developed theory of the formation of evaluation criteria, the researcher might well be advised to perform both analyses in search of a convergent picture of the market.

Models of Attitude and Preference Formation

The basic concept behind attitude measurement and modeling is that the way we feel about something determines how we act when we are presented with a purchase opportunity. Advertising expenditures are often justified on the basis that such investments can modify attitudes and, hence, behavior.

An attitude can be defined as an overall tendency to consistently respond favorably or unfavorably toward an object. While an attitude is an overall measure, most models of attitude formation assume that choice behavior, as well as attitudes, are determined by judgments on specific attributes of the choice object. These models, then, transform consumer cognitions (beliefs) on a variety of attribute dimensions to a single-dimensional scale of brand attitude. The product attributes must be salient;

that is, they must be the ones that are considered important by consumers and the ones in which the various brands or products are believed to differ. [See Hughes (1974) for an overview of methods for attitude identification and measurement.]

Models of attitude structure can generally be classified by whether they are compensatory or noncompensatory. In a compensatory model the weakness of a brand on one attribute can be compensated for by strength on another, and the attributes are summed to determine the favorability or unfavorability of the attitude toward the brand. On the other hand, in noncompensatory models only two or three attributes are used to evaluate a product, and if a brand is not adequate on any one attribute, the brand is eliminated. Examples of both compensatory and noncompensatory models are given below.

Compensatory Models

The Fishbein Model. Fishbein (1963) developed a theory of attitude formation and change based on behavioral-learning theory, which can be summarized as

$$A_0 = \sum_{i=1}^{N} b_i a_i \qquad (7.7)$$

where A_0 = attitude toward any psychological object
       b_i = belief (subjective likelihood) that object possesses attribute i
       a_i = evaluation (goodness or badness) of attribute i
       N = number of salient attributes

In this model the overall attitude toward a brand is viewed as the product of the beliefs about a brand along a particular attribute and the value of the attribute summed over all attributes. For example, consider a facial cleanser. We would consider the degree to which a respondent believes a brand supplies moisturizing and the relative goodness or badness of moisturizing as an attribute.

The Fishbein model has seen a number of studies evaluating its relevance to marketing situations. [See Lutz and Bettman (1977) and Wilkie and Pessemier (1973) for reviews.] However, marketing researchers have had difficulty in actually applying it to marketing situations. The use of a probability scale to measure brand attributes proved cumbersome in many market research studies, and simple scales were proposed as measures of beliefs (e.g., the rating of *degrees* of moisturizing from 7 = very moisturizing to 1 = not moisturizing). But as Lutz and Bettman (1977) note, this modification compromises the theory behind the Fishbein model.

Belief/Importance Model. This model was first proposed in marketing by Bass and Talarzyk (1972). They state that the overall evaluation of a brand is a function of beliefs about the attributes possessed by the brand (b_i) weighted by the importance of each attribute (I_i):

$$A_0 = \sum_{i=1}^{N} b_{0i} I_i \qquad (7.8)$$

Evidence comparing this model to the Fishbein model is mixed: Bettman, Capon, and Lutz (1975) report superior results from the Fishbein model, while Mazis and Ahtola (1975) report superior results from the beliefs/ importance model.

Extended Fishbein Model. The ambiguous results obtained from these multiattribute models has prompted Fishbein and others to reassess the beliefs/evaluation model to make it more relevant to marketing (Fishbein and Ajzen, 1975). The most widely known extension has others, apart from the person making the purchase, influencing the decision in some decision circumstances. In particular,

$$BI = \sum_{i} a_i b_i + \sum_{j} SNB_j MC_j \qquad (7.9)$$

where BI = behavioral intent
a_i, b_i = defined as before
SNB_j = social normative belief, which relates what an individual considers is expected of him by an external social group on scale j
MC_j = motivation to comply with these expectations

EXAMPLE: SNB_j and MC_j could be measured as follows:

(SNB):

My professional col- leagues think I should buy a foreign car..	My professional col- leagues think I should *not* buy a foreign car.

(MC):

I want to do what my colleagues think I should do regarding a car..	I do *not* want to do what my colleagues think I should do regarding a car.

The extended Fishbein model has been applied in recent years and generally has been shown to perform better than the original model. In addition, Wilson, Matthews, and Harvey (1975) and others found that attitudes toward the purchase of a brand were more closely related to behavior than were attitudes toward the brand itself. Thus it may be more relevant to ask consumers whether their teeth will get white if they use Ultra Brite than to ask whether they think Ultra Brite whitens teeth.

Ideal-point Model.   An offshoot of the belief/importance model, the ideal-point model, requires a consumer's rating of an ideal brand along with his ratings of the actual brands being analyzed.

EXAMPLE: Lehmann (1971a) modeled television-show choice as follows:

$$A_0 = \sum_i v_i |B_{i0} - I_i|^k$$

where A_0 = overall attitude (preference for a TV show)
  v_i = weight attached to TV-show characteristic i
    (action, suspense, humor, etc.)
  B_{i0} = belief about show on dimension i
  I_i = ideal position in dimension i
  k = distance measure

His model is shown to be substantially more powerful in predicting behavior than are models based on demographic variables.

Beliefs-Only Model.   Sheth and Talarzyk (1972) developed a beliefs-only model when researchers found that ratings on the importance of attributes were not related to brand attributes. In a study of six consumer products they found that satisfaction ratings on specific attributes of each brand (taste, price, nutrition, etc.) were related to the overall evaluation of the brand. However, there was little relationship between the importance assigned to each attribute and brand evaluation.

Some research supports beliefs alone as the key influence on brand evaluation and behavior (Sheth, 1973), while other research supports including the importance terms (Bass and Wilkie, 1973; Weddle and Bettman, 1973). Here, as with most conflicting findings, the best model appears to depend on what and who are being tested and how the test is conducted.

Noncompensatory Models

The multiattribute models described above assume that individuals evaluate brands across a number of different attributes and then determine the most preferred brand by summing across these attributes. Nakanishi and Bettman (1974) suggest that such an evaluation process may be too complex for many consumer goods; consumers may evaluate brands on two or three key attributes and eliminate brands if they are not adequate on any one attribute. We review several of the more important noncompensatory models below.

Conjunctive Model.   Here it is assumed that a consumer will consider a brand only if it meets certain minimum, acceptable standards on key dimensions. If any one attribute is deficient, the product is eliminated from consideration.

As an example, Exhibit 7.10 shows rating scales for an evoked set of

EXHIBIT 7-10   **Ratings of brands for use in noncompensatory-attitude models: breath mint and hard-roll candy.**

	Certs	Life Savers Mints	Trident	Sugarless Breath Savers
Taste/Flavor	4	7	4	7
Breath Effectiveness	6	4	5	4.5
Contains Sugar	Yes	Yes	No	No

Note: 7 = highly satisfied with brand's performance on attribute, . . . , 1 = highly dissatisfied with brand's performance on attribute.

brands of breath-freshening candy. Assume that consumer A wants a sugarless breath freshener; thus he immediately eliminates Certs and Life Savers Mints. Then if the consumer finds taste more important than breath freshening, he will choose sugarless Breath Savers; if the reverse is true, Trident will be chosen.

Disjunctive Model.   In a disjunctive model one or two attributes stand out as the selection criteria. As an example, suppose one consumer sees taste as the dominant dimension. Then Certs and Trident are immediately eliminated, and the choice is made on other dimensions between Life Savers Mints and Sugarless Breath Savers.

Lexicographic Model.   A lexicographic model assumes that all attributes are used but in a stepwise manner. Brands are evaluated on the most important attributes first; then if there are ties, a second attribute is used, and so forth.

In our example suppose taste is followed by sugarlessness as key attributes. Certs and Trident are eliminated first; then Life Savers Mints are eliminated, leaving Sugarless Breath Savers as the chosen brand.

A number of other noncompensatory models have been proposed, including elimination by aspects, lexicographic semiorder, additive difference, and others. See Bettman (1979) for a more detailed discussion of these and other models.

In general, noncompensatory models require individuals to process information by attribute across brands, while compensatory models require consumers to process information by brand across attributes. Since evaluations are simple and faster in noncompensatory models, it is likely that they are better representations of decision processes for low-involvement goods while compensatory models more accurately describe brand evaluations for high-involvement products in more complex decision-making settings.

Incorporating Uncertainty

In some ways the models of this section are related to the determination of objectives in Chapter 3. We have assumed, as in Chapter 3, that we have multiple criteria of varying importance that we wish to combine into an overall value or preference function. In the literature on decision theory all these functions would be called value functions. They translate (map) a set of attributes, known with certainty, into a function called value.

But what about a new product? Is it reasonable to use the same model to predict choice when the attributes of some products are known with more certainty than others? Here, again, *utility theory* and the direct assessment of a utility function across attributes are useful. Exhibit 7.11 illustrates how risk can be measured in the direct assessment of a consumer's utility function. The methods of Chapter 3 apply here. [See Keeney and Raiffa

Instruction to Consumer:

Imagine you can only choose between two health plans, plan 1 and plan 2. In both plans personalness convenience, and value are good (rated 5). You are familiar with plan 1 and know that quality is satisfactory plus (rated 4). You are not sure of the quality of plan 2. If your choose plan 2, then the wheel is spun and the quality you will experience for the entire year depends on the outcome of the wheel. If it comes up yellow, the quality is very good (rated 6); and if it comes up blue, the quality is just adequate (rated 2). Graphically this is stated:

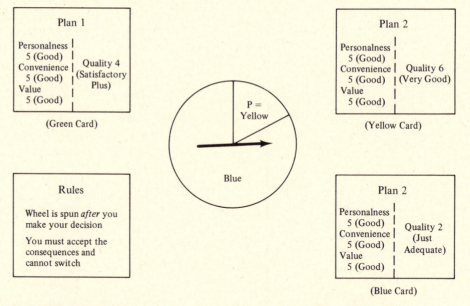

Instruction to Consumer:

At what setting of the odds (size of the yellow area) would you be indifferent between plan 1 and plan 2? (Respondent is given wheel and adjusts it until size of yellow area is appropriate. He is challenged by being given the choice with his setting. If he prefers one plan or the other, the interview iterates the question until a true indifference setting is determined.)

EXHIBIT 7-11   Schematic of lottery question for direct utility function assessment. (Source: Glen L. Urban and John R. Hauser, *Design and Marketing of New Products,* © 1980, p. 274. Adapted by permission of Prentice-Hall, Inc., Englewood Cliffs, N.J.)

(1976) for detailed development and Hauser and Urban (1979) for application in marketing.]

Finally, it should be noted that most of the models dealt with here are stated-importance models; that is, the respondent rates the attribute importance. In revealed-preference models the importance ratings are inferred. This issue is addressed below for the logit model and in Chapter 11 in the discussion on conjoint analysis and preference regression.

Choice Models

During the last decade or two a wide range of models has been developed to address the problem of consumer choice. As in all consumer behavior modeling, the appropriate model is a function of the specific choice situation and the objectives of the analysts. We focus on two main categories of models: high-involvement choice models—essentially logit-type models—and low-involvement (stochastic) choice models. Although the logit-type models include stochastic elements and many of the stochastic models include control variables, this categorization appears to be a useful way to separate these two different research traditions.

High-Involvement Choice Models

Most high-involvement choice models derive from Luce's (1959) choice axiom:

$$p_i(j, m_i) = \frac{V_i(j)}{\displaystyle\sum_{k \in m_i} V_i(k)} \tag{7.10}$$

where $p_i(j, m_i)$ = probability that individual i chooses brand j
$V_i(j)$ = consumer i's ratio-scaled preference for brand j
$k = 1, 2, \ldots, m_i$
m_i = set of brands in a respondent's set of alternatives

Axelrod (1968) suggests the use of the constant-sum technique for eliciting preference judgments for consumers. Allaire (1973) recommends these judgments be obtained only from among those brands an individual would actually consider buying. Torgerson (1958, pp. 108, 112) provides a least-squares method for estimating ratio-scale values from paired-comparison data.

EXAMPLE: Suppose there are three brands, A, B, and C, to be evaluated and a consumer is given the following task: "Allocate 20 chips to each pair of brands in a manner that reflects your overall preference for those brands."

$$
\begin{array}{ccccc}
\text{A} & 16 & \text{A} & 16 & \text{B} & 10 \\
\text{B} & \underline{4} & \text{C} & \underline{4} & \text{C} & \underline{10} \\
& 20 & & 20 & & 20
\end{array} \qquad (7.11)
$$

This allocation is called a *paired comparison.*

Ratio-Scaled Preferences: p_A, p_B, and p_C should satisfy (at least approximately) these relationships:

$$
\frac{p_A}{p_B} = \frac{16}{4} \qquad \frac{p_A}{p_C} = \frac{16}{4} \qquad \frac{p_B}{p_C} = \frac{10}{10} \qquad (7.12)
$$

resulting in one solution of $p_A = \frac{2}{3}$, $p_B = p_C = \frac{1}{6}$.

Luce's model is an example of what is referred to as a *constant-utility model.* In such a model the decision rule is subject to randomness (hence the probability of purchase measure is the dependent variable), but individuals' subjective evaluations of the alternatives are assumed constant. According to these models, choice probabilities are defined by a function of the distance between the preference scores of the product alternatives that form the individual's choice set.

An approach that has been more popular and seen more marketing applications is that of a *random-utility* model, in which the preference scores (the product-utility-values) undergo random fluctuations, while the choice mechanism is deterministic. In these models some true utility measure $V_{ij}{}^T$ is assumed such that

$$
V_{ij}{}^0 = V_{ij}{}^T + \epsilon_{ij} \qquad (7.13)
$$

where $V_{ij}{}^0$ = observed preference or utility measure
ϵ_{ij} = uncertainty in preference measure

These models further assume that an individual will choose the brand with the highest *true* utility, $V_{ij}{}^T$. If p_{ij} is an estimate of the probability that consumer i will choose brand j, then the random-utility model yields

$$
p_{ij} = p(V_{ij}{}^0 > V_{ik}{}^0) \qquad \text{for all } k \text{ in } m_i \text{ not equal to } j \qquad (7.14)
$$

$$
= p(V_{ij}{}^T + \epsilon_{ij} > V_{ik}{}^T + \epsilon_{ik}) \qquad \text{for all } K \text{ in } m_i \text{ not equal to } j \qquad (7.15)
$$

Most random-utility models differ in their assumptions about the structure of the error term. We review the assumptions leading to the multinomial logit model here.

Multinomial Logit Model.   The assumptions required for the multinomial logit model are as follows:

1. $\{\epsilon_{ij}\}$ for all j are independently and identically distributed.
2. The distribution of the $\{\epsilon_{ij}\}$ is double exponential (extreme value):

$$
p(\epsilon_{ij} > x) = e^{-e^{-bx}} \qquad (7.16)
$$

Because the ϵ_{ij} are assumed independent, the joint cumulative distribution for the ϵ_{ij}, $j = 1, \ldots, J$, is the product of the J univariate-cumulative-distribution functions:

$$p(\epsilon_{i1} \leq x, \epsilon_{i2} \leq x, \ldots, \epsilon_{ij} \leq x) = \prod_{j=1}^{J} e^{-e^{-bx_j}} \tag{7.17}$$

Now for a given value of ϵ_{i1}, this equation is the joint-cumulative-distribution function of $\{\epsilon_{ij}\}$ for $j = 2$ to J at the values $V_{i1} - V_{ij} + \epsilon_{i1}$. Integrating ϵ_{i1} out of the above equation yields

$$p_{i1} = \frac{e^{bV_{i1}^T}}{\displaystyle\sum_{j=1}^{J} e^{bV_{ij}^T}} \tag{7.18}$$

The logit model can be used directly with a linear compensatory model as follows:

$$V_{ij}^T = \frac{1}{K} \sum_{k=1}^{K} b_{ijk} I_k \tag{7.19}$$

where b_{ijk} = respondent i's evaluation of product j with respect to attribute k

I_k = importance weight associated with attribute k

If we substitute eq. (7.19) into eq. (7.18), we get

$$p_{i1} = \frac{e^{\sum_k b_{i1k} I_k}}{\displaystyle\sum_j e^{\sum_k b_{ijk} I_k}} \tag{7.20}$$

Similarly, equations for $p_{i2}, \ldots, p_{iJ}$ can be defined. The importance weights I_k can be derived from maximum-likelihood procedures, as explained in Chapter 5. These weights are often called revealed importances because they are revealed by choice behavior rather than from direct-preference analysis. Furthermore, they are interpreted in much the same way as regression coefficients. In most computer packages the statistical significance of each I_k is determined through a t test based on asymptotic values of the standard errors of the estimates. Chapman and Staelin (1982) suggest a procedure that exploits the information content of the complete rank-order choice set.

EXAMPLE: Suppose that a survey of shoppers has been performed in an area in order to understand their shopping habits and to determine the share of shoppers a new store might attract. Three existing stores and one proposed store (described in a written concept statement) were rated on a number of dimensions: (1) variety, (2) quality, (3) parking, and (4) value for the money. The ratings on these dimensions are given in Exhibit 7.12.

EXHIBIT 7-12   **Ratings and importance data for the store-selection example.**

Store	Attribute Ratings			
	Variety	Quality	Parking	Value for the Money
1	0.7	0.5	0.7	0.7
2	0.3	0.4	0.2	0.8
3	0.6	0.8	0.7	0.4
4 (new)	0.6	0.4	0.8	0.5
Importance Weight	2.0	1.7	1.3	2.2

By a fit of shoppers' choices of existing stores to their ratings through the logit model, the coefficients $\{a_d\}$ have been estimated:

$$V_i = \sum_{d=1}^{4} a_d X_{id} \qquad (7.21)$$

where V_i = attractiveness of store i
X_{id} = rating for store i on dimension d
a_d = importance weight for dimension d

The data in Exhibit 7.12 come from a group of relatively homogeneous consumers. The share of the old stores with and without the new store, the potential share of the new store, and the draw estimated from this group are given in Exhibit 7.13.

Two things should be clear from this example. The first is that the logit model is useful for a variety of applications, such as new-product/concept evaluations, as well as for understanding choice behavior. However, a very particular form of choice behavior is specified. The draw [column (e) in Exhibit 7.13] is proportional to share [column (c)]. Thus the logit model includes special assumptions that may weaken its applicability in certain marketing situations.

Model Limitations and Extensions.   There are two main criticisms of the logit model. The first has to do with the (postulated) form of the error

EXHIBIT 7-13   **Logit-model analysis for the store example.**

Store	(a) $U_i = \Sigma a_d X_{id}$	(b) e^{U_i}	(c) Share Estimate Without New Store	(d) Share Estimate With New Store	(e) Draw [(c) − (d)]
1	4.70	109.9	0.512	0.407	0.105
2	3.30	27.1	0.126	0.100	0.026
3	4.35	77.5	0.362	0.287	0.075
4	4.02	55.7		0.206	

EXHIBIT 7-14   **Logit-model analysis:
                store example with a
                change in the evoked set.**

Store	e^{U_i}	Share Estimate
1	109.9	0.376
2	27.1	0.092
3	77.5	0.266
4	77.5	0.266

function. Although McFadden (1970) gives some support for the soundness of that particular distributional form, other forms, particularly normally distributed errors, may be more reasonable. The second criticism is that changes in the evoked set, as noted above, cause proportional changes in probability estimates. For example, assume that the new store (store 4) was in the same chain and right next door to store 3. With the logit model we would then have the estimates shown in Exhibit 7.14, but it would be more reasonable in this case to expect that store 4 would draw proportionally more from store 3 (its twin) and less from the other stores.

This latter problem is referred to as Luce's axiom, or the problem of independence of irrelevant alternatives. To overcome it, one must define the choice set so that the detrimental effect of the axiom can be minimized. In particular, proper definition of market hierarchies, when they exist, can minimize the problem. Some work on the generalized extreme-value/ nested logit model (McFadden, 1980) handles these problems directly.

A model that explicitly addresses evoked-set effects is the multinomial probit model. This model uses a normally distributed error structure and allows the covariance between error terms to be nonzero. But it is not possible to write a general analytical expression for the choice probabilities, and estimation and evaluation are quite complex. However, recent developments have led to practical computer programs for this model (Daganzo, 1979).

For marketing applications of the logit model, see Berkowitz and Haines (1982), Gensch and Recker (1979), Punj and Staelin (1978), and Urban and Hauser (1980). For more detailed discussion and derivations of other choice models, see McFadden (1976, 1980).

Low-Involvement (Stochastic) Choice Models

As noted earlier, stochastic models of consumer behavior are most appropriate where a major element of the choice process involves uncertainty (versus rational choice), as in the case of low-involvement goods. Partly because frequently purchased consumer-packaged goods are often low-involvement items and partly because a large quantity of brand-switching

EXHIBIT 7-15   **Characteristics of stochastic models.**

Brand Choice	Which brand will be chosen next? How many alternatives are considered (us versus them)?
Purchase Timing	When and how frequently will purchases occur?
Impact of Decision Variables	What will be the effect on choice of price, advertising, and so on?
Heterogeneity	Is the population considered homogeneous or heterogeneous with respect to purchase probability, consumption, or response?
Stationarity	Do the probability laws change over time or as a result of consumer- or marketer-controlled actions? If so, what is the probability law?
Store Bought from	Where was the purchase made?
Measures of Interest	Does the model compute expected brand shares, penetration, market structure, and so on?

data is available for such products, packaged goods have formed the focus of stochastic choice modeling.

These models differ in a number of ways, as illustrated in Exhibit 7.15. For example, they can be classified by whether or not they consider brand choice, purchase timing, store of purchase, and the impact of marketing variables. They also differ on how they handle consumer heterogeneity. Some models segment individuals into homogeneous subsets and analyze these subsets separately. Others perform measurements at the level of the individual household. But the most popular approach toward the heterogeneity problem is through the explicit inclusion of a measurement of the heterogeneity, called a mixing distribution.

DISCUSSION: A mixing distribution is an explicit representation of the way a parameter or a set of parameters varies across the population. For example, assume a population with the following choice model in a market with two brands A and B at the prices P_A and P_B:

$$p(\text{purchase A} \mid k_0) = \left(\frac{P_B}{P_A + P_B}\right)^{k_0} \tag{7.22}$$

where k_0 is a (price-sensitivity) parameter that varies over the population. Assume also that the population is heterogeneous so that

$$k_0 = \begin{cases} 1 & \text{for 80\% of the population} \\ 2 & \text{for 20\% of the population} \end{cases}$$

Then what is the likelihood that a randomly chosen customer will buy brand A?

For the population as a whole, that likelihood is

$$E[p(A)] = p(\text{purchase } A \mid k_0 = 1) \cdot p(k_0 = 1)$$
$$+ p(\text{purchase } A \mid k_0 = 2) \cdot p(k_0 = 2)$$
$$= 0.8 \left(\frac{P_B}{P_A + P_B} \right) + 0.2 \left(\frac{P_B}{P_A + P_B} \right)^2 \tag{7.23}$$

Suppose k_0 has some more-complex continuous distribution across the population, $f_k(k_0)$. Then

$$E[p(A)] = \int_{k_0} \underbrace{p(\text{purchase } A \mid k_0)}_{\substack{\text{conditional probability} \\ \text{of purchase given } k_0}} \underbrace{f_k(k_0)dk_0}_{\substack{\text{mixing} \\ \text{distribution}}} \tag{7.24}$$

This approach has important implications for the structure of stochastic consumer choice.

In addition, a model may (or may not) allow for updating in some way due to effects of the environment, purchase feedback, controllable variables, and so on. Finally, models also differ in the number of brands they consider and in the information they give back to the analyst such as expected brand shares, penetration, and market structure.

There are a number of important problems associated with model building in general that are particularly acute when the models are stochastic. The first of these is that a number of different models may represent a set of data equally well. This implies, as Morrison (1969a) notes, that stochastic models of brand choice are unlikely to provide unique theories of consumer behavior. In fact, given enough data, any model can be shown to be *incorrect*. This problem is compounded by the fact that all consumers may not follow the same model (Blattberg and Sen, 1976; Givon and Horsky, 1979; Jones, 1970).

Another important problem, first discussed by Frank (1962), is that what appears to be a high-order behavior (i.e., nonstationarity of response, learning, etc.) may simply be the result of heterogeneity when behavior is studied at an aggregate level. This problem is called the spurious effect of heterogeneity and can be best understood through the following example.

EXAMPLE: Assume we have a market with two brands (A and B) and that the buying population is made up of two subpopulations (I and II). Assume also that there are five times as many I's as II's; that is, $p(\text{customer in I}) = \frac{1}{6}$ if a customer is randomly chosen from the population. Further assume that these subpopulations are homogeneous with given and constant (but different) probabilities of purchasing each of the brands:

$$p(A \mid I) = 0.6 \qquad p(A \mid II) = 0.06 \tag{7.25}$$

If we sample from this population, what is the probability that brand A will be purchased? This probability can be calculated as

$$p(A) = p(A \mid I)p(I) + p(A \mid II)p(II)$$
$$= (0.6)(\tfrac{1}{6}) + (0.06)(\tfrac{5}{6}) = 0.15 \tag{7.26}$$

Now let us consider the likelihood that the population that buys A on a given purchase repeats it on the next purchase:

$$p(A \text{ on } 2 \mid A \text{ on } 1) = \frac{p(A_2 \text{ and } A_1)}{p(A_1)}$$
$$p(A_2 \cap A_1) = p(A_2 A_1 \mid I) \, p(I) + p(A_2 A_1 \mid II)p(II)$$
$$= (0.6^2)(\tfrac{1}{6}) + (0.06^2)(\tfrac{5}{6}) = 0.063 \tag{7.27}$$

With eqs. (7.26) and (7.27) we get $p(A_2 \mid A_1) = 0.063/0.15 = 0.42$! Now compare $p(A_1) = 0.15$ to $p(A_2 \mid A_1) = 0.42$. Thus in this example the purchase of A on a given occasion apparently increases the probability that the brand will be purchased next. The increase is real, but the cause is due to *selective selection* (i.e., the spurious effect of heterogeneity) rather than learning.

Finally a third problem, not addressed by most stochastic models, is that the process itself may change because of the effect of internal or external events.

In the discussion that follows we review stochastic brand-choice (analyzing the brand chosen) and purchase-incidence (purchase-timing) models separately. Although these models appear to be different, they overlap in their use: one can study the choice of a brand on the basis of its incidence of purchase. Herniter (1971) produced one of the first models to create a joint purchase-timing–brand-choice model. Since then, Zufryden (1978), Jeuland, Bass, and Wright (1980), and Bemmaor (1978) have all extended his results, using different assumptions about the structure of the process.

Brand-Choice Models

Brand-choice models can usually be distinguished by how they deal with (1) population heterogeneity, (2) purchase-event feedback, and (3) exogenous market factors.

As discussed above, the mixing distribution, the most popular approach for dealing with population heterogeneity, has each individual in the population make a random choice from some distribution of response. Although conceptually difficult, this approach has a distinct advantage: the identification and the measurement of specific discriminating characteristics of households need not be done explicitly.

Models differ according to how they deal with purchase-event feedback, the influence of present purchase behavior on future purchase probabilities. Models that assume no purchase-event feedback are called *zero-order models*; the name refers to the fact that the purchase probability of the brand on the $(n + k)$th occasion, p_{n+k}, is equal to the purchase probability on the nth occasion, p_n. On the other hand, *Markov models* assume that only the previous brand choice affects the present purchase probability, while *learning models* assume that the entire purchase history affects current choice, with more-recent purchases having more effect.

Market factors are the third determinant of brand-choice behavior and are most frequently accounted for in one of two ways: (1) explicitly including the influence of specific market factors in the model and (2) postulating that the effects of all such forces can be accounted for with a time trend or structural shift in the model. Models whose parameters do not change over time are referred to as stationary-in-parameters models; such models do not necessarily include stationary purchase probabilities, which may change because of purchase feedback.

Much of the information used in a number of popular brand-choice models can be extracted from a *brand-switching matrix*. The elements in this matrix are obtained from purchase information on two choice occasions separated in time, where the time between the two purchases may differ considerably for different consumers.

Exhibit 7.16 gives some data on the brand-switching habits of 513 consumers over two purchase occasions. In this exhibit parts (b) and (c) show transition probabilities expressed as joint and conditional probabilities, respectively. Let

$p(i|j)$ = conditional probability that a customer will purchase brand i on the second purchase occasion given that brand j was purchased on the first occasion

$p(i, j)$ = joint probability that a consumer will purchase brand i on the second purchase occasion and brand j on the first purchase occasion

These purchase probabilities are related as follows:

$$p(i|j) = \frac{p(i, j)}{p(j)} \tag{7.28}$$

where $p(j)$ = probability of purchasing brand j on the first purchase occasion; so $p(j) = m_j$, the market share of brand j. It also follows from the definition of joint and conditional probabilities that

$$\sum_j p(i, j) = m_i \tag{7.29}$$

EXHIBIT 7-16   **Brand-switching habits of 513 consumers over two purchase occasions.**

		Brand Bought on Occasion 2			
		A	B	C	
Brand Bought on Occasion 1	A	137	47	19	203
	B	41	179	12	232
	C	22	10	46	78
		200	236	77	513

(a) Purchases of Brands A, B, and C over Two Purchase Occasions

		Brand Bought on Occasion 2			
		A	B	C	
Brand Bought on Occasion 1	A	0.267	0.092	0.150	0.396
	B	0.080	0.349	0.023	0.452
	C	0.043	0.019	0.090	0.152
		0.390	0.460	0.150	1.00

(b) Joint-probability Matrix

		Brand Bought on Occasion 2			
		A	B	C	
Brand Bought on Occasion 1	A	0.674	0.232	0.093	1.00
	B	0.177	0.772	0.051	1.00
	C	0.283	0.125	0.592	1.00

(c) Conditional-probability Matrix

and

$$\sum_i p(i|j) = 1 \qquad (7.30)$$

In the example in Exhibit 7.16, the joint- and conditional-probability measures are obtained from information in part (a).

Zero-order Models. We review several zero-order models here that differ in (1) the assumptions they make about consumer preferences and choice and (2) the number of brands they consider.

The *heterogeneous Bernoulli model* assumes that (1) in a population of customers each has a (constant) probability p_i of buying one of the two brands in the market (brand 1) and (2) p is distributed as $f(p)$ in this

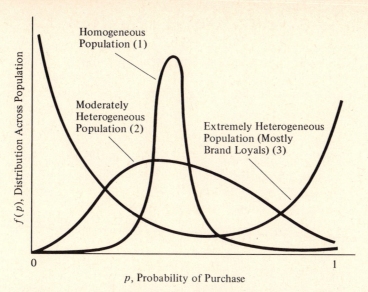

EXHIBIT 7-17   Three types of population-heterogeneity distributions.

population. Exhibit 7.17 illustrates this second assumption. In the exhibit distribution 1 represents a relatively homogeneous population with almost all consumers having nearly the same probability of purchasing brand 1; distribution 2 represents a situation where there is substantial heterogeneity, with probability of purchase distributed widely across the population; and, finally, distribution 3 represents an extremely heterogeneous population where, in effect, there appear to be two distinct market segments, one loyal to each of the two brands.

EXAMPLE: A flexible distribution that is frequently used in this context is the beta distribution:

$$f(p) = k_1 p^{\alpha-1}(1 - p)^{\beta-1} \qquad (7.31)$$

This distribution has two shape parameters, α and β [the third value, K_1, in eq. (7.31) is a constant of integration that forces $\int_0^1 f(p)dp = 1$], and can accommodate any of the shapes in Exhibit 7.17.

To illustrate the use of this model, we note that for a given value of p, the likelihood of r purchases of brand 1 in n purchase occasions is

$$\ell(n, r \,|\, p) = k_2 p^r (1 - p)^{n-r} \qquad (7.32)$$

Now by Bayles' rule, the posterior distribution of p is proportional to the likelihood given p [eq. (7.32)] times the initial (prior) distribution of p [eq. (7.31)]. So the posterior distribution of p is given by

$$\text{Posterior}(p) = k_3 p^{\alpha+r-1}(1 - p)^{\beta+n-r-1} \qquad (7.33)$$

Note that eq. (7.33) is also a beta distribution with parameters $\alpha + r$ and $\beta + n - r$.

Consider now an individual who, indeed, makes r purchases of brand 1 out of n purchase occasions. What is his likely probability of next purchase? It is the expected value of p given n and r, or the mean of the distribution in eq. (7.33):

$$E(p \,|\, n, r) = \frac{\alpha + r}{\alpha + \beta + n} \qquad (7.34)$$

To be specific, consider individual A, who has a purchase history of 1111:

$$E_A(p) = \frac{\alpha + 4}{\alpha + \beta + 4} \qquad (7.35)$$

For individual B, whose purchase history is 0000, we get

$$E_B(p) = \frac{\alpha}{\alpha + \beta + 4} \qquad (7.36)$$

These posterior expectations give us a method for estimating α and β. [Note also that the differences in $E(p)$ are due solely to the spurious effect of heterogeneity; no learning as such is occurring.]

Now assume we look only at purchase strings of length 3; the possibilities are given in Exhibit 7.18. If we index the observation by ijk (where i, j, $k = 0$ or 1), then we might consider structuring the estimation of α and β in such a way as to force $E(p \,|\, ijk)$ to be close to n_{ijk}/N, the empirical frequency. Formally, we might set up the problem as follows.

Find α and β to

$$\text{Minimize} \sum_{ijk} \left[E(p \,|\, ijk) - \frac{n_{ijk}}{N} \right]^2 \qquad (7.37)$$

In practice, the estimation procedure for α and β is somewhat different. A χ^2 statistic is usually minimized, with

$$\chi^2 = \sum_{ijk} \frac{E(p \,|\, ijk) - n_{ijk}/N}{E(p \,|\, ijk)} \qquad (7.38)$$

However, the idea is the same: use the expected and observed proportions in each purchase-sequence string to estimate the parameters α and β. These parameters then give complete information about the distribution of p (i.e., the distribution of brand loyalty in the market).

The number of observations in a purchase string will vary from study to study: the longer the purchase string, the more degrees of freedom there will be for estimation, but the greater the likelihood will be of a shift in market structure. In addition, the longer the purchase string, the fewer will be the individual consumers usually retained for estimation, because of turnover in the panel (the usual data source) and differences in purchase frequency.

EXHIBIT 7-18 **Observed and theoretical proportions in each purchase category: Bernoulli model.**

Purchase Strings	$E(p)$	Observed Number	Example
111	$\dfrac{\alpha + 3}{\alpha + \beta + 3}$	n_{111}	123
110		n_{110}	137
101	$\dfrac{\alpha + 2}{\alpha + \beta + 3}$	n_{101}	202
011		n_{011}	214
100		n_{100}	127
010	$\dfrac{\alpha + 1}{\alpha + \beta + 3}$	n_{010}	116
001		n_{001}	92
000	$\dfrac{\alpha}{\alpha + \beta + 3}$	n_{000}	36
		N	1047

A *simple multiple-brand model* is the next zero-order model we consider. On the basis of extensive empirical research, Ehrenberg (1972) postulated that the joint probability of a consumer purchasing brands i and j on successive purchase occasions is given by

$$p_{ij} = km_i m_j \tag{7.39}$$

where $\{m_i\}$ are the market shares of the respective brands. With eqs. (7.29) and (7.39) it is easy to show that

$$p(i, i) = m_i - km_i(1 - m_i) \tag{7.40}$$

Then summing eq. (7.39) over brands, we get an equation for k:

$$k = \frac{1 - \sum p_i(i, i)}{1 - \sum_i m_i^2} \tag{7.41}$$

Noting again that $p(i) = m_i$, we get, from eqs. (7.28), (7.39), and (7.40),

$$p(i|j) = \begin{cases} km_i & j \neq i \\ 1 - k(1 - m_i) & j = i \end{cases} \tag{7.42}$$

which shows that the conditional probabilities of purchasing brand i are independent of brand j.

Kalwani and Morrison (1977) show that two assumptions—(1) a zero-order process applies and (2) switching is proportional to share—are sufficient to derive the above results. Alternatively, Kalwani (1979) shows that if the purchase-probability density function of consumers in a choice category is given by the Dirichlet distribution (the multivariate extension of the beta distribution), then eq. (7.39) holds as well. Bass, Jeuland, and Wright (1976) have shown that eq. (7.39) can be derived by starting with individual consumer preferences and combining them with Luce's choice axiom.

Using the data from Exhibit 7.16, we construct, in Exhibit 7.19, the theoretical brand-switching matrix following eqs. (7.39), (7.40), and (7.41). The observed and expected switching proportions are quite close, suggesting that this model adequately describes this switching behavior.

The *Hendry model* (The Hendry Corporation, 1970, 1971) is closely related to the above model. The main difference is in the calculation of the switching constant. It is derived from the concept of entropy, a measure of

EXHIBIT 7-19   Computations of theoretical switching levels: Hendry and Ehrenberg.

Brand	Shares	$\dfrac{m_i^2 \ln(1/m_i)}{1 + m_i \ln(1/m_i)}$	$m_i(1 - m_i)$
A	0.390	0.105	0.238
B	0.460	0.121	0.166
C	0.150	0.033	0.134
		0.259	**0.538**

$$k_w = \frac{0.259}{0.538} = 0.481 \text{ (Hendry)}$$

$$k = \frac{1 - \sum_i p_{ii}}{1 - \sum_i m_i^2} = \frac{0.294}{0.614} = 0.479 \text{ (Ehrenberg)}$$

Expected/Observed Brand-Switching Matrix
Brand Bought on Occasion 2:

		A	B	C
Brand Bought On Occasion 1	**A**	0.275 / 0.267	0.086 / 0.092	0.028 / 0.037
	B	0.086 / 0.080	0.341 / 0.349	0.033 / 0.023
	C	0.028 / 0.043	0.033 / 0.019	0.089 / 0.090

Note: Theoretical switching values are in the upper left in each box; observed switching values are in the lower right. k and k_w are so close in this example that differences would hardly be discernible. Ehrenberg's k was used for calculating theoretical switching.

the disorder or randomness of a probabilistic system. The entropy of a system consisting of n possible states is

$$S = -k_W \sum_{i=1}^{n} p_i \log p_i \qquad (7.43)$$

where p_i is the probability that the system is in state i.

EXAMPLE: Consider a situation where we have two brand markets (brands 1 and 2) and a customer has a certain probability p of purchasing the brand. From eq. (7.43) (assume $k_W = 1$ for simplicity), if $p = 0$, $S = 0$; if $p = 0.2$, $S = 0.500$; if $p = 0.3$, $S = 0.611$; and if $p = 0.5$, $S = 0.693$. So as the likelihood of purchase of the brand increases toward 0.5, the entropy increases. In fact, the entropy of this (unconstrained) system is maximized when $p = 0.5$. This result corresponds to intuition about the randomness of behavior being greatest when p is far from both 0 and 1.

In the Hendry model the switching constant (known as k_w) is calculated to maximize the system entropy subject to knowledge of brand shares:

$$k_w = \frac{\sum_i m_i^2 \ln(1/m_i)/[1 + m_i \ln(1/m_i)]}{\sum m_i(1 - m_i)} \qquad (7.44)$$

As shown in Exhibit 7.19, the value of k_w for these data is quite close to the value of k from Ehrenberg's formulation. Ehrenberg and Goodhart (1973) report on a comparative test of these two models in an analysis of the breakfast-cereal market; the Hendry model tended to overstate repeat purchases and understate brand switching relative to Ehrenberg's formulation.

The major use of the Hendry model is as a tool to study competition and market structure. Two alternatives are said to be in direct competition if the switching to (and between) them from any other alternative is guided by eq. (7.39). A key output of the Hendry system is a hierarchical market structure. The underlying assumption is that consumer choice follows a hierarchy of differentiating characteristics. A commonly used example is margarine where the product comes in two forms: sticks and tubs. Do consumers primarily make their choice first on the basis of form and then on the basis of brand, or vice versa? Exhibit 7.20 illustrates the alternatives.

The procedure is as follows. First, a hypothetical market structure is set up on the basis of expert judgment. According to Hendry, if a market structure is correct, then brand switches between entities at the end of a branch will be consistent with theoretical levels for a constant k_w. If the theoretical and observed switching levels are consistent, the hierarchy is said to represent the market adequately. If there are significant differences,

Form–Specific Margarine Market

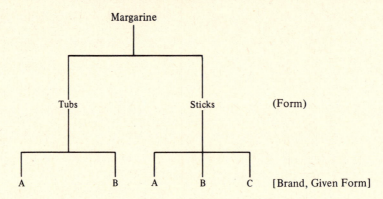

(Form)

[Brand, Given Form]

Brand–Specific Margarine Market

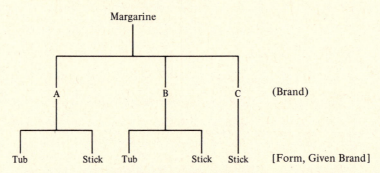

(Brand)

[Form, Given Brand]

EXHIBIT 7-20   **Alternative market hierarchies: margarine market.**

then alternative hypothetical structures are tested. After several attempts, a partitioning structure that provides a reasonably good fit to the data is identified. The implications of the market-structure hierarchy for product/ market planning will be discussed in Chapter 17.

The significance of the Hendry (and related) models is that important insight into the structure of market competition can be obtained from them. For example, type-primary structures call for promotional and new-product strategies that are different from those for form-primary structures.

Kalwani (1979) points out the need for detailed empirical testing, as well as an improved theoretical basis for the Hendry partitioning approach. In related work Herniter (1973) also developed a brand-purchasing model based on the concept of entropy. As with Hendry, the Herniter model is determined by market shares. Herniter (1974) reports an empirical test of the two models, with the Hendry model providing a superior fit in a four-brand market. Herniter's approach becomes analytically difficult for more than three brands because of the difficulty of solving his general entropy equations. Bass (1974a) simplifies the results so that fewer segments are needed ($n + 1$ versus $2^n - 1$ for Herniter) by assuming that all switching is done by a segment of the market called the stochastic preference group. This procedure also expands on Herniter's entropy problem by allowing different product categories to have different loyalty patterns.

Markov Models. While zero-order models assume that brand choice is independent of past purchase behavior, Markov models (of the first order) assume that only the last brand chosen affects the current purchase. Specifically, there are two properties that characterize a stationary (probabilities do not change) first-order Markov process. Let Y_t denote the brand chosen on the tth purchase occasion and N denote the number of brands. Then the stationary Markov process satisfies the following conditions:

$$p(Y_t = k \,|\, Y_{t-1}, Y_{t-2}, \ldots, Y_0) = p(Y_t = k \,|\, Y_{t-1}) \qquad (7.45)$$
$$\text{(one period memory)}$$

$$p(Y_t = k \,|\, Y_{t-1}) = p(Y_1 = k \,|\, Y_0) \qquad (7.46)$$
$$\text{(stationary for all } t, k)$$

All the information needed to characterize brand choice in a Markov model is contained in the probability transition matrix (Exhibit 7.16). Let us denote such a matrix as $\mathbf{P} = \{p_{ij}\}$, where p_{ij} is the probability of purchasing j next, given i was last purchased. As a so-called stochastic matrix, $\mathbf{P}$ has the following properties:

$$0 \le p_{ij} \le 1 \qquad (7.47)$$

$$\sum_i p_{ij} = 1 \qquad (7.48)$$

Given current market shares, a Markov model can be used to predict how market shares change over time. Suppose we know $\{m_{it}\}$; then market shares for all brands (i) at time $t + 1$ can be calculated as

$$m_{j,t+1} = \sum_{i=1}^{n} p_{ij} m_{it} \qquad (7.49)$$

EXAMPLE: Consider a two-brand example, A and B, with the following switching matrix:

$$t + 1$$

	A	B
A	0.7	0.3
B	0.5	0.5

t where $m_{At} = 0.5$; $m_{Bt} = 0.5$

By eq. (7.49), we get

$$\hat{m}_{At+1} = m_{At}p_{AA} + m_{Bt}p_{BA}$$
$$= (0.5)(0.7) + (0.5)(0.5) = 0.6 \tag{7.50}$$

Similarly,

$$m_{Bt+1} = 1 - 0.6 = 0.4$$
$$\hat{m}_{At+2} = \hat{m}_{At+1}p_{AA} + \hat{m}_{Bt+1}p_{BA}$$
$$= (0.6)(0.7) + (0.4)(0.5) = 0.62$$

and so on, until

$$\hat{m}_{A\infty} = \text{long-run market share} = 0.625$$

This example demonstrates two uses of the Markov model. First, it shows that forecasting of market shares can be performed by using the transition matrix. Second, it shows how the effect of a change in market structure can be evaluated.

Suppose in this example that the transition matrix was calculated following a price shift. What is the effect of the shift on brand A? In the long run, it can be expected to lead to a share change of $\hat{m}_{A\infty} - m_{At} = 0.625 - 0.50 = 0.125$. That increase in share can then be evaluated for cost effectiveness.

As with other stochastic models, the calculation of transition probabilities is usually based on panel data.

Several critical assumptions are present in this development, including purchase timing (one purchase per time period), homogeneity, and stationarity, that is, $p_{ijt} = p_{ijt+k}$ for all k. This latter assumption is often unrealistic; a firm losing market position will take corrective action. A number of models in the literature, including Maffai (1960a), Harary and Lipstein (1962), Ehrenberg (1965), and Montgomery (1969), allow for varying transition probabilities. Other researchers, such as Telser (1962b), Hartung and Fisher (1965), Lee, Judge, and Zellner (1970), and Horsky (1976, 1977), relate the transition probabilities to decision variables.

EXAMPLE: Telser (1962) specified the following simple functional form for his transition matrices:

$$p_{ii} = \alpha_{ii} + \beta_{ii}p_{it}$$
$$p_{ki} = \alpha_{ki} + \beta_{ki}^{*}p_{it} \tag{7.51}$$

Substituting eq. (7.51) into eq. (7.49), he gets equations of the form

$$m_{it} = \alpha + \beta m_{it-1} + \gamma p_{it} + \mu_{it} \tag{7.52}$$

where μ_{it} is the residual and the parameters α, β, and γ are functions of previously specified parameters. Using MRCA national consumer-diary-panel data, he derives price-elasticity estimates for three product categories:

−5.7 for frozen orange juice, −5.5 for instant coffee, and −4.4 for regular coffee. Although some questions can be raised about the statistical properties of these estimates, the approach shows the viability of using stochastic choice models to make inferences about market response to changes in decision variables.

Although quite flexible, the one-period learning effect and implicit homogeneity of most Markov models have limited their use somewhat. [See Morrison (1966) for a discussion of the problems of including heterogeneity in a general Markov structure; Morrison et al., 1982, provide an application of a heterogeneous Markov model.] Also, more-flexible mechanisms for incorporating learning are clearly desirable. We deal with one such mechanism next.

Learning Models. To express the reinforcement effects of past brand choices, Kuehn (1962) applies a learning model, developed by Bush and Mosteller (1955), to a consumer-choice problem. Learning models are based on the idea that at the individual level each purchase of a given brand enhances the likelihood of future purchases of the brand.

To understand the model in its simplest form, consider a two-brand market where

$$Y_t = \begin{cases} 1 & \text{if the brand of interest is purchased on occasion} \\ 0 & \text{otherwise} \end{cases}$$

and

p_t = probability of purchasing brand on occasion t [i.e., $p_t = p(Y_t = 1)$]

The basic equations of the simple linear learning model are a pair of operators called the acceptance operator and the rejection operator:

$$p_t = \alpha_1 + \lambda_1 p_{t-1} \qquad \text{if brand } i \text{ is purchased at } t \qquad (7.53)$$
(acceptance operator)

$$p_t = \alpha_2 + \lambda_2 p_{t-1} \qquad \text{if brand } i \text{ is not purchased at } t \qquad (7.54)$$
(rejection operator)

EXAMPLE: Assume that the acceptance and rejection operators have equal slopes (i.e., $\lambda_1 = \lambda_2$), as displayed in Exhibit 7.21. The horizontal axis represents the probability of choosing brand j in period t, and the vertical axis represents the probability of choosing brand j in period $t + 1$. The figure contains a positively sloped 45° line as a norm. The figure also contains two positively sloped lines representing the acceptance and rejection operators from eqs. (7.53) and (7.54).

For example, suppose the probability of purchasing brand j this period is 0.60. Suppose it is actually what he buys. The probability that the buyer will buy brand j again, assuming that he is satisfied, is found by running a dotted line up from the horizontal axis at 0.60 to the purchase-operator line (because brand j was purchased) and going across the vertical axis and

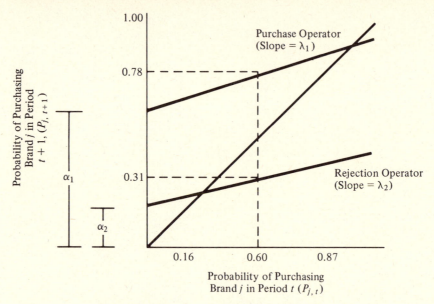

EXHIBIT 7-21   The simple linear learning model. (Source: Adapted from Kuehn, 1962.)

reading the new probability. In this illustration the new probability is 0.78. If the buyer had not purchased j, the dotted line from 0.60 would have been run up only to the rejection operator and been read on the vertical axis. In that case the probability of the person buying j next time would have fallen from 0.60 to 0.31.

If the consumer continues buying brand j, the probability of buying brand j approaches 0.87 as a limit. This upper limit, given by the intersection of the purchase-operator and the 45° lines, represents a phenomenon known as *incomplete habit formation*. No matter how much brand j is bought, some probability still remains that the consumer may buy another brand. On the other hand, if the consumer does not buy brand j for a long time, the probability of buying this brand falls continuously but never to zero. This is the phenomenon of *incomplete habit extinction*. There is always some positive probability that a consumer may buy a previously neglected brand.

The incomplete-habit-formation aspect of this model is seen by successive substitutions of eq. (7.53):

$$p_t = \alpha_1 + \lambda_1 p_{t-1} = \alpha_1 + \lambda_1(\alpha_1 + \lambda_1 p_{t-2})$$
$$= \alpha_1 + \lambda_1\alpha_1 + \lambda_1^2\alpha_1 + \cdots$$
$$= \alpha_1(1 + \lambda_1 + \lambda_1^2 + \cdots) \tag{7.55}$$

$$p_U = \frac{\alpha_1}{1 - \lambda_1} \qquad \text{upper limit of } p \tag{7.56}$$

Similarly, when the brand is never bought,

$$p \rightarrow p_L = \frac{\alpha_2}{1 - \lambda_2} \qquad \text{lower limit}$$

For a two-brand market, if $\lambda_1 = \lambda_2 = 0$, the linear learning model reduces to a Markov model with constant transition probabilities:

$$t + 1$$

t	α_1	$1 - \alpha_1$
	α_2	$1 - \alpha_2$

$$\tag{7.57}$$

Applications of the learning model have been reported by Kuehn (1962) with data on the purchase of frozen orange juice, by Carman (1966) with dentifrice data following the American Dental Association's endorsement of Crest, by Kuehn and Rohloff (1967a) in the context of evaluating promotions (Chapter 15), and in a modified form by Haines (1964). More recent applications include those of Lawrence (1975) and Wierenga (1974). In the latter work the linear learning model produces results superior to those of the homogeneous and heterogeneous, zero-order and first-order Markov models. In another study Massy, Montgomery, and Morrison (1970) show that the linear learning model may account for population heterogeneity; the approach works essentially through the introduction of a mixing distribution on the initial probability levels, as reviewed earlier.

In the form described above the linear learning model does not contain any decision variables. Lilien (1974a) introduces price into the model:

$$p_{t+1} = (1 - c)(\alpha + \beta Y_t + \lambda p_t) + c\phi(\delta_{t+1}) \tag{7.58}$$

where
c = price consciousness of consumer
δ_t = price measure
$\phi(\cdot)$ = price-response function

He uses the model to measure the effect of price on brand choice/learning behavior and to derive pricing policies under given assumptions about competitive behavior in the marketplace. His results in the gasoline market are generally supportive of this model form.

The linear learning model and its derivatives generally face three problems. First, the model is well suited for two-brand markets (us versus them) only; when more-detailed market descriptions are needed, it is not easily extended. Second, the model is structured to give only positive feedback for brand purchase and, hence, may not be useful in new-product situations. Third, the model is analytically more complex than the others cited here, limiting its accessibility.

Purchase-Incidence Models*

The primary contributor to the study of purchase-incidence models is Ehrenberg with his negative-binomial-distribution (NBD) theory and model. The work by Chatfield, Ehrenberg, and Goodhardt (1966), Ehrenberg and Pyatt (1971), and Ehrenberg (1972, 1975) and their references indicate that the NBD model fits a wide variety of purchase data very well. The primary emphasis of this work has been on the number of units purchased of a particular size of a given brand in some specified time period, often 4, 12, or 13 wk. Goodhardt and Ehrenberg (1967) show that under a stationary environment the number of purchases made by individuals in a given period can be used to predict the complete probability distribution for the purchases in the next period. If the market is, in fact, nonstationary, as it would be during a promotional campaign, then the predictions under the stationarity assumption can be used as a norm or a yardstick to assess the observed changes in purchasing behavior.

This latter use of the NBD model—its calibration under stationary conditions to evaluate the effect of market changes—gives it most of its power but has also been the subject of controversy: ". . . Ehrenberg assumes the market is stationary, but this is a weakness of the model" (Blattberg, 1981, p. 197).

The NBD Model. The aggregate distribution of r, the number of units purchased in a unit time period, will be negative binomial under the following conditions:

1. if each individual purchases in a Poisson manner with rate λ per unit time (say, 4 wk)
2. if the purchasing rate λ is distributed according to a gamma distribution across the population of consumers:

$$g(\lambda \mid k, m) = \frac{e^{-\lambda(k/m)} \lambda^{k-1}(k/m)^k}{\Gamma(k)} \qquad m, k > 0, \lambda > 0 \qquad (7.59)$$

where
$$E(\lambda) = m \qquad (7.60)$$

$$\text{Var}(\lambda) = \frac{m^2}{k} \qquad (7.61)$$

Poisson Purchasing. The purchase rate is said to be governed by a Poisson process under the following assumptions:

1. The likelihood of purchase in any period of short duration is independent of the time when the last purchase was made.
2. The likelihood of purchase does not change over time.

*This section draws on notes developed by Manohar Kalwani, Spring 1980.

Under these assumptions the distribution of the time until the next purchase is exponential with parameter λ:

$$f(t \mid \lambda) = \lambda e^{-\lambda t} \tag{7.62}$$

where $\lambda > 0$

        $f(t \mid \lambda)$ = density function for time until next purchase

Under these conditions the probability that in a period of unit length (4 wk, say) a consumer with purchasing rate λ will make r purchases is

$$p(r \mid \lambda) = \frac{e^{-\lambda} \lambda^r}{r!} \tag{7.63}$$

a Poisson distribution.

Clearly, the selection of the time period is critical if the Poisson assumption is to hold: it must not be so short (such as 1 wk) that purchases of an individual consumer on successive days are negatively correlated. Chatfield and Goodhardt (1973) provide some empirical support in favor of purchasing behavior more regular than is consistent with the Poisson assumption, and suggest an Erlang distribution.

Gamma Mixing Distribution. The gamma distribution is a flexible two-parameter distribution that can take on a variety of shapes, defined on $\lambda > 0$. The use of the gamma as a mixing distribution, the measure of population heterogeneity, has not been challenged to any significant degree.

Following the two assumptions above, the proportion of consumers who purchase r units (the particular package size) of the brand is given by

$$
\begin{aligned}
p(r; k, m) &= \int_0^\infty p(r \mid \lambda) g(\lambda \mid k, m) d\lambda \\
&= \int_0^\infty \frac{e^{-\lambda} \lambda^r}{r!} g(\lambda \mid k, m) d\lambda \\
&= \frac{\Gamma(k + r)}{\Gamma(k) r!} \left(\frac{k}{k + m} \right)^k \left(\frac{m}{m + k} \right)^r
\end{aligned} \tag{7.64}
$$

where $E(r) = m \tag{7.65}$

$$\mathrm{Var}(r) = m \left(1 + \frac{m}{k} \right) \tag{7.66}$$

The NBD parameters are commonly estimated by equating the observed mean and proportion of nonbuyers to their theoretical values. This technique is called fitting by mean and zeros. If the sample mean is denoted by $\overline{x}$ and the proportion of buyers by b, we find

$$\overline{x} = \hat{m} \tag{7.67}$$

and

$$1 - b = \left(1 + \frac{\bar{x}}{\hat{k}}\right)^{-k} \tag{7.68}$$

[Note that $\hat{k}$ must be calculated numerically by successive approximations or by trial and error from eq. (7.68).] The estimates of m and k are used to construct a frequency distribution of consumers in the sample who buy 0, 1, 2, ..., or, in general, r units in some specified time period.

The NBD method constructs two key measures of market response to the brand: *penetration* and *purchase frequency*. Penetration b is defined as the proportion of consumers who buy this brand at least once in the given time period; purchase frequency w is the average number of times these buyers purchase the brand in the specified time period.

The NBD Model Predictions.   Under stationary conditions the distribution of purchases in a time period T is an NBD as long as the unit time period (say, 4 or 12 wk) is also negative binomial with parameters $m_T = Tm$ and $k_T = k$. Thus the proportion of buyers in such a time period is given by

$$b_T = 1 - \left(1 + \frac{Tm}{k}\right)^{-k} \tag{7.69}$$

Recall that b_T is called penetration. The longer the time period, the larger the penetration will be.

An important use of the NBD model is in the study of *repeat-buying behavior*. This field is concerned with purchasing behavior in two consecutive and equal time periods, say I and II. A repeat buyer is one who buys at least once in both time periods. A lost buyer purchases in period I but not in period II. Conversely a new buyer purchases in period II but not in period I.

Under stationary conditions the proportion of new buyers in the sample, b_N, is equal to the proportion of lost buyers, where the proportion of new buyers is computed as the difference between the proportion of buyers in the combined period and the proportion of buyers in period I. Therefore,

$$
\begin{aligned}
b_N = b_L &= \left[1 - \left(1 + \frac{2m}{k}\right)^{-k}\right] - \left[1 - \left(1 + \frac{m}{k}\right)^{-k}\right] \\
&= \left(1 + \frac{m}{k}\right)^{-k} - \left(1 + \frac{2m}{k}\right)^{-k}
\end{aligned} \tag{7.70}
$$

where the distribution of purchases in period I is an NBD with parameters m and k. The proportion of repeat buyers b_R is given by

$$
\begin{aligned}
b_R = b - b_N &= \left[1 - \left(1 + \frac{m}{k}\right)^{-k}\right] - \left[\left(1 + \frac{m}{k}\right)^{-k} - \left(1 + \frac{2m}{k}\right)^{-k}\right] \\
&= 1 - 2\left(1 + \frac{m}{k}\right)^{-k} + \left(1 + \frac{2m}{k}\right)^{-k}
\end{aligned} \tag{7.71}
$$

For the data included in Exhibit 7.22 ($m = 3.43$ and $k = 0.42$), $b_N = b_L = 0.093$ and $b_R = 0.513$.

The amounts bought by each class of buyer are obtained as follows. Because the purchases of a particular consumer in successive time periods are independent Poisson variates, a person with purchase rate λ will, on average, buy λ units in period II regardless of how much he happened to buy in period I. Consider the new buyers who did not buy in period I. In period II the mean amount bought by this subgroup on a per-consumer basis is given by

$$m_N = \int_0^\infty e^{-\lambda} \lambda g(\lambda \mid k, m)d\lambda = \frac{m}{[1 + (m/k)]^{k+1}} \tag{7.72}$$

since $e^{-\lambda}$ is the probability of not buying in period I given purchase rate λ. Under stationary conditions this amount will be the same as the mean amount bought in period I by the lost buyers, m_L. Then the mean amount bought by repeat buyers, m_R, is given by

$$m_R = m - m_N = m\left[1 - \left(1 + \frac{m}{k}\right)^{-(k+1)}\right] \tag{7.73}$$

The quantities m, m_N, and m_R are calculated on a per-consumer basis. In practice, it is often more useful to calculate quantities analogous to w, the

EXHIBIT 7-22   Illustration of NBD model.

Number of Purchases	0	1	2	3	4	5	6	7	8	9	10	11	12	13
Households Buying	193	71	49	28	20	22	14	16	11	9	12	7	7	4

Number of Purchases	14	15	16	17	18	19	20	21	22	23	24	29	36	37
Households Buying	1	3	5	4	2	2	2	2	2	1	2	1	1	4

(a) Number of Purchases of Cornflakes Made in 24 Wk by 491 Households

$$\hat{m} = \overline{x} = 3.43$$

$$\left(\frac{193}{491}\right) = 1 - b = \left(1 + \frac{\overline{x}}{\hat{k}}\right)^{-k} \rightarrow \hat{k} = 0.42$$

$$b = 0.607 \qquad w = \frac{\hat{m}}{b} = 5.65$$

(b) Estimation of Parameters and Statistics

	Number of Purchases										
	0	1	2	3	4	5	6	7	8	9	10+
Observed %	39	14	10	6	4	4	3	3	2	2	11
NBD	39	15	9	7	5	4	3	3	2	2	11

(c) The Fit of the Negative Binomial Distribution

DATA SOURCE: Charlton, Ehrenberg and Pymont. (1972).

rate of buying per buyer. The average rates of buying per new, lost, and repeat buyer are obtained as follows:

$$w_N = w_L = \frac{m_N}{b_N} \tag{7.74}$$

$$w_R = \frac{m_R}{b_R} \tag{7.75}$$

For the illustration $m_N = m_L = 0.15$, $m_R = 3.28$, $w_N = w_L = 1.59$, and $w_R = 6.39$.

While other authors have challenged the assumptions underlying the NBD model, Ehrenberg's contribution is in showing the importance of brand penetration in explaining behavior. "The fundamental finding in the study of buying behavior is that there are simple and highly generalizable patterns" (Ehrenberg, 1972, p. 17). He argues that these simple rules of behavior explain far more about a brand's purchase behavior than do assumptions about loyalty, specially segmented brands, marketing effects, and so on. More research looking for and explaining such marketing generalizations would provide an important contribution to this field.

Future of Stochastic Choice Modeling

From our discussion here it appears that stochastic models have the potential to provide some important information. They are useful constructs for obtaining both static and time-trend information about the structure of the marketplace and buying patterns. They also allow the development of norms to compare the future (during a promotional period) with what would have been expected given the events of the past. Some stochastic models also incorporate decision variables and can be used directly for decision making, although not with the degree of simplicity of aggregate-response models.

Then what is the future and use of this area of investigation? Blattberg (1981) and Jones (1979) give their views. On the plus side:

Insight into market behavior and market structure not available on an aggregate level can be derived from these models.

The penetration of electronic point-of-purchase scanning will provide a major and more readily available, valid, and representative source of consumer panel data in the future, making these modeling techniques more readily accessible.

However, more work is needed in the following areas:

the incorporation of decision variables into brand-choice and purchase-incidence models (Jones and Zufryden, 1980, 1982; Zufryden 1981, 1982) the empirical and theoretical generalizations of market behavior, for a better understanding of which models are appropriate where (Hauser and Wisniewski, 1982a, b)

the development of aggregate counterparts to the stochastic models of individuals

better communication of the benefits of stochastic modeling to the managers who are the consumers of the information these models provide

Summary

In a field both as vast and diffuse as that of consumer behavior and consumer markets, it is difficult to develop a synthesis. In this chapter we have tried to structure and highlight important knowledge that exists about consumer behavior, consumer markets, and the associated models. The consumer market is the set of all individuals who are actual or potential buyers of a product or service. To understand a market, we ask six questions: (1) Who is in the market (occupants)? (2) What do they buy (objects)? (3) When do they buy (occasions)? (4) Who does the buying (organization)? (5) Why do they buy (objectives)? (6) How do they buy (operations)? (7) Where do they buy (locations)?

The buying situation may vary from one of routinized purchase (often the case with low-involvement goods) to extensive problem solving (the case with high-involvement goods). The type of buying situation will determine the type of behavior, in terms of product evaluation and selection strategies that a consumer is likely to make, and the appropriate model.

Consumer behavior models are usefully viewed by their level of detail and by what part of the consumer purchasing process they address. Large-system models provide an integrating framework to understand the complexities of consumer behavior. However, they are difficult to operationalize and test. Perceptual-evaluation models focusing on the evaluation stage (multidimensional scaling, and factor analysis) map the way individuals perceive brands. Models of attitude and preference formation relate beliefs and evaluations about products to overall attitudes (preferences or purchase intentions) toward the product. Choice models can be viewed as one of two types: high-involvement models and low-involvement (stochastic) models. Of the high-involvement models the multinomial logit model is perhaps the most widely used. Finally, stochastic models deal mainly with brand choice and purchase timing. Brand-choice models include zero-order models, such as Bernoulli models and the Hendry model, and higher-order models, such as Markov and learning models. The major contribution to the field of purchase-timing models has come from Ehrenberg with his negative-binomial-distribution theory and model.

The consumer behavior field is currently somewhat disjoint; more-integrated effort is needed to bring it together. The research rift between economists, behavioral scientists, and operations researchers has to be bridged: behavioral-science models should consider more of the stochastic model's parsimony and operationality, while stochastic models should better incorporate the phenomenon included in the behavioral models.

Finally, there is clearly a need for better communication of the variety of important theories, concepts, and tools developed here to the marketing manager, who is the ultimate user of these ideas.

Problems

7.1 A group of consumers is asked to rate five different brands of coffee according to two characteristics: strength and body. Each brand is rated on a scale from 1 to 7 for each characteristic. Each consumer is also asked to rate his ideal coffee. The brands are rated by the consumers in the following way:

Brand	Strength	Body
A	3	5
B	5	2
C	6	3
D	2	3
E	3	1
I (ideal)	5	5

Assume that the above perceptions are typical of the consumer group and that preference falls equally fast in all directions from the ideal brand.

a. Represent these perceptions in euclidian two-space, and order the different brands according to their probable market share if product characteristics were the only factor that counted.

b. Suppose that the consumer is only one-third as concerned with body as he is with the strength of his coffee. Compute the weighted distances, and reorder the brands according to their probable market shares.

7.2 A large marketing research firm pays a large group of households to keep a diary of their weekly grocery purchases. Suppose the record of 20 such households is examined with respect to the purchases of a particular product of which there are three brands: A, B, and C. The table below shows the brands chosen by these 20 households in 2 successive weeks.

House	1	2	3	4	5	6	7	8	9	10	11	12	13	14	15	16	17	18	19	20
Week 1	A	A	A	A	A	A	A	A	A	A	B	B	B	B	B	B	C	C	C	C
Week 2	A	A	A	A	A	A	A	B	B	C	A	B	B	C	C	C	B	B	C	C

Develop a matrix of brand-switching probabilities on the basis of these 2 wk of data.

7.3 Consider this brand-switching matrix:

$$
\begin{array}{c}
 & & \text{To} \\
 & & \text{A} \quad \text{B} \quad \text{C} \\
\text{From} & \begin{array}{c} \text{A} \\ \text{B} \\ \text{C} \end{array} &
\begin{pmatrix} 0.7 & 0.2 & 0.1 \\ 0.3 & 0.6 & 0.1 \\ 0.1 & 0.4 & 0.5 \end{pmatrix}
\end{array}
$$

a. The initial brand shares are (0.10, 0.40, 0.50). What is brand A's expected share next period?

b. What is brand A's ultimate market share if the switching probabilities remain constant?

7.4 Using the first-order Markov matrix shown in Problem 7.3, determine the following:

a. the probability that A will be purchased in period $t + 1$, given that C was purchased in period t

b. the probability of A_{t+1}, given B_t

c. the probability of B_{t+1} and C_{t+2} given A_t

d. the probability of A_{t+1} and A_{t+2}, given A_t

7.5 Mrs. Smith just moved into town, and on her first trip to the supermarket she enters the store with a 0.4 probability of buying brand B. Suppose she buys brand B this time and also on her second trip. Assume that her learning operators are

$$p_{t+1} = 0.3 + 0.6p_t \qquad \text{for a purchase}$$
$$p_{t+1} = 0.1 + 0.6p_t \qquad \text{for a rejection}$$

a. What is the probability that she will buy brand B on her *third* trip to the store?

b. If she keeps buying brand B, what is her probability of buying brand B in the limit?

7.6 A buyer may choose from three competing brands of laundry detergent, A, B, and C. The unadjusted repurchase probabilities for each brand (i.e., the unadjusted probability that the buyer who has purchased the brand at time t will repurchase that brand at time $t + 1$) are $r_A = 0.70$, $r_B = 0.40$, and $r_C = 0.20$. The relative merchandising attractiveness of each brand is $a_A = 0.25$, $a_B = 0.35$, and $a_C = 0.40$. Construct a model that describes the buyer's switching and staying behavior.

7.7 Consider a three-brand market where the following brand switching has been observed between two successive purchase occasions per consumer:

First Purchase	Second Purchase Brand A	Brand B	Brand C	
Brand A	0.41	0.11	0.04	0.56
Brand B	0.09	0.15	0.01	0.25
Brand C	0.03	0.03	0.13	0.19
	0.53	0.29	0.18	1.00

    a. Estimate the Hendry coefficient k_W and the theoretical switching rates based on the Hendry model.

    b. Estimate the value of the coefficient k of eq. (7.41) and the associated theoretical switching probabilities.

    c. Brand C ran a temporary price reduction, which occurred generally between the first and second purchase occasions. Comment on the effectiveness of this price reduction.

7.8 A frequent exercise among builders of stochastic models of brand choice is to test whether a model fits observed behavior well or to test which of two models fits best. A frequent test of the presence of a homogeneous Bernoulli process is a chi-square test.

    a. We observe, for each consumer, two successive purchases of the product. It appears that the same percentage of all buyers buy A on the first and second of those purchases. Suppose this percentage is 70%. Assume that the underlying process is homogeneous Bernoulli.

        i. What is p_A?

        ii. Determine the percentage of the buyers who should have the following sequences of purchases if the process is, indeed, homogeneous Bernoulli: AA; AB; BA; BB.

        iii. We observe 100 consumers for two purchases and find the following sequences of purchases:

Last Purchase	Current Purchase	
	A	B
A	52	18
B	18	12

    Do a chi-square test. Is the homogeneous Bernoulli model fitting?

        iv. We now observe 500 customers for two purchases and find the following sequences of purchases:

Last Purchase	Current Purchase	
	A	B
A	260	90
B	90	60

    Do a chi-square test. Is the homogeneous Bernoulli model fitting?

        v. Compare the observed frequencies of each sequence of purchase in parts iii and iv. What do you conclude about the chi-square test?

    b. Suppose now we observe the following frequencies for each sequence of purchase:

Last Purchase	Current Purchase	
	A	B
A	42.5%	12.5%
B	12.5%	32.5%

How does a homogeneous Bernoulli model fit? How does a homogeneous Markov model fit?

c. Suppose that the consumer's population is made up of two subgroups. In subgroup I (which comprises 50% of the consumers), consumers prefer brand A and follow a Bernoulli model: they buy A 90% of the time, regardless of their previous purchase. In subgroup II (which comprises the remaining 50% of the population), consumers prefer brand B and follow a Bernoulli model: they buy B 80% of the time, regardless of their previous purchases.

    i. What is the expected frequency of each of the sequences of purchase (AA, AB, BA, BB) in subgroup I?

    ii. What is the expected frequency of each of the sequences of purchase (AA, AB, BA, BB) in subgroup II?

    iii. Assume a market analyst has data only on the frequency of purchases in the total market, and that he does not know about subgroups I and II. What frequencies of purchase should he be expected to observe?

    iv. Compare the results here with the frequencies observed in part b. Any comments?

7.9 In the linear learning model each consumer has his own probability of purchasing A on his t^{th} purchase $p_{A,t}$. This probability depends on the corresponding probability of the preceding purchase, $p_{A,t-1}$, and on whether A was indeed bought on the last purchase, as follows:

$p_{A,t} = a + b + cp_{A,t-1}$ if A was purchased on occasion $t - 1$

$p_{A,t} = a + cP_{A,t-1}$ if B was purchased on occasion $t - 1$

Assume $a = 0.0052$, $b = 0.4393$, and $c = 0.5448$.

a. Construct a graph showing on the abscissa $p_{A,t-1}$ and on the ordinate $p_{A,t}$ (the graph should comprise two lines, one corresponding to the case where A was bought on occasion $t - 1$, the other to the case where A was not bought).

b. What is the highest value that p_A can take if it starts from an intermediate value and, because of repeated purchases, increases? Assume a consumer has initially this value for $p_{A,t}$; what is his expected number of purchases before he buys B? How will his p_A change during that time?

c. What is the lowest value that p_A can take if it starts from an intermediate value and, because of repeated purchases, decreases? Assume a consumer has this value for p_A; what is his expected number of purchases before he buys A for the first time? How will his p_A change during that time?

d. Assume a consumer has initially a p_A of 0.5. If one considers his next three purchases, eight patterns are possible: AAA, AAB, ABA, ABB, BAA, BAB, BAA, BBB. What is the probability of occurrence of each of these patterns? What would be the final p_A for each of the patterns? Would you say that the situation of having a p_A equal to 0.5 is stable?

e. Given the results of parts b, c, and d, try to give an intuitive answer to the following question. Suppose we make a histogram of the distribution of initial p_A's over the population. Which one of the following three patterns is more likely to appear? Why?

H_1

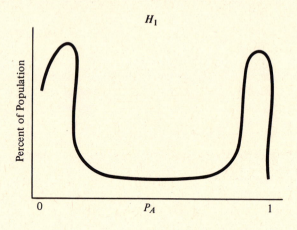

H_2

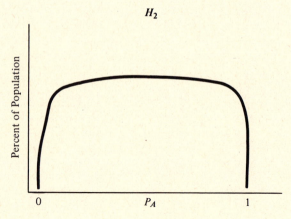

H_3

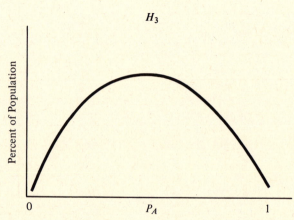

    f. The basic assumption of the heterogeneous Bernoulli model is that each consumer has a constant p_A (the p_A's being different from consumer to consumer). Considering your answers to parts b, c, and d, would you say that it is frequent, or not, for a consumer to have a constant p_A during several successive purchases? How well should a heterogeneous Bernoulli model be expected to fit if the true process is a linear learning model and vice versa?

7.10 Analysis of panel data for a breakfast cereal reveals that the penetration for the given brand over a 4-wk period is 0.04 and the average number of purchases per buyer is 1.6.

    a. We know that the proportion of nonbuyers in the population over the period for the NBD is

$$p_0 = \left(1 + \frac{m}{k}\right)^{-k}$$

We have observed that $p_0 = 1 - 0.04 = 0.96$ and $m = bw = 0.04(1.6) = 0.064$. Estimate k by approximation.

    b. A heavy buyer is defined as one who purchases twice or more during the period. Estimate the proportion of heavy buyers and proportion of sales due to heavy buyers.

    c. Taking 4 wk as the time unit, compute the predicted penetration of the brand over 24 wk. Compare with the observed value, 9%.

    d. Consider two periods of 24 wk each. Estimate the proportion of new buyers, consumers who do not buy the brand during the first 24-wk period and who buy it at least once during the next 24-wk period. What is the predicted average number of purchases of the brand per new buyer over the period of 24 wk? Compare with the observed value, 1.4.

7.11 Consider two competing brands X and Y. It is observed that over a quarter their penetrations are 42% for brand X and 6% for brand Y. The average numbers of purchases per buyer of the brand are 3.7 for brand X and 2.5 for brand Y.

    a. Over a year, what are the predicted penetrations of brands X and Y?

    b. Over a year, what are the predicted number of purchases per buyer of brands X and Y?

    c. Over a year, what is the predicted ratio of sales of brand X and brand Y?

7.12 Compare Bettman's model, the linear learning model, the logit model, and the Fishbein model as models of consumer behavior. First define an analytic need, evaluate the models along your criteria, and compare them. For what purposes might each model be best?

Organizational-Buying Models

To market effectively to organizations (rather than to consumers), one must understand the way organizations buy. Organizational purchasing reflects a complex set of activities engaged in by many members of the buying organizations, including information search and acquisition processes, the development of choice criteria, and, finally, supplier choice and ultimate purchase, which become the same event. Much work has appeared in the literature on particular aspects of organizational buying (vendor-selection criteria, source loyalty, etc.), which, along with more-general models or conceptual frameworks, are applicable to a wide variety of organizations, regardless of objectives, ownership, or organizational structure.

Organizational and consumer buying behavior have two attributes in common: a purchase is the usual outcome of the process and the decision is a result of decision-making activities. Because of these similarities, some naive attempts have been made to apply the same structures and concepts to organizational buying as to consumer buying. However, in spite of this superficial similarity, organizational buying must be handled differently from consumer buying for several important reasons.

First, organizational demand is *derived* demand. Products are purchased by organizations to meet the needs of their customers. Impulse buying is far less common; objective criteria—such as meeting production needs and schedules with a minimum-cost product—often drive the choice process.

Second, more than one individual and, often, many individuals are involved in the purchasing-decision process; as Wind (1976) points out, purchasing managers rarely make a buying decision independent of the influence of others in the organization.

Third, because of (1) the often high dollar volume involved, (2) the number of individuals affected, and (3) the technical nature of the products under consideration, the purchasing process may take a long time. This extended purchase process, which may take months (or sometimes even years), makes it difficult to determine a functional relationship between marketing effort and buyer response.

Finally, as Hudson (1971) and others have noted, organizational buyers are not as interested in a physical product as in the satisfaction of a total need. Thus the offering may include such items as technical support, training, delivery dates, and financial terms. This method of satisfying the total need is part of the trend toward systems selling (Mattssons, 1973).

Thus to analyze marketing opportunities when customers are other organizations requires an understanding of organizational-buying behavior. In other words, to make effective use of industrial-marketing resources requires an understanding of (1) *who* is involved in the purchasing process, (2) *how* they buy (i.e., what the stages of the process are and how the individuals involved influence one another), and (3) *why* they buy (what the forces influencing the decisions are and what the relative significance of those forces is).

Two types of models of organizational buying have appeared in the literature:

1. **Models of elements of organizational buying.** Because of the complexity of organizational buying and the difficulty involved in developing operational models of the processes, research in the field has often had limited objectives, looking at one or another aspect of the process. Although limited in scope and approach, these studies provide specific results that can support certain decisions for sales and marketing managers.

2. **Integrative models of organizational buying.** Several models that attempt to structure the whole organizational-buying process have appeared in the literature in the last few years. The value of these models varies from providing conceptual insight to supplying operational results for marketing management.

In this chapter we review these models and briefly summarize other work in the field, concluding with a perspective on future developments.

The Structure of Organizational Buying

Group Influence

A number of empirical studies (Buckner, 1967; *Scientific American,* 1970) have clearly and effectively demonstrated that a single decision maker does *not* exist. Rather, a number of individuals influence the purchase decision.

EXAMPLE: A survey performed by *Purchasing Magazine* (1965), of 603 chemical-industry purchasing executives showed that the purchasing agent *alone* chose the source of supply in only 13% of the cases. In 10% of the cases the purchasing agent was not even involved! Across the sample the average number of personnel involved in purchase decisions was about five, but in a

EXHIBIT 8-1   Modeling the stages of the organizational-buying process.

Robinson and Faris (1967)	Ozanne and Churchill (1971)	Webster and Wind (1972)	Kelley (1974)	Bradley (1977)	Wind (1978a)
1. Problem (need) recognition	1. Awareness	1. Identify needs	1. Recognize need	1. Purchase initiation	1. Identification of needs
2. Determine characteristics		2. Establish specifications			2. Establish specifications
3. Describe characteristics					
4. Search for sources	2. Interest	3. Identify alternatives	2. Information search	2. Survey of alternatives	3. Search for alternatives
5. Acquire proposals					4. Establish contact
6. Evaluate proposals	3. Evaluation	4. Evaluate alternatives	3. Evaluate alternatives	3. Supplier short listing	5. Set purchase and usage criteria
					6. Evaluate alternatives
			4. Approval of funds		7. Budget availability
					8. Evaluate specific alternatives
					9. Negotiate
7. Select order routine	4. Trial	5. Select supplier	5. Decision	4. Award contract	10. Buy
	5. Adoption				11. Use
8. Performance feedback					12. Postpurchase evaluation

SOURCE: Wind and Thomas, 1980, p. 7.

few cases over 50 people were involved. [See also Harding (1966) and O'Rourke, Shea, and Solley (1973)].

Owing to the number of individuals involved and the resultant complexity of the buying process, a number of researchers have tried to structure organizational buying by the phases and the roles played by individuals in the process. The steps involved have been characterized by a number of authors in somewhat different ways, as shown in Exhibit 8.1. The stages are shown sequentially, although in some purchase situations two or more stages occur simultaneously. In other cases a number of partial or complete iterations may occur before a choice of suppliers is made. In fact, the purchasing process has been characterized by Goodman (1971) as one of "creeping commitment," a series of incremental choices that gradually reduce the number of alternatives.

Another analytical result of the multiperson nature of the buying process has been the concept of the *buying center*. A buying center, which includes all organizational members involved in a purchase situation, is an "informal, cross-sectional decision unit in which the primary objective is the acquisition, importation and processing of relevant purchasing-related information" (Spekman and Stern, 1979, p. 56).

Throughout the procurement process different members of the buying center assume different roles; these roles include users, influencers, buyers, deciders, and gatekeepers (Webster and Wind, 1972, pp. 77–80). In a particular organization one individual might assume all the roles, while in another a separate individual might assume each different role.

Fisher (1969) has proposed a simple model for integrating the factors influencing the buying process and the degree of involvement of different functional areas of the firm. In his model, illustrated in Exhibit 8.2, commercial uncertainty increases with the size of the investment, the average order size, the time space of the commitment, the potential effect on profit, and the ease of forecasting the effect of the purchase. Product complexity increases with the degree of custom ordering of the product, the technological sophistication of the product, the shortness of previous-

EXHIBIT 8-2   **Nature of involvement in the purchasing-decision process.**

		Product Complexity	
		High	Low
Commercial	**High**	All-individuals involved	Top-management involvement
Uncertainty	**Low**	Engineering functions involved	Procurement involvement

SOURCE: Drawn from Fisher, 1969, p. 25.

purchase history, the newness of the product, the importance of after-sales service, and the difficulty of installation.

In a recent study Lilien and Wong (1981) developed a model of the buying center in the metalworking industries, quantifying and clarifying some of these qualitative hypotheses.

Buying Situations

Three types of buying situations have been delineated by Robinson and Faris (1967): (1) the new task, (2) the straight rebuy, and (3) the modified rebuy. The individuals involved in the buying-decision process are likely to vary depending on the type of purchase situation (Brand, 1972).

In new-task situations the problem or need is perceived by members of the buying center to be different from past experiences. A significant amount of information is required, and the organizational decision makers undertake extensive problem-solving activities (Howard and Sheth, 1969).

On the other hand, a straight-rebuy situation involves a continuing or recurring requirement. The buyers have substantive experience dealing with the need and require little or no new information. The approach that most purchasing organizations take in these situations is called routinized-response behavior, where organizational buyers have well-developed choice criteria that can be applied to the purchase decision.

A modified-rebuy situation is one in which organizational buyers feel that significant benefits could be derived from a reevaluation of alternatives, and it is most likely to occur when a firm is displeased with the performance of its current suppliers. Buyers have relevant experience in satisfying the continuing or recurring requirement but believe it may be worthwhile to seek additional information before a decision is made. The decision-making process here is best described as limited problem solving.

Individual Forces

Individuals, not organizations, make decisions. Therefore attention must be given to individual behavior within the buying center. Each member of the buying center has a unique personality, a different organizational function, and a different set of personal goals and objectives. Thus each individual will hold different perceptions of the same buying situation. According to Sheth (1973b), industrial-product users generally value prompt delivery and efficient service; engineering personnel value product quality, standardization of the product, and product pretesting; while purchasing personnel assign the most importance to maximum price advantage and economy in shipping and forwarding. Where multiple individuals are involved with different preferences and perceptions, marketing management must satisfy these individuals simultaneously.

Models of Elements of Organizational Buying

It is not surprising that the complexity of organizational buying has led many researchers to focus on single aspects of it. In this section we consider two such aspects: supplier selection and loyalty source.

Supplier Selection

Lehmann and O'Shaughnessy (1974) performed a study of the relative importance of 17 attributes of the purchasing situation among a sample of 19 United States and 26 United Kingdom companies. However, they focus on the purchasing agent and therefore limit use of their results to those situations where a purchasing agent has primary influence in purchasing decisions.

The study provided a set of attribute-importance weights (w_i) for a vendor-selection model of the following sort:

$$\text{Supplier score} = \sum_{i=1}^{I} w_i R_i \qquad (8.1)$$

where R_i is a supplier's score on attribute i.

Seventeen attribute dimensions, listed in Exhibit 8.3, were considered for evaluation. The authors assumed that the relative importance of the product and supplier attributes varies by the product type, and they classified products on the premise that purchasing agents would weight

EXHIBIT 8-3   Seventeen attributes rated by purchasing agents.

1. Overall reputation of the supplier
2. Financing terms
3. Supplier's flexibility in adjusting to your company's needs
4. Experience with the supplier in analogous situations
5. Technical service offered
6. Confidence in the salesmen
7. Convenience of placing the order
8. Data on reliability of the product
9. Price
10. Technical specifications
11. Ease of operation or use
12. Preferences of principal user of the product
13. Training offered by the supplier
14. Training time required
15. Reliability of delivery date promised
16. Ease of maintenance
17. Sales service expected after date of purchase

SOURCE: Lehmann and O'Shaughnessy, 1974, p. 38.

attributes to minimize problems associated with adoption. Their product classification is as follows:

Type I: Routine-order products. These products are frequently ordered and used. There is no problem in learning to use the product nor is there any question about whether the product will work.

Type II: Procedural-problem products. For these products there is no question that the product will do the job, but personnel must be trained to use the product.

Type III: Performance-problem products. These products are characterized by doubt about whether the product will perform adequately in the application considered.

Type IV: Political-problem products. For these products there is difficulty in reaching agreement on product choice among those affected. They are often associated with large capital outlays and are frequently inputs to several departments.

Each respondent was asked to rate, on a six-point semantic-differential scale, the relative importance of each of the 17 attributes in choosing a supplier for the four product types. Exhibit 8.4 gives the resulting average scores. Clearly, the importance of the various attributes varies by product type. For example, price is the most important attribute for type IV, political products (apparently as a tie-breaking criterion), but is only eighth in importance for type III products, those with performance problems; technical service is critical for types II and III but less important for other products. However, there is consistency across product types: "... all ... suppliers should place heavy emphasis on reliability of delivery. Purchasing agents ... will favor the source which always delivers as promised" (Lehmann and O'Shaughnessy, 1974, pp. 41–42).

Although limited to purchasing agents and including no test for external validity (do these weights reproduce *actual* choice?), the analysis reveals important issues for supplier selection, particularly reliability of delivery. More generally, the analysis shows that a model-based development of marketing strategy must be tuned to the situation—that the elements of importance will vary dramatically depending on the buyers' perceptions of problems presented by the purchase situation. The results of this study are generally consistent with those reported elsewhere, particularly those of Banville and Dornaff (1973) and Saleh and LaLonde (1972).

Source Loyalty

In a model that eventually became a component of the Webster and Wind (1972) model, reviewed in the next section, Wind (1970) explains industrial source loyalty. Operationally, source loyalty is the proportion of purchases

EXHIBIT 8-4 **Average attribute importance for the four product types.**

	Product Type[a]							
	I		II		III		IV	
Attribute	Mean	Rank	Mean	Rank	Mean	Rank	Mean	Rank
1. Reputation	4.84 (1.09)	4	5.33 (0.80)	7	5.29 (0.82)	5	5.53 (0.69)	2
2. Financing	4.51 (1.39)	9	4.07 (1.29)	16	3.91 (1.31)	16	4.91 (1.24)	13
3. Flexibility	5.07 (1.12)	3	5.40 (0.62)	5	5.42 (0.62)	2	5.51 (0.59)	5
4. Past experience	4.71 (0.94)	6	4.93 (0.86)	13	5.07 (0.69)	9	5.04 (0.93)	10
5. Technical service	4.36 (1.28)	12	5.53 (0.66)	1	5.38 (0.89)	3	5.40 (0.62)	7
6. Confidence in salesmen	3.96 (1.35)	14	4.73 (12.3)	15	4.42 (1.20)	15	4.58 (1.20)	16
7. Convenience in ordering	3.80 (1.32)	15	3.73 (1.29)	17	3.71 (1.34)	17	4.08 (1.24)	17
8. Reliability data	4.47 (1.24)	11	5.16 (1.07)	11	5.33 (0.67)	4	5.53 (0.59)	3
9. Price	5.60 (0.62)	2	5.29 (0.70)	8	5.18 (0.94)	8	5.56 (0.69)	1
10. Technical specifications	4.73 (1.25)	5	5.22 (0.67)	9	5.27 (0.69)	6	5.42 (0.72)	6
11. Ease of use	4.51 (1.29)	10	5.53 (0.59)	2	5.24 (0.80)	7	5.18 (0.83)	8
12. Preference of user	4.00 (1.19)	13	4.76 (1.11)	14	4.53 (1.14)	13	4.84 (0.90)	14
13. Training offered	3.22 (1.18)	16	5.42 (0.87)	3	4.73 (1.19)	12	5.00 (0.83)	11
14. Training required	3.22 (1.22)	17	5.11 (1.23)	12	4.44 (1.22)	14	4.69 (1.02)	15
15. Reliability of delivery	5.64 (0.53)	1	5.42 (0.72)	4	5.44 (0.66)	1	5.53 (0.69)	4
16. Maintenance	4.60 (1.05)	8	5.20 (0.69)	10	4.82 (0.96)	11	5.00 (0.74)	12
17. Sales service	4.64 (1.25)	7	5.36 (0.77)	6	5.07 (0.84)	10	5.09 (0.70)	9
Product Type Mean	4.46		5.07		4.90		5.11	

[a]Values given are mean (standard deviation).

SOURCE: Lehmann and O'Shaughnessy, 1974, p. 39.

from a given supplier. Managerially, however, it can be interpreted as a sense of commitment to a brand or supplier.

Wind hypothesized that loyalty was a function of four major sets of variables:

1. task variables: price, quality, delivery, service
2. the buyer's past experience with the various sources (assumed to be summarized in his attitude toward various sources)
3. organizational variables, such as pressure for cost savings or number of complaints
4. work-simplification variables: those factors perceived by the buyer as simplifying his task

Exhibit 8.5 reproduces Wind's conceptualization of the determinants of source loyalty. Operationally, the variables used in his model are as follows:

Task Variables
1. price of favorite source relative to others
2. price at time *t* relative to previous price

Past Experience
1. attitude toward source relative to ideal
2. attitude toward source relative to other sources

Organization Variables
1. dollar value of an order
2. current, relative divisional cost savings
3. cumulative divisional cost savings

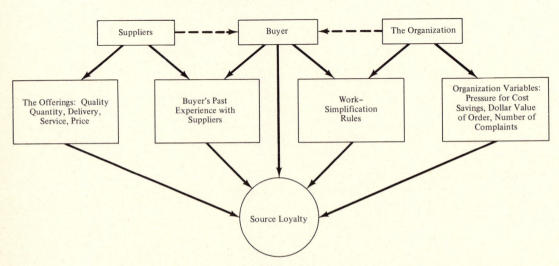

EXHIBIT 8-5   **A simplified model of industrial source loyalty.** (Source: Wind, 1970, p. 451.)

4. recommendation of brand by user
5. buyer identification (used to identify whether a buyer changed when a source changed)

Work-Simplification Variables
1. change of supplier to a geographically closer source
2. previous-purchase history—purchase inertia

It is somewhat puzzling that price is the only task variable included. In fact, Wind states: "[other task variables] do not determine which suppliers will be selected" (p. 451). This omission may not be too serious because the attitudinal and work-simplification variables pick up the effect of delivery and terms. The latter variables are justified by the hypotheses that buyers prefer suppliers who are nearby and will stay with a favored source unless there is strong pressure to shift.

Wind operationalized his model as a multiple-regression equation:

$$SL = a_0 + \sum_{i=1}^{I} a_i F_i \tag{8.2}$$

where

SL = number of purchases from the favorite source as a percentage of the total number of purchases from all sources

F_i = task, past-experience, organizational, and work-simplification variables

$a_0, a_1, \ldots$ = regression coefficients

Attitudinal data were collected from buyers at an advanced-electronics firm. In addition, purchase-history cards and weekly cost-savings memos were coded for 394 data-point transactions. An initial set of regressions led to the best reduced model, which included all statistically significant variables, shown in Exhibit 8.6.

Although this study has some definitional and methodological problems (the bounded dependent variable leads to some problems, and multicollinearity and heteroscedasticity were reported as significant difficulties), the results are quite clear. At least in this industry—electronics—products characterized by low price and high cost savings have high levels of loyalty. User specification, positive attitudes toward the supplier, and a previous history of buying the product from the given supplier are important as well.

Another interesting look at the importance of loyalty in the supplier-choice process was reported by Bubb and van Rest (1973), who developed a model of the supplier-choice process on the basis of their experience with European companies purchasing a new material. They proposed a hierarchical model in which a list of acceptable suppliers is evaluated with supply criteria in sequence until only one is left. In about 30 percent of the decisions studied, loyalty was considered the first factor in the selection process—that is, it was the most important factor.

EXHIBIT 8-6   Regression-analysis results for source loyalty.

Variable Type	Independent Variable[a]	Standardized Regression Coefficient[b]
I. Task	Price relative to previous price	-0.315 (-3.08)
II. Attitudinal	Attitude toward a given source relative to other sources	0.191 (3.73)
III. Organizational	Dollar value of the order	-0.224 (-2.68)
	Divisional cost saving relative to savings of other divisions	0.343 (4.54)
	Recommendation of brand by user	0.204 (3.82)
IV. Work Simplification	Previous-purchase history	0.131 (2.59)

[a]Dependent variable = number of purchases from favored source as percentage of purchases from all sources.

[b]$R^2 = 0.94$; $F = 70.27$; t statistic in parentheses.

SOURCE: Wind, 1970, p. 453.

Large-System Models of Organizational Buying

Webster (1979) cites three general models of the organizational-buying decision process, which are described below. These models focus on the entire process and are applicable to a wide spectrum of industrial products. As simplifications of the true process, they identify the most important variables and suggest the relationships between these variables. The first two of these models, the Sheth model and the Webster-Wind model, are similar in structure and goals to the large-system models described in the previous chapter.

The Sheth Model

Sheth (1973b) has adapted the Howard-Sheth model of consumer buying behavior for industrial organizations. It is an overall model, focusing on the important elements in the decision process and their interactions. The form of the model, shown in Exhibit 8.7, is a block or flow model in which the variables and their effects are suggested, but functional relationships are not identified.

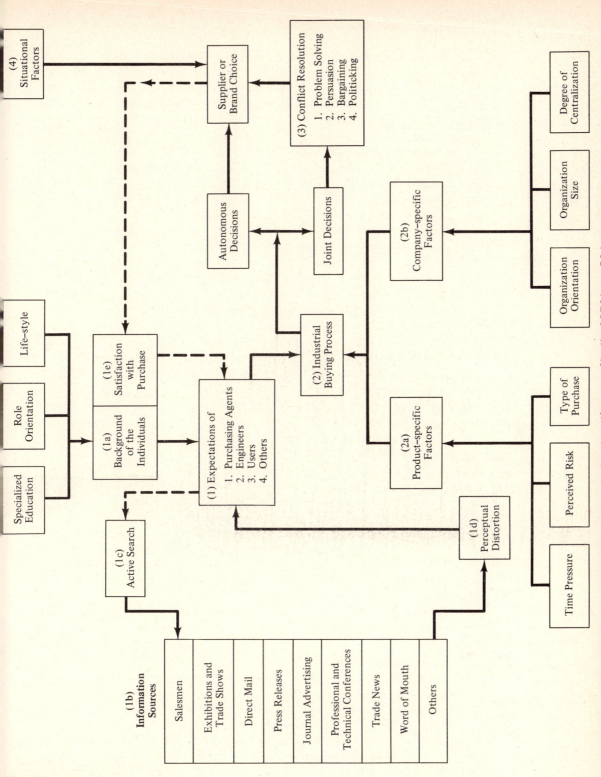

EXHIBIT 8-7   Sheth's model of Industrial-buyer behavior. (Source: Sheth, 1973*b*, p. 51.)

The model assumes there are three major elements in the organizational-buying process: (1) the so-called psychological world of the individuals involved in the buying process, (2) the conditions that precipitate joint decision making, and (3) when the purchasing process is a joint decision, the process of conflict resolution. In addition, Sheth identifies situational factors that influence the final choice of supplier or brand.

Psychological Characteristics.   A primary component of the psychological aspect of the Sheth model is the concept of expectations, which he defines as "the perceived potential of alternative suppliers and brands to satisfy a number of explicit and implicit objectives in any particular buying situation" (p. 52). Because many individuals, including the purchasing agent, may be involved in the buying process, Sheth identifies several factors that cause individual members of the buying process to hold different expectations. These include the background of the individuals, their information sources, their individual attempts at active search, perceptual distortions, and satisfaction with past purchases.

Background variables include education, role orientation, and lifestyle. Sheth notes that different educational backgrounds of the purchasing agents, engineers, and plant managers may generate substantially different goals and values. This view is consistent with that of Scott and Wright (1976), who show that different individuals often use different buying criteria to select and evaluate their purchase decisions.

Sheth's second and third factors, information sources and search processes, create unique expectations among buying-center members. This concept is consistent with the notion of the gatekeeping function or the delegation of responsibility to certain individuals to search and gather relevant information. The fourth factor, perceptual distortion, is the interpretation of incoming information by individuals to make it consistent with their existing knowledge and beliefs. The last factor, satisfaction with past purchases, causes different expectations among the individuals involved; for example, production personnel may have been pleased with the performance of a previously purchased item, but purchasing personnel may believe it was too costly.

Joint Decision Making.   Sheth distinguishes between purchasing processes that involve only one individual and those that involve a group of people. The number of persons involved is determined from factors classified as either product-specific—time pressure, perceived risk, and type of purchase—or company-specific—company orientation and size and degree of centralization. According to the model, the more nonroutine the purchase, the higher the perceived risk, and the less the time pressure, the more likely it is that the decision process will include more people. Similarly, the larger the organization and the more highly centralized the organizational structure, the more likely is joint decision making.

Conflict Resolution.   The process of conflict resolution is relevant in a joint-decision-making process when goals, perceptions, and value systems vary. Following completion of early phases of the buying process, including need identification, information gathering, and evaluation of suppliers, the participants will become involved in a conflict-resolving task. Sheth posits two types of rational conflict resolution: problem solving, in which information acquisition and deliberation play key roles, and persuasion, where an attempt is made to influence dissenting members by highlighting incongruities between purchase criteria and overall corporate goals. Both of these techniques can be utilized when all parties agree on goals and objectives. However, when fundamental differences exist, trade-offs and bargaining may be necessary, and when disagreement in goals and objectives is coupled with disagreement on decision-making styles, conflict resolution may only result from politicking. These approaches are both nonrational methods of conflict resolution and are likely to negatively affect the organization. Therefore, a problem-solving approach is generally preferred.

Finally, Sheth notes that ad hoc situational factors, beyond the control of participants, such as changes in economic conditions, reorganization, and strikes, may influence the purchasing decision.

Webster-Wind Model

A key contribution of the Webster-Wind (1972a,b) model is its view of organizational-buying behavior as a special case of organizational decision making. In their view a buying situation is created when members of the organization perceive a problem that can be solved through purchasing action. To address the buying problem, then, they introduce the concept of a buying center, which consists of those members of the organization who will be involved in the buying-decision process.

Webster and Wind's model, represented in block-diagram form in Exhibit 8.8, considers four sets of variables: environmental factors (E), organizational factors (D), group factors (G), and individual factors (I), all influencing buying behavior (B):

$$B = f(I, G, D, E) \tag{8.3}$$

These four sets of variables are developed as follows:

1. *Environmental factors* include legal, cultural, technological, economic, and physical-environment variables, serving primarily as constraints on action. These variables are assessed to affect general business conditions, as well as the flow of marketing information.
2. *Organizational characteristics*, given special prominence in this model, are divided into four sets of variables: technology, structure, goals and tasks, and actors. Technology affects what is purchased and the nature of the buying process itself. Organizational structure is defined in terms of five subsystems—communication, authority, status, reward, and

work flow—that shape the buying process. Goals and tasks are associated with the phases of the decision process and the possible roles of the actors involved.

3. *Interpersonal variables* are defined within the structure of the buying center. These variables include task (related to the specific buying

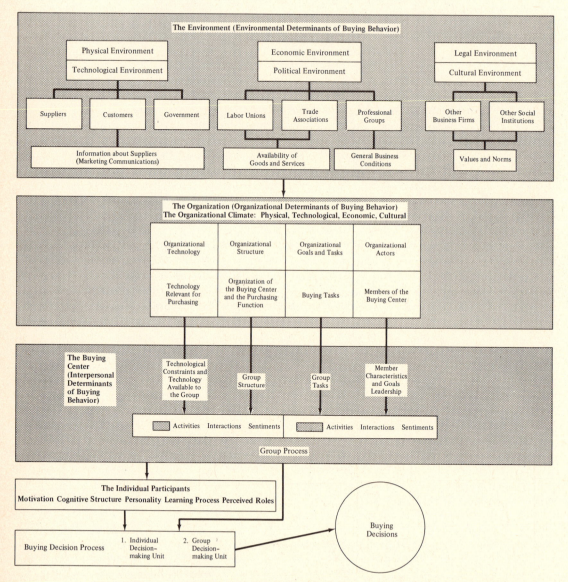

EXHIBIT 8-8   **A model of organizational-buying behavior. (**Source: Frederick E. Webster, Jr., Yoran Wind, *Organizational Buying Behavior,* © 1972, p. 15. Adapted by permission of Prentice-*Hall, Inc.* Englewood Cliffs, N.J.)

situation) as well as nontask variables (related to the general structuring and functioning of the group).

4. *Individual variables* are critical, since Webster and Wind assert that in the final analysis all organizational-buying behavior is individual behavior. The variables affecting the individual's decision process include motivation, cognitive structure, personality, learning, perceived roles, and preference structure.

In evaluating a product, Webster and Wind realize that the organizational buyer makes a decision over multiple attributes. They examine several classes of decision models—conjunctive, disjunctive, lexicographic, and compensatory—and conclude that buyers may use any one of them in their individual decision processes.

The strength of the Webster-Wind model—its generality—is its weakness as well. The model attempts to be comprehensive and thus, like the Sheth model, is weak on the specifications of the relationships between key variables and on the measurements needed to make the model operational. In addition, neither model clearly states the special role of marketing variables and the way those variables can change buyer behavior. The key contributions of both these models, then, are their identification of key variables and relationships and the stimulus they have provided for the development and understanding of high-quality research in the field.

The Choffray-Lilien Model*

Building upon the important conceptual work described above, Choffray and Lilien developed a model of the organizational adoption process for new capital equipment. Relative to the Webster-Wind and Sheth models, it is short and simple, focusing on those variables with a consistent, major influence across decision classes and organizations.

The model deals explicitly with the links between the characteristics of an organization's buying center and the major stages in the industrial-purchasing decision process through the following:

1. the elimination of evoked product alternatives that do not meet organizational requirements
2. the formation of decision participants' preferences
3. the formation of organizational preferences and choices

It handles three types of customer heterogeneity:

1. **Need-specification heterogeneity.** Potential-customer organizations may differ in their need-specification dimensions, that is, the criteria used to specify requirements. For example, company A uses payback period as a criterion, while company B uses initial cost only. Further-

*Much of the material in this section is drawn from Choffray and Lilien (1980c)

more, they may also differ in their specific requirements: company A requires a 3-yr payback, while company C finds 4 yr satisfactory.

2. **Buying-center heterogeneity.**   Potential customers may differ in the composition of their buying centers. Who is involved? What are their responsibilities? For instance, company A has a purchasing agent and an engineer involved in the buying process for industrial cooling equipment, where the engineer screens alternatives and the purchasing agent buys. Meanwhile, in company B top management is also involved.

3. **Evaluation-criteria heterogeneity.**   Decision participants may differ in their sources of information, as well as in the number and nature of the criteria they use to assess alternatives: engineers are concerned about reliability, while purchasing agents are concerned about price.

The consideration of these sources of heterogeneity requires members of the buying center be grouped. To this end, the model assumes the following:

1. Within potential-customer organizations the composition of the buying center can be characterized by the job categories of participants involved in the purchasing process.

2. Decision participants who belong to the same job category share the same set of product-evaluation criteria and the same information sources.

The operational sequence of measurements and models are specified in Exhibit 8.9. The first two stages define the market technically and perform a first-level segmentation, called macrosegmentation, which characterizes organizations likely to react differently to the product offering because of their industry or other observable characteristics.

The next step is called microsegmentation. Here macrosegments are divided into smaller groups with similar decision-process structure. A survey tool, called a decision matrix, is used to measure the involvement of different categories of individuals in a particular organization at each stage of the purchasing procedure. Organizations with similar structures across individuals and decision-process phases are clustered together. A procedure for performing these tasks is discussed in Chapter 9.

Following this target-market definition, there are five submodels: an awareness model, a feasibility model, an individual-choice model, a group-choice model, and a growth model. The procedure assumes that organizations in a microsegment (having similar decision-making units) use the same dimensions for screening product alternatives. Similarly, the model assumes that individuals with similar backgrounds and job responsibilities structure preferences in the same manner.

Stated analytically, the probability that product a_0 in evoked set A is the organization's choice at time t (given that the organization is in the market to

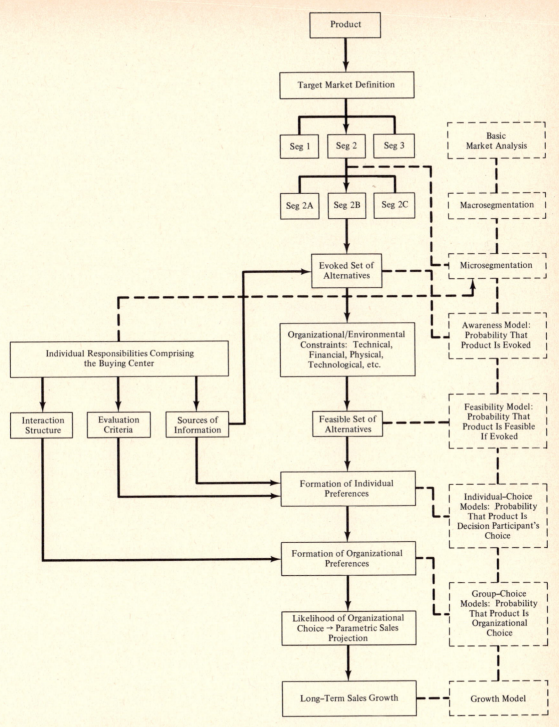

EXHIBIT 8-9   **General structure of industrial-market-analysis model.** (Source: Choffray and Lilien, 1980*c*, p. 36.)

purchase a product in the class) can be written as

$p(a_0 = \text{organizational choice})$

$$= p(a_0 = \text{group choice}\,|\,\text{interaction, feasible, evoked}) \qquad (8.4)$$
$$\times\ p(a_0 = \text{feasible}\,|\,\text{evoked}) \times p(a_0 = \text{evoked})$$

The Awareness Submodel. The awareness model links the level of marketing support for product a_0—measured in terms of spending rates for activities such as personal selling, technical service, and advertising—to the probability that a decision participant belonging to category i (say production and maintenance engineers) will evoke a_0 as a potential solution to the organizational-purchasing problem. Let $p_i(a_0 = \text{evoked})$ denote this probability. Hence we postulate that

$p_i(a_0 = \text{evoked}) = f_i(\text{marketing spending})$

$$\text{for } i = 1, \dots, \text{number of categories}$$

When several decision-participant categories are involved in the purchasing process, the probability that product a_0 will be evoked as an alternative is the probability that at least one member of the buying center will evoke it. Thus,

$$p_G(a_0 = \text{evoked}) = 1 - \prod_i [1 - p_i(a_0 = \text{evoked})] \qquad (8.5)$$

where index i covers all decision-participant categories in the purchasing process of the organization's microsegment. (This equation assumes independence, and the model form can be relaxed.) The functional form of each of the awareness functions $f_i(\cdot)$'s can be either derived empirically through a field study or provided by the product manager judgmentally.

The Feasibility Submodel. The feasibility model accounts for the process by which organizations eliminate products outside their range of acceptability. They do so by setting bounds on price, criteria for reliability, specifications on the number of successful prior installations, minimum values for payback periods, and so forth.

Development and calibration of the market acceptance or feasibility function assumes the following:

1. There exist a number of need-specification dimensions for screening new-product alternatives, which are either continuous (cost must be less than $X) or discrete (product must contain feature Y) variables. For a given company only a subset of these dimensions may be relevant.
2. For relevant dimensions, organizations are capable of specifying either the minimum or maximum acceptable level of their requirements on a continuous specification or whether or not a discrete feature is required.

Let

$$\mathbf{X} = \{X_j\} = X_1, \ldots, X_{J_d} = \text{set of need-specification dimensions}$$

where $j = 1, \ldots, J_c$ are continuous dimensions

$j = J_{c+1}, \ldots, J_d$ are discrete dimensions

Then the set of dimensions $j = 1, \ldots, J_d$ is an exhaustive set of dimensions relevant for product choice in the class. Thus,

X_{ij} = maximum or minimum value of dimension j acceptable to organization i for $j = 1, \ldots, J_c$

$$= \begin{cases} 1 & \text{if company } i \text{ requires discrete attribute } j, \text{ for } j = J_{c+1}, \ldots, J_d \\ 0 & \text{otherwise} \end{cases}$$

If we assume a sample population of potential buying organizations, then our problem is to determine

$g(\mathbf{X}^0)$ = proportion of organizations that find product design

$$\mathbf{X}^0 \text{ acceptable} \qquad (8.6)$$

For a particular organization a product is acceptable if it satisfies all of its requirements. Hence $\mathbf{X}^0$ is acceptable if and only if

$$X_1^0 < X_{i1}, X_2^0 < X_{i,2}, \ldots, X_{J_c}^0 < X_{iJ_c} \qquad (8.7)$$

(We can assume that X_{ij} is a maximum value without loss of generality.) Note that for $j = J_{c+1}, \ldots, J_d$, an acceptable product design $\mathbf{X}^0$ is of the form $X_j^0 = 1$ if X^0 contains attribute j and if

$$\sum_{j \in \Delta^0} X_{ij} = 0 \qquad (8.8)$$

where Δ^0 = set of all discrete criteria that the product does not possess

(Note that if $\sum_{j \in \Delta^0} X_{ij} > 0$, the company requires at least one attribute the product does not possess.)

At the organization level, acceptance of a product alternative follows a conjunctive decision rule. The purpose of the acceptance function is to approximate the process probabilistically for a segment of potential-customer organizations.

Let $x_{r\ell}$ be the level of dimension ℓ for design r, and let $t_\ell(x_{r\ell})$ be the fraction of organizations finding $x_{r\ell}$ acceptable, independent of other dimensions. Then market or segment response is modeled as

$$T(\mathbf{x}_r) = \alpha \prod_{\ell=0}^{n} [t_\ell(x_{r\ell})]^{\alpha_\ell} \qquad (8.9)$$

where α_ℓ, $\ell = 0, \ldots, n$, are parameters to be estimated and T is the fraction of the market finding $\mathbf{x}_r$ acceptable.

This approach allows development of complex market-response models that are nonlinear in design features and parameters. High-level interactions among design options may be tested and their impact on market acceptance assessed. Furthermore, the procedure can be adapted to group organizations with similar buying criteria and can be modified to account for measurement errors. [For details, see Choffray and Lilien (1982).]

Individual-Evaluation Submodel.   As noted in the previous chapter, a prevailing model of the individual-choice process proceeds through stages from perception to evaluation, to preference, and to choice.

In industrial-purchasing situations, product-perception differences are likely to occur among decision participants because of differences in background and job responsibilities (Sheth, 1973b; Choffray and Lilien, 1980c). Consideration of these differences is important in developing carefully targeted communication programs.

Evaluation deals with the reduction of a perceptual space to a subspace of a lower dimension, whose axes represent basic performance dimensions used by individuals to assess products in this class. An individual's evaluation of a new product's position may then be viewed as a point in this reduced space. For example, an individual may rate a product as a 7 on reliability and a 6 on quality. If analysis shows these dimensions are, in fact, similar, the product might be rated 6.5 on a joint dimension of reliability quality.

The identification of differences in evaluation criteria across decision-participant groups is important for understanding industrial-purchasing behavior. We would not expect production and maintenance engineers to use the same criteria as members of purchasing departments: engineers are more concerned with product reliability and efficiency, while purchasing officers are most concerned about cost. Factor analysis is usually used to perform this task.

Preference formation concerns the relationship between individual *i*'s evaluation of a product and his preference for it. Consider two individuals,

EXHIBIT 8-10   **Preference-formation example.**

	Engineer			Purchasing Agent		
	Reliability Score	Cost-Value Score	Preference Score[a]	Reliability Score	Cost-Value Score	Preference Score
Relative Importance	0.83	0.17		0.17	0.83	
Product A	6	2	5.33	3	3	3.00
Product B	3	3	3.00	4	2	2.33
Product C	1	5	1.67	1	4	3.50

[a]The higher the score, the better is the evaluation of the product.

SOURCE: Choffray and Lilien, 1980c, p. 115.

an engineer and a purchasing agent, evaluating three different products (A, B, and C). Assume that we have already determined their evaluation criteria and have developed composite rating scores. Exhibit 8.10 gives their evaluation scores and their stated product preferences.

Here we see that the engineer prefers the high-reliability product, but the purchasing agent likes the high-cost-value product. With statistical analysis across several engineers and purchasing agents, we determine that the relative importance of reliability to cost for the engineer is 5:1 (0.83/0.17 in Exhibit 8.10); the situation is reversed for purchasing agents. This type of result is very important for determining issues to be stressed in communications programs targeted at different groups.

Several industrial-marketing studies have addressed the relative power of models of decision participants' preference formation (Lavin, 1969; Scott and Bennett, 1971; Wildt and Bruno, 1974).

Finally, *choice* formation deals with the mapping of each participant's product preferences into an estimate of his likelihood of endorsing each. However, it is usually agreed that the higher an individual's preference for a product, the higher will be the probability that he will choose it when placed in a purchase situation. Again, the methods and models of Chapter 7 apply here.

Group-interaction Submodel.   There are frequently several individuals involved in the purchase of an industrial product, individuals who have their own preferences for organizationally feasible alternatives. Individual preferences then must be translated into organizational choices.

Empirical study of joint decision making has been difficult, since neither a theoretical framework nor research tools in marketing appear geared to group-decision processes. As a result, marketing practitioners and researchers have generally considered group decision making as a process that cannot be observed or measured but that must be inferred from observations of response to specific marketing stimuli. There are no formal models for characterizing and understanding organizational-buying interaction, although some progress has been made in this direction (Krapfel, 1978 and Spekman, 1979).

Choffray and Lilien propose four models of group choice: the weighted-probability model, the voting model, the minimum-endorsement model, and the preference-perturbation model. We present the weighted-probability model in detail here for illustration.

The weighted-probability model assumes that the group, as a whole, is likely to adopt a given alternative, say a_0 in product class A, proportionally to the relative importance of those members who choose it. Let

$p_G(a_j)$ = probability that group chooses a_j

w_d = relative importance, on average, of decision participant d, $d = 1, \ldots, D$, in choice process for microsegment investigated

So

$$\sum_{d=1}^{D} w_d = 1$$

Then the weighted-probability model postulates that

$$p_G(a_0) = \sum_{d=1}^{D} w_d p_d(a_0) \tag{8.10}$$

This model can be interpreted as a two-step sampling process where, in step one, the organization samples a single decision maker from the set of decision participants in proportion to each participant's relative importance in the choice process. Then in step two, the retained decision maker selects an alternative according to his own choice probabilities, $p_d(a_j)$.

There are two interesting special cases of the weighted-probability model:

1. **Autocracy.** If $w_L = 1$, then all other $w_{i \neq L} = 0$, and a single participant L is the only one responsible for the group choice.
2. **Equiprobability.** If $w_d = 1/D$ for all d, then every decision participant has an equal chance of making the final decision.

The equiprobability form of the weighted-probability model has received some empirical support in dyadic decision making (Davis et al., 1973). Moreover, the model was found to accurately describe group-risk shifts (Davis, 1973).

Consider an organization with three decision participants (1, 2, and 3) and three alternatives, $A = \{a_0, a_1, a_2\}$, as shown in Exhibit 8.11. Then $p_G(a_0) = 0.2w_1 + 0.3w_2 + 0.7w_3$. An equiprobability model with $w_i = \frac{1}{3}$, $i = 1, 2, 3$, will yield $p_G(a_0) = 0.4$. An autocratic model with $w_1 = 1$ yields $p_G(a_0) = 0.2$; with $w_3 = 1$, it will yield $p_G(a_0) = 0.7$. These values are upper and lower bounds on $p_G(a_0)$ for the weighted-probability model. In terms of our example, $0.7 \geq p_G(a_0) \geq 0.2$.

Another group-interaction model, the voting model, attributes the same weight to all individuals involved in the decision process. It states that the probability that the organizations will choose an alternative among those feasible is equal to the probability that the alternative receives the endorse-

EXHIBIT 8-11   Example of individual-choice probabilities $p_d(a_j)$.

a_j	$p_1(a_j)$	$p_2(a_j)$	$p_3(a_j)$
a_0	0.2	0.3	0.7
a_1	0.5	0.2	0.2
a_2	0.3	0.5	0.1

ment (that is the vote) of the largest number or majority of decision participants.

The third model type, the minimum-endorsement model, assumes that to be accepted by a firm, a product alternative must be the choice of a prespecified number (quota) of participants involved in the process. Conceptually, the model considers interaction in the purchasing process as a dynamic voting scheme in which the participants vote over and over until the quota is reached.

Finally, the preference-perturbation model assumes that a group is most likly to choose the alternative that perturbs individual preferences least. The probability that a given product be chosen by a firm's buying center is inversely proportional to the number of preference shifts needed to make that alternative the first choice of every decision participant.

These four models correspond to different assumptions about group-choice behavior. However, they are not exhaustive, and many other models could be developed.

The Growth Submodel.   This model, in its present form, is static. It gives a prediction of the likely sales of a product if it were established in the marketplace. However, because of risk-averse purchasing behavior, the so-called word-of-mouth effect, and other factors, a marketer is unlikely to see these projected sales immediately. Therefore the model's output should be considered as the product's sales potential. The rate at which a new product grows toward its potential is discussed in Chapter 19 in the context of diffusion models.

Use of The Model.   Starting with the microsegmentation analysis, we can characterize each microsegment by a set of decision-participant categories, along with their relative involvement in the purchasing-decision process. Let these microsegments be represented by z, where $z = 1, \ldots, Z$, and the volume-weighted percentage of companies in the target market that fall in each of them by ψ_z, for $z = 1, \ldots, Z$.

The individual-choice models provide the distribution of individual-choice probabilities $p_d(a_j)$ for organizationally feasible alternatives within each category of decision participants.

Then for each microsegment the manager in charge of the new product specifies what models of multiperson interaction best reproduce his understanding of the adoption process. This method of judgmental calibration guarantees that the manager's prior knowledge of the market is incorporated in the market-assessment procedure. For segment z his estimates might be ω_{1z} for the weighted-probability model, ω_{2z} for the voting model, ω_{3z} for the minimum-endorsement model, and ω_{4z} for the preference-perturbation model, and $\Sigma_\ell \, \omega_{\ell z} = 1$. In a specific case one ω may be one and the rest zero, suggesting that the manager views that microsegment as homogeneous in terms of the interaction process taking place within potential-customer firms.

If we let $S_z(a_0)$ denote the estimated market share of microsegment z that finally adopts new products a_0, we get

$$S_z(a_0) = \sum_{\ell} \omega_{\ell z} p_G(a_0 | \ell)$$ (8.11)

where $p_G(a_0 | \ell)$ is the probability that a_0 is the organizational choice given interaction model ℓ.

Microsegment response can then be aggregated by computing

$$V(a_0) = V \sum_{z=1}^{Z} \psi_z S_z(a_0)$$ (8.12)

where V is total market potential.

EXAMPLE: The procedure above was used to assess the market potential for solar-powered cooling systems. The objective of the study was to determine (1) the current (and projected) market potential for solar-powered cooling systems, (2) the type of marketing programs most likely to be effective in supporting solar cooling, and (3) the performance solar cooling had to achieve to meet market needs.

Microsegmentation.   Analysis of the decision process in the participating companies led to the identification of four microsegments. Exhibit 8.12 gives the sizes of these microsegments, as well as the key decision participants in the equipment-selection phase of the decision process. Companies in segment 4 are smaller, more satisfied with their current cooling system, and more concerned with the economic aspects of cooling. They are characterized by a more frequent involvement of managerial functions and rely on external sources of expertise (HVAC, Heating, Ventilating and Air Conditioning consultants) to assist them. Segments 1 and 3 do not differ much by size of firm, but segment 3 companies have more plants, have larger cooling needs, and are more concerned with reliability of cooling than segment 1 is. Thus companies in segment 3 rely on engineering functions for air-conditioning assessment, while those in segment 1 rely on management functions. Finally, segment 2 consists of large companies with a small number of plants. Such companies tend to have decisions made at the plant level, as indicated by the high frequency of involvement of plant managers and engineers.

Market-potential assessment.   Discussions with decision makers in the industry suggested that the use of a weighted-probability model to evaluate the interaction process between participant categories would be generally acceptable. Thus to get conditional probability of choice given feasibility, we use the following equation:

$$p_G(a) = \sum_{i} w_i p_i(a)$$ (8.13)

EXHIBIT 8-12   **Microsegments of organizations in the potential market for solar air conditioning.**

Item	Segment 1	Segment 2	Segment 3	Segment 4
Microsegment size in potential market	12%	31%	32%	25%
Major decision participants in a/c equipment-selection decision (frequencies of involvement)	Plant managers (1.00) HVAC consultants (0.38)	Production engineers (0.94) Plant managers (0.70)	Production engineers (0.97) HVAC consultants (0.60)	Top management (0.85) HVAC consultants (0.67)
Satisfaction with current a/c system	Medium High	Low	Medium Low	High
Consequence if new a/c less economical than projected	Medium High	Low	Medium Low	High
Consequence if new a/c less reliable than projected	Medium High	Low	High	Medium low
Company size	Medium	Large	Large	Small
Percentage of plant area requiring a/c	Medium Large	Small	Large	Medium
Number of separate plants	Medium Large	Small	Large	Medium Small

NOTE: Abbreviation a/c means air conditioning.

where i = decision-participant category and $p_i(a)$ = fraction of responding individuals indicating first preference for solar. Exhibit 8.13 gives the conditional probability of group choice for each segment.

The model suggests putting these pieces together as

Penetration potential = choice level given feasibility

$\times$ feasibility given awareness $\times$ awareness

For awareness it was found that 15% of company people and 41% of HVAC consultants were aware of solar cooling. Thus the probability that the group will be aware is 1 − (no one is aware), or $1 - \Pi[1 - p(\text{aware})]$. Hence we get awareness by segment:

Segment 1: $1 - 0.85 \times 0.59 = 0.50$

Segment 2: $1 - (0.85)^2 = 0.28$

EXHIBIT 8-13   **Microsegment response in solar-cooling study.**

Segment	Size	Conditional Probability of Group Choice Given Feasibility $(p_1 w_1 + p_2 w_2)$
1	0.12	$0.44 \times 0.72 + 0.15 \times 0.28 = 0.359$
2	0.31	$0.50 \times 0.57 + 0.44 \times 0.43 = 0.474$
3	0.32	$0.50 \times 0.62 + 0.15 \times 0.38 = 0.367$
4	0.25	$0.45 \times 0.56 + 0.15 \times 0.44 = 0.318$

$$\text{Segment 3: } 1 - 0.85 \times 0.59 = 0.50$$

$$\text{Segment 4: } 1 - 0.85 \times 0.59 = 0.50$$

considering only the two major decision participant groups.

To develop total market response, we take feasibility = 0.02, as calculated from the study, and calculate likely response as 0.32%. (See Exhibit 8.14.) A similar calculation assuming 100% awareness (perhaps on the basis of a heavy media campaign) would yield an expected share of 0.77%.

Applying these numbers against projected total air-conditioning sales gives estimates of total solar-air-conditioning potential of $15 million in 1980 and $17.9 million in 1985.

Critique.   This new-product-assessment procedure has costs as well as benefits. The market-potential figure reported above is very low and could have been derived in a much simpler manner. Here, as with many other models reviewed in this book, the value of the procedure lies in its diagnostics. The analysis allows managers to identify and evaluate product-design trade-offs. In the solar-cooling study a 25 percent system-cost reduction led to a model-projected 75 percent increase in market potential.

In terms of communications programs the separate analysis of the different decision participants leads to information about communication targeting not otherwise available. In the solar-cooling study, if only one of the four major categories of decision participants could have been reached with a communications program, the most leverage (assuming equal mes-

EXHIBIT 8-14   **Calculation of expected response.**

Segment	Size	×	Awareness	×	Feasibility	×	Group Choice	=	Response
1	0.12	×	0.50	×	0.02	×	0.359	=	0.00043
2	0.31	×	0.28	×	0.02	×	0.474	=	0.00082
3	0.32	×	0.50	×	0.02	×	0.367	=	0.00117
4	0.25	×	0.50	×	0.02	×	0.318	=	0.00080
							Response	=	0.0032

sage impact) would have been seen by targeting at HVAC consultants. With this group a 10 percent improvement in preference leads to a projected share increase of 8.1 percent, compared with a 5.3 percent improvement from the next-highest group.

Applications of this model to smart computer terminals, copiers, thermic-diode solar panels, photovoltaic cells, airline meals, and industrial heating equipment have been reported. The model is an example of an operational, organizational-buying-behavior model that can aid in decision making. However, it is in an early stage of development and awaits further testing.

Organizational-buying Models: Current Status and Research Needs

In this section we briefly review the research status and some research needs in the field of organizational buying. More comprehensive reviews of the field are available in Bonoma, Zaltman and Johnson (1977), Sheth (1976), Webster (1979), and Wind and Thomas (1980).

Two types of research have addressed purchasing behavior in industrial markets: adoption research and behavior research.

Adoption research, performed mainly by economists, deals with the organization's final choice and relates this choice to characteristics of the product and the market. This research generally addresses technical innovations and includes the work of Mansfield (1968), who investigated the speed of adoption of fourteen innovations in four industries as a function of product and of a potential-customer firm characteristics; Ozanne and Churchill (1971), who investigated the adoption of a new, automatic machine tool; Peters and Venkatesan (1973), who looked at the diffusion of a new small computer; and Czepiel (1976), who studied the diffusion of continuous casting in the American steel industry.

On the other hand, *behavioral research* has produced the general models reviewed above, as well as some additional, detailed empirical studies. For example, Hillier (1975) attempted to provide an integrated, conceptual model, while empirical studies have generally dealt with certain aspects of industrial-buying behavior:

- observation of actual purchase situations (Brand, 1972; Cyert et al., 1956)
- analyses of the involvement of various organizational functions in industrial purchasing (Buckner, 1967; Harding, 1966; *Scientific American*, 1970; Spekman and Stern, 1979)
- studies of the behavior and decision style of individual decision participants (Cardozo and Cagley, 1971; Crow, Olshavsky, and Sum-

mers, 1980; Hakansson and Wootz, 1975; Lehmann and O'Shaughnessy, 1974; Scott and Bennett, 1971; Scott and Wright, 1976; Sweeney et al., 1973; Wildt and Bruno, 1974; Wilson, 1971).

From the standpoint of decision-making support, organizational-buying-behavior research provides the marketing manager with (1) general conceptual models, identifying important variables and providing a check-list of important issues, (2) much detailed, situation-specific research, suggesting the type and direction of effects in certain situations, and (3) the beginning of the development of some comprehensive model-based methodologies to support industrial-marketing decision making.

Eckert (1981) outlines major research needs in this area. She notes that there are several important issues that need to be addressed for progress in the area, including (1) the focus or unit of analysis, (2) the changing nature of the buying group, (3) the relationship between buying and selling organizations, and (4) the operational specification of variables and relationships implied in the construction of buying models. These issues lead to some interesting research questions:

How can the variables and relationships in models such as Webster and Wind's and Sheth's be put into equation form? What data are required to calibrate such models? How can these models be empirically tested?

What does "influence" mean? How can we determine, validly and reliably, *who* is involved (or likely to be involved) in a decision process and *what influence* those persons are likely to have? Research in this area must encompass the dynamics of the structure of influence over time and must relate it to the stages of the buying process. (Krapfel, 1982; Moriarty and Bateson, 1982; Silk and Kalwani, 1982).

Related to the concepts of influence is a need to know how individuals in organizations become aware and knowledgeable about product information. Operational models relating personal and impersonal marketing-communications strategies to information flows within organizations are needed to determine the role of informal communications on organizational-purchasing behavior.

Are there product, market, and environmental characteristics that can predict, across industries, the structure of the buying process (Who will be involved? How many individuals?) within purchasing organizations? Such research would provide a means of developing much more carefully targeted marketing programs.

Finally, with the key unit of measurement being the group, or buying center, what research tools—decision matrices (Chapter 9), buying panels, protocol studies, gaming/laboratory procedures—can be developed to measure and reflect the richness of industrial-buying situations?

In summary, this chapter shows that relative to the work that has gone on in modeling consumer behavior, organizational-buying models are in an early stage of development. Although many key concepts and some models exist, the complexity and diverseness of organizational buying has slowed the development of a systematic operational set of models that can be used for decision making.

Summary

Organizational buying represents a complex set of activities by a number of individuals in the buying organization. The process takes place over time, has a number of phases, and is influenced by a number of individual, group, organizational, and environmental factors.

Organizational-buying models have generally been one of two types: they have focused on a limited aspect of the buying process and studied that aspect in depth, or they have attempted to characterize the process as a whole. Models of the former type provide specific (if limited) information for decision making, while models of the latter type provide more perspective, structure, and understanding.

Recent progress in the field has focused on the development of more operational models and associated situation-specific measurement procedures. These models and procedures are more primitive than their counterparts in the consumer-marketing area but are beginning to show promise of operational applicability. Of key importance is the trend toward developing models and associated measurements that are custom-designed or adapted for the industrial-purchasing area, rather than borrowing less-appropriate tools from the consumer area.

Problems

8.1 Suggest an operational definition of source loyalty that differs from Wind's.

8.2 Compare the Sheth, Webster-Wind, and Choffray-Lilien models in terms of comprehensiveness and operationality.

8.3 Are industrial buyers more rational than consumer buyers? If so, what are the implications of this observation for modeling industrial-buying behavior.

8.4 The Merton Company, which sells bearings, has identified three individuals who influence decisions in a given customer firm. Let the influence of these three individuals on the purchase decision be denoted by $a_i = f(t_i)$. The probability of receiving an order is then given by

$$p = \Sigma \, a_i f(t_i)$$

where $f(t_i) = 1 - e^{-b_i t_i}$ $(i = 1, 2, 3)$ and t_i is the time devoted to the ith decision influence.

a. What is the optimum allocation of salesperson time to each decision influence?
b. Suggest a procedure for measuring the parameters $\{a_i\}$.
c. How would you interpret a high value versus a low value of b_i?
d. Does the model in its present stage incorporate a brand-loyalty component? If not, develop the extension to the model to include this component.

8.5 The Widget Fittings Manufacturing Company has classified its customers according to whether they are current or prospective customers. Current customers are characterized by the phenomenon of source loyalty, and for an average customer the probability of retention is given by

$$R(t) = 0.2 + 0.8(1 - e^{-2t})$$

where t is the time per month spent with the account. For new accounts the relation between time spent and the probability of conversion is given by

$$S(t) = 0.43t + 1.5t^2 - t^3$$

a. What time should be spent with a new account to maximize the conversion probability per time spent [i.e., the ratio $S(t)/t$]?
b. Assuming new accounts and current accounts are equally profitable, what time should be spent with an existing account so that the marginal returns from existing accounts are equal to those from new accounts?

8.6 Those involved in organizational-purchasing decision processes are often referred to as decision-participants. Suggest a valid measure or set of measures for the following:
a. whether a particular individual is involved in a decision process
b. the level of involvement (importance) of a particular decision influence

8.7 An industrial-source-loyalty study was conducted in the chemical-feedstocks market. A sample of 400 companies was classified in terms of total annual sales (1 = low to 5 = high) and source loyalty (1 = low to 4 = high). The following data were collected:

	Degree of Source Loyalty				
Annual Sales	**1**	**2**	**3**	**4**	**Total**
1	11	9	18	27	65
2	8	15	25	31	79
3	15	28	25	28	96
4	28	24	20	8	80
5	33	20	19	8	80
	95	96	107	102	400

Is there a relationship between the size of the company and source loyalty?

8.8 Is the nature of the product or the nature of the customer more fundamental in distinguishing between consumer and industrial marketing?

CHAPTER

Market Segmentation

Markets, whether consumer or industrial, are heterogeneous. Customers have different constraints, needs, and incentives. Products compete with one another imperfectly in satisfying those needs. Market segmentation, then, is the "adjustment of product and marketing effort to differences in consumer or user requirements" (Smith, 1956, p. 3).

As a theory, market segmentation is the grouping of potential customers into sets that are homogeneous in response to some elements of the marketing mix. As a strategy, it is the allocation of marketing resources, given a heterogeneous customer population. Thus the identification of segments, homogeneous in response, allows the refinement of marketing strategy.

These theoretical and strategic definitions of segmentation highlight two interrelated components. The strategic definition involves the development of a marketing strategy for a segment or for allocating resources to several segments; the theoretical definition involves the development of tools to identify distinct subgroups in the market and to characterize the differences in their response functions.

Since Smith's article, segmentation has become an important, dominant concept in the marketing literature mainly because it can increase the expected profitability of a firm's marketing strategy. This theme is developed in detail in Frank, Massy, and Wind (1972).

The practical importance of segmentation is reflected in the frequency with which firms undertake segmentation studies. In addition, the literature on segmentation is quite broad. [See Michman, Gable, and Gross (1977) and Wind (1978b) for comprehensive reviews.] Yet while academic segmentation research has been one of the most advanced areas of research in marketing, very little has been published on management's use of these research

289

results. Wind (1978*b*) maintains that there is a significant gap between academic research on segmentation and its real-world application and calls for (1) a reevaluation of traditional segmentation studies in light of new academic developments in design and analysis and (2) a reexamination of academic work on segmentation to better reflect management's information needs.

In this chapter we define the segmentation problem both in theory and in practice and outline the most frequently applied approaches. We conclude with a perspective on current developments in the field and a view on narrowing the theory-practice gap.

Segmentation: Problem Definition and Model Development

The concept of segmentation has been widely accepted by marketing management. Segmentation research has been used to answer a wide variety of questions about the varying response of market segments to marketing strategies (price changes, new product offerings, promotional plans, etc.), as well as about the selection and definition of target segments for these planned offerings. Some typical management problems addressed by segmentation studies are the following:

> Which new-product concepts evoke the highest respondent interest, and how do the evaluations of these concepts differ by respondent group—heavy versus light product users and users versus nonusers of the company's brand?
>
> In terms of target markets for a new-product concept, how do interested and disinterested respondents differ by demographic and socioeconomic characteristics, attitudes, and product-use characteristics?
>
> Can the market for new-product concepts be segmented in terms of the respondents' price sensitivity (or other benefits sought), and what are the concept evaluations, attitudes, product use, demographic, and other background characteristics of the various price-sensitive segments (Wind, 1978*b*, p. 318)?

However, such questions have little to do with the normative theory of segmentation, which focuses on the relationship between customer characteristics, varying response receptivity, and the optimal development of a marketing strategy. As we show below, the discrepancy between management needs and normative developments can be attributed, at least partially, to difficulties in measurement and in the implementation of the theory.

To answer the management questions raised above, we can develop a segmentation model. The market segments identified in the model should satisfy three conditions: homogeneity, parsimony, and accessibility. Homogeneity is the measure of the degree to which potential customers in a segment have similar responses to some variable of interest. Unfortunately, there is no perfect segmentation, resulting frequently in considerable overlap in responses to marketing variables. Parsimony is the degree to which the segmentation would make every potential customer a unique target. If the study is to be managerially useful [a requirement not met by most segmentation studies; see Guiltman and Sawyer (1974)], a small set of groupings of substantial size should be identified. Finally, accessibility is the degree to which segments are characterized by observable descriptor variables for differentiated marketing strategies.

The segmentation model requires a dependent variable, usually called a segmentation *basis*, and independent variables, or segment *descriptors*. In practice, the distinction between bases and descriptors is often blurred. Descriptors are used for predicting a basis after segmentation is performed on a representative sample of the potential market. Analytical methods, such as regression or discriminant analysis, relate segment membership to descriptors. The resulting model is used to predict if a potential customer will belong to a specific segment.

Given an objective of interest, say "purchase likelihood," a relevant segment descriptor is one that discriminates between segments of the population along the criterion (basis) of interest. Exhibit 9.1(a) shows a relevant segmentation basis. There, individuals from different climates—solar regions—have different responsiveness to solar water-heating systems. In Exhibit 9.1(b) we see that for the same product the educational level of the potential buyer is an irrelevant segmentation basis.

Frank, Massy, and Wind (1972) describe alternative variable types that can be used to segment markets, as illustrated in Exhibit 9.2. For most of these variables there is a trade-off between accessibility and relevance. The situation-specific variables, the bases (boxes 3 and 4), are generally customers' product requirements and responses to marketing stimuli. As such, they are generally most closely related to the response variable of interest and, hence, are the most relevant. The general variables, the descriptors (boxes 1 and 2), are often not as directly or closely related to the response variable but are more accessible for marketing-strategy formulation.

Geographic and Demographic Variables

With geographic segmentation the market is divided into different locations, such as nations, states, counties, cities, or neighborhoods. The marketer recognizes that market potential and cost vary with market location. Other typical geographic segmentation variables are region, size of county, size of city or SMSA (Standard Metropolitan Statistical Area), population density, and climate.

Demographic and socioeconomic variables are among the most frequently reported indicators for classifying potential consumers. Chief among them are age, sex, marital status, family life cycle, family size, income, education, occupation, religion, race, nationality, and social class.

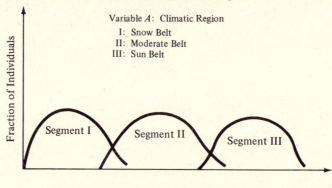

Relevant Segmentation Descriptor

Variable *A*: Climatic Region
   I: Snow Belt
  II: Moderate Belt
 III: Sun Belt

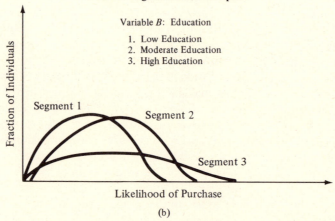

Fraction of Individuals

Segment I   Segment II   Segment III

Response Variable of Interest:
Likelihood of Purchasing Solar Water Heater

(a)

Irrelevant Segmentation Descriptor

Variable *B*: Education

1. Low Education
2. Moderate Education
3. High Education

Fraction of Individuals

Segment 1   Segment 2

Segment 3

Likelihood of Purchase

(b)

EXHIBIT 9-1   Relevant and irrelevant segment descriptors.

Geographic, demographic, and socioeconomic variables have long been the most popular segmentation bases, partly because consumer wants and usage rates are often highly associated with them, although Frank (1968), among others, has concluded that these variables are not particularly good bases for segmentation. However, they are easier to measure than most other types of variables, which may help explain their broad use.

The reasons that demographics do not always work well can be subtle. For example, Ford Motor Company used age as a key segmentation variable when developing a target market for the Mustang: the car was designed to appeal to young people who wanted a sporty, inexpensive car. Therefore

EXHIBIT 9-2   Characterization of alternative segmentation-variable types.

		Characteristics of Customer	
		General (Descriptor)	Situation-Specific (Basis)
Type of Measure	Objective	1. Demographic geographic	3. Brand use/ consumption
	Inferred	2. Psychographic	4. Behavioristic attitudes/preferences/ perceptions/market-factor sensitivity

Ford was surprised to find that the car was being purchased by all age groups. Subsequent research showed that its target market was not the chronologically young but those who were psychologically young.

Psychographic Variables

Under psychographic segmentation, buyers are divided into different groups according to life-style or personality differences. People in the same demographic group often differ remarkably in their psychographic profiles. Life-style refers to the distinctive mode of orientation an individual or group has toward consumption, work, and play. Terms such as "swingers," "hippies," or "jet-setters" are descriptive of different life-styles.

Furthermore, marketers try to endow their products with brand personalities (brand image, brand concept) designed to correspond with consumer personalities.

Brand-Use/Consumption Variables

The brand-use/consumption category and the next category comprise groups that are brand-specific or product-class-specific. Many markets can be segmented into nonusers, past users, potential users, new users, and regular users of a product. This categorization is called user-status segmentation. High-market-share firms, like Kodak in the film market, are interested in converting potential users into new users, while a lower-market-share competitor is more interested in attracting regular users of other products to its brand.

In volume segmentation, markets are segmented into light-, medium-, and heavy-user groups of the product. Heavy users may constitute a small fraction of the customers but a large fraction of the volume. For example, Twedt (1964) reports that 50 percent of beer drinkers account for 88 percent of beer consumption. The targeting of light beers for the heavy-user half is a recent and highly visible strategy pursued in the marketing arena.

Buyers may also be segmented by purchase occasion. For example, airline companies direct very different marketing programs and offer different benefits to business travelers and to vacationers.

Behavioristic Variables

Consumers may also be segmented on the basis of inferred measures of their attitudes, awareness, status, or response to the actual product or its attributes. Many marketers believe that these behavioristic variables are the proper starting point for most segmentation studies.

Buyers are drawn to different brands for different reasons. Take toothpaste, for example; customers may seek decay prevention, bright teeth, good taste, or low price. Haley (1968) has characterized those seeking decay prevention as "worriers," bright teeth as "sociables," good taste as "sensuous," and low price as "independents."

EXHIBIT 9-3   Preferred segmentation bases.

For General Understanding of a Market
Benefits sought (in industrial markets the criterion used is purchase decision)
Product-purchase and -use patterns
Needs
Brand-loyalty and -switching patterns
A hybrid of the variables above

For Positioning Studies
Product use
Product preference
Benefits sought
A hybrid of the variables above

For New-Product Concepts (and New-Product Introduction)
Reaction to new concepts (intention to buy, preference over current brand, etc.)
Benefits sought

For Pricing Decisions
Price sensitivity
Deal-proneness
Price sensitivity by purchase/use patterns

For Advertising Decisions
Benefits sought
Media use
Psychographic/life-style
A hybrid (of the variables above and/or purchase/use patterns)

For Distribution Decisions
Store loyalty and patronage
Benefits sought in store selection

SOURCE: Wind, 1978*b*, p 320.

But operationalizing the concept of benefit segmentation leads to some problems. First, it may be difficult to estimate the size of the different benefit groups in the population as a whole. Second, the cited benefit may be related to a deeper-seated psychological need. Finally, some buyers are interested in a benefit bundle rather than a single benefit; thus marketers must segment by benefit-bundle groups (Green, Wind, and Jain, 1972).

In addition, at any point in time consumers differ in readiness toward buying the product. Some members of the potential market are unaware of the product, some are aware, some are interested, some prefer it, and, finally, some are ready to buy. The particular distribution of people over these stages of readiness makes a big difference in designing marketing programs. For example, several years ago an advertising campaign for Alka Seltzer was an artistic success but a marketing flop because it aimed at recognition and awareness, whereas the brand needed to convert people who knew the brand to people who would prefer it to alternatives.

Finally, Frank and Massy (1975) contend that a crucial criterion for determining the desirability of segmenting a market along a particular dimension is whether different submarkets have different elasticities with respect to the price and promotion policies of the firm. The essence of the normative approach to market segmentation, then, is the identification of segments that respond differently to marketing resources.

To conclude this section, we reproduce a preferred list of variables in Exhibit 9.3 that Wind (1978*b*) suggests for segmentation bases. But as he maintains, the choice of such variables should be situation-specific.

The Normative Theory of Segmentation

Claycamp and Massy (1968) developed a normative theory of market segmentation that draws on the concept of varying-response elasticities and the consequent allocation of marketing resources.

Their approach aggregates individuals until the incremental value of further aggregation is no longer justified. They suggest five stages of aggregation, where the final stage represents nonsegmentation or mass marketing and will not be discussed here.

Stage I: Perfect Segmentation.   Let

$f(p_i, X_{i1}, \ldots, X_{im})$ = customer-demand functions, $i = 1, \ldots, N$ (number of customers)

$\qquad p_i$ = price to customer i

$\qquad X_{ij}$ = nonprice promotional variable j offered to customer i, (where there are m such promotional variables)

$\qquad c_i$ = cost to distribute to customer

$$g(\cdot) = \text{production cost function}$$

$$V_{ij} = \text{unit cost of promotional level } X_{ij}$$

Then the profit to the firm is

$$Z = \sum (p_i - c_i) f_i(p_i, X_{i1}, \ldots, X_{im})$$

$$- g\left(\sum_i f(p_{ij} X_{i1}, \ldots, X_{im})\right) - \sum_i \sum_j V_{ij} X_{ij} \qquad (9.1)$$

with the profit-maximizing levels of p_i and X_{ij} found in theory by differential calculus. In practice, both institutional and informational constraints preclude this approach, and therefore we advance to the next stage.

Stage II: Institutional Constraints. There will usually be a fixed set of promotional vehicles of size n through which the firm exercises nonprice marketing efforts. Call the level of effort placed in these vehicles Y_k ($k = 1, \ldots, n$). Then we have

$$X_{ij} = \sum_{k=1}^{n} b_{ijk} y_k \qquad (9.2)$$

where b_{ijk} = contribution of the kth promotional input for the ith customer

If we assume that the price to each customer must be the same and that distribution costs are the same, eq. (9.1) becomes

$$Z = (p - c) \sum_i f_i\left(p, \sum_k b_{ijk} y_k\right) - \sum w_k y_k - g\left(\sum f_i\right) \qquad (9.3)$$

Equation (9.3) can now be maximized for p and $y_1, \ldots, y_n$. Although containing fewer decision variables now, eq. (9.3) still requires that response at the individual level be known.

Stage III: Microsegmentation. If we assume that media-circulation information is only available for M mutually exclusive and exhaustive classes, then we need to aggregate individuals into these classes. At this level, media-characteristic coefficients need to be made constant for a media class. We do this with $b_{\ell jk}$, where $\ell = 1, \ldots, M$, and eq. (9.1) becomes

$$Z = (p - c) \sum_\ell \sum_{i \in \ell} f_i\left(p, \sum_k b_{\ell jk} y_k\right) - \sum w_k y_k - g\left(\sum_\ell \sum_{i \in \ell} f\right) \qquad (9.4)$$

At this level individuals have been aggregated up to a point where calibrating response functions may be possible from time-series or survey data. For example, response data from automated checkout counters and similar data-collection devices might be used.

Stage IV: Macrosegmentation. To the extent that either the samples in the microsegments are too small for calibrating a response function or the response functions for several sets of segments are essentially equivalent, then microsegments can be aggregated to form macrosegments. A macrosegment h contains customers in media-descriptive cells, $\ell \in h$, so eq. (9.1) now becomes

$$Z = (p - c) \sum_h \sum_{\ell \in h} \sum_{i \in \ell} f_i \left(p, \sum_k b_{hjk} y_k \right) - \sum w_k y_k - g \left(\sum_h \sum_{\ell \in h} \sum_{i \in \ell} f_i \right) \quad (9.5)$$

Here the coefficients b_{hjk} can be found by aggregating the $b_{\ell jk}$ from before for $\ell \in h$. In this latter case the promotion rule associated with optimizing eq. (9.5) is the solution to

$$(p - c - \text{MC}) \sum_j \sum_h \left(\sum_{\ell \in h} b_{\ell jk} \right) \left(\sum_{\ell \in h} \sum_{i \in \ell} \frac{\partial f_i}{\partial X_{ij}} \right) = w_k \qquad k = 1, \ldots, n \quad (9.6)$$

where MC is the marginal production cost associated with the optimal demand level. Equation (9.6) can now, theoretically at least, be solved for promotional strategies of an optimal segmentation scheme.

Although this approach has not been applied, it has made several contributions. First, it shows segmentation to be an agglomorative process: customers are grouped together until it becomes economically feasible to collect response-function information. Second, the authors point out that the criterion for macrosegmentation formation should be to minimize within-group response-function variance relative to between-group variance. Aggregation should continue until the reduction in research costs associated with demand-function calibration equals the reduction in profits associated with the level of aggregation.

The model in its present form requires a large amount of data to be operationalized and is both a deterministic and a static model. Furthermore, model extensions have been made by Frank, Massy, and Wind (1972), who incorporated uncertainty, and by Tollefson and Lessig (1978), who considered other forms of aggregation criteria that are more likely to maximize profit.

Mahajan and Jain (1978) extend the approach to allow for simultaneous development of segments and allocation of marketing resources. In one formulation they consider the problem of determining the profit-maximizing price to charge to different market segments. If

p_{iq} = price charged to individual i if he is assigned to segment q, $i = 1, \ldots, n$, $q = 1, \ldots, K$

$D_i(p_{iq})$ = demand function

$b_{iq} = \begin{cases} 1 & \text{if subject } i \text{ is in segment } q, q = 1, \ldots, K \\ 0 & \text{otherwise} \end{cases}$

$h(\cdot)$ = production cost function

then the problem is to find the $\{p_{iq}\}$ that maximizes

$$Z = \sum_q \sum_i b_{iq} p_{iq} D_i(p_{iq}) - h\left(\sum_q \sum_i b_{iq} D_i(p_{iq})\right) \qquad (9.7)$$

subject to

$$\Sigma b_{iq} = 1$$

(i.e., a subject can be grouped in one and only one segment). Other possible constraints include minimum and maximum numbers of subjects in a segment, the maximum distance between a subject in a group and its centroid (average value on segment descriptors—a measure of segment homogeneity and accessibility), and the like. [An approach toward solving this constrained clustering problem was developed by Klastorian (1973).] Finally, the authors show how to extend this model to incorporate promotional allocation and media expenditures. But as with the Claycamp and Massy model, it awaits empirical testing.

Market Segmentation in Practice

In practice, segmentation techniques are either people-oriented (as in boxes 1 and 2 of Exhibit 9.2) or product-oriented (as in boxes 3 and 4), although some approaches mix the two. A review of the literature published in the past decade reveals a host of articles on the comparative advantage of one technique over another. Most of these arguments are moot: a clear understanding of the uses and limitations of the techniques and an evaluation of the techniques according to the objectives of the specific study usually clarify the problems. The choice of technique must be closely related to the objectives of the problem, the quantity of available data and their structure, the budget for the study, and the purpose of the study. We review and illustrate the use of some of the most widely used techniques in consumer markets below and develop an approach for industrial markets in the next section.

Cross-Classification Analysis

In spite of the proliferation of more-sophisticated techniques, cross-classification remains the most widely used segmentation technique. Interactions and nonlinearities are frequently visible from the cross-tabulation tables, and they are useful tools for viewing the data.

However, cross-classification becomes unwieldy if there are more than two or three classification variables. In addition, if potential segmentation bases are continuous, the selection of breaking points for cross-classification

EXHIBIT 9-4   **Conditional probability of purchase of frozen orange juice and beer.**

		0	1	2–4	5+
Education	Grade school or less	0.67	0.12	0.14	0.07
	1–3 yr of high school	0.62	0.16	0.13	0.09
	graduated high school	0.61	0.13	0.14	0.12
	1–3 yr of college	0.51	0.16	0.22	0.11
	Graduated college	0.40	0.17	0.20	0.23

(a) Frozen Orange Juice/Monthly Use Level

		0	1–18	19–24	25+
Age of Head of Household	18–24	0.45	0.15	0.17	0.24
	25–34	0.33	0.08	0.24	0.35
	35–49	0.36	0.09	0.22	0.33
	50–64	0.42	0.07	0.23	0.27
	65+	0.61	0.04	0.22	0.13

(b) Beer/Monthly Use Level

SOURCE: Bass, Tigert, and Lonsdale, 1968, p. 269.

may obscure important effects. Furthermore, the procedure is not appropriate if significant interactions exist among the variables.

EXAMPLE: Bass, Tigert, and Lonsdale (1968) report on correlates of use rates for several consumer products. Their results, shown in Exhibit 9.4, indicate that the probability that a household in which the head is a college graduate will buy five or more cans of frozen orange juice is about twice the probability for a household in which the head is a high-school graduate. In the same exhibit a nonlinear relationship is evident between beer consumption and age.

Automatic Interaction Detection (AID)

Automatic interaction detection (Sonquist, 1970) has been touted as a method of screening a large number of alternative bases. In essence, it is a multivariate technique for determining what variables and splits within variables produce the greatest discrimination in group means for the dependent variable (purchase frequency, price elasticity of demand, etc.).

The procedure works as follows: group means are determined for each classification of the independent variables, and all dichotomous groupings of each variable are examined. Suppose that there are four categories of job classification—professional, clerical, blue-collar, and other. The group means for all *dichotomous* groupings are then examined: blue-collar versus the other three categories, blue-collar plus professional versus the other two categories, and so on.

Then each prediction variable is split into two nonoverlapping subgroups providing the largest reduction in unexplained variance. The split is chosen to maximize the between sum of squares (BSS) for the ith group (the group to be split):

$$BSS = N_1\overline{Y}_1^{\,2} + N_2\overline{Y}_2^{\,2} - N_i\overline{Y}_i^{\,2} \tag{9.8}$$

where Y = independent variable
       1, 2 = split subgroups $(N_1 + N_2 = N_i)$
           i = parent group

The procedure then splits the sample on the variable yielding the largest between sum of squares, and the new groups formed become candidates for further splitting. The output can take the shape of a tree diagram, each branch splitting until terminated by one of three stopping rules: (1) a group becomes too small to be of further interest, (2) a group becomes so homogeneous that further division is unnecessary, or (3) there is no further possible division that significantly reduces BSS.

The following comments on AID are found in the literature:

> Both regression and cross classification analysis are inadequate means of segmenting markets. . . . The AID program is a significant improvement over standard cross tabulation analysis. It is capable of analyzing and reducing large combinations of data to produce the greatest discrimination between subgroups (Assael, 1970, p. 158).

> As prevalently employed and interpreted, AID is both misleading and unreliable to an unexpected degree. Further, even when used correctly at a preliminary stage of data analysis, it is subject to considerable bias and its use without validation tests can never be justified (Doyle and Fenwick, 1975, p. 408).

Therefore AID can be used for segmentation studies and can handle many forms of independent and dependent variables (but always reduces them to dichotomous values). It can help determine good forms for dummy variables to be used in regression analyses. It can also be used, profitably, along with regression analysis (Armstrong and Andress, 1970). But it does present problems. Doyle and Fenwick (1975) identify the need for large samples, problems with skewed variables and intercorrelated predictors, lack of robustness (multiple samples from the same population result in different trees), lack of significant tests, and the arbitrary nature of the stopping rules.

EXAMPLE: Assael and Roscoe (1976) report on a market-segmentation study for AT&T to identify heavy- and light-long-distance callers. A sample of 1750 individuals was studied, all from the southern region. The output of the AID analysis is shown in Exhibit 9.5, with the tree and intermediate splits presented in Exhibit 9.6.

EXHIBIT 9-5   **Final output of AID analysis of the long-distance-telephone market.**

Segment Profile	Average Long-Distance Bill	Percent of Sample	Percent of Total Long-Distance Billing Accounted for by Segment
1. Income $15,000 and over	$11.10	15.4	29.0
2. Income less than $15,000, one or more extensions, higher socioeconomic status based on education and occupation	7.56	15.6	20.1
3. Same as 2 but medium to low socioeconomic status	5.16	18.6	16.2
4. Income under $15,000, no extensions, and family has teenage children	7.38	5.1	6.4
5. Same as 4 but no teenage children	3.69	45.3	28.3

SOURCE: Assael and Roscoe, 1976, p. 70.

This analysis shows that segments of the long-distance market can be identified on the basis of demographic and telephone-equipment bases. Exhibit 9.5 shows that the most-concentrated-use segment, those with incomes over $15,000, represent 29% of long-distance billing but account for only 15.4% of the sample. In addition, there is a three-to-one difference in expenditures between the most- and the least-concentrated-use segment.

In terms of marketing strategy this study suggests that income alone is a sufficient criterion for reaching the heavy-use segment. It also identifies a relatively heavy-use segment (box 6, Exhibit 9.6) among those who have low incomes but are above average by socioeconomic status and have extension phones.

Regression Analysis

Multiple-regression-based procedures overcome many of the problems involved in cross-classification. In a typical multiple-regression study, the dependent variable is usually some measure of a consumption rate, and the independent variables are socioeconomic and demographic variables postulated to vary with consumption.

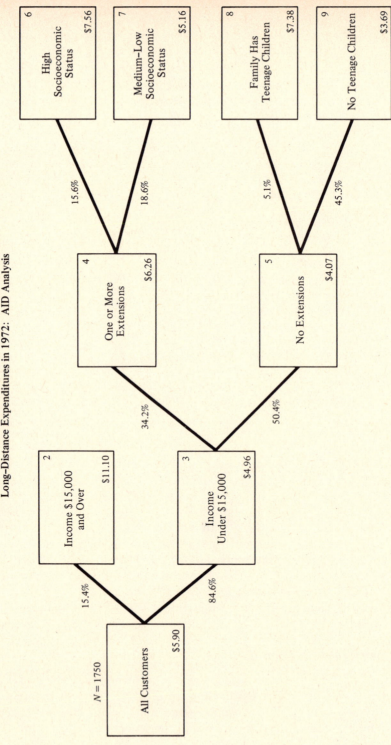

Segmentation of the Long-Distance Market by Average Monthly Long-Distance Expenditures in 1972: AID Analysis

All Customers $5.90

N = 1750

15.4% — Income $15,000 and Over $11.10 (2)

84.6% — Income Under $15,000 $4.96 (3)

34.2% — One or More Extensions $6.26 (4)

50.4% — No Extensions $4.07 (5)

15.6% — High Socioeconomic Status $7.56 (6)

18.6% — Medium–Low Socioeconomic Status $5.16 (7)

5.1% — Family Has Teenage Children $7.38 (8)

45.3% — No Teenage Children $3.69 (9)

EXHIBIT 9-6 **AID tree: long-distance-market study.** (Source: Assael and Roscoe, 1976, p. 70.)

Frank, Massy, and Boyd (1966) studied the importance of socioeconomic and demographic variables on purchase behavior. Data from the *Chicago Tribune* panel on purchase histories of 491 households in 57 grocery fields were related to 14 socioeconomic and demographic variables. Owing to the low level of explanatory power of these variables, Frank (1968) concluded that socioeconomic factors are not particularly useful bases for segmentation.

Morrison (1973) and Beckwith and Sasieni (1976) argue that although a regression model may accurately predict a consumer's average purchase rate, it may do a very poor job of predicting the exact number of purchases in a given period. Wildt (1976) shows how the standard regression assumptions of independent, identically normally distributed errors are violated in this context, and in a later paper Wildt and McCann (1980) show that reasonable assumptions lead to a model in which the error term is heteroscedastic across purchasing units and correlated within purchasing units. They develop an appropriate model and show how to estimate it with iterative, generalized least squares (Zellner, 1962).

One well-known, successful use of regression analysis in market segmentation is described in the following example.

EXAMPLE: McCann (1974) set out to show that differences in response rates do exist among readily identifiable market segments. The data used are from MRCA purchasing records for 7500 individuals over 29 brands of a frequently purchased consumer product in 28 bimonthly periods. He postulates the following model form:

$$MS_{it} = a_{0i} + a_{1i}\,AS_{it} + a_{2i}\,P_{it} + a_{3i}\,D_{it} + a_{4i}\,MS_{it} + \mu_{it} \qquad (9.9)$$

where MS_{it} = market share of brand i at t
         AS = advertising share
          P = price
         D = dealing activity
         μ = disturbance

He develops what he refers to as the average-coefficient regression method, pooling information about segment elasticities after individual brand-response models have been calibrated.

Each of 13 segmentation bases was tested as a candidate for significant differences in response coefficients. The results are summarized in Exhibit 9.7. That exhibit shows that 5 of the 13 segmentation bases resulted in significant differences for the advertising coefficient, and 5 bases showed significant differences for the price coefficient. McCann's results confirm Frank's observations: when the bases are examined for at least one significant difference among the 3 variables, 6 of the 8 buyer-behavior segments emerge while only 1 out of 5 demographic segments showed a significant difference.

EXHIBIT 9-7 **Summary of segment response coefficients.**

Segmentation Base	Segment	Variable[a]		
		Advertising	Price	Deal
Use rate	High (1A)	L	L	—
	Low (1C)	H	H[b]	—
Price	High (2A)	H[b]	H[b]	—
	Low (2B)	L	L	H
Innovativeness	High (3A)	H[b]	H[b]	—
	Low (3B)	L	—	—
Multiple-brand buying	High (4A)	H	L	H[b]
	Low (4B)	L	H	—
Brand loyalty	High (5A)	H	H	—
	Low (5B)	L	L	—
Brand switching	High (6A)	M	L	—
	Low (6B)	M	H	—
Store loyalty	High (7A)	L	H	—
	Low (7B)	H[b]	L	—
Deal-proneness	High (8A)	H[b]	H[b]	H
	Low (8B)	L	L	—
Household income	High (9D)	L	L	H
	Low (9A)	H[b]	H[b]	—
Housewife age	High (10C)	M	H	—
	Low (10A)	M	L	—
Area size	Small (11A)	M	H	—
	Large (11C)	M	L	—
Household size	Small (12A)	H	H	H
	Large (12D)	L	L	—
Housewife employed	No (13A)	M	L	H
	Yes (13B)	M	H	—

SOURCE: McCann, 1974, p. 410.

[a]H = high response coefficient; L = low response coefficient; M = response coefficient equal to market response; — = response coefficient not significantly different from zero at 0.10 level.

[b]Significant difference at 0.10 level.

McCann also develops a segmentation coefficient, the product of the relative size, level of demand, and response rate of the segment. The coefficient helps indicate which of the segments are managerially (as opposed to statistically) significant.

Although there are statistical problems with this approach—the specified model is questionable, and only the main effects of each segmenting variable are measured—this study indicates that regression analysis can be used to measure differential responsiveness of various market segments.

One reason that regression-based studies may not work well is that only one measure of consumption is used. This single measure fails to encompass elements of consumer behavior, such as total consumption, the number of purchases of the preferred brand, or the number of brands purchased.

An alternative is canonical analysis, in which a vector of independent variables is related to a vector of dependent variables (Green and Tull, 1975). Frank (1972) used canonical analysis to identify socioeconomic and life-style segments that showed significantly different consumption patterns across a wide range of product fields. Assael and Roscoe (1976) identify two main segments of telephone-service-use patterns.

Cluster Analysis

Cluster analysis is a group of procedures used to aggregate objects that are close to one another according to some criterion. The objective essentially is to partition a heterogeneous set of entities—consumers in our case—into mutually exclusive, homogeneous subsets. To solve this problem, many cluster-analysis procedures portray entities as points in metric space and search for regions in that space characterized by a high density of points. Clusters are then formed from entities that are close to one another, while distant points become members of different clusters. [See Hartigan (1975) for a review.]

Most marketing applications have used agglomerative hierarchical-clustering methods, at each stage grouping the most-similar entries into the same clusters. The solutions they generate can be graphically presented as dendrograms or trees, such as the one in Exhibit 9.8.

At each stage of the clustering process, agglomerative methods form new clusters that minimize some function of intercluster distance. The dissimilarity matrix is recomputed after each aggregation step, and the process is repeated. Procedures differ by the measure of similarity or dissimilarity they use and by the rule they use for clustering.

If each entity is represented by a vector of metric information, distance-type measures can be used; when the measurements are nonmetric or of differing dimensions, a class of measures called matching coefficients is usually used (Bijnen, 1973). These coefficients measure association between vectors of binary variables.

Most cluster-analysis segmentation studies proceed through several steps, including measurement and definition of a similarity or dissimilarity measure, identification of outliers, tests for nonrandomness of the data structure, cluster invariance analysis, and cluster profiling. [See Choffray (1977) for a discussion of these steps.]

The selection of a clustering algorithm is not simple because, except with very stable clusters, different methods lead to different cluster compositions. One solution, proposed by Everitt (1974), is to use several clustering methods in parallel and analyze the compositions of the resulting clusters. If the clusters or segments are real, their composition will vary little across methods.

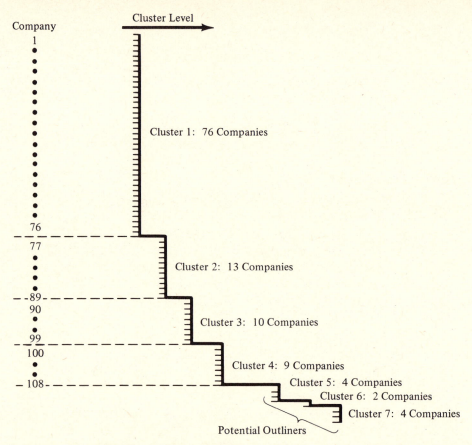

EXHIBIT 9-8   Sample cluster-analysis tree: organizations in HVAC–equipment-purchasing market.

Some of the more popular clustering methods are single-linkage clustering, complete-linkage clustering, average-linkage clustering, and minimum-variance cluster analysis. [See Anderberg (1973), Dalziel (1974), and Hartigan (1975) for complete descriptions.]

To give a flavor of the clustering process, we consider the approach for complete-linkage cluster analysis. Here a cluster is defined as a group of entities in which members are more similar to each other than to members of any other cluster. At each stage after cluster u and v have been merged, the dissimilarity between the new cluster, say t, and some other cluster w is determined by

$$d_{tw} = \max(d_{uw}, d_{vw}) \qquad (9.10)$$

A new cluster is formed by finding those two entities or clusters for which d_{tw} is smallest and merging them.

Most clustering algorithms are fast and simple to use. But there is no single, good model or theory of cluster analysis; existing cluster analysis is simply a set of numerical procedures. Problems such as the number of variables to use, the dissimilarity measure, the clustering approach, and the number of clusters to retain must be answered by marketing management. Lessig and Tollefson (1971) address some of these issues in a segmentation application. For an excellent, comprehensive discussion of cluster analysis in marketing, see Chandon (1980).

Discriminant Analysis

The objective of discriminant analysis is the classification of individuals (or objects) into two or more mutually exclusive and exhaustive groups on the basis of several observable variables.

A classical, two-category discriminant-analysis problem in marketing is the segmentation of the market for loans, credit cards, and the like into good and bad credit risks on the basis of age, income, and other such variables. The model is used to classify individuals into these categories for decisions about whether to grant credit or loans.

Discriminant analysis provides a scoring system that is a weighted average of the numerical values of the independent variables:

$$Z_i = a_0 + \sum_j a_j X_{ij} \qquad (9.11)$$

where X_{ij} = ith individual's value of jth independent variable (age, income, etc.)

a_j = discriminant coefficients for jth variable

Z_i = discriminant score of ith individual

The estimation and the use of discriminant analysis are similar to those of regression. Furthermore, the coefficients $\{a_i\}$ are analogous to regression coefficients, but instead of explaining variance in the dependent variable (as in regression), in discriminant analysis the object is to correctly classify as many people as possible. This classification is done by maximizing the ratio of within-group to between-group variances.

Methodologically, the space of explanatory variables is collapsed into a single dimension, where the axis is found through a set of weights applied to the original axes.

The classification procedure (for two groups) is as follows:

If $Z_i > K_{crit}$, classify i as group I.

If $Z_i < K_{crit}$, classify i as group II.

When there are two groups, this classification procedure is simple and only one equation is generated; when $n = 3$, a two-dimensional partitioning of

3-space is needed and two equations are generated; and, in general, $n - 1$ equations are produced when classifying individuals into n groups.

The magnitude of the coefficients of the discriminant function depends on the measurement scale. Therefore in an assessment of the variable value for a segmentation basis, standardized variables are used:

$$a_j^* = \frac{a_j}{\sigma_j} \qquad (9.12)$$

where σ_j is the standard deviation of variable a_j. If $|a_j^*| > |a_k^*|$, then variable j is a better segmentation basis than variable k.

As with regression analysis, there are a number of critical assumptions associated with (linear) discriminant analysis, including the appropriateness of a linear classification rule, sample-size effects on estimation and classification, and so on. [See Lachenbruch (1975) or Morrison (1974) for detailed discussion.]

EXAMPLE: Johnson (1971) reports a discriminant analysis of the structure of the Chicago beer market. Approximately 500 male beer drinkers described 8 brands of beer on 35 dimensions. Two dimensions were found to account for approximately 90% of discrimination among the images of these 8 products.

Exhibit 9.9 shows the space with the location of each brand indicated on

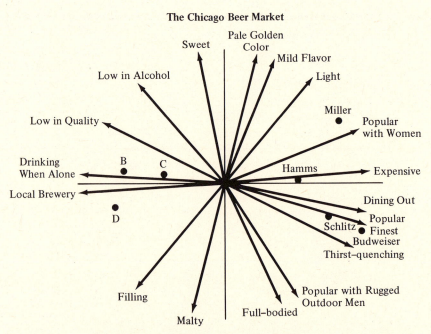

EXHIBIT 9-9 **Discriminant-analysis-based picture of the Chicago beer market.** (Source: Johnson, 1971, p. 14.)

two dimensions. The horizontal dimension contrasts premium price on the right with popular price on the left, while the vertical dimension reflects relative lightness. The mean rating on each of the attribute vectors (the centroid) is shown via its relative position in each attribute vector. Miller, for example, is perceived as being most popular with women, followed by Budweiser, Schlitz, Hamms, and four unnamed popularly priced beers.

Johnson also shows how to plot and cluster consumer ideals, showing where consumer-need segments suggest new-brand/marketing opportunities.

We have presented a sampling of the more widely discussed techniques that can be used for market segmentation. Other techniques, such as factor analysis and multidimensional scaling, while sometimes used for segmentation are more widely used in deriving product spaces. These tools are widely applied as support for product-design decisions and are discussed in Chapters 7 and 11.

An Approach for Industrial-market Segmentation

As we noted in the previous chapter, industrial marketing has many fundamental differences from consumer marketing. Segmentation strategies and variables are quite different from the consumer-oriented variables used in the studies described above.

Cardozo and Wind (1974) review how segmentation analysis is carried out in industrial markets. The results of a survey they performed reveal that segmentation strategies are used primarily after the fact, to assess a product's past performance, rather than to develop effective marketing programs, and that relevant, applicable segmentation strategies are generally lacking in industrial markets. Segmentation bases deemed most appropriate by managers, such as the characteristics of the buying organization's decision-making unit (DMU), do not lend themselves easily to analysis. Therefore second-choice bases are used instead.

Exhibit 9.10 shows how industrial marketing managers view segmentation bases. Organizational-characteristic bases, the most frequently used criteria, are intermediate in terms of appropriateness but highest in ease of implementation. On the other hand, DMU characteristics are viewed as the most appropriate but also the most difficult to implement.

Cardozo and Wind recommend a two-stage approach. The first stage calls for identifying *macrosegments* through the use of such characteristics as (1) end-use market, (2) product application, (3) customer size, (4) use rate, and (5) geographic location. The second stage calls for dividing macrosegments into *microsegments* through the use of such characteristics as (1) position in authority, (2) personal characteristics, (3) perceived product

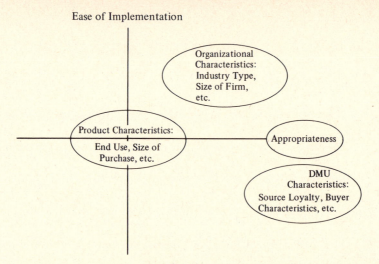

EXHIBIT 9-10   **How industrial marketers view various segmentation bases.** (Source: Reprinted by permission of the publisher from "Industrial Market Segmentation" by Yoram Wind and Richard Cardozo, *Industrial Marketing Management*, vol. 3, pp. 153–166, 1974, by Elsevier Science Publishing Co., Inc.)

importance, (4) attitudes toward vendor, (5) buying-decision criteria, and (6) stage in the buying process. Exhibit 9.11 outlines this hierarchical approach toward industrial-market segmentation.

EXAMPLE: In a study of the market for satellite copiers, sponsored by the 3M Company and the Chilton Company, Lilien and Fried (1978) implemented the above procedure. They used organizational size and geographic area as the primary macrosegmentation variables. In one geographic area with primarily medium-sized firms, a field study was performed on an exploratory basis. They studied 95 individuals from 57 organizations, all of whom were designated as prospects by 3M sales representatives.

Within the macrosegment defined above, they performed a microsegmentation of the market with a cluster-analysis approach (Choffray and Lilien, 1980b) based on similarities in the structure of the decision-making unit. As long as all buying organizations are in the same macrosegment, if they have the same responsibility structures, they are assumed to respond similarly to marketing stimuli.

The Choffray-Lilien procedure has four phases: (1) measuring decision-making-unit (DMU) composition, (2) defining a similarity measure across firms, (3) clustering/segmenting firms into microsegments, and (4) characterizing microsegments.

Step 1:   *Measuring DMU composition.* The measurement tool proposed is a decision matrix aimed at measuring involvement in the buying process. As

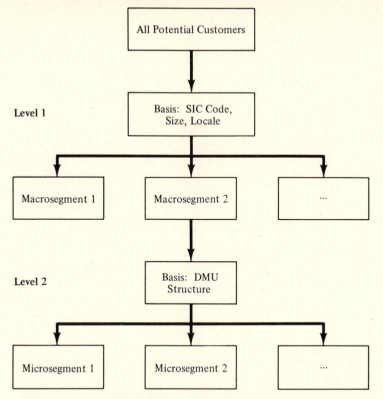

EXHIBIT 9-11   A hierarchy of industrial-market segmentation.

shown in Exhibit 9.12, a decision matrix is a two-way table in which the columns correspond to phases of the purchasing-decision process (needs evaluation, product assessment, etc.) and the rows correspond to the categories of individuals involved in the process (engineering, purchasing, top management, etc.).

Administration of the decision matrix calls for two-stage sampling procedures. In each target organization a senior management member is

EXHIBIT 9-12   Outline of a decision matrix.

	Phases of Purchasing-Decision Process		
Decision-participant categories	**Description of Phase 1**	**•••**	**Description of Phase n**
Decision-participant category 1	% of responsibility		
•			
•			
•			
Decision-participant category m			
	100%	•••	100%

identified first. He is asked to name those people in his organization most likely to participate in the decision to purchase a product in the class identified. Then only those individuals so identified are contacted to complete the decision matrices (and provide other measurements).

In completing the matrices, respondents indicate the percentage of task responsibilities in each phase of the process associated with each participant category. The request for constant-sum information develops a relative-influence measure and avoids such answers as "in our firm all categories of decision participants are involved in all stages of the decision process."

Development of a specific decision matrix follows analysis of the purchasing process in a pilot sample of organizations. [Choffray and Lilien (1980b) discuss the development of decision matrices and their responsibility and validity as measurement tools.]

Step 2: Defining a similarity measure across firms. Many indices of interorganizational similarity or dissimilarity can be used. Choffray (1977) suggests the following approach. Let

X_{ijh} = entry in row j, column h of the decision matrix completed by company i

Then

$$X_{ijh} \geq 0 \quad \text{and} \quad \sum_j X_{ijh} = 1 \quad \text{for all } i, h$$

A participant may be said to be involved if $X_{ijh} > \epsilon$ for some value of ϵ. Empirically, ϵ may be set to zero or some other value greater than zero depending on the reliability of the measurements from the decision matrix. Now define

$$\delta_{ijh} = \begin{cases} 1 & \text{if } X_{ijh} > \epsilon \\ 0 & \text{if } X_{ijh} \leq \epsilon \end{cases}$$

A dissimilarity measure that reflects the dissimilarity between two firms r and s, using decision-matrix data, is

$$D_{rs}^2 = \sum_j \sum_h (\delta_{rjh} - \delta_{sjh})^2 \tag{9.13}$$

This coefficient belongs to a more general class of distance functions between sets of 0–1 entities (Curry, 1976) and can be used as metric input in subsequent analyses.

Step 3: Segmenting firms into microsegments. Following the development of a matrix of dissimilarities $\{D_{rs}\}$, groups of firms can be clustered together that are similar in the structure of their purchasing-decision process. Cluster-analysis methods can be used for this purpose.

Step 4: Characterizing microsegments. The last step of the procedure describes each microsegment by patterns of involvement in the purchasing process. Categories of individuals most likely to participate in the various stages of the process are identified. Each group of organizations is also characterized on the basis of factors external to the buying center. Multiple discriminant analysis can be used here.

Thus this procedure yields the following:

a set of microsegments along with their relative importance in the target macrosegment

a description of the major categories of individuals involved in purchasing decision making within each macrosegment

a microsegment-membership equation, taking characteristics of the firm and predicting the microsegment

Results. The results of the segmentation analysis produced two fundamentally different patterns in the decision process for selecting copiers—that is, two microsegments that were stable under three different clustering algorithms. The first showed high involvement of purchasing agents in all stages of the decision process. This pattern was primarily characteristic of private-sector firms. The second microsegment showed high involvement of administrative staff—that is, product users—and was characteristic of public-sector organizations. In addition, preference/attribute-importance analysis showed that purchasing agents were primarily price-oriented, while users were interested in features (plain-paper bypass, automatic feed, sorting, etc.). These findings suggested a possible segmentation strategy in the market, useful for targeting selling messages and for assessing the market for segment-specific product offerings and strategies.

This example shows that adaptation, of well-known approaches to segmentation used primarily in the consumer area can lead to a customized approach viable for industrial markets.

Segmentation Theory, Practice and Future

Published segmentation studies can be classified (Frank, Massy, and Wind, 1972) by whether their main thrust is understanding consumer behavior (behavioral school) or developing marketing implications (decision-oriented school).

Behavioral School

The behavioral school generally focuses on demographics, psychographics, product attributes, loyalty groups, and DMU characteristics. The use of psychographics, popularized in the early 1970s, is illustrated by the work of Kinnior, Taylor, and Ahmed (1972) who studied personality traits of the "ecologically concerned citizen" and found him to be a tolerant, understanding individual with a high desire to avoid harm. In another large study concerned with life-styles, Ziff (1971) classifies housewives into six segments. [See Wells (1975) for a critical review of psychographics.]

The use of product attributes for segmentation—benefit segmentation— has also been quite fashionable. Haley (1968) segmented the market for toothpaste by the principal benefits sought by the consumer, and Green, Wind, and Jain (1972) segmented the market for a new line of aerosol floor cleaners by consumer evaluation of five product benefits.

Brand loyalty has also seen some interesting applications. Blattberg and Sen (1974, 1975, 1976) defined market segments in terms of brand-loyalty patterns and have developed a methodology to characterize each segment in terms of a different model of stochastic choice. In another article (with Buessing and Peacock, 1978), they assign consumers to loyalty groups and then develop a model to explain the behavior of the deal-prone segment.

Although much effort has gone into developments in the behavioral school, and many useful insights about market structure have been drawn, it is not clear that the derived segments will respond differently to marketing efforts.

Decision-oriented School

The decision-oriented school focuses on differences in response elasticities in order to guide marketing decision making. The theoretical foundation of this school was laid by Claycamp and Massy (1968), reviewed earlier, and was expanded by Frank, Massy, and Wind (1972), Mahajan and Jain (1978), and Tollefson and Lessig (1978).

Assael (1976) reports on three studies for AT&T that use response elasticities as the basis for segmentation. Martin and Wright (1974) have integrated a cost/profit model into AID for isolating segments that are profitable to address separately. This idea is related to McCann's (1974) idea of a segmentation coefficient. Finally, Starr and Rubinson (1978) segment consumers on the basis of brand loyalty. The price elasticities of the resulting groups varied and provided a relevant basis for segmentation. Thus the developments in the decision-oriented school are fewer and harder to come by.

Further work in this area requires a careful blending of the behavioral and decision-oriented approaches. Interestingly, management seems to conduct behaviorally oriented segmentation studies and then makes decisions on the basis of their results. This situation reinforces the need to bridge the theory-practice gap, described earlier. Wind (1978b) gives a detailed discussion of research needs that exist in this area, such as developing the associated measurements and implementation strategy required to operationalize the normative theory of market segmentation. This need is at the heart of the theory-practice gap.

Summary

Market segmentation is the division of a market into distinct subsets of customers, where each subset reacts to media or product offerings differently. Marketing opportunities increase when these differences among groups are recognized and measured. Market segmentation, as a theory, explains these differences while, as a strategy, it exploits the differences.

To be operationally useful, market segments should be homogeneous, relatively few in number, and accessible. However, these objectives are conflicting. Segmentation models are used to help structure segments. Segmentation bases and descriptors differ from model to model, with bases normally being situation-specific while descriptors are more general. A good descriptor separates consumers on the basis of interest.

The normative theory of segmentation has its roots in the literature of microeconomics. Normative-segmentation models suggest grouping consumers by their elasticity of demand to various marketing instruments (price, promotion, and advertising, in particular). The normative theory awaits further operationalization and practical use.

A number of multivariate techniques have been used to address segmentation problems, such as cross-tabulation, AID, regression, cluster analysis, and discriminant analysis. Here, as with most marketing problems, there is no best technique, but there are techniques that are more appropriate for particular marketing problems. The wise analyst must analyze his problem and select an analytical approach that is most appropriate.

Although most segmentation studies have dealt with consumer markets, the industrial-marketing area has seen some application. One approach is a two-step procedure: macrosegmentation (segmenting on more-traditional, readily measured variables) followed by microsegmentation (segmenting on the basis of structure of the decision-making unit).

A major challenge in segmentation theory and practice today appears to be developing the measurement methods and the selling strategy that will make normative-segmentation models useful to management.

Problems

9.1 Suggest some major benefit segments of the market for cameras.

9.2 What ways might the markets for each of the following products be segmented?
   a. household detergents
   b. animal feed
   c. jet airplanes
   d. automobile tires

9.3 Apply the Wind-Cardozo two-stage approach to segmenting industrial markets to a new word processor with a larger memory, but a higher price, than its closest competitors.

9.4 A study of consumers' perceptions of coffee revealed that they could be described in terms of two dimensions, X_1 and X_2, which were described as flavor and aroma. The location of the three bands in the market are shown below, as is the location of four consumer segments, described in terms of their ideal points.

	Product			Segment (Ideal Point)			
	1	2	3	A	B	C	D
X_1, Flavor	2	-1	-3	1	-2	-2	2
X_2, Aroma	1	2	-3	2	1	-1	-2
Segment Share				40%	30%	20%	10%

Assume that the probability of purchase of a brand is given by $p = a/d^2$, where d is the distance of the ideal point to the brand and a is a normalizing constant.

a. Estimate the expected market shares for each brand in each segment.

b. Suggest a marketing strategy for product 3.

9.5 The credit firm of MRI has expressed interest in the possible use of discriminant analysis in the preliminary screening of credit applications. From past records the company has assembled information on two classes of married credit grantees: (1) poor risks and (2) good risks. Additional information about a sample of credit grantees has also been obtained and appears below:

	Annual Income (in $1000s)	No. of Credit Cards	Age	No. of Children
Poor Risks				
1	9.2	2	27	3
2	10.7	3	24	0
3	8.9	1	32	2
4	11.2	1	29	4
5	9.9	2	31	3
6	10.7	4	29	1
7	8.6	3	28	1
8	9.1	0	31	5
Good Risks				
1	18.6	7	42	3
2	17.4	6	47	5
3	22.6	4	41	1
4	24.3	5	39	0
5	19.4	1	43	2
6	14.2	12	46	3
7	12.7	8	42	4
8	21.6	7	48	2

    a. After standardizing variables to mean zero and unit standard deviation, compute a linear discriminant function for two-way analysis.

    b. Which variables appear to discriminate best among the groups?

    c. How might bayesian procedures be used in segmentation problems involving discriminant analysis?

9.6 What marketing strategies would you suggest be used after the following?

    a. Assael and Roscoe's AID analysis of the long-distance phone market

    b. Johnson's discriminant analysis of the Chicago beer market

    c. Lilien and Fried's cluster analysis of the satellite-copier market

9.7 What related set of measurements are required to operationalize Claycamp and Massy's or Mahajan and Jain's normative-segmentation models?

10 Demand Assessment and Forecasting

A key input into models of market behavior are quantitative estimates of demand by product, territory, and type of customer. The planning process requires estimates of the present level and the future course of market demand. These estimates are the output of *demand assessment* and *demand forecasting*, respectively, which are integral parts of three key management functions—the analysis of market opportunities, the planning of marketing effort, and the control of marketing performance. In this chapter we develop methods and approaches for both assessing and forecasting demand.

Concepts in Demand Assessment and Forecasting

Demand assessment is the development of quantitative estimates of demand, which can vary by product level (product item, product form, product line, company sales, industry sales, and national sales), space or region (customer, sales territory, region, United States, world), and time frame (short term, medium term, long term). Its major elements are market demand and company demand. Within each the distinction among a demand function, a potential, and a forecast is important.

In the evaluation of marketing opportunities the first step is to estimate total market demand.

Definition: Market demand for a product is the total volume that would be bought by a defined customer group in a defined geographical area in a defined time period in a defined marketing environment under a defined marketing program.

This definition needs qualification. For example, "product" requires a careful product-class definition; "volume" can be measured in physical units or in dollars; "customer group" implies that market demand can be measured for the whole market or for any segment.

Two other key concepts needed here are *market potential*—the greatest amount that could be sold (under current environmental conditions) if industry marketing effort were made arbitrarily large—and *demand forecast*—a specific value of market demand (sometimes outside the scope of past observations) that we expect to reach with a given marketing effort. It is important to distinguish between these concepts. If we let

D_i = company *i*'s demand in product class
S_i = company *i*'s share of market
D = total market volume

then we get

$$D_i = S_i \times D \qquad (10.1)$$

Assessing Current Demand

There are two main types of current-demand estimates in which a seller might be interested: total market potential and territorial or sectoral potential.

Total Market Potential

Total market potential is the maximum amount of sales (in units or dollars) available to firms in an industry during a given period under a given level of industry marketing effort and given environmental conditions. A common way to estimate it is as follows:

$$Q = n \times q \times p \qquad (10.2)$$

where Q = total market potential
         n = number of buyers in specific product/market under given assumptions
         q = quantity purchased by average buyer
         p = price of average unit

The most difficult component to estimate in eq. (10.2) is *n*, the number of buyers in the specific product/market. One can usually start with the total population, called the suspect pool, and then eliminate groups that obviously would not buy the product. For example, if we were estimating the potential for a solar heating system, we might take the fraction of the population that owns a single-family house (about 20 percent) and multiply that by the fraction of unobstructed south-facing roofs (say 25 percent) to get 5 percent of the population as the number of potential buyers.

A variation on eq. (10.2) is known as the chain-ratio method, which is based on the notion that it may be easier to estimate the separate components of a magnitude than to estimate the magnitude directly (Armstrong, Denniston, and Gordon, 1975). Suppose a brewery is interested in estimating the market potential for a new dietetic beer. An estimate can be made by the following calculation (Ackoff, 1970, pp. 36–37):

$$
\begin{Bmatrix} \text{Demand} \\ \text{for the} \\ \text{new} \\ \text{dietic} \\ \text{beer} \end{Bmatrix} = \begin{Bmatrix} \text{(population)} \times \text{(personal discretionary income} \\ \text{per capita)} \times \text{(average percentage of discre-} \\ \text{tionary income spent on food)} \times \text{(average percent-} \\ \text{age of amount spent on food that is spent on} \\ \text{beverages)} \times \text{(average percentage of amount spent} \\ \text{on beverages that is spent on alcoholic beverages)} \\ \times \text{(average percentage of amount spent on alcoholic} \\ \text{beverages that is spent on beer)} \times \text{(expected} \\ \text{percentage of amount spent on beer that will be} \\ \text{spent on dietetic beer)} \end{Bmatrix} \quad (10.3)
$$

Once the total market potential is estimated, it should be compared with current market size, the actual volume (in units or dollars) that is currently being purchased. Current market size is always smaller than the total market potential.

The remaining factor is the company's current market share. For share we introduce another concept, that of the served market. A company's served market is comprised of all those buyers for whom the company's product is available, accessible, and attractive. If the company distributes its product in only one part of the country and if its price would not appeal to many of its competitors' customers, then the company would not penetrate its competition very much. A company may have a low share of the current market but a high share of its served market.

Territorial or Sectoral Potential

All companies are concerned with (1) identifying the geographic buying-sector breakdown of potential sales, (2) allocating their marketing budget optimally among those markets, and (3) evaluating their performance in the different markets. A key input into these decisions is the market potential of the different territories or sectors. Two main methods for estimating these potentials are available: the first, the market-buildup method, is used primarily in the industrial sector, while the second, the index-of-buying-power method, is used mainly by consumer-goods firms.

Market-buildup Method.   The market-buildup method calls for identifying all the potential buyers for the product in each market and adding up the estimated potential purchases of each. If a list of all potential buyers and a good estimate of what each will buy are available, this method is straightforward.

In industrial markets most market-buildup procedures rely on the standard industrial classification (SIC) system, in which each major type of economic activity is classified with a two-digit code and further divided into three- and four-digit categories. For example, major group 38 is instruments and related products, which has a subgroup 383, measuring and controlling devices, and a detailed industry category 3824, totalizing fluid meters and counting devices. The detailed definition of SIC 3824 covers about a page in the SIC-code guide and specifies the products that are included. All of these classifications are based primarily on the product manufactured or handled or on the service performed.

In addition, the Bureau of the Census has developed the product classification system, designed primarily for industry categories containing a variety of different products (machine tools, for example). A product class then is a group of relatively similar products within an industry category. They are assigned a seven-digit code: the first four digits are those in the four-digit SIC code; digit five represents the product class; and digits six and seven represent the individual product. For example, detailed industry category 3533, oilfield machinery, has 4 product classes, including 3533 1, rotary oilfield and gasfield drilling machinery and equipment, which is further divided into 12 products, including 35331 11, Christmas tree assemblies, and 35331 13, casing and tubing heads and supports. The product-classification information is collected every 5 yr and is updated by the Annual Survey of Manufacturers, a minicensus available between census periods.

Within the SIC system the basic unit of classification is an establishment, not the legal entity or corporation. A corporation may be a legal association of different businesses located in different areas performing different functions. Suppose the XYZ Company has a paper mill, a printing plant, and a (separate) publishing operation. For the purpose of the SIC code, XYZ represents at least three establishments classified under different categories.

An establishment is classified into a code on the basis of its major economic activity. For manufacturing operations the value of production establishes the classification. For example, assume that an establishment reported the following:

Total Value of Shipment and Other Receipts	$1000
Miscellaneous Receipts (resales, etc.)	15
Total Value of Products Shipped	985
32721 Concrete Pipe Products	100
32722 Precast Concrete Products	785
32730 Ready-mixed Concrete	100

This plant would be coded into SIC industry 3272, concrete products, with a product specialization ratio (see below) of 90 percent (885/985); it would be subclassed into the five-digit class 32722, precast concrete, with a primary-product-class specialization rate of 80 percent (785/985).

To use the SIC code for assessing demand, we must recognize that each category may comprise a heterogeneous set of establishments, small and large, diverse in manufacturing methods and, perhaps, even in products produced. One establishment producing household cooking equipment may also produce microwave transmitters, but a second may not. Certain establishments may be automated; others may use hand labor extensively. Some establishments may have integrated fabrication and production facilities; others may assemble final products from components. The differences in purchasing needs among these different organizations may be dramatic. Therefore in analyses that use the SIC code, several important assumptions must be checked.

The first is that all establishments in the same category engage in similar activities. A check on this assumption is given by the *specialization ratio*, the proportion of an industry's output accounted for by the products in the industry's classification. This ratio can vary dramatically. For example, the specialization ratio for SIC 3822, environmental controls, is 86 percent; for SIC 3691, storage batteries, it is 98 percent; and for SIC 3586, measuring and dispensing pumps, it is 71 percent. The higher the specialization ratio, the more homogeneous the output of the industry is and, consequently, the closer it conforms to its SIC classification. For most manufacturing industries the ratio is usually high.

Another key assumption is that the establishments in a given category account for all or a large proportion of the total activity occurring in that category. This assumption can be checked with the *coverage ratio*, the share of total national output of a product that is produced by establishments in the industry classification for which it is the primary product. These ratios also vary greatly. For example, the coverage ratio for SIC 3822, environmental controls, is 90 percent; for SIC 3732, ship building and repairing, it is 98 percent; but for SIC 3412, metal panels, drums, and pails, it is 11 percent. The coverage ratio is low when the primary product of an industry is classified under another industry category. For instance, SIC 3317, steel pipe and tubes, has a coverage ratio of only about 38 percent. Many establishments in other SIC codes also produce steel pipe and tubes, although not as their major output. Thus the large variation in these two ratios suggests the caution needed when one is using SIC codes.

The specialization ratio and the coverage ratio are important indicators of analytical reliability, but other problems exist that are not so easily measured. For example, problems arise from establishments owned by other establishments that consume their entire output. These interplant transfers, included along with all other shipments, can be a significant source of analytical bias. Another difficulty arises in the all-other or not-elsewhere-classified categories. Farm equipment (SIC 3522), for example, includes a variety of products that are too small to warrant separate classification.

As a source of data, then, the SIC code is an extremely powerful data base that, like all powerful tools, must be used with care.

But how can we use these data for assessing demand for a product? The first step in a market-buildup method is sometimes called an SIC search, where each four-digit SIC code is studied to determine whether establishments making that product or performing that service are potential customers. This process acts as a screening procedure, eliminating from consideration those codes unlikely to produce significant market potential. The industries that emerge provide a first, crude defintion of the largest potential market for the product investigated.

After tentative identification of a few SIC codes, the next step is the development of a market profile, including those measurable characteristics of a market affecting the way demand is derived.

If markets are defined in terms of SIC codes, the following characteristics, among others, are available from the U.S. Census:

1. total number of establishments
2. breakdown by state
3. value of shipments
4. value added by manufacture
5. number of employees
6. total capital expenditures
7. specialization ratio
8. coverage ratio

Quantities 3–6 above are often best understood on a per-establishment or per-employee basis. For example, a high value of shipments per establishment means big firms, while a high value of shipments per employee may mean automated facilities, especially if combined with high total capital expenditures per employee and high value added per employee.

EXAMPLE: Assume we are interested in the market for a separation process that can be used to filter malt beverages or, alternatively, can be used for milk separation. What did these industries look like in 1972? Data from the 1972 Census of Manufacturers, summarized in Exhibits 10.1 and 10.2, provide an answer.

Of the two alternative markets for the product, milk is more than twice as large according to value of shipments, but new capital expenditures are about the same for milk and malt beverages, with no significant difference in trends.

In addition, there are many fewer establishments in the malt beverage

EXHIBIT 10-1 **Sample market profile: fluid milk and malt beverages.**

	2026 Fluid Milk	2082 Malt Beverages
Total establishments	2,507	167
New England	252	9
Maine	44	0
New Hampshire	20	1
Vermont	27	0
Massachusetts	94	4
Rhode Island	23	2
Connecticut	44	0
Middle Atlantic	534	42
East North Central	480	41
West North Central	337	15
South Atlantic	228	17
East South Central	123	3
West South Central	141	12
Mountain Division	130	5
Pacific Division	282	23
Number of establishments with 20 or more employees	1,287	130
Number of employees	126,100	51,000
Per establishment	50.3	308.3
Value added by manufacture ($ millions)	2,552.4	1,993.6
Per employee (in $)	20,241	38,711
Capital expenditures (in $ millions)	149.2	155.6
Per establishment	0.0593	0.931
Per employee	0.0011	0.0030
Specialization ratio	88	100
Coverage ratio	96	100
Value of shipments (in $ millions)	9,395.8	4,054.4
Per establishment	3.74	24.3
Distribution of Establishment Size		
1–4 employees	657	22
5–9	243	3
10–19	320	12
20–49	499	17
50–99	405	18
100–249	313	32
250–499	53	39
500–999	6	15
1000–2499	0	6
2500+	1	3

SOURCE: 1972 Census of Manufacturers.

EXHIBIT 10-2 **Profile trends**

	(New) Capital Expenditures		Assets Per Employee	
Year	2026 Fluid Milk	2082 Malt Beverages	2026 Fluid Milk	2092 Malt Beverages
1972	149.2	155.6	—	—
1971	146.3	160.2	12,900	41,020
1970	151.8	177.7	11,900	39,290
1969	119.2	249.8	11,310	36,380
1968	110.4	193.6	10,900	32,340
1967	120.3	140.4	10,280	29,110
1966	105.2	168.8	—	—
1965	114.6	115.4	—	—

SOURCE: 1972 Census of Manufacturers.

industry, geographically concentrated in the Middle Atlantic and East North Central. This feature may make the malt-beverage industry easier to enter than the milk industry in terms of required selling resources.

The exact size and location of the individual establishments can generally be determined through state industrial directories. These directories are an invaluable first step in developing territorial market potentials and sales estimates. For example, considering a sales territory of Massachusetts, there are 94 establishments in SIC 2026 and 4 in SIC 2082. Assuming that separators account for an average of 5% of capital expenditures, we get (from Exhibit 10.1)

$$\text{SIC 2026: } 94 \times 0.05 \times 59,300 = \$278,000$$
$$\text{SIC 2082: } 4 \times 0.05 \times 31,000 = \underline{186,000}$$
$$\text{TOTAL} = \$464,200$$

or an annual potential in the state of just under $0.5 million.

In a similar way, the company can estimate the market potential for other territories in the country. Suppose the market potentials for all the markets sum up to $49 million. In this case the company concludes that the Massachusetts market contains about 1% of the total market potential.

If the company decides to sell in Massachusetts, it needs a system for identifying the best prospect companies. State industrial directories usually have this information. An alternative source is *Dun's Market Identifiers*, which lists 27 key facts for over 3.25 million establishments in the United States and Canada in manufacturing, wholesaling, retailing, transportation, communications, public utilities, agriculture, mining, and services.

Index-of-buying-power Method. Consumer companies must also estimate territorial market potentials. The method most commonly used is a straightforward index method.

One of the best-known, general-purpose, multiple-factor indices of area demand is the Annual Survey of Buying Power published by Sales and Marketing Management. The index is designed to reflect the relative buying power in the different regions, states, and metropolitan areas of the nation and is computed by

$$B_i = 0.5y_i + 0.3r_i + 0.2p_i \qquad (10.4)$$

where B_i = percentage of total national buying power found in area i
y_i = percentage of national disposable personal income originating in area i
r_i = percentage of national retail sales in area i
p_i = percentage of national population located in area i

For example, suppose Virginia has 2.00 percent of the United States disposable personal income, 1.96 percent of United States retail sales, and 2.28 percent of United States population. Then the buying-power index for Virginia would be

$$0.5(2.00) + 0.3(1.96) + 0.2(2.28) = 2.04 \qquad (10.5)$$

That is, 2.04 percent of the nation's sales for a specific product might be expected to take place in Virginia. Sales and Marketing Management holds that these weights reflect market potential for many consumer goods that are neither low-priced staples nor high-valued luxury goods. However, the weights vary in their appropriateness for different products, and an individual firm should rely on a regression-based approach for finding the best weights to estimate market potential for its products.

Forecasting Demand

Predicting the course of a company's or an industry's sales is essential for the planning and control of all business operations. As business markets become more unstable and subject to fluctuation, it becomes a more and more critical task for marketing management. Lacking some form of projection, firms have no reasonable starting point for many forms of routine business analysis.

Vital as they are, forecasts are estimates, at best. Some firms do better jobs than others, but no one has come up with a perfect method. Many companies are beginning to rely on several independent forecasting methods, leading to more-frequent checks for reasonableness and more-reliable diagnostics.

Hurwood, Grossman, and Bailey (1978) provide the following characteristics of a superior forecasting system:

The system encourages an open-minded weighing and testing of alternatives. Its predictive power and cost are well matched to its purposes.
Its input data are appropriate, consistent, and reliable, and they are protected from contamination and misuse.
Its procedures discourage aimless intervening and tinkering while encouraging the adjustments of first approximations in light of new facts.
It has adequate provisions for tracking, updating, and self-correction.
Its management users are alert to the possibilities of forecast error, they understand the underlying assumptions, they are familiar with and accept the forecasting methodology, and their own contribution and involvement at critical points are assured.
For many companies, flexibility is now emerging as perhaps the most distinguishing feature of their forecasting program. . . . And, more than ever before, the primary mission has become that of finding and applying the right combination of methods for the particular forecasting job at hand (p. iii).

For aid in the search for forecasting systems, there have been numerous recent works on demand and sales forecasting; all provide some guidelines for choosing among the vast array of methods (e.g., Chambers, Mullick, and Smith, 1974; Makridakis and Wheelwright, 1978; Wood and Fildes, 1976). The main thrust of these guidelines is to separate causal from noncausal methods and qualitative from quantitative methods.

Exhibit 10.3 classifies many of the more prominent techniques by whether they are judgmental, market and survey analyses, time series, or causal analyses.

Before discussing these methods in detail, we must put them in perspective by considering their use in practice. Several studies have reported the managerial use and acceptance of the different methods, including the work of Pokemper and Bailey (1970), Dalrymple (1975), Wheelright and Clarke (1976), and Pan, Nichols, and Joy (1977). In each case

EXHIBIT 10-3   A classification of market-forecasting approaches.

Judgmental	Market and Survey Analysis	Time Series	Causal Analysis
Salesforce composite	Buyer intentions	Naive methods	Regression analysis
Delphi methods	Product tests	Moving averages	Econometric models
Jury of executive opinion		Exponential smoothing	Input-output analysis
		Box-Jenkins method	New-product forecasting
		Decompositional methods	

the studies involved mailing questionnaires to a sample of the relevant population.

The results of one study (Dalrymple, 1975), reporting the specific methods used, are shown in Exhibit 10.4. These results were derived from a mailed questionnaire sent to 500 midwestern businessmen with a return rate of 35 percent. They show judgmental methods to be by far the most widely used, followed by the simplest time-series methods. However, data on the use of forecasting methods classified by the forecaster's placement of the firm in the industry show that the more sophisticated techniques (Box-Jenkins, econometric methods, etc.) are used significantly more often by those firms placed ahead of industry, possibly pointing to the technological diffusion of forecasting techniques (Wheelright and Clark, 1976).

Although conducted on different samples, with different analytical techniques, these studies do point to some important trends. First, the technological sophistication of the techniques surpasses their use in practice; quantitative techniques are not as widely used as judgmental methods. In addition, the study by Pan, Nichols, and Joy (1977) suggests that those firms with a commitment to and a need for accurate results tend to achieve them, with the likely use of multiple procedures. On the whole, these studies point to significant progress in the implementation of forecasting in various firms by the mid 1970s.

EXHIBIT 10-4   Data on industry use of selected forecasting methods.

Method	Percent of Companies Using the Method Regularly	Average Percent Forecasting Error for Firms Using the Method Regularly
Time-series Analysis		
Trend projections	28	6.2
Moving average	24	6.2
Exponential smoothing	13	7.3
Econometric Analysis		
Regression	17	6.4
Input-output model	6	6.2
Judgmental Methods		
Salesforce-composite method	48	6.8
Jury of executive opinion	52	7.0
Survey-analysis Methods		
Intention-to-buy survey	15	8.5
Industry survey	22	6.7

SOURCE: Adapted from Dalrymple. Copyright, 1975, by the Foundation for the School of Business at Indiana University. Reprinted by permission, Tables 2 and 6, pp. 71 and 73.

We now discuss the methods in Exhibit 10.3 in turn. Those methods reviewed in detail elsewhere in this book receive more cursory coverage.

Judgmental Methods

The procedures for judgmental calibration, developed in Chapter 5, apply to judgmental forecasting. There are three strategies for collecting such information—through salesforce-composite estimates, jury of executive opinion, and Delphi and related methods—each discussed in turn below.

Salesforce-composite Estimates. Many company managements turn to members of the salesforce for help when assembling clues about future sales. However, few companies use their estimates without some adjustments. In the first place, sales representatives are biased observers. They may be characteristically pessimistic or optimistic, or they may go to one extreme or another because of a recent sales setback or success. Furthermore, they are often unaware of larger economic developments and of marketing plans of their company that will influence future sales in their territory. They may understate demand so that the company will set a low sales quota, or they may not have the time or concern to prepare careful estimates.

Under the assumption that these biasing tendencies can be countered, a number of benefits can be gained by involving the salesforce in forecasting. Being closest to the customers, sales representatives may have more knowledge of or better insight into developing trends than any other single group. This situation is especially likely when the product is fairly technical and subject to a changing technology. Second, with their participation in the forecasting process, the sales representatives may have greater confidence in the derived sales quotas, and this confidence may increase their incentive to achieve those quotas. Finally, a grass-roots forecasting procedure results in estimates broken down by product, territory, customer, and sales representative.

EXAMPLE: At Jones and Loughlin Steel separate sets of quarterly forecasts are prepared independently by district sales managers and by product marketing managers. These forecasts are then reconciled and annualized by commercial-planning specialists.

Jury of Executive Opinion. A common judgmental approach is combining the view of key executives in hopes of gaining a sounder forecast than might be made by a single estimator. It is a method employed by all kinds of companies but is somewhat more likely to be adopted by a service firm or a manufacturer of consumer goods than by an industrial marketer.

The procedures used for executive-opinion juries vary from independent assessments to direct confrontations. (Chapter 5 elaborates on the advantages and problems associated with each.) The key problems with executive-opinion juries relate to (1) giving too much weight to opinion, (2) infringing on executives' time, and (3) weighting the estimates of the individual forecasts. Therefore juries are usually used as one input into a larger forecasting system.

EXAMPLE: Hurwood, Grossman, and Bailey (1978) report that an equipment manufacturer uses ". . . judgment of sales and marketing executives, aided by time series projections (based on inventory department analysis) and reports from the field, along with comparisons with earlier forecasts and with the previous year's sales to date" (p. 21).

Delphi and Related Methods.   In gathering informed opinion, an increasing number of companies are relying on the Delphi method for forecasting, especially for medium- or long-term forecasting. [See Chapter 5 for details, and see Linstone and Turoff (1975) and Sackman (1975) for fuller discussion and critique.]

EXAMPLE: Johnson (1976) reports on the experience of Corning Glass with the Delphi method to develop a 10-yr market forecast for certain electronic components. He reports excellent results with respect to the quantity of data obtained from experts from many disciplines, and satisfaction with the movement of panel members' opinions toward consensus, with the rationale of the panelists for their answers, and with the commitment they gave to the study.

Judgmental forecasting methods have been critically examined in several recent studies. Staelin and Turner (1973) examined the salesforce-composite method and postulated two principal causes of error: the error associated with each particular estimate and the error associated with the covariance between estimates. They suggest that management should obtain trial forecasting data and analyze them to determine the relative magnitudes of the two types of error.

Jolson and Rossow (1971) and Best (1974) studied the Delphi method and suggest that results can be improved when experts are separated from nonexperts in the forecasting task. Judges with high self-rated expertise gave better judgments and were also able to translate their uncertainty into reasonable probabilistic terms.

Market and Product Analysis

Buying Intentions.   Forecasting is essentially the art of anticipating what buyers are likely to do under a given set of conditions. This definition immediately suggests that a most useful source of information would be the buyers themselves. Ideally, a probability sample of potential buyers would be drawn up; each buyer would be asked how much he would buy of a product in a given, future time period under stated conditions. The buyers would also be asked to state what proportion of their total projected purchases would be bought from a particular firm, or at least what factors would influence supplier choice. With this information the firm would have an ideal basis for forecasting its sales.

Unfortunately, this method has a number of limitations in practice, the most important of which are (1) the relationship between stated intentions and actual behavior and (2) potential nonresponse bias. (The latter problem is particularly critical in industrial markets composed of relatively few buyers.) The value of this method then depends on the extent to which the buyers have clearly formulated intentions and then carry them out. [See Haley and Case (1979) and Morrison (1979) for discussion of stated intentions versus actual behavior.]

Two areas where buyer-intention surveys have proven to be of value are major consumer durable goods and industrial goods. With regard to major consumer durables, such as automobiles, new housing, furniture, and applicances, several sampling services (such as the Survey Research Center at the University of Michigan, Sindlinger & Company of Norwood, Pennsylvania, The Conference Board, Inc., and the Commercial Credit Corporation) regularly produce reports on consumer buying intentions. In some form they ask the consumer whether he intends to buy each of several different durables within a stated period of time.

In the realm of industrial buying, intention surveys regarding plant equipment and materials have been carried out by various agencies. The two best-known, capital-expenditures surveys are the one conducted by the U.S. Department of Commerce in collaboration with the Securities and Exchange Commission and the one conducted annually in the late fall by McGraw-Hill through *Business Week*. Most of the estimates have been within a 10 percent error band of the actual outcomes. In addition, many industrial firms find it useful to carry on their own survey of customer buying intentions.

Market Tests. The usefulness of opinions, whether those of buyers, sales representatives, or other experts, depends on their cost, availability, and reliability. In cases where buyers do not plan their purchases carefully or are very erratic in carrying out their intentions or where experts are not very good guessers, a more direct market test of likely behavior is desirable. A direct market test is especially desirable in forecasting the sales of a new product or the likely sales of an established product in a new channel of distribution or territory. Where a short-run forecast of likely buyer response is desired, a small-scale market test is usually a good solution. This approach is explored in more detail in Chapter 19.

Time-Series Methods

As an alternative (or complement) to surveys, opinion studies, and market tests, many firms prepare forecasts on the basis of statistical analysis of past data. The logic of this approach is that past data incorporate enduring causal relationships that will carry forward into the future and that can be uncovered through quantitative analysis. Thus the forecasting task becomes, in essence, a careful study of the past plus an assumption that the same relationships will hold in the future.

There are a number of time-series analysis and forecasting methods, differing mainly in the way past observations are related to the forecast values. We illustrate the comparative performance of a few of these methods with data from the National Bureau of Economic Research Series MDSMS on shipments for fabricated metal products. The quarterly data for 1969–1977 are shown in Exhibit 10.5(a), and forecasts for the four quarters of 1978, computed with the naive, moving-average, the moving-average with trend adjustment, the exponential-smoothing, and the optimal Box-Jenkins methods are shown in Exhibit 10.5(b), along with the actual data for that period.

Naive Methods.   The simplest time-series forecasting procedure uses the most recently observed value as a forecast: a naive forecast is equivalent to giving a weight of one to the most recent observation and zero to all other observations. Other naive methods may modify this procedure by adjusting for seasonal fluctuations. These methods are used mainly as a basis for comparing alternative forecasting approaches.

Slightly more sophisticated methods include the following:

Freehand projection, which is a visual exploration of a plot of time-series observations. This method has the advantage of delivering a

EXHIBIT 10-5   Forecasting comparison for fabricated metal products.
                 (a) Data for Forecasting Comparison

Year	Q1[a]	Q2	Q3	Q4
1969	11,445	11,573	11,516	11,990
1970	11,704	11,050	11,069	10,705
1971	10,729	10,931	11,832	12,172
1972	12,472	12,840	12,865	13,491
1973	14,324	14,684	14,689	15,473
1974	16,483	16,634	17,245	17,177
1975	16,230	16,562	17,614	18,318
1976	19,148	19,730	19,184	19,424
1977	20,774	21,184	21,052	22,121

[a]Q1 = quarter 1, and so on.

SOURCE: National Bureau of Economic Research Series MDSMS.

EXHIBIT 10-5 **Forecasting comparison for fabricated metal products.**
(b) Comparison of Forecasting Methods

1978	(1) Actual	(2) Naive	(3) Averaged on Four Previous Quarters, Moving Average	(4) Moving Average with Trend Adjustment
Q1	22,433	22,121	21,283	22,666
Q2	23,792	22,433	21,698	23,219
Q3	23,980	23,792	22,350	23,772
Q4	25,840	23,980	23,082	24,325
MAPD[a]	3.78	3.78	7.85	2.53

1978	Exponential Smoothing (5) $\rho = 0.90$	(6) $\rho = 0.50$	(7) Optimal Box-Jenkins
Q1	22,014	21,397	23,168
Q2	22,391	21,915	23,509
Q3	23,652	22,853	24,133
Q4	23,947	23,416	25,141
MAPD[a]	4.10	6.65	1.95

[a]MAPD = mean-absolute-percent deviation = $\frac{1}{n} \sum (|\text{actual} - \text{forecast}|/\text{actual}) \times 100$.

forecast quickly and cheaply, and it is easy to understand. However, it is of low accuracy, especially for nonlinear series, and is not reproducible.

Semiaverage projection, in which the time series is divided in half, averages are calculated for each half, and a line is then drawn between the average points and the projected points. This method has the same advantages and disadvantages as freehand projection.

Smoothing Techniques. The notion underlying smoothing methods is that there is some pattern in the values of the variables to be forecast, which is represented in past observations, along with random fluctuations. Smoothing methods try to distinguish the underlying pattern from the random fluctuations by eliminating the latter.

One way to lessen the impact of randomness in individual short-range forecasts is to average several of the past values. The *moving-average* approach is one of the simplest procedures for doing so. It weights the past N observations with the value 1/N, where N is specified by the analyst and remains constant. The larger N, the greater will be the smoothing effect on the forecast. If a year's worth of monthly data were available, the moving-average method would forecast the next period as $\frac{1}{12}$ of the total for the past year. When new data become available, they are used, with the newest observation replacing the oldest. In this sense the average is moving.

Typically, the method of moving averages is used for forecasting only one period in advance. It does not adapt easily to pattern changes in the data.

Formally, for *simple moving averages*, let

$$S_t = \text{forecast for time } t$$

$$X_t = \text{actual value at time } t$$

$$N = \text{number of values included in average}$$

Then forecasting with moving averages can be represented as

$$S_{t+1} = \frac{1}{N} \sum_{i=t-N+1}^{t} X_i = \frac{X_t - X_{t-N}}{N} + S_t \tag{10.6}$$

This equation makes it clear that the new forecast S_{t+1} is a function of the preceding moving-average forecast S_t. Furthermore, if X_t corresponds to a change (e.g., step change) in the basic pattern of variable X, it is difficult for the method to account for that change. Note also that the larger N, the smaller $(X_t - X_{t-N})/N$ will be and the greater the smoothing effect will be.

Advantages of the technique are that a forecast can be produced in little time, at low cost, and with little technical knowledge. Low accuracy and an arbitrary choice of the number of observations in calculating forecasts are among its disadvantages. Furthermore, simple moving averages are not very effective in the presence of complex data patterns such as trend, seasonal, and cyclical patterns.

Another procedure, the *double moving average*, starts by computing a set of single moving averages and then computes another moving average based on the values of the first. Let

$$S'_{t+1} = \text{single moving-average forecast for time } t$$

$$S''_{t+1} = \text{double moving-average forecast for time } t$$

Then

$$S'_{t+1} = \frac{1}{N} \sum_{i=t-N+1}^{t} X_i \tag{10.7}$$

$$S''_{t+1} = \frac{1}{N} \sum_{i=t-N+2}^{t+1} S'_i \tag{10.8}$$

With a trend, a single or double moving average lags the actual series. Also, the double moving average is always below the simple moving average. Thus it is possible to forecast by taking the difference between the single moving average and the double moving average and adding it back to the single moving average. This forecasting technique is called the *double moving averages with trend adjustments*. Specifically, if

$$S_{t+m} = \text{forecast } m \text{ periods in advance}$$

$$b = \text{adjustment to forecast}$$

then

$$a = 2S'_{t+1} - S''_{t+1} \tag{10.9}$$

$$b = \frac{2}{N-1}(S'_{t+1} - S''_{t+1}) \tag{10.10}$$

and

$$S_{t+m} = a + bm \tag{10.11}$$

The *exponential-smoothing* approach is very similar to the moving-average method, differing in that the weights given to past observations are not constant—they decline exponentially so that more recent observations get more weight than earlier values. Choice of the smoothing factor is left to the analyst. Most often a value is selected experimentally from a set of two or three different trial values. As with moving-average methods, exponential smoothing has limitations when basic changes are expected in the data pattern. These methods cover a variety of procedures, some of which make adjustment for trends and for seasonality. In essence, most adjust the data in some way before applying an exponential-smoothing procedure.

With the notation above the procedure can be represented by

$$S_{t+1} = \alpha X_t + (1 - \alpha)S_t \tag{10.12}$$

where $0 \le \alpha \le 1$ is selected on an empirical basis by the analyst. By successive substitution, we get

$$S_{t+1} = \alpha X_t + \alpha(1 - \alpha)X_{t-1} + \alpha(1 - \alpha)^2 X_{t-2} + \alpha(1 - \alpha)^3 X_{t-3} + \ldots \tag{10.13}$$

Hence the procedure is termed exponential because the $(n + 1)$th term above is

$$\alpha(1 - \alpha)^n X_{t-n} \tag{10.14}$$

A high value of α gives past forecasts and past data (included in S_t) little weight, while a low value of α weights the most recent period very little compared with all other past observations.

The method of *double exponential smoothing* is analogous to that of double moving averages. Thus

$$S'_{t+1} = \alpha X_t + (1 - \alpha)S'_t \tag{10.15}$$

$$S''_{t+1} = \alpha S'_{t+1} + (1 - \alpha)S''_t \tag{10.16}$$

$$a = 2S'_{t+1} - S''_{t+1} \tag{10.17}$$

$$b = \frac{\alpha}{1 - \alpha}(S'_{t+1} - S''_{t+1}) \tag{10.18}$$

$$S_{t+m} = a + bm \tag{10.19}$$

where α is the exponential-smoothing constant and m is the number of periods ahead we wish to forecast. Double exponential smoothing easily adapts to changes in patterns, such as step changes.

Smoothing methods are based on the idea that a forecast can be made by using a weighted sum of past observations. In the case of simple moving averages, the individual weights are $1/N$. For exponential smoothing the analyst has to postulate the declining weighting factor. *Adaptive filtering* is another approach for determining the most appropriate set of weights. It is based on an iterative process that determines weights that minimize forecasting error.

Specifically, all the methods reviewed so far are based on the idea that a forecast can be made as a weighted sum of past observations:

$$S_{t+1} = \sum_{i=t-N+1}^{t} W_i X_i \qquad (10.20)$$

where S_{t+1} = forecast for period $t + 1$
  W_i = weight assigned to observation i
  X_i = observed value at i, as before,
  N = number of observations used in computing S_{t+1} (and, so, the number of weights required)

Adaptive filtering attempts to determine a best set of weights. The usual criterion used is that the weights should minimize the average mean-squared forecasting error. The result of applying this procedure is a very simple updating rule:

$$\mathbf{W}' = \mathbf{W} + 2ke\mathbf{X} \qquad (10.21)$$

where $\mathbf{W}'$ = revised vector of weights
  W = old set of weights
  k = scalar, learning constant
  e = forecasting error in last period
  $\mathbf{X}$ = vector of observed values

This equation states that the revised weights should equal the old set of weights adjusted for the most recently observed error. The adjustment is based on the error for that forecast, the observed values, and the learning constant k.

As an initial set of weights, $1/N$ will generally suffice, where N corresponds, for example, to the length of a complete cycle in the data pattern. Specification of k, the learning constant, requires more thought. Several rules of thumb are available to help in that choice (Wheelright and Makridakis, 1977).

The procedures to revise weights use nonlinear-optimization methods and usually require computer support for implementation.

The *Box-Jenkins (ARMA) method* is a philosophy for approaching forecasting problems. It is the most general of the short-term forecasting techniques and one of the most powerful available today. It can develop an adequate model for almost any pattern of data. However, its complexity requires that its users have a certain amount of expertise.

Box and Jenkins propose three general classes of models for describing any type of stationary process (processes that remain in equilibrium about a constant mean level): (1) autoregressive (AR), (2) moving average (MA), and (3) mixed autoregressive and moving average (ARMA). A series with a trend is frequently made stationary by taking first or second differences prior to applying the procedure.

An AR model is of the form

$$Y_t = \phi_1 Y_{t-1} + \phi_2 Y_{t-2} + \cdots + \phi_p Y_{t-p} + \nu_t \qquad (10.22)$$

where the ν_t are independent, random shocks with constant variance (usually assumed to be independent and normally distributed with mean zero and constant variance σ^2). This model is called autoregressive because Y_t is in some way regressed on its past values.

An MA model is of the form

$$Y_t = \mu_t - \theta_1 \nu_{t-1} - \theta_2 \nu_{t-2} - \cdots - \theta_q \nu_{t-q} \qquad (10.23)$$

where ν_t is the current error and $\nu_{t-1}, \ldots, \nu_{t-q}$ are the values of lagged errors. This model implies that the variable of interest is a linear function of previous values of the error, rather than of the variable itself.

Finally, an ARMA model is of the form

$$Y_t = \underbrace{\phi_1 Y_{t-1} + \cdots + \phi_p Y_{t-p}}_{\text{AR}} + \underbrace{\nu_t + \theta_1 \nu_{t-1} + \cdots + \theta_q \nu_{t-q}}_{\text{MA}} \qquad (10.24)$$

This model represents the combination of an AR and an MA model. It expresses future values of a variable as a linear combination of both past values and forecasting errors.

The structure of an ARMA model can be characterized by its autocorrelation function:

$$\rho_j = \frac{\text{cov}(Y_t, Y_{t-j})}{\sqrt{\text{var } Y_t \text{ var } Y_{t-j}}} \qquad (10.25)$$

If the series is stationary, then var y_t = var y_{t-j}, and we obtain

$$\rho_j = \frac{\text{cov}(Y_t, Y_{t-j})}{\text{Var } Y_t} \qquad (10.26)$$

For a general ARMA model, ρ_j will be a complex function of $\{\theta_i\}$ and $\{\phi_i\}$. Exhibit 10.6 sketches some autocorrelation functions; these functions are used below to specify an ARMA model.

EXHIBIT 10-6 **Some autocorrelation functions.** (Source: Wonnacott and Wonnacott, 1979, p. 239.)

For Moving Averages

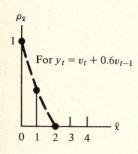

For $y_t = v_t + 0.6v_{t-1}$

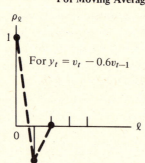

For $y_t = v_t - 0.6v_{t-1}$

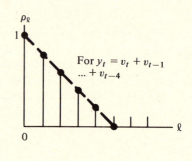

For $y_t = v_t + v_{t-1}$
$... + v_{t-4}$

For Autoregressions

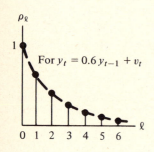

For $y_t = 0.6y_{t-1} + v_t$

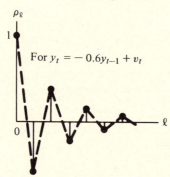

For $y_t = -0.6y_{t-1} + v_t$

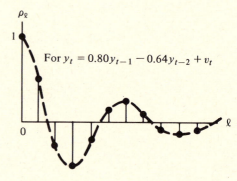

For $y_t = 0.80y_{t-1} - 0.64y_{t-2} + v_t$

For Mixtures

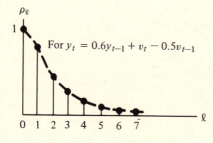

For $y_t = 0.6y_{t-1} + v_t - 0.5v_{t-1}$

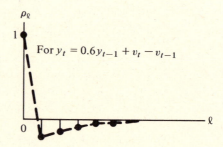

For $y_t = 0.6y_{t-1} + v_t - v_{t-1}$

If a series is increasing or decreasing with time, we can remove this (trend) by taking differences,

$$\Delta Y_t = Y_t - Y_{t-1} \tag{10.27}$$

and then developing an ARMA model for ΔY_t. The original series Y_t can be recovered by successively adding in the ΔY_t, starting at Y_0. If the trend is nonlinear, several differences (d) may be required to produce a stationary ARMA series. Again, the original series can be recovered by summing d times. Such a series is called an integrated ARMA series, denoted as ARIMA (p, d, q), where p is the order of the AR part, q is the order of the MA part, and d is the level of difference used to produce stationarity.

In the actual building of an ARIMA model, there are three stages:

1. specification (determining p, d, and q)
2. estimation of $\{\phi_i\}$ and $\{\theta_j\}$
3. diagnostic checking

In the first stage the most usual procedure, after differencing to achieve stationarity, is to calculate the population autocorrelation function,

$$\hat{\rho}_j = \frac{\displaystyle\sum_{t=j+1}^{n} Y_t Y_{t-j}}{\displaystyle\sum_{t=1}^{n} Y_t^2} \tag{10.28}$$

(where the Y's here are assumed to be centered at zero) and compare it with expected patterns of different ARMA models (such as those displayed in Exhibit 10.6). For estimation a variety of programs are available, most of which combine a search procedure over some of the parameters with an OLS estimate of others. Box and Jenkins (1976) discuss estimation farther. Diagnostic checking involves checking that (1) the estimated residuals are indeed uncorrelated and (2) a bigger model with another parameter would not fit the data significantly better.

Finally, to forecast with an ARMA model, we plug the estimated future values of Y_t into the equation. Future values of ν_t are usually assumed to be zero and therefore eventually drop out, with the forecast becoming purely autoregressive.

Multivariate extensions of the ARMA models, known as multivariate ARMA, or MARMA (Box and Jenkins, 1976; Makridakis and Wheelright, 1978), which combine powerful time-series forecasting techniques with explanatory variables and causal models, have been developed. For an application in estimating the dynamic elements in a competitive, market-response framework, see Hanssens (1980).

Completeness and versatility are the main advantages of the Box-Jenkins approach. In practice, however, the analytical complexity of the models and the expertise needed in selecting the most appropriate ones have limited its use.

Decomposition Methods.   The forecasting methods described thus far are based on the idea that when an underlying pattern exists in a data series, it can be distinguished from randomness by smoothing (averaging) past values. The smoothing eliminates randomness so that the pattern can be projected into the future and used as a forecast. These methods make no attempt to identify individual components of the basic underlying pattern. However, in many cases the pattern can be broken down (decomposed) into subpatterns that identify each component of the series separately. Such a breakdown can frequently produce improved accuracy in forecasting and aid in better understanding the series.

Decompositional methods assume that all series are made up of patterns plus error. The objective is to decompose the pattern of the series into trend, cycle, and seasonality:

$$X_t = f(I_t, T_t, C_t, E_t) \tag{10.29}$$

where X_t = time series at time t
I_t = seasonal component (or index) at t
T_t = trend component at t
C_t = cyclical component at t
E_t = error or random component at t

The exact functional form of eq. (10.29) depends on the decompositional method used. The most common form is a multiplicative model:

$$X_t = I_t \times T_t \times C_t \times E_t \tag{10.30}$$

An additive form is used often, as well.

Although there are a number of decompositional methods, they all seem to follow the same basic process:

1. For the series X_t, compute a moving average of length N, where N is the length of the seasonality (e.g., N = 12 with monthly data). This averaging will eliminate seasonality by averaging seasonally high periods with seasonally low periods; and because random errors have no systematic pattern, it reduces randomness as well.
2. Separate the outcome of the N-period moving average from the original data period to obtain trend and cyclicality. If the model is multiplicative, this step is done by dividing the original series by the smoothed series, leaving seasonality and error:

$$\frac{X_t}{T_t + C_t} \, (= \text{moving average}) = I_t \times E_t \tag{10.31}$$

3. Isolate the seasonal factors by averaging them for each of the periods making up the complete length of the seasonality.

4. Specify the appropriate form of the trend (linear, quadratic, exponential) and calculate its value at each period T_t. This step may be done by regression analysis or by moving averages with trend adjustments.
5. Use the results to separate out the cycle from the trend + cycle (i.e., the moving average).
6. When the seasonality, trend, and cyclicality are separated from the original data series, the remaining randomness, E_t can be identified.

The most widely used decompositional method is known as the Census II method, developed at the Bureau of the Census. [See Shiskin, Young, and Musgrave (1967) for complete details.] The Census II method (in its X–11 version) considers such items as trading days (the number of Mondays, say, in a month may be critical if Monday is a traditional sale day), smoothing for extreme points, varying-length moving averages for random components with different average levels, and so on. This method was developed empirically and tested on thousands of series. As such, although it does not have a sound statistical base, it is intuitive and geared to the practitioner and, therefore, the opposite of procedures such as the Box-Jenkins approach, which is derived from theory. However, the method appears to be most appropriate for short- or medium-term forecasting and is mainly suited to macroeconomic series.

Another widely used decompositional method is the FORAN system (McLaughlin and Boyle, 1968), which has the advantage of being able to handle more than one independent variable (i.e., it can handle independent variables other than time) and is oriented toward the forecasting needs of business organizations. A system called FORAN II with a more complete range of forecasting options and diagnostics was introduced in 1977.

Causal Methods

In the models described above it is assumed that little is known about the underlying cause of demand and that the future will be pretty much like the past. As such, these time-series methods are most useful for short- or medium-term extrapolations (usually less than a year in the future).

An alternative approach, especially useful when market conditions are not inherently stable, is to express demand as a function of a certain number of factors that determine its outcome. Such forecasts are not necessarily time-dependent, which makes them useful for longer-term predictions. In addition, developing an explanatory or causal model facilitates a better understanding of the situation.

Regression and Econometric Models. Regression and econometric models typically specify the structure between demand and its underlying causes. Strictly speaking, multiple-regression equations fall in the realm of econometrics, although generally econometrics refers to sets of two or more regression equations. Chapter 5 develops regression and econometric models and estimation procedures in detail.

EXAMPLE: In industrial markets, firms often wish to relate product-demand needs with published data for those SIC codes considered high potential. In these analyses, number of employees is frequently used as the most readily available surrogate for customer size.

The Machinco Company makes high-technology components and currently has 17 customers. Exhibit 10.7 gives the number of employees and volume of purchases from Machinco of each of its customers.

If we use number of employees as a rough predictor of sales potential, we might relate

$$\text{Sales} = a_0 + a_1 \text{ (number of employees)} \qquad (10.32)$$

Then through linear regression, we find that $a_0 = 8.52$ and $a_1 = 0.061$. The U.S. Census of Manufacturers reports that prospective customers for Machinco's product have a total of 126,000 employees. With this information and eq. (10.32) above, we find

$$\text{(Potential) sales} = 8.52 + 0.061 \times 126{,}000 = 7695 \qquad (10.33)$$

EXHIBIT 10-7   Machinco's customers and current sales levels.

Customer Number	No. of Employees	Sales in $1000s[a]
1	110	9.8
2	141	21.2
3	204	14.7
4	377	22.8
5	395	48.1
6	502	42.3
7	612	27.8
8	618	40.7
9	707	59.8
10	721	44.5
11	736	77.1
12	856	59.2
13	902	52.3
14	926	77.1
15	1045	74.6
16	1105	81.8
17	1250	69.7
		Total = 823.0

[a]Regression of sales versus employees gives sales = $8.52 + 0.61$ × no. of employees, $R^2 = 0.77$.

This value is nearly ten times the current sales of Machinco (823), which indicates substantial possibilities for expanding sales to other prospects.

Suppose that the company has two prospects. Company A has 1600 employees, and B has 500 employees. A good guess for the sales potential for company A is $8.52 + 0.061 \times 1600$, or 106 units. Similarly, we get 39 units as the potential for company B.

For a description of another analysis similar to this one in operation, see Cox and Havens (1977).

Input-Output Analysis. In many instances there are insufficient data for time-series or causal (regression) methods, in which case approaches known as aggregate procedures may be used. These methods link demand to economic factors that reflect the capacity of a market or market segment to consume a product. A number of such techniques are available; they differ mainly in the economic indicators used and in the way the relationships are constructed. The best-known and most widely used is input-output analysis.

In our economy firms produce products and sell them to other firms that add value to them, sell them, and so on, until at last the finished product is in the hands of the consumer. Such transactions—a sort of economic system of shipments—are studied in the discipline known as input-output analysis. [See Leontief (1951, 1966).]

The input-output principle is the conservation of mass. Everything that is produced has to go somewhere, and when demand for finished products increases, this derives demand for other intermediate (industrial) products.

In a complex and diversified economy, direct consumer sales frequently represent only a portion of the output of a given industry. The rest are intermediate products used by its purchasers for input into other production processes. Final demand is that output of an industry not sold to another industry but rather to consumers, government, inventory, or export. The sum of final demand in a national input-output table is the gross national product.

Thus we can develop a series of accounting equations:

Output of any industry = sales to intermediate users + final demand

Mathematically, we let

X_i = sales of any industry, $i = 1, \ldots, n$

x_{ij} = sales of industry i to industry j, $j = 1, \ldots, n$

Y_{ik} = sales by industry i to ultimate consumer k, $k = 1, \ldots, K$

Now an equation can be written for each industry:

$$\underbrace{X_i}_{\substack{\text{Output} \\ \text{sector}}} = \underbrace{x_{i1} + \cdots + x_{in}}_{\substack{\text{Intermediate} \\ \text{demand}}} + \underbrace{Y_{i1} + \cdots + Y_{iK}}_{\substack{\text{Final} \\ \text{demand}}} \qquad (10.34)$$

A system of such equations, one for each industry, is called a transactions matrix. It can be understood through an example of a simple economy with three sectors: agriculture, manufacture, and consumers. Consider Exhibit 10.8.

The agricultural sector produces 200 sacks of flour, the manufacturing sector produces 100 bars of soap, and consumers provide 600 person-years of labor. The elements in Exhibit 10.8 show the intersectoral flows. For example, agriculture turned out 200 sacks of flour but used up 50 in the process and sent 50 to the soap manufacturers. The consumers got the rest. Manufacturing sent 28 bars of soap to agriculture, used 12 itself, and sent the remaining 60 bars to consumers.

Each column represents the input structure of the sector. To produce 200 sacks of flour, the farmers needed to consume 50 sacks, to use 28 bars of soap, and to absorb 160 person-years of labor. Manufacturing needed 40 sacks of flour, 12 bars of its own soap, and 360 person-years of labor to produce the 100 bars of soap. And consumers spent the incomes that they received for supplying 600 person-years of labor on 110 sacks of flour, 60 bars of soap, and 80 person-years of direct services of labor.

Of course, to be useful, an input-output table must have many more entries. Various countries have developed input-output tables; the most recent include more than 360 sectors in the United States and 56 (through Eurostat) in Europe. In a larger table manufacturing would be much more disaggregated; typical products might be yards of cotton cloth, yards of woolen cloth, reams of newsprint, and the like. Furthermore, in practice, the intersectoral flows are generally represented in a common unit (dollars) for convenience.

If we now take the output of sector i as absorbed by sector j per unit of total output, we get the input coefficient of a product of sector i into sector j. Mathematically, we get

$$a_{ij} = \frac{x_{ij}}{X_j} \tag{10.35}$$

A complete set of input coefficients for all sectors of a given economy—arranged in the same way as the transactions matrix—is the structural matrix of an economy. Exhibit 10.9 gives the structural matrix for our

EXHIBIT 10-8　**Example of transactions matrix.**

		Outputs			
		Processing Sector		Final Demand	Output
		Agriculture	Manufacture	Consumers	Total
Inputs	Agriculture	50	40	110	200 Stacks of Flour
	Manufacture	28	12	60	100 Bars of Soap
	Consumers	160	360	80	600 Person-Years

EXHIBIT 10-9   **Structural matrix.**

From	Agriculture	To Manufacture	Consumers
Agriculture	0.25	0.16	0.37
Manufacture	0.35	0.12	0.50
Consumers	0.40	0.72	0.13
	1.00	**1.00**	**1.00**

three-sector economy with a sack of flour = $2, a bar of soap = $5, and a person-year of labor = $1.

To interpret this table, we note that an input coefficient measures the input required from one industry to produce $1 of output in another industry. For example, for every dollar in manufacturing, we need 16¢ from agriculture, 12¢ from manufacturing itself, and 72¢ from consumers (labor). The assumption is that larger outputs need more inputs. In terms of our prior notation,

$$x_{ij} = F(X_j) = a_{ij}X_j \qquad (10.36)$$

This equation assumes that the relationship between inputs and outputs is linear, at least in a range.

In the short run, this linearity appears to be a reasonable assumption. [See Leontief (1951) and Shapiro (1972).] There is reasonable evidence that the level of technology for a given industry changes rather slowly. Consequently, if we let

$$Y_i = Y_{i1} + \cdots + Y_{iK}$$

$$= \text{sales of industry } i \text{ to all ultimate consumer groups} \qquad (10.37)$$

then the following relationship is valid:

$$X_i = a_{i1}X_1 + a_{i2}X_2 + \cdots + a_{in}X_n + Y_i \qquad (10.38)$$

where i = industry.

More formally, a set of input-output equations can be displayed as follows:

$$(X_1 - x_{11}) - x_{12} \cdots - x_{1n} = Y_1$$
$$-x_{21} + (X_2 - x_{22}) \cdots - x_{2n} = Y_2$$
$$\vdots \qquad (10.39)$$
$$-x_{n1} - x_{n2} + (X_n - x_{nn}) = Y_n$$

If we define $a_{ij} = x_{ij}/X_j$ = input coefficient of product i into sector j, we get

$$(1 - a_{11})X_1 - a_{12}X_2 - \cdots - a_{1n}X_n = Y_1$$
$$\vdots \qquad (10.40)$$
$$- a_{n1}X_1 - a_{n2}X_2 - \cdots + (1 - a_{nn})X_n = Y_n$$

If the set of final demands, $Y_1, \ldots, Y_n$, is known, the system can be solved for the n total outputs, $X_1, \ldots, X_n$. The general solution for the unknown X's can be represented as

$$
\begin{aligned}
X_1 &= A_{11}Y_1 + A_{12}Y_2 + \cdots + A_{1n}Y_n \\
X_2 &= A_{12}Y_1 + A_{22}Y_2 + \cdots + A_{2n}Y_n \\
&\;\;\vdots \\
X_n &= A_{n1}Y_1 + A_{n2}Y_2 + \cdots + A_{nn}Y_n
\end{aligned}
\qquad (10.41)
$$

where A_{ij} indicates how much output X_i of the ith sector would be affected by a unit increase in the consumption of good j.

Furthermore, when it exists,

$$
\begin{bmatrix} A_{11} \cdots A_{1n} \\ \cdots \cdots \\ A_{n1} \cdots A_n \end{bmatrix} = \begin{bmatrix} (1 - a_{11}) - a_{12} - \cdots - a_{1n} \\ \cdots \cdots \cdots \cdots \cdots \cdots \\ -a_{n1} - a_{n2} - \cdots - (1 - a_{nn}) \end{bmatrix}^{-1}
\qquad (10.42)
$$

Thus the matrix A_{ij} is the inverse of the matrix of input coefficients.

For there to be a set of outputs $X_1, \ldots, X_n$ capable of satisfying any set of final deliveries $Y_1, \ldots, Y_n$, it is necessary that all elements of A_{ij} be nonnegative.

Finally, input-output theory can be made dynamic by considering intersectoral dependence involving lags or rates of change over time. [See Leontief (1966) for more details.]

Practically, input-output forecasts provide estimates of industrial growth, of the markets that account for that growth, and of the inputs the industry will require if that growth is to be achieved. However, many firms are not in a single industry and must adapt the input-output analysis. One way of achieving this goal (Tiebout, 1967) is to insert the product of an organization as a row in the available tables. Then the company can estimate sales to the various sectors specified in the input-output study and can calculate how much each industry requires from it per dollar of output. Row coefficients are suitably adjusted. The firm can enter itself as a column, and the new structure can be used as an individual company or product forecast. Alternatively, the input-output matrix can be expanded by detailed analysis of a firm's target markets, inserting them as sectors in the economy. This technique may require customized data collection.

EXAMPLE: Rippe, Wilkinson, and Morrison (1976) discuss input-output-demand forecasting with anticipation data, which are reports on expected future sales and capital spending for an industry. The empirical justification for using anticipation data in demand forecasts comes from several sources. Muth (1961) notes that averages of anticipations for an industry are as accurate as elaborate equation models and better than naive models. [See also Rippe and Wilkinson (1974).]

Rippe, Wilkinson, and Morrison (1976) also propose an extension of the usual input-output framework by including purchases of goods on capital accounts. Let

$$X_k = S_k + I_k \qquad (10.43)$$

where S_k = sales on current account for industry k
   I_k = sales on capital account for industry k

(Current accounts use the input for each unit of output; capital accounts generally use the input in production equipment, and therefore purchases of capital-account inputs are not directly related to output.)

Then similar to the above,

$$X_i = a_{i1}S_1 + \cdots + a_{in}S_n + c_{i1}I_1 + \cdots + c_{in}I_n + Y_i \qquad (10.44)$$

The anticipations method of forecasting uses $S_1, \ldots, S_n, I_1, \ldots, I_n$, available at two-digit SIC-code accuracy, h time periods into the future.

If X_i^0 is current demand, then X_i^h is demand h time periods in the future. Assume that Y_i^h can be modeled as

$$\hat{Y}_i^h = f(Y_i^0, Y_i^{-1}, \ldots) \qquad (10.45)$$

perhaps as an autoregressive model. Then

$$\hat{X}_i^h = a_{i1}\hat{S}_1 + \cdots + a_{in}\hat{S}_n + c_{i1}\hat{I}_1 + \cdots + c_{in}\hat{I}_n + \hat{Y}_{ih} \qquad (10.46)$$

where $\hat{S}_1$ and $\hat{I}_n$ are derived from anticipations data.

As an example, the American Iron and Steel Institute (1974) publishes an industry breakdown of shipments each year that can be used as a starting point in the forecast. These numbers must be adjusted to correspond with two-digit SIC codes. The complete details of the example are found in Rippe, Wilkinson, and Morrison (1976). In terms of mean-absolute forecast error, the method does more than 50% better than a simple model derived by assuming the same change as between the two most recent years.

In sum, this method looks promising. It can be extended to industry sales by product line, company sales, and company sales by product line as long as the appropriate technical coefficients (the a's and the c's) can be estimated at the product or company level. The use of industry anticipatory data allows for more direct and easy use than exogenous forecasts of each industry's demand. The interested reader might also consult Ranard (1972) for a description of a sales-forecasting system using input-output analysis.

New-product Forecasting Methods.   New-product/new-business analysis causes several significant problems for forecasters. First, by definition, new products have little sales history, and therefore most time-series-based procedures are not viable. In addition, the structure of new-product sales tends to be considerably less stable than that for existing products. An important objective is the prediction of the terminal share of a product or the product's performance after its sales have settled down.

The information at the marketer's disposal varies by product class and includes diary panel data, pretest-market evaluations, usage rates, relative penetrations, first-purchase and repeat rates, and so on.

Methods for new-product forecasting are varied, based on different behavioral assumptions and different data sources. They include brand-switching analysis, trial-repeat analysis, microflow simulation models, conjoint-analysis-based and utility-theory-based approaches, and diffusion analyses. These methods are explored in detail in Chapters 11 and 19.

Accuracy of Forecasting Methods

Although a wide choice of demand forecasting procedures are available, there have been a relatively small number of empirical attempts to compare their accuracy. In Exhibit 10.5(b) we presented an illustrative comparison of the forecasting accuracy for Box-Jenkins, two single exponential-smoothing models, moving averages, moving averages with trend adjustments, and a naive model (last-period's sales). The optimal Box-Jenkins procedure produced the best forecasts in this comparison.

Newbold and Granger (1974) report an empirical comparison of Box-Jenkins with two fully automatic procedures—the Holt-Winter and a stepwise autoregressive scheme—for a single-period time horizon. Box-Jenkins forecasts were found to be more accurate than the Holt-Winter forecasts in 73 percent of the cases and more accurate than the stepwise autoregressive forecasts in 68 percent of the cases. These percentages drop to 58 percent and 63 percent, respectively, when the time horizon is extended to eight periods. Reid (1971) also concludes that the Box-Jenkins approach gives more accurate results than exponential-smoothing or stepwise-regression methods.

In terms of times-series versus econometric approaches, Naylor, Seaks, and Wichern (1972) made a detailed comparison of the Box-Jenkins approach in comparison with the Wharton econometric model for the years 1963–1967 (Exhibit 10.10). The results show that the accuracy of the ARMA models is superior to that of the Wharton econometric model.

Nelson (1972) compared the FRB-MIT-PENN model with ARMA models, using a longer time period. He concludes, "The simple ARMA models are relatively more robust with respect to past sample predictions than the complex FRB-MIT-PENN models. . . . An unweighted assessment clearly indicates that a decision maker would be better off relying simply on ARMA predictions [for forecasting]" (p. 915). The results of Cooper (1972)

EXHIBIT 10-10   **Comparison of the Wharton econometric model with the Box-Jenkins approach (1963–1967).**

	Wharton (Average Absolute error)	Box-Jenkins (Average Absolute Error)
I_p (investment in billions)	1.09	0.59
P (GNP price deflator in percentages)	0.22	0.11
Un (unemployment in percentages)	0.186	0.109
GNP (in billions)	2.51	2.01

SOURCE: Naylor, Seaks, and Wichern, 1972, p. 831.

confirm these findings as well. Thus it seems that time-series methods can do as well on accuracy as causal models, and other criteria—such as believability and the inclusion of control variables—must be considered in discriminating between them. Spivey and Wrobleski (1981) conclude that United States econometric models in the first half of the 1970s have been unreliable for periods three or more quarters into the future, casting doubt on their value even for policy assessment.

Therefore for the choice among forecasting methods, a number of issues must be considered. For example, the number of historical (and relevant!) data points is critical in making a decision. Furthermore, cost effectiveness, a crucial factor, has been ignored in the published comparisons. A useful qualitative evaluation, prepared by Chambers and colleagues (1974) and summarized in Exhibit 10.11, suggests which forecasting techniques are most accurate for short-, medium-, and long-range forecasts. The X–11 model and simultaneous-equation systems were judged best in the ability to identify structural changes in the data series (turning points). Hogarth and Makridakis (1981) provide a thorough review of the uses, limitations, and inherent biases in forecasting.

EXHIBIT 10-11   **Most-accurate forecasting techniques.**

Forecasting Period		
Short-Term, 0–3 mo	**Medium-Term, 3 mo to 2 yr**	**Long-Term, 2+ yr**
Exponential smoothing	X–11 (Bureau of the Census)	Trend-line projection
Box-Jenkins	Trend-line projection	Simultaneous-equation systems
X–11 (Bureau of the Census)	Simultaneous-equation systems	Input-output models
Trend-line projection	Input-output models	
Simultaneous-equation systems		

SOURCE: Chambers et al., 1974.

Summary

No firm can conduct its business successfully without trying to measure the actual size of present and future markets. Quantitative measurements are essential for the analysis of market opportunities and the planning of market programs, varying in the level of product aggregation, the time dimension, and the space dimension. However, in all its studies the company should be clear about its demand-measurement concepts, particularly the distinction between market demand and company demand, and the corollary concepts of forecasts and potentials.

Current demand may be estimated for the market as a whole or for various territories. In the latter case the market-buildup method is commonly used for industrial goods and the index-of-buying-power method for consumer goods.

For forecasting future demand a company may rely on expert opinion, buyer surveys, times-series methods, or causal demand analysis. These methods vary in their appropriateness to the purpose of forecast, the type of product, and the availability and reliability of data. Current thinking has firms using a combination of independent forecasts to confirm one another and to provide important forecasting diagnostics.

The selection of a forecasting method must carefully weigh the use of the forecast. Time-series models do as well as causal models in recent tests but are not useful for policy evaluation. The length of the forecasting period is also critical in choosing a forecasting model.

Problems

10.1 A manufacturer of printing equipment estimates sales by first asking the district sales managers for district forecasts. How can these initial forecasts be refined at higher company levels to arrive at a final companywide sales forecast?

10.2 What are the differences between time-series analysis and causal analysis? What are the major advantages and weaknesses of the two approaches in demand assessment and forecasting?

10.3 "It is reasonable to expect in most practical situations that the best available combined forecast will outperform the best individual forecast—it cannot, in any case, do worse." Comment.

10.4 What kinds of information can be derived from standard industrial classifications for demand forecasting? What are some limitations of SIC analysis?

10.5 A brand manager expects his new-product sales to grow continuously so that he will sell $100 + 4t$ units of the product per day, t days after introduction. [That is, on the initial day ($t = 0$) he will sell 100 units, on the next day ($t = 1$) he will sell 104 units, etc.] Set up the appropriate equations and solve for the day that the 10,000th unit will be sold.

10.6 A firm has collected the following historical data concerning its past sales performance:

Year	Company Product Sales (in $000s), y	Industry Sales (in $millions), x_1	Index of Industrial Production, x_2
1973	408	9.0	103.1
1974	419	9.5	108.0
1975	398	9.3	101.7
1976	399	10.1	99.4
1977	418	12.3	98.6
1978	415	11.6	99.8
1979	459	10.5	101.2
1980	429	9.1	96.1
1981	461	11.5	98.9
1982	467	10.7	103.5

It is recommended that sales forecasts be made by one of the three following equations:

$$y = b_0 + b_1x_1 + b_2x_2$$
$$y = b_0x_1^{b_1}x_2^{b_2}$$
$$y = b_0 + b_1x_1^{1/2} + b_2x_2$$

Which of these equations would you recommend and why?

10.7 The company whose sales data are shown in Problem 10.6 undertook a product-quality-improvement program, which first had an impact in 1979. Can the effect of this program be ascertained? What forecast equation would you now recommend? For your recommended forecast equation, interpret the relative effects of the independent variables.

10.8 The weekly sales of a cutting tool are shown below. Simulate a one-week-ahead forecast for these data, using (a) simple exponential smoothing with $\alpha = 0.10$ and (b) double exponential smoothing with $\alpha = 0.20$. Compare the results obtained using appropriate criteria.

Week	Sales	Week	Sales
1	50	5	66
2	65	6	69
3	63	7	62
4	58	8	70

10.9 You are given the values $X_1 = 2$, $X_2 = 1$, $X_3 = 5$, $X_4 = 1.5$, $X_5 = 2.2$, $X_6 = 2$.

a. Use an AR(1), model and calculate ϕ_1 by trial and error in such a way as to minimize MSE (mean square error).

b. Use the adaptive-filtering rule, $W' = W + 2ke_t X_{t-1}$, in order to find the optimal W value.

10.10 A company selling agricultural fertilizers wants to forecast market sales for one of its major products. The market research department has collected data on total industry sales for the past 8 yr:

Year	Industry Sales (in 1000s of tons)
1973	7.1
1974	17.1
1975	33.2
1976	37.4
1977	47.0
1978	72.8
1979	59.0
1980	62.7

a. Forecast industry sales for 1981, using at least two methods. Choose a selection criterion and retain the better one.

b. Forecast industry sales for 1986, also using at least two methods, and retain the better.

c. Have you used the same forecasting model in parts a and b? Why (or why not)?

10.11 A marketing researcher sought a multiple-regression equation to explain past sales in an industry. Good industry data on the dependent and independent variables only went back 5 yr. He fitted the following equation:

$$Y = 5241 + 31X_1 + 12X_2 + 50X_3$$

where Y = yearly sales, $1000s
        X_1 = United States disposable personal income, $ billions
        X_2 = United States population, millions of households
        X_3 = time, yr (1976 = 0)

He was pleased to find that this equation accounted for 98% of the yearly variations in industry sales. List any reservations you would have about using this equation in forecasting future industry sales.

4

Micromarketing Decision Models

11 Product Design and Development Models

The long-term health of many organizations, both consumer and industrial, is intimately tied to their ability to innovate—to provide existing and new customers with a continuing stream of new products and services. Under modern conditions of competition, it is becoming increasingly hazardous not to innovate; the firm that does not maintain a program of managed innovation can quickly find itself well behind competition.

Although innovation is important, it is risky and costly as well. Ford lost an estimated $350 million on its ill-fated Edsel, and duPont lost an estimated $100 million on its Corfam product (synthetic rubber). Further, Xerox's venture into computers was a disaster, and the French Concorde aircraft will probably never recover its investment.

A survey of 125 companies by Hopkins and Bailey (1971) indicated that the median percentage of major new products and services whose performance fell short of expectations was 20 percent for industrial-product manufacturers, about 18 percent for service industries, and about 40 percent for consumer-product manufacturers. Good statistics on new-product failure are not readily available or comparable, but in another widely referenced study, Booz, Allen and Hamilton (1971) report that of 366 new products in 54 prominent companies, approximately a third were not successful. In some areas, such as consumer products, the failure rate is even higher, with 50 to 60 percent of the products failing in national introductions or in major test markets (A. C. Nielsen, Inc., 1971, 1979; Silk and Urban, 1978).

The resources allocated to new-product failures are substantial: Booz, Allen and Hamilton report that 70 percent of the resources spent on new products are allocated to products that are not successful in the market. Urban and Hauser (1980, p. 49) have estimated that the average design cost for a new consumer product is about $200,000, and for an industrial product it is $620,000. Therefore if we factor in failure rates, the average cost to produce a *successful* new product is several times higher.

In addition, there are many reasons to believe that successful new-product development will be even harder in the future than it has been in the past. These factors include the shortage of new-product ideas, the fragmentation of markets, increasing social and governmental constraints, capital shortages, and shorter product life cycles.

Thus management faces a dilemma: it must develop new products to survive, yet the odds are heavily weighted against their success. The solution lies in developing new products in a systematic, scientific way that controls and reduces the risk of failure. Urban and Hauser (1980) provide an excellent integrated treatment of an analytical approach to new-product development and marketing. In this chapter we discuss the new-product development and design process, leaving the presentation of more-integrated, new-product and market-planning models for Part 5.

Product Design in Perspective

Exhibit 11.1 displays one view of the product-design process. It contains a managerial side (the action component) and a consumer side (the response component). The managerial side categorizes the decisions required in new-product development, while the consumer-response side categorizes market measurements and models to assist in that process.

Although this process is perceived as iterative, the initial driving force is *opportunity identification*. Procedures, such as the Hendry (1970, 1971) and Prodegy (Urban, Johnson, and Brudnick, 1979) approaches, provide quantitative support to aid such searches.

Consumer measurements are required for understanding consumers' responses to alternative product offerings. Qualitative measurements put management in touch with the market by providing insight into the consumer's perception, evaluation, and choice processes. It is at this stage that management gains insight into how consumers see product alternatives, how the products relate as complements or substitutes, and what types of consumers and use combinations are the most viable targets. Focus-group interviews are usually used to obtain these data. Then, following qualitative analysis, quantitative measurements are required to assess likely consumer response with some level of confidence. These measurements are usually obtained from mail, telephone, or personal-interview surveys designed to measure attitudes, preferences, and likely choices in given decision situations for a representative sample of consumers.

Consumer models, detailed in Chapters 7 and 8, reflect the diversity of

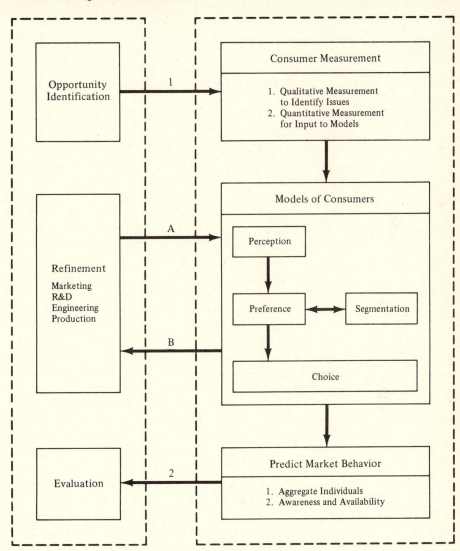

EXHIBIT 11-1 **The new-product-design process.** (Source: Glen L. Urban, and John R. Hauser, *Design and Marketing of New Products,* © 1980, p. 158. Adapted by permission of Prentice-Hall, Inc., Englewood Cliffs, N.J.)

choice situations and choice-making processes. Product-design models frequently rely on rational-choice models. The physical features of the product as well as its psychological features and promises (communicated by advertising) are believed to influence the consumer-choice process at all levels. This type of model suggests that a product with the right *physical* features that does not communicate them properly will not get past the perception-preference stage, and a product whose advertising communicates benefits it does not deliver will get poor purchase feedback and no repeat sales, along with negative word-of-mouth effects. (An ad agency executive once said, "Good advertising is the fastest way to kill a poor product.")

Exhibit 11.1 highlights the several points of leverage where product design or positioning changes are most likely to be influencial, including perception, preference, and choice. *Perception* is the identification of the key physical or psychological dimensions of importance to the consumer; *preference* refers to the way consumers use their perceptions to evaluate products; and *choice* encompasses the external events (availability, for example) required for translating product preferences into an actual purchase situation. Exhibit 11.1 also introduces the concept of *segmentation*; managers need to know whether consumers are sufficiently homogeneous in their perceptions and preferences for a single-product strategy or whether a number of products are required, each targeted at a different customer group.

Other elements in Exhibit 11.1 are *predictions* of market behavior (what will most likely occur under a given competitive scenario); managerial-*refinement* actions, design and marketing *adjustments* needed to improve the product; and *evaluation,* the managerial-analysis process, which determines the potential profitability of the venture and quantifies the political, technological, and environmental constraints affecting a market-entry decision.

At the center of the design process is the *consumer;* product opportunities are focused at filling existing or latent consumer needs. A number of studies on new-product failures (Angelus, 1969; Booz, Allen and Hamilton, 1971; Briscoe, 1973; Cooper, 1975; Crawford, 1977; Davidson, 1976; Rothwell et al., 1974) have found that although there are often many causes, a predominant reason that products fail is for lack of a clear understanding of market needs. For example, the Davidson study showed that of 100 new grocery products introduced in Great Britain, 74 percent of the successful products offered superior consumer benefits while only 20 percent of the failures did. Calentone and Cooper (1977), in a study of new-industrial-product failures, found that the largest category, 28 percent, included products that met a nonexistent need while only 15 percent of the product failures were "bad" products—that is, did not do what they were supposed to do.

A successful product-design process, then, is *proactive* (as opposed to reactive)—the organization actively initiates efforts to change the status quo. Reactive strategies tend to produce imitative, second-to-the-market products. Proactive marketing strategies require methods for understanding and satisfying consumer needs better. This type of strategy is a key element in the success of such companies as Procter and Gamble, General Foods, and McDonalds.

Idea Sources and Generation

In the development and design of products, a number of potential new-product ideas must be generated and screened. These ideas are not yet products but, rather, preproducts. There are a number of sources for generating such ideas, including customers, scientists, competitors, company salespeople and dealers, and top management. Their functions vary by the type of product and market.

Customers.   The marketing concept suggests that customer needs and wants are the logical starting point for new-product ideas. These can be identified through surveys, projective tests, focused group discussion, suggestion systems, and preference and perceptual mapping.

Scientists.   R&D programs are designed with the concept of developing fundamentally new ideas and products.

Competitors.   Not everyone can be first into the market, and a competitive-product launch is often a spur to new-product development.

Sales representatives and dealers.   These individuals have direct customer contact, know customers' needs, and are often excellent idea sources.

Top management.   For better or worse, company top management may take personal responsibility for developing and promoting new-product ideas in their companies.

Other sources.   Other new-product idea sources include inventors, patent attorneys, university and commercial laboratories, industrial consultants, advertising agencies, marketing research firms, and industrial publications.

In addition, a number of methods have been developed to aid the idea-generation process. Most are techniques for breaking the current mode of thinking and putting pieces of ideas (and often individuals with disparate backgrounds) together. Some of these techniques are called attribute listing, forced relationships, morphological analysis, problem analysis, brainstorming, and synectics [see Parnes and Harding (1962), and Tauber (1972)].

A key element of the idea-generation process for new products is the wedding of consumer input and technology. The information flow within the R&D department and between technical fields must be functioning properly (Allen, 1977). Furthermore, technological forecasting can help predict when a new product or technology will be able to meet customer needs and achieve economic impact (Bright, 1970; Utterback and Braun, 1972).

A growing body of literature (von Hippel, 1977a, 1977b, 1978) suggests that, particularly in industrial markets, there are systematic ways to generate and tap successful new-product ideas from users. Exhibit 11.2 summarizes the level of involvement by users in new-product development observed by a variety of researchers in several industries.

von Hippel has observed that in industrial markets innovative users are frequently the source of successful new products, a source that an efficient market-analysis operation should tap.

IBM designed and built the first printed circuit card component insertion machine of the X–Y Table type to be used in commercial production. IBM needed the machine to insert components into printed circuit cards which were, in turn, incorporated into computers. After building and testing the design in-house, IBM, in 1959, sent engineering drawings of their design to a local machine builder along with an order for 8 units. The machine builder completed this and subsequent orders satisfactorily and later (1962) applied to IBM for permission to build essentially the same machine for sale on the open mar-

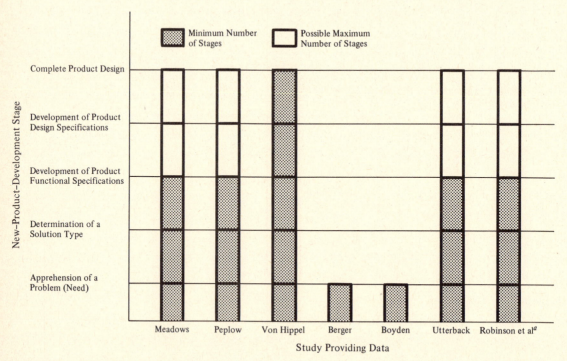

[a]Scale valid for new-product portion of study sample only.

EXHIBIT 11-2   **New-product-development data supplied by customer to manufacturer.** (Source: von Hippel, 1978, p. 43.)

ket. IBM agreed and the machine builder became the first commercial manufacturer of X–Y Table component insertion machines extant. This episode marked the firm's entry into the component insertion equipment business. They are a major factor in the business today (von Hippel, 1977*a*, pp. 64–65).

On the basis of his observations, von Hippel proposes three paradigms for industrial-product development, reproduced in Exhibit 11.3. Paradigm 1, customer-active, reflects a situation in which customer surveillance is most likely to yield an efficient stream of potentially successful new-product ideas. Paradigm 2, manufacturer-active, reflects a situation where inferred needs through careful, conventional market research is most likely to yield a new-product success. Finally, paradigm 3 reflects a situation awaiting an R&D breakthrough, such as an advance in computer-memory speed or development of superior plastic resiliency.

von Hippel's observations suggest that three separate sources are responsible for successful new ideas in different organizations. Consider the problem of allocating organizational resources to different sources. Let

X_1 = annual spending rate in traditional market-research-based studies, including product development (manufacturer-active generation)

X_2 = annual spending rate in customer-surveillance work, including product development (customer-active generation)

X_3 = annual spending rate on R&D for unfilled known needs

$f_i(X_i)$ = return in terms of expected number of successful products per year from investment level X_i in activity i

a_i = relative profitability of a success from source i

B = annual budget level

With no interactions, the idea-search-and-product-development problem is to find X_1, X_2, X_3 that

$$\text{Maximize } Z = a_1 f_1(X_1) + a_2 f_2(X_2) + a_3 f_3(X_3) \qquad (11.1)$$

subject to

$$X_1 + X_2 + X_3 \le B$$

Lower bounds on the $\{X_i\}$ could be imposed as well to keep at least maintenance-level efforts going in each of these areas.

One reason to develop this equation is that firms are making qualitative decisions of this type each day. Furthermore, von Hippel and others are beginning to provide the data needed to specify the form of the f_i's—that is, identifying industries in which users are likely to be most influential, for example. Retrospective analysis of R&D/marketing ratios in an industry, combined with managerial judgment, can go a long way toward calibrating this equation.

Therefore we expect this model to be used in one form or another for

EXHIBIT 11-3 **Three proposed paradigms for industrial-product idea generation.** (Source: von Hippel, 1978, p. 48.)

Paradigm	Sequence of Activities			Universe of Standard Industrial Products
1. Customer-Active	Product Request from Customer →	Custom Industrial Product →	Adoption by Others →	% NA
2. Manufacturer-Active	Needs Research by Manufacturer →	Idea Generation →	Idea Testing →	% NA
3. Unfilled Known Need	Generally Known User Need →	Advance in Technology →	Development of Responsive Product →	% NA

structuring the budget of new-product-development programs over the next few years.

Product-Design Techniques

In this section we outline some of the approaches and techniques most frequently used in the product-design process. Similar to the other types of models we have reviewed, the approaches differ by their assumptions, data requirements, model structure, uses, limitations, availability of computer support, and other dimensions. We focus on two sets of techniques: perceptual-mapping procedures and preference/choice models. The former consider the structure of individual's perceptions of products in a given product class, while the latter focus on the linkage between perceptions, preferences, and/or choice.

Perceptual Mapping

As an aid in understanding how consumers think about products in existing markets, a group of procedures called perceptual mapping is used. In perceptual maps, products are represented (mapped) by locations in a space of several dimensions (such as "value for the money," "gentleness," and "effectiveness" for pain relievers), which distinguish among the products.

Perceptual theory suggests that although consumers can be questioned about literally hundreds of different product attributes, they generally use a small number (two to four) when they think about a particular product or product class. Thus an objective of perceptual-mapping procedures is to identify the relevant dimensions and to locate the positions of existing and potential new products along these dimensions.

Although a number of approaches have been suggested for the perceptual-mapping task, most fall into one of two categories: attribute-based procedures (factor analysis) and similarity-based procedures (multidimensional scaling). Chapter 7 reviews and compares these techniques; later on in this chapter we show how the perceptual map is used as part of the new-product-design-and-positioning process in several model-based methodologies.

Preference/Choice Models

Urban and Hauser (1980) suggest that while early work in most product categories may concentrate on the mapping of existing product spaces to identify potential opportunities, later work should concentrate on estimating how products with given physical features are likely to perform in the marketplace. This estimation is done with preference models. Most product-design approaches use preference data because of the loss of information when one is considering only choice (Shocker and Srinivasan, 1979): when preference is used as a criterion variable, the entire preference ranking is available as data input.

In this section we discuss three widely used preference models: expectancy value, preference regression, and conjoint analysis. In each case the product design can be considered a vector of attributes $\{y_k^*\}$, where $k = 1, \ldots, K$, the number of attributes. We also consider Y_{ijk} as individual i's *perception* of product j along dimension k.

Expectancy-value Models.   Wilkie and Pessemier (1973) review the development and use of expectancy-value models in marketing. These models are based on a compositional or buildup principal, where an object's total utility is the weighted sum of its perceived attribute level and the associated value ratings as judged explicitly by the respondent:

$$p_{ij} = \sum_{k=1}^{K} w_{ik} y_{ijk} \qquad i = 1, \ldots, I, j = 1, \ldots, J \qquad (11.2)$$

where p_{ij} = (inferred) value or utility of product j for individual i
  w_{ik} = importance placed by individual i on attribute k

EXAMPLE: A new-product study has determined that the attribute "moisturizing" is important in the purchase of a facial cleanser. Suppose a new product is being compared against an existing product (Ponds). The perceptual and importance weights might be measured from responses to the following questions.

Perception.   On the scale of 1 to 7 below, indicate how well you feel this product moisturizes.

	Moisturizing						
	Poorly		Moderately Well			Extremely Well	
	1	**2**	**3**	**4**	**5**	**6**	**7**
PONDS	[ ]	[ ]	[ ]	[ ]	[ ]	[ ]	[ ]
New Product X	[ ]	[ ]	[ ]	[ ]	[ ]	[ ]	[ ]

Importance.   Now we would like to know how *important* the attribute "moisturizing" is to you when you make a decision about purchasing a facial cleanser. How important is it to have a facial cleanser that moisturizes?

Of No Importance	Moderately Important	Important	Very Important	Extremely Important
[ ]	[ ]	[ ]	[ ]	[ ]

Generally, there would be a number of attributes and associated product and importance ratings. Other measurements of attribute importance can be used as input; in particular, paired comparison of scales by their importance eliminates having all scales rated very or extremely important.

For predicting use of a new product or concept, the expectancy-value approach is low in cost and easy both to administer and to evaluate. Furthermore, it gives a quick early guide to the likely success of the product.

However, it has several disadvantages. First, it is not as accurate as other methods in predicting preference. Second, it deals with the attributes themselves, rather than the underlying perceptual dimensions. Third, it is subject to halo effects (Beckwith and Lehmann, 1975), in which an individual rates his most-preferred product high on all scales, biasing the results. In addition, the model is a linear additive model and therefore is appropriate only for use as a guide in early design work, especially in those categories, such as frequently purchased products, where the consumer-choice process is relatively simple. Another possible, significant problem is that of scale redundancy. If two scales are, in fact, measuring the same underlying attribute, this model double-counts the weight. And because the weights are specified by the respondent, their reliability and validity are questionable.

Preference Regression. On the surface, preference regression looks a lot like an expectancy-value model. However, there are several important differences: (1) overall preferences for alternative products are measured directly and used as dependent variables; (2) importance weights are inferred from consumer-preference ratings; (3) importance weights are assumed homogeneous across a response group; and (4) perceptual or evaluation dimensions (resulting from, say, a factor analysis) are used rather than the attribute items in the analysis.

The linear model for preference regression is

$$p_{ij} = \sum_{k=1}^{K^*} w_k x_{ijk} + \text{error} \tag{11.3}$$

where w_k = (inferred) importance weight

x_{ijk} = individual i's rating of product j along evaluation dimension k, for $k = 1, \ldots, K^*$ (note that $K^* \leq K$, the number of original attributes)

p_{ij} = (rank-order) preference judgments for product j by individual i

Several algorithms are available for determining the model weights. In general, the $\{p_{ij}\}$ are rank orders, and a number of techniques have been developed to find the $\{w_k\}$ that best reproduce the original preference ranks. These include monanova (Green and Wind, 1973) and monotone regression (Johnson, 1975).

However, empirical results by Green (1975), Hauser and Urban (1977), and others have demonstrated that in most cases it is sufficient to use simple regression analysis with the preference rank as the dependent variable. This procedure is less expensive and more widely available than the monotonic procedures and therefore puts preference regression within reach of more analysts.

EXAMPLE: In a study of the market for industrial solar cooling systems, the following question was used to elicit preference information:

> You have just rated three alternative industrial air-conditioning (a/c) systems. Now we would like to know your overall preferences for these systems.
>
> Write a 1 next to the one that would be your first choice, a 2 next to your second choice, and a 3 next to your third choice.
>
> Conventional Absorption a/c system _____
> Conventional Compression a/c system _____
> Solar Absorption a/c system _____

These rank orders were then regressed against product evaluations for homogeneous groups of individuals to determine their preference functions (Choffray and Lilien, 1980b, p. 44).

In the preference-regression process, factor analyses of the original attribute ratings are performed first to obtain evaluation dimensions. Then individuals' evaluations of each product (the factor scores) are made and regressed against the rank order of preferences. Because of insufficient degrees of freedom for estimation at the individual level, the regression is usually run across a group of individuals perceived to be homogeneous in the importance they place on evaluation dimensions. The estimated $\{w_k\}$ are the importance weights (revealed preferences) individuals have for evaluation criteria. In particular, note that

$$\frac{\partial p_{ij}}{\partial x_{ijk}} = w_k \tag{11.4}$$

that is, w_k represents the sensitivity of preference to a change in attribute j for individual i. If the $\{x_{ijk}\}$ are standardized, then the larger values of $\{w_k\}$ are associated with the more important dimensions for affecting consumer choice.

Advantages of the preference-regression approach are that (1) it is easy to use because most installations have regression packages, (2) it is more accurate than the expectancy-value approach, and (3) the derived importance weights $\{w_k\}$ can be used to guide both product-design modification and advertising-copy development.

Disadvantages of preference regression are (1) a linear-model form is usually used, so nonlinear-threshold-saturation effects are not handled well; (2) it should not be used with the basic attributes because of intercorrelations; and (3) importance weights are average weights and do not reflect differences at the individual level.

Conjoint Analysis. Conjoint analysis is a set of methods designed to predict consumer preferences for a multiattribute product. The respondent is asked to react to a total product profile, and then the resulting total preference score is decomposed into a set of utilities for each of the attributes. The procedure treats combinations of attributes set at discrete levels.

EXAMPLE: This study (Green and Tull, 1975, p. 641 ff) used conjoint analysis to evaluate consumers' utilities for various types of retail discount cards that differ in (1) size of discount, (2) number of cooperating stores in the respondent's trading area, and (3) annual cost of the card. Each card was described as a three-component profile, and each component had three levels:

1. size of discount—5%, 10%, and 15% off regular retail prices
2. number of cooperating stores in the subject's shopping area—10, 20, and 30 stores
3. annual cost of the card—$10, $15, and $25 annual cost

The above design, known as a complete 3^3 factorial design, produced 27 separate combinations, which were presented to subjects in random order. Each subject sorted the cards into four groups, ordered the cards within a group, and then was asked to make certain the poorest of a better group was better than the best of a poorer group. This procedure resulted in a strict rank order of the 27 cards from "poorest" to "best buy for the money."

Monanova was applied to each respondent's data to obtain individual utility functions for each level of each attribute that best reproduced the original rank order. Exhibit 11.4 shows one individual's part worths (individual attribute-level utilities). Note that the major contributors to total utility are size of discount and annual cost, with number of cooperating stores essentially flat over the relevant range.

These part worths are interval-scaled with a common unit, allowing for comparison of utility ranges across the factors making up the product profiles.

As seen in the above example, individual utility functions are not considered linear. Generally, in this form of conjoint analysis, indicator variables are used to represent each level of each feature:

$$d_{mkp} = \begin{cases} 1 & \text{if product } m \text{ has feature } k \text{ at level } p \\ 0 & \text{otherwise} \end{cases}$$

EXHIBIT 11-4   Part-worth functions: conjoint-analysis study. (Source: Paul E. Green, and Donald S. Tull, *Research for Marketing Decision,* 3rd ed., © 1975, p. 644. Reprinted by permission of Prentice-Hall, Inc., Englewood Cliffs, N.J.)

Then the utility function of feature k for product m is

$$\mu_{ik} = \sum_{p=1}^{P} \lambda_{ikp} d_{mkp} \qquad (11.5)$$

where i refers to the individual respondents, and P is the number of possible levels of the feature. Note that because $d_{mkp} = 1$ for only one level, eq. (11.5) sets μ_{ik} equal to product m's utility at that level of feature k.

With all K attributes, then the conjoint-analysis estimating equation is

$$R_{im} = \sum_{k=1}^{K} \sum_{\ell=1}^{L} \lambda_{ik\ell} d_{mk\ell} + \text{error} \qquad (11.6)$$

where R_{im} is the rank-order preference given by individual i for product m ($m = 1, \ldots, 27$ in the example). Note that although the utilities in eq. (11.6) are additive, interactions of any order can be included by defining a set of $d_{mkpk'p'}$, where this indicator would be one only when feature k was at level p *and* k' was at level p'. In practice, degrees of freedom for estimation usually prevent inclusion of many interaction items, and the linear additive form is used almost exclusively.

In eq. (11.6) the $\lambda_{ik\ell}$'s, called part worths, can be estimated with monanova, regression, or linear programming (Srinivasan and Shocker, 1973).

One difficulty with conjoint analysis is that it becomes unwieldy if the number of attributes and/or levels is high, because the consumer must then rank a large number of combinations. For example, four attributes at four levels would lead to $4^4 = 256$ combinations! An alternative is to use fractional factorial procedures (Green and Wind, 1973), in which only a subset of the alternatives is given to the consumer. Depending on the desired level of interaction effects, the analyst can employ different procedures; a common design is the so-called Latin square, which is appropriate if no interaction effects are to be measured (Cochran and Cox, 1957). Another approach involves trade-off analysis, in which consumers are asked to evaluate pairs of features independently of the other features (Johnson, 1974).

An extension of conjoint analysis uses constant-sum paired comparisons instead of rank orders for preference measures. In this approach a consumer is given, say, 100 chips to allocate between two alternatives in a way that reflects his overall relative preference. Hauser and Shugan (1980) develop the associated theoretical basis for using the resulting (ratio-scaled) data. Under appropriate conditions the preference model is

$$p_{ij} = \mu_{i1}(x_{ij1})\mu_{i2}(x_{ij2}) \cdot \cdot \cdot \mu_{ik}(x_{ijK}) \tag{11.7}$$

If, say, 100 chips are allocated between two products m and n, such that $a_m =$ the number of chips allocated to product m, then if we use a similar dummy-variable convention to that developed above, we get

$$\log \frac{a_m}{100 - a_m} = \sum_k \sum_\ell (d_{mk\ell} - d_{nk\ell}) \log \lambda_{k\ell} \tag{11.8}$$

Again, the consumer is given a fractional factorial of design pairs, and regression can be used to estimate the log $\lambda_{k\ell}$'s from eq. (11.8).

In summary, conjoint measurement is most useful in evaluating design trade-offs when a small number of important, discrete, physical alternatives are being considered. Analysis is normally done at the individual level, and market response is estimated by aggregation of individual responses. In fact, a useful output of a conjoint analysis study can be a benefit segmentation of the market, where individuals are grouped according to similarities in their attribute scoring. Cattin and Wittink (1982) review commercial uses of conjoint analysis. Green, Carroll, and Goldberg (1981) discuss the POSSEE system, a decision support system for conjoint analysis studies.

Conjoint analysis has several important limitations. First, no statistical-inference procedures exist, which is a serious drawback for fitting a model form. Second, the procedure assumes that the appropriate experimental factors (the product attributes or features) are known in advance, are small in number, and are constant across respondents. Third, when the dimensions of choice are psychological—or, at least, not easily quantifiable (flavorful, tart-sweet, etc.)—the procedure is difficult to use. Finally, the approach assumes that either the rank-ordered or paired-comparison data about individual preferences provide reliable information about likely consumer actions. Products are often designed to maximize share of first preference, where that preference is predicted from the individuals' estimated utility functions. Under what circumstances such a measure reliably predicts future purchases or future market share is unclear.

EXHIBIT 11-5   **Summary of the preference-analysis methods as they are used in new-product design.**

Properties	Expectancy Value	Preference Regression	Conjoint Analysis
Underlying theory	Psychology	Statistics	Mathematical psychology
Functional form	Linear	Linear and non-linear	Additive
Level of aggregation stimuli presented to respondent	Individual attribute scales	Group actual alternatives or concepts	Individual profiles of attributes
Measures taken	Attribute importances	Attribute ratings and preference	Rank-order preference
Estimation method	Direct consumer input	Regression	Monotonic analysis of variance or linear programming
Use in new-product design	Early indications	Core-benefit proposition	Selection of product features

SOURCE: Glen L. Urban, John R. Hauser, *Design and Marketing of New Products,* © 1980, p. 256. Adapted by permission of Prentice-Hall, Inc., Englewood Cliffs, N.J.

Evaluation of Approaches.   Exhibit 11.5 summarizes the properties of the three techniques used for product-design/preference analysis. Urban and Hauser (1980) summarize their evaluation of these techniques as follows:

> Each of these models plays an effective role in new product design. If cost is a constraint, expectancy value models offer an inexpensive way to get a rough idea of the linear effects of product attributes in forming preferences. In defining the positioning of a new product for the core benefit proposition [a short statement describing the key physical and psychological benefits the product provides], preference regression excels in analyzing the importance of psychological dimensions used to define perceptual maps. Conjoint analysis is best when physical features of products are the focus of the design problem (p. 255).

Model-based Procedures for Product Design

In this section we review two widely referenced methods for new-product design: Urban's (1975b) PERCEPTOR model and Shocker and Srinivasan's (1974) LINMAP-based approach. Because PERCEPTOR focuses on perceptual dimensions and the trial-repeat process, it is most appropriate for frequently purchased packaged goods, while LINMAP, based on conjoint analysis, is more appropriate for consumer durables or other products where attributes are actionable.

PERCEPTOR

The PERCEPTOR model and measurement methodology was developed for the design and positioning of new, frequently purchased consumer products. The main idea is the specific linkage of the distance from an ideal brand to trial-repeat estimates for a new product in an existing market. As such, the structure provides a basis for evaluating, refining, and selecting among alternative product concepts.

Long-run-share Model.   Urban postulates a trial-repeat framework similar to that of Parfitt and Collins (1968):

$$m = ts \tag{11.9}$$

where m = long-run market share
t = fraction of target market that *ever tries* the new brand
s = long-run share of purchases among those who have ever tried the brand

Trial Model.   Ultimate trial is modeled as

$$t = qwv \tag{11.10}$$

where q = ultimate probability of trial given awareness and availability
w = long-run awareness of the brand
v = long-run availability (volume-weighted percent of stores carrying the brand)

Note that at the design stage w and v are managerial inputs: brand management is expected to have some feel for the probable levels of v and w. In general, w will be higher with heavier advertising, and v will be higher with more dealer promotions.

Share Among Those Who Tried.   Urban models long-run share as the equilibrium of a two-state Markov process:

		Purchase at $t + 1$	
		New Brand	**Other Brands**
Purchase at t	**New Brand**	p_{11}	$1 - p_{11}$
	Other Brands	p_{21}	$1 - p_{21}$

The steady-state share in the process above is

$$s = p_{21}/(1 + p_{21} - p_{11}) \tag{11.11}$$

where only those who have tried the brand are considered.

Probability of Purchase (Trial).   The basic probability-of-purchase model is

$$q = \alpha_0 + \alpha_1 d_B^2 \tag{11.12}$$

where q = as defined in eq. (11.10)
            d_B^2 = squared distance of the new brand to the average ideal brand on the perceptual map for those who are aware of but who have not yet tried the brand
         α_0, α_1 = parameters to be estimated

Specifically, assume that a reduced perceptual space has K dimensions and that the new brand is perceived to occupy position $\{X_k\}$ and an ideal brand is perceived to occupy position $\{I_k\}$ in that space. Essentially, d_B^2 is modeled as

$$d_B^2 = \sum_k h_k(X_k - I_k)^2 \tag{11.13}$$

where h_k is the relative importance of dimension k. Note that $\{X_k\}$ can be obtained from PREFMAP (Carroll and Chang, 1967), a preference-regression procedure.

Probability of Repeat.   Following use of a product, consumers' perceptions of it may change. Denote $\{X_k^*\}$ as the perceptions among those who have tried the brand. Then

$$p_{11} = \tilde{\alpha}_0 + \tilde{\alpha}_1 \tilde{d}_B^2 \tag{11.14}$$

where $\tilde{d}_B^2 = \sum_k h_k(X_k^* - I_k)^2 \tag{11.15}$

that is, distance from the ideal *after* use. Urban stated that p_{21}, the probability of repeat purchase if the new product is not chosen, is determined empirically for each case.

Source of New-brand Share.   Urban postulates that new-brand share is obtained from the other brands, proportional to their appearance in consumer evoked sets and inversely proportional to their (squared) distance from the new brand:

$$V_b = \frac{m(e_b/D_{bB}^2)}{\sum_{j=1}^{B-1} \dfrac{e_j}{D_{jB}^2}} \tag{11.16}$$

where V_b = estimated loss in share by existing brand b, $b = 1, \ldots, B - 1$
         m = estimated share of new brand
         e_b = fraction of people having brand b in their evoked set
       D_{bB}^2 = squared distance from brand b to new brand B in the perceptual map

Measurements and Estimation. After exploratory work to determine market boundaries and relevant dimensions (usually conducted by personal interviews at a central location), a survey is conducted to elicit individuals' (1) evoked set of brands, (2) similarity judgments (if multidimensional scaling is to be used), (3) ratings of brands on perceptual scales, (4) brand preferences, and (5) brand choice, which is obtained by giving the respondent a small sum of money and asking him to select a desired brand. In each case one or more new-brand concepts or prototypes are included along with the descriptions of other recognizable brands. If the brand looks reasonable, a group of people is given the product to try for a while, and postuse measurements are taken, much as above. For those who did not want to rebuy the brand after use, a five-point, intent-to-repeat scale is used to estimate p_{21}.

Regression analysis is used to estimate the parameters. The dependent variable for each product in the class is the percent who choose the product at the end of the survey (divided by the percent who evoke the brand), and the independent variable is the standardized distance to the ideal point. Exhibit 11.6 gives the estimates reported for four new-product cases, all of which fit quite well.

Evaluation. Several empirical tests of the individual elements, as well as of the overall model structure, are presented by Urban with the following results: the average absolute deviation for observed versus predicted *trial* rates across 8 products was 0.07, and for repeat rates the average absolute deviation for 5 products was 0.067. Of these 13 cases only one difference was statistically significant at the 0.10 level. In a macrotest of the market-structure equations, (11.9)–(11.11), test-market data were used for 6 products, and the average absolute difference between actual and predicted shares was less than 1 percent. Other tests on the cumulative trial structure and on the source of new-brand share were similarly satisfactory.

The model has a number of apparent uses, including (1) identification of potential new-product opportunities, (2) evaluation of a number of new-product concepts, and (3) diagnosis of needs for product redesign/repositioning for frequently purchased consumer-packaged goods. Urban reports several applications, including (1) diagnosing and correcting differences between product claims and performance for a personal-care prod-

EXHIBIT 11-6   PERCEPTOR-distance-function fits.

	R^2	α_0	α_1	t	df
Beer	0.87	12.5	−13.3	6.9	6
Skin-Care Product	0.68	21.0	−16.9	6.25	11
Over-the-Counter Medicinal	0.94	36.3	−15.8	9.63	5
Pain-Relief Product	0.84	28.7	−16.1	5.71	6

SOURCE: Urban, 1975, p. 867. Reprinted by permission of the Institute of Management Sciences, *Management Science*, Vol. 21, No. 8, April, 1975.

uct, which led to a projected share increase of between 1 and 3 percent, and (2) identifying a new-product opportunity in the medicinal-care field.

The PERCEPTOR model is an intuitively appealing model that is easy to use. However, it has several problems, which limit its value. First, the concept of relating share and draw to squared distance from an ideal point is not without its critics. In later work Hauser and Urban (1977) use a multinomial logit approach to model individual choice, which suggests a different method for developing individual-choice behavior based on utility theory. However, the data-collection procedure for PERCEPTOR is somewhat simpler than the utility-theory-based model. The PERCEPTOR approach is also limited by the fact that it is deterministic and that analysis is performed at the market level. Again, later work (Urban and Hauser, 1980) focuses more on the issues of individual-measurement and benefit segmentation. Finally, the estimation of the long-run repeat rate with short-run switching probabilities, while innovative, ignores changes in those probabilities over time (Kalwani and Silk, 1980).

Shocker and Srinivasan's LINMAP Procedure

Shocker and Srinivasan (1974) propose a four-stage procedure to identify new-product alternatives that address specific firm objectives. At the heart of the procedure are a consumer-choice model, relating product choice to distance to the individual's ideal brand, LINMAP, a linear-programming procedure that jointly derives individual ideal points and attribute-importance weights, and a firm's objective function, which guides the search for new-product opportunities. The four stages of the procedure are (1) identify the market, (2) represent products in attribute space, (3) estimate utility functions and likely product choices, and (4) identify the best new opportunity.

Identification of the Relevant Market.   The authors note that the first stage of their procedure is to identify the relevant market as determined by interproduct competition *perceived by users* rather than by manufacturers. Brand-similarity ratings and/or analysis of brand-switching behavior in the marketplace can be used (Stefflre, 1972).

Representation of Brands in Attribute Space.   The authors stress that whatever the procedure used to derive an attribute space, the dimensions must be "actionable." Thus the attributes must be important to consumers, and movements along those dimensions must clearly specify actions to be taken by the manufacturer in developing the product as a physical and psychological entity. In this model the authors assume that each individual shares the same product perceptions while differing in preferences and, hence, in importance weights and ideal points. Stefflre (1971) supports this position.

Estimation of Consumer Response to New-Product Ideas.   In developing a consumer-response model *at the individual level,* the authors assume the following:

1. A set of attributes exist that are known and relevant to brand preferences.
2. Each brand j can be characterized by its position in multiattribute space as $\{y_{jp}\}$ for $p = 1, \ldots, T$.
3. For each individual there is a set of ordered pairs of brands $\Omega = \{(j,i)\}$ where, in each pair (j, k), j is preferred to k on a forced-choice/paired-comparison basis.
4. Each individual has an idiosyncratic ideal brand, as well as attribute saliences, representing the importance of each attribute dimension. We define $\{w_p\}$ as the importance of dimension p $(w_p > 0)$ and $\{X_p\}$ as the ideal brand positions along dimension p.
5. Likelihood of consumer choice of a brand is a function of its distance to the ideal brand, with the individual preferring the product nearer his ideal.

The authors define a distance function:

$$s_j = \sum_p (y_{jp} - X_p)^2 w_p \quad j = 1, \ldots, J \quad \text{(number of brands)} \quad (11.17)$$

where s_j is the importance-weighted squared distance between brand j and the ideal brand. In eq. (11.17) there are two quantities that are unknown, the $\{X_p\}$ and the $\{w_p\}$. If those quantities were known, then, ideally, following assumptions 3 and 5,

$$s_k \geq s_j \quad \text{for all } (j, k) \text{ in } \Omega \quad (11.18)$$

The authors suggest the use of LINMAP (Srinivasan and Shocker, 1973) for calculating the unknowns. In essence, a set of $\{X_p\}$ and $\{w_p\}$ is sought such that eq. (11.18) most nearly holds for all pairs of brands. Formally, the problem is to find $\{X_p\}$ and $\{w_p\}$ that

$$\text{Minimize} \sum_{(j,k) \in \Omega} z_{jk} \quad (11.19a)$$

[i.e., minimize discrepancies from eq. (11.18)] subject to

$$s_k - s_j + z_{jk} \geq 0 \quad (11.19b)$$

(equations defining discrepancies) for all (j, k) in Ω, and

$$\sum_{(j,k) \in \Omega} (s_k - s_j) = 1 \quad \text{(scaling factor)} \quad (11.19c)$$

In the formulation above, model (11.19) serves to eliminate the acceptability of the otherwise feasible solution $w_p = 0$ for all p. Although the formulation is perhaps best understood as detailed in model (11.19), a number of transformations and additional constraints are needed to put the problem into the linear-programming form used by LINMAP.

Once values of $\{w_p\}$ and $\{X_p\}$ have been determined, the relationship between distance and choice must be specified. The authors suggest the form

$$\pi_j = \frac{a}{s_j^b} \qquad a > 0, b \geq 0 \tag{11.20}$$

where π_j is the probability of choosing brand j and a is a normalization constant such that $\Sigma_j \pi_j = 1$ (i.e., an individual must choose some brand). The parameter b can be estimated by using historical data from a number of users in the product class. Pessemier and colleagues (1971) show that it is more a function of the product market and less one of individual differences. They also suggest an estimation procedure.

Search for New-product Ideas. The firm may have one of a number of different objectives; the authors suggest considering total incremental revenue for all products in the specific market. From eq. (11.20) π_j is known for every brand j for every individual. If we index individuals by i, then

$$\pi_{ij} = \frac{a_i}{s_{ij}^b} \tag{11.21}$$

where j ranges over brands available to individual i. Then if we denote the new brand as r and ψ as the set of the firm's brands, q_i, the likelihood that individual i buys some brand from the firm is

$$q_i = \frac{\pi_{ir} + \sum_{j \in \psi} \pi_{ij}}{\pi_{ir} + \sum_{j} \pi_{ij}} \tag{11.22}$$

That is, the numerator of eq. (11.22) is all the company's brands, while the denominator reflects all the brands in the market. [Equation (11.2) is equivalent to recalculating a in eq. (11.20).] If we let $\Sigma_{j \in \psi} \pi_{ij} = h_i$, then h_i represents the share of individual i's purchases that the firm received before the new-brand introduction. The incremental revenue associated with the new product then is

$$\text{Incremental revenue} = \sum_i (q_i - h_i)V_i \tag{11.23}$$

where V_i represents the purchasing power of individual i.

Finally, if variable costs can be associated with $\{y_{rp}\}$, the new-brand position, then a profit equation can be constructed:

$$Z = \sum_i (q_i - h_i)Q_i[P - c(y_{r1}, \ldots, y_{rt})] \tag{11.24}$$

where Q_i = annual volume (in units) associated with individual i
P = unit price
c = incremental manufacturing costs per unit associated with product design $\{y_{rp}\}$

The authors suggest nonlinear-programming or grid-search methods to find the product design $\{y_{rp}\}$ (or set of designs) that maximizes eq. (11.23), eq. (11.24), or another appropriate objective.

Assessment. The new-product-design procedure developed here has a number of advantages. First, analysis is at the individual level, and therefore multiple-product designs appealing to different market segments can easily be generated. Second, the procedure specifically incorporates the firm's objectives (profit, revenue, etc.) and considers the total impact on the firm of the new-product decision, including cannibalization and other factors. In addition, this work helped serve to introduce linear programming as a procedure for calibrating utility functions in conjoint analysis. The approach has been gaining in popularity: it has been used in health care, communications services, razor blades, and other product categories. [See Braun and Srinivasan (1975), Hauser and Shugan (1980), Parker and Srinivasan (1976) and Pekelman and Sen (1979) for examples.]

This approach has several drawbacks as well. First, the model is static, and the market is assumed nonreactive. There is no trial-repeat structure like PERCEPTOR, and competitive response is not considered, making the revenue and/or profit calculations suspect. In addition, the model of choice behavior, although intuitively attractive, is not without criticism. And, finally, because of the structure of solutions to linear-programming problems in general, there will be only as many nonnegative $\{X_p, w_p\}$ as there are preference pairs calibrated for an individual. Thus the ideal points and/or importance weights will be determined by the number of paired comparisons generated, an undesirable property.

Other Product-Design Models

PERCEPTOR and LINMAP are but two of a growing number of model-based procedures for the product-design process. In Shocker and Srinivasan's (1979) review of the literature, they find, on the positive side, that methodologies are being developed that fulfill the promise of the marketing concept—integration of consumer wants and desires into the product-design process. On the negative side, they report that ". . . the frameworks reviewed represent unfulfilled promises. . . . Will managements use them?" (p. 178). Clearly, the use of such procedures calls for changes in organizational decision-making styles. As with any innovation, the greater the change required for implementation, the greater will be the benefits that must be promised for diffusion. These procedures need more compelling demon-

EXHIBIT 11-7 Summary of alternative methods to aid in the search for new-product designs.

	Approaches			
Stages	Johnson (1971)	Lehmann (1971a)	Shocker and Srinivasan (1974)	Rao and Soutar (1975)
1. Determination of relevant product markets	Competitive products assumed known	Not discussed	(Stefflre's) products-by-uses analysis	Not discussed
2. Identification of determinant attributes	Direct questioning	Direct questioning Executive judgment MDS—multidimensional scaling of similarity judgments	Kelly's repertory grid MDS Direct questioning Regression	Functional attributes determined judgmentally
3. Creation of perceptual product space	Multiple discriminant analysis	Direct measurement of attribute levels	Direct measurement of attribute levels	Direct measurement of attribute levels
4. Modeling individual or segment decision making	Interval-scaled preferences Direct scaling of ideal points Regression to estimate attribute weights Choice not modeled	Direct scaling Probabilistic choice model	Ordinal preferences LINMAP First-choice model Probabilistic choice model (Luce)	Interval-scaled preferences using Thurstone's law Regression Probabilistic choice model (Luce)

Approaches				
Hustad, Mayer, and Wipple (1975)	Pessemier (1975)	Urban (1975*b*)	Hauser and Urban (1977)	Other Approaches
Ad hoc situations used Evoked set of products	Evoked set of products	Evoked set of products	Evoked set of products	Three-mode factor analysis (Belk, 1975) and principal-components analysis (Srivastava, Shocker, and Day, 1978) to define situational typologies Review of methods (Day, Shocker, and Srinivastava, 1979)
Direct questioning Judgment Hustad's procedure to determine optimal number of attributes	No specific techniques suggested	Direct questioning Kelly's repertory grid MDS	Direct questioning Kelly's repertory grid MDS	Review of methods (Alpert, 1971; Myers, 1970; Wilkie and Weinreich, 1973)
MDS	Multiple discriminant analysis	Factor analysis MDS	Factor analysis MDS	MDPREF (Green and Carmone, 1970; Green and Rao, 1972)
Ordinal preferences PREFMAP Choice not modeled	Ratio (dollar metric) preferences PREFMAP Probabilistic choice model (Luce)	Ordinal preferences PREFMAP or LINMAP Prediction of long-run market share	Ordinal preferences PREFMAP or LINMAP Utility theory Probabilistic choice model (multinominal logit)	Review of methods (Green and Srinivasan, 1978; Green and Wind, 1973)

EXHIBIT 11-7   Continued

	Approaches			
Stages	Johnson (1971)	Lehmann (1971a)	Shocker and Srinivasan (1974)	Rao and Soutar (1975)
4. Modeling individual or segment decision making (*Continued*)				
5. Evaluation of search for new product-concepts	Heuristic—locate new products near concentrations of ideal points	Subjective—generate arbitrary new concepts and use framework to predict market share/present value of sales	Nonlinear program Heuristic search through coarse and fine grids Modified gradient search Costs explicitly considered	Nonlinear program
Remarks		Based on expectancy-value theory	First overall approach to recognize importance of all steps in conceptual framework	Uses only functional product attributes

		Approaches		
Hustad, Mayer, and Wipple (1975)	Pessemier (1975)	Urban (1975b)	Hauser and Urban (1977)	Other Approaches
				Multiplicative models (Nakanishi, Cooper, and Kassarjian, 1974) Conjunctive, disjunctive models (Wright, 1975) Choice models (McFadden, 1970; Pessemier et al, 1971; Punj and Staelin, 1978) Brand-specific effects (Srinivasan, 1976)
Not discussed	Heuristic-search (STRATOP) gradient procedure Costs explicitly considered	Subjective (product refinement)	Subjective (product refinement)	Nonlinear programming (Albers and Brockhoff, 1977; Zufryden, 1976) Gradient search (Morgan and Purnell, 1969)
First approach explicitly using situations	Mentions need to consider competitive reactions to moves by the firm	Uses multistage data collection to predict ultimate trial and brand-switching behaviors and long-term market share	Models manager's decision process as well as customer's and integrates the two	

SOURCE: Shocker and Srinivasan, 1979, p. 164.

strations of their comparative advantage over alternative procedures for wider use.

We are beginning to see successful applications. Stefflre (1971) reports having fully developed six products. Wind (1973), Myers (1976), Johnson (1974), Pessemier (1975), and Hustad, Mayer, and Wipple (1975) all hint that clients have used their approaches successfully. Green and Srinivasan (1978) report increasing use of conjoint analysis for product design, and, as reviewed earlier, Urban (1975b) reports use for eight new products, while Parker and Srinivasan (1976) report a successful application in the design of rural health-care facilities. Furthermore, Hauser and Urban (1977) report good results for design of a health-maintenance organization, of financial-service packages, and of several new, frequently purchased consumer goods. Urban and Hauser (1980) also report a number of applications. Finally, Choffray and Lilien (1982) report that their procedure for industrial products has been applied in several cases.

In evaluating alternatives, Shocker and Srinivasan (1979) have found it useful to summarize methods according to (1) product-market determination, (2) identification of attributes, (3) creation of perceptual product space, (4) choice modeling, and (5) search process for new product concepts. Their summary is reproduced in Exhibit 11.7.

All the noted approaches are proactive—using consumer input in active search of new-product opportunities. Furthermore, they all assume the new product enters an existing market; a new product that creates a new market or a new market dimension is not addressed. Truly novel products generally do not come from consumer ideas; consumers tend to be interpolators (within existing markets) rather than extrapolators. The research of Mansfield and Wagner (1975) and others suggests that, at least for industrial markets, the level of economic success of new products is higher for products that originated in R&D than for those created in response to market needs. However, those products had a higher failure rate as well: consumer-based product-design modeling is likely to lower the risk of innovation but also lowers the return.

The methods also assume that a product can be decomposed and analyzed as a vector of attributes. Most methods assume a single use and/or use situation; they do not allow for variety seeking and/or the maintenance of a portfolio of products (breakfast cereals, beers, soft drinks, etc.). Customer decision models need more work. The material in Chapter 7 suggests that a single choice model is unlikely to be applicable to all decision situations or even to all consumers for a given product category. The structure, dynamics, and competitive nature of the marketplace need to be addressed more completely. However, to keep these procedures in perspective, we must view them not as complete answers to product-design questions but rather as decision support for the design process. As such, they suggest the advisability of multiple methods of data collection and analysis, and they provide a structure to explore and learn about market opportunities and the sensitivity of the marketplace to errors in analysis and marketing. As these methods gain acceptance, we should get a better understanding of consumer wants and the consumer-choice process and should be better prepared to meet those needs with lowered risks of product failures.

Organizing for Product Design and Development

The product design and development process, as discussed above, is an integrated series of steps, which can be loosely classified into opportunity identification, design, testing, and introduction. These steps must be taken by all organizations in one way or another, formally or informally. However, larger organizations, with the ability to allocate significant resources, can proceed more formally and perform more-detailed analyses than can smaller companies or entrepreneurs.

Variations in the process associated with the scale or size of the organization are outlined in Exhibit 11.8. The large firm or division minimizes risk by performing analytical studies in the market-definition, -design, and -testing phases. In particular, there is an active relationship between the development of a core-benefit proposition (CBP) to meet consumer needs and the model-based link of that CBP to product features in the design stage. The large firm also more actively explores segment differences in the market. The smaller firm (third column) goes through the same steps but in a less formal manner. For example, proportionally more resources are allocated to qualitative research (focus groups and the like). However, product design is supported by concept and product tests with some formal modeling. On the other hand, entrepreneurs rarely have the resources for formal analysis. They are often wedded to an idea and desperately want to see it work. But exposure to customer feedback early in the design process can help reduce their failure rate as well.

By Product Type

The activities involved in new-product design and development will differ by product type. Exhibit 11.9 highlights some basic differences. For example, in the opportunity-identification phase, the rate of market definition and creative groups is much higher for frequently purchased consumer goods; R&D and actual-user design input is greater for industrial goods. In the design phase itself, preference/perception/choice models are most appropriate for consumer products, while models of the buying process and diffusion models (Chapter 19) are well suited for industrial and high-technology products. Finally, users are employed far more extensively in the development and delivery of important features for industrial products than for other types of products.

EXHIBIT 11-8 Variations in new-product-development activities by size of organization.

Phase of Development	Size of Organization		
	Large Firm or Division	Small Business	Entrepreneur
Opportunity identification	Analytic market definition and segmentation study Creative group sessions R&D	Focus groups Creative groups	Look to consumers Generate alternatives
Design	Development of CBP[a] Models of perception, preference, and choice Product features to fulfill CBP[a] Benefit segmentation R&D marketing link	CBP orientation[a] Concept test Product placement Engineering	CBP concept[a] Consumer relations Engineering Financial support
Testing	Formal advertising testing Lab and consumer product testing Pretest-market-model analysis Test market	Product testing Pretest-market-model analysis Monitor roll out and improve	Prototype and in-use tests Sell some Revise product Sell more
Introduction	National launch Adaptive control	National penetration	Build business

SOURCE: Glen L. Urban, John R. Hauser, *Design and Marketing of New Products*, © 1980, p. 554. Adapted by permission of Prentice-Hall, Inc., Englewood Cliffs, N.J.
[a]CBP = core-benefit proposition.

EXHIBIT 11-9   Variations in new-product-development activities by product type.

Phase of Development	Product Type				
	Consumer Frequently Purchased	Consumer Durable	Industrial	High Technology	Service
Opportunity identification	Market definition Creative groups	Market definition Engineering/ marketing Creative groups	User identification Needs analysis Technology/ marketing R&D	R&D Technical forecast Users	Needs analysis Service plans
Design	CBP Psychological Perception/ preference/ choice Features Advertising	CBP Psychological and physical Perception/ preference/ choice Features Advertising Diffusion	CBP Physical and psychological Buying process Features Engineering Selling	CBP Physical buying process R&D Communication Selling Diffusion	CBP Benefits delivery Perception/ preference/ choice Communication
Testing	Consumer pre-test market Test market	Laboratories and consumer pre-test models	Laboratory tests In-use tests	laboratory tests In-use tests	Demonstration or pilot programs
Introduction	Launch Adaptive control	Launch Adaptive control	Launch Adaptive control	Launch Adaptive control	Launch Adaptive control

SOURCE: Glen L. Urban, John R. Hauser, *Design and Marketing of New Products,* © 1980, p. 557. Adapted by permission of Prentice-Hall, Inc., Englewood Cliffs, N.J.

Organizational Structure

Although many alternative new-product organizations exist [see Conference Board (1974) for a review], there appears to be an emerging consensus on an efficient way to organize the process. For a large firm a frequent structure is a growth-and-development department with a small staff, supplemented by venture team members on a project basis from R&D, marketing, and so on—the department usually has funds to buy supplemental services from inside or outside the organization. On the other hand, small companies rely more on a task force or a new-product committee, purchasing most services from outside suppliers. New-product development in a small firm is often intermittent, not warranting a separate, formal department.

Summary

In the past decade we have seen an exciting development of techniques and models to support the product-design process. As this process has become more risky and costly, the impetus to control those risks and costs via analytical methods has increased.

The modeling approaches reviewed here are proactive—they actively seek consumer-based information to aid in the search for new-product opportunities. There are a number of sources for new ideas, both inside and outside the firm. Customers are often the source of new-product ideas, particularly for industrial products, and therefore resources should be allocated in many industries to monitor customer activities.

A number of techniques exist to support product-design decisions. We separate perceptual-mapping techniques (factor analysis and multidimensional scaling) from preference/choice models (expectancy-value models, preference regression, and conjoint analysis), where the former methods structure perceptual space, suggesting product opportunities, while the latter techniques are most useful for evaluating opportunities in those perceptual spaces.

Two model-based procedures for product design were reviewed; PERCEPTOR, useful for frequently purchased goods, and LINMAP, most useful for durables. While both procedures have seen application, they are part of an evolution in the development of product-design models.

With the variety of techniques available and the difficulty of the problem, firms need to use different procedures depending on their size and the type of product they wish to market. Furthermore, different organizational structures for new-product development are appropriate for different-sized firms.

Thus there are a number of valuable aids available for supporting product-design decisions. These procedures give incomplete answers to complex questions and therefore must be applied with care and wisdom to be of most use.

Problems

11.1 Suggest a method for collecting the data to operationalize model (11.1). For what firms would such a procedure be practical?

11.2 In a large sample, people were asked to rate how much they liked each of five beverages: milk, coffee, tea, fruit juice, and soda pop. Through factor analysis the following table of factor loadings was obtained. What might each of the three factors be?

| | Factors | | |
Beverage	I	II	III
Milk	0.504	−0.213	−0.217
Coffee	−0.209	0.373	−0.328
Tea	−0.137	0.682	0.307
Fruit juice	0.475	−0.107	0.110
Soda pop	−0.368	−0.645	0.534

11.3 In a segment of the coffee market two main dimensions have been identified: flavor (F) and richness (R). Three brands share this market, with market shares and positions as follows (including a rating for an ideal brand):

| | Position | | |
Brand	F	R	Market Share
A	1	−2	15%
B	2	1	45%
C	1	2	40%
Ideal	3	3	

a. Use this information to estimate α_0 and α_1 in eq. (11.12). What assumptions are you making?

b. A new brand, positioned at F = 1, R = 1, is considering market entry. Assuming that $w = 100\%$ in eq. (11.10), that $\tilde{\alpha}_0 = \alpha_0$ and $\tilde{\alpha}_1 = \alpha_1$, and that $p_{12} = p_{21}$, use the PERCEPTOR model to estimate this brand's long-run market share. What is the source of that share?

11.4 Compare the conjoint-analysis approach with the feasibility submodel of the Choffray-Lilien methodology in Chapter 8 for designing a new industrial durable product. What are the strengths and the weaknesses of the two approaches?

11.5 What differences would you expect to see in new-product-development activities between a small industrial-goods manufacturer and a large packaged-food firm?

11.6 A new product X is being evaluated for entry into the detergent market. A laboratory test was performed on a sample of housewives, who were clustered on the basis of a battery of attitude and life-style variables, as follows:

Group	Group Description	Percent of Housewives	Percent of Product Class Used
1	Old-fashioned	45	50
2	Swingers, like new things	20	5
3	Cleaning, like clothes/house spotless	35	45

Blind product tests for X and the remaining three brands yielded the following results, where each brand was rated on a scale from 1 to 10:

Group	Brand X	Other Brands
1	8.5	8.0, 7.5, 7.0
2	6.0	6.5, 7.5, 8.0
3	6.5	6.0, 6.5, 8.0

When the groups were shown advertising for the product, and where all the other brands were made known, brand X's share of expected net purchases was 10% in group 1, 14% in group 2, and 22% in group 3. Assume that $r_i / \Sigma\, r_j$ is a measure of product preference, where r_i is the rating of brand i.

a. How does the blind preference for brand X vary across segments?

b. How does this preference compare to expected-purchase share?

c. What are the implications for redesigning/repositioning product X for market entry?

CHAPTER 12

Pricing Models

Pricing is but one element of the marketing mix that affects product demand. Yet it has probably been studied more heavily than any other marketing variable, especially by economists, and with good reason. Few marketing (or investment) decisions within a firm have more critical consequences than those made in pricing products and services. In addition, setting and adapting prices in competitive markets calls for high levels of quantitative and intuitive skills.

With an area of such importance and with so much at stake, it might be assumed that a great deal of continuing research and planning would by now underlie the formulation of pricing strategy and the setting of prices. One might also expect that a well-developed body of experience would have resulted in rules of thumb to guide pricing decisions. But this does not appear to be the case:

> Many pricing decisions still have a distinctly "ad hoc" appearance, as if made without much prior thought and analysis. And much discussion of pricing practice these days still retains a theoretical flavor (Randall, in Bailey, 1978, p. iv).

In this chapter we first review key pricing phenomena and their effects, focusing on classical economic theory and the phenomena the theory does and does not explain. Then we discuss pricing in practice and indicate the differences between the theoretical results and the real-world problems they are designed to address. Next, we review several recent modeling efforts in marketing that extend the classical theory. Finally, we briefly discuss other developments in pricing research in the marketing area and conclude with an assessment of the current status and future of price modeling.

The Classical Economic Model: Consumer Behavior, Elasticity, and the Law of Demand

From the viewpoint of the classical economist, price allocates goods and services in the marketplace. For the consumer it represents the cost of a purchase in monetary terms. For the seller it motivates a level of supply and acts to allocate economic resources on the production side.

A basic relationship in economic theory is known as the Law of Demand, which states that the quantity demanded per period (also known as the time rate of demand) is negatively related to price. The basis for this law is the postulate of a rational consumer who has full knowledge of the available goods and substitutes, a limited budget, and a singular drive to maximize his utility. For a given structure of relative prices, he will allocate his income over goods (including savings) so as to maximize his utility. If the price relations change, he will normally substitute less-expensive goods for more-expensive goods; this action will increase his utility. [See Henderson and Quandt (1958).]

Rational Consumer Behavior

The rational consumer is postulated to have a utility function (u), a set of possible commodities to purchase $(Q_1, \ldots, Q_n)$, and a budget (B). His problem then is to

$$\text{Maximize } u = f(q_1, \ldots, q_n) \tag{12.1}$$

subject to

$$\sum_{i=1}^{n} p_i q_i \le B$$

where q_i = quantity of commodity Q_i consumed
p_i = price of commodity i

The consumer's demand curve is found by solving eq. (12.1) for q_i as a function of price. The Law of Demand implicitly incorporates (and aggregates) consumers' demand curves into a demand function. [See Lancaster (1979, 1980) for a more contemporary view, incorporating issues of segmentation and product positioning.]

Elasticity

Central to these developments is the concept of *price elasticity,* defined as the ratio of the percentage change in demand to a percentage change in price:

$$\epsilon_{qp} = \frac{\text{fraction change in demand}}{\text{fraction change in price}} = \frac{(Q_1 - Q_0)/Q_0}{(P_1 - P_0)/P_0}$$

$$= \frac{\Delta Q/Q}{\Delta P/P} = \frac{\Delta Q}{\Delta P}\frac{P}{Q} \qquad (12.2a)$$

or in continuous form

$$\epsilon_{qp} = \frac{\partial Q}{\partial P}\frac{P}{Q} \qquad (12.2b)$$

where ϵ_{qp} = elasticity of quantity demanded with respect to change in price

Q_1 = quantity demanded per period after price change

Q_0 = quantity demanded per period before price change

P_1 = new price

P_0 = old price

$\Delta Q = Q_1 - Q_0$

$\Delta P = P_1 - P_0$

Normally, price elasticities are understood to be negative (we drop the sign in further discussion). A price elasticity of one means that demand rises (falls) by the same percentage that price falls (rises). In this case total revenue is left unaffected. A price elasticity greater than one means that demand rises (falls) by more than price falls (rises) in percentage terms, and total revenue rises (falls). A price elasticity less than one means that demand rises (falls) by less than price falls (rises) in percentage terms, and total revenue falls (rises).

The price elasticity of demand gives more precision to the question of whether the firm's price is too high or too low. For revenue maximization the price is too high if the demand elasticity at that price is greater than one and too low if demand elasticity at that price is less than one. Whether this rule is also true for profit maximization depends on the behavior of costs.

Another important elasticity concept is *income elasticity*. If a substantial price reduction occurs on an item, it amounts to an increase in real income for those households consuming it in substantial quantities. With the greater purchasing power, they may decide to switch to more-expensive products instead of consuming more of the former product. In such cases we say the income effect outweighs the substitution effect, and the product they abandon is called an inferior good. For example, if poor families consume a lot of potatoes, and the price of potatoes falls, these families might use the resulting savings to buy more meat and cut down on their potato consumption. Meat, a more desired good, replaces potatoes because of the income effect of the price cut.

This concept is formalized as the *income elasticity of demand*, defined as $(\partial Q/\partial I)\,(I/Q)$, where I is a measure of consumer income. Most products have an income elasticity between zero and one and are called normal goods. Those goods with income elasticity greater than one are called superior goods, while those with income elasticity less than zero are inferior goods.

Another measure of demand sensitivity is the relationship between the price of one good and the quantity demanded of another. This measure is known as the *cross-price elasticity of demand* and is computed for product X as $(\partial Q_x/\partial P_y)\,(P_y/Q_x)$, where Y is any other good. If the cross-price elasticity is positive, then goods X and Y are substitutes; if it is negative, they are complements.

As we will see in later sections, the relationship of price elasticity to time and to stage of the life cycle are two important topics of recent work. Furthermore, both behavioral research and industry experience suggest that price elasticities are likely to be different for price increases than for decreases and for the degree a given price is away from the average market price.

Finally, the relationship between elasticity and marginal revenue should be noted:

$$\text{Total revenue} = \text{TR} = PQ$$

Therefore,

$$\text{Marginal revenue} = \text{MR} = \frac{\partial \text{TR}}{\partial Q} = P + Q\frac{\partial P}{\partial Q}$$

$$= P\left(1 + \frac{Q}{P}\frac{\partial P}{\partial Q}\right) = P\left(1 - \frac{1}{\epsilon_{qp}}\right) \qquad (12.3)$$

Equation (12.3) shows that marginal revenue varies with both price and the price elasticity of demand.

Two Demand Models

The Law of Demand does not specify the shape of the price-quantity relationship. In fact, it varies with the particular product or product class. However, two equation forms have become particularly popular for representing this relationship: the linear and constant-elasticity forms.

Linear Demand-price Function.   Exhibit 12.1 shows the linear form of the demand-price relationship. Mathematically, the general linear equation is

$$Q = a - bP \qquad (12.4)$$

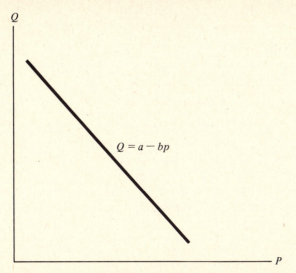

EXHIBIT 12-1   The linear demand-price function.

where a and b are constants. This linear relationship need not apply throughout the domain of possible prices but should be approximately true in the neighborhood of the prevailing price.

How can the price elasticity be determined in the neighborhood of a particular price, say P_1, on a linear demand curve? For the linear demand function shown in eq. (12.4), $\partial Q / \partial P = -b$ and

$$\epsilon_{qp} = \frac{\partial Q}{\partial P}\frac{P}{Q} = -b \cdot \frac{P}{a - bP} = -\frac{bP}{a - bP} \tag{12.5}$$

Following from eq. (12.5), we note the following:

1. The price elasticity will be one when $P = a/2b$.
2. The price elasticity is high (in absolute terms) at high prices, making it desirable to lower price.
3. The price elasticity is low at low prices, making it desirable to raise price.

All of this discussion pertains to a linear demand function and is subject to the usual qualifications about the use of the elasticity concept in practice. First, in practice, a price is changed not by an infinitesimal amount but by a finite amount, and the magnitude of this change makes a difference in the level of response. Second, the effect of the price change depends on the current level of the price—that is, whether it is high or low. Third, the short- and long-run elasticities may be quite different. For instance, buyers may have to continue with the present supplier immediately after his price increase because choosing a new supplier takes time, but they may eventually stop purchasing from him. In this case demand is more elastic in the long run than in the short run. Stigler (1952) suggests that demand is generally more elastic in the long run because the short run is marked by the difficulty of rapid adjustment, the existence of market imperfections, and the presence of habit. Alternatively, in some situations the reverse may happen: buyers may drop a supplier in anger after he increases prices but return to him later. The significance of the distinction between short- and long-run elasticities is that the seller may not learn the effects of his price revision until some time after the change.

Constant-elasticity Demand-price Function.   Another popular shape for the demand function is based on the notion of constant elasticity. This function, shown graphically in Exhibit 12.2, is

$$Q = aP^{-b} \qquad\qquad (12.6)$$

As we have shown in Chapter 4, the exponent b is the price elasticity, which is constant for all prices. This form of demand has been popular among analysts because it includes an explicit term for elasticity, produces curvilinearity, and is easy to manipulate mathematically.

There are many other negative-sloping demand functions related to different hypotheses about model response; the theory of price response in a particular market and the relationship of that theory to observation should dictate the choice of the function.

In its simplest form the classical model introduces a cost function $C(Q)$

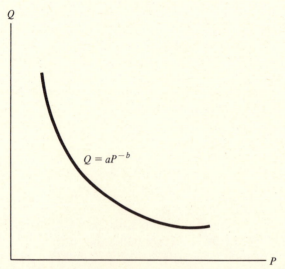

EXHIBIT 12-2   Constant-elasticity, price-demand function.

and a profit function Z, where $Z = PQ - C(Q)$. Price P^* is then chosen to maximize Z.

Limitations of the Classical Model

The classical model has several key assumptions that limit its applicability, including the following:

The firm's objective in setting a price is to maximize short-run profits on the particular product.

The only parties to consider in setting the price are the firm's immediate customers.

Price can be set independent of the levels set for the other marketing variables.

The demand and cost equations can be estimated with sufficient accuracy.

The firm has true control over price.

Market responses to price changes are well understood.

We consider these limitations in turn.

The Problem of Objectives

The theoretical pricing model usually assumes a single product for which the seller must determine the price that maximizes current profits. Current profits, rather than long-run profits, are at issue because of stable-demand and -cost assumptions. In reality, demand can be expected to change over time (because of changes in tastes, population, and income). Costs can change as well (because of changes in technology and input price). Pricing to maximize long-run profits would have to utilize projections of the likely long-run courses of demand and cost. Furthermore, a more sophisticated model is required for determining optimal pricing over the product's life cycle.

A detailed discussion of the selection and evaluation of objectives is given in Chapter 3. Here we want to emphasize that, in practice, the firm usually has several different, more concrete pricing objectives.

Some companies are interested in penetrating a market and therefore set a relatively low price to stimulate the growth of the market and to capture a large share of it. In many cases long-run profitability seems to rise with market share. (See Chapter 17 for a discussion of this view.) For example, Texas Instruments often sets out to dominate a market by initially pricing below cost while building up production experience and market share. Any of several conditions might favor setting a low price:

1. The market appears to be highly price-sensitive—that is, many additional buyers would come into the market if the product were priced low.
2. The unit costs of production and distribution fall with increased output (whenever a product is favored by scale economies, it is desirable to give serious consideration to all measures that would stimulate sales, including a low price).
3. A low price would discourage actual and potential competition.

Other firms take advantage of the fact that some buyers are willing to pay a much higher price than others because the product, for one reason or another, has high value to them. With this objective of *skimming pricing*, the firm initially sets a high price to gain a premium from these buyers and only gradually reduces it to draw in the more-price-elastic segments of the market. This practice is a form of price discrimination over time rather than over space. It is most often applied under the following conditions:

1. There is a sufficiently large number of buyers whose demand is relatively inelastic (were the company to set a low price initially, it would forgo the potential premium from this segment of the market).
2. The unit production and distribution costs of producing a smaller volume are not so much higher that they cancel the advantage of charging what some of the traffic will bear.
3. There is little danger that the high price will stimulate the emergence of rival firms (where barriers to entry are high, because of patents, high development costs, raw-material control, or high promotion costs, the innovating firm can proceed with relative safety to pursue a market-skimming pricing policy).

DuPont practices market-skimming pricing, particularly for patent-protected discoveries; the company used it with cellophane and nylon, for instance. Polaroid is another practitioner; it introduces an expensive version of a new camera and only gradually introduces lower-priced models in a bid for the mass market. Simon (1982) develops a model that distinguishes between skimming and penetration pricing strategies, and Dolan and Clarke (1981) discuss the two strategies in a new product setting.

Other objectives that firms have include *current-revenue pricing*, used when a firm is strapped for funds; *target-profit* or *cost-plus pricing*, discussed below; and *promotional pricing*, used to enhance or publicize the sale of an entire line rather than to yield a profit on the singular product. Two examples are *loss leader pricing*, designed to attract a large number of buyers who can be expected to buy the firm's other products, and *prestige pricing,* in which a high price is set on a product to enhance the quality image of the product line.

The Problem of Multiple Parties

In addition to taking a narrow view of pricing objectives, the classical pricing model assumes that the only significant group to consider in the pricing of a product is the firm's customers. But several other parties must be considered in setting the price, including intermediate customers, competition, suppliers, government, and other company executives.

Intermediate Customers.   The firm must think through its pricing not only for its ultimate customers but for its intermediate customers as well. In fact, some companies set a price for distributors and allow them to set whatever final price they wish. Alternatively, the manufacturer determines both the final price and the distributor's margin necessary to provide sufficient distributor incentive.

Competition.   The classical pricing model does not consider competitive reactions explicitly. But the price set by the manufacturer influences the rate of entry of new rivals and the pricing policies of existing rivals. The traditional demand curve is too inflexible to represent the dynamic reactions and counterreactions occasioned by a pricing policy.

Suppliers.   The company's suppliers of materials, funds, and labor must also be considered in setting the price. For many suppliers the product's price indicates the level of the firm's revenues (and profits) from the product, and for labor unions a high price or a price increase constitutes grounds for higher wages.

Government.   Another interested party is the government. Under the Robinson-Patman Act the seller cannot charge different prices to comparable customers unless the price differences are based strictly on cost differences. Under the Miller-Tydings Act, depending on state laws, the seller may or may not be able to require retailers to sell the branded product at a uniform list price. In addition, public utilities must justify their rates before regulatory commissions; the steel industry must move cautiously with price increases because of the government's interest in price stability; the prices of agricultural goods and of imported goods are affected by agricultural and tariff legislation, respectively; and various state and local governments pass legislation and rulings affecting the prices that can be set by sellers.

Other Company Executives.   Price concerns many different parties within the company. The sales manager wants a low price so that his salespeople can talk price to customers. The controller wants a price that leads to an early payout. Furthermore, price makes an important difference in copy and media tactics to the advertising manager. Finally, the production-scheduling manager is interested because price affects the rate of sales.

The Problem of Marketing-Mix Interaction

In determining the effect of price on sales, the classical pricing model assumes that other marketing variables are held at some constant level. This assumption is evident in the usual treatment of the demand function as a relationship only between quantity demanded (Q) and price (P). But this assumption begs the question of how optimal values are set for advertising, personal selling, product quality, and other marketing variables before price is set.

The Problem of Estimating Demand and Cost Functions

Some statistical problems seriously hamper the determination of actual demand and cost functions. In the case of a new product, there is no experience upon which to base the estimates. Unless data are available on a similar established product, estimates are likely to take the form of guesses rather than hard facts. Moreover, data on established products are usually not much more satisfactory.

Johnston (1963) has described econometric techniques for estimating cost functions from existing data. However, demand functions are more difficult to determine because (1) several of the variables are not quantifiable; (2) they are typically highly intercorrelated; (3) both demand and cost may have been shifting during the period; and (4) the random errors tend to be large. Furthermore, because some of the independent variables are also dependent (sales depends on advertising, and advertising depends on sales), a system of simultaneous equations, rather than a single-equation estimate of demand, is required. Finally, even if these hurdles were to be overcome, there will always be lingering doubts about whether the relationships measured from historical data apply to today's situation.

The Problem of Price Discretion

The seller's degree of price discretion is largely determined by the buyer's concern with price and the degree of product differentiation. Exhibit 12.3

EXHIBIT 12-3   **Marketers' degree of price discretion.**

	Product Differentiation	
	High	**Low**
Buyers' Concern with Price High	Medium	Low
Low	High	Medium

SOURCE: © 1976 McGraw-Hill Book Co. (UK) Ltd. From: Fitzroy: *Analytic Methods for Marketing Management.* Reproduced by permission of the publisher.

illustrates this variability. Furthermore, price is not the sole determinant of purchase behavior; other factors, such as reliability and service, have a substantial influence on choice. Gross (1978) discusses the concept of a premium-price differential as something that is "granted" to the product by the marketplace. He is concerned with price as an *output* of the product's position and with how well it delivers value, rather than price as a *control variable*, as viewed by many marketing theorists and economists.

Price discretion depends on, among other things, (1) the buyers' willingness to pay, (2) the firm's costs, (3) competition, and (4) corporate objectives. Moreover, real or potential governmental regulation further determines pricing discretion.

The Problem of Varying Buyer Reactions to Price Changes: Information and Expectations

Classical microeconomic theory usually assumes near-perfect information about market prices and a downward-sloping demand curve. However, consumers are not always in agreement. A price reduction that would normally attract more buyers may not be known by many buyers. To other buyers it might signify the following (Oxenfeld, 1961, p. 28):

> The item is about to be superseded by a later model.
> The item has some fault and is not selling well.
> The firm is in financial trouble and may not stay in business to supply future parts.
> The price will come down further and it pays to wait.
> The quality has been reduced.

Conversely, a price *increase* that would normally deter sales may carry a variety of different meanings to buyers:

> The item is hot and may be unobtainable unless it is bought soon.
> The item represents an unusually good value.
> The seller is greedy, is charging what the traffic will bear, and may charge more if the potential buyer waits.

Thus demand is affected not only by current price but by the information carried by the price and by expectations about future prices.

Extensions of the Classical Model

Pricing research is leading to modifications of the classical model in several areas.

Price Consciousness and Price Image

Underlying the concept of price as an important marketing variable is the assumption that customers are price-conscious enough to use a price cut to guide purchase decisions. As noted by Gabor (1977), the price setter must know the extent of price consciousness to determine the importance of pricing in the marketing mix. While price consciousness itself is not measurable, price recall has been used in the past as a reasonable substitute. However, this substitution leads to problems, because price recall is an indicator of price awareness while price consciousness represents a deliberate effort on the part of buyers to search for lower prices. Thus a price-aware buyer may not necessarily be a price-conscious buyer.

Gabor and Granger (1961) studied the extent to which housewives were aware of the prices of goods that they regularly purchase. From a sample of 425 housewives, the prices of 82 percent of recent purchases of 15 household products and food items were remembered (irrespective of whether the price quoted was correct or not). This price awareness was found to be inversely correlated with social class. Furthermore, branded products tended to be associated with lower price awareness than unbranded products. Similarly, the percentage of purchases correctly priced was higher for the lower social groups and for unbranded products. The majority of erroneous prices given were not more than 10 percent different from the actual price. Thus Gabor and Granger concluded that a substantial portion of housewives take cognizance of current prices and *can* therefore behave in a way that conforms to demand theory.

The difference between actual price and recall price (or price image) is of concern to the seller because it provides insight into the buyers' perception of value, as well as the potential response to actual price adjustments. Especially for less frequently purchased items, during an inflationary period price image tends to lag behind actual price, and thus there may be a stronger reaction to upward price adjustments. In instances in which price image leads actual price, an upward price adjustment may be accepted with little or no adverse reaction.

The degree of price awareness has been studied repeatedly over the years.

EXAMPLE: One of the companies in the Bell chain was considering a rate reduction on the extension (or second) phone, which it installed in a home for an extra monthly charge of 75¢. The company had been heavily promoting second phones with limited success and was wondering how many additional phones would be ordered if the charge was reduced to 50¢.

In a direct-attitude survey potential extension users were asked what they thought the extension service cost. Over 80% of the respondents named a price over 75¢/mo—in some cases as high as $2. Here the amount of price misinformation was profound and could have been an important deterrent to purchase.

The Relationship Between Price and Quality

Under classical economic theory, price's main role is to indicate the cost of acquiring a good or service. If perfect information is assumed in the marketplace, price in itself has no informational content. Thus, except for several recognized irregularities, economic theory prescribes a downward-sloping demand curve, indicating increasing quantities demanded at lower prices.

Seminal work by Stoetzel (1954), Adam (1958), and Gabor and Granger (1966) has modified this view of demand, suggesting that because the product-selection process has certain risks, price may be taken as a quality cue to reduce the perceived risk of purchase.

In the work of Gabor and Granger (1966) and Sowter, Gabor, and Granger (1971), the relationship between price and quality is specified via a "limit concept." (This relationship is known in the economic literature as a reservation price.) A consumer intent on purchasing a product in a particular class has two price limits in mind: an upper limit above which purchase will not be made because the good or service is too expensive and a lower limit below which purchase will not be made because the quality of the item is suspect. Within the range created by these limits, price does not act as an absolute barrier to purchase, as it does outside the range.

We formalize these concepts as follows:

$L(p)$ = probability that randomly chosen member of target population finds price p of the good too low

$H(p)$ = probability that randomly chosen member of population will find price too high

$B(p)$ = probability that randomly selected customer will not see price as obstacle to purchase

The authors call $B(p)$ the *buy-response curve* and, by definition,

$$B(p) = 1 - H(p) - L(p) \qquad (12.7)$$

On the basis of extensive analysis of a number of low-priced, frequently purchased products, the authors demonstrate that $1 - L(p)$ and $H(p)$ can be approximated by the cumulative log-normal distribution. If $p^* = \ln p$, then $1 - L(p^*)$ and $H(p^*)$ can be represented by a cumulative normal distribution, as illustrated in Exhibit 12.4.

The theory of the buy-response curve can be used to predict brand choice in the marketplace in the following way.

EXAMPLE: Consider a product field in which the consumer is familiar with all the brands. In such a case the effect of price as an indicator of quality becomes

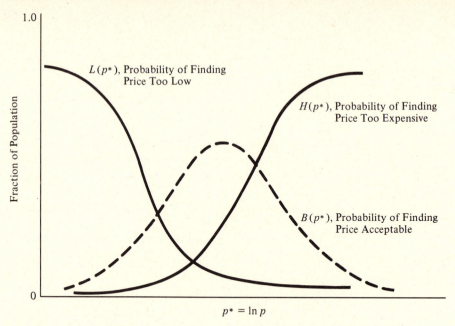

EXHIBIT 12-4   **Distribution of price-acceptability curves.**

less important, and $L(p)$ vanishes, although $H(p)$ remains. Consider two brands, X and Y, with associated prices p_X and p_Y and quantities sold Q_X and Q_Y. Define

$S(p_X, p_Y)$ = probability that randomly chosen member of homogeneous population will choose X over Y when prices are p_X and p_Y

Assume that $S(p_X, p_Y)$ can be approximated by $S(p_X/p_Y) = S(V)$; that is, brand preference is a function of the price ratio V.

From the theory of the buy-response curve and empirical tests, $1 - S(V)$ is approximately log-normal with mean μ and variance σ^2. This result has key marketing implications, because market-share predictions are made on the basis of V, μ, and σ^2. In addition, note that $1 - S(V)$ has a value of 0.5 when $\ln V = \mu$; thus the mean is a measure of absolute brand preference. If $\mu = 0$, brand preferences are equal when $p_X = p_Y$; if $\mu > 0$, preferences are equal when $p_X > p_Y$; and if $\mu < 0$, preferences are equal when $p_X < p_Y$. The variance σ^2 can be interpreted as a measure of brand loyalty: if σ^2 is low, then a relatively small change in the price ratio will cause a large shift in brand preferences, while a high value of σ^2 indicates that consumers do not respond to small changes in the price ratio.

Granger and Bittson (1972) report a number of applications of this theory with good results. However, it is costly to apply because market surveys and retail audits are required to provide the data for estimating μ and σ^2 (Gabor, Granger, and Sowter, 1970).

Studies eliciting quality ratings of unbranded, undifferentiated products with varying prices from test groups have supported the price-quality relationship. Other testing has focused on the behavioral and attitudinal characteristics of subjects judged price-reliant. On the basis of selections from seven products, each offered in three identical but disguised brands priced at low, medium, and high levels, Lambert (1972) obtained the following results:

1. In all product categories individuals selecting the high-priced brand had greater confidence in price as an indicator of quality.
2. Perceived experience in purchasing the product appeared to be greater among those selecting the higher price.
3. Those selecting the high-priced brand tended to have greater confidence in their ability to judge product quality.
4. Those selecting the high-priced brands perceived a greater range of variation in quality among brands within the product category.
5. More-serious consequences from making a bad selection were envisioned by those selecting the high-priced brand.
6. There was no support for the hypothesis that those selecting the high-priced brand were generally more cautious or exhibited greater uncertainty in selection.
7. For five of the seven products tested, those who selected the high-priced brand tended to believe that brand choice was likely to affect social image.

Shapiro (1973) attempted to correlate price reliance with personal attitudes and behavioral characteristics. He found the following characteristics significantly and positively correlated with price reliance: trust in the honesty of the price maker, trust in the competency of the price maker, snobbery, generalized risk, financial risk, performance risk, psychosocial risk, desire for shopping speed, desire for convenience, and perception of quality differences among brands.

Other research found price-reliance and price-quality perceptions present for some types of consumer goods but not for others. And some have challenged the existence of price-quality reliance in a realistic market setting in which brand names and product differentiation are present. Jacoby, Olson, and Haddock (1971) tested students' quality perceptions of beer samples, finding a strong price-quality relationship when no other cues were available. When compositional differences (use of different beer brands) and brand names entered the test, the strength of the price cue relative to quality rating greatly diminished and was generally found to be insignificant. The results of other multicue tests have been mixed, and therefore this area needs further research.

Most work investigating a price-quality relationship reveals a nonlinear form, generally consistent with the buy-response curve. For instance,

Peterson (1970) tested quality responses of students to soft-drink concentrates. He found a relationship between price and quality of the form

$$U = a + bP + cP^2 \tag{12.8}$$

where U is the mean score on a seven-point quality rating and P is the price level. In a similar experiment McConnell (1968) found a nonlinear quality-price interaction in students' assessments of beer quality. However, these research results are mixed, at best. For example, as Peterson notes, a likely explanation for his quadratic price-quality relationship is the product reference the subjects used in his experiment. Riez (1980) retested McConnell's data and found a lack of significance in the major price-quality finding. In a reply McConnell (1980) sums up by saying, "A number of researchers have studied the price-quality relationship over the years. . . . Yet we still lack substantive knowledge about the phenomenon" (p. 264).

Variations and Extensions of the Concept of Elasticity

Short- and long-run differences in elasticity have been observed. Therefore for the concept of elasticity to be functionally useful, it must be depicted as varying in time.

Many other factors affect demand elasticity. For example, demand is more elastic when there are functionally adequate substitutes available, when the good is a luxury item, or when its purchase represents a large share of a consumer's disposable income. Conversely, when there are few or no substitutes available, when the good represents a necessity, or when its purchase price is low (and thus represents a small share of disposable income), demand tends to be less price-elastic.

Another factor related to price elasticity, which plays an important role in pricing strategy, is the phase of the life cycle. Simon's (1979) study of the relationship between the brand life cycle and price elasticity shows a pattern of decreasing price elasticity in the introduction, growth, and maturity stages of the life cycle and increasing price elasticity during the decline stage. As discussed in detail later, this relationship supports a market penetration pricing strategy in general.

In summary, while the classical Law of Demand incorporates some of the most important phenomena in a supply-demand relationship, its simplicity limits its applicability. Dynamics of elasticity, as well as those of demand and cost, have not generally been included. In addition, the price-quality relationship and the competitive nature of markets that limits flexibility in pricing strategy have frequently been overlooked. However, these elements have been the focus of recent research, which is reviewed in later chapters.

Setting Price in Practice

Thus in spite of the conceptual neatness and intuitive appeal of the classical model, there are difficulties in its application, especially in the estimation of demand parameters. Methods used or suggested for obtaining parameter estimates include surveys and questionnaires, economic techniques on past data, laboratory-controlled experimentation, and field experimentation. However, surveys and questionnaires are not always considered reliable. "Consumer intent to purchase data related to price—whether that data be qualitative or quantitative—should be used only for directional or guidance purposes" (Nault, 1978, p. 4). Econometric methods often are applied to historical series with insufficient pricing variation to read meaningful effects. Laboratory experiments may not be valid when extrapolating to the real world, while field experimentation often does not control enough real-world variables. In addition, price often acts as a cue beyond expression of the purchase cost of a good, limiting the applicability of simple model concepts. Thus the problem with most economic pricing models is that they oversimplify reality and are not readily implementable.

But the pricing models and procedures used in practice tend to be based on a limited view of pricing problems and opportunities, also. They tend to emphasize one of the factors, such as cost, demand, or competition, and neglect the others. Nevertheless, they meet some of the more practical requirements for price determination in the presence of imperfect information and multiple parties. Below, we briefly examine cost-oriented, demand-oriented, and competition-oriented pricing.

Cost-oriented Pricing

A great number of firms set their prices largely or even wholly on the basis of their costs. Typically, all costs are counted, including a usually arbitrary allocation of overhead made on the basis of expected operating levels.

Markup Pricing. The most elementary examples of cost-oriented pricing are markup pricing and cost-plus pricing. They are similar in that price is determined by adding some fixed percentage to the unit cost.

Does the use of a rigid, customary markup over cost make logical sense in the pricing of products? Generally, the answer is no. Any model that ignores current demand elasticity in setting prices is not likely to lead, except by chance, to the achievement of maximum profits, either in the long or the short run. As demand elasticity changes—as it is likely to do seasonally, cyclically, and over the product life cycle—the optimum markup should also change. If markup remains a rigid percentage of cost, then under ordinary conditions it would not lead to maximum profits. However, under special conditions a rigid markup at the right level may lead to optimum profits. The two conditions are that average (unit) costs be fairly constant for different points on the demand curve and that costs be constant over time.

EXAMPLE: We saw earlier in eq. (12.3) that marginal revenue is related to price:

$$MR = \left(1 - \frac{1}{\epsilon}\right) P \tag{12.9}$$

where ϵ = price elasticity of demand, expressed as a positive number. Profits are maximized when marginal revenue is equated to marginal cost (MC). Therefore the optimality condition is

$$MC = \left(1 - \frac{1}{\epsilon}\right) P \tag{12.10}$$

Suppose that average costs (AC) are constant. Then AC = MC, and the condition for optimality is

$$AC = \left(1 - \frac{1}{\epsilon}\right) P \tag{12.11}$$

Equation (12.11) can be rearranged to yield a formula for the optimal markup:

$$\frac{P}{AC} = \frac{1}{1 - (1/\epsilon)} = \frac{\epsilon}{\epsilon - 1}$$

Subtracting AC/AC from both sides and simplifying, we obtain

$$\frac{P - AC}{AC} = \frac{\epsilon}{\epsilon - 1} - 1 = \frac{1}{\epsilon - 1}$$

or

$$\text{Optimal markup} = \frac{1}{\epsilon - 1} \tag{12.12}$$

According to eq. (12.12), the optimal markup is inversely related to price elasticity. If brand-price elasticity is high, say 5.0, as it might be in the case of branded sugar, then the optimal markup is relatively low (25%). If brand elasticity is low, say 2.0, as it might be in the case of branded frozen pastry, the optimal markup is relatively high (100%). Furthermore, if the price elasticity remains fairly constant over time, then a fairly rigid markup would be consistent with optimal pricing.

Both required conditions—constant costs and constant elasticity—are likely to roughly characterize many retailing situations. This situation may explain why fairly rigid markups are in widespread use in retailing and why they may not be inconsistent with optimal-pricing requirements. However, in manufacturing it is less likely that the two special conditions hold, and fixed-markup pricing is more difficult to justify on logical grounds.

Target Pricing. A common cost-oriented approach used by manufacturers is known as target pricing, in which the firm tries to determine the price that would give it a specified target rate of return on its total costs at an estimated standard volume. This pricing approach has been most closely associated with General Motors, which has stated that it prices its automobiles so as to achieve a long-run average rate of return of 15–20 percent on its investment. It is also closely associated with the pricing policies of public utilities, which have a large investment and are constrained by regulatory commissions.

Demand-oriented Pricing

Cost-oriented approaches rely on the idea of a standard markup over costs and/or a conventional level of profits. Demand-oriented approaches look instead at the intensity of demand. A high price is charged when or where demand is intense, and a low price is charged when or where demand is weak, even though unit costs may be the same in both cases.

Sellers face a strong temptation to set different prices in different markets to take advantage of varying demand intensities. Whether they practice price discrimination in fact depends on certain conditions holding true (Stigler, 1952). First, the market must be segmentable, and the segments must show different intensities of demand. Second, there should be no chance that the members of the segment paying the lower price could turn around and resell the product to the segment paying the higher price. Third, there should be little chance that competitors will undersell the firm in the segment being charged the higher price. Fourth, the cost of segmenting and policing the market should not exceed the extra revenue derived from price discrimination. Fifth, price discrimination would have to be permissible under the law, a condition that is generally not satisfied. Finally, there should be little chance that the higher-paying customers will be alienated and react negatively to the company in the long run.

Competition-oriented Pricing

When a company sets its prices chiefly on the basis of what its competitors are charging, rather than on the basis of cost or demand, its pricing policy can be described as competition-oriented.

The most popular type of competition-oriented pricing occurs when a firm tries to keep its price at the average level charged by the industry. This type is called going-rate or imitative pricing.

Going-rate pricing is practiced primarily in homogeneous-product markets, although the market structure itself may vary from pure competition to pure oligopoly. The firm selling a homogeneous product in a purely competitive market actually has very little choice in setting its price. In pure oligopoly, in which a few large firms dominate the industry, firms also tend to charge the same price as competition, although for different reasons. Because there are only a few firms, each firm is aware of the others' prices, and so are the buyers. Price differences are likely to favor the lower-priced firm, discouraging price increases by a single firm.

On the other hand, in markets characterized by product differentiation, the individual firm has more latitude in its price decision. Product differences, whether in styling, quality, or functional features, serve to desensitize the buyer to existing price differentials. Product and marketing programs are made compatible within a chosen pricing zone, and firms respond to competitive changes in price to maintain their pricing zone.

Recent Contributions to the Pricing Literature

Numerous contributions to the literature on pricing have been made in the last several decades. In this section we examine critical, but often ignored, considerations in pricing strategy and models—demand and cost dynamics and competitive response. Other developments are reviewed in less depth in the next section.

Most companies do not excel at the pricing function because sufficient account of demand intensity and customer psychology is not made. Price is not revised often enough to capitalize on changed conditions in the marketplace. Price is too often set independently of the rest of the marketing mix rather than as an intrinsic element of market-positioning strategy. Finally, price is not varied enough to read differential response by different product items and market segments.

Pricing models fail for many of the same reasons. The chief criticism of pricing models—their static (nondynamic) nature—precludes their giving cognizance to changes in the marketplace. A key parameter for modeling change over time is price sensitivity, or the price elasticity of demand. Simon (1979) addresses this issue empirically and derives optimal-pricing policies for a model with price elasticities varying over the life cycle. A second, frequently overlooked issue is competitive interactions. Rao and Shakun (1972) operationalize Gabor and Granger's (1966) price-limit theory in a competitive-market environment and derive optimal-pricing strategies. A final criticism of the classical model is its neglect of dynamic costing. Dolan and Jeuland (1981) propose pricing strategies based on experience-curve price declines in a diffusion environment. These models are described in detail below.

Simon's Model

A key parameter in brand-pricing decisions is the change in consumer demand, which is a function of the price elasticity. Simon (1979) looks at the dynamics of price elasticity over the life cycle and reviews the implications of those dynamics for strategic price determination. Following Polli and Cook (1969) and others, he argues that while much evidence is available in regard to the life cycle of the product class, few empirical studies have focused on the life cycle at the brand level. However, this issue is precisely what is most important to marketing managers in pricing decisions.

Data. Forty-three brands in seven West German markets for three basic product classes form the empirical basis of Simon's study. The products are frequently purchased consumer nondurables in the pharmaceutical, detergent, or household cleanser classes. A minimum of five brands, representing at least 55 percent of the market, are included for study in each market. The analysis (and, perhaps, Simon's model) is most appropriate for well-established product classes.

Models. Simon suggests that dynamic-sales-response models can be represented by the following form:

$$q_{it} = A_{it} + B_{it} + C_{it} \tag{12.13}$$

where A_{it} = carry-over and obsolescence effects of nonprice factors on brand i at time t (this term establishes the brand-life-cycle parameters)

B_{it} = absolute-price-effect term for brand i at time t

C_{it} = effect of price differential between brand i and all other brands in market at time t (in effect, it represents the cross-price-elasticity effect)

q_{it} = quantity of brand i sold at time t

Term A_{it} represents a combination of the life-cycle obsolescence factor and carry-over effects, due to lagged advertising response and the lagged sales variable. Then the pattern of life cycle, such as growth and decline, which is not directly affected by price considerations, is defined by this term. Two versions of the term are

(A1): $A_{it} = a_1 + a_2 q_{i,t-1} (1 - a_3)^{t-\bar{t}}$ (12.14)

and

(A2): $A_{it} = (a_1 + a_2 q_{i,t-1}) (1 - a_3)^{t-\bar{t}}$ (12.15)

where $\bar{t}$ is time of introduction. In eq. (12.14) initial demand potential for the brand is not subject to obsolescence, while in eq. (12.15) obsolescence occurs. Exhibit 12.5 illustrates the flexibility of these specifications. (Two additional versions of A, which include seasonal variables, are provided in the exhibit.)

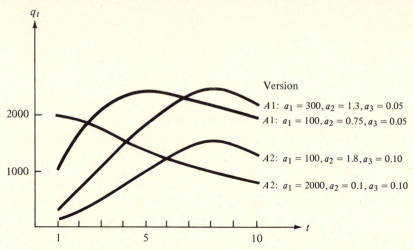

q_t

2000 —

1000 —

Version

$A1: a_1 = 300, a_2 = 1.3, a_3 = 0.05$

$A1: a_1 = 100, a_2 = 0.75, a_3 = 0.05$

$A2: a_1 = 100, a_2 = 1.8, a_3 = 0.10$

$A2: a_1 = 2000, a_2 = 0.1, a_3 = 0.10$

1   5   10 t

EXHIBIT 12-5 Brand-life-cycle curves. (Source: Simon, 1979, p. 441.)

Term B_{it} represents the relationship between sales quantity and the absolute price level. Simon hypothesized a linear relationship of the form

$$B_{it} = bP_{it} \qquad (12.16)$$

where the parameter b is less than zero and P_{it} is the price of brand i at time t.

The C_{it} term represents the effect of the price differential between brand i and all other brands in the market on sales brand i. The desired effect is an underproportional sales response for a relatively small price differential and an overproportional sales effect for a large price differential. The price differential is the excess of the price of brand i over the mean price of all other brands in the market (or the excess of all other brands over i). Models representing these effects are

$$(C1): \qquad C_{it} = c_1 \sinh{(C_2 \, \Delta P_{it})}^- \qquad (12.17)$$

and

$$(C2): \qquad C_{it} = c_1 \sinh{(C_2 \, \Delta P_{it})}\overline{q}_{t-1} \qquad (12.18)$$

where $\Delta P_{it} = \dfrac{\overline{P}_{it} - P_{it}}{\overline{P}_{it}}$ = price differential

$\overline{P}_{it} = \displaystyle\sum_{\substack{j=1 \\ j \neq i}}^{n} \dfrac{m_{jt}P_{it}}{1 - m_{it}}$ = average price of all other brands in market

m_{it} = market share of brand i at time t

$$\bar{q}_{t-1} = \sum_{j=1}^{n} q_{i,t-1} = \text{total market demand at } t-1$$

$$\sinh(x) = \frac{e^x - e^{-x}}{2}$$

c_1, c_2 = parameters

Version $C2$ differs from $C1$ by its assumption that a response to a price differential is proportional to total market demand.

Empirical Results.   Simon applied the different versions of these terms to market data and used ordinary (and, where appropriate, generalized) least squares to determine the best-fit combination for each brand. Parameters a_2 and c_2 were set in limited intervals, making the sales-response function linear in all other parameters. Simon reports interpretable results for all but 8 of the brands. On the remaining 35 brands, 82 percent of the coefficients are significant at the 90 percent level, and 83 percent of the regressions yielded R^2's of greater than 0.60. Simon concludes that the brand-life-cycle dynamics and cross-price-elasticity effects are appropriately modeled.

Visual inspection of brand-growth and -decline patterns is then used to classify the observations into stages of the life cycle. With the best model version for each brand and the resultant parameters, price elasticities and rates of growth (or decline) are computed for each brand and for each life-cycle phase. Exhibit 12.6 illustrates the results (the abbreviation BLC on

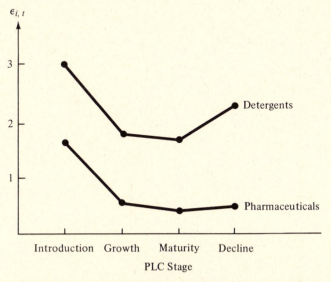

EXHIBIT 12-6   **Average price elasticities at different stages of the life cycle.** (Source: Simon, 1979, p. 449.)

the horizontal axis represents brand life cycle), summarized as follows:

In 95 percent of the cases, $\epsilon_{\text{introduction}} \geq \epsilon_{\text{growth}}$.

In 71 percent of the cases, $\epsilon_{\text{growth}} \geq \epsilon_{\text{maturity}}$.

In 100 percent of the cases, $\epsilon_{\text{maturity}} \leq \epsilon_{\text{decline}}$.

Pricing-strategy Implications. Simon's chief result is the implication of these changing price elasticities for optimal brand-price-setting policy. With a goal of maximum net present value of the profit stream over the brand's life horizon, management's objective becomes

$$\text{Maximize } Z = \sum_{\tau=0}^{T-t} [P_{t+\tau}Q_{t+\tau} - C(Q_{t+\tau})](1 + r)^{-\tau} \tag{12.19}$$

where $C(Q)$ = cost function
r = discount rate
P = price
Q = quantity sold
$T - t$ = (remaining) brand life

If competitive brands' prices are given, the optimal price at time t, derived from taking the derivative of eq. (12.19) with respect to P_t, is

$$P_t^* = \left[\frac{1}{1 - (1/\epsilon_t)}\right] C_t'$$

$$- \left[\frac{1}{1 - (1/\epsilon_t)}\right] \sum_{\tau=1}^{T-t} \cdot (P_{t+\tau} - C_{t+\tau}') a_2^\tau (1 - a_3)^{\tau t + \tau(\tau-1)/2} (1 + r)^{-\tau} \tag{12.20}$$

where ϵ_t = brand's own price elasticity at time t
C_t' = per-unit (marginal) cost at time t

To compare the above price to that of static economic theory, we set marginal cost C_t' equal to marginal revenue from the static model:

$$C_t' = MR = P_t\left(1 - \frac{1}{\epsilon_t}\right) \tag{12.21}$$

or

$$P_t^* = \left[\frac{1}{1 - (1/\epsilon_t)}\right] C_t' \tag{12.22}$$

Thus the static model's optimal price is equal to the first term in Simon's model. However, the dynamic model considers the effects of future price changes due to changes in elasticity and nonprice influence over the brand life cycle. If $a_2 > 0$, $0 \leq a_3 \leq 1$, and $P_{t+j} > C_{t+j}'$, then the dynamic price is below the optimal static price, and the dynamic model yields higher profits. The optimal-price trend in the dynamic model tends to increase as price elasticity decreases. The optimal-price path is most easily obtained by means of a branch-and-bound algorithm (Chapter 6) and depends on the relative magnitude of demand and cost factors. Exhibit 12.7 illustrates the optimal strategy for one brand. In general, Simon's model and his empirical results support a penetration-type pricing strategy for brands introduced into markets with existing substitutes.

Assessment. Simon's model is an important extension of the static economic model, yielding pricing-strategy implications for different stages in the product's life cycle. However, his model has several important limitations. The independence of his A, B, and C terms is subject to question. For example, aspects of the marketing mix that determine obsolescence and psychological superiority of products should incorporate price as a factor that can affect, but not halt or control, the life cycle. Simon keeps the C terms constant over time, fixing the cross-price elasticity of the brand over the life cycle. This condition is in contradiction to effects suggested by Parsons (1975).

Furthermore, his objective function assumes a set of given competitive-brand prices, and therefore the model is not truly dynamic. This problem can be corrected by establishing a cross-price-elasticity effect that is dependent on the life-cycle stage, although data limitations may preclude this tack.

Finally, although success has been seen in historical analyses, it is not clear how a brand should be treated early in its life cycle. The variation in parameters within a product class is quite large, suggesting large differences in life-cycle processes, even among brands within the same market.

On net, however, by demonstrating analytically and empirically how

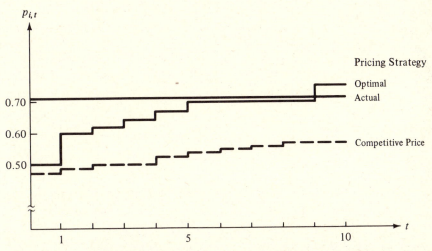

EXHIBIT 12-7   **Optimal and actual pricing strategy of brand 4.2.** (Source: Simon, 1979, p. 451.)

the dynamics of time-varying price elasticities can be incorporated into a life-cycle pricing model, Simon's model makes an important contribution to the theory, and, it is hoped, to the practice of dynamic marketing decision making.

The Rao-Shakun Model

The Rao-Shakun (1972) model is reviewed for two reasons. First, they operationalize the Gabor and Granger (1966) price-limit model in the context of developing an entry strategy for a new brand in the marketplace. Second, they explicitly consider the structure of the market as well as the objective of the brand and the competitors in reaching a price strategy.

Model Assumptions.   The Rao-Shakun model is based on the following hypotheses and assumptions:

1. A homogeneous group of customers is considered.
2. The minimum price that a member of the group is willing to pay for the product is a log-normally-distributed random variable, having mean μ and variance σ^2.
3. For each customer there is a fixed interval on the log-price scale of constant length a, which defines his range of acceptable prices. Thus as a consequence of the first two assumptions, the maximum price that a member of the group is willing to pay is also log-normal, with mean $\mu + a$ and variance σ^2.

These hypotheses are consistent with the findings of Gabor and Granger (1966). While the third hypothesis was not explicitly tested by Gabor and Granger, it will not distort the model's reasonableness on an aggregate basis.

EXHIBIT 12-8   Brand objectives from Rao and Shakun (1972).

1. $\max\limits_{p_i} S_i$	Price is set to maximize sales of brand i
2. $\max\limits_{p_i}(S_i + S_j)$	Price is set to maximize sales of brands i and j (for instance, when both brands are offered by the same seller)
3. $\max\limits_{p_i}\left(S_i + \sum\limits_{j\neq i} S_j\right)$	Price is set to maximize sales of all brands in the market
4. $\min\limits_{p_i}(\max S_j)$	Price of brand i is set to minimize the maximum possible sales of brand j (competitive strategy)

SOURCE: Rao and Shakun, 1972. Reprinted by permission of the Institute of Management Sciences. *Management Science*, Vol. 18, No. 5 Part 2, January 1972.

Four objectives, reproduced in Exhibit 12.8, are considered. Although these objectives—sales rather than profit maximization, in particular—are chosen for their analytical tractability rather than their managerial usefulness, they are helpful indicators for developing structural insight.

Let

P_i = price of brand i

p_i = ln P_i

ρ_i = probability that randomly chosen customer chooses brand i

$\phi(x)$ = cumulative distribution function of a standard normal random variable

The One-brand Case. If only brand i is selling in a market with price P_i, then the probability that a randomly chosen customer buys brand i is

$$\rho_i = 1 - \text{Prob}(P_i \text{ found too high}) - \text{Prob}(P_i \text{ found too low})$$

$$= \phi\left(\frac{p_i - \mu}{\sigma}\right) - \phi\left(\frac{p_i - \mu - a}{\sigma}\right) \qquad (12.23)$$

that is, the probability that the price is neither too high nor too low. By differentiating ρ_i with respect to p_i and setting the result equal to zero, we get the optimal one-brand price:

$$p_i = \mu + \frac{a}{2} \qquad (12.24)$$

The Two-brand Case. To determine consumer choice in a multibrand market, Rao and Shakun introduce additional behavioral assumptions. In particular, they assume the following:

1. A proportion λ of customers, the quality-conscious group, will buy the higher-priced brand in their acceptable range.
2. A proportion $(1 - \lambda)$, the price-conscious group, will buy the lower-priced brand in their acceptable range.

By simple logical arguments following their assumptions, the authors show that the probability that a randomly chosen individual within the group will purchase brand 1 when $0 < p_2 - p_1 < a$ and $p_1 < p_2$ is

$\rho(1) = \text{Prob} (p_2 \text{ too high but } p_1 \text{ is acceptable})$

$\qquad + (1 - \lambda)\text{Prob (both brands are acceptable)}$

$$= \phi\left(\frac{p_2 - a - \mu}{\sigma}\right) - \phi\left(\frac{p_1 - a - \mu}{\sigma}\right)$$

$$+ (1 - \lambda)\left[\phi\left(\frac{p_1 - \mu}{\sigma}\right) - \phi\left(\frac{p_2 - a - \mu}{\sigma}\right)\right] \qquad (12.25)$$

Similarly,

$$\rho(2) = \phi\left(\frac{p_2 - \mu}{\sigma}\right) - \phi\left(\frac{p_1 - \mu}{\sigma}\right) + \lambda\left[\phi\left(\frac{p_1 - \mu}{\sigma}\right) - \phi\left(\frac{p_2 - a - \mu}{\sigma}\right)\right] \quad (12.26)$$

When $p_2 - p_1 \geq a_1$, then eqs. (12.25) and (12.26) are evaluated at $\lambda = 1$.
Four observations can be made at this point:

1. A proportion π_i, where

$$\pi_i = \phi\left(\frac{p_2 - a - \mu}{\sigma}\right) - \phi\left(\frac{p_1 - a - \mu}{\sigma}\right) \quad (12.27)$$

will *not* switch to brand 2 because they regard p_2 as too high a price.
This proportion is the brand-loyal or unswitchable segment.
2. If $p_2 - p_1 \geq a$, then the brands are noncompetitive because they do not
share a common population of buyers. This condition provides an
operational measure for market-structure analysis and a way of determining if a new brand will cannibalize a manufacturer's existing
brands.
3. Brand 1 can capture some of brand 2's business by emphasizing its
quality; this has the effect of lowering λ. A similar argument holds for
brand 2.
4. The market share of the ith brand is

$$S_i = \frac{\rho_i}{\rho_1 + \rho_2} \quad i = 1, 2 \quad (12.28)$$

Brand Entry.   Suppose brand 1 is already established in the market and
brand 2 wishes to enter. With the equations above, equilibrium prices can be
obtained for most combinations of brand objectives.
First, consider the situation where both brands wish to maximize sales.
If there is no long-run penalty for entering the market late, the result can be
derived by differentiating eqs. (12.25) and (12.26) with respect to p_1 and p_2
and setting the results equal to zero:

$$p_1 = \frac{\sigma^2}{2} \ln(1 - \lambda) + \mu + \frac{a}{2} \quad (12.29)$$

and

$$p_2 = -\frac{\sigma^2}{2} \ln \lambda + \mu + \frac{a}{2} \quad (12.30)$$

where these equations give the results under competitive conditions. Under
cooperative strategy (item 3 in Exhibit 12.8), optimal prices for maximization

of market sales are

$$p_1 = a \tag{12.31}$$

and

$$p_2 = \mu + a \tag{12.32}$$

The authors go on to explore other entry- and equilibrium-pricing rules for other combinations of brand objectives. They also show extensions of the model to three brands by introducing fractions of individuals who will purchase highest- or middle-priced brands when three brands are available.

Assessment.   The approach suggested by Rao and Shakun is a unique one for pricing in a multiple-seller market. Their model incorporates the price-limit theory of consumer choice, thereby explicitly recognizing the price-quality relationship. In addition, the pricing strategies are shown to vary by the number of sellers, as well as by the objectives of the marketer and his competitors in the marketplace. Thus a structure is presented for evaluating price-setting strategies in a dynamic competitive environment.

The model has a number of significant weaknesses. First, for analytical ease they use sales maximization as the brand objective rather than profit maximization, which limits the usefulness of their results. Second, the model ignores the complexities of market structure and market power by dealing with homogeneous groups. To operationalize this concept, the seller must set different prices (via different-priced brands) for each of the homogeneous groups within the market. Unless sufficient market power by the seller exists, this approach will not be viable. Third, it is not clear how one incorporates dynamics within the model. Simon (1979) showed that brand price elasticity varies over the product life cycle; this condition indicates that the price-limit distribution's mean and variance may vary over time. Fourth, the authors essentially ignore data gathering, estimation, and other empirical issues, deferring to Gabor and Granger. Yet their model includes other parameters—price and quality-conscious proportions of the population, as well as competitive objectives. In particular, their solutions require competitors (at least implicitly) to act according to given objectives and to have the same model parameters in mind. Finally, the model does not incorporate the effect of price on the quantity of goods purchased.

In conclusion, the Rao-Shakun approach reflects the limitation of our understanding and our methodology in this area. It addresses two key pricing problems: the price-quality relationship and market competition. But in doing so, its usefulness is compromised because of the restrictiveness of its assumptions. The fact that the model has not been applied points to the need for related empirical work.

The Dolan-Jeuland Model*

A third extension of the classical economic model, increasingly popular in marketing literature, incorporates cost and diffusion-process dynamics. That is:

Current sales of a product are related to past levels of sales. Bass (1969a) showed that the probability of an individual adopting a (durable) product at t can be represented as a linear function of the previous number of adopters.

Production costs, especially the labor component, decline with accumulated output—the more that is produced, the lower will be the unit production cost (Abell and Hammond, 1979; Yelle, 1979).

A common functional form of the experience-curve cost model is

$$MC(t) = MC(0)\left[\frac{V(t)}{V(0)}\right]^{-b} \tag{12.33}$$

where $MC(t)$ = marginal production cost at time t
$MC(0)$ = marginal production cost at beginning of commercialization
$V(t)$ = accumulated volume at time t
$V(0)$ = pilot production quantity

Static Demand.   The authors investigate several cases; the first is that of static demand, in which the sales rate at time t is a function of price only:

$$\frac{dV}{dt} = ae^{-dP(t)} \tag{12.34}$$

where $P(t)$ = price at time t
a, d = constants

The full model is then formed by introducing the following variables:

$Z(t)$ = cumulative discounted profit at t
r = discount rate
t_f = end of planning period
$C = MC(0)/V(0)^{-b}$ = unit cost at beginning of commercialization

By definition,

$$MC(t) = MC(0)\left[\frac{V(t)}{V(0)}\right]^{-b} = CV(t)^{-b} \tag{12.35}$$

---

*The reader wishing to review this model should consult the section of Chapter 17 on cost dynamics and the section of Chapter 19 on new-production diffusion.

With the objective of maximizing cumulative discounted profits, the optimization model becomes

$$\max_{P(t)} Z(t_f) \tag{12.36}$$

subject to

$$\frac{dV}{dt} = ae^{-aP(t)} \qquad \text{(demand)}$$

$$\frac{dZ}{dt} = [P(t) - CV(t)^{-b}] \frac{dV(t)}{dt} e^{-rt} \qquad \text{(profit)}$$

$$V(0) > 0 \qquad Z(0) = 0 \qquad P(t) > 0 \qquad \text{for all } t$$

The optimal price at time t, $P^*(t)$, obtained by solving system (12.36), is

$$P^*(t) = \frac{1}{d} + Ce^{-r(t-t_f)}V(t_f)^{-b} + re^{-rt} \int_t^{t_f} Ce^{-rz} V(z)^{-b} \, dz \tag{12.37}$$

Equation (12.37) is most easily interpreted if we consider the case where a zero discount rate is used ($r = 0$). Then it reduces to

$$P^*(t) = \frac{1}{d} + CV(t_f)^{-b} \tag{12.38}$$

or $P^*(t) = 1/d + MC$; that is, pricing is a constant (but dynamically changing) markup over unit costs, clearly declining with time.

Dynamic Demand. In the case of dynamic demand the authors investigate a modification of Bass' (1969*a*) model suggested by Robinson and Lakhani (1975). In this model the market rate of penetration is

$$\frac{dX(t)}{dt} = [\alpha + \beta X(t)][1 - X(t)] e^{-dP(t)} \tag{12.39}$$

where $X(t)$ = proportion of market penetrated at time t
[so $V(t) - V(0) = mX(t)$]
α = coefficient of innovation (impetus to purchase regardless of previous number of adopters)
β = coefficient of imitation (impact of previous adopters on probability of purchase)

Then the optimization problem with no discounting is

$$\max_{P(t)} Z(t_f) \tag{12.40}$$

subject to

$$\frac{dX}{dt} = (\alpha + \beta X)(1 - X)e^{-dP(t)} \qquad \text{(penetration)}$$

$$\frac{dV}{dt} = m\frac{dX}{dt} \qquad \text{(demand)}$$

$$\frac{dZ}{dt} = [P(t) - CV(t)^{-b}]\frac{dV}{dt} \qquad \text{(profit)}$$

where m = market potential.

The solution to system (12.40) yields

$$P^*(t) = \frac{1}{d} + CV(t_f)^{-b} + \frac{1}{d}\ln\left\{\frac{[\alpha + \beta X(t_f)][1 - X(t_f)]}{[\alpha + \beta X(t)][1 - X(t)]}\right\} \qquad (12.41)$$

Note that eq. (12.41) is identical to eq. (12.38) except for the last term. This last term, along with the length of the planning horizon, determines the shape of the optimal time path of price. (See Exhibit 12.9.)

A review of eq. (12.41) and Exhibit 12.9 gives important insight into the structure of dynamic pricing policies. For example, Dean (1969) discusses two pricing strategies for the innovative firm likely to face eventual competition: market skimming and a penetration policy. This analysis shows the following (for the innovative firm's monopoly period):

A skimming policy (high initial prices followed by lower prices) is optimal if the demand curve is stable over time (no diffusion) and production costs decline with accumulated value.

Penetration pricing (low initial costs as an entering wedge into the marketplace) is optimal if a durable's demand is characterized by a diffusion process.

Assessment.   In particular situations the actual price levels will have to be calculated numerically [Robinson and Lakhani (1975) use dynamic programming], and situations of discounted profit, especially in a competitive (nonmonopoly) situation, must be considered. In addition, handling the price-decline effect as specified in eq. (12.39) leads to some intuitive model difficulties. [See Kalish (1982) for a review of further developments and a generalization of these results.]

Despite its limitations, this paper points to the importance and viability of developing pricing policies based on the elasticity of demand, the evolution of production costs, and demand-side dynamics. Although much more needs to be accomplished in fine-tuning such models, the basic structures developed here appear to be adaptable to a wide range of situations, filling a gap felt by Monroe and Della Bitta (1978), who said "... no models are available for the new product pricing decision" (p. 426).

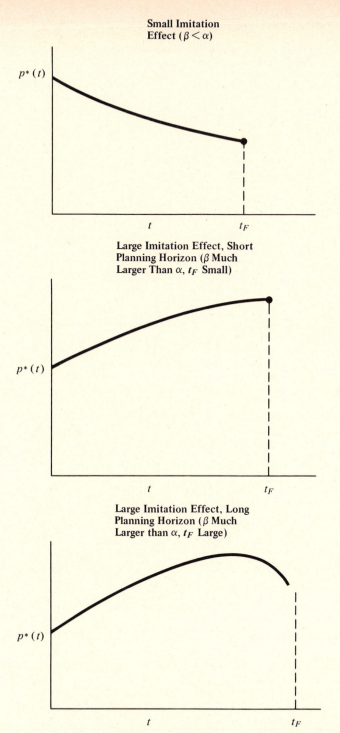

EXHIBIT 12-9   **Optimal time path for diffusion-demand cases (nondiscounted profits).** (Source: Dolan and Jeuland, 1981, p. 60.)

Other Pricing Models

In this section we review how some major issues discussed above have been addressed in other recent pricing models.

Market-pricing Models

In Exhibit 12.10 a summary of the features of recent pricing models is given. From this exhibit we note that a diversity of market settings and conditions are considered.

The dynamics of demand continues to be a critical issue. Thomas and Chabria (1975) specify a time-varying, stochastic demand function and use a bayesian procedure to update the parameter values of the demand distribution. They then derive pricing policies with dynamic programming. A similar stochastic demand function is used by Lodish (1980a) and is applied to the case of pricing broadcast spots.

Landau (1976) considers a single seller in a market in which demand increases with the amount already sold up to the point of saturation. He

EXHIBIT 12-10   **Recent market-pricing models.**

	Competitive Dynamics	Demand Dynamics	Cost Dynamics	Price-Quality Considerations	Profit Maximizing
Simon (1979)	−	+	−	−	+
Rao and Shakun (1972)	+	−	−	+	−
Braverman (1971)	−	−	−	−	+
Thomas and Chabria (1975)	−	+	−	−	+
Davis and Simmons (1976)	+	+	+	−	+
Robinson and Lakhani (1975)	−	+	+	−	+
Mesak and Clelland (1979)	+	−	−	−	−
Parsons and Price (1972)	−	−	−	−	−
Lodish (1980a)	−	+	−	−	+
Kunreuther and Richard (1971)	−	−	−	−	+
Brooks (1975)	−	−	−	−	−
Thomas (1970)	−	+	+	−	+
Kunreuther and Schrage (1973)	−	+	−	−	+
Glickman and Berger (1976)	−	−	−	−	+
Doland and Jeuland (1981)	−	+	+	−	+
Landau (1976)	−	+	+	−	+

NOTE: + means a feature of the model; − means not a feature of the model.

shows that the optimal long-term price path leads to lower prices, greater output, and higher profit than the myopic one-period maximization.

On the side of cost dynamics, Davis and Simmons (1976) suggest a dynamic-programming approach to pricing strategy in an oligopolistic market characterized by cost/volume relationships. Under a series of restrictive assumptions about the setting of market prices and the uses of production capacity, they show that profitability is tied to pricing to gain market share for a market leader.

Competitive response has been addressed in a number of ways aside from that of Rao and Shakun (1972) but without notable success. Mesak and Clelland (1979) propose a model to predict the impact of a vector of price changes on sales of a brand of a low-priced, frequently purchased product. Each consumer is assumed to have a perceived value for each of the brands. Then his regular brand is the one for which the excess of this value over market price is highest, and he switches brands when the excess value of another brand becomes greater. The model presents a structure for assessing the likely effect of price changes on sales and brand share, but it is difficult to use in an empirical setting given the data and assumptions needed about competitive activities.

Sales—Market-Share Maximizing	Stochastic	One Seller in Market	Other Marketing Variables	Emphasis on Entry Pricing	Inventory/Holding Costs Considered	Multiperiod
−	−	−	+	−	−	+
+	+	−	−	+	−	−
−	+	−	−	−	−	−
−	+	−	−	+	+	+
−	−	−	−	−	−	+
−	−	+	−	−/+	−	+
+	−	−	−	−	−	−
+	+	−	−	−	−	−
−	+	−	−	−	+	+
−	−	−	−	−	+	−
−	−	−	−	−	−	−
−	−	+	−	−	+	+
−	−	−	−	−	+	−
−	−	−	+	−	−	−
−	−	+	−	−/+	−	+
−	−	−	−	−	−	+

This latter model highlights a need for integration. Current models either integrate demand and cost dynamics into a formula for long-term profit maximization, or they focus on the competitive dynamics of the market (particularly in the short run). An integrative effort is needed that treats market realities and data limitations at the same time.

Competitive-bidding Models

Competitive bidding is a common form of pricing in markets where the firm is in competition with an unknown number of suppliers and has no deterministic knowledge of their prices. Many manufacturers and service organizations, selling to the Defense Department, municipal governments, original-equipment producers, and so forth, must bid against others for the work; the contract usually goes to the lowest bidder. Therefore, the seller must carefully think through two issues regarding each bidding opportunity: (1) should he bid at all (the decision to bid), and (2) if so, what bid should he make (the bid-size problem)?

If the supplier decides to make a bid on a particular job, he must search for a price that is somewhere above his costs but below competitors' bids. The higher the seller sets his price above his costs, the greater will be the conditional profit but the smaller will be the probability of getting the contract. These considerations have been formalized in a simple model in which bids are calculated to maximize the company's expected profits. The expected profit in a potential bid is the product of the probability of getting the contract and the estimated profit on the contract:

$$E(Z_p) = f(P)(P - C) \tag{12.42}$$

where $E(Z_p)$ = expected profit with a bid of P
$f(P)$ = probability of winning contract with a bid of P
P = bid price
C = estimated cost of fulfilling contract

Each possible price, then, is associated with a certain probability of winning the contract. A company may logically choose the expected profit-maximizing price. Exhibit 12.11 shows four alternative bid levels and the associated probabilities and profits for a hypothetical situation. In this example the firm will be tempted to bid $10,000 because its associated expected profit is highest ($216) at this level.

However, the chief problem with this model is guessing the probabilities of winning the contract at various bidding levels. Where price is the buyer's only concern, this probability is the probability of submitting a lower bid than those of all the other competitors, and the probability of submitting the lowest bid is the joint probability that the company's bid is lower than each competitor's bid (assuming competitors' bids are independently

EXHIBIT 12-11   Effect of different bids on expected profit.

Company's Bid	Company's Profit	Probability of Getting Award with This Bid (Assumed)	Expected Profit
$ 9,500	$ 100	0.81	$ 81
10,000	600	0.36	216
10,500	1100	0.09	99
11,000	1600	0.01	16

formed):

$$f(P) = f_1(P)f_2(P) \cdots f_j(P) \cdots f_n(P) \qquad (12.43)$$

where $f_j(P)$ is the probability that a bid of P is lower than competitor j's bid.

Competitors' bids are uncertain but may be derived from past bidding behavior, as follows. Assume competitor j has bid on a number of past contracts and that data are available. Then for each bid,

$$r_j = \frac{P_j}{C} \qquad (12.44)$$

where r_j = ratio of competitor j's bid to company cost
P_j = past bid by j
C = company's cost at time of bid

The ratios for several past bids of a competitor form a distribution $g_j(y)$, where y is competitor j's bid.

If for a given contract our cost is C, then we might guess that the probability of j's bid price being greater than ours is $\int_r^\infty g_j(y)dy$, where $r = P/C$. With k competitors our likelihood of winning is

$$\prod_{j=1}^{K} \int_r^\infty g_j(y)dy \qquad (12.45)$$

If each competitor has the same bid density $g(\cdot)$, eq. (12.45) reduces to

$$f(P) = \left[\int_r^\infty g(y)dy\right]^k \qquad (12.46)$$

and the expected profit of bid price P is

$$E[Z(P)] = (P - C)\left[\int_r^\infty g(y)dy\right]^k \qquad (12.47)$$

Given knowledge of g and C, eq. (12.47) can be solved for an optimal value of P.

In the last step we knew that there would be exactly k bidders. If k is only known probabilistically, then eq. (12.47) is modified as follows. Suppose a distribution $h(k)$ is found that describes well the past number of bidders (which may correlate with the size of the contract). Then the probability that a company bid of P will win is

$$f(P) = \sum_k h(k) \left[\int_r^\infty g(y) dy \right]^k \tag{12.48}$$

and eq. (12.48) is used in eq. (12.42) to determine an optimal bid.

Like the pricing model of classical demand theory, the bid model has a nice intuitive structure. But for practical use it clearly needs modification. Realistically, the company may be missing an adequate past history for certain competitors. In this case, for each potential competitor management will have to develop a subjective probability distribution for r, based on whatever information is available. Furthermore, the company may believe that competitors will depart from their past pattern of bidding, in which case management will again want to replace historical probability distributions with ones that more accurately reflect its subjective expectations.

The model may need further modifications to meet other special circumstances present in the competitive-bidding situation. For example, the company may expect a sequence of opportunities to open up, one at a time and with different values, and because of limited resources, it cannot afford to win all the contracts. Here the company must decide when to bid and how much. Clearly, the availability of further opportunities will influence the company's bid in a particular case. Another circumstance that would modify the bidding process occurs when the buyer is known to take other factors into consideration besides the bid, such as the bidder's reputation for reliability, service, quality, proximity, past relations with buyer, and so forth. In this situation a supplier with a good reputation may set a bid higher than his competitors by the amount of superior reputation he enjoys (Simmonds, 1968).

Competitive-bidding situations have been analyzed with a variety of other mathematical methods. For instance, game theory has been used as a mode of analysis when the company has no idea of the probability distribution of the possible bids by competitors and chooses to bid on the basis of a maximum criterion (Greismer and Shubik, 1963). In other situations bayesian decision theory has been used to assess the expected value of perfect information for a player seeking information about the value of the contract or a competitor's likely bid (Lavalle, 1967). Further-more, payoff tables have been extensively used by Edelman (1965) of RCA to array the payoffs of each possible RCA bid against possible bids by each competitor as a prelude to determining a best bid. In general, each company that does competitive bidding faces particular variables that require adaptations of the models reviewed here.

Recent work on competitive bidding has focused on two important issues. The first is the use of appropriate costs to reflect forgone opportunities when setting bids, and the second is the development of tools to assign bids to multiple contracts in an environment of limitations and constraints.

Kortanek, Soden, and Sodaro (1973) develop models of varying complexity to deal with the utilization of constrained resources. The models are based on the formula

Optimal bid price = direct costs + opportunity costs

$$+ \text{ competitive-advantage fee} \qquad (12.49)$$

The authors construct a multiple-contract bidding process in which no one competitor consistently has an advantage and a competitor's efficiency depends on the relationship between the contracts he obtains. The objective function is the contribution over direct cost per capacity unit. The model employs linear programming with two key dual variables, machine resources and the competitive-advantage fee, which represents how well the contract fits with the remaining resources.

The optimal bid price b_k^* is determined by

$$b_k^* = \frac{d_k + \lambda_k(C_k) - g_k(b_k^*)}{g_k'(b_k^*)} \qquad (12.50)$$

where d_k = direct costs

$\lambda_k(C_k)$ = opportunity costs (shadow prices) of scarce resources used, defined as the value of the resources if the contract were lost

$g_k(b_k)$ = probability density function of winning project k with bid b_k

$g_k'(b_k)$ = derivative of g_k at b_k

Attanasi (1974) provides an explanation of the above model. He demonstrates that it maximizes expected contributions over direct costs by equating the rate of proportionate increase in the probability of losing the contract with the proportionate increase in contract contribution over full costs.

Goodman and Baurmeister (1976) develop an algorithm for determining bids for multiple contracts under constraint with a decision-tree approach. The process starts with individual models of expected returns on contracts based on predetermined probability distributions of competitors' bids. An n-stage decision model is then developed combining the n contracts in chronological order into a decision tree. The algorithm is then used to determine bid prices that optimize returns over the contract set given minimum and maximum utilization constraints.

Grinyar and Whittaker (1973) look at a different issue in competitive bidding, that of cost-estimation bias. They note that the nature of the process is such that a bidder who underestimates costs tends to increase his probability of winning the bid, and, consequently, winning bids are more likely to be based on improper costing—the "winner's curse." [Oren and Williams (1975) provide a detailed theoretical explanation for this phenomenon.] By examining bid data in the construction industry, they develop a multiplier to increase cost estimates so that this bias may be incorporated in the competitive-bid process. The authors claim that the model had been adopted by at least one firm in the industry.

Thus recent developments in competitive bidding tend to be centered on the cost side, emphasizing appropriate use of opportunity costs and explicit considerations of constraints in multicontract settings. Further development of methods to assist the manager in deriving probability densities for competitors' bids is needed to make the area more useful for management applications. [See Monroe (1979) for discussion of how to operationalize competitive-bidding procedures.]

Product-Line-pricing Models

The interdependence of individual brands in a firm's product line complicates the development of appropriate pricing models and strategies. Certain brands may act as substitutes, while others act as complements to each other. When such interdependencies exist, it is impossible to determine optimal pricing for each brand without taking the others into consideration.

The Rao-Shakun (1972) model developed a framework under which optimal prices for separate brands could be derived when a firm introduces multiple brands of a product to capture the maximum sales from buyers with widely distributed price-limit ranges.

Urban (1969) proposed an early but comprehensive model for analysis of product-line decisions, including pricing. He proposes a brand-sales response, which is a function of the marketing variables for the brand, its complements, and its substitutes:

$$X_j = a P_{jI}^{\text{EPI}} A_{jI}^{\text{EAI}} D_{jI}^{\text{EDI}}$$

$$\left(\prod_m P_{Im}^{\text{CP}_{jm}} A_{Im}^{\text{CA}_{jm}} D_{Im}^{\text{CD}_{jm}} \right) \left(\frac{P_{1j}^{\text{SP}_i} A_{1j}^{\text{SA}_i} D_{1j}^{\text{SD}_i}}{\sum_{i=1}^{n} P_{ij}^{\text{SP}_i} A_{ij}^{\text{SA}_i} D_{ij}^{\text{SD}_i}} \right) \qquad (12.51)$$

where
X_j = firm 1's sales of product j
a = constant
P_{jI}, A_{jI}, D_{jI} = average price level and total advertising and distribution levels of all brands of product j
EPI, EAI, EDI = industry, advertising, and distribution elasticities for product j

P_{Im}, A_{Im}, D_{Im} = average price level and total advertising and distribution levels of all brands of product m, $m \neq j$

$CP_{jm}, CA_{jm}, CD_{jm}$ = cross-price, -advertising, and -distribution elasticities for products j and m

m = product indexed over m

P_{ij}, A_{ij}, D_{ij} = price and advertising and distribution levels for product j by firm i

SP_j, SA_j, SD_j = competitive-price, -advertising, and -distribution sensitivities for firm i and product j

The first three terms on the right in eq. (12.51) develop industry demand as a function of price, advertising, and distribution, holding these decision variables fixed for all other products. The next three terms adjust the industry demand for changes in the decision variables of interrelated products. The last term determines the market share of firm 1's brand of product j based on the levels and sensitivities of each brand's price, advertising, and distribution. The model specifies the response-function form and requires a large amount of data for its estimation. Furthermore, it ignores the dynamics of competitive response and is computationally difficult to evaluate. Finally, although it has been referenced frequently, it has not been widely used.

Monroe and Della Bitta (1978) discuss models with interdependent demand, which also yield single-period, profit-maximizing prices. Such models have been developed for linear, nonlinear, and stochastic demand relationships. Their model considers only the interactions of products within the firm (and thus fixes the parameters of competitive products), and it yields a one-period, profit-maximizing price for the product line. However, the empirical estimation of the joint-cost matrix required for this model would be a major challenge for most managers.

For the most part these studies represent the extent of research in the product-line-pricing area. This limited development is likely caused by the need for more fully developed, single-product pricing models before adding product-line considerations.

Monroe and Zoltners (1979) discuss the conceptual problem associated with product-line pricing. Although theoretical solutions for five theoretical product-line-pricing situations can be found (Palda, 1971), they report few attempts to develop analytical models. In fact, Monroe and Zoltners argue that the decision objective of maximizing profit contribution is inappropriate and demonstrate the effectiveness of a criterion they call "contribution per resource unit." They state, "When the volume of products that could be sold is greater than the resource capacity to produce those products, the largest contribution (and profit) results from producing those products that generate the greatest contribution per resource unit used" (p. 55). Their procedure represents an attempt to quantify and structure this difficult area.

Summary

While nonprice factors continue to grow in importance in the modern marketing process, price remains a key element and pricing is especially challenging in certain types of situations.

For setting an initial price, a firm can draw guidance from the classical, theoretical pricing model of economics. This model indicates how the firm can find a short-run, profit-maximizing price when estimates of demand and cost are available. However, the model leaves out several factors that must be considered in actual pricing situations, such as the presence of other objectives, multiple parties, marketing-mix interactions, and uncertainties surrounding the estimates of demand and cost. In practice, companies tend to orient their pricing toward either cost (as in markup pricing and target pricing), demand (as in price discrimination), or competition (as in going-rate pricing).

Recent research has focused on the dynamics of pricing decisions. Empirical testing of life-cycle and diffusion-type models has shown that the incorporation of market dynamics leads to different strategies and policies from those of static models.

In the context of entry pricing and price changes, competitive-interaction dynamics have also been addressed. These models have been intuitively interesting but have not been sufficiently specific and data-based to be operationally useful as yet. Competitive-bidding models have been developed to structure the decisions in such contexts, but most of these models still require significant amounts of subjective input.

Major challenges in the pricing area include the development of general market-pricing models that integrate competitive interactions with market dynamics and measurement and estimation procedures to make these models operational. In conclusion, the literature presents many theoretical pricing models, but more reports of their proven value from marketing managers are required to guide future developments.

Problems

12.1 What is price elasticity? Differentiate elasticity, inelasticity, unit elasticity, and cross elasticity.

12.2 Differentiate among cost-oriented pricing, demand-oriented pricing, and competition-oriented pricing with regard to the company's goals, the degree of competition, and the stage of the product life cycle.

12.3 The marketing management of a firm has suggested a price increase of $0.74 on a product currently selling at $8.95. Current unit variable costs are $4.65, while the elasticity of demand is estimated to be -1.75. Would you recommend that the price increase be adopted?

12.4 The ABC Plumbing Company is invited to bid for a contract to install the plumbing system in a new apartment building. The company estimates that the cost of installation as specified in the contract will be $10,000. From past experience the company has determined that the probability of winning the contract is

$$f(P) = e^{-P/10,000}$$

Should the company make a bid? At what price? What is the company's expected profit at this price?

12.5 A manufacturer sells its product in two distinct markets, A and B. The demand equations associated with each market are

$$Q_A = 400 - 2p_A$$
$$Q_B = 150 - 0.5p_B$$

The firm's total cost equation is

$$C = 10,000 + 20(Q_A + Q_B)$$

The current selling price is $120 in both markets. Assuming that the conditions necessary for the successful practice of price discrimination hold, could the company benefit by charging different prices in markets A and B? If so, what prices should be set in each market?

12.6 A caterer is about to submit a sealed bid to run a restaurant concession at a municipal airport for the next 5 yr. He must state the fixed rent that he is prepared to pay annually. He estimates that gross profits, before rent is paid, will be $100,000 the first year and will increase by 10%/yr. Past experience shows that if R is the annual rent offered by a winning bid and G is his own estimate of the total gross profit of a contract running n years, the ratio nR/G is normally distributed about 0.5 with a standard deviation of 0.07. What should be bid so as to maximize his expected net profit?

12.7 Suppose that in the circumstance of Problem 12.6 the caterer wishes to bid so that, on average, the money left on the table does not exceed 10% of his bid. What should the bid be? (The money left on the table is the difference between the winning and the second bid. When all bids are published, the winner does not wish to appear foolish for having bid way above his competitors. The average value is computed only over the cases in which the caterer wins the concession.)

12.8 Consider the problem of developing a two-product pricing strategy given a linear price-interaction model:

$$Q_i = k_i - a_i P_i + b_i P_j$$
$$Q_j = k_j - a_j P_j + b_j P_i$$

where Q = quantity demanded
$\qquad\quad\;\; P$ = price

and k, a, and b are positive constants. Assume a cost function of the form

$$C = F + c_i Q_i + c_j Q_j$$

a. Interpret the terms k, a, and b.
b. Form a total profit function.
c. Differentiate the profit function to determine optimal prices P_i and P_j.
d. Suggest some more-realistic functions for Q and C.

12.9 How does Simon's model handle the issue of competitive pricing? Suggest an alternative.

12.10 Can Dolan and Jeuland's model be used for pricing in an oligopoly? Why or why not? Comment on their use of a multiplicative form of diffusion effect × price effect. Does it seem appropriate?

CHAPTER 13

Distribution Decision Models

The distribution decision is the determination of the most profitable ways to reach the market. The seller may either distribute or sell his product directly or indirectly through middlemen. If he decides to sell directly, this action has implications for, among other things, the size and type of the salesforce, the size of the advertising budget, and prices. If he decides to sell through middlemen, a different plan of salesforce activity, advertising, and pricing is needed. Thus the distribution decision is an important input to the planning of the other marketing efforts.

Physical distribution accounts for about 25 percent of the retail dollar and for more than a sixth of the United States GNP (Joubert, 1972). In some firms, distribution costs account for more than 50 percent of all operating expenses. Transportation costs alone are 20 percent of total costs in the pulp-and-paper industry, and in food manufacturing, physical distribution costs are more than 30 percent of sales. For all United States corporations, costs of physical distribution are double net profit. Heskett (1973) estimates that almost half of every dollar Americans spend on material items covers distribution-related costs. Perreault and Russ (1976), in a survey of industrial purchasing managers, found that physical distribution services were second only to product quality and more important than price in influencing industrial-purchase decisions.

Distribution channels, like other elements of the marketing mix, are not necessarily fixed or permanent, and innovators in the marketplace often adopt more efficient ways of making goods available to buyers (e.g., automated, 24-hr tellers). In addition, channels of distribution may not even be directed by manufacturers. The traditional standard channel—manufacturer → wholesaler → retailer—is being preempted by alternative channels, such as the following:

corporate channels,   which are centrally owned and operated *vertical* marketing systems, characterized by a combination of successive stages of production and distribution under a single ownership

administered channels,   where coordination of successive stages of production and distribution are achieved not through common owner- ship but through the size and economic power of one of the parties in the system (e.g., manufacturers of dominant brands in certain markets are able to secure strong trade support and cooperation from retailers)

contractual channels,   which are a group of independent firms at different levels of the production or distribution system integrating their programs on a contractual basis to achieve more economies or impact than they could achieve alone

This third type of channel, the so-called contractual vertical marketing systems (McCammon, 1970), constitutes one of the most important develop- ments in distribution in recent years and can be classified under three major subcategories:

Wholesaler-sponsored voluntary chains.   These chains originated in the effort of wholesalers to save the independent retailers they served from the competition of large chain organizations. IGA (Independent Growers Association) is an example.

Retailer cooperatives.   In these groups, which arose in defense against corporate chains, retailers organize a new business entity to carry on wholesaling and, sometimes, production as well.

Franchise organizations.   These organizations have several succes- sive stages in the production-distribution process linked under an agreement with one entity of the system, considered the franchiser. [See Izraeli (1972) and Vaughn (1974) for detailed discussion of franchising systems.]

There is polarity in both the selection of a distribution system and the related issue of market positioning. Those independents that do not join a system become specialty-store operators, serving special segments of the market that are not available or attractive to mass merchandisers. Then manufacturers face a dilemma in channel decisions; should they align themselves with large buying organizations or pursue the more traditional channels? Competition in retailing develops not just among independent business units but among whole systems of centrally programmed networks seeking to achieve the best economies and customer response.

In general, distribution comprises those functions of the firm involved in getting products from the manufacturer to the customer, including the following:

distribution planning with its related activities of production planning and materials procurement inventory management and related problems of receiving, inbound transportation, and order processing

packaging

in-plant warehousing

shipping

outbound transportation

field warehousing

retail-outlet planning, operations, and control

For simplicity, we divide the distribution decision into four components. The first is *distribution strategy,* which is the determination of the method for selling products to designated end markets. The company has options ranging from direct selling to bulk supply to the use of a variety of intermediaries (manufacturers' agents, brokers, jobbers, wholesalers, retailers, etc.). The second decision category is *distribution location,* which is the determination of the number and location of outlets that the seller wants to work through. Here the company considers how many outlets will maximize return and what their best locations are. The third is *distribution logistics,* which is the determination of the best way to supply products to intermediary sellers or final buyers. Here the company seeks to balance high service to customers with low inventory, warehousing, and transit costs. Finally, the fourth is *distribution management,* which is the development, management, and control of a trade mix (a mix of gross margins, allowances, and services) that will motivate the distribution system to perform at peak level. Most analytical tools handle these components separately. [For an ambitious, integrative effort, see Corstjens and Doyle (1979).]

Although we discuss all of the above problem areas, we focus proportionally more attention on distribution location and distribution logistics. These areas are the ones that are more frequently under the control of the marketing function and are also more amenable to model-based approaches.

We observe several things about distribution decisions. First, there is nothing sacrosanct or permanent about the particular institutions that constitute a company's distribution system at a point in time. The important thing about a distribution channel is not the institutions that make it up but the functions they perform. These functions can be performed in different ways by different distribution channels, operating at different levels of costs and generating different levels of sales. The major reason for a channel change is a discovery of more effective or efficient ways to accomplish the same work.

EXAMPLE: Consider the circumstances under which it would be cost-effective for producers to benefit by working through middlemen, and how many middlemen may arise in a given market.

Although simplistic, the following model and analysis (originally suggested by Balderston, 1958) illustrates how to calculate the equilibrium number of middlemen that will grow to serve a channel in the presence of full information, freedom of entry and exit, and a given set of costs. The equilibrium number of middlemen is that number that minimizes the average cost of distribution to the participating producers.

Assume a market in which there are m producers and n customers and where each producer separately contacts each of the n customers. Since there are m producers, there will be

mn contacts per period in the system in the absence of a middleman

If each contact costs b, then

bmn is the cost of contacts per period in the system with no middlemen

If costs are borne equally, for any one producer,

bn is the producers' cost of contact per period in the absence of middlemen

Now assume a middleman is established and all producers sell through him. Then there will be

$m + n$ contacts in the system per period with one middleman

Exhibit 13.1 illustrates the reduction in the number of contacts in the system brought about by a middleman, where there are three producers and three customers. The middleman effects a reduction in the number of required contacts from 9 to 6.

Suppose the cost of a contact between a producer and the middleman or the middleman and a customer is $\bar{b}$. Then

$\bar{b}(m + n)$ is the total cost of contacts in the system in the presence of one middleman

Then for any one producer, when the costs are borne equally,

$\bar{b}(m + n)/m$ is a producer's cost of contacts per period with one middleman

Therefore, a producer would prefer to work through a middleman if

$$\frac{\bar{b}(m + n)}{m} < bn \qquad (13.1)$$

If $b = \bar{b}$, eq. (13.1) reduces to

$$m + n < mn \qquad (13.2)$$

Inequality (13.2) is satisfied if $m > 2$ and $n \geq 2$ or if $m \geq 2$ and $n > 2$—that is, there must be more than two producers and/or two customers before a

**Number of Contacts with Three Producers (m)
Selling Directly to Three Customers (n):
$mn = 3 \times 3 = 9$**

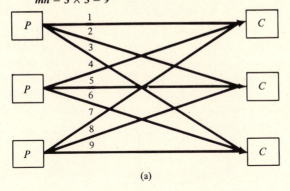

(a)

**Number of Contacts with Three Producers
Selling through One Wholesaler Who Sells to
Three Customers: $m + n = 6$**

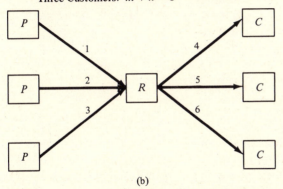

(b)

**EXHIBIT 13-1   How a middleman reduces the number of required customer
contacts in a system.**

middleman is able to perform the customer-contact function at less cost than
the producer can.

Now let w^* denote the equilibrium number of middlemen. Then the
condition for a producer to prefer to work through middlemen is

$$w^*(m + n) = mn \tag{13.3}$$

or

$$w^* = \frac{mn}{m + n} \tag{13.4}$$

Equation (13.4) says that the equilibrium number of middlemen is equal to
the ratio of total customer-contact cost without a middleman to that with
middlemen.

If $b \neq \bar{b}$, then eq. (13.4) becomes

$$w^* = \frac{bmn}{\bar{b}(m + n)} \qquad (13.5)$$

However, this formulation is quite simplistic. It assumes that all producers sell to all customers (no segmentation), that contact costs are the same independent of customer or producer, that all contacts are equally effective, and that only one level of intermediary can be formed. [See Baligh and Richartz (1967) for discussion and extensions.] For a real-world situation, it can be appropriately modified.

The importance of this illustration is to show that the use of middlemen and their equilibrium number are determined primarily by the extent to which they can perform the channel work more efficiently than producers can on their own.

A second important point about channels is that a firm cannot always put together the channel it wishes. For example, a firm producing a new food product will find it extremely difficult to obtain shelf space unless it has considerable economic power or the new product appears to be a sure winner. Furthermore, a seller may finally arrive at a sound distribution strategy only to learn that the particular middlemen are not available at all or not available on the terms contemplated.

A third point is that even after they have agreed to work with the seller, middlemen do not always perform in the expected way. The seller has to recognize, especially in individualistic marketing channels, that middlemen are independent profit-seeking firms that will behave in their own self-interest. Many middlemen are more oriented toward the satisfaction of their customers than the satisfaction of their suppliers, especially when the various suppliers each account for small shares of their business.

Fourth, the seller must select the channels of distribution with an eye not only on the economics but also on the control aspects of channels and their adaptability. A channel decision is a long-term commitment to a way of doing business, and it influences product development, marketing-communication strategy, salesforce territories and plans, pricing, and so forth. The company must consider how much control it is likely to achieve through the desired channels.

Distribution Strategy

Distribution strategy is the determination of the chief way a company will sell its products to designated end markets. It is not simply a matter of whether to sell through one type of retailer versus another (say department versus discount stores) but whether the firm should use retailers at all in relation to other possible systems of distribution. The management must try to distinguish all of its major channel alternatives and use some method of analysis to evaluate the relative value of each.

Specific models have not been developed for all aspects of distribution-strategy planning. Hutt and Speh (1981) view the channel-design process as illustrated in Exhibit 13.2. Although specifically developed for industrial firms, the structure has more general applicability. The stages of their model are as follows:

1. *channel objectives*—integrating the channel decision into the overall marketing plan and strategy
2. *channel-design constraints*—recognizing that, practically, channel options may be severely limited by constraining factors, such as the availability of good middlemen, traditional channel patterns, product

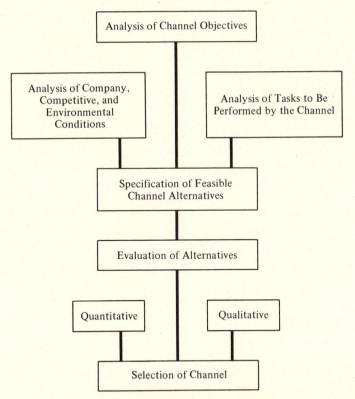

EXHIBIT 13-2 **The channel-design process.** (From *Industrial Marketing Management* by Michael D. Hutt and Thomas W. Speh, p. 235. Copyright © 1981 by CBS College Publishing. Reprinted by permission of CBS College Publishing.)

characteristics, company finances, competitive strategies, and customer dispersion (Stern and El-Ansary, 1977)

3. *specification of channel tasks*—recognizing that a channel is a sequence of activities
4. *evaluation of channel alternatives*—evaluating (a) the number of steps or levels to be included in the channel, (b) the number of intermediaries to employ, (c) the types of intermediaries to employ, and (d) the number of distinct channels to use
5. *channel selection*—selecting the alternative that is "best," where best incorporates both short- and long-run aspects

There have been some quantitative studies of the channel-evaluation-and-selection process for industrial products. Exhibit 13.3 depicts the 6 most

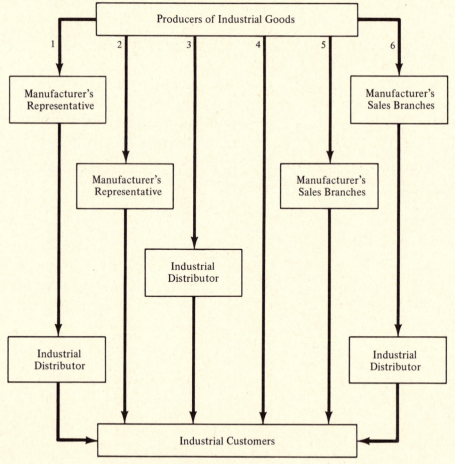

EXHIBIT 13-3   **The six most common industrial channels.** (Source: Haas, 1976, p. 153.)

common channels. Diamond's (1963) study of 167 industrial manufacturers, covering 220 product lines, found that these 6 channels accounted for all sales in his sample. Note that of the 6 basic channels, 3 represent captive or totally company-controlled channels (paths 2, 4, and 5) while the remaining 3 are independent or company-external channels.

To study the impact of product and market factors on the selection of internal versus external channels, Lilien (1979) ran a discriminant analysis with data from a sample of 125 industrial products. The most important variables that he found for classifying and predicting the channel of distributors are given below. [See Barefoot (1978) for the literature review leading to variable selection.]

1. **Size of the firm.** Size is the most important variable for determining the directness of distribution. As firms grow larger, they are better able to support a company-owned distribution channel.

2. **Size of average order.** As the average order size increases, direct distribution becomes more economical.

3. **Technical-purchase complexity.** The greater the importance of technical service to the product's success and the more important the buyer views the purchase, the more likely is direct distribution.

4. **Stage in the product life cycle.** A new or growing product is more likely to use a captive form of distribution than a product whose sales have leveled off or are declining.

5. **Degree of standardization.** A product that is complex, unique, or made to order is more frequently sold directly.

6. **Purchase frequency.** Frequently purchased products require less selling effort to make a sale and are therefore less frequently sold directly.

These results are descriptive, giving an understanding of the factors that, historically, have led to selection of certain channel strategies. The model can serve as a checklist of variables and their relative importance for decisions concerning the directness of distribution for industrial products. In addition, Lilien shows how to develop a classification function for predicting channel membership for a product with given characteristics. [See Lilien (1979), for variable definitions and results of these analyses.]

One way to appreciate the variety and complexity of distribution strategy decision problems and associated model-based support is to consider the following case (Bursk and Greyser, 1968).

EXAMPLE: ***Commodity Chemical Company: Choosing Distribution Strategy for a New Product.*** The Commodity Chemical Company is an old-line manufacturer of chemicals that had enjoyed a period of high profits but more recently has experienced a profit slump. To combat this slump, management sought new products and in this connection has expanded its research and development program. The first fruits of its new research program are perchlorotrombones (name fictitious), a new class of chlorinated organic chemicals that function as bleaches, germicides, and oxidants. The diversification committee of the Commodity Chemical Company is considering marketing a product based on this chemical for the swimming pool germicide market. It believes that its product has qualities superior to existing pool-germicidal chemicals. At the same time, the company has never done any previous consumer marketing, and its present channels of distribution are far from ideal for tapping the swimming pool market. During the committee's discussion, the research director, sales manager, commercial development manager, advertising agency representative, and company consultant all came up with different proposals for the marketing of this product.

Exhibit 13.4 lists five ways that the company could sell its product. The seller will want to study the implications of these five alternative retailing channels, especially their relative volumes of pool germicides, their relative rates of growth, and their relative profitability. Management has the option of concentrating on one of the channels or utilizing several of them.

Exhibit 13.5 illustrates five different distribution strategies the company can follow.

Strategy 1 (the present-distributors alternative) would have the company use its present distribution channels to market the product to retailers and service people in the swimming pool market. This approach was

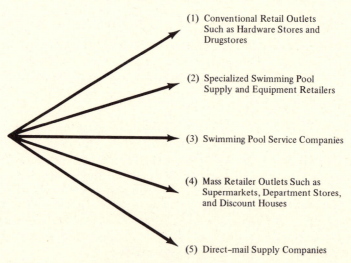

(1) Conventional Retail Outlets Such as Hardware Stores and Drugstores

(2) Specialized Swimming Pool Supply and Equipment Retailers

(3) Swimming Pool Service Companies

(4) Mass Retailer Outlets Such as Supermarkets, Department Stores, and Discount Houses

(5) Direct–mail Supply Companies

EXHIBIT 13-4   **Commodity Chemical Company: alternative retailing strategies.**

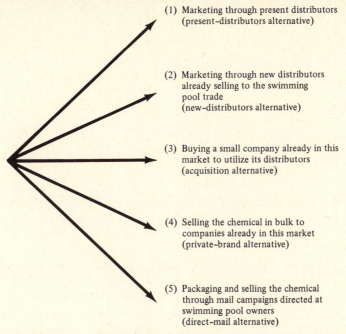

(1) Marketing through present distributors
(present–distributors alternative)

(2) Marketing through new distributors
already selling to the swimming
pool trade
(new–distributors alternative)

(3) Buying a small company already in this
market to utilize its distributors
(acquisition alternative)

(4) Selling the chemical in bulk to
companies already in this market
(private–brand alternative)

(5) Packaging and selling the chemical
through mail campaigns directed at
swimming pool owners
(direct–mail alternative)

EXHIBIT 13-5 Commodity Chemical Company: alternative distribution strategies.

advocated by the sales manager, who felt that the present distributors would be upset if they were bypassed by the company and not allowed to participate in the potential profits on this new product.

Strategy 2 (the new-distributors alternative) would have the company use swimming pool supply distributors to bring its new product into the various retail channels. The commercial development manager favored this alternative because he felt that the company's present chemical distributors lacked contacts and experience in dealing with the kinds of retailers who sold swimming pool germicides.

Strategy 3 (the acquisition alternative) calls for acquiring a small company that is already well entrenched in the swimming pool supply market and using its established distribution system. The research director favored this method of breaking into the market.

Strategy 4 (the private-brand alternative) would have the company sell the new chemical in bulk to companies that are already in the pool supply business. This alternative is likely to yield lower profits but at the same time reduces the company's risk. The company's consultant suggested that this alternative be given serious consideration.

Strategy 5 (the direct-mail alternative) calls for packaging the chemical under a company brand name and using a direct-mail approach to sell it.

This strategy would be evaluated through a preliminary test in some major cities. It was advocated by the advertising agency representative as a sound way to evaluate the size and interest of the market in the new germicide.

These strategies and their advocates obviously hold a broad range of viewpoints. What is required in resolving these differences is an analytical framework.

Three widely used analytical approaches are available for resolving distribution-strategy problems; they are, in order of complexity, the weighted-factor-score method, direct utility assessment, and simulation.

The weighted-factor-score approach uses analysis of company objectives, distribution tasks, and constraints to evaluate each channel alternative. The approach involves five steps: (1) the important factors for achieving channel objectives are defined; (2) each of these factors is assigned a weight to reflect its relative importance (the sum of these weights must equal 1.0); (3) they are rated on a 0.0–1.0 scale for each channel alternative; (4) they are multiplied by the associated factor score; (5) the individual scores are added to get a composite score for the strategy. When data are available, this approach is useful at an early stage of evaluation. It is widely used in screening new-product proposals and has undergone numerous refinements [see Freimer and Simon (1967)]. Its limitations include (1) using interval scales for what may be ordinal data, (2) using factor weights that may be related to factor scores, (3) using factors that may not be independent, and (4) dependence on rater competence and lack of bias.

There are numerous sophisticated techniques based on formal decision analysis (Keeney and Raiffa, 1976) for performing these evaluations, but these techniques are time-consuming and require more accurate measures of channel desirability. In addition, as Freimer and Simon (1967) point out, there are statistical procedures that can be used to ensure that the factors are independent and to derive weights statistically.

Our experience is that when screening a number of options like this, managerial discussions on the selection of weights are most valuable. They ensure that the same issues and the same factors are used in evaluating alternatives. Then once the number of alternative strategies has been reduced to a small number, a more careful, *economic* analysis should be performed. A frequently used approach to perform the economic analysis is computer simulation, often of the stochastic Monte Carlo type (see Chapter 6). This approach forces managers to specify the likely market and competitive and environmental consequences of their channel decisions, as well as the probability of those events occurring. [See Kotler (1971, pp. 296–297) for an illustration of simulation applied to this problem.] Although the most time-consuming of the suggested methods, the simulation approach allows managers to project the logical consequences and risks of their estimates and provides a framework to test the effect of introducing new assumptions.

Distribution Location

As part of determining its distribution strategy, a company must decide on the degree of market exposure desired. Specifically, it must decide on the number of sales outlets to use and their locations. The company could decide on a policy of intensive distribution in which it places its product in every available outlet, a policy of selective distribution in which it places its product in a more limited number of outlets, or a policy of exclusive distribution in which it places its product in the hands of a few exclusive agents.

Consider a national company (automobile manufacturer, gasoline retailer, food chain, national franchiser, etc.) that has adopted a particular market-exposure policy and presently operates a network of sales outlets. Each year this company has to consider new investment in facilities improvement and expansion. Suppose it establishes a budget for investment in facilities. The company finds that it can invest this money in four possible ways or in any mixture of the four:

1. The money can be spent in expanding the size of the present outlets.
2. The money can be spent in remodeling the present outlets.
3. The money can be spent in relocating some of the present outlets.
4. The money can be spent in opening up new outlets.

In principle, the company allocates the budget over the four alternatives in such a way that the marginal dollar yields the same return in all uses. In practice, management feels compelled to make certain specific facility investments out of what appears to be necessity or indisputable soundness. Some stores have to be expanded, renovated, or relocated, and some new sites are too good to pass up. Actually, the company faces a sequence of four decisions:

1. Of all the potentially promising areas in the country for locating one or more new outlets, which areas should be selected (market-selection decision)?
2. How many new outlets should be located in each selected area (number-of-outlets decision)?
3. In which particular sites should the new outlets be located (site-selection decision)?
4. What size and characteristics should each particular outlet have (store-size and -characteristics decision)?

This sequence of decisions is illustrated in Exhibit 13.6.

Market-Selection Decision

A company planning to develop n new outlets must determine in which market areas to place them. A market area is a city, country, state, or region

Key Concepts   Outputs

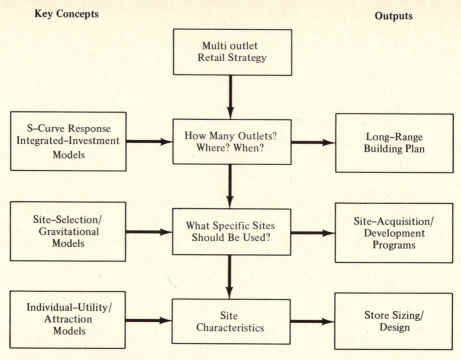

EXHIBIT 13-6   **Structuring some key problems in retail-outlet management.**

in which company outlets can be opened. This problem can be called the macroproblem, in contrast to site location, which is a microproblem. Some of the outlets may be placed in market areas in which the company is already established and wants to increase its market share; the others can be placed in new market areas deemed promising by the company. In both cases the company is guided by the profit potential. The task, then, is one of developing a good measure of market-area profit potential.

Most practitioners are able to list numerous indicators of market-area profit potential. According to a Sears executive:

> I could easily fill a book describing the full extent of the field work, statistical analysis and projections that go into the study of a single Sears market. All important factors which bear on how customers spend their retail dollars are carefully examined and evaluated. Briefly, I can tell you that we analyze not only our existing stores in a market, but we carefully study competition, population density and growth (which includes age distribution), housing growth (past and future), the diversity and stability of the local economy, unemployment, and a long list of other factors, some major, some minor, that might influence retail business (statement by Arthur Rosenbaum, director of Sears Business Research Department, in a company news brochure).

But what is rarely found is an explicit formula that combines all of the important indicators of profit potential into a specific profit measure for the area. Here we propose such a measure.

The proposed measure involves the following three concepts:

S_i = company sales potential of market area i
Z_i = company profit potential of market area i
$V(Z_i)$ = present value of company profit potential in market area i

The basic approach is to estimate the company's sales potential in market area i and then to subtract estimated selling costs to find the company profit potential of the area. The profit potential is assumed to grow or decline at a certain rate over a given number of years, which yields a projected earnings stream for n years that is then discounted at the company's target rate of return to find the present value of the company profit potential in market area i. These steps are described below.

Estimating Company Sales Potential in Market Area i. The first step is to estimate the probable sales that a new or additional company store of average size and average location is likely to realize in this market area. Suppose the company examines the statistics on its other stores and calculates the average annual household expenditures spent by each income class at a typical company outlet. This average provides a starting point for estimating the expected sales of a new outlet in this market area. Suppose that the market area has a known frequency distribution of households by income class. Then the company can estimate that unadjusted sales of a new company store in this market area would be S_i dollars:

$$S_i = \sum_{j=1}^{n} s_j p_{ij} N_i \qquad (13.6)$$

where S_i = estimated annual sales of new company outlet in market area i (unadjusted)
s_j = average annual household expenditures of income class j at company outlet
p_{ij} = percentage of total households of market area i in income class j
N_i = number of households in market area i

At this point the company introduces certain adjustments in the sales estimate to compensate for the oversimplifications. Because this figure was based on the spending patterns of different income classes at any average company store now existing in the system, it should be adjusted for any factors present in the market area that are likely to increase or decrease this (average) level of expenditure. The most important factor to adjust in this figure is the amount of competition that exists in this market area relative to that in an average market area. Let I represent an index of competitiveness that normally stands at 1.00. Then adjusted, estimated company sales potential in market area i for a new store of average size is given by

$$S_i' = I_i S_i \qquad (13.7)$$

This figure should be similarly adjusted for any additional factors that could cause sales to be different from those in an average company store.

Estimating Company Profit Potential in Market Area i.   The company now estimates its expenses of doing business in this market area. A good way to proceed is to express each major category of expense as a percentage of sales. Several expenses are likely to be in the same relation to sales in all market areas, such as depreciation, heat, light, and salaries. These items can be lumped together as a single percentage of sales. However, at least three other expenses may vary considerably from the normal percentage and should be stated separately. The first is the shipment cost to this market area. If the company has its major plant in market area k, then the cost of operating an outlet in market area i is directly related to the distance between k and i, the cost of transportation between these points, the issue of whether estimated sales support carload shipments, and so forth. Thus shipping cost to market area i may turn out to be more or less than the average percentage of sales. A second expense deserving separate estimation is advertising and promotion. If the company is already well established in this area, the advertising cost may be relatively low as a percentage of estimated sales. Alternatively, if the company is new in the area, the advertising cost may be relatively high. A third cost that might warrant separate treatment is real estate costs, which may be unusually high or low in this market area relative to the average market area.

The profit potential of market area i can now be expressed as

$$Z_i = S_i' - (n_i + t_i + a_i + f_i)S_i' \qquad (13.8)$$

where Z_i = profit potential in market area i

S_i = adjusted company sales potential in market area i

n_i = estimated normal expenses of selling in market area i as percentage of sales (excluding transportation, advertising, and real estate)

t_i = transportation expense of selling in market area i as percentage of sales

a_i = advertising expense of selling in market area i as percentage of sales

f_i = real estate expense of selling in market area i as percentage of sales

Estimating the Present Value of Company Profit Potential in Market Area i.   The final step calls for forming an estimate of the expected trend in profit in market area i over the planning horizon. An area that is growing rapidly in population and income may mean healthy and growing profits for a number of years; a more stable area may mean profits will continue at their first-year level. The estimation of future profits can be made in some detail through separate estimates of sales growth and the growth of each cost item. For our purposes we assume that future profits will grow or decline at the rate g for n years and that the company discounts future profits at the rate r. Therefore the net present value of the company's future profit potential for market area i is estimated as

$$V(Z_i) = \frac{\sum_{k=1}^{n} (1 + g_i)^k Z_{ik}}{(1 + r)^k} - C_i \tag{13.9}$$

where $V(Z_i)$ = net present value of company's future profit potential in market area i

Z_{ik} = profit potential of market area i in year k

g_i = growth rate of profit potential in market area i

r = company discount rate

I_i = present value of outlet-investment cost in market area i

Armed with these net present value estimates, the company can rank the market areas in order of attractiveness. In principle, the company should open a new or additional outlet in every market area in which the net present value is positive. If the sum of the investments exceeds the original budget for new-outlet development, the company can either borrow the additional funds needed or cut off new-store openings at the point where the budget is exceeded.

Number-of-Outlets Decision

Among the key assumptions underlying the market-area evaluation above is that share of market equals share of outlets.

But empirical studies have shown the relationship between outlet share and market share to be nonlinear and generally S-shaped (Hartung and Fisher, 1965; Lilien and Rao, 1976). Small outlet shares produce smaller market shares; as outlet share grows, market share grows at a faster rate until it exceeds outlet share. Then as outlet share continues to increase, the rate of market-share growth decreases. Few cases of very high outlet shares have been observed, but the lower part of the curve (below an outlet share of 50 percent) is well documented. But because market share must equal one when outlet share equals one, the upper part of the curve can be hypothesized with a great deal of confidence. Exhibit 13.7 graphically illustrates the S-shaped curve, with the hypothesized portion shown by the dotted curve.

A number of hypotheses concerning consumer and/or corporate behavior have been offered to justify the S-shaped relationship. However, the explanation is still the subject of debate. Nonetheless, this empirically verified relationship is an important finding for decision makers.

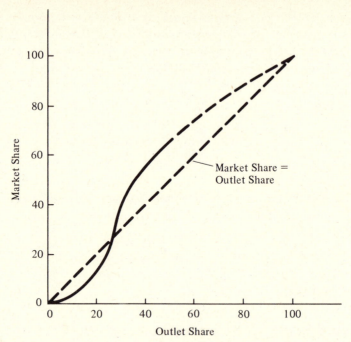

EXHIBIT 13-7   **Typical outlet-share/market-share relationship.**

The first attempt to operationalize this concept in the form of a planning model was reported by Hartung and Fisher (1965). They model the sequence of purchases by a customer as a two-state Markov chain. The states are "purchase company brand" and "purchase some other brand." The probability that a customer will buy the company's brand on the tth occasion, given that he bought it at $t - 1$, is assumed to be k_1s (where s is outlet share), and the probability that the customer buys the brand at t, given that he bought some other brand at $t - 1$, is k_2s, where k_1 and k_2 are constants. This model implies that market share m is

$$m = \frac{k_2s}{(1 - s) + (1 + k_2 - k_1)s} \tag{13.10}$$

The values of k_1 and k_2 are estimated from aggregate data and found to be 4.44 and 0.64, respectively. Although this model provides a good fit in the range of available data, it breaks down for s greater than about 0.20—that is, for $s = 1/k_1$ and $m = 1$. Thus the model is of limited use for allocation planning, especially where a firm is contemplating a penetration strategy.

In more-recent work Naert and Bultez (1975) relax some of these assumptions and develop more-robust results. But they still rely on the basic markovian assumption.

Lilien-Rao Model. Lilien and Rao (1976) rely on a different set of assumptions. They assume that in addition to share of outlets, the share of market would be closely related to the age of outlets relative to competition. New outlets are likely to be better situated relative to population centers and traffic patterns. In addition, most firms tend to support markets that have a

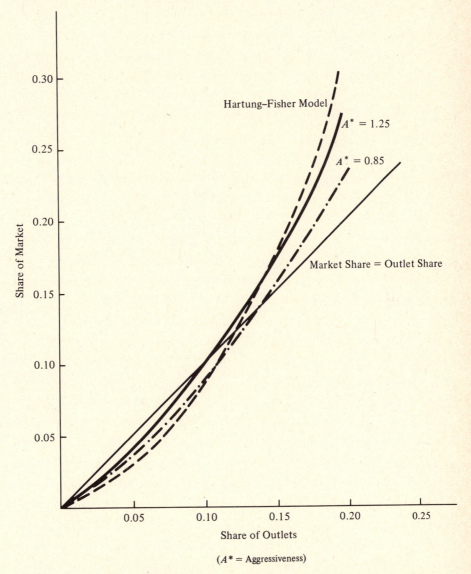

EXHIBIT 13-8 **Market share as a function of outlet share and aggressiveness (A^*) estimated from Mobil Corporation data.** (Source: Lilien and Rao, 1976. p. 6.)

large share of new outlets with more-aggressive advertising and promotional policies.

The authors define the following measure of building activity and call it aggressiveness a:

$$a = \frac{\text{(number of recently built company outlets)} \div \text{(total company outlets)}}{\text{(number of recently built industry outlets)} \div \text{(total industry outlets)}}$$

(13.11)

They relate market share to outlet share and aggressiveness as $g = (a, s)$. Exhibit 13.8 gives an example estimated from Mobil Corporation data.

The authors then incorporate this market-share/outlet-share model into an allocation procedure. The objective is to maximize the total net present value (NPV) of a Y-year building program, subject to restrictions on the total number of outlets that can be built (1) within a market, (2) across all markets in a given year, and (3) during the Y years:

$$\text{NPV} = \sum_{j=1}^{J} \sum_{i=1}^{S} \frac{\text{CF}_{ij}}{(1 + r)^{i-1}}$$

(13.12)

where CF_{ij} = cash flow associated with market area j in year i
r = discount rate
J = number of market areas considered in plan
S = planning horizon $(S > y)$

The maximization procedure first selects the group of outlets in the market with the highest average NPV per outlet and then the next highest NPV group and so on until all allowable outlets have been allocated.

To calculate cash flows and, hence, associated NPVs, the authors suggest that knowledge is required of the firm's building/investment plan, current market share, market-growth rate, discount rate, margins, competitive-building/investment plans, current age distribution of firm and industry outlets, and other financial information, such as land costs, improvement and equipment costs, depreciation methods, and working capital needs. Furthermore, before one can proceed, two additional assumptions are required: (1) "new" outlets are 4 yr old or newer, and (2) after Y years the firm will build enough outlets to maintain its ending market share. Assumption (1) is arbitrarily set at 4 yr and could easily be changed; assumption (2) is an approach for handling end-off problems.

The problem, then, is to find $\{X_{it}\}$, the number of outlets to be built in market i at time t to

$$\text{Maximize } Z = \sum_{i=1}^{M} \sum_{t=1}^{Y} \sum_{j=1}^{X_{it}} V_{ijt} \qquad \text{(NPV of profit)}$$

(13.13)

subject to

$$\sum_{k-1}^{t} \sum_{i-1}^{M} X_{ik} \leq T_t \qquad \text{(cumulative building constraints)}$$

$$0 \leq X_{it} \leq n_{it} \quad \text{(annual building constraints)}$$

where V_{ijt} is the incremental net present value of the ith outlet in market j given that it is opened at time t.

EXAMPLE:　A two-market, 1-yr example will illustrate how the solution algorithm works. Exhibit 13.9 gives the data.

Assume here that $n_1 = n_2 = 5$ and $T = 5$, and define average NPV of next j outlets in market as:

$$W_{ij} = \begin{cases} \sum_{k-1}^{j} V_{ikj} & i, j = 1, \ldots n_i \\ -B & \text{for } j > n_i \, (B \text{ is a large positive number}) \end{cases} \qquad (13.14)$$

The procedure is to sequentially select maximum NPV entries in the $\{W_{ij}\}$ tables and update them. Initially,

$$W_{ij} = \begin{bmatrix} 5 & 4 & 4 & 3.5 & 3 \\ 4 & 4.5 & 5.3 & 5.1 & 4.4 \end{bmatrix} \quad \text{and} \quad \begin{matrix} X_1 = 0 \\ X_2 = 0 \end{matrix} \qquad (13.15)$$

The maximum entry is 5.3 for market 2 with three outlets. Therefore three outlets are added to X_2, and W_{ij} is updated:

$$W_{ij} = \begin{bmatrix} 5 & 4 & 4 & 3.5 & 3 \\ 4.5 & 3 & -B & -B & -B \end{bmatrix} \quad \text{and} \quad \begin{matrix} X_1 = 0 \\ X_2 = 3 \end{matrix} \qquad (13.16)$$

Note that the $-B$ values prevent the allocation of more than two additional outlets to market 2 and that $W_{21} = 20.5 - 16 = 4.5$, which is the incremental NPV of the fourth outlet (the *next* one) in market 2. The maximum current entry in the $\{W_{ij}\}$ table is 5 for market 1. Updating, we

EXHIBIT 13-9　Data for sample problem.

Number of Outlets	Cumulative NPV, Market 1	Cumulative NPV, Market 2
1	5	4
2	8	9
3	12	16
4	14	20.5
5	15	22

get

$$W_{ij} = \begin{bmatrix} 3 & 3.5 & 3 & 2.5 & -B \\ 4.5 & 3 & -B & -B & -B \end{bmatrix} \quad \text{and} \quad \begin{matrix} X_1 = 1 \\ X_2 = 3 \end{matrix} \qquad (13.17)$$

The highest entry now is 4.5 for market 2 with one outlet. We now have allocated five outlets ($X_1 = 1$, $X_2 = 4$), and the procedure stops.

For a multiyear problem an additional check is needed after each allocation to make certain no single-year constraint is violated. Otherwise, the procedure is identical.

Application and Assessment.   The algorithm is simple and efficient. A 170-market, 5-yr problem allocating 3000 outlets was run in under 5 min on an IBM 360-75. The bulk of the time was spent on input/output and NPV calculation; the allocation procedure itself took under a minute. This approach was far superior to an initial dynamic-programming approach that offered a more exact solution but was not computationally efficient for more than 20 markets. The system was used as an aid to outlet-building planning at Mobil from 1969–1972 (a peak outlet-building period) and became an integral part of the planning process.

The model demonstrates that the response parameters, constraints, and economic calculations needed to develop and evaluate a major outlet-expansion plan can be quantified and that useful results for management can be developed. However, the applicability of this approach to problems other than those of the franchise-type-outlets kind is not clear. And the theoretical underpinnings and generality of the market-share/outlet-share relationship need to be more completely developed.

Site-Selection Decision

Once the commitment to locate in a market area or city has been made, a second key problem faced by the multioutlet business is new-outlet placement. Approaches to this problem vary. Applebaum (1968) reports that 10 percent of a sample of 170 large retail chains performed no systematic analysis for location of retail outlets. The same study showed that research expenditures varied widely; the average research expenditure per new location was about 1 percent of the site-investment cost.

A variety of different methods have been suggested to assist in the evaluation and measurement of site potential. Some of these have been published and are briefly reviewed below. [Green and Applebaum (1975) review quantitative approaches to this problem.] Many other approaches are commercially available, but their details are usually closely guarded and unavailable for critical review and publication. The large number of commercial and academically published models suggest that researchers (and managers) feel a need for rational and formal use of information in this area. However, most of the models appear to be ad hoc in nature. They consider neither the synergistic influences of other outlets (the company's or a competitor's) nor any well-developed theory of consumer motivation or behavior.

The problem of site selection is actually two problems: one of site search and one of site evaluation. Site search is the procedure used by the company to discover potentially good sites for its outlets. Large companies usually work through real estate agents or through a company real estate department to search out good sites. This process usually produces a number of new real estate opportunities each period. However, some of these sites will fail immediate tests, and the others will have to be evaluated more thoroughly. Our discussion centers on site evaluation, which can be distinguished by at least three different approaches: the checklist method, the analog method, and the gravitational method. Each of these are examined below.

Checklist Method of Site Selection.   The most elementary method of evaluating a potential site is to visit it, observe the various factors likely to affect sales and costs, and make an intuitive judgment of its potential success.

Because of the large number of pertinent factors, real estate advisors have developed checklists to assist firms in evaluating the potential success of sites. Nelson (1958) has published one of the most thorough checklists, which includes eight major site factors (trading-area potential, accessibility, growth potential, business interception, cumulative attraction potential, compatibility, competitive hazards, and site economics), each of which is divided into several subfactors. Then with these lists management checks each factor separately for a proposed site and gives a rating of excellent, good, fair, or poor. The result of these ratings, based on as much hard data collection as possible, is a profile of the strengths and weaknesses of the proposed sites.

Analog Method of Site Selection.   This method of site evaluation represents a more sophisticated research procedure than checklists for estimating the potential sales at a site. [See Applebaum (1966).] In it, zones are developed around the proposed site, and the sales that the proposed store is likely to attract from each zone are estimated on the basis of the drawing-power rates of similar stores in the company's chain. Hence it is called the analog method.

EXAMPLE: Exhibit 13.10 illustrates the analog approach. The area surrounding the proposed site is divided into quarter-mile zones (column 1). Census tract data are used to estimate the population residing in each zone (column 2). The first use of analogs comes into play to estimate per capita sales from each zone (column 3). The analyst chooses a subset of other stores in the chain that are located at sites resembling the proposed new site. Presum-

EXHIBIT 13-10   **Illustration of Applebaum's site-evaluation method applied to location X.**

(1) Zone (in mi)	(2) Population in Zone	(3) Estimated per Capita Sales	(4) Estimated Weekly Sales	(5) Computed Drawing Power (in %)
0.00–0.25	4,700	$2.00	$ 9,400	28
0.25–0.50	12,900	0.76	9,804	29
0.50–0.75	23,000	0.22	5,060	15
0.75–1.00	36,300	0.12	4,356	13
Beyond	—	—	5,051	15
			$33,671	**100**

SOURCE: Applebaum, 1966, p. 140.

ably, customer-spotting techniques have been applied at other sites, which have revealed the drawing power and per capita expenditures for different zones surrounding each of these other stores. In practice, customer spotting involves taking a random sample of 300–400 customers of an existing store and finding out the customers' addresses, weekly food expenditures, and so forth. This technique allows one to construct a prospectus for each store of the percentage of customers who come from each quarter-mile zone surrounding the store and their weekly expenditures. This information is averaged for the subset of analogous stores chosen by the analyst and is used to develop column 3. The figures in column 3 may be the literal average-per-capita sales of the analogous stores or they may be these data adjusted to compensate for factors not found in the other stores.

Column 4, estimated weekly sales by zone, is then found by multiplying zone population by zone-per-capita expenditures. The total of these figures provides the estimated weekly sales for the new outlet—$33,671 in this example. As a check, column 5 is computed by recasting column 4 as percentages. It says that the new store is expected to draw 28% of its total sales from the nearest zone, 29% of its total sales from the second zone, and so forth. These drawing-power percentages are compared to the average of the analogous stores (not shown); to the extent that they match, the analyst has increased confidence in the sales estimate.

Gravitational Models of Site Selection.   This approach was pioneered by Huff (1962, 1963, 1964) and is based on the theory of individual, discrete choice originally developed by Luce (1959).

In most forms the model is defined as

$$p_{ij} = \frac{V_{ij}}{\sum_{n \in N_i} V_{in}} \qquad (13.18)$$

where p_{ij} = probability that individual i chooses jth alternative on next choice alternative

V_{ij} = individual i's utility for jth alternative

$N(i)$ = choice set of individual i

Huff's specification of this general concept held that the attraction (utility) exercised on any consumer in small area i by a retail center at location j is directly proportional to the size of the retail center and inversely proportional to the customer's distance from the center.

The reasoning is as follows. Suppose stores or shopping centers are pretty much alike, except for size and distance. A larger center means a larger product assortment and hence a greater utility for the consumer. On the other hand, distance represents a cost or disutility to the consumer. On the assumption that the consumer wants to be an efficient shopper, he will be attracted to any particular center in proportion to the ratio of utility to disutility. Huff expressed the consumer's attraction in the following form:

$$p_{ij} = \frac{S_j/D_{ij}^\lambda}{\displaystyle\sum_{n \in N_i} (S_n/D_{in}^\lambda)} \tag{13.19}$$

where p_{ij} = probability of consumer in area i shopping at a particular location j

S_j = size of retail center in location j

D_{ij} = distance between i and j

λ = estimated sensitivity parameter relating kinds of shopping trips and distance

N_i = choice set of retail locations from area i

EXAMPLE: Suppose $\lambda = 2$ and the consumer is able to shop at two retail centers, the first consisting of 100,000 ft^2 at a distance of 1 mi from his home and the second consisting of 50,000 ft^2 at a distance of 2 mi. According to Huff's formula, the probabilities of the consumer shopping at each store are 0.89 and 0.11, respectively, as shown by the following calculation:

$$p_{i1} = \frac{100,000/1^2}{100,000/1^2 + 50,000/2^2}$$

$$p_{i2} = \frac{50,000/2^2}{100,000/1^2 + 50,000/2^2} \tag{13.20}$$

Although, in practice, both lead to the same analytical results, these probabilities are subject to two different interpretations:

1. Each consumer in location i will shop 89% of the time at center 1 and 11% of the time at center 2.
2. Eighty-nine percent of the consumers in location i will shop at center 1, while 11% will shop at center 2.

To estimate the key parameter λ, we develop the following quantity:

$$E_{ij} = p_{ij}(\lambda)C_i \qquad (13.21)$$

where E_{ij} = expected number of consumers originating at i and terminating at j
   C_i = total number of consumers at i

Estimates of parameters of this type of model are discussed in Nakanishi and Cooper (1974). Huff's approach and its extensions (Gautschi, 1981; Gautschi and Corstjens, 1979; Stanley and Sewall, 1976) are most applicable for shopping centers.

A more general structure for these models, applicable to a wider range of outlets, can be summarized as follows:

Site potential = local sales component + transient sales component

$$(13.22)$$

Equation (13.22) says that sales potential at a particular site has two separate components: sales to people who live nearby and sales to people who are driving through (i.e., who do not live in the area). The nature and importance of these two components vary considerably by product class, but the basic structure serves as a starting point for model development.

Reinitz Model.   Reinitz (1968) proposes an assessment procedure that has been used for a number of years to assess site potential for gasoline stations. In his model the local sales component is a simplified version of the Huff procedure, extended to incorporate attributes other than distance and size. Then the estimation of local potential for site i, f_i, has four steps:

1. Choose a local-area radius, usually 1 mi. (Model results are generally not sensitive to the size of this radius as long as it is not too small.) Obtain car population, gasoline use, and other descriptive information of the area.
2. Obtain a census of existing outlets, and rate them by a number of predetermined attributes. Let

   r_{ij} = rating of outlet i in trading area, along attribute j
         (e.g., j may be ease of accessibility)

One key attribute to include here is brand image or market presence, linking this model with the S-curve model reviewed in the previous section.

3. Obtain importance weights for these attributes from consumers. Let

   w_j = average importance weight of attribute j

4. Now estimate local potential f_i:

$$f_i = \frac{\sum_i w_i r_{ij}}{\sum_i \sum_j w_i r_{ij}} \, GL \qquad (13.23)$$

where G = annual product (gasoline) consumption in area
         L = fraction of sales average customer buys locally
         i = index covering all outlets in local area

Functional forms other than eq. (13.23) have been used with different normative results (Gautschi, 1981), but none have shown significant improvements in predictive power.

Next, the transient sales potential is estimated. Transient trading routes are composed of portions of roads passing the key site and along which the transient traffic flows. The potential customer may or may not stop. Two questions need to be addressed: (1) how many potential transient customers are there, and (2) what fraction will stop.

Identify all routes past the site and index those roads by k. (Note that at an intersection with two-way traffic in each direction, there are 16 possible routes through the intersection; so k would range from 1 to 16.) Define

    L = road length, as a standard of measure (L usually equals a few miles)
$\{R\}$ = set of road legs among transient trading routes (index k identifies specific element in $\{R\}$)
  L_0 = average distance between refuelings
   q = average gasoline consumption rate (units of product per mile per customer)

Assuming that the amount of gasoline left in the tank is a random variable, we would expect that for a randomly selected customer,

$$p(\text{needing fuel}) = \frac{L}{L_0} \qquad (13.24)$$

and the average quantity purchased is

$$Q = L_0 q \qquad (13.25)$$

If traffic flow along route k is T_k cars per day, then the expected amount purchased per day is

$$G_k = T_k Q p(\text{needing fuel}) \qquad (13.26)$$

Along each leg (route) this site should see the share of this potential relative to its attractiveness, so

$$g_{ik} = \frac{\sum_j w_j r_{ij}}{\sum_{i \in R_k} \sum_j w_j r_{ij}} T_k L_o q \qquad (13.27)$$

where g_{ik} = potential along leg k
          R_k = set of indices of stations along route k

Finally,

$$g_i = \sum_k g_{ik} \qquad (13.28)$$

where g_i = total transient potential for site i
          k = ranges over all transient routes that are associated with outlet i

Thus with eq. (13.22), site potential = $f_i + g_i$, where f_i is determined from eq. (13.23) and eq. (13.28) determines g_i.

A number of judgments and measurements are needed to calibrate and use this model, such as the boundaries of local trading areas, the length of transient trading routes, area-population measures, transient traffic flows, the fraction of sales bought locally, and strength and importance weights for the proposed and existing sites.

Application and Assessment.   This model was in regular use for national and international site evaluations of a major oil company for a period of about a decade. It serves as a structure for defining the data-gathering needs, as well as the evaluation steps, required to support site-location decisions.

In terms of extensions Stanley and Sewall (1976) replace the size variable in Huff's model with an image variable obtained through multidimensional scaling. Hlavacek and Little (1970), in a study of auto-dealership selection, use an approach that considers the distance customers travel, as well as the attractiveness (image) of the automobiles offered for sale. As Gautschi (1981) points out, these approaches are extensions of the multiplicative competitive-interaction (MCI) Model of Nakanishi and Cooper (1974), and all may suffer to some extent by omitted attributes and heterogeneity of individual choice sets.

The transient model is an important addition to the basic MCI structure, especially in such product classes as gasoline and fast foods. There, a great deal of brand-to-brand substitution is possible, and the purchase trip is often a secondary part of another journey.

In terms of predictive validity (Do any of the models predict site sales accurately?), two issues have clouded reports to date: lack of controlled evaluation and prediction of sales potential.

Model validation has usually been done by checking how well the model fits data from outlets used in its development or from a small holdout sample. Since many of the models have been implemented, these tests must have produced acceptable results. For example, Reinitz's model was subjected to extensive testing of this type; had the model's predictions been used, most of the unprofitable outlets and only a few of the profitable ones would have been eliminated.

The more rigorous type of testing—predicting the sales of unconstructed outlets and comparing these predictions with actual sales—has rarely been conducted in practice because sales potential is a long-range concept. Outlets may approach their potential in only 6 mo or reach it over a period of several years.

In work by Kinberg and Rao (1978), data for checking and savings accounts for branch banks were analyzed to identify when a steady-state level of business was reached. It was found that the time required to reach the steady-state level varied from 2 yr to over 7 yr, depending on such area characteristics as population-turnover rate. Because of such large time lags, substantial changes occur in traffic patterns and neighborhood characteristics, which invalidate many original model assumptions and, thus, the forecasts of sales potential. Therefore evaluation of a model's predictive power is a long-range task, requiring the kind of effort and dedication to validation that many commercial organizations are unwilling to undertake.

All of the models predict sales *potential*. Actual sales achieved by a site depend critically on the management of the outlet. Once an outlet earns a reputation for poor service, it is almost impossible for it to reach a target sales level that approaches the predicted potential. Conversely, sites with good management consistently exceed their potential. Therefore because there is no method for estimating the *ex ante* quality of an individual manager, there is a large uncontrollable source of error intrinsic to every forecast. Site-selection models will remain incomplete and inaccurate unless they incorporate management quality into the model specifications.

In conclusion, compared with the analog approach, the gravitational approach to site selection is more analytical. However, a shortcoming of the approach is that it requires site-by-site evaluations; it does not consider the impact of one site on the others. The S curve relating market share to outlet share provides at least a starting point for analyzing such interactions. Also, the S curve provides a way to incorporate brand strength directly into site potential.

More importantly, a behavioral approach to the modeling of site potential is required. Some interesting work reported by Ackoff (1962) relates the probability of a consumer stopping at a particular outlet to the perceived time it will take to obtain service, and it relates perceived time to actual time in a nonlinear fashion. This cognitive-distance approach has been explored by McKay, Olshavsky, and Sentell (1975) but needs further analysis. For a critical review of this and other research in a retailing setting, see Hirschman (1981).

Store-Size and -Characteristic Decisions

Closely related to the analysis of site potential are the store characteristics that influence its attractiveness. In the analysis of a location opportunity, management considers not so much the effect of an average company store in that location but that of a store of a particular size, layout [see Farley and Ring (1966)], product assortment, decor, parking capacity, and so forth. Management seeks those levels of these factors that have a maximum impact on profits.

Of all the outlet characteristics, store size is traditionally singled out as most important. The larger the store is, the greater its product assortment and neighborhood conspicuousness will be, and therefore the larger its trading area and sales penetration will be. Yet sales may not increase with store size in a proportional manner. To build stores of the right size, management needs some measure of the relationship between store size and store sales. If small stores yield higher returns on investment than large stores, the company may be better off building several small stores, instead of a few large ones, with a given budget.

Baumol and Ide (1956) developed a model in which store size had both positive and negative effects on store sales as size increased. Instead of using store size directly, they focused on a correlated variable, the number of different items N that the retailer carried. They argued that the greater the number of different items there are, the more likely it is that the shopper will be attracted because he would have greater confidence in finding the items he wanted. On the other hand, the greater the number of different items there are, the more will be the time required by the shopper to get to the spot in the store where the items he wants are kept. Their particular formulation of the two effects of the number of items is as follows:

$$f(N, D) = k_1 p(N) - k_2(c_d D + c_n \sqrt{N} + c_i) \qquad (13.29)$$

where $f(N, D)$ = measure of consumer's expected net benefit from shopping at store with N different items and distance D
$p(N)$ = probability that consumer will find some set of items in store that will make his trip successful
c_d, c_n, c_i = cost parameters
k_1, k_2 = respective weights for benefit and cost of shopping, $0 \leq k_i \leq 1$ and $k_1 + k_2 = 1$

Their formulation permits a number of conclusions to be drawn. First, the expected net benefit of shopping in a store with very few items may be negative. Second, the expected net benefit of shopping in a store with a tremendous number of items may also be negative because the first term in eq. (13.29) can never exceed k_1 while $k_2 c_n \sqrt{N}$ grows indefinitely large. (For example, this result explains why a Sears store is never built so large that it carries all the items listed in its catalog.) Third, sales are likely to increase with store size at an increasing and then a diminishing rate, which eventually becomes negative. The exact shape depends on the parameters in the equation. [Corstjens and Doyle (1981) present a review of the literature on retail-shelf-space allocation and an associated model.]

Many manufacturers collect data on a large number of site-specific variables for equations that determine the relative importance of the various site characteristics. In a case study Dufton (1958) describes such an analysis for the Rayco Manufacturing Company. He included 37 variables in his regression model, which accounted for 92 percent of the sales variations. However, Ackoff and Sasieni (1968, pp. 61–62) describe the methodological and conceptual flows in such an approach. Their analysis suggests that such models often do not predict well, nor do they yield useful managerial insights.

If a large-scale study of the importance of site characteristics is performed, it is essential that (1) the dynamics of buyer behavior (as in the last section on transient outlet sales) be incorporated in the model, (2) the dimensions be complete and independent, and (3) the choice set (set of outlet alternatives) be properly specified.

Distribution Logistics

In addition to establishing locations for its outlets, a company must also design an efficient physical-distribution system for getting goods to its outlets and customers. This system consists of decisions on warehouse location, inventory levels, packaging and handling procedures, and transportation carriers. These decisions have both cost and demand aspects. The cost aspect of physical distribution has received the most attention, and many successful operations-research models have been developed in this area. However, the demand aspect has come to the foreground more recently and deserves the serious attention of designers of physical-distribution systems.

Of course, marketing executives are particularly interested in the demand aspect of physical distribution. Each component decision can affect company sales. Warehouse locations are a promotional tool in that they give confidence to local buyers of better availability and faster service. Inventory-level policies affect availability and hence sales. Packaging and handling procedures, insofar as they affect the damaged-goods rate, affect the number of customers. Transportation modes, insofar as they can mean faster or slower arrival of goods, affect buyer satisfaction and sales.

In Exhibit 13.11 a comprehensive distribution-planning system is outlined. According to Geoffrion (1975, pp. 18–19), such a system should satisfy the following primary questions:

1. How many warehouses should there be?
2. Where should they be located (given a list of current and plausible candidate locations)?
3. What size should each warehouse be (including selection among specific expansion and contraction projects under consideration)?
4. Which warehouse should service what customer?
5. How should each plant's output be allocated among warehouses and customers for each product?
6   What should the transportation flows be on an annual basis throughout the entire distribution system?
7. What is the breakdown of cost-savings and customer-service implications associated with the best distribution-system design compared with a projection of the current system to the target period?

He does not include inventory control, order processing, packaging-materials handling, vehicle routing, and other operational problems in the model. For planning it is sufficient to assume that these tactical functions are performed as economically as possible and are consistent with desired levels of customer service. Their cost consequences should be woven into the individual cost elements of the planning model.

Furthermore, because they all interact with one another, the above questions should be resolved simultaneously, not piecemeal. The cost elements of the model include the following:

1. transportation costs between plants, warehouses, and customers
2. all warehouse and inventory costs
3. costs and savings of expanding, opening, and closing warehouses
4. production costs by product at the plants

When the above questions have a significant influence on demand, revenues from sales must be incorporated into the model (as negative costs). The sum of all these costs must then be minimized subject to all necessary restrictions, including the following:

1. The stipulated production capacities of each plant must not be exceeded.
2. The size of each open warehouse must be between prescribed lower and upper limits.
3. (Often) Each customer must be served by a single warehouse for certain products.
4. A warehouse is eligible to serve a customer only if it is sufficiently close that the transit times under economical delivery modes are in accord with the desired level of customer service.

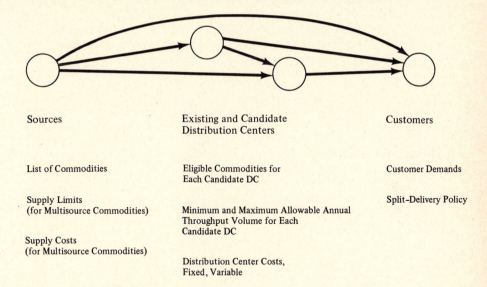

Sources   Existing and Candidate   Customers
Distribution Centers

List of Commodities   Eligible Commodities for   Customer Demands
Each Candidate DC

Supply Limits   Split–Delivery Policy
(for Multisource Commodities)   Minimum and Maximum Allowable Annual
Throughput Volume for Each
Candidate DC
Supply Costs
(for Multisource Commodities)

Distribution Center Costs,
Fixed, Variable

Freight Rates: Inbound, Direct, Interwarehouse Transfer, Outbound

MAIN FUNCTION OF THE SOLVER

Determine
    How Many DCs, Where, and What Size
    DC Territories
    All Transportation Flows
    Source Loadings

                     So as to Minimize Total Costs
                        Supply (e.g., Manufacturing)
                        Transportation
                        Warehousing
                        Inventory
                        System Reconfiguration

                                        Subject to All Appropriate Constraints
                                         Supply Capacity
                                         DC Throughput Capacity
                                         Demands to be Met
                                         Single Sourcing of Customers
                                         Customer Service

EXHIBIT 13-11   **Sketch of a comprehensive distribution-planning system.** (Source: Geoffrion and Powers, 1980, p 24.) Reprinted by permission of the Institute of Management Sciences. *Interfaces*, V. 10, No. 2, april 1980.

5. All forecast customer demands must be satisfied (any undesirable demands would be eliminated from the forecast).
6. Any other desired constraints on configuration, such as lower and upper limits on the number of open warehouses; subsets of warehouses, among which at least one or at most one should be open; more-complex constraints on warehouse capacity; and desired levels of customer service.

A solution strategy for this problem has been formulated by Geoffrion and Graves and is described below.

Geoffrion-Graves Model

Geoffrion and Graves (1975) state the problem as follows:

$$\text{Find } \{X_{ijkl}\} \, \{Y_{kl}\} \, \{Z_k\}$$

to minimize

$$\underbrace{\sum_l \sum_k \sum_j \sum_i c_{ijkl} X_{ijkl}}_{\substack{\text{(production and} \\ \text{shipping costs)}}} + \sum_k \Big[\underbrace{f_k Z_k}_{\substack{\text{fixed} \\ \text{charge}}} + \underbrace{V_k \sum_i \sum_l D_{il} Y_{kl}}_{\substack{\text{variable costs} \\ \text{(inventory and} \\ \text{holding)}}} \Big] \qquad (13.30a)$$

subject to

$$\sum_l \sum_k X_{ijkl} \le S_{ij} \qquad \text{(supply constraints)} \qquad (13.30b)$$

$$\sum_i X_{ijkl} = D_{ik} Y_{kl} \qquad \text{(demand constraints)} \qquad (13.30c)$$

$$\sum_k Y_{kl} = 1 \qquad \begin{array}{l}\text{(each customer zone} \\ \text{must be served by} \\ \text{a warehouse or dis-} \\ \text{tribution center, DC)}\end{array} \qquad (13.30d)$$

$$V_k Z_k \le \sum_i \sum_l D_{il} Y_{kl} \le \overline{V}_k Z_k \qquad \begin{array}{l}\text{(upper and lower} \\ \text{throughput constraints} \\ \text{for open DC's)}\end{array} \qquad (13.30e)$$

Plus other configurational constraints on Y and/or Z   (13.30f)

In this model no customer zone is serviced by more than one distribution center (DC). Constraint (13.30f) allows incorporation of the idiosyncrasies of most real applications, such as upper/lower bounds on the number of DCs open, precedence relations among the DCs (not A unless B), mandatory service constraints (if DC A is open, it must serve customer zone B), and so on.

However, most real-life problems are too large to be solved by conventional codes (Geoffrion and Marsten, 1972). In an illustration from Hunt-Wesson Foods, with several hundred distinguishable commodities produced at 14 locations and distributed nationally through a dozen distribution centers, the formulated problem had over 11,000 rows, over 700 binary variables, and over 23,000 continuous variables.

The authors show how these problems can be decomposed so that the multicommodity aspect becomes less burdensome: when the binding variables are temporarily held fixed so as to satisfy eqs. (13.30d), (13.30e), and (13.30f), the remaining optimization separates into as many independent classical-transportation problems as there are commodities. To solve their problem, they adopt Benders' (1962) decomposition method, which allows efficient solutions of the original problem, solutions that are as close to optimal as desired. (Most runs took less than a minute on an IBM 360-91.)

Application and Assessment

The actual details of the optimization above are beyond the scope of this book. The point is that true optimization of full problems as formulated in model (13.30) is currently possible by using an approach like that of Geoffrion and Graves. But because true optimization has been difficult until recently, most problems of this type have been solved by nonoptimizing heuristics. Geoffrion and VanRoy (1979) present an excellent in-depth discussion on the risks of using heuristics in distribution planning. Optimization is needed to permit reliable comparisons between different runs of the model. Without optimization, sensitivity analysis becomes unreliable. And there are other risks. Geoffrion (1975) relates a situation in which the results of a $75,000 consulting project were improved upon by management *by hand!*

The main points here are as follows:

The methodology exists and *should be used* to develop comprehensive distribution models that treat interdependent decisions simultaneously.

Only systems that truly optimize permit reliable comparisons of the results of multiple computer runs and therefore allow reliable and responsible sensitivity analyses and answers to "What if . . . ?" questions.

Geoffrion (1975) has produced a summary of his evaluation of available distribution logistics optimization models and methods, which is reproduced as Exhibit 13.12. Note that the decomposition method described above does well along the key relevant dimensions.

Analytical support for the design and operation of distribution systems using computer simulators has also been developed recently. The distribution-system simulator (Aggarwal, 1973; Connors et al., 1972; Hax, 1975),

EXHIBIT 13-12 Summary evaluation of available optimizing model/methods.

		Geoffrion and Graves (1974)	Mathematical-Programming System Extended IBM UMPIRE (1970) OPHILIE/LP (1970)	Geoffrion and McBride (1972)	Akinc and Khumawala (1974)	Khumawala Users Manual (1972)	Polignani (1970) SIA Depot Location (1971)	Haverly (1970) Fieldhouse and Fieldhouse (1974)
Important Problem Features Treated Properly	1. Multiple Products	Yes	Yes	Yes (with the Help of a Simple Trick) →→→			Yes (In the Absence of Problem Feature 2)	Yes (In the Absence of Problem Feature 2)
	2. Two Stages of Distribution Plants, Warehouses, and Customers	Yes	Yes	No	No	No	Yes (In the Absence of Problem Feature 1)	Yes (In the Absence of Problem Feature 1)
	3. Capacities for Plants and Size Limits for Warehouses	Yes	Yes	Yes	Yes (Upper Limits Only)	No	Yes (Upper Limits Only)	Yes (Upper Limits Only)
	4. Warehouse Economies of Scale and Fixed Charges	Yes	Yes	Yes	Yes	Yes	Yes	Yes
	5. Each Customer Serviced by a Single Warehouse	Yes	Yes (but Usually Impractical)	Yes (optional)	No	No	No	Doubtful
	6. Shipments to Customers: Preserve Identity of Originating Plant	Yes	Yes	←——— Not Applicable ———→			No	No
	7. Optional Restrictions on System Configuration	Yes	Yes	Yes	No	No	No	Yes
Computational Criteria	1. Capable of True Optimization	Yes	Yes	Yes	Yes	Yes	Yes	Yes
	2. Probable Computational Efficiency for Problems of *Moderate Size*	Good	Poor to Adequate	←— Good to Adequate —→			Probably Adequate	Probably Adequate
	3. Suitability for Multiple Secondary-Optimization Runs: Fast, Reliable, Easy to Use	Good	Poor	←— Good to Adequate —→			Probably Adequate	Uncertain

LREPS (Bowersox et al., 1972), and several other simulation packages have been designed specifically for distribution. In addition, many firms have programmed their own simulation studies by using specialized simulation languages, such as GPSS and SIMSCRIPT.

With simulation a *fully specified* system is evaluated in great detail, and therefore simulation is a logical complement to the optimization approach (albeit, optimization at a more macrolevel) specified above. In this context inventory-control and waiting-line problems can be studied in detail. Practical applications of simulation-based studies have included supermarket sizing, bank-office design, and airline ticket offices.

Another key element of physical distribution is inventory management. Although the marketer does not usually have control over inventory policy, he is inclined to seek a strong voice in setting that policy. The marketer's chief concern is in providing a high level of customer service, and inventory policy is a tool in the demand-creation-and-satisfaction process. But while marketers would like all their customers' orders to be filled immediately, such an inventory is often very costly. Inventory-control decisions balance ordering and storage costs against the cost and likelihood of run-out and, hence, potential lost sales. Heskett (1977) points out that many companies have higher inventory-carrying costs than necessary because they try to offer their customers the same service standard on all their goods. But customers expect to wait longer for nonstandard items than for faster-moving ones. Therefore savings are available (at no loss in overall customer satisfaction) by developing different inventory policies for products with different demand profiles. For a review of the state of the art in inventory control and a guide to the related literature, see Wagner (1980).

Distribution Management

We have examined the successive questions of distribution strategy, location, and logistics and reviewed the analytical techniques available to aid decision making in these areas. Let us assume that the company's distribution system is now designed, implemented, and operating. Then the company's task is to motivate its outlets—both company-owned and independent—to operate at the highest level of performance. The company would like to see the outlets order as much as possible, give the most prominent display space to its merchandise, cooperate wholeheartedly in special promotions, boost its products over competitors' products, and provide excellent customer service. To encourage these practices, the company has available a certain number of sales tools, the more important ones of which are retail margin, special retail allowances, number of company service calls, cooperative-advertising allowances, dealer-training programs, dealer literature and sales aids, and so on. Each tool has a certain incentive value that varies with its own level and the level of the other tools. The company's challenge is to find the proper mix of incentives that optimizes its profits through the dealer. Fortunately, the appropriate decision models do not differ substantially from those developed for other marketing tools. At the same time some specific comments on model building in this area are offered to suggest the types of problems encountered.

Companies would like to obtain as much dealer shelf space for their products as possible. Shelf space, and price and image of the product are major factors affecting the level of retail sales. To the extent that the dealer has latitude in setting the price, he will be influenced by the manufacturer's price and any allowances offered at the time. Allowances can lead the dealer to set a lower retail price or devote more shelf space to the product or both. Shelf space is also influenced by the amount of retail advertising; dealers expect products with higher advertising to sell more units and therefore may allocate more shelf space for these products. Finally, shelf space is also influenced by any overstock held by the dealer. Some salesmen deliberately seek to overstock the dealer so that he will devote more space to the product to reduce stock. If additional shelf space increases sales substantially, the dealer will be led to increase his order level for the product; then, in a circular manner, the company's share of total sales through this dealer will rise. A dynamic model of these interactions can be developed as a tool for determining effective marketing policies with respect to retail margins, allowances, advertising, and overstocking.

One large company (private communication) developed a simulation model to clarify the complicated effects of trade and consumer promotions on its sales. The product was flashbulbs for use in amateur photography, and distribution was through approximately 2000 wholesalers, who sold the product through approximately 100,000 retail stores. The need to study its promotional policies in more detail arose from the observation that the company shipments ranged from 5 million to 75 million units a month, while incentives to distributors, retailers, and consumers ranged from 0 to 8 percent a month. An analysis of the gross data on sales and promotions revealed no consistent relationship. The same promotion seemed to have different effects at different times and in different situations. It was suggested that a simulation model be constructed to represent the industry, particularly the response differences of various channels associated with their volume, cost of money, and min-max inventory rules. The model was developed and tested against historical data on company promotion with good results. The analyst concluded:

> Some past programs now began to make sense as to why they succeeded and why they failed. In some areas, the sales promotion activity thought to be ef-fective had failed because it had points in it that were not appealing to the channels of distribution as far as carrying inventory was concerned. The price

weighted by the volume was not in accordance with their needs or desires. It was also found that, in the trade, the capital structure of the channels of distribution was such that terms were more appealing than discounts.

The company has used this simulator to pretest alternative sales plans consisting of allowances, terms, and discounts and is satisfied that its value as an analytical device has more than justified the cost of developing it.

Summary

A company's channels of distribution represent a foundation for its other marketing policies. For this reason management will want to exercise great care in its decisions on distribution strategy, location, logistics, and management. The first of these, distribution strategy, is the determination of the basic way in which the company sells to buyers. Here the company should carefully distinguish all of the alternatives and evaluate them, either through the weighted-factor-score method, decision analysis, or simulation-based methods.

The second decision area, distribution location, is concerned with four interrelated decisions: market selection, number of outlets, site location, and the size and other characteristics of the store. The first task is to determine the most attractive market areas in the country in which to locate new outlets. A good procedure is to estimate discounted cumulative profits on a new average-size outlet that might be opened in each area and then to rank the locations from the most to the least profitable. In this way the company can concentrate its store-location research in the highest-ranking areas. The company should then turn to the question of the optimal number of outlets per market area. Quantitative approaches to this question incorporate an S-shaped, market-share/outlet-share relationship. As for site location, current techniques range from primitive checklists to the analog method to gravitational models. Also, store size was shown to be an important factor in affecting the level of sales. Other characteristics of the outlet, such as its decor, caliber of management, product assortment, and so forth, also affect demand. One way to examine the relative influence of all these factors on demand is by a regression-type analysis performed on data for existing company stores. However, this approach has methodological risks.

Distribution logistics, the third area of distribution decision making, is concerned with determining the best way to supply company outlets with product. This decision involves four major variables: the number of warehouses, inventory levels, packaging and handling procedures, and transportation carriers. For an optimal physical-distribution system, an appropriate cost function must be formulated, which includes the cost of lost sales. Once this cost is included with the other physical-distribution costs, the task is to minimize the distribution cost function subject to certain constraints. New linear-programming routines based on the decomposition principle can now handle problems of realistic size; analysts no longer have to rely on heuristics. Simulation and inventory theory can be used to deal with shorter range-problems of the operational design and control of the distribution system.

The fourth area, distribution management, concerns the motivation of the outlets to perform at the highest possible level. Here management can formulate a dynamic analysis of the interaction of trade allowances, advertising, and overstocking and use the power of computer simulation to pretest the effects of alternative promotional programs to the trade.

Problems

13.1 Suppose you are the marketing manager of a medium-sized manufacturing company. The president has just made the following statement: "The distribution activity is not a concern of the marketing department. The function of the marketing department is to sell the product . . . let the rest of the company handle production and distribution." How would you reply to this statement? Can you expect any support for your answer from the quantitative (modeling) approach discussed in this chapter?

13.2 Find an optimal outlet decision by using the algorithm of the Lilien-Rao model for the situation given by following data:

Number of Outlets	Cumulative NPVs		
	Market 1	Market 2	Market 3
1	5	4	6
2	8	9	7
3	12	16	13
4	15	21	14

13.3 What are major trade-offs to be considered in developing a logistics model? What are the merits and weaknesses of the optimization approach for the logistics problem in comparison with the heuristics?

13.4 The ABC Corporation currently sells one of its products directly to retailers through its own salesforce. Present sales are 100,000 units per year, and the company's profit margin is $2 per unit. Management estimates that the cost of maintaining the salesforce is $1 per unit. The company is considering the use of wholesalers, rather than selling directly to retailers. The wholesaler's commission would be 75¢ per unit, but salesforce costs per unit sold would be cut by one-half.

a. The initial cost of converting to the wholesaler distribution system is $18,000. How many additional units would the company have to sell to cover its transition costs in 1 yr?

b. Management's estimates of the pessimistic, most likely, and optimistic levels of sales for the coming year under the wholesaler strategy are 100,000, 110,000, and 120,000, respectively. Should the company change its distribution channels?

13.5 A large fish-and-chips restaurant franchiser is considering opening a new outlet in a large metropolitan area. There are presently 200 fish-and-chips outlets in the area, of which 20 hold his company's franchise. Each outlet in the area has average monthly sales of $10,000.

a. Using the Hartung-Fisher model, determine the amount of additional sales that would be created by opening up a new outlet in this area (assume $k_1 = 4.44$ and $k_2 = 0.64$).

b. What would be the amount of additional sales if 30 of the 200 stores in the area were company franchises?

13.6 A men's shoe manufacturer plans to establish a new outlet in one of its two major market areas; A_1 or A_2. The company and its competitors currently sell a total of 100,000 pairs of shoes in each area. There are 250 outlets in A_1 (of which 25 are company outlets) and 200 outlets in A_2 (40 of which are company outlets). In a recent study the company found that it was able to retain about 30% of its customers in A_1 and about 40% in A_2 from purchase to purchase. It was also found that the company was able to persuade 10% of its competitor's customers in A_1 (8% in A_2) to switch to its own brand. Should the new outlet be established in A_1 or A_2?

13.7 A company is considering the development of one of two new market areas. Estimates of potential sales, expenses, and growth rates for each area are presented in the following table:

	Area 1	Area 2
Adjusted annual sales potential S_t	$500,000	$750,000
Transportation expenses (percent of sales) d_t	0.20	0.15
Advertising expenses (percent of sales) a_t	0.25	0.30
Real estate expenses (percent of sales) l_t	0.10	0.12
Other expenses (percent of sales) n_t	0.29	0.35
Expected growth rate of profit potential	0.04	0.06

It is estimated that it would cost the same amount to develop either area ($150,000). Suppose the company's cost of capital is 10%. Which area offers the more attractive rate of return over a 3-yr planning horizon?

13.8 Huff's gravitational model assumes that the consumer's marginal utility with respect to distance varies according to the value of the exponent λ. For instance, $\lambda = 2$ indicates that the consumer experiences diminishing marginal utility with respect to increases in distance. The model, however, assumes that the consumer experiences constant marginal utility with respect to increases in store size.

Suppose that the consumer actually experiences diminishing marginal utility with respect to increases in store size. Using an exponent as the parameter that accounts for the consumer's marginal utility of store size, modify Huff's formulation to accommodate this diminishing marginal utility.

13.9 You manufacture mattresses. The amount of mattresses you sell at the retail level is a function of all the elements in the marketing mix, including the commission you give to retailers. Currently, all manufacturers give a commission of 4%. You are thinking about changing your commission rate. Your (constant) profit per mattress sold is 10% of the mattress retail price, *before* the commission is deducted from your profits.

Your current (stable) market share is 5%. You assume your market share, with a different commission, would be

$$5\% \times \frac{\text{your commission}}{\text{other brands' commissions}}$$

a. What happens if you decrease your commission (e.g., to 2%) and other manufacturers do not? What will be your market share and profit?

b. What happens if you increase your commission (e.g., to 6%) and other manufacturers do not?

c. What happens if you increase your commission (e.g., to 6%) and other manufacturers follow your move?

d. You assume that competitors will follow your move if you increase your commission but will not if you decrease it. Graph a curve of your share against possible commission levels between 0 and 8%. Graph a curve of your profit against possible commission levels.

e. What should you do?

13.10 Consolidated Oil Company is considering developing an integrated program to plan their retail-location activities.

a. Construct a consolidated flow diagram relating the strategy, location, and site-relocation decisions. What models would you suggest for each stage?

b. Propose a related data-collection scheme.

c. Modify the location model you suggested in part a so that it can handle divestment (as well as building) decisions.

CHAPTER

14

Advertising Decision Models

One of the most important and bewildering promotional tools of modern marketing management is advertising. No one doubts that it is effective in presenting information to potential buyers. There is also widespread agreement that it can be persuasive to some extent and can reinforce buyer preference for a company's product. These potential values of advertising are attested to by the fact that in 1980 the top 100 advertisers raised their advertising spending 11 percent over 1979 to an estimated $13 billion. Procter and Gamble, the number-one advertiser, spent $650 million and Sears Roebuck, Inc., spent $600 million (*Advertising Age*, September 10, 1981, p. 1).

Advertising is bewildering because, among other reasons, its effects typically play out over time, may be nonlinear, and interact with other elements in the marketing mix in creating sales. Currently, no one knows what advertising really does in the marketplace. However, what advertising is supposed to do is fairly clear: advertising is undertaken to increase company sales and/or profits over what they otherwise would be. However, it is rarely able to create sales by itself. Whether the customer buys also depends on the product, price, packaging, personal selling, services, financing, and other aspects of the marketing process.

More specifically, the purpose of advertising is to enhance potential buyers' responses to the organization and its offerings by providing information, by channeling desires, and by supplying reasons for preferring a particular organization's offer.

For advertising, even more than for other elements of the marketing mix, it is important to keep in mind that advertising decisions and their effectiveness are influenced to a great extent by their interaction with marketing objectives, with product characteristics, and with other elements of the marketing mix. For example:

Personal selling. When personal selling is an important element in the marketing mix (in industrial markets, for example), the role of advertising is diminished. Personal selling is a far more effective (but expensive) communication method than advertising. But because of its extra expense, it can be used more effectively when the expected level of sales to a single prospect is large (generally, sales to industrial customers, wholesalers, and retailers).

Branding. If a company produces several variations of its product under a family or company name (Kelloggs, Campbell Soup), advertising is appropriated to the entire line, with special-brand attention given from time to time. When different brand names exist (Tide at Procter and Gamble, for example), each brand and the advertising budget and copy and media decisions associated with it can be addressed independently.

Pricing. The copy or message of the advertising must reinforce and be consistent with the brand's price position. A premium-priced brand should emphasize differentiating qualities, while a low-priced brand should stress the price differential.

Distribution. The length of the distribution channel and the overall marketing strategy dictates different targets for advertising messages. If wholesalers or retailers are involved, two different strategies are generally available: push versus pull. A push strategy is aimed at salesmen or the trade, and the objective is to push the product through channels; a pull strategy is aimed at the ultimate consumer, and its objective is to have consumer interest pull the merchandise through the distribution channnels.

The differences among product characteristics, marketing-program objectives, and marketing strategies explain to an extent the differences in advertising-spending levels of products. The median advertising-spending level for a large sample of industrial products was found to be 0.7 percent of sales (Lilien, 1978a), while *Advertising Age* annually reports rates of around 2 percent of sales for industries like automobiles, tires, oil, and appliances and over 7 percent for soaps, cleansers, drugs, and cosmetics. These wide variations reflect differences in the relative importance and efficiency of advertising.

Aaker and Myers (1975) define three decision areas for advertising: (1) objective setting and budgeting (i.e., how much to spend), (2) copy decisions (i.e., what message), and (3) media decisions (i.e., what media should be used). Although these three points are addressed separately here, they are closely interrelated: advertising objectives drive copy decisions, and copy effects, varying by response group, affect media decisions. In addition, time is an issue for all three decision areas. For budgeting, dollars must be spent over time, and pulsing versus more-continuous spending patterns must be evaluated. Furthermore, advertising copy varies in its effectiveness over time, eventually wearing out. Thus the creation of new copy must be phased in. Finally, media decisions are closely connected with the timing and scheduling of messages, as well as with the selection of media.

To guide our discussion, we first review what is known about the effects of advertising—that is, what does advertising seem to do? This review aids the discussion and evaluation of advertising models for the three decision areas given in the following sections.

The Effects of Advertising

Response Phenomena

Little (1979b) identifies three sets of controversies for aggregate-advertising response models:

Shape. This notion refers to the long-term level of sales expected at each different level of advertising. Is the relationship linear? S-shaped? What are sales when advertising is zero? Is there a supersaturation point, where large amounts of advertising depress sales?

Dynamics. This notion refers to the speed of sales increase when advertising is increased and the rate of decay when advertising is decreased. Another question is whether hysteresis exists—that is, whether advertising can move sales to a new level at which it will stay without further advertising input.

Interaction. Two main questions exist here. The first is, What type of market (strong or weak market-share markets) is a more appropriate target for advertising? The second is, What is the appropriate structure of the interaction of advertising with other elements in the marketing mix?

Little (1979b) also reviews many empirical examples in an all-too-infrequent attempt to unify and generalize what we have observed. Exhibit 14.1 illustrates several of the observed phenomena. First, we note that advertising increases sales here: there are considerable increases in sales after the introduction of substantial new-advertising dollars. We also note that the sales rate increases within a month or so, substantially faster than many managers purport to be the case. Bloom, Jay, and Twyman (1977) and Pekelman and Tse (1976) report similar results with a change in copy, indicating that dollar spending may be the same as effective spending.

EXHIBIT 14-1   **Sales rate of a packaged good rose quickly under increased advertising but declined slowly after it was removed. Vertical axis shows the ratio of sales in test areas to sales in control areas not receiving the heavy advertising.** (Source: Little, 1979b. Reprinted with permission from *Operations Research*, Vol. 27, Issue 4, 1979b, p. 63, Operations Research Society of America. No further reproduction without the consent of the copyright owner.)

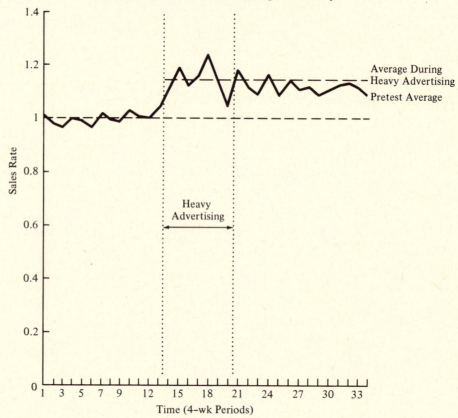

The exhibit also shows sales leveling off under the new spending regime: apparently, the total effect of the advertising was seen before spending stopped. Little (1979b) in other studies and the Bloom, Jay, and Twyman (1977) article show these effects as well. Haley (1978) refines this observation by demonstrating that the magnitude of the sales increase actually decreases over time. Thus the increased advertising may lead a group of nonusers to buy the product for a change, and then some of these customers continue to purchase.

Finally, Exhibit 14.1 shows the beginning of decay following the lowering of advertising. Furthermore, this sales decay seems to take place more slowly than sales growth. Hence two separate phenomena are involved: the rise is related to advertising communications [Krugman (1972) argues that three exposures may be enough to stimulate action], while the decline is related to product experience, a different phenomenon, and should be expected to occur at a different rate.

Exhibit 14.2 shows the sales of a line of products that have never been advertised. Supermarkets and department stores are literally stocked with house brands, price brands, and others that see quite healthy sales in the absence of advertising. Therefore an advertising-response model should admit the possibility of sales with zero advertising.

Perhaps the most interesting set of controversies in advertising deal with nonlinearities in the response curve. Logic suggests that a linear response curve is unreasonable: a product with a linear response would have an optimal advertising rate of either zero or infinity, and its sales could be made increasingly large with continuing increases in advertising spend-

EXHIBIT 14-2 **The healthy sales of a line of unadvertised food products show that advertising is not always required in order to sell something.** (Source: Little, 1979b. Reprinted with permission from *Operations Research*, Vol. 27, Issue 4, 1979b, p. 637, Operations Research Society of America. No further reproduction permitted without the consent of the copyright owner.)

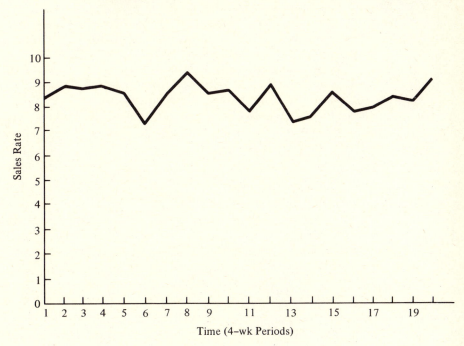

EXHIBIT 14-3 **Two examples of nonlinear response exhibit the phenomenon of diminishing returns at high advertising rates.** (Source: Little, 1979b. Reprinted with permission from *Operations Research*, Vol. 27, Issue 4, 1979b, p. 638, Operations Research Society of America. No further reproduction permitted without the consent of the copyright owner; and reprinted with permission from *Operations Research Quarterly*, Vol. 9, B. Benjamin and J. Maitland, "Operational Research and Advertising: Some Experiments in the Use of Analogies," copyright 1958. Pergamon Press, Ltd.)

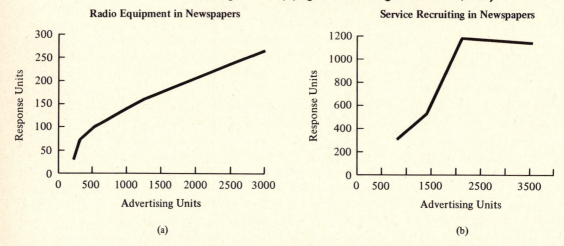

ing. On the other hand, nonlinearity covers many alternatives, the two most important of which are diminishing returns and an S shape.

Exhibits 14.3(a) and 14.3(b) show two products that display concavity (diminishing returns). Although there is some argument to the contrary (Simon, 1969), both the practice of pulsing (justified on the theory that small advertising rates do little good but that medium rates are effective) and empirical evidence support the S-shaped hypothesis. Though not all products display an S-shaped sales response, Rao (1978) and Rao and Miller (1975) present a series of examples that do show such a shape. Wittink (1977) also finds larger advertising-sales slopes at higher advertising rates, supporting a region of increasing returns consistent with the S-shaped-response hypothesis.

Little (1979b) shows the results of a series of tests of the impulse response of advertising—the response over time to a short but heavy increase in advertising spending—which is reproduced in Exhibit 14.4. These data [as well as similar results from Bass and Clarke (1972)] show that advertising response is fairly quick (within 1 to 2 mo) and that there is negative sales reaction about 4 mo after the pulse. This effect, common in consumer promotions, reflects the borrowing of future sales. [See Clarke (1976) for a more complete evaluation of this phenomenon.]

EXHIBIT 14-4   **A large impulse of advertising in month 0 yields substantial sales increases in months 0, 1, and 2 for an infrequently purchased consumer durable.** (Source: Little, 1979b. Reprinted with permission from *Operations Research,* Vol. 27, Issue 4, 1979b, p. 641, Operations Research Society of America. No further reproduction without the consent of the copyright owner.)

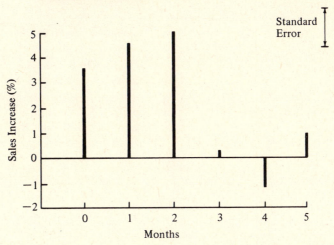

Other effects reviewed by Little (1979b) are the (relatively rapid) sales response for infrequently purchased goods (those people react who are in the market), the market-depletion phenomena for such goods, and competitive effects. Where the evidence is weak or nonexistent is on the question of where to advertise (in strong markets? in weak markets?), on the existence and pervasiveness of hysteresis, and on the structure of interactions. The issue of interactions is particularly difficult, and such effects are harder to measure than main effects (Eskin and Baron 1977; Swinyard and Ray 1977; Wildt, 1977). Effects also differ over the product's life cycle and from market to market.

Finally, Little summarizes his observations with a list of five phenomena that a good advertising response model should admit:

1. Sales respond dynamically upward and downward, respectively, to increases and decreases of advertising and frequently do so at different rates.
2. Steady-state response can be concave or S-shaped and will often have positive sales at zero advertising.
3. Competitive advertising affects sales.
4. The dollar effectiveness of advertising can change over time as the result of changes in media, copy, and other factors.
5. Products sometimes respond to increased advertising with a sales increase that falls off even as advertising is held constant (Little, 1979b, p. 644).

All of these phenomena have implications for action, and although other phenomena clearly exist (the effect of uncertainty, for example; Holthausen and Assmus, 1982), this list sets minimum requirements for model validity. In the next section we explore several advertising models to see if and in what way they handle these phenomena.

Copy Research

Copy research involves investigations of a myriad of phenomena from how the physical and mechanical aspects of ads relate to recognition, recall, and other measures (Hendon, 1973) to the humor and seriousness of TV commercials (Wells, Leavitt, and McConnell, 1971). In his review of a large number of copy-testing studies, Ramond (1976) provides the following principles, where the term "principle" implies a basic finding with implications for future practice. These principles, like the observations above, hold in many circumstances, all other things being equal:

> The *bigger* the print ad, the more people will recognize it later (Starch 1966; Trodahl and Jones, 1965; Twedt, 1952; Yamanaka, 1962), possibly as a function of the square root of the size increase.
>
> *Color* ads are recognized by more people than black-and-white ads (Gardner and Cohen, 1966; Twedt, 1952).
>
> The *shorter its headline,* the greater the recognition of an ad (Leo Burnett bulletin, unpublished).
>
> Because TV commercials vary in more ways than print ads and have been studied for a shorter time, less is known about their copy tests (McGuire, 1976).
>
> *Shorter TV commercials* are recalled as well as longer ones.
>
> *Product class* has a significant effect on recognition or recall of both TV and print ads.
>
> *Sex, humor, and fear* have no consistent effect in what advertising communicates.
>
> *Awareness and attitude* changes are sensitive to differences in TV-commercial execution and can predict changes in brand choice (Assael and Day, 1968; Axelrod, 1968).
>
> Ads need not be believed to be remembered (Leavitt, 1962; Maloney, 1963).

While these observations have not been sufficiently understood or generalized to justify the term "theory," they do represent what appears to be general agreement about the effects of advertising copy. Research in this area continues. For example, Hanssens and Weitz (1980) reported that industrial-ad recall and readership scores were strongly related to a variety of characteristics, such as size and position in magazines; Goodwin and

Etgar (1980) have reported on relationships between communication effects and the type of advertising appeals, and Rossiter (1981) reports on regression analysis, reproducing Starch readership scores.

Frequency Phenomena

For media planning and scheduling, knowledge of the effect of advertising exposures over time is critical. In an important effort at consolidating the literature, Naples (1979) summarizes theoretical and empirical research related to effective advertising frequency.

The theoretical foundations of the effects of frequency are based on laboratory research in psychology and can be traced to the work of Ebbinghaus in the late 1800s in which he showed that the forgetting rate is made slower by repeated learning of the same lessons. Later work by Zielski (1959) applied Ebbinghaus' findings to ads for grocery products.

The work of Appel (1971) and Grass (1968) shows that response to a simple stimulus first increases, then passes through a maximum, and finally declines, as shown in Exhibit 14.5. From studies for a number of duPont products, Grass concludes that attention increases and maximizes at two exposures, while the amount of learned information increases and maximizes at two or three exposures. Krugman (1972), on the basis of his brain-wave and eye-movement studies, has been a strong advocate of the three-exposure rule for the past decade.

In an important paper on the results of a unique data-collection exercise, McDonald (1971) reports on the effects of frequency. In this study,

EXHIBIT 14-5 **Attention paid to TV commercials versus exposure frequency.** (Source: Grass, 1968.)

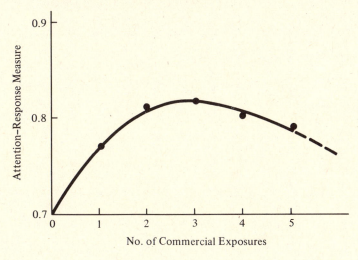

EXHIBIT 14-6   **The effect of advertising exposure (opportunity to see, OTS) on brand switching.** (Source: McDonald, 1971.)

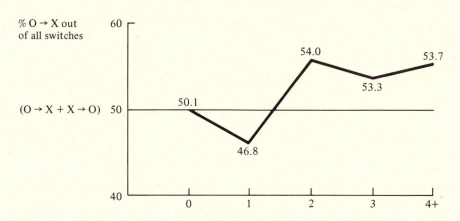

OTS in Interval

% O → X out of all switches

(O → X + X → O)

60

50.1

54.0

53.3

53.7

50

46.8

40

0   1   2   3   4+

purchasing records and newspaper-, magazine-, and media-exposure records for 50 product fields were kept for 255 housewives over a 13-wk period. The main result was that over 9 product fields studied in depth, housewives were, on average, 5 percent more likely to switch into, rather than out of, a particular brand if, between the two purchases, they saw two or more ads for that brand than if they saw zero or one ad. Exhibit 14.6 reproduces the main results, showing that the added value of more than two ads is marginal. McDonald also found that the effect is stronger for advertising seen within four days of the last purchase.

In a study conducted for four advertisers, Ogilvy and Mather (1965), using television viewing diaries, tracked brand preference and related it to number of exposures. The results of their study showed (1) no more than minimal effects for one exposure in an 8-wk period, (2) major differences by time of day, and (3) major differences by brand. (See Exhibit 14.7.) In another study using diary recorded purchasing within a split-cable television market, the results were pretty much consistent with the suggestion of at least two exposures for maximum effectiveness (Naples, 1979). An interesting additional finding was that the brands that showed the greatest response were those with the highest share of advertising in their categories.

On the basis of these studies and a review of others, Naples (1979, pp. 63–81) offers the following conclusions:

1. Optimal exposure frequency appears to be at least three exposures within a purchase cycle.
2. Beyond three ad exposures, effectiveness increases but at a decreasing ratio.
3. Frequency by itself does not cause wear-out, although it can advance the decline of an effective campaign.

EXHIBIT 14-7   **Brand-preference change induced by frequency of exposure to daytime television (food products).** (Source: Ogilvy and Mather, 1965.)

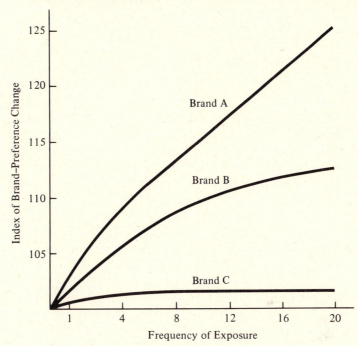

4. Response to advertising appears smaller for the brand with dominant market share.

These conclusions relate to consumer ads. Our knowledge of industrial advertising frequency is even poorer (Cort, Lambert, and Garrett, 1982).

In summary, although our knowledge about advertising response, effective frequency, and effective copy is limited, some principles clearly exist. These principles must be validated in specific situations and product areas prior to making advertising decisions.

Objectives Setting and Budgeting: Practice and Models

Objectives

Advertising decisions must be made with a realistic appraisal of what advertising can actually accomplish for the advertiser. In some situations effective advertising can trigger actual purchases; in others it can only lay groundwork for favorable attitudes. Furthermore, different effects may ensue, depending on whether the stimuli are single advertisements or major advertising campaigns. Thus setting objectives for advertising requires an understanding of the advertising process. This process is discussed first in terms of the influence of the single advertisement on a potential buyer and then in terms of the influence of a whole advertising campaign.

The Influence of a Single Ad.   Consider a single ad inserted in a particular medium. The difficulty of estimating the resulting exposure varies for the different media. In the case of TV the exposure value of the ad is related to audience size, which can be measured, albeit with some error, by various TV-media-rating services. We will ignore for the present the desirability of weighting the exposures differently for the buying power of the persons exposed, a refinement that will be taken up later in the media-decision section.

Then only a fraction of the number of persons who are exposed to the media vehicle carrying the advertisement will actually see the advertisement, where seeing the advertisement is measured by finding out whether the person recognizes or can recall it. Let this fraction be f_1. Furthermore, only a fraction of those who see the advertisement register it, where registering the advertisement is measured by finding out whether the person correctly recalls some of the content, such as the message or appeals used in the advertisement. Let this fraction be f_2. Although the advertisement has some value if it is only seen (in creating or maintaining brand identification), it has more value if the person can recall the appeals. Finally, some fraction of those who register the advertisement will be moved by the appeals (which will be related to the quality of the advertisement). Let this fraction be f_3. It is this effect that finally enters into the effective value of the advertising insertion, $V(E_A)$. In summary, the actual effective value of a single advertisement is given by

$$V(E_A) = f_1 f_2 f_3 E_A \qquad (14.1)$$

where $V(E_A)$ = effective value of single advertising insertion
  f_1 = percent of persons exposed to medium who have seen advertisement (exposure value)
  f_2 = percent of persons seeing advertisement who registered message
  f_3 = percent of persons registering message who were favorably impressed
  E_A = average number of persons exposed to medium carrying advertisement

Thus the effective value of a single advertising insertion is not given by its exposure value but possibly by much less, depending on the values of the various downward adjustments for audience shrinkage. Advertising-readership-measurement services tend to supply management with some measure of f_1 and f_2 based on controlled-sampling techniques. The fraction f_3 is harder to define and measure, although field surveys aim to provide this information as well.

The Influence of an Ad Campaign.   As noted earlier, the timing of ads and their spacing within a purchase cycle may influence the buyer: there may be too few repetitions for an ad to rise above a threshold, and too many ads may be counterproductive. Thus a central objective of advertising decision makers is to determine the minimum exposure frequency per period that will accomplish the advertising objectives of the advertiser.

To clarify the conceptual issues posed by exposure frequency, we consider the effects of two or more exposures to an advertisement with a fixed time between exposures. Assume that there are three thresholds for a consumer: a trial threshold (T), a repurchase threshold (R), and a loyalty threshold (L) (Langhoff, 1967). The effect of repetition is represented in Exhibit 14.8. The horizontal axis shows time, and the vertical axis shows the propensity to buy, where the propensity to buy is assumed to be a positive function of the level of cognition and feelings resulting from an exposure. Exhibit 14.8(a) shows how the repetition of an advertisement, when it is effective, raises the person's propensity to buy. Between exposures, there is some decay in the propensity to buy. In this illustration four exposures were necessary to raise the propensity to buy to the trial threshold, and a diminishing rate of increase is evident. Exhibit 14.8(b) shows the difference made by a short spacing versus a long spacing between exposures. The former is known as concentrated advertising (also intensive or burst advertising), and the latter is known as dispersed advertising (also uniform or paced advertising). In this case the concentrated advertising brought about trial in four exposures because of the short spacing between them, whereas the dispersed advertising failed to do so in four exposures. In Exhibit 14.8(c) we see the case in which advertising led to product trial and the product was disappointing. Finally, Exhibit 14.8(d) underscores how proportionately greater increases in competitive advertising can erode the propensity to buy the company's product.

Setting Advertising Goals

To the extent that the advertiser has realistically appraised the manner in which advertising might influence the sales of his brand, he is able to decide on goals for the advertising program. As an example, consider a company that is preparing to set advertising objectives for two of its brands, A and B. For each brand the company has conducted marketing research to determine the number of persons in the market and the percentage distribution of these persons in three classes: awareness, brand trial, and satisfaction. The results for the two brands are displayed in Exhibit 14.9. As for brand A, 80 percent of the total market is aware of the brand, 60 percent of those who are

EXHIBIT 14-8   The effect of repetition on the propensity to buy. (Source: Langhoff, 1967, p. 47.)

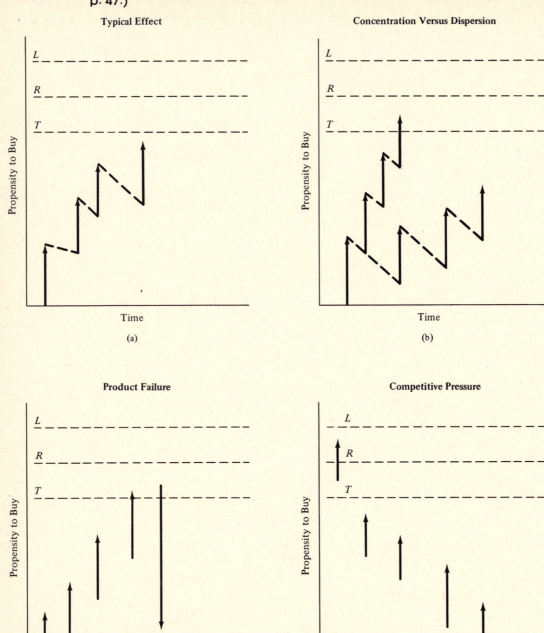

EXHIBIT 14-9   Current consumer states for two brands.

Current Consumer States, Brand A

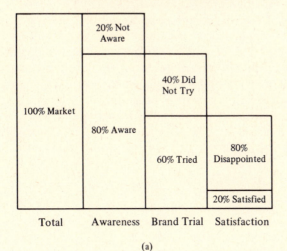

(a)

Current Consumer States, Brand B

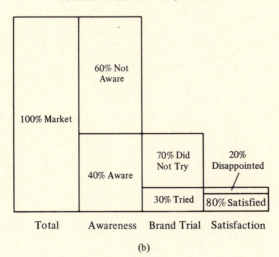

(b)

aware of it have tried it, and 20 percent of those who have tried it are satisfied. The distribution is quite different for brand B. Only 40 percent of the total market is aware of brand B, and only 30 percent of those who are aware of it have tried it, but 80 percent of those who have tried it are satisfied. Clearly, these two profiles have very different implications for advertising objectives and strategy. The market is highly aware of brand A, but a substantial portion of those who have tried it are disappointed. This result indicates that the advertising-exposure schedule and the creative message are effective in creating awareness, but the product fails to live up to the claims. Brand B has the opposite problem. The advertising has only produced 40 percent awareness, and only 12 percent of the market has tried the product. But of those who have tried brand B, satisfaction is very high. In this case the entire advertising program, including the media, the message, and the level of expenditure, may be much too weak to take advantage of the satisfaction-generating power of the brand.

The company's advertising goals for a brand are suggested by this type of analysis; the company can identify the type of advertising job it must do and the cost of doing it.

Setting the Advertising Budget

Each year the firm must decide how much to spend on advertising. Four of the more common methods for making this decision are described below (Hurwood and Brown, 1972; Lilien et al., 1976).

Affordable Method.   Many companies set the advertising budget on the basis of what they think the company can afford. As explained by one advertising executive:

> Why it's simple. First, I go upstairs to the controller and ask how much they can afford to give us this year. He says a million and a half. Later, the boss comes to me and asks how much we should spend, and I say, "Oh, about a million and a half." Then we have an advertising appropriation (Seligman, 1956, p. 123).

Setting budgets in this manner is tantamount to saying that the relationship between advertising expenditure and sales results is at best tenuous: whatever funds the company has available it should spend on advertising as a form of insurance. The basic weakness of this approach is that it leads to a fluctuating advertising budget that makes it difficult to plan for long-range market development.

Percentage-of-Sales Method.   Many companies set their advertising expenditures at a specified percentage of sales (either current or anticipated) or of the sales price. For example, a railroad company executive once said:

> We set our appropriation for each year on December 1 of the preceding year. On that date we add our passenger revenue for the next month, and then take 2 percent of the total for our advertising appropriation for the new year (Frey, 1955, p. 65).

Furthermore, automobile companies typically budget a fixed percentage for advertising based on the planned price of each car, and oil companies tend to set the appropriation as some fraction of a cent for each gallon of gasoline sold under their own label.

A number of advantages are claimed for this method. First, advertising expenditures are likely to vary with what the company can afford. Second, it encourages management to think in terms of the relationship between advertising cost, selling price, and profit per unit. Third, to the extent that competing firms spend approximately the same percentage of their sales on advertising, it encourages competitive stability.

In spite of these advantages, the percentage-of-sales method has little to justify it. It uses circular reasoning in viewing sales as the cause of advertising rather than as the result, and it leads to an appropriation set by the availability of funds rather than by the opportunities. Furthermore, the method does not provide a logical basis for the choice of a specific percentage, except what has been done in the past, what competitors are doing, or what the costs will be. Finally, it does not encourage the constructive development of advertising appropriations on a product-by-product and territory-by-territory basis but instead suggests that all allocations be made at the same percentage of sales.

Competitive-Parity Method. Some companies set their advertising budgets specifically to match competitors' outlays—that is, to maintain competitive parity. This thinking is illustrated by the executive who asked a trade source, "Do you have any figures that other companies in the builders' specialities field have used that would indicate what proportion of gross sales should be given over to advertising?" (Frey, 1955, p. 49).

Two arguments are advanced for this method. One is that competitors' expenditures represent the collective wisdom of the industry. The other is that maintaining a competitive parity helps to prevent advertising wars. But neither of these arguments is valid. There are no a priori grounds for believing that the competition is using more logical methods for determining outlays. Advertising reputations, resources, opportunities, and objectives are likely to differ so much among companies that their budgets are hardly a guide for another firm to follow. Furthermore, there is no evidence that appropriations based on the pursuit of competitive parity do, in fact, stabilize industry advertising expenditures.

Knowing what the competition is spending on advertising is undoubtedly useful information. But it is one thing to have this information and another to follow it blindly.

Objective-and-Task Method. The objective-and-task method calls upon advertisers to develop their budget by (1) defining their advertising objectives as specifically as possible, (2) determining the tasks that must be performed to achieve these objectives, and (3) estimating the costs of performing these tasks. The sum of these costs is the proposed advertising budget (Colley, 1961; Wolfe, Brown, and Thompson, 1962).

Advertising goals should be formulated as specifically as possible in order to guide the copy development, the media selection, and the measurement of results. The stated goal "to create brand preference" is much weaker than "to establish 30 percent preference for brand X among Y million housewives by next year." Colley listed as many as 52 specific communication goals, including the following:

Announce a special reason for buying now (price premium, etc.).

Build familiarity and easy recognition of the package or trademark.

Place advertiser in a position to select preferred distributors and dealers.

Persuade the prospect to visit a showroom and ask for a demonstration.

Build morale of the company's salesforce.

Correct false impressions, misinformation, and other obstacles to sales.

This method has strong appeal and popularity among advertisers. Its major limitation is that it does not indicate how the objectives themselves should be chosen and whether they are worth the cost of attaining them.

Model-based Approaches

In recent years there has been significant research in the development of decision models for setting advertising budgets. Although many of the related articles focus on the intricacies of the optimization, most of the decision models have a form related to the following. Find $\{A_i(t)\}$ to

$$\max Z = \underbrace{\sum_t \sum_t S_i(t \,|\, \{A_i(t)\}, \{C_{ij}(t)\}) \cdot m_i}_{\text{Gross profit}} - \underbrace{\sum_i \sum_t A_i(t)}_{\substack{\text{Advertising} \\ \text{spending}}} \qquad (14.2)$$

subject to

$$\sum_i \sum_t A_i(t) \le \text{budget constraint}$$

$$L_i \le \sum A_i(t) \le U_i \qquad \text{(regional constraint)}$$

where $S_i(t \,|\, \{A_i(t)\}, \{C_{ij}(t)\})$ = sales in area i at time t as function of current and historical brand and competitive advertising.

$C_{ij}(t)$ = competitive advertising for competitor j in area i

$A_i(t)$ = advertising level in area i at time t

EXHIBIT 14-10   **Steady-state sales response is affected by competitive advertising in a Lanchester model.** (Source: Little, 1979b. Reprinted with permission from *Operations Research*, Vol. 27, Issue 4, 1979b, p. 651, Operations Research Society of America. No further reproduction without the consent of the copyright owner.)

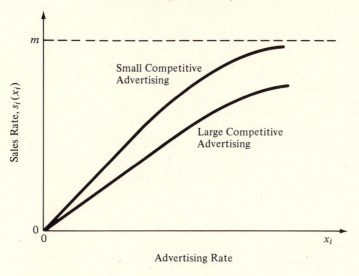

Advertising Rate

with the steady-state solution

$$S_i = \frac{m\rho_i X_i^{\epsilon_i}}{\displaystyle\sum_{j=1}^{n} \rho_j X_j^{\epsilon_j}} \qquad i = 1, \ldots, n \tag{14.10}$$

Note that this equation is a form of the attraction model analyzed in Chapter 4 and is quite versatile, being S-shaped in X_i for $\epsilon_i > 1$ and concave for $0 \le \epsilon_i < 1$. Thus if ρ_i carries copy and media effectiveness, the Lanchester model displays the properties of the first four phenomena observed by Little, except for nonzero sales at zero advertising. This latter condition is easily addressed here (and in other models with this difficulty) by defining the model only over that portion of the market that is attractable to advertising, as illustrated in Exhibit 14.11. Finally, like the other models, this model does not display erosion of incremental sales under constant advertising (the fifth phenomenon).

The model can easily be generalized to include ρ_{ij} terms—that is, where each firm's advertising has different effects on advertising by other firms. This form captures commonly occurring market structures where differential competition exists. Furthermore, many applications may replace m with $m(\Sigma X)$, allowing the market size to depend on total industry advertising.

This structure has been used in an industrial context for six products by

EXHIBIT 14-11   **The advertising-attractable region represents only a portion of the total market sales.**

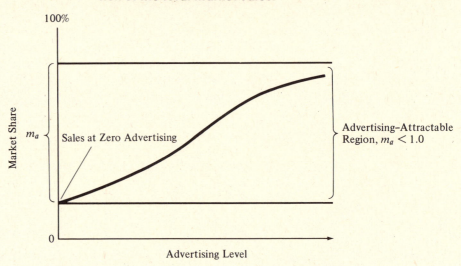

Lilien and Ruzdic (1982), and its use is compared to other specifications by Naert and Weverbergh (1981) with good empirical results. Furthermore, it has many of the desirable properties suggested by Little, and the transformations suggested in Chapter 4 allow model parameters to be estimated by standard methods. Finally, although it does not possess the erosion property suggested by Little, the model is intuitively appealing, rather complete, and logically consistent. Its major drawback is its requirement for complete competitive information on share and advertising spending—a drawback that is less formidable when competitors are collapsed into one or two categories. However, its apparent intractability to estimation has limited its use, but as this perceived (as opposed to real) difficulty is surmounted, the model should see more application, allowing a fuller evaluation as a useful model of advertising response.

Rao and Miller's Approach.   An interesting example of the econometric type that makes clever use of data in multiple markets is that of Rao and Miller (1975). The main idea behind their approach is that many national advertising campaigns provide a quasi-experimental set of conditions due to natural market-to-market variations in exposure rates and other characteristics. The idea is to derive an advertising-response coefficient from each of a number of sales districts and then to combine those coefficients in a way that produces a general sales-response function.

The authors assume that advertising has an immediate and a lagged effect and that the lagged effect decays exponentially. Although they show how to handle price offers and other trade promotions, we concentrate here only on the aspects of the model that relate to advertising. Their individual-market model is

$$S_t = c_0 + c_1 A_t + c_1 \lambda A_{t-1} + c_1 \lambda^2 A_{t-2} + \cdots + \mu_t \qquad (14.11)$$

where $\qquad S_t$ = market share at t

A_t = advertising spending at t

c_0, c_1, λ = constants $(\lambda < 1)$

μ_t = random disturbance

This equation means that an incremental expenditure of one unit of advertising in a given period will yield c_1 share points that period, $c_1 \lambda$ in the following period, $c_1 \lambda^2$ the period after that, and so on.

As in Chapter 4, the distributed lag form in eq. (14.11) can be simplified by multiplying λ times S_{t-1},

$$\lambda S_{t-1} = \lambda c_0 + \lambda c_1 A_{t-1} + \lambda^2 c_1 A_{t-2} + \cdots + \lambda \mu_{t-1} \qquad (14.12)$$

and subtracting eq. (14.12) from eq. (14.11):

$$S_t = c_0(1 - \lambda) + \lambda S_{t-1} + c_1 A_t + \mu_t - \lambda \mu_{t-1} \qquad (14.13)$$

Note that the short-run effect of advertising here is

$$\frac{dS_t}{dA_t} = c_1 \qquad \text{(short-run effect)} \qquad (14.14)$$

while the long-run effect is c_1 in the first period, then λc_1, $\lambda^2 c_1 + \cdots$ in subsequent periods, or

$$c_1 + \lambda c_1 + \lambda^2 c_1 + \cdots = \frac{c_1}{1 - \lambda} \qquad \text{(long-run effect)} \qquad (14.15)$$

Now if

I = industry sales per year in district

P = district population

AV = average rate of advertising during period

then with six periods per year (as with Nielsen data), by eq. (14.15), a \$1000 increase in advertising produces a share increase of $c_1/(1 - \lambda)$. Thus the sales increase of an additional \$1000 in advertising is

$$y_i = \Delta \text{sales}_i = \left(\frac{c_1}{1 - \lambda} \right) \frac{I}{6} \qquad \text{(in market } i\text{)} \qquad (14.16)$$

at a per capita advertising rate of $AV_i/P = x_i$. In other words, eq. (14.16) can be interpreted as the derivative of a general response curve at the per capita spending rate AV/P.

This procedure gives a set of values (y_i, x_i) for each market i, where the

$\{y_i\}$ are the derivatives of a more general response function $g(x)$, so $y = dg/dx$. Assuming that $g(x)$ is S-shaped, the authors propose using a polynomial in x to approximate it; specifically, they assume that $g(x)$ can be modeled as a cubic function in x, while $y(x)$ is a quadratic function in x:

$$y = k_1 + k_2 x - k_3 x^2 + k_4 z \tag{14.17}$$

where $\qquad z =$ percent share of premium brands (an empirical adjustment factor that accounted for variability in marginal response)

$\qquad k_1, \ldots, k_4 =$ parameters to be estimated

Given a set of $\{y_i\}$ and $\{x_i\}$ (as well as $\{z_i\}$), the coefficients in eq. (14.17) can be estimated with the approaches described in Chapter 5. The total advertising-response function can be obtained simply by integrating eq. (14.17). Note that after integration we obtain

$$g(x) = k_0 + k_1 x + \frac{k_2}{2} x^2 - \frac{k_3}{3} x^3 + k_4 z \tag{14.18}$$

with k_0 unspecified. The authors assume $k_0 = 0$ (zero advertising equals zero sales), but this model can clearly accommodate a nonzero sales level at zero advertising, in line with Little's second phenomena. Then eq. (14.18) can be used in eq. (14.2) to allocate an advertising budget over districts and over time.

The basic procedure is illustrated with applications to five brands. The average value of the coefficients of determination (R^2) for the within-market models, eq. (14.13), was 0.69; and the average R^2 for the response curves, eq. (14.17), was 0.60. Thus the fits appear adequate. Exhibit 14.12(a) graphs the relationship between marginal sales due to advertising and average expenditure levels for one of the five brands reported (brand B), while Exhibit 14.12(b) reproduces the associated advertising-response function. The authors show how this model can be used to evaluate alternative advertising policies, making a case for pulsing in most circumstances.

The method appears to have been widely applied, incorporating dealing and price effects as well (Rao, 1978, 1979). Some products show S-shaped responses, while others show concave responses. On the other hand, this modeling approach, like most other econometric models, has a variety of weaknesses. Of Little's desirable phenomena, only the second, a possible S-shaped response, is included. However, the model could be extended to include competitive effects (phenomenon three), and copy/media effectiveness could be included as an effectiveness factor in the x's. However, eq. (14.13) does not readily admit differing rise and decay times. And as with all econometric-based models, the data quality and its variability determine the acceptability of the model fit.

In conclusion, this approach is both interesting and useful. It uses

EXHIBIT 14-12   Rao and Miller's econometric model for advertising decisions. (Source: Rao and Miller, 1975, p. 13.)

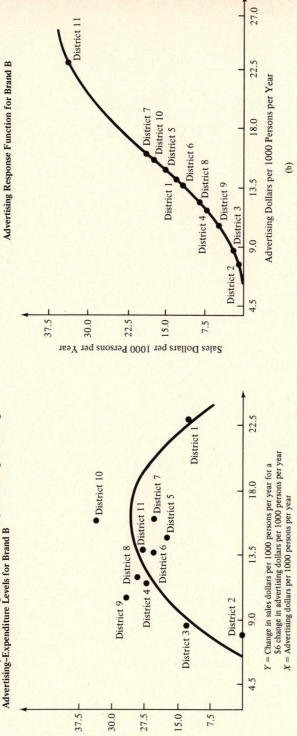

Relationship between Marginal Sales Created by Advertising and Average Advertising–Expenditure Levels for Brand B

Advertising Response Function for Brand B

Y = Change in sales dollars per 1000 persons per year for a
$6 change in advertising dollars per 1000 persons per year
X = Advertising dollars per 1000 persons per year

econometric methods to estimate local conditions of a (postulated) global response curve. Furthermore, it blends well with the type of data typically collected for frequently purchased packaged goods. Although it has theoretical problems and reports of its use are incomplete, it appears to have considerable applicability.

Assessment and Other Approaches.   A priori models of interest include those of Sasieni (1971) and Schmalensee (1972), who introduce general functions and derive the characteristics of optimal policies. As such, they specify little about the mechanism of advertising. Little (1979b) reviews other models of this type, finding that most lack flexibility in rise and decay rates and have inflexible, concave steady-state responses. In general, most of these latter developments are embellishments of the Vidale-Wolfe model.

In the *econometric* area the amount of work is large. Clarke (1976) reviews over 70 studies, restricting himself to those amenable to inferences about the cumulative effects of advertising. Lambin (1976) alone reports analyses of 107 brands. Aaker and Carman (1982) review studies involving 176 brands. However, these studies rely on existing historical data and therefore generally suffer from the lack of large changes in advertising required to draw clear inferences. Most of the econometric models are either linear or log-linear and often lag some of the variables. Furthermore, simultaneous-equation studies are common, and explanatory variables are added as available, covering other marketing activities, economic indicators, and dummy variables for special circumstances. In general, these models lack flexibility in the shape of the response curve, not allowing for different rise and decay rates. In addition, they have difficulty handling many of the other desirable characteristics.

According to Little (1979b), these standard econometric forms are not so much models for advertising as convenient functional forms for fitting the advertising response in the neighborhood of historical operation. As such, they are useful locally and may be combined with other sources of information to fit responses over a wider region. They are also useful for theory building and generalization; for example, Clarke (1976) makes a case for the short-term effect of advertising being of the order of a couple of weeks.

Mixed-mode models, which draw on theoretical response structures and attempt to calibrate them with specific historical data bases, are providing important contributions. But most of the more elaborate models are nonlinear in some of the parameters and present calibration problems. Kuehn, McGuire, and Weiss (1966) present a BRANDAID-type model (Chapter 18) form with price embedded in the structure; they derive a response function that is S-shaped. Horsky (1977) builds a discrete-time Lanchester model for cigarette data, which is driven by exponentially weighted past advertising and requires nonlinear estimation. Parsons (1975) adds time-varying advertising effectiveness to a model of advertising response for a household cleanser and finds that advertising effectiveness changes over the product life cycle. This model also requires nonlinear estimation, as does an approach by Turner and Wiginton (1976), in which the Vidale-Wolfe model is calibrated on aggregate industry sales and advertising for filter cigarettes. Simon (1982) adds the phenomenon of advertising wearout and derives an optimal advertising policy that calls for pulsing.

Finally, because of this lack of understanding about the effectiveness of advertising response, *industry-norm* models are gaining acceptance. The basic premise is that, on average, market factors will drive competitors to advertise at efficient levels and that careful study of those norms can be used to guide budget-setting practice. Lilien (1979) and Farris and Buzzell (1979) provide examples of this model-based approach, which is particularly appropriate for industrial markets.

In conclusion, then, advertising is rich with phenomena, many of which occur regularly in reported empirical studies. But more needs to be known about the dynamics of the effects and their estimation. Although there are apparently a large number of models, most are variations on a theme. The discrete-time Lanchester model or the BRANDAID model provide generalizations of most of the existing models.

Advances in measurement, particularly from the point-of-sale equipment in retail stores, promise to refine our understanding of advertising phenomena, leading to further refinements of advertising models. However, at the moment we appear to be faced with a priori models, which are more conceptually sound but see little use, and econometric models, which fail to represent advertising effects adequately (except possibly over a limited range) yet see wide use. More integration of data from different sources, perhaps combining judgmental and empirical estimation procedures, and creative use of existing data (as with Rao and Miller) offer important opportunities for integration and model improvements.

Message and Copy Decisions

Much of the effect of an advertising exposure depends on the creative quality of the ad itself. But rating the quality of the ad is extremely difficult, and much controversy surrounds the area of copy testing. An advertisement may have very good aesthetic properties and win awards, and yet it may not do much for sales. Another advertisement may seem crude and offensive, and yet it may be a major force behind sales. Such properties in advertisements as humor, believability, informativeness, simplicity, and memorability have not shown consistent relationships with sales generation. In this section we discuss three issues: copy testing and the measurement of copy effectiveness, the rating of the creative quality of ads, and the proper number of ads to screen.

Copy Testing and Measures of Copy Effectiveness

Copy strategy is based on advertising objectives. For a new brand, copy is oriented toward building broad awareness and inducing trial, while for established brands it focuses on reminding individuals to use the brand, increasing the rate of use, and distinguishing the brand from other brands. According to Aaker and Myers (1975), in the choice of an ad message consideration should be given to the credibility, the attractiveness, and the power of the source. Then the creative process involves finding the facts and ideas that match a brand's message with its copy objectives.

The basis of copy testing is to determine if an ad is likely to work. There are two elements involved in copy testing: the dependent-variable measure and the measurement setting. The possible measures of response include the following:

1. *attention and impression*, the ability of the ad to attract attention and be memorable
2. *communication/understanding*, the ability of the ad to convey the message clearly and unambiguously to the target market
3. *persuasion*, the ability of the ad to modify attitudes and beliefs about the product on certain key attributes or to change overall purchase intentions
4. *purchase*, the ability of the ad to generate a positive impact on purchasing behavior

The latter two measures, while most appropriate, are the most difficult to measure, and, in fact, most copy tests are concerned with the first two constructs.

Copy tests can also be classified by whether they use a laboratory setting, a simulated natural environment, or a totally natural environment (i.e., market tests). Laboratory and simulated-natural-environment methods include focus-group interviews as well as a variety of physiological recording devices, including eye cameras (measuring eye movement), polygraphs and related devices (measuring emotional/psychological responses), pupilometers (measuring pupil dilation, which occurs when something interesting is seen), and the like.

In simulated natural environments subjects are usually brought to a theater, and measures of interest, liking, and often likelihood of purchase before and after exposure are obtained from them. Some procedures provide on-line measurements during exposure. For example, ASI (Audience Studies, Inc.) measures galvanic skin resistance; Schwerin shows ads in a program environment and measures changes in liking arising from the ad.

Market tests are provided by a number of companies. Usually, the campaign is limited to a small region, and various measures of recall and preference are asked of those exposed/not exposed to the ad. Burke, Inc., and BBDO, Inc., provide such services. Ad-Tel uses split-cable techniques and personal interviews, plus a mail panel, to measure the effects of ads.

These methods provide some measures that may (or may not) be related to product sales. In an interesting cross-cultural comparison of attitudes toward copy testing, Boyd and Ray (1971) found that emphasis is placed on predictive validity, explanatory power, and reliability and that sales should not be used as a criterion because of measurement problems.

Recent reports on the techniques, design, value, and limitations of copy-testing procedures include the work of Young (1972), Dunn and Ziff (1974), Roshwalb (1975), Silk (1977), Bloom, Jay, and Twyman (1977), Ostlund, Clancy, and Sapra (1980), and Hodock (1980).

Estimating the Creative Quality of Ads

Several studies have attempted to relate desirable characteristics of ads to quantifiable mechanical and message elements. Most of these studies have focused on readership or recall scores for print ads, the easiest types of ads and response variables to measure. An interesting early study of this type, performed by Twedt (1952), regressed readership scores of 151 advertisements in *The American Builder* against a large number of variables and found that the parameters of size of the advertisement, size of illustration, and number of colors accounts for over 50 percent of the variance in advertising readership. Interestingly, these mechanical variables explained advertising-readership variation better than many of the content variables that were also tried out in the regression.

A well-known regression study of the effect of advertising-format variables on readership scores was performed by Diamond (1968). His data were 1070 advertisements that appeared in *Life* between February 7 and July 31, 1964. For each advertisement he had 6 different Starch readership scores: men-readers noted, seen-associated and read most and women-readers noted, seen-associated and read most. In addition to these 6 Starch scores, he measured 12 variables related to each ad: product class, past advertising expenditure, number of ads in issue, size, number of colors, bleed/no bleed, left or right page, position in magazine, layout, number of words, brand prominence, and headline prominence. Each of the readership models was of the form

$$R_n = h + \sum_i a_i x_i + \sum_j \sum_k d_{jk} y_{jk} \tag{14.19}$$

where R_n = one of set of 6 readership measures (percent)
       h = constant term
      x_i = level of ith continuous variable

a_i = contribution of ith continuous variable

d_{jk} = level of jth discrete variable, where k is either 0 or 1, representing the two possible levels

y_{jk} = contribution of kth state of jth discrete variable

Diamond fitted several regression models and used the coefficients to draw conclusions about the effect of different variables on readership score. For example, he found that the Starch score was higher the larger the advertisement, the greater the number of colors, and the fewer the number of advertisements in the issue; he found that right-hand-page advertisements gained more attention than left-hand-page advertisements; and that advertisements with photographs did better than advertisements with illustrations, and both did better than nonpictorial advertisements. To validate these conclusions, Diamond used his model to predict scores for 43 advertisements in the February 26, 1965, issue of *Life*; his equations had coefficients of determination for prediction as high as 0.74. With this degree of success, he then placed the model on an on-line, time-sharing computer system for planning and testing alternative advertising formats. Such a system provides norms for existing ads as well as diagnostics for improving ads.

In a study of the effectiveness of industrial print ads, Hanssens and Weitz (1980) related 24 ad characteristics to recall, readership, and inquiry generation for 1160 industrial ads in *Electronic Design*. They used a model of the form

$$y_i = e^a \prod_{j=1}^{p_1} x_{ij}^{b_i} \prod_{j=p_1+1}^{p} (1 + x_{ij}')^{b_i} e^{\mu_i} \qquad (14.20)$$

where y_i = effectiveness measure for ith ad

x_{ij} = value of jth nonbinary characteristic of ith ad (page number, ad size)

x_{ij}' = value (0 or 1) of jth binary characteristic of ith ad (bleed, color, etc.)

e^a = scale factor

μ_i = error term

They segmented 15 product groups into three categories—routine purchase items, unique purchase items, and important purchase items—by factor analysis of purchasing-process similarity ratings obtained from readers of the magazine. Their results are similar to those of Twedt (1952) and Diamond (1968): advertising characteristics were found to account for more than 45 percent of the variance in the *seen* effectiveness measure, more than 30 percent of the *read-most* effectiveness measure, and between 19 and 36 percent of the variance in *inquiry generation*. Thus the variance explained by the seen measure is significantly greater than that explained by the read-most measure, which, in turn, is greater than that explained by the inquiry measure. These results are consistent across the three product categories. They are also in line with a hierarchy-of-effects model, which postulates that communication variables typically have a greater effect on lower-order responses (awareness) than on higher-order responses (behavior).

Both recall and readership were found to be strongly related to format and layout variables (ad size, colors, bleed, use of photographs/illustrations, etc.), while the effects were weaker for inquiry generation. The effects of some factors, such as ad size, were consistently related across product groups and effectiveness measures, while others, such as the use of attention-getting methods (woman in ad, size of headline, etc.), were specific to the product category and the effectiveness measure.

Interestingly, while there have been a number of speculations in the literature (Ramond, 1976), there have been no major reported studies, comparable to those of either Diamond or Hanssens and Weitz, for broadcast ads.

How Many Advertisements Should Be Created and Pretested?

When an advertising agency undertakes an advertisement for a client, the agency generally does not stop with the first idea it develops. The first creative idea may be the best, but typically it is not. Often, the client wants the agency to create and test a few alternative ideas before making a selection. The more advertisements that the agency creates and pretests, the higher is the probability that it will find a really first-rate one. But the more time it spends trying to create alternative advertisements, the higher its costs are. Therefore there must be some optimal number of alternative advertisements that an agency should try to create and test for the client.

If the agency were reimbursed by the client for the cost of creating and pretesting more advertisements, then the agency might create the optimal number of advertisements for pretesting. Under the normal commission system, in which the agency's income is mainly a 15 percent commission on media billings, the agency does not have an incentive to go through the expense of creating and pretesting many alternative advertisements. This question has been studied in an ingenious way by Gross (1972), who concluded that agencies generally create too few advertisements for pretesting. This result means that the advertiser does not typically get the best ad for his money but only the best (it is hoped) of the few that have been created. Here we examine his reasoning.

Gross developed three models for (1) the creation of alternative advertisements, (2) the screening of advertisements, and (3) the determination of the optimal expenditures. In the first model he visualizes each of n creative men given the same data on a product and asked to create an advertisement independently. He assumes that each resulting advertisement has a certain level of effectiveness that must be measured by a pretest measure and that the individual effectivenesses of the n advertisements are normally distributed. An advertisement at the center of the distribution has an average effectiveness, and the other advertisements are better or worse than this one. Let E stand for the relative effectiveness of an advertisement—that is, its effectiveness relative to an average advertisement—which can be defined as the discounted present value of the increment in net profits over the profits from an average advertisement that would accrue with that advertisement. Therefore the distribution of the relative effectiveness of all possible advertisements has a mean relative effectiveness of zero—that is, $\mu_E = 0$—and a standard deviation of relative effectiveness of σ_E, as shown in Exhibit 14.13.

Thus creating n different advertisements independently is like making n independent draws from the relative-effectiveness distribution. Presumably, the greater the number of advertisements generated, the better the best one will be. At the same time it is assumed that the average cost of creating an advertisement is c. Therefore the cost of creating n independent advertisements is

$$C_{cn} = cn \qquad (14.21)$$

where C_{cn} = cost of creating n advertisements at average cost of c
        c = average cost of creating advertisements
        n = number of advertisements created

The second model deals with the pretesting of the n advertisements to determine the best one. There are many different ways to pretest advertisements, and each may differ in its reliability and its validity. The observed

EXHIBIT 14-13   **Probability distribution of the relative effectiveness E of advertisements generated independently.**

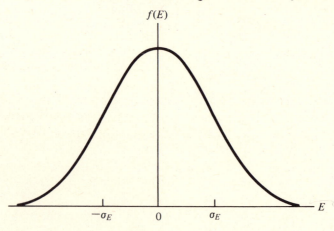

pretest score of advertisement j on the ith replication of the pretest is given by

$$O_{ij} = \mu_o + T_{ij} + t_{ij} \qquad j = 1, 2, \ldots, n; \qquad i = 1, 2, \ldots, r \qquad (14.22)$$

where O_{ij} = observed score of advertisement j on ith replication of pretest

μ_o = mean pretest score for all advertisements generated by independent process

T_{ij} = true deviation of jth advertisement's score from mean of all scores

t_{ij} = deviation from true score of advertisement j introduced by random error in ith replication of testing procedure

Thus the observed score of advertisement j of the ith replication of the pretest is equal to the sum of the mean score of all advertisements, the true deviation of this advertisement's quality from the average quality, and the error occurring on this replication. Replication error arises from differences between samples and the administration of the sampling procedure. It is assumed that this error is normally distributed with a mean of zero and a variance of σ_t^2.

The range of variation in the quality of advertisements can also be assumed to be normally distributed with a mean of zero and a variance of σ_T^2. If a number of advertising alternatives were independently generated and tested just once each with the pretest, the observed variance σ_o^2 would be

$$\sigma_o^2 = \sigma_T^2 + \sigma_t^2 \qquad (14.23)$$

The relationship in eq. (14.23) enables us to use the following measure of reliability for a particular pretest:

$$R = \left(1 - \frac{\sigma_t^2}{\sigma_o^2}\right)^{1/2} \qquad (14.24)$$

This measure produces a number between zero and one. When there is no measurement variance—that is, $\sigma_t^2 = 0$—the reliability of the pretest is one, as it should be. When there is a considerable measurement variance in relation to true quality variance—that is, $\sigma_t^2 \rightarrow \sigma_o^2$—the reliability of the pretest approaches zero. This formula for reliability is quite operational, because σ_t^2 may be estimated empirically by testing the same advertisement several times and σ_o^2 may be estimated by observing the scores achieved by a number of alternative advertisements.

Gross defines the validity of the particular pretesting procedure to be the correlation ρ between the advertisement's true pretest score and its relative profit effectiveness. A correlation of ± 1 means that the pretest measure correlates perfectly with the advertisement's relative effectiveness, and a correlation of 0 means that the pretest measure is really of no use in identifying the better advertisements.

With these definitions of the reliability and validity of a particular pretesting procedure, Gross shows that the expected relative profitability of the advertisement that achieves the highest pretest score is

$$E_n = e_n \sigma_E \rho R \tag{14.25}$$

where E_n = expected relative profitability of advertisement that achieves highest score on pretest when sample size is n

e_n = expected value of advertisement having greatest relative effectiveness in sample of size n from standardized normal distribution of relative effectiveness (values for different sample sizes are shown in Exhibit 14.14)

σ_E = standard deviation of relative-effectiveness distribution

ρ = validity of particular pretesting procedure, that is, correlation between true score on pretest and relativeness of advertisement

R = reliability of particular pretesting procedure, as defined earlier

According to eq. (14.25) the expected relative profitability of the best-scoring advertisement on the pretest is higher: (1) the higher the expected value of the advertisement (which is a function of the number of advertisements independently drawn), (2) the higher the standard deviation in the quality of the possible advertisements, and (3) the higher the validity and reliability of the particular pretesting procedure. If the validity and reliability of the pretest were perfect, then the relative profitability of the advertisement would depend only on the number of advertisements drawn and the dispersion of advertising quality.

EXHIBIT 14-14   **Expected value of largest observation of a sample of size _n_.**

n	e_n	n	e_n
1	0.564	7	1.423
2	0.846	8	1.485
3	1.029	9	1.538
4	1.163	10	1.586
5	1.267	11	1.629
6	1.352	12	1.668

SOURCE: Donald B. Owen, _Handbook of Statistical Tables,_ © 1962. U.S. Department of Energy, p. 152. Published by Addison-Wesley Publishing Company, Inc., Reading, Mass. Reprinted with permission of the publisher.

Each pretesting procedure will have its particular cost, which can be assumed to have the form

$$C_{sn} = C_F + c_s n \qquad n \geq 2 \tag{14.26}$$

where C_{sn} = cost of screening n advertising alternatives over and above cost of screening one advertisement
C_F = fixed costs of setting up for screening
c_s = marginal screening cost per alternative
n = number of alternatives to be screened

Gross is now able to bring together the two descriptive models into a decision model for determining the number of advertising alternatives to create and screen. The decision model must compare the increases in expected value and in costs from creating and testing more advertisements. At the point at which the incremental expected return is no longer sufficient to cover the incremental cost, the optimal point is reached. Analytically, we find that

$$P_1 = 0 \tag{14.27}$$
$$P_n = E_n - C_{c(n-1)} - C_{sn} \qquad n \geq 2 \tag{14.28}$$

where P_n = expected contribution to profits of generating and screening n advertising alternatives instead of just generating one
E_n = expected relative profitability of advertising alternative achieving highest score, exclusive of costs of testing and costs of creating all but first advertisement
$C_{c(n-1)}$ = cost of generating alternatives except first
C_{sn} = cost of screening n alternatives

Using difference relationships, Gross is able to show that the optimal n^* is the smallest value of n for which the following relationship is satisfied:

$$\Delta e_n < \frac{c + c_s}{\sigma_E \rho R} \tag{14.29}$$

where Δe_n = increment of expected value of advertisement having greatest relative effectiveness in sample of size n from standardized normal distribution of relative effectiveness
c = average cost of creating advertisement
c_s = average cost of screening advertisement
σ_E = standard deviation of relative-effectiveness distribution
ρ = validity of pretest
R = reliability of pretest

The result in eq. (14.29) can be shown as follows. By substituting eqs. (14.25) and (14.26) into eq. (14.28), we get

$$P_n = e_n \sigma_E \rho R - C_{c(n-1)} - C_F - C_{sn} \tag{14.30}$$

Similarly, the expected profits from generating $n - 1$ ads is

$$P_{n-1} = e_{n-1} \sigma_E \rho R - C_{c(n-2)} - C_F - C_{s(n-1)} \tag{14.31}$$

Then the expected contribution to profits of generating n versus $n - 1$ ads is

$$P_n - P_{n-1} = \Delta e_n \sigma_E \rho R - c - c_s \tag{14.32}$$

where c is the average cost of creating an ad.

The optimal value of n (n^*) occurs when the expected contribution to profits of creating one more ad becomes negative:

$$0 > \Delta e_n \sigma_E \rho R - c - c_s \tag{14.33}$$

which simplifies to eq. (14.29).

The implications of eq. (14.29) for the size of the advertising budget for creating and screening advertisements are illustrated with an example described by Gross. He chose conservative values for eq. (14.29) to derive a conservative estimate, making the following assumptions:

1. Suppose the cost of creating and screening one advertisement is about 5 percent of the media budget D; that is,

    $$c + c_s = 0.05D$$

2. An outstanding advertisement is one that is at the 2σ level in probability and in the long-run returns a profit equal to the media expenditure (whereas an average advertisement only recovers the media expenditure). This assumption means that

    $$2\sigma_E = D \qquad \text{or} \qquad \sigma_E = 0.5D$$

3. The correlation between the true pretest score and the true profitability—that is, the pretest's validity—is

    $$\rho = 0.63$$

    In other words, the pretest can account for 40 percent (ρ^2) of the variance in relative profitability.

4. The reliability of the pretest is

    $$R = 0.71$$

    In other words, $\sigma_t^2 / \sigma_o^2 = 0.5$, which means that at least 50 percent of the observed variance in scores on alternative advertisements is due to measurement error.

Placing the above estimates in eq. (14.29), we find

$$\frac{c + c_s}{\sigma_E \rho R} = \frac{0.05D}{(0.5D)(0.63)(0.71)} = 0.224 \tag{14.34}$$

The value of 0.224 for Δe_n, using Exhibit 14.14, indicates an optimal n^* of 3; that is, the increment Δe_2 in that table is $0.846 - 0.564 = 0.232$, and the increment Δe_3 is $1.029 - 0.846 = 0.183$. Thus under these conservative assumptions, the advertising agency should create and pretest at least three advertisements.

The optimal creative expenditure d^* as a proportion of the media expenditure is given by

$$d^* = \frac{n^*(c + c_s)}{D} \tag{14.35}$$

For the previous example this value is

$$d^* = \frac{3(0.05D)}{D} = 0.15 \tag{14.36}$$

Therefore under these conservative estimates of the variables, the optimal expenditure turns out to be 15 percent of the media budget.

Although these specific results have been challenged [see Longman (1967) for example],* Gross' basic result yields important implications for pretesting procedures. He found that the value of pretesting depended more on the validity of the pretest than on its reliability. Furthermore, he found that the higher the validity of the pretest, the greater was the justification for a large sample size to increase reliability.

Media Selection and Scheduling

There are two major areas in which advertising agencies specialize: one is the creative decision, reviewed previously, and the other is the media decision. Media selection is the problem of finding the best way to deliver the desired number of exposures to the target audience and to schedule the delivery of those exposures over the planning period.

The concept of "desired number of exposures" needs elaboration. Presumably, the advertiser is seeking a response to its advertising from the target audience. Assume that the desired response is a certain level of product trial, which depends, among other things, on the level of audience

---

*In an unpublished communication Gross reports that a leading New York ad agency offered a "lifetime supply of martinis" to the analyst who could refute these results. His analyses obviously struck a nerve.

brand awareness. Suppose the rate of product trial increases at a diminishing rate with the level of audience awareness, as shown in Exhibit 14.15(a).
Then if the advertiser wants to achieve a product trial rate of (say) T^*, it must
achieve a brand-awareness rate of A^*, and the task is to find out how many
exposures E^* are needed to produce this awareness.

The effect of exposures on audience awareness depends on the
exposures' reach, frequency, and impact. These factors are defined as
follows:

> *reach (R)*, the number of different persons or households exposed to a
> particular media schedule at least once during a specified time
> period
>
> *frequency (F)*, the number of times within the specified time period that
> an average person or household is exposed to the message
>
> *impact (I)*, the qualitative value of an exposure through a given medium
> (thus a food ad would have a higher impact in *Good Housekeeping* than
> it would have in *Popular Mechanics*)

Exhibit 14.15(b) shows the relationship between audience awareness
and reach. Audience awareness is greater the higher the exposures' reach,
frequency, and impact. Furthermore, there are important trade-offs among
reach, frequency, and impact. For example, suppose the media planner has
an advertising budget of $1 million and the cost per thousand exposures of
average quality is $5. Then he can buy 200 million exposures (equal to

EXHIBIT 14-15   Relationship among trial, awareness, and the exposure function.

Relationship Between Product Trial Rate and Audience–
Awareness Level

Relationship Between Audience–Awareness Level
and Exposure Reach and Frequency

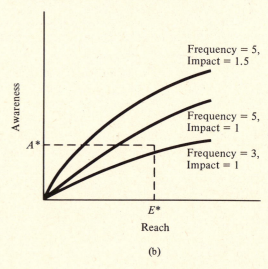

(a)

(b)

$1,000,000 × 1000/$5). If he seeks an average exposure frequency of 10, then he can reach 20 million people (equal to 200,000,000 ÷ 10) with the given budget. But if he wants higher-quality media, costing $10 per thousand exposures, he can reach only 10 million people, unless he is willing to lower the desired exposure frequency.

The relationship among reach, frequency, and impact is captured in the following concepts:

Total number of exposures (E) is the reach times the average frequency, that is, $E = R \cdot F$. It is also called the gross rating points (GRP). If a given media schedule reaches 80 percent of the homes with an average exposure frequency of 3, the media schedule is said to have a GRP of 240 (equal to 80 · 3). If another media schedule has a GRP of 300, it can be said to have more weight, but we cannot tell how this weight breaks up into reach and frequency.

Weighted number of exposures (WE) is the reach times the average frequency times the average impact, that is,

$$WE = R \cdot F \cdot I \tag{14.37}$$

The media-planning problem can now be viewed as follows. With a given budget, what is the most cost-effective combination of reach, frequency, and impact to buy?

In practice, many media planners often review each major media type for its capacity to deliver particular objectives. The major media types and their percentages of allocated advertising expenditures in 1976 were newspapers (30 percent), television (20 percent), direct mail (14 percent), radio (7 percent), magazines (5 percent), outdoor (1 percent), and miscellaneous (23 percent). These major media types vary in their reach, frequency, and impact values. For example, television delivers much more reach than magazines, outdoor delivers much more frequency than magazines, and magazines deliver more impact than newspapers.

In choosing a combination of media types, the media planner considers (1) target-audience media habits, (2) the characteristics of the product, (3) the message, and (4) the relative cost. On the basis of media impacts and costs, the media planner chooses specific media within each media type (women's magazines, daytime TV, daily newspapers in 20 major markets) that delivers the desired response in the most *cost-effective* way. He then makes a final judgment on which specific vehicles will deliver the best communication of reach, frequency, and impact for the money.

A number of agencies (and firms) use mathematical models to aid in making media plans. In more quantitative terms the media-decision problem can be stated as follows:

Given a media budget, an advertising message and copy, a set of media alternatives, and data describing the audiences and costs of the media alternatives, decide on (1) the media alternatives to use, (2) the number of insertions in each and their timing, and (3) the size and color of the media options in each case, in such a way that these decisions maximize the effect (measured in some way) of the media budget.

The output of the media-decision process is called the *media schedule.*

The Choice of an Objective Function

The most desirable measure of the effect of alternative media schedules is the impact on company profits. Because the media budget is assumed to be fixed, the profit-maximizing schedule is the same as the sales-maximizing schedule. However, most media models do not presume a knowledge of the current or long-run sales that will be generated by advertisements placed in different media. (MEDIAC, reviewed below, is an exception.) Various communication surrogates are commonly used to measure the effectiveness of advertising when sales would be difficult or impossible to measure. In media models the surrogate that is used most often is the number of exposures to relevant members in the target audience—that is, the weighted number of exposures, defined above.

To determine the total weighted-exposure value of a media schedule, we must know two things: (1) the net cumulative audience of each media vehicle as a function of the number of exposures and (2) the level of audience duplication across all pairs of vehicles. In the case of two media alternatives we would typically have an equation for net coverage as follows:

$$E = r_1(X_1) + r_2(X_2) - r_{12}(X_{12}) \qquad (14.38)$$

where
$$E = \text{reach of media schedule (i.e., total weighted-exposure value with replication and duplication removed)}$$
$$r_i(X_i) = \text{number of persons in audience of media } i$$
$$r_{12}(X_{12}) = \text{number of persons in audience of both media vehicles}$$

[The $r_i(X_i)$ are typically concave; an old study of the *Saturday Evening Post* showed only 55 percent more families are reached with 13 issues than with 1 issue.] With three media alternatives their reach would be

$$E = r_1(X_1) + r_2(X_2) + r_3(X_3) - r_{12}(X_{12})$$
$$- r_{13}(X_{13}) - r_{23}(X_{23}) + r_{123}(X_{123}) \quad (14.39)$$

In this case net coverage is found by summing the separate reaches of the three vehicles with the triplicated group and subtracting all the duplicated audiences. This equation can be generalized to the case of n media alternatives.

Obtaining data on the size of audience overlap for different sets of media vehicles requires large and expensive samples. Agostini (1961) has developed a useful estimation formula based on data from a French study of media-audience overlap, showing that total reach for magazine insertions may be estimated by

$$C = \left[\frac{1}{K(D/A) + 1}\right] A \qquad (14.40)$$

where C = total reach

K = constant, estimated as 1.125

$A = \Sigma_{j=1}^{n} r_j(X_j)$ = total number of persons in audiences of media 1, 2, . . ., n

$D = \Sigma_{j=1}^{n}\Sigma_{k=j+1}^{n} r_{jk}(X_{jk})$ = total of all pairwise duplicated audiences (if D_{ab} is number of people simultaneously covered by a and b, then $D = D_{ab} + D_{ac} + \cdots + D_{an} + D_{bc} + \cdots + D_{bn} \ldots$)

This relationship with parameter K = 1.125 has been shown to be a useful approximation for American and Canadian magazines as well (Bower, 1963). [See Claycamp and McClelland (1968) for an analytical interpretation of the formula. For an alternate approach, see Metheringham (1964).]

Because either the GRPs or the weighted number of exposures (WE) is normally available for any campaign, eq. (14.40) can be used in eq. (14.37) to estimate the *implied* frequency of a schedule. Media-scheduling models have the option of working with a sales objective function, an effective-exposure value, or with reach and frequency separately. The more appropriate sales and effective-exposure measures are also more difficult to operationalize, calling for model-analytic trade-offs. We treat some of these trade-offs below.

Modeling Approaches

There are generally three components in models for media decisions: (1) the *objective function,* which assigns a value (profit/effective exposures, etc.) to an insertion schedule, (2) the *solution strategy* (heuristic, optimization, etc.), and (3) the *constraints* (budget, other).

According to Aaker and Myers (1975), there are generally five principle components of the objective function:

1. the vehicle exposure measure—used to measure the net reach, schedule exposure, or GRPs
2. repetition effect—What is the relative impact of successive exposures on the same person? (The material reviewed earlier suggests this function should be S-shaped.)
3. the forgetting effect—What forgetting occurs between exposures and what is the nature of the decay?
4. the media-option source effect—What is the relative impact exposure from a given source?
5. the segmentation effect—Who is exposed and what is the fraction of the audience that represents target segments?

Media models can usefully be classified by their solution approach: optimizing models and nonoptimizing approaches. Under the optimizing-model category are several classes of mathematical-programming models, and within the area of nonoptimizing approaches there are heuristic-programming, stepwise or marginal-analysis procedures, and simulation models.

Optimization Methods   Much of the work on media models in the early and middle 1960s focused on linear-programming approaches. The main constraints in the programs were the size of the advertising budget, the minimum and maximum uses of specific media vehicles and media categories, and the desirable, minimum exposure rates to different target buyers. Then the choice of a best plan requires the specification of an effectiveness criterion, which, in media selection, most frequently is the weighted number of exposures.

Exhibit 14.16 shows a linear-programming statement of the media-selection problem, both in abstract form and in terms of an example. The problem is to find the combination of media that maximizes the weighted number of exposures, subject to the constraints. In the sample problem the

EXHIBIT 14-16   Formulation of a linear-programming model for a media-selection problem.

Model[a]		A Sample Problem
Maximize $E = e_1X_1 + e_2X_2 + \cdots + e_nX_n$	effectiveness function	$E =$ $3100X_1 + 2000X_2 + \cdots + 2400X_n$
subject to $c_1X_1 + c_2X_2 + \cdots + c_nX_n$ $\leq B$	budget constraint	$15{,}000X_1 + 4000X_2 + \cdots + 5000X_n$ $\leq 500{,}000$
$c_1X_1 + c_2X_2 + \cdots + c_nX_n$ $\geq B_1$	media-class-use constraint	$15{,}000X_1 + 4000X_2 + \cdots + 5000X_n$ $\geq 250{,}000$
$X_1 \geq k_{1L}$ $X_1 \leq k_{1U}$ $X_2 \geq k_{2L}$ $X_2 \leq k_{2U}$ . . . $X_n \geq k_{nL}$ $X_n \leq k_{nU}$	individual medium-use constraints	$X_1 \geq 0$ $X_1 \leq 52$ $X_2 \geq 1$ $X_2 \leq 8$ . . . $X_n \geq 6$ $X_n \leq 12$

[a] E = total exposure value (weighted number of exposures); e_1 = exposure value of one ad in medium i; X_1 = number of ads placed in medium i; c_1 = cost of one ad in medium i; B = total advertising budget; B_1 = part of advertising budget; k_{iL} = minimum number of units to purchase of medium i; k_{iU} = maximum number of units to purchase of medium i.

total advertising budget is $500,000, of which at least $250,000 must be spent on media class 1 (say magazines). Media vehicle 1 gives 3100 (in thousands) effective exposures with each use and costs $15,000. It is possible to place up to 52 advertisements in this media over a year's time. The other values are similarly interpreted. Given these concrete values, the linear-programming problem can be solved for the best media mix.

Linear-programming applications to media-scheduling problems include the works of Miller and Starr (1960), Day (1963), Learner (1961), Engel and Warshaw (1964), and others. [See Stewart and Blackwell (1980) for a more complete review.]

The problem as stated above has several important limitations (Kotler, 1965*b*):

1. Linear programming assumes that each exposure has a constant effect.
2. It further assumes constant media costs (no discounts).
3. It cannot handle audience duplication and replication.
4. It fails to say anything about when the advertisements should be scheduled.

Some of these problems can be addressed by using more-advanced programming techniques, such as goal programming (Charnes et al., 1968), separable programming (Brown and Warshaw, 1965), and dynamic programming (Little and Lodish, 1966; Maffai, 1960*b*). But this tack has not proven fruitful:

> . . . attempts to use optimizing methods for the media selection decision have fallen far short of their intended mark. . . . A clear trend away from optimization methods and toward nonoptimizing procedures has been evident for some time now (Stewart and Blackwell, 1980, p. 8).

Nonoptimizing Methods Simple approaches to solving the media-scheduling problem, which are popular with advertising media planners but have attracted little enthusiasm from academic researchers, are the *stepwise or marginal-analysis models*. These procedures construct a media schedule in steps, at each step introducing the insertion that gives the greatest increase in effectiveness for the money (a so-called greedy algorithm). An example of this approach is the high-assay model (Moran, 1963). It starts with the media available in the first week and selects the single, best buy. After this selection is made, all the remaining media choices are reevaluated to take into account audience duplication and potential media discounts. Then a second selection is made for the same week if the achieved exposure rate for the week is below the optimal rate. The latter is a complex function of several marketing and media variables. This selection continues until the optimal exposure rate for the week is reached, at which point new media choices are considered for the following week.

Although this approach handles many of the objections to the mathematical-programming approaches, it suffers from the following difficulties (Gensch, 1973):

1. It does not guarantee an optimal or even a near-optimal solution.
2. It does not handle advertising timing.
3. The criterion function is limited.
4. Data demands are somewhat unrealistic.
5. It does not handle carry-over effects.

Both mathematical programming and marginal analysis are designed to discover good or optimal media schedules. *Simulation* models, on the other hand, are designed to estimate the exposure characteristics of a given media schedule. Typically, they utilize a hypothetical sample of persons who are exposed in a Monte Carlo fashion to the media schedule.

A simulation model was developed by Gensch (1973). The input stage of his model requires the following data: (1) the proposed media plan and schedule, (2) a set of weights for the effectiveness of different media, (3) a set of weights for the effectiveness of alternative sizes and colors in advertising forms, (4) a set of weights showing the value of different patterns of exposure frequency, (5) a list of the media cost and volume discounts, (6) a set of weights showing the value of an exposure to different types of persons in the target population, and (7) data from the Brand Rating Research Corporation showing the reading and viewing patterns over time of a real sample of individuals.

From these inputs his computer program is able to generate weekly and cumulative output on several important variables bearing on the overall impact of the proposed media schedule, including (1) the number and percentage of people in the target population reached by the proposed media schedule and its cost, (2) the number of persons reached zero, one, two, and so on times during the period of the proposed media schedule, and (3) an adjusted exposure number representing the overall impact of the proposed media schedule, which takes into account all of the objective and subjective evaluations of the media and the value of exposures to different members of the target audience.

Gensch tested the applicability of his model to a media-selection problem of the advertising agency handling the account of Ken-L-Ration canned dog food. The target population was defined as female heads of households in the nation. Information on past purchases was obtained from the Brand Rating Research Corporation, and subjective media weights were obtained from media planners in the company's advertising agency. Two alternate media plans had been drawn up by the agency before Gensch's model was applied. The media experts considered both plans to be good but held that one had an edge over the other. Gensch simulated the two plans, and the one that achieved higher overall impact agreed with the agency's judgment. Gensch also tested the sensitivity of the overall impact values to variations in the subjective weights.

The final step utilized a heuristic procedure that led to an improved, though not necessarily optimal, schedule. The result of this attempt was a schedule that the experts at the advertising agency felt was clearly superior to those they themselves had drawn up.

Other simulation-based approaches include those of Simulamatics Corporation (1962), the University of London's DYNAMO (1972) system, and Intermarco's (1971) Planex model.

The two most critical difficulties with all simulation models are validation, the relationship between the simulated sample and the real world, and optimization—that is, simulation models are designed to be used as evaluative tools, not optimization tools. As such, they complement rather than compete with optimization and stepwise procedures.

Dissatisfaction with the optimization approaches encouraged modelers in the late 1960s and the 1970s to relax the optimization criterion in an attempt to develop more-realistic model structures. We discuss one of the best-known models of this heuristic type, Little and Lodish's MEDIAC model, below.

MEDIAC Model   MEDIAC (Little and Lodish, 1969) assumes an advertiser is seeking to buy media for a year with B dollars that will maximize his sales. He can identify S different segments of his market, and for each segment he can estimate its sales potential in time period t:

$$\overline{Q}_{it} = n_i q_{it} \tag{14.41}$$

where $\overline{Q}_{it}$ = sales potential of market segment i in time period t (potential units per time period)

n_i = number of people in market segment i

q_{it} = sales potential of person in segment i in time period t (potential units per capita per time period)

The sales potential represents the maximum attainable sales in a segment in a given time period if advertising and other company marketing resources are used maximally. Actual sales are likely to be below potential sales and depend on the per capita–advertising-exposure level in the segment and time period. The more dollars spent on advertising in media reaching that segment, the higher the per capita exposure level and the higher the percentage of sales potential that will be realized. Thus the percentage of sales potential realized is a function of the per capita exposure level:

$$r_{it} = f(y_{it}) \tag{14.42}$$

where r_{it} = percent of sales potential of market segment i that is realized in time period t

y_{it} = exposure level of average individual in market segment i in time period t (exposure value per capita)

As an example of one possible sales function for eq. (14.42), Little and Lodish suggest the modified exponential, which shows diminishing marginal returns to increased advertising exposure:

$$r = r_0 + a(1 - e^{-by}) \qquad 0 \le y \tag{14.43}$$

where r_0, a, and b are nonnegative constants specific to the product.

Returning to the more general function in eq. (14.42), we find that the total sales for the year is given by

$$Q = \sum_{i=1}^{s} \sum_{t=1}^{T} n_i q_{it} f(y_{it}) \tag{14.44}$$

that is, the realized sales potentials in each time period summed over all the market segments.

The next task is to indicate how y_{it}, the per capita exposure level in segment i in time period t, is determined. In the absence of new advertising reaching this segment in time period t, the per capita exposure level will be some fraction α of last period's exposure level:

$$y_{it} = \alpha y_{i,t-1} \tag{14.45}$$

The fraction α represents the percentage of the advertising that is remembered from one period to the next by an average person in the segment. If there is new advertising in time period t, then the exposure level this period will be given by the more general expression

$$y_{it} = \alpha y_{i,t-1} + \Delta E_{it} \tag{14.46}$$

where ΔE_{it} is the increase in per capita exposure level in market segment i in time period t due to new advertising reaching this segment.

The net effect of eq. (14.46) is a pattern for per capita exposure level over time that resembles that shown in Exhibit 14.17. Between periods of new advertising, the exposure value falls at a diminishing rate because of forgetting. New advertising, on the other hand, increases the exposure value in the segment.

Now we must show the relationship of the increase in exposure value, ΔE_{it}, to purchases of specific media options. The advertiser must decide how many insertions he wants to buy in each available media vehicle in each time period. The increase in per capita exposure value is related to the number of these insertions in the following fashion:

$$\Delta E_{it} = \sum_{j=1}^{n} e_{ij} k_{ijt} x_{jt} \tag{14.47}$$

where $\quad e_{ij}$ = exposure value of one exposure in media vehicle j to person in market segment i

$\quad k_{ijt}$ = expected number of exposures produced in market segment i

EXHIBIT 14-17   **Per capita exposure level over time in a market segment.** (Source: Little and Lodish, 1969, p. 12.)

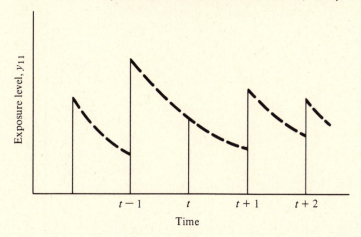

by one insertion in media vehicle j in time t (exposure efficiency)

x_{jt} = number of insertions in media vehicle j in time period t

Thus the advertiser's decision variable is x_{jt}.

Suppose that he decides to buy x_{jt} insertions. Each insertion in media j will yield an exposure value e_{ij}, where

$$e_{ij} = f(\text{media class, editorial climate of media vehicle } j, \text{ media option, market segment})$$ (14.48)

Different media classes have different potentials for demonstration, believability, color, and informativeness. Thus if a food product is involved and color is important, magazines may be given a higher-rated exposure value than newspapers or radio. Furthermore, the editorial climate recognizes that readers have images of particular vehicles that may add or subtract from the tone of believability of the advertisement. For example, *Good Housekeeping* may lend more credibility to an advertised product claim than *True Confessions* may. In addition, advertising impact increases with the size and use of color in ads and should be reflected in the exposure value. This impact is reflected in the "media option" factor. Thus the exposure value of an insertion may be assumed to rise with the square root or some other function of the size of the ad. Finally, the exposure value of an insertion can vary by market segment.

The exposure value of any particular insertion in media j is a number showing how good this insertion is in relation to a reference insertion in some media. Suppose that the highest exposure value is arbitrarily called one and is achieved for a particular segment by a two-page, four-color ad in

Time. Then every other possible media option that might reach this segment is assigned value relative to this ideal value.

The exposure value of a particular insertion in media j is further modified by the exposure efficiency k_{ijt} in the particular market segment in the particular time period [see eq. (14.47)]. The exposure efficiency depends on the following factors:

$$k_{ijt} = h_j g_{ij} n_i s_{jt} \tag{14.49}$$

where h_j = probability of exposure to advertisement in vehicle j, given that person is in audience of vehicle

g_{ij} = fraction of people in market segment i who are in audience of vehicle j (average value over year)

n_i = number of people in market segment i

s_{jt} = seasonal index of audience size for vehicle j in period t (average value − 1.00)

Thus exposure effectiveness reflects the size of the media vehicle's audience at that time of the year, modified by the percent that are likely to be exposed to the advertisement if they are in the audience of the vehicle.

The description of the MEDIAC model given above must now be embodied in a mathematical-programming statement designed to find the best media plan. The problem can be stated as one of trying to find the x_{jt}, for all j and t, that will maximize

$$\sum_{i=1}^{S} \sum_{t=1}^{T} n_i q_{it} f(y_{it}) \tag{14.50}$$

subject to current exposure-value constraints

$$y_{it} = \alpha y_{i,t-1} + \sum_{j=1}^{N} k_{ijt} e_{ij} x_{jt} \tag{14.51}$$

lower and upper media-use-rate constraints

$$l_{jt} \le x_{jt} \le u_{jt} \tag{14.52}$$

a budget constraint

$$\sum_{j=1}^{N} \sum_{t=1}^{T} c_{jt} x_{jt} \le B \tag{14.53}$$

and nonnegativity constraints

$$x_{jt}, y_{it} \ge 0 \tag{14.54}$$

In this form the problem has a nonlinear but separable objective function that is subject to linear constraints. If the nonlinear objective function is assumed concave [as in eq. (14.41)], the problem can be solved by piecewise linear-approximation techniques. If it is assumed to be S-shaped and the problem is of modest size, Little and Lodish show that it can be solved by dynamic programming. If the problem is not of modest size, then the authors show that satisfactory, though not necessarily optimal, solutions can be obtained through the use of heuristic methods.

The model was extended by Lodish (1971a) to consider the effect of competitors' schedules. This extension is the only reported attempt to incorporate the effect of competition into a media-decision model.

The model formulation, while quite complete, has several weaknesses. It assumes a linear cost structure for media [eq. (14.53)], while actual rates are considerably more complex and often subject to negotiation. Also, the exposure value in eq. (14.47) depends on whether the exposure is the first, second, or nth exposure.

MEDIAC represents an important attempt to include the dimensions of market segments, sales potentials, diminishing marginal returns, forgetting, and timing into a media-planning model. Its availability for on-line access via a remote terminal presents a complete, usable model for this decision area. However, its use has been limited by its sophistication: it may be too complex for most media planners.

Other heuristic procedures include those by Urban (1975a), the SOLEM model (Bimm and Millman, 1978), and Aaker's ADMOD (1975) model, designed to deal simultaneously with budget, copy, and media-allocation decisions. ADMOD's main distinguishing feature is its focus on the behavioral and attitudinal states of individuals in the target audience without simulation. It deals with many of the same issues as MEDIAC, but it has greater data needs.

Evaluation   Since the surge of the 1960s there has been a marked decline in the development of media-decision models. The reason appears to be that satisfactory tools are available for practitioners and that the more complete models bring with them added complexity, which makes them difficult to understand and use (Simon and Thiel, 1980). Therefore these more complete models must prove their superiority in value to the media scheduler. For them to do so, both a more complete understanding of the advertising process and a better packaging of media models are required. [The objectives of ad agencies may not necessarily coincide with their clients' objectives. See Schmalensee, Silk, and Bojanek (1981).] Improved media models should be built partly to aid in decision making but, more importantly, also to aid in the research process, guiding our investigations of advertising's effects. In the meantime, tools appear to be available that meet the level of sophistication of almost any user, and the more complete ones must be customized to the needs of those users. In this vein, Wilson, Vice President and Director of Marketing Science at BBDO (private communication, 1981) comments:

> In order for modeling specialists to increase their rate of success in media applications, it is imperative that modelers approach their task from the user's (i.e., the media planner's) perspective. In other words, the modeler must arrive

at a better understanding of the planner's organizational environment, planning constraints, and built-in complexities such as scheduling within television day parts, the influence of timing on the costs of insertions, widely varying costs among vehicles, and serious difficulties in measuring audience reach and frequency. With this in mind, efforts to provide accurate and usable media models should be viewed as a classic implementation problem. The resulting challenge to marketing modelers is to pay close attention to the needs of the model user and then build models accordingly.

Summary

Advertising is one of the most potent tools available to the modern marketer for informing and possibly persuading buyers of the virtues of his product. However, its actual communication effects and sales impact are hard to establish outside of an experimental situation in which everything extraneous is held constant. To guide their budgeting, advertisers need whatever theoretical assistance they can get on how advertising works and what its effect depends on.

A number of general effects of advertising phenomena that impact on advertising-spending-policy development, media selection, and copy-development strategies were reviewed. Advertising goals should be set with an understanding of the conditions under which an advertising exposure is likely to have an effect. The effect of advertising depends on several qualities of the ad (its creative quality, media class, media vehicle, media option, and time of appearance) and several qualities of the potential buyer (buyer class, buyer state, advertising attentiveness of buyer, and buyer's frequency of exposure to media j). The sales impact of an advertising campaign depends on the number of people in the market in such states as brand awareness, brand acceptability, and brand satisfaction and the power of the campaign to improve the ratios of triers to potential buyers and of users to triers.

Quite a few advertising-response models have been built over the last several years; they fall into two general classes: a priori models and econometric models. A priori models (such as the Lanchester type and Vidale-Wolfe models) provide a more conceptually sound set of characteristics, while the econometric models are better related to available data. Better data collection, as well as improved and eclectic estimation methods, should lead to a synthesis of these different approaches.

Advertisers are concerned with measuring the quality of the message and the copy making up the advertisement. Various measures have been developed to evaluate the impact of an advertisement or advertising campaign on sales, comprehension, and awareness. The sales impact is the most desirable effect to measure, but most of the successful work has measured the market's awareness of the advertisement. In addition, statistical analyses of readership scores on various content and mechanical features of an ad have been able to show the contribution of different variables to the size of the readership score. An advertising agency usually prepares some alternative ads before testing and selecting one as the most effective. Gross developed a model based on the premise that the more ads an agency prepares, the better the best one will be. He came to the conclusion that advertising agencies tend to spend far too little in creating and screening ads in relation to the amount they spend on media purchases.

The media decision received much early attention from model builders. Most of the resulting models use the weighted number of exposures for judging the merit of a media plan. These media models have been built along the lines of optimizing and nonoptimizing methods. One of the most complete models is MEDIAC, which incorporates many realistic facets of the media problem, such as market segments, sales potentials, exposure probabilities, diminishing marginal-response rates, forgetting, and seasonality.

Problems

14.1 A company's advertising expenditures average $5000/mo. Current sales are $29,000, and the saturation sales level is estimated at $42,000. The sales response constant is $2, and the sales decay constant is 6% per month. Use the Vidale-Wolfe formula in Chapter 4, eq. (4.55), to estimate the probable sales increase next month.

14.2 A firm has determined that the actual effective value of a single advertising insertion for its brand A in a particular medium is 2160. It has also found that the percent of people exposed to the medium who have seen the ad (f_1) is 0.9, the percent seeing the ad who register the message (f_2) is 0.6, and the percent registering the ad who are favorably impressed is 0.4. Determine the following:
  a. the percent of the people exposed to the medium who saw the ad, registered the message, but were not favorably impressed
  b. the percent of those exposed who saw the ad but did not register the message
  c. the average number of persons exposed to the medium

14.3 An advertising agency plans to create a number of advertisements for one of its clients and pretest them in order to select the best one. It wishes to know how many advertisements to create and test. The following information has been obtained:
  (a) The average cost of creating and screening one advertisement is about $0.025D$.
  (b) An outstanding advertisement is one that is at the 3σ level in probability, and in the long run it will return in profits an amount equal to the media expenditure.
  (c) The pretest's validity is 0.7.
  (d) The reliability of the pretest is 0.8.

Determine the optimal number of advertisements to be created and pretested, using the Gross formulation.

14.4 A manufacturer wishes to determine the level of advertising that will maintain its current sales growth rate at 4%. Current sales are $50,000, and it is estimated that sales could reach a level of $150,000 at saturation. Sales response to advertising dollars is estimated at 1.1, and it has been determined that the company would lose 0.2 of its sales per period if no advertising expenditure were made.
   a. How much advertising is needed to maintain the desired growth?
   b. What rate of growth would be sustained if $20,000 was spent per period for advertising?

14.5 An executive recently recommended allocating advertising expenditures to various markets in proportion to sales in these markets. His reasons were as follows. In the absence of further company advertising a fixed (but unknown) percentage of sales in each market would be lost to competitors. The role of advertising is to hold present customers to replace them. Therefore the promotional level in each market should be proportional to the sales level. Do you agree?

14.6 Suppose the probability equation for any person watching the "Tonight Show" is

$$p = 0.04 + 0.20X_1 + 0.44X_2$$

where p = probability of watching "Tonight Show"
   X_1 = sex, with 1 for male and 0 for female
   X_2 = education, with 1 for college and 0 for high school

What is the probability that a high-school-educated male is watching the show on a particular evening?

14.7 A company wishes to know how many successive advertisements it should place in each of three magazines (A, B, and C) in order to obtain the greatest total reach. Two alternative strategies are under consideration. Alternative 1 is (A, B, C) = (3, 2, 2). That is, the company would place 3 advertisements in magazine A, 2 in B, and 2 in C. Alternative 2 is (A, B, C) = (2, 3, 2). The table below shows the net cumulative audience for 1, 2, or 3 exposures in each magazine. Also shown are the pairwise-duplicated audiences for each alternative.

	Net Cumulative Audience (in 1000s)		
Exposures	A	B	C
1	100	150	75
2	125	180	85
3	140	200	90

	Pairwise Duplication (in 1000s)		
Alternative	D_{12}	D_{13}	D_{23}
1	30	15	20
2	32	10	25

Using Agostini's estimation formula, determine which alternative offers the greatest total reach.

14.8 A company plans to place advertisements in two different magazines, A and B. A total budget of $250,000 has been established for these advertisements over the coming year, and the company does not wish to spend less than $100,000 of the budgeted amount. Magazine A gives 1,500,000 effective exposures with each use, and costs $7000. Magazine B gives 800,000 effective exposures with each use, and costs $3000. Magazine A is a weekly publication, while magazine B is published monthly. State this problem as a linear-programming problem, and solve it to find the optimal number of advertisements to be placed in magazines A and B in the coming year.

14.9 Retail sales of a product are given by

$$s = \alpha \ln \beta x$$

where s is the sales rate and x is the advertising rate. Let

g_1 = retailer's incremental profit as fraction of *retail* sales
g_2 = manufacturer's incremental profit as fraction of *retail* sales

The manufacturer has made contracts with its retailers for cooperative advertising. Under the contract the retailer advertises the manufacturer's product in local media and the manufacturer pays part of the cost. Consider the following case: (a) The retailer decides the amount of advertising. (b) The retailer pays a fraction w of the cost. (c) The manufacturer pays a fraction $(1 - w)$ of the cost. (d) The manufacturer sets w. Suppose that the retailer spends to maximize his profit and the manufacturer picks w to maximize his, knowing how the retailer is going to act. What will w be?

14.10 A company buys weekly television spots in the New York market. Each quarter the company reviews the ratings, drops spots that have a high cost per exposure, and adds any spots it can find with low cost per exposure in an effort to maximize profit. No budget restriction is set. Sales response is

$$s = \alpha + \beta(1 - e^{-\gamma v})$$

where v is total exposures per week in the market and s is sales per week in the market. Each spot can be characterized by Δv, its audience; Δx, its cost per week; and $k = \Delta x / \Delta v$, its cost per exposures.
a. Find a procedure for rearranging the spot schedule so as to maximize profit rate. (Ignore the discrete nature of spots if you wish.)
b. Express the decision rules of part a as a control curve, that is, a plot of maximum tolerable cost per exposure, k, versus accumulated exposures per week bought, v.

14.11 The reach of a media schedule is the fraction of the target population that receives at least one exposure. Consider a series of n advertising insertions in a certain publication. Let

p = probability that member of population receives exposure with one insertion
$f(p)$ = probability density function of p over target population (beta density)
$$= \frac{\Gamma(\alpha + \beta)}{\Gamma(\alpha)\Gamma(\beta)} p^{\alpha-1}(1 - p)^{\beta-1} \qquad 0 < p < 1; \alpha, \beta > 0$$

a. Suppose that the exposures to the n successive insertions are independent events. Calculate the reach of the schedule.

b. Suppose that the fraction of the population receiving an exposure from one issue is 0.3 and the fraction receiving exposures from successive issues is 0.1. Assume the beta density and independence assumptions are correct. What will be the reach of four insertions? *Note:*

$$\Gamma(\alpha) = \int_0^\infty e^{-x} x^{\alpha-1} \, dx = (\alpha - 1)\Gamma(\alpha - 1)$$

If α is an integer, then

$$\Gamma(\alpha) = (\alpha - 1)!$$

15 Sales-Promotion Models

Relative to the emphasis given in practice to advertising and personal selling as major tools of the marketer, sales promotion is often perceived as playing a secondary role. As such, quantitative analyses of sales-promotion activities have not led to the same level of sophistication as that found in advertising-decision models. In addition, historically, sales promotion has been viewed primarily as a short-run phenomenon; some recent literature challenges this view.

In this chapter we define categories of sales promotion and their reported effects. We then review methods for evaluating promotional-program-modeling approaches that have led to tools for promotional decision making. The last section assesses the field and discusses what can (and should) be accomplished in furthering our understanding of the effects of promotions.

Sales Promotion: Types and Effects

Sales promotion comprises a wide variety of tactical promotion tools of a short-term incentive nature designed to stimulate earlier and/or stronger target-market response. Among the more popular forms are coupons, premiums, and contests for consumer markets; buying allowances, coopera-tive-advertising allowances, and free goods for distributors and dealers; discounts, gifts, and extras for industrial users; and sales contests and special bonuses for members of the salesforce.

A key factor associated with most types of promotions is that, properly applied, they are *complementary* with other elements of the marketing mix and therefore involve a coordinated effort among retailers, wholesalers, salesmen, advertising, and (often) manufacturing and distribution. This issue is often overlooked in studies of manufacturer-based deals, which neglect temporary retailer specials and other activities by the retailer or distributor. Exhibit 15.1 shows the flow of promotion and suggests the importance of understanding and modeling the individual and combined effects of promotional activity at several levels.

Thus to model promotional effects, we must determine (1) the objectives of the promotion, (2) characteristics of different promotion types and their purported effects on the objectives, (3) the effectiveness of different promotions, and (4) the range of promotion decisions.

Objectives of Promotions

Because sales-promotion tools are so varied in form, no single purpose can be advanced for them. For example, a free sample stimulates consumer trial, while a free management-advisory service cements a long-term relationship

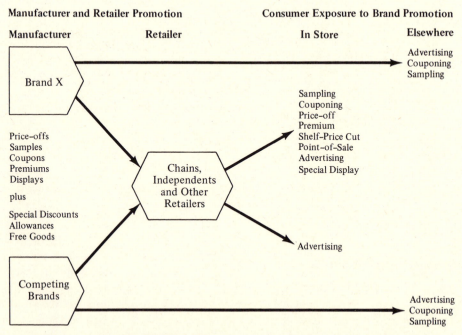

EXHIBIT 15-1   **The flow of promotion.** (Source: Robinson, et al. *Promotional Decision Using Mathematical Models,* Allyn and Bacon, Inc., 1967, p. 7. Reprinted by permission.)

with a retailer. Sales-promotion techniques make three contributions to exchange relationships:

1. **Communication.** They gain attention and usually provide information that may lead the consumer to the product.
2. **Incentive.** They incorporate some concession, inducement, or contribution designed to represent value to the receiver.
3. **Invitation.** They include a distinct invitation to engage in the transaction now.

Although the primary purpose is usually to attract nonbrand users to the brand, incentive promotions are adopted by sellers also to reward brand-loyal users for their loyalty. Because both types of buyers buy during the promotion period, both purposes are served. The nonbrand users are of two types: those who are loyal to other brands and those who are brand switchers. Incentive promotions primarily attract the brand switchers; the brand-loyal users of other brands do not always notice or act on the promotion. But because brand switchers are what they are, sales promotions are unlikely to turn them into loyal brand users. Therefore incentive promotions used in markets of high brand similarity produce a high sales response in the short run but little permanent gain. However, in markets of high brand dissimilarity, incentive promotions are more likely to alter market shares permanently.

Thus it is important to set objectives for the particular promotion, whether they relate to the level of retail inventory, to increased retail distribution, to coupon-redemption rates, or to sales effects. A further complicating factor is that even for the same brand, objectives for promotional activity may vary over time. Occasionally, a promotion may be aimed at countering the advertising or promotions of a competitive brand, especially if the competitor is new to the market. Promotions that require an individual to save coupons or package labels aim at building a high degree of purchase loyalty among buyers. But most promotions (Kuehn and Rohloff, 1967a, p. 46) are aimed at attracting consumers who are not regular users of the brand—called obtaining trial. A more difficult factor to evaluate is how customers alter their subsequent purchasing behavior (and brand perceptions) on the basis of having bought a brand on a deal.

Characteristics of Promotions

Marketing managers choose promotions for their cost effectiveness given the task at hand. Some of the key considerations vary with promotional type.

For *sampling*, implementation can be door to door, by mail, or free with the purchase of another product. Furthermore, the size of the sample can vary. (The promotion for the introduction of Gainesburgers by General

Foods, which included, in a sample pack, *half* the recommended size of a dog's meal, had less than ideal results.) Because the number and type of households vary by area, different variables may be important for different situations. For example, the package size of the sample may target the product to one particular usage group and not another. In theory, marketers should target samples at prospects that hold the greatest potential (conversion rate, usage, or both) for future sales.

For a *manufacturer-price-off offer* the total quantity of the promotion must be determined, which, in turn, is affected by the amount the retailer will accept—too small a deal quantity may not motivate the retailer to feature the item. Furthermore, the price-off offer can cover one size, all sizes, or a selected set of sizes. Finally, the percentage of the price off must be carefully determined, as must the frequency. A too-frequent price-off offer may lead the consumer to expect a continuation and to perceive the regular price as an increase.

For *couponing*, the redemption rate is key, which, in turn, depends on the value of the coupon (Reibstein and Traver, 1982). As with sampling, the manufacturer has partial control of the type of household reached.

For *in- and on-pack premiums* the selection of premium type and duration is important. The premium should be consistent with the quality image of the brand and, if appropriate, should be in place long enough (as with glassware) so that a set can be obtained by a regular buyer.

In-store displays are recognized as effective means of moving merchandise, but display space is limited and the display must pay for itself by the retailer's standards. Many promotions of this type fail because the materials provided to retailers are not used.

In sum, each promotion type has some different dimension that makes it unique and that affects its cost and its impact on short- and long-term brand sales differently. When several promotions are introduced simultaneously, the situation is even more complicated. Furthermore, costs vary widely—door-to-door sampling is exceedingly expensive while mail-away premiums can be quite cheap. The execution and effectiveness of promotions also vary widely, differentially affecting sales as well as profitability.

Evidence of Promotional Effects

There is lack of agreement among researchers about what promotions do and how they should be viewed. Many researchers feel that promotions, in contrast to advertising, do not build up a long-term consumer franchise. Brown (1974) studied 2500 instant-coffee drinkers and offers these conclusions (pp. 36–37):

1. Sales promotions yield faster sales responses than advertising does.

2. Sales promotions do not tend to yield new long-term buyers in mature markets because they attract mainly deal-prone consumers who switch among brands as deals become available.
3. Loyal brand buyers tend not to change their buying patterns as a result of competitive promotion.
4. Advertising appears to be capable of increasing the prime franchise of a brand.

On the other hand, in an intriguing study Seipel (1971) found that housewives who had taken advantage of a premium in the past increased their purchases of that brand even though they didn't have a higher opinion of that brand than other subjects did.

Strang, Prentice, and Clayton (1975) suggest that sales-promotion tools can be divided into two groups: those that are consumer-franchise building and those that are not. The former imparts a selling message along with the deal, as with free samples, coupons (when they include a selling message), and premiums related to the product. Sales-promotion tools that are not consumer-franchise building include price-off packs, consumer premiums not related to a product, contests and sweepstakes, consumer refund offers, and trade allowances. Sellers are urged to use the former promotions when possible because they enhance the brand's value in the mind of the consumers.

The interaction of promotions with other elements in the marketing mix must not be ignored. Strang (1976) reports that in one study a point-of-purchase display referring to a current TV commercial produced 15 percent more sales than comparable displays without the advertising tie-in. In another study Brown (1973) suggested that in terms of evaluating promotions, the impact on the producer's inventory levels should be considered and that inventory control should be another aim of promotional activity. In a third study Hinkle (1965) studied price deals covering 19 brands in 3 product categories and concluded that price dealing is more effective for new brands than for established brands. In addition, he concluded that off-season price reductions are more profitable, a high frequency of promotions makes consumers overly price-conscious, and deals do *not* appear to be a good way to counter competitor-brand-introduction effects. Cotton and Babb (1978) confirm Hinkle's findings for dairy products, showing that promotional response is lower for more-familiar products. They also show that promotional response is much greater than an equivalent price increase, at least in the short term.

Shoemaker (1979) studied panel data for three products, looking at the impact of promotions on purchase timing, purchase quantities, and brand choice. He concluded that promotions affected the brand selected and the quantity purchased but did not have an impact on the timing of purchases—consumers did not appear to alter their purchase-timing patterns to take advantage of a promotion. However, these effects varied by whether or not the product was perishable.

In terms of the effect of promotion type, Dodson, Tybout, and Sternthal (1978) found that for two consumer-packaged goods, media-distributed coupons and cents-off deals induced brand switching and resulted in *less* loyalty when they were retracted than in cases where no deals were offered. In contrast, package coupons were found to stimulate brand loyalty, which was maintained when the coupons were retracted.

Implementation of promotions varies considerably, influencing their effects drastically. Chevalier and Curhan (1976), in a study of promotional activity in a large regional supermarket chain, concluded that slow-moving products are unlikely to be displayed whatever the inducement—that is, retailers absorb the deals without passing them on to consumers. Kuehn and Rohloff (1967a) report that retailer fraud in coupon redemption may be as high as 80 percent.

Hallaq (1977) performed an interesting study aimed at sizing premiums. His subjects—elementary schoolchildren—were given two sets of premiums to see if their selection of cereals could be influenced. Large premiums seemed to have an impact, while small ones did not. This result suggests a possible threshold size for promotional activities.

In an experiment on price advertising (a form of price promotion), Della Bitta, Monroe, and McGinnis (1981) report that as the size of the discount increased, there was a greater perception of value, less interest to search for other brands, and greater interest in the brand. In general, these effects were proportionally stronger the lower the price of the brand.

Wilkinson, Mason, and Paksoy (1982) studied several promotional types combined with newspaper advertising. They found that price reductions and in-store promotions were more effective than newspaper advertising in temporarily affecting unit sales of supermarket products.

Finally, promotional timing and spacing are critical. Kuehn and Rohloff (1967b) show that the average time between promotions has an effect on consumers' repurchase probabilities. Kinberg and Rao (1975) present plausible theoretical arguments suggesting that consumers respond differently to a promotion if they know its length than if they do not.

Sales-Promotion Decisions

A sales-promotion program typically involves a number of management decisions, including the size of incentive, conditions for participation, distributor vehicle, duration, timing, and the overall promotion budget.

For the size of the incentive the usual assumption is that for most products there are threshold and saturation effects: a certain minimum size is needed for response, and past a certain point higher incentives produce sales increases at a diminishing rate. This sales-response function varies with the type of product and delivery medium.

In addition, conditions for participation may vary. By carefully choosing these conditions, the seller can selectively discourage those who are unlikely to become regular users of the product.

Furthermore, distribution vehicles for the promotion vary in terms of cost and reach. Options include in or on the package, in the store, in the mail, and in the advertising media. In-package coupons reach current users, while mailed coupons can be directed at nonusers at a greater cost.

The duration of the promotion also plays an important part in its effect. If the promotion is too short, many prospects will not have a chance to take advantage because they may not be repurchasing at the time. On the other hand, a promotion that lasts too long is perceived as a long-term price concession, and the deal loses its act-now character.

Closely tied to a promotion's duration is its timing and frequency. The timing of a promotion requires the coordination of production, salesforce, and distribution personnel.

Finally, the size of the budget for promotions, as with that for advertising, is most frequently determined by a rule of thumb and not on the basis of cost effectiveness. The rules for advertising budgeting discussed in Chapter 14 are often applied here as well.

Evaluating the Effects of Promotions

The evidence cited above leads to the following observations for evaluating promotional results:

Brand loyalty may (or may not) be affected.

New triers may (or may not) be attracted.

Promotions interact with other elements of the marketing mix (advertising, in particular).

Promotional results interact with production and distribution, affecting inventory levels in a rapid and dramatic manner.

Promotional frequency influences promotional effects and is linked to the average length of the product's purchase cycle.

The type of promotion selected may have differential effects on brand loyalty and promotional attractiveness.

Promotion size may have threshold and saturation effects, suggesting an S-shaped sales-response relationship.

Finally, different promotions may be implemented with different degrees of success, resulting in ambiguous measures of market response.

With the effects summarized above, it is not surprising that there is little agreement about how to evaluate promotions.

> Evaluation of promotion programs receives . . . little attention. Even where an attempt is made to evaluate a promotion, it is likely to be superficial. . . . Evaluation in terms of profitability is even less common (Strang, 1976, p. 120).

The most common consumer-promotion evaluation technique is to compare sales or market share before, during, and after a promotion. Increased sales then are attributed to the impact of the sales-promotion program, all other things being equal. Exhibit 15.2 shows an example of results that manufacturers would like to see. In the promotion period the company's brand share rose to 10 percent. This share gain of 4 percent is made up of (1) deal-prone consumers, who switched to this brand to take advantage of the deal, and (2) brand-loyal customers, who increased their purchases in response to the price incentive. Immediately after the promotion ended the brand share fell to 5 percent because consumers were overstocked and they were working down their inventory. After this stock adjustment brand share went up to 7 percent, showing a one-percentage-point increase in the number of loyal customers. This pattern is likely to occur when the brand has good qualities that many nonbrand users did not know about.

In many cases the results are less satisfactory. Consider two different situations. In the first one, brand share jumps up to 10 percent in the promotion period, falls to 2 percent in the immediate postpromotion period, and then returns to 6 percent. This pattern suggests that the existing customers were the main buyers during the promotion period and that they

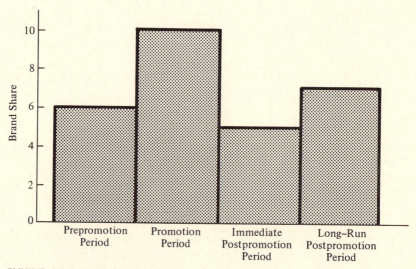

EXHIBIT 15-2   **Ideal effect of a consumer deal on brand share.**

stocked up on this brand, then consumed from their own stock immediately after the promotion period, and ultimately returned to their normal rate of purchase. Thus the effect of the deal was largely to alter the time pattern of purchase rather than the permanent level of purchase. This pattern is not necessarily unwanted. For instance, if inventories are excessive, a company may want to clear them and, in the meantime, cut production.

In the second case brand share rises little or not at all during the promotion period and then falls and remains below the normal level after the promotion period. This situation suggests a brand that is on a downward sales trend, which the promotion slowed down but did not halt or reverse. Peckham (1973) gives some examples in which this pattern occurred.

Thus a thorough understanding of the market, the promotional objectives, and the alternatives employed is required to model and evaluate sales promotions. No general integrated effort has appeared in marketing literature; rather, more limited approaches are reported, which follow different behavioral assumptions in different markets and focus on different aspects of the problem.

Promotional Models

A number of models have been developed and proposed in the marketing literature. They generally fall into three categories: (1) theoretical models without empirical support, (2) regression-type models without theoretical justification, and (3) empirically supported models derived from some behavioral hypotheses. Models in the first category, while interesting, are by definition untested and will be briefly reviewed later. The second types of models, while widely used by many firms, do not provide much general insight. Therefore, we review three models of the third type below, in the order in which they entered the literature: the Kuehn-Rohloff (1967b) model, the Rao-Lilien (1972) model, and the Little (1975) model.

The Kuehn-Rohloff Model

Kuehn and Rohloff (1967b) address the problem of assessing promotions from a model-based, yet practical, viewpoint. In general, they suggest a four-step procedure:

1. Compute the gross profit on the sales volume moved by the promotion. This amount is computed by multiplying the sales volume by the gross margin, where the gross margin is the selling price minus the cost of the goods sold. The authors believe that this figure is easily arrived at for price-off promotions and on-pack-premium promotions. However, they

caution that for coupon promotions, adjustments must be made for fraudulent coupon redemption.

2. Subtract the gross profit that the brand being promoted would have realized if there had been no promotion. This estimate is computed by multiplying the gross profit (from step 1) by the probability that the brand purchased in a particular promotion would have been purchased even if it were not available on deal. The model reviewed below is used to estimate this probability.

3. Subtract the direct cost of promotion. This value includes both fixed costs of promotions, such as coupon mailing, and variable costs, such as lost revenues per unit due to a price-off promotion.

4. Add gross profit from conversion. This estimate is an estimate based on projected future sales resulting from customers using the promotion. As a rule of thumb, Kuehn and Rohloff state that these estimates can be obtained by examining the increase in consumers' purchase probabilities over a time period of approximately three times the average purchase cycle of the product class. This assumption about the effective life of promotional effects appears to be drawn from the authors' experience.

The Modeling Approach. Essentially, the authors use Kuehn's (1958) linear learning model to evaluate promotions. This model requires diary panel data that explicitly recognize the timing of a particular brand's and the competitors' promotions. As presented by Kuehn and Rohloff, it can be specified as two equations:

gain equation: if brand i is purchased on the nth purchase,

$$p_{i,n+1} = (1 - \lambda)p_{i,n} + \phi s_i + (\lambda - \phi) \tag{15.1}$$

loss equation: if brand i is not purchased on the nth purchase,

$$p_{i,n+1} = (1 - \lambda) p_{i,n} + \phi s_i \tag{15.2}$$

where $p_{i,n}$ = probability that brand i will be purchased on nth purchase occasion.
s_i = equilibrium (projected) market share for brand i, $\Sigma s_i = 1$
λ, ϕ = product- and class-specific constants, $\lambda > \phi$, $\lambda \in (0, 1)$.

Exhibit 15.3 illustrates the brand-shifting model. The uppermost, solid sloping line is the gain equation for brand i, while the lower solid line is the loss equation. In each case $p_{i,n+1}$ is a linear function of $p_{i,n}$ with a slope of $(1 - \lambda)$. The exhibit also shows the rate at which an individual, starting at $p_i = A$, will approach $(\phi s_i/\lambda) + [(\lambda - \phi)/\lambda]$ with repeated purchase of brand i.

Now aggregating over the population yields

$$\overline{p}_{i,n+1} = \overline{p}_{i,n}[(1 - \lambda)\overline{p}_{i,n} + \phi s_i + \lambda - \phi] + (1 - \overline{p}_{i,n})[(1 - \lambda)\overline{p}_{i,n} + \phi s_i]$$

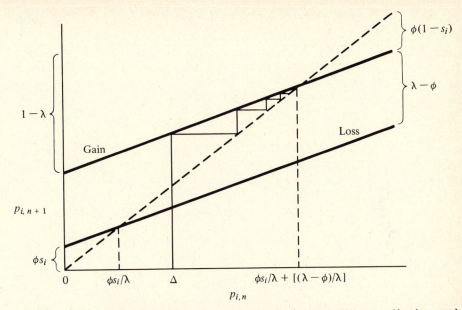

EXHIBIT 15-3   **The graph of the brand-shifting model.** (Source: Kuehn and Rohloff, "What Are Promotions?" in *Promotional Decision Using Mathematical Models,* Allyn and Bacon, Inc., 1967b, p. 45. Reprinted by permission.)

or

$$\bar{p}_{i,n+1} = (1 - \phi)\bar{p}_{i,n} + \phi s_i \qquad (15.3)$$

where $\bar{p}$ is the average (expected) value of p.

Thus this trend model assumes that the purchase probabilities of various families lie away from an equilibrium position, which they approach on subsequent purchases. Equation (15.3) shows that the rate at which $\bar{p}_{i,n}$ approaches s_i, the equilibrium market share, depends only on ϕ (i.e., it is independent of λ). Therefore knowledge of ϕ and $p_{i,n}$ should provide the key pieces of information for determining the effect of a particular promotion.

A promotion is viewed here as a market disturbance, and the rate at which the disturbed share $\bar{p}$ returns to equilibrium s is governed by ϕ. Then the gain (or loss) over the equilibrium share s is the promotional effect.

The authors feel that, rather than being a model of consumer behavior, their model specifies the expected value of $p_{i,n}$ over a population of families. In this case the relevant equation is eq. (15.3), as plotted in Exhibit 15.4. In this exhibit the value of s_i is at the intersection of the line $\bar{p}_{i,n+1}$ and the diagonal, where $p_{i,n} = p_{i,n+1}$.

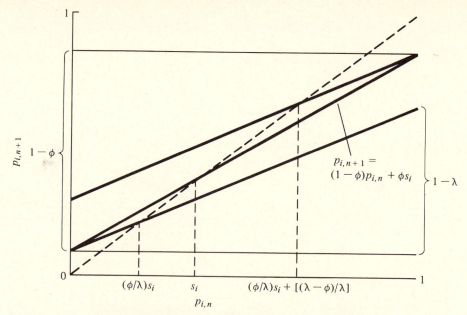

EXHIBIT 15-4   **The graph of the expected value of $p_{i,n+1}$ given $p_{i,n}$.** (Source: Kuehn and Rohloff, "Evaluating Promotions Using a Brand Shifting Model," in *Promotional Decision Using Mathematical Models*, Allyn and Bacon, Inc., 1967a, p. 58, Reprinted by permission.)

On the basis of some of Kuehn's (1962) past work, Kuehn and Rohloff argue that ϕ and λ differ depending on the average time between successive purchases for a group of consumers. Kuehn's timing model is

$$p_{i,T} - s_i = (p_{i0} - s_i)e^{-aT - bA} \tag{15.4}$$

where T = time period
         A = average time between purchases
         a, b = parameters of product class

From eq. (15.4) we see that if the time between successive purchases is large (i.e., A is large), then p_{iT} approaches s_i very quickly. Thus the value of p_{iT} will stay in the neighborhood of its equilibrium value. Conversely, heavy buyers for whom p_{iT} is far from s_i will show a relatively slower return to their equilibrium share.

This information is summarized by the authors in the following relationship, which is obtained by subtracting eq. (15.2) from eq. (15.1):

$$\lambda - \phi = p_{i,n+1}(\text{from gain}) - p_{i,n+1}(\text{from loss}) \tag{15.5}$$

Now both λ and ϕ are functions of the time between the nth and the $(n + 1)$st purchase. As the purchase interval (T) gets large, both $\lambda(T)$ and $\phi(T)$ will tend toward one. Furthermore, the authors assert that a reasonable approximation, as $T \to 0$, is

$$\lambda(T) \to \lambda c \qquad \phi(T) \to \phi c$$

where c is a constant. Exhibit 15.5 presents the relationship between λ and ϕ as an implicit function of t, the time between purchases.

To estimate the increase in volume for a particular deal k, the authors propose the following relative measure:

$$W_k = \frac{\Sigma f_i V_i Q_{ik}}{\Sigma f_i} \qquad (15.6)$$

where f_i = panel-family projection factor (used for projecting to national results)

V_i = volume for family

Q_{ik} = relative increase in volume for deal

and the sum is over families who purchased on the deal.

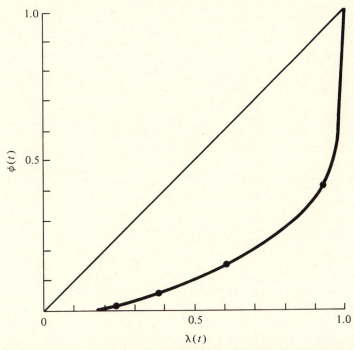

EXHIBIT 15-5   **The functional relationship between λ and ϕ.** (Source: Kuehn and Rohloff, "Evaluating Promotions Using a Brand Shifting Model," in *Promotional Decision Using Mathematical Models,* Allyn and Bacon, Inc., 1967a, p. 63. Reprinted by permission.)

The term Q_{ik} is the key term. In general, it measures the difference between the predeal probability of purchase and the postdeal probability of purchase. The difficulty is in aggregation over time. For example, the authors consider the following raw measure of conversion.

If the deal was purchased on the nth purchase, the predeal purchase probability for the promoted brand is estimated by $p_{i,n}$ from eqs. (15.1) and (15.2). The postdeal purchase probability $\hat{p}_{i,n+2}$ depends only on the single purchase following the deal and can be found with the expected-value method:

$$p_{i,n+1} = (1 - \phi)p_{i,n} + \phi s_i \qquad (15.7)$$

and

$$\hat{p}_{i,n+2} = \begin{cases} (1 - \lambda)p_{i,n+1} + \phi s_i + \lambda - \phi & \text{if } i \text{ is purchased at } n + 1 \qquad (15.8) \\ (1 - \lambda)p_{i,n+1} + \phi s_i & \text{if } i \text{ is not purchased at } n + 1 \quad (15.9) \end{cases}$$

Then

$$Q_{ik} = \hat{p}_{i,n+2} - p_{i,n} \qquad (15.10)$$

Equation (15.10) is clearly too simplistic, and perhaps a more reasonable approach is to take a weighted conversion factor, extrapolating the effect of the deal into all future periods. As an approximation, the authors recommend tracking all purchases during a 3-mo period following the deal.

Empirical Results.   The authors use the learning model to evaluate promotions in several ways. First, they show who is attracted to the deals. Exhibit 15.6 shows the distribution of prepurchase probabilities for households buying a certain brand (V) on deal and not on deal. Fifty-three percent of the purchases for the brand could have been expected from consumers with low prepurchase probabilities of purchasing the brand (20 percent). However, of those who purchased on deal type 17, only 27 percent had such low prepurchase probabilities, indicating that the deal attracted steady customers (higher prepurchase probabilities of purchase) and that the attraction to new triers was low.

The authors also demonstrate how to use the model to study the relationship among deal type, brand, and product-to-product repurchase for both new buyers and for existing customers. Furthermore, they illustrate the phenomenon of size loyalty, showing that the phenomenon is occasionally stronger than brand loyalty.

Assessment.   The use of a brand-switching model (in this case a learning model) before the deal to predict "what would have happened" is a useful innovation. The linear learning model is relatively flexible and implementable, and it appears to identify the relative effectiveness of different promotional types. Although the authors do not stress it, their model, in a sense, provides a means of evaluating selective promotional response according to predeal brand loyalty. Finally, because the approach is flexible and extendable, the analyst can adapt it easily.

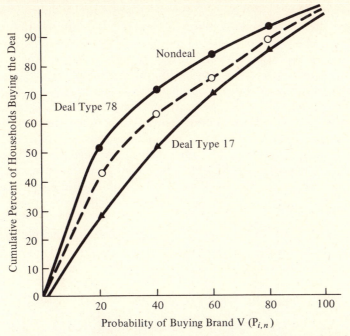

EXHIBIT 15-6 **Distribution of the prepurchase probability of brand V for households buying various brand V deals and nondeals.** (Source: Kuehn and Rohloff, "Evaluating Promotions Using a Brand Shifting Model," in *Promotional Decision Using Mathematical Models,* Allyn and Bacon, Inc., 1967a, p. 73. Reprinted by permission.)

However, there are several problems with the approach. The model is never justified, either theoretically or empirically, nor is its value compared with that of other models that might have presented different normative implications. Furthermore, it requires panel data for its use. Also, it is a descriptive model and therefore requires careful further analysis to determine what promotions should be run. Its key contribution is as an early demonstration of how a model could be used to help evaluate a promotion. In conclusion, the model perhaps does not go far enough in proving its generality and applicability; in the 14 yr since the models' publication, few similar approaches have been reported.

Rao-Lilien Model

We investigate the Rao-Lilien (1972) model for several reasons. First, the model was developed in a franchised-retail environment—gasoline in particular—and demonstrates model customization for this type of market. Second, the model demonstrates how a set of behavioral assumptions lead to a reasonable model form. Third, the modeling includes competitive effects explicitly. And fourth, the model deals with multiple, simultaneous promotions and shows how joint effects of multiple promotions can be handled.

Problem Setting.   The incentive for model development arose from the need to improve a sales-forecasting system for Mobil Corporation in the late 1960s. Two main types of promotions were leading to highly erratic retail-sales patterns: competitive games and unsolicited credit card mailings (legal at the time). In addition, many markets showed rather drastic price fluctuations, and price variation was modeled as promotional activity as well.

Gasoline games were offered in many varieties in the late sixties, but they all had certain common elements. A customer would obtain a game form with a number or other identification from the promoting brand, and, periodically, winners would be selected by random drawings. Initially, the objective was to draw customers from competitors' brands, who would then become regular customers. Later, however, the games took on a more defensive flavor and were instituted more to avoid a loss than to acquire new customers.

Credit cards were mailed to residents in certain neighborhoods who satisfied specific demographic and socioeconomic criteria. Again, a shift of customers to the mailing brand was the objective.

Note that in both of these cases it was not expected that customers would buy more than their normal quantity; rather, sales gains were seen as coming only through acquisition of new customers.

Modeling Approach.   Because of the lack of knowledge about customer heterogeneity, the authors chose an aggregate-modeling approach. In the given franchised-retail setting they hypothesized that incremental gains in sales from a promotion depend on three factors:

1. **Promotion potential.**   The potential of a promotion is related to the fraction of individuals not currently participating in a promotion. If the promoting brand(s) has a joint market share of m, then $(1 - m)$ can be switched, and potential P, the likelihood of a randomly chosen customer being in the target market, is an increasing function of $(1 - m)$.

2. **Promotion reach.**   The more outlets the promoting brand (or brands) has, the easier a willing individual will find it to participate. Thus if m is defined as above, then reach R, the likelihood that a randomly chosen customer can reach the promoting outlet, is an increasing function of m.

3. **Promotion strength.**   The more interesting the promotion, the more likely an individual will be to take advantage of it. The strength S of the promotion is modeled as $K(x, t)$, where x represents the characteristics of the promotion and t is time. The analyst might hypothesize that K is S-shaped in x (as in a price promotion) and decreasing in t (as the novelty wears off).

From these assumptions we find that the probability that a randomly chosen customer will respond to the promotion is PRS, and the expected gain, V^* per customer in the market for a promotion is

$$V^* = PRSg \tag{15.11}$$

where g is the average quantity purchased per customer during the promotional period. If there are C customers in the market, then

$$V = PRSG \tag{15.12}$$

where V is the incremental sales gain to promoting brands and $G = Cg$.

Application to Gasoline Games. The authors argue that reasonable forms for the terms in eq. (15.12) are

$$P = 1 - m \tag{15.13}$$

$$R = m^\alpha \tag{15.14}$$

$$S = K \qquad \text{(at least in the short term)} \tag{15.15}$$

These separate functional forms and the way they fit together are illustrated in Exhibit 15.7. Exhibit 15.7(c) shows that for all promoting brands the percentage volume gain is small when the share of those involved is very small (reach is low) or where share is very large (potential is low). Plugging eqs. (15.13)–(15.15) into eq. (15.12) yields

$$V = KG(1 - m)m^\alpha \tag{15.16}$$

where V is the volume gained by all game-playing brands.

Similarly, consider a nonpromoting brand with share m_0. If we let V_L be the loss to that brand, and assume loss is proportional to share, the loss is

$$V_L = KGm^\alpha(1 - m)\frac{m_0}{1 - m} \tag{15.17}$$

$$= KGm^\alpha m_0 \tag{15.18}$$

Because the expected sales volume with no promotions is $m_0 G$, the *promotional loss* P_L is

$$P_L = \frac{V_L}{m_0 G} = Km^\alpha \tag{15.19}$$

Similarly, a proportional gain P_G to a game-playing brand is modeled as

$$P_G = KGm^\alpha(1 - m)\frac{m_0}{m}\frac{1}{m_0 G} \tag{15.20}$$

$$= Km^{\alpha-1}(1 - m) \tag{15.21}$$

Note that as $m \to 1$, $P_L \to K$; therefore K is the largest proportional loss that a company can incur by not participating in the promotion.

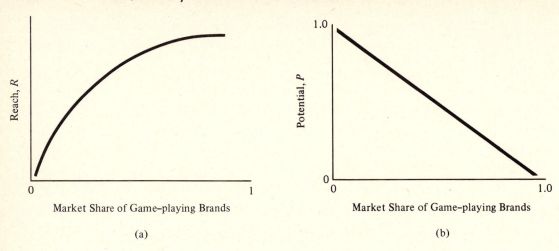

Reach, R

Market Share of Game–playing Brands

(a)

Potential, P

Market Share of Game–playing Brands

(b)

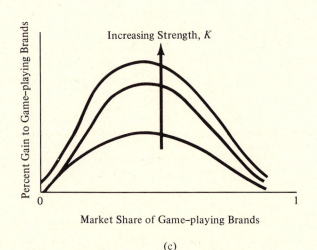

Increasing Strength, K

Percent Gain to Game–playing Brands

Market Share of Game–playing Brands

(c)

EXHIBIT 15-7   The structure of the Rao-Lilien game-promotion model.

Other Promotions. A similar development leads to a model for price changes and for credit card mailings. In gasoline markets in the 1960s, most price competition was between the group of majors (national brands) and the independents (local brands). From the standpoint of the majors, then, an increase in the price differential can be viewed as a promotion by the independents against the majors. The price model is similar to the game-promotion model:

$$P = 1 - m_I \tag{15.22}$$

$$R = m_I^{\alpha} \tag{15.23}$$

$$S = f(\delta) \tag{15.24}$$

where m_I = market share of independents

           δ = change in usual price difference between majors and independents

The approach for credit card mailings is analogous, although slightly more complicated.

Multiple Promotions and Interactions. Suppose that there were a game and a credit card mailing in a market at the same time. Then we need to calculate the joint effect of the promotion, $V_G \cup V_C$, which can be decomposed as

$$V_G \cup V_C = V_G + V_C - V_G \cap V_C \qquad (15.25)$$

If the effects are not synergistic, the intersection $V_G \cap V_C$ can be bounded logically by min (V_G, V_C) from above (all people attracted by the game, say, would have been attracted by the mailing) and from below by $V_C V_G / G$ (assuming that the proportions of the population attracted to each type of promotion are independent). Because the populations are unlikely to be independent, this latter term should understate the interaction.

     The authors suggest modeling the intersection as a convex combination of the bounds:

$$V_G \cap V_C = \lambda \min(V_G, V_C) + (1 - \lambda)\frac{V_G V_C}{G} \qquad 0 < \lambda < 1 \qquad (15.26)$$

Estimation of Parameters. The approach for estimating parameters of this model assumes that some past periods of no promotional activity exist for forecasting sales during the promotional period:

$$Y = \mu + \text{promotion effect} + \epsilon \qquad (15.27)$$

where Y = actual sales divided by forecast sales for the period

        μ = $E(Y | \text{no promotions})$ = 1 + promotional forecasting bias

        ϵ = random error

The promotion model gives the promotion effect in each market as a function of $\{K_i\}$, α, λ, and so on. Historical experience with the forecasting procedure yielded estimates of μ which were approximately one. Parameters of the model were then estimated with a nonlinear estimation procedure from the equation

$$Y^* = Y - \mu = \text{promotion effect} + \epsilon \qquad (15.28)$$

Implementation. The authors also report the results of introducing the model into the existing sales-forecasting system. Exhibit 15.8 compares the results of the time-series forecasts alone (the alternative system in use at the time) with the results after the addition of the promotion model in a market used for validation. The lag in pickup of the July–August 1967 sales spurt was attributed to an advertising campaign, not treated in the model structure. In a test of 19 markets the variance in error between 12 actual and

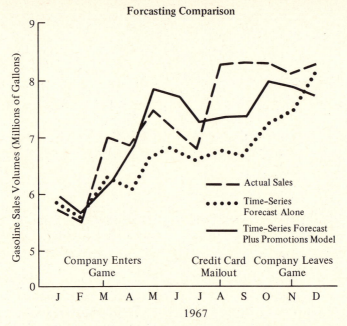

Forcasting Comparison

EXHIBIT 15-8   **Rao-Lilien model's prediction results.** (Source: Rao and Lilien, 1972, p. 159. Reprinted by permission of the Institute of Management Sciences. *Management Science,* Vol. 19, No. 2, October 1972.)

predicted monthly sales figures was reduced by over 50 percent with the use of the model.

In updating the parameters, the authors found that the game-strength parameter K was approximately half its original value 1 yr after games were introduced. Furthermore, the strength of a credit card mailing was found to peak about 4 mo after the original mailing and then gradually decline until, after 1½ yr, its value was half that at its peak. Finally, the pricing-model parameters were reported to be the least stable, suggesting that the price-model structure might be too simplistic.

The authors report using this model as a simulation tool as well. In addition to providing improved sales forecasts, a real-time version of the model was available to marketing planners to experiment (on the model) with different promotional plans and competitive assumptions.

Assessment.   This modeling approach has the advantage of providing a modular structure that can be applied to many promotional types. Furthermore, it appears to be a logical model development and has been used.

However, it is not clear whether the modeling assumptions and approach are widely applicable outside a franchise-retailing environment with nondifferentiated products. But it is one of few promotional models that deals with competitive effects and with the joint effects of several promotions explicitly.

Little's BRANDAID Promotional Model

Little's (1975) BRANDAID model contains a promotional submodel that is investigated separately here because of its unique approach. BRANDAID, as developed in Chapter 18, is an aggregate-marketing model, and Little's structure and model calibration is based on past observation rather than specific theory.

Background.   Little notes that for a typical promotion stores stock up on the product, often reduce shelf price, and sell much more of the product than they normally do. He also notes that the period of high sales is often followed by a period of reduced sales or, at least, reduced factory shipments, caused by stocking up by retailers and, often, by consumers (Blattberg, Eppen, and Lieberman, 1981). Furthermore, when retailers discover that a promotion is coming, they may hold back on their orders, causing sales to be depressed in advance of the promotion. Finally, sales of promoted packs may reduce the sales of other packs via cannibalization.

Little's model incorporates these phenomena through two constructs: a promotional time pattern and a promotional response function. The *promotional time pattern* (Exhibit 15.9) is characteristic of the given type of

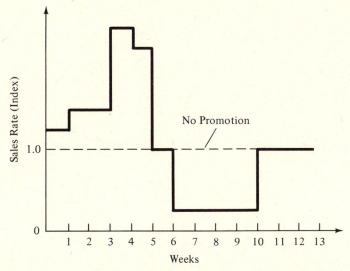

EXHIBIT 15-9   **Time pattern of response to reference promotion (from an application).** (Source: Little, 1975. Reprinted with permission from *Operations Research,* Vol. 23, Issue 4, 1975, p. 641, Operations Research Society of America.)

promotion and may include a prepromotion period of depressed sales, a postpromotion depression of varying time and intensity, and so forth. The *promotional response function* acts as a scale factor for the basic or reference promotion. It depends on the promotional intensity and produces a promotional-amplitude value of one for a reference promotional intensity of one. (See Exhibit 15.10.) The argument here is that at small values of a price-off, say, the promotion works poorly because of its lack of visibility or reluctance by retailers to accept it. Then after a certain level of intensity, the promotion reaches a peak because most retailers have accepted the promotion and are doing as much with it as they possibly can.

Modeling approach.   Little proceeds as follows. Let

$q(\tau)$ = reference index per time pattern (as in Exhibit 15.9) for reference promotion in τth period after start

$a(t)$ = promotional intensity of promotion starting in t ($a = 1$ for reference promotion and $a = 0$ for no promotion)

$r(a)$ = sales response to promotional intensity, a scale factor of time pattern [$r(1) = 1$ and $r(0) = 0$]

Q_{np} = sales expected when there is no promotion

With the above we can build up a promotional effect as follows:

Net sales gain from reference promotion at t_p

$$= Q_{np}[q(t - t_p) - 1] \qquad (15.29)$$

Net sales gain from promotion of intensity a

$$= Q_{np}[q(t - t_p) - 1]r(a(t_p)) \qquad (15.30)$$

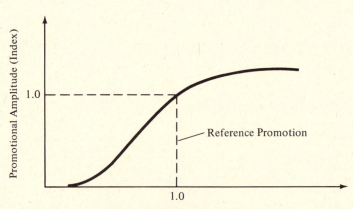

EXHIBIT 15-10   **Sales response to promotional intensity, a scale factor on the amplitude of the time pattern (hypothetical curve).** (Source: Little, 1975. Reprinted with permission from *Operations Research*, Vol. 23, Issue 4, 1975, p. 641, Operations Research Society of America.)

With no promotion for the full line, as well as cannibalization, we have

Sales gain at t from promoted portion of line

$$= Q_{np}\ell\{[q(t - t_p) - 1]r(a(t_p))\} \quad (15.31)$$

and

Total sales of line under given promotion

$$= Q_{np}\{1 + \ell(1 - b)[q(t - t_p) - 1]r(a(t_p))\} \quad (15.32)$$

where ℓ = fraction of line promoted
   b = fraction of sales gain due to cannibalization (so $1 - b$ is true gain for total product line)

When a series of promotions, indexed by subscript p, occurs, we obtain

Total sales of line under promotion schedule p

$$= Q_{np}\left\{1 + \sum_p \ell_p[1 - b_p][q_p(t - t_p) - 1] \, r_p(a_p(t_p))\right\} \quad (15.33)$$

Equation (15.33) suggests that each promotion can have its own set of parameters, but, in practice, the same time pattern and response function will usually apply to all promotions of a given type.

To account for different levels of promotional intensity, Little suggests incorporating factors similar to those for copy or media efficiency:

$x(t)$ = promotional size at t (in dollars per sale unit)
$h(t)$ = coverage efficiency at t (function of customers reached by promotion)
$k(t)$ = consumer effectiveness at t (effect of point-of-display premium quality or other consumer-oriented enhancements of basic offer)

Using the subscript zero to denote the reference promotion, we get

$$a(t) = \frac{h(t)k(t)x(t)}{h_0 k_0 x_0} \quad (15.34)$$

This equation allows for more detailed examination of promotional intensity by decomposing it into several components before applying it to eq. (15.33). **Model Calibration and Use.** The performance of the promotional submodel is not discussed separately but, rather, as an integrated part of the calibration and use of the BRANDAID model (Chapter 18). Calibration of this model includes an unspecified combination of historical, statistical-analysis, and managerial judgment as first steps, followed by tracking and, if possible, field measurement and adaptive control. In a reported case study—GROOVY—the BRANDAID model as a whole tracked sales well both during the period of calibration and afterward. Because the promotional submodel was an important element in this market, we can infer that the promotional model performed adequately.

This promotional model has been used as part of the BRANDAID structure for brand promotional planning in a number of companies, reportedly with success, especially in diagnosis and tracking. There the brand-management team is concerned with understanding why an effect is taking place and with determining which of several alternative actions are best. The model appears well suited to this purpose.

Assessment. Little's model is the most modular and flexible model reviewed here and, in that sense, the most useful. Its reliance on a template of past promotional patterns as a base to adjust from is innovative and quite realistic because promotional effects are bumpy. The weakness of the model is that it is not based on theory—a future promotion is assumed to be a modified form of a past promotion. In addition, because the calibration is part statistical and part judgmental, it is not clear how to determine if the model is adequate in a specific situation. Furthermore, this model would be difficult to adapt to situations other than consumer packaged goods. In conclusion, however, it is probably the most managerially useful model in the published literature to date.

Other Promotional Models

A number of other interesting modeling efforts in this area have appeared in the literature, with varying degrees of success and applicability.

Aaker (1973) uses a stochastic choice model, similar to that of Kuehn and Rohloff, to describe predeal and postdeal behavior. His major innovation is the normative nature of his model: he breaks up the value of a promotion into the short-term value (the increased loyalty among existing customers) and the long-run value associated with switchers. Most of his effort is the derivation of the long-run value of switchers, which is shown to depend on new triers' buying potential, brand profitability, brand acceptance, and the firm's discount factor. Although it is an interesting and potentially valuable modeling effort, no application of the model is reported, and it is not used with any empirical data.

Blattberg and colleagues (1978) treat household purchasing and inventory decisions like those of a firm, assuming that purchasing decisions are based on transaction costs, holding costs, and stockout costs, in addition to product characteristics. Household characteristics are then related to these cost parameters to identify those households most likely to be deal-prone. Empirical tests on panel data from five frequently purchased products show that deal-prone households can be identified with variables such as home ownership and automobile ownership.

In later work Blattberg, Eppen, and Lieberman (1981) develop an inventory-control model which incorporates retailer and consumer costs and yields different implications for the manufacturer from those of brand-switching models. In particular, this work assumes that consumers purchase to minimize total cost (purchase cost plus holding cost) and that the retailer sets price to maximize profit. The authors conclude that dealing increases sales primarily through stockpiling, resulting in a sales trough after the deal [consistent with Little's model and with the work of Brown (1973)]. This is a different view than the brand-switching view, and "... both explanations can be true and the cause of dealing. Theoretical and empirical work needs to be done comparing the inventory model ... with other explanations for dealing" (p. 129).

Keon (1980a), in an extension of his (1980b) bargain-value model, relates probability of purchase of a brand to its bargain value, which is defined as its monetary worth (to the individual) divided by its price. A price promotion affects the brand's bargain value directly. In addition, Keon assumes that consumers associate different utilities with different package sizes, independent of price or brand, and that purchase quantity is a function of normal purchase habits, inventory, and price discount (if any).

Keon's approach is first to examine the frequency distributions of purchase probability, on the basis of his model and assumptions, and then the direction and magnitude of the change in the distribution following certain promotions. The model examines and relates four significant variables—price, purchase quantity, package size, and brand loyalty—in a consistent framework and, as such, could be a useful tool. However, the model—called PROMODEL—is still in a developmental stage and awaits testing.

Other well-known promotional-modeling efforts include Magee's (1953) analysis of the relationship between sales volume and frequency of promotional attention in an industrial setting. His definition of promotional effort mainly encompasses sales calls, so his effort is not directly applicable to our more limited definition. Massy and Frank (1965) use a (transformed) linear-regression model, in distributed lag form, to model the effect of relative price and dealing activity on different market segments. The results indicate general success in measuring promotional effects and in identifying differential effectiveness of different market segments. Hopkins and Parsons (1981) provide a detailed literature review, related primarily to the behavioral effects of couponing.

Finally, to sum up the need for better theory and models, Wilson (1980) provides a set of model-testing procedures for promotional evaluation. He recommends the combination of objective and subjective testing procedures, the use of multiple models for comparison purposes, and the use of multiple criterion variables.

Thus the term "promotions" covers a heterogeneous set of activities with potentially different impacts in different markets and for different product classes. For these reasons a dominant theory and a dominant model of promotional effects have not emerged. With our present state of knowledge, we must first try to understand the effects the specific promotion(s) are likely to have and then choose a model to deal with those effects. The several models analyzed in depth provide three different approaches to modeling promotions; the other references present other views.

There is clearly a need for an integrating theory—perhaps in the form of a taxonomy—to help the marketer choose the right promotion and the right promotional model for his needs. In the meantime, some important, useful, and applicable tools have been developed, which, with suitable application of managerial judgment, can be of significant help in making promotional decisions.

Summary

Sales promotions are a mixed set of activities that are often not as well understood in their role in the marketing mix as are, for example, advertising and salesforce decisions. Included as promotions are a wide variety of short-term-incentive tools, such as coupons, premiums, contests, and buying allowances, designed to stimulate earlier and/or stronger market response. They can be used to stimulate consumer markets or the trade, as well as to support the organization's own salesforce.

Models for sales-promotion evaluation have considered several different phenomena. One is the long-term-profit effect from brand switchers. Another is the short-term phenomena among regular buyers of stocking up. A third phenomenon, the capture of deal-prone users, is dealt with in several models as well. The models reviewed here provide both insight into promotional effects and practical tools for assessing and planning sales promotions. Modeling approaches have dealt with short-term and long-term effects, both at the individual and at the aggregate level, with proven effectiveness.

Therefore model-based tools to assist in making promotional decisions are available. They depend, as do all good models, on an insightful manager to blend his decision needs, data, and understanding of the marketplace in choosing an appropriate analytical approach. Although modeling in this area is in need of an integrating theory, practical and usable tools are currently available and need only minor customization for many immediate applications.

Problems

15.1 Why is sales promotion less frequently modeled than advertising or personal-selling activities?

15.2 What differences between sales response to media advertising and to a cents-off coupon would lead to different modeling strategies?

15.3 Joe Prince, marketing manager of XYZ Snack, is considering offering a case allowance to the trade. He expects sales to be 40,000 cases in the absence of promotion. The case price is $10 and the gross profit contribution is 40%. He is considering a $1 case allowance. He expects sales of 20,000 cases during the promotional period. The estimated cost of developing this promotion is $12,000.
a. Will he make a profit on this promotion?
b. What is the break-even sales increase that will justify this case allowance?

15.4 The Market Research Department of the *Boston Globe* has determined that a Bostonian has a probability p_i of buying its Sunday edition. It has also been established that these probabilities have a distribution $f(p)$ across the population. This purchase probability distribution may be approximated as

$$f(p) = \begin{cases} a + bp & 0 \le p \le 1, 0 < a < 2 \\ 0 & \text{otherwise} \end{cases}$$

The parameter a is related to the level of promotion (in thousands of dollars) as

$$a = \begin{cases} 2 - x^{1/2} & 4 \ge x \ge 0 \\ 0 & x > 4 \end{cases}$$

Suppose that there are 500,000 Bostonians and that the *Globe* price is 20¢. Furthermore, assume that the incremental profit is 12% of retail sales.

a. What are the maximum and minimum values of the *Globe*'s expected reach?
b. Find the level of promotion that maximizes the *Globe*'s expected profit.
c. What is the expected reach and profit at this level?

15.5 A manufacturer of men's dress shirts has a promotional budget of $80 (in thousands of dollars) and wishes to determine which allocation of this budget between its two territories will maximize profits. The demand functions for territories 1 and 2 are

$$Q_1 = 10X_1^{1/2} \qquad Q_2 = 5X_2^{1/2}$$

where X_i is the amount of promotional dollars spent in territory i. The respective cost functions are

$$C_1 = 100 + 6Q_1 + X_1, \qquad C_2 = 30 + 4Q_2 + X_2$$

a. Suppose $P_1 = \$7$ and $P_2 = \$8$. What is the optimal allocation of the budget between the two territories?
b. Could additional profits be made by increasing the budget?
c. What is the optimal budget?

15.6 An interesting situation develops between a manufacturer and an independent distributor over promotional effort to the final customer. Let

$i = 1$ refer to manufacturer, 2 to distributor
z_i = profit rate, $/yr

x_i = promotional effort, \$/yr
g_i = incremental profit as fraction of *retail* sales
c_{0i} = fixed-cost rate, \$/yr
 s = retail-sales rate, \$/yr
 $s = \alpha \ln \beta (x_1 + x_2)$

a. What will x_1 and x_2 be if the manufacturer and the distributor independently try to maximize profit? Are you sure?

b. What value of $x_1 + x_2$ will maximize total profit in the system?

15.7 Use the Rao-Lilien model:

a. At what market share of game-playing brands is the total volume gained by game-playing brands maximized? (Assume $\alpha = 0.2$.)

b. Consider a gasoline market. You are the manager at Pepgas who is in charge of deciding whether or not to have a game. You have determined that the market is stable with respect to price, there will be no credit card mailouts in the near future, and total market gasoline-sales volume (G) is stable. Right now a share of the market, m, is involved in games. Determine under what circumstances to have a game if π = profit margin per sales unit and K, the cost of running the game, is fixed.

c. Assume that two brands (major, independent) exist in a gasoline market. Independent has set his price at P_I and has market share m_I; the cost to companies at the pump is C per gallon.

   i. Compare and contrast the Rao-Lilien price model with the Gabor-Granger model (Chapter 12) (model assumptions, robustness, etc.).

   ii. What are the implications of the two models for sales-maximizing policies? For profit-maximizing policies? Which seems more relevant to this situation?

15.8 The drug industry has been subject to considerable public criticism. It faces some interesting promotional problems. Suppose that a group of N pharmaceutical firms selling indistinguishable products for the same price are competing with one another by promotion. The market is of fixed size and is insensitive to price. For sales response assume the steady state of a Lanchester model with equal promotional effectiveness, that is,

$$s_i = \frac{x_i}{\sum_{j=1}^{N} x_j} M$$

Let

x_i = promotional spending rate of company i, \$/yr
s_i = sales rate of company i
M = total market for product, units per year
p = selling price
c_1 = incremental cost of producing unit, dollars per unit
c_0 = fixed-cost rate for company, exclusive of promotion \$/yr

Each company manipulates its x_i to try to maximize its own profit.

a. What will be the spending, sales, and profit rates for each?

b. If each company raises its price until its profit is a fraction r of sales, what will the price be?

c. With the price as in part b, what will be the fraction f of the customer's dollars that is being spent on promotion?

d. Suppose $r = 5\%$, $N = 4$, and $c_0 = 0.15c_1 M/N$ for each company. What will f be?

CHAPTER 16

Salesforce Models

Every organization has one or more individuals who have direct responsibility for interacting with prospects and customers. This group of individuals is called the salesforce. Their role in the marketing mix varies from firm to firm. Furthermore, anyone is a company salesperson when he is trying to win business for the company, including officers and servicemen, as well as salespersons who are hired to do full-time selling. We restrict the term "salesperson" here to those who earn their livelihood primarily through selling.

In this chapter we concentrate on field selling, which is found in almost every industry and involves a salesforce that travels to actual and potential buyers. Salespersons may all work out of a central office, or they may be located in the different territories for which they have individual responsibility. Furthermore, they may report to district managers, who report to regional or general sales managers.

Sales management is involved in two main areas: administration and strategy. Administration includes recruiting, selection, training, assigning, compensating, motivating, and controlling the salesforce, while strategy deals with issues of force sizing, territory design, and call-planning procedures. Although administration and strategy are not completely separate, our focus in this book is on normative approaches to strategy questions, and our coverage emphasizes that focus.

Personal Selling: Tasks, Importance, and Models

The Role of the Salesforce

Narrowly defined, the objective of the salesforce is to sell. But the role of the salesperson has many dimensions. Selling is a communications process in which information is transmitted and persuasive messages applied. But it is a two-way process, and communications can be modified or adjusted during the process. As the link between the buying and the selling organization, the salesperson provides what Spekman (1979) refers to as boundary-spanning activities:

Represents and transacts.   The salesperson is the face of the organization but is charged with representing the needs of two organizations: his firm and the customer's organization.

Buffers.   The salesperson has to promote environmental stability, smoothing irregularities between production cycles in his organization and the sales-ordering cycle of the customer.

Processes information and monitors.   The salesperson provides a continual flow of information about market and environmental conditions that is vital to the activities of the producing firm.

Links and coordinates.   The salesperson guides informal coordination efforts between the producing and client firms or through middlemen to the client firm.

The salesperson must act as a problem solver, understanding the customer's problem and how it can be solved through the use of the firm's products. His role varies widely depending on the industry. In consumer-goods companies the salesperson calls on retail outlets, services the accounts, arranges for displays and shelf positions, and so on, while in many industrial-product situations the salesperson also has to identify and solve a unique customer problem, a job requiring substantial independence and creativity.

Thus the salesperson performs a large number of functions, the impacts and influences of which may be difficult to quantify, presenting a challenge for the quantitative model builder.

Salesforce Decision Problems

Exhibit 16.1 shows the four main phases of the management of the personal-selling function. First, the role of personal selling in the firm's marketing mix must be defined by establishing goals or criteria for use in salesforce decision making. Second, a resource commitment to the effort must be established, which involves developing a salesforce budget and determining

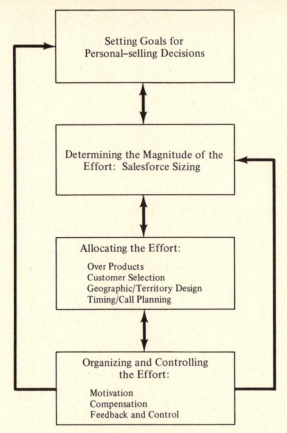

EXHIBIT 16-1 **The structure of salesforce decision problems.** (Source: David B. Montgomery and Glen L. Urban, *Management Science in Marketing*, 1969, p. 244. Reprinted by permission of Prentice-Hall, Inc., Englewood Cliffs, N.J.)

the size of the salesforce. Third, resources must be allocated to establish how effort is spread over the dimensions of customers, products, sales territories, and time (i.e., scheduling of calls). Finally, organization, motivation, and control of selling effort must be considered: the structure of the salesforce and the levels of reporting responsibility must be set; motivation and compensation schemes must be established; training and assignment of salespersons must be considered; and the results of the selling effort—sales performance—must be monitored and fed back into these other decision areas to assist the firm in adapting to changing market conditions.

The two-directional flows in Exhibit 16.1 suggest that this process is cyclical rather than sequential. Salesforce goals affect the magnitude of the effort, but the size of the effort limits possible goals as well. The size of the salesforce affects its allocation, but at the allocation stage the firm may discover that sales response is greater (or less) than expected, and therefore profitability may be enhanced by allocating more (or fewer) resources to personal selling. The initial-salesforce-size decision may also be updated in light of customer and territory allocations. Simultaneous determination of these management problems would be ideal, but, in practice, firms usually allocate resources sequentially across the dimensions.

The Importance of Salesforce Planning

The salesforce represents a large investment for most firms, especially in the industrial-goods area. According to the annual McGraw-Hill survey, the average cost of an industrial sales call in 1981 was $137, while the average cost to close a sale (the average cost of a sales call times the reported number of visits required to close a sale) was $589. These costs vary considerably by industry, with a closing cost for transportation equipment at $1121.

Exclusive of the cost of sales management and overhead, the median cost of the salesforce was 6.3 percent of sales for a sample of 125 United States industrial products and 9.9 percent for a sample of 80 European products (Lilien and Weinstein, 1983). In aggregate, salesforce-related expenditures exceed those of other marketing functions; Lambert (1968) estimated that salesforce spending is between 1.6 and 3.0 times the amount allocated to advertising.

In addition, as pointed out by Zoltners and Gardner (1980), these large expenditures are directed at a dynamic internal and external environment. They report that a "leading consumer products firm recently increased a divisional salesforce by 50 percent when it introduced a single new product" (p. 2). New products, in particular, are most often sold through the company's salesforce; when these products mature, they are often removed from the salesforce's portfolio and sold through distributors (Lilien, 1979).

The nature and structure of the salesforce will change with changes in the internal environment. Zoltners and Gardner (1980) report that an industrial firm recently tripled its salesforce for a particular division when the products of that division were classified as stars. Mergers of several firms often require a new territory alignment or reallocation of sales calls.

In addition, changes in the external environment of the firm affect salesforce decisions in important ways. Changes in customers' purchasing organizations may necessitate salesforce restructuring: a centralized purchasing facility can change with the location and the magnitude of the sale, requiring modification in sales call frequency, as well as potential reassignment of sales personnel.

Finally, salesforce decisions, once made, are more difficult to change than decisions in other functional areas; people are affected by salesforce decisions, and this human investment is not as easily changed as decisions in advertising, promotion, or pricing. Controlled experimentation and shifts in allocations are risky, expensive, and hard to justify. Shifts in salesforce allocations may break old, favorable customer relationships. Furthermore, the long lead time involved in recruiting, hiring, and training new salespeople makes increases in sales resources a gradual process, and once a salesperson is a firm's employee, termination and replacement costs lobby against releasing the individual during short-term economic downturns.

Modeling Salesforce Problems

There are a range of management-science models aimed at salesforce decision problems. A review by Zoltners and Gardner (1980) covers over 60 articles in the field, Cravens (1979) reviews 22 models, and Zoltners and Sinha (1980) produce 48 references for integer-programming models of sales resource allocation alone.

On the surface the types of problems that face sales management— sizing of the force, allocating the salesforce, scheduling calls, structuring sales territories—appear well suited to many of the quantitative approaches that characterize the methodology of management science and operations research, such as integer programming, dynamic programming, assignment problems, and transportation problems. In fact, developments in the field are numerous, and both integrative models [Beswick and Cravens (1977) for example] and empirical model tests (Fudge and Lodish, 1977) have been reported. But implementation rates, although not reported systematically, appear to be low: a small number of organizations are using isolated pieces of methodology. Improvements in implementation rates will occur when the role and activity of the salesperson are better understood and when management-science approaches are no longer felt to be threatening and intimidating to sales managers.

In the following sections we present model-based approaches for salesforce sizing, sales resource allocation, territory design, and quota and compensation setting, as well as integrative-modeling approaches to salesforce problems.

Salesforce Sizing

The size of the salesforce is one of the most important decisions facing executives in many industries. In practice, this decision is affected by other elements in the marketing mix and influences the overall marketing strategy. The specific options chosen—salesforce size versus the use of wholesalers, distributors, agents, and so forth—depend on the relative costs and the selling tasks required [See Corey (1976, chap. 4) for a discussion of the trade-offs here.]

Breakdown and Work-Load Methods

To address the problem of salesforce sizing, many firms use one of several relatively simple approaches: the breakdown, or percentage-of-sales, approach and the work-load approach.

In the *percentage-of-sales approach* a sales forecast is prepared, a historical (or otherwise justified) percentage of sales is applied against the forecast, and the average cost of a salesperson is divided into this figure to get the salesforce size.

In the *breakdown method* the average revenue generated by a salesperson is divided into the sales forecast to get a salesforce-size figure. Neither the breakdown nor the percentage-of-sales variation have much to recommend it (besides simplicity) because each ignores the interaction between the number of salespersons and sales, as well as the factors that influence salespersons' productivity.

Talley (1961) recommends another approach based on *equalizing the work load* of sales representatives. His approach assumes management has determined the optimum number of calls to make on accounts of different types and has the following steps:

1. Customers are grouped into classes according to size (although other criteria may be used).
2. The desired call frequencies (number of sales calls per account per unit time) are established for each class.
3. The number of accounts of each class are multiplied by the corresponding call frequency to arrive at the total work load for the region or county.
4. The average number of calls a sales representative can make per year is determined.
5. The number of sales representatives needed is determined by dividing the total annual calls required by the average annual calls made by a sales representative.

EXAMPLE: Suppose the firm has three classes of customers, as described in Exhibit 16.2. The product requires 4200 calls per year. If an average representative can make 700 calls per year, then six sales representatives are required.

As with the breakdown method, the work-load method is easy to use and has had wide application. [See Fogg and Rokus (1973) for an adaptation used to decide the mix of direct salespersons and manufacturers' representatives.] But, again, no account is taken of the influence of the call rate on the sales of a given customer, and it ignores the issue of how call rates are determined. Furthermore, the approach does not view salesforce-size determination as an investment that should yield the highest possible profitable return.

EXHIBIT 16-2   **Work-load-approach example for salesforce sizing.**

Customer Category	Number of Customers	Calls per Year	Total Calls
A	30	24	720
B	90	12	1080
C	400	6	2400

Total Calls Required $= 4200$

$$\text{Number of Salespeople} = \frac{\text{Total Calls Required}}{\text{Number of Calls per Salesperson per Year}}$$

$$= \frac{4200}{700} = 6$$

Industry-Guidelines Methods

An increasing number of firms are relying on new quantitative industry guidelines to support their selling (and communications) expenditure decisions. The basic idea is that budgeting expenditures are related to a number of product and market characteristics. Two main efforts have attempted to explain differences in marketing-spending levels by studying a cross section of business situations. One comes from the ADVISOR project and is specifically aimed at industrial firms (Lilien, 1979). The other is based on the PIMS project (Buzzell and Farris, 1976). The uses and limitations of this cross-sectional approach for setting a selling budget are discussed in Chapter 18.

Market-Response Methods

To determine the most profitable salesforce size, one must recognize that the salesforce budget, the number of salespersons to employ, and the compensation scheme are intimately interconnected. The compensation scheme affects the quality of the people that can be attracted to a position, as well as the way they perform (i.e., the sales response to selling effort). With this simultaneity in mind, and with the recognition that all steps in Exhibit 16.1 may have to be performed iteratively, consider the following simplistic approach (from Montgomery and Urban, 1969).

Assume that the best level of salesforce size is one that maximizes the profit rate. Then the salesforce-sizing problem is to find X*, the level of selling effort that maximizes Z, profit:

$$\max Z = PQ(X) - C_1(Q) - C_2(X) \tag{16.1}$$

where Z = profit
           P = selling price
           Q = number of units sold as function of selling effort

$C_1(Q)$ = total cost of producing and merchandising Q units
$C_2(X)$ = total cost of selling effort of level X

Equation (16.1) assumes all other elements in the marketing mix are fixed (price, advertising, etc.), no carry-over or competitive effects exist, a single product is sold by the salesperson, a compensation scheme for the salesperson is well established, and so on. It also assumes that the salespersons have a given average quality that is linked to the (given) compensation scheme.

This equation is naive, yet it points out the key unknown variable: the elements P, $C_1(Q)$, and $C_2(X)$ are likely to be known (or at least readily estimable), but $Q(X)$, the sales response to selling effort, is not. Several approaches for estimating $Q(X)$ have been proposed, including analysis of historical data, field experimentation, and simulation. The first two of these are discussed below. [Montgomery and Urban (1969, pp. 253 ff) discuss the simulation approach in this context, but little use of that approach has been reported.]

Under the assumption that the future will in some way be like the past, historical sales records in many firms may form the basis to infer the relationship between selling effort and sales. A widely discussed approach by Semlow (1959) requires (1) a good measure of the sales potential of each sales territory and (2) historical sales-performance records of salespersons in territories of different potential. He postulates that territories having greater sales potential would also have more (but not proportionately more) sales, and he graphs a set of data for 25 territories relating sales volume as a fraction of market potential to percentage of (national) sales potential represented by that sales territory:

$$\frac{Q_i}{P_i} = f(P_i) \tag{16.2}$$

where P_i = percent of total potential in territory i
Q_i = actual sales in territory i

The relationship in Semlow's example approximates a hyperbola and, at first glance, appears quite powerful. Although Semlow does not suggest a function form for f, Weinberg and Lucas (1977) propose

$$\frac{Q_i}{P_i} = kP_i^{\alpha} \tag{16.3}$$

and fit it to his data, yielding

$$\frac{Q_i}{P_i} = 233P_i^{-0.985} \tag{16.4}$$

with adjusted $R^2 = 0.79$ and $t(\alpha) = 9.66$.

The problem with Semlow's analysis is that P_i is present on both sides of the equation (i.e., plotting $Y = 1/X$ against X will yield a hyperbolic relationship). In reanalyzing Semlow's data, Weinberg and Lucas consider

$$Q_i = kP_i^\alpha \tag{16.5}$$

which yields $K = 231$ and $\alpha = 0.022$ with adjusted $R^2 = 0.00$ and $t(\alpha) = 0.22$. They conclude that "Semlow's results have no explanatory power" (p. 147). This result does not suggest that "potential" cannot be an important determinant of sales level, but in this case it is not (or at least the measure used by Semlow was not).

A more careful analysis by Lucas, Weinberg, and Clowes (1975) related sales level to territorial potential and work load. Using both linear and log-linear structures, the authors show that significant variation in sales can be explained by potential and work load. However, the relationships vary somewhat by region.

They suggest the following normative analysis for determining sales-force size:

$$\max Z = mXf\left(\frac{P}{X}, \frac{W}{X}\right) - CX \tag{16.6}$$

where m = profit margin per unit sold
  X = number of salespersons
  C = cost per salesperson
  P = corporate potential
  W = corporate work load

They illustrate the optimization by specifying

$$f(P, W) = aP_i^{b_1}W_i^{b_2} \tag{16.7}$$

and show that an optimal salesforce size can be determined by

$$X = \left[\frac{maP^{b_1}W^{b_2}(1 - b_1 - b_2)}{C(b_1 + b_2)}\right] \tag{16.8}$$

The limitations of this approach include the difficulty of evaluating equal-potential or equal-work-load markets. Furthermore, the controllable variables are not independent, all salespersons are not alike, and short-term variations in salesforce size are limited. These problems suggest that the results be used with caution:

> The impact of these limitations does not make the optimization procedure meaningless, but it does affect the way the solution should be used. Given the limitations, the results only provide directional information. For example, if the optimum size of the salesforce is substantially larger than the current size of the salesforce, then the implication is that the firm should reduce the average size of its territories and increase the number of salespersons it employs. Depending upon the specific problem this may imply that the firm should in-

crease its capacity for training new salespersons or merely that the company should seek to reallocate its existing salesforce (Lucas, Weinberg, and Clowes, 1975, p. 304).

In sum, some successful historical analyses of the relationship between sales level and potential have been completed that can lead to normative implications for salesforce-sizing decisions. However, in this approach aggregate relationships are derived that assume that the firm's current sales-effort-allocation program will remain unchanged, but sales revenues are also a function of how the sales effort is allocated across products markets, sales regions, and so forth.

Alternatively, the relationship between selling effort and sales can be inferred by experimental procedures. In theory, this method is best, but, practically, experimentation is a costly and time-consuming procedure. Furthermore, because changes in the size of the salesforce for experimental purposes require changing the number and locations of people, it may be organizationally infeasible.

Nevertheless, several experimental studies have been reported. Brown, Hulswit, and Kettelle (1956) report on a study where salespersons were to allocate varying levels of effort to three groups of accounts, and response measures were inferred. The particular design allowed salespersons to choose which accounts would receive medium effort and which would receive low effort, while large accounts received the highest level of effort. This approach violates the random-assignment assumption necessary for a good experimental design and contributes to an overstatement of market response to sales effort.

In another study Waid, Clark, and Ackoff (1956) report on experimental variations in the level of calling frequency. The results suggest that the company was operating in a saturation region of an (assumed) S-shaped sales-response curve. The Lamp Division of General Electric reduced the number of calls per customer and reported significant cost savings without increasing its salesforce.

However, these examples of experimentation in salesforce size are the exception. In general, experimentation is most likely to enter the salesforce-size decision indirectly, through the results of allocation studies or frequency-and-scheduling studies. Meidan (1982) provides an overview and evaluation of these and other methods for salesforce sizing.

Allocation of Selling Effort

In the allocation of selling effort we address the following basic questions:

How can salespersons best utilize their time, allocating it between customers and prospects?

How should selling effort be allocated to products?

Here we assume that sales territories are fixed; we relax this assumption in the next section.

Time Allocation: Salesperson Call Planning (CALLPLAN)

In most markets all customers are not identical. Therefore three types of questions generally must be asked about a salesperson's call-selection procedure: (1) How much time should be spent with each prospect? (2) How much time should be spent with each current customer? (3) How should time be allocated between customers and prospects?

CALLPLAN (Lodish, 1971b, 1974) is an interactive salesperson's call-planning system. Its objective is to determine call-frequency norms for each client (current customer) and each prospect (account not currently buying from the salesperson). Call frequencies are the numbers of calls per effort period, which is the time period on which the allocations are based (usually 1–3 mo).

The model is based on the assumption that the expected sales to each client and prospect over a response period (usually a year) is a function of the average number of calls per effort period during that response period. The response period is assumed to be long enough so that phenomena such as carry-over in call effort from one period to the next are considered.

The CALLPLAN procedure has two phases:

1. the calibration stage, in which the expected profit associated with different call policies for each customer and prospect is determined
2. the optimization phase, in which optimal allocation of time to customers and prospects is established

Calibration Phase.   Lodish suggests a decision-calculus approach for calibrating the response function with each salesperson's own best estimate of customer response to changes in call frequency, as follows. For each customer i, let $r_i(X_i)$ be the expected sales to account i during the response period if X_i calls are made during the effort period.

In practice, Lodish recommends asking for five discrete levels of X_i, where X_{ic} is the current level: (1) no calls $(0, r_0)$; (2) half the current rate $(X_{ic}/2, r_{0.5})$; (3) the current rate (X_{ic}, r_1); (4) 1.5 times the current rate $(1.5X_{ic}, r_{1.5})$; and (5) a saturation rate (∞, r_∞). Furthermore, he suggests the following functional form to represent $r(X)$.

$$r_i(X_i) = r_0 + (r_\infty - r_0)\frac{X_i^{a_1}}{a_2 + X_i^{a_1}} \qquad (16.9)$$

The values of a_1 and a_2 can be fit globally over the full range by nonlinear regression. A simple procedure fits the parameters in two steps:

first over the call rates $X_i \le X_{ic}$ and then over the call rates $X_i > X_{ic}$. The curve in eq. (16.9) can either be concave or S-shaped, as displayed in Exhibit 4.12.

The expected sales to a client or prospect are multiplied by an adjustment factor f_i, specific to the account, to obtain an adjusted number that reflects the contribution of sales to that customer.

The salespersons's territory is divided into J mutually exclusive geographic areas. A certain time per call is assumed that takes into consideration the average travel time to account i when in geographic area j. The number of trips to a geographic area is assumed to be the maximum number of times any one account is called upon during the effort period.

Optimization Phase. If we let

t_i = time spent with customer i (call length)
n_j = number of trips per effort period made to geographic area j
U_j = time it takes to get to geographic area j
C_j = out-of-pocket expenses involved in getting to geographic area j
e = number of effort periods per response period
T = selling plus travel time available per effort period

then

$t_i X_i$ = time spent with customer i during effort period
$n_j U_j$ = time getting to geographic area j during effort period

The problem is to find integer values $\{X_i\}$ to

$$\max Z = \sum_i f_i r_i(X_i) - e \sum_j n_j C_j \quad \text{(profit)} \qquad (16.10)$$

subject to

$$\sum_i X_i t_i + \sum_j n_j U_j \le T \quad \text{(time constraint)}$$

$$n_j = \max(X_i \text{ in geographic area } j)$$

$$LB_i \le X_i \le UB_i \quad \begin{array}{l}\text{(minimum and maximum} \\ \text{bounds on calling frequency)}\end{array}$$

Lodish (1971b) describes an intricate dynamic-programming approach to solve system (16.10). However, when $r_i(X_i)$ is replaced by its linear concave envelope (see Exhibit 16.3), an incremental-analysis search procedure provides very efficient solutions. The CALLPLAN approach is usually interactive, with salesmen putting in input values, looking at the results, modifying the input values, and so on. Therefore this fast, approximate approach is quite adequate.

Application. The CALLPLAN procedure is usually applied in an organization through a 1- or a 1½-day seminar including salespersons, salesforce

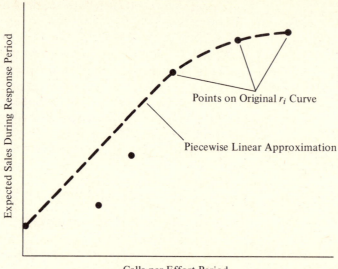

EXHIBIT 16-3   **Sales-response levels and piecewise, linear, concave approximation.**

managers, and a corporate staff person (leader). The leader introduces the model concepts and explains the data input needed for the model. Most of the time (2–4 h) is needed to estimate the effects of changes in call frequency on sales to each account. Lodish contends that the very process of having salespersons and their managers evaluate alternative call frequencies for each account is beneficial by itself, even if no computer analysis is done with the data, but that it would be difficult to motivate them to spend so much time on such a task without a goal. Most of the rest of the time is spent fine-tuning estimates, discussing results, and doing sensitivity analyses of call-policy alternatives. The procedure is reportedly in regular use (updating done quarterly to annually depending on the application) in over twenty firms.

Experimental Test.   Interestingly, a controlled experiment was run at United Airlines on the use of CALLPLAN (Fudge and Lodish, 1977). United Airlines has a salesforce to promote passenger travel and another to promote air freight operations. Account call frequency determines, to a large degree, the efficiency of their time allocation.

Twenty salespersons (16 passenger representatives and 4 cargo representatives) participated in the experiment; 10 pairs of salespersons (5 in New York and 5 in San Francisco) were matched by local management. Ten CALLPLAN participants were chosen randomly, one from each pair. Then the remaining 10 salespersons comprised the control group. This group was told they were participating in an experiment and manually estimated call-frequency policies and anticipated sales for each account to compare with CALLPLAN. Therefore major sources of potential contamination were largely controlled for.

After 6 mo the CALLPLAN group had an 11.9 percent increase in sales from the previous year, while the control group had only a 3.8 percent increase; thus the CALLPLAN users realized an 8.1 percent higher level of sales. This difference was significantly different from 0 at the 0.025 level. The actual sales improvement over that of the control group for just these ten people was "well into seven figures" (p. 104).

According to the evaluation committee at United Airlines, the observed benefits of CALLPLAN are as follows:

> prepares a formal forecast and builds an account-by-account analysis, giving it authority.
>
> formalizes the planning process and gives it a long-range character not now present.
>
> redirects calls to more susceptive accounts to get more revenue.
>
> highlights selling time versus time spent on other tasks.
>
> emphasizes a planned call with predetermined objectives over a drop-in type (p. 105).

Assessment.   The CALLPLAN model provides several important contributions. First, it is an operational procedure for salesperson's time allocation. Second, its value has been experimentally tested with success. And third, it points out the value of modeling and computer analysis in this context. Because the judgments were made by the salespersons themselves, they could clearly be inaccurate or biased. Therefore the value of the approach is to provide the salesperson—the decision maker here—with a means of evaluating his decisions by using the available information (his judgment); the computer and the model provide a systematic way of evaluating that information, identifying inconsistencies and allowing for sensitivity analysis.

The model appears to be best suited for repetitive selling situations with single (or at most a few) products. In these situations the amount of time with the client may well relate to the amount of sales generated. In addition, the model seems best suited for rather mature product lines where knowledge of the customer base and sales potential is greatest.

Allocation of Selling Resources Across Products (DETAILER)

Quite often a single salesforce must handle a range of products. Under these circumstances selling time must be allocated across the products in a cost-effective manner. This decision is a difficult one. New products often need several years of selling before sales reach potential. During this time selling effort is an investment, and short-term measures of effectiveness, like sales volume or profitability, lobby against promoting them heavily. Yet effort on behalf of such products ties in closely with the long-term health of the firm. Thus the strategic direction of the firm—the longer-term commitment to a changing product and market mix—must be carefully considered in setting time allocations for certain products. The longer-term perspective may necessitate the salesforce allocating a disproportionate amount of time to a certain set of products at the expense of short-term profits.

Management can take one of two main approaches to this allocation question. The first treats the problem directly while the second deals with the problem indirectly through the compensation system. Ideally, the salesperson's compensation should reward him for acting optimally *for the firm*. The compensation issue is explored in some depth later; we deal with a direct allocation model here.

Montgomery, Silk, and Zaragoza (1971) developed DETAILER, a decision-calculus model for the salesforce-allocation question, which deals with the carry-over effect of sales effort. Their approach assumes that the firm sells a group of products with a salesforce of fixed size and for which cross elasticities of demand are minimal, and their objective function is the maximization of total company profits. Furthermore, they assume the salespersons are not compensated on commission.

Model Background.   The model was developed for an ethical drug company, whose salespersons (known as detail men) call mainly on doctors. Territories were designed so that there were approximately the same number of doctors (N) for each detail man.

The authors assume that no more than three products can be effectively presented in a single sales visit. Then the key decision variables in planning time allocation are the number of times and the number of customers to whom a product should be promoted in a given period. Therefore the authors further assume that there are four discrete, alternative policies for coverage:

N calls per period (complete coverage)

$N/2$ calls per period (half coverage)

$N/4$ calls per period (quarter coverage)

0 calls per period (no coverage)

Because each detailman contacts N customers and promotes three products on each call, there is a total effort of $3N$ product calls available. Thus

$$3N = ND_c + \frac{N}{2} D_h + \frac{N}{4} D_q \tag{16.11}$$

where D_c = number of products receiving complete coverage
D_h = number of products receiving half coverage
D_q = number of products receiving quarter coverage

Therefore as many as 12 products receiving quarter coverage or as few as 3 products receiving complete coverage could be promoted in any given period. The solution approach is similar to that of CALLPLAN in that it involves two stages: a response-function/calibration stage and an allocation/optimization stage.

Response-Function Development and Calibration. To operationalize a response model, the authors define the *relative exposure value* R_t as an index of the relative effectiveness of alternative call policies in the current period. Specifically,

$$R_t\left(\frac{N}{2}\right) = 1$$

$$R_t(0) = 0$$

$$R_t\left(\frac{N}{4}\right) = q \qquad 0 < q < 1$$

$$R_t(N) = c \qquad c > 1 \tag{16.12}$$

This scaling of R_t, a dimensionless property, eliminates effects such as seasonality and allows them to be added back separately. The scaling of $R_t(N/2) = 1$ implies that $N/2$ is equivalent to "saturation" detailing in the long term.

Then to accommodate forgetting and carry-over effects, they define the *accumulated exposure level A_t*:

$$A_t = f(R(X_t)) + (1 - \lambda)A_{t-1} \tag{16.13}$$

where A_t = exposure value in period t, resulting from current and past detailing

X_t = current detailing level $\left(\text{equal to } 0, \frac{N}{4}, \frac{N}{2}, \text{ or } N\right)$

$f(\cdot)$ = current effect of $R(\cdot)$ and A_t

λ = forgetting parameter

The specific form of $f(\cdot)$ used was $\lambda R(\cdot)$. Therefore,

$$A_t = \lambda R(X_t) + (1 - \lambda)A_{t-1} \tag{16.14}$$

For a value of sales in period t, a sales model is introduced:

$$Q_t = P(t)I(A_t) \tag{16.15}$$

where $Q(t)$ = unit sales in period t
$P(t)$ = sales potential in period t (saturation sales)
$I(\cdot)$ = sales index in t, fraction of sales potential that will be seen, a function of accumulated exposure value A_t

Then for specification of the form of $I(A_t)$, certain constraints must be met. For instance, $I(0) = 0$, $I(\infty) \le 1$, and $I(A)$ should generally be nondecreasing in A. In addition, as saturation is approached, there should be decreasing returns to additional effort, and the relationship should allow for increasing returns at low-exposure levels, suggesting threshold effects. A simple cubic function was proposed as a form that would handle these restrictions and also provide few parameters for judgmental calibration:

$$I_t = \begin{cases} a_0 + a_1 R_t^2 - a_2 R_t^3 & \text{if } a_0 + a_1 R_t^2 - a_i R_t^3 \le 1.0 \\ 1.0 & \text{otherwise} \end{cases} \tag{16.16}$$

The model is now complete, requiring the specifications of six parameters for each salesperson: c, q, λ, a_0, a_1, and a_2. For c and q, salespersons are asked to estimate the value of quarter and complete coverage relative to half coverage, and the value of λ is derived by asking them for a short-term sales forecast if no detailing effort is provided. Then for a_0, a_1, and a_2, managers are asked to make forecasts of sales at different levels of (constant) detailing effort over an extended period of time. Other questions are asked of the managers to help check these values.

Allocation and Optimization.   The objective function suggested by the authors is to maximize total gross product-line profits over the planning horizon: find $\{X_{it}\}$ to

$$\max Z = \sum_{i=1}^{n} m_i \sum_{t=1}^{T} P_{it} I(A_{it}) \tag{16.17}$$

subject to $X_{it} = 0$, $N/4$, $N/2$, or N and eq. (16.11),

where Z = total gross product-line profits summed over planning horizon
$\quad\quad m_i$ = gross margin for product i, $i = 1, \ldots, n$
$\quad\quad n$ = number of products
$\quad\quad T$ = planning horizon

The problem above could be formulated as a dynamic program. However, as with CALLPLAN, a fast, simple procedure that achieves good results is preferred to a computationally complex one.

The heuristic approach the authors suggest starts with an initial detailing plan for each product in each period. The solution procedure zeros out the plan for each product in the first period. Then it incrementally allocates detailing effort based on marginal improvement in long-run profit until detailing capacity is exhausted. The resulting values of $\{A_{it}\}$ are then used in calculating detailing levels for the second period, and the procedure is repeated until the end of the planning period. The search procedure starts at period 1 again and cycles until the results of two passes over all t periods give the same results.

Assessment.   DETAILER appears to be a conceptually sound, easy-to-use procedure for allocating selling effort across a line of products. As with

CALLPLAN and all decision-calculus approaches, judgmental calibration plays a key role in deriving the results. A fixed number of salespersons is assumed, and no product-line interdependencies are included. These simplifications are balanced by the model's parsimony and usability—it helps the salesperson and the sales manager develop a plan by allocating calls to products that result in substantially improved levels of sales. One division of a firm reported a 1-yr profit improvement of $85,000 with the model; another application reported a profit improvement of over $1 million over a 2-yr planning horizon.

However, the approach suffers from the same problems as CALL-PLAN: judgmental data are used for calibration, and it ignores interaction with other elements of the selling mix.

Allocation-Model Extensions and Related Work

The CALLPLAN model has been extended by Lodish in several ways. In one article (Lodish, 1975), he extends the concept to aid in designing salesforce territories. A CALLPLAN analysis is used to find optimal-profit call frequencies for given territories. From this initial solution the marginal profit of an additional hour of sales effort is found. Sales territory boundaries are then restructured to equalize marginal profitability. Five firms have reportedly used this procedure successfully.

A further extension of CALLPLAN (Lodish, 1976) deals with assigning salespersons to accounts. In this extension the manager judges the effectiveness of each salesperson with each account and incorporates these judgments into the analysis of call frequency and territory alignment. The effectiveness of salesperson k on account i is called V_{ik}, and new variables $\{y_{ik}\}$ are set to one if salesperson k handles account i and to zero otherwise. This problem is now formulated: find $\{y_{ik}\}$ and $\{X_i\}$ to

$$\max Z = \sum_i f_i r_i(X_i) \sum_k y_{ik} V_{ik} \qquad (16.18)$$

subject to

$$\sum_i y_{ik} X_i \le T_k \qquad \text{(salesman } k\text{'s time constraint, } k = 1, \ldots, K)$$

$$\sum_k y_{ik} \quad \le 1 \qquad \text{(assignment constraints)}$$

Lodish reports that this problem was solved with a piecewise linear approximation to the V_{ik} and a linear-programming code. This model does not handle the y_{ij} as 0–1 variables as would seem appropriate in most applications. However, Lodish reports good results in an application involving a firm selling advertising to agencies, advertisers, and media-buying services in a single geographic area.

In a similar vein, Lodish (1980*b*) develops a more integrated treatment dealing with salesforce size, as well as the allocations of effort to the product and market segments. Furthermore, Zoltners, Sinha, and Chong (1979) have addressed a problem similar to CALLPLAN and propose an integer-programming solution. Theirs is one of a number of models that address salesforce-allocation decisions.

In addition, Zoltners and Sinha (1980) review the issues addressed by recent models, and they categorize the approaches along the following dimensions:

1. sales resource (such as budget, number of representatives, and time)
2. sales entities (accounts, market, and products)
3. method of development of sales-response functions
4. optimization/search procedure
5. enhancements: multiple criteria/multiple resources, carry-over effects/multiple time periods, sales-entity interaction, and deterministic versus stochastic response-function formulation

Their classification is reproduced in Exhibit 16.4.

This stream of research has been extending and generalizing basic models, some of which were developed more than a decade ago. Although some authors continue to develop and argue for more-general model structures and improved solution algorithms, it appears as if the greatest short-term benefits could be achieved by studying two key problems:

1. routes (and barriers) to implementation of salesforce-allocation models
2. the characterization of the determinants of salesforce—sales-response functions

For the first research area, more tests like that of Fudge and Lodish (1977) are required. Detailed reports of successful implementation strategies (perhaps as case studies), as well as failures, would help enormously in bridging the theory-practice gap. Many good models are available, but few are seeing use and we need to understand why.

In terms of characterizing factors that should be considered in developing sales revenue functions, more research, such as that of Ryans and Weinberg (1979), is required. They developed a framework for specifying the major constructs that account for territory sales revenue, including the following:

1. company marketing activities
2. salesforce policies and procedures
3. field sales manager
4. salesperson characteristics
5. territory characteristics
6. competition

They built a sales-response function, in multiplicative form, for each of three firms. Their results and their review of the related literature show the following:

1. Sales potential seems to be more important than measures such as work load in explaining variation in territory sales response.
2. Work load is difficult to operationalize and does not always yield consistent results.
3. The influence of the field sales manager, operationalized as span of control, was usually significant, with sales decreasing as span of control increased.
4. Competitive strength appeared to relate to territory sales response, suggesting the need for further work in this area.

Finally, their work shows that models of territory sales response can be developed and that results achieved in one setting can be replicated in others. This result suggests that more work is needed to further develop these findings and integrate them into response-function estimation procedures.

Sales Territory Design

Most companies assign sales representatives to geographic entities called *territories,* which are aggregated into large groupings called *districts,* which, in turn, may be aggregated into major sales regions.

In designing a system of territories either for a new salesforce or to update the territorial structure for an existing salesforce, companies generally try to meet the following objectives:

The territories should be easy to administer.

Sales potential should be easy to estimate.

Total travel time should be kept under careful control.

Territories should provide a sufficient and equitable work load and sales potential for each salesperson.

These characteristics are achieved through decisions about the size and shape of territorial units.

In terms of territory size two main approaches are used: one forms territories of *equal sales potential* and the other forms territories of *equal work load.* Each principle has pluses and minuses.

The logic of creating territories of equal potential is to provide each sales representative with the same income opportunities and to permit the firm to evaluate performance more readily. Persistent differences in sales yield by territory are assumed to be due to differences in ability or effort. Thus this approach creates a competitive environment among salespersons.

EXHIBIT 16-4   A summary of sales-resource-allocation models.

	Structural Components		
1 **Reference**	**2** **Sales Resource**	**3** **Sales Entity**	**4** **Sales-Response Function:** **(a) Functional form,** **(b) Estimation**
Brown (1937)	Number of sales representatives	Sales territories	(a) Linear function with territory market potential as an upper bound
Wellman (1939)	Sales dollars	Geographic areas	Theoretical article; several functions were suggested; linear, concave, nonconcave
Nordin (1943)	Selling expense	Sales districts	(a) Power function (b) Historical data, subjective judgment
Magee (1953)	Promotional effort	Dealers	(a) Probabilistic function; Poisson distribution (b) Historical data
Brown, Hulswit, and Kettelle (1956)	Sales time	Conversion group, holding group	(a) Probabilistic function derived by using probability of holding or conversion functions (b) Experimentation
Waid, Clark, and Ackoff (1956)	Number of sales calls	Accounts	(a) S-shaped (b) Historical data
Buzzell (1964)	Number of sales representatives	Channels of distribution	(a) Modified exponential (b) Historical data; single-point fit
Thompson and McNeal (1967)	Sales-representative call time	Customers in each of several nonabsorbing markovian states	(a) Expected profit for each markovian state; not expressed as a function of sales effort (b) Historical data

Modeling Enhancements				
5	6	7	8	9
Search Procedure	Multiple Decision Criteria and/or Multiple Resources	Carry-over Effects/Multiple Time Periods	Sales-Entity Interactions	Stochastic Response Function
Optimization				
LaGrange multiplier technique when possible				
LaGrange multiplier technique				
Analysis of probabilistic model				X
Managerial decision rules				
Concluded that accounts were being saturated				
LaGange multiplier technique				
Ranking procedure				

EXHIBIT 16-4   **A summary of sales-resource-allocation models (*Continued*).**

	Structural Components		
1	**2**	**3**	**4** **Sales-Response** **Function:** **(a) Functional form,**
Reference	**Sales** **Resource**	**Sales** **Entity**	**(b) Estimation**
Lambert (1968)	Number of sales representatives	Sales districts	(a) Power function (b) Historical data; multiple-regression analysis
Layton (1968)	Sales effort available to a sales team	Prospective customers	(a) Discrete sales-response functions resulting from a decision-tree analysis (b) Subjective judgment
Lodish (1971*b*, 1975), Fudge and Lodish (1977)	Sales-representative call time	Clients, prospects	(a) Logit function (b) Subjective judgment
Montgomery, Silk, and Zaragoza (1971)	Sales calls	Products	(a) Cubic response function and exponential forgetting function (b) Subjective judgment
Comer (1974)	Sales territory, sales effort	Customers, prospects	(a) Discrete functions based on probability estimates (b) Historical data, subjective judgment
Darmon (1975)	Sales-representative call time	Customers, prospects	(a) Probabilistic function based on the linear learning model (b) Historical data, subjective judgment
Armstrong (1976)	Sales-representative call time	Current and prospective accounts	(a) Probabilistic functions, modified exponential (b) Subjective judgment

	Modeling Enhancements			
5	**6**	**7**	**8**	**9**
Search Procedure	**Multiple Decision Criteria and/or Multiple Resources**	**Carry-over Effects/Multiple Time Periods**	**Sales-Entity Interactions**	**Stochastic Response Function**
LaGrange multiplier technique				
Dynamic program-ming	X			X
Optimal solution to approximate prob-lem			X	
Heuristic		X	X	
Heuristic		X		
Single-period knap-sack models		X		
Nonlinear program-ming plus round-ing to nearest in-teger	X			X

EXHIBIT 16-4   **A summary of sales-resource-allocation models (*Continued*).**

	Structural Components		
1	**2**	**3**	**4**
Reference	**Sales Resource**	**Sales Entity**	**Sales-Response Function:** (a) Functional form, (b) Estimation
Lodish (1976)	Sales time available to several sales representatives	Accounts	(a) Concave, piece-wise, linear approximations to nonlinear functions (b) Subjective judgment
Beswick (1977) Beswick and Cravens (1977)	Sales time	Control units: individual customers, groups of customers, small geographic units	(a) Class of multivariate response functions, primarily exponential (b) Historical data, subjective judgment
Parasuraman and Day (1977)	Call time	Customer groups	(a) Logit function (b) Subjective judgment
Glaze and Weinberg (1978)	Sales-representative call time	Clients, prospects	(a) Modified exponential (b) Subjective judgment
Zoltners, Sinha, and Chong (1979)	Sales-representative call time	Clients, prospects	(a) Arbitrary, discrete (b) Arbitrary
Lodish (1980b)	Call time	Products and market segments	(a) Logit function (b) Subjective judgment
Zoltners and Sinha (1980)	Arbitrary	Arbitrary	(a) Arbitrary, discrete (b) Arbitrary

Modeling Enhancements				
5	6	7	8	9
Search Procedure	Multiple Decision Criteria and/or Multiple Resources	Carry-over Effects/Multiple Time Periods	Sales-Entity Interactions	Stochastic Response Function
Linear programming and rounding to integer solution				
Dynamic programming	X			
Heuristic		X	X	
Combination of the Lodish algorithm and heuristic			X	
Integer programming			X	
Optimal solution to approximate problem			X	
Integer programming	X	X	X	X

SOURCE: Zoltners and Gardner, 1980, pp 7–8

But customer geographic density almost always varies, and so territories with equal potential can cover vastly different areas. For example, the potential for a large drill press is as large in Detroit as it is in a number of western states. A sales representative assigned to Detroit can cover that same potential with far less effort than the sales representative covering the several western states.

Alternatively, then, the firm can try to equalize work loads, which requires that territories be designed so that each representative can adequately cover his territory. In general, this approach leads to variations in sales potential. This latter approach may not present a problem when the salesforce is on straight salary, but it is unfair to a commissioned salesforce.

Operationally, any approach requires blending salary and commission structures and also trading off potential against work load. In practice, better territories are often assigned to better or more senior salespersons.

Territories are usually formed by combining smaller units, such as census tracts, or counties until they add up to a territory of a given potential or work load. They are put together with reference to the location of natural barriers, the compatibility of adjacent areas, adequacy of transportation, and so forth.

In recent years a number of automatic procedures, generally based on linear or integer programming, have been developed. We review one below.

GEOLINE Model

Hess and Samuels (1971) developed a model, called GEOLINE, based on the REDIST program used for legislative districting. Their procedure builds sales and service territories that satisfy three principles: (1) equal sales work load (or some other, single criterion); (2) contiguity, that is, each territory must consist of adjacent areas; and (3) compactness, that is, the territories should be as easy as possible to cover from a travel standpoint.

A measure of a territory's compactness is the *moment of inertia*, the sum of the squares of the distances from the home base to all customers weighted by the customers' volume of business, or

$$M = \sum_i V_i d_{hi}^2 \qquad (16.19)$$

where M = moment of inertia of territory
V_i = sales volume of customer i
d_{hi} = distance of customer i from home base h

The building up of sales territories starts with a large number of small areas, called standard geographic units (SGUs), usually census tracts or something of similar size. These units are considered as points, with the coordinates of each unit j being n_j (the north/south or y coordinate) and e_j

(the east/west or x coordinate), for $j = 1, \ldots, J$. Then for each of these SGUs there is an activity measure a_j. Initially, a number of territories and a starting set of area centroids, N_i and E_i, for $i = 1, \ldots, I$ (number of territories), must be established.

Hess and Samuels report that the homes or offices of existing salespersons provide excellent starting points. Alternatively, centroids of existing territories have been used.

Model Formulation. The problem (or sequence of problems) that they formulate is to find $\{X_{ij}\}$ to

$$\min \sum_j \sum_i c_{ij} X_{ij} a_j \qquad \text{(moments of inertia)} \qquad (16.20)$$

subject to

$$\sum_j X_{ij} a_j = \frac{1}{I} \sum a_j \qquad \text{(equal-activity constraint)}$$

$$\sum_i X_{ij} = 1 \qquad \text{(assignment requirement)}$$

where $c_{ij} = (N_i - n_j)^2 + (E_i - e_j)^2$ the cost (contribution to moment of inertia) of assigning the geographic unit i to territory j) and   (16.21)

X_{ij} = proportion of geographic unit j assigned to territory i

Equation (16.20) is a linear program that results in split territories—that is, some SGUs are assigned to more than one territory. In practice, this situation is handled by assigning the SGU to the territory for which its share of actiivity is the largest:

$$X_{ij} = \begin{cases} 1 & \text{if } X_{ij}^o = \max_i [X_{ij}^o] \\ 0 & \text{otherwise} \end{cases} \qquad (16.22)$$

where the superscript in X_{ij}^o indicates that it is the optimal solution to eq. (16.20). As an example, suppose that $X_{14}^o = 0.4$, $X_{54}^o = 0.3$, $X_{84}^o = 0.3$ and all other $X_{i4}^o = 0$. The procedure above would modify the solution by setting $X_{14} = 1$ and all other $X_{i4} = 0$.

The authors report that minor deviations from equality of work load result from recombinations of these split territories. In practice, about one geographic area is split per territory. Thus by making the number of SGUs large relative to the number of territories, these deviations will be small. With about twenty SGUs per territory, they report deviations of ± 10 percent on average.

The solution algorithm is not finished after the solution of eq. (16.20).

The original centroids were set arbitrarily. Therefore the next stage of the solution procedure requires recalculation of territory centroids:

$$N_i = \frac{\sum\limits_j X_{ij} a_j n_j}{\sum\limits_j a_j X_{ij}} \qquad (16.23)$$

$$E_i = \frac{\sum\limits_j X_{ij} a_j e_j}{\sum\limits_j a_j X_{ij}} \qquad (16.24)$$

where the $\{X_{ij}\}$ used in eqs. (16.23) and (16.24) are the values from the previous linear-programming solution rounded off to integers.

The calculation sequence then continues: centroids $\rightarrow$ linear-programming allocations $\rightarrow$ integerize solution $\rightarrow$ new centroids, and so on. The calculation ends when successive linear programs give identical solutions or when a predetermined number of iterations have been performed. Careful examination of intermediate solutions is required to prevent looping, reported to occur in 10 percent of the cases. Managerial intervention is easy with this procedure, which allows special considerations, assignments, and adjustments to be made. Because the final solution is a local rather than a global solution, in practice, the procedure is restarted with other initial centers.

Application. The GEOLINE model represents a practical, flexible, and useful tool. The model is not restricted to any specific activity measure; rather, the selection of this measure is up to sales management. In the seven applications reported by the authors, the activity measures used included customer count, calls, potential, and a weighted measure.

In terms of application the authors report the following results with IBM world trade:

IBM found that the computer prepared better districts than they could by hand. The field test involved locating typewriter servicemen territories in a northern city. As more and more typewriters are sold and as machines age, more service time and men are required. Realigning the service territories required several days of the branch manager's time.

IBM wished to equalize the workload from serviceman to serviceman. Estimates of maintenance time per machine were already available and geographically located in units of approximately 50 typewriters. For each geographic area estimates of service hours per month were computable.

The branch manager and the operations research analyst estimated coordinates of each geographic area. (These same coordinates can be used for subsequent applications.) The capacities of some of the service territories were increased or decreased by 10 percent to recognize slower or faster repairmen. The branch manager picked approximate centers for the territories. Total data preparation required one and a half days.

The total problem required constructing seven territories from 80 small areas. The first solution was so good that no further starting centers were needed. The system is being implemented in other cities now (Hess and Samuels, 1971, p. 52).

Assessment. Although a useful procedure, this model is not without its limitations. The selection of an activity measure, while flexible, is ambiguous. The objective function is to minimize a weighted moment of inertia, but it is not clear how this measure relates to other, more objective criteria, such as cost and profit. Furthermore, SGUs may be split between territories, but the model does not consider accessibility or compatibility with geographic considerations, such as highways, mountains, and waterways. Finally, the model does not recognize the interaction between sales territory design, salespersons call planning, and salesforce sizing.

Related Work

A number of other models have been developed that deal with problems of territory design. Easingwood (1973) has developed a heuristic procedure that looks at average work load in an attempt to equalize that work load among regions or territories. Richardson (1979) presents a linear-programming-based procedure that permits the balancing of up to five measures of sales potential. Zoltners (1979) presents an integer-programming-based approach, allowing for single or multiple activity centers. Segal and Weinberger (1977) incorporate accessibility into their model, but SGUs may still be split between territories. Finally, Sinha and Zoltners (1982) present a customized solution procedure that performs quite well compared to those of Hess and Samuels (1971) and Segal and Weinberger (1977), satisfies the accessibility criteria, and does not split SGUs. In addition, in a reported application it produced more-balanced territorial alignments than the other two models.

Other models integrate territory design, along with other components of the salesforce decision. Lodish (1975) includes territory realignment along with call planning; Comer (1974) deals with call planning and territory design jointly. Beswick and Cravens (1977) and Glaze and Weinberg (1979) have both incorporated territory alignment in their models, allowing for the use of the Hess-and-Samuels procedure. Shanker, Turner, and Zoltners (1975) integrate territory design and salesperson call planning into one procedure that maximizes the total sales from all territories. Exhibit 16.5 gives the graphical output of the Shanker-Turner-Zoltner procedure.

In sum, there appear to be a number of sales-territory-design procedures that are user-oriented, capture many real-life complexities, and are relatively easy to apply. In addition, there continue to be reports of the use of these procedures.

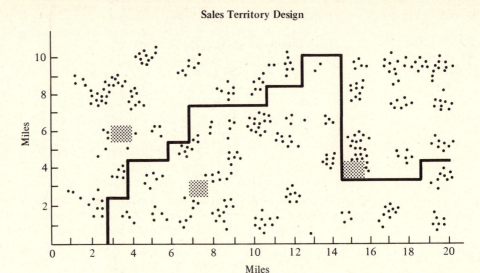

Sales Territory Design

Dots represent individual customers. Shaded blocks represent optimal
resident locations. Solid lines represent optimal boundaries for
sales territory.

EXHIBIT 16-5   **Optimal boundaries and resident locations for three sales
territories.** (Source: Shanker, Turner, and Zoltners, 1975, p.
319. Reprinted by permission of the Institute of Management
Sciences. *Management Science,* Vol. 22, No. 3, November
1975.)

Setting Commissions and Quotas: Indirect Control of the Salesforce

The approaches toward helping the salesperson allocate time among customers and products reviewed here present mechanistic models of the
time-and-effort-allocation process. In practice, every salesperson has a
significant amount of control over how he spends his time. Aside from direct
control in the form of guidelines, firms develop quota and commission
systems to help motivate the salesperson to allocate his or her time in an
optimal way for the firm.

The literature on salesperson performance and its relationship to a
number of personal and job-related factors is large, and a number of articles
in a volume edited by Bagozzi (1979a) as well as an article by Ford, Walker,
and Churchill (1981), deal with the issue in some detail. Of particular
interest are articles by Bagozzi (1978, 1980) in which he demonstrates that
self-esteem is a key determinant of salesperson performance:

> Management should enhance self-esteem by regularly providing positive feedback . . . as soundly visible acknowledgment of good performance . . . it is essential that accurate and complete feedback be provided as to attainment of goals (Bagozzi, 1980, p. 71).

This analysis points to the need for an intelligently designed quota system.

Typically, field managers take their annual quotas and divide them up among sales representatives. There are three schools of thought on how this quota setting should proceed. The *high-quota school* sets quotas above what most sales representatives will achieve but which are possible for all. Advocates of this system believe that high quotas spur extra effort. The *modest-quota school* sets quotas that a majority of the salesforce can attain, believing that salespersons will accept the quotas as fair and will gain confidence from attaining them. Finally, the *variable-quota school* contends that individual differences among sales representatives warrant high quotas for some and modest quotas for others. The components of self-esteem will vary by individual: representative A may get no satisfaction from achieving an easily attainable result, while representative B may be discouraged by a target that appears too difficult to achieve. Thus the variable-quota approach appears to have much to recommend it if it is not too difficult to apply.

Many different types of incentives can be structured around attainment of sales quotas: gifts, awards, sales contests, trips, and so on are common. The most widely studied form of financial incentive discussed in the literature has been the commission. Most firms compensate salespersons by some combination of salary (for income security) plus commission (for motivation).

How the commission portion of the compensation structure should be set has been the subject of several important articles over the last few years. The fundamental work in this area is a paper by Farley (1964) in which he showed that a commission-rate policy based on the product's gross margin will motivate the salesperson to allocate time to maximize company profits. In a later article, reviewed below, Davis and Farley (1971) extend and qualify Farley's original arguments.

Davis and Farley

Consider a company that produces several products and pays its salespersons through commissions. Davis and Farley (1971) look at the profit-maximizing problem as it appears to the firm and the income-maximization problem as it appears to the salesperson and consider under what conditions these expressions can be jointly optimized.

Consider the salesperson first; his optimization problem is set t_{ij} to

$$\text{Maximize } W_j = \sum_i r_i p_i f_{ij}(t_{ij}) \qquad \text{(commission income)} \qquad (16.25)$$

subject to

$$\sum_i t_{ij} \le T_j \qquad \text{(time constraint)} \tag{16.26}$$

$$t_{ij} \ge 0$$

where W_j = total commission earned by salesperson j
r_i = commission rate paid on total sales of product i
p_i = price of product i
t_{ij} = amount of time spent on product i by salesperson j
$f_{ij}(t_{ij})$ = quantity sold of product i by salesperson j
T_j = total time available to salesperson j

Thus the salesperson's problem is to determine how much time to spend selling each product within the limits of his total time to maximize his commission (the commission rate times sales summed for all products).

The conditions for the salesperson to maximize his total commission can be found by combining eqs. (16.25) and (16.26) into the lagranigian expression:

$$L(W_j) = \sum_i r_i p_i f_{ij}(t_{ij}) + \lambda_j \left(T_i - \sum_i t_{ij} \right) \tag{16.27}$$

where λ_j are the lagrangian multipliers. A necessary condition for maximization of $L(W_j)$ is for the first derivative of eq. (16.27) to equal zero:

$$\frac{dL(W_j)}{dt_{ij}} = r_i p_i \frac{df_{ij}}{dt_{ij}} - \lambda_j = 0 \tag{16.28}$$

or

$$r_i p_i \frac{df_{ij}}{dt_{ij}} = \lambda_j \tag{16.29}$$

This condition says that the marginal increase in commissions with an extra application of effort should equal the marginal cost of increasing the selling time.

The firm's optimization problem is set r_i to

$$\max Z = \sum_i \left\{ (1 - r_i) p_i \left[\sum_j f_{ij}(t_{ij}) \right] - C_i \left[\sum_j f_{ij}(t_{ij}) \right] \right\} \quad \text{(net revenue)} \tag{16.30}$$

subject to

$$\sum_i t_{ij} \le T_j \tag{16.31}$$

$$t_{ij} \ge 0$$

where $C_i \left[\sum_j f_{ij}(t_{ij}) \right]$ = total cost to firm of producing product i

Thus the firm's problem is to set commissions to motivate salesmen to allocate their selling time to maximize firm profits. The firm's profits are shown in eq. (16.30) as the difference between its total revenue after commissions and its total costs, which are some function (not necessarily linear) of its respective levels of output of the various products.

The condition for an optimal solution to this problem is given by combining eqs. (16.30) and (16.31) into the lagrangian expression:

$$L(Z) = \sum_i \left\{ (1 - r_i)p_i \left[\sum_j f_{ij}(t_{ij}) \right] - C_i \left[\sum_j f_{ij}(t_{ij}) \right] \right\} + \gamma_j \left(T_j - \sum_i t_{ij} \right) \quad (16.32)$$

where γ_j are lagrangian multipliers (not the same as λ_j). Again, a necessary condition for maximization is for the first derivative of eq. (16.32) to equal zero:

$$\frac{dL(Z)}{dt_{ij}} = (1 - r_i)P_i \frac{df_{ij}}{dt_{ij}} - \frac{\partial C_i}{\partial f_{ij}} \frac{df_{ij}}{dt_{ij}} - \gamma_j = 0 \quad (16.33)$$

or

$$\left[(1 - r_i)P_i - \frac{\partial C_i}{\partial f_{ij}} \right] \frac{df_{ij}}{dt_{ij}} = \gamma_j \qquad \text{for all } i \text{ and } j \quad (16.34)$$

This condition says that the company should encourage salespersons to allocate their time among the company products in such a way that, at the margin, the company's profit on each product is the same and equal to γ_j, the marginal return on additional selling time beyond $\Sigma_i t_{ij}$. (γ_j = marginal cost of relieving the time constraint, i.e., increasing T_j.)

Now under what circumstances will salespersons allocate their time among products to maximize their commissions and the company's profits at the same time? For this result to happen there must be some time allocation that satisfies both eqs. (16.29) and (16.34). This result is very unlikely to happen because two improbable conditions must exist. The first is that r_i in eq. (16.29) must equal $(1 - r_i)$ in eq. (16.34) for all i, and this could only happen if $r_i = 0.50$. But it is very unlikely that the commission rate of all products will be 0.50. The second condition is that the marginal cost of production must equal zero, that is, $\partial C_i/\partial f_{ij} = 0$, which is also unlikely.

The implication of this analysis is that a system of commission rates paid on sales is unlikely to lead salespersons to allocate their time in a way that maximizes the firm's profits. The firm might attempt to set sales quotas for the various products for individual salespersons based on its profit-maximizing solution, but salespersons are not likely to heed these quotas if they prevent them from maximizing their commissions.

A system that may reconcile the conflicting interests of salespersons and the company calls for setting the commission rates on product gross margin instead of sales. The lagrangian expression for the salesperson's optimization problem becomes

$$L(W_j) = \sum_i r_i \left\{ p_i f_{ij}(t_{ij}) - C_i \left[\sum_j f_{ij}(t_{ij}) \right] \right\} - \lambda_j (T_j - \sum_i t_{ij}) \qquad (16.35)$$

And the lagrangian expression for the company's optimization problem becomes

$$L(Z) = \sum_i \left((1 - r_i) \left\{ p_i \sum_j f_{ij}(t_{ij}) - C_i \left[\sum_j f_{ij}(t_{ij}) \right] \right\} \right) + \gamma_j (T_j - \sum_i t_{ij}) \qquad (16.36)$$

The first expression is maximized when

$$r_i \left(p_i - \frac{\partial C_i}{\partial f_{ij}} \right) \frac{df_{ij}}{dt_{ij}} = \lambda_j \qquad (16.37)$$

and the second is maximized when

$$(1 - r_i) \left(p_i - \frac{\partial C_i}{\partial f_{ij}} \right) \frac{df_{ij}}{dt_{ij}} = \gamma_j \qquad (16.38)$$

Then the interests of the salesperson and the company are reconciled if there is some time allocation that can satisfy eqs. (16.37) and (16.38) simultaneously. Suppose that the marginal cost of producing each product is constant (though not necessarily identical) and known by each salesperson. The firm's problem, then, is to determine a set of commission rates on the various products that will maximize its total profits, taking into account how its salespersons will respond to these rates.

However, the problem of reconciling the interests of salespersons and the company is complicated if marginal costs are increasing instead of constant. Under increasing marginal costs, the salesperson no longer knows the marginal cost of selling a product in his portfolio. The marginal cost will be determined by the product's output level, which will be determined by the separate decisions of all salespersons on how much time to spend in selling that product. Furthermore, the separate decisions of the salespersons will be influenced by the commission rates set by the company. If the company had full information about the individual salespersons' time-effectiveness functions df_{ij}/dt_{ij}, it could determine the profit-maximizing commission rates with eq. (16.38). But the company usually does not have this information.

These difficulties have been the motivating force behind the search for decentralized solutions to the problem. Quotas imposed on the salesforce represent centralized solutions; yet if they do not conform to commission-maximizing sales levels for the salespersons, they are not likely to be fulfilled.

Davis and Farley have suggested a decentralized solution that, in principle, would reconcile the salespersons' and firm's interests. In their solution the firm determines alternate sets of commission rates on the various products, on the basis of its knowledge of cost behavior (which it may not wish to reveal to the salespersons) and its price-setting capabilities. These sets of rates are transmitted to the salespersons, who transmit back desired quotas under each set of commissions. The company examines the discrepancies between what it would like to see sold of each product and what the salespersons indicate they would sell. The company then adjusts the commission rates to bring salesforce intentions into line with company intentions. Specifically, the commission rates are raised on products for which the planned sales levels are too low and are lowered on products for which the planned sales levels are too high. After several iterations a final set of commission rates on gross margins is found that brings planned sales into equilibrium with the company's desired rates.

Assessment and Related Work

Even Davis and Farley, while identifying the problem, recognized that their proposed solution is cumbersome. Farley and Weinberg (1975), working with response functions, show that the sales-response function can be related to the commission rate. Each salesperson is given various commission rates and asked to specify quotas. A profit equation is derived by aggregating commission-response functions and incorporating cost data. Optimal commission rates are derived by differentiating the profit equation with respect to the commission rates.

These models have been extended in several ways. Weinberg (1975) showed that under constant marginal costs, when salespersons are paid commissions on gross margin and also given control over price, then they should set prices to simultaneously maximize their commission income and firm profit. In another paper Weinberg (1978) extends the idea of equal commission rates based on gross margin to situations where products are interdependent and the salesperson has other objectives, such as minimizing work subject to an income constraint.

In addition, there is an interesting stream of research on the assumptions of the model, specifically the assumption of the commission-maximizing salesperson. Winer (1973) ran an experiment and found that most salespersons were not dollar maximizers but "quota-achievers." In another study Darmon (1974) found that a model in which a salesperson minimizes work to reach an acceptable income level best explains his behavior and proposed models that allow development of commissions based on different goals.

Srinivasan (1979) shows that the optimal solution of Farley's (1964) problem is a commission rate infinitesimally greater than zero. This result follows from the assumption that salespersons work for a certain time T regardless of their realized income. However, following Darmon's (1974) work, he considers a salesperson who maximizes his utility, which is a function of his leisure time. He shows that in this case optimal commisson rates are unequal fractions of gross margin and suggests that they be set higher for products with greater elasticities.

Albers (1981a) extends these results further, showing that the optimal commission rate should be both salesperson- and product-specific. The author argues that this seemingly impractical suggestion can be carried out through a quota system with bonuses for achievement. Albers (1981b) extends this analysis to include salesperson turnover in a dynamic framework.

In conclusion, there is a stream of theoretical evidence that suggests circumstances under which an equal-gross-margin commission system is optimal. However, more empirical studies are required to investigate the effect of commission systems in directing sales effort for determining the situations favoring one compensation system over others.

Integrative Models for Salesforce Decisions

Most of the approaches analyzed thus far have focused on one problem element—salesforce size, allocation, territory alignment, or commission rate. However, because these decisions are highly interrelated, it is unreasonable to expect that optimizing them separately will lead to an overall optimization of the system.

We earlier reviewed some integrative efforts: allocation strategy and territory alignment have been considered by Shanker, Turner, and Zoltners (1975), Lodish (1975), and Glaze and Weinberg (1979). Each of these models is broken into two stages and iteratively solves the allocation problem with fixed territory alignment and then the territory-alignment problem with fixed allocation. Zoltners (1976, 1979) has shown how to incorporate these two decision problems into a single model. Lodish (1980b) has also incorporated allocation strategy and salesforce size into a single model. However, several more ambitious attempts at integrating strategy, size, and alignment elements have been developed. We review one below.

Beswick-Cravens Model

Beswick and Cravens (1977) view salesforce decisions as a sequential, multistage optimization problem as presented in Exhibit 16.6. They see this process broken into five stages (assuming allocation of effort among products is external to the model).

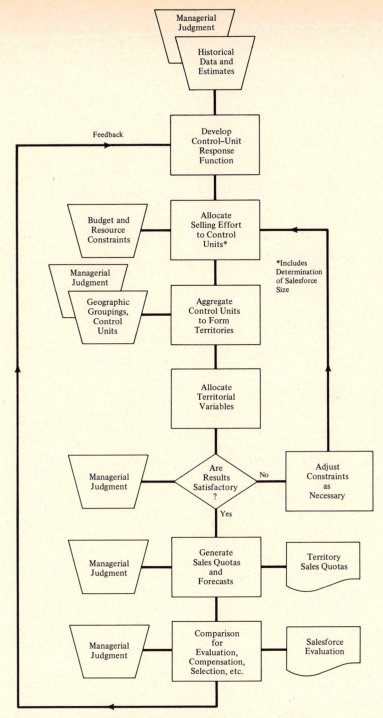

EXHIBIT 16-6 **Beswick-Cravens model: a multistage decision model for salesforce management.** (Source: Beswick and Cravens, 1977, p. 136.)

Stage I: Developing Market-Response Functions. The authors postulate that the way a control unit, the smallest unit of a market, responds to selling effort can be structured as

$$SR = f(E, W, P, C, Q) \tag{16.39}$$

where SR = sales response
E = selling effort
W = work load
P = potential
C = company effort
X = company experience
Q = salesperson quality

Following Beswick (1973), they suggest that a multiplicative form be used for eq. (16.39):

$$SR = a_0 E^{a_1} W^{a_2} P^{a_3} C^{a_4} X^{a_5} Q^{a_6} \tag{16.40}$$

Either managerial judgment or statistical analysis can be used to develop parameter estimates for eq. (16.40).

Stage II: Allocating Selling Effort and Salesforce Sizing. Given the response functions in stage I, the allocation and salesforce-sizing problem is formulated as follows: find $\{N, t_i\}$ to

$$\text{Maximize } Z = Sm - NV - F \qquad \text{(profit)} \tag{16.41}$$

subject to

$$NV \le L_i \qquad \text{(personal-selling budget)}$$

$$N = \sum_i t_i \qquad \text{(time constraint)}$$

$$S \le L_2 \qquad \text{(capacity constraint)}$$

$$S = \sum_i SP_i \qquad \text{(sales-level equation)}$$

where S = total sales dollars
m = margin
N = number of salespersons
V = variable cost associated with average salesperson
F = fixed cost, assumed constant (as long as L_2 is not exceeded)
t_i = time allocated to control unit i [roughly the same as E in eq. (16.40)]

For the response functions considered by the authors, eq. (16.41) is very simple to solve (Beswick, 1977) assuming all variables except t_i are constant. The output of this stage is optimal or near-optimal salesforce size and effort allocation for a given territory design.

Stage III: Territory Design. Two approaches are suggested for realigning territories: one employs managerial judgment while the other uses the t_i from stage II as activity measures in the Hess-Samuels procedure, which then realigns the sales territories.

Stage IV: Allocation of Territorial Variables and Comparison with Objectives. Once stage III is completed, the variables that were held constant during stage II can be incorporated into the analysis. Territorial-level variables that changed during the territory-design process, such as salesperson ability and experience, are updated and computed to change eq. (16.40). Other variables, such as advertising, can also be included in the model at this level. In addition, the output of previous stages needs careful review to see if the total system response (sales, profit, salesforce size) and the proposed territory alignment are consistent with managerial objectives. Normally, several cycles through stages II, III, and IV are required.

Stage V: Forecasting, Evaluation, and Control. Equation (16.40) provides sales forecasts that can be used to set quotas and can also be used as controls. Furthermore, the results of stage II can be used for call planning. In essence, the model can be used at this stage as an outside benchmark for performance comparison. Large discrepancies between actual and forecast performance lead to model adjustments and/or performance feedback for the salesperson.

Application and Evaluation. The authors report using the model for a manufacturer of a high-priced consumer good with a national salesforce of 100 salespersons, who call primarily on retailers. Groups of counties were used as control units; the test involved 38 sales territories and 232 control units.

The complete response-function form, eq. (16.40), was calibrated with historical data; all but one term was significant at the 0.05 level, and 75 percent of variation in sales response was explained.

Applications of several stages of the model led to identification of two major alternatives:

1. By reallocation of the existing salesforce, the company can expect to see a $831,000 sales increase, an improved distribution of income, and a $119,000 improvement in pretax profits associated with a commission rate decrease.
2. By expansion of the salesforce from 38 to 42 salespersons, the firm can expect to see a total sales increase of $1,400,000.

This model is an understandable and managerially useful tool. Rather than treating salesforce decisions part by part, it treats the problem globally (albeit in an iterative, hierarchical manner). Although it does not ensure global optimality, it gives a practical example of the value of incorporating interdependencies.

The flexibility of the modeling procedure is its weakness as well as its strength. How much customization this procedure needs in any specific application is not clear. How significant the role of management should be in model calibration and application is also unclear. Furthermore, the issues of salesforce organization and allocation of effort across products are not considered either.

Other Multiple-Resource Models

In addition to the aforementioned work of Shanker, Turner, and Zoltner (1975) and Lodish (1980b), the most ambitious recent development is by Zoltners and Gardner (1980). Their model integrates salesforce organization, size, and allocations over prospects, time and products, and sales territory design. Their approach, while exciting, has yet to see reported use and is currently in the proposal stage.

Comer (1974) has examined the assumptions underlying salesforce decision models and demonstrates how the basic assumptions and constraints imposed by these models affect their structure. He develops some expressions that are more consistent with observed behavior in the area and that can be used in model building. He also underscores the need for understanding the following:

variations in effort quality

product, profit, and production effects and product-line interdependencies

interactions with other elements of the marketing mix

Summary

Most companies use a salesforce to reach their intermediate and/or final customers. Salespersons perform a number of useful functions, including locating new prospects, communicating product information to customers, persuading customers to close a sale, learning of customers' changing needs, and bringing this and other market information back to the company. Many companies make a considerable investment in selecting, training, and motivating salespersons to perform these tasks effectively.

Marketing management faces a hierarchy of decision problems ranging from selling and salesforce objectives to salesforce sizing, effort allocation, territory design, and motivation and compensation. A number of model-based approaches have been developed that deal with each of these problems individually.

In recent years two streams of development have proven most promising. The first deals with understanding differences in observed customer- or territory-response rates to selling effort. The response curve is at the heart of most operational models in this area. Recent developments have borrowed concepts from the behavioral literature on salesforce effectiveness to determine the elements in response models. The second development has been in integrative model structures. Without significantly altering the valuable individual-subdecision models, recent efforts have focused on piecing these models together in a logically consistent way. By recognizing the interdependencies among territory design, salesforce-time allocation, and salesforce sizing, these models have added considerable credibility to the decision-support structures available in the area.

It does not appear that a fundamental breakthrough in modeling will occur in this area: the groundwork and basic constructs exist. The best existing models allow for an easy blending of judgmental and objective calibration and balance the value of optimization with the computational efficiency of heuristics. These models are tools that can be used and appear widely applicable in a large number of situations.

Why, then, isn't the use of these models pervasive? Partially, this problem is a diffusion phenomenon. Where the problem is important to the firm and where the firm is innovative, the approaches are being used, as with the Fudge and Lodish experience. But many more reports of such applications are desirable to aid in model credibility and to accelerate the diffusion of use; more empirical work is required to identify the important generalizations about market response to selling effort, relating variability in response to territory characteristics, span of control, level of effort, and so on.

In sum, tools are available and are being used by some. The challenge now is to integrate these concepts into the thinking and decision processes of more organizations.

Problems

16.1 The sales manager of the Midwest Paper Company would like to determine how many sales calls per month the salesforce should make to average-size accounts. Suggest an experiment to answer this question.

16.2 An automobile-parts manufacturer sells its product to three types of customers: (a) automobile manufacturers for use as original equipment (OE) (b) wholesale distributors who in turn distribute to parts retailers (WD) (c) parts retailers, primarily jobbers and service stations (PR). From past experience the company has found it most efficient to have three salesmen selling in each territory, one for each type of customer. In a particular territory the sales manager asks each salesman what he expects to be able to sell to each type of customer. These estimates are shown in the following table:

Salesman	Customer Type		
	OE	WD	PR
A	100,000	90,000	80,000
B	92,000	92,000	85,000
C	102,000	95,000	75,000

To which customer type should each salesman be assigned in order to maximize sales in the territory?

16.3   A salesman has four open calls in the next period that he would like to devote to one of three prospects. The probabilities that these prospects will be converted to customers after four calls are 0.6, 0.8, and 0.4, respectively (for prospects 1, 2, and 3). If converted to customers, the respective prospects will yield the following profits to the firm in the coming 3 yr:

Prospect	Year		
	1	2	3
1	2,000	2,000	3,000
2	4,000	1,000	1,000
3	2,000	2,000	6,000

The cost of each call is $500. Compute the expected rate of return for each prospect. In which prospect should the salesman invest his four calls? (Assume a time discount of 5%.)

16.4   A salesman calculates that he will be able to make approximately 720 sales calls during the coming year and wants to know how he can best allocate these calls between current customers and prospects in his territory. He has estimated his customer holding rate in the absence of sales calls at 0.6 and for a very large number of calls at 0.9. Total sales in his territory last year were $200 (in thousands). The maximum possible sales to prospects in the territory for the coming year are estimated at $100 (in thousands). All 720 sales calls allocated to customers would be expected to yield $175; if they were allocated to prospects, they would be expected to yield $80. Determine the optimal allocation of calls between customers and prospects.

16.5   The XYZ Company is interested in finding out what makes a superior salesman. The company decides to try to identify its own superior salesmen and study their common characteristics. (a) Are its superior salesmen those men who rank highest in annual sales? (b) Are its superior salesmen those men whose sales have shown the fastest rate of growth? (c) Are its superior salesmen those men who score highest on self-confidence and energy? (d) Are its superior salesmen those men who work well without supervision? Suggest an approach for answering these questions.

16.6 An industrial firm has analyzed its sales territories and obtained the data below. Its total market can be divided into 12 small geographic regions, with (x, y) coordinates as shown. Also shown is the number of calls

Unit j	x-Axis Coordinate, x_j	y-Axis Coordinate, y_j	No. of Calls	I	II	III
1	48	35	56		1	
2	53	11	44	1		
3	20	56	48			1
4	34	64	51		1	
5	20	22	45			1
6	29	31	51			1
7	44	75	46		1	
8	25	71	43		1	
9	78	31	63	1		
10	30	8	58			1
11	15	18	69			1
12	80	26	71	1		

required by each unit and the existing allocation of units to each of three sales territories. Can you suggest a new set of sales territories? (Fitzroy, 1976)

16.7 The Three-by-Five Company has tried two different sales pitches for its door-to-door salesmen. The old pitch was basically a demonstration. The new pitch is basically a verbal sales pitch. Each of the two salesmen, Brown and Green, used the new and the old pitch in two suburbs of Grand Rapids, Michigan, which is a popular city for test marketing. The salesmen alternated between two suburban areas known locally as Leerview and Gimsee. Each salesman made 200 calls in each suburb, using each sales pitch. The number of calls that resulted in sales were as follows:

Sales Pitch	Suburb Leerview	Gimsee
Demonstration	70, 60	80, 90
Verbal	80, 70	90, 100

In each cell the left-hand number represents Brown's sales and the right-hand number is Green's sales. For example, using the demonstration pitch on 200 calls in Leerview, Brown made 70 sales. Both salesmen prefer to continue using the old demonstration pitch unless the new verbal pitch is really better. What advice would you give to the Three-by-Five salesmen?

16.8 Gerald is a salesman who currently plans to spend five days in Plains, Georgia, where he has three customers: firms A, B, and C. He has determined that his sales to each customer depend on the time spent with him, following the functions

$$S_A = 20{,}000 \log(x_A + 1)$$

where S_A = sales to firm A, \$/mo
          x_A = time spent in firm A,

and, similarly,

$$S_B = 40{,}000 \log (x_B + 2)$$
$$S_C = 50{,}000 \log (x_C + 2)$$

a. Assume Gerald can go from one firm to another in no time. How should he allocate his time between the three firms so as to maximize his sales? What will be his sales then?
b. Gerald wonders whether he should spend less time (4 days) or more time (6 days) or spend 5 days as scheduled in Plains discussing with these firms. What would be his time allocations and sales in the case of 4 days? of 6 days?
c. Gerald works only 10 days a month as a salesman (assume that is an absolute constraint), which he allocates between Plains, Georgia, and Grand Rapids, Michigan. He has determined, by means similar to those employed in parts a and b, that his sales in Grand Rapids would be as follows:

   for 4 days in Grand Rapids, sales of \$131,000
   for 5 days in Grand Rapids, sales of \$140,000
   for 6 days in Grand Rapids, sales of \$149,000

   How should Gerald allocate his monthly 10 days of work between Grand Rapids and Plains to maximize his sales?
d. Gerald thinks about spending one more day a month working as a salesman and one less day doing consulting (his other occupation). If Gerald were to work one more day as a salesman, how should he allocate his 11 working days between Grand Rapids and Plains?
e. Gerald is paid, as a salesman, 10% of the sales he makes. His consulting fee is \$1000/day. Should he keep his monthly salesman schedule to 10 days or increase it to 11 days?

5

Market-
Planning
Models

Market Planning and Strategy

Previous chapters have discussed and compared developments in marketing modeling, focusing almost exclusively on short-term, tactical issues. In this chapter we broaden the scope to include issues that until recently have been considered outside the domain of traditional marketing analysis. In the last few years there has been a burst of interest in model-building approaches for more integrative efforts addressing broader business-planning issues.

In later chapters we discuss model-based approaches to marketing-mix issues and new-product planning and analysis. Here we develop a framework for analysis of strategic-marketing and -planning problems. In the next section we define market planning and relate it to the more general business-planning function. Next we review phenomena that underlie most of the analytic approaches used in this area. Then we review a series of approaches, varying in objectives and analytic style, for integrating these concepts into procedures to support business-planning decisions.

However, before proceeding, we want to point out that this area is at the same time the most diverse and the most dynamic in the marketing-modeling area. As such, the material presented here is likely to become outdated somewhat sooner than that in most other chapters.

Marketing-Planning and Strategy Decisions

In this chapter we assume that we deal with a large organization with several business divisions and several product lines within each division. Marketing plays a role at each level. At the organizational level, marketing contributes perspectives and estimates to help top management decide on the corporation's mission, opportunities, growth strategy, and product portfolio. Corporate policies then provide the context for strategy formulation in each of the business divisions by the divisional managers. Finally, the managers of each product and/or market within each division develop their marketing strategy within the context of the policies and constraints developed at the higher divisional and corporate levels.

The term *strategic-management process* is often used to describe the steps taken at the corporate and divisional levels to develop long-run strategies for organizational survival and growth, while the parallel *strategic-marketing process* refers to the steps taken at the product and/or market level to develop viable marketing positions and programs. The strategic-marketing process takes place within the larger strategic-management process of the corporation.

In the areas of planning and strategy there is little agreement on what the problems are and much less on how they break down functionally. A more traditional view of marketing in an organizational-planning context has both marketing- and production-planning models feeding into financial models. According to Naylor (1979, p. 19), "marketing planning models provide the revenue projections which drive the business planning models." In other words, such models are looked upon as inputs into a system, in which financial considerations provide the driving force.

A more marketing-oriented planning structure, proposed by Wind (1981a), is presented in Exhibit 17.1. It is based on seven interrelated phases (Wind, 1981a, p. 5):

1. determination of corporate objectives, resources, and constraints
2. monitoring of the current and anticipated environment
3. situation analysis
4. market/product-portfolio analysis and decisions
5. generation of tentative product/marketing programs
6. evaluation of alternative programs and selection of the best one
7. organization for marketing action, implementation, and control

The first three phases of this process provide input to all the product/marketing activities of the firm; the objectives-setting process can be specified with methods outlined in Chapter 3. The last three phases are common to all planning models and are covered in a number of other chapters. The fourth phase, the market/product-portfolio analysis and decision problem, is a major focus of the contemporary planning literature. This phase requires a series of decisions, broadly covering three major areas:

1. **Product/market-mix decision.** In its simplest form this decision deals with the degree to which the firm chooses to grow through existing

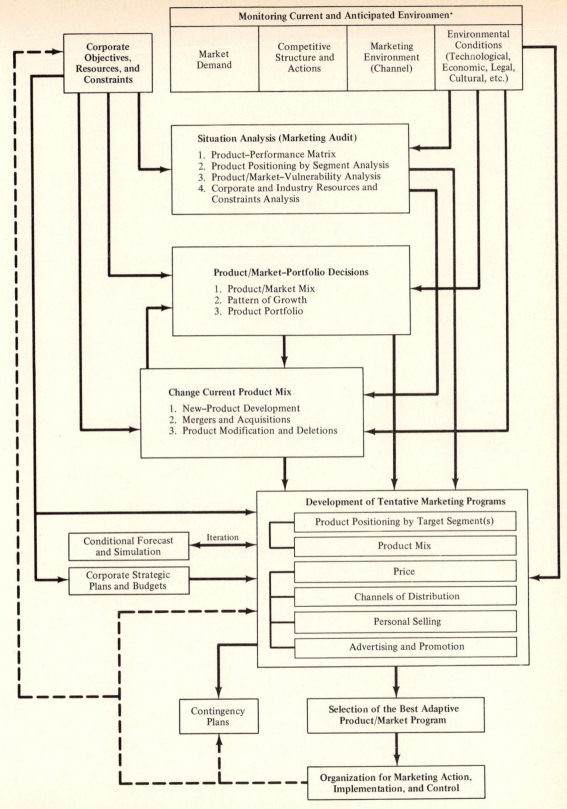

Monitoring Current and Anticipated Environment

| Market Demand | Competitive Structure and Actions | Marketing Environment (Channel) | Environmental Conditions (Technological, Economic, Legal, Cultural, etc.) |

Corporate Objectives, Resources, and Constraints

Situation Analysis (Marketing Audit)
1. Product–Performance Matrix
2. Product Positioning by Segment Analysis
3. Product/Market–Vulnerability Analysis
4. Corporate and Industry Resources and Constraints Analysis

Product/Market–Portfolio Decisions
1. Product/Market Mix
2. Pattern of Growth
3. Product Portfolio

Change Current Product Mix
1. New–Product Development
2. Mergers and Acquisitions
3. Product Modification and Deletions

Development of Tentative Marketing Programs
- Product Positioning by Target Segment(s)
- Product Mix
- Price
- Channels of Distribution
- Personal Selling
- Advertising and Promotion

Conditional Forecast and Simulation

Iteration

Corporate Strategic Plans and Budgets

Contingency Plans

Selection of the Best Adaptive Product/Market Program

Organization for Marketing Action, Implementation, and Control

EXHIBIT 17-1 **A product/marketing-planning model.** (Source: Wind, 1981a, p. 6.)

(versus new) products in existing (versus new) markets. The selection of these directions requires analysis of the firm's resources, likely competitive and environmental conditions, and rates of market growth.

2. **Patterns of growth analysis.**   When a new-product option is chosen, the question raised is whether the firm should attempt to develop it internally or go the route of merger/acquisition/licensing. Wind (1979) discusses the design of a program to guide such decisions.

3. **Product-portfolio analysis.**   Following the above two decisions, the firm is faced with determining a best portfolio of products or businesses and allocating resources to them. In the past many firms encouraged all their business units to grow year after year by giving them all a large budget each year, and all were held to goals of increased sales and profits. In recent years organizations have been more selective because cash is scarce and opportunities differ greatly by business area. Organizations view themselves as managing a portfolio of businesses, and a major company objective is to keep refreshing its portfolio by flushing out poor businesses and adding promising new ones.

Thus strategic marketing planning can be viewed as the process of analyzing market opportunities and choosing marketing positions, programs, and controls that create and support viable businesses consistent with the firm's objectives. See Bettis and Hall (1981) and Haspeslagh (1982) for review of the state of portfolio planning and management practice.

We now review three concepts that underly most of the analytical approaches to the planning problem: the product life cycle, the experience curve, and the definition of the market.

The Product Life Cycle

One of the most important concepts underlying most business-planning models is the product life cycle. Because sales position and profitability can be expected to change over time, a product's strategy needs periodic revision. The concept of the life cycle is an attempt to recognize distinct phases in the sales history of the product. Its importance is that, because of these changes over time, it can be "used prescriptively in the selection of marketing actions and planning" (Polli, 1968, p. 67).

Most discussions of the product life cycle (PLC) portray the sales history of a typical product as following an S-shaped sales curve, as illustrated in Exhibit 17.2. This curve is typically divided into four stages known as introduction, growth, maturity, and decline. *Introduction* is a period of slow growth as the product is introduced in the market. The profit curve in Exhibit 17.2 shows profits as low or negative in this stage because of the

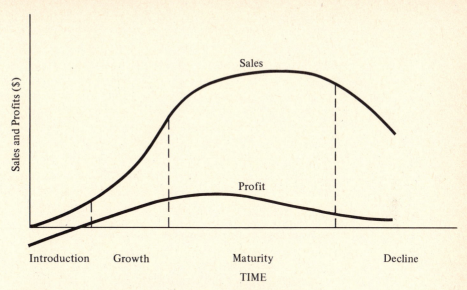

EXHIBIT 17-2   **Stages in the sales and profit cycles.**

heavy expenses of product introduction. *Growth* is a period of rapid market acceptance and substantial profit improvement. *Maturity* is a slowing-down period of sales growth because the product has achieved acceptance by most of the potential buyers. Profits peak in this period and start to decline because of increased marketing outlays needed to sustain the product's position against competition. Finally, *decline* is the period when sales continue a strong downward drift and profits erode toward zero.

The empirical evidence of the existence and pervasiveness of the product-life-cycle concept is quite uneven. In a literature review Rink and Swan (1979) were able to identify 12 types of product-life-cycle patterns. For example, Cox (1967) studied the life cycles of 754 ethical drug products and found the most typical form was a cycle-recycle pattern, shown in Exhibit 17.3(a). He explains that the second hump in sales is caused by a promotional push during the decline phase. In another study Buzzell (1966) reports a scalloped life-cycle pattern, shown in Exhibit 17.3(b), representing a succession of life cycles based on the discovery of new-product characteristics, new uses, or new markets.

In addition to these differences in shape, there are clearly differences in cycle length between products. Rink and Swan (1979) report on 12 studies of consumer nondurables, 9 of consumer durables, and 4 of industrial products and suggest that not enough empirical research has been done to lead to generalizable conclusions within and across these product types.

Studies by Harrell and Taylor (1981) and by Thorelli and Burnett (1981) add data from ten consumer-durable establishments and from over 1000

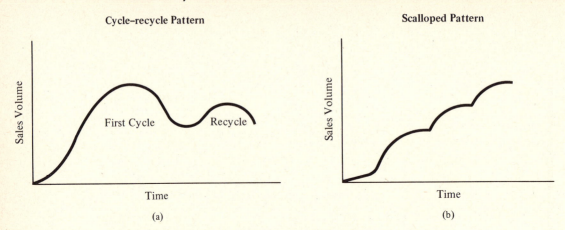

EXHIBIT 17-3   **Some anomalous product-life-cycle patterns.**

industrial firms to the set of data on consumer durables and industrial products, respectively. Both these papers conclude that growth rates are only one aspect of the product life cycle: elements such as market innovation, market concentration, competitive structure, economic cycles, and supply constraints, as well as the influence of replacement sales, affect the structure of the life cycle as well.

In fact, research is further confused by differences in the level of product aggregation and by difficulties with the definition of a new product. Typically, there are three possible levels of aggregation: product class (cigarettes), product form (plain filter cigarettes), and brand (Philip Morris, regular or nonfilter). (See Exhibit 17.4.)

The PLC concept is applied differently in these three cases. Product classes have the longest life histories, longer than particular product forms, and certainly longer than most brands. The sales of many product classes can be expected to continue in the mature stage for an indefinite duration because they are highly related to population (cars, perfume, refrigerators, and steel). Product forms tend to exhibit the standard PLC histories more faithfully. Product forms, such as the dial telephone and cream deodorants, seem to pass through a regular history of introduction, rapid growth, maturity, and decline. On the other hand, a brand's sales history can be erratic because changing competitive strategies and tactics can produce substantial ups and downs in sales and market shares, even to the extent of causing a mature brand to suddenly exhibit another period of rapid growth.

Another difficulty in life-cycle studies is the definition of a new product. How "new" must a product be to be considered a new product? Furthermore, is a variation in an established product a new product? This difficulty is more than semantic and has not been resolved.

Two problems frequently tackled by life-cycle researchers are the

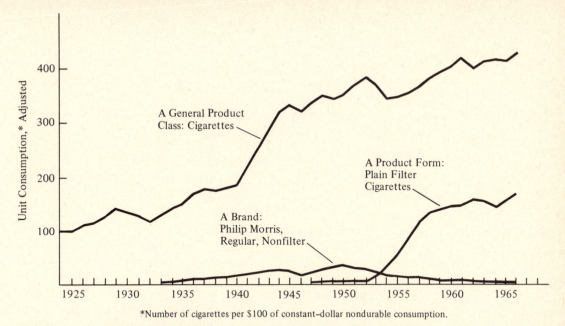

*Number of cigarettes per $100 of constant–dollar nondurable consumption.

EXHIBIT 17-4 **Product-life-cycle curves for product class, product form, and brand. (Source: Reprinted from "Validity of the Product Life Cycle," Journal of Business, Vol. 42, No. 4, October 1969, p. 389, by Rolando Polli and Victor Cook by permission of The University of Chicago Press. Copyright © 1969 by the University of Chicago. All rights reserved.)**

forecasts of stage transitions and phase duration. Chapter 19 reviews a number of new-product growth models useful for the early stage of the life cycle. Wilson (1969) suggests using a series of leading indicators for the timing of the maturity and decline phases, such as declining industry profits or overcapacity in the industry, while Cooke and Edmundson (1963) recommend using a time-series-based analysis developed on early data points.

Although some success has been claimed for these methods, they typically use data from one phase to forecast the timing and length of the next stage. Accurate long-range forecasting is quite difficult and therefore little is known about the length and sequence of life-cycle phases.

Day (1981a) summarizes the evidence on phase length and transition as follows:

Initial trajectory stage. The initial trajectory is profoundly affected by the factors influencing innovation diffusion in general. The most important factors include perceived advantage, perceived risk, barriers to adoption (incompatibility with existing operations or values), and information and availability. Pricing strategies in anticipation of experience-curve price declines can increase the comparative advantage.

Transition to rapid growth.   A number of factors, latent during introduction, become critical as growth accelerates. They include (1) change in the relationship with substitute products, reflecting changes in price-performance ratios, which, perhaps, result from variation in raw-material prices; (2) competitive entry strategies, reflecting increased ease of entry after initial risks have been reduced by the innovating firms; (3) the influence of repeat buying, which, as Midgeley (1981) shows, affects the shape of the life-cycle curve for consumer nondurables, and, as Harrell and Taylor (1931) show, affects the life cycle for durables; and (4) growth itself, or the bandwagon affect, resulting from rapid market expansion, which may uncover unsatisfied segments and open up new market opportunities.

Evolution to maturity.   Three factors affect the rate at which cumulative sales penetration approaches ultimate market capacity. First, the time rate of change of market potential, due either to price variation or to demographic trends, can affect the time of evolution. Second, as buyer learning increases, the impact on market potential becomes more important. As products take on more of a commodity status, buyers become more price-sensitive and less responsive to advertising and promotion (Erickson and Montgomery, 1980). Third, as a slowdown in the rate of market growth occurs, excess capacity may trigger a competitive battle for market share (Wasson, 1978).

The onset of decline.   Although decline is a neglected area of research, Harrigan (1980) has observed that some environments appear to be more favorable than others in terms of long-run sales, prices, and profit stability. In general, less favorable environments were brought to decline by fashion or demographic changes, while more favorable environments seemed to have pockets of enduring demand that could be protected from incursion by displaced competitors.

The problems of forecasting phase change and phase length, outlined here, are made more difficult by the widely held belief that life cycles are becoming shorter; Qualls, Olshavsky, and Michaels (1981) provide empirical support for this notion.

What then, is the value or use of the product-life-cycle concept in planning and strategy formulation? Clearly, a single life cycle does not exist; neither does a single life-cycle strategy. A realistic view is that life-cycle analysis is only one important element in the overall analysis of marketing opportunities. The life cycle acts as a classification device and suggests conditions under which market growth, for example, may occur. During market growth, competitors are better able to enter the market, and new opportunities for product offerings are available in selected market segments. Price and advertising elasticities are believed to change over the product life cycle as well [see Michwitz (1959) and Parsons (1975), or see

Simon (1979) as reviewed in Chapter 12]. However, other writers feel that the product-life-cycle concept is a dependent variable, determined largely by marketer action, rather than an independent variable to which firms should adapt their marketing programs (Wind and Claycamp, 1976; Dhalla and Yuspeh, 1976).

In summary, it appears that the product-life-cycle concept can provide a framework for organizing strategy alternatives and some limited input into operational marketing-planning models.

Cost Dynamics: Scale and Experience Effects

A second key phenomen affecting marketing strategy is cost dynamics. One of the most widely discussed findings of the PIMS program (reviewed later in this chapter) is that market share is a primary determinant of business profitability: the PIMS results show that, on average, a difference of market share between competitors of 10 percent translates into a 5 percent difference in pretax return on investment. One reason for this increase in profitability is that firms with larger market shares have lower costs, due partly to *economies of scale*—where very large plants cost less per unit of production to build and run—and partly to the *experience effect*—where the cost of many products decline 10–30 percent in real terms each time the company's experience in producing and selling them doubles.

Economies of Scale

Economists have identified a number of factors that affect the way the size of a production operation affects unit costs (Bain, 1952; Mansfield, 1975):

Lower building costs. Large manufacturing facilities can be constructed at a lower cost per unit of capacity than smaller ones. In industries such as petroleum and chemical, where process plants are frequently built at different sizes, the "six-tenths" rule is common: capital costs increase by the six-tenths power of capacity. According to this rule, doubling capacity increases building costs by $2^{0.6} \simeq 1.5$.

Lower operating costs. Large-scale plants are also more efficient to operate. For example, it usually takes less than twice the labor force to run a plant twice the size of another.

Other value-added cost decreases. A number of other elements decline on a unit-cost basis with increases in scale. These include marketing, sales, distribution, R&D, and service, all of which have a fixed-cost component for a firm wishing to maintain a market position. For example, the number of potential customers that must be reached with a salesforce or by advertising is not affected by the scale of the production operation. But when such (fixed) costs are spread over more units, their impact per unit is less.

Purchasing economies.   Unit prices for raw materials are also lower when they are purchased in larger quantities.

Careful cost accounting and engineering analysis can often lead to relationships among production volume, plant size, and unit costs for a particular product.

Experience-Curve Effects

Although it has long been known that costs fall with cumulative experience, it is only recently that this phenomenon has been studied carefully and quantified (Yelle, 1979). Initially, it was believed that only the labor portion of manufacturing costs decreased with cumulative production. The commander of the Wright-Patterson Air Force Base noted in the 1920s that the number of hours required to assemble a plane decreased as the total number of aircraft increased. The relationship between cumulative production and labor costs became known as the *learning curve*.

In the 1960s evidence began mounting that the phenomenon was broader. The Boston Consulting Group (1970), in particular, showed that each time cumulative volume of production of a product doubled, total value-added costs—including sales, administration, and so on—fell by a constant percentage. This relationship between total costs and cumulative production became known as the *experience curve*.

The simplest form of the learning or experience curve is the log-linear model:

$$C_q = C_n \left(\frac{q}{n} \right)^{-b} \tag{17.1}$$

where q = cumulative production to date
   n = cumulative production at particular, earlier time
   C_n = cost of nth unit (in constant dollars)
   C_q = cost of qth unit (in constant dollars)
   b = learning constant

In general, experience curves are characterized by their *learning rate*. Suppose that each time experience doubles, cost per unit drops to 80 percent of the original level. Then the 80 percent is known as the *learning rate*. The learning rate is related to the *learning constant* as follows:

$$r = 2^{-b} \times 100 \tag{17.2}$$

or

$$b = \frac{\ln 100 - \ln r}{\ln 2} \qquad (17.3)$$

where r = learning rate (percentage)
  b = learning constant

Exhibit 17.5 shows how costs fall with experience for various learning rates and levels of experience.

Many alternative models of the experience curve have been proposed [see Carlson (1961, 1973) for discussion], including the plateau model, the Stanford-B model, the DeJong model, and the S model (Exhibit 17.6). Furthermore, the Boston Consulting Group (1970) has been active in providing evidence of the pervasiveness of the experience-curve effect. Exhibit 17.7 gives some examples.

If one is to make strategic use of this phenomenon, it must be understood and *predicted*. The major reasons for the experience effect are as follows.*

1. **Labor efficiency.** As workers repeat a particular task, they become better at it, learning improvements and shortcuts. Maintenance personnel, supervisors, and marketing, sales, and administrative personnel all improve their efficiency.

EXHIBIT 17-5 **Sample cost reductions due to increased experience.**

Ratio of Old Experience to New Experience	Experience Curve (in %)					
	70%	75%	80%	85%	90%	95%
1.1	5	4	3	2	1	1
1.25	11	9	7	5	4	2
1.5	19	15	12	9	6	3
1.75	25	21	16	12	8	4
2.0	30	25	20	15	10	5
2.5	38	32	26	19	13	7
3.0	43	37	30	23	15	8
4.0	51	44	36	28	19	10
6.0	60	52	44	34	24	12
8.0	66	58	49	39	27	14
16.0	76	68	59	48	34	19

SOURCE: Derek F. Abell, John S. Hammond, *Strategic Market Planning: Problems and Analytical Approaches,* © 1979, p. 109. Adapted by permission of Prentice-Hall, Inc., Englewood Cliffs, N.J.

*Derek F. Abell, John S. Hammond, *Strategic Market Planning: Problems and Analytical Approaches,* ©1979, pp. 112–113. Adapted by permission of Prentice-Hall, Inc., Englewood Cliffs, N.J.

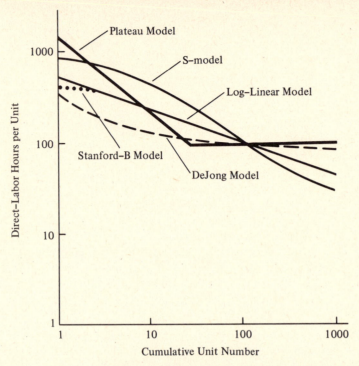

EXHIBIT 17-6   **Various learning-curve models all having the same direct-labor input at 100 units.** (Source: Yelle, 1979, p. 304, *Decision Sciences* journal.)

2. Work specialization and method improvement. As workers handle fewer individual operations, they are able to accumulate experience faster. Redesign of work methods also improves efficiency.

3. New production processes. A large number of process innovations and improvements occur as experience accumulates, especially in capital-intensive industries. The semiconductor industry—a low-labor-content manufacturing operation—sees experience curves of 70–80 percent, primarily through process improvements.

4. Getting better performance from production equipment. Experience often reveals innovative ways of increasing output from production equipment. Hirschman (1964) points out that the capacity of a fluid catalytic-cracking unit increases by about 50 percent over a 10-yr period.

5. Changes in resource mix. As experience accumulates, producers can often replace more-expensive resources (labor or raw materials) with less-expensive resources. Automation may replace labor; lower-grade chemical feedstocks may replace higher-cost grades.

6. Product standardization. Product standardization allows for the replication of tasks necessary for worker learning. Even when a wide product line is

Integrated Circuits

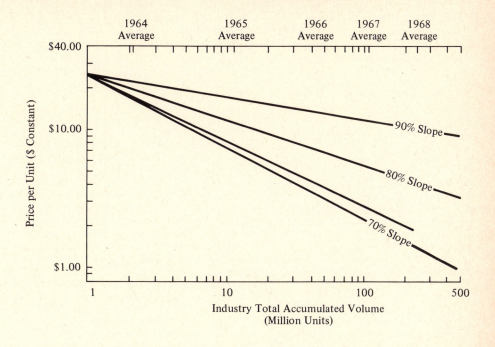

Motor Gasoline

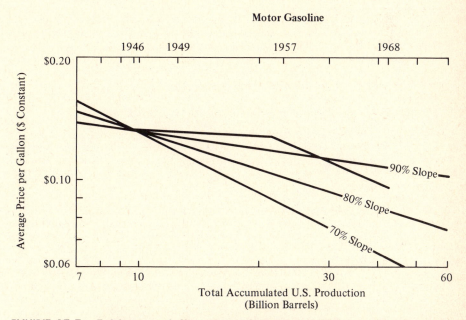

EXHIBIT 17-7 **Evidence of the pervasiveness of the experience-curve effect.** (Source: *Perspectives on Experience*, The Boston Consulting Group, Inc., 1970, pp. 75, 77.)

important, modularization of subcomponents (as in the auto industry) can produce the effects of standardization.

7. Product redesign. As experience is gained with producing and using a product, a greater understanding of true performance requirements is gained. Products may be redesigned to conserve material, substitute less costly material, produce more efficiency in manufacturing and so forth.

These observations suggest that experience by itself does not cause cost declines but, rather, provides the opportunity for such declines. Many of the above effects (work specialization, for example) may become possible because of the size of the operation and therefore are part of a scale effect. In fact, growth in experience usually occurs at the same time the size of an operation grows, although scale effects can be used to bypass experience (as the Japanese did in the steel industry). But it is often difficult (and not too important for planning) to separate the effects.

While the experience concept is rather simple, its application in a model requires ingenuity. It is important to (1) adjust prices for inflation; (2) plot cost versus experience (not time); (3) consider cost components separately, because each may have different learning rates; (4) correct for *shared experience*, when two or more products share a common resource or activity; (5) adjust for different experience rates between competitors (firm A, a late entry, may benefit from B's experience, may be able to exploit shared experience that B cannot, may have a different proportion of value added than B, etc.); (6) begin at the right starting point [choosing n and C_n in eq. (17.1)]; (7) measure costs properly over a reasonably long-term time frame; and (8) properly define the unit of analysis (a firm may have a large share of a small market yet have less experience than a competitor with a small share in a much larger market!). These and other practical considerations in developing and using the experience curve are discussed by Abell and Hammond (1979) by the Boston Consulting Group (1970) and by Hax and Majluf (1982).

The experience-curve concept is of strategic importance in business planning for many industries. In stable industries, where profit margins remain at a constant percentage of cost, the experience curve allows for long-range cost, price, and profit projections. Many situations are similar to the one illustrated in Exhibit 17.8. In phase A, costs exceed prices, as is often the case in a *start-up* situation. In phase B the market leader maintains a *price umbrella* over higher-cost producers entering the market, trading future market share for current profit. In phase C, the *shakeout period*, one producer begins lowering prices faster than costs, perhaps because of overcapacity. In phase D *stability* occurs when profit margins return to normal levels, following industry costs again. This illustration suggests the importance (as well as the risks) associated with a market-dominance strategy. While being the market leader and operating at a low-cost position

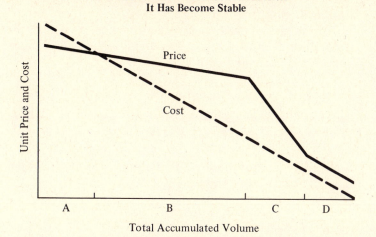

A Characteristic Unstable Pattern After It Has Become Stable

EXHIBIT 17-8 **Typical price-cost relationship.** (Source: *Perspectives on Experience,* The Boston Consulting Group, Inc., 1970, p. 21).

are desirable, a shakeout period (phase C) can be precipitated in a market by aggressively pursuing market share.

EXAMPLE: Assume a firm with a 5% share of a market growing at 10% wishes to catch the market leader, a firm with a 20% share. To do so in, say, 8 yr would require a 31% annual growth rate and a capacity increase of 860%, assuming the market leader holds its share. These simple (but striking) calculations raise important questions about the use of experience-curve concepts in strategy:

> Can the expansion be funded? What strategy will achieve such a large share gain? From which competitor(s) will the share come? Will the smaller one be squeezed out by an aggressive strategy? What competitive reaction can be expected? Will the market be worth leading 8 yr from now?
>
> The importance of doing these calculations and heeding their implications was underscored by the withdrawal of RCA, Xerox, and GE from the mainframe computer business; all three firms experienced multimillion dollar losses in computers. An appropriate set of calculations, done at the outset, might have dissuaded these companies from even entering the market [Abell and Hammond (1979). pp 118–119]

In Chapter 12 the use of the experience curve in developing an optimal *monopoly*-pricing strategy was discussed. The more difficult question raised here suggests that informed strategic decisions in the face of experience-curve cost declines require information about market growth, competitive costs, and likely competitive reaction. However, many of these considerations have yet to find their way into operational strategic-marketing/planning models.

In conclusion, the experience-curve cost declines, where they can be carefully *modeled* and *forecast*, provide an essential piece of information for informed business planning.

Market Definition and Market Structure

We have assumed throughout that a market is well defined or understood. But what is a market? And how is it structured?

Methods for Market Definition

Key strategic issues, such as the basic business definition, opportunity assessment, threat analysis, and the like, are closely tied to the breadth or the narrowness of the market. When attainment of market share represents a desirable objective, market boundaries must be defined to determine the extent to which the objective is met.

The traditional approach for describing markets has been by generic title and then by physical properties. For example, in the *auto* market (generic title), the size of the car (subcompact, compact, midsize, full size) has been used. The main idea behind the traditional approach is that there is relatively more (actual or perceived) competition within markets than across markets. Conceptually, the definition of a market is analogous to the development of a consumer market segment (Chapter 9). In fact, most economists and marketing analysts argue that the definition of a market should depend on how consumers view it.

Day, Shocker, and Srivastava (1979) define a product market as follows:

> The *set of products* judged to be substitutes within those usage segments in which similar patterns of benefits are sought and the *customers* for whom such usages are relevant (p. 10).

That is, a product market is a group of physical products perceived to be substitutes by a particular group of customers for specific occasions.

Day, Shocker, and Srivastava classify methods for identifying product markets by whether they rely on behavioral or judgmental data (Exhibit 17.9). Their classifications are reviewed below.

Cross Elasticity of Demand.   This approach is considered by most economists to be the standard one against which other approaches should be judged. Mathematically, the cross elasticity of demand is $(\partial Q_i / \partial X_j)(X_j / Q_i)$,

EXHIBIT 17-9   Analytic methods for defining product markets.

A: **Purchase or Use- Behavior Approaches**		B: **Customer-Perceptions/ Judgmental Approaches**	
A1.	Cross Elasticity of Demand	B1.	Decision-Sequence Analysis
A2.	Similarities in Behavior	B2.	Perceptual Mapping
A3.	Brand Switching	B3.	Technology-Substitution Analysis
		B4.	Customer Judgment of Substitutability

SOURCE: Day, Shocker, and Srivastava, 1979, p. 11.

where X_j represents some marketing activity (price generally) associated with brand j, and Q_i is the volume of brand i. In essence, if this term is large, i and j are said to be in the same market. This approach, despite its seeming logic, is frequently criticized and rarely used because (1) it assumes no response by one firm to price variations of another, (2) it is static and cannot accommodate changing product market composition, and (3) it is difficult to estimate in relatively stable markets, where there is frequently insufficient data variation.

Similarities in Use Behavior.   A study by Cocks and Virts (1975) addressed the question of substitutability of drugs with different chemical makeup but of similar therapeutic value. The data required information on the need for the drug (the diagnosis), as well as the drug prescribed to treat the problem. A unique panel of 3000 physicians produced these data. As yet, few consumer panels have tracked use occasions for products, limiting the applicability of this approach.

Brand Switching.   This approach suffers from some of the same limitations as the cross-elasticity method—the measures can only be used *after* a set of competitive products has been established. In general, the approach breaks down a matrix of brand-switching probabilities or proportions into competitive markets. The Hendry approach (Chapter 7) is an example.

Brand-switching data as potential measures of market boundaries are flawed because of (1) their limitations to markets with high repeat rates, (2) the need to assume stable switching behavior, and (3) their inability to handle multiple-use occasions, multiple users, and multiple, simultaneous purchases.

Furthermore, all the approaches that use behavioral data suffer from analyzing what was rather than focusing on what might be. For instance, problems, such as lack of availability, may prevent substitution of one brand for another when they might otherwise be substitutes. Unless data are collected in a laboratory-based setting, these approaches, at best, provide a partial solution to the problem of market definition. To complement them, consumer perceptions and judgments are useful.

Decision-Sequence Analysis.   Decision-sequence analysis considers protocols of the consumer decision-making process that indicate the sequence in which decision criteria are used for final product choice (Bettman, 1971). For example, a potential customer might be asked, when choosing a margarine, whether he chose a form first (stick versus tub), a raw material first (corn oil, safflower oil, etc.) or a brand first. Because respondents are not used to this type of introspection, the approach has several empirical problems. There is also a problem of declaring two decision processes similar.

Perceptual Mapping.   As discussed in Chapters 7 and 11, perceptual mapping is a set of approaches used to represent the position of brands in geometric space. Those brands close together are considered to form a market and be substitutes. The approach is flexible and has seen wide use in market-definition studies.

Technology Substitution.   Technology substitution is an approach for determining how products (industrial products, generally) are likely to compete. The rate at which one material substitutes for another (e.g., polyvinyl for glass in bottles) is related to its relative utility in each situation (Stein, Ayers, and Shapeneso, 1975). The result is a quantitative measure of relative utility that can be used to estimate substitutability among competing products or technologies in certain situations.

Consumer Judgments of Substitutability.   There are a variety of ways to gather information on substitutability from consumers, ranging from simply asking consumers to methods with more diagnostic power. [See Day, Shocker, and Srivastava (1979) for a critical review of these other methods.]

An interesting addition to the above list of alternatives is a model that combines switching data and behavioral data, called Prodegy (Urban, Johnson, and Brudnick, 1979). The approach is hierarchical, as is the Hendry model, but branches can be defined not only by physical product attributes but by use occasions and users. Perceptual information is integrated by providing a perceptual map for each branch at the bottom of the tree. Exhibit 17.10 illustrates the results for coffee. First, coffee is divided into ground and instant; instant coffee, in turn, is divided into caffeinated and decaffeinated brands; and each of these is then divided into freeze-dried and regular varieties. For each branch a perceptual map describes the relative positions of brands on the dimensions of "taste" and "mildness." The model is developed and calibrated with data from a laboratory-based, simulated-purchase situation, in which the favorite brand is "out of stock," so that there is another measure of what is substitutable. Statistical analysis is used to select a hierarchical tree that best fits substitution data. Although this approach has had limited use, its combination of behavioral and perceptual data in a model-and-measurement methodology appears to provide a new alternative to define market boundaries, at least for frequently purchased products.

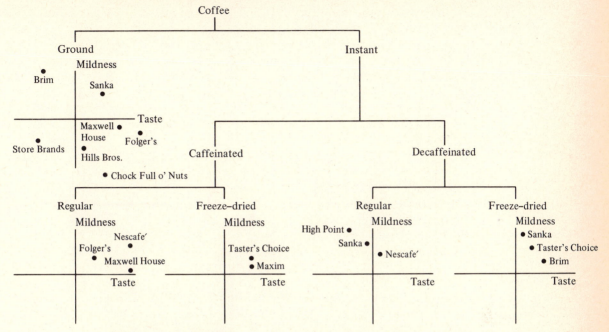

EXHIBIT 17-10   Hierarchical definition of the coffee market. (Source: Urban and Hauser, 1980, p. 94, Fig. 5.7.)

In conclusion, the method for choosing market boundaries and the boundaries themselves will differ depending on the time frame and the use to which the information will be put.

Regardless of the method, the most persistent problem is the lack of defensible criteria for recognizing [market] boundaries (Day, Shocker, and Srivastava, 1979, p. 18).

Market Structure

The field of industrial economics has had, as one of its foci, the nature of competition. Recently, much of the work has been brought together in a manner that is comprehensible to management, primarily by Porter (1980). According to this view, industry structure is determined by the nature of five competitive forces (see Exhibit 17.11):

1. **Threat of competitive entry.** This factor depends on the barriers to entry that are present in the market, as well as the reaction from existing competitors, that an entrant can expect. If the barriers are high and/or the newcomer can expect sharp retaliation from entrenched competitors, the threat of entry is low. Major barriers to entry include econo-

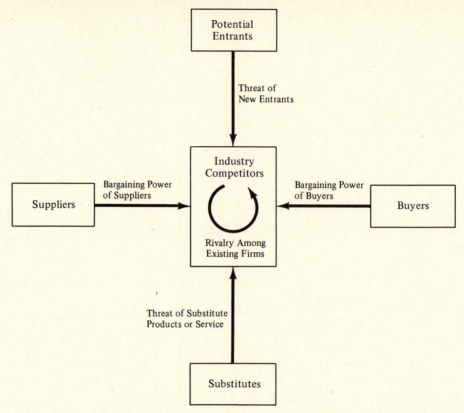

EXHIBIT 17-11   **Forces driving industry competition.** (Source: Redrawn with permission of Macmillan Publishing Co., Inc. from *Competitive Strategy: Techniques for Analyzing* by Michael E. Porter. Copyright © 1980 by The Free Press, a Division of Macmillan Publishing Co., Inc.)

mies of scale, product differentiation, capital requirements, switching costs, access to distribution channels, and the like.

2. **Intensity of rivalry among existing competitors.**   Factors associated with intense rivalry include slow industry growth, balanced share position (lack of a market leader), high fixed costs, lack of differentiation, and high exit barriers.

3. **Pressure from substitute products.**   The greater the extent of substitute products providing an attractive price-performance alternative to suppliers is, the lower is the potential for industry profits.

4. **Bargaining power of buyers.**   The greater the power of buyers, the lower are industry profits. Buyers are powerful if (1) their sales are high relative to seller sales, (2) they earn low profits (Chrysler exerts

effective price pressure on its suppliers), (3) they pose a threat of direct competition through backward integration, and (4) they have full information about demand, market prices, and so forth.

5. **Bargaining power of suppliers.** Powerful suppliers can exert power over participants in an industry by threatening to raise prices or reduce the quality of purchased goods and services. The conditions for powerful suppliers mirror those for powerful buyers, extending to the threat of forward integration.

Porter (1980) argues that a competitive strategy is one that takes offensive or defensive action in order to create a defensible position against these five competitive forces. The alternatives are as follows:

positioning the business so that its capabilities provide defense against competitive forces

improving the firm's position through strategic moves

anticipating shifts in the underlying factors affecting market structure and preemptively adjusting to them

Porter maintains that the collective strength of these forces determines the ultimate profit potential of an industry and hence guides market strategy. In their present form, however, these results provide more of a checklist of forces, with a few measurement guidelines, rather than a complete theory of competitive-market structure.

Buzzell (1981) has shown that the pervasive pattern of market share across a wide range of businesses is highly skewed and is well represented by a semilogarithmic distribution:

$$\log ms_i = k_0 + k_1 i \tag{17.4}$$

where ms_i = market share of ith largest competitor
         k_0, k_1 = distribution parameters

He also shows that large-share businesses have a tendency to lose share over time and notes that this basic pattern is so nearly universal that is seems appropriate to call it a "natural" market structure. However, he concludes that "there is no satisfactory theory that would account for the observed common pattern of market share distribution or for the tendency of large-share businesses to lose share" (p. 50).

Integration, quantification, and theoretical development is needed to make use of market-structure analysis in strategic-market-planning models. A further discussion of the nature of competition in marketing models is included in Chapter 18.

Analytic Approaches to Market-Strategy Development

A wide variety of tools are used for market-strategy and portfolio-analysis problems. Although other classifications have been used, these approaches can roughly be classified as follows:

> shared-experience models: the PIMS approach
> product-portfolio models
> > standardized
> > customized
> > financial
> normative-resource-allocation models

All of these approaches, explicitly or implicitly, incorporate life-cycle analysis, experience-curve effects, market-definition and market-structure effects. Each approach is discussed in turn below.

The Shared-Experience Approach: PIMS

The PIMS (profit impact of marketing strategy) project began in 1960 at General Electric as an intrafirm analysis of the relative profitability of its businesses. It is based on the concept that the pooled experiences from a diversity of successful and unsuccessful businesses will provide useful insights and guidance about the determinants of business profitability. The term "business" refers to a strategic business unit, which is an operating unit selling a distinct set of products to an identifiable group of customers in competition with a well-defined set of competitors. In early 1981 the data base of about 100 data items per business included more than 2000 businesses from about 215 participating firms.

Perhaps the most publicized use of the PIMS data is in the form of the PAR regression model, which relates return on investment (ROI = pretax income/average investment over 4 yr of data) to a set of 37 independent variables (Schoeffler, 1977; Schoeffler, Buzzell, and Heany, 1974). Although the precise form of the model has not been made public, selected findings are available. In Exhibit 17.12 the PIMS independent variables are listed and classified by their degree of management control; in Exhibit 17.13 a comparison of the relationship among market share, investment intensity, and profitability is given. The PIMS conclusion is that "low market share plus high investment intensity equals disaster." Exhibit 17.13 also shows a clear and significant trend upward in profitability with increases in market share. Another interesting result, presented in Exhibit 17.14, is the relationship among product quality, the marketing/sales ratio, and profitability: the PIMS conclusion is that "high marketing expenditure damages profitability when quality is low."

EXHIBIT 17-12   **Categorization of PIMS independent variables by the degree to which they may be controlled by management.**

Directly Controllable by Management (Goals/Strategies)	Partially Controllable by Management	Largely Uncontrollable by Management (Environmental)
Market position	Instability of market share	Industry long-run growth
Price relative to competition	Relative pay scale[a]	Short-run market growth
Product quality	Capacity utilization[b]	Industry exports
New-product sales	Corporate size	Sales direct to end user
Manufacturing costs/sales	Change in market share	Share of four largest firms
Receivables/sales	Change in selling-price index	Buyer-fragmentation index
Vertical integration	Change in vertical integration	Investment intensity[c]
Inventory/purchases	Market-position impact	Fixed-capital intensity[c]
Sales/employee		Competitive-market activity
Marketing less sales-force expenses/sales		Change in capital activity
R&D expenses/sales		Investment-intensity impact
Corporate payout		
Degree of diversification		
Growth of sales		
Change in product quality		
Change in advertising and promotion/sales		
Change in salesforce Expenses/sales		
Change in return on sales		

SOURCE: Anderson and Paine, 1978, p. 607.

[a]Only controllable by increasing.

[b]Only controllable in the short run.

[c]Only controllable at the entry level.

A number of other results of this nature are available on the impact of strategic variables on ROI, cash flow, and other elements of interest to the firm (Gale, 1978, 1980; Gale and Swire, 1980; Schoeffler, 1977a, 1977b, 1978, 1979). These results are generally available as 3×3 matrices, which compare the effects of two variables at a time on a single criterion variable.

The PAR model alluded to above is used to produce a PAR report, the key management report from the PIMS program. The report specifies the ROI and cash flow environment that could be expected for a business with a

EXHIBIT 17-13   **Impact of strategic planning on profit performance: investment intensity and market share.**

Investment Intensity	Market Share (in %)		
	Under 12%	**12–26%**	**Over 26%**
Under 45%	21.2	26.9	34.6
45–71%	8.6	13.1	26.2
Over 71%	2.0	6.7	15.7

PIMS Conclusion   Low market share plus high investment intensity equals disaster.

SOURCE: Reprinted by permission of the Harvard Business Review. An exhibit from "*Impact of Strategic Planning on Profit Performance*" by Sidney Schoeffler, Robert D. Buzzell, and Donald F. Heany. (March/April 1974), pp. 137–145. Copyright © 1974 by the President and Fellows of Harvard College; all rights reserved.

EXHIBIT 17-14   **Impact of strategic planning on profit performance: product quality and ratio of marketing expenditures to sales.**

Product Quality	Ratio of Marketing Expenditures to Sales (in %)		
	Low: Under 6%	**Average: 6–11%**	**High: over 11%**
Inferior	15.4	14.8	2.7
Average	17.8	16.9	14.2
Superior	25.2	25.5	19.8

PIMS Conclusion   A high marketing expenditure damages profitability when quality is low.

SOURCE: Reprinted by permission of the Harvard Business Review. An exhibit from "*Impact of Strategic Planning on Profit Performance*" by Sidney Schoeffler, Robert D. Buzzell, and Donald F. Heaney (March/April 1974), pp. 137–145. Copyright © 1974 by the President and Fellows of Harvard College; all rights reserved.

given kind of market environment, market position, degree of competitive differentiation, and the like.

EXAMPLE: Exhibit 17.15 gives a sample PAR summary report, showing how the PAR ROI compares with the PAR ROI for all businesses in the PIMS sample. This product has an actual ROI of 25.4%. The average for all PIMS business is 16.7%. However, the use of strategic variables available to this business suggests that its PAR ROI should exceed the average by 9.6%, yielding a PAR ROI of 26.3%. The reason for the difference is associated primarily with the attractiveness of the business environment and the effective use of investment. Other, more detailed reports reveal that the specific elements leading to the positive effects are a high-level, long-run industry growth

EXHIBIT 17-15   **Sample PAR summary report.**

P
I
M
S

PAR RETURN ON INVESTMENT (PRETAX) 1972–1974

PAR RETURN ON INVESTMENT IS AN ESTIMATE OF THE PRETAX
RETURN ON INVESTMENT (ROI) THAT IN 1972–74 WAS NORMAL
FOR BUSINESSES FACING MARKET AND INDUSTRY CONDITIONS
EQUIVALENT TO THOSE OF YOUR BUSINESS AND OCCUPYING A
SIMILAR MARKET POSITION.

FOR BUSINESS NO. 87041, PRETAX

PAR ROI	26.3%
ACTUAL ROI	25.4

IMPACT ON PAR ROI OF THE FACTORS BY CATEGORY

PAR ROI EQUALS THE SUM OF THE TOTAL IMPACT AND THE
AVERAGE ROI OF ALL BUSINESS IN THE PIMS DATA BASE.

CATEGORY	IMPACT ON PAR ROI (PRETAX) %
ATTRACTIVENESS OF BUSINESS ENVIRONMENT	3.1
STRENGTH OF YOUR COMPETITIVE POSITION	0.1
DIFFERENTIATION OF COMPETITIVE POSITION	1.2
EFFECTIVENESS OF USE OF INVESTMENT	13.4
DISCRETIONARY BUDGET ALLOCATION	−6.8
COMPANY FACTORS	−1.2
CHANGE/ACTION FACTORS	−0.2
TOTAL IMPACT	9.6
AVERAGE ROI, ALL PIMS BUSINESSES	16.7
PAR ROI, THIS BUSINESS	26.3%

SOURCE: Tex-Fiber Industries-Petroloid Products, 9-577-040, Copyright © 1976 by the President
and Fellows of Harvard College, in Derek Abell and John Hammond, *Strategic Market
Planning: Problems and Analytical Approaches,* by Abell and Hammond. Englewood Cliffs,
N.J.: Prentice-Hall, Inc., 1979, p. 330. Reprinted by permission of the Harvard Business
School.

(21.3% for this business compared with an 8% industry average) and a relatively high degree of vertical integration and capacity utilization.

This type of analysis provides an auditing tool, displaying the deviation of actual ROI from PAR ROI, and yields insights into how well and why the business has met its strategic potential.

In addition, three other types of reports appear to be useful for management:

The *strategy sensitivity report* predicts what would happen (in the short and long term) if certain strategic changes were made. This report relies on future values, provided by the user, of industry sales, costs, and prices.

Optimum-strategy reports predict what combination of strategic sources results in the best ROI, discounted net income, or discounted cash flow. The choice of several objectives allows a look at potential suboptimal strategies: a strategy to maximize cash flow may result in a drop in market share, resulting in lower long-run net income and ROI.

The *limited-information model (LIM) report* uses an abbreviated set of factors (18 versus 37 for the PAR model) to predict and evaluate PAR ROI and cash flow. This type of report is useful when quick analysis of one's own business is required, and it is increasingly being used for evaluating the positions of competitors. It also is a useful tool for screening and evaluating acquisition candidates.

A large number of other analyses have been and are being explored with the PIMS data base. For example, over the past half decade it has generally been accepted that a few key factors account for the largest part of the variability in profitability and cash flow. These key factors and the situations that influence their effect are being explored in more detail with the PIMS data. Some of the more important work is described below.

The Determinants of Market Share.   There seems to be general agreement that high market share and high profitability are related. Therefore investigators are studying how market share can be changed. Buzzell and Wiersema (1980) studied the percentage change in market share over a 4-yr period with regression analysis. They found that three categories of variables reflected market-share changes: (1) initial share level and rank; (2) relative product quality and new product activity, reflecting past product development and marketing activities; and (3) the exit and entry of competitors.

Strategic Trade-offs.   The PAR model is a compensatory model that can be used to investigate how a low-share business (for example) can be made profitable with a balance of strategic factors. Some work in this area includes that of Chussil and Downs (1979), which shows that high volume (quality above that expected at a given price) can help businesses gain share in slow-growth markets. Furthermore, Chussil (1978) showed that spending on R&D of more than 0.75 percent of sales above PAR has a significant depressing effect on profit when market share is low. These and other findings should help provide the beginning of an empirical base upon which to develop theories of strategy development.

Product-life-cycle Analysis.   Thorelli and Burnett (1981) showed that as the product aged (a surrogate for stage in its life cycle), there were decreases in market concentration, decreases in share movements by competitors, fewer new-product introductions, and so forth. However, the relationships were weak, calling for better measurement of life-cycle stages.

Evaluation.   Although of apparent value to planners and marketing strategists, the results of the PIMS program have come under criticism. Few of the criticisms have questioned the value of inferential analysis from shared-business experience because the data base is far richer than any current or prospective alternatives. Rather, the criticisms of PIMS generally fall into three categories: specification problems, measurement error, and interpretation. Most of these criticisms are summarized in Anderson and Paine (1978) and in Lubatkin and Pitts (1982).

In terms of *specification,* questions have been raised about the structure of the regression model—whether additive effects, multiplicative effects, interactions, multicollinearity, or heteroscedasticity exist. Furthermore, the use of ROI forces a short-term focus on strategy questions, and there is misspecification resulting from the presence of an investment term (investment intensity) among the independent variables, leading inevitably to a significant relationship with the dependent variable. In addition, the omission of business goals and the structure of the organization may be a problem, and the disguising of sales data and other units only allows the modeling of operating ratios. For some analyses this feature may lead to spurious relationships (Lilien, 1979).

In terms of *measurement error,* it is inevitable that different firms, with different accounting methods, interpretations, and levels of understanding of the data requirements, will provide noisy data. The potential significance of this problem was underscored by Rumelt and Wensley (1980), who report little stability in market-share estimates when different measures were correlated over different time periods. These types of problems are inherent in shared data; users of the results need to be made aware of the extent of the possible problem.

Potentially the most serious problem is in the *interpretation.* The PIMS results are norms; therefore the equations do not have a causal interpretation. High market share and high profit occur together. Although it is tempting to predict the consequences on profitability of changes in the independent variables of the PAR model, it is not reasonable to do so. Lack of information about goals and the extent to which certain strategies, exercised over time, were able to achieve those goals makes the problem

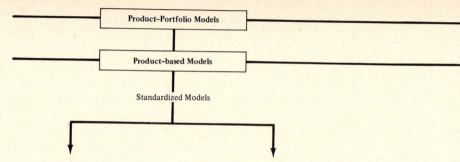

Product–Portfolio Models

Product–based Models

Standardized Models

Univariate Dimensions:
Boston Consulting Group's Growth–Share Matrix

		Relative M/S	
		H ◄——► L	
Market Growth	H	"Star"	Problem child
	L	Cash cow	Dog

Composite Dimensions:
The McKinsey/GE Business–Assessment Array

		Industry Attractiveness		
		High	Medium	Low
Business Strengths	High	Investment and Growth (C)	Selective Growth (G)	Selectivity (Y)
	Medium	Selective Growth (G)	Selectivity (Y)	Harvest (R)
	Low	Selectivity (Y)	Harvest (R)	Harvest (R)

A.D. Little's Business–Profile Matrix

		Stage of Industry Maturity			
		Embryonic	Growth	Mature	Aging
Competitive Position	Dominant				
	Strong				
	Favorable				
	Tentative				
	Weak				

Shell International's Directional–Policy Matrix

		Prospects for Sector Profitability		
		Unattractive	Average	Attractive
Company's Competitive Capabilities	Weak	Disinvest	Phased Withdrawal / Custodial	Double or Quit
	Average	Phased Withdrawal	Growth	Try Harder
	Strong	Cash Generation	Growth / Leader	Leader

EXHIBIT 17-16 Portfolio models. (Source: Reprinted by permission from "Marketing-Oriented Strategic Planning Models," by Yoram Wind, *Marketing Decision Models*, pp. 220–221. Copyright © 1981 by Elsevier Science Publishing Co., Inc.)

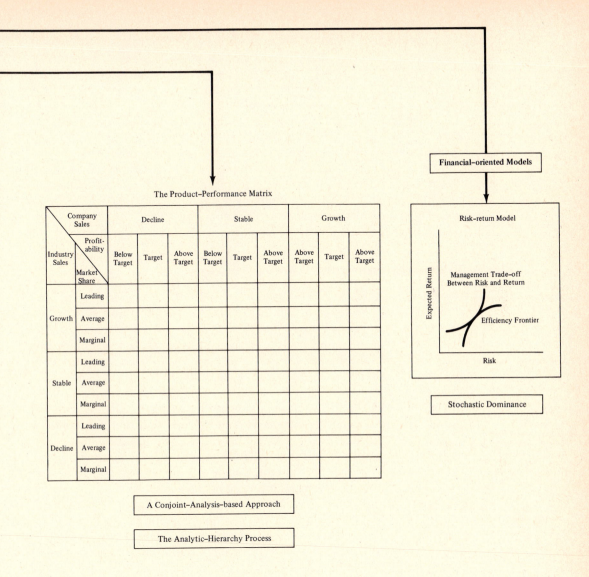

The Product–Performance Matrix

Industry Sales	Company Sales → Profit-ability / Market Share ↓	Decline			Stable			Growth		
		Below Target	Target	Above Target	Below Target	Target	Above Target	Above Target	Target	Above Target
Growth	Leading									
	Average									
	Marginal									
Stable	Leading									
	Average									
	Marginal									
Decline	Leading									
	Average									
	Marginal									

A Conjoint–Analysis–based Approach

The Analytic–Hierarchy Process

Financial–oriented Models

Risk–return Model

Management Trade-off Between Risk and Return

Efficiency Frontier

Expected Return

Risk

Stochastic Dominance

more severe. At the moment we must be careful about drawing a causal conclusion from the relationship between market share and profitability because the models used do not yet have a sound empirical or theoretical justification. [For example, see Hameresh, Anderson, and Harris (1978) for evidence of a negative share/profitability relationship.]

In conclusion, the PIMS models and data base provide an important empirical base and structure for asking intelligent questions about strategy. The results should not be ignored, but neither should they be used as a substitute for informed judgment and analysis of a specific situation. As a complement to other approaches and as a tool for describing and explaining market phenomena, PIMS is extremely valuable. Problems are likely to occur when the results are used to replace situation-specific analysis instead of providing decision support.

Product-Portfolio Classification and Analysis Models

In recent years there has been an emergence of a number of product-portfolio models. Following Wind (1981c), we classify these models as standardized models, customized models, and financial models. Some of the key dimensions of the major portfolio approaches are shown schematically in Exhibit 17.16 and are summarized in Exhibit 17.17. Wind and Mahajan (1982) provide detailed discussions of these models. We discuss one from each category below.

Standardized Models (BCG: Boston Consulting Group).   Common to all standardized product-portfolio models is the recognition that the value of market position or market share depends on the structure of competition and the stage of the product life cycle. This recognition is consistent with our discussion of the importance of the product life cycle, the experience curve, and market structure in providing input into strategic decisions.

The earliest and most widely implemented standard approach is the growth/share matrix developed by the Boston Consulting Group (BCG). In this approach the company classifies all of its strategic business units (SBUs) in the business-portfolio matrix (also called the growth/share matrix), shown in Exhibit 17.18. There are several things to notice:

1. The vertical axis, the market-growth rate, shows the annualized rate at which the various markets in which each business unit is located are growing. Market growth is arbitrarily divided into high and low growth by a 10 percent growth line.

2. The horizontal axis, relative market share, shows the market share for each SBU relative to the share of the industry's largest competitor. Thus a relative market share of 0.4 means that the company's SBU stands at 40 percent of the leaders' share, and a relative market share of 2.0 means that the company's SBU is the leader and has twice the share of

EXHIBIT 17-17   **Key characteristics of nine portfolio models.**

Model	Degree of Adaptability	Specific Dimensions	Allocation Rules	Comments
1. BCG growth/ share matrix	None; a rigid framework	1. Relative market share (cash generation) 2. Market growth (cash use)	1. Allocation of resources among the four categories (move "cash" to "problem child," etc.) 2. Consideration for product deletion (e.g., "dogs") 3. No explicit portfolio recommendation except with respect to the balance of cash flows	Widely used but conceptually questionable, given the forcing of two dimensions, the unique operational definition, and lack of rules for determining a portfolio of "dogs," "stars," et cetera. No consideration of risk, no weighting of dimensions.
2. McKinsey/GE business-assessment array	Limited through the selection of variables used to determine the two composite dimensions	1. Industry attractiveness 2. Business strengths	In its simplistic use, it offers a slightly greater precision than BCG (nine cells versus four and better definition of dimensions). In its more sophisticated uses (as by GE), the classification of products on these two dimensions is used only as input to an explicit resource-allocation model.	Forcing of two dimensions, which might not be the appropriate ones. The empirical determination of the correlates of the two dimensions is superior to the BCG approach, yet given the tailoring of factors to each industry, comparability across the industries is difficult. No consideration of risk.
3. A. D. Little business-profile matrix	Same as McKinsey/GE	1. Competitive-market position 2. Industry maturity	Same as McKinsey/GE	Same as McKinsey/GE

EXHIBIT 17-17   **Key characteristics of nine portfolio models.** (*Continued*)

Model	Degree of Adaptability	Specific Dimensions	Allocation Rules	Comments
4. Shell International directional-policy matrix	Same as McKinsey/GE	1. Profitability of market segment 2. Competitive position in the segment	Same as McKinsey/GE	Same as McKinsey/GE
5. Product-performance matrix	Considerable; the specific dimensions are selected by management	1. Industry sales 2. Product sales 3. Market share 4. Profitability all by market segment	Same as BCG but based on projected results in response to alternative marketing strategies	Limited applications (major user: International Harvester), yet it offers the conceptual advantage of management-determined performance dimensions and allocation of resources based on projected rather than historical performance. No weighting of dimensions.
6. Conjoint-analysis-based approach	Fully adaptable to management needs	No general dimensions; the dimensions determined by management judgment	Based on computer simulation, which incorporates management utility functions (for the dimensions of the portfolio) and product-performance data (supplemented to the extent needed by mangement perceptions of current and new products and businesses)	Limited applications; very demanding of management time

EXHIBIT 17-17   **Key characteristics of nine portfolio models.** (*Continued*)

Model	Degree of Adaptability	Specific Dimensions	Allocation Rules	Comments
7. Analytic-hierarchy process	Fully adaptable to management needs	As with conjoint analysis, determined by management judgment	Optimal allocation among all items of the portfolio (e.g., products, market segments) determined algorithmically	Limited applications. Conceptually and mathematically very appealing. Allows management to evaluate strategic assumptions and allocate resources across products, market segments, and distribution networks optimally under different scenarios of market and competitive conditions. Weighting of dimensions explicitly considered.
8. Risk/return model	None; a theory-derived model	1. Expected return (mean) 2. Risk (variance)	Determination of optimal portfolio	Conceptually the most defensible, yet difficult to operationalize for the product-portfolio decision. Limited real-world applications.
9. Stochastic dominance	Same as risk/return model	The entire distribution of return	Same as risk/return	Same as risk/return

SOURCE: Reprinted by permission from "Marketing-Oriented Strategic Planning Models," by Yoram Wind, *Marketing Decision Models*, pp. 222–223, 1981, by Elsevier Science Publishing Co., Inc.

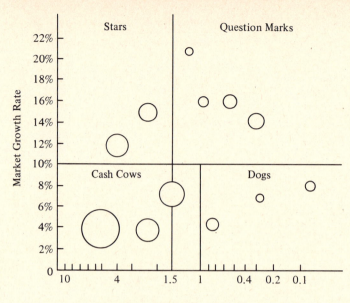

EXHIBIT 17-18   **The BCG business-portfolio matrix.**

the next-strongest company in the market. Relative market share gives more information about competitive standing than absolute market share; an absolute market share of 15 percent may or may not mean market leadership until we know the leader's share. The more SBUs with a relative market share greater than 1.5 that a company has, the more markets it is a leader in. The relative market share is drawn on a logarithmic scale.

3. The circles depict the growth/share standings of the company's various SBUs. The areas of the circles are proportional to the SBUs' dollar sales.

4. Each quadrant represents a distinct type of cash flow situation, leading to the following classification of SBUs:

   a. *Stars* are high-growth, high-share SBUs. They often use cash because cash is necessary to finance their rapid growth. Eventually, their growth will slow down, and they will turn into cash cows and become major cash generators supporting other SBUs.

   b. *Cash cows* are low-growth, high-share SBUs. They throw off a lot of cash that the company uses to meet its bills and support other SBUs that are cash using.

   c. *Question marks* (also called problem children or wildcats) are low-share SBUs in high-growth markets. They require a lot of cash to maintain and increase their share. Management has to think hard about whether to spend more to build these question marks into leaders; if not, the question marks will have to be phased down or out.

   d. *Dogs* (also called cash traps) are low-growth, low-share SBUs. They may generate enough cash to maintain themselves but do not promise to be a large source of cash.

5. The higher an SBU's market share, the higher its cash-generating ability because higher market shares are accompanied by higher levels of profitability. On the other hand, the higher the market-growth rate, the higher are the SBUs cash-using requirements for it to grow and maintain its share.

6. The distribution of the SBUs in the four quadrants of the business-portfolio matrix suggests the company's current state of health and desirable future strategic directions. The company in Exhibit 17.19 is fortunate in having some large cash cows to finance its question marks, stars, and dogs.

7. As time passes, SBUs will change their positions in the business-portfolio matrix. Many SBUs start out as question marks, move into the star category if they succeed, later become cash cows as market growth falls, and, finally, turn into dogs toward the end of their life cycle.

8. Management's job is to project a future matrix showing where each SBU is likely to be, assuming no change in its strategy. By comparing the current and future matrices, management can identify the major strategic issues facing the firm. The task of strategic planning is then to determine what role should be assigned to each SBU in the interest of efficient resource allocation. Four basic strategies are usually evaluated:

   a. *build*—improve market position and forgo short-term earnings to achieve this goal
   b. *hold*—preserve the market position
   c. *harvest*—get a short-term increase in cash flow regardless of the long-term effect
   d. *divest*—sell or liquidate the business because resources can be used better elsewhere

The main concept behind the BCG approach is that of *cash balance*—that the long-run health of the corporation depends on some products generating cash (and profits) and others using the cash to support growth. Unless a company has an unusually favorable cash flow, it cannot afford to sponsor too many products with large cash appetites. On the other hand, if resources are spread too thin, the company may end up with a number of marginal businesses and reduced capacity to finance promising future opportunities.

Evaluation.   In spite of their popularity, the BCG and other standardized approaches are limited by their attempt to boil down business strategy to the interplay of two or a small number of standardized dimensions, potentially ignoring important problems. The BCG approach gives market share (relative experience) and market growth (stage in the life cycle) fundamental positions in the development of strategy. But as we discussed earlier, market definition and market structure are difficult and often ill-defined quantities. Furthermore, the approach assumes that all competitors have the same overhead structures and experience curves, and that position on the experience curve corresponds to market position. Also, the firm may have a number of other objectives besides cash flow balancing. Wind, Mahajan, and Swire (1982) studied the matrix positioning of 15 SBUs for a *Fortune* 500 firm and found that the same businesses could be classified as dogs, cash cows, stars, or question marks depending on the specific operational definition of the matrix dimension. To the extent that this finding is symptomatic of a general nonrobustness of these approaches, it "strongly questions the advisability of using standardized portfolio models as a basis for classifying businesses and providing strategic guidelines" (p. 28).

In conclusion, while standardized approaches are widely used and clearly of value in helping to think about the problem, the use of only two dimensions, the lack of rules for portfolio formation, the lack of dimension weighting, and the lack of consideration of risk raise serious questions about the appropriateness of these approaches. (See Wensley (1982) for an interesting comparison of PIMS and BCG).

Customized Approaches.   In contrast to the standardized portfolio approaches, there are a series of customized approaches that do not prespecify dimensions or objectives.

The *product-performance-matrix* approach (Wind and Claycamp, 1976) allows management to choose specific dimensions. Reportedly, International Harvester uses four: industry sales, product sales, market share, and profitability. In allocating resources, this approach follows that of BCG but is based on projected results in response to alternative marketing strategies. Although used by International Harvester, it has seen limited application elsewhere.

Conjoint analysis (Green and Wind, 1973) lets management select dimensions and their relative importance, combined in a utility function. On the basis of these functions together with product-performance data, any portfolio can be combined with another in terms of its overall performance. The approach has seen little application to date, perhaps because it is time-consuming in application.

The *analytic-hierarchy process (AHP)* is a recent addition to the set of methodologies for assessing and allocating resources in a portfolio. [This discussion comes from Wind (1981c) and Wind and Saaty (1980).]

With the AHP the analyst structures a problem hierarchically and then, through an associated measurement-and-decomposition process, determines the relative priorities consistent with overall objectives of all entities at the lowest level of the hierarchy. These priorities can then be used as guidelines in allocating resources among these entities.

The basic idea behind the AHP is that pairwise comparisons can be used to recover the relative weights (importance) of items or objects at any level of a hierarchy. Suppose we have n objects, labeled $A_1, \ldots, A_n$, and that we *know* the vector of corresponding weights $w = (w_1, \ldots, w_n)$. We can then form a matrix of pairwise comparisons of weights:

$$A = \begin{array}{c} A_1 \\ \vdots \\ A_n \end{array} \begin{bmatrix} \begin{array}{ccc} A_1 & \cdots & A_n \end{array} \\ \dfrac{w_1}{w_1} \quad \cdots \quad \dfrac{w_1}{w_n} \\ \\ \dfrac{w_n}{w_1} \quad \cdots \quad \dfrac{w_n}{w_n} \end{bmatrix} \tag{17.5}$$

We can recover the scale of weights $w_1, \ldots, w_n$ by multiplying A on the right by w and solving the eigenvalue problem:

$$Aw = \lambda w \tag{17.6}$$

Equation (17.6) has a nontrivial solution because $\lambda = n$ is the largest eigenvalue of A. This result follows because A has unit rank and, therefore, one and only one nonzero eigenvalue:

$$\sum_{i=1}^{n} \lambda_i = \text{trace}(A) = n \qquad \lambda_{\max} = n \tag{17.7}$$

In application, w_i / w_j are not known but must be estimated. Wind and Saaty (1980) suggest comparing objects via a nine-point scale, where 1 signifies two activities that contribute equally to the attainment of an objective and 9 represents one activity having the highest possible priority over another. The reciprocal of the rating is then entered in the transpose position of A. The solution to eq. (17.6), where $\lambda = \lambda_{\max}$, now gives an estimate of the weights.

EXAMPLE: This example is adapted from Wind and Saaty (1980, pp. 649–652).* The AHP approach was used at the Colonial Penn Insurance Company to investigate whether the company should continue to focus its efforts only on insurance products or should diversify into other products and markets. Furthermore, given the firm's historical strength in a direct-mail operation, should they focus their operation on products and markets that can be

*Reprinted by permission of The Institute of Management Sciences, *Management Science*, V. 26, No. 7, July 1980.

reached effectively by mail or should they consider developing new distribution vehicles such as telephone, stores, and agents?

The AHP was used to help guide the selection of the desired target portfolio of products/markets and distribution outlets and direct the allocation of resources among the portfolio's components. A hierarchy was developed jointly with the company president and is presented (in a disguised form) in Exhibit 17.19. This hierarchy is based on three major levels:

1. Environmental scenarios are summarized as follows:
   a. an optimistic environment (low-risk and potentially high-return environment conditions)
   b. continuation of the status quo
   c. a pessimistic scenario (high-risk and potentially low-return environmental conditions)
2. Corporate objectives are the criteria for the evaluation of the various courses of action. Five objectives are identified:
   a. profit level
   b. sales growth
   c. market share
   d. volatility
   e. demand on resources
3. The courses of activities include the three sets of products, markets, and distribution outlets that branch into a great number of specific potential activities, including various new distribution outlets not currently used by the firm, new market segments, and specific new-product activities.

Having selected the hierarchical structure, outlined in Exhibit 17.19, the president evaluated all pairwise comparisons by using the nine-point scale discussed earlier. These evaluations resulted in reciprocal matrices of the components of each level against the items in the level above. For example, consider the evaluation of the three major sets of activities against the objectives. This evaluation involved five matrices, one for each objective. (Exhibit 17.20 gives the matrix for the profit-level objective.)

In this case the president judged distribution to be of strong importance (5) over products in leading to the achievement of the firm's target profit level, but somewhat less important when compared to customers (4). Furthermore, he judged customers to be of weaker importance over products (3). The reciprocals of the three judgments were added, and the president continued with the pairwise-comparison tasks of other matrices. These tasks included the evaluation of the following:

scenarios against the overall objectives of the firm

objectives against each scenario

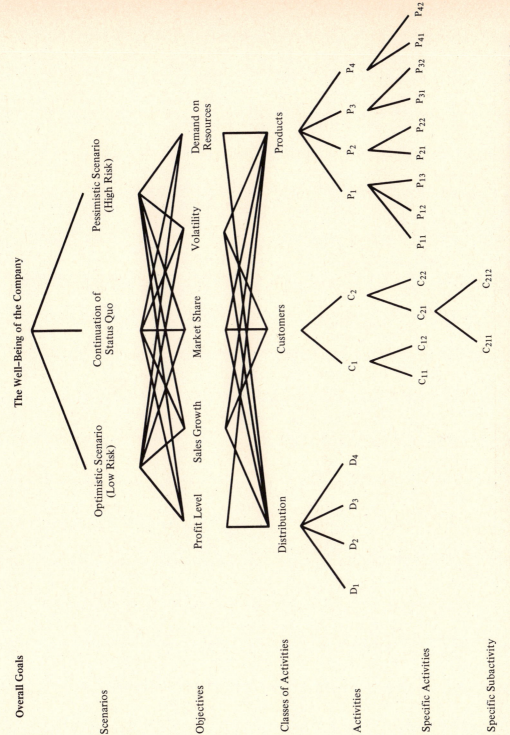

EXHIBIT 17-19 **A disguised analytical hierarchy for the selection of a target product/market/distribution portfolio for Colonial Penn Insurance Company.** (Source: Wind and Saaty, 1980, p. 650.)

EXHIBIT 17-20   Pairwise-importance matrix example for profit objective

	Products	Customers	Distribution
Products	1	$\frac{1}{3}$	$\frac{1}{5}$
Customers	3	1	$\frac{1}{4}$
Distribution	5	4	1

the classes of activities and subactivities against each of the objectives

the cross-impact evaluation of the likely occurrence and impact of each component given each of the other components at the same level of the hierarchy

These data provided the input to the eigenvalue analysis (Saaty, 1977), and a resulting partial hierarchy is presented in Exhibit 17.21.

An examination of this exhibit reveals rules for allocating the firm's resources in developing products, markets, and distribution vehicles under three alternative scenarios. In the example presented in Exhibit 17.21, the

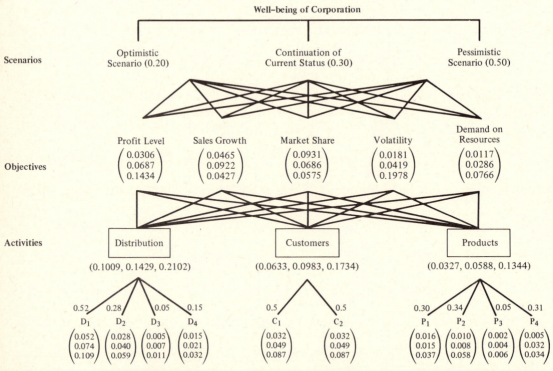

EXHIBIT 17-21   An analytical hierarchy of the products/customers/distribution portfolio at Colonial Penn Insurance. (Source: Wind and Saaty, 1980, p. 651.)

president has a strong preference for the development of distribution outlets. In fact, the allocation of the developmental resources of the firm under this example should be 0.45 to (current and new) distribution outlets, 0.35 to (current and new) market segments, and 0.22 to (current and new) products. This rule suggests allocating resources in proportion to the priorities. [Other resource-allocation rules, such as the ratio of priorities (benefits) to costs, can also be used.] The output as presented in Exhibit 17.21 provides other information as well:

The perceived likelihood of occurrence of the three scenarios is as follows:

optimistic	0.2
status quo	0.3
pessimistic	0.5

The relative importance of the five objectives is as follows:

profit level	0.2427
sales growth	0.1814
market share	0.2192
volatility	0.2578
demand on resources	0.1169

The overall weight of each objective reflects the importance of the objective under the three scenarios (e.g., the overall importance of profit level is 0.2427, which is based on 0.0306 under optimistic scenarios, 0.0687 under the status quo, and 0.1434 under pessimistic conditions). An examination of the results suggests that the relative importance of the various objectives varies considerably by the anticipated scenario. For example:

Sales growth is twice as important under continuation of the status quo as under the other two scenarios (0.092 versus 0.045 and 0.042).

Market share is most important under an optimistic scenario (0.093 versus 0.068 and 0.057).

Profit level, volatility, and demand on resources are most important under pessimistic scenarios.

As this illustration shows, the AHP can be of aid in structuring and analyzing hierarchical problems in general and portfolio-analysis problems in particular. Although having been somewhat limited in application to date, its flexibility and simplicity suggests that it will be used widely in the future, probably in conjunction with other model-and-measurement procedures. It is limited now to linear-type objectives and cannot handle the interactive, multiple-criteria objectives analyzed in Chapter 3. Furthermore, it does not provide either a sound rationale for or a reasonable alternative to allocating resources proportionally to their relative importance. In conclusion, though, the AHP approach represents new methodology with applications in portfolio analysis and selection, in new-product planning and development, and in evaluation of marketing-mix strategies (Wind and Saaty, 1980).

Financial Models. Financial-portfolio analysis deals with investments in holdings of securities generally traded through financial markets. It typically takes as its objective the creation of an efficient (productive) portfolio—one that maximizes return for a given level of risk or minimizes risk for a specified level of return [see Van Horne (1980), for example]. In the model as applied to business portfolios, we assume management is able to assess the expected rate of return and the variance of that return, as well as the covariance between returns for any pair of businesses.

Let

$$r_i = \text{(actual) annual return of product } i$$
$$E(r_i) = \text{expected annual return of business } i$$
$$V(r_i) = \text{variance of return for business } i$$
$$= E[r_i - E(r_i)]^2$$
$$V(r_i r_j) = \text{covariance of return between product } i \text{ and product } j$$
$$= E\{[r_i - E(r_i)][r_j - E(r_j)]\}$$

The fundamental theorem of portfolio analysis is that it is possible to select an investment subset that would yield a given return at less risk (variance) than the lowest risk of a single investment yielding that return.

To see this result, we consider n potential businesses to invest in and a vector of expected returns,

$$E(r_1), \ldots, E(r_n) \tag{17.8}$$

a vector of their relative shares of the total investment,

$$a_1, \ldots, a_n \qquad \text{where } \Sigma \, a_i = 1 \tag{17.9}$$

a vector of the return variances,

$$V(r_1), \ldots, V(r_n) \tag{17.10}$$

and the matrix of covariances between the returns from all pairs of businesses,

$$\{V(r_i r_j)\} \qquad i, j = 1, \ldots, n \tag{17.11}$$

With this information, the expected return and variance of any subset of m businesses can be estimated, where $m < n$. The expected return from any portfolio is

$$E\left(\sum_{i=1}^{m} a_i r_i\right) = \sum_{i=1}^{m} a_i E(r_i) \tag{17.12}$$

and the variance (risk) associated with the portfolio is

$$V\left(\sum_{i=1}^{m} a_i r_i\right) = \sum_{i=1}^{m} a_i^2 V(r_i) + \sum_{\substack{i=1 \\ i \neq j}}^{m} \sum_{j=1}^{m} a_i a_j V(r_i r_j) \tag{17.13}$$

Equation (17.13) gives the key to the fundamental result found earlier, which we can see with the following example.

Consider two businesses with equal returns and equal risks but with returns not perfectly correlated [i.e., $V(r_i r_j) < V(r_j)$]. Then by eq. (17.13),

$$V(a_1 r_1 + a_2 r_2) = a_1^2 V(r_1) + a_2^2 V(r_2) + 2 a_1 a_2 V(r_1 r_2) \tag{17.14}$$

But we have assumed that $V(r_1) = V(r_2)$; so

$$V(a_1 r_1 + a_2 r_2) = (a_1^2 + a_2^2) V(r_1) + 2 a_1 a_2 V(r_1 r_2) \tag{17.15}$$

We have also assumed $V(r_1 r_2) < V(r_1)$; so

$$(a_1^2 + a_2^2) V(r_1) + 2 a_1 a_2 V(r_1 r_2) < (a_1^2 + a_2^2) V(r_1) + 2 a_1 a_2 V(r_1) \tag{17.16}$$

The right side of eq. (17.16) is $(a_1 + a_2)^2 V(r_1) = V(r_1)$ because $a_1 + a_2 = 1$. Thus

$$V(a_1 r_1 + a_2 r_2) < V(r_1) = V(r_2) \tag{17.17}$$

This argument easily extends to n businesses.

Now assume the firm can find the minimum-risk portfolio for any specified return level. This procedure can be done as follows.

Where $m = 3$, eqs. (17.13) and (17.14) imply that the isomean (constant-return) curves are a system of straight lines and the isovariance curves are a system of concentric ellipses of which the minimum variance corresponds to the center. See Exhibit 17.22. For the specific return E_1, the last-risk portfolio corresponds to the point of tangency (A) with the lowest-value isovariance ellipse. This value defines the proportions of businesses 1 and 2 directly, and through $\sum_{i=1}^{3} a_i = 1$, it defines the proportions of product 3. This portfolio has minimum risk corresponding to ellipse V_1.

The set of all minimum-risk portfolios is called the *efficient set*. The shape of the efficient set is illustrated on the risk-return chart in Exhibit 17.23. It shows that higher-return portfolios are accompanied by proportionally higher risk.

The final question is which portfolio of products is the best one for the company to select. To answer this question, a company must determine its risk-return utility function and construct an indifference curve. The risk-return portfolio that maximizes management's utility is the one at the point of tangency of the efficient set and the risk-return indifference curve.

This procedure can be used when the expected-return variances and covariances can be estimated, when they are stable over the planning

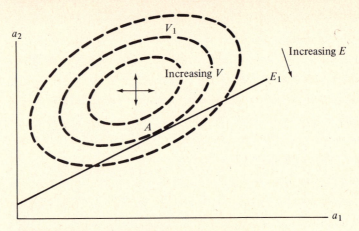

EXHIBIT 17-22   **Isovariance return curves.**

horizon, and when the company's objectives can be reduced to a risk-return utility function.

Assessment.   This approach, while theoretically appealing, is somewhat inflexible and is apparently difficult to operationalize. [See Anderson (1979, 1981) for further development and discussion.] Cardozo and Wind (1980) show how the approach was used for one company. Recently, a more general approach has been proposed for product-portfolio analysis: the stochastic dominance approach. This approach provides greater flexibility than the mean-variance approach by not requiring specific information about the business's utility function and by considering the entire distribution of returns. Mahajan, Wind, and Bradford (1982) discuss the approach and its potential application to business-portfolio analysis.

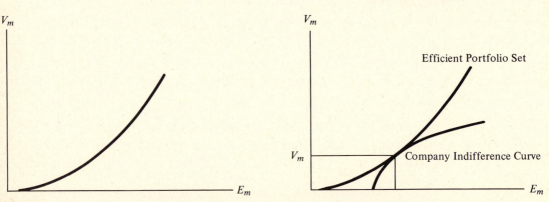

EXHIBIT 17-23   **Efficient set of portfolios and company indifference curve.**

Normative Models

As theory and understanding about the factors underlying effective strategies are emerging, normative-product-portfolio models that incorporate those ideas are also emerging. The STRATPORT model of Larréché and Srinivasan (1981, 1982) is an example of an integrative, normative approach.

STRATPORT.   The unit of analysis in STRATPORT is the business unit, and its main focus is the allocation of marketing resources across these units; it is not concerned with the allocation of resources within business units. The business units are assumed to be independent of one another—they share no experience-curve synergies or marketing synergies. The model is structured around two time frames: the planning period and the postplanning period, common to all business units. Changes in market shares are assumed to be accomplished during the planning period, while the postplanning period captures the long-term-profit impacts of the strategy implemented during the planning period, and market shares are treated as if they had remained constant during this time. Marketing expenditures are set at maintenance levels, while capacity expenditures and changes in working capital follow the evolution of sales. The basic components of the model for a single business unit are outlined in Exhibit 17.24. In the model the following notation is used. Time is at the end of period t. Flow variables (cost, revenue, production) have a start time and end time. So $_{t_1}C_{t_2}$ is the cost from t_1 to t_2, and C_t is the cost from 0 to t. Also, T is the length of the planning period, and $S - T$ is the length of the postplanning period.

The driving force behind the model is the set of business-unit market shares $\{m_{T_i}\}$, $i = 1, \ldots, N$. The problem is then to find $m_{T_1}, \ldots, m_{T_N}$ to

$$\text{Maximize } \pi = \sum_{i=1}^{N} \pi_i(m_{T_i}) \tag{17.18}$$

subject to

$$ML_i \leq m_{T_i} \leq MV_i \qquad i = 1, \ldots, N \tag{17.19}$$

and

$$F = \sum_{i=1}^{N} F_i(m_{T_i}) \leq \Delta \tag{17.20}$$

Equation (17.18) represents total profit during the planning horizons (in constant dollars), eq. (17.19) represents the upper and lower limits on market share, and eq. (17.20) represents the cash flow constraint. In effect, eq. (17.20) is not fixed since the value of Δ can be affected by borrowing.

We now consider the components of the model for a single business unit, dropping the i subscript (business-unit notation). The effect of market-

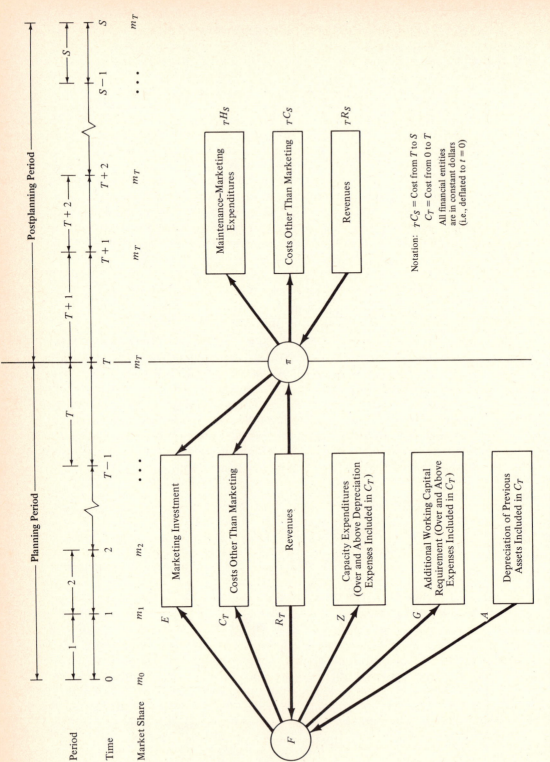

$F = $ Cash Flow need during Planning Period $= E + C_T - R_T + Z + G - A$

$\pi = $ Long-Term Profit $= (R_T + {}_T R_S) - (C_T + {}_T C_S) - (E + {}_T H_S)$

EXHIBIT 17-24 Components of long-term profit and short-term cash flow needed for a single business unit. (Source: Larréché and Srinivasan, 1982, p. 982. Reprinted by permission of The Institute of Management Sciences. *Management Science,* Vol. 28, No. 9, September 1982.)

ing investment during the planning period is modeled by the market-response function:

$$m_T = L + (U - L)\left(\frac{E^\alpha}{B + E^\alpha}\right) \qquad (17.21)$$

where L, U = lower and upper limits on m_T
       α, B = parameters to be estimated
       E = marketing expenditures

This function was described in Chapter 4. The parameters are usually chosen judgmentally.

The evolution of market share from m_0 at 0 to m_T at T is modeled as

$$m_t = m_{0t} + (m_T - m_0) f(t) \qquad (17.22)$$

where
$$f(t) = \left(\frac{t}{T}\right)^\beta \qquad \beta > 0 \qquad (17.23)$$

Thus values of β greater than one lead to a slow approach to m_T, while values of β near zero lead to a rapid approach to ultimate shares.

The model assumes that industry demands are exogenous, given by $\{M_t\}$. Then the total production for the firm is given by

$$P_T = \sum_{t=1}^{T} \left(\frac{m_{t-1} + m_t}{2}\right) M_t \qquad (17.24)$$

where the market share during a period is approximated by its average value.

Combining eqs. (17.22), (17.23), and (17.24) yields

$$P_t = k_1 + k_2 m_T \qquad (17.25)$$

where k_1 and k_2 are constants that can be evaluated numerically following some algebra (Larréché and Srinavasan, 1982).

Total costs are driven by the experience curve and are modeled as

$$C_T = \frac{c}{(1 - \lambda)} [({}_{tF}P_T)^{1-\lambda} - ({}_{tF}P_0)^{1-\lambda}] \qquad (17.26)$$

where C_T = total cost of units sold
       λ = learning or experience constant
       ${}_{tF}P_T$ = total production from time of product introduction ($tF < 0$) to end of planning horizon (similarly for $tF > 0$)

A similar expression is derived for costs during the postplanning period.

Industry unit price is assumed to fall with industry cumulative experience as

$$P_I = pI^{-\eta} \qquad (17.27)$$

where P_I = average industry unit price
  I = industry cumulative value (in units)
  p = constant
  η = industry learning constant, which potentially changes over time

Now following the reasoning in eq. (17.26), we get

$$_{tI}Q_{t2} = \frac{p}{1 - \eta} [(_{tI}I_{t2})^{1-\eta} - (_{tI}I_{t1})^{1-\eta}] \qquad (17.28)$$

where $_{tI}Q_{t2}$ = industry revenue from start time for industry (t_1) to present (t_2)

The price set by the firm may be higher or lower than the industry price, so the firm's revenue during the time period t is modeled as

$$_{t-1}R_t = \omega_{t-1}Q_t \left(\frac{m_t + m_{t-1}}{2}\right) \qquad (17.29)$$

where ω = ratio of firm's price to industry average price

Revenue during the postplanning period is modeled similarly.
  A market share of m_T at T requires production capacity of

$$X = m_T M_T \qquad (17.30)$$

If the current plant capacity is X_0 and $X_0 < X$, capacity expansion expenditures will be incurred during the planning period; if $X < X_0$, then liquidation of excess capacity can generate a cash inflow. The capacity expenditures corresponding to X are modeled as

$$Y = \left(\frac{bX^\gamma}{a + X^\delta}\right) - q \qquad (17.31)$$

where Y = capacity-expansion expenditures
  q = cash value of divesting entire current capacity
  a, b, γ, δ = positive constants, with $0 < \gamma - \delta < 1$

Expenditures above what is spent (through C_T and $_TC_S$ in the form of depreciation) during the planning period are expressed as a fraction (θ_1) of Y: $Z = \theta_1 Y$.
  We also need to adjust C_T by an amount A, which represents the depreciation over the period 0 to T of assets acquired prior to $t = 0$.
  In general, a change in market share calls for a change in working capital, modeled as a function of revenue in period t:

$$g_t = \alpha(_{t-1}R_t)^\beta \qquad (17.32)$$

The change in working capital corresponding to the change in market share is given by $g_T - g_0$. To avoid double-counting the working capital expenses included in C_T, we only take a fraction θ_2 of $g_T - g_0$:

$$G = \theta_2(g_T - g_0) \tag{17.33}$$

where G is the additional required working capital.

Let V denote the proportion of the firm's revenue spent to maintain market share at m_T; V is modeled as

$$V = d - e(m_T - L) \tag{17.34}$$

where d and e are constants to be determined. The cost of maintaining share from t to $t + 1$ $(t \geq T)$ is

$$_tH_{t+1} = V_tR_{t+1} \tag{17.35}$$

and from eqs. (17.34) and (17.35), we get

$$_TH_S = d_TR_S - e\,_TR_S(m_T - L) \tag{17.36}$$

The value of profit from the business unit can now be calculated as

$$\pi = (R_T + {}_TR_S) - (C_T + {}_TC_S) - (E + {}_TH_S) \tag{17.37}$$

where expressions for terms on the right-hand side of eq. (17.37) are developed above. Similarly, the cash flow need for the business unit during the planning period is

$$F = E + C_T - R_T + Z + G - A \tag{17.38}$$

where, again, the expressions are given above, and discounted dollars are used in all expressions. To account for taxes, we must multiply eq. (17.37) by $(1 - \text{tax rate})$, as we must also do for E, C_T, and R_T in eq. (17.38). Risk can be handled by discounting business units at different discount rates, reflecting their different risk profiles. The risk-return (variance-covariance) approach developed in the last section is not included because of the desire for simplicity and modest data demands.

Given a specific portfolio strategy, the model described above can evaluate its profit implications and cash flow needs. In addition, STRAT-PORT has an optimization module to determine the allocation of resources among business units with the maximum net present value over the time horizon, subject to market-share and cash flow constraints. The cash flow constraint can be evaluated over ranges of borrowing activity, if desired. For details of the solution algorithm and an illustrative run of the model, see Larréché and Srinivasan (1981, 1982).

Evaluation. As with any model as ambitious as STRATPORT, there are flaws. The model focuses on the most quantifiable aspect of strategy and does not deal with R&D investments or personnel, financial, and manufac-turing policies. Qualitative aspects of management policy (political, environmental) are not handled either. Furthermore, the objective function and the use of subjectively calibrated marketing-response models as the driving force behind the model are questionable. In addition, the model assumes no marketing or production synergies, making it untenable at low levels in a business hierarchy, and it ignores competitive response, which some feel is the essence of business strategy. The model is quite complex and uses a number of response functions without theoretical or empirical justification. Finally there are no reports of its implementation.

The significance of the model is its honest attempt to structure the cash flow considerations, experience-curve concepts, and portfolio-analysis problem in a coherent, operational form. The fact that a structured, explicit model exists, developed in the form of a decision-support system, should provide a spur for future developments in this field. We feel that STRAT-PORT, while far from the last word in the field of normative-marketing-planning models, at least provides an explicit foundation for current experimental applications and future developments.

Two other recent efforts that provide normative guidance for looking at the product-portfolio problem are those of Corstjens and Weinstein (1982) and of Choffray (1981). The Corstjens and Weinstein approach uses the risk-return concept and incorporates learning-curve cost economies and a BCG-type matrix, center-of-gravity constraint to structure a portfolio. However, the model is static in nature and does not consider the dynamic complexities of marketing strategy addressed by STRATPORT. It has reportedly been used to evaluate portfolio strategies for a firm with ten strategic business units. Choffray's approach, based on risk decomposition, has been used to handle divestment as well as acquisition decisions.

Summary

An understanding of several basic phenomena in market-planning strategy is developing, which is leading to important models in this area. Marketing planning loosely covers resource allocation among businesses under a firm's control (portfolio). The objectives of the firm, the nature of the environment, and the development, evaluation, selection, and implementation of portfolios are the interrelated phases of the planning process.

The product life cycle is a key concept underlying portfolio planning. Because of changes in a product's sales position and profitability over time and because of associated changes in price and advertising elasticity, the concept can be used in the selection of marketing actions and in planning. Although difficult to define and operationalize, the product life cycle provides a useful framework for organizing thinking about strategic alternatives.

The dynamics of cost—economies of scale and experience-curve cost declines—are at the heart of modern business strategy. Related in many ways, these concepts explain how declines in cost can be planned for, opening up important strategic opportunities and providing rationale for the relatively high profitability of high-market-share companies.

Market strategy depends on the definition of a market and on the analysis of its structure. Modern theory suggests that markets should be considered as the set of products that are substitutes in use segments in which similar benefits are sought. A number of methods are available to define markets with either historical (use patterns or cross-elasticity data) or perceived similarity (judgmental) data.

The field of industrial economics is developing hypotheses that explain why certain markets are more competitive than others. Factors such as threat of competitive entry, intensity of existing rivalries, pressures from substitute products, and buyers' and suppliers' power are instrumental in determining the competitive nature of a market.

There are three classes of analytical approaches to marketing-strategy development. They include the shared-experience approach, typified by the PIMS program; product-portfolio models, including standardized, customized, and financial approaches; and a few recent normative-resource-allocation approaches. All of these approaches make use of the life cycle, cost dynamics, and market-structure analysis.

The field of model development for business strategy is in its infancy: it essentially did not exist a decade ago. Within the next decade the methods outlined here should be superseded. Current methods provide both the operational tools and the working hypotheses that can support expected future developments.

Problems

17.1 What are the implications of the PIMS findings for marketing strategy? In particular, under what circumstances does it pay to buy market share?

17.2 Draw the risk-return relationship for a product portfolio with the following characteristics. Product 1 has an expected return of 7.5 with a standard deviation of 3. Product 2 has an expected return of 15.7 with a standard deviation of 5, and there is a correlation of -0.7 between the two returns.

17.3 In analyzing its product mix, a firm has collected the following data. In the firm the sales effort is the only important marketing expense, and contribution is defined as the product contribution to selling expenses, overheads, and profit. (Fitzroy, 1976)

Pro-duct	Annual Sales (in $1000s)	Market Share (in %)	Sales Growth per Year (in %)	Market Growth (in %)	Product Contri-bution (in $1000s)	Selling Effort (in $1000s)	Assets Employed (in $1000s)	Incremental Sales per $1000 Increase in Selling Effort (in $1000s)
1	37	45	24	25	6.7	5.5	168	10.1
2	75	32	3	−1	15.8	6.1	310	9.5
3	148	12	8	7	56.2	7.5	393	18.6
4	18	53	28	26	2.9	3.1	60	12.6
5	195	19	7	8	74.1	8.9	537	21.3

    a. If the firm wanted to reduce its product line, which product would you eliminate and why?

    b. Write an overall evaluation of the current product mix. Specify any additional data that may be required.

    c. Assume that the firm has available an extra $6000 of selling effort, which can be applied to any product. For any product, however, the minimum increment in selling effort is $2000. How would you allocate this $6000 across the product mix? On what assumptions is your recommendation based?

17.4 Assuming that the product life cycle is a viable, operational concept, suggest how to measure the stage in the life cycle for (a) a snack food, (b) sulfuric acid, and (c) a main-frame computer.

17.5 The experience-curve concept suggests that total costs decline with experience. The usual experience-curve form is exponential decline. Suggest behavioral assumptions and derive this result from those assumptions.

17.6 A firm with an 8% market share in a market growing at 15% per year wishes to catch the market leader in 5 yr. The market leader holds an 18% market share. Assuming the market leader holds its market share, how much must the firm's product capacity increase to meet these objectives? What is the firm's compound growth rate?

17.7 What would appear to be the best method to define the market for (a) a breakfast cereal, (b) a new machine tool, (c) a microcomputer? Why? Would any of these methods have shown an increase in swimming pool sales during the last oil crisis?

17.8 The analytic-hierarchy process can be of aid in structuring and analyzing portfolio problems. How can it be used to allocate resources?

17.9 What are the main strengths and weaknesses of the STRATPORT model? Do you expect that many firms will use the model?

18 Modeling the Marketing Mix and Competitive Response

Throughout Part 4 we assumed that we could investigate the effect on product sales of only one variable at a time. Clearly, the firm has control of many, if not all, of the marketing-mix variables. Furthermore, and most importantly, the whole (the net effect of the combination of marketing variables) may well be different than the sum of its parts. Product profitability is affected by price, advertising, promotion, selling effort, and the like; in turn, the effect of selling effort may be influenced by advertising spending, the effect of promotions may be related to the level of competitive promotional spending, and so on.

In this chapter we proceed as follows. First, we review the elements of the marketing mix and some historical and theoretical investigations concerning the mix. Next, we consider some empirical results regarding interactions between mix elements. Following that, we discuss some approaches to the problem of introducing competitive response into marketing-mix models. Then we investigate several marketing-mix models in some detail.

The Marketing Mix: Definition and Theoretical Approaches

We define *marketing-decision variables* as those variables under the firm's control that can affect the level of demand. They are distinguished from *environmental variables*, which also affect demand but are not under the control of the firm, at least not totally and directly. (To the extent that competitive prices react to changes in the firm's price, for example, those prices can be considered *partially* under the *indirect* control of the firm.)

We classify the marketing-mix variables by the "four P's" (McCarthy, 1981): (1) product, (2) place, (3) promotion, and (4) price. Some of the particular instruments summarized by each of the four P's are listed in Exhibit 18.1.

The marketing-mix problem can be generally stated as to find $\{X_t\}$, $t = 1, \ldots, T$, that optimize product objectives subject to

$$Q_t = f_t(\mathbf{X}_t, \mathbf{C}_t, \mathbf{E}_t, Q_{t-1}) + \epsilon_t \qquad (18.1)$$

and budget and other constraints,

where Q_t = product sales at time t

          $\mathbf{X}_t$ = vector of marketing-mix variables at time t (level of variables in Exhibit 18.1)

          $\mathbf{C}_t$ = vector of competitive-marketing-mix variables at time t (which may include other products of firm)

          $\mathbf{E}_t$ = vector of environmental variables at time t

      Q_{t-1} = lagged sales, representing effect of past company and competitive advertising

         ϵ_t = stochastic error

EXHIBIT 18-1   Marketing mix-instruments: the four P's

Product variables
Quality
Models and sizes
Packaging
Brands
Service

Place variables
Channels of distribution
Outlet location
Sales territories
Warehousing system

Promotion variables
Advertising
Sales promotion
Personal selling
Publicity

Price variables
Allowances and deals
Distribution and retailer markups
Discount structure

The basic market-response model in eq. (18.1) is quite general; even the functional form (f_t) is viewed as potentially varying in time. The general marketing-mix problem, then, is to find values for the $\{\mathbf{X}_t\}$ in each time period that optimize a profit function, say. In general, this problem involves a multivariable, multi-time period, nonlinear, stochastic function with interactions.

Historically, economists dealing with the theory of the firm have focused most of their attention on the single variable, price. In a monopoly, where competition is absent, the optimal product price is found where marginal revenue equals marginal cost. In the marketing-mix problem multiple competitors are generally involved, and nonprice competition is considered.

An early theoretical extension of economic theory to other marketing-mix elements was developed by Dorfman and Steiner (1954). They considered price, advertising, and quality and show that a necessary condition for profit maximization is that the price elasticity, the marginal-product revenue of advertising, and the quality elasticity times price over unit cost be equal. (See Chapter 6.) Note that the Dorfman-Steiner results do *not* suggest an optimal policy; rather, they state conditions that are satisfied when optimal values are found. To find the optimal values, the analyst must know the form of the demand function.

Nerlove and Arrow (1962) extended the analysis to consider the effects of marketing variables over time. They introduce the concept of advertising goodwill to model dynamic characteristics: they assume that advertising does not influence sales directly but rather serves to increase the level of goodwill. In the absence of advertising, goodwill declines at a constant rate, representing the phenomenon of forgetting. Sales are assumed to be influenced by the level of goodwill—not directly by advertising—in addition to price and an environmental variable. The authors develop dynamically optimal conditions for price and advertising; the Dorfman-Steiner conditions result when goodwill decays immediately—that is, when there are no carry-over effects—in which case their formulation simplifies to a sequence of independent, single-period problems. An interesting result of their analysis is that with (1) no competitive effects, (2) no changes in the environment, (3) constant marginal costs of production, and (4) a log-linear demand function, the optimal advertising strategy is a constant percentage of sales.

Lambin, Naert, and Bultez (1975) generalized the Dorfman-Steiner theorem to the case of (1) an oligopoly with multiple competitive reactions and (2) expansible industry demand. They consider two kinds of competitive reaction: simple competition, in which a price change by the firm sparks a competitive price change, and multiple competition, in which a price change may cause a competitive increase in advertising spending. Their optimality conditions for the marketing mix relate the demand elasticity for the product to industry elasticity, market-share elasticity, and both industry and market-share-reaction elasticities. Monopoly, oligopoly with no competition or simple competition, stable or expansible industry demand, as well as the Dorfman-Steiner conditions, all result as special cases of their more general results. This approach is discussed in more detail later.

The importance of these theoretical results is that under general conditions they allow an investigation of whether the firm is operating at or near an optimum point. From an operational standpoint they do not suggest what form the market-response model should take. To evaluate specific response functions, we must consider how the various elements of the marketing mix interact.

Marketing-Mix Interactions

Elements of the marketing mix can be expected to interact with one another. A number of studies have addressed this issue with varying results. In this section we review some hypotheses on marketing-mix interactions and the supporting evidence.

Elements of the Marketing-Mix Interact

Marketing modelers certainly seem to think marketing-mix interactions exist. One way to test this conjecture is by comparing the results of market share or sales models with and without interactions. Weiss (1968), Sexton (1970), and Wildt (1974) studied multiplicative models of market share and found that these models fit their data better than additive models. Weiss' (1968) analysis of market-share movements for a low-cost, frequently purchased consumer product included price and advertising variables as ratios to mean product-class price in log-linear form. Of nine models tested, the log-linear form with price measured relative to volume-weighted market price fit the data best. However, the structure of the log-linear form only allows positive interactions. Sexton (1970) used a negative-exponential-type model:

$$S = k(1 - e^{-f(q,a,d,p)}) \tag{18.2}$$

where S = sales or share
            k = constant
            f = some function
q, a, p, d = elements of marketing mix

He found that it fit the data better than linear and log-linear alternatives. But this form again only allows for positive interactions, and, furthermore, advertising was not found to be a significant determinant of market share. Wildt (1974) studied three firms selling infrequently purchased goods in a competitive system, employing a log-linear form. There was no reported attempt to investigate other functional forms. His results suggest that, by a test for the conditions for short-term optimality, the firms were overspending by 50–300 percent on advertising. However, in the long term only one firm was considerably overspending. In sum, these studies (and others cited below) suggest that the elements of the marketing mix do interact.

Advertising Reduces Price Sensitivity

A common justification among marketing managers for heavy advertising is lower price elasticities; advertising is assumed to create barriers against competitive effects, including price. Eskin and Baron (1977) examined the effect of price and advertising on new-product sales in four test-market experiments. They found three out of four significant interactions—with higher responsiveness to advertising associated with lower price levels. They provide a number of explanations for this phenomenon, among which are an increase in the number of consumers effectively aware of the product, especially among the low-need (price-sensitive) group. They speculate that "if increases in advertising expenditures increase sales, then such increases are greater under low price conditions than under high price conditions" (p. 507).

Prasad and Ring (1976) studied an experimental setup where the market-share response to advertising depended on the brand's relative price. In particular, consistent with Eskin and Baron, advertising is found to be more effective at lower price levels. An implication of their model is that, in one market studied, once a brand's price is 7 percent above competitive price levels, the effect of increased TV advertising is a decrease in market share! Interactions among media (TV, magazines, and newspapers) were also found to be significant, and the authors speculate that these effects and interactions may be closely related to the advertising-copy platform.

Wittink (1977) investigated territorial differences in the relationship between price elasticity and advertising expenditures with a lagged, exponential-form, market-share response model. By estimating response elasticities over 25 territories, he found that the relative price elasticity increases as advertising share increases. The levels of price were not presented to permit a check on the conjecture of the effect of price level on advertising elasticity; however, Wittink did encounter a region of increasing advertising elasticity over a limited range of increases in advertising share (in support of an S-shaped advertising-response curve).

Sasieni (1981) showed data on advertising elasticities for a number of brands and found that while some showed a more sensitive response at high prices, others were more sensitive at lower prices. He suggested that without a clear understanding of the nature of the advertising appeal and the structure of the market (Where are brands concentrated? At higher prices? At lower prices?), a clear direction for such interactions could not be predicted a priori.

In conclusion, many practitioners believe that advertising reduces price elasticity and also that advertising is more effective at higher prices. However, empirical evidence does not support this view. It seems that the specific structure of the market studied, as well as the nature of the advertising (medium, message), may affect the sign and the magnitude of the interaction. [See Farris and Albion, (1980) for a more complete review.]

Promotional Interactions Vary

Because of the diverse nature and effectiveness of sales-promotional tools, their effects and interactions with other elements in the mix can be expected to vary. Best and Hozier (1980) found no main or interaction effects of advertising for a frequently purchased branded good. However, promotional effects were significant with the store, as well as the firm, running the promotions. The interaction between the two effects was significant, reducing market share. However, the interaction was smaller than either of the two main effects, suggesting a cannibalization (share comes from either one of the promotions) rather than a true negative interaction. Rao and Lilien (1972) found a similar effect for two forms of gasoline promotions.

Response Varies by Market Segment and over Time

The conjecture that response varies by market segment and over time covers several important areas in marketing decision making. McCann (1974) analyzed panel data to measure differential effectiveness of market segments to advertising, price, and promotion and found significant differences by segment. Moriarty (1975) demonstrates significant differences in responsiveness to advertising and price by region and market position for a frequently purchased good sold through supermarkets. Rao and Lilien (1972) report a decay in the effectiveness of promotions over time.

Advertising and Selling Interact

It has long been a contention in industrial markets that advertising reduces the total cost of selling. Studies by Morrill (1970) and Kolliner (1963) generally support this notion. In a study of blood donations Swinyard and Ray (1977) found that the interaction between selling and advertising depends on the order of exposure.

This discussion leads to some suggested properties for a marketing-mix model. A good marketing-mix model (one that incorporates the most important phenomena) should have the following properties: it should

1. allow for interactions among marketing-mix elements in general
2. permit advertising to increase or decrease price sensitivity
3. permit price to increase or decrease advertising effectiveness
4. permit positive or negative interactions among promotional vehicles
5. permit varying effectiveness over time and across market segments
6. incorporate advertising/selling interactions that are positive and that include order effects
7. incorporate advertising and promotional effectiveness explicitly

These seemingly reasonable properties are not trivial for an operational marketing-mix model, as we will see. In addition, we add the following property:

8. A good marketing-mix model should incorporate competitive effects.

Competitive Response: Evidence and Models

Substitutes exist for most products, and it is naive to assume that an investigation of the optimal marketing mix can be performed without regard to competition. Marketing scientists have focused almost exclusively on consumer response to marketing actions, disregarding competitive response, which is one of the least understood areas in marketing. Dolan (1981) presents an overview of approaches to competition from microeconomics and marketing, as well as empirical evidence about the type of competition from various industry studies.

Microeconomic Approaches

The central focus of microeconomics is the price system, so competitive models in microeconomics center on price competition. In the monopoly and perfect-competition cases, price theory provides a rich theoretical structure with unambiguous results for optimal pricing. But for oligopoly the problem of specifying competitors' behavior has limited the implications that can be derived from price theory. Singer (1968) points out that the models of oligopoly provide no single solution or strategy for a firm to follow.

The actual difficulty is that different assumptions about competition lead to different normative results. Chamberlain (1957) shows that, depending on the behavioral assumptions underlying a model of duopoly, the competition between two firms may lead to a price anywhere between the monopoly price and the perfectly competitive price. Or the price may perpetually oscillate.

Baumol (1972) agrees that consideration of the entire sequence of moves and countermoves by competitors is a problem that is hopelessly complex. Instead, he proposes one of two approaches: (1) ignore the interdependence or (2) assume each competitor is a rational economic agent and then determine, as a likely set of actions, those that will allow him to maximize his expected utility.

These two approaches are akin to the early work on *reaction functions*, proposed by Cournot in 1838, and to *game-theory* models. The classical reaction-function hypothesis is that each seller assumes the output (action) of rival firms to be fixed and then sets price to determine profit-maximizing output. This approach leads to unrealistic results that are clearly nonoptimal (Mansfield, 1979; Scherer, 1980).

Dolan (1981) points out that many in marketing seem to feel that game-theory models would solve many competitive issues if only some critical mathematical hurdles could be overcome. This is unlikely to be the case: game theory has "insuperable problems as a prescriptive theory of rational decisions in conflict situations [and] the prescriptive aspect of game theory ought to be written off" (Rapoport, 1966, pp. 202–203). The main problem is that the important normative contributions of game theory are for zero-sum games (market share, say), while the important marketing problems are in the non-zero-sum area (market sales and profits). Therefore the value of game theory is most likely to remain at the level of insight rather than prescription.

Thus microeconomic models and approaches to competition in oligopoly, developed for gaining insight into the basic structure and workings of markets, seem inappropriate for the situation-specific normative interests of marketers. Most marketing scientists and practitioners would agree with Joskow (1975) "that not only aren't [these formal models] particularly useful but also that they aren't even used" (p. 273).

Empirical Evidence

One of the focuses of research in the area of industrial organization is the nature of the structural variables that influence competitive behavior. The type and intensity of competition are attributed to eight major factors (Porter, 1980):

1. number and size distribution of competitors
2. industry growth rate
3. cost structure and storage costs
4. extent of product differentiation
5. divisibility of capacity additions

6. diversity of competitors
7. importance of the market to firms and
8. height of exit barriers

Dolan (1981) has examined a number of industry studies to determine the extent to which these structural variables determined the mode of competition. He summarizes his results in a set of four lessons:

1. High fixed costs promote competitive responses to share gain attempts.
2. Low storage costs reduce competitive reactions.
3. Growing primary demand reduces competitive reactions.
4. Large firms avoid price competition.

Exhibit 18.2 gives the details of the studies he compared. His observations suggest that structural dimensions of the market affect the likelihood of market response as well as the form of that response. These observations also suggest the major factors affecting response and show the need to incorporate the measurement and use of those factors in marketing models of competitive response.

Marketing-Model Approaches

Recall from Chapter 4 the argument in favor of decomposing a brand-sales share model (Q) into market demand (V) times market share (S). The best marketing models that incorporate competitive effects separate these two

EXHIBIT 18-2   Four comparisons of industry behavior.

Major Lesson	Interacting Factors	Industries Studied
High fixed costs promote competitive response to share gain attempts	Cost structure Number of firms Size distribution of firms	Steel Aluminum Coal
Low storage costs reduce competitive reactions	Cost structure Storage costs	Aluminum Rayon Airline
Growing primary demand reduces competitive reaction	Industry growth Product differentiation Number of Firms	Cigarette Motorcycle
Large firms avoid price competition	Size distribution of firms Diversity in cost positions	Farm machinery Electrical equipment

SOURCE: Dolan, 1981, p. 231.

components of demand. Marketers have handled competitive behavior in three ways: (1) by ignoring it, (2) through the judgmental-model approach, and (3) through the reaction-matrix approach.

The *judgmental* approach to calibrating response functions has been discussed in Chapter 5; its use for developing competitive-response estimates is less widely reported. Little (1975) uses this approach, and a case by Buzzell (1964), based on a model at duPont, employs a probabilistic model of competitive response to find an optimal pricing strategy. In addition, the General Electric Company (1980) uses a pricing model based on deterministic judgments of (1) the timing of a competitive response to a GE price move and (2) the degree to which the competition follows the GE price move (degree is defined as percentage change in competitive price divided by percentage change in GE price). On the basis of these inputs the model simulates marketing activity to determine the effect of price changes. The procedure, not aimed at optimal decision making, provides a tool to answer "what if" questions about GE's pricing behavior.

The judgmental approach, while used in many firms, has not been subject to rigorous empirical or theoretical testing in general. Most applications have been in the competitive-bidding area, characterized by price competition only and by little data analysis to infer the nature of competitive activity. [See Engelbrecht-Wiggins (1980) for a state-of-the-art review.]

An important new direction in marketing is the use of *reaction matrices* (not to be confused with reaction functions), pioneered by Lambin, Naert, and Bultez (1975). The reaction-matrix idea can be best understood with an example. Assume there are two competitors in the market, competing on price (P) and advertising (A). Their reaction matrix is shown in Exhibit 18.3. Under the assumption that these elasticities are constant and stable over time and that a multiplicative function is a reasonable representation of the structure of interaction, equations, such as (18.3a) and (18.3b), can be used to estimate the $\{\eta\}$ in Exhibit 18.3:

$$\log P_1(t) = a_1 + b_1 \log P_2(t) + b_2 \log A_2(t) \qquad (18.3a)$$

$$\log A_1(t) = a_2 + b_3 \log P_2(t) + b_4 \log A_2(t) \qquad (18.3b)$$

Then b_1 is an estimate of $\eta_{P_1 P_2}$, b_2 estimates $\eta_{A_1 P_2}$, and so on. A portion of the reaction matrix for the application reported in Lambin, Naert, and Bultez is reproduced in Exhibit 18.4. That exhibit shows that all diagonal elements are significantly different from zero, signifying that firm 2 reacts directly to any change in the marketing mix of firm 1 (it changes price in response to a price change, for example). In addition, the lagged advertising-price elasticity is also significant, showing that indirect responses are important as well. This example shows that reaction behavior is complex, involving multiple responses and potential lags in time; therefore tracking direct responses could lead to mistaken inferences.

Firm 2

		P_2	A_2
Firm 1	P_1	$\eta_{P_1P_2}$	$\eta_{P_1A_2}$
	A_1	$\eta_{A_1P_2}{}^a$	$\eta_{A_1A_2}$

EXHIBIT 18-3 **Reaction matrix: two firms, two marketing variables.**

$^a\eta_{A_1P_2}$ = percentage change in A_1 with a 1% change in P_2.

		Firm 2	
		Price	**Advertising (Lagged)**
Firm 1	**Price**	0.664^a (0.030)	1.898^a (0.825)
	Advertising	0.008 (0.005)	0.273^a (0.123)

EXHIBIT 18-4 **Partial reaction-function example.**

SOURCE: Lambin, Naert, and Bultez, 1975, p. 119.
^{a}Significant at the 0.05 level.

This approach has been used by Bensoussan, Bultez, and Naert (1978) to optimize marketing-mix decisions in a competitive environment. Lambin (1976) and Schultz and Hanssens (1976) report additional applications of the approach for assessing competitive behavior. Hanssens (1980) extends the basic model to explicitly represent multiple competitors and to develop interrelationships among the marketing elements within a particular firm.

Proponents of the reaction-matrix approach stress the need for incorporating managerial judgment here as well:

> The econometric measures should be regarded as reference values rather than as constants, given the instability of competitive behavior in most cases. The relevant reaction elasticities should then be obtained by subjective adjustment of the econometric estimates (Lambin, Naert, and Bultez, 1975) p. 127.

Hanssens (1980) concurs, calling for the integration of three types of information: judgment, marketing and economic theory, and statistical procedures.

Assessment

The reaction-matrix approach provides a rich direction for analyzing marketing-mix issues in a competitive environment. One of its main contributions has been the development of a tool to decompose sales elasticity:

$$\text{Sales elasticity} = \text{share effect} + \text{size effect} \qquad (18.4)$$

$$\text{Share effect} = \text{direct effect} + \text{competitive-response effect} \quad (18.5)$$

$$\text{Size effect} = \text{direct effect} + \text{competitive-response effect} \quad (18.6)$$

This decomposition permits a more careful assessment of the firm's marketing-mix options as well as their direct and indirect effects.

However, the approach is currently limited by difficulties in estimating the reaction matrix. Improved sources of competitive-data collection may allow for better estimation in many markets. But for the foreseeable future, managerial judgment clearly will continue to be required for the approach to be viable, both descriptively and predictively. In addition, models have currently been limited to log-linear forms, primarily for ease of estimation.

In conclusion, we concur with Simon (1982a): "It is extremely difficult to explain the actual observed reactive behavior by means of a mathematically simple and econometrically measurable reaction function" (p. 32). If this is the case with historical data, the prediction problem is clearly even more difficult. The development of the reaction matrix is a step in the right direction. However, the competitive component will be the weak link in most marketing-mix models for some time to come.

Descriptive Models of the Industrial-Marketing Communications Mix

Our focus has been primarily on normative or decision-making models. However, in the absence of clear analytical guidance or a good normative framework, decisions still get made, and we can learn a great deal from how they do. When faced with developing an operating rule in a dynamic situation, managers often rely on guidelines, rules of thumb, and coefficients of industry behavior. There are at least two arguments to support this approach.

The first argument deals with the concept of shared experience. Managers dealing with similar problems over a period of time may develop some equilibrium behavior that appears to be reasonable. Bowman (1963) suggests that through experience managers learn what the critical variables are that affect their decisions and acquire reasonable implicit models of these problems. However, in a specific decision situation they may respond selectively to particular information clues and organizational pressures,

Thus Bowman argues that experienced managers make good decisions on the average but may display considerable variance in behavior. Therefore managers' decisions could be improved by making them more consistent. In a series of studies Bowman (1963) and Kunreuther (1969) show that significant cost savings can be realized by consistently applying decision rules from the managers' own past behavior.

A second, related argument takes a Darwinian view of management practice: by and large, those products in place have survived, and therefore they are successfully managed. Efficient-market theory suggests that marketing behavior on average will be pushed toward optimal behavior or the enterprise will fail. With this motivation we consider quantitative descriptions of marketing practice, specifically in the industrial-marketing area. Two separate efforts have attempted to explain differences in marketing-spending levels by studying a cross-section of business situations: the ADVISOR models (Lilien, 1978a,b,c, 1979) and PIMS-based models (Buzzell and Farris, 1976).

The ADVISOR Models

Partially in response to the lack of quantified information about industrial-marketing communications decisions, the ADVISOR studies were begun in 1973. ADVISOR 1 (Lilien, 1978a) established that the factors involved in marketing budgeting for industrial products are quite general. The cross-sectional approach used was partially motivated by the success of the PIMS program (Chapter 17).

Early in 1977 a larger study—ADVISOR 2—began with 22 companies participating (including AT&T Long Lines, duPont, General Electric, Goodyear, International Harvester, International Paper, 3M, Norton, Owens Corning, Union Carbide, U.S. Steel, and others). The objectives of the study were to duplicate the earlier ADVISOR results with a larger data base and a better theoretical structure.

Analyses of the budgeting-decision process and results of ADVISOR 1 suggest that the models of marketing communications spending should have the following properties:

1. incorporate the effect of interactions between product characteristics
2. allow product characteristics to reflect proportional changes in the marketing level
3. check the form of the relationship between marketing spending and sales (Are marketing/sales or advertising/sales ratios constant?)

The level of advertising (or marketing) spending is dictated primarily by the size of the product (as measured by last year's sales) and by the number of customers the marketing effort must reach. That spending is then modified by such factors as stage in the life cycle of the product, customer concentration, and technical complexity of the product.

A simple model that reflects these concepts is log-linear:

$$\text{marketing}_t = \beta_0 \, \text{sales}_{t-1}^{\beta_1} \, \text{users}^{\beta_2} \prod_i C_{\text{var}_i}^{\beta_i} \prod_j D_{\beta_j}^{\text{var}_j} \qquad (18.7)$$

where   marketing = marketing spending, \$
        sales = sales dollars (lagged 1 yr)
        users = number of customers (individuals) marketing program must reach
        C_{var_i} = continuous, independent variable i, transformed to be greater than one
        D_{var_j} = 0–1 indicator for discrete, independent variable j

Two things should be noted about this postulated log-linear form. First, the coefficient of sales (β_1) allows a test for constant returns to scale. Second, the model allows for interactions between the variables. Then a multiplicative error term of log-normal form permits the use of ordinary least squares on the logarithm of eq. (18.7).

The main explanatory variables for industrial-marketing-spending levels [see Lilien (1979) for complete definitions] were identified by prior correlation analysis, as guided by the first ADVISOR analyses, and a qualitative review of the budgeting process in participating companies. Exhibit 18.5 gives the results of the regressions.

In the first column of this exhibit, sales, we see that both advertising and marketing are strongly and positively related to sales. We also note that the coefficient of advertising (0.618, standard error = 0.07) is significantly less than one. This suggests that the A/S and M/S ratios should not be modeled as constants, independent of the sales level. Furthermore, from the A/M row, we see that as sales goes up, advertising gets less of the marketing dollar. This situation may result from a limit on possible media spending because of the limited number of trade journals while no such limit exists on the salesforce.

In the second column we see that the more users, the more money is spent on marketing and on advertising, and that there is no obvious effect on the A/M ratio. The other effects in this exhibit can be similarly explained.

Other models have been developed to consider media selection, distribution-channel choice, dynamic changes in spending patterns, and trade-show use (Lilien, 1979, 1981). Furthermore, the results of these studies have been replicated for a sample of 80 products in Europe, with remarkably consistent results (Lilien and Weinstein, 1983).

The ADVISOR models fit well and give results that are intuitively understandable and internally consistent.

EXHIBIT 18-5 Norm-model results of the ADVISOR study.

Dependent Variable	Continuous Variables						Dichotomous Variables			Constant	R^2 / F	SEE / N
	Sales (LSLS)	No. of Users (LUSERS)	Customer Concentration (LCONC)	Fraction of Sales Made to Order (LSPEC)	Prospect/ Customer/ Product Attitudes Difference (DIFF)	Sales Direct to Users (LDIR-USER)	Stage in Life Cycle (LCYCLE)	Product Plans (PLANS)	Product Complexity (PROD)			
Advertising (LADV)	+0.618 [9.1]	+0.104 (3.6)	−1.881 (3.1)	−1.989 (4.4)	a	a	−0.892 (3.2)	−1.503 (6.0)	a	−0.651	0.59 / - - - / 25.0	1.12 / - - - / 110
A/M [Logit [A/M]]	−0.232 (4.5)	a	a	a	+0.383 (2.0)	−0.255 (2.1)	a	a	−0.230[b] (1.2)	+0.544	0.24 / - - - / 7.5	0.91 / - - - / 100
Marketing (LMKTG)	+0.712 (12.6)	+0.082 (3.1)	−1.633 (3.1)	−0.993 (2.8)	−0.305 (1.7)	−0.194[b] (0.6)	−0.424 (2.0)	−0.809 (3.9)	+0.528 (2.5)	+0.185	0.72 / - - - / 28.2	0.91 / - - - / 110

SOURCE: Lilien, 1979, p. 195. Reprinted by permission of the Institute of Management Science, *Management Science,* Vol. 25, No. 2, February 1979.

Note: *t* statistics in ( ); all equations significant at $\alpha < 0.001$.

[a]Variable insignificant and logically irrelevant.

[b]Variable retained for logical consistency.

The PIMS/Buzzell-Farris Models

Buzzell and Farris (1976) analyzed the 386 businesses in the PIMS data base that were primarily industrial. Four ratio measures of marketing expenditure were used as dependent variables: advertising and sales promotions to sales, advertising to sales, salesforce to sales, and total marketing to sales. The analysis was divided into three broad product categories: capital goods, supplies, and raw materials and components. A series of independent variables, classified into product, market, customer, strategy, and cost categories, were used in the 12 different multiple-regression models evaluated.

All the models in the 1976 study used a linear-regression equation to explain the ratios A/M, A/S, and so on. For example,

$$\frac{M}{S} = a_0 + a_1 X_1 + a_2 X_2 + \cdots \tag{18.8}$$

Therefore these models have structural as well as predictive problems. In later work, using better model forms and improved justification for their structure, Farris and Buzzell (1979) analyze a sample of 791 industrial businesses and use the logarithm of the ratio of advertising and promotion to sales as the dependent variable. Their results are shown in Exhibit 18.6.

In evaluating their results, the authors conclude: "In spite of some evidence for instability of a few regression coefficients, ... the overall pattern seems to be one of consistent relationships across a wide variety of industrial businesses" (pp. 119–120).

Evaluation and Use

How do these studies with similar objectives compare? In evaluating these models, Galper (1979) reports:

> The descriptive analyses of total marketing communications expenditures that have recently been completed on the PIMS data base and under the AD-VISOR project represent major contributions to the field. These studies have demonstrated that there are discernible underlying product, market, behavioral, and strategic characteristics that are related to the communications spending decisions of industrial marketers. Furthermore, the results of these two studies reinforce each other. Four of the eight significant variables determined in the ADVISOR model were found to be significant in the Buzzell and Farris models. More importantly, five out of six signs were also determined to be the same. In addition, the development of "guideline" models that permit marketing practitioners to calibrate their current spending practices is a valuable operational tool (p. 9).

A discussion of the differences and similarities between these two studies appears in a series of notes (Farris and Buzzell, 1980; Lilien, 1980) that may entertain the curious reader.

EXHIBIT 18-6 **Farris-Buzzell advertising-model results: regression analyses of cross-sectional variations in the logarithm of *A* and *P/S* ratios.**

Independent Variables	Regression Coefficients (Estimated Standard Deviations)[a]
Produced to order (dummy variable)	−3.59
(× 10)[b]	(0.71)
Number of end users (scale) (× 100)	6.54
	(3.07)
Purchase frequency (reverse scale)	1.72
(× 10)	(0.26)
Purchase amount (scale) (× 10)	−1.75
	(0.26)
Importance of auxiliary services	1.66
(scale) (× 10)	(0.46)
Percent of sales direct to end users[c]	−5.15
(× 1000)	(0.93)
Market share[c] (× 1000)	−7.26
	(1.84)
Relative price[c] (× 100)	1.47
	(0.46)
Contribution margin on sales[c]	2.34
(× 100)	(0.27)
Percent capacity utilized[c] (× 1000)	−7.12
	(1.95)
Percent sales from new products	7.19
(× 1000)	(1.69)
Constant	−1.77
	(0.56)
$R^2 =$	0.416
$N =$	791
$F =$	50.44[d]

SOURCE: Farris and Buzzell, 1979 p. 119.

[a] All coefficients significant at the 0.05 level.

[b] For ease of reading the tables, coefficients have been multiplied by the noted numbers: either 10, 100, or 1000.

[c] 4-yr average.

[d] Significant at the 0.01 level.

These models are different in their user orientation from most of the other models discussed in this book: they can be used directly to give norms for products that were not studied or included in the original data base. Thus they can be tools for managerial control. Characteristics for an existing product can be collected and input to a computer program, which feeds back guidelines that are then compared with the actual budget. (Exhibit 18.7 gives part of a sample par report. The center is the point prediction and the ranges are prediction intervals with a user-specified tolerance limit.) If the guidelines agree with the budget, no further analysis is performed. If they disagree, reasons for the differences are sought. Then the model acts as a control procedure for exception analysis—to find those product cases most in need of more detailed review.

Consider the following discussion of the value of these models.

EXAMPLE: Jack Frey, ADVISOR representative from duPont, notes, "ADVISOR is best used as a tool to ask questions. When a product's spending level is outside of the norm range, that's a signal that a question might be asked: is there a good reason for the product to be so far above (or below) the norm?"

He also talks about auditing: "While comparisons on a product-by-product basis are useful, the most value frequently is in generating norms for a group of products and comparing them. That comparison (see Exhibit 18.8) serves as a focus for discussion about how well marketing plans balance. Again, the tool should be used to focus attention on what question should be asked and is not meant to provide a direct answer."

The exhibit illustrates Frey's cross-product-comparison approach. Here we see products A and B within the range estimate both for advertising/marketing as well as for marketing/sales. Therefore there is no apparent reason to question their budgets.

Consider product C, which is very high on marketing/sales and very high on advertising/marketing. Both selling and advertising spending are high here, advertising disproportionately so. Is there a good explanation?

Product D is also very high on marketing/sales but low on advertising/marketing. Here the level of personal-selling spending is very high relative to the ADVISOR norm. If that selling level is reasonable, perhaps more support might be given to advertising. Product E has an advertising/marketing level in range but its marketing/sales level is low. Again, is there a good reason for the spending level to be this low?

In sum, Frey sees ADVISOR as a tool to help focus management attention on questions that should be asked about the budgeting process.

In spite of the value of these models, they have limitations. First, inferences were made with cross-sectional data bases collected over a short

EXHIBIT 18-7   Sample portion of par report: ADVISOR study.

Variable	Actual Budget	Industry Norms	
		Center	Range
Advertising (in $1000s)	20.000	24.000	19.200–28.800
Advertising/marketing	0.020	0.025	0.020–0.030
Marketing (in $1000s)	1000.000	950.000	760.000–1140.000

Advertising Expense/Marketing Expense

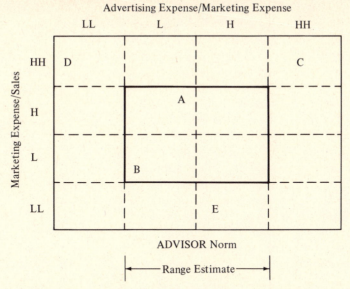

EXHIBIT 18-8 **Comparing actual levels with model norms for five business-es.**

time interval. Pooling of cross-sectional data for analysis assumes homo-geneity of observations—that is, that all cases in the pooled data base have essentially the same kind of relationship between the dependent and independent variables. Bass (1974b) and Bass, Cattin, and Wittink (1977) discuss these issues in detail and show that the significance of particular independent variables may change dramatically, depending on the observa-tions making up the pooled data set.

The second and most significant limitation concerns causality: we must not confuse correlation with causation here. Furthermore, from the stand-point of use, the industrial-marketing manager would most like to know what he should spend (to maximize profit), not what others in similar situations have spent in the past.

Normative-Marketing-Mix Models

An Industrial-Marketing Approach

The guideline models reviewed above are valuable, but they do not say how much *should* be spent. There have been few examples of causal analyses of industrial-marketing-spending effectiveness in the published literature [Weinberg (1960) is an exception] because of the nature of most industrial-marketing situations. Industrial markets differ dramatically: products may be high- or low-ticket items, frequently or infrequently purchased, with many or few customers. Such diversity suggests that a single analysis approach is unlikely to fit all situations.

Consider a range of product-market settings. At one extreme products such as copiers have almost all organizations as potential customers. Therefore potential volume is large, and much variation occurs in the marketing mix (use of broadcast media, frequent sales programs, targeted direct-mail campaigns, etc.). These markets, with large customer bases and high numbers of purchases per year, have many properties of consumer markets and include office supplies, business forms, word-processing equipment, and telecommunications products and services.

At the other extreme are products like offshore oil rigs, whose potential customers are few and well defined, where no two products are identical—each meets a specific set of demand dimensions—and where the purchase takes months and often years of negotiation. We refer to this situation as a custom-purchase situation, where a specially designed marketing effort may be developed for each sale.

Suppose we wish to model sales response to marketing spending for these two extreme types of situations. For general situations where there are a large number of purchase occasions, market experimentation is a feasible and suitable approach. On the other hand, custom situations do not usually provide data bases sufficient for statistical inference, which requires grouping at one stage or another; instead, customer-by-customer, situation-specific analyses are required.

But what of the situations in between, characterized by a moderate number of customers and a moderate sales rate? With relatively small markets, if a proposed expenditure for marketing experimentation is compared with its value in terms of added information, the cost may not justify the expense. Other organizational reasons, including a need for competitive security, may also preclude field experimentation. In addition, buyer-seller relationships are often long term, so the historical variability needed to read response to marketing-strategy variation is usually missing.

However, some of these products do permit analysis. They have markets that have gone through a significant disruption—a major competitive entry, a product modification, or some similar event. This disruption gives knowledge both of causality and of the magnitude of the effect. Lilien and Ruzdic (1982) refer to the event as a *natural experiment* and the resulting product market as a *market in transition*.

Exhibit 18.9 illustrates two markets in transition. In case 1 [Exhibit 18.9(a)], the company "discovered" marketing as a means of improving sales. Its major product line consists of a construction material for a variety of applications, made from a proprietary substance. The products meet a specialized need of restaurants and fast-food outlets and have been used for

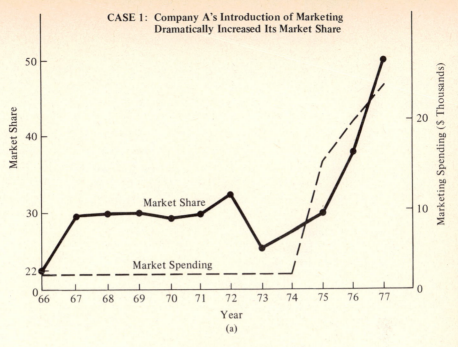

CASE 1: Company A's Introduction of Marketing
Dramatically Increased Its Market Share

(a)

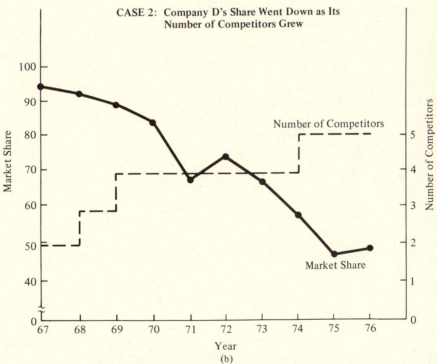

CASE 2: Company D's Share Went Down as Its
Number of Competitors Grew

(b)

EXHIBIT 18-9   **Two illustrations of natural experiments.** (Source: Lilien, Gary L. and A. Api Ruzdic. "Analyzing Industrial Markets with Natural Experiments," ed. by A. A. Zoltners. TIMS Studies in the Management Sciences, Vol. 18, New York: North-Holland Publishing Co., 1982, p. 244. Reprinted with permission.)

this purpose since 1966. However, the company did not begin a formal marketing effort until 1975. The result of this marketing-spending program was a dramatic increase in market share.

In case 2 [Exhibit 18.9(b)], new competition entered the market. The company manufactures a diverse line of specialty chemicals produced from renewable natural fats and oils. The product under study, used in a wide variety of applications, was sold exclusively by the company from 1950 to 1968. During the period from 1968 to 1974, four additional firms entered the market, cutting this company's share from about 95 percent of the market to about 50 percent.

Intuitively, a natural experiment can be said to have occurred when some dramatic change in the company's historical behavior or in the competitive environment has happened that affects the company's market position. The event or events should be identifiable and the cause-and-effect relationship clear, both intuitively and statistically, for a situation to be amenable for analysis.

The Model.   For the analysis of these situations we need an industrial-market-response model. A model that is simple and flexible, and incorporates many of the eight properties suggested earlier, can be derived from the following equations (in a market with two competitors):

$$\frac{dQ_1}{dt} = h_1 Q_2 - h_2 Q_1 \qquad \frac{dQ_2}{dt} = h_2 Q_1 - h_1 Q_2 \qquad (18.9)$$

where Q_i = sales of firm i
h_i = marketing effectiveness of firm i at t
V = market sales = $Q_1 + Q_2$

If h_1 and/or h_2 varies significantly over time, the transient solution to eq. (18.9) is fairly complex. If the response takes place fairly quickly and does not vary a great deal during any period of analysis, we can use the steady-state solution:

$$\frac{Q_1}{V} = \frac{h_1}{h_1 + h_2} \qquad (18.10)$$

In the general case, with I competitors,

$$\frac{Q_1}{V} = \frac{h_1}{\sum_{i-1}^{I} h_i} \qquad (18.11)$$

There are several ways to interpret eqs. (18.10) and (18.11). If we consider a changing market, these equations suggest how changes in $h_1, \ldots, h_I$ affect long-term market-share structures. If we assume the market comes to equilibrium each year, then annual data can be used with them to model market response.

To do so, we need a functional form for $\{h_i\}$, the "effectiveness" parameters. Evidence suggests that the response should generally be modeled as S-shaped (Lilien and Ruzdic, 1982). A form that permits computational efficiency is the logistic form:

$$h_i = \exp\left(a_0 + \sum_{j=1}^{J} a_j X_{ij} + \text{interactions}\right) \tag{18.12}$$

where X_{ij} = marketing-effectiveness component j (advertising spending, for example) for firm i

a_j = coefficients to be determined

This form leads to the following model for two competitors (excluding interaction terms):

$$\frac{Q_1}{V} = \frac{\exp\left(a_0 + \sum_{j=1}^{J} a_j X_{1j}\right)}{\exp\left(a_0 + \sum_{j=1}^{J} a_j X_{ij}\right) + \exp\left(\sum_{j=1}^{J} a_j X_{2j}\right)} \tag{18.13}$$

In the cases investigated to date, the X's have included marketing spending, inertia (lagged sales), and nonmarketing factors, such as product innovations (e.g., a clear quality change) and competitive-market entries.

Application. Estimates of the coefficients for the two cases described above are given in Exhibit 18.10. In these cases [as well as in the others reported in Lilien and Ruzdic (1982)], all coefficients have the expected sign—a marketing-spending increase leads to a share increase, for example.

EXHIBIT 18-10   **Parameter-estimation results on two cases.**

Independent Variable	Case 1[a]	Case 2[a]
Marketing spending	0.659×10^{-5}	0.318×10^{-5}
	(2.56)	(2.05)
Sales inertia	0.361×10^{-6}	0.194×10^{-7}
(lagged sales)	(1.76)	(1.81)
Competitive-marketing	-0.217×10^{-5}	-0.871×10^{-6}
spending	(1.73)	(2.01)
Competitive-sales inertia	-0.123×10^{-6}	-0.128×10^{-7}
	(1.26)	1.42
Number of competitors	—	-0.967×10^{-1}
		(1.96)
Overall fit: ℓ^2	0.92	0.90
Number of observations	12	11

SOURCE: Lilien, Gary L. and A. Api Ruzdic. "Analyzing Industrial Markets with Natural Experiments, ed. by A. A. Zoltners. TIMS studies in the Management Sciences, vol. 18. New York: North-Holland Publishing Co., 1982. p. 257. Reprinted with permission.

[a]Corrected t statistics in parentheses.

The majority of the adjusted t-statistics indicate that the coefficients are significant above the 90 percent level, and the ℓ^2's [roughly analogous to R^2 (Richardson and Ben-Akiva, 1975)] show that the models fit reasonably well.

However, the small samples used in these estimates limit the confidence in the results; small errors in measurement could lead to large errors in the estimated coefficients, and therefore care is required in their use. Furthermore, these models indicate the importance of the various components of company market share but do not tell us how much *should* be spent in marketing.

Conceptually, we can look at eq. (18.13) as having one control variable—marketing spending—and can construct a profit equation:

$$Z = Z(X) = Vmf(X) - X \tag{18.14}$$

where m = margin
Z = profit
V = industry volume
$f(X)$ = market share [from Eq. 18.13) as a function of marketing spending

This formula ignores effects over time but again, conceptually, could be maximized to yield a marketing-spending level X^* that is optimal.

This approach has important implementation problems, especially if X^* is far from the current spending level. In such a case the optimum spending is a risky recommendation because the prediction interval for these models widens with the distance from the center of the data and the models do not incorporate competitive-marketing response explicitly.

Thus while profit maximization may be unworkable, an appropriate use of eq. (18.14) is as a tool to suggest the *direction* that marketing spending should move in. For example, the profit response from a small addition in the marketing budget can be analyzed. [Six cases are discussed in Galper (1979).] It is assumed that this small amount will not upset competition and is readily implementable.

Exhibit 18.11 illustrates this concept. Point X is the starting point. If we increase marketing a small amount ΔX, our model predicts a profit change ΔZ. Suppose $\Delta Z / \Delta X = 1.40$. That says that a small increase in marketing yields a 140 percent return on investment—a go decision for most companies. If $\Delta Z / \Delta X$ is less than zero, then increased marketing investment does *not* pay. In fact, as long as $\Delta Z / \Delta X$ is less than the company's internal rate of return, marketing spending should be decreased.

This concept was applied to sample cases 1 and 2. For case 1 the marginal effect of marketing spending on profitability is positive (a $1.75 return for each extra dollar invested). In addition, this slope *increases* with greater increases in marketing effort. The recommendation to the company

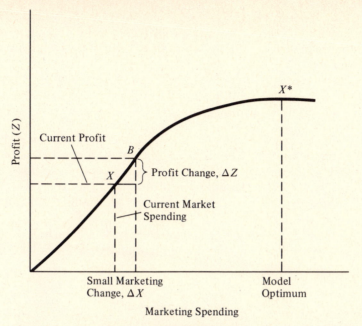

EXHIBIT 18-11 **The marginal value of increasing marketing spending.**

was that the company would benefit from a sizable increase in its marketing budget, a recommendation that management concurred with.

For case 2 the marginal effect of additional marketing spending was much lower than for case 1 ($0.38 return on an additional dollar of marketing spending). The recommendation to the firm was that a small return might be available from increased marketing spending at this time but that competitive response (not included in this analysis) could quickly erode any gains. Therefore this situation appeared to be one where a hold strategy in terms of marketing spending was in order. Management agreed.

Assessment. The approach described here for normative modeling of response to industrial-marketing spending appears to have promise. In the two cases described [and in the four others described in detail in Galper (1979)], causally sound recommendations for marketing-spending policies were made on the basis of the analysis. The approach provides a general model structure that is adaptable to a variety of market situations. In terms of the properties outlined earlier, this model form allows for either positive or negative interactions, permits price to increase advertising sensitivity and vice versa, and incorporates advertising and promotional effectiveness explicitly.

However, the approach requires a natural experiment for application, and many industrial markets will not find it viable for that reason. Furthermore, the models assume stable coefficients in changing environments.

Also, competitive response was not explicitly included: competitive firms were aggregated into a single competitor (nonresponsive). Finally, the parameters were estimated from small data bases, which are the rule in such markets.

A Consumer Approach: BRANDAID

BRANDAID (Little, 1975) is a flexible marketing-mix model not linked to a specific data base. The model is different from other published efforts in that (1) its structure is generally inclusive (at the expense of leaving many parts of the model calibration to the manager) and (2) it is modular and flexible, providing specific, customized submodels that can be used or not used as desired.

Exhibit 18.12 shows the marketing system to be modeled. The elements are a manufacturer, competitive manufacturers, retailers, consumers, and

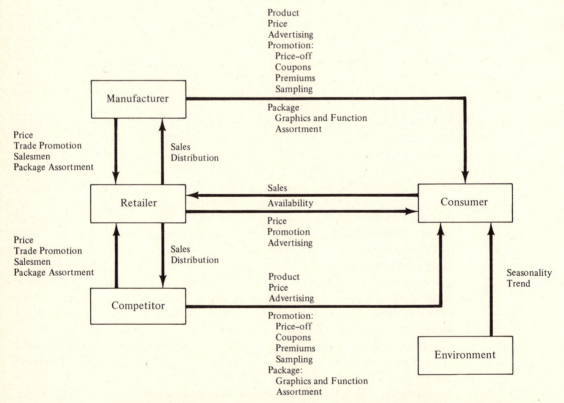

EXHIBIT 18-12   **The BRANDAID view of the marketing system to be modeled.** (Source: Little, 1975. Reprinted with permission from *Operations Research*, Vol. 23, Issue 4, 1975, p. 632, Operations Research Society of America)

the general environment. The model is clearly addressed at consumer packaged goods.

Model Structure. The model structure is based on the concept of a product-class and sales rate:

$$m_i(t) = \frac{s_i(t)}{S(t)} = \text{market share of } i \text{ at } t \qquad (18.15)$$

where $s_i(t)$ = sales of brand i at t
          $S(t)$ = product-class sales at t

In addition, the model develops an annual profit rate, $z_i(t)$:

$$z_i(t) = g_i(t)s_i(t) - \text{marketing-cost rate} \qquad (18.16)$$

where $g_i(t)$ is the contribution of brand i (in dollars per sales unit).

For a given brand (dropping the subscript i), the brand sales rate $s(t)$ is expressed as a reference value modified by the effect of marketing activities and other sales influences. The structure of the model is

$$S(t) = S_0 \prod_{i=1}^{I} e_i(t) \qquad (18.17)$$

where S_0 = reference-brand sales rate, dollars per customer per year
          $e_i(t)$ = effect index in brand sales of ith sales influence,
          $i = 1, \ldots, I$ (I = number of sales indices).

Two points should be made about eq. (18.17). First, each e_i refers to a different marketing-mix activity. Under reference conditions the advertising index would be 1.0. With a new program that index might be changed to 1.1, indicating a (current) 10 percent sales increase due to advertising. Second, the structure of the model says that an improvement in the effect of one marketing variable increases the improvement that can be obtained from another. Thus a price improvement of 30 percent (relative to reference conditions) together with an advertising improvement of 20 percent yields an improvement of $(1.3)(1.2) = 1.56$, or 56 percent. Little points out that other degrees of interaction can be provided by adding effect indices that depend on more than one marketing activity. However, that would likely reduce the model's applicability and ease of use somewhat. The model can also be adjusted for geographic or other forms of market segmentation by providing different parameters and control variables for each segment.

The specific submodels are described below, in turn. In each case we drop the subscript i in $e_i(t)$ for the particular promotional activity because it will be clear from the context.

Advertising Submodel. The advertising submodel starts with the brand's sales at a reference value and assumes that there exists some advertising rate that will maintain sales at that level. This rate is called the maintenance or reference advertising rate. When advertising is above reference, sales are assumed to increase; below reference, they decrease. Exhibit 18.13 shows the idea graphically. Steady-state sales at each advertising rate defines a curve of long-run sales response to advertising. Exhibit 18.14 plots r(a), the set of asymptotes from Exhibit 18.13.

The dynamics of the process are captured in the following equation:

$$e(t) = \alpha[e(t - 1)] + (1 - \alpha)r(a(t)) \tag{18.18}$$

where $e(t)$ = advertising-effect index
$r(a)$ = long-run sales response to advertising (index)
α = carry-over effect of advertising per period

The value of α determines how quickly a long-run sales rate is reached; if $\alpha = 0$, this rate is reached immediately, but if $\alpha = 1$, it is never reached. When α depends on the level of advertising, it can be viewed as $\alpha(a)$.

Operationally, the advertising rate is the rate of messages delivered to individuals by exposure in media paid for in dollars. Thus

$$a(t) = \frac{h(t)k(t)X(t)}{h_0 k_0 X_0} \tag{18.19}$$

where $X(t)$ = advertising spending rate
$h(t)$ = media efficiency at t
$k(t)$ = copy effectiveness at t
X_0, h_0, k_0 = reference values of the above quantities

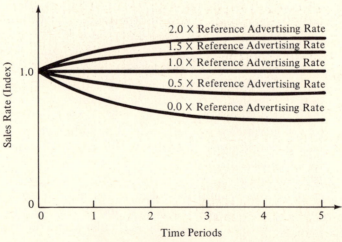

EXHIBIT 18-13 **Sales response over time to different advertising rates (curves adapted from an application).** (Source: Little, 1975. Reprinted with permission from *Operations Research*, Vol. 23, Issue 4, 1975, p. 637, Operations Research Society of America.)

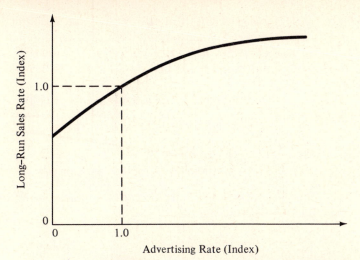

EXHIBIT 18-14 **Long-run sales response to advertising corresponding to Exhibit 18.13.** (Source: Little, 1975. Reprinted with permission from *Operations Research*, Vol. 23, Issue 4, 1975, p. 638, Operations Research Society of America.)

The model can be customized to incorporate a memory effect:

$$\hat{a}(t) = \beta\hat{a}(t-1) + (1-\beta)a(t) \tag{18.20}$$

where $\hat{a}(t)$ = effective advertising at t
β = memory constant for advertising (fraction for period)

The effective-advertising equation can also be customized by making advertising a weighted sum of different types of advertising.

Price Submodel. BRANDAID assumes there will be an overall price effect, plus perhaps an effect due to price ending (where a jump from 97¢/lb to 99¢/lb produces a smaller loss than the jump from 99¢ to $1.01). The price-index submodel has the form

$$e(t) = r(a(t))\,\psi(X(t)) \tag{18.21}$$

where $a(t) = \dfrac{X(t)}{X_0}$ = relative price
$X(t)$ = manufacturer's brand price
$r(a)$ = response function
$\psi(X)$ = price-ending effect

Note that the price model includes a response function $r(a)$.

Salesforce Submodel. The salesforce submodel is also structured in the form of a response function. Salesperson effort is defined as

$$a(t) = \frac{h(t)k(t)X(t)}{h_0 k_0 X_0} \tag{18.22}$$

where $X(t)$ = salesperson-effort rate, dollars per customer per year
$\quad\quad\quad h(t)$ = coverage efficiency, calls per dollar
$\quad\quad\quad k(t)$ = effectiveness in store, effectiveness per call
$\quad\quad\quad a(t)$ = index of normalized salesperson-effort rate

To account for memory and carry-over effects, we use $\hat{a}(t)$:

$$\hat{a}(t) = \beta\hat{a}(t-1) + (1-\beta)a(t) \tag{18.23}$$

where $\hat{a}(t)$ = effective effort at t
$\quad\quad\quad \beta$ = carry-over constant (fraction per period)

Finally, the salesperson-effect index includes a carry-over (loyalty) constant α, as well as a response function:

$$e(t) = \alpha e(t-1) + (1-\alpha)r(\hat{a}(t)) \tag{18.24}$$

Other Influences.   Other influences, such as seasonality, trends, package changes, and the like, can be handled by direct indices. For example, trend can be treated as a growth rate. In this case a trend would be modeled as

$$e(t) = e_0 \prod_{\tau=1}^{t} [1 + r(\tau)] \tag{18.25}$$

where $r(\tau)$ is growth rate in period τ. The promotion submodel was presented in Chapter 15.

Competition.   In BRANDAID, competition is handled in the same way as direct sales effects; each effect (competitive advertising, competitive pricing, etc.) goes into the model either as an index or as an additional submodel, depending on the level of detail available. Individual brands generate unadjusted incremental sales, while competitive interactions produce adjusted sales. Consider a brand b and a single sales influence (price, for example) for which

$$S_b' = S_{0b}e_b' \tag{18.26}$$

where S_b' = unadjusted sales
$\quad\quad\quad S_{0b}$ = reference sales
$\quad\quad\quad e_b'$ = unadjusted-effect index

Let

γ_{bc} = fraction of brand c's unadjusted incremental sales that comes from b
Because brand c's unadjusted sales relative to reference are $S_c' - S_{0c}$, adjusted sales for b become

$$S_b = S_b' - \sum_{c \neq b} \gamma_{bc} (S_c' - S_{0b}) \tag{18.27}$$

By dividing eq. (18.27) through by S_{0b}, we get

$$e_b = e_b' - \sum_{c \neq b} \frac{S_{0c}}{S_{0b}} \gamma_{bc} (e_c' - 1) \qquad (18.28)$$

which can be used in the general multiplicative form [eq. (18.17)]. Equation (18.28) generalizes to arbitrary sales influences, allowing a separate index for each influence. Without knowledge of market structure, a useful assumption is that a brand draws sales from competing brands proportionally to their sales. Thus

$$\gamma_{bc} = \frac{S_{0b}(1 - \gamma_{cc})}{\displaystyle\sum_{c \neq b} S_{0c}} \qquad (18.29)$$

where $\quad \gamma_{cc} = 1 - \displaystyle\sum_{b \neq c} \gamma_{bc} \qquad (18.30)$

= fraction of unadjusted incremental sales of brand c coming from product-class sales gain

Exhibit 18.15 lists the models and submodels that are available in BRANDAID.

Use. "A model is not productive until people use it and take different actions because of it" (Little, 1975, p. 656). The implementation of BRANDAID can be viewed as the development of a decision-support system for aiding brand management decisions. (See Chapter 20.) Little recommends a team approach to implementation; the ideal team involves an internal sponsor, a marketing manager, a models person on location, and a top-management unbrella. Implementation is viewed as passing through an introductory, then an on-going period, following the guidelines in Chapter 21.

Calibration of the model involves two types of data: state data (reference values of sales, share, product class sales, etc.) and response information. The former are easy to obtain; the latter require a creative blending of judgment, historical analysis, tracking (running the model on past data and getting managers to review the results and, if necessary, refine parameters), field experimentation, and adaptive control (the formal processes of using marketing activities to refine parameter estimates through an on-going measurement process).

Little describes a case, called GROOVY, for a well-established brand of packaged goods sold through grocery stores. Exhibit 18.16 shows GROOVY sales (warehouse shipments) by month for months 1 to 36 (1966–1968). Clearly, there are many fluctuations in these figures.

Response curves were first estimated judgmentally and then were checked econometrically. Exhibit 18.17 shows the calibrated indices of the

EXHIBIT 18-15   **Principal sales influences and their treatment in BRANDAID (any sales influence can depend on brand, package type, time, segment, or a combination of these).**

Sales Influences	Model Options	
	Direct Index	Response Submodel
Manufacturer's Control Variables		
M1. Product characteristics	✓	
M2. Price	✓	✓
M3. Advertising	✓	✓
M4. Consumer promotion		
(a) Price-off	✓	✓
(b) Sampling	✓	✓
(c) Coupons	✓	✓
(d) Premiums	✓	✓
(e) Other	✓	
M5. Trade promotion		
(a) Price-off	✓	✓
(b) Other	✓	
M6. Salesman effort	✓	✓
M7. Package		
(a) Graphics and function	✓	
(b) Assortment	✓	
M8. Production capacity	✓	✓
M9. Other	✓	
Environmental Influences		
E1. Seasonality	✓	
E2. Trend	✓	✓
E3. Other	✓	
Retailer Activities		
R1. Availability	✓	✓
R2. Price	✓	
R3. Promotion	✓	
R4. Advertising	✓	
R5. Consumer sales at fixed distribution		✓
R6. Other	✓	

SOURCE: Little, 1975, p. 653. Reprinted with permission from *Operations Research*, Vol. 23, Issue 4, 1975, p. 653, Operations Research Society of America.

individual effects. Exhibit 18.18 shows the results of using the calibrated model to predict future effects. The major deviations are due to a strike and the introduction of a new package size. After adjusting for these (unexpected) factors, the model tracked well over the next 5 yr and has proved useful for advertising, pricing, and promotional planning. For example, by tracking months 72 to 78, analysis made it clear that year-to-date sales were

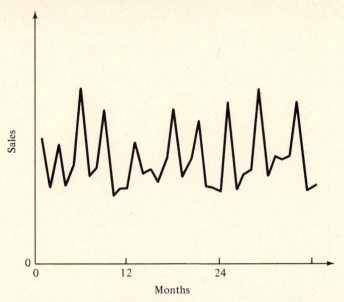

EHXIBIT 18-16 **GROOVY sales for 1966–1968.** (Source: Little, 1975. Reprinted with permission from *Operations Research*, Vol. 23, Issue 4, 1975, p. 663, Operations Research Society of America.)

good. However, since (1) most of the year's advertising was spent, (2) most of the promotional activity was over, and (3) price had been increased, the prospects for the rest of the year were bleak. The brand manager used this analysis to support a request for additional promotional funds, a proposal accepted by management. This action is one that "almost certainly would not have been taken without the tracking and forecasting of the model."

Assessment. BRANDAID provides a sound and usable approach to support marketing-mix decisions for frequently purchased packaged goods. The richness of its model structure calls for an eclectic blend of calibration procedures. It has demonstrated value in use and, in fact, because of its blend of models, data bases, and understandable software (it is written in a specially designed software language, EXPRESS, that allows on-line model development), should be viewed in the larger sense as a decision-support system.

Nevertheless, it has several weaknesses. Because of the model's richness, it can be "overcalibrated" (Welsch, private communication); in other words, different calibrations may provide equally good fits with different policy implications. Furthermore, it is a complicated structure that requires heavy involvement from the user, a potential barrier to implementation. In addition, it does not explicitly consider some of the elements of competitive response reviewed earlier, although, as noted, such elements are difficult to measure. Also, as with any marketing-mix model, it assumes that the firm's

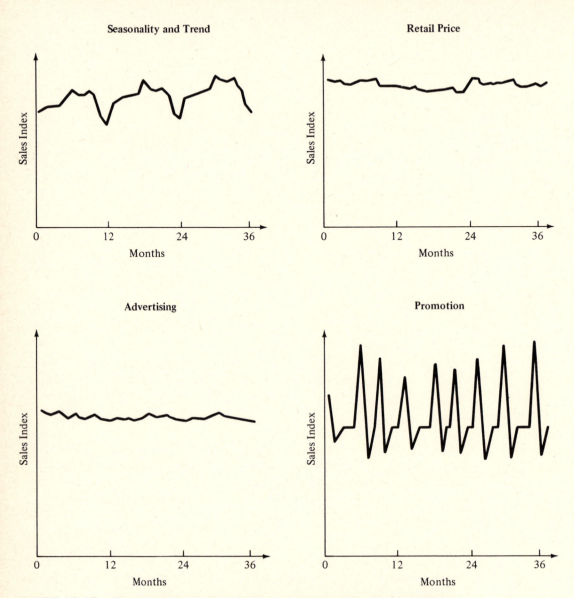

EXHIBIT 18-17 **The individual-effect indices calculated by the model from historical company actions (these are submodel *outputs*, not inputs) for the GROOVY case.** (Source: Little, 1975. Reprinted with permission from *Operations Research*, Vol. 23, Issue 4, 1975, p. 666, Operations Research Society of America.)

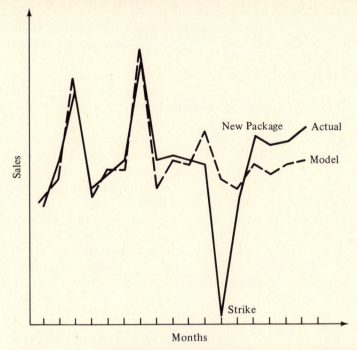

EXHIBIT 18-18 **Tracking of the model for the GROOVY case when the calibration of Exhibit 18.17 is continued into 1969.** (Source: Little, 1975. Reprinted with permission from *Operations Research*, Vol. 23, Issue 4, 1975, p. 668, Operations Research Society of America.)

decision-making structure corresponds to the model structure. To the extent that pricing is a product-line decision and different model components are managed at different levels of the firm, the model will be of less use.

In terms of the properties of a marketing-mix model developed earlier, it handles interactions in general, allows for positive/negative interactions among promotional vehicles, permits time-varying/segment-varying effectiveness, and incorporates advertising and promotional effectiveness explicitly. Some other effects, such as nonmultiplicative-type interactions, could be incorporated, while order effects, such as advertising-selling order, are more difficult to include.

In conclusion, BRANDAID provides a useful approach to marketing-mix decisions and shows that a model-based–decision-support system can aid in the management of mature products.

Other Marketing-Mix Models

We divide other marketing-mix models into decision-support systems and optimization models.

Decision-Support Systems (DSS). There is an increasing awareness that a good data base and flexible software are required for model implementation. In the marketing-mix area there are several examples other than Little's approach.

Lambin (1972) developed a DSS, called SIMAREX, to support marketing-mix decisions for a major oil company. The model is based on parameter estimates of a linear-regression model of market share as a function of share of service stations, share of other outlets for gasoline, current and lagged advertising shares, and lagged market share, as well as service station and advertising goodwill. The parameter estimates are used for simulating the effects of marketing strategies. The system encourages the adjustment of these estimates for new factors and changing relationships. Lambin reports a 2-yr development time for the system and suggests that the value of the econometric analysis was to provide organized prior information upon which managers could base judgments. Although the model has a number of technical weaknesses (linearity of response, nonconsideration of active competitive efforts, etc.), it represents an effort to provide decision support for marketing-mix decisions, blending empirical and judgmental information.

An intriguing attempt to deal with competitive effects in detail is the COSMOS system (Dutta and King, 1980). In an example of price-quality decision making with interactions, they develop a competitive system using metagame analysis. Starting with existing competitive scenarios, each firm in the market tries to anticipate the others' competitive moves and decides on the best course of action related to its anticipation. The competitive-analysis portion of the system then analyzes the stability of the competitive situation. The system, incorporating brand and competitive data bases, was used to analyze competitive situations for a business-products firm. No report of its operational results are presented, although system users report a high degree of satisfaction.

In an ambitious proposal Rao and Sabavala (1981) propose an integrative framework to deal with marketing-mix issues for existing brands, as well as market-share predictions for new brands. The model is a micromodel, dealing with choice among evoked brands by an individual or by members of a homogeneous market segment. The model, while clearly more complete than BRANDAID, would require a great deal of data for calibration and might approach a microsimulation model (Amstutz, 1967) in complexity. It is currently more useful for future research needs than as an operational replacement for BRANDAID. In addition, their paper contains a useful literature review on sales-response analyses, preference- (utility-) response models, and the relationship between controllable variables and perceptions.

Optimization Models. As noted earlier, Bensoussan, Bultez, and Naert (1978) have incorporated the reaction-matrix concept into an optimization procedure.

Balachandran and Gensch (1974) developed a sales-response model with a linear form and interactions. The model described the situation of a large midwestern brewery, including as variables relative advertising, relative promotion, relative price, and several others (salesperson's effort, trade discounts, etc.). They then applied geometric programming to maximize sales. Although this procedure attempts to provide insight (optimization information) about the marketing mix, the use of sales as the objective function and stepwise regression to specify the response functions limits its credibility.

In a more limited study Gensch and Welam (1974) show how convex programming can be used to provide guidance for price and promotional decisions for a consumer-goods firm. Optimal price and promotional spending and allocation are determined. But the model uses a rather inflexible constant-elasticity response function, which limits its use somewhat.

On net, the most successful approaches toward market-mix modeling have stressed evaluation over optimization and have blended judgmental assessment with empirical data to permit calibration of more-realistic response functions.

Summary

The firm has control of many if not all of the marketing-mix variables and can set them jointly. This chapter presented the evidence of marketing-mix effects and approaches to modeling those effects.

Beginning with the early efforts of Dorfman and Steiner, we traced the conditions for optimality in the marketing mix. More-recent theoretical approaches have dealt with competitive effects, changes over time, and expansive industry demand, and some of these newer approaches are empirical.

The evidence on the interactions of elements of the marketing mix is not vast but does suggest that (1) significant interactions exist, (2) advertising affects price sensitivity, (3) promotional interactions vary, (4) response varies by market segment and over time, (5) advertising can reduce the cost of selling, and (6) the order of the advertising-selling effort exposure can influence effectiveness.

The modeling of competition has drawn attention from game theorists, economists in the industrial-organization area, and marketing modelers. Game-theory approaches appear to have limited use. However, some relevant empirical work has begun to appear in the literature on industrial organization, but a theory has yet to emerge. Furthermore, a promising new approach is the use of reaction matrices.

Descriptive marketing-mix models, based on the ADVISOR and the PIMS data bases, can provide guidelines for industrial-communication-budgeting decisions. Normative-marketing-mix modeling in the industrial area is beginning to emerge.

In the consumer area the BRANDAID model, a marketing decision-support system, provides a modular set of components, each developed individually, that can be drawn upon in the customization of a marketing mix-model for a particular application.

The future of the marketing-mix area appears rather fruitful if the foundation that has been laid can be built upon. The major limitations in modeling in this area include gaps in our knowledge about mix interactions and the way to handle competition. The interactions problem is slowly being resolved, but an integrative theory is not on the horizon. Furthermore, the problem of competition is inherently difficult. With a longer-term view we foresee a reaction matrix with elements that vary by the levels of the marketing-mix components.

For a marketing-mix model to be viable, it must be a decision-support system with associated data, statistical analysis, and understandable software. Successful models will be used to answer "what-if" questions and are unlikely to be used for optimization. The focus on evaluation rather than optimization parallels the way managers currently address these problems; the future success of marketing-mix models depends on their ability to correspond to real management questions.

Problems

18.1 The Elkton Company designs, manufactures, installs, and services pneumatic, electric, and hydraulic environmental-control systems for large buildings. The Elkton Company currently has 50% of the large-building, environment-control-system market. Its four competitors have 30, 10, 6 and 4% respectively. Contracts are obtained on a bid basis. Each salesman bids as high a price as he thinks he can get and is rated on the average markup he is able to attain.

a. List as many company marketing-decision variables as you can for the company.

b. Conjecture the relative importance of each of the four P's to the Elkton Company.

18.2 Consider a firm marketing a particular product. Let

π = profit rate, \$/yr
p = price, dollars per unit
c = incremental cost, dollars per unit
x = advertising rate, \$/yr
$s = s(p, x)$ = sales rate, units/yr
c_0 = fixed-cost rate, \$/yr

a. State conditions on the derivatives of $s(p, x)$ such that it will be profitable to increase advertising. Do the same for price.

b. Let

$$y = y(p, x) = -\frac{p}{s}\frac{ds}{dp} = \text{price elasticity of demand}$$

What is the implication of $y < 1$?

c. Let

$$\mu = \mu(p, x) = p\frac{ds}{dx} = \text{marginal-revenue product of advertising}$$

Show that under some circumstances the firm maximizes profit when it chooses p and x so that

$$\mu = y$$

What are those circumstances?.

18.3 A large-appliance manufacturer, dissatisfied with its current market share, decides to increase its marketing effort substantially. As a result, the marketing budget is increased by 20% over a 2-yr period. What assumptions could be drawn under the following conditions?

a. After a sufficient length of time, the company had increased its sales volume but not its market share.

b. After a sufficient length of time, the company's market share had increased, but its sales volume was unchanged. In which of these cases does the increase in marketing effort appear to have had the greatest effect?

c. Interpret the results in parts a and b in terms of the effects used in the reaction-matrix approach.

18.4 An experiment was performed by a local retailer in which the price of an item varied between 30¢ and 40¢ during eight weekly periods. During some of these periods an advertisement was also run. The sales of the product in each period are tabulated below:

Week	1	2	3	4	5	6	7	8
Price	30	40	30	40	30	40	30	40
Ad	Yes	No	Yes	No	No	Yes	No	Yes
Sales	7	7	9	5	1	13	3	11

What can you conclude about the sales response to the different prices?

18.5 Is it reasonable to expect that there is a relationship between the level of a company's advertising and the effectiveness of its salesmen? Illustrate this effect in a demand equation.

18.6 An industrial-equipment manufacturer is trying to decide between making additional investments in advertising for its product or using this investment to improve product quality. At present it is spending about $4 (in units of $10,000) on advertising and nothing on the improvement of product quality. The relationship between profits and advertising has been determined as

$$Z(A) = 0.3 + 0.4A - 0.06A^2$$

where $Z(A)$ = profits, units of $10,000 per period
         A = advertising expenditures, units of $10,000 per period

Similarly, the effect of improvements in product quality is expressed as

$Z(R) = 0.3R - 0.1R^2$

where R = expenditures on improvement in quality, units of $10,000 per period

The joint effect of these two variables is estimated as

$Z(A, R) = Z(A) + Z(R) + 0.06AR$

a. Determine the amount the manufacturer should be spending on advertising and product-quality improvement, respectively, to obtain maximum profits.
b. If the manufacturer can increase its total marketing budget to $7 (in units of $10,000), how should it be split between advertising and quality improvement?
c. Determine the marginal profit on increasing the budget of $7 (in units of $10,000) by $1.

18.7   On the basis of an analysis of past data, a firm has developed the following market-share model:

$\ln m_t = b_0 + b_1 \ln p_t + b_2 \ln a_t + b_3 \ln m_{t-1}$

with $b_1 = -2.85$; $b_2 = 0.356$, and where

m_t = level of market share at time t
p_t = price level at time t
a_t = advertising share at time t

a. If total industry demand and total industry advertising can be assumed constant, show that

$$\frac{\partial m}{\partial a} = b_2 \frac{m}{a}$$

b. Sales of the firm have averaged 156,000 units per year at an average selling price of $8.95, and their current market share is 15%. The firm's average advertising expenditures have been $426,000/yr, with total industry advertising of $2,130,000. Past analysis has indicated an advertising retention rate of 0.6. The cost of capital for the firm is 12%. Investigate the short-term and long-term profitability of advertising.

18.8   The Delicious Donut Stores face the following planning problem: they would like to be able to tell their individual franchise dealers how their sales are related to pricing variation. Products are denoted by i, where i = 1 might be donuts, i = 2 might be coffee, i = 3 might be minidonuts, and so on. Assume the following, for a product i:

Product effect.   Sales of i are affected by the difference between the price of i at t [$P_i(t)$] and the expected price at t [$\overline{P}_i(t)$], perhaps as projected from past history. If $P_i(t) = \overline{P}_i(t)$, sales are as projected by a linear trend. Sales go up when $P_i(t) < \overline{P}_i(t)$, and vice versa. Sales have upper and lower bounds.

Cross-line effect.   Sales of i are affected by the difference between the prices of products *other* than i and the expected price of those products. (A volume-weighted average of prices for products other than i may be relevant here.) If the price of products other than i increases, sales decrease. Again, sales are bounded above and below.

Competitive effect. Sales of product i are affected by changes in the difference between Delicious' price for the product and the (volume) weighted, average market price for the product, $Q_i(t)$. As the difference $P_i(t) - Q_i(t)$ increases from its normal amount, sales decrease, and vice versa. Sales again are bounded above and below.

a. Formulate a mathematical model relating sales to each of the above effects for a particular product. Try to use no more than three parameters per effect. Graph the expected form, given the function you used.
b. Put the models together in an additive form and in a multiplicative form for the joint effects.
c. From part b for each of, say, three products (coffee, donuts, other), what parameters of the model need to be estimated? Suggest a method of estimation.
d. Assuming the parameters of your model are known, as is whatever competitive information you need, use your model to develop an expression for outlet profit per period. Solve the model for optimal product prices. What assumptions have you made? What additional data did you need to assume was available?

18.9 We hear much from industrial-advertising practitioners about their rules of thumb for budgeting advertising. It is of interest to find some situations under which it is optimal to budget a constant percent of sales for advertising. Consider a monopoly model. Let profit Z be

$$Z = PQ(A, P) - C[Q(A, P)] - AT$$

where Q = quantity sold, a function of A and P
A = number of advertising messages bought by firm
P = prevailing price of product
C = total production cost
T = cost/ad message

a. Set the first derivative of Z with respect to A equal to 0.
b. Let a be the elasticity of demand with respect to advertising, and

$$a = \frac{\partial Q / \partial A}{Q / A}$$

Substitute this equation into the result from part a and solve for AT/PQ (the advertising-to-sales ratio). Interpret the result.
c. Refer to part a. Differentiate the relationship with respect to P, set the derivative equal to 0 and obtain the condition for monopoly pricing,

$$\frac{P - \partial C / \partial Q}{P} = ?$$

letting $e = -(\partial Q / \partial P)(Q/P)$ = price elasticity of demand.
d. Substitute the result in part c into the result you got from part b. What does it say about the ratio of dollar advertising to dollar sales if a and e are constant? What if the price of ad message changes?

18.10 Generalize Problem 18.9 a little. Let $Q = Q(A, \overline{A}, P)$, where

$\overline{A}$ = number of messages purchased by competitors

Then

$Z = PQ(A, \overline{A}, P) - C[Q(A, \overline{A}, P)] - AT$

a. Set the derivative of Z with respect to A equal to 0 and solve for T. What does the relationship say?

b. Let

a = elasticity of Q with respect to A
$\overline{a}$ = elasticity of Q with respect to $\overline{A}$
η = elasticity of $\overline{A}$ with respect to A

Resolve part a for AT/PQ. What conditions must hold now for the optimal ratio of dollar sales to dollar advertising to be constant?

c. Under what conditions will profit as a percentage of sales (Z/PQ) rise with P?

Sales Models for New Products

In Chapter 11 we reviewed the importance of having a systematic process of new-product design and development to ensure long-term organizational health. Companies recognize that innovation is accompanied by high costs and risks. These risks can be controlled through a well-conceived and professionally managed program of new-product development. The key ingredients of such a program are (1) effective organizational arrangements for new-product research and development, (2) professional staffing, (3) adequate expenditures for marketing research, and (4) the use of sound, explicit models for planning and forecasting new-product sales.

This chapter will focus on the last ingredient: new-product planning and forecasting models. A number of new-product decision models have been developed recently, varying in the number and type of variables considered, the level of aggregation, and the method of solution. All of these models attempt to explain and/or control the level of sales of a new product over time.

The first section of this chapter establishes some basic distinctions of new-product problems, based on the product's newness and its repurchasability. The second section focuses on the theory of the consumer-adoption process and the underlying behavioral phenomena during the sales of new products. The third section examines first-purchase models—that is, models designed to predict the cumulative number of new-product triers over time. These models are used to forecast sales of durable goods and novelty items. The fourth section examines repeat-purchase models—that is, models designed to predict the repeat-purchase rate of those buyers who have tried the product. Predicting the sales of a repurchasable new product requires combining an appropriate first-purchase model with a repeat-purchase model. This section deals primarily with test-market models and pretest-market models, both of which attempt to forecast product sales prior to national introduction.

Types of New-Product Situations

Presumably, a new product is introduced by a company when a favorable estimate has been made of its future sales and profits. A new product's sales are shaped by many factors, including the size of the potential market, the nature of competition, and the company's marketing plan and resources. The appropriate sales-forecasting model varies with the type of new-product situation. These situations are distinguished by the degree of newness of the product and the degree of product repurchasability.

Product Newness

We do not rigorously attempt to define a new product but instead distinguish among three categories.

The first category, new-product innovation, is composed of products that are new both to the market and to the company. These are the really new products that establish new-product classes to compete against other product classes.

The second category is the new brand, consisting of products that are new to the company but not very new to the market. The new brand represents the effort of a company to add its own entry into an established product class. Consumers recognize the brand as part of the established product class, and less learning has to take place compared with the case of innovations.

The third type of new product is the new model, style, or package size. Here the company's product is only superficially new to the company and to the market and is immediately recognized and understood as an extension or deepening of the company's product line.

Product Repurchasability

In addition to distinguishing degrees of product newness, it is also helpful to distinguish among products that buyers are likely to purchase only once, those they are likely to purchase occasionally, and those they are likely to purchase frequently.

In a population of a given size, once all the potential buyers have brought a product in the first category, there are no more sales. The expected sales over time for a nonrepurchasable new product are illustrated in Exhibit 19.1(a). The number sold in each period rises at the beginning and

Sales Volume, Noncumulative

Sales Volume, Cumulative

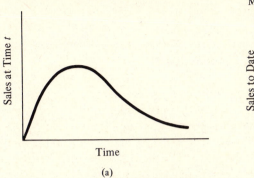

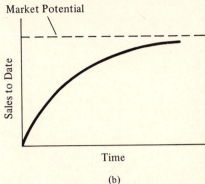

EXHIBIT 19-1   **Sales life cycle for a nonrepurchasable new product in a fixed-size market.**

later falls, until no potential buyers are left. If the curve is recast in terms of cumulative sales of the product, it would resemble the curve in Exhibit 19.1(b). In this form the curve illustrates the rate of market penetration, which is shown approaching a limiting value representing total possible sales—that is, market potential. If the number of potential buyers is not fixed, then the curves must be modified.

Products that are purchased occasionally are exemplified by many durable goods, such as automobiles, toasters, industrial equipment, and certain clothing items. These goods exhibit replacement cycles, dictated either by their physical wearing out or their psychological obsolescence from changing styles and tastes. Most sales forecasting for these products consists of separately estimating sales to first-time buyers and replacement sales. Replacement sales are usually estimated from data on the age distribution of existing goods and product mortality data. Exhibit 19.2 shows the sales life cycle of an infrequently purchased product made up of new sales and replacement sales. (Models for replacement sales are not studied in this chapter as such.)

New products that are likely to be repurchased frequently, such as consumer nondurables, have a different-looking sales life cycle, as shown in Exhibit 19.3. The number of persons buying the product for the first time increases and then decreases, since there are fewer persons left who have not tried it (assuming a fixed population). Superimposed on the first-purchase sales volume is the repeat-purchase sales volume, assuming that the product satisfies some fraction of triers, who then became steady customers. The sales curve eventually falls to a plateau, a level of steady repeat-purchase volume; by this time the product is no longer in the class of new products.

The reason for the characteristic early peak and then decline to a

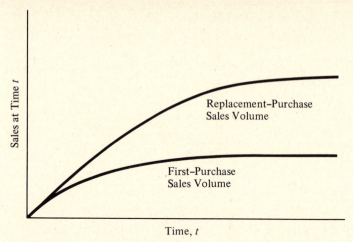

EXHIBIT 19-2   **Sales life cycle for an infrequently purchased product.**

(steady-state) sales or share position is not necessarily due to any inherent product weakness; it simply reflects that any new product will only be able to satisfy and convert from other brands a fraction of those who try. The long-term share is made up of satisfied triers.

Because all new products, whether they are purchased once, occasionally, or frequently, must be adopted by a purchasing population who initially do not know about them, we next review some basic concepts of the consumer-adoption process.

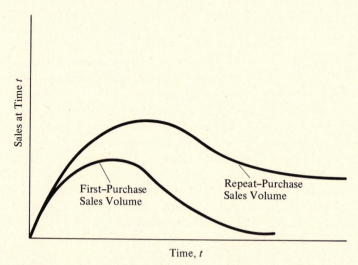

EXHIBIT 19-3   **Sales life cycle for a repurchasable new product.**

The Consumer-Adoption Process for New Products

The theory of the *diffusion of innovations* addresses how a new idea, a good, or a service is assimilated into a social system over time. This topic has been studied in depth by scientists from different disciplines, including sociologists, economists, and marketers.

The *diffusion process* is the spread of an idea or the penetration of a market by a new product from its source of creation to its ultimate users or adopters, while the *adoption process* is the steps an individual goes through from the time he hears about an innovation until final adoption, the decision to use an innovation regularly. The differences among individuals in their response to new ideas is called their innovativeness; it represents the degree to which an individual is relatively early or late in adopting a new product or idea. Individuals are often classified into different adopter categories on the basis of their innovativeness, as illustrated in Exhibit 19.4.

Individuals can also be classified by their influence on others with respect to innovation. *Opinion leaders* are those individuals from whom others seek information and advice and who therefore influence the action of late adopters. These concepts have important implications for modeling the adoption process. In the early stage of the process innovators alone are involved in purchase decisions. Later, word of mouth from innovators (if they are also opinion leaders) increases the likelihood of trial. However, as more try, there are fewer left who have not tried, and the rate of trial decreases. Bass' (1969a) model operationalized these concepts in a marketing framework.

There have been many studies on how individuals react to new ideas

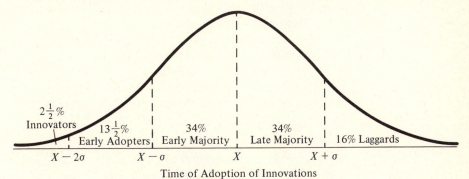

Time of Adoption of Innovations

EXHIBIT 19-4   Adopter categorization on the basis of relative time of adoption of innovations. (Source: Redrawn with permission of Macmillan Publishing Co., Inc. from *Diffusion of Innovations* by Everett M. Rogers, p. 162. Copyright © 1962 by The Free Press, a Division of Macmillan Publishing Co., Inc.)

and new products. In seminal work Rogers (1962) and his colleagues collected and generalized a great deal of diffuse literature about the adoption process. Some key generalizations are given below as propositions.

The *first proposition* is that the individual consumer goes through a series of stages of acceptance in adopting a new product. The stages are classified by Rogers as follows:

1. *awareness,* in which the individual becomes cognizant of the innovation but lacks information about it
2. *interest,* in which the individual is stimulated to seek information about the innovation
3. *evaluation,* in which the individual considers whether it would make sense to try the innovation
4. *trial,* in which the individual tries the innovation on a small scale to improve his estimate of its utility
5. *adoption,* in which the individual decides to make full and regular use of the innovation

The *second proposition* is that people differ markedly in their likelihood of trying new products. Rogers has characterized the five groups of adopters in Exhibit 19.4 by ideational values. For example, the dominant value of *innovators* is *venturesomeness*—they like to try new ideas even at some risk and are cosmopolitan (oriented outside their social system). The dominant value of *early adopters* is *respect*—they adopt new ideas early but with discretion and enjoy a position in the community as opinion leaders.

From a normative standpoint an innovating firm should target its communications and marketing efforts toward those people most likely to be early in adopting the innovations, because messages reaching late adopters and laggards are likely to be wasted.

But who are the innovators? The identification of innovativeness as a general personality trait has proven elusive; individuals may be innovative in some areas, laggards in others. To understand the characteristics of innovators, Rogers and Stamfield (1968) have classified over 2400 research studies. A summary of their general findings on correlates of innovativeness follows.

Social characteristics. Education, literacy, income and standard of living are positively related to innovativeness, while there is no consistent relationship between age and innovativeness.

Attitudes. We know that knowledgeability, attitude toward change, achievement motivation, and educational aspirations are positively related to innovativeness, but there is currently insufficient evidence about variables such as business orientation, satisfaction with life, empathy, and rigidity to change conditions.

Social relations. Variables such as cosmopolitanism, mass-media exposure, and contact with change agencies are positively related to innovativeness, as are deviancy from social-system norms and participation in social-group activities.

Once the characteristics of early adopters in a particular marketplace are known, they can act as a guide for developing early marketing-communications programs.

The *third proposition* about the adoption process of a new product is that personal influence plays a large role. Personal influence is the effect of statements by one person on another's attitudes or probability of purchase. Such opinion leadership is an integral part of the diffusion process (Coleman, Katz, and Menzel, 1957; Katz and Lazarsfeld, 1955; Midgeley, 1977; Robertson, 1971). Innovators and early adopters communicate their experiences to others; later adopters look to these persons for opinion leadership, which either encourages or discourages them from adopting the product. The role of personal influence varies across individuals and decision situations, and it is more important in the evaluation stage of the decision process than in other stages, for late adopters than for early adopters, and in risky situations than in safe situations. In general, the traits of opinion leaders have been difficult to identify. Some opinion leaders are innovators while others are not. Furthermore, opinion leadership appears to be product-area specific (Silk, 1966) and is a relative phenomenon, because leaders have more information than followers (Robertson, 1978).

The *fourth proposition* is that the character of the product itself affects its rate of adoption. Several product characteristics seem to have a significant influence on the relative rate of diffusion. All other things being equal, an innovation will diffuse more quickly under the following conditions:

It has a strong *relative advantage*—a greater perceived advantage in terms of higher profitability, reliability, ease of operation, or whatever the relevant dimensions.

It has a high degree of *compatibility*—it is consistent with the existing attitudes and values of the individual in the social system.

It *fulfills felt needs*.

It is not *complex*.

It is *divisible*—it may be tried on a limited basis.

It is *communicable*—the result and benefit are easily observable and describable to others.

It is *available*.

It pays an *immediate or short-term benefit*.

The relative importance of these factors in any new innovation should be quantified with a marketing program developed around the key areas.

The generalizations outlined above for consumer markets (hypothesized to apply to industrial markets as well), provide the behavioral foundation for new-product sales modeling.

Diffusion Models: Models of First Purchase

The task of a diffusion model is to produce a life-cycle sales curve based on (usually) a small number of parameters, which may or may not have behavioral content. The presupposition is that these parameters may be estimated either by analogy to the histories of similar new products introduced in the past, by consumer pretests, or by early sales returns as the new product enters the market. In the past two decades a great deal of work on diffusion modeling has been done, which largely draws from the more well-developed theory of contagious diseases or the spread of epidemics (Bailey, 1975).

Prior to 1969 most diffusion models could be classified as pure innovative or pure imitative. A pure innovative model assumes that innovative or external influences are operative in the diffusion process, while a pure imitative model assumes that the only effects on the process are driven by imitation or word of mouth. We give an example of each below.

A Pure Innovative Model

One of the earliest market-penetration models was the exponential one proposed by Fourt and Woodlock (1960), which was tested against several new products. Their retrospective observation of many market-penetration curves showed that (1) the cumulative curve approaches a limiting penetration level of less than 100 percent of all households and frequently far less and (2) the successive increments of gain declined. They found that an adequate approximation to these observations was provided by a curve of the following form:

$$Q_t = r\overline{Q}(1 - r)^{t-1} \qquad (19.1)$$

where Q_t = increment in cumulative sales (i.e., sales at time t) as fraction of potential sales

r = rate of penetration of untapped potential (a constant)

$\overline{Q}$ = potential sales as fraction of all buyers

t = time period

The formula is completely specified by the two parameters r and $\overline{Q}$.

As an illustration of how it works, we assume that a new product is about to be introduced. It is estimated that 40 percent of all households will eventually try the new product ($\overline{Q}$ = 0.4). Furthermore, it is believed that in each period 30 percent of the remaining new-buyer potential is penetrated (r = 0.3). Therefore the first-period increment in new-buyer penetration of this market is

$$Q_1 = r\overline{Q}(1 - r)^{1-1} = r\overline{Q} = 0.3(0.4) = 0.12 \qquad (19.2)$$

And the second-period increment in new-buyer penetration of this market is

$$Q_2 = r\overline{Q}(1 - r)^{2-1} = r\overline{Q}(1 - r) = r(\overline{Q} - r\overline{Q})$$
$$= 0.3[0.4 - 0.3(0.4)] = 0.084 \quad (19.3)$$

Note that eq. (19.1) produces an (exponentially) declining curve of new-buyer sales over time. Exhibit 19.5 displays the shape of this curve. To use the model, we need an estimate of $\overline{Q}$, the ultimate penetration, usually derived from market research studies. The second parameter r can be derived from the cumulative decline in the penetration rate observed in several periods of sales data.

In theory, the model can be used normatively by setting $r = r(x)$, where x is some controllable marketing variable. However, in its present form, diffusion is purely a function of time and incorporates few of the adoption-process characteristics outlined above.

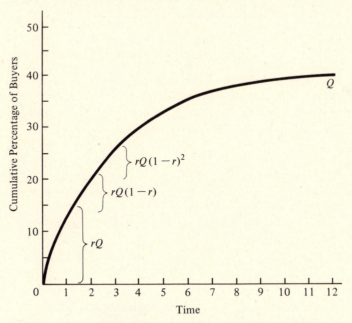

EXHIBIT 19-5   Increments of new-buyer penetration. (Source: Fourt and Woodlock, 1960, pp. 33–34.)

Pure Imitative Diffusion Models

A model that has been widely applied to industrial product data is that of Fisher and Pry (1971). The underlying hypothesis of their model is that when a new product or process replaces an older one, the rate of adoption is proportional to the interaction of the fraction of the older one still in use and the current level of penetration. Mathematically, this relationship is expressed as follows:

$$\frac{df}{dt} = b(1 - f)f \tag{19.4}$$

where f = fraction of market having adopted new product, $Q/\overline{Q}$
        b = constant characterizing growth to potential associated with particular technology

Integrating eq. (19.4) yields a logistic curve:

$$f = \frac{1}{1 + e^{b(t - t_0)}} \tag{19.5}$$

where t_0 = time when adoption of new product has penetrated half the market
        t = time since introduction, yr

Equation (19.5) can be conveniently rewritten:

$$\left(\frac{f}{1 - f}\right) = e^{b(t - t_0)} = e^{b_0 + bt} \tag{19.6}$$

Exhibit 19.6 demonstrates how the (log-linear) form of eq. (19.6) fits the data for a number of products and processes. The Fisher-Pry model has been demonstrated to work quite well retrospectively with data from a new technology that completely replaced an older one. As a predictive tool, when little data are available and when it is unclear that one technology completely substitutes for another, its value is more questionable.

The work of Blackman, Seligman, and Solgliero (1973) and Blackman (1974), building on the work of Mansfield (1961, 1968), provides a means of making projections for substitution in the *absence* of an adequate, historical data base. The Mansfield-Blackman model, written in the same form as eq. (19.6), is as follows:

$$\left(\frac{f}{L - f}\right) = e^{b_0 + bt} \tag{19.7}$$

where L is the upper limit in the market share that the new innovation can capture in the long run.

Mansfield's important contribution was the decomposition of the constant b above. He argued that b should be higher when (1) the relative

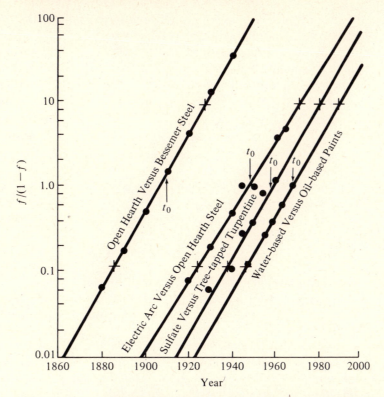

EXHIBIT 19-6   Substitution data and their fit to the model for a number of products and processes. (Source: Reprinted by permission of the publisher from "A Simple Substitution Model of Technological Change," by J. C. Fisher and R. H. Pry, *Technological Forecasting and Social Change,* Vol. 3, pp. 75–88. Copyright © 1971 by Elsevier Science Publishing Co., Inc.)

profitability associated with the new product is high and (2) the initial investment is low. In studies of diffusion in disparate industrial sectors, including railroads, coal, steel, and breweries, he found an empirical expression for b:

$$b = Z + 0.53\pi - 0.27S \qquad (19.8)$$

where Z = industry specific constant

π = estimated rate of return of innovation divided by minimum rate of return for investment (i.e., hurdle rate)

S = initial investment in innovation times 100 divided by total assets of average firm adopting innovation

This equation is consistent with Mansfield's hypothesis: the more profitable the innovation is to the adopting firm and the smaller the (relative) cost of adoption, the more quickly the product will diffuse.

A critical term is still Z, the industrial-innovation coefficient in eq. (19.8). Blackman, Seligman, and Solgliero (1973) relate this coefficient to more-general industry coefficients and create an *industry-coefficient index* (I), which is derived as follows:

1. They create a matrix of eight general measures of industry innovativeness—such as current and planned R&D expenditures, new-product sales as a percentage of total sales, value added—for each of a dozen industrial sectors.
2. They factor-analyze this matrix to obtain a set of factor scores for each industry.
3. They regress the score for the first factor (I) against the value of Z to obtain

$$Z = 0.222I - 0.316 \tag{19.9}$$

They get a t statistic for the coefficient of I of 3.38, and the coefficient of determination (R^2) is 0.85. Thus, in general, the fit appears quite good. Exhibit 19.7 gives the values of the innovation index in a number of industrial sectors.

To use this model for prediction, we must know the current level of market penetration (i.e., the initial conditions), the ultimate level of penetration, and the economic consequences of adopting the innovation. The initial conditions will specify b_0 and b. The coefficient of the time-dependent term in eq. (19.7) is developed from economic calculations involving eq. (19.8) plus an industry-innovation factor derived from Blackman, Seligman, and

EXHIBIT 19-7   Ranking of industrial sectors by the innovation index.

Industrial Sector	Innovation Index
Aircraft and missiles	2.29
Electrical machinery and communication	1.76
Chemicals and allied products	0.60
Autos and other transportation equipment	0.29
Food and kindred products	−0.35
Professional and scientific instruments	−0.37
Fabricated metals and ordinance	−0.60
Petroleum products	−0.64
Stone, clay, and glass	−0.70
Paper and allied products	−0.75
Textile-mill products and apparel	−0.75
Rubber products	−0.76

SOURCE: Reprinted by permission of the publisher from "An Innovation Index Based upon Factor Analysis." by A. Wade Blackman, E. J. Seligman and G. C. Solgliero, *Technological Forcasting and Social Change*, Vol. 4, p. 301–316, 1973, by Elsevier Science Publishing Co., Inc.

Solgliero (1973) and used in eq. (19.9). Note that π, S, and I may all vary with time over the life of the innovation.

This approach has significant limitations. A reasonable measure of the ultimate market must be known, while the model generally deals with a single market segment. It is a purely imitative approach and is apparently most applicable in industrial markets. Finally, it deals only with economic variables as the forces driving the diffusion process. However, in a customized form the model represents a usable tool. [Downey, et al. (1981) is a recent example of the use of this approach.]

Bass' Model

Fourt and Woodlock model a process of pure innovation. The Fisher-Pry/Mansfield-Blackman efforts represent pure imitation models. In an important integrative effort Bass (1969a) combined the innovative and imitative components (in discrete-time form):

$$Q_t = p\,(\overline{Q} - Q_T) + \underbrace{r\left(\frac{Q_T}{\overline{Q}}\right)(\overline{Q} - Q_T)}_{\text{imitation effect}} = \left(p + r\frac{Q_T}{\overline{Q}}\right)(\overline{Q} - Q_T) \quad (19.10)$$

$$\underbrace{\qquad}_{\substack{\text{innovation} \\ \text{effect}}}$$

where
- Q_t = number of adopters at time t
- $\overline{Q}$ = ultimate numbers of adopters
- Q_T = cumulative number of adopters to date
- r = effect of each adopter on each nonadopter (imitation rate)
- p = individual conversion ratio in the absence of adopters' influence (innovation rate)

In each period there will be both innovators and imitators buying the product. The innovators are not influenced in their purchase timing by the number of persons who have already bought, but they may be influenced by the steady flow of promotions. As the process continues, the relative number of innovators diminishes monotonically with time. However, imitators are influenced by the number of previous buyers and increase relative to the number of innovators as the process continues.

The combined rate of first purchasing by innovators and imitators is given by the term $p + rQ_T/\overline{Q}$ and increases through time because Q_T increases through time. In fact, the rate of first purchasing is a linear function of the cumulative number of previous first purchases. But the number of remaining nonadopters, given by $\overline{Q} - Q_T$, decreases through time. The shape of the resulting sales curve of new adopters depends on the relative rates of these two opposite tendencies. In the case of a successful new product, when the coefficient of imitation is likely to exceed the coefficient of innovation—that is, $r > p$—the sales curve will first rise and then fall. When $r < p$ the sales curve will fall continuously. Exhibit 19.8 illustrates both cases.

Bass applied his model to the sales time series of eleven major-appliance innovations, including room air conditioners, electric refrigerators, home freezers, black-and-white televisions, power lawn mowers, and so forth. In each case he used annual sales data from the year of the new product's introduction to the year when replacement sales began to be important. The equation was estimated by least-squares regression after eq. (19.10) was rewritten as follows:

$$Q_t = p\overline{Q} + (r - p)Q_T - \frac{r}{\overline{Q}}Q_T^2 \qquad (19.11)$$

This equation is simply a second-degree polynomial in Q_T, the cumulative sales to time T. Thus

$$Q_t = a + bQ_T + cQ_T^2 \qquad (19.12)$$

where
$$a = p\overline{Q}$$
$$b = r - p$$
$$c = \frac{r}{\overline{Q}} \qquad (19.13)$$

The data are time series of Q_t and Q_T. Equation (19.12) can be estimated as soon as data are available for the first 3 yr of the new product's sales because three parameters—a, b, and c—have to be estimated. After they are estimated, it is simple to work back to p, r, $\overline{Q}$ in eq. (19.11). Bass points out that the estimates for $\overline{Q}$, p, and r are biased and should be corrected as

$$r = \frac{0.97r^1}{1 + 0.4(1 + 4\theta)r^1}$$

$$p = \frac{0.97p^1}{1 + 0.4(1 + \theta)p^1}$$

$$\overline{Q} = \frac{\overline{Q}^1}{0.97 - 0.4(p + r)}$$

where $\theta = r^1/p^1$ and the values r^1, p^1, and $\overline{Q}^1$ are the values calculated from eq. (19.13). The equation can be reestimated each year as new sales data become available.

The results are illustrated for room air conditioners in Exhibit 19.9. The fitted sales matched the pattern of actual sales quite well, with $R^2 = 0.92$. The estimated parameters of the equation, $p = 0.0104$, $r = 0.4186$, and $\overline{Q} = 16,895,000$, make it possible to predict (1) the time when sales would reach its peak (t^*) and (2) the magnitude of peak sales (Q_t^*) from eq. (19.10) or its continuous analog:

$$t^* = \frac{1}{p + r} \ln \frac{r}{p} \qquad (19.14)$$

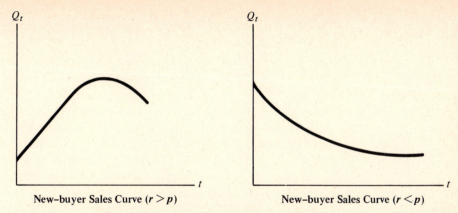

New-buyer Sales Curve ($r > p$)   New-buyer Sales Curve ($r < p$)

EXHIBIT 19-8 **New-buyer sales curve, Bass' model.** (Source: Bass, 1969*a*, pp. 217–218. Reprinted by permission of the Institute of Management Sciences. *Management Science,* Vol. 15, No. 5, January 1969.)

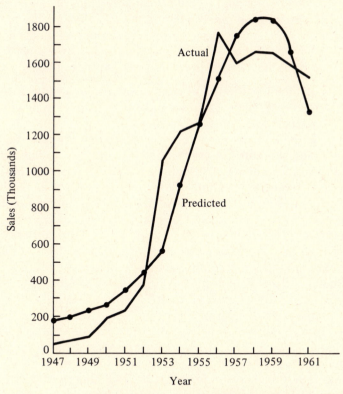

EXHIBIT 19-9 **Actual sales and predicted sales for room air conditioners (Bass model).** (Source: Bass, 1969*a*, p. 219. Reprinted by permission of the Institute of Management Sciences. *Management Science,* Vol. 15, No. 5, January 1969.)

and

$$Q_t{}^* = \frac{\overline{Q}(p + r)^2}{4r} \tag{19.15}$$

For room air conditioners the predicted time of peak was 8.6 yr while the actual time was 7 yr, and the predicted magnitude of peak was 1.8 million while the actual was 1.7 million. Furthermore, the Bass model produced reasonable good fits for most of the other 11 innovations studied. If it is necessary to estimate p, r, and $\overline{Q}$ before a product is extensively introduced, the following possibilities exist:

1. If the new product is expected to go through the same history as some previous new product in the same product class, then the parameters for the earlier product may be used as an approximation.
2. A study of many past-product introductions might reveal predictive relationships among the parameters p, r, and $\overline{Q}$ and features of the product class and/or buyer characteristics of the new product, which can be plugged into the predictive equations to find p, r, and $\overline{Q}$.
3. Data may be collected from a sample of households either in a laboratory setting, through in-home, product-use tests or in limited test markets that suggest the relative magnitudes of p, r, and $\overline{Q}$.

The resulting equation can then be used for long-range forecasting, particularly to predict the time of peak sales and the magnitude of peak sales for the new product.

The Bass model is one of the most frequently referred to models in the marketing literature. As such, it has more than its share of champions, as well as critics. Dodds (1973) reported reasonable results in the application of the Bass model to the cable-TV market. Nevers (1972) reported the successful extension of the model to retail services, industrial technology, agriculture, and consumer durables. Furthermore, Lekvall and Wahlbin (1973) derive a model that in reduced form is identical to Bass', but they offer a different behavioral interpretation of its parameters, calling p a coefficient of external influence (promotional activities) while q remains the imitation effect (the coefficient of internal influence). The Bass model was also recast by Mahajan and Schoeman (1977), whose formulation makes the model assumptions more transparent.

A number of critics have leveled attacks on the basic Bass model. In the original paper Bass noted that the parameter estimates are very sensitive to small variations in the data when there are only a few observations and suggested subjective or intuitive adjustments, particularly of $\overline{Q}$. Furthermore, the applicability of the model is limited to new generic classes of infrequently purchased products during the period when repeat purchases are negligible. It also does not incorporate seasonality. Other problems with the model include the following:

1. Diffusion is considered a function of time only and marketer-controlled variables are neglected. The model developed by Dolan and Jeuland (1981) (Chapter 12), as well as one by Bass (1980), addresses the issue of price in a diffusion framework; the paper by Horsky and Simon (1983) (described next) incorporates advertising, as does Simon and Sebastian (1982) and Kalish (1982) integrates several of these effects.
2. The number of potential adopters is assumed constant over time. Several researchers, such as Mahajan and Peterson (1978) and Sharif and Ramanathan (1981), have shown how a time-varying adopter population can be accommodated into such a modeling framework.
3. The diffusion parameters (r, p) are assumed constant. Bass (1980), Robinson and Lakhani (1975), Kalish (1982), and others have relaxed that assumption.
4. As a single-product model, it ignores the influence of other products on the timing of adoption. Peterson and Mahajan (1978) address this issue.
5. The model does not incorporate cognitive states such as unawareness $\rightarrow$ awareness prior to adopting. The paper by Dodson and Muller (1978) (described below) incorporates this issue.
6. The model assumes a homogeneous population. Jeuland (1979b, 1981) points out the problems associated with such assumptions.

In addition, Heeler and Hustad (1980) question its use in an international setting, finding systematic underreporting of the predicted time to peak sales for over 60 introductions of durable goods. Jeuland (1981) proposes a more generalized model to correct for these and other systematic biases. But the strength and number of these criticisms underscore the importance of the original Bass contribution—it served as a starting point for the use and development of conceptually sound diffusion models in marketing. As a model with an understandable structure and simple data needs, it is readily usable. Its current applicability may be limited, but, often, modifications for specific situations are relatively easy to make.

Kalish (1982) provides a critique of these models (and others), derives a more general diffusion-model framework from basic economic principles, and develops associated, general, normative implications.

Horsky-Simon Model

Horsky and Simon (1983) essentially use the original Bass model but explicitly incorporate the effect of advertising in Bass' innovation coefficient p. Specifically, they assume

$$p = a_1 + a_2 \ln A(t) \qquad (19.16)$$

where $A(t)$ = level of advertising at time t
   a_2 = coefficient reflecting effectiveness of advertising

a_1 = coefficient reflecting part of information conveyed to innovators by alternative means such as samples, displays, publicity

Thus eq. (19.10) becomes

$$Q_t = [a_1 + a_2 \ln A(t)] (\overline{Q} - Q_T) + r\frac{Q_T}{\overline{Q}}(\overline{Q} - Q_T) \qquad (19.17)$$

Note that eq. (19.17) incorporates both diminishing returns to advertising (through the logarithm function) and the lagged and carry-over effects of advertising through the innovation term. The authors point out that in industries within the capital-goods sector, the level of selling effort would probably be used in place of advertising as the conveyor of information.

The authors tested their model with data on the diffusion of a telephone-banking service, introduced independently by five banks. Each of the banks was isolated geographically from the others and essentially did not face competition from rival products during the period under test. Furthermore, none of the banks changed other elements of their marketing mix during the period analyzed. The parameters of the models were estimated for the five banks in much the same way as described by Bass, with the result that the effect of advertising (the coefficient a_2) was found to have the correct logical sign in each case and to be statistically significant in three out of five cases.

The authors also show how to incorporate this model in a procedure for an optimal advertising policy. They show that this policy is decreasing over time, which is consistent with intuition. This result shows that the heaviest spending is required when the product needs to become known.

This model is a straightforward extension of the basic Bass model. By incorporating an advertising term, it transforms the descriptive Bass model into a normative framework. However, in its current form it allows unbounded values for innovation for $A(t)$ large and, thus, better provides a local rather than a global evaluation for marketing policies. It is an important attempt, however limited, at incorporating a normative framework in the basic Bass model structure.

Dodson-Muller Model

The Dodson-Muller (1978) model is the only one reviewed here proposing a three-stage, consumer-adoption process: unaware → aware (potential customer) → adoption. Exhibit 19.10 displays this structure and the associated controls. The system is governed by a set of four equations regulating the flows between the states:

$$\frac{dX(t)}{dt} = -\beta X(t)[Y(t) + Z(t)] - \mu X(t) \qquad (19.18)$$

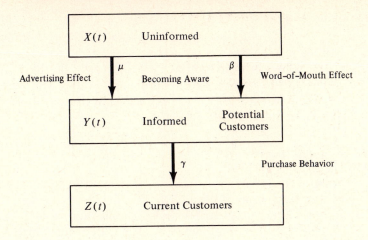

EXHIBIT 19-10 **Structure of Dodson-Muller, three-stage model.** (Source: Redrawn from Dodson and Muller, 1978, p. 1572. Reprinted by permission of the Institute of Management Sciences. *Management Science*, Vol. 24, No. 15, November 1978.)

$$\frac{dY(t)}{dt} = \beta X(t)[\,Y(t) + Z(t)] + \mu X(t) - Y(t) \qquad (19.19)$$

$$\frac{dZ(t)}{dt} = \gamma Y(t) \qquad (19.20)$$

$$X(t) + Y(t) + Z(t) = N(t) \qquad (19.21)$$

where $N(t)$ = number of current or potential adopters in the system at t
$X(t)$ = number of people *unaware* of product at t
$Y(t)$ = number of those *aware but who have not yet purchased* product by t
$Z(t)$ = number of customers *who have purchased* product by t
β = constant reflecting word-of-mouth effect
μ, γ = constants reflecting impact of firm's marketing effort

This model structure is drawn from the work of Lavidge and Steiner (1961) and others, who postulate a "hierarchy of effects" leading to product purchase. Although it is a step beyond the Bass model in structural realism, it is more complex and more difficult to operationalize.

Equations (19.18)–(19.21) are developed as follows. First, the people who know about the product, $Y(t) + Z(t)$, contact and inform a total of

$b[Y(t) + Z(t)]$, of which only a fraction, $X(t)/N(t)$, are newly informed. Therefore, $\beta = bN(t)$ in eq. (19.18). Similarly, those informed through advertising are $\mu N(t)$, but only $X(t)/N(t)$ are newly informed. Second, those who know but did not buy are *increased* by the newly informed, $\beta X(t) [Y(t) + Z(t)] + \mu X(t)$, and *decreased* by those who buy, $\gamma Y(t)$. Third, those who buy in any period are a fraction of those who are aware, $\gamma Y(t)$. Note also that the sales rate $S(t)$ is

$$S(t) = \frac{dZ(t)}{dt} = \gamma Y(t) \tag{19.22}$$

Bass' model is a special case when $Y(t) = 0$ for all t (everyone who becomes aware adopts the product) and $N(t) = N$. The Horsky-Simon model is also a special case, as are the Fourt-Woodlock model and many others.

The authors use their model to show that here, in general, as with Horsky-Simon, the higher the advertising effort, the higher and earlier is the time to peak sales.

Depending on how the form $N(t)$ is specified and how μ and γ are related to marketing activities, this model shows great flexibility and can be used for a variety of purposes. Its main limitation is data availability and estimation—data regarding the time paths of $X(t)$ and $Y(t)$ are frequently unavailable. The authors suggest searching an exhaustive list of parameters for those that best replicate existing sales data. This approach, not demonstrated to be either viable or efficient in their work, seriously compromises the applicability of their model.

The authors extend their model to incorporate both a forward flow—repurchase—and backward flows—purchase of rival brands and forgetting—to handle repeat sales. They show that under suitable circumstances their model yields as special cases the models of Gould (1970), Nerlove and Arrow (1962), Vidale and Wolfe (1957), and others.

The significance of the Dodson-Muller model is its generality—its ability under specific conditions to give rise to simple, more readily operationalized models—rather than its direct applicability. By starting with such a model and then making simplifying assumptions, trade-offs between realism and operationality may be made clearer.

Other Diffusion Models

The model structures described here are far from the only ones that have addressed diffusion phenomena. For example, Floyd (1968) adds a linear patch to the Blackman-Fisher-Pry model, which tends to overpredict near the end of the forecast period; his model underpredicts. Sharif and Kabir (1976) modify Floyd's patch with some success, while Stapleton (1976) suggests the use of a cumulative normal curve to model the S-shaped diffusion phenomenon. Nelson, Peck, and Kalacheck (1967) postulate that new-product diffusion is caused by movement from one form of equilibrium to another. A mathematical formulation of this phenomenon assumes that the percentage adjustments in any period is proportional to the percentage difference between the current and ultimate adoption levels. This assumption leads to the derivation of a Gompertz function.

Sahal (1976) summarized this proliferation of S curves for examining diffusion phenomena by stating that many S-shaped functions will fit data retrospectively, but

> the value of such a model is limited because it sheds little light on the nature of the underlying mechanism. More important, such a model is likely to be of little help in *prediction* because of the difficulty in choosing (especially at an early stage in the process of diffusion) a specific form from a variety of S-shaped curves that would be appropriate (p. 230).

EXHIBIT 19-11   First-purchase diffusion models of new-product acceptance.

Work By	Coefficient of Internal Influence	Coefficient of External Influence	Total Number of Potential Customers
Basic Models			
Bass (1969*a*)	Constant	Constant	Constant
Fourt and Woodlock (1960)	0	Constant	Constant
Mansfield (1961)	Constant	0	Constant
Gompertz curve (e.g., Hendry, 1972)	Constant	0	Constant
Lekvall and Wahlbin (1973)	Constant	Constant	Constant
Extensions			
Robinson and Lakhani (1975)	f (price)	Constant	Constant
Horsky and Simon (1980)	Constant	f (advertising)	Constant
Lilien, Rao, and Kalish (1981)	Constant	f (personal selling)	Constant
Bass (1980)	f (demand elasticity, learning parameters, price)	f (demand elasticity, learning parameters, price)	Constant
Peterson and Mahajan (1978)	f (product relationships)	Constant	Constant
Mahajan and Peterson (1978)	Constant	Constant	f (all relevant variables)
Mahajan et al. (1979)	Constant	0	f (housing starts)
Dodson and Muller (1978)	0	Constant	f (advertising, word of mouth)
Chow (1967)	Constant	0	f (price)
Lackman (1978)	Constant	0	f (profit/sales)

SOURCE: Mahajan and Peterson, 1979, p. 64.

Mahajan and Muller (1979) point out limitations in our current portfolio of diffusion models that must be addressed for the models to be more theoretically sound and of more practical use. They stress that these models must be used at a time when little data are available. Therefore calibration must be creative, either using other similar products (Dodds, 1973; Lilien, Rao, and Kalish, 1981) or using experience surveys.

A unified theory to incorporate marketing variables and exogenous factors into diffusion models is not apparent. Exhibit 19.11 summarizes work on first-purchase diffusion models. From this exhibit it is clear that even the model extensions have dealt only with price and promotion and not in a consistent fashion.

Furthermore, only the models of Dodson and Muller (1978) and Lilien, Rao, and Kalish (1981) incorporate repeat purchase. Also, virtually all models assume a complete social network—all adopters interacting with all nonadopters—which is clearly unrealistic. A model by Midgley (1977) attempts to address the point. In addition, few recent diffusion models allow negative and/or time-varying feedback. Finally, these models are deterministic, whereas the process is stochastic; and although the models have been available for some time, little material exists about their validity and reliability. More published reports are required about when models work and when they do not. (See Lawrence and Lawton, 1981, for an exception)

In summary, many tools of varying levels of complexity and applicability are available for aiding in forecasting and controlling the rate of diffusion of new products and new technologies. The next several years should see both increased reporting of the uses and limitations of models of these phenomena and a theoretical integration of model structures.

Repeat-Purchase Models for New Products

Many new products are of the repurchasable kind. These include virtually all the nondurables consumed by the household and the factory. The sellers of these products are even more interested in the repurchase rate than in the trial rate. A low trial rate could be attributable to poor distribution, promotion, or packaging, all of which are correctable. Trial of a new product can be stimulated by distributing free samples, introductory pricing, and so on. But a low repurchase rate may suggest a product that does not meet the consumer's expectations, which is harder to correct. Unfortunately, early aggregate sales figures do not distinguish between the two rates. A rising sales curve could mean a high trying rate with a low rebuying rate (a bad situation) or a low trying rate with a high rebuying rate (a correctable situation).

Exhibit 19.12 outlines most of the phenomena that are modeled in the efforts reviewed in this section. From the exhibit we see that individual consumers, facing a new, frequently purchased product:

1. **must be made aware** (advertising, promotion and sampling are marketer controls here)
2. **must be induced to try** (advertising, promotion, and samples are useful here; distribution and product price may also affect likelihood of trial)
3. **must be induced to repeat once** (product quality, relative price, and distribution affect repeat likelihood)
4. **must be induced to repeat regularly (become a loyal customer)** (product quality, relative price, and distribution affect this likelihood as well)

As noted earlier, the costs and risks of introducing a new, frequently purchased consumer product are high. To help reduce those costs, consumer-goods manufacturers have instituted a series of methods for investigating how the market is likely to react to the new-product offering. The major

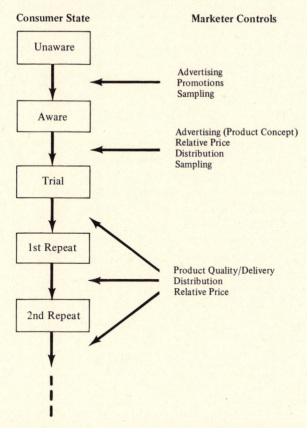

EXHIBIT 19-12   The structure of repeat purchasing and marketer controls.

methods of market testing are, from least to most costly (Tauber, 1977), (1) sales-wave research, (2) pretest markets or purchase labs, (3) controlled test marketing, and (4) test markets.

Sales-wave research is an extension of home-use testing in which consumers who initially try the product are given an opportunity to obtain more of the product or any competitor's product at reduced prices. They may be offered the product as many as three to five times (sales waves), while each time the company notes how many consumers selected its product. Sales waves permit some estimates of repeat-purchase rates under marketer-controlled conditions and the testing of different advertising-copy programs under conditions secure from competitive scrutiny. However, they do not simulate the actual shopping situations well, nor are they able to reproduce the effects of advertising media other than print.

Pretest markets (purchase labs) provide a simulated shopping situation, usually involving intercept interviews with several hundred shoppers and inviting them to participate in the test. After some measurements the shopper is exposed to a series of ads (one for the new product) and then given some money to keep or use in a simulated store environment where the advertised brands are available for purchase. These measures give an indication of product trial. Repeat is usually measured through a call-back and an offer to buy more of the product. This method has the advantage of giving quick results (especially for trial) at a cost usually under 5 percent of that for a full test market. We review below the ASSESSOR model, which uses pretest-market-generated data to project market results.

Controlled test marketing (minimarket testing) involves several panels of stores that have agreed to carry new products for a certain fee. After specification of the number, types, and locations of the stores, a test is set up for the new product. Sales results are audited both from shelf movements and from consumer diaries kept by consumers who frequent the stores, and the company can also do small-scale advertising tests in local newspapers. This approach has the advantage of providing a true in-store environment. The procedure is usually handled by a research firm, so the manufacturer does not have to use its salesforce, give trade allowances, or develop distribution. Its disadvantage is that the minitests may not adequately represent the difficulties of the marketplace, including problems of distribution, and, furthermore, these minimarkets are carefully monitored by competitors.

Test markets provide the ultimate forum for testing a new consumer product short of national introduction. A number of representative markets are chosen, and the company's salesforce tries to sell the trade on carrying the product and giving it good shelf exposure. The company also puts on full advertising and promotional campaigns in the test markets, similar to those anticipated to accompany national introduction. The primary motive for test marketing is usually to obtain a reliable forecast of future sales. A second motive is to pretest alternative marketing plans. Firms often use multiple

EXHIBIT 19-13 **Test-market results and marketer actions.**

Test-Market Result		Marketer Actions
Trial Rate	Repurchase Rate	
High	High	Commercialize the product
High	Low	Redesign/drop product
Low	High	Redesign/increase advertising and sales promotion
Low	Low	Drop the product

test-market sites to test different positioning strategies or entire marketing-mix alternatives. Test marketing calls for several key decisions, including the number and location of test cities, the level of the test, the type of information to collect, and the action to take (Cadbury, 1975; Klompmaker, Hughes, and Haley, 1976). Generally, actions following test marketing can be categorized as described in Exhibit 19.13.

In spite of their advantages, test markets have some problems, including (1) finding representative markets, (2) quantifying the impact of competitive and/or extraneous and uncontrolled factors, and (3) the problem of competitive scrutiny (Achenbaum, 1964). Because of these problems and the over $1 million reported average cost (Urban and Hauser, 1980), some companies are skipping test marketing, preferring to go national after earlier pretest marketing. Such a decision often appears reasonable: the expected savings associated with test marketing a product that has been successfully pretest marketed is about equal to the expected cost (Urban and Hauser, 1980, pp. 56–57).

Given the large costs that are associated with new-consumer-product introduction and testing, it is not surprising that a number of models have been developed that are of considerable help in evaluating and interpreting test-market and pretest-market results. We now focus on three of these models in some detail: the Parfitt-Collins (1968) model and the Tracker model (Blattberg and Golanty, 1978), both used for test-market evaluation, and ASSESSOR (Silk and Urban, 1978), used for pretest-market evaluation. We then review other approaches and developments in the field.

Parfitt-Collins Model

The Parfitt-Collins (1968) model is reviewed here primarily because its development exerted influence on the structure and development of later models. The objective of their effort was to develop a simple method for obtaining an early prediction of ultimate market share with panel data.

Parfitt and Collins see ultimate brand share as the product of three factors:

$$s = prb \qquad (19.23)$$

where s = ultimate brand share
p = ultimate penetration rate of brand (percentage of new buyers of this product class who *try* this brand)
r = ultimate *repeat*-purchase rate of brand (percentage of repurchases of this brand to all purchases by persons who once purchased this brand)
b = *buying-rate* index of repeat purchase of this brand (average buyer = 1.00)

The definitions of these variables and the working of this model can be conveyed by an example. Assume that a company launches a new brand in an established product field.

Trial Rate. Its share of new buyers in this product field will rise from zero to some ultimate percent as weeks pass. Exhibit 19.14(a) illustrates this situation with the cumulative penetration of a new brand in the toilet-soap field.

The penetration rate increases at a decreasing rate beginning at time zero. A curve can be fit to these data after a few weeks; the authors recommend

$$p(t) = p(1 - e^{-at}) \qquad (19.24)$$

where $p(t)$ = cumulative trial by t
p = ultimate (long-run) trial in eq. (19.23)
a = growth-rate parameter

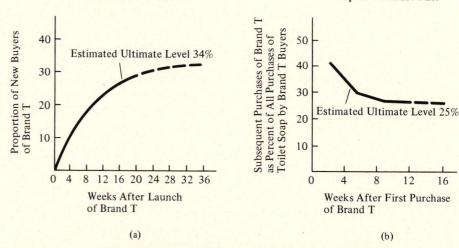

(a)

(b)

EXHIBIT 19-14   Cumulative penetration and repeat-purchasing rate for brand T (Parfitt-Collins model). (Source: Parfitt and Collins, 1968, pp. 132–133.)

Alternatively, a free-hand extrapolation can be performed to yield the ultimate penetration rate p—the rate that would apply between 12 and 18 mo after the product is launched.

Repeat Rate. The repeat rate for this brand will also be monitored as data come in. This rate shows the percentage of repurchases of this brand relative to purchases of all brands by those who have tried the brand. Exhibit 19.14(b) shows the repeat-purchase rate for the new brand of toilet soap, which is approximately 40 percent in the first 4 wk after purchase—that is, four out of ten purchases of toilet soap by triers of brand T were again brand T. The exhibit shows this rate as falling with the passage of time toward an asymptote of 25 percent; the earlier triers of a new product tend to like it more than later triers.

Use Rate. If purchasers of the new brand buy at the average volume of purchasers of all brands in this product class, then $b = 1.00$.

We are now ready to predict the ultimate brand share. According to eq. (19.23)

$$s = 0.34 \, (0.25) \, (1.00) = 0.085$$

That is, if 34 percent of new buyers in this market ultimately try this brand, if 25 percent of their subsequent repurchases go to this brand, and if those buying the brand buy an average quantity, the brand share should settle at an equilibrium level of 8.5 percent. If this brand attracts heavier-than-average buyers, say with an index of 1.20, then the share prediction would be 10.2 percent $(0.34 \times 0.25 \times 1.20)$.

The nice feature of this model is that ultimate-share prediction can be made as soon as the penetration curve and the repeat-purchase curve tend toward clear asymptotic values, which usually occurs before a stable brand share is achieved.

Assessment. Parfitt and Collins report on the accuracy of their market-share forecasts for 24 products that were successfully introduced. From six 4-wk reporting periods 1 yr after introduction, the predicted market share in all but two cases was within the range of market shares observed during this period. The actual level of market share was, of course, far from stable.

The Parfitt-Collins model assumes that market conditions do not change during or after the test period and that the new product has entered an existing and well-defined product category; clearly, trial and repeat rates are category-dependent.

Its other limitations include (1) lack of consideration of an aware state prior to trial, (2) no effects of advertising, promotion, or distribution, and (3) no consideration of different repeat rates for different repeat classes (first repeat, second repeat, etc.) A correlate of the latter limitation is an assumed lack of development of loyalty with different levels of repeat purchase. This result is in conflict with the observations of Massy (1969), Eskin (1973), and others.

In summary, the Parfitt-Collins model is a useful starting point for modeling in this area; it is simple and appealing. Later models have extended this basic structure.

The Tracker Model

The Tracker (Blattberg and Golanty, 1978) model uses survey data to predict year-end, test-market sales. The model is relatively inexpensive to implement, with the cost reported at $15,000. Potential users are tracked through an awareness stage to trial and, finally, to various repeat levels. The method requires three waves of questionnaires of 500–1000 respondents, launched once every 4 wk, to support estimation of parameters in the awareness, trial, and repeat submodels.

Awareness Model.   Total brand awareness is developed as

$$A_t = \frac{\text{UR} + \text{AR}}{N} \tag{19.25}$$

where A_t = awareness at t
UR = unaided recall of new brand
AR = aided recall of new brand given lack of unaided recall
N = sample size

The model relates the change in awareness at t to advertising spending as

$$\ln\left[\frac{1 - A_t}{1 - A_{t-1}}\right] = a - b(\text{GRP}_t) \tag{19.26}$$

where GRP_t = gross-rating points of advertising at t
a, b = parameters

Note that eq. (19.26) shows diminishing returns to advertising spending and that, without advertising, awareness may be stable ($a = 0$), it may grow ($a < 0$), or it may decline ($a > 0$). The parameter b is a measure of the awareness response to advertising: the greater b, the greater the advertising effectiveness is.

Forgetting is not explicitly included in this formulation. The authors estimate A_0, the initial awareness level, and a and b by regressing previous introductions in the same product class against advertising spending. A problem may be that a and b should not be constant over a period of time; in particular, the authors recommend that b be adjusted downward after a period of time.

Trial Model.   In this model, trial rates are estimated with two separate populations: the newly aware and those aware for more than one period. In particular, the authors specify trial rates as

$$T_t - T_{t-1} = \underbrace{c(A_t - A_{t-1})}_{\text{newly aware}} + \underbrace{d(A_{t-1} - T_{t-1})}_{\substack{\text{past aware but} \\ \text{not yet trying}}} \qquad \text{for } 0 < d < c < 1 \qquad (19.27)$$

where T_t = cumulative percentage of triers by period t
A_t = percent aware in period t
c = probability of trial by consumers who became aware this period
d = probability of trial by consumers aware last period or earlier but who have not yet tried

Here the model postulates a greater conversion rate among the newly aware.

The trial rate in eq. (19.27) is adjusted for relative price:

$$(T_t - T_{t-1})^* = (T_t - T_{t-1})RP_t^\gamma \qquad (19.28)$$

where RP_t = relative price at t
γ = price-elasticity parameter

Similarly, an error term is added to eq. (19.27) for estimation; it is both autocorrelated and heteroscedastic (where the heteroscedasticity is related to relative price). Parameters of the model are assumed constant in a product class and are estimated by a nonlinear procedure, pooling data for a number of products in the class.

Repeat Model and Projection Model.   The projection model for market share or sales is based on tracing the percentage of triers who become first-time users, second-time users, and so on. Triers or repeat users who discontinue use are classified as nonusers. Triers are assumed to have a constant, average purchase rate TU, and repeaters are assumed to have a different use rate RU. Total sales per potential trier is then given as

$$TS_t = (T_t - T_{t-1})TU + \sum_{i=1}^{t-1} UC_{it}RU \qquad (19.29)$$

where   TS = total sales per potential trier
T_t = new triers during period t
TU = trial-use rate
RU = repeat-use rate
UC_{it} = percentage of new triers in period i who are still users during period t

To model UC_{it}, the authors use a depth-of-repeat model. For simplicity it is assumed that

$$UC_{t-1,t} = r(T_t - T_{t-1}) \qquad (19.30)$$

that is, that the percentage (r) of triers who repeat at least once is independent of time. The rest of the structure of UC_{it} develops as follows:

$$UC_{t,t+i+1} = k_i(UC_{t,t+1}) \tag{19.31}$$

where k_i is the percentage of triers in period t who continue to purchase after period $t + i$. Note that the $\{k_i\}$ are also assumed independent of time.

According to the authors, r and RU are estimated with telephone surveys, while the $\{k_i\}$ are estimated subjectively with product-satisfaction data from the questionnaires; the trial rate TU is set equal to one by definition. The reason for the subjective estimates of the $\{k_i\}$ is that no quantitative, long-term, depth-of-repeat information is available; this problem exists in all cases where a short purchase history is used to project future sales.

If sampling is instituted during the test market, the model must be replicated for the sampled and nonsampled potential customers.

Assessment.   The authors report 11 new-product introductions evaluated with Tracker. The predictions appear reasonable, being within 10–15 percent of actual in 8 of the cases. In 2 of the other cases the model predicted an early failure.

The model provides a relatively complete, practical structure that is apparently being applied with success in evaluating test markets. Its weaknesses are that numerous parameters (the $\{k_i\}$, for example) are subjectively estimated and based on little data. In addition, the estimation procedures are somewhat ad hoc; for example, the awareness model often will not discriminate between company and brand identification. Furthermore, parameters are often estimated partially from related products; this feature limits the model's use in cases where a product is relatively unique.

ASSESSOR

ASSESSOR (Silk and Urban, 1978) is a pretest market model designed to give a market-share projection for the new brand and the source of the new brand's share. In addition, it produces diagnostic information about the new brand's positioning and permits low-cost screening of various marketing-mix elements (copy, price, package, etc.).

One of the innovative features of ASSESSOR is its *convergent approach* to modeling. For greater confidence in the results, it uses a trial-repeat structure and a parallel preference model. The disadvantage of the convergent measurement is its increased cost. However, this disadvantage may not prove serious, because input for more than one model can be obtained from the same consumer measures. Exhibit 19.15 shows the overall structure of the ASSESSOR system. The measurements for both models are obtained from a research design with laboratory and use tests.

Research Design and Measurements.   Exhibit 19.16 outlines the basic

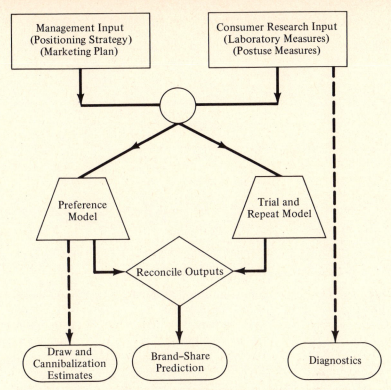

EXHIBIT 19-15 **Structure of ASSESSOR system.** (Source: Silk and Urban, 1978, p. 173.)

steps of the research design and identifies the main types of data required at each stage. The idea is to parallel the basic stages of consumer response to a new product from awareness through trial and to repeat. For simulation of awareness a sample of consumers (usually recruited through an interview conducted in the immediate vicinity of a shopping center) is exposed to advertising for the new product and a small set of competing products already established in the marketplace. Following this step, for simulation of *trial*, the consumers enter a simulated shopping facility where they have an opportunity to purchase quantities of the new and/or established products. Those who do not try (purchase) are given a sample of the product to simulate product sampling. *Repeat* is assessed by one or more follow-up interviews with the same respondents conducted after enough time has passed for them to consume a sufficient quantity of the new product at home.

Trial-repeat Model.   Awareness for the ASSESSOR model is developed as a managerial input. Long-run market share is calculated with the basic trial-repeat model from Parfitt and Collins (1968), without the use-rate term:

$$s = pr \qquad (19.32)$$

where s = ultimate market share
p = ultimate penetration rate (long-run trial)
r = ultimate repeat rate among triers

The ASSESSOR model decomposes these quantities:

$$p = \underbrace{FKD}_{\substack{\text{those} \\ \text{who} \\ \text{try}}} + \underbrace{CU}_{\substack{\text{those} \\ \text{sampled}}} - \underbrace{(FKD)(CU)}_{\substack{\text{adjustment} \\ \text{for double} \\ \text{counting}}} \qquad (19.33)$$

EXHIBIT 19-16   ASSESSOR research design and measurement.

Design[a]	Procedure	Measurement
O_1	Respondent screening and recruitment (personal interview)	Criteria for target-group identification (e.g., product-class use)
O_2	Premeasurement for established brands (self-administered questionnaire)	Composition of relevant set of established brands, attribute weights and ratings, and preferences
X_1	Exposure to advertising for established brands *and* new brand	
$[O_3]$	Measurement of reactions to the advertising materials (self-administered questionnaire)	Optional (e.g., likability and believability ratings of advertising materials)
X_2	Simulated shopping trip and exposure to display of new and established brands	
O_4	Purchase opportunity (choice recorded by research personnel)	Brand(s) purchased
X_3	Home use/consumption of new brand	
O_5	Postuse measurement (telephone interview)	New-brand use rate, satisfaction ratings, and repeat-purchase propensity; attribute ratings and preferences for relevant set of established brands plus the new brand

SOURCE: Silk and Urban, 1978, p. 174.

[a]O = measurement; X = advertising or product exposure.

where F = long-run probability of trial given unlimited distribution and
      awareness

K = long-run probability of awareness

D = long-run probability of availability in consumer's retail outlet
      (weighted average of retail outlets carrying brand)

C = probability of consumer receiving sample

U = probability that a consumer who receives sample uses it

The first item in eq. (19.32), FKD, represents those consumers who will
be aware of the brand, have it available, and then try it. The second term,
CU, represents those who will try a sample. The third term (FKD) (CU),
represents the intersection of these first two populations and is subtracted to
eliminate double counting in the trial estimate. The parameter F is
measured as the proportion of laboratory shoppers who buy the brand,
while the rest of the parameters are estimated on the basis of past
experience with similar products and by managerial judgment.

The repeat rate r is modeled as the equilibrium share of a two-state
Markov process [see Urban (1975b), discussed in Chapter 11]:

$$r = \frac{q(k,z)}{1 + q(k, z) - q(z, z)} \qquad (19.34)$$

where $q(k, z)$ = probability that consumer who last purchased some estab-
            lished product k will switch to new brand z on next
            purchase occasion

$q(z, z)$ = probability that consumer who last purchased new brand
            will repurchase it on next buying occasion

The transition probabilities above are estimated from the postuse
survey. If those sampled display a different repeat rate from those who
made a purchase in the laboratory, separate repeat rates are calculated and
applied to the trial model.

Preference Model.   Following Luce (1959) and an adaptation and operationalization by Pessemier and colleagues (1971), ASSESSOR assumes that
brand preferences obtained in a laboratory situation can be used to predict
consumer purchase behavior. The preference model is a variation of the
logit model discussed in Chapter 7, which is derived from a constant-sum,
paired-comparison task in which consumers allocate a fixed number of
chips between each pair of brands in their evoked set. A scaling technique
developed by Torgerson (1958) transforms these constant-sum measures into
a ratio-scaled preference V_{ij}, indicating consumer i's preference for brand j.
These preferences are linked to purchase probabilities:

$$L_{ij} = \frac{(V_{ij})^b}{\sum_{\ell \in m_i} (V_{i\ell})^b} \qquad (19.35)$$

where L_{ij} = probability of choice by consumer of product
$\qquad$ V_{ij} = preference measure
$\qquad$ m_i = brands in consumers i's evoked set
$\qquad$ b = parameter to be estimated

In practice, the b coefficient, reported in the range of 1.5 and 3.0 for most applications, increases the relative distance between the more- and less-preferred products relative to the simple Luce model (where $b = 1$).

Two main assumptions are required for the use of this model. The first is that the set of brands be *true* competitors; if choices are first made between groups of products within a class and then between products within groups, the choice process is hierarchical and the model is inappropriate. (This assumption is equivalent to the brands being at the bottom of a branch in the Hendry system. See Chapter 7.) The second required assumption is that the market has stabilized; if it has not stabilized, preferences will be changing.

ASSESSOR assumes that the b coefficient does not change with the introduction of the new product. This assumption is equivalent to assuming that the product is entering an existing product category. The coefficient can be estimated by a maximum-likelihood procedure using paired-comparison data for existing brands, with the brand last bought or bought most often as the dependent variable.

The model for choice after trial of the new brand (z) is given by

$$L_{iz} = \frac{(V_{iz})^b}{(V_{iz})^b + \sum\limits_{\ell \in m_i} (V_{i\ell})^b} \qquad (19.36)$$

where $\qquad$ L_{iz} = probability that consumer i chooses brand z after having tried it
$\qquad$ m_i = brands in i's evoked set
$\qquad$ $V_{iz}, \{V_{i\ell}\}$ = preference scores after trying new brand

Thus eq. (19.35) is used *before* trial to calibrate coefficient b, and eq. (19.36) is used *after* the new product is tried to estimate purchase probabilities.

The market-share calculation takes into account that not all consumers have the new product in their relevant or evoked set of choices:

$$s = \frac{E_z \sum\limits_{i=1}^{N} L_{iz}}{N} \qquad (19.37)$$

where $\qquad$ s = estimated market share
$\qquad$ E_z = proportion of consumers who evoke new brand
$\qquad$ N = number of consumers measured

When significant variation in use rates exist, each L_{iz} is weighted by a use-level index. Similarly, the L_{iz} are weighted differently if they are not representative of the market demographically or in other ways.

Silk and Urban (1978) develop a relationship between E, the fraction of consumers who eventually evoke the new brand and include it in their relevant set of brands, and both the unaided-brand-awareness and the advertising-recall measures, which are collected on the premeasurement questionnaires.

Draw and Cannibalization Estimates. It is important for the multibrand manufacturer to develop an estimate of cannibalization and draw—the effect of the new brand on existing brand shares. After the new product is introduced, the market consists of two subpopulations: those who include the new brand in their relevant set of brands and those who do not. Let these population sizes be E_z and $1 - E_z$, respectively. Under a suitable set of assumptions, the effect of the new brand on any other brand j can be estimated:

$$L_{ij} = \begin{cases} \dfrac{(V_{ij})^b}{\displaystyle\sum_{\ell \in m_i} (V_{k\ell})^b} & \text{if } z \text{ is \textit{not} included in evoked set} \\[2em] \dfrac{(V_{ij})^b}{(V_{iz})^b + \displaystyle\sum_{\ell \in m_i} (V_{i\ell})^b} & \text{if } z \text{ is included in evoked set} \end{cases} \quad (19.38)$$

Now consider two populations: the brand z evokers (of which there are n^*) and the nonevokers (n^{**}), where $n^* + n^{**} = N$. Suppose we order the consumers so that the brand z evokers come first. Then for $i = 1, \ldots, n^*$ individual i evokes the brand; for $i = n^* + 1, \ldots, N$ the individual does not evoke the brand. The market shares for these two populations are

$$S_j^* = \sum_{i-1}^{n^*} \frac{L_{ij}}{n^*} \quad (19.39)$$

$$S_j^{**} = \sum_{i-n^*+1}^{N} \frac{L_{ij}}{N - n^*} \quad (19.40)$$

where the appropriate value of L_{ij} in eqs. (19.39) and (19.40) is taken from eq. (19.38). Now the evoking proportion E_z is a controllable quantity that depends on advertising, and the total share of brand j after introduction of the new brand is

$$S_j = E_z S_j^* + (1 - E_z) S_j^{**} \quad (19.41)$$

while the draw from brand j for z is

$$\text{draw}_j = S_j^{**} - S_j \quad (19.42)$$

Note that the draw_j in eq. (19.42), when summed over all competitors' brands, equals the share estimate for the new brand.

Assessment.   The ASSESSOR model makes two contributions. The first is a proposal for a convergent methodology, providing for increased diagnostics and checks of consistency for the pretest-market procedure. The second is the development of theoretical support for a modeling system for pretest-market evaluation.

Urban and Hauser (1980) report that 120 new packaged goods were tested with ASSESSOR. Some 60 percent of these products went to market, and data were available on 25 completed new-product test markets (p. 403). A share-point upward bias of 0.6 point was found. Without a correction for the bias the standard deviation of the difference between actual and predicted shares was 2.0 points. After a correction for the bias the standard deviation was 1.0 share point. The standard deviation of the share estimate permits a probability statement about test-market success and therefore provides an important managerial tool.

For example, suppose management required a minimum share for break-even of 6.0 percent, and ASSESSOR predicted 9.1. If we account for the model bias, the required share is 1.25 standard deviations above the predicted share: $(9.1 - 6.0 - 0.6)/2.0 = 1.25$. Under the assumption of appropriate normality, this result translates into about a 90 percent probability of achieving the minimum required share.

The procedure, while providing key benefits, has several significant weaknesses. Although trial is probably adequately measured, it is questionable whether repeat rates can be adequately measured by telephone questioning and/or purchasing. In addition, the repeat model, eq. (19.34), only considers first repeat and does not consider any of the depth-of-repeat information incorporated in Tracker or Eskin (1973). Also, the selection of a distribution index (D) is somewhat arbitrary and may serve more as a tuning factor than a control variable. A well-defined and relatively homogeneous market class and choice set are clearly required here, or the draw and cannibalization estimates will be inappropriate, due to the independence of irrelevant alternatives assumption. Furthermore, extension of the procedure beyond grocery items is questionable.

The model also does not explicitly include positioning information, marketing-mix diagnostics, or competitive effects, although model adjustments are possible. However, on net, the procedure is quite complete, is fundamentally sound, and is clearly being used.

Other Models

A number of repeat-purchase models for new products are available; they differ widely in assumptions, structure, and reported applicability. Exhibit 19.17 summarizes the more well-known, applied models along a variety of key dimensions. We note their key features briefly below.

Ahl (1970) simplifies the Parfitt-Collins procedure to forecast test-market share from panel data. He concentrates on volume and on a procedure to go from test-market data to national data. His model makes a number of overly simplistic assumptions.

Assmus (1975) developed the NEWPROD model, which is basically a simulation procedure for tracking potential buyers through stages of the adoption process to forecast new-product market shares. The model is easy to understand but may be too simplistic for broad use and is not based on extensive empirical experience.

Blackburn and Clancy's (1982) LITMUS model provides pretest-market sales forecasts and informal diagnostics, derived from laboratory-test-market and telephone-call-back data. The model includes a number of behavioral states and marketing-mix variables. Variable but encouraging performance was noted for 20 new-product introductions.

Burger, Lavidge, and Gundee's (1978) COMP model is a pretest-market model that uses a set of measurements similar to those in ASSESSOR. Trial, purchase, and repurchase intent are linked to the planning advertising and distribution effort and to probabilities-of-purchase estimates. Regression analyses and data manipulation are performed to obtain the desired estimates without sound theoretical or behavioral foundation. Validation results for 11 products are reported.

Choffray and colleagues's (1979) pretest-market procedure also uses data-collection techniques similar to those of ASSESSOR. The model relies on a critical preference ratio to relate relative new-brand preference to purchase likelihood. It uses discriminant analysis to derive trial estimates and provides a quantitative link between product perceptions and market-share estimates with detailed diagnostics. Good results for five products are reported.

Claycamp and Liddy (1969) developed a model relating a series of critical decision and exogenous variables to awareness and trial. Independent variables, estimated by experts, are input into the model to predict awareness and trial. The model does not include a repeat stage.

Eskin (1973) focuses on the structure of repeat rates for accurate test-market forecasts. He derives several empirical generalizations but focuses solely on the repeat model, neglecting trial and awareness stages. His empirical generalizations have been studied more rigorously by Kalwani and Silk (1980). Good predictive accuracy is reported.

Eskin and Malec (1976) derive a model relating the growth rate and sales potential of new products to distribution, promotion, and potential consumer-class size with a data base of 50 recent new-product introductions. Repeat rate is a simplification of Eskin's (1973) model. The model has not been validated.

Massy's (1969) STEAM model is a detailed simulation model for predicting postintroduction equilibrium sales volume from diary panel data. The model incorporates heterogeneous purchase behavior at the household level, but validation results are unsatisfactory.

EXHIBIT 19-17 **Test- and pretest-market models.**

	1. Ahl (1970)	2. Assmus (1975), NEWPROD	3. Blackburn and Clancy (1982), LITMUS	4. Blattberg and Golanty (1978), TRACKER	5. Burger, Lavidge, and Gundee (1978), COMP
Model Focus					
Pretest			X		X
Test	X	X		X	
Validation Reports					
number	7	3	20	11	11
accuracy[a]	G	?	S	G	G
Features					
Awareness		X	X	X	X
initial awareness					
decay over time		X	X	X	
distinctiveness of product concept					
advertising effects		X			
threshold				X	
diminishing returns		X	X	X	
sampling effect		X	X		
coupon/promotion effect		X	X		
Trial Stage	X	X			
distinctiveness of product					X
differentiation over time		X	X		
price sensitivity				X	
distribution sensitivity		X			
advertising effects			X		
sampling effects		X	X	X	
coupon/promotion effect		X	X		
word-of-mouth effect					
Repeat Stage	X	X			
product satisfaction					X
depth of repeat		X	X	X	
differentiation by time since last purchase					
price sensitivity					

6. Choffray et al. (1979)	7. Claycamp and Liddy (1969)	8. Eskin (1973)	9. Eskin and Malec (1976)	10. Massy (1969), STEAM	11. Parfitt and Collins (1968)	12. Pringle, Wilson and Brody (1982) NEWS	13. Silk and Urban (1978), ASSESSOR	14. Urban (1970), SPRINTER MOD III
X	X		X			X	X	
		X		X	X	X		X
5	7	—	—	1	24	28	25	1
G	G	G	—	U	S	G	G	G
X						X	X	X
						X		X
	X							
X								
	X					X		
X						X		
	X					X		
X								
	X				X			
X		X	X		X	X		X
								X
X	X	X				X	X	X
								X
X						X	X	X
	X					X		
								X
X	X	X	X	X	X	X	X	X
X								
	X			X	X		X	
	X			X	X	X		X
								X

EXHIBIT 19-17   **Test- and pretest-market models (*Continued*).**

	1. Ahl (1970)	2. Assmus (1975), NEWPROD	3. Blackburn and Clancy (1982), LITMUS	4. Blattberg and Golanty (1978), TRACKER	5. Burger, Lavidge and Gundee (1978), COMP
distribution sensitivity		X			
Buying Level	X		X	X	
differentiated by trial/repeat			X	X	
time of or depth of repeat					
consumer groups					
Competitive Response					
Product Design Diagnostics[b]	N	N	I	I	I

[a]U = unsatisfactory; S = satisfactory; G = good.

[b]N = none; I = informal; F = formal.

BBDO's NEWS model (Pringle, Wilson, and Brody, 1982) is a detailed model that provides profitability analysis for a given market plan or for early test-market rents. Individuals are traced through a number of behavioral states with a variety of market influences. A large data base of normative values, collected by BBDO, is used as a diagnostic aid. Validation data on market share for 28 products are provided.

Urban's (1970) SPRINTER MOD III is a model-based information system that analyzes test-market results and aids in improving marketing-mix variables by simulating awareness, intent, search, choice, and postpurchase behavior. It is a detailed, deterministic, multiperiod model that incorporates competitive response, as well as an explicit go/no-go decision framework. Although conceptually appealing and complete, its framework of over 500 equations and its large data needs have limited its application.

Other models have been developed and are being used, but their success and applicability have not been reported. As is clear from Exhibit 19.17, a wide range of capabilities has been included in these models. Significantly, the most successful procedures balance complexity with parsimony. Furthermore, a sounder theoretical base is gradually being developed for these procedures. It is encouraging to note that this area appears to be in an advanced state of development and that the models are being widely used.

Interested readers should see Assmus (1981), Narasimhan and Sen (1983), Robinson (1981), Urban and Hauser (1980) and Wilson and Pringle (1981) for up-to-date reviews of this area. Clearly, a critical need here is for uniform and understandable standards of validation and of reporting of

6. Choffray et al. (1979)	7. Claycamp and Liddy (1969)	8. Eskin (1973)	9. Eskin and Malec (1976)	10. Massy (1969), STEAM	11. Parfitt and Collins (1968)	12. Pringle, Wilson and Brody (1982) NEWS	13. Silk and Urban (1978), ASSESSOR	14. Urban (1970), SPRINTER MOD III
X								
X						X	X	X
						X		
								X
X								X
								X
F	N	N	N	N	N	I	I	I

model performance (Urban and Katz, 1982). Different measures are used, and therefore the results of the different models are difficult to compare. Another need is for procedures that can be used for a truly new product.

Summary

Decision making is most hazardous in new-product development and introduction. This is an age in which companies must introduce new products to survive and yet do so with the knowledge that a substantial number will fail. The costs involved are considerable, and alert management is taking whatever steps will help reduce the risks in the way of organization, professional staffing, marketing research, and model construction.

The variety of current models for new-product forecasting and planning reflects to a large extent the variety of new-product situations in which companies engage. New-product situations can be distinguished by the degree of newness of the product and the degree of product repurchasability. Product newness ranges from the truly new-product innovation to the new brand to the new model, style, or package size of an existing brand. Product repurchasability ranges from those that are bought only once to those that are bought occasionally to those that are bought frequently.

This last distinction enables us to separate the analyses of the first-time purchase from the repeat purchases, under the assumption that different factors are involved. The occurrence of first-time purchases can be analyzed as a diffusion process. Such a process uses a few macroparameters to locate a curve that describes the spread of the innovation through a population over time.

A number of different models have been developed that treat the diffusion as an imitation, an innovation, or a combination of processes. Recently, control variables that influence the rate of diffusion have been incorporated into these models. In addition, important work is continuing on ways of predicting the parameters of these models so that product success and sales forecasts can be developed earlier and more accurately.

Frequently purchased products require that attention be paid to the repeat-purchase phenomenon. The modeling and estimation of repeat rates is a key feature in the models that were developed for analyzing test-market and pretest-market (laboratory-simulation) results. More-recent models incorporate and operationalize the concept of depth of repeat, because the probability of repeat purchase appears to vary with the number of past purchases.

Both for frequently and for infrequently purchased products a number of clearly useful models are available. The major needs in the area are better reporting and consolidation of results for improved comparative analysis and attention to market situations in which the product is clearly new.

Problems

19.1 Using the Fourt-Woodlock market-penetration model, compute the increments in penetration for the first five periods for a company whose rate of penetration of untapped potential is 0.4 and whose potential sales as a percent of all buyers is 0.6. Verify mathematically that the sum of the individual increments approaches 0.6 as t goes to infinity.

19.2 For a particular product, the coefficient of innovation p (for the Bass model) is 0.05 and the coefficient of imitation r is 0.2. The total number of potential buyers is 100,000.
  a. Determine the time when sales will reach its peak.
  b. Calculate the magnitude of peak sales.
  c. Suppose that the Bass model is fitted to empirical data, resulting in the following expression:

$$Q_t = 410 + 0.39Q_T - 10^{-6}Q_T^2$$

  From this equation, determine the total number of potential adopters $\overline{Q}$.

19.3 What limitations do you see in the ASSESSOR trial model? In the repeat model? What is the benefit of the convergent approach? What is the applicability of the approach to consumer durables? To industrial products?

19.4 A group of consumers is asked to rate five different brands of coffee on two characteristics: strength and body. Each brand is rated on a scale of 1 to 7 for each characteristic. Each consumer is also asked to rate an ideal coffee. The average brand ratings are as follows:

Brand	Strength	Body
A	3	4
B	6	2
C	6	3
D	2	3
E	1	1
Ideal	5	5

a. Represent these perceptions in euclidean 2-dimensional space and order the brands according to their probable market share if product characteristics were the only factor that counted.

b. Suppose that a regression analysis found the following relationship to be true:

$$M_i = \frac{K}{d_{iS}^2} + \frac{3K}{d_{iB}^2}$$

where M_i = market share of brand i
   K = constant
   d_{iS} = distance for brand i from ideal on strength
   d_{iB} = distance for brand i from ideal on body

   i. Find K. (*Hint:* What does ΣM_i equal?)
   ii. Calculate the shares of brands A through E from the model.

c. Suppose a new brand F was found to be rated as

   Strength = 3;   Body = 3

   What would the estimate of its market share be? How would it draw that share from other brands? (*Hint:* Remember that market shares *must* sum to 1.)

19.5 The ABC Company recently introduced a new product. The product has been on the market for 7 wk, and the sales manager wishes to determine the product's long-run share of the market. The research department has provided data on the cumulative-penetration and repeat-purchase rates for the product to date. These data are presented in the following table:

Week	1	2	3	4	5	6	7
Cumulative Penetration	0.13	0.20	0.26	0.30	0.33	0.35	0.36
Repurchase Rate		0.48	0.42	0.37	0.33	0.30	0.28

A test-market survey has estimated that product awareness in the market is 73% and that 92% of the outlets are carrying the brand. Company customers tend to be somewhat lighter users than average product-class users (index = 0.92, where 1.0 is average). Provide a long-term market-share projection for the product.

a. Assuming test-market conditions are duplicated nationally.

b. Assuming national awareness is 62% and only 80% of the outlets are carrying the brand.

c. Suppose that management has found that

Awareness = 0.4 ln (advertising dollars)

where advertising dollars are measured in millions. Assume 90% distribution, $10,000,000 in sales per market-share point, and gross margin, before advertising, is 15% of sales. How much should be spent on advertising to maximize profit? (*Hint:*

Profit = market size · share · margin − advertising dollars

Share = awareness (advertising dollars) · other factors

Find the profit-maximizing level of advertising.)

19.6 A firm has been evaluating new products on the basis of three criteria: growth, stability, and production factors. It has recently collected data on the success or failure of 10 products, each of which had been rated on these three criteria. Use a discriminant-analysis program to determine the weights for each criterion. Which criterion is the most important? Evaluate the success of the discriminant function in terms of the number of misclassifications. (Fitzroy, 1976, p. 307)

Products	Stability Factors	Growth Fractors	Production Factors
Successful			
1	9	8	6
2	8	7	5
3	7	7	5
4	10	8	3
5	9	6	4
6	8	7	2
Unsuccessful			
1	4	3	2
2	2	2	3
3	3	1	4
4	2	3	3

19.7 After a number of weeks in the test market, a consumer product has reached a penetration level of 42% with repeat purchases of 32%. For the product field in question, total annual sales are estimated to be 186,000 units in the test-market area, and the test area contains 12.3% of all households. What is the predicted national sales of the product if it is further estimated that while it is in the national market, distribution efficiency will be at a level of 82% of that reached during test? On what assumptions is your estimate based? (Fitzroy, 1976, p. 308)

19.8 A new product has been tested by 607 housewives who were asked to indicate their buying intentions. The housewives were then classified by age and the following results were obtained:

Buying Intentions	Age of housewife			
	16–24	25–34	35–44	45+
Definitely intend buying	18	16	41	16
Intend to buy	26	33	30	10
Might or might not buy	37	18	52	23
Do not intend buying	31	25	55	28
Definitely do not intend buying	36	21	60	31

From these data, would you expect the appeal of the product to vary widely depending on the age of the housewife? (Fitzroy, 1976, p. 308)

19.9 The government wishes to stimulate the growth of photovoltaics (solar cells) in order to reduce dependence on fossil fuels. We assume that PV (photovoltaic) sales will increase according to a diffusion-of-innovation process with the following characteristics.

1. The potential market is determined by the value in use of PV products, expressed as the cost per kilowatt-hour of the best competitive fuel minus the cost per kilowatt-hour of PV. (The latter is an imputed cost since the sun is free and the expense is largely a fixed investment.)

2. The sales of PV will follow a growth curve in which sales rate will be proportional to the following: (a) the number of units already installed; (b) the visibility (publicity and advertising) given to the installed units; (c) a function of the cost-per-kilowatt-hour difference between PV and the best competitive fuel; (d) the amount of the potential PV market not yet converted.

3. The cost, and therefore, the price, of PV will follow a learning curve, that is, will decrease as a function of total units produced, rapidly at first and then slowly.

   To model the process, let

y = cumulative amount of PV capacity installed at time t, MW (megawatts)

m = maximum potential demand for PV, MW

a. As a sample first model, suppose

$$\frac{dy}{dt} = ay\left(1 - \frac{y}{m}\right)$$

Find $y(t)$ for this model. Starting from an initial installation of y_0 megawatts, sketch $y(t)$. *Note:*

$$\int \frac{dx}{x(ax^n + c)} = \frac{1}{cn} \log \frac{x^n}{ax^n + c}$$

b. For a second model we go to discrete time and include more phenomena. Consider a particular PV application (e.g., irrigation). Let

y_t = cumulative installed capacity at t, MW
p_t = installed price of PV, \$/kWh (kilowatt-hour)
c_t = delivered price of best competitive fuel, \$/kWh
$u_t = c_t - p_t$ price advantage of PV at t

$g(u)$ = attractiveness function for buying PV
m = total market potential of application
$p(y)$ = unit price after y units have been built and installed

i. Sketch what $g(u)$ and $p(y)$ might look like. To take specific analytic forms, suppose that the attractiveness function for buying PV is exponential, with relative price

$$g(u) = e^{u/a}$$

Take a = \$0.10/kWh. For a learning curve, assume

$$p_t = p_0 e^{-y_{t-1}/b}$$

Currently, a peak kilowatt (i.e., a photovoltaic cell that generates a kilowatt with the sun shining on it) costs \$50,000. Suppose that after 10,000 MW of PVs has been produced, the price will be \$500/kW. Assuming the current amount of installed PV is 1 MW, find p_0 and b.

ii. Suppose the process follows the following growth model:

$$y_t = y_{t-1} + \alpha y_{t-1} g(u_t) \left(1 - \frac{y_{t-1}}{m}\right)$$

where m = total potential sales, MW
          = 20,000
       α = proportionality constant determining basic growth rate of process; represents new PV sales as a fraction of cumulated sales to date under conditions of price parity (fraction per year)
          = 0.5

Starting with y_0 = 1 MW, follow the process for 2 yr, determining y. Assume c_t = \$0.05/kWh for all t.

c. The government proposes to intervene and buy the initial production up to y such that $u = 0$ and give it away or otherwise see that it is installed.

i. How much will it cost to buy that production?
ii. Starting with y_0 at the production found in part i, run the process 5 yr.
iii. Suppose the government also conducts a publicity program that increases α by 50%. Run the process for 3 yr.

d. What improvements would you suggest in the model?

6

Making It Happen

CHAPTER 20

The Marketing Decision-Support System

The main purpose of this book has been to organize and synthesize the theory and associated models relevant for marketing decision making. In this chapter and the next we concentrate on issues of introducing and using marketing models for decision making. In the next chapter we discuss implementation; in this chapter we discuss an emerging problem-solving technology that consists of people, knowledge, and computer software and hardware wired into the management process. We believe that this technology will be seen in retrospect as the result of an evolution in the use of computer systems for management decisions.

In the first two sections we trace the need for marketing information and the evolution of business systems, from electronic-data-processing (EDP) systems that have become essential for the efficient operation of large-scale business and government enterprises to the set of software tools designed to support managers who are making and implementing decisions. Following Gorry and Scott Morton (1971), we call these latter tools decision-support systems (DSS) or, more specifically, marketing decision-support systems (MDSS). General business problems are handled first; the focus is then narrowed to marketing problems. Following that, we illustrate the MDSS concept with three sample cases. We then collect and develop guidelines for successful system design, and conclude with remarks on implementation and the future of DSS, forming a bridge to Chapter 21.

Information Needs

The 1980s have been called the age of information, and over the past several decades business has increased its mastery over the resources of the firm. But it is hard to find company executives anywhere who are substantially satisfied with their marketing information. Typical complaints include the following:

There is too much information of the wrong kind.

There is not enough information of the right kind.

Information is too dispersed to be useful.

Information arrives too late to be useful.

Information often arrives in a form that leaves no idea of its accuracy and, therefore, lacks credibility.

Most firms are anxious to adapt their information supply to the needs of the modern economy. Three trends make the need for marketing information stronger than ever before. The first is a shift from local and regional to national and international marketing. The international firm requires quick access to information from areas where their products are sold, which may be removed from the location of management. A second trend is a transition from buyer needs to buyer desires. As society becomes increasingly affluent, buying becomes a highly personal expressive act, and sellers must depend on systematic research data (rather than common sense) to understand the latent, as well as the overt, desires of consumers. The third trend is the transition from price to nonprice competition. As trends toward market segmentation take hold and as sellers increase their reliance on competitive weaponry such as branding, product differentiation, advertising, and sales promotion, they require timelier and increased information on the effectiveness of these marketing tools.

On the supply side these explosive information needs are being met by the comparable explosion in electronic technology. Computer hardware and software of increasing sophistication, linked to broader and more accurate data-collection capabilities, have provided an opportunity for better information processing. Other devices for the handling and transmitting of data (closed circuit/split-cable TV, copying machines, tape recorders, etc.) have created a revolution in information-handling capabilities.

The Evolution of Business Systems: From TBS to DSS

Cohen (1981) suggests that decision-support systems are emerging as the result of an evolution in the development and the use of computer hardware and software for business problems. Roughly speaking, business-application systems can be grouped into four classes: transaction-based systems (TBS), data-based systems (DBS, or data-based management systems, DBMS), management-information systems (MIS), and decision-support systems (DSS). Of these four system types, three are application systems that directly relate to business functions, while the fourth, DBS, is designed to support and improve the performance of application systems by providing better storage, maintenance, and access to data.

Transaction-based Systems

Dating from the late 1950s and early 1960s, transaction-based systems represent the earliest use of computers in business applications. Their functions are to collect and report data generated by business transactions in standard business functions, such as accounting, finance, and marketing. TBSs, such as accounting and reporting programs, production-control programs, sales-reporting programs, and the like, emphasize essentially clerical activities and are aimed toward automating the storage and retrieval of regularly generated data. The focus is on reducing costs, improving accuracy, and allowing quicker access to data concerning day-to-day operations. The output of these systems is usually a set of standard reports produced on a periodic basis. The systems are usually expensive to design (tens to hundreds of thousands of dollars) and must be extensively redesigned when there are major changes in transaction patterns.

Management-Information Systems

After the introduction of DBSs for coordinating disparate files of transaction data, MISs were developed to facilitate management use of the diverse sets of data. Their purpose is to process data into information for more complete use of multiple data sources within the same firm. MISs represent an evolution from TBS, more because of the way data from diverse sources can be processed than because of the way reporting occurs. Examples of MISs include financial-control systems, material-requirements planning systems, and the like. As with TBSs, the system must be extensively redesigned if the DBS changes or if management's information needs change.

Decision-Support Systems

As the "significant current frontier in the use of computers in business organizations" (Alter, 1980, p. 3), DSSs emphasize ad hoc use and flexibility in facilitating line-management, planning, and staff functions. In contrast to TBSs, which activate and facilitate data storage, DSSs aim to improve and expedite the processes by which people make and communicate decisions. Thus the emphasis in DSSs is on increasing individual and organizational effectiveness rather than improving data-processing effectiveness.

From a survey of 114 users and data-processing managers, Alloway (1980) found that about 85 percent of installed business systems can be classified as TBSs, about 10 percent MISs, and about 5 percent DSSs.

It is useful to think of business systems on a continuum of increasing user flexibility. Because a TBS collects and reports on transaction-generated data, it must closely parallel the firm's business operations. While this characteristic simplifies the initial system design, changes in business operations necessitate changes in the TBS. This process, known as system maintenance, can run as high as 40 percent of the system's total annualized cost (Wolverton, 1974).

An MIS's link to business operations is less direct because it operates through a data base and a DBS. Only if the data base changes will every MIS in the firm need alteration. Although a complete overhaul of all MIS systems in a firm is rare, it is not uncommon for a single manager's information needs to change with time. When the rate of change of such needs is slow, an internal data-processing group can provide adequate system maintenance. However, when those needs change rapidly, an MIS may need to be altered so frequently that it will be uneconomical to run (Morgan and Soden, 1973).

A DSS is essentially a rapidly changing MIS. When designed properly, a DSS can evolve rapidly, whether the need for change comes from new users, new data, new models, or new applications. It is designed so that on-going design and maintenance represent a closed loop between the user and the system. This technique eliminates the need for corporate data-processing involvement, although the design and maintenance are often performed by a systems-liaison person working out of either the users' or the systems' department.

Before addressing marketing DSSs, we review the range of DSS users and applications. Alter (1980) develops a taxonomy along a single dimension called the "degree of action implication of system output"—that is, the degree to which the system output can directly determine a decision. Exhibit 20.1 categorizes types of DSSs along this dimension and relates them to a spectrum of generic operations.

Alter reports that the 56 systems he reviewed fell into seven reasonably distinct types:

1. *File-drawer systems* allow immediate access to data items. An example is a system for facilitating the production of integrated circuits, in which daily work reports by more than 1000 machine operators on more than 50 manufacturing steps are assessed via a cathode ray tube to monitor work flow and avoid bottlenecks.
2. *Data-analysis systems* allow manipulation of data, typically by non-managerial line or staff personnel, for analysis of historical data files. An example is a budget-analysis system used by division controllers in a bank to expedite reviews of budgetary performance. A CRT allows

EXHIBIT 20-1   **Parallels between generic operations and types of DSSs.**

Generic Operations	Types of DSS
Retrieving a single item of information	
	A. File-drawer systems allow immediate access to data items
Providing a mechanism for ad hoc data analysis	B. Data-analysis systems allow the manipulation of data by means of operators tailored to the task and setting of operators of a general nature
	C. Analysis-information systems provide access to a series of data bases and small models
Providing prespecified aggregations of data in the form of reports	D. Accounting models calculate the consequences of planned actions on the basis of accounting definitions
	E. Representational models estimate the consequences of actions on the basis of models that are partially nondefinitional
Estimating the consequences of proposed decisions	F. Optimization models provide guidelines for action by generating the optimal solution consistent with a series of constraints
Proposing decisions	G. Suggestion models perform mechanical work leading to a specific suggested decision for a fairly structured task
Making decisions	

SOURCE: Alter, *Decision Support Systems: Current Practice and Continuing Challenges,* © 1980. Addison-Wesley, Reading, Mass. Figure 16, p. 75. Reprinted with permission.

controllers to review data in budget reports and only annotate (and hard-copy) variances that are significant.

3. *Analysis-information systems* provide easy access to a series of data bases and small models. An example is a system in a consumer-products company, which deals with data bases on sales, advertising, promotion, pricing, and related data. The system is used, in conjunction with a statistical package, for a variety of ad hoc analyses.

4. *Accounting models* project the consequences of planned action with

accounting definitions. They typically generate income statements, balance sheets, or other outcome measures, while inputs are usually estimates of costs and revenue by a firm's business unit.

5. *Representational models* estimate the consequences of actions with models that are, at least partly, nondefinitional. Most simulation models fall into this category. A major manufacturing company uses a risk-analysis system to analyze acquisition and expansion decisions. After the selection of factors that have major impact on the project, the relationship between those factors and profit and other output measures is established. For each factor a probability distribution reflects the range of uncertainty, and simulation generates the probability distribution of rate of return, net present value, and the like.

6. *Optimization models* provide guidelines for managerial actions by generating an optimal solution to a problem consistent with a series of constraints. A large oil company uses a linear-programming system to integrate its production and marketing efforts for long-range planning.

7. *Suggestion models* generate suggested action from mathematical procedures, which range from decision rules to optimization methods. These systems bypass other procedures for generating suggestions and therefore are even more structured than optimization methods. A cardboard-box manufacturer prices its products on the basis of factors such as dimensions, type of joint, coatings, reinforcement, and so on, which are input for a suggestion model that produces the base prices.

Alter's taxonomy can be compared to Keen and Scott Morton's (1978) spectrum of decision and task types, in which decisions and tasks are divided into three zones by the degree of environmental structure. At one extreme are "unstructured" tasks, like hiring and firing. Data to support these tasks are rarely available, and the decision-making mechanisms are too poorly understood for effective modeling. Thus unstructured tasks rarely receive computer decision support. At the other end of the spectrum are well-understood and institutionalized "structured" tasks, which change slowly over time. Managers rarely spend much time on these decisions (e.g., when should a stock item be reordered?) because the data and the solution process are readily available. More-standard data-processing systems are appropriately used here. In the middle are "semistructured" tasks and decisions, supported by subjective data and implicit models. Here a manager and a support system can be mutually beneficial. Many marketing decisions fall into this category.

In summary:

Decision support systems are small-scale interactive systems designed to provide managers with flexible, responsive tools that act, in effect, as a staff assistant, to whom they can delegate more routine parts of their job. DSS's support, rather than replace, a manager's judgment. They do not impose solutions and methods, but provide access to information, models and reports and help extend the manager's scope of analysis (Keen, 1980d, p. 1).

The Marketing Decision-Support System

How can this concept be applied to marketing decisions? Little (1979a) feels that a *marketing* decision-support system (MDSS) is

> a coordinated collection of data, systems, tools and techniques with supporting software and hardware by which an organization gathers and interprets relevant information from business and environment and turns it into a basis for marketing action (p. 11).

In his view a manager uses an MDSS to learn about the business environment and to take action with respect to it. Little's artistic view of the inanimate part of this process is reproduced in Exhibit 20.2. This process has five components: data, models, statistics, optimization, and Q/A (communication with the system). We review them in turn.

Data

Organizations face an often bewildering stream of data and information, which arises from a number of sources: personal contacts, business publications, and marketing research data, as well as the multitude of business transactions, such as orders, shipments, and records of internal actions (advertising expenditures). Decision making requires certain information, which either may or may not currently exist. Data that already exist are called *secondary* data, while data that the firm must gather are called *primary* data.

Secondary Data.   Before going to the trouble and expense of gathering primary data, existing sources should be examined. Although secondary data are not always available in as accurate and complete a form as would be ideal and are often gathered for different purposes than the current one, they are often very useful. The challenge is to be familiar with the major sources of data and to use them critically. Two classes of existing information useful for marketing analysis are internal-accounting files and marketing-intelligence sources. The former provides executives with *results data*, while the latter provides *happenings data*.

The earliest and most basic source of information is the *internal-accounting system*. This system reports orders, sales, inventories, receivables, payables, and so on and allows management to compare actual and expected levels of performance and to spot opportunities and problems. The heart of the system is the order-shipping-billing cycle. Sales representatives,

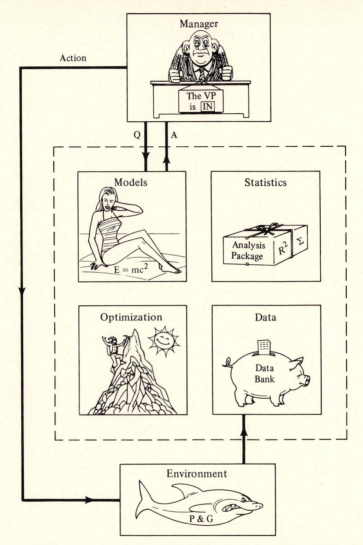

EXHIBIT 20-2   **A manager uses a marketing decision-support system (MDSS) to learn about the business environment and take action with respect to it.** (Source: Little, 1979a, p. 10.)

dealers, and customers dispatch orders to the firm. Then the order departments prepare multicopy invoices and dispatch them to various departments. Items that are out of stock are back-ordered. Items that are shipped are accompanied by shipping and billing documents, which are also sent to multiple departments.

The time marketing executives have to wait for reports on sales activity varies. In retailing operations like Sears and J. C. Penney, electronic cash registers and automatic data entry allow daily (or even more frequent) reporting of sales levels. In consumer-food companies warehouse-withdrawal reports are issued with fair regularity, but actual retail-purchase reports, which are based on special store or consumer-panel audits, take about 2 mo. Many companies are using sophisticated systems to improve the timeliness of this type of data reporting.

Sources of *marketing intelligence* provide information about changing conditions in both the macro- and task environments. Companies can improve their use of these sources in several ways: (1) systematizing data-collection efforts by the salesforce, (2) using additional intelligence sources, and (3) buying information from specialized marketing research services.

The salesforce is in a good position to pick up significant bits of information that would never appear in the usual summary statistics of company sales activity. To utilize this source properly, sales representatives should be trained to be intelligence gatherers for the firm. Furthermore, call reports that are easy to fill out should be used by the salesforce, and an intelligence office should be established to receive and disseminate the information. Finally, sales managers should review the intelligence performance of their representatives and make it a factor in pay raises.

Similar steps should be taken to motivate and utilize *additional intelligence sources*. Sales managers, dealers, advertising agencies, and others can systematically produce intelligence information. In addition, it is often desirable to hire full-time specialists to gather marketing intelligence through such means as (1) pricing or purchasing competitors' products, (2) attending open houses and trade shows, (3) reading competitors' published reports and attending stockholders' meetings, (4) talking to competitors' former employees and present employees, dealers, distributors, suppliers, and freight agents, (5) hiring a clipping service, and (6) reading business and trade-association publications. [See Boyd, Westfall, and Stasch (1977) and Choffray and Lilien (1980c) for examples and guides to domestic and international information sources.]

There are a variety of *special marketing-intelligence services* that collect data that can be purchased by marketers. For example, the A. C. Nielsen Company sells bimonthly data, based on a sample of 1600 stores, on brand shares, retail prices, percentage of stores stocking items, and percentage of stockout stores. The Market Research Corporation of America (MRCA) sells reports, based on the purchase diaries of a representative panel of 7500 households across the country, on weekly movements of brand shares, sizes, prices, and deals. Clipping services may be hired to report on competitive-advertising expenditures, media mixes, and advertising appeals. Recently, some more creative data-collection systems have been emerging, including UPC data, TELLUS, and X/Market.

Universal product codes (UPCs or scanner data) are rapidly increasing in popularity in retailing environments. Scanner data may be the best available solution to collecting decentralized consumer spending data. Especially when linked to credit card purchases (as they have been in several experimental markets), scanner data provide an unobtrusive source of accurate diary-panel data. Another key advantage of UPC data is their ability to be aggregated as desired by product, package size, brand, price, store, or market.

TELLUS (MSI Data Corporation) is an "electronic pushbutton questionnaire that can conduct in-store interviews at a fraction of the cost and time of mall intercepts" (Cadotte, 1980). It is a freestanding microcomputer capable of prompting and storing answers for up to a dozen questions. Usually the unit is positioned in a heavily trafficked area. Its novelty has the potential to attract a broader cross section of respondents than traditional data-collection methods.

X/Markets (from Economic Information Systems, Inc.) is an interactive, on-line, time-sharing computer system that processes and distributes industrial-marketing information. As a marketing tool, it allows the user to identify, measure, and analyze marketing potential at a corporate or industry level. The system aggregates data to provide information by SIC code on employment, sales volume, and market penetration by geographic region (Berger, 1980).

Primary Data.   When secondary data are not available or are of questionable quality, researchers must collect primary data. There are four basic methods of primary collection: observation, experimentation, the survey method, and judgmental assessment.

In *observation* the researcher attempts to learn about the problem by observing the relevant actors. This method has been used to study (1) the movement of shoppers through department stores, (2) the percentage of shoppers who stopped in front of a particular display, (3) the eye movements of shoppers who looked at the display, and (4) the selling appeals used by sales personnel with customers. Thus it can be used to study both sales techniques and consumer responses. Its main advantage is that it generally leads to a more objective picture of overt behavior than can be expected from personal accounts: it avoids the problem of response bias.

However, observation introduces two new biases. It assumes that the investigators are accurate and diligent observers. Instruments, such as tape recorders and cameras, are usually included to improve observational accuracy. It also assumes that the act of observing the marketing process does not change the behavior of those being observed, which is why concealed observation is often attempted. Nevertheless, the method yields little or no information about consumers' state of mind, buying motives and images.

At the other extreme is *experimentation*. One of the major weaknesses of the observational method is that there is little or no control over the behavior or environment being observed. Behavior is observed in its natural setting with all the unique and uncontrollable factors that go with it. Therefore plain observation rarely gives conclusive proof of cause-and-effect relationships in marketing.

To test hypotheses about the effects of particular marketing stimuli on behavior, the experimenter must introduce some controls. The experimental method introduces selected stimuli into a controlled environment and systematically varies them. To the extent that extraneous factors are eliminated or controlled, the observed effects can be related to the variations in the stimuli. The control eliminates competing hypotheses that might also explain the observed phenomena.

The most effective use of funds for market experimentation requires careful experimental design, which involves decisions on the number of subjects, the length of the experiment, and the types of control. These are technical problems and are treated in depth in Banks (1965). Experimentation is probably the best way to parameterize many models—and probably the least utilized. DSS developments are making microlevel experiments possible. For an excellent treatment of the theory of experimental design and its application in a marketing context, see Churchill (1979).

The most common method of generating primary data is through *surveys.* Compared with either direct observation or experimentation, surveys yield a broader range of information and are effective for a large number of research problems. They can produce information on socioeconomic characteristics, attitudes, opinions, motives, and overt behavior and are an effective way of gathering information for planning product features, advertising copy, advertising media, sales promotions, channels of distribution, and other marketing variables.

A good survey requires expert planning. The research director faces many alternative ways to collect the information and must decide among survey methods, research instruments, and sampling plans. These decisions constitute the research strategy.

Suppose a company wants to draw a sample of people and interview them about their knowledge and attitudes toward the company's products. There are a large number of possible research strategies. Exhibit 20.3 shows four of the more common ones. The first strategy is to collect a limited amount of information by making telephone calls to a sample of households chosen in a systematic way by telephone. The second is to send questionnaires to a group of magazine subscribers. The third strategy is to take a large-scale national probability sample, and the fourth is to carry out some in-depth interviews with a small group of product users.

Another way to gather primary data is through *subjective estimation,* soliciting and pooling estimates from company consultants and knowledgeable executives. It is useful where numbers do not exist but where there are experts who can produce better-than-average estimates. This approach to data gathering was discussed in Chapter 5.

In summary, an MDSS must capture and make accessible key market-

EXHIBIT 20-3   **Some alternative research strategies for collecting consumer information about a product.**

Elements of the Strategy	Strategy 1	Strategy 2	Strategy 3	Strategy 4
Survey method	Telephone interviews ↓	Mail interviews ↓	Personal interviews ↓	Personal interviews ↓
Research instrument	with a few factual questions ↓	with a 2-page questionnaire ↓	with many questions ↓	with projective tests ↓
Sampling plan	to a small sample of households chosen by random-digit dealing in the target area	to all subscribers to a magazine	to a large sample of subjects chosen on a national probability-sampling basis	to a dozen people found using the product

ing variables, such as sales, price, advertising, promotion, and perceptual/attitudinal information, in sufficient detail and in readily accessible form. Few companies do an adequate data-collection-and-maintenance job. Data are often costly to collect and maintain and are worthless by themselves. The other elements of the MDSS and the interface with marketing management create the value.

Models

The main focus of this book has been the second element of the MDSS, the set of *models*. Models can range from a way of looking at and structuring data (implicit models) to the more-explicit models discussed in this book. Models aid in planning, decision making, and a range of less publicized supporting tasks required for market analysis and understanding. We believe that explicit models are more valuable because of their direct relationship with data, statistics, and the optimization/policy-evaluation elements in the MDSS.

Statistics

Statistics is the process of relating models to data. Statistical operations range from the simple (addition, subtraction, etc.) to the most sophisticated multivariate techniques (factor analysis, nonlinear parameter estimation, etc.). In the DSS the simpler statistical functions are frequently the most useful. Simple statistical functions include adding (making significant figures from many smaller, trivial numbers), segregating numbers into groups, taking ratios, making comparisons, plotting relationships, identifying exceptional cases, and the like. These manipulations provide the basic information needed for many of the models reviewed here, as well as for the production of standard managerial models, such as forecasting and budgeting, pro forma profit and loss and balance sheets.

This discussion should not be taken to minimize the importance of the statistical methods reviewed earlier but rather to point out the importance of the accessibility of simple, more basic statistical operations in the normal course of decision making.

Optimization

The decision maker seeks to improve the operation of his organization. The model-based method for doing so is loosely called optimization or policy evaluation (Chapter 6). The most frequently used approach to optimization is case analysis, in which different numbers are calculated and compared. As the problem becomes more complicated, ranking a series of numbers may be required. Finally, as discussed in Chapter 6, there are many cases where the more formal analytical-optimization and mathematical-programming techniques of management science become appropriate.

Q/A

The last and in many ways the most critical element in the DSS is the user interface. The manager and his staff must communicate with the system. "Computers are impossible to work with, but are getting better" (Little, 1979a, p. 23). The right software (programs), interfaces (terminals), data files, and other information can be used in ways that are highly effective. The increasing speed and decreasing cost of computation are pushing the frontier of DSS application. Hardware costs are plummeting, and a revolution in software is making MDSSs accessible to an increasingly wide range of users.

The current software philosophy is to let the computer solve its own problems. For example, suppose I have two sets of data—SALES and ADVERTISING—and want to plot the relationship. Earlier computer systems required the user to build elaborate programs for this purpose. Good contemporary software systems handle this task automatically. A command like PLOT SALES, ADVERTISING is sufficient in many of the new systems to produce a sales-advertising plot on an $8\frac{1}{2} \times 11$ sheet of paper, with axes labeled and a grid that has gradations in rounded numbers. The computer has done the work of a rather efficient (if not intelligent) clerk. If you don't like the results, you can override the command, but the point is that the new software allows results to be returned faster and more efficiently than traditional FORTRAN programming.

A number of such systems are becoming more readily available commercially. A system whose emphasis is scientific is APL, while business-oriented systems include EXPRESS, PROBE, TSAM, and XSIM. Many of these systems are extendable so that subroutines in more primitive languages (FORTRAN, for example) can be introduced as new commands. See Keen and Scott Morton (1978) for a further discussion of interactive Q/A systems and their uses. In summary, an MDSS includes data, models, statistics, optimization, and an efficient procedure (software system) for communicating with the computer in a simple but powerful way.

MDSSs in Practice: Three Cases

In this section we describe three MDSSs: the first, more anecdotal than the others, illustrates the key points.

The Marketing Manager, The Management Scientist, and the MBA (Little, 1979a, pp. 11–12)

Once upon a time (1973), an MBA student took a summer job with a large food manufacturer. He reported to a management scientist in the principal division of the company and was assigned to enter key marketing information, basically store audit data, on a time-shared computer. The goal was an easy-to-use retrieval system, essentially the DATA box of Exhibit 20.3.

OK. He did this.

By the end of the summer, word of the system had reached the marketing manager of the division's major product, who asked for a demonstration, and so the three met. The MBA and the management scientist showed the marketing manager how simple, conversational commands could retrieve data items, such as sales, share, price, distribution level, and so on, by brand, package size, and month.

The marketing manager was impressed. "You must be fantastically smart," he told the MBA. "The people downstairs in MIS have been trying to do this for years, and they haven't gotten anywhere. You did it in a summer."

It was hard for the MBA to reject this assessment out of hand, but he did acknowledge, and this is a key point, that the software world had changed. There are now high-level analytic languages available on time-sharing that facilitate data retrieval and processing.

The MBA and the management scientist, flushed with success, now said to the marketing manager, "OK. Ask us anything!" (Famous last words.)

The marketing manager thought a minute and said, "I'd like to know how much the competition's introduction of a 40-oz package in Los Angeles cut into the sales of our 16-oz package."

The MBA and the management scientist looked at each other in dismay. What they realized right away is that there isn't going to be any number in the machine for sales that didn't occur. This isn't a retrieval question at all, it's an analysis question.

Here then is another point. The marketing manager had no idea the number would not be in the machine. To him, it was just a fact no different from other facts about the market. Notice also that the question is a reasonable one. One can visualize a whole string of managerial decisions that might be triggered by the answer, possibly even culminating in the introduction of a new package by the company.

What is needed to answer the question is a model—probably a rather simple model. For example, one might extrapolate previous share and use it to estimate the sales that would have happened without the competitor's introduction. Then subtraction of actual sales would give the loss.

The three discussed possible assumptions for a few minutes and agreed on how to approach the problem. Then the management scientist typed in one line of high-level commands. Out came the result, expressed in dollars, cases and share points.

The marketing manager thought the answer was fine, a good demonstration. The MBA and the management scientist thought it was a miracle! They had responded to the question with speed and accuracy unthinkable a few months earlier.

The story is simple but contains several important lessons. The same points come up again and again in various organizations, although not always so neatly and concisely:

Managers ask for analysis, not retrieval.   Sometimes retrieval questions come up, of course, but most often the answers to important questions require nontrivial manipulation of stored data. Knowing this tells us much about the kind of software required for an MDSS. For example, a data-based management system is not enough.

Good data are vital.   If you haven't done your homework and put key data on the system, you are nowhere. Thus a powerful analytical language alone is not enough.

You need models.   These are often simple, but not always. Some can be prepackaged. Many are ad hoc.

The management scientist is an intermediary.   He connects the manager to the MDSS. The manager does not use the system directly. The management scientist interprets questions and formulates problems in cooperation with the manager and then creates models and uses them to answer the questions and analyze issues.

Speed is important.   If you can answer people's questions right away, you will affect their thinking. If you cannot, they will make their decisions without you and go on to something else.

Muscular software cuts out programmers.   New high-level languages on time-sharing permit a management scientist or recently trained MBA to bring up systems and do analyses single-handedly for efficient problem solving. Furthermore, the problem solver identifies and deals directly with marketing management so that his understanding and motivation are high. Time-sharing costs more than batch processing, but an army of programmers is eliminated, and, far more importantly, problems get solved on time.

Interactive Marketing Systems: A Media Decision-Support System
(Adapted from Alter, *Decision Support Systems: Current Practice and Continuing Challenges,* © 1980. Addison-Wesley, Reading, Mass., pp: 225–246. Reprinted with permission.)

The problem of allocating advertising dollars to media is important to three groups of people:

advertisers, who have money for advertising and want to reach potential consumers of their product

media representatives, who have advertising space they want to sell

agencies, who are principally involved in getting advertisers and media people together in an effective and efficient way

This case describes a series of advertising-analysis programs that are among the principal products of Interactive Marketing Systems, Inc. (IMS). The system here is a data base of market research information and a series of programs that apply specialized types of analysis to that data base.

As seen by IMS, there are three basic problems that they can help an advertiser address:

Who are the potential customers for the product?

What are their media habits (e.g., magazine readership)?

How can the media be effectively used to reach the consumers?

The thrust of the IMS system is to identify potential customers and analyze their media habits to determine the overall thrust of a campaign. Their system does not deal with questions, such as copy programs, timing, and the like.

A number of data bases are available to support the decision problem. The "Simmons Sample," collected annually by W. R. Simmons and Associates Research, Inc., provides information on more than 15,000 consumers with respect to demographic characteristics, consumption habits, media-use habits, and psychographic information. One purpose of the IMS system is to provide simple, quick access to this rather large data base for the purpose of analysis.

The original IMS system is simple to operate so that it will be used. It leads the user through the typing of all information required for specifying a desired report. A cross-tabulation would require a description of the report itself, a definition of the population to be scanned, and a specification of the portions of the population that fall into each column or category. For example, a row specification might be MIDINC MEN: MEN AND INC 25–35,000, which defines MIDINC MEN (middle-income men) as those men with incomes in the $25,000–$35,000 range.

Four important analyses are performed by IMS:

1. *Cross-tabulation* is used to gain an understanding of the target population and its habits or demographics.
2. *Market-segmentation analysis* uses AID (see Chapter 9) to segment consumers into groups with relatively homogeneous characteristics (consumption habits, for example).
3. *Reach and frequency analyses* evaluate a given advertising program in terms of its *reach* (number of people who are exposed to the campaign) and *frequency* (the average number of exposures during the analysis period) and provide statistics for each segment of the target population.
4. *Optimization* procedures, given a target population and an advertising budget, select a media schedule that maximizes any linear combination of reach and frequency or minimizes cost subject to a reach goal.

IMS serves three groups of users. Advertisers (the least frequent users) use the system to identify target markets. Advertising agencies can use the system to aid in developing (and supporting) their recommendations for a media strategy. Finally, media people, the most frequent users, employ the system to help persuade advertisers and agencies to allocate advertising dollars to their media.

The IMS system provides on-line capability for handling a wide range of media and marketing questions. The on-line/real-time capability, coupled with easy-to-use campaigns, is important for meeting four critical needs:

speed and convenience (next-day service is unacceptable for many applications)

monitoring results and testing alternatives (the system encourages customized searches of the data bases)

personnel development (many clients see value in having their own staffs act as the liaison between information and decision)

privacy (customers do not like to publicize what they are doing and the private on-line nature of the system minimizes the chances of information leakage)

IMS is representative of the new breed of MDSSs that provide the software and analytical tools to extract information from large data bases. The system is evolving in the direction of a balance between managerial judgment and computer power and is evolutionary in design, typical of MDSSs.

A Retailing Decision-Support System

Lodish (1981) describes a decision-support system designed and developed over a period of a year to help the manager of a large mass retailer improve its marketing-planning activities. Exhibit 20.4 outlines the structure of the decision-support system.

The evolution of the system provides insight into successful MDSS development. The first system component to be developed was the yearly market-

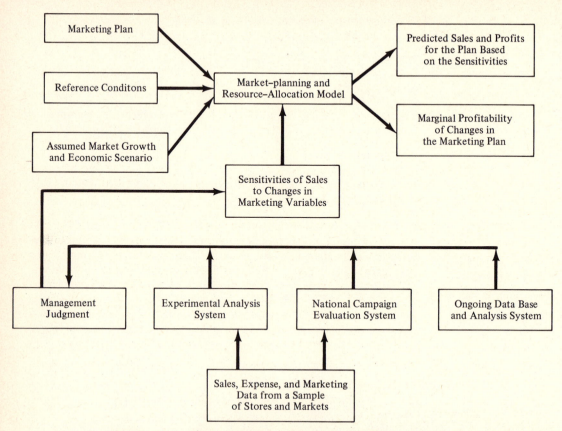

EXHIBIT 20-4 **The retailing decision-support system: an overview.** (Source: Reprinted by permission of the publisher from "Experience with Decision Calculus Models and Decision Support Systems," by Leonard M. Lodish, *Marketing Decision Models,* p. 171. Copyright © 1981, by Elsevier Science Publishing Co., Inc.

planning and resource-allocation model, which inputs reference conditions, marketing-plan alternatives, assumed market-growth and economic scenarios, and managerial estimates of the sensitivity of sales to changes in marketing variables. The system provides two types of output:

1. sales and profits anticipated for the marketing plan based on the system inputs
2. an evaluation of the marginal profitability of changes in the marketing plan

It was designed to run modularly so that it could produce analyses for a department or group of departments independently or in the aggregate or for different subgroups of stores involved separately or together.

As management gained experience with the system, it found that it was not as confident of its estimates of the response elasticities as it would have liked to have been. Therefore, management added three other components to the system as methods for evaluating these elasticities:

1. *A national campaign and event evaluation system* was designed to estimate the sales effectiveness of large national campaigns or events seen periodically by the retailer. This system takes internal sales data from a sample of stores and examines the promoted items before, during, and after the national event.

2. *A market-experiment system* was designed to be used when the national campaign and event system did not provide high-quality estimates of sensitivities. Typically, the sample of stores used here is specific to the design of the particular experiment being conducted.

3. *An interactive data base and analysis system* was developed to provide managers with a continuous picture of how well the marketing activities were doing. The data base is a nationally representative sample of stores, used to track the effectiveness of past decisions, providing rapid response to ad hoc managerial questions and acting as a general working system for identifying problems early.

The system has proved to be an important tool for assessing and improving company profitability. The result of one experiment provided an estimate of incremental sales per $1000 of TV expenditures as $11,700 versus $4200 for magazines (the current, most heavily used medium). The item, following the shift to TV, became one of the most successful in the history of the store.

According to Lodish, the decision model has caused managers of many departments to become much more rational in their market-planning procedures. The firm's top management called for development of a longer-term version of the model so that strategic-planning scenarios could be evaluated over a 5-yr planning horizon.

A critical ingredient in the success of this system was the interface person who related managers' needs to the MDSS and translated the output into the manager's terminology. The real-time, interactive system made this interface person as effective as possible, allowing rapid response to critical questions. Subjective data were often used to parameterize models where empirical data were not available.

Lodish notes that this (and other examples he cites) did not have "optimization or statistical parity as a primary goal. The goal of all was helping managers to consider and evaluate more alternatives than they had prior to the model" (p. 82).

For other examples of MDSSs, see Lodish (1981); the discussion of BRANDAID in Chapter 18 could also be reviewed in the context of an MDSS. Furthermore, Alter (1980) provides detailed case discussions of seven other DSSs.

MDSS Design: Some Guidelines

An MDSS should be designed so that it can be used. It will be used if it provides users with flexible decision-making leverage at moderate cost (in time and dollars). A number of authors have provided extensive guidelines for DSS design (Barbosa and Hirko, 1980; Huber, 1981; Keen, 1981; Keen and Scott Morton, 1978; Lucas, 1978; Schonberger, 1980; Sprague, 1980). We briefly synthesize these views, following Keen and Scott Morton (1978), into a three-step design process: the predesign stage, the design stage, and the postdesign stage.

Predesign Stage

The purposes of the predesign stage are to make certain that the right problem is worked on (decision analysis) and to involve users in a contract for action (entry). The decision analysis clearly establishes how the current decision process takes place and how it can be supported, while entry builds the commitment and rapport that sets the stage for later implementation.

Generally, in the predesign phase several designs for evaluation should be developed. Analysis at this stage may suggest that only a small subset of the decisions being made in the area justify the use of a DSS, and a value analysis may suggest that no payoff exists for support of those decisions. In general, while the steps leading to a final design are often judgmental, the issues to be considered revolve around risk and payoff (Keen and Scott Morton, 1978, p. 176):

> Which alternative(s) offer the most improvement to the existing decision process? What are the likely economic payoffs? What is the cost of the organizational or behavioral gains?
>
> How difficult will it be to implement this degree of change? Are we ready to commit the dollars, time, prestige, and support necessary?
>
> What are the downside risks—if the system falls behind schedule or meets resistance, what are the costs (financial, behavioral, political, etc.)? Does the system permit a phased evolutionary development?

Design Stage

A DSS cannot be designed by a cookbook recipe, but it can be outlined with flow diagrams (Exhibit 20.5), which can be used as a checklist. When the predesign cycle is complete, the design specification is a statement of intention, focusing on what the DSS should do, not what it should look like. Answers to a number of key questions guide the design:

> What should the DSS accomplish? Design must be based on use. What can users reasonably expect to do with the system?

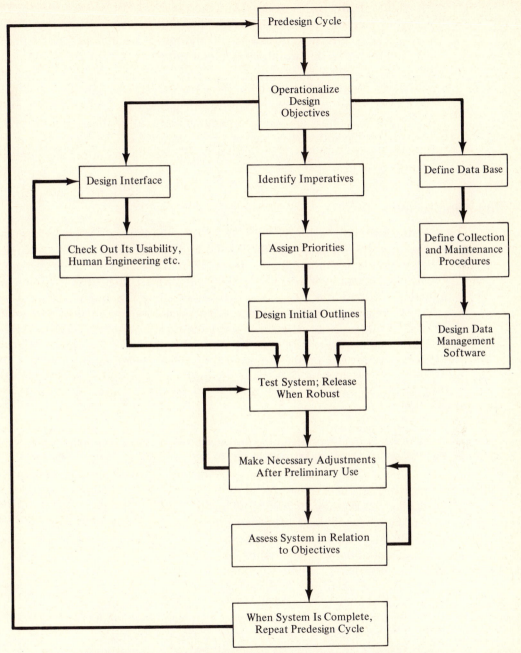

EXHIBIT 20-5 **The DDS design cycle.** (Source: Keen and Scott Morton, *Decision Support Systems: An Organizational Perspective.* Figure 6-5, p. 186. Copyright © 1978 by Addison-Wesley, Reading, Mass. Reprinted with permission.)

What should the user see? This feature is the interface, the software, the means through which the user communicates with the system. A good software interface must be (1) truly conversational, (2) robust (bomb-proof and reliable), and (3) easy to control (a user's system, not an analyst's system).

How should the supporting data base be structured? A difficulty for many DSSs is that they require fairly large data bases and complex retrieval facilities with infrequent access to all of the data. It is difficult to develop software to perform such retrieval efficiently. It may be easy to specify a data base but next to impossible to collect and maintain those data.

Postdesign Stage

A distinguishing aspect of a DSS is its evolutionary design. Competent managers learn from using the system and extend their analyses, requiring additional levels of support. The evolution of the DSS design is also one of change in a manager's decision process. But for a DSS to affect management action, evaluation must be incorporated as part of the design strategy.

In summary, by its very nature of adaptability, a DSS must be designed to meet the evolving needs of a particular application. As such, the typical development process follows the steps of analysis (predesign), design and construction, and implementation (including evolutionary redesign). The design focus must be on system use and usability, and system design and implementation must be recognized as being inseparable.

MDSS: A Bridge to Implementation for Marketing Models

The purpose of this book is to provide a model-building approach for making marketing decisions. The MDSS makes the model-building approach accessible. Furthermore, implementation, MDSS system design, and good marketing modeling should be inseparable. Thus the design, implementation, and evaluation of MDSSs is best treated as an integrated whole. Practically, such a treatment would result in a long clumsy chapter here, and therefore the discussion of implementation and cost/benefit analyses of system uses are presented in the next chapter.

To foreshadow that discussion, we must recognize that implementation (whether of a DSS, a marketing model, or any new management technique) constitutes a change in the organization's work environment. Then implementation is a process of organizational change, and the process of planning for and introducing that change can critically affect its ultimate chance of acceptance. For a discussion of an evolutionary strategy for implementing a DSS see Alavi and Henderson (1981).

A View Ahead for MDSSs

There are six trends that are affecting and will continue to affect the development and use of MDSSs: hardware trends, software trends, hardware-software trade-offs, communications technology, data-collection trends, and human development.

Hardware Trends

The driving force behind the computer revolution has been astounding. The trend toward more powerful and inexpensive computation is expected to continue:

> Today's microcomputer, at a cost of perhaps $300, has more computing capacity than the first large electronic computer, ENIAC. It is 20 times faster, has a larger memory, consumes the power of a light bulb rather than that of a locomotive, occupies 1/30,000 the volume and costs 1/10,000 as much. It's available by mail order or at your local hobby shop (Noyce, 1977, p. 65).

Software Trends

Software trends are leading to a wider, more flexible array of user-oriented languages. The trends in this direction are intended to make the interface even friendlier. Development efforts are underway to (1) redesign keyboards with a simpler, more sensible array of key positions, (2) permit frequently used phrases or commands to be assigned to any key at any time, and (3) allow the keyboard to be supplemented by voice input of simple, frequently used phrases. Advances in artificial intelligence that permit us to teach a computer how to understand our language will allow more flexibility in command structure in the future.

Hardware-Software Trade-offs

We will see an increasing fraction of total system costs assigned to software, with hardware-cost declines outstripping the rate of software improvement. Boehm (1973) suggested that by 1985 software should account for over 90 percent of the system costs.

Communications-Technology Trends

Two trends in communications technology, which barely affect most DSS users today, will have major impacts in the future. One is the advance of communications and computer-network development. The other is the rapid advance of microelectronics, which is turning the hand-held calculator boom of the 1970s into the personal-computer explosion of the 1980s.

These trends will increasingly permit local control and entry of data, centralized control of data standards and data entry, and centralized access to almost any data in computer-readable form.

Data-Collection Trends

Closely related to the above, data-collection trends are profoundly affecting the way MDSSs can be used. The electronic cash register, the universal product code, the automated checkout, and the credit card diary panel are making a vast array of high-quality and timely data available for marketing decision making.

Human-Development Trends

Human-development trends should not be overlooked in terms of system use. Two trends are important here. The first is penetration and use through familiarity. As DSSs became more widely used, they became less threatening. Furthermore, developers are learning to design friendlier systems to further reduce the threat. The second trend is evolutionary, through education. Most students in business and engineering are heavily exposed to computers and quantitative techniques. As they develop and rise through their companies, they will prove more receptive than many current managers, who were trained very differently.

In sum, the trends in MDSS can be characterized by faster and friendlier systems meeting the needs of more receptive and more knowledgeable users.

Summary

The use of marketing models for decision making calls for access to data and tools for manipulating the models and the data. The structure for performing this task—for making marketing models work—is a marketing decision-support system (MDSS).

An MDSS is viewed as having five components: a data bank, a models bank, statistical packages, optimization routines, and a user-directed interface. Data come from many sources. The best starting point is usually an examination of secondary sources. Further data can be gathered through observation, experimentation, surveys, and expert-questioning methods. Models, statistics, and optimization have been dealt with extensively in other sections of this book.

Major recent developments have taken place with respect to the user interface—the software/hardware system interacting with the user. New software permits data and files to pass easily between analyses and allows a wide scope of studies to be performed quickly and efficiently.

Two functions are vitally important for a DSS: meeting user needs and evolving with those needs. The system must be designed so that, as the application evolves and the company's needs grow, the system can grow as well.

Important developments in decision-support systems for marketing will continue to be seen in the next few years. Those developments will be driven by cheaper and faster hardware, friendlier and more efficient software, improved computer-communication capabilities, better data collection, and more receptive and better-educated users.

Problems

20.1 Some marketers view the emergence of computer models in marketing with hostility. They will make the following statements: (a) we don't use computer models; (b) computer models are typically unrealistic; (c) anyone can build a computer model; (d) a computer model is of no help unless you can get the data and you have a complicated, high-cost computer. How would you answer these objections considering the basic structure of an MDSS?

20.2 There has been a recent trend toward the centralization of information activities in large companies. What developments have led to this centralization? What are some of the advantages and disadvantages of a centralized information system?

20.3 One of the telephone companies in the Bell chain is considering a rate reduction. The company noticed that the percentage of homes with one or more extension phones was approaching a stable level of around 30%. There was some evidence that many families whose dwelling units were large resisted two phones because the 75¢ monthly charge seemed too high to them. The company was wondering how many additional extension phones would be ordered if the charge were reduced to 50¢. Discuss four ways in which the company can obtain this information.

20.4 For what type of situations would you think a marketing MIS might be more appropriate than an MDSS? Why?

20.5 A packaged-food manufacturer collects monthly sales, revenue, advertising, and promotional data on all six of its products (plus competitive products) in three markets. How might you design an MDSS for this firm? How would you justify its cost?

CHAPTER 21 Implementation

Most of this book has dealt with the problem of building useful models of marketing processes and decision situations. In this chapter we explicitly consider how management science in marketing can be marketed (implemented).

Management science and model building still have a strange sound to many marketing practitioners in spite of the number of companies that have undertaken projects in this area. Those who spend their days managing a salesforce, reviewing an advertising campaign, dealing with customers, and developing budgets for product lines and sales territories see a great deal in marketing that defies classification and analysis. They therefore develop a natural suspicion about the proclaimed contributions that mathematics and the scientific method can make toward the understanding and solution of marketing problems. There are many facets of the marketing process that rely heavily on creativity, human relations, and the like that may never be quantifiable. But at the same time there are other facets of marketing that have responded well to systematic observation and analysis.

The attempt to get marketing executives to support the development of formal marketing models that aid in planning is unfortunately still greeted with feelings that range all the way from intense suspicion and hostility to naive and uncritical acceptance. The introduction of management science into the marketing area shares the difficulties found in its introduction into other parts of the company. In addition the implementation of marketing models faces the added handicap that the validity of marketing models is not yet proven to the same extent as models in other functional areas such as production or finance. Nevertheless, there are some sound strategies for demonstrating the potential value of management science to marketing practitioners.

Significantly, literature is emerging on the personal, structural, and organizational aspects of the management sciences, which has many lessons for implementing marketing models. Some of this research, which we will review, is specific to marketing. In this chapter we first discuss the meaning of implementation and then briefly review reported case studies. The following sections focus on the lessons from the literature on implementation. We close with a discussion of implementation strategies.

The Meaning of Implementation

The value of models in marketing, as in any area of application, should be measured by their impact on organizational effectiveness. According to Schultz and Slevin (1979), implementation is the bridging of the gap between theory and practice and the improvement of organizational effectiveness through organizational change. In a recent article Schultz and Henry (1981) distinguish between implementation and successful implementation. They contend that implementation means changed decision making, while successful implementation means improved decision making. A *successful model,* on the other hand, is one that adequately represents the modeled phenomena and is used for the purpose for which it was designed. However, it may or may not result in successful implementation. Consider the development of a product-design model. Its goal is to optimize the design of product features. If it does so and is used for this purpose, it is successful. However, the process of model building and calibration might identify a new market segment, leading to a reassessment of marketing strategy. This is implementation success. Thus for management-science work to be successful in the broad sense (implementation success), it need not be associated with the success of a specific model (model success).

Schultz and Henry (1981) posit three stages of management-science activity: (1) *intervention,* when management-science activity takes place (a model gets built); (2) *implementation,* when decision making is changed as a result of intervention; and (3) *improvement,* when there is a positive change in decision making. These three stages roughly correspond to the different views of implementation held by analysts, managers, and implementation researchers. Many management scientists view implementation as getting the results of their work into the hands of managers. To the manager, it is technical assistance in problem solving, so the specific problem must be successfully solved. Implementation researchers focus on the broader dimension of organizational change.

Many other perspectives exist, perhaps as many as there are interested analysts and practitioners in the field. A commonsense synthesis of these positions might hold that the objective of all interested parties is to improve organizational effectiveness. Implementation is the change needed to bring about such improvement.

What Is Being Used?

In many books and professional and popular journals, marketing models are referred to as if they were being used pervasively. Schultz and Slevin (1979) report that management-science/operations-research (MS/OR) applications have been around for over thirty years and that the field apparently is in a period of consolidation. Exhibit 21.1 suggests the historical evolution of OR/MS implementation. The level of top-management support has waned; for implementation success this result requires reduction of the user's tendency to resist change—the user and the organization must work together as change agents.

Larréché and Montgomery (1977) performed one of the few comparative analyses of marketing models. Unfortunately, they focused on model builders' rather than users' perceptions of viable models, and no information about the level of use was collected.

Pokemper (1977), in a survey of the level of implementation of management-science methods in nearly 500 business firms, reports on the types and levels of uses and applications. One such report is given below.

EXAMPLE:

A Major-Style Goods Manufacturer (Pokemper, 1977, p. 22).
While this firm's MS unit has worked in all areas of the firm, much of its effort is concentrated in the marketing or sales, general-management, and finance areas. Some of its major projects have involved (1) inventory and production analyses for closer control of the firm's widespread production and distribution facilities; (2) experimentation with computer-readable product labeling for more efficient data generation and control of sales and distribution-information needs; and (3) a data-exchange program with buyers for a faster and more sensitive response to changing market conditions, as well as for improved customer services. In addition, the MS unit has aided the company in projects that run the gamut from improved planning procedures to designing specific quality-control procedures.

The OR/MS manager of the firm indicates that much of the unit's success has been based on its own market orientation: "We work hard at being responsive, recognizing our clients' needs, doing a good professional job, being innovative, taking a corporate view—in short, bringing many factors from many areas to bear on a problem and adding our own technical expertise and ability to work with others in a mutually pleasant way." He noted that his unit avoided oversophisticated models because of a conviction that the softness of data in the apparel industry would not support such efforts with the requisite accuracy or reliability.

EXHIBIT 21-1   **Historical evolution of OR/MS.**

Era	Examples	Top-management Support	Radicalness of Implementation as Seen by User
Yankee ingenuity, (1950)	Military: Plane deployment Aircraft maintenance PERT LP—oil refinery LP—lumber mill	Very high	High
Sophisticated, 1960s	Inventory models Production scheduling Forecasting Advertising effectiveness	Moderate	High
Soporific, 1970s	MIS Interactive models Data retrieval Capacity simulations	Low	High

SOURCE: Reprinted by permission of the publisher from "Introduction: The Implemention Problem," by Randall L. Schultz and Dennis P. Slevin, *The Implementation of Management Science*, p. 5, copyright © 1979 by Elsevier Science Publishing Co., Inc.

Pokemper reports that three-fourths of all management-science units are actively engaged in working with their clients to ensure the implementation of successful project results. As a result, an increasing amount of management-science group time is spent in unglamorous maintenance activities, and their work cannot be implemented in the ordinary sense because it constitutes counseling and advice.

A total of 74 percent of the responding firms reported having sales/marketing applications in the last 5 yr. Exhibit 21.2 gives details. Marketing

EXHIBIT 21-2   **Management-science applications in marketing.**

Application Area	Percent Engaged in in Past 5 Yr	Percent Expected to Engage in in Next 5 Yr
Advertising management	11	13
Competitive analysis	27	28
Competitive bidding	18	14
Marketing-information systems	32	34
Marketing-strategy analysis	31	35
Marketing search	41	41
New-Product analysis	26	27
Product-life-cycle analysis	19	28
Pricing studies	41	39
Product or line strategy	19	27
Sales territory analysis	19	21

SOURCE: Pokemper, 1977, p. 55.

research, pricing, MIS, and strategy analyses are the most frequently reported application areas, with strategy problems and sales territory analyses among the growth areas. The most prevalent management-science technologies and methodologies reported are forecasting, regression, simulation, and various statistical procedures (Pokemper, 1977, pp. 66–67).

Pokemper's results correspond closely with those of Schultz and Slevin: management science in marketing, as in other functional areas, is facing an adolescent crisis. Its level of use and implementation is reasonable but much lower than earlier expectations. We now explore some reasons for these unmet expectations.

The Dimensions of Implementation Success

If we consider the implementation of a model as a diffusion process, then the theory of innovation diffusion, developed in Chapter 19, becomes relevant. In particular, Mansfield (1968) and Blackman (1974) found that a product or process (a model?) will diffuse more rapidly if (1) the profitability of its adoption is high, (2) the capital investment of its adoption is low, and (3) the industry in which the adoption takes place is innovative. The implications of these observations for studying the rate of implementation of marketing models are that there may be characteristics of the model that allow it to show large expected profitability, that there may be required characteristics for implementation, and that there may be characteristics of the firm or organization that predispose it more or less well to model adoption.

Interestingly, this view matches well with Larréché and Montgomery's (1977) study of the likelihood of model acceptance, which identified three sets of dimensions related to model success: model, organization, and implementation-strategy dimensions. We discuss the first two in this section and treat implementation strategy in the next.

Model-related Dimensions

In Chapter 2 we identified a number of model dimensions related to implementation. Little (1970) suggests that decision models should be simple, robust, easy to communicate with, adaptive, and complete on important issues. These characteristics are seemingly in conflict: simple models are rarely complete, and vice versa. Urban's (1974) view of evolutionary model building, along with Little's concept of a model's being adaptive, provides clues for resolving this conflict: "simple" and "complete" are understood to be relative concepts.

Little's most controversial dimension is that of ease of control. This feature means that the model is constructed in such a way that it can behave as a manager wants it to. But combined with subjective-calibration procedures, the easy-to-control model can potentially be self-serving, bearing out the manager's prejudices rather than performing well.

Naert and Leeflang (1978) downplay this concern:

> The manager has to keep control over the model, otherwise it is unlikely that he will ever use it. This view might be dangerous in the sense that the model can be manipulated at will by the manager. This, however, does not usually represent a real problem. After all, the manager is looking for help and not a fancy toy to play with. The manager who manipulates the model and its parameters thoughtlessly is only fooling himself (p. 548).

However, this view may be wishful thinking. Parsons and Schultz (1976) question the view and argue for extending it by adding an additional dimension to the set of model criteria: validity.

> . . . we would extend the idea of decision calculus by imposing another requirement on models, namely that they be evaluated in terms of the *representativeness* of the mechanism describing market behavior. This additional requirement guarantees that at least the sales response component of the decision model faces a rigorous test of its validity as a theory of market response. We would argue that a test of a theory is its validity, while a test of a model is its utility and so it is possible for a model to be useful even though it is based on an inadequate theory of sales response. But it is better to have both a valid and useful model (p. 33).

We concur and append the notion of validity to the requirements for a successful model.

In line with the argument at the beginning of this section, we also add the notion of *potential cost-effectiveness*. Formal marketing models rarely become implemented in small organizations because they have a certain fixed-cost component in terms of managerial and analyst time, as well as expenditure. If the problem (and the organization) is too small, the model-building exercise will not be a valuable investment. The small-firm manager who says he "doesn't have the time for models" is probably right insofar as the size of his problems and the potential for improvement will not justify the cost of analysis. (The microcomputer may be changing his mind now, however.)

Model Validity. Validity or validation is a catchall that means different things in different scientific disciplines. Faivre and Sanchez (1973) review the meaning of validity in philosophy, behavioral science, economics, operations research, and management science. Even within specific disciplines, validity may have varied and special meanings. For example, Zaltman, Pinson, and Angelmar (1973) distinguish seven types of "concept validity": observational, content, criterion-related, construct, systematic, semantic, and control validity.

We discuss this issue briefly here, introducing and illustrating several key concepts. An excellent treatment of the issue of validation of marketing models is found in Naert and Leeflang (1978, chap. 12).

Four main criteria for validation relevant for marketing models are measure reliability and validity, face validity, statistical validity, and use validity.

Measure validity is the extent to which an instrument measures what it is supposed to measure. A measure with little validity has little value. However, even if a measure is valid, it may not be possible to measure it without error. *Measure reliability* is the extent to which a measure is error-free.

Measure validity has two parts: convergent and discriminant validity. *Convergent validity* is the extent to which an instrument correlates highly with other measures of the variable of interest; *discriminant validity* is the extent to which an instrument shows low correlation with other instruments supposedly measuring other variables.

EXAMPLE: As an example in which both reliability and validity impact decision making, consider Gross' (1972) copy-testing model (Chapter 14). He derives a rule on the optimum number of ads to screen. In the case he illustrates, the optimum number of ads to screen is three. However, for a copy-testing instrument that was perfectly reliable (test-retest correlation equals one) and perfectly valid (sales-response-instrument correlation equals one), the optimum number of ads to screen can be shown to be six. Conversely, for a measure that is either completely unreliable or completely invalid, it does not pay to perform any copy testing at all.

Face validity is the *reductio ad absurdum* principle in mathematics, which shows the falsity of an assumption by deriving from it a manifest absurdity. The idea is to question whether the model's structure and its output are believable. Face validity is based on theory, common sense, and known empirical facts (experience). Massy (1971) describes four areas for face validity: model structure, estimation, information contribution, and interpretation of results.

The validity of the *model structure* means that the model should do sensible things. Sales should be nonnegative and have a finite upper bound. Market shares should sum to one. Sales response to advertising spending might account for decreasing returns or first increasing and then decreasing returns to scale. This type of validity, closely akin to Little's concept of robustness, is essential for model credibility. If it is easy to make a model do things that are not consistent with managerial experience or intuition, the model is unlikely to be used.

The choice of *estimation method* is another essential aspect of face validity. For example, if a reasonable set of assumptions about the process generating the data (or previous studies) suggests that residuals are autocorrelated, then the use of ordinary least squares is inappropriate and generalized least squares (Chapter 5) may be the appropriate and valid estimation procedure.

The *amount of information* contributed by the model also dictates its value as well as its validity. For example, Kuehn and Rohloff (1967a) (Chapter 15) suggest calibrating the promotional-response models before and after the promotional period to assess its impact. If model-parameter changes are insignificant, the model is of limited value in assessing promotional impact, and different measures may be required.

Finally, the *level and interpretation of results* impact model implementability and validity in much the same way as model structure does. If the price or advertising elasticity of demand has the wrong logical sign, the model loses validity and hence implementability. In some areas there have been a sufficient number of cases to approach a consensus of at least order-of-magnitude estimates for parameters. For example, Lambin (1976, p. 93) found that in 38 cases studied the market share/advertising elasticity was 0.100 with a standard deviation of 0.108, which gives a rough indication of whether a particular estimated coefficient is reasonable.

Another criterion for validating marketing models is *statistical validity,* the criterion employed to evaluate the quality of a relationship estimated by econometric methods. The important issues in a marketing context usually relate to goodness of fit, reliability of the estimated coefficients, multicollinearity, and assumptions about the disturbance term (homoscedasticity and autocorrelation). For discussion of these issues, see any good text on econometrics [e.g., Thiel (1971), Wonnacott and Wonnacott (1979); or see Naert and Leeflang (1978) or Parsons and Schultz (1976) for a treatment specifically related to marketing problems].

Validation also relates to the *intended use* of the model. Chapter 2 described a number of model-based uses, including descriptive, predictive, and normative. The validity criteria vary in their appropriateness for specific uses. Validity for descriptive models would seem to place heavy requirements on face validity and goodness of fit. For a normative model the reliability of a model's response coefficients, those that enter into policy calculations, would seem most critical. For predictive validity a goodness-of-fit measure, such as R^2 or mean squared deviation, is often used on a holdout or validation sample. The use of such a sample makes the validation task predictive, while measuring goodness of fit on the estimation data gives information useful only for descriptive validity.

Most econometric studies include two sets of validity tests. The first set deals with checking the model's assumptions for problems, such as multicollinearity, autocorrelation, nonnormality, and the like. This task is called *specification-error analysis.* If no violations are identified, the model as a whole can be tested and, most importantly, *discrimination tests* between alternative models can be performed (Parsons and Schultz, 1976, chap. 5).

Two additional points on validation should be made. First, any good model-implementation exercise incorporates updating. Markets are dynamic, and model parameters, as well as entire model structures, may change. As model predictions become less reliable over time, a review of model structure and/or parameters is in order. Second, just as Little's decision-calculus criteria involve trade-offs, no model may dominate all alternatives (perform better on all relevant dimensions). This notion can lead to important practical problems. Often a model with more variables will prove to fit better but to forecast less accurately than its rejected rivals. It is quite common in marketing models to find statistical-fit criteria in conflict with predictive criteria. This result points to the importance of establishing criteria for validity that are in line with the intended use of the model.

Model Costs and Benefits. Our discussion earlier suggested that the overall rate of diffusion of a model partly depends on its costs relative to its benefits. This is on an aggregate basis, of course. On an individual basis a particular company might decide to implement a model for noneconomic reasons. By and large, however, modeling in marketing must be viewed as an investment. The ability of that investment to prove its value can frequently be estimated with some reliability.

A thoughtful treatment of cost/benefit considerations in relationship to marketing models is found in Naert and Leeflang (1978, chap. 14). We draw heavily on their discussion here.

Model-development costs, in time and dollars, are generally of three types: development costs, maintenance costs, and costs inherent to use.

Development costs are usually fixed costs, incurred once when the project is undertaken. If these development costs alone are greater than the expected benefits (as may be the case for a small firm), the modeling task cannot be justified. One way to control development costs is to use an existing model, usually on a rental basis from a consulting firm.

Maintenance costs are those costs incurred in keeping a model up to date. For large-scale accounting systems maintenance costs are often many times greater than development costs. For marketing models the level of maintenance costs is usually determined by two factors: the level/frequency of model use and the rate of structural change in the marketplace. Infrequently used models in relatively stable markets generally have low maintenance costs.

The *costs of use* have two main components: computer time and managerial time. Computer time is usually well accounted for, while managerial time is often perplexingly difficult to allocate. If a model takes two person-days of managerial time per month to run, should that time be allocated to the model? Suppose the model is a promotional-allocation model, and the manager needs to set promotional budgets. He may be spending more time on this task than he would have otherwise because he now has the ability to consider more alternatives. Is the net cost positive or negative—that is, should the time for evaluation of the new alternatives (those he would not have evaluated without the model) be attributed to the model? What about the freeing up of managerial time by routinizing what was formerly a nonroutine task? And how does one account for a manager's time? Salary only? Salary plus overhead? In most cases he is a fixed asset, and the company may decide no incremental costs are being incurred.

These cost issues need to be assessed on a case-by-case basis. We recommend the following approach. Start off by making a worst-case analysis for costs (as well as benefits). If the model shows value when burdened most heavily with allocated costs, its use is clearly justified. If it is only marginally profitable, a more refined analysis may be required. This worst-case approach may greatly reduce the effort required to perform the cost/benefit analysis.

Finally, it is important that the costs of the decision-support system be allocated to or charged against the model. A model often requires special data or at least data in a specific form. But as those same data may be used for production planning and/or inventory control, it is important that the costs not only be acknowledged but also properly allocated. Cost of collection, storage, maintenance, and retrieval of data need to be assessed for the model. The communications component—that portion of the decision-support system allocated to support this model—needs to be considered as well.

In general, model *benefits* are of two types: tangible and intangible. Models in some areas have almost all their benefits in the intangible category; many planning models—and, in fact, the entire planning function—in many firms have this characteristic. *Intangible* benefits often accrue from having the model ask the right questions.

EXAMPLE: One of the firms participating in the ADVISOR study (Chapter 18) used the questionnaire developed there as a basis for forming a product-market information system for the firm. A representative from another company (private correspondence) maintains that the largest benefit from the modeling procedure is the data-collection task. He maintains that "the ADVISOR approach forces the same vocabulary and the same data-collection questions on our different product managers. Having them focus their attention on these key questions and having them compare their responses with one another has helped us uncover inconsistencies in reasoning in our historical-budgeting process." This benefit occurs *before* the model is run and is a frequent occurrence.

This example shows that building a model in marketing is akin to any scientific investigation. It requires specification of the following:

what is known
what data should be collected
what hypotheses/theories exist

what past observations exist

what we know about the laws of motion of the system in question

Thus the modeling task brings along with it a questioning process that systemizes managerial decision making, uncovers inconsistencies in reasoning, and generally makes assumptions, objectives, and performance more overt. To the extent that these goals are desirable within an organization, the model-building task may have considerable intangible or side benefits.

For the measurement of *direct benefits* either profitability or cost savings are most appropriately used. Except in a few experimental situations, particularly where decisions are frequent and repetitive, a direct measure of profit is usually difficult to obtain. In Chapter 16 we reviewed the experiment of Fudge and Lodish (1977) ascribing an expected dollar benefit to the use of the CALLPLAN model in an application for United Airlines. However, such examples are rare, and the modeler must often use creative estimates of expected profitability, with and without the use of the model, to estimate benefits.

EXAMPLE: This example is adapted from Urban and Hauser (1980). Urban and Hauser collected information about the costs of new-product failures. They present cost and benefit figures for the ranges of stages in the analysis process for new consumer products. They point out that the way to evaluate the benefits of these phases of analysis is to assess the decrease in cost resulting from increased spending on market modeling. They show that the added investment in pretest-market analysis reduces the cost of bringing one successful new product to market on average from $9,642,000 to $8,556,000—a savings of over $1,000,000. The major portion of this savings is gained by reducing the number of required test markets at $1,000,000 per test market. Without pretest markets, $1/(0.45 \times 0.85) = 2.6$ test markets on average are needed, [average attempts = 1/(probability of success)], while with pretest markets, only $1/(0.80 \times 0.85)$, or 1.47, test markets are required per market success. A cost of $50,000 per pretest market and an average requirement of $1/(0.60 \times 0.60 \times 0.65) = 2.45$ such analyses per actual market success yields an expected total cost of $2.45 \times \$50,000$, or $123,000. Thus the case for pretest-market modeling and analysis is quite strong. (See Exhibit 21.3 for details.)

EXAMPLE: This example is adapted from Edelman (1965). Edelman reviewed bidding for government contracts under closed-bidding situations. The company bidding the lowest for the contract gets the bid (see Chapter 13). If we let

C = expected cost of carrying out the contract
X = bid price
$g(X)$ = likelihood of winning with a price of X
$Z(X)$ = profit expected from bidding X.

EXHIBIT 21-3 **The cost of bringing one successful product to market, showing the benefit of pretest-market investment.**

Phase of New-Product-Introduction Process	Average Cost (in $1000s)	Without Pretest Market		With Pretest Market	
		Probability of Success	Expected Cost (in $1000s)	Probability of Success	Expected Cost (in $1000s)
Opportunity identification	100	—	100	—	100
Design	200	0.50	1046[a]	0.50	980
Testing					
Pretest market	50	—	—	0.60	123
Test market	1000	0.45	2614[b]	0.80	1471
National introduction	5000	0.85	5882	0.85	5882
Total cost			9642		8556

Net benefit of pretest market = 9,642,000 − 8,556,000 = $1,086,000

SOURCE: Redrawn from Glen L. Urban, John R. Hauser, *Design and Marketing of New Products,* © 1980, pp. 56–57. Adapted by permission of Prentice-Hall, Inc., Englewood Cliffs, N.J.

[a]200 (0.50 × 0.45 × 0.85) = $1046.

[b]1000 (0.45 × 0.85) = $2614.

then

$$E[Z(X)] = (X - C)g(X) \tag{21.1}$$

and the optimal bid price X is the one that maximizes eq. (21.1). Edelman presents the information in Exhibit 21.4 as evidence for the value of the model, comparing model-based bids with company-based procedures. The measurement of benefit here is quite simple because the company has

EXHIBIT 21-4 **Benefit of using a competitive-bidding model.**

Case	Bid Without Model	Bid with Model	Lowest Competitor	Performance Without Model[a]	Performance with Model
1	44.53	46.00	46.49	4.2	1.1
2	47.36	43.68	42.93	(10.3)	(0.6)
3	62.73	59.04	60.76	(3.2)	2.8
4	47.72	51.05	53.38	10.6	4.4
5	50.18	42.60	44.16	(13.7)	3.1
6	60.39	54.61	55.10	(9.6)	0.9

SOURCE: Reprinted by permission of the Harvard Business Review. An exhibit from "Art and Science of Competitive Bidding" by Franz Edelman (July/August 1965). Copyright © 1965 by the President and Fellows of Harvard College. All rights reserved.

[a]Percent under (over) lowest competitive bid.

already calculated an expected profit without the model; the expected profit with the model allows a monetary evaluation of the difference to be ascribed as the benefit of the model.

Several other points about benefits need to be made. First, an offshoot of the model-development process may be an overall improvement in the understanding of marketing phenomena that benefits *all* firms in the industry. However, the benefit to the developing firm may not justify the investment. These are situations in which multicompany-sponsored modeling activities (PIMS and ADVISOR, for example) are appropriate. A similar problem arises from the internal-external model-development question. A model developed in-house may have lower operating costs than a consultant's model, but the fixed cost must be spread over a sufficiently large number of applications to justify its construction.

EXAMPLE: Suppose it takes a $100,000 in-house development effort to produce a pretest-market procedure but only $25,000 to run each application. How many new-product introductions are required to justify in-house development? Assuming a consultant's price of $50,000, the break-even calculation is

$$50,000X = 100,000 + 25,000X$$
$$X = 4$$

In other words, more than four pretest-market evaluations of new-product introductions would justify the $100,000 investment.

There are a series of experience-based and quality-based arguments that may be made either for or against in-house model development. In general, the greater the level and frequency of model use, the more beneficial in-house development is and the greater the justifiable sophistication in model development (the fixed-cost component) is.

Organizational Dimensions of Implementation Successes

The discussion above focuses on the model-specific dimensions that are relevent to implementation success. A research stream of growing importance has focused on model building and related organizational dimensions. We focus here first on the manager/management scientist interface and then on the importance of the organization and its assets.

The Manager/Management Scientist Interface.   C. P. Snow's two-culture problem is at the heart of the implementation issue in marketing. A key dimension of the problem is the relationship between line management and staff. Line management holds the basic responsibility for making or improving decisions on product, price, advertising, and so on. It could, in principle, proceed solely on its own intuition. In practice, most managers rely to some degree on staff resources. In some cases they may have already made up their minds and are seeking confirmation. In others they are honestly seeking input. In still other cases they seek insurance for their decision in the event that it turns out to be incorrect.

On the other hand, the staff may have quite a different view of its roles and contributions to the decision-making process. Instead of seeing themselves as offering services to the line manager, they may believe that their technical skills qualify them to give sound advice on the various courses of action facing the firm, and, in fact, that the best decision is often implicit in the results of their research and not something to be arbitrarily considered by the manager. In the more extreme cases they would like to see the responsibility for policy making in the hands of a planning staff and the manager's task as carrying out these policies.

In addition to role conflict between line management and staff regarding the responsibility for decision making, there tends to be personality conflict since the two jobs tend to attract different types of minds: the practical versus the theoretical. Beldo (1961) listed four conflicts in the fundamental outlook of mangers and researchers that get in the way of productive relationships: simplicity versus complexity, certainty versus probability, immediacy versus futurity, and concreteness versus abstraction. (See Exhibit 21.5) Basically, the manager has a job to do and is of a more practical frame of mind with little tolerance for uncertainty, equivocation, and delay. Meanwhile, the analyst sees gray areas, listing different recommendations arising from different assumptions and generally attempting to qualify his results. This orientation contributes to the impression on the part of many managers that management scientists are either incapable or unwilling to give clear answers. Thus both role conflicts and personality conflicts often plague the relationship between the manager and the management scientist.

Opinions differ about what the proper and most productive relationship is between the two. Churchman and Schainblatt (1965) distinguished among four possible types of manager/management scientist interfaces. The first,

EXHIBIT 21-5   Fundamental conflicts between managers and researchers.

Management Demands	Research Offers
Simplicity (Can't you just answer yes or no?)	Complexity (The variability of response indicates . . .)
Certainty (It is or it isn't)	Probability (Maybe)
Immediacy (Now)	Futurity (It appears that by the end of the year . . .)
Concreteness (Aren't we number one yet?)	Abstraction (Our exponential gain indeed appears favorable)

SOURCE: Beldo, 1961.

or *separate-function position,* holds that the researcher's function is to develop a good, technical research design and solution, and the manager's function is to develop a good operational solution. Neither has an obligation to understand the details of the other's job. The second, or *communication position,* holds that the manager must understand the researcher and communicate his problem carefully to him but that the researcher does not have the corresponding obligation. The third, or *persuasion position,* holds that the researcher must understand the manager's needs and gear his work toward helping the manager make and recognize better decisions, while the busy manager does not have the corresponding obligation. Finally, the fourth, or *mutual-understanding position,* holds that the most productive relationship is achieved when both parties set about to understand each other's work and requirements.

In separate follow-up studies addressing the appropriateness of these communication patterns, Dyckman (1967) and Duncan (1974) surveyed groups of managers and researchers. In each case members of the groups were asked whether they agreed, disagreed, or were neutral about whether each of these four positions was appropriate. The studies give somewhat different results, which might be explained by wording or sampling differences. Interestingly, in the Dyckman study the view of managers and researchers were more divergent: when asked about the separate-function position, managers split about equally on the issue, while management scientists disagreed with it strongly by a rate of about 5:1. In Duncan's study disagreement was over 90 percent for both groups. Furthermore, Dyckman's results show a level of agreement with the other three positions (communication, persuasion, and mutual understanding) that are about equal across groups and across positions, while Duncan's sample strongly agrees with the other three.

If these differences are, in fact, real (i.e., they reflect a shift during the years between studies), they show a growing appreciation, especially on the part of managers, of the importance of the close connection between managers and researchers.

The difference between modelers and managers has been explored by Hammond (1974), who sees eight dimensions of difference: (1) goal orientation, (2) time horizon, (3) comparative expertise, (4) interpersonal style, (5) cognitive style, (6) problem definition, (7) validation of analysis, and (8) degree of structuredness.

In terms of *goal orientation,* the manager may see his personal goal or the departmental goal as primary, while the model builder is more inclined to work toward achieving organizational goals. The model builder is also more likely to be an optimizer, while the manager is interested in achieving a target.

The *time horizon* of the manager is shorter than that of the modeler. Furthermore, their *comparative expertise*—the manager in marketing and the modeler in the methodology of model building—may lead to different jargon and related communication problems.

In terms of *interpersonal style,* the manager is more relationship-oriented, while the modeler may be more task-oriented, aiming at getting the job done, and with respect to *cognitive style,* the modeler is more analytical while the manager is more intuitive (heuristic). Work by Huysmans (1970*a*, 1970*b*) and Doktor and Hamilton (1973) has shown that the more heuristic the individual, the less likely he is to accept recommendations from model builders.

The *problem definitions* of modelers tend to be more explicit and limited to dimensions most readily quantifiable, while the manager's definitions will often be vague and include a number of qualitative dimensions. Furthermore, managers and modelers differ in their approach toward *analysis validation,* with modelers often more interested in validation of model structure and managers interested in knowing how well the model performs. Finally, in terms of *degree of structuredness,* the manager sees his environment as relatively less structured than the modeler, who often imposes structure on the environment.

Recently, research has focused on the measurement of the specific behavioral aspects of implementation that affect its success. The research on *factor studies* (Schultz and Henry, 1981) concentrates on identifying key behavioral factors.

Huysmans (1970*a*) has studied differences in cognitive style between researchers and managers and concludes that an understanding of the manager's style (heuristic versus analytic) will affect the likely success of the model-building approach. For example, only analytical managers are found to accept models that require explicit understanding. Thus the model-building approach and the communication process should adapt to the manager's cognitive style.

Larréché (1979) argues for the use of Schroder, Driver, and Treufort's (1967) integrative-complexity theory. Integrative complexity is an individual's ability to absorb and structure complex relationships and multidimensional information. He suggests that the level of information processing obtained is dependent both on the manager's integrative complexity and the model's environmental complexity. This notion is akin to Lilien's (1975) concept of model relativism, where the best model is the one that best matches the use (and user).

A number of other research studies are reviewed by Schultz and Henry (1981) and are included in the volume by Doktor, Schultz, and Slevin (1979). Many of these studies focus on identifying dimensions of congruence and dissonance between the manager and the model builder and how they relate to implementation success. In some cases managerial attitude may not be changed, and functionally related intermediaries (interpreters?) may be required to provide the communications link (Bean and Radnor, 1979).

Organizational Factors.   Implementation requires the adoption of new ideas by the organization, and therefore a change process must occur in the organization. Sorensen and Zand (1979) posit that there are three stages in a change process: unfreezing, changing, and refreezing. Unfreezing entails overcoming resistance to change; changing means the introduction of new ideas and procedures; and refreezing occurs when these new ideas become part of the normal, day-to-day, decision-making process. Ginzberg (1979), in a study of 29 computer-based, management-science projects, found that researchers have a marked tendency to terminate a project before complete refreezing occurs. Organizations then tend to retrogress. The implication for successful implementation is that more emphasis is required on refreezing—continuing involvement with the firm longer than was previously believed necessary.

Galbraith (1979) suggests introducing "management islands" to differentiate the new technology from daily operations and protect it from short-run considerations. These islands should be autonomous units, receiving funding and expertise from high-level corporate sources. As the new technology (the model) matures in this environment, young managers (change agents) can be sent out to other parts of the firm to spread the word. This process may be very useful for implementation since support is nurtured internally.

A number of organizational factors seem to affect the likelihood of implementation success, including stage in the life cycle of the management-science group, level of top-management support for management science, and congruence between organizational and management-science goals.

In the early stages of a management-science group's life cycle, where strong organizational support has not developed, implementation is more difficult, and therefore proportionally more attention and resources must be dedicated to it. Because top-management support is essential for long-term acceptance, educational programs and seminars about management-science benefits may be required when such support is lacking. When organizational goals and management-science-group goals conflict, the likelihood of implementation is low. In any case it is the researcher's responsibility to ensure a match between the goal of his group, the newly built model, and the goals of the organization.

The amount of disruption the model creates in small, socially important organizational groups will affect implementation success; significant impact on structures of social importance creates barriers to implementation. Therefore the model should be designed to preserve as much of an organization's interpersonal structure as possible.

To the extent that models represent a change in historical patterns, they are a threat to many operating managers. The model may be perceived as disturbing the existing equilibrium in the organization, perhaps affecting status, prestige, and power. Managers may believe the model represents a threat to their jobs (Turban and Meredith, 1977). If such fears represent fear of the unknown—they are more perceived than real—resistance to change may be overcome by careful preparation. Little (1975) recommends orientation seminars, while Montgomery, Silk, and Zaragoza (1971) report success with giving managers access to on-line models for hands-on experience.

Finally, the greater the extent that the models represent the way decisions *actually* get made in the organization (versus how they should theoretically get made), the more successful they will be. If the pricing function is separate from brand management, then a marketing-mix model that includes price controls is not organizationally relevant and is less likely to be used. If advertising-budgeting and media-selection decisions are made at different levels of the organizational hierarchy, then an advertising model should separate the two decisions.

Implementation Strategy

The material reviewed so far is only useful if it provides suggestions for implementation success. Such success will always have a number of factors that are specific to the situation and organization. However, much can be learned from the wisdom of others. The work of Little (1970, 1975), Doktor, Schultz, and Slevin (1979), Schultz and Henry (1981), Urban (1974), Hammond (1974), Berry, Christenson, and Hammond (1980), and Naert and Leeflang (1978) forms part of the basis for the synthesis outlined here.

We consider here how management science can effectively be introduced into the marketing organization. This problem is viewed as having five aspects:

1. What kinds of persons make effective management scientists in marketing?
2. Where should these persons be placed in the organization?
3. What educational programs should they run for the management?
4. What marketing problems should be analyzed first?
5. What involvement should managers have in the design of the model?

Effective Management Scientists in Marketing

Early management scientists working in marketing were trained in other application areas—production, physical distribution, and the like—and often marketing problems were made to comply with the structure of the problems of these other areas. It soon became clear that marketing problems have their own special structure and need customized methodology and thinking.

The newer marketing management scientists realize this problem and spend as much time observing marketing processes in their full complexity as they do in learning the niceties of existing mathematical methodologies. The company seeking an effective person to do management-science work in marketing must search for a person who knows marketing. He can be proportionally stronger on methodology, or proportionally stronger in marketing, but he must know both.

As part of the individual's training, he should be exposed to a formal treatment of the implementation problem. Just as we do not expect management scientists to develop models by brute force, neither should we expect them to approach implementation without formal instruction. Schultz and Henry (1981) contend that a well-trained MBA with the usual education in individual and social behavior is better prepared to sell OR than an operations researcher!

Organizational Placement of the Marketing Management Scientist

A frequent issue is whether the marketing management scientist should be located in a separate department along with other management scientists or in the marketing department, either in a staff planning position serving the marketing vice-president or in the marketing research department. All of these locations are used in actual practice. Many large companies have a sizable management-science department, and one or more of the professionals specialize in making their services available to the marketing department. The advantage of this arrangement is that the marketing management scientist has active interaction with other management scientists and can keep abreast of ideas that are being developed in the other areas. The disadvantage is that he is removed from the scene of daily marketing decision making, which will mean that he will miss some opportunities to propose research where needed and also may be less knowledgeable about actual marketing processes. For this reason, in more and more companies the marketing management scientist works in the marketing group.

There is also the issue of level of authority. When the marketing management scientist is placed close to the vice-president of marketing, he can be highly influential in infusing management-science thinking into the marketing organization. At the other extreme, the management scientist might be placed within the marketing research department as a resource for model building. In this position his skills and influence may be less visible to line management, and he may be less free to choose the problems on which to work.

A mixed strategy that some larger companies have used with success is to maintain both types of groups. The internal-department group is responsible for small-scale developments, interaction with management, and most implementation problems, while the central group is responsible, much as an outside consulting firm is, for larger special situations and a limited amount of postsolution involvement.

Regardless of the placement of the group, to ensure success, the management scientist must accept responsibility for implementation (follow through in refreezing), and the modeling activity must have top-management support.

Educational Programs for Line Management

Fear of the unknown is one of the key barriers to implementation. Whether informally, through interactive hands-on sessions, or formally, through company-sponsored courses, managers must be kept abreast of what modeling can and cannot do for them.

Yet many current courses are less than successful because they focus on the tools and techniques of interest to the management scientist and not on the important issues for the manager. Whatever the format of the program (weekly seminar, three-day intensive program, or whatever), it is important to stress that *the value of the modeling approach is the process, not the resulting model.* In addition, the model-building activity is individualistic, people-dependent, and customized to the organization. Its effect on the analytical or thought process that goes into decision making is its major value. The model must not presume to replace management intuition or thought or to substitute for it. Rather, it must provide input into the decision process, clarifying analysis and (it is hoped) providing the information and the discipline that makes decision making easier.

Thus company-sponsored education is critical because it reduces concern about what is in the management scientist's black box and because expectations about how the contents of the black box will be used are clarified.

Choice of Problems

The management scientist who has undertaken to work with marketing line management will recognize a large number of marketing problems deserving study. However, he must be judicious about selecting problems that are *thought to be important* and for which there is a *reasonable chance for early solution* and payoff. For example, it would be fatal for the beginner to choose as his first assignment to build a marketing-planning simulator because such a simulator requires a tremendous number of person-hours for model design and data collection; a few years would pass before any practical results would be possible. Before this time someone is sure to question his value to the firm. Such a problem choice is also absurd because it is highly desirable to diversify the portfolio of studied problems to minimize risk; it would be better to work on several problems and achieve some successes than to rest everything on one problem, no matter how important.

There are two particular areas in marketing in which study is likely to produce improved procedures or solutions in a reasonable amount of time. The first is in the evaluation of nonrecurrent major-policy proposals. Where a company is facing a marketing decision of some importance, such as shifting from one marketing channel to another or dropping a price in an oligopoly situation, management will find simple decision-tree analysis or simulation models, both of which are easy to understand, useful. These techniques have an intuitive appeal and are helpful in the broadest range of situations. On the other hand, problems that involve linear programming, queueing theory, or calculus are likely to be harder for management to grasp.

The second area is in the improvement of routine management decision systems and procedures. Most companies can benefit from objective studies of their current procedures for making sales forecasts, developing budgets for territories and products, developing sales quotas for salespersons, and so on. Studies of the present systems can yield clues to alternative decision procedures that can lead to substantial improvements in performance.

Especially early in the life cycle of the management-science group, it is important to (1) be opportunistic, (2) keep it simple, and (3) score early victories.

By being *opportunistic* we mean to select problems where there is a high likelihood of success and where management attention is focused. Axioms for new-product success are relevant here: a new product (a management-science group?) is most likely to succeed where it fulfills an obvious, felt need.

Keep it simple is a rule that cannot be overemphasized, especially where there is management skepticism. A strategy that one successful consulting firm uses is to start all projects as information-retrieval/report-generation exercises. After capturing the company's data and reporting it regularly in a clear and timely format, managers begin to ask additional questions, which require analysis, not data retrieval, and which form the basis of the first round of (still simple) model building.

Few groups in industry have true long-term leases on life. Therefore *scoring an early victory* is important. This goal can be achieved in one of two ways. First, judicious problem selection may lead to a short, simple, but highly important project that shows clear benefits as a first effort. Alternatively, a project may be divided into phases, each of which produces information useful to management, perhaps long in advance of project completion. As an example, a pricing- and-promotional-evaluation system, built for a large packaged-foods manufacturer, produced a series of sales forecasts as an early product. These forecasts, needed for later modeling efforts, were found extremely valuable in themselves by the firm's management, and therefore the likelihood of success of the longer-term project was enhanced.

Early victories are usually easier (and success higher, in general) when (1) the process/operation being modeled is *well understood*, (2) the data are both *ample* (they exist) and *accessible* (some one knows an easy way to get them), and (3) the problem is found in company areas where *structured decision procedures* already exist.

This last point suggests that if the current decision framework is highly intuitive and unstructured, then a change is required for implementation. This added requirement lowers the likelihood of implementation success. An area where innovative, formal techniques have prospered previously is a good target.

Degree of Management Participation in Model Building

Management scientists tend to be divided over how much involvement the manager should have in the model-building and data-gathering phases of the research process. In the area of production and physical distribution, the management scientist generally listens to the manager's definition of the problem, goes away and builds a model, and then presents his solution and evidence some months later to the manager, with a few progress reports in between. This practice reflects the straightforward nature of many of the problems in these areas and the highly technical and standardized nature of the mathematical analysis. Its main weakness is that the manager rarely gets to understand the technical details of the model and often has to accept it on blind faith. In the marketing area this approach is deadly. Management-science practitioners are increasingly of the opinion that marketing managers should be involved as much as possible in the model-building process. First, it is important that the manager and management scientist come to a sound conclusion about what is the real problem; this conclusion may be more elusive in marketing than in other areas. Second, the participation of the manager will keep the management scientist from building the wrong model or omitting important factors. Third, the manager will achieve a feeling that he understands the model, rather than feeling that the model is a threat or a mystery. Fourth, he will feel that it is *his* model. Fifth, his participation is a form of education that will increase his ability to understand and use more-sophisticated models.

Those who believe that management involvement is highly desirable hold that it is more important to develop models that managers understand and by implication will use than to develop sophisticated models they cannot understand and will reject. By first building simple models that the manager understands and then adding refinements as the manager himself calls for them, the management scientist achieves a maximum amount of management motivation and education (Urban, 1974).

The degree of management participation involves other dimensions as well. The goals of the modeling exercise must be agreed on by both manager and management scientist. This task means timing as well as output. Late results create bad impressions. When a comfortable schedule, including contingencies up front, is established, the likelihood of timely delivery will be enhanced.

The roles of the manager and the management scientist must be clearly defined. Managers make decisions; modelers make models. This condition may appear to be in conflict with the call for involvement and interaction above, but a clear separation of certain responsibilities is important so that each individual's domain is established.

The manager and the management scientist must develop a joint plan for long-term model management and maintenance. As new data become available, the model may quickly become obsolete, leading to a new loss of credibility if systematic updating does not take place.

In conclusion, it is useful to highlight a few "don't"s along with the "do"s:

Don't make unnecessary changes.   If a manager has been receiving a report in a given format, continue to give him the same format he is used to even if the information is being generated by a new model. By changing as little as possible in a short time frame, barriers to implementation will be lowered.

Beware of false accuracy.   A wise manager we know sends back any computer-generated results with more than two significant digits. Multi-digit precision ("our market share in this market will be 12.372 percent if we introduce the new ad campaign according to plan") gives a false sense of security and discourages asking hard questions of the model.

Don't use models for advocacy.   Models should be used to *explore* options for the future. Unfortunately, they are often misused to justify a favored set of actions.

Don't be afraid to modify.   After the model is built, programmed, and documented, there is a tendency to treat it as an icon. The model should be continuously subjected to tests, should be updated, and should be treated as an *evolving* entity.

Every practicing management scientist has his own set of strategies and ideas about implementation that he has found helpful. Summarizing implementation needs, Grayson (1973) contends: "What we need to do is humanize the scientist and simonize the humanist." (p. 41)

Summary

In this chapter we have defined and reviewed some of the collective wisdom about implementation. Implementation means bridging the gap between theory and practice and improving organizational effectiveness. Current feelings about management-science applications in marketing are still mixed, with the field currently in a period of consolidation. Management feels that in the next few years there will be increasing use of models for product-line and strategic planning and continuing heavy use of models for market research and pricing decisions.

Implementation can be thought of as having three sets of dimensions: those related to the model itself, those related to the human and organizational-related aspects of implementation, and those related to the strategy for implementation.

The model-related dimensions deal with the overall utility of the model (its cost/benefit ratio), as well as characteristics relating to its validity, completeness, and ease of use. These model benefits can often be estimated explicitly.

Organizational dimensions related to successful implementation focus primarily on differences in background and perceptions between the manager and the management scientist. There is a growing view on both sides that a clear, mutual understanding is required to help ensure implementation success.

To effect these ends, the company must employ management scientists with good mathematical training and, even more importantly, a good understanding of the complexities of the marketing process, so that their models are relevant to the manager. The management scientist working on marketing problems can be placed either in a central management science department or in a marketing department, each possibility offering a number of advantages and disadvantages. Wherever he is based, he should develop educational seminars for managers that are endorsed and supported by top management. In addition, he should carefully select as first problems to work on those that can be finished in a reasonable amount of time with clear payoff. Finally, the management scientist should seek to involve the manager in the model building as a means of motivating and educating him about the potential values of the management-science approach.

The key point is that implementation doesn't just happen. It must be planned for and worked for, and the likelihood of success can be enhanced through attention to the lessons of implementation studies.

Problems

21.1 Distinguish among measure validity, face validity, statistical validity, and use validity.

21.2 "The diffusion and use of marketing models is inevitable; a creative analyst can only accelerate or forestall inevitable trends." Comment.

21.3 What differences would you suggest between implementation strategies for marketing models for (a) a large packaged-foods manufacturer, (b) a small industrial-component-parts manufacturer, and (c) a public-sector agency interested in marketing an issue? How would you evaluate cost/benefits?

21.4 Urban and Hauser suggest the net benefit of pretest analysis is over $1 million. Comment on the assumptions underlying that calculation. Is the approach applicable for other models?

21.5 What does Grayson mean when he says: "What we need to do is humanize the scientist and simonize the humanist"?

21.6 Top management in a large manufacturing company felt that the marketing department could benefit greatly from the implementation of management-science (MS) methods in the marketing operation. A group of operations-research experts from the firm's centralized MS group was assigned to study marketing problems and activities. After a number of months of independent work, the MS group came up with a lengthy report, which included recommendations for a comprehensive restructuring of the marketing operation and the implementation of a number of sophisticated operations-research models. The report was passed along to the company's marketing management with a recommendation to implement the recommended actions as soon as possible. Upon reading the report, the marketing manager claimed that the recommendations were highly unrealistic and completely unworkable. He further stated that the department personnel lacked the understanding and technical ability to implement the MS proposal. Discuss the problems highlighted in this situation. What should top management do to deal with these problems and to prevent their recurrence in the future?

21.7 The management of a company is considering the introduction of a new product. The research department is called on to provide information that management can use to make the necessary decision. In light of the fundamental differences in the outlooks of the two groups, what specific answers are typically sought by management in this situation, and what answers are likely to be provided by the research department?

21.8 A marketing manager hired an MS expert into his department, although he was doubtful of the value of MS methods in marketing operations. The management scientist immediately set to work to develop an elaborate consumer behavior simulation model. Six months later, just as the model was beginning to take shape, the marketing manager fired the MS expert, convinced that his original thoughts concerning the value of MS in marketing were justified, since the man had wasted 6 mo on a project that promised little in the way of practical operating results. Where did the management scientist go wrong?

22 Marketing Models Today and Tomorrow

In the preceding chapters we saw that decision making is a complex and difficult task that is becoming even more difficult, and that a subset of decision problems can be clarified in a timely and valuable way by the model-building approach. Here we first sketch the state of the art today, and then we describe some views about putting what we know to work. Finally, we discuss our views and those of others in the field about the role of marketing models in the years ahead.*

Marketing Models Today

Marketing modeling, as viewed here, is a blending of the strengths of several disciplines to aid in marketing decision making. The area is one of high opportunity but requires individuals with a highly eclectic set of talents:

> In order to attain the advantages attributed to marketing models, corporations (including advertising agencies and consulting firms) seek skilled people to (1) build, test, and implement marketing models and (2) serve as liaisons with marketing management to assure that these models actually fit the needs of the

*The quotations cited in this chapter are generally presented without reference. They come from private correspondence, from transcripts of addresses delivered at the EURO/TIMS/ORSA Marketing Science Conference at ESSEC/Paris, June 1980, or from transcripts of addresses at the Marketing Measurement and Analysis Conference at the Wharton School, March 1982.

managers who intend to rely on them. Such individuals, almost by definition, must approach their task both as a *scientist* and as an *artisan*. A marketing modeler must be well-heeled in areas such as marketing management, management science and statistics, econometrics, computer science, scientific method, behavioral science and communication and persuasion. (R. Dale Wilson, BBDO, Inc.).

Wilson calls for a tall order in his marketing modeler and the skills and knowledge he needs. Let us take the point of view of the *scientist* first. Our approach has stressed a multistage process for addressing marketing problems. What is the science of marketing modeling? How can problems be recognized? How can they be structured in model form? How can firms characterize their objectives and goals and state those goals quantitatively? How can data be integrated into the model structure in the form of parameter estimates? How can the model be tested on data (resulting, perhaps, in new theories or new models) and how can the model be manipulated to help analyze marketing-decision alternatives? The theory and some approaches to answering these questions are addressed in Part 1 of this book.

The marketing scientist must base his model on scientific theories. Two main publics respond to marketing actions: consumers and competitors. *Consumer* behavior theory is a vast and continually growing area. Consumer response to marketing activity needs to be incorporated in most marketing-modeling efforts. But who is in the market and where, how, why, and what do they buy? In any purchase situation the characteristics of the buyer, the product, the seller, and the selling situation (including other known alternatives) interact to influence the buying outcome. In *organizational* buying the problem of multiple decision makers—with varying personal (versus organizational) objectives—complicates the set of issues. The fields of consumer and industrial-buying behavior, although diverse in their findings, are beginning to provide the theoretical foundation required to build sound marketing models.

The reaction to competitive effort is less well understood. Nevertheless, new approaches based on reaction matrices and empirical studies from industrial organization are beginning to provide a basis for modeling competitive response.

Other disciplines also contribute to marketing modeling. Market-segmentation theory, whose operationalization is one of the key advances in marketing practice over the past 15 yr, provides tools for defining target markets. Forecasting theory provides an all-other-things-equal view of the future and gives a systematic basis against which the results of marketer actions can be compared. In addition, the tools of economics, operations research, and statistics provide building blocks, modeling approaches, and analysis procedures to aid in the marketing-model-building process. These fields have provided some important structure for approaching and building marketing models.

But here is where the *artisan* comes in. What type of model should be chosen? The theories of consumer behavior/consumer response are not unambiguous, and the artistic model builder must choose among the sometimes incomplete and often conflicting theories and empirical evidence. Furthermore, he must consider the ultimate user and use in building the model.

Many models of individual elements of the marketing mix are currently well developed. In some areas (salesforce, advertising, distribution, etc.), off-the-shelf models are available that, with a little modification and some customization, can be used directly. Some of these models (e.g., Fudge and Lodish, 1977) have even had their values proven experimentally! Thus the value and the methods are there, at least for individual elements of the marketing mix.

The most exciting areas in marketing modeling are the emerging integrative efforts. Marketing-planning models, integrating product life cycle, product portfolio, and experience-curve concepts, are being developed into usable tools. Marketing-mix models, with simultaneous control of the elements, are providing an evolving view of marketing-mix interactions and competitive-response analysis. Such models are showing value more as evaluation tools (what if?) than as optimization tools (what is best?).

Furthermore, new-product models, especially for pretest and test-market analysis for consumer packaged goods, have proven their value in the marketplace. Few firms bear the risk of entering competitive consumer markets without using some type of formal analysis.

Models for industrial-product planning are coming into use as well: ". . . researchers have the packaged goods problem pretty well licked; now we can go on to the hard problems, the industrial marketing area, which is an order of magnitude more complex than most of the consumer marketing problems" (Irwin Gross, Du Pont). Models for developing norms for marketing spending, for evaluating new-product sources, and for assessing markets for new industrial products are available and are increasingly being used.

These models are being made available more and more often through decision-support systems, which blend models, data, statistics, and optimization in a user-oriented system, responding to manager needs with friendly software. The art of modeling comes in when trying to make it happen.

Marketing decision model builders should show their knowledge of marketing by *applying the marketing concept* to their model building activities. Very often, they have been model-oriented (i.e., product-oriented) and they have been more interested in mathematical elegance than in fulfilling the needs of decision makers. A consumer orientation to model building should start with a clear recognition of model users' needs and these needs typically include: making better decisions, reducing decision risks, understanding the decision making environment and keeping control of the situation and of the decision making process itself (Rene Darmon, McGill University).

Marketing modeling today has a number of weak links, especially with regard to understanding the phenomena being modeled. The field is not unlike the field of agriculture in the late 1800s and early 1900s, with empirical results, experimentation, and theoretical and methodological developments proceeding cyclically and where improvements in one area stimulate developments in another. Or, perhaps, marketing modeling is in a position similar to evolution at the time of Darwin, where regularities in certain structural patterns are observed and are used to formulate theories.

Marketing modeling is neither the answer to all problems nor is it the ivory-tower waste of time that some may feel it is. Rather, there exists in the field considerable theory, a large amount of methodology, and proven value in many instances. However, the theory is uneven, and more must be done both in terms of theory development and in terms of improving the practice of marketing modeling.

The Inevitability of Implementation

The case was developed in the last chapter for viewing implementation of marketing models as a diffusion process. Given that view, the eventual implementation process is *not controllable;* if marketing models provide value to decision makers, they will be adopted and used; but if they do not, they will not be used. By better design and packaging (communication), we can accelerate the process; by overpromising and losing sight of user needs, we can delay implementation. But the value of implementation itself will determine what areas (if any) will prove fruitful for marketing modeling.

We believe that the modeling approach to marketing decision making is inevitable. There are several trends that are driving the process:

1. **DSS development.**   The amount of data is exploding, the reporting of data is becoming more timely, and the quality of marketing data is improving. Marketing models provide tools to summarize, interpret, and make normative use of those data. This trend will *accelerate* diffusion.
2. **Diffusion of microprocessors.**   Apart from DSS development, microprocessors put vast amounts of analytic power *on the manager's desk.* Modeling is required (although not presented in those terms) to harness that power, and the associated modes of thinking will routinize the use of marketing models. This trend will *accelerate* diffusion.
3. **Quantitative MBAs becoming managers.**   Normal personnel development in firms is leading to a generation of managers trained in and receptive to model-based decision support. This evolution will *accelerate* diffusion.

4. **Improvement in marketing theory.** As more experiences are shared by marketers through the marketing literature, improved theories will develop. The sharing of experience through case studies will help identify prevalent phenomena in marketing. These observations will act as the driving force for improved model development. As theory improves and models become better founded, implementation *will accelerate*.

5. **Improved reporting of value and experience.** As we continue to catalogue success stories and thereby learn what works and what doesn't (an important trend in the area of new-product models), we lower the risk of implementation. As firms document model uses and values, implementation will *accelerate*.

This list of trends could be expanded, but the result would be the same—the process of using marketing models will be accelerated in the future. For example, if we add to the above the need to respond to market conditions more rapidly than ever before, model-based analysis in many fields of marketing appears even more inevitable. Foolish overselling of model values, rigidity of model structures, and stress on optimization versus evaluation can slow the thrust but not stop it. Marketing models are taking their place among the standard tools of management decision making.

A final comment about the diffusion process: if model adoption is a diffusion phenomenon, then patience is required of model builders. Model-based decision making in marketing requires a change in business practice, where model builders must become model customers and then model implementors. Such changes take place slowly, even if the change is inevitable. The time from model conception to broad use may be measured in 5-yr units. These changes in business practices cannot be accelerated too greatly. However, once implementation occurs and marketing modeling is established as standard business practice, the likelihood of it falling out of use becomes small.

A Look Ahead

What should we look for in marketing modeling developments in the next decade? John Little (1979a, p. 25) foresees the following:

An order-of-magnitude increase in the amount of marketing data used.

Through MDSS development the internal data of a company will become accessible on a rather detailed basis. Automatically collected point-of-sale information from the marketplace (e.g., universal-product-code data from supermarkets) will replace most current store audits. Much better longitudinal data on customers (e.g., panels) will be generally available and will include such currently missing information as media use. The monitoring of competitive advertising, promotion, and price will be vastly improved.

A similar tenfold increase in computer power available for marketing analysis. The hardware is already built; it is out there and purchasable, and the price is going to break. The only problem will be for marketing to absorb computer power in a useful way.

Widespread adoption of analytic computer languages. These make data accessible and greatly facilitate analysis. Some exist now, more will be introduced, and all will improve.

A shift from market-status reporting to market-response reporting. This is an important change. SAMI, Nielsen, and other market-monitoring systems, including internal sales reporting, emphasize market status, that is, how things are—what are sales, share, price, advertising, and so on?

Tomorrow's system will report response, that is, how things react—what are price elasticity, advertising response, promotional effectiveness, and so on? Companies will even do a reasonably good job of monitoring competitor's market response.

Much work lies ahead for marketing scientists for this result to come to pass. We need well-designed data sources and many new tools. How do we handle eclectic data sources in developing and calibrating models? What are the best underlying models to represent marketing phenomena? We can expect a flowering of new work.

New methodology for supporting strategy development. Marketing scientists will further advance our understanding of product-market boundaries. Better response measurements will expose more clearly the nature of competitive interaction and give rise to game-theoretic strategy development.

A shortage of marketing scientists. You know what that means—higher salaries, more fun, exciting new toys. From this I conclude that marketing is the right field to be in.

Some related views are as follows:

This explosion of data can be likened to Leeuwenhoek's introduction of the microscope. The microscope permitted observation and measurement of a whole new world, the world of the infinitesimal, vastly advancing theory in the field of biology. Theory, data and methodology advance together; the electronic revolution in data collection, information processing and data communication will enable us to make vast strides in understanding and controlling marketing phenomena (David Learner, MRCA).

In the future we must employ methodologies that bring data and theory together. Data without theory results in raw empiricism. Theory without data is speculation. Only the combination of the two leads to scientific knowledge (Claes Fornell, University of Michigan).

A number of other areas besides data and computer support, such as industrial marketing, will provide other important developments in the 1980s. Irwin Gross at Du Pont describes some of the things that his company is working on:

> . . . one of our projects is to develop an *inventory of markets* to which Du Pont has access. This sounds simple, but it isn't. All our businesses are product-oriented. In one instance we had a record of a company being called upon by eleven different Du Pont salesmen. . . . Another area we are studying is *pricing*. We have come to view price in two parts—the price premium and the commodity price. There are many products that Du Pont sells which are granted a price premium by the market. We are trying to understand the underlying factors associated with such perceived values. As for the commodity price, a breakthrough in our thinking occurred when we stopped thinking about price as a controllable variable. Price is an output of the system, not an input; it is the result of market forces. . . . In the *salesforce* area, we are planning to do experimental work on measuring the sales response to sales calls. We have plenty of models in this area, but a shortage of data, so we hope we can generate some data, generalize and develop some theory in this area. . . . In the *advertising* area, one of the exciting things we are looking into is the effect of advertising on price. We always think of advertising's effect on sales. But we have done some hypothesis testing that shows that a major effect of advertising in the industrial area is to sustain the perceived values leading to a premium price in the market. This puts a whole new light on justifying advertising expenditures for well established products in the middle or latter stages of their life cycle, where conventional wisdom suggests there is no good reason to advertise. If these products can maintain a price premium, then maintaining advertising may be worthwhile . . . In the *organizational buying area*, we are trying to understand the impact of Du Pont's marketing, production and R&D services on large customers. These customers often have hundreds of people involved in purchasing processes. How do we allocate resources under these conditions? . . . And, finally, if more of my academic colleagues would shift their attention from applying methodology to problems as they would like to see them and pay attention to problems as they really are, we could make some real strides in understanding industrial market phenomena and improving marketing practice.

This is a tall order and an intriguing list of potential developments! In addition, we see potential, important strides in understanding and controlling the rate of diffusion of new industrial products—quantifying the product, market, and competitive and environmental factors that must come together to help ensure diffusion success.

Data and Data Analysis

To follow up on John Little's remarks on data, we present the following comments on the close relationship between data and methodology:

> Industry is seeing exploding costs of data collection and the day of the personal interview as we know it may rapidly be fading. This suggests that future research will make much greater use of combined mail and telephone interviewing. For people with an interest in data analysis, this means developing procedures that use more simple kinds of data, analyzed in more relevant ways (Paul Green, The Wharton School).

Interactions and Competitive Response

The revolution in measurement should have a major impact on the modeling of individual elements of the marketing mix. Furthermore, as these problems become more routine (we assume they will), increasing attention will be placed on the measurement of interactions in the marketing mix and of competitive response. Marketing managers say they don't know about interactions and competition. Yet a manager we know always runs an advertising campaign when he runs a promotion in a certain market; another hesitates varying price except within certain ranges because of his experience with one large competitor. Thus managers know much more about the behavior of the marketplace than they realize. The job of the marketing modeler, then, is to quantify this knowledge and combine it with more and better data for improved models in these areas.

Dynamics

There has been a burst of interest in diffusion models, especially those that incorporate control variables. This interest has arisen from the difficulty, particularly early in the life cycle, of modeling and predicting the impact of marketer and competitive activities on sales. Furthermore, this area is becoming increasingly important as new-product development becomes both a more risky and a more costly endeavor in the 1980s.

Diffusion models are being extended in several ways. They are incorporating marketing-mix variables (price and advertising, in particular) and are being used to develop policies. Furthermore, they are being extended for use in oligopolistic markets and are incorporating time-varying production costs. Finally, they are being extended to include wear-out effects on word-of-mouth, goodwill, and the like.

Consumer Behavior

Will the gap among behavioral scientists, stochastic modelers, economists, and other professionals be bridged? Will a coherent theory of consumer behavior develop in the decade ahead? We think not. On the other hand, there is increasing evidence that we are reading one another's literature and that some consolidation is beginning to emerge. But a complete and consistent theory of consumer behavior must await many more advances in our understanding of human behavior in general. What is beginning to emerge is a growing foundation for empirical hypotheses upon which marketing models can be built. To the extent that that foundation of knowledge grows in the 1980s and 1990s, we will have a better understanding of the action and reaction of those important participants in our modeling exercises, the consumers.

Bargaining Theory

In the 1980s the development and application of bargaining theory as an alternative to market-response analysis when the numbers of buyers and sellers are small should evolve. This theory has application in industrial markets and will affect the development of models of channel relationships in consumer markets as well.

Market Planning

Market planning is in its infancy. As we saw in Chapter 17, we are just beginning to put the tools together. New models incorporating more than financial synergy will be built to help plan marketing strategy at the multiproduct or firm level.

Other Marketing Applications

Several years ago marketing in the public sector was an area of new interest. Today, marketing's impact in the public sector is small but growing. Nonprofit organizations need customer and competitive analysis as much as do their for-profit associates, although their objectives are more difficult to specify. As we develop more and better measurements and models, marketers will increasingly be drawn into the regulatory process, helping to resolve issues about the impact of industrial activities on market structure and market share. For example, how can deceptive advertising be compensated? New theories and better measurements and models in marketing can help provide answers.

Implementation

The research on implementation, especially for decision-support systems, will provide increasingly better guidelines for operationalizing models.

Furthermore, as that research becomes more developed, the success rate for marketing-modeling efforts will become higher.

The 1980s and 1990s will see broad strides forward for marketing models. As data become available more rapidly and more systematically and as decision-support systems make the potential of such data manifest for marketing decision makers, the economic driving force behind marketing models will become stronger and better theories will emerge. Models provide a means to structure thinking and to structure data, and therefore decisions in fast-moving environments are made more systematic:

> Whether we are conscious of it or not, we are all builders of models. We all make assumptions, develop hypotheses, and collect data of one sort or another. Out of this process we develop certain expectations about the behavior of others and the world we live in. What makes the builder of formal models different is the necessity to make explicit assumptions, hypotheses, expectations and to submit these to systematic, empirical testing. It is by this systematic testing that we learn about the world.
>
> The builder of formal models can make his/her greatest contribution by helping others to be more explicit about the assumptions they are making and by assisting in developing a suitable test for a particular model. It is never a question of whether we will use a model to help us make a decision but how explicit and testable we are willing to make the model (David W. Stewart, Owen Graduate School of Management, Vanderbilt University).

Finally, we present this view from industry on the implication for careers:

> The tremendous growth in computer and modeling technology during the past few years translates into a huge potential for applications to marketing problems. Such potential means nearly unbounded career opportunities for individuals who have a firm mastery of the principles related to marketing modeling and who, at the same time, are effective in communicating their knowledge (R. Dale Wilson, BBDO, Inc.).

These last points, when tied in with knowledge of emerging technologies—scanners, interactive cables, personal computers, and advances in artificial intelligence—promise to help make the 1980s and beyond an exciting period to be involved with marketing models.

Summary and Commencement

The reader no doubt will appreciate a brief ending to this long book. The field of marketing models, we feel, is healthy and is too broad to sketch in compact form. This book may have erred by valuing comprehensiveness over conciseness. But, it is hoped, the book provides a firm foundation both for immediate applications as well as for future developments in the field.

The field of marketing models is growing in importance, in impact, and in the conceptual soundness of its methods. The literature is beginning to see documented reports of the value of using marketing models. More importantly, empirical evidence is slowly being collected in many marketing fields that provide a sound basis for theory and should lead to the development of better models.

In the 1980s and 1990s there should be considerable advances in many areas of marketing models. Those developments will be driven by better data, by faster and friendlier access to information via decision-support systems and microprocessors, and by a receptive generation of managers, trained to use the newly available information to help make decisions. The next decade promises to be exciting for all those involved, academics and practitioners alike.

Problems

22.1 What areas would you add to the list of future development trends listed in this chapter?

22.2 What impact do you expect microcomputers to have on the development and implementation of marketing models? Give some examples.

22.3 "The builder of formal models can make his/her greatest contribution by helping others to be more explicit about the assumptions they are making and by assisting in developing a suitable test for a particular model." Comment.

22.4 What trends do you see in the consumer behavior area to suggest convergence in a theory of behavior? Is the area convergent or divergent? Will a theory or model of consumer behavior be developed in your lifetime?

Bibliography

Aaker, David A. "Toward a Normative Model of Promotional Decision Making." *Management Science* Vol. 19, No. 6 (February 1973), pp. 593–603.

———. "ADMOD: An Advertising Decision Model." *Journal of Marketing*, Vol. 12 (February 1975), pp. 37–45.

Aaker, David A., and James M. Carman. Are You Overadvertising?" *Journal of Advertising Research*, Vol. 22, No. 4 (August/September 1982), pp. 57–70.

Aaker, David A., and John G. Myers. *Advertising Management*. Englewood Cliffs, N.J.: Prentice-Hall, 1975.

Aaker, David A., and Charles B. Weinberg. "Interactive Marketing Models." *Journal of Marketing*, Vol. 39 (October 1975), pp. 16–23.

Abell, Derek F., and J. S. Hammond. *Strategic Marketing Planning*. Englewood Cliffs, N.J.: Prentice-Hall, 1979.

Achenbaum, Alvin A. "The Purpose of Test Marketing." In *The Marketing Concept in Action*, ed. R. M. Kaplan. Chicago: American Marketing Association, 1964.

Ackoff, Russell L. *Scientific Method: Optimizing Applied Research Decisions*. New York: Wiley, 1962.

———. *A Concept of Corporate Planning*. New York: Wiley, 1970.

———. *The Art of Problem Solving*. New York: Wiley, 1978.

Ackoff, Russell L., and Maurice W. Sasieni. *Fundamentals of Operations Research*. New York: Wiley, 1968.

Adam, D. *Les Reactions du Consommoteur Devant le Prix*. Paris: Sedesp, 1958.

Adler, Lee. "Systems Approach to Marketing." *Harvard Business Review* Vol. 45 (May–June 1967), p. 166.

Advertising Age, September 10, 1981, p. 1.

Aggarwal, Sumer. "A Critique of 'The Distribution Simulator' by M. M. Connors et al." *Management Science*, Vol. 20, No. 4, Part 1 (December 1973), pp. 482–486.

Agostini, M. M. "How to Estimate Unduplicated Audiences." *Journal of Advertising Research* Vol. 1, No. 3 (March 1961), pp. 11–14.

Ahl, David H. "New Product Forecasting Using Consumer Panels." *Journal of Marketing Research*, Vol. 7 (May 1970), pp. 159–167.

Ahtola, Olli. "The Vector Model of Preferences: An Alternative to the Fishbein Model." *Journal of Marketing Research*, Vol. 12 (February 1975), pp. 52–59.

Akinc, U., and B. M. Khumawala. "An Efficient Branch and Bound Algorithm for the Capacitated Warehouse Location Problem." Working paper, Graduate School of Business Administration, University of North Carolina, July 1974.

Albers, Sonke. "Incorporation of Turnovers and Long-Run Planning Periods in Compensation Schemes for Controlling a Sales Force." Working Paper No. 8, The Marketing Science Group of Germany, March 1981a.

———. "Controlling a Salesforce with the Help of Compensation Schemes." Working paper no. 4, The Marketing Science Group of Germany, November 1981b.

Albers, Sonke, and Klaus Brockhoff. "A Procedure for New Product Positioning in an Attribute Space." *European Journal of Operational Research*, Vol. 1 (1977), pp. 230–238.

Alexander, Ralph S. *Marketing Definitions: A Glossary of Marketing Terms.* Chicago: American Marketing Association, 1960.

Alexander, Ralph S., James S. Cross, and Ross M. Cunningham. *Industrial Marketing.* Rev. ed. Homewood, Ill: Irwin, 1961.

Alford, Charles L., and Joseph B. Mason. "Generating New Product Ideas." *Journal of Advertising Research* Vol. 15 (December 1975), pp. 27–32.

Allaire, Yvan. "The Measurement of Heterogeneous Semantic, Perceptual and Preference Structures." Ph.D. thesis, MIT, 1973.

———. "A Model for the Evaluation of Tests and Additional Information in New Product Decisions." *INFOR*, Vol. 13 (February 1975), pp. 36–47.

Alavi, Maryam, and John C. Henderson. "An Evolutionary Strategy for Implementing a Decision Support System." *Management Science*, Vol. 27, No. 11 (November 1981), pp. 1309–1323.

Allen, T. J. *Managing the Flow of Technology.* Cambridge, Mass.: MIT Press, 1977.

Alloway, Robert M. "User Managers' System Needs." CISR working paper no. 56, Sloan School of Management, 1980.

Alpert, Mark I. "Definition of Determinant Attributes: A Comparison of Methods." *Journal of Marketing Research*, Vol. 8 (May 1971), pp. 184–191.

Alter, Steven. "A Taxonomy of Decision Support Systems." *Sloan Management Review* (Fall 1977), pp. 39–56.

———. *Decision Support Systems: Current Practice and Continuing Challenges.* Reading, Mass.: Addison-Wesley, 1980.

Alter, Steven, and Michael Ginzberg. "Managing Uncertainty in MIS Implementation." *Sloan Management Review* Vol. 20 (Fall 1978), pp. 23–31.

American Iron and Steel Institute. *Annual Statistical Report, 1973.* Washington, D.C.: 1974.

Amstutz, Arnold E. *Computer Simulation of Competitive Market Response.* Cambridge, Mass.: MIT Press, 1967.

Anderberg, Michael R. *Cluster Analysis for Applications.* New York: Academic Press, 1973.

Anderson, Carl R., and Frank T. Paine. "PIMS: A Reexamination." *Academy of Management Review*, No. 3 (July 1978), pp. 602–612.

Anderson, Paul. "The Marketing Management/Finance Interface." In *1979 Educator Conference Proceedings*, eds., N. Beckwith, M. Houston, R. Mittelstaedt, K. B. Monroe, and S. Ward, pp. 325–329. Chicago: American Marketing Association, 1979.

———. "Marketing Investment Analysis." In *Research in Marketing*, Vol. 4, ed. J. N. Sheth, pp. 1–38. Greenwich, Conn.: JAI Press, 1981.

Anderson, Ralph E. "Consumer Dissatisfaction: The Effect of Disconfirmed Expectancy on Perceived Product Performance." *Journal of Marketing Research*, Vol. 10 (February 1973), pp. 38–44.

Angelus, T. L. "Why Do Most New Products Fail?" *Advertising Age*, Vol. 40 (March 24, 1969), pp. 85–86.

Ansoff, H. Igor. "The State of Practice in Planning Systems." *Sloan Management Review* (Winter 1977), pp. 1–24.

Appel, Valentine. "On Advertising Wear-Out." *Journal of Advertising Research*, Vol. 11 (February 1971), pp. 11–14.

Applebaum, William. "Methods for Determining Store Trade Areas, Market Penetration, and Potential Sales." *Journal of Marketing Research* (May 1966), pp. 127–141.

———. "Survey of Store Location by Retail Chains." In *Guide to Store Location Research*, ed. C. Kornblau. Reading, Mass.: Addison-Wesley, 1968.

Armstrong, G. M. "The SCHEDULE Model and the Salesman's Effort Allocation." *California Management Review*, Vol. 18, No. 4 (Summer 1976), pp. 43–51.

Armstrong, J. Scott. *Long Range Forecasting: From Crystal Ball to Computer.* New York: Wiley, 1978.

Armstrong, J. Scott, and J. G. Andress. "Exploratory Analysis of Marketing Data: Trees vs. Regression." *Journal of Marketing Research*, Vol. 7, No. 4 (November 1970), pp. 487–492.

Armstrong, J. Scott, William B. Denniston, Jr., and Matt M. Gordon. "The Use of the Decomposition Principle in Making Judgments." *Organizational Behavior and Human Preference*, Vol. 14 (1975), pp. 257–63.

Arrow, Kenneth J. *Social Choice and Individual Values.* 2nd ed. New York: Wiley, 1963.

Assael, Henry. "Segmenting Markets by Group Purchasing Behavior: An Application of the AID Technique." *Journal of Marketing Research*, Vol. 7 (May 1970), pp. 153–158.

———. "Segmenting Markets by Response Elasticity." *Journal of Advertising Research*, Vol. 16, No. 2 (April 1976), pp. 27–35.

———. *Consumer Behavior and Marketing Action.* Boston: Kent, 1981.

Assael, Henry, and George S. Day. "Attitudes and Awareness as Predictors of Market Share." *Journal of Advertising Research*, Vol. 8, No. 4 (December 1968), pp. 3–10.

Assael, Henry, and A. Marvin Roscoe, Jr. "Approaches to Market Segmentation Analysis." *Journal of Marketing*, Vol. 40 (October 1976), pp. 67–76.

Assmus, Gert. "Newprod: The Design and Implementation of a New Product Model." *Journal of Marketing*, Vol. 39 (January 1975), pp. 16–23.

———. "New Product Models." In *Marketing Decision Models*, eds. R. Schultz and A. Zoltners, pp. 125–146. New York: North Holland, 1981.

Attanasi, Emil. "Some Interpretations of Sequential Bid Pricing Strategies." *Management Science*, Vol. 20, No. 11 (July 1974), pp. 1424–1427.

Axelrod, Joel N. "Attitude Measures that Predict Purchase." *Journal of Advertising Research*, Vol. 8 (March 1968), pp. 3–17.

Bagozzi, Richard P. "Marketing As Exchange: A Theory of Transactions in the Marketplace." *American Behavioral Scientist*, Vol. 21 (April 1978a), pp. 535–556.

———. "Salesforce Performance and Satisfaction as a Function of Individual Difference, Interpersonal and Situational Factors." *Journal of Marketing Research*, Vol. 15 (November 1978b), pp. 517–531.

———. ed. *Sales Management: New Developments from Behavioral and Decision Model Research.* Cambridge, Mass.: Marketing Science Institute, 1979a.

———. *Causal Models in Marketing.* New York: Wiley, 1979b.

———. "Performance and Satisfaction in an Industrial Salesforce: An Examination of their Antecedents and Simultaneity." *Journal of Marketing*, Vol. 44 (Spring 1980), pp. 65–77.

Bagozzi, Richard P., Claes Fornell, and David F. Larchen. "Canonical Correlation Analysis: A Special Case of a Structural Relations Model." *Multivariate Behavioral Research*, Vol. 16 (October 1981), pp. 437–454.

Bailey, Earl, ed. *Pricing Practices and Strategies.* Report 751. New York: The Conference Board, 1978.

Bailey, N. T. J. *The Mathematical Theory of Infectious Diseases and Its Applications.* 2nd ed. New York: Homer Press, 1975.

Bain, Joe S. *Price Theory.* New York: Holt, Rinehart and Winston, 1952.

Balachandran, V., and Dennis H. Gensch, "Solving the 'Marketing Mix' Problem Using Geometric Programming." *Management Science,* Vol. 21, No. 2 (October 1974), pp. 160–170.

Balderston, F. E. "Communication Networks in Intermediate Markets." *Management Science,* Vol. 4 (January 1958), pp. 154–171.

Baligh, Helmy, and Leon E. Richartz. *Vertical Market Structures.* Boston: Allyn & Bacon, 1967.

Banks, Seymour. *Experimentation in Marketing.* New York: McGraw-Hill, 1965.

Banville, Guy R., and Ronald J. Dornaff. "Industrial Source Selection Behavior—An Industrial Study." *Industrial Marketing Management,* Vol. 2, No. 3 (June 1973), pp. 251–259.

Baker, Michael J. *Marketing New Industrial Products.* London: Macmillan, 1975.

Barbosa, L. C., and R. G. Hirko. "Integration of Algorithmic Aids into Decision Support Systems." *MIS Quarterly* (March 1980), pp. 1–12.

Bard, Yonathan. *Nonlinear Parameter Estimation.* New York: Academic Press, 1974.

Barefoot, Donald L. "An Analysis of Distribution Channel Strategy for Industrial Markets." Master's thesis, Sloan School of Management, MIT, February 1978.

Barnett, Arnold I. "More on a Market Share Theorem." *Journal of Marketing Research,* Vol. 13 (1976), pp. 104–109.

Barten, A. P. "The Systems of Consumer Demand Functions Approach: A Review." *Econometrica,* Vol. 45 (1977), pp. 23–51.

Bass, Frank M. "Marketing Research Expenditures—A Decision Model." *Journal of Business,* Vol. 36, No. 1 (January 1963), pp. 77–96.

———. "A New Product Growth Model for Consumer Durables." *Management Science,* Vol. 15 (January 1969a), pp. 215–227.

———. "A Simultaneous Equation Regression Study of Advertising and Sales of Cigarettes." *Journal of Marketing Research,* Vol. 6 (1969b), pp. 291–300.

———. "The Theory of Stochastic Preference and Brand Switching." *Journal of Marketing Research,* Vol. 11 (1974a), pp. 1–20.

———. "Profit and the A/S Ratio." *Journal of Advertising Research,* Vol. 14 (December 1974b), pp. 9–19.

———. "The Relationship Between Diffusion Rates, Experience Curves, and Demand Elasticities for Consumer Durable Technological Innovations." *Journal of Business,* Vol. 53 (July 1980), pp. 551–567.

Bass, Frank M., Phillipe J. Cattin, and Dick R. Wittink. "Market Structure and Industry Influence on Profitability." In *Strategy + Structure = Performance,* ed. Hans R. Thorelli. Bloomington: Indiana University Press, 1977.

Bass, Frank M., and D. G. Clarke. "Testing Distributed Lag Models of Advertising Effects." *Journal of Marketing Research,* Vol. 9 (1972), pp. 298–308.

Bass, Frank M., A. P. Jeuland, and G. P. Wright. "Equilibrium Stochastic Choice and Market Penetration Theories: Derivations and Comparisons." *Management Science,* Vol. 22 (June 1976), pp. 1051–1063.

Bass, Frank M., and Ronald T. Lonsdale. "An Exploration of Linear Programming in Media Selection." *Journal of Marketing Research,* (May 1966), pp. 179–188.

Bass, Frank M., and Leonard J. Parsons. "A Simultaneous Equation Regression Analysis of Sales and Advertising." *Applied Economics,* Vol. 1 (1969), pp. 103–124.

Bass, Frank M., Edgar A. Pessemier, and Donald R. Lehmann. "An Experimental Study of Relationships Between Attitudes, Brand Preference and Choice." *Behavioral Science,* Vol. 17 (November 1972), pp. 532–541.

Bass, Frank M., and Thomas L. Pilon. "A Stochastic Brand Choice Framework for Econometric Modeling of Time Series Market Share Behavior." Working paper 668,

Krannert, Graduate School of Management, Purdue University, 1979.

Bass, Frank M., and W. Wayne Talarzyk. "An Attitude Model for the Study of Brand Preference." *Journal of Marketing Research,* Vol. 9 (February 1972), pp. 93–96.

Bass, Frank M., Douglas Tigert, and Ronald Lonsdale. "Market Segmentation: Group vs. Individual Behavior." *Journal of Marketing Research*, Vol. 5 (August 1968), pp. 264–270.

Bass, Frank M., and William L. Wilkie. "A Comparative Analysis of Attitudinal Predictions of Brand Preference." *Journal of Marketing Research,* Vol. 10 (August 1973), pp. 262–269.

Bass, Frank M., and Dick R. Wittink. "Pooling Issues and Methods in Regression Analysis with Examples in Market Research." *Journal of Marketing Research,* Vol. 12 (1975), pp. 414–425.

Bass, Frank et al., eds. *Mathematical Models and Methods in Marketing.* Homewood, Ill.: Irwin, 1961.

Bauer, Raymond A. "Consumer Behavior as Risk Taking." In *Risk Taking and Information Handling in Consumer Behavior,* ed. Donald F. Cox. Boston: Harvard Business School, Division of Research, 1967.

Baumol, W. *Economic Theory and Operations Analysis.* Englewood Cliffs, N.J.: Prentice-Hall, 1972.

Baumol, William J., and Edward A. Ide. "Variety in Retailing." *Management Science,* Vol. 3 (October 1956), pp. 93–101.

Bean, Alden S., and Michael Radnor. "The Role of Intermediaries in the Implementation of Management Science." In *The Implementation of Management Science,* eds. Robert Doktor, Randall L. Schultz, and Dennis P. Slevin. New York: North-Holland, 1979.

Beckwith, Neal E. "Multivariate Analysis of Sales Response of Competing Brands to Advertising." *Journal of Marketing Research,* Vol. 9 (May 1972), pp. 168–176.

Beckwith, Neal E., and D. R. Lehmann. "The Importance of Halo Effects in Multi-Attribute Attitude Models." *Journal of Marketing Research,* Vol. 12 (August 1975), pp. 265–275.

Beckwith, Neal E., and Maurice W. Sasieni. "Criteria for Market Segmentation Studies." *Management Science,* Vol. 22 (April 1976), pp. 892–903.

Beldo, Leslie A. "Introduction to Attitude Research and Management Decision." In *Effective Marketing Communication,* ed. George L. Baker. Chicago: American Marketing Association, 1961.

Belk, Russell W. "Situational Variables and Consumer Behavior." *Journal of Consumer Research,* Vol. 2 (December 1975), pp. 157–164.

Bell, David E., Ralph L. Keeney, and John D. C. Little. "A Market Share Theorem." *Journal of Marketing Research,* Vol. 12 (1975), pp. 136–141.

Bellman, Richard, and Stuart Dreyfus. *Applied Dynamic Programming.* Princeton University Press, 1962.

Bem, D. "Attitudes as Self Descriptions: Another Look at the Attitude-Behavior Link." In *Psychological Foundations of Attitudes,* ed. A. G. Greenwald, T. C. Brock, and T. M. Ostrom, New York: Academic Press, 1968.

Bemmaor, A. "Stochastic Models of Product Usage and Brand Choice: An Empirical Study." Ph.D. thesis, Purdue University, 1978.

Benders, J. F. "Partitioning Procedure for Solving Mixed Variables Programming Problems." *Numerische Mathematik,* Vol. 4 (1962), pp. 238–252.

Benjamin, B., and J. Maitland. "Operational Research and Advertising: Some Experiments in the Use of Analogies." *Operational Research Quarterly,* Vol. 9 (1958), pp. 207–217.

Bensoussan, A., Alain Bultez, and Philippe Naert. "Leader's Dynamic Marketing Behavior in Oligopoly." *TIMS Studies in the Management Sciences,* Vol. 9 (1978), pp. 123–145.

Berger, A. W. "New Computer Systems Provide Accurate Industrial Market Data." *Marketing News,* Vol. 14, No. 2 (1980), p. 7.

Berger, P. D. "On Setting Optimal Sales Commissions." *Operational Research Quarterly*, Vol. 23 (June 1972), pp. 213–215.

———. "Optimal Compensation Plans: The Effect of Uncertainty and Attitude Toward Risk on the Salesman Effort Allocation Decision," in *Proceedings of the 1975 Marketing Educator's Conference*, ed. E. Mazze. Chicago: American Marketing Association, 1975.

Berkman, H. W., and Christopher C. Gilson. *Consumer Behavior: Concepts and Strategies*. Ecino, Calif.: Dickenson, 1978.

Berkowitz, M. K., and G. H. Haines. "Predicting Demand for Residential Solar Heating: An Attribute Method." *Management Science*, Vol. 28, No. 7 (July 1982), pp. 717–727.

Berle, Adolph A., Jr., and Gardiner C. Means. *The Modern Corporation and Private Property*. New York: Macmillan, 1932.

Bernhardt, Irwin, and Kenneth D. Mackenzie. "Some Problems in Using Diffusion Models for New Products." *Management Science*, Vol. 19 (October 1972), pp. 187–200.

Berrisford, Thomas, and James Wetherbe. "Heuristic Development: A Redesign of Systems Design." *MIS Quarterly* (March 1979), pp. 11–19.

Berry, William L., C. J. Christenson, and J. S. Hammond III. *Management Decision Sciences: Cases and Readings*. Homewood, Ill.: Irwin, 1980.

Best, Roger J. "An Experiment in Delphi Estimation in Marketing Decision Making." *Journal of Marketing Research*, Vol. 11, Nov. 4 (November 1974), pp. 448–452.

Best, Roger J., and George C. Hozier, Jr. "Relating Market Share Behavior to the Main and Interactive Components of a Firm's Marketing Mix." *Marketing Measurement and Analysis*, eds. D. Montgomery and D. Wittink. Cambridge, Mass.: Marketing Science Institute, 1980.

Beswick, C. A. *An Aggregate Multistage Decision Model for Sales Force Management*. Ph.D. thesis, University of Tennessee, 1973.

———. "Allocating Selling Effort Via Dynamic Programming." *Management Science*, Vol. 23, No. 7 (March 1977), pp. 667–678.

Beswick, C. A., and D. W. Cravens. "A Multistage Decision Model for Salesforce Management." *Journal of Marketing Research*, Vol. 14 (May 1977), pp. 135–144.

Bettis, Richard A., and William K. Hall. "Strategic Portfolio Management in the Multibusiness Firm." *California Management Review*, Vol. 24, No. 1 (Fall 1981), pp. 23–38.

Bettman, James R. "The Structure of Consumer Choice Processes." *Journal of Marketing Research*, Vol. 8 (November 1971), pp. 465–471.

———. "Perceived Price and Product Perceptual Variables." *Journal of Marketing Research*, Vol. 10 (February 1973), pp. 100–102.

———. *An Information Processing Theory of Consumer Choice*. Reading, Mass.: Addison-Wesley, 1979.

Bettman, J. R., N. Capon, and J. R. Lutz. "Cognitive Algebra in Multiattribute Attitude Models." *Journal of Marketing Research*, Vol. 12 (1975), pp. 151–164.

Bijnen, E. J. *Cluster Analysis*. The Netherlands: Tilburg University Press, 1973.

Bimm, E. B., and A. D. Millman. "A Model for Planning TV in Canada." *Journal of Advertising Research*, Vol. 18, No. 4 (1978), pp. 43–48.

Blackburn, Joseph D., and Kevin J. Clancy. "LITMUS: A New Product Planning Model." In *Marketing Planning Models*, ed. A. A. Zoltners. TIMS Studies in the Management Sciences, Vol. 18. New York: North-Holland, 1982, pp. 43–61.

Blackman, A. Wade, Jr. "The Market Dynamics of Technological Substitutions." *Technological Forecasting and Social Change*, Vol. 6, No. 1 (1974), pp. 41–63.

Blackman, A. Wade, Jr., E. J. Seligman, and G. C. Solgliero. "An Innovation Index Based Upon Factor Analysis." *Technological Forecasting and Social Change*, Vol. 4 (1973), pp. 301–316.

Blake, Robert R., and Jane S. Mouten. *The Grid for Sales Excellence: Benchmarks for Effective Salesmanship.* New York: McGraw-Hill, 1970.

———. "Evaluation of Stochastic Brand Choice Models." In *Marketing Decision Models,* ed. R. Schultz and A. Zoltners. New York: North Holland, 1981.

Blattberg, Robert C., Thomas Buessing, Peter Peacock, and Subrata Sen. "Identifying the Deal Prone Segment." *Journal of Marketing Research,* Vol. 15, No. 3 (August 1978), pp. 369–377.

Blattberg, Robert C., Gary D. Eppen, and Joshua Lieberman. "A Theoretical and Empirical Evaluation of Price Deals for Consumer Non-Durables." *Journal of Marketing,* Vol. 45, No. 1 (Winter 1981), pp. 116–129.

Blattberg, Robert C., and John Golanty. "Tracker: An Early Test Market Forecasting and Diagnostic Model for New Product Planning." *Journal of Marketing Research,* Vol. 15 (May 1978), pp. 192–202.

Blattberg, Robert C., and Abel P. Jeuland. "A Micro-Modeling Approach to Determine the Advertising-Sales Relationship." *Management Science,* Vol. 27, No. 9 (September 1981), pp. 988–1004.

Blattberg, Robert, and Subrata K. Sen. "An Evaluation of the Application of Minimum Chi Square Procedures to Stochastic Models of Brand Choice." *Journal of Marketing Research,* Vol. 10 (1973), pp. 421–427.

———. "Market Segmentation Using Models of Multidmensional Purchasing Behavior." *Journal of Marketing,* Vol. 38 (October 1974), pp. 17–28.

———. "A Bayesian Technique to Discriminate Between Stochastic Models of Brand Choice." *Management Science,* Vol. 21, No. 6 (February 1975), pp. 682–696.

———. "Market Segments and Stochastic Brand Choice Models." *Journal of Marketing Research,* Vol. 13 (February 1976), pp. 34–45.

Bloom, Derek, Andrea Jay, and Tony Twyman. "The Validity of Advertising Pretests." *Journal of Advertising Research,* Vol. 17, No. 2 (April 1977), pp. 7–16.

Boehm, Barry. "Software and Its Impact: A Quantitative Assessment." *Datamation* (May 1973), pp. 48–59.

Bonczek, Robert H., Clyde W. Holsapple, and Andrew B. Whinston. "A Generalized Decision Support System Using Predicate Calculus and Network Data Base Management." *Operations Research,* Vol. 29, No. 2 (March–April 1981), pp. 263–281.

Bonoma, Thomas V., G. Zaltman, and W. Johnson. *Industrial Buying Behavior.* Cambridge, Mass.: Marketing Science Institute, 1977.

Boot, T. *Quadratic Programming Algorithms: Anomalies and Applications.* Skokie, Ill.: Rand McNally, 1964.

Booz, Allen and Hamilton. *Management of New Products.* New York: 1971.

Bordley, Robert F. "A Multiplicative Formula for Aggregating Probability Assessments." *Management Science,* Vol. 28, No. 10 (October 1982), pp. 1137–1148.

The Boston Consulting Group. *Perspectives on Experience.* Boston: 1970.

Bower, John. "Net Audiences of U.S. and Canadian Magazines: Seven Tests of Agostini's Formula." *Journal of Advertising Research* (March 1963), pp. 13–21.

Bowersox, D. J., O. K. Helferich, E. J. Marien, P. Gilmour, M. L. Lawrence, F. W. Morgan, and R. T. Rogers. *Dynamic Simulation of Physical Distribution Systems.* East Lansing: Michigan State University Business Studies, 1972.

Bowman, E. H. "Consistency and Optimality in Managerial Decision Making." *Management Science,* Vol. 9 (January 1963), pp. 310–321.

Box, George E. P., and Gwilym M. Jenkins. *Time Series Analysis: Forecasting and Control.* 2nd ed. San Francisco: Holden-Day, 1976.

Boyd, Harper W., Jr., and Michael L. Ray. "What Big Agency Men in Europe Think of Copy Testing Methods." *Journal of Marketing Research,* Vol. 8 (May 1971), pp. 219–223.

Boyd, Harper W., Jr., Ralph Westfall, and Stanley F. Stasch. *Marketing Research: Text and Cases.* 4th ed. Homewood, Ill.: Irwin, 1977.

Bradley, M. F. "Buying Behavior in Ireland's Public Sector." *Industrial Marketing Management,* Vol. 6 (August 1977), pp. 251–258.

Bradley, Stephen P., Arnoldo C. Hax, and Thomas L. Magnanti. *Applied Mathematical Programming.* Reading, Mass.: Addison-Wesley, 1977.

Brand, Gordon T. *The Industrial Buying Decision.* London: The Institute of Marketing and Industrial Marketing Research, 1972.

Braun, M. A., and V. Srinivasan. "Amount of Information as a Determinant of Consumer Behavior Toward New Products." Reprint Series, Report No. 220. Stanford University, 1975.

Braverman, Jerome D. "A Decision Theoretic Approach to Pricing." *Decision Sciences,* Vol. 2, No. 1 (January 1971), pp. 1–16.

Brigham, Eugene F. *Fundamentals of Financial Management.* Hinsdale, Ill.: Dryden Press, 1980.

Bright, J. R. "Evaluating Signals of Technological Change." *Harvard Business Review,* Vol. 8, No. 1 (January–February 1970), pp. 62–79.

Briscoe, C. "Some Observations on New Industrial Product Failures." *Industrial Marketing Management,* Vol. 2 (February 1973), pp. 151–162.

Brooks, Douglas G. "Cost Oriented Pricing: A Realistic Solution to a Complicated Problem." *Journal of Marketing,* Vol. 39, No. 2 (April 1975), pp. 72–74.

Brown, A. A., and A. Deaton. "Surveys in Applied Economics: Models of Consumer Behavior." *The Economic Journal,* Vol. 82 (1972), pp. 1145–1236.

Brown, A. A., F. T. Hulswit, and J. D. Kettelle. "A Study of Sales Operations." *Operations Research Quarterly,* Vol. 4 (June 1956), pp. 296–308.

Brown, D. B., and M. R. Warshaw. "Media Selection by Linear Programming." *Journal of Market Research,* Vol. 2 (February 1965), pp. 83–88.

Brown, L. O. "Quantitative Market Analysis: Scope and Uses." *Harvard Business Review,* Vol. 15, No. 2 (Winter 1937), pp. 233–244.

Brown, Robert G. "A Model for Measuring the Influence of Promotion on Inventory and Consumer Demand." *Journal of Marketing Research* (November 1973), pp. 380–389.

———. "Sales Response to Promotions and Advertising." *Journal of Advertising Research* (August 1974), pp. 33–39.

Brown, R. V. *Research and the Credibility of Estimates.* Cambridge, Mass.: Harvard University Press, 1969.

Bubb, P. L., and D. J. van Rest. "Loyalty as a Component of the Industrial Buying Decision." *Industrial Marketing Management,* Vol. 3 (1973), pp. 25–32.

Buckner, Hugh. *How British Industry Buys.* London: Hutchinson, 1967.

Bunge, Mario. *Scientific Research: The Search for Information.* New York: Springer-Verlag, 1967.

Burger, Philip C. "COMP: A New Product Forecasting System." Working paper 123–72, Graduate School of Management, Northwestern University, 1972.

Burger, Philip C., Robert J. Lavidge, and Howard N. Gundee. "COMP: A Comprehensive System for the Evaluation of New Products." Working paper. Chicago: Elrich and Lavidge, October 1978.

Bursk, Edward D., and Stephen A. Greyser. *Advanced Cases in Marketing Management.* Englewood Cliffs, N.J.: Prentice-Hall, 1968.

Bush, R., and F. Mosteller. *Stochastic Models for Learning.* New York: Wiley, 1955.

Buzzell, R. D. *Mathematical Models and Marketing Management.* Boston: Harvard University, Division of Research, 1964.

Buzzell, Robert. "Competitive Behavior and Product Life Cycles." In *New Ideas for Successful Marketing.* ed. J. S. Wright and J. L. Goldstucker. Chicago: American Marketing Association, 1966.

———. "Are There 'Natural' Market Structures?" *Journal of Marketing,* Vol. 45 (Winter 1981), pp. 42–51.

Buzzell, Robert D., and Paul W. Farris. "Industrial Marketing Costs." Working paper, Marketing Science Institute, December 1976.

Buzzell, Robert D., and Frederik D. Wiersema. "Modeling Changes in Market Shares: A Cross Sectional Analysis." Working paper, Harvard Business School, 1980.

Cadbury, N. D. "When, Where and How to Test Market." *Harvard Business Review* (May-June 1975), pp. 96–105.

Cadotte, E. R. "TELLUS Computer Lets Retailers Conduct In-Store Market Research." *Marketing News,* Vol. 14, No. 2 (1980), p. 17.

Calentone, Roger J., and Robert G. Cooper. "A Typology of Industrial New Product Failures." In *1977 Educator's Conference Proceedings,* ed. B. Greenberg and D. Bellenger, pp. 492–497. Chicago: American Marketing Association, 1977.

Cardozo, Richard N., and James W. Cagley. "An Experimental Study of Industrial Buyer Behavior." *Journal of Marketing Research,* Vol. 8 (August 1971), pp. 329–334.

Cardozo, Richard, and Yoram Wind. "Industrial Market Segmentation." *Industrial Marketing Management,* Vol. 3 (1974), pp. 153–166.

Cardozo, Richard, and Yoram Wind. "Portfolio Analysis for Strategic Product Market Planning." Working paper, Wharton School, 1980.

Carlson, J. G. "How Management Can Use the Improvement Phenomenon." *California Management Review,* Vol. 3, No. 2 (1961), pp. 83–94.

―――. "Cubic Learning Curves: Precision Tools for Labor Estimating." *Manufacturing Engineering and Management.* Vol. 71, No. 5 (1973), pp. 22–25.

Carman, J. M. "Brand Switching and Linear Learning Models." *Journal of Advertising Research,* Vol. 6 (June 1966), pp. 23–31.

Carmone, F. J., P. E. Green, and A. K. Jain. "Robustness of Conjoint Analysis: Some Monte Carlo Results." *Journal of Marketing Research,* Vol. 15 (May 1978), pp. 300–303.

Carroll, J. D., and J. J. Chang. "A General Index of Nonlinear Correlation and Its Applications to the Interpretation of Multidimensional Scaling Solutions." *American Psychologist* 19 (1964), pp. 540–549.

―――. "Relating Preference Data to Multidimensional Scaling Solutions via a Generalization of Coombs Unfolding Model." Bell Telephone Laboratories Report. Murray Hill, N.J.: 1967.

―――. "Analysis of Individual Differences in Multidimensional Scaling via an N-way Generalization of the Eckart-Young Decomposition." *Psychometrika,* 35 (1970), pp. 283–319.

Cattin, Philippe and Dick R. Wittink. "Commercial Use of Conjoint Analysis: A Survey." *Journal of Marketing,* Vol. 46 (Summer 1982) pp. 44–53.

Chakravarti, D., A. A. Mitchell, and R. Staelin. "Judgemental Based Marketing Decision Models: An Experimental Investigation." *Management Science,* Vol. 25 (March, 1979), pp. 251–263.

―――. "Two Experiments Assessing the Efficiency of Judgement Based Models in Aiding Marketers' Decisions." In *Proceedings, First Market Measurement and Analysis Conference,* ed. D. Montgomery and D. Wittink, pp. 531–550. Cambridge, Mass.: Marketing Science Institute, 1980a.

Chakravarti, D., A. A. Mitchell, and R. Staelin. "A Procedure for Parameterizing Decision Calculus Models of Dynamic Market Response." In *Proceedings from the Second ORSA/TIMS Special Interest Conference on Market Measurement and Analysis,* ed. R. Leone, pp. 182–193. Providence, R.I.: The Institute of Management Sciences, 1980.

―――. "Judgement Based Marketing Decision Models: Problems and Possible Solutions." *Journal of Marketing,* Vol. 45, No. 4 (Fall 1981), pp. 13–23.

Chamberlain, E. *The Theory of Monopolistic Competition.* Cambridge, Mass.: Harvard University Press, 1957.

Chambers, John C., Satinder K. Mullick, and Donald D. Smith. *An Executive's Guide to Forecasting*. New York: Wiley, 1974.

Chandon, Jean-Louis. "Cluster Analysis in Marketing Research." Paper presented at EURO/TIMS/ORSA Marketing Science Conference, ESSEC/Paris, 1980.

Chapman, Randall G. "Retail Trade Area Analysis: Analytics and Statistics." In *Proceedings from the Second ORSA/TIMS Special Interest Conference on Market Measurement and Analysis*, ed. R. Leone, ed. Providence, RI. The Institute of Management Sciences, 1980, pp. 50–53.

Chapman, Randall G., and Richard Staelin. "Exploiting Rank Ordered Choice Set Data Within the Stochastic Utility Model." *Journal of Marketing Research*, Vol. 19 (August 1982), pp. 288–301.

Charlton, P., A. S. C. Ehrenberg, and B. Pymont. "Buyer Behavior under Mini-Test-Conditions." *Journal of the Market Research Society*, 14 (1972) pp. 171–183.

Charnes, A., and W. W. Cooper. "Chance-Constrained Programming." *Management Science*, Vol. 6 (October 1959), pp. 73–80.

Charnes, A., W. W. Cooper, J. K. Devoe, D. B. Learner, and W. Reinecke. "A Goal Programming Model for Media Planning." *Management Science* 14 (April 1968), pp. 431–436.

Chatfield, C., A. S. C. Ehrenberg, and G. J. Goodhardt. "Progress on a Simplified Model of Stationary Purchasing Behavior." *Journal of the Royal Statistical Society*, Series A (1966), pp. 317–367.

Chatfield, C., and G. J. Goodhardt. "A Consumer Purchasing Model with Erlang Inter-Purchase Times." *Journal of the American Statistical Association* (December 1973), pp. 828–835.

Chevalier, Michael, and Ronald C. Curhan. "Retail Promotions as a Function of Trade Promotions: A Descriptive Analysis." *Sloan Management Review*, Vol. 18 (Fall 1976), pp. 19–32.

Choffray, Jean-Marie. "A Methodology for Investigating the Structure of the Industrial Adoption Process and the Differences in Perception and Evaluation Criteria Among Potential Decision Participants." Ph.D. thesis, MIT, April 1977.

———. "A Normative Methodology to Support Corporate Diversification Decisions." Paper presented at the Intensive Advanced Course in Marketing—Corporate Diversification and the Management of the Industrial Innovation Process, European Institute for Advanced Studies in Management, Brussels, November 1981.

Choffray, Jean-Marie, and Gary L. Lilien. "Assessing Response to Industrial Marketing Strategy." *Journal of Marketing*, Vol. 42, No. 2 (April 1978a) pp. 20–31.

———. "The Market for Solar Cooling: Perceptions, Response and Strategy Implication." In *Energy Policy, Studies in the Management Series*, Vol. 10, eds. J. Aronofsky, A. Rao, and M. Shakun, pp. 209–226. New York: North Holland, 1978b.

———. "Industrial Market Segmentation by the Structure of the Purchasing Process." *Industrial Marketing Management*, Vol. 9, No. 4 (October 1980a), pp. 331–342.

———. "A Model-Based Methodology for Assessing Market Response for New Industrial Products." In *Research in Marketing*, Vol. 3, ed. J. Sheth, pp. 37–81. Greenwich, Conn.: JAI Press, 1980b.

———. *Market Planning for New Industrial Products*. New York: Wiley, 1980c.

———. "DESIGNOR: A Decision Support Procedure for Industrial Product Design." *Journal of Business Research*, Vol. 10, No. 2 (September 1982), pp. 185–197.

Choffray, Jean-Marie, Gary L. Lilien, Paul E. Johnston, and Murray Wolinsky. "A Pre-Test Market Model and Measurement Procedure for New Packaged Goods." Working paper, Marketing Science Center, ESSEC, France, 1979.

Chow, G. C. "Technological Change and the Demand for Computers." *American Economic Review*, Vol. 57, No. 5 (December 1967), pp. 1117–1130.

Churchill, Gilbert A., Jr. *Marketing Research: Methodological Foundations*. 2nd ed., Hinsdale, Ill.: Dryden Press, 1979.

Churchman, C. West, Russell L. Ackoff, and E.

Leonard Arnoff. *Introduction to Operations Research.* New York: Wiley, 1957.

Churchman, C. West, and A. H. Schainblatt. "The Research and the Manager: A Dialectic of Implementation." *Management Science,* Vol. 11 (February 1965), pp. B69–87.

Chussil, Mark J. "How Much to Spend in R and D?" *Pimsletter,* No. 13 (1978).

Chussil, Mark J., and Steve Downs. "When Value Helps." *Pimsletter,* No. 18 (1979).

Clarke, Darral G. "Sales-Advertising Cross-Elasticities and Advertising Competition." *Journal of Marketing Research,* Vol. 10 (August 1973), pp. 250–261.

————. "Economic Measurement of the Duration of Advertising Effects on Sales." *Journal of Marketing Research,* Vol. 18 (1976), pp. 345–357.

Claycamp, Henry J., and Lucien E. Liddy. "Prediction of New Product Performance: An Analytical Approach." *Journal of Marketing Research,* Vol. 6 (November 1969), pp. 414–420.

Claycamp, Henry J., and William F. Massy. "A Theory of Market Segmentation." *Journal of Marketing Research,* Vol. 5 (November 1968), pp. 388–394.

Claycamp, Henry J., and C. W. McClelland. "Estimating Reach and the Magic of K." *Journal of Advertising Research,* Vol. 8 (June 1968), pp. 44–51.

Clee, M. A., and R. A. Wicklund. "Consumer Behavior and Psychological Reactance." *Journal of Consumer Research,* Vol. 6 (March 1980), pp. 389–405.

Clemons, E. K. "Data Base Design for Decision Support." Ph.D. thesis, The Warton School, University of Pennsylvania, 1980.

Clowes, G. A. "Data Management Should be No. 1 Priority in Developing On-Line Marketing Information Systems." *Marketing News,* Vol. 14, No. 12 (1980), pp. 1–10.

Cochran, W. G., and G. M. Cox. *Experimental Design.* 2nd ed., New York: Wiley, 1957.

Cochrane, D., and G. H. Orcutt. "Application of Least Squares Regression to Relationships Containing Autoregressive Error Terms." *Journal of the American Statistical Association,* Vol. 44 (1949), pp. 32–61.

Cocks, Douglas L., and John R. Virts. "Market Diffusion and Concentration in the Ethical Pharmaceutical Industry." Internal memorandum, Eli Lilly & Co., 1975.

Cohen, Jason N. *Decision Support Systems for Marketing Models.* Master's thesis, MIT June 1981.

Coleman, J. C., E. Katz, and A. Menzel. "The Diffusion of an Innovation Among Physicians." *Sociometry,* Vol. 20, No. 4 (December 1957), pp. 253–270.

Coleman, Richard P. "The Significance of Social Stratification in Selling." In *Marketing: A Maturing Discipline,* ed. M. L. Bell. Chicago: American Marketing Association, 1961.

Colley, Russel H. *Defining Advertising Goals for Measured Advertising Results.* New York: Association of National Advertisers, 1961.

Comer, J. M. "ALLOCATE: A Computer Model for Sales Territory Planning." *Decision Sciences,* Vol. 5 (July 1974), pp. 323–338.

Conference Board. "Options in New Product Organization." Report No. 613. New York, 1974.

Connors, M. M., C. Coray, C. J. Cuccaro, W. K. Green, D. W. Low, and H. M. Markowitz. "The Distribution System Simulator." *Management Science,* Vol. 18, No. 8 (April 1972), pp. B425–453.

Cooke, Ernest, and Ben Edmundson. "Computer Aided Product Investment Decisions." In *Increasing Marketing Productivity and Conceptual and Methodological Foundations of Marketing,* ed. T. Greer. Chicago: American Marketing Association, 1963.

Cooper, R. G. "Why New Industrial Products Fail." *Industrial Marketing Management,* Vol. 4, No. 2 (December 1975), pp. 315–326.

Cooper, R. L. "The Predictive Performance of Quarterly Econometric Models of the United States." In *Econometric Models of Cyclical Behavior,* ed. B. C. Hickman. New York: National Bureau of Economic Research, 1972.

Copland, B. D. *The Study of Attention Value.* London: Business Publications, 1958.

Corey, E. Raymond. *Industrial Marketing: Cases and Concepts.* 2nd ed. Englewood Cliffs, N.J.: Prentice-Hall, 1976.

Corstjens, M., and Peter Doyle. "Channel Optimization in Complex Marketing Systems." *Management Science,* Vol. 25, No. 10 (October 1979), pp. 1014–1025.

————. "A Model for Optimizing Retail Space Allocations." *Management Science,* Vol. 27, No. 7 (July 1981), pp. 822–833.

Corstjens, Marcel, and David Weinstein. "Optimal Strategic Business Unit Portfolio Analysis." In *Marketing Planning Models,* ed. A. Zoltners. TIMS Studies in the Management Sciences, Vol. 18. New York: North-Holland, 1982, pp. 141–160.

Cort, Stanton G., David R. Lambert, and Paula L. Garret. *Frequency in Business-to-Business Advertising—A State-of-the-Art Review.* Presented at the 4th Annual Business Advertising Research Conference, April 21, 1982. New York: The Advertising Research Foundation, 1982.

Cotton, B. C., and Emerson M. Babb. "Consumer Response to Promotional Deals." *Journal of Marketing,* Vol. 42 (July 1978), pp. 109–113.

Cowling, K., and J. Cubbin. "Price, Quality and Advertising Competition: An Econometric Investigation of the United Kingdom Car Market." *Economica,* Vol. 38 (1971), pp. 378–394.

Cox, D. R. *Analysis of Binary Data.* London: Methuen, 1970.

Cox, Donald F., and Robert E. Good. "How to Build a Marketing Information System." *Harvard Business Review,* Vol. 45 (May–June 1967), pp. 145–154.

Cox, William, Jr. "Product Life Cycles as Marketing Models." *Journal of Business,* Vol. 40 (October 1967), pp. 375–384.

Cox, William E., Jr., and George N. Havens. "Determination of Sales Potential and Performance for an Industrial Goods Manufacturer." *Journal of Marketing Research,* Vol. 14, No. 4 (November 1977), pp. 574–578.

Crafton, Steven M. "Convenience Store Pricing and Value of Time: A Note on the Becker-Devany Full Price Model." *Southern Economic Journal,* Vol. 45, No. 4 (April 1979), pp. 1254–1260.

Cravens, David W. "Salesforce Decision Models: A Comparative Assessment." In *Sales Management: New Developments from Behavioral and Decision Model Research,* ed. R. Bagozzi, pp. 310–324. Cambridge, Mass.: Marketing Science Institute, 1979.

Crawford, C. M. "Marketing Research and the New Product Failure Rate." *Journal of Marketing,* Vol. 41 (April 1977), pp. 51–61.

Crissy, W. J. E., W. H. Cunningham, and I. C. M. Cunningham. *Selling: The Personal Force in Marketing.* New York: Wiley, 1977.

Crow, Lowell E., Richard W. Olshavsky, and John O. Summers. "Industrial Buyers' Choice Strategies: A Protocol Analysis." *Journal of Marketing Research,* Vol. 17 (February 1980), pp. 34–44.

Curry, David J. "Some Statistical Considerations in Clustering with Binary Data." *Multivariate Behavioral Research* (Arpil 1976), pp. 175–189.

Cyert, Richard M, Herbert A. Simon, and Donald B. Trow. "Observation of a Business Decision." *Journal of Business,* Vol. 29 (October 1956), pp. 237–248.

Czepiel, John. "Decision Group and Firm Characteristics in an Industrial Adoption Decision." In *Marketing: 1776–1976 and Beyond,* ed. K. L. Bernhardt. Chicago: American Marketing Association, 1976.

D'Abro, A. *The Rise of the New Physics.* New York: Dover, 1951.

Daganzo, Carlos. *Multinomial Probit.* New York: Academic Press, 1979.

Dalkey, Norman C. "The Delphi Method: An Experimental Study of Group Opinion." RM-5888 PR, Rand Corporation, June 1969.

Dalkey, Norman C., and Olaf Helmer. "An Experimental Application of the Delphi Method to the Use of Experts." *Management Science,* Vol. 9 (April 1963), pp. 458–467.

Dalrymple, D. J. "Sales Forecasting Methods and Accuracy." *Business Horizons* (December 1975), pp. 69–73.

Dalziel, Murray M. "Using AGCLUS: A Program to Do Hierarchical Clustering Analysis." Harvard University, Cambridge, Mass. Center for the Behavioral Sciences Computing Facility, January 1974.

Darmon, R. Y. "Salesmen's Response to Financial Incentives; An Empirical Study." *Journal of Marketing Research*, Vol. 9 (November 1974), pp. 418–426.

———. "Scheduling Sales Calls with a Communication Response Model." In *Marketing in Turbulent Times* and *Marketing: The Challenges and Opportunities*, AMA Combined Proceedings Series, No. 37, ed. E. Mazze, pp. 530–533. Chicago: American Marketing Association, 1975.

———. "Setting Sales Quotas with Conjoint Analysis." *Journal of Marketing Research*, Vol. 16 (February 1979), pp. 133–140.

Davidson, J. H. "Why Most New Consumer Brands Fail." *Harvard Business Review*, Vol. 54 (March–April 1976), pp. 117–121.

Davis, Harry L. "Dimensions of Marital Roles in Consumer Decision-Making." *Journal of Marketing Research*, Vol. 7 (May 1970), pp. 168–177.

Davis, J. H. "Group Decision and Social Interaction: A Theory of Social Decision Schemes." *Psychological Review*, Vol. 80, No. 2 (March 1973), pp. 97–125.

Davis, J. H., J. L. Cohen, J. Hornik, and K. Rissman. "Dyadic Decision as a Function of the Frequency Distribution Describing the Preferences of Members' Constituencies." *Journal of Personality and Social Psychology*, Vol. 26, No. 2 (1973), pp. 178–195.

Davis, K. Roscoe, and L. F. Simmons. "Exploring Market Pricing Strategies Via Dynamic Programming." *Decision Sciences*, Vol. 7, Nov. 2 (April 1976), pp. 181–193.

Davis, Otto A., and John U. Farley. "Allocating Sales Force Effort with Commissions and Quotas." *Management Science*, Vol. 18, No. 4, Part II (December 1971), pp. 55–63.

Dawes, R., and B. Corrigan. "Linear Models in Decision-Making." *Psychological Bulletin*, Vol. 81 (February 1974), pp. 95–106.

Day, George. "The Product Life Cycle: Analysis and Applications Issues." *Journal of Marketing*, Vol. 45, No. 4 (Fall 1981a), pp. 60–67.

———. "Analytical Approaches to Strategic Market Planning." In *Review of Marketing*, ed. B. Enis and K. Roering. Chicago: American Marketing Association, 1981b.

Day, George S., Allan D. Shocker, and Rajendra K. Srivastava. "Consumer-Oriented Approaches to Identifying Product Markets." *Journal of Marketing*, Vol. 43, No. 4 (Fall 1979), pp. 8–19.

Day, Ralph L. "Linear Programming in Media Selection." *Journal of Advertising Research* (June 1963), pp. 40–44.

Deal, K. R., and S. Zionts. "A Differential Game Solution to the Problem of Determining the Optimal Timing of Advertising Expenditures." In *Proceedings of the Second Annual Northeast Regional AIDS Conference. Kingston, R.I., April 13–14, 1973*, ed. Sherman Chottiner. Atlanta: American Institue of Decision Sciences, 1973.

Dean, J. R. "Pricing Pioneering Projects." *Journal of Industrial Economics*, Vol. 17 (July 1969), pp. 165–179.

Della Bitta, Albert J., Kent B. Monroe, and John M. McGinnis. "Consumer Perceptions of Comparative Price Advertisements." *Journal of Marketing Research*, Vol. 18 (November 1981), pp. 416–427.

Departmental Merchandising and Operating Results of 1962. New York: National Retail Merchants Association, 1963.

Dhalla, Nariman, and Sonia Yuspeh. "Forget the Product Life Cycle Concept." *Harvard Business Review*, Vol. 54 (January–February 1976), pp. 102–112.

Diamond, Daniel S. "A Quantitative Approach to Magazine Advertisement Format Selection." *Journal of Marketing Research* (November 1968), pp. 376–387.

Diamond, William T. *Distribution Channels for Industrial Goods.* Columbus: Ohio State University Press, 1963.

Dillon, William R., Donald G. Frederick, and Vanchai Tangpanichdee. "A Note on Accounting for Sources of Variation in Perceptual Maps." *Journal of Marketing Research*, Vol. 19 (August 1982), pp. 302–311.

Dodds, Wellesley. "An Application of the Bass Model in Long-Term New Product Forecasting." *Journal of Marketing Research*, Vol. 10 (August 1973), pp. 308–311.

Dodson, Joe A., Jr., and Eitan Muller. "Models of New Product Diffusion Through Advertising and Word-of-Mouth." *Management Science*, Vol. 24 (November 1978), pp. 1568–1578.

Dodson, Joe A., Jr., Alice M. Tybout, and Brian Sternthal. "Impact of Deals and Deal Retractions on Brand Switching." *Journal of Marketing Research*, Vol. 15 (February 1978), pp. 72–81.

Doktor, R. H., and W. F. Hamilton. "Cognitive Style and the Acceptance of Management Science Recommendations." *Management Science*, Vol. 19, No. 8 (April 1973), pp. 884–894.

Doktor, R. H., R. L. Schultz, and D. P. Slevin, eds. *The Implementation of Management Science*. TIMS Studies in the Managements Sciences, Vol. 13. New York: North Holland, 1979.

Dolan, Robert J. "Models of Competition: A Review of Theory and Empirical Evidence." In *Review of Marketing*, eds. B. Enis and K. Roering, pp. 224–234. Chicago: American Marketing Association, 1981.

Dolan, Robert J. and Darral G. Clarke. "Definition and Choice of New Product Pricing Strategies." In *Proceedings from the Third ORSA/TIMS Special Interest Conference on Market Measurement and Analysis, 1981*, ed. J. Keon, pp. 108–116. Providence, R.I.: The Institute of Management Sciences, 1981.

Dolan, Robert J., and Abel P. Jeuland. "Experience Curves and Dynamic Demand Models: Implementation for Optimal Pricing Strategies." *Journal of Marketing*, Vol. 45, No. 1 (Winter 1981), pp. 52–73.

Dorfman, R., and P. O. Steiner. "Optimal Advertising and Optimal Quality." *The American Economic Review*, Vol. 44 (1954), pp. 826–836.

Downey, William T., *et al.*, *The Effect of Government Economic Incentives on the Industrial Market Penetration of Capital Intensive Solar Thermal and Wind Energy Systems*. Lexington, Mass.: Arthur D. Little, 1981.

Doyle, Peter, and Ian Fenwick. "The Pitfalls of AID Analysis." *Journal of Marketing Research*, Vol. 12 (November 1975), pp. 408–413.

Doyle, S. X. "The Motivation and Compensation of Field Sales Representatives." Ph.D. thesis, Harvard Business School, 1976.

Draper, Norman, and Harry Smith. *Applied Regression Analysis*. New York: Wiley, 1966.

Dufton, Charles. "Rayco Manufacturing Company, Inc.: Pinpointing Store Locations by Electronic Computer." Case 3M38, Intercollegiate Case Clearing House. Boston: Harvard Graduate School of Business Administration, 1958.

Duncan, W. J. "The Researcher and the Manager: A Comparative View of the Need for Mutual Understanding." *Management Science*, Vol. 20, No. 8 (April 1974), pp. 1157–1163.

Dunn, Theodore F., and Ruth Ziff. "PREP: A New Copytesting System." *Journal of Advertising Research*, Vol. 14, No. 5 (October 1974), pp. 53–59.

Dutta, Biplab K., and William R. King. "A Competitive Scenario Modeling System." *Management Science*, Vol. 26, No. 3 (March 1980), pp. 261–273.

Dyckman, Thomas R. "Management Implementation of Scientific Research: An Attitudinal Study." *Management Science*, Vol. 13 (June 1967), pp. B612–620.

Easingwood, C. "Heuristic Approach to Selecting Sales Regions and Territories." *Operations Research Quarterly*, Vol. 24, No. 4 (December 1973), pp. 527–534.

Eckert, Ann. "Models of Industrial Buyer Behavior: A State-of-the-Art Review." Master's thesis, Sloan School of Management, MIT, 1981.

Edelman, Franz. "Art and Science of Competitive Bidding." *Harvard Business Review* (July–August 1965), pp. 53–66.

Ehrenberg, A. S. C. "The Pattern of Consumer Purchases." *Applied Statistics*, Vol. 8 (1959), pp. 26–46.

————. "An Appraisal of Markov Brand Switching Models." *Journal of Marketing Research*, Vol. 2 (1965), pp. 347–363.

————. *Repeat-Buying: Theory and Applications.* Amsterdam: North-Holland, 1972.

————. *Data Reduction.* London: Wiley, 1975.

Ehrenberg, A. S. C., and G. J. Goodhart. "The Hendry Brand Switching Coefficient." *ADMAP*, Vol. 10, No. 4 (1973), pp. 232–238.

Ehrenberg, A. S. C., and F. G. Pyatt. *Consumer Behavior.* London: Penguin Books, 1971.

Eliashberg, Joshua. "Consumer Preference Judgements: An Exposition with Empirical Applications." *Management Science*, Vol. 26, No. 1 (January 1980), pp. 60–77.

Elrod, Terry, and Russel S. Winer. "An Empirical Evaluation of Aggregation Approaches for Developing Market Segments." *Journal of Marketing*, Vol. 46 (Fall 1982), pp. 65–74.

Engel, James F., D. T. Kollat, and R. D. Blackwell. *Consumer Behavior.* New York: Holt, Rinehart and Winston, 1968.

Engel, James F., and Martin R. Warshaw. "Allocating Advertising Dollars by Linear Programming." *Journal of Advertising Research*, Vol. 4 (September 1964), pp. 42–48.

Engelbrecht-Wiggans, Richard. "Auctions and Bidding Models: A Survey." *Management Science*, Vol. 26, No. 2 (February 1980), pp. 118–142.

Erickson, Gary M. "Advertising in Dynamic Markets." In *Proceedings from the Second ORSA/TIMS Special Interest Conference on Market Measurement and Analysis*, ed. R. Leone, pp. 110–120. Providence, R.I.: The Institute of Management Science, 1980.

————. "Using Ridge Regression to Estimate Directly Lagged Effects in Marketing." *Journal of the American Statistical Association*, Vol. 76, No. 376 (December 1981), pp. 766–773.

Erickson, Gary, and David B. Montgomery. "Measuring the Time-Varying Response to Market Communication Instruments." In *Market Measurement and Analysis*, eds. D. Montgomery and D. Wittink. Cambridge, Mass.: Marketing Science Institute, 1980.

Eskin, Gerald J. "Dynamic Forecasts of New Product Demand Using a Depth of Repeat Model." *Journal of Marketing Research*, Vol. 10 (May 1973), pp. 115–129.

Eskin, Gerald J., and Penny H. Baron. "Effects of Price and Advertising in Test Market Experiments." *Journal of Marketing Research*, Vol. 14 (November 1977), pp. 499–508.

Eskin, Gerald J., and John Malec. "A Model for Estimating Sales Potential Prior to Test Marketing." In *Proceedings of the American Marketing Association Educators' Conference*, ed. K. L. Bernhardt, pp. 230–233. Chicago: American Marketing Association, 1976.

Everitt, B. S. *Cluster Analysis.* London: Halsted Press, 1974.

Ewers, Jack, and Iris Vessey. "The Systems Development Dilemma—A Programming Perspective." *MIS Quarterly* (June 1981), pp. 33–45.

Faivre, J. P., and C. Sanchez. "The Validation of Marketing Models." In *Proceedings of ESOMAR Seminar on Marketing Models, Noordwijk-aan-zee: The Netherlands 1973*, pp. 133–191.

Farley, John U. "An Optimal Plan for Salesmen's Compensation." *Journal of Marketing Research*, Vol. 1 (May 1964), pp. 39–43.

Farley, John U., and H. J. Leavitt. "A Model of the Distribution of Branded Personal Products in Jamaica." *Journal of Marketing Research*, Vol. 5 (1968), pp. 362–368.

Farley, John U., and L. Winston Ring. "A Stochastic Model of Supermarket Traffic Flow." *Operations Research* (July 1966), pp. 555–567.

————. "An Empirical Test of the Howard-Sheth Model of Consumer Buying Behavior. *Journal of Marketing Research*, Vol. 7 (November 1970), pp. 427–435.

———. "Empirical Specification of a Buyer Behavior Model." *Journal of Marketing Research*, Vol. 11, No. 1 (February 1974), pp. 89–96.

Farley, John U., and C. B. Weinberg. "Inferential Optimization: An Algorithm for Determining Optimal Sales Commissions in Multiproduct Sales Forces." *Operations Research Quarterly*, Vol. 25 (June 1975), pp. 413–418.

Farris, Paul W., and Mark S. Albion. "The Impact of Advertising on the Price of Consumer Products." *Journal of Marketing*, Vol. 44, No. 3 (Summer 1980), pp. 17–35.

Farris, Paul W., and Robert D. Buzzell. "Relationship Between Changes in Industrial Advertising and Promotion Expenditures and Changes in Market Share." Marketing Science Institute working paper, No. 76–119. Cambridge, Mass.: Marketing Science Institute, December 1976.

———. "Why Advertising and Promotional Costs Vary: Some Cross Sectional Analyses." *Journal of Marketing*, Vol. 43, No. 4 (Fall 1979), pp. 112–122.

———. "A Comment on 'Modeling the Marketing Mix Decision for Industrial Products.'" *Management Science*, Vol. 26, No. 1 (January 1980), pp. 97–100.

Feldman, W., and R. Cardozo. "The 'Industrial' Revolution and Models of Buyer Behavior." *Journal of Purchasing* (November 1969), pp. 77–88.

Fiacco, A. V., and G. P. McCormick. *Nonlinear Programming: Sequential Unconstrained Minimization Techniques.* New York: Wiley, 1968.

Fieldhouse, M. "The Depot Location Problem." Paper presented at the 17th International Conference of TIMS, London, July 1970.

Fishbein, Martin. "An Investigation of Relationship Between Beliefs About an Object and the Attitude Toward the Object." *Human Relations*, Vol. 16 (1963), pp. 233–240.

———. "Attitude and Prediction of Behavior." In *Readings in Attitude Theory and Mea-surement*, ed. Martin Fishbein, pp. 477–492. New York: Wiley, 1967.

Fishbein, Martin, and I. Ajzen. *Belief, Attitude, Intention and Behavior.* Reading, Mass.: Addison-Wesley, 1975.

Fishburn, Peter C. "A Survey of Multiattribute/ Multicriterion Evaluation Theories." In *Multiple Criterion Problem Solving*, ed. S. Zionts. New York: Springer-Verlag, 1977.

Fisher, Frank M. *The Identification Problem in Econometrics.* New York: McGraw-Hill, 1966.

Fisher, J. C., and R. H. Pry. "A Simple Substitution Model of Technological Change." *Technological Forecasting and Social Change*, Vol. 3 (1971), pp. 75–88.

Fisher, L. *Industrial Marketing.* London: Business Books, 1969.

Fitzroy, Peter T. *Analytic Methods for Marketing Management.* New York: McGraw-Hill, 1976.

Floyd, A. "Trend Forecasting: A Methodology for Figure of Merit," In *Proceedings of the First Annual Technology and Management Conference*, ed. J. Bright. Englewood Cliffs, N.J.: Prentice-Hall, 1968.

Fogg, C. D., and J. W. Rokus. "A Quantitative Method for Structuring A Profitable Sales Force." *Journal of Marketing*, Vol. 37, No. 3 (July 1973), pp. 8–17.

Ford, Neil M., Orville C. Walker, Jr., and Gilbert A. Churchill, Jr. "Differences in the Attractiveness of Alternative Rewards among Industrial Salespeople: Additional Evidence." Working paper. Cambridge, Mass.: Marketing Science Institute, 1981.

Fornell, Claes, and Fred L. Bookstein. "A Comparative Analysis of Two Structural Equation Models: LISREL and PLS Applied to Market Data." University of Michigan working paper 271, September 1981.

Fornell, Claes, and Daniel R. Denison. "A New Approach to Nonlinear Structural Modeling by Use of Confirmatory Multidimensional Scaling." Working paper. The University of Michigan, December 1981.

Fourt, Louis A., and Joseph W. Woodlock. "Early Prediction of Market Success for

New Grocery Products." *Journal of Marketing,* Vol. 24 (October 1960), pp. 31–38.

Frank, Ronald E. "Brand Choice as a Probability Process." *Journal of Business,* Vol. 32 (1962), pp. 43–56.

_____. "Market Segmentation Research: Findings and Implications." In *Applications of the Sciences in Marketing Management,* eds. F. Bass, C. King, and E. Pessemier, pp. 39–68. New York: Wiley, 1968.

_____. "Predicting New Product Segments." *Journal of Advertising Research,* Vol. 12, No. 3 (June 1972), pp. 9–13.

Frank, Ronald E., and William F. Massy. "Noise Reduction in Segmentation Research." In *Control of 'Error' in Market Research Data,* eds. J. Farley and J. Howard, pp. 145–205. Lexington, Mass.: Heath, 1975.

Frank, Ronald E., William Massy, and Harper Boyd, Jr. "Correlates of Grocery Product Consumption Rates." Working paper, April 1966.

Frank, Ronald E., W. F. Massy, and Y. Wind. *Market Segmentation.* Englewood Cliffs, N.J.: Prentice-Hall, 1972.

Freimer, Marshall, and Leonard Simon. "The Evaluation of New Product Alternatives." *Management Science,* Vol. 13 (February 1967), pp. 279–292.

Frey, Albert Wesley. *How Many Dollars for Advertising?* New York: Ronald Press, 1955.

Fudge, W. K., and L. M. Lodish. "Evaluation of the Effectiveness of a Model Based Salesman's Planning System by Field Experimentation." *Interfaces,* Vol. 8, No. 1, Part 2 (November 1977), pp. 97–106.

Gabor, A. *Pricing: Principles and Practice.* London: Heineman Educational Books, 1977.

Gabor, A., and C. W. J. Granger. "On the Price Consciousness of Consumers." *Applied Statistics,* Vol. 10, No. 3 (November 1961), pp. 170–188.

_____. "Price as an Indicator of Quality: Report on an Inquiry." *Economica,* Vol. 33, No. 129 (February 1966), pp. 43–70.

Gabor, A., C. W. J. Granger, and A. P. Sowter. "Real and Hypothetical Shopping Situations in Market Research—A Study of Method." *Journal of Marketing Research,* Vol. 7 (August 1970), pp. 335–339.

Galbraith, Jay R. "A Change Process for the Introduction of Management Information Systems: A Successful Case." In *The Implementation of Management Science,* eds. Robert Doktor, Randell L. Schultz, and Dennis P. Slevin, pp. 219–233. Amsterdam: North-Holland, 1979.

Gale, Bradley T. "Planning for Profit." *Planning Review,* Vol. 4, No. 7 (1978), pp. 30–32.

_____. "Can More Capital Buy Higher Productivity?" *Harvard Business Review,* Vol. 58 (July–August 1980), pp. 78–86.

Gale, Bradley T., and Ben Branch. "The Dispute about High-Share Businesses." *Pimsletter,* No. 19 (1979).

_____. "Cash Flow Analysis: More Important than Ever." *Harvard Business Review,* Vol. 59, No. 4 (July–August 1981), pp. 131–136.

Gale, Bradley T., and Donald J. Swire. *The Limited Information Report.* Cambridge, Mass.: Strategic Planning Institute, 1980.

Galper, Morton. "Communication Spending Decisions for Industrial Products: A Literature Review." Working paper. Cambridge, Mass.: Marketing Science Institute, 1979.

Gardner, David M. "Is There a Generalized Price-Quality Relationship?" *Journal of Marketing Research,* Vol. 8 (May 1971), pp. 241–243.

Gardner, Yehudi A., and Burleigh B. Cohen. "ROP Color and Its Effect on Newspaper Advertising." *Journal of Marketing Research,* Vol. 3 (November 1966), pp. 365–371.

Garfinkel, R. S., and G. L. Nemhauser. *Integer Programming.* New York: Wiley, 1972.

Gatignon, Hubert, and Dominique M. Hanssens. "Modeling the Impact of Seasonality on the Effectiveness of the Marketing Variables." In Proceedings from the Second ORSA/TIMS Special Interest Conference on Market Measurement and Analysis, ed. R. Leone. Providence, R.I.: Institute of Management Science, 1980.

Gautschi, David A. "Specification of Patronage Models for Retail Center Choice." *Journal of Marketing Research*, Vol. 18 (May 1981), pp. 162–174.

Gautschi, David A., and M. Corstjens. "Retail Patronage Models: An Empirical Testing of Specification and Trip Heterogeneity Issues." In *Proceedings of the Sixth International Research Seminar in Marketing, Senoinque, France, 1979*, ed. J. P. Leonardi. Aix en Provence: ARP I.A.E./FNEGE, 1979.

General Electric Company. "Price-Share-Margin Computer Model." Internal memorandum, 1980.

Gensch, Dennis H. *Advertising Planning*. New York: Elsevier, 1973.

Gensch, Dennis H., and W. W. Recker. "The Multinominal, Multiattribute Logit Choice Model." *Journal of Marketing Research*, Vol. 16 (February 1979), pp. 124–132.

Gensch, Dennis H., and Ulf Peter Welam. "Optimal Price and Promotion for Interdependent Market Segments." *Operations Research*, Vol. 22, No. 4 (July–August 1974], pp. 746–755.

Geoffrion, Arthur M. "A Guide to Computer-Assisted Methods of Distribution Systems Planning." *Sloan Management Review*, Vol. 16, No. 2 (Winter 1975), pp. 17–38.

Geoffrion, A. M., and G. W. Graves. "Multicommodity Distribution System Design by Benders Decomposition." *Management Science*, Vol. 20, No. 5 (January 1974), pp. 822–844.

Geoffrion, A. M., and R. D. McBride. "The Capacitated Plant Location Problem with Additional Constraints." Paper presented at the Joint National Meeting of AIIE, ORSA, and TIMS, Atlantic City, N.J., November 1972.

Geoffrion, A. M., and R. E. Marsten. "Integer Programming Algorithms—A Framework and State of the Art Survey." *Management Science*, Vol. 18, No. 9 (May 1972), pp. 465–491.

Geoffrion, Arthur M., and Richard F. Powers. "Facility Location Is Just the Beginning." *Interfaces*, Vol. 10, No. 2 (April 1980), pp. 22–30.

Geoffrion, A., and J. J. VanRoy. "Caution: Common Sense Planning Methods Can Be Hazardous to Your Corporate Health." *Sloan Management Review*, Vol. 20 (Summer 1979), pp. 31-42.

Gibson, C. F., and R. L. Nolan. "Managing the Four Stages of EDP Growth." *Harvard Business Review*, Vol. 52, No. 1 (1974), pp. 76–88.

Gibson, Paul. "Procter and Gamble: It's Got a Little List." Vol. 121, No. 6 *Forbes* (March 20, 1978), pp. 33–34.

Giddings, F. H. *The Scientific Study of Human Society*. Chapel Hill: University of North Carolina Press, 1924.

Ginzberg, Michael J. "A Study of the Implementation Process." In *The Implementation of Management Science*, ed. Robert Doktor, Randall L. Schultz, and Dennis P. Slevin, pp. 85–102. Amsterdam: North-Holland, 1979.

———. "Early Diagnosis of MIS Implementation Failure: Promising Results and Unanswered Questions." *Management Science*, Vol. 27, No. 4 (April 1981a), pp. 459–478.

———. "Key Recurrent Issues in the MIS Implementation Process." *MIS Quarterly* (June 1981b), pp. 47–59.

Givon, Moshe, and Dan Horsky. "Market Share Models as Approximators of Aggregate Heterogeneous Brand Choice Behavior." *Management Science*, Vol. 26 (September 1978), pp. 43–56.

———. "Application of a Composite Stochastic Model of Brand Choice." *Journal of Marketing Research*, Vol. 16 (1979), pp. 258–267.

Glaze, R., and C. B. Weinberg. "A Sales Territory Alignment Program and Account Planning System." In *Sales Management: New Developments from Behavioral and Decision Model Research*, ed. R. Bagozzi. Cambridge, Mass.: Marketing Science Institute, 1979.

Glickman, Theodore S., and Paul D. Berger. "Optimal Price and Protection Period

Decisions for a Product Under Warranty." *Management Science*, Vol. 22, No. 12 (August 1976), pp. 1381–1390.

Goldberger, A. S. *Econometric Theory*. New York: Wiley, 1964.

Gonik, J. "Tie Salesmen's Bonuses to Their Forecasts." *Harvard Business Review*, Vol. 56 (May–June 1978), pp. 116–123.

Goodhardt, G. J., and A. S. C. Ehrenberg. "Conditional Trend Analysis: A Breakdown by Initial Purchasing Level. *Journal of Marketing Research*, Vol. 4 (May 1967), pp. 155–162.

Goodman, C. S. *Management of the Personal Selling Function*. New York: Holt, Rinehart and Winston, 1971.

Goodman, David, and Hans Baurmeister. "A Computational Algorithm for Multi-contract Bidding Under Constraint." *Management Science*, Vol. 22, No. 7 (March 1976), pp. 788–798.

Goodwin, Stephen, and Michael Etgar. "An Experimental Investigation of Comparative Advertising: Impact of Message Appeal, Information Load and Utility of Product Class." *Journal of Marketing Research*, Vol. 17 (May 1980), pp. 187–202.

Gorry, G. Anthony, and Michael S. Scott Morton. "A Framework for Management Information Systems." *Sloan Management Review*, Vol. 13 (Fall 1971), pp. 55–70.

Gottlieb, Maurice J. "Segmentation by Personality Types." In *Advancing Marketing Effectiveness*, ed. L. H. Stackman. Chicago: American Marketing Association, 1959.

Gould, J. P. "Diffusion Processes and Optimal Advertising Policy." In *Microeconomic Foundation of Employment and Inflation Theory*, eds. E. S. Phelps et al. New York: Norton, 1970.

Granger, C. W. J., and A. Bittson. "Consumer Attitudes Toward Package Size and Price." *Journal of Marketing Research*, Vol. 9 (August 1972), pp. 239–248.

Grass, Robert C. "Satiation Effects of Advertising." 14th Annual Conference, Advertising Research Foundation, 1968.

Grass, Robert C., and Wallace H. Wallace. "Advertising Communication: Print vs TV." *Journal of Advertising Research*, Vol. 14 (October 1974), pp. 19–23.

Grayson, C. Jackson, Jr. "Management Science and Business Practice." *Harvard Business Review*, Vol. 51, No. 4 (July–August 1973), pp. 41–48.

Green, H. L., and W. Applebaum. "The Status of Computer Applications to Store Location Research." Paper delivered at the Seventy-First Annual Meeting of the Association of American Geographers, Milwaukee, Wis., April 23, 1975.

Green, Paul E. "Marketing Applications of MDS: Assessment and Outlook." *Journal of Marketing*, Vol. 39 (January 1975), pp. 24–31.

Green, Paul E., and Frank Carmone. *Multidimensional Scaling and Related Techniques in Marketing Analysis*. Boston: Allyn & Bacon, 1970.

Green, Paul E., J. Douglas Carroll, and Stephen M. Goldberg. "A General Approach to Product Design Optimization via Conjoint Analysis." *Journal of Marketing*, Vol. 45 (Summer 1981), pp. 17–37.

Green, Paul E., and W. S. Desarbo. "Componential Segmentation in the Analysis of Consumer Tradeoffs." *Journal of Marketing*, Vol. 43 (Fall 1979), pp. 83–91.

Green, Paul E., and Ronald E. Frank. "Bayesian Statistics and Marketing Research." *Applied Statistics*, Vol. 15, No. 3 (1966), pp. 173–190.

Green, Paul E., and Vithala R. Rao. *Applied Multidimensional Scaling*. New York: Holt, Rinehart and Winston, 1972.

Green, Paul E., and V. Srinivasan. "Conjoint Analysis in Consumer Research: Issues and Outlook." *Journal of Consumer Research*, Vol. 5 (September 1978), pp. 103–123.

Green, Paul E., and Donald S. Tull. *Research for Marketing Decisions*. 3rd ed. Englewood Cliffs, N.J.: Prentice-Hall, 1975.

Green, Paul E., and Y. Wind. *Multi-Attribute Decisions in Marketing.* Hinsdale, Ill.: Dryden Press, 1973.

Green, Paul E., Yoram Wind, and Arun Jain. "Benefit Bundle Analysis." *Journal of Advertising Research,* Vol. 12, No. 2 (April 1972), pp. 31–36.

Greiner, L. E. "Evolution and Revolution as Organizations Grow." *Harvard Business Review,* Vol. 50, No. 4 (1972), pp. 37–46.

Griesmer, James H. and Martin Shubik. "Toward a Study of Bidding Processes: Part I, Some Constant-Sum Games; Part II, Games with Capacity Limitations; Part III, Some Special Models." *Naval Research Logistics Quarterly,* Vol. 10, Nos. 1, 2, and 3 (1963) pp. 11–21; 151–173; 199–217.

Grinyar, Peter H., and John D. Whittaker. "Managerial Judgement in a Competitive Bidding Model." *Operational Research Quarterly,* Vol. 24, No. 2 (1973), pp. 181–191.

Gross, Irwin. "The Creative Aspects of Advertising." *Sloan Management Review,* Vol. 14 (Fall 1972), pp. 83–109.

————. "Insights from Pricing Research." In *Pricing Practices and Strategies,* ed. Earl Bailey, pp. 34–39. New York: The Conference Board, 1978.

Gruber, William, and John S. Niles. *The New Management.* New York: McGraw-Hill, 1976.

Guiltman, J., and A. Sawyer. "Managerial Considerations for Market Segmentation Research." In *American Marketing Association Combined Proceedings, 1974,* ed. Ronald C. Curhan, Chicago: American Marketing Association, 1975.

Hass, Robert W. *Industrial Marketing Management.* New York: Petrocelli/Charter, 1976.

Haines, G. "A Theory of Market Behavior After Innovation." *Management Science,* Vol. 10 (July 1964), pp. 634–658.

Hakansson, Hakan, and Bjorn Wootz. "Supplier Selection in an Industrial Environment—An Experimental Study." *Journal of Marketing Research,* Vol. 12 (February 1975), pp. 46–51.

Haley, Russell I. "Benefit Segmentation: A Decision-Oriented Research Tool." *Journal of Marketing,* Vol. 32 (July 1968), pp. 30–35.

————. "Sales Effects of Media Weight." *Journal of Advertising Research,* Vol. 18 (1978), pp. 9–18.

Haley, Russell I., and Peter B. Case. "Testing Thirteen Attitude Scales for Agreement and Brand Discrimination." *Journal of Marketing,* Vol. 43, No. 4 (Fall 1979), pp. 20–32.

Hallaq, John H. "Children's Reactions to Premiums: An Experimental Approach." In *Contemporary Marketing Thought, 1977 Educators Proceedings,* eds. B. Greenberg and D. Bellinger, pp. 65–67. Chicago: American Marketing Association, 1977.

Hamerish, R. G., M. J. Anderson, Jr., and J. E. Harris. "Strategies for Low Market Share Business." *Harvard Business Review,* Vol. 56 (May–June 1978) pp. 95–102.

Hammond, John S. "The Do's and Don'ts of Computer Models for Planning." *Harvard Business Review,* Vol. 52, No. 2 (March–April 1974), pp. 110–123.

Hampel, F. E. "The Influence Curve and Its Use in Robust Estimation." *Journal of the American Statistical Association,* Vol. 69 (1974), pp. 383–393.

Hanan, Mark. *Life Styled Marketing.* New York: American Management Association, 1972.

Hansen, F. "Psychological Theories of Consumer Choice." *Journal of Consumer Research,* Vol. 3 (December 1976), pp. 117–142.

Hanssens, Dominique M. "Marketing Response, Competitive Behavior, and Time Series Analysis." *Journal of Marketing Research,* Vol. 17 (November 1980), pp. 470–485.

Hanssens, Dominique M., and Barton A. Weitz. "The Effectiveness of Industrial Print Advertisements Across Product Categories." *Journal of Marketing Research,* Vol. 17 (August 1980), pp. 294–306.

Harary, F., and B. Lipstein. "The Dynamics of Brand Loyalty: A Markovian Approach." *Operations Research*, Vol. 10 (1962), pp. 19–40.

Harding, Murray. "Who Really Makes the Purchasing Decision?" *Industrial Marketing*, Vol. 51 (September 1966), pp. 76 ff.

Harman, Harry H. *Modern Factor Analysis*. University of Chicago Press, 1976.

Harrell, Stephen G., and Elmer D. Taylor. "Modeling the Product Life Cycle for Consumer Durables." *Journal of Marketing*, Vol. 45, No. 4 (Fall 1981), p. 68–75.

Harrigan, Kathryn Rudie. "Strategies for Declining Industries." *Journal of Business Strategy*, 1 (Fall 1980), pp. 20–34.

Harsanyi, J. C. "Cardinal Welfare, Individualistic Ethics and Interpersonal Comparison of Utility." *Journal of Political Economy*, Vol. 63 (1955), pp. 309–321.

Hartigan, John A. *Clustering Algorithms*. New York: Wiley, 1975.

Hartung, P. H., and J. C. Fisher. "Brand Switching and Mathematical Programming in Market Expansion." *Management Science*, Vol. 11 (August 1965), pp. B231–243.

Haspeslagh, Philippe. "Portfolio Planning: Uses and Limits." *Harvard Business Review*, Vol. 60, No. 1 (January–February 1982), pp. 58–73.

Hauser, John R., and F. S. Koppelman. "The Relative Accuracy and Usefulness of Alternative Perceptual Mapping Techniques." *Journal of Marketing Research*, Vol. 14, No. 3 (November 1979), pp. 495–507.

Hauser, John R., and Steven M. Shugan. "Intensity Measures of Consumer Preference." *Operations Research*, Vol. 28, No. 2 (March–April 1980), pp. 278–320.

Hauser, John R., and Glen L. Urban. "A Normative Methodology for Modeling Consumer Response to Innovation." *Operations Research*, Vol. 25, No. 4 (July–August 1977), pp. 579–619.

———. "Assessment of Attribute Importances and Consumer Utility Functions: Von Neuman-Morganstern Theory Applied to Consumer Behavior." *Journal of Consumer Research*, Vol. 5 (March 1979), pp. 251–262.

Hauser, John R., and Kenneth J. Wisniewski. "Dynamic Analysis of Consumer Response to Marketing Strategies." *Management Science*, Vol. 28, No. 5 (May 1982a), pp. 455–486.

Hauser, John R., and Kenneth J. Wisniewski. "Application, Predictive Test, and Strategy Implications for a Dynamic Model of Consumer Response." *Marketing Science*, Vol. 1, No. 2 (Spring 1982b), pp. 143–179.

Haverly, C. A., and M. Fieldhouse. "Warehouse Location Calculations." Notes distributed at a mathematical-programming-project session at the SHARE XLII Meeting in Houston, March 1974.

Hax, Arnoldo. "A Comment on 'The Distribution System Simulator.'" *Management Science*, Vol. 21, No. 2 (October 1975), pp. 233–236.

Hax, Arnoldo C., and Nicolas S. Majluf. "Competitive Cost Dynamics: The Experience Curve." *Interfaces*, Vol. 12, No. 5 (October 1982), pp. 50–61.

Heeler, Rodger M., and Thomas P. Hustad. "Problems in Predicting New Product Growth for Consumer Durables." *Management Science*, Vol. 26 (October 1980), pp. 1007–1020.

Heilbroner, R. L. *The Worldly Philosophers*. New York: Simon & Schuster, 1967.

Henderson, James M., and Richard E. Quandt. *Microeconomic Theory: A Mathematical Approach*. New York: McGraw-Hill, 1958.

Hendon, Donald W. "How Mechanical Factors Affect Ad Perception." *Journal of Advertising Research*, Vol. 13, No. 4 (1973), pp. 39–46.

Hendry Corporation. *Hendrodynamics: Fundamental Laws of Consumer Dynamics*. Hendry Corporation Mimeo, Chapters 1 and 2, 1970, 1971.

Hendry, I. "The Three Parameter Approach to Long Range Forecasting." *Long Range Planning*, Vol. 5 (March 1972), pp. 40–45.

Herbst, P. G. "Conceptual Framework for

Studying the Family." In *Social Structure and Personality in a City*, eds. O. A. Oeser and S. B. Hammond, chap. 10. London: Routledge & Kegan Paul, 1954.

Herniter, J. D. "A Probabilistic Model of Purchase Timing and Brand Selection." *Management Science*, Vol. 18 (1971), pp. 102–113.

————. "An Entropy Model of Brand Purchase Behavior." *Journal of Marketing Research*, Vol. 10 (1973), pp. 361–375.

————. "A Comparison of the Entropy Model and the Hendry Model." *Journal of Marketing Research*, Vol. 11 (February 1974), pp. 21–29.

Herniter, J. D., and J. F. Magee. "Customer Behavior as a Markov Process." *Operations Research*, Vol. 9 (1961), pp. 105–122.

Hershey, John C., Howard C. Kunreuther, and Paul J. H. Schoemaker. "Sources of Bias in Assessment Procedures for Utility Functions." *Management Science*, Vol. 28, No. 8 (August 1982), pp. 936–954.

Hertz, David B. "Risk Analysis in Capital Investment." *Harvard Business Review* (January–February 1964), pp. 95–106.

Heschel, M. S. "Effective Sales Territory Development." *Journal of Marketing*, Vol. 41, No. 2 (April 1977), pp. 39–43.

Heskett, James L., Nicholas A. Glaskowsky, Jr., and Robert M. Ivie. *Business Logistics*. 2nd ed. New York: Ronald Press, 1973.

————. "Logistics—Essential to Strategy." *Harvard Business Review* (November–December 1977), pp. 85–96.

Hess, S. W., and S. A. Samuels. "Experiences with a Sales Districting Model: Criteria and Implementation." *Management Science*, Vol. 18, No. 4, Part II (December 1971), pp. 41–54.

Hillier, T. J. "Decision-Making in the Corporate Industrial Buying Process." *Industrial Marketing Management*, 4 (1975), pp. 99–106.

Hinkle, Charles L. "Temporary Price Reductions as an Element of Marketing Strategy." Ph.D. thesis, Graduate School of Business Administration, Harvard University, 1964.

————. "The Strategy of Price Deals." *Harvard Business Review* (July–August 1965), pp. 75–84.

Hinkle, Charles L., and Patrick J. Robinson. "The Nature of the Sales Promotion Process." In *Promotional Decisions Using Mathematical Models*, ed. P. Robinson, pp. 3–18. Boston: Allyn & Bacon, 1967.

Hirschman, Elizabeth C. "Retail Research and Theory." In *Review of Marketing*, ed. B. Enis and K. Roering, pp. 120–133. Chicago: American Marketing Association, 1981.

Hirschman, Winifried B. "Profit from the Learning Curve." *Harvard Business Review*, Vol. 42, No. 1 (January–February 1964), pp. 125–139.

Hlavac, T. E. Jr., and J. D. C. Little. "A Geographic Model of an Urban Automobile Market." In *Applications of Management Sciences in Marketing*, eds. D. B. Montgomery and G. L. Urban. Englewood Cliffs, N.J.: Prentice-Hall, 1970.

Hodock, Calvin J. "Copy Testing and Strategic Positioning." *Journal of Advertising Research*, Vol. 20 (February 1980), pp. 33–38.

Hoerl, Arthur E., and Robert W. Kennard. "Ridge Regression: Applications to Non-Orthogonal Problems." *Technometrics*, Vol. 12, No. 7 (February 1970), pp. 69–81.

Hoffer, George, James Marchand, and John Albertine. "Pricing in the Automobile Industry: A Simple Econometric Model." *Southern Economic Journal*, Vol. 43, No. 1 (July 1976), pp. 948–951.

Hogarth, Robin M., and Spyros Makridakis. "Forecasting and Planning: An Evaluation." *Management Science*, Vol. 27, No. 2 (February 1981), pp. 115–138.

Holthausen, Duncan M., Jr., and Gert Assmus. "Advertising Budget Allocation under Uncertainty." *Management Science*, Vol. 28, No. 5 (May 1982), pp. 487–499.

Hopkins, David S. *New Product Winners and Losers*. New York: The Conference Board, Report No. 773 (1979).

Hopkins, David S., and Earl L. Bailey. *New Product Pressures*. The Conference Board Record (June 1971), pp. 16–24.

Hopkins, Patricia M., and Leonard J. Parsons. "The Impact of a Cents-Off Coupon on Attitude, Preference and Intention." Working paper, College of Management, Georgia Institute of Technology, November 1981.

Horsky, Dan. "An Empirical Analysis of the Optimal Advertising Policy." *Management Science,* Vol. 23 (1976), pp. 1037–1049.

———. "Market Share Response to Advertising: An Example of Theory Testing." *Journal of Marketing Research,* Vol. 14 (1977), pp. 10–21.

Horsky, Dan, and Leonard S. Simon. "Advertising and the Diffusion of New Products." *Marketing Science,* Vol. 2 (Winter 1983) pp. 1–10.

Howard, John A. *Consumer Behavior: Application of Theory.* New York: McGraw Hill, 1977.

Howard, John A., and Jagdish N. Sheth. *The Theory of Buyer Behavior.* New York: Wiley, 1969.

Howard, Ronald A. *Dynamic Programming and Markov Processes.* Cambridge, Mass.: MIT Press, 1960.

Huber, George P. "The Nature of Organizational Decision Making and the Design of Decision Support Systems." *MIS Quarterly* (June 1981), pp. 1–10.

Hudson, C. L. "Buying-Selling: Greater Integration in the Seventies." *Industrial Marketing Management,* Vol. 1, No. 1 (1971), pp. 59–79.

Huff, D. L. *Determination of Inter-Urban Retail Trade Areas.* Los Angeles: University of California, Real Estate Research Program, 1962.

———. "A Probabilistic Analysis of Consumer Spatial Behavior." In *Emerging Concepts in Marketing,* ed. W. S. Decker. Chicago: American Marketing Association, 1963.

———. "Defining and Estimating a Trading Area." *Journal of Marketing,* Vol. 28 (July 1964), pp. 34–38.

———. "Retail Location Theory." In *Theory in Retailing: Traditional and Non-Traditional Sources,* ed. E. C. Hirschman. Chicago: American Marketing Association, 1981.

Hughes, G. David. "The Measurement of Beliefs and Attitudes." In *The Handbook of Marketing Research,* ed. R. Ferber, pp. 3.16–3.43. New York: McGraw-Hill, 1974.

———. *Marketing Management: A Planning Approach.* Reading, Mass.: Addison Wesley, 1978.

Hull, Clark L. *A Behavior System.* New Haven, Conn.: Yale University Press, 1952.

Hurter, Arthur P., Jr., and Albert H. Rubenstein. "Market Penetration by New Innovations: The Technological Literature." *Technological Forecasting and Social Change,* Vol. 11 (1978), pp. 197–221.

Hurwood, David L., and James K. Brown. *Some Guidelines for Advertising Budgeting.* New York: The Conference Board, 1972.

Hurwood, David L., Elliott S. Grossman, and Earl L. Bailey. *Sales Forecasting.* The Conference Board Report No. 730. New York: The Conference Board, 1978.

Hustad, Thomas P., Charles S. Mayer, and Thomas W. Wipple. "Consideration of Context Differences in Product Evaluation and Market Segmentation." *Journal of the Academy of Marketing Science,* Vol. 3 (Winter 1975), pp. 34–47.

Hutt, Michael D., and Thomas W. Speh. *Industrial Marketing Management.* New York: Dryden Press, 1981.

Huysmans, Jan H. B. M. "The Effectiveness of the Cognitive-Style Constraint in Implementing Operations Research Proposals." *Management Science,* Vol. 17 (September 1970a), pp. 92–104.

———. *The Implementation of Operations Research.* New York: Wiley, 1970b.

Huxley, Thomas H. "Education Value of Natural History Sciences." In *Readings in Philosophy of Science,* ed. P. P. Wiener. New York: Scribner, 1953.

Intermarco, Ltd. "Advertising Planning by Media-Planex." London: 1971.

Intriligator, Michael D. *Mathematical Optimization and Economic Theory.* Englewood Cliffs, N.J.: Prentice-Hall, 1971.

Izraeli, Dov. *Franchising and the Total Distribution System*. London: Longman Group, 1972.

Jacoby, J., J. C. Olson, and R. A. Haddock. "Price, Brand Name, and Product Composition Characteristics as Determinants of Perceived Quality." *Journal of Applied Psychology*, Vol. 55, No. 6 (December 1971), pp. 570–579.

Jeuland, Abel P. "Brand Choice Inertia as One Aspect of the Notion of Brand Loyalty." *Management Science*, Vol. 25 (July 1979*a*), pp. 671–682.

――――. "Epidemiological Modeling of the Diffusion of Innovation: Evaluation and Future Directions of Research." In *Educators' Conference Proceedings*, eds. N. Beckwith, M. Houston, M. Mittelstaedt, K. Monroe, and S. Ward. pp. 274–278. Chicago: American Marketing Association, 1979*b*.

――――. "The Interaction Effect of Preference and Availability on Brand-Switching and Market Share." *Management Science*, Vol. 25, No. 10 (October 1979*c*), pp. 953–965.

――――. "Empirical Investigation of Price and Advertising Competition Using a Market Share Model." In *Marketing Measurement and Analysis*, eds. David Montgomery and Dick Wittink. Cambridge Mass.:Marketing Science Institute, 1980.

――――. "Parsimonious Models of Diffusion of Innovation, Part A: Derivations and Comparisons." Working paper, University of Chicago, June 1981.

Jeuland, Abel P., Frank Bass, and Gordon Wright. "A Multibrand Stochastic Model Compounding Heterogenous Erlang Timing and Multinomial Choice Processes." *Operations Research*, Vol. 28, No. 2 (March–April 1980), pp. 255–277.

Jeuland, Abel P., and Robert J. Dolan. "An Aspect of New Product Planning: Dynamic Pricing." In *Marketing Planning Models*, ed. A. A. Zoltners. pp. 1–21. TIMS Studies in the Management Sciences, Vol. 18; New York: North-Holland, 1982.

Johansson, J. K., Leigh McAlister, and Douglas L. Maclachan. "Do Not Aggregate! A Comment on the Implications of Recent Research in Normative Segmentation Theory." In *Proceedings from the Third ORSA/TIMS Special Interest Conference on Market Measurement and Analysis*, ed. J. Keon. pp. 184–196. Providence, RI: The Institute of Management Sciences, 1981.

Johnson, Jeffrey L. "A Ten Year Delphi Forecast in the Electronics Industry." *Industrial Marketing Management*, Vol. 5, No. 1 (March 1976), pp. 45–56.

Johnson, Richard M. "Market Segmentation: A Strategic Management Tool." *Journal of Marketing Research*, Vol. 8 (February 1971), pp. 13–18.

――――. "Tradeoff Analysis of Consumer Values." *Journal of Marketing Research*, Vol. 11 (May 1974), pp. 121–127.

――――. "A Simple Method for Pairwise Monotone Regression." *Psychometrika*, Vol. 40 (June 1975), pp. 163–168.

Johnston, Jack. *Statistical Cost Analysis*. New York: McGraw-Hill, 1963.

Jolson, M. A., and G. L. Rossow. "The Delphi Process in Marketing Decision Making." *Journal of Marketing Research*, Vol. 8 (1971), pp. 443–448.

Jones, C. "Let There Be Light with Sound Analysis." *Harvard Business Review*, Vol. 54, No. 3 (May–June 1976), pp. 6–7.

Jones, J. M. "A Dual-Effects Model of Brand Choice." *Journal of Marketing Research*, Vol. 7 (1970), pp. 458–464.

――――. "A Composite Heterogeneous Model for Brand Choice Behavior." *Management Science*, Vol. 19 (January 1973), pp. 499–509.

――――. "Whither Stochastic Choice Models?" Working paper No. 79, University of California at Los Angeles, August 1979.

Jones, J. M., and F. S. Zufryden. "Adding Explanatory Variables to a Consumer Purchase Behavior Model: A Exploratory Study." *Journal of Marketing*, Vol. 17 (August 1980), pp. 323–334.

――――. "An Approach for Assessing Demographic and Price Influences on Brand Purchase Behavior." *Journal of Marketing,* Vol. 46 (Winter 1982), pp. 36–46.

Jöreskog, K. "A General Approach to Confirmatory Maximum Likelihood Factor Analysis." *Psychometrica,* Vol. 34 (1969), pp. 183–202.

———. "A General Method for the Analysis of Covariance Structures." *Biometrika,* Vol. 57 (1970), pp. 239–251.

———. "A General Method for Estimating A Linear Structural Equation System." In *Structural Equations in the Social Sciences,* eds. A. Goldberger and O. D. Duncan, pp. 85–112. New York: Academic Press, 1973.

———. "Analyzing Psychological Data by Analysis of Covariance Matrices." In *Contemporary Developments in Mathematical Psychology,* eds. R. Atkinson, D. H. Krantz, R. D. Lucet, and P. Suppes, pp. 1–56. San Francisco: Freeman, 1974.

Jöreskog, K. G., and D. Sörbom. *Advances in Factor Analysis and Structural Equation Models.* Cambridge, Mass.: Abt Books, 1979.

———. *LISREL V: Analysis of Linear Structural Relationships by Maximum Likelihood and Least Square Methods.* Chicago: National Educational Resources, 1981.

Jöreskog, K. G., and Herman Wald, eds. *Systems Under Indirect Observation: Causality, Structure, Prediction.* Amsterdam: North-Holland, 1981.

Joskow, Paul L. "Firm Decision-Making Processes and Oligopoly Theory." *American Economic Review,* Vol. 65, No. 2 (May 1975), pp. 270–279.

Joubert, William. *Profit Potentials of Physical Distribution.* Chicago: American Marketing Association, 1972.

Juster, F. T. "Consumer Buying Intentions and Purchase Probability: An Experiment in Survey Design." *Journal of the American Statistical Association,* Vol. 61 (September 1966), p. 658–696.

Kalish, Shlomo. "Models of the Diffusion of Innovation and Their Implications for Government Policies." Master's thesis, MIT, June 1980.

———. "Modeling the Effect of Price, Advertising and Word of Mouth on the Diffusion of New Consumer Durables." Paper presented at the TIMS/ORSA National Meeting, Houston, October 1981.

———. "Control Variables in Models of Innovation Diffusion." Ph.D. thesis, MIT, 1982.

Kalwani, Manohar. "The Entropy Concept and the Hendry Partitioning Approach." Working paper, Sloan School of Management, MIT, 1979.

Kalwani, Manohar. "Notes on the Negative Binomial Distribution." Massachusetts Institute of Technology, Spring 1980.

Kalwani, M. U., and D. G. Morrison. "A Parsimonious Description of the Hendry System." *Management Science,* Vol. 23 (1977), pp. 467–477.

Kalwani, Manohar U., and Alvin J. Silk. "Structure of Repeat Buying for New Packaged Goods." *Journal of Marketing Research,* Vol. 18 (August 1980), pp. 316–322.

Kaplan, A. D. H., Joel B. Dirlam, and Robert F. Lanzillotti. *Pricing in Big Business.* Washington, D.C.: Brookings Institution, 1958.

Kassarjian, Harold H., and Waltraub M. Kassarjian. "Attitudes Under Low Commitment Conditions." In *Attitude Research Plays for High Stakes,* ed. John C. Mahoney and Bernard Silverman. Chicago: American Marketing Association, 1979.

Kassarjian, Harold H., and T. S. Robinson. *Perspectives in Consumer Behavior.* Glenview, Ill.: Scott, Foresman, 1973.

Katz, E., and P. F. Lazarsfeld. *Personal Influence.* New York: Free Press, 1955.

Keen, Peter G. W. "Computer-Based Decision Aids: The Evaluation Problem." *Sloan Management Review,* Vol. 16 (Spring 1975), pp. 17–29.

———. " 'Interactive' Computer Systems for Managers: A Modest Proposal." *Sloan Management Review,* Vol. 18 (Fall 1976), pp. 1–17.

———. "Decision Support Systems: A Research Perspective." CISR working paper no. 54,

Sloan School of Management, MIT, March 1980*a*.

———. "Decision Support Systems: Translating Analytic Techniques into Useful Tools." *Sloan Management Review*, Vol. 21 (Spring 1980*b*), pp. 33–44.

———. "The Mythical Man Month Revisited: Building A Decision Support System in APL." Presented at APL Users Meeting, Toronto, (September 1980*c*), Toronto, Canada.

———. "Decision Support Systems and Managerial Productivity Management." CISR working paper no. 60, Sloan School of Management, MIT, October 1980*d*.

———. "Value Analysis: Justifying Decision Support Systems." *MIS Quarterly* (March 1981), pp. 1–15.

Keen, Peter G. W., and Michael S. Scott Morton. *Decision Support Systems: An Organizational Perspective*. Reading, Mass.: Addison-Wesley, 1978.

Keeney, Ralph. "Analyisis of Preference Dependencies Among Objectives." *Operations Research*, Vol. 29, No. 6 (November–December 1981), pp. 1105–1120.

Keeney, Ralph L., and Craig W. Kirkwood. "Group Decision Making Using Cardinal Social Welfare Functions." *Management Science*, Vol. 22, No. 4 (December 1975), pp. 430–437.

Keeney, Ralph L., and Howard Raiffa. *Decisions with Multiple Objectives: Preferences and Value Tradeoffs*. New York: Wiley, 1976.

Kelley, Patrick. "Functions Performed in Industrial Purchase Decisions with Implications for Marketing Strategy." *Journal of Business Research*, Vol. 2 (October 1974), pp. 421–433.

Keon, John. "The Bargain Value Model and a Comparison of Managerial Implications with the Linear Learning Model." *Management Science*, Vol. 26, No. 11 (November 1980*a*), pp. 1117–1130.

———. "The Design of a Stochastic Model for the Analysis of Price Promotions." In *American Marketing Association Educa-*

tors Conference Proceedings. eds. R. P. Bagozzi, K. L. Bernhardt, P. S. Busch, D. W. Cravens, J. F. Hair, Jr., and C. A. Scott, Chicago: American Marketing Association, 1980*b*.

Khumawala, B. M. "An Efficient Branch and Bound Algorithm for the Warehouse Location Problem." *Management Science*, Vol. 18, No. 12 (August 1972), pp. B718–B731.

Kinberg, Yoram, and Ambar G. Rao. "Stochastic Models of a Price Promotion." *Management Science*, Vol. 21 (April 1975), pp. 897–907.

———. "Branch Bank Expansion Planning." Unpublished manuscript, 1978.

Kinberg, Yoram, Ambar G. Rao, and Melvin F. Shakun. "A Mathematical Model for Price Promotions." *Management Science*, Vol. 20, No. 6 (February 1974), pp. 984–959.

King, William R. *Quantitative Analysis for Marketing Management*. New York: McGraw-Hill, 1967.

King, William R., and Jamie I. Rodriguez. "Participative Design of Strategic Decision Support Systems: An Empirical Assessment." *Management Science*, Vol. 27, No. 6 (June 1981), pp. 717–726.

Kinnear, Thomas C., James R. Taylor, and Sadrudin A. Ahmed. "Socioeconomic and Personality Characteristics as They Relate to Ecologically Constructive Purchasing Behavior." In *Proceedings, 3rd Annual Conference, Association for Consumer Research 1972*, ed. M. Venkatesan, pp. 34–60. Atlanta: Association for Consumer Research, 1972.

Klabir, D. "A Monte Carlo Investigation of the Statistical Significance of Kruskal's Non-Metric Scaling Procedure." *Psychometrica*, Vol. 34, No. 3 (September 1969), pp. 319–330.

Klastorian, T. *A Clustering Approach to Systems Design*. Ph.D. thesis, University of Texas at Austin, 1973.

Klompmaker, Jay E., G. D. Hughes, and P. I. Haley. "Test Marketing in New Product Development." *Harvard Business Review*, Vol. 54 (May–June 1976), pp. 128–138.

Kolliner, Sim A., Jr. "New Evidence of Ad Values." *Industrial Marketing*, Vol. 48 (August 1963), pp. 81–84.

Kornbluth, Jonathan S., and Ralph Stever. "Multiple Objective Linear Fractional Programming." *Management Science*, Vol. 27, No. 9 (September 1981), pp. 1024–1039.

Kortanek, K. O., J. V. Soden, and D. Sodaro. "Profit Analyses and Sequential Bid Pricing Models." *Management Science*, Vol. 20, No. 3 (November 1973), pp. 396–417.

Kotler, Philip. "Competitive Strategies for New Product Marketing over the Life Cycle." *Management Science*, Vol. 12, No. 4 (1965*a*), pp. B104–B109.

———. "Computerized Media Planning: Techniques, Needs, and Prospects." In *Occasional Papers in Advertising*. Urbana, Ill.: American Academy of Advertising, 1965*b*.

———. *Marketing Decision Making: A Model Building Approach*. New York: Holt, Rinehart and Winston, 1971.

———. *Marketing Management: Analysis Planning and Control*. 4th ed. Englewood Cliffs, N.J.: Prentice-Hall, 1980.

Koyck, L. M. *Distributed Lags and Investment Analysis*. Amsterdam: North-Holland, 1954.

Krapfel, R. "A Decision Process Approach to Modeling Organizational Buying Behavior." In *Research Frontiers in Marketing: Dialogue and Directions*, ed. S. Jain. Chicago: American Marketing Association, 1978.

Krapfel, Robert E., Jr. "An Extended Interpersonal Influence Model of Organizational Buyer Behavior." *Journal of Business Research*, Vol. 10, No. 2 (1982), pp. 147–157.

Krugman, Herbert E. "The Impact of Television Advertising: Learning Without Involvement." *Public Opinion Quarterly*, Vol. 29 (Fall 1965), pp. 349–356.

———. "Why Three Exposures May Be Enough." *Journal of Advertising Research*, Vol. 12 (December 1972), pp. 11–14.

Kuehn, Alfred A. "An Analysis of the Dynamics of Consumer Behavior and Its Implications for Marketing Management." Ph.D. thesis, Graduate School of Industrial Administration, Carnegie-Mellon University, 1958.

———. "Consumer Brand Choice—A Learning Process?" *Journal of Advertising Research*, Vol. 2 (December 1962), pp. 10–17.

Kuehn, Alfred A., and Michael J. Hamburger. "A Heuristic Program for Locating Warehouses." *Management Science*, Vol. 9 (July 1963), pp. 643–666.

Kuehn, Alfred A., T. W. McGuire, and D. L. Weiss. "Measuring the Effectiveness of Advertising." In *Proceedings, Fall Conference, American Marketing Association*, ed. R. M. Haas, pp. 185–194. Chicago: American Marketing Association, 1966.

Kuehn, Alfred A., and A. C. Rohloff. "Evaluating Promotions Using a Brand Switching Model." In *Promotional Decisions Using Mathematical Models*, ed. P. Robinson, pp. 50–85. Boston: Allyn & Bacon, 1967*a*.

———. "What Are Promotions?" In *Promotional Decisions Using Mathematical Models*, ed. P. Robinson, pp. 41–49. Boston: Allyn & Bacon, 1967*b*.

Kunreuther, Howard. "Extensions of Bowman's Theory of Scientific Decision-Making." *Management Science*, Vol. 15 (April 1969), pp. B415–N439.

Kunreuther, Howard, and Jean Francois Richard. "Optimal Pricing and Inventory Decisions for Non-Seasonal Items." *Econometrica*, Vol. 39, No. 1 (January 1971), pp. 173–175.

Kunreuther, Howard, and Linus Schrage. "Joint Pricing and Inventory Decisions for Constant Priced Items." *Management Science*, Vol. 19, No. 7 (March 1973), pp. 732–738.

Lachenbruch, P. *Discriminant Analysis*. New York: Hesner Press, 1975.

Lackman, C. L. "Gompertz Curve Forecasting: A New Product Application." *Journal of the Market Research Society*, January 20, 1978, pp. 45–47.

Laczniak, Gene R. "An Empirical Study of Hospital Buying." *Industrial Marketing Management*, Vol. 8, No. 1 (January 1979), pp. 57–62.

Lambert, Z. V. *Setting the Size for the Sales Force.* University Park: Pennsylvania State University Press, 1968.

——. "Price and Choice Behavior." *Journal of Marketing Research,* Vol. 9 (February 1972), pp. 35–40.

Lambin, Jean-Jacques. *Modeles et Programmes de Marketing.* Paris: Press Universitaires de France, 1970.

——. "A Computer On-Line Marketing Mix Model." *Journal of Marketing Research,* Vol. 11 (May 1972), pp. 119–126.

——. *Advertising, Competition and Market Conduct in Oligopoly Over Time.* Amsterdam: North-Holland, 1976.

Lambin, Jean-Jacques, Phillipe Naert, and Alain Bultez. "Optimal Marketing Behavior in Oligopoly." *European Economic Review,* Vol. 6 (1975), pp. 105–128.

Lancaster, Kelvin. *Variety, Equity and Efficiency.* New York: Columbia University Press, 1979.

——. "Competition and Product Variety." *Journal of Business,* Vol. 53, No. 3, Part 2 (July 1980), pp. S79–S104.

Landau, H. J. "Pricing in a Dynamic Model with Saturation." *Econometrica,* Vol. 44, No. 6 (November 1976), pp. 1153–1155.

Langhoff, Peter. "Options in Campaign Evaluation." *Journal of Advertising Research* (December 1967), pp. 41–47.

Lankau, W. E. "Software Requirements for Marketing Decision Support Systems." Paper presented at INFO 80, Chicago, 1980.

Larréché, Jean-Claude. "Integrative Complexity and the Use of Marketing Models." In *The Implementation of Management Science,* eds. Robert Doktor, Randall L. Schultz, and Dennis P. Slevin, pp. 171–187. Amsterdam: North-Holland, 1979.

Larréché, Jean-Claude, and David B. Montgomery. "A Framework for the Comparison of Marketing Models: A Delphi Study." *Journal of Marketing Research,* Vol. 14, No. 4 (November 1977), pp. 487–498.

Larréché, Jean-Claude, and V. Srinivasan. "STRATPORT: A Decision Support System for Strategic Planning." *Journal of Marketing,* Vol. 45, No. 4 (Fall 1981), pp. 39–52.

——. "STRATPORT: A Model for the Evaluation and Formulation of Business Portfolio Strategies." *Management Science,* Vol. 28, No. 9 (September 1982), pp. 979–1001.

Lavalle, I. H. "A Bayesian Approach to an Individual Player's Choice of Bid in Competitive Sealed Auctions." *Management Science* (March 1967), pp. 584–597.

Lavidge, Robert J., and Gary A. Steiner. "A Model for Predictive Measurement of Advertising Effectiveness." *Journal of Marketing* (October 1961), pp. 59–67.

Lavin, Milton L. "A Comparison of Descriptive Choice Models." Ph.D. thesis, MIT, 1969.

Lawler, E., and J. Rhode. *Information and Control in Organizations.* New York: McGraw-Hill, 1976.

Lawrence, Kenneth D., and William H. Lawton. "Applications of Diffusion Models: Some Empirical Results." In *New-Product Forecasting: Models and Applications,* eds. Yoram Wind, Vijay Mahajan, and Richard N. Cardozo, pp. 529–541. Lexington, Mass.: D. C. Heath and Co., 1981.

Lawrence, R. J. "Consumer Brand Choice: A Random Walk?" *Journal of Marketing Research,* Vol. 12 (1975), pp. 314–324.

Layton, R. A. "Controlling Risk and Return in the Management of a Sales Team." *Journal of Marketing Research,* Vol. 5 (August 1968), pp. 277–282.

Lazo, Hector. "Emotional Aspects of Industrial Buying." In *Dynamic Marketing for a Changing World,* ed. R. S. Hancock, pp. 258–266. Chicago: American Marketing Association, 1960.

Leal, Antonio, Stevin Levin, Steven Johnston, Marcy Agman, and Gershon Weltman. "An Interactive Computer Aiding System for Group Decision Making." Report from Perceptronics Inc., Woodland Hills, Calif., February 1978.

Learner, D. "Mathematical Programming for Better Media Selection." Paper delivered at the 1961 Regional Convention, American Association of Advertising Agencies, New York, 1961.

Leavitt, Clark. "The Application of Perception Psychology to Marketing." In *Marketing Precision and Executive Action*, ed. Charles H. Hindersman, pp. 430–437. Chicago: American Marketing Association, 1962.

Lee, T. C., G. Judge, and A. Zellner. *Estimating the Parameters of the Markov Probability Model from Aggregate Time Series Data.* Amsterdam: North-Holland, 1970.

Leeflang, P. S. H. "The Allocation of Shelf Space over Article Groups: A Portfolio Problem." In *Proceedings, ESOMAR Seminar, Breukelen, The Netherlands*, pp. 37–73. Amsterdam: ESOMAR, 1975.

Lehmann, Donald R. "Television Show Preference: Application of A Choice Model." *Journal of Marketing Research*, Vol. 8 (February 1971a), pp. 47–55.

————. "Evaluating Marketing Strategy in a Multiple Brand Market." *Journal of Business Administration*, Vol. 3 (Fall 1971b), pp. 15–26.

Lehmann, Donald R., and J. O'Shaughnessy. "Differences in Attribute Importance for Different Industrial Products." *Journal of Marketing*, Vol. 35, No. 2 (April 1974), pp. 36–42.

Lehmann, Donald R., William L. Moore, and Terry Elrod. "The Development of Distinct Choice Process Segments over Time: A Stochastic Modeling Approach." *Journal of Marketing*, Vol. 46 (Spring 1982), pp. 48–59.

Lekvall, Per, and Clas Wahlbin. "A Study of Some Assumptions Underlying Innovation Diffusion Functions." *Swedish Journal of Economics*, Vol. 75 (1973), pp. 362–377.

Leone, Robert P. "Constructing Models of Competition: An Alternative to Traditional Economic Analysis." In *Marketing Measurement and Analysis*, eds. D. Montgomery and D. Wittink, pp. 250–270. Cambridge, Mass.: Marketing Science Institute, 1980.

Leontief, W. W. *The Structure of the American Economy 1919–1939.* 3rd ed. New York: Oxford University Press, 1951.

————. *Input-Output Economics.* New York: Oxford University Press, 1966.

Lessig, V. Parker, and John O. Tollefson. "Market Segmentation Through Numerical Taxonomy." *Journal of Marketing Research*, Vol. 8 (November 1971), pp. 480–487.

Lilien, Gary L. "A Modified Linear Learning Model of Buyer Behavior." *Management Science*, Vol. 20 (March 1974a), pp. 1027–1036.

————. "An Application of a Modified Linear Learning Model of Buyer Behavior." *Journal of Marketing Research*, Vol. 11 (August 1974b), pp. 279–285.

————. "Model Relativism: A Situational Approach to Model Building." *Interfaces*, Vol. 5 (1975), pp. 11–18.

————. "Advisor 1: A Descriptive Model of Advertising Budgeting for Industrial Products." Working paper WP 974–978, Sloan School of Management, MIT, February 1978a.

————. *A Study of Industrial Marketing Budgeting Descriptive Analysis—Final Report.* Cambridge, Mass.: MIT, February, 1978b.

————. "Advisor 2: A Study of Industrial Marketing Budgeting. Part 2: Change Models, Distribution Channel Models, Uses." Working paper no. 992–78, Sloan School of Management, MIT, May 1978c.

————. "Advisor 2: Modeling the Marketing Mix for Industrial Products." *Management Science*, Vol. 25, No. 2 (February 1979), pp. 191–204.

————. "Reply to Farris and Buzzell's Comment on ADVISOR 2 Paper." *Management Science*, Vol. 26, No. 1 (January 1980), pp. 101–105.

————. "A Descriptive Model of the Trade-Show Budgeting Decision Process." *Industrial Marketing Management*, Vol. 12, No. 1 (February 1983) pp. 25–29.

Lilien, Gary L., and L. Jo Fried. *Results and Recommendations from a Pilot Study of*

Industrial Buying Panels and the Copier Market. MIT report, May 1978.

Lilien, Gary L., and Paul E. Johnston. *A Market Assessment for Active Solar Heating and Cooling Products.* Report to U.S. Department of Energy, Active Building Systems Branch, September 1980.

Lilien, Gary L., and John D. C. Little. "The ADVISOR Project: A Study of Industrial Marketing Budgets." *Sloan Management Review,* Vol. 17, No. 3 (Spring 1976), pp. 17–31.

Lilien, Gary L., and Ambar G. Rao. "A Model for Allocating Retail Outlet Building Resources across Market Areas." *Operations Research,* Vol. 24 (January–February 1976), pp. 1–14.

Lilien, Gary L., Ambar G. Rao, and Shlomo Kalish. "Bayesian Estimation and Control of Detailing Effort in a Repeat Purchase Environment." *Management Science,* Vol. 27, No. 5 (May 1981), pp. 493–507.

Lilien, Gary L. and A. Api Ruzdic. "Analyzing Natural Experiments in Industrial Markets." In *Marketing Planning Models,* ed. A. A. Zoltners, pp. 241–269. TIMS Studies in the Management Sciences, Vol. 18, New York: North-Holland, 1982.

Lilien, Gary L., Alvin J. Silk, Jean-Marie Choffray, and Murlidhar Rao. "Industrial Advertising Effects and Budgeting Practices." *Journal of Marketing,* Vol. 40, No. 1 (1976), pp. 16–24.

Lilien, Gary, and David Weinstein. "An International Comparison of the Determinants of Industrial Marketing Expenditures." *Journal of Marketing* (September 1983, forthcoming).

Lilien, Gary L., and M. Anthony Wong. "Modeling the Structure of the Buying Center: Some Empirical Results." The Pennsylvania State University Working Series in Marketing Research, No. 115, October 1981.

Linstone, Harold, and Murray Turoff, eds. *The Delphi Method: Techniques and Applications.* Reading, Mass.: Addison-Wesley, 1975.

Lipstein, B. "A Mathematical Model of Consumer Behavior." *Journal of Marketing Research,* Vol. 2 (1965), pp. 259–265.

Little, John D. C. "A Model of Adaptive Control of Promotional Spending." *Operations Research,* Vol. 14 (1966), pp. 1075–1097.

———. "Models and Managers: The Concept of A Decision Calculus." *Management Science,* Vol. 16 (1970), pp. B466–B485.

———. "BRANDAID: A Marketing Mix Model, Part I: Structure; Part II: Implementation." *Operations Research,* Vol. 23 (1975), pp. 628–673.

———. "Decision Support Systems for Marketing Managers." *Journal of Marketing,* Vol. 43, No. 3 (Summer 1979a), pp. 9–27.

———. "Aggregate Advertising Models: The State of the Art." *Operations Research,* Vol. 27, No. 4 (July–August 1979b), pp. 629–667.

Little, John D. C., and Leonard M. Lodish. "A Media Selection Model and Its Optimization by Dynamic Programming." *Industrial Management Review,* Vol. 8 (Fall 1966), pp. 15–23.

———. "A Media Planning Calculus." *Operations Research,* Vol. 17 (January–February 1969), pp. 1–34.

———. "Commentary on 'Judgement Based Marketing Decision Models.'" *Journal of Marketing,* Vol. 45, No. 4 (Fall 1981), pp. 24–29.

Lodish, Leonard M. "Considering Competition in Media Planning." *Management Science,* Vol. 17 (February 1971a), pp. B293–306.

———. "CALLPLAN: An Interactive Salesman's Call Planning System." *Management Science,* Vol. 18, No. 4, Part II (December 1971b), pp. 25–40.

———. "'Vaguely Right' Approach to Sales Force Allocations." *Harvard Business Review,* Vol. 52 (January–February 1974), pp. 119–124.

———. "Sales Territory Alignment to Maximize Profit." *Journal of Marketing Research,* Vol. 12 (February 1975), pp. 30–36.

———. "Assigning Salesmen to Accounts to Maximize Profit." *Journal of Marketing Research,* Vol. 13 (November 1976), pp. 440–444.

———. "Applied Dynamic Pricing and Production Models with Specific Application to Broadcast Spot Pricing." *Journal of Marketing Research,* Vol. 17 (May 1980*a*), pp. 203–211.

———. "A User Oriented Model for Sales Force Size, Product and Market Allocation Decisions." *Journal of Marketing,* Vol. 44 (Summer 1980*b*), pp. 70–78.

———. "Experience with Decision Calculus Models and Decision Support Systems." In *Marketing Decision Models,* eds. R. Schultz and A. Zoltners, pp. 165–182. New York: North Holland, 1981.

Longman, Kenneth A. "Remarks on Gross' Paper." In *Proceedings of the 13th Annual Conference of the Advertising Research Foundation, New York City, November 14, 1967.* New York: Advertising Research Foundation, 1968.

Lubatkin, Michael and Michael Pitts. "PIMS: Fact or Folklore?" *The Journal of Business Strategy* (Winter, 1982) pp. 38–43.

Lucas, Henry C., Jr. "The Evolution of an Information System: From Key-Man to Every Person." *Sloan Management Review,* Vol. 20 (Winter 1978), pp. 39–52.

Lucas, Henry C., C. B. Weinberg, and K. Clowes. "Sales Response as a Function of Territorial Potential and Sales Representative Workload." *Journal of Marketing Research,* Vol. 12 (August 1975), pp. 298–305.

Luce, R. Duncan. *Individual Choice Behavior.* New York: Wiley, 1959.

Luss, H., and S. K. Gupta. "Allocation of Effort Resources Among Competing Activities." *Operations Research Quarterly,* Vol. 23, No. 2 (March–April 1975), pp. 360–365.

Lussier, A. A., and R. W. Olshavsky. "Task Complexity and Contingent Processing in Brand Choice." *Journal of Consumer Research* (September 1979), pp. 154–165.

Lutz, Richard J., and James R. Bettman. "Multiattribute Models in Marketing: A Bicentennial Review." In *Consumer and Industrial Buying Behavior,* eds. A. Woodside, J. Sheth, and P. Bennett, pp. 137–149. New York: North-Holland, 1977.

McAlister, L. "Choosing Multiple Items from a Product Class." *Journal of Consumer Research,* Vol. 6 (March 1979), pp. 389–405.

McCammon, Bert C., Jr. "Perspectives for Distribution Programming." In *Vertical Marketing Systems,* ed. Louis P. Bucklin, pp. 32–51. Glenview, Ill.: Scott, Foresman, 1970.

McCann, John M. "Market Segment Response to the Marketing Decision Variables." *Journal of Marketing Research,* Vol. 11 (November 1974), pp. 399–412.

McCarthy, E. Jerome. *Basic Marketing.* Seventh Edition. Homewood, Ill.: Irwin, 1981.

McClelland, D. C. *Personality.* New York: Holt, Rinehart and Winston, 1951.

McConboy, C. A., and M. Suly. "A Case Study of OR/MS Implementation in an Industrial Environment." In *The Implementation of Computer-Based Decision Aids,* ed. P. Keen. Cambridge, Mass.: MIT, 1975.

McConnell, J. D. "The Price-Quality Relationship in an Experimental Setting." *Journal of Marketing Research,* Vol. 5, No. 3 (August 1968), pp. 300–303.

———. "Comment on 'A Major Price-Perceived Quality Study Re-examined.'" *Journal of Marketing Research,* Vol. 17 (May 17, 1980), pp. 262–264.

McDonald, Colin. "What Is the Short-Term Effect of Advertising?" Special Report No. 71–142, Cambridge, Mass.: Marketing Science Institute, February 1971.

McFadden, D. "Conditional Logit Analysis of Qualitative Choice Behavior." In *Frontiers in Econometrics,* ed. P. Zarembka, pp. 105–142. New York: Academic Press, 1970.

———. "Quantal Choice Analysis: A Survey." *Annals of Economic and Social Measurement* (May 1976), pp. 363–369.

———. "Econometric Models for Probabilistic Choice Among Products." *Journal of Busi-*

ness, Vol. 53, No. 3, Part 2 (July 1980), pp. 513–530.

McGuire, William. "A Bibliography of TV Copy Research." New York: Advertising Research Foundation, unpublished manuscript, 1976.

McIntyre, Shelby H. "An Experimental Study of the Impact of Judgment-Based Marketing Models." *Management Science*, Vol. 28, No. 1 (January 1982), pp. 17–33.

McIntyre, Shelby H., and Imran S. Currim. "Evaluating Judgment-Based Marketing Models: Multiple Measures, Comparisons and Findings." In *Marketing Planning Models*, ed. A. A. Zoltners, pp. 185–207. TIMS Studies in the Management Sciences, Vol. 18, New York: North-Holland, 1982.

McKay, David B., Richard W. Olshavsky, and Gerald Sentell. "Cognitive Maps and Spatial Behavior of Consumers." *Geographical Analysis*, Vol. 7, No. 1 (January 1975), pp. 19–34.

MacLachlan, D. "A Model of Intermediate Market Response." *Journal of Marketing Research*, Vol. 9 (November 1972), pp. 378–384.

McLaughlin, R. L., and J. J. Boyle. *Short Term Forecasting*. Chicago, Ill.: American Marketing Association, 1968.

Maffai, R. B. "Brand Preference and Simple Markov Processes." *Operations Research*, Vol. 8 (1960*a*), pp. 210–218.

———. "Planning Advertising Expenditures by Dynamic Programming Methods." *Industrial Management Review*, Vol. 1 (December 1960*b*), pp. 94–100.

———. "Advertising Effectiveness, Brand Switching, and Market Dynamics." *Journal of Industrial Economics*, Vol. 9 (1961), pp. 119–131.

Magee, J. "The Effect of Promotional Effort on Sales." *Operations Research Quarterly*, Vol. 1 (February 1953), pp. 64–74.

Mahajan, Vijay, and Arun K. Jain. "An Approach to Normative Segmentation." *Journal of Marketing Research*, Vol. 15 (August 1978), pp. 338–345.

Mahajan, Vijay, and Eitan Muller. "Innovation Diffusion and New Product Growth Models in Marketing." *Journal of Marketing*, Vol. 43 (Fall 1979), pp. 55–68.

Mahajan, Vijay, and Robert A. Peterson. "Innovation Diffusion in a Dynamic Potential Adopter Population." *Management Science*, Vol. 24 (November 1978), pp. 1589–1597.

———. "First-Purchase Diffusion Models of New-Product Acceptance." *Technological Forecasting and Social Change*, Vol. 15 (1979), pp. 127–146.

Mahajan, Vijay, R. A. Peterson, A. K. Jain, and N. Malhotra. "A New Product Growth Model with a Dynamic Market Potential." *Long Range Planning*, Vol. 12 (August 1979), pp. 51–58.

Mahajan, Vijay, and Milton E. F. Schoeman. "Generalized Model for the Time Pattern of the Diffusion Process." *IEEE Transactions on Engineering Management*, Vol. EM-24 (February 1977), pp. 12–18.

Mahajan, Vijay, Yoram Wind and John W. Bradford. "Stochastic Dominance Rules for Product Portfolio Analysis." In *Marketing Planning Models*, ed. A. Zoltners, pp. 161–183. TIMS Studies in the Management Sciences, Vol. 18. New York: North-Holland, 1982.

Makridakis, Spyros, and Steven C. Wheelwright. *Forecasting: Methods and Applications*. New York: Wiley, 1978.

Maloney, John C. "Copy Testing: What Course Is It Taking?" In *Proceedings, Ninth Annual Conference*. New York: Advertising Research Foundation, 1963.

Mansfield, Edwin. "Technical Change and the Rate of Imitation." *Econometrica*, Vol. 29, No. 4 (October 1961), pp. 741–765.

———. *Industrial Research and Technological Innovation*. New York: Norton, 1968.

———. *Microeconomics: Theory and Applications*. New York: Norton, 1975.

———. *Microeconomics: Theory and Applications*. New York: Norton, 1979.

Mansfield, Edwin, and Samuel Wagner. "Organizational and Strategic Factors Associated with Probabilities of Success in Industrial R&D." *The Journal of Business*, 48 (April 1975), pp. 179–198.

Martin, Claude R., and Roger L. Wright. "Profit Oriented Data Analysis for Market Segmentation: An Alternative to AID." *Journal of Marketing Research*, Vol. 11 (August 1974), pp. 399–412.

Maslow, A. H. *Motivation and Personality*. New York: Harper & Row, 1954.

Massy, William F. "Forecasting Demand for New Convenience Products." *Journal of Marketing Research*, Vol. 6 (November 1969), pp. 405–412.

———. "Statistical Analysis of the Relationship Between Variables." In *Multivariate Analysis in Marketing: Theory and Application*, ed. D. A. Aaker. Belmont, Calif.: Wadsworth, 1971.

Massy, William, and Ronald Frank. "Short Term Price and Dealing Effects in Selected Market Segments." *Journal of Marketing Research*, Vol. 2 (May 1965), pp. 171–185.

Massy, W. F., D. B. Montgomery, and D. G. Morrison. *Stochastic Models of Buying Behavior*. Cambridge, Mass.: MIT Press, 1970.

Mathematical Programming System Extended, Mixed Integer Programming. Manual SH20-0908, IBM Corporation, White Plains, N.Y.

Mattssons, L. G. "Systems Selling as a Strategy in Industrial Markets." *Industrial Marketing Management*, Vol. 3, No. 2 (1973), pp. 107–120.

Mazis, Michael B., and Olli T. Ahtola. "A Comparison of Four Multi-Attribute Models in the Prediction of Consumer Attitudes." *Journal of Consumer Research*, Vol. 2 (June 1975), pp. 38–52.

Meidan, Arthur, "Optimizing the Number of Industrial Salespersons." *Industrial Marketing Management*, 11 (1982), pp. 63–74.

Mesak, Hani I., and Richard C. Clelland. "A Competitive Pricing Model." *Management Science*, Vol. 25, No. 11 (November 1979), pp. 1057–1068.

Metheringham, R. A. "Measuring the Net Cumulative Coverage of a Print Campaign." *Journal of Advertising Research*, Vol. 4, No. 4 (December 1964), pp. 23–28.

Meyer, Carl F. "Long Range Selection and Timing Analysis System for Facility Location: Implementation." *Management Science*, Vol. 20, No. 3 (November 1973), pp. 261–273.

Michman, Ronald D., Myron Gable, and Walter Gross. *Market Segmentation: A Selected and Annotated Bibliography*. Chicago: American Marketing Association, 1977.

Mickwitz, Gosta. *Marketing and Competition*. Helsingfors: Central Tryckeriet, 1959.

Midgley, D. F. *Innovation and New Product Marketing*. London: Croom Helm, 1977.

———. "Toward a Theory of the Product Life Cycle: Explaining Diversity." *Journal of Marketing*, Vol. 45, No. 4 (Fall 1981), pp. 97–108.

Mihram, G. Arthur. *Simulation: Statistical Foundations and Methodology*. New York: Academic Press, 1972.

Miller, D. W., and M. K. Starr. *Executive Decisions and Operations Research*. Englewood Cliffs, N.J.: Prentice-Hall, 1960.

Miller, William B. "Building An Effective Information Systems Function." *MIS Quarterly* (June 1980), pp. 21–30.

Mitroff, Ian I., Frederick Betz, Louis Pondy, and Francisco Sagasti. "On Managing Science in the Systems Age: Two Schemas for the Study of Science as a Whole Systems Phenomenon." *Interfaces*, Vol. 4, No. 3 (May 1974), pp. 46–58.

Monroe, K. B. *Pricing: Making Profitable Decisions*. New York: McGraw-Hill, 1979.

Monroe, K. B., and A. J. Della Bitta. "Models for Pricing Decisions." *Journal of Marketing Research*, Vol. 15 (August 1978), pp. 413–428.

Monroe, K., and Andris A. Zoltners. "Pricing the Product Line During Periods of Scarcity." *Journal of Marketing*, Vol. 43, No. 3 (Summer 1979), pp. 49–59.

Montgomery, David B. "A Stochastic Response Model with Application to Brand Choice."

Management Science, Vol. 15 (1969), pp. 323–337.

———. "The Outlook for MIS." *Journal of Advertising Research*, Vol. 13, No. 3 (June 1973), pp. 5–11.

Montgomery, D. B., and A. B. Ryans. "Stochastic Models of Consumer Choice Behavior." In *Consumer Behavior*, eds. S. Ward and T. Robertson. Englewood Cliffs, N.J.: Prentice-Hall, 1973.

Montgomery, D. B., and A. J. Silk. "Estimating Dynamic Effects of Marketing Communications Expenditures." *Management Science*, Vol. 18 (June 1972), pp. B485–B501.

Montgomery, D. B., A. J. Silk, and C. E. Zaragoza. "A Multiple-Product Sales Force Allocation Model." *Management Science*, Vol. 18, No. 4, Part II (December 1971), pp. 3–24.

Montgomery, David B., and Glen L. Urban. *Management Science in Marketing.* Englewood Cliffs, N.J.: Prentice-Hall, 1969.

———. "Marketing Decision-Information Systems: An Emerging View." *Journal of Marketing Research*, Vol. 7 (May 1970), pp. 226–234.

Montgomery, D. B., and F. E. Webster, Jr. "Applications of OR to Personal Selling Strategy." *Journal of Marketing*, Vol. 32 (January 1968), pp. 50–57.

Mood, Alexander M., and Franklin A. Graybill. *Introduction to the Theory of Statistics.* 2nd ed. New York: McGraw-Hill, 1963.

Moran, William T. "Practical Media Decisions and the Computer." *Journal of Marketing* (July 1963), pp. 26–30.

Morgan, H. L., and J. V. Soden. "Understanding MIS Failures." *Database*, Vol. 5, No. 2 (1973), pp. 157–171.

Morgan, James N., and John A. Sonquist. "Problems in the Analysis of Survey Data and a Proposal." *Journal of the American Statistical Association*, Vol. 58 (September 1963), pp. 415–434.

Morgan, Nigel, and Janet Purnell. "Isolating Openings for New Products in a Multidimensional Space." *Journal of the Market Research Society*, Vol. 11 (July 1969), pp. 245–266.

Moriarty, Mark. "Cross-Sectional, Time-Series Issues in the Analysis of Marketing Decision Variables." *Journal of Marketing Research*, Vol. 12 (May 1975), pp. 142–150.

Moriarty, Rowland T., and John E. G. Bateson. "Exploring Complex Decision Making Units: A New Approach." *Journal of Marketing Research*, Vol. 19 (May 1982), pp. 182–191.

Moriarty, Mark, and Gerald Salamon. "Estimation and Forecast Performance of a Multivariate Time Series Model of Sales." *Journal of Marketing Research*, Vol. 27 (November 1980), pp. 558–564.

Morrill, John E. "Industrial Advertising Pays Off." *Harvard Business Review*, Vol. 48 (March–April 1970), pp. 4–14.

Morrison, Donald G. "Testing Brand Switching Models." *Journal of Marketing Research*, Vol. 3 (1966), pp. 401–409.

———. "The Uses and Limitations of Brand Switching Models." Paper presented to the Center for Continuing Education Symposium, Chicago, June 1969*a*.

———. "Conditional Trend Analysis: A Model That Allows for Nonusers." *Journal of Marketing Research*, Vol. 6 (November 1969*b*), pp. 342–346.

———. "Evaluating Market Segmentation Studies: The Properties of R^2." *Management Science*, Vol. 19 (July 1973), pp. 1213–1221.

———. "Discriminant Analysis." In *Handbook of Marketing Research*, ed. R. Ferber. New York: McGraw-Hill, 1974.

———. "Purchase Intentions and Purchase Behavior." *Journal of Marketing*, Vol. 43, No. 2 (Spring 1979), pp. 65–74.

Morrison, Donald G., Richard D. H. Chen, Sandra L. Karpis, and Kathryn E. Britney. "Modelling Retail Customer Behavior at Merrill Lynch." *Marketing Science*, Vol. 1, No. 2 (Spring 1982), pp. 123–141.

Moskowitz, H. R. "Computer Modeling Can Help Develop New Consumer Products Faster, and Cheaper." *Marketing News*, Vol. 14, No. 12 (1980), p. 8.

Muth, John F. "Rational Expectations and the Theory of Price Movements." *Econometrica*, Vol. 29, No. 3 (July 1961), pp. 315–335.

Myers, James H. "Finding Determinant Buying Attitudes." *Journal of Advertising Research*, Vol. 1 (December 1970), pp. 9–12.

————. "Benefit Structure Analysis: A New Tool for Product Planning." *Journal of Marketing*, Vol. 40 (October 1976), pp. 23–32.

Myers, James H., and Mark I. Alpert. "Semantic Confusion in Attitude Research: Salience vs. Importance vs. Determinance." In *Advances in Consumer Research*, Vol. IV. Proceedings of the Seventh Annual Conference of the Association of Consumer Research, October 1976, ed. W. D. Perreault, Jr., pp. 106–110. Atlanta: Association for Consumer Research, 1977.

Naert, Philippe, and Alain V. Bultez. "Logically Consistent Market Share Models." *Journal of Marketing Research*, Vol. 10 (1973), pp. 334–340.

————. "A Model of a Distribution Network Aggregate Performance." *Management Science*, Vol. 21, No. 10 (June 1975), pp. 1102–1112.

Naert, Philippe, and Peter Leeflang. *Building Implementable Marketing Models*. Boston: Leiden Press, 1978.

Naert, Philippe, and M. Weverbergh. "On the Prediction Power of Market Share Attraction Models." *Journal of Marketing Research*, Vol. 18 (May 1981), pp. 133–145.

Nakanishi, Masao. "Measurement of Sales Promotion Effect at the Retail Level: A New Approach." Working paper, Graduate School of Management, University of California of Los Angeles, 1972.

Nakanishi, Masao, and James R. Bettman. "Attitude Models Revisited: An Individual Level Analysis." *Journal of Consumer Research*, Vol. 1 (December 1974), pp. 20–21.

Nakanishi, Masao, and Lee G. Cooper. "Parameter Estimation for a Multiplicative Competitive Interaction Model—Least Squares Approach." *Journal of Marketing Research*, Vol. 11 (August 1974), pp. 303–311.

Nakanishi, Masao, Lee G. Cooper, and Harold H. Kassarjian. "Voting for a Political Candidate Under Conditions of Minimal Information." *Journal of Consumer Research*, Vol. 1 (September 1974), pp. 36–43.

Naples, M. J. *Effective Frequency*. New York: Association of National Advertisers, 1979.

Narasimhan, Chakravarthi, and Subrata K. Sen. "New Product Models for Test Market Data." *Journal of Marketing*, Vol. 47 (Winter 1983) pp. 11–24.

Narayana, Chem L., and Rom J. Markin. "Consumer Behavior and Product Performance: An Alternative Conceptualization." *Journal of Marketing*, Vol. 39 (October 1975), pp. 1–6.

Nault, James P. "Common Fallacies." In *Pricing Practices and Strategies*, ed. Earl L. Bailey. New York: The Conference Board, Report 751, 1978.

Naylor, T. H. *Corporate Planning Models*. Reading, Mass.: Addison-Wesley, 1979.

Naylor, T. H., T. G. Seaks, and D. W. Wichern. "Box-Jenkins Methods: An Alternative to Econometric Forecasting." *International Statistical Review*, Vol. 40, No. 2 (1972), pp. 123–137.

Nelson, Charles R. "The Prediction Performance of the FRB–MIT–PENN Model of the U.S. Economy." *The American Economic Review*, Vol. 62, No. 5 (December 1972), pp. 902–917.

————. *Applied Time Series Analysis for Managerial Forecasting*. San Francisco: Holden-Day, 1973.

Nelson, Richard. *The Selection of Retail Locations*. New York: F. W. Dodge Corporation, 1958.

Nelson, R. R., M. J. Peck, and E. D. Kalacheck. *Technology, Economic Growth and Public Policy*. Washington, D.C.: Brookings Institution, 1967.

Nerlove, M., and K. J. Arrow. "Optimal Advertising Policy Under Dynamic Conditions." *Econometrica,* Vol. 29 (May 1962), pp. 129–142.

Nevers, John V. "Extensions of a New Product Growth Model." *Sloan Management Review,* Vol. 13 (Winter 1972), pp. 77–91.

Newbold, P., and C. W. J. Granger. "Experience with Forecasting Univariate Time Series and Combinations of Forecasts." *Journal of the Royal Statistical Society,* Series A, Vol. 137, Part 2 (1974), pp. 131–165.

Nicosia, F. M. *Consumer Decision Processes.* Englewood Cliffs, N.J.: Prentice-Hall, 1966.

Nielson, A. C., Inc. "New Brand or Superbrand?" *The Nielson Researcher* (Marketing Service), No. 5 (1979), pp. 4–10.

————. "New Product Success Ratios." *The Nielson Researcher* (Marketing Service), (1979), pp. 2–9.

Noble, Ben. *Applied Linear Algebra.* Englewood Cliffs, N.J.: Prentice-Hall, 1969.

Nolan, Richard L., and James C. Wetherbe. "Toward a Comprehensive Framework for MIS Research." *MIS Quarterly* (June 1980), pp. 1–19.

Nordin, J. A. "Spatial Allocation of Selling Expenses." *Journal of Marketing,* Vol. 7 (January 1943), pp. 50–57.

Noyce, Robert N. "Microelectronics." *Scientific American,* Vol. 237, No. 3 (September 1977), pp. 62–69.

Office of Economic and Cultural Development. *Gaps in Technology: Scientific Instruments.* Third Ministerial Meeting in Science, Paris, 1968.

Ogilvy and Mather Research Department. "An Experimental Study of the Relative Effectiveness of Three Television Dayparts." New York, 1965.

Olshavsky, R. W., and A. H. Granbois. "Consumer Decision Making—Fact or Fiction?" *Journal of Consumer Research,* Vol. 6 (September 1979), pp. 93–100.

OPHELIE/LP Addendum: Mixed Integer Capability of OPHELIE/LP System. Publication No. D0001507032, Control Data Corporation, Minneapolis, 1970.

Oren, M. E., and A. C. Williams. "On Competitive Bidding." *Operations Research,* Vol. 23, No. 6 (November–December 1975), pp. 1072–1079.

O'Rourke, Rita, J. M. Shea, and W. Solley. "Survey Shows Need for Increased Sales Calls, Advertising and Updated Mailing Lists to Reach Buying Influences." *Industrial Marketing,* Vol. 58 (April 1973), p. 38.

Ostlund, Lyman E., Kevin J. Clancy, and Rakesh Sapra. "Inertia in Copy Research." *Journal of Advertising Research,* Vol. 20, No. 1 (February 1980), pp. 17–23.

Owen, Donald B. *Handbook of Statistical Tables.* Reading, Mass.: Addison-Wesley, 1962.

Oxenfeld, Alfred R. *Pricing for Marketing Executives.* Belmont, Calif.: Wadsworth, 1961.

Ozanne, Urban B., and Gilbert A. Churchill. "Five Dimensions of the Industrial Adoption Process." *Journal of Marketing Research,* Vol. 8 (August 1971), pp. 322–328.

Palda, Kristian S. *The Measurement of Cumulative Advertising Effects.* Englewood Cliffs, N.J.: Prentice-Hall, 1964.

————. *Pricing Decisions and Marketing Policy.* Englewood Cliffs, N.J.: Prentice-Hall, 1971.

Pan, Judy, D. R. Nichols, and O. M. Joy. "Sales Forecasting Practices of Large U.S. Industrial Firms." *Financial Management,* Vol. 6, No. 3 (Fall 1977), pp. 72–77.

Parasuraman, A., and R. L. Day. "A Management-Oriented Model for Allocating Sales Effort." *Journal of Marketing Research,* Vol. 14 (February 1977), pp. 22–33.

Parfitt, J. H., and B. J. K. Collins. "Use of Consumer Panels for Brand Share Prediction." *Journal of Marketing Research,* Vol. 5 (May 1968), pp. 131–146.

Park, C., and T. M. Sheth. "Impact of Prior Familiarity and Cognitive Complexity on Information Processing Rules." *Communication Research,* Vol. 2 (July 1975), pp. 260–266.

Parker, Barnett R., and V. Srinivasan. "A Consumer Preference Approach to the Planning of Rural Primary Health Care Facilities." *Operations Research*, 24 (September-October 1976), pp. 991–1025.

Parnes, Sidney J., and Harold F. Harding. *Source Book for Creative Thinking*. New York: Scribner, 1962.

Parsons, Leonard J. "The Product Life Cycle and Time Varying Advertising Elasticities." *Journal of Marketing Research*, Vol. 12, No. 3 (August 1975), pp. 476–480.

Parsons, Leonard J., and W. Bailey Price. "Adaptive Pricing by a Retailer." *Journal of Marketing Research*, Vol. 9 (May 1972), pp. 127–133.

Parsons, Leonard J., and Randall Schultz. *Marketing Models and Econometric Research*. New York: North-Holland, 1976.

Peckham, James O., Sr. *The Wheel of Marketing*. Chicago: A. C. Nielson, 1973.

Pegram, Roger M., and Earl L. Bailey. *The Marketing Executive Looks Ahead*. New York: The Conference Board, No. 13, 1967.

Pekelman, Dov, and Subrata Sen. "Improving Prediction in Conjoint Measurement." *Journal of Marketing Research*, Vol. 16 (May 1979), pp. 211–220.

Pekelman, Dov, and E. Tse. "Experimentation and Control in Advertising—An Adaptive Control Approach." Working paper 76-04-01, Wharton School, University of Pennsylvania, 1976.

Perreault, William D., Jr., and Frederick A. Russ. "Physical Distribution in Industrial Purchase Decisions." *Journal of Marketing*, Vol. 40 (April 1976), pp. 3–10.

Pessemier, Edgar A. *New Product Decisions: An Analytical Approach*. New York: McGraw-Hill, 1966.

————. "Market Structure Analysis of New Product and Market Opportunities." *Journal of Contemporary Business* (Spring 1976), pp. 35–67.

————. "Strategy Development for New Product Introductions: Predicting Market and Financial Success." In *Marketing Planning Models*, ed. A. Zoltners, pp. 85–98. TIMS Studies in the Management Sciences, Vol. 18. New York: North-Holland, 1982.

Pessemier, Edgar A., Philip Burger, Richard Teach, and Douglas Tiger. "Using Laboratory Brand Preference Scales to Predict Consumer Brand Purchases." *Management Science*, Vol. 17 (February 1971), pp. B371–B385.

Peters, Michael P., and M. Venkatesan. "Exploration of Variables Inherent in Adopting an Industrial Product." *Journal of Marketing Research*, Vol. 10 (August 1973), pp. 312–315.

Peterson, Robert A. "The Price-Perceived Quality Relationship: Experimental Evidence." *Journal of Marketing Research*, Vol. 7 (November 1970), pp. 525–528.

Peterson, Robert A., and Alain J. P. Jolibert. "A Cross-National Investigation of Price and Brand as Determinants of Perceived Product Quality." *Journal of Applied Psychology*, Vol. 61, No. 4 (August 1976), pp. 533–536.

Peterson, Robert A., and V. Mahajan. "Multi-Product Growth Models." In *Research in Marketing*, Vol. 1, ed. J. Sheth, pp. 201–232. Greenwich, Conn.: JAI Press, 1978.

Pindyck, Robert S. "Gains to Producers from the Cartelization of Exhaustive Resources." *The Review of Economics and Statistics*, Vol. 60, No. 2 (May 1978), pp. 238–251.

Pokemper, Stanley J. *Management Science in Business*. New York: The Conference Board, 1977.

Pokemper, Stanley J., and Earl L. Bailey. *Sales Forecasting Practices: An Appraisal*. Experiences in Marketing Management Report, No. 25. New York: The Conference Board, 1970.

Poligami User's Manual. London: S.I.A. Ltd., April 1970.

Polli, Rolando. *A Test of the Classical Life Cycle by Means of Actual Sales Histories*. Ph.D. thesis, University of Pennsylvania, 1968.

Polli, R., and V. Cook. "Validity of the Product Life Cycle." *The Journal of Business*, Vol. 42, No. 4 (October 1969), pp. 385–400.

Porter, Michael E. *Competitive Strategy: Techniques for Analyzing Industries and Competitors*. New York: Macmillan, 1980.

Prasad, Kanti V. "A Brand Choice Model with Store as an Intervening Variable." Paper presented at the ORSA/TIMS/AIEE Joint

National Meeting, Atlantic City, November 1972.

Prasad, Kanti V., and L. Winston Ring. "Measuring Sales Effects of Some Marketing Mix Variables and Their Interactions." *Journal of Marketing Research,* Vol. 13 (November 1976), pp. 391–396.

Pratt, John. "Risk Aversion in the Small and the Large." *Econometrica,* Vol. 32, (1964), pp. 122–136.

Preston, Lee E. *Profits, Competition, and Rules of Thumb in Retail Food Pricing.* Berkeley: University of California Institute of Business and Economic Research, 1963.

Pringle, Lewis G., R. Dale Wilson, and Edward I. Brody. "News: A Decision-Oriented Model for New Product Analysis and Forecasting." *Marketing Science,* Vol. 1, No. 1 (Winter 1982), pp. 1–29.

Punj, G. N., and R. Staelin. "The Choice for Graduate Business Schools." *Journal of Marketing Research,* Vol. 15 (November 1978), pp. 588–598.

Purchasing Magazine. "Purchasing Magazine Readers Have Something to Tell You About Chemicals." Report No. 10-A. New York: Purchasing Magazine, 1965.

Qualls, William, Richard W. Olshavsky, and Ronald E. Michaels. "Shortening of the PLC—An Empirical Test." *Journal of Marketing,* Vol. 45, No. 4 (Fall 1981), pp. 76–80.

Raiffa, Howard. *Decision Analysis: Introductory Lectures on Choices Under Uncertainty.* Reading, Mass.: Addison-Wesley, 1968.

Raiffa, Howard, and Robert Schlaifer. *Applied Statistical Decision Theory.* Boston: Harvard University, Division of Research, 1961.

Ramond, Charles. *Advertising Research: The State of The Art.* Association of National Advertisers, New York, 1976.

Ranard, Elliot D. "Use of Input-Output Concepts in Sales Forecasting." *Journal of Marketing Research,* Vol. 9, No. 1 (February 1972), pp. 53–58.

Rao, Ambar G. "Productivity of the Marketing-Mix: Measuring the Impact of Advertising and Consumer and Trade Promotions on Sales." Paper presented at ANA Advertising Research Workshop, New York, 1978.

Rao, Ambar G., and Gary L. Lilien. "A System of Promotional Models." *Management Science,* Vol. 19, No. 2 (October 1972), pp. 152–160.

Rao, Ambar G., and P. B. Miller. "Advertising/Sales Response Functions." *Journal of Advertising Research,* Vol. 15 (1975), pp. 7–15.

Rao, Ambar G., and Melvin F. Shakun. "A Quasi-Game Theory Approach to Pricing." *Management Science,* Vol. 18, No. 15 (January 1972), pp. 110–123.

Rao, R. C., and R. E. Turner. *Sales Force Specialization and Selling Effectiveness.* Kingston, Ontario: Queen's University, January 1976.

Rao, Vithala R., and James E. Cox, Jr. *Sales Forecasting Methods: A Survey of Recent Developments.* Report No. 78–119. Cambridge, Mass.: Marketing Science Institute, December 1978.

Rao, Vithala R., and Darius J. Sabavala. "Allocation of Marketing Resources: The Role of Price Promotions." *In Proceedings from the Second ORSA/TIMS Special Interest Conference on Market Measurement and Analysis,* ed. R. Leone, pp. 110–120. Providence, R.I.: The Institute of Management-Science, 1980.

———. "Some Issues in the Construction of Models for Marketing Decisions." In *Research in Marketing,* Vol. 4, ed. J. Sheth, pp. 251–272. Greenwich, Conn.: JAI Press, 1981.

Rao, Vithala, and Geoffrey N. Soutar. "Subjective Evaluations for Product Design Decisions." *Decision Sciences,* Vol. 6 (January 1975), pp. 120–134.

Rapoport, A. *Two-Person Game Theory.* Ann Arbor: University of Michigan Press, 1966.

Ratchford, Brian T. "Cost-Benefit Models for Explaining Consumer Choice and Information Seeking Behavior." *Management Science,* Vol. 28, No. 2 (February 1982), pp. 197–212.

Ray, Michael L. "Sequence Analysis of Developments in Marketing Communications."

Journal of Marketing, Vol. 37 (January 1973), pp. 29–38.

Reeves, Gary R., and Kenneth D. Lawrence. "Combining Sales Forecasts Using Multiple Objectives." In *Proceedings from the Third ORSA/TIMS Special Interest Conference on Market Measurement and Analysis*, ed. J. Keon, pp. 209–213. Providence, R.I.: The Institute of Management Science, 1981.

Reibstein, David J., and Phillis A. Traver. "Factors Affecting Coupon Redemption Rates." *Journal of Marketing*, Vol. 46 (Fall 1982), pp. 102–113.

Reid, D. J. "A Comparison of Forecasting Techniques in Economic Time Series." Paper presented at the Operations Research Society's Long Range Planning and Forecasting Session, May 5–7, 1971, Dallas, Texas.

Reinitz, R. C. "A Sales Forecasting Model for Gasoline Service Stations." Private Correspondence, 1968.

Reisman, D., N. Glazer, and R. Denny. *The Lonely Crowd*. New Haven, Conn.: Yale University Press, 1961.

Resnick, Robert, and David Halliday. *Physics, Part I*. New York: Wiley, 1960.

Richardson, M. G., and M. Ben-Akiva. *A Disaggregate Travel Demand Model*. Lexington, Mass.: Heath, 1975.

Richardson, R. J. "A Territory Realignment Model—MAPS." Paper presented at the New Orleans ORSA/TIMS Meeting, May 1, 1979.

Riez, Peter C. "A Major Price-Perceived Quality Study Reexamined." *Journal of Marketing Research*, Vol. 17 (May 17, 1980), pp. 259–262.

Rink, David R., and John E. Swan. "Product Life Cycle Research: A Literature Review." *Journal of Business Research*, Vol. 7, No. 3 (September 1979), pp. 219–242.

Rippe, Richard D., and Maurice Wilkinson. "Forecasting Accuracy and the McGraw-Hill Anticipations Data." *Journal of the America Statistical Association*, Vol. 69, No. 348 (December 1974), pp. 849–858.

Rippe, Richard D., Maurice Wilkinson, and Donald Morrison. "Industrial Market Forecasting with Anticipations Data." *Management Science*, Vol. 22, No. 6 (February 1976), pp. 639–651.

Robertson, T. S. *Innovative Behavior and Communication*. New York: Holt, Rinehart and Winston, 1971.

————. "Diffusion Theory and the Concept of Personal Influence." In *Behavioral and Management Science in Marketing*, ed. A. Davis and A. Silk, pp. 214–236. New York: Wiley, 1978.

Robinson, Bruce, and Chet Lakhani. "Dynamic Price Models for New-Product Planning." *Management Science*, Vol. 21, No. 10 (June 1975), pp. 1113–1122.

Robinson, Patrick J., ed. *Promotional Decisions Using Mathematical Models*. Boston: Allyn & Bacon, 1967.

Robinson, Patrick J. "Comparison of Pre-Test-Market New-Product Forecasting Models." In *New-Product Forecasting: Models and Applications*, eds. Yoram Wind, Vijay Mahajan, and Richard N. Cardozo, pp. 181–204. Lexington, Mass.: Heath, 1981.

Robinson, Patrick J., and Charles W. Faris. *Industrial Buying and Creative Marketing*. Boston: Allyn & Bacon, 1967.

Rogers, E. M. *The Diffusion of Innovation*. New York: Free Press, 1962.

Rogers, E. M., and J. D. Stamfield. "Adoption and Diffusion of New Products: Emerging Generalizations and Hypotheses." In *Applications of the Sciences in Marketing Management*, eds. F. Bass, C. King, and E. Pessemier, pp. 227–250. New York: Wiley, 1968.

Rosenberg, M. J. "Cognitive Structure and Attitudinal Affect." *Journal of Abnormal and Social Psychology*, Vol. 53 (1956), pp. 367–372.

Roshwalb, Irving. "How Much Is an Ad Test Worth?" *Journal of Advertising Research*, Vol. 15, No. 1 (February 1975), pp. 17–23.

Ross, G. T., and A. A. Zoltners. "Weighted Assignment Models and Their Application." *Management Science*, Vol. 15, No. 7 (July 1979), pp. 683–696.

Rossiter, John R. "Predicting Starch Scores." *Journal of Advertising Research*, Vol. 21, No. 5 (October 1981), pp. 63–68.

Rothchild, Michael L. "Advertising Strategies for High and Low Involvement Situations." In *Attitude Research Plays for High Stakes*, eds. John Maloney and Bernard Silverman, pp. 74–93. Chicago: American Marketing Association, 1979.

Rothwell, R., C. Freeman, A. Horsley, V. T. P. Jervis, A. B. Robertson, and J. Townsend. "SAPPHO Updated—Project SAPPHO Phase II." *Research Policy*, Vol. 3 (1974), pp. 258–291.

Rumelt, Richard P., and Robin Wensley. "In Search of the Market Share Effect." UCLA, working paper, 1980.

Ryan, M. J., and E. H. Bonfield. "Fishbein's Intentions Model: A Test of External and Pragmatic Validity." *Journal of Marketing*, Vol. 44 (Spring 1979), pp. 82–95.

Ryans, A. B., and C. B. Weinberg. "Sales Territory Response." *Journal of Marketing Research*, Vol. 16 (November 1979), pp. 453–465.

_____. "Salesforce Management: Integrating Research Advances." *California Management Review*, Vol. 24, No. 1 (Fall 1981), pp. 75–89.

Saaty, Thomas. "A Scaling Method for Priorities in Hierarchical Structures." *Journal of Mathematical Psychology*, Vol. 15, No. 3 (June 1977), pp. 234–281.

Sackman, Harold. *Delphi Critique*. Lexington, Mass.: Heath, 1975.

Sahal, D. "The Multidimensional Diffusion of Technology." In *Technological Substitution: Forecasting Technologies and Applications*, eds. H. Linstone and S. Sahal, pp. 223–244. New York: Elsevier, 1976.

Saleh, F., and B. J. LaLonde. "Industrial Buying Behavior and the Motor Carrier Selection Decision." *Journal of Purchasing*, Vol. 8, No. 1 (February 1972), pp. 18–34.

Sasieni, Maurice W. "Optimal Advertising Expenditures." *Management Science*, Vol. 18, No. 4, Part II (December 1971), pp. 64–72.

_____. "Pricing and Advertising for Profit." Paper presented at Pennsylvania State University, October 1981.

Scherer, F. *Industrial Market Structure and Economic Performance*. Skokie, Ill.: Rand McNally, 1980.

Schlaifer, Robert. *Analysis of Decisions Under Uncertainty*. New York: McGraw-Hill, 1969.

Schmalensee, Richard. *The Economics of Advertising*. Amsterdam: North-Holland, 1972.

_____. "A Model of Advertising and Product Quality." *Journal of Political Economics*, Vol. 86 (1978), pp. 485–503.

Schmalensee, Richard, Alvin J. Silk, and Robert Bojanek. "The Impact of Scale and Media Mix on Advertising Agency Cost." Working paper. Boston, Mass.: Massachusetts Institute of Technology, 1981.

Schoeffler, Sidney. "Cross Sectional Study of Strategy, Structure and Performance: Aspects of the PIMS Program." In *Strategy + Structure = Performance: The Strategic Planning Imperative*, ed. H. B. Thorelli. Bloomington: Indiana University Press, 1977a.

_____. "Nine Basic Findings on Business Strategy." *Pimsletter*, No. 1, 1977b.

_____. "Capital Intensive Technology vs. ROI: A Strategic Assessment." *Management Review* (September 1978), pp. 8–14.

_____. "SPI Seeks Science, Not Single, Oversimplistic Strategic Variables." *Marketing News* (February 9, 1979), pp. 1–4.

Schoeffler, Sidney, Robert D. Buzzell, and Donald F. Heany. "Impact of Strategic Planning on Profit Performance." *Harvard Business Review*, Vol. 52, No. 2 (March–April 1974), pp. 137–145.

Schonberger, Richard J. "MIS Design: A Contingency Approach." *MIS Quarterly* (March 1980), pp. 13–20.

Schroder, H. M., M. J. Driver, and S. Treufort. *Human Information Processing*. New York: Holt, Rinehart and Winston, 1967.

Schultz, R. L., and D. Hanssens. "Logical Implications of Competitive Behavior: An

Approach to Model Specification." Working paper no. 561, Krannert Graduate School of Management, 1976.

Schultz, R. L., and M. D. Henry. "Implementing Decision Models." In *Marketing Decision Models*, eds. R. Schultz and A. Zoltners, pp. 275-296. New York: North-Holland, 1981.

Schultz, Randall L., and Dennis P. Slevin. "Introduction: The Implementation Problem." In *The Implementation of Management Science*, eds. Robert Doktor, Randall L. Schultz, and Dennis P. Slevin, pp. 1-15. Amsterdam: North-Holland, 1979.

Schultz, R. L., and A. A. Zoltners. *Marketing Decision Models*. New York: North-Holland, 1981.

Scientific American. *How Industry Buys*. New York: 1970.

Scott, Jerome E., and Peter D. Bennett. "Cognitive Models of Attitude Structure: 'Value Importance' Is Important," In *Relevance in Marketing: Problems, Research Action*, p. 33. Chicago: American Marketing Association, 1971.

Scott, Jerome E., and Peter Wright. "Modeling an Organizational Buyer's Product Evaluation Strategy: Validity and Procedural Consideratons." *Journal of Marketing Research*, Vol. 13 (August 1976), pp. 211-224.

Segal, M., and D. B. Weinberger. "Turfing." *Operations Research*, Vol. 25, No. 3 (May-June 1977), pp. 367-386.

Seipel, Carl-Magnus. "Premiums—Forgotten by Theory." *Journal of Marketing*, Vol. 35 (April 1971), pp. 26-34.

Seligman, Daniel. "How Much for Advertising?" *Fortune* (December 1956), pp. 120-126.

Semlow, W. J. "How Many Salesmen Do You Need?" *Harvard Business Review*, Vol. 37 (May-June 1959), pp. 126-132.

Senn, A. "Essential Principles of Information Systems Developments." *MIS Quarterly* (June 1978), pp. 17-26.

Sethi, Suresh P. "Optimal Control of the Vidale-Wolfe Advertising Model." *Operations Research*, Vol. 21, No. 4 (July-August 1973), pp. 998-1013.

Sethi, Suresh P., and Gerald L. Thompson. *Optimal Control Theory: Applications to Management Science*. Boston: Marinus Nijuff, 1981.

Sewall, Murphy A. "A Decision Calculus Model for Contract Bidding." *Journal of Marketing*, Vol. 40, No. 4 (October 1976), pp. 92-98.

Sexton, Donald E., Jr. "Estimating Marketing Policy Effects on Sales of a Frequently Purchased Product." *Journal of Marketing Research*, Vol. 7 (August 1970), pp. 338-347.

Shanker, R. J., R. E. Turner, and A. A. Zoltners. "Sales Territory Design: An Integrated Approach." *Management Science*, Vol. 22, No. 3 (November 1975), pp. 309-320.

Shapiro, Arlene. *Input-Output Analysis as a Predictive Tool*. Washington, D.C.: Bureau of Economic Analysis, 1972.

Shapiro, Arthur. "Promotional Effectiveness at H. J. Heinz." *Interfaces*, Vol. 6, No. 2 (February 1976), pp. 84-86.

Shapiro, Benson P. "Price Reliance: Existence and Sources." *Journal of Marketing Research*, Vol. 10, No. 3 (August 1973), pp. 286-294.

————. "Account Management and Sales Organization: New Developments in Practice." In *Sales Management: New Developments from Behavioral and Decision Model Research*, ed. Richard P. Bagozzi, pp. 265-294. Cambridge, Mass.: Marketing Science Institute, 1979.

Sharif, M. N., and C. Kabir. "A Generalized Model for Forecasting Technological Substitutions." *Technological Forecasting and Social Change*, Vol. 8, No. 4 (1976) pp. 353-364.

Sharif, M. N., and K. Ramanathan. "Binomial Innovation Diffusion Models with Dynamic Potential Adopter Population." *Technological Forecasting and Social Change*, Vol. 20, No. 1 (August 1981) pp. 63-87.

Sharif, C. W., M. Sharif, and R. W. Nebergati. *Attitude and Attitude Change.* Philadelphia: Saunders, 1965.

Sheth, Jagdish N. "Brand Profile from Beliefs and Importances." *Journal of Advertising Research,* Vol. 13 (February 1973a), pp. 37–42.

_____. "A Model of Industrial Buyer Behavior." *Journal of Marketing,* Vol. 37 (October 1973b), pp. 50–56.

_____. "An Investigation of Relationships Among Evaluative Beliefs, Affect, Behavioral Intention, and Behavior." In *Consumer Behavior: Theory and Application,* eds. John U. Farley, John A. Howard, and L. Winston Ring. pp. 89–114. Boston: Allyn & Bacon, 1974.

_____. "Recent Developments in Organizational Buying Behavior." Working paper no. 317, College of Commerce and Business Administration, University of Illinois, August 1976.

Sheth, Jagdish N., and W. Wayne Talarzyk. "Perceived Instrumentality and Value Importance as Determinants of Attitudes." *Journal of Marketing Research,* Vol. 9 (February 1972), pp. 6–9.

Shiskin, J. A., H. Young, and J. C. Musgrave. "The X–11 Variant of the Census II Seasonal Adjustment Program." Technical Paper No. 15, Bureau of the Census, February 1967.

Shneiderman, B. "Human Factors Experiments in Designing Interactive Systems." *Computer* (December 1979), pp. 9–19.

Shocker, Allan D., and V. Srinivasan. "A Consumer-based Methodology for the Identification of New Product Ideas." *Management Science,* Vol. 20, No. 6 (February 1974), pp. 921–937.

_____. "Multi-attribute Approaches for Product Concept Evaluation and Generation: A Critical Review." *Journal of Marketing Research,* Vol. 16 (May 1979), pp. 159–180.

Shoemaker, Robert W. "An Analysis of Consumer Reactions to Product Promotions." In *Conceptual and Theoretical Developments in Marketing,* eds. O. C. Ferrell, S. W. Brown, and C. W. Lamb, Jr., pp. 244–248. Chicago: American Marketing Association, 1979.

Shoemaker, Robert W., and F. R. Shoaf. "Repeat Rates of Deal Purchases." *Journal of Advertising Research,* Vol. 17 (1977), pp. 47–53.

Shubik, Martin. "Oligopoly Theory, Communication, and Information." *American Economic Review,* Vol. 65, No. 2 (May 1975), pp. 280–283.

Shugan, S. "The Cost of Thinking." *Journal of Consumer Research* (September 1980), pp. 99–111.

Sicherman, Alan. "An Interactive Computer Program for Assessing and Using Multiattribute Utility Functions." Technical Report No. 111, Operations Research Center, MIT, 1975.

Silk, Alvin J. "Overlap Among Self-Designated Opinion Leaders: A Study of Selected Dental Products and Services." *Journal of Marketing Research,* Vol. 3, No. 3 (August 1966), pp. 255–259.

_____. "Preference and Perception Measures in New Product Development: Exposition and Review." *Industrial Management Review* (Fall 1969), pp. 21–36.

_____. "Test-Retest Correlations and the Reliability of Copy Testing." *Journal of Marketing Research,* Vol. 14 (November 1977), pp. 476–486.

Silk, Alvin J., and Manohar U. Kalwani. "Measuring Influence in Organizational Purchase Decisions." *Journal of Marketing Research,* Vol. 19 (May 1982), pp. 165–181.

Silk, Alvin J., and Glen L. Urban. "Pre-Test Market Evaluation of New Packaged Goods: A Model and Measurement Methodology." *Journal of Marketing Research,* Vol. 15 (May 1978), pp. 171–191.

Simmonds, Kenneth. "Competitive Bidding: Deciding the Best Combination of Non-Price Features." *Operational Research Quarterly* (March 1968), pp. 5–14.

Simmons, D. M. *Nonlinear Programming for Operations Research.* Englewood Cliffs, N.J.: Prentice-Hall, 1975.

Simon, Herbert A. "A Behavioral Model of Rational Choice." *Quarterly Journal of Economics*, Vol. 89 (1952), pp. 99–118.

Simon, Hermann. "An Analytical Investigation of Kotler's Simulation Model." *Management Science*, Vol. 24, No. 14 (October 1978), pp. 1462–1473.

———. "Dynamics of Price Elasticity and Brand Life Cycles: An Empirical Study." *Journal of Marketing Research*, Vol. 16, No. 4 (November 1979), pp. 439–452.

———. "Pricestrat—An Applied Strategic Pricing Model for Nondurables." In *Marketing Planning Models*, ed. A. A. Zoltners, pp. 23–41. TIMS Studies in the Management Sciences, Vol. 18. New York: North-Holland, 1982a.

———. "ADPULS: An Advertising Model with Wearout and Pulsation." *Journal of Marketing Research*, Vol. 19 (August 1982b), pp. 352–363.

Simon, Hermann, and Karl-Heinz Sebastian. "Diffusion and Advertising: The German Telephone Campaign." Working paper, The Marketing Science Group of Germany, August 1982.

Simon, Hermann, and Michael Thiel. "Hits and Flops Among German Media Models." *Journal of Advertising Research*, Vol. 20, No. 6 (December 1980), pp. 25–29.

Simon, J. L. "New Evidence for No Effect of Scale in Advertising." *Journal of Advertising Research*, Vol. 9 (1969), pp. 38–41.

Simulmatics Corporation. *Simulmatics Media-Mix, Technical Description.* New York, October 1962.

Singer, E. *Antitrust Economics: Selected Legal Cases and Economic Models.* Englewood Cliffs, N.J.: Prentice-Hall, 1968.

Sinha, Prabhakant, and Andris A. Zoltners. "Sales Territory Alignment: A Review and a Model." Working paper, Marketing Science Center, Northwestern University, January 1982.

Sinha, Prabharkant, and Andris A. Zoltners. "Integer Programming Model and Algorithmic Evolution: A Case from Sales Resource Allocation." In *Marketing Planning Models*, ed. A. A. Zoltners, pp. 99–116. TIMS Studies in the Management Sciences, Vol. 18. New York: North-Holland, 1982.

Slovic, P., and D. MacPhillamy. "Dimensional Communicability and Cue Utilization in Comparative Judgment." *Organizational Behavior and Human Performance*, Vol. 11 (1974), pp. 172–194.

Smith, Wendell R. "Product Differentiation and Market Segmentation as Alternative Marketing Strategies." *Journal of Marketing*, Vol. 20, No. 3 (July 1956), pp. 3–8.

Sonquist, John A. *Multivariate Model Building.* Ann Arbor, Mich.: Survey Research Center, 1970.

Sorenson, Richard E., and Dale E. Zand. "Improving the Implementation of OR/MS Models by Applying the Lewin-Schein Theory of Change." In *Implementing Operations Research/Management Science*, eds. Randall L. Schultz and Dennis P. Slevin, pp. 217–235. New York: Elsevier, 1975.

Sowter, A. P., A. Gabor, and C. W. J. Granger. "The Effect of Price on Choice." *Applied Economics*, 3 (1971) pp. 167–181.

Spekman, Robert E., "Organizational Boundary Behavior: A Conceptual Framework for Investigating the Industrial Salesperson." In *Sales Management: New Developments from Behavioral and Decision Model Research*, ed. R. Bagozzi, pp. 133–144. Cambridge, Mass.: Marketing Science Institute, 1979.

Spekman, Robert E., and Louis W. Stern. "Environmental Uncertainty and Buying Group Structure: An Empirical Investigation." *Journal of Marketing*, Vol. 43, No. 2 (Spring 1979), pp. 54–64.

Spivey, Allen W., and William J. Wrobleski. "Forecasting Experiences of Major U.S. Econometric Models in the 1970's." Working paper, Division of Research, University of Michigan, July 1981.

Sprague, Ralph H., Jr. "A Framework for the Development of Decision Support Systems." *MIS Quarterly* (December 1980), pp. 1–26.

Srinivasan, V. "Network Models for Estimating Brand Images." Research paper no. 344, Graduate School of Business, Stanford University, December 1976.

————. "The Nonoptimality of Equal Commission Rates in Multi-Product Salesforce Compensation Schemes." Research paper no. 529, Graduate School of Business, Stanford University, December 1979.

————. "An Investigation of the Equal Commission Rate Policy for a Multi-Product Salesforce." *Management Science*, Vol. 27, No. 7 (July 1981), pp. 731–756.

Srinivasan, V., and A. D. Shocker. "Linear Programming Techniques for Multidimensional Analysis of Preferences." *Psychometrika*, Vol. 38, No. 3 (September 1973), pp. 337–369.

Srivastava, Rajendrak, Allan D. Shocker, and George Day. "An Exploratory Study of Situational Effects on Product-Market Definition." In *Advances in Consumer Research*, ed. H. Keith Hunt. Atlanta: Association for Consumer Research, 1978.

Staelin, Richard, and Ronald E. Turner. "Error in Judgmental Sales Forecasts: Theory and Results." *Journal of Marketing Research*, Vol. 10, No. 1 (February 1973), pp. 10–16.

Stafford, James E., and Ben M. Enis. "The Price-Quality Relationship—An Extension." *Journal of Marketing Research*, Vol. 6 (November 1969), pp. 456–458.

Stanley, T., and M. Sewall. "Image Inputs to a Probabilistic Model: Predicting Retail Potential." *Journal of Marketing*, Vol. 33 (July 1976), pp. 48–53.

Stapleton, E. "The Normal Distribution as a Model of Technological Substitution." *Technological Forecasting and Social Change*, Vol. 8, No. 3 (1976), pp. 325–334.

Starch, Daniel. "How Does Shape of Ads Affect Readership?" *Media/Scope*, Vol. 10, No. 7 (July 1966), pp. 83–85.

Starr, Martin K., and Joel R. Rubinson. "A Loyalty Group Segmentation Model for Brand Purchasing Simulation." *Journal of*

Marketing Research, Vol. 15 (August 1978), pp. 378–383.

Stefflre, Volney J. *New Products and New Enterprises: A Report of an Experiment in Applied Social Science.* Irvine: University of California, March 1971.

————. "Some Applications of Multi-Dimensional Scaling to Social Science Problems." In *Multi-dimensional Scaling: Theory and Applications in the Behavioral Sciences*, ed. Roger N. Shepard, A. K. Romney, and Sarah B. Nerlove. New York: Seminar Press, 1972.

Stein, M. O., R. V. Ayers, and A. Shapeneso. "A Model for Forecasting the Substitution of One Technology for Another." *Technological Forecasting and Social Change*, Vol. 7 (February 1975), pp. 57–79.

Stern, Louis W., and Abel I. El-Ansary. *Marketing Channels.* Englewood Cliffs, N.J.: Prentice-Hall, 1977.

Stern, Mark. *Marketing Planning: A Systems Approach.* New York: McGraw-Hill, 1966.

Stewart, David N., and Joan Blackwell. "Media Decision Models: A Review and Evaluation." Paper presented at the TIMS/ORSA Meeting, Washington, D.C., May 1980.

Stigler, George. *The Theory of Price.* Rev. ed. New York: Macmillan, 1952.

Stobaugh, Robert, and Daniel Yergin, eds. *Energy Future.* New York: Random House, 1979.

Stoetzel, J. "Le prix comme limite." In *La Psychologie Economique*, ed. P. L. Reynaud. Paris: Librairie Marcel Riviere et Cie, 1954.

Strang, Roger A. "Sales Promotion-Fast Growth, Faculty Management. *Harvard Business Review*, Vol. 54, No. 4 (July–August 1976) pp. 115–124.

Strang, Roger A., Robert M. Prentice, and Alden G. Clayton. *The Relationship Between Advertising and Promotion in Brand Strategy.* Cambridge, Mass.: Marketing Science Institute, 1975.

Swan, John E., and Linda Jones Combs. "Product Performance and Consumer Satisfaction: A New Concept." *Journal of Market-*

ing Research, Vol. 13 (April 1976), pp. 25–33.

Sweeney, Timothy W., H. Lee Mathews and David T. Wilson. "An Analysis of Industrial Buyers' Risk Reducing Behavior: Some Personality Correlates." In *Increasing Marketing Productivity*, ed. Thomas V. Greer. Chicago: American Marketing Association, 1974.

Swinyard, W. R., and M. L. Ray. "Advertising-Selling Interactions: An Attribution Theory Experiment." *Journal of Marketing Research*, Vol. 14 (1977), pp. 509–516.

Taggart, William M., and Valdur Silbey. "A 'Balanced' Orientation for the Information Systems Manager." *MIS Quarterly* (June 1979), pp. 21–33.

Taha, H. *Integer Programming: Theory, Application and Computations*. New York: Academic Press, 1975.

Talley, W. J., Jr. "How to Design Sales Territories." *Journal of Marketing*, Vol. 25 (January 1961), pp. 7–31.

Tapiero, C. S., and J. U. Farley. "Optimal Control of Sales Force Effort in Time." *Management Science*, Vol. 21, No. 9 (May 1975), pp. 976–985.

Tauber, Edward M. "HIT: Heuristic Ideation Technique—A Systematic Procedure for New Product Search." *Journal of Marketing*, Vol. 36 (January 1972), pp. 58–70.

Tauber, Edward M. "Forecasting Sales Prior to Test Market." *Journal of Marketing*, Vol. 41 (January 1977), pp. 80–84.

Taylor, James W. "The Role of Risk in Consumer Behavior." *Journal of Marketing*, Vol. 38 (April 1974), pp. 54–60.

Telser, L. G. "Advertising and Cigarettes." *Journal of Political Economy*, Vol. 60 (1962a), pp. 471–499.

———. "The Demand for Branded Goods as Estimated from Consumer Panel Data." *Review of Economics and Statistics*, Vol. 44 (1962b), pp. 300–324.

———. "A Theory of Innovation and Its Effects." *Bell Journal of Economics*, Vol. 13, No. 1 (Spring 1982), pp. 69–92.

Theil, Henri. *Principles of Econometrics*. New York: Wiley, 1971.

———. *Theory and Measurement of Consumer Demand, Vol. 1*. New York: North-Holland, 1975.

———. *Theory and Measurement of Consumer Demand, Vol. 2*. New York: North-Holland, 1976.

Thomas, Joseph. "Price Production Decisions with Deterministic Demand." *Management Science* Vol. 16, No. 11 (July 1970). pp. 747–750.

Thomas, Joseph, and Prem Chabria. "Bayesian Models for New Product Pricing." *Decision Sciences*, Vol. 6, No. 1 (January 1975), pp. 51–64.

Thompson, W. W., and J. U. McNeal. "Sales Planning and Control Using Absorbing Markov Chains." *Journal of Marketing Research*, Vol. 4 (February 1967), pp. 62–66.

Thorelli, Hans B., and Stephen C. Burnett. "The Nature of Product Life Cycles for Industrial Goods Businesses." *Journal of Marketing*, Vol. 45, No. 4 (Fall 1981), pp. 97–108.

Tiebout, Charles M. "Input-Output and the Firm: A Technique for Using National and Regional Tables." *The Review of Economics and Statistics*, Vol. 49, No. 2 (May 1967), pp. 260–262.

Tinter, G., and J. K. Sengupta. *Stochastic Economics*. New York: Academic Press, 1972.

Tollefson, John O., and V. Parker Lessig. "Aggregation Criteria in Normative Segmentation Theory." *Journal of Marketing Research*, Vol. 15 (August 1978), pp. 348–355.

Torgerson, Warren S. *Theory and Method of Scaling*. New York: Wiley, 1958.

Trodahl, Verling C., and Robert L. Jones. "Prediction of Newspaper Advertisement Readership." *Journal of Advertising Research*, Vol. 5 (March 1965), pp. 23–27.

Turban, E., and J. R. Meredith. *Fundamentals of Management Science*. Dallas: Business Publications, 1977.

Turner, R. E. "Product Priorities Within a Multiple-Product Marketing Organization."

Journal of Marketing Research, Vol. 9 (May 1974), pp. 143–150.

Turner, R. E., and J. C. Wiginton. "Advertising Expenditure Trajectories: An Empirical Study for Filter Cigarettes 1953–1965." *Decision Sciences,* Vol. 7 (1976), pp. 496–509.

Twedt, Dik W. "A Multiple Factor Analysis of Advertising Readership." *Journal of Applied Psychology* (June 1952), pp. 207–215.

———. "How Important to Marketing Strategy Is the Heavy User?" *Journal of Marketing,* Vol. 28 (January 1964), pp. 71–72.

UMPIRE: Unified Mathematical Programming System Incorporating Refinements and Extensions: User's Guide. Publication S00037-00-00. Los Angeles: Computer Sciences Corporation, 1970.

University of London Atlas Computing Service. *DYNAMO—Media Scheduling Suite of Programs.* University of London, Atlas Computing Service, 1972.

Urban, Glen L. "A Mathematical Modeling Approach to Product Line Decisions." *Journal of Marketing Research,* Vol. 6 (February 1969), pp. 40–47.

———. "SPRINTER Mod III: A Model for the Analysis of New Frequently Purchased Consumer Products." *Operations Research,* Vol. 18 (September–October 1970), pp. 805–853.

———. "Building Models for Decision-Makers." *Interfaces,* Vol. 4, No. 3 (May 1974), pp. 1–11.

———. "National and Local Allocation of Advertising Dollars." *Journal of Marketing Research,* Vol. 15, No. 6 (1975a), pp. 7–16.

———. "PERCEPTOR: A Model for Product Positioning." *Management Science,* Vol. 21, No. 8 (April 1975b), pp. 858–871.

Urban, Glen L., and John R. Hauser. *Design and Marketing of New Products.* Englewood Cliffs, N.J.: Prentice-Hall, 1980.

Urban, Glen L., R. Johnson, and R. Brudnick. "Market Entry Strategy Formulation: A Hierarchical Model and Consumer Measurement Approach." Working paper, Sloan School of Management, MIT, 1979.

Urban, Glen L., and Gerald M. Katz. "Pre-Test-Market Models: Validation and Managerial Implications." Working Paper, Sloan School of Management, MIT, April, 1982.

Utterback, J. M., and J. W. Braun. "Monitoring Technological Opportunities." *Business Horizons* (October 15, 1972), pp. 5–15.

Van Horne, J. C. *Financial Management and Policy.* 5th ed. Englewood Cliffs, N.J.: Prentice-Hall, 1980.

Vaughn, Charles L. *Franchising: Its Nature, Scope, Advantages and Development.* Lexington, Mass.: Heath, 1974.

Venkatesan, M. "Cognitive Consistency and Novelty Seeking." In *Consumer Behavior: Theoretical Sources,* eds. Scott Ward and Thomas Robertson. Englewood Cliffs, N.J.: Prentice-Hall, 1973.

Vidale, H. L., and H. B. Wolfe. "An Operations Research Study of Sales Response to Advertising." *Operational Research Quarterly,* Vol. 5 (1957), pp. 370–381.

Von Hippel, Eric A. "Has a Customer Already Developed Your Next Product?" *Sloan Management Review,* Vol. 18 (Winter 1977a), pp. 63–74.

———. "Transferring Process Equipment Innovations from User Innovators to Equipment Manufacturing Firms." *R & D Management,* Vol. 8, No. 1 (October 1977b), pp. 13–22.

———. "Successful Industrial Products from Customer Ideas." *Journal of Marketing,* Vol. 42, No. 1 (January 1978), pp. 39–49.

Wagner, Harvey M. "Research Portfolio for Inventory Management and Production Planning Systems." *Operations Research,* Vol. 28, No. 3 (May–June 1980), pp. 445–475.

Waid, C., D. F. Clark, and R. L. Ackoff. "Allocation of Sales Effort in the Lamp Divisions of the General Electric Company." *Operational Research Quarterly,* Vol. 4 (December 1956), pp. 629–647.

Walters, C. G. *Consumer Behavior: Theory and Practice.* Homewood, Ill.: Irwin, 1978.

Warren, E. H., Jr. "Solar Energy Market Penetration Models: Science or Number Mysticism?" *Technological Forecasting and Social Change,* Vol. 16, No. 2 (February 1980), pp. 105–118.

Warshaw, P. "Predicting Purchase and Other Behavior from General and Contextually Specific Intentions." Journal of Marketing Research, Vol. 17 (February 1980*a*), pp. 26–33.

———. "A New Model for Predicting Behavioral Intentions: An Alternative to Fishbein." *Journal of Marketing Research* (May 1980*b*), pp. 153–172.

Wasson, Chester R. *Dynamic Competitive Strategy and Product Life Cycles.* St. Charles, Ill.: Challenge Books, 1978.

Webster, Frederick E., Jr. "Management Science in Industrial Marketing." *Journal of Marketing,* Vol. 42, No. 1 (January 1978*a*), pp. 21–27.

———. Is Industrial Marketing Coming of Age?" In *Review of Marketing,* eds. G. Zaltman and T. Bonoma. Chicago: American Marketing Association, 1978*b*.

———. *Industrial Marketing Strategy.* New York: Wiley, 1979.

Webster, Frederick E., Jr., and Yoram Wind. *Organizational Buying Behavior.* Englewood Cliffs, N.J.: Prentice-Hall, 1972*a*.

———. "A General Model for Understanding Organizational Buying Behavior." *Journal of Marketing,* Vol. 36 (April 1972*b*), pp. 12–19.

Weddle, David E., and James R. Bettman. "Marketing Underground: An Investigation of Fishbein's Behavioral Intention Model." In *Advances in Consumer Research,* Vol. 1, eds. S. Ward and P. Wright, pp. 310–318. Atlanta: Association for Consumer Research, 1974.

Weinberg, Charles B. "An Optimal Commission Plan for Salesmen's Control Over Price." *Management Science,* Vol. 21 (April 1975), pp. 937–943.

———. "Jointly Optimal Sales Commissions for Nonincome Maximizing Sales Forces."

Management Science, Vol. 24 (August 1978), pp. 1252–1258.

———. "Marketing Mix Decision Rules for Nonprofit Organizations." In *Research in Marketing,* Vol. 3, ed. J. Sheth, pp. 191–234. Greenwich, Conn.: JAI Press, 1979.

Weinberg, Charles B., and H. C. Lucas, Jr. "Letter to the Editor." *Journal of Marketing,* Vol. 41, No. 2 (April 1977), p. 147.

Weinberg, R. S. *An Analytical Approach to Advertising Expenditure Strategy.* New York: Association of National Advertisers, 1960.

Weiss, Doyle L., "Determinants of Market Share." *Journal of Marketing Research,* Vol. 5 (August 1968), pp. 290–295.

Wellman, H. R. "The Distribution of Selling Effort Among Geographic Areas." *Journal of Marketing.* Vol. 3, No. 3 (January 1939), pp. 225–239.

Wells, William D. "Psychographics: A Critical Review." *Journal of Marketing Research,* Vol. 12 (May 1975), pp. 196–213.

Wells, William D., Clark Leavitt, and Maureen McConnell. "A Reaction Profile for TV Commercials." *Journal of Advertising Research,* Vol. 11, No. 2 (December 1971), pp. 11–17.

Wenig, P. W. "Media Schedule Operations." *Data,* Vol. 1 (December–April 1964), pp. 16–24.

Wensley, Robin. "PIMS and BCG: New Horizons or False Dawn?" *Strategic Management Journal,* Vol. 3 (1982) pp. 147–158.

Westfall, Ralph. "Psychological Factors in Predicting Product Choice." *Journal of Marketing,* Vol. 26 (April 1962), pp. 34–40.

Wheatley, John J., and John S. Y. Chiu. "The Effects of Price, Store Image, and Product and Respondent Characteristics on Perceptions of Quality." *Journal of Marketing Research,* Vol. 14 (May 1977), pp. 181–186.

Wheelwright, Steven C., and Darral G. Clarke. "Corporate Forecasting: Promise and Reality." *Harvard Business Review,* Vol. 54, No. 6 (November–December 1976), pp. 40 ff.

Wheelwright, Steven C., and Spyros Makrida-kis. *Forecasting Methods for Management.* 2nd ed. New York: Wiley, 1977.

Wiederhold, G. *Database Design.* New York: McGraw-Hill, 1977.

Wierenga, B. *An Investigation of Brand Choice Processes.* Rotterdam: Rotterdam University Press, 1974.

Wildt, Albert R., "Multi-firm Analysis of Competitive Decision Variables." *Journal of Marketing Research,* Vol. 11 (February 1974), pp. 50–62.

———. "On Evaluating Market Segmentation Studies and the Properties of R^2." *Management Science,* Vol. 22 (April 1976), pp. 904–908.

———. "Estimating Models of Seasonal Marketing Response Using Dummy Variables." *Journal of Marketing Research,* Vol. 14, No. 1 (February 1977), pp. 34–41.

Wildt, Albert R., and Albert V. Bruno. "The Prediction of Preference in Capital Equipment Using Linear Attitude Models." *Journal of Marketing Research,* Vol. 11 (May 1974), pp. 203–205.

Wildt, Albert R., and John M. McCann. "A Regression Model for Market Segmentation Studies." *Journal of Marketing Research,* Vol. 17 (August 1980), pp. 335–340.

Wilkie, William L., and Edgar A. Pessemier. "Issues in Marketing's Use of Multi-Attribute Models." *Journal of Marketing Research,* Vol. 10 (November 1973), pp. 428–441.

Wilkie, W. L., and Rolf P. Weinreich. "Effects of the Number and Type of Attributes Included in an Attitude Model: More Is Not Better." Institute Paper No. 385, Krannert Graduate School of Industrial Administration, Purdue University, 1973.

Wilkinson, J. B., J. Barry Mason, and Christie H. Paksoy. "Assessing the Impact of Short-Term Supermarket Strategy Variables." *Journal of Marketing Research,* Vol. 19 (February 1982), pp. 72–86.

Wilson, Aubrey. "Industrial Market Research in Britain." *Journal of Marketing Research,* Vol. 6 (February 1969), pp. 15–28.

Wilson, David T. "Industrial Buyers' Decision-Making Styles." *Journal of Marketing Research,* Vol. 8 (November 1971), pp. 433–436.

Wilson, David T., H. L. Matthews, and J. W. Harvey. "An Empirical Test of the Fishbein Behavioral Intention Model." *Journal of Consumer Research,* Vol. 1 (1975), pp. 39–48.

Wilson, R. Dale. "A Model Testing Procedure for Evaluating the Influence of Short-Term Promotions on Patterns of Consumer Behavior: Literature Review and Methodology." In *Proceeding, Special Interest Conference on Market Measurement and Analysis, Proceedings,* ed. R. Leone, pp. 54–60. Providence, R.I.: The Institute of Management Science, 1980.

Wilson, R. Dale, and Lewis G. Pringle. *Modeling New Product Introductions: A Comparison of NEWS, SPRINTER, and TRACKER.* Paper presented at the Analytic Approaches to Product and Marketing Planning Conference, Nashville, October 1981.

Wind, Yoram. "Industrial Source Loyalty." *Journal of Marketing Research,* Vol. 7 (November 1970), pp. 450–457.

———. "A New Procedure for Concept Evaluation." *Journal of Marketing,* Vol. 37 (October 1973), pp. 2–11.

———. "Preference of Relevant Others and Individual Choice Models." *Journal of Consumer Research,* Vol. 3 (August 1976), pp. 50–57.

———. "Organizational Buying Behavior." In *Review of Marketing,* eds. G. Zaltman and T. Bonoma, pp. 160–193. American Marketing Association, 1978a.

———. "Issues and Advances in Segmentation Research." *Journal of Marketing Research,* Vol. 15 (August 1978b), pp. 317–337.

———. "A Research Program for a Marketing Guided Approach to Mergers and Acquisitions." Wharton School working paper, January 1979.

———. "Product-Market Planning Models: Concepts, Techniques and Needed Development." Wharton School working paper, 1981*a*.

———. "Marketing-Oriented Strategic Planning Models." In *Marketing Decision Models*, eds. R. Schultz and A. Zoltners, pp. 207–250. New York: North-Holland, 1981*b*.

———. "Marketing and Corporate Strategy: Problems and Perspectives." Presented at the 13th Annual Albert Wesley Frey Lecture, The University of Pittsburgh, March 1981*c*.

———. *Product Policy: Concepts, Methods and Strategy*. Reading, Mass.: Addison-Wesley, 1982.

Wind, Yoram, and Henry Claycamp. "Planning Product Line Strategy: A Matrix Approach." *Journal of Marketing*, Vol. 40 (January 1976), pp. 2–9.

Wind, Yoram and Vijay Mahajan. "Measurement Issues in Portfolio Analysis." In *Proceedings, Special Interest Conference on Market Measurement and Analysis, 1980*, ed. R. Leone, pp. 50–53. Providence, R.I.: The Institute of Management Sciences, 1980.

Wind, Yoram, Vijay Mahajan, and Donald J. Swire. *Portfolio Analysis and Strategy*. Reading, Mass.: Addison-Wesley, 1982.

Wind, Yoram, and Thomas L. Saaty. "Marketing Applications of the Analytic Hierarchy Process." *Management Science*, Vol. 26, No. 7 (July 1980), pp. 641–658.

Wind, Yoram, and Robert Thomas. "Organizational Buying Behavior: Problems and Opportunities." Working paper No. 8–81, Wharton School, University of Pennsylvania, 1980.

Winer, R. L. "The Effect of Product Sales Quotas on Sales Force Productivity." *Journal of Marketing Research*, Vol. 10 (May 1973), pp. 180–183.

Winkler, R. L. "The Assessment of Prior Probabilities in Bayesian Analysis." *Journal of the American Statistical Association*, Vol. 62 (1967*a*), pp. 776–800.

———. "The Quantification of Judgment: Some Methodological Suggestions." *Journal of the American Statistical Association*, Vol. 62 (1967*b*), pp. 1105–1120.

———. "The Quantification of Judgment: Some Experimental Results." *Proceedings of the American Statistical Association* (1967*c*), pp. 386–395.

———. "The Consensus of Subjective Probability Distributions." *Management Science*, Vol. 15 (1968), pp. B-61–B-75.

Wittink, D. R. "Exploring Territorial Differences in the Relationship Between Marketing Variables." *Journal of Marketing Research*, Vol. 14 (1977), pp. 145–155.

Wolfe, H. B., J. K. Brown, and G. C. Thompson. *Measuring Advertising Results*. Studies in Business Policy, No. 102. New York: The Conference Board, 1962, pp. 62–68.

Wolverton, R. W. "The Cost of Developing Large-Scale Software." *IEEE Transactions on Computers*, Vol. C–23, No. 6 (1974), pp. 615–636.

Wonnacott, Ronald J., and Thomas H. Wonnacott. *Econometrics*. 2nd ed. New York: Wiley, 1979.

Wood, Douglas, and Robert Fildes. *Forecasting for Business: Methods and Application*. New York: Longman Group, 1976.

Wright, P. L. "The Harassed Decision Maker: Time Pressures, Distractions, and the Use of Evidence." *Journal of Applied Psychology*, Vol. 59 (October 1974*a*), pp. 555–561.

———. "The Use of Phased, Noncompensatory Strategies in Decisions Between Multiattribute Products." Research Paper 223, Graduate School of Business, Stanford University, 1974*b*.

———. "Consumer Choice Strategies: Simplifying Versus Optimizing." *Journal of Marketing Research*, Vol. 11 (February 1975), pp. 60–67.

Wright, P. L., and B. Weitz. "Time Horizon Effects on Product Evaluation Strategies." *Journal of Marketing Research*, Vol. 14 (November 1977), pp. 429–443.

Yamanaka, Jiro. "The Prediction of Ad Readership Scores." *Journal of Advertising Research*, Vol. 2 (March 1962), pp. 18–23.

Yelle, L. E. "The Learning Curve: Historic Review and Comprehensive Survey." *Decision Sciences*, Vol. 10 (April 1979), pp. 302–327.

Young, Shirley. "Copy Testing Without Magic Numbers." *Journal of Advertising Research*, Vol. 12, No. 1 (February 1972), pp. 3–12.

Zaltman, G., C. R. A. Pinson, and R. Angelmar. *Metatheory and Consumer Research*. New York: Holt, Rinehart and Winston, 1973.

Zaltman, G., and M. Wallendorf. *Consumer Behavior: Basic Findings and Management Implications*. New York: Wiley, 1979.

Zangwill, Willard I. *Nonlinear Programming: A Unified Approach*. Englewood Cliffs, N.J.: Prentice-Hall, 1969.

Zellner, Arnold. "An Efficient Method of Estimating Seemingly Unrelated Regressions and Tests for Aggregation Bias." *Journal of the American Statistical Association*, Vol. 57 (June 1962), pp. 348–368.

Zentler, A. P., and D. Ryde. "An Optimum Geographic Distribution of Publicity Expectation in a Private Organization." *Management Science*, Vol. 2 (1956), pp. 337–352.

Zielski, Hubert A. "The Remembering and Forgetting of Advertising." *Journal of Marketing*, Vol. 23 (January 1959), pp. 239–243.

Ziff, Ruth. "Psychographics for Market Research." *Journal of Advertising Research*, Vol. 11, No. 2 (April 1971), pp. 3–9.

Zoltners, Andris A. "Integer Programming Models for Sales Territory Alignment to Maximize Profit." *Journal of Marketing Research*, Vol. 13 (November 1976), pp. 426–430.

——. "A Unified Approach to Sales Territory Alignment." In *Sales Management: New Developments from Behavioral and Decision Model Research*, eds. R. Bagozzi, pp.

360–376. Cambridge, Mass.: Marketing Science Institute, 1979.

——. "Normative Marketing Models." In *Marketing Decision Models*, ed. R. Schultz and A. Zoltners, pp. 55–76. New York: North-Holland, 1981.

Zoltners, Andris A., and Kathy S. Gardner. "A Review of Sales Force Decision Models." Working paper, Northwestern University, July 1980.

Zoltners, Andris A., and P. Sinha. "Integer Programming Models for Sales Resource Allocation." *Management Science*, Vol. 26, No. 3 (March 1980), pp. 242–260.

Zoltners, Andris A., P. Sinha, and P. S. C. Chong. "An Optimal Algorithm for Sales Representative Time Management." *Management Science*, Vol. 25, No. 12 (December 1979), pp. 1197–1207.

Zufryden, Fred S. "Media Scheduling: A Stochastic Dynamic Model Approach." *Management Science*, Vol. 19, No. 12 (August 1973), pp. 1395–1406.

——. "ZIPMAP—A Zero-One Integer Programming Model for Market Segmentation and Product Positioning." Working paper, Graduate School of Business Administration, University of Southern California, 1976.

——. "An Empirical Evaluation of a Composite Heterogenous Model of Brand Choice and Purchase Timing." *Management Science*, Vol. 24 (1978), pp. 761–773.

——. "A Logit-Markovian Model of Consumer Purchase Behavior Based on Explanatory Variables: Empirical Evaluation and Implications for Decision Making." *Decision Sciences*, Vol. 12, No. 4 (October 1981), pp. 645–660.

——. "A General Model for Assessing New Product Marketing Decisions and Market Performance." In *Marketing Planning Models*, ed. A. Zoltners, pp. 63–83. TIMS Studies in the Management Sciences, Vol. 18. New York: North-Holland, 1982.

Name Index

A

Aaker, David A., 476, 500, 502, 515, 523, 552
Abell, Derek F., 418, 615, 618–619, 629
Achenbaum, Alvin A., 723
Ackoff, Russell L., 28, 31, 34–35, 41, 320, 461, 463, 567, 578
Adam, D., 401
Adler, Lee, 8
Aggarwal, Sumer, 467
Agostini, M. M., 514
Ahl, David H., 734, 736, 738
Ahmed, Sadradin A., 313
Ahtola, Olli, 221
Ajzen, I., 221
Alavi, Maryam, 768
Albers, Sonke, 594
Albion, Mark S., 662
Allaire, Ivan, 179, 225
Allen, T. J., 359
Alloway, Robert M., 750
Alpert, Mark I., 199
Alter, Steven L., 749–751, 762, 765
Amstutz, Arnold E., 692
Anderberg, Michael R., 306
Anderson, Carl R., 627, 631
Anderson, M. J., Jr., 634
Anderson, Paul, 648
Anderson, Ralph E., 201
Andress, J. G., 300
Angelmar, R., 777
Angelus, T. L., 358

Appel, Valentine, 483
Applebaum, William, 454–456
Armstrong, G. M., 580
Armstrong, J. Scott, 129, 300, 320
Arnoff, E. Leonard, 34, 35
Arrow, Kenneth J., 61, 493, 659, 718
Assael, Henry, 202, 300–302, 305, 314, 482
Assmus, Gert, 482, 735, 736, 738
Attanasi, Emil, 427
Axelrod, Joel N., 225, 482
Ayers, R. V., 622

B

Babb, Emerson M., 533
Bagozzi, Richard P., 29, 126–128, 588, 589
Bailey, Earl L., 327, 330, 355, 389
Bailey, N. T. J., 706
Bailigh, Helmy, 438
Bain, Joe S., 613
Baker, Michael J., 5
Balachandran, V., 693
Balderston, F. E., 436
Banks, Seymour, 757
Banville, Guy R., 264
Barbosa, L. C., 766
Bard, Yonathan, 75, 119
Barefoot, Donald L., 441
Barnett, Arnold I., 95

Baron, Penny H., 481, 661
Barten, A. P., 92
Bass, Frank M., 83, 85, 87, 89, 113, 125, 162, 179, 205, 220, 222, 232, 238, 241, 299, 418, 419, 480, 493, 675, 703, 711–716
Bateson, John E. G., 286
Bauer, Raymond A., 200
Baumol, William J., 462, 664
Baurmeister, Hans, 427
Bean, Alden S., 787
Beckwith, Neal E., 95, 303, 365
Beldo, Leslie A., 785
Bell, David E., 95
Bellman, Richard, 181
Bemmaor, A., 232
Ben-Akiva, M., 680
Benders, J. F., 467
Benjamin, B., 480
Bennett, Peter D., 277, 286
Bensoussan, A., 172, 667, 692
Berger, A. W., 756
Berkowitz, M. K., 229
Berle, Adolph A., Jr., 44
Berry, William L., 789
Best, Roger J., 330, 662
Beswick, C. A., 562, 582, 587, 594–596
Bettis, Richard A., 608
Bettman, James R., 204, 206–208, 220–223, 622
Bijnen, E. J., 305
Bimm, E. B., 523

Bittson, A., 402
Blackburn, Joseph D., 735, 736, 738
Blackman, A. Wade, Jr., 708, 710, 711, 718, 776
Blackwell, Joan, 517
Blattberg, Robert C., 181, 205, 231, 246, 250, 314, 549, 552, 723, 726, 736, 738
Bloom, Derek, 477, 478, 503
Boehm, Barry, 769
Bojanek, Robert, 523
Bonoma, Thomas V., 285
Bookstein, Fred L., 128
Boot, T., 169
Bordley, Robert F., 139
Bower, John, 515
Bowersox, D. J., 469
Bowman, E. H., 26, 129, 668, 669
Box, George E. P., 338, 339
Boyd, Harper W., Jr., 303, 503, 755
Boyle, J. J., 341
Bradford, John W., 648
Bradley, Stephen P., 121, 162
Brand, Gordon T., 262, 285
Braun, J. W., 360
Braun, M. A., 162, 377
Brigham, Eugene F., 52
Bright, J. R., 360
Briscoe, C., 358
Brody, Edward I., 737–739
Brown, A. A., 92, 567, 578
Brown, D. B., 517
Brown, James K., 490, 491
Brown, L. O., 578
Brown, Robert G., 532, 533, 553
Brown, R. V., 129
Brudnick, R., 356, 622
Bruno, Albert V., 277, 286
Bubb, P. L., 267
Buckner, Hugh, 259, 285
Buessing, Thomas, 314, 552
Bultez, Alain V., 94, 95, 125, 172, 450, 659, 666, 667, 692
Bunge, Mario, 26, 29, 30
Burger, Philip C., 376, 731, 735, 736, 738
Burnett, Stephen C., 609, 631
Bursk, Edward D., 441
Bush, R., 243

Buzzell, Robert D., 501, 564, 578, 609, 625, 626, 628, 630, 666, 669, 672, 673

C

Cadbury, N. D., 723
Cadotte, E. R., 756
Cagley, James W., 285
Calentone, Roger J., 358
Capon, Noel, 221
Cardozo, Richard N., 285, 309, 310, 648
Carlson, J. G., 615
Carman, James M., 245, 500
Carroll, J. D., 213, 369, 372
Case, Peter B., 331
Cattin, Philippe, 369, 675
Chabria, Prem, 422
Chakravarti, D., 129, 134
Chamberlain, E., 663
Chambers, John C., 327, 349
Chandon, Jean-Louis, 307
Chang, J. J., 213, 372
Chapman, Randall G., 227
Charnes, A., 182, 183, 517
Chatfield, C., 188, 246, 247
Chevalier, Michael, 534
Choffray, Jean-Marie, 273, 275–277, 305, 310, 312, 366, 382, 654, 735, 737, 739, 755
Chong, P. S. C., 576, 582
Christenson, C. J., 789
Churchill, Gilbert A., Jr., 285, 588, 757
Churchman, C. West, 34, 35, 785
Chussil, Mark J., 630, 631
Clancy, Kevin J., 503, 735, 736, 738
Clark, D. F., 567, 578
Clarke, Darral G., 83, 328, 396, 480, 493, 500
Claycamp, Henry J., 295, 314, 515, 613, 640, 735, 737, 739
Clayton, Alden G., 533
Clelland, Richard C., 423
Clowes, K., 566, 567
Cochran, W. G., 369
Cochrane, D., 113
Cocks, Douglas L., 621

Cohen, Burleigh B., 482
Cohen, Jason N., 748
Coleman, J. C., 705
Colley, Russell H., 491, 492
Collins, B. J. K., 371, 723–726, 729, 734, 737, 739
Combs, Linda Jones, 200
Comer, J. M., 580, 587, 598
Connors, M., 467
Cook, V., 409, 611
Cooke, Ernest, 611
Cooper, Lee G., 458, 460
Cooper, R. L., 348
Cooper, Robert G., 358
Cooper, W. W., 182, 517
Corey, E. Raymond, 562
Corstjens, Marcel, 435, 458, 463, 654
Cort, Stanton G., 485
Cotton, B. C., 533
Cowling, K., 125
Cox, D. R., 77
Cox, G. M., 369
Cox, William E., Jr., 343, 609
Cravens, David W., 562, 582, 587, 594, 595
Crawford, C. M., 358
Crow, Lowell E., 285
Cubbin, J., 125
Cuccaro, C. J., 467
Curhan, Ronald C., 534
Currim, Imram S., 134
Curry, David J., 312
Cyert, Richard M., 285
Czepiel, John, 285

D

D'Abro, A., 29
Daganzo, Carlos, 229
Dalkey, Norman C., 137, 139
Dalrymple, D. J., 327, 328
Dalziel, Murray M., 306
Darmon, R. Y., 580, 593
Davidson, J. H., 358
Davis, J. H., 280
Davis, K. Roscoe, 423
Davis, Otto A., 172, 589, 592, 593

Day, George S., 482, 611, 620–623
Day, Ralph L., 162, 517, 582
Deal, K. R., 493
Dean, J. R., 420
Della Bitta, Albert J., 420, 429, 534
Denison, Daniel R., 213
Denniston, William B., Jr., 320
Devoe, J. K., 517
Dhalla, Nariman, 613
Diamond, Daniel S., 503–505
Diamond, William T., 441
Dillon, William R., 217
Dirlam, Joel B., 44
Dodds, Wellesley, 714, 720
Dodson, Joe A., Jr., 534, 715–718, 720
Doktor, R. H., 787, 789
Dolan, Robert J., 396, 408, 421, 663–665, 715
Dorfman, R., 152, 659, 693
Dornaff, Ronald J., 264
Downey, William T., 711
Downs, Steve, 630
Doyle, Peter, 300, 435, 463
Draper, Norman, 116
Dreyfus, Stuart, 181
Driver, M. J., 787
Dufton, Charles, 463
Duncan, W. J., 786
Dunn, Theodore F., 503
Dutta, Biplab K., 692
Dyckman, Thomas R., 786

E

Easingwood, C., 587
Eckert, Ann, 286
Edelman, Franz, 426, 782, 783
Edmundson, Bea, 611
Ehrenberg, A. S. C., 188, 237–239, 242, 246, 250, 252
El-Ansary, Abel I., 439
Eliashberg, Joshua, 60
Elrod, Terry, 211
Engel, James F., 162, 517
Engelbrecht-Wiggans, Richard, 666
Eppen, Gary D., 549, 552
Erickson, Gary M., 116, 612

Eskin, Gerald J., 481, 661, 725, 734, 735, 737, 739
Etgar, Michael, 483
Everitt, B. S., 305

F

Faivre, J. P., 777
Faris, Charles W., 262
Farley, John U., 125, 172, 209, 462, 589, 592, 593
Farris, Paul W., 501, 564, 662, 669, 672, 673
Fenwick, Ian, 300
Fiacco, A. V., 121, 170
Fildes, Robert, 327
Fishbein, Martin, 200, 220, 221
Fishburn, Peter C., 55
Fisher, Frank M., 124
Fisher, J. C., 242, 449, 450, 708, 709, 711, 718
Fisher, L., 261
Fitzroy, Peter T., 398
Floyd, A., 718
Fogg, C. D., 563
Ford, Neil M., 588
Fornell, Claes, 128, 213, 803
Fourt, Louis A., 706, 707, 711, 718
Frank, Ronald E., 179, 231, 289, 291, 292, 295, 297, 303, 305, 313, 314, 553
Frederick, Donald G., 217
Freeman, C., 358
Freimer, Marshall, 444
Frey, Albert Wesley, 490, 491
Fried, L. J., 310
Fudge, W. K., 134, 562, 570, 576, 580, 782, 799

G

Gable, Myron, 289
Gabor, A., 400, 401, 402, 408, 414, 417
Galbraith, Jay R., 788
Gale, Bradley T., 627
Galper, Morton, 672, 680, 681
Gardner, Kathy S., 561, 562, 583, 598
Gardner, Yehudi A., 482
Garfinkel, R. S., 165

Garret, Paula L., 485
Gautschi, David A., 458–460
Gensch, Dennis H., 120, 229, 518, 693
Geoffrion, Arthur M., 165, 464–467
Gibson, Paul, 4
Giddings, F. H., 28
Ginzberg, Michael J., 788
Givon, Moshe, 205, 231
Glaze, R., 582, 587, 594
Golanty, John, 723, 726, 736, 738
Goldberg, Stephen M., 369
Goldberger, A. S., 113, 116
Goodhardt, G. J., 188, 239, 246, 247
Goodman, C. S., 261
Goodman, David, 427
Goodwin, Stephen, 482
Gordon, Matt M., 320
Gorry, G. Anthony, 747
Gould, J. P., 718
Granger, C. W. J., 348, 400–402, 408, 414, 417
Grass, Robert C., 483
Graves, G. W., 165, 466, 467
Graybill, Franklin A., 107
Grayson, C. Jackson, Jr., 795, 796
Green, H. L., 454
Green, Paul E., 29, 138, 179, 213, 295, 305, 314, 365–369, 382, 640, 804
Green, W. K., 467
Greyser, Stephen A., 441
Griesmer, James H., 426
Grinyar, Peter H., 427
Gross, Irwin, 399, 505, 507–511, 525, 778, 799, 803
Gross, Walter, 289
Grossman, Elliot S., 327, 330
Gruber, William, 5
Guiltman, J., 291
Gundee, Howard N., 735, 736, 738

H

Haas, Robert W., 440
Haddock, R. A., 403
Haines, G., 229, 245

Hakansson, Hakan, 286
Haley, P. I., 723
Haley, Russell I., 294, 314, 331, 478
Hall, William K., 608
Hallaq, John H., 534
Halliday, David, 88
Hamburger, Michael J., 162
Hamerish, R. G., 634
Hamilton, W. F., 787
Hammond, J. S., III, 418, 615, 618, 619, 629, 786, 789
Hampel, F. E., 116
Hanssens, Dominique M., 339, 482, 504, 505, 667
Harary, F., 242
Harding, Murray, 261, 285
Harding, Harold F., 359
Harman, Harry H., 116, 217
Harrell, Stephen G., 609, 612
Harrigan, Kathryn Rudie, 612
Harris, J. E., 634
Harsanyi, J. C., 61
Hartigan, John A., 305, 306
Hartung, P. H., 242, 449, 450
Harvey, J. W., 221
Haspeslagh, Philippe, 608
Hauser, John R., 60, 120, 163, 179, 211, 215, 217, 218, 219, 224, 225, 229, 251, 355–357, 363, 366, 369, 370, 374, 377, 382, 384, 385, 623, 723, 734, 738, 782, 783, 796
Havens, George N., 343
Hax, Arnoldo C., 121, 162, 467, 618
Heany, Donald F., 626, 628
Heeler, Rodger M., 715
Helmer, Olaf, 139
Henderson, James M., 390
Henderson, John C., 768
Hendon, Donald Wayne, 482
Henry, M. D., 773, 787, 789, 790
Herniter, J. D., 232, 240
Hertz, David B., 186, 187
Heskett, James L., 433, 469
Hess, S. W., 584, 585, 587, 597
Hillier, T. J., 285
Hinkle, Charles L., 533
Hirko, R. G., 766
Hirschman, Elizabeth C., 462
Hlavac, T. E., Jr., 460
Hodock, Calvin L., 503

Hoerl, Arthur E., 116
Hogarth, Robin M., 349
Holthausen, Duncan M., Jr., 482
Hopkins, David S., 355
Hopkins, Patricia M., 553
Horlsey, A., 358
Horsky, Dan, 205, 231, 242, 500, 715, 718
Howard, John A., 204, 210, 211, 262
Howard, Ronald A., 181
Hozier, George C., Jr., 662
Huber, George P., 766
Hudson, C. L., 259
Huff, David L., 456–458, 460
Hughes, G. David, 220, 723
Hull, Clark L., 209
Hulswit, F. T., 567, 578
Hurwood, David L., 327, 330, 490
Hustad, Thomas P., 382, 715
Hutt, Michael D., 439
Huxley, Thomas H., 26
Huysmans, Jan H. B. M., 34, 787

I

Ide, Edward A., 462
Intriligator, Michael D., 172
Izraeli, Dov, 434

J

Jacoby, J., 403
Jain, Arun, 295, 297, 314
Jay, Andrea, 477, 478, 503
Jenkins, Gwilym M., 338, 339
Jervis, V. T. P., 358
Jeuland, Abel P., 205, 232, 238, 408, 421, 715
Johnson, Jeffrey L., 330
Johnson, Richard M., 308, 309, 356, 365, 369, 382, 622
Johnson, W., 285
Johnston, Jack, 122, 398
Johnston, Paul E., 735
Jolson, M. A., 139, 330
Jones, J. Morgan, 205, 231, 250
Jones, Robert L., 482
Jöreskog, K. G., 127, 128, 217
Joskow, Paul L., 664

Joubert, William, 433
Joy, O. M., 328
Judge, G., 242

K

Kabir, C., 718
Kalacheck, E. D., 718
Kalish, Shlomo, 420, 715, 720
Kalwani, Manohar, 237, 240, 246, 286, 374, 735
Kaplan, A. D. H., 44
Kassarjian, Harold H., 201, 204
Kassarjian, Waltraub M., 201
Katz, E., 705
Katz, Gerald M., 739
Keen, Peter G. W., 752, 753, 760, 766, 767
Keeney, Ralph L., 36, 54–58, 60–62, 95, 174, 224, 444
Kennard, Robert W., 116
Keon, John, 553
Kettelle, J. D., 567, 578
Kinberg, Yoram, 461, 534
King, William R., 163, 692
Kinnear, Thomas C., 313
Kirkwood, Craig W., 61
Klabir, D., 213
Klastorian, T., 298
Klompmaker, Jay E., 723
Kolliner, Sim A., Jr., 662
Koppelman, F. S., 219
Kornbluth, Jonathan S., 171
Kortanek, K. O., 427
Kotler, Philip, 184, 444, 517
Koyck, L. M., 82, 83
Krapfel, Robert E., Jr., 277, 286
Krugman, Herbert E., 479, 483
Kuehn, Alfred A., 95, 162, 243–245, 500, 531, 534, 537–541, 543, 552, 779
Kunreuther, Howard, 26, 129, 669

L

Lachenbruch, P., 308
Lakhani, Chet, 181, 419, 420, 715
LaLonde, B. J., 264
Lambert, David R., 485
Lambert, Z. V., 403, 561, 580

Lambin, Jean-Jacques, 92, 95, 125, 493, 500, 659, 666, 667, 692, 779
Lancaster, Kelvin, 390
Landau, H. J., 422
Langhoff, Peter, 487, 488
Lanzillotti, Robert F., 44
Larchen, David F., 128
Larréché, Jean-Claude, 139, 649–651, 653, 774, 776, 787
Lavalle, I. H., 426
Lavidge, Robert J., 12, 717, 735, 736, 738
Lavin, Milton L., 277
Lawrence, Kenneth D., 720
Lawrence, R. J., 245
Lawton, William H., 720
Layton, R. A., 580
Lazarsfeld, P. F., 705
Leal, Antonio, 61
Learner, D. B., 517, 802
Leavitt, Clark, 482
Leavitt, H. J., 125
Lee, T. C., 242
Leeflang, Peter, 12, 67, 72, 91, 93, 119, 777–780, 789
Lehmann, Donald R., 89, 211, 222, 263–265, 286, 364
Lekvall, Per, 714
Leontief, W. W., 343, 345, 346
Lessig, V. Parker, 297, 307, 314
Liddy, Lucien E., 735, 737, 739
Lieberman, Joshua, 549, 552
Lilien, Gary L., 38, 245, 262, 273, 275–277, 310, 312, 366, 382, 441, 449, 451, 476, 490, 493, 496, 501, 537, 543, 546, 548, 561, 564, 631, 662, 669, 670–672, 676, 677, 679, 720, 735, 755, 787
Linstone, Harold, 330
Lipstein, B., 242
Little, John D. C., 12–14, 79, 95, 129, 131, 134, 181, 460, 477–481, 493, 495, 496, 498, 500, 517, 519–522, 537, 549, 550, 552, 553, 666, 682–685, 687–692, 753, 754, 759, 760, 776–778, 780, 789, 801, 804
Lodish, Leonard M., 134, 181, 422, 517, 519–523, 562, 568–570, 575, 576, 580, 582, 587, 594, 598, 763–765, 782, 799

Longman, Kenneth A., 511
Lonsdale, Ronald T., 162, 299
Low, D. W., 467
Lubatkin, Michael, 631
Lucas, Henry C., Jr., 566, 567, 766
Luce, R. Duncan, 225, 456, 731
Lutz, J. R., 221
Lutz, Richard J., 220

M

McCammon, Bert C., Jr., 434
McCann, John M., 303, 304, 314, 662
McCarthy, E. Jerome, 658
McClelland, C. W., 515
McConnell, J. D., 404
McConnell, Maureen, 482
McCormick, G. P., 121, 170
McDonald, Colin, 483, 484
McFadden, D., 120, 229
McGinnis, John M., 534
McGuire, T. W., 95, 500
McGuire, William, 482
McIntyre, Shelby H., 134
McKay, David B., 462
McLaughlin, R. L., 341
McNeal, J. U., 578
Maffai, R. B., 242, 517
Magee, J. F., 553, 578
Magnanti, Thomas L., 121, 162
Mahajan, Vijay, 297, 314, 634, 640, 648, 714, 715, 719, 720
Maitland, J., 480
Majluf, Nicolas S., 618
Makridakis, Spyros, 327, 336, 339, 349
Malec, John, 735, 737, 739
Maloney, John C., 482
Mansfield, Edwin, 285, 382, 613, 664, 708, 709, 711, 776
Markowitz, H. M., 467
Marsten, R. E., 165, 467
Martin, Claude R., 314
Mason, J. Barry, 534
Massy, William F., 90, 245, 289, 291, 295, 297, 303, 313, 314, 553, 725, 735, 737, 739, 778
Matthews, H. L., 221
Mattssons, L-G., 259
Mayer, Charles S., 382
Mazis, Michael B., 221

Means, Gardiner C., 44
Meidan, Arthur, 567
Menzel, A., 705
Meredith, J. R., 789
Mesak, Hani I., 423
Metheringham, R. A., 515
Meyer, Carl F., 165
Michaels, Ronald E., 612
Michman, Ronald D., 289
Mickwitz, Gosta, 612
Midgeley, David, 612, 705, 720
Mihram, G. Arthur, 188
Miller, D. W., 517
Miller, P. B., 480, 493, 496, 499, 501
Millman, A. D., 523
Mitchell, A. A., 129, 134
Mitroff, Ian I., 34
Monroe, Kent B., 420, 428, 429, 534
Montgomery, David B., 90, 139, 242, 245, 493, 560, 564, 565, 572, 580, 612, 774, 776, 789
Mood, Alexander M., 107
Moore, William L., 211
Moran, William T., 517
Morgan, H. L., 750
Moriarty, Mark, 113, 662
Moriarty, Rowland T., 286
Morrill, John E., 662
Morrison, Donald G., 90, 231, 237, 243, 245, 303, 308, 331, 346, 347
Mosteller, F., 243
Muller, Eitan, 715–718, 720
Mullick, Satinder K., 327, 349
Musgrave, J. C., 341
Muth, John F., 346
Myers, James H., 199, 382
Myers, John G., 476, 502, 515

N

Naert, Philippe, 12, 67, 91, 93–95, 119, 125, 172, 450, 496, 659, 666, 667, 692, 777–780, 789
Nakanishi, Masao, 95, 222, 458, 460
Naples, M. J., 483, 484
Narasimhan, C., 738
Nault, James P., 405

Naylor, T. H., 348, 349, 606
Nelson, Charles R., 348
Nelson, Richard, 455, 718
Nemhauser, G. L., 165
Nerlove, M., 493, 659, 718
Nevers, John V., 714
Newbold, P., 348
Nichols, D. R., 328
Nicosia, F. M., 204
Niles, John S., 5
Noble, Ben, 151
Nordin, J. A., 578
Noyce, Robert N., 769

O

Olshavsky, Richard W., 285, 462, 612
Olson, J. C., 403
Orcutt, G. H., 113
Oren, M. E., 428
O'Rourke, Rita, 261
O'Shaughnessy, J., 263–265, 286
Ostlund, Lyman E., 503
Owen, Donald B., 508
Oxenfeld, Alfred R., 399
Ozanne, Urban B., 285

P

Paine, Frank T., 627, 631
Paksoy, Christie H., 534
Palda, Kristian S., 429
Pan, Judy, 328
Parasuraman, A., 582
Parfitt, J. H., 371, 723–726, 729, 734, 737, 739
Parker, Barnett R., 377, 382
Parnes, Sidney J., 359
Parsons, Leonard J., 82, 83, 125, 413, 500, 553, 612, 777, 779
Peacock, Peter, 314, 552
Peck, M. J., 718
Peckham, James O., Sr., 537
Pekelman, Dov, 163, 377, 477
Perreault, William D., Jr., 433
Pessemier, Edgar A., 89, 186, 220, 364, 376, 382, 731
Peters, Michael P., 285
Peterson, Robert A., 404, 715, 719
Pilon, Thomas L., 205
Pinson, C. R. A., 777

Pitts, Michael, 631
Pokemper, Stanley J., 327, 774–776
Polli, Rolando, 409, 608, 611
Porter, Michael E., 623–625, 664
Powers, Richard F., 465
Prasad, Kanti V., 661
Pratt, John, 53
Prentice, Robert M., 533
Pringle, Lewis G., 737, 738, 739
Pry, R. H., 708, 709, 711, 718
Punj, G. N., 120, 229
Pyatt, F. G., 246

Q

Qualls, William, 612
Quandt, Richard E., 390

R

Radnor, Michael, 787
Raiffa, Howard, 36, 37, 54–58, 60, 62, 141, 179, 224, 444
Ramanathan, K., 715
Ramond, Charles, 482, 505
Ranard, Elliot D., 347
Rao, Ambar G., 408, 414, 415, 417, 423, 428, 449, 451, 461, 480, 493, 496, 498, 499, 501, 534, 537, 543, 546, 548, 662, 720
Rao, Vithala R., 213, 692
Rapoport, A., 664
Ratchford, Brian T., 208
Ray, Michael L., 481, 503, 662
Recker, W. W., 120, 229
Reibstein, David, 532
Reid, D. J., 348
Reinecke, W., 517
Reinitz, R. C., 458, 461
Resnick, Robert, 88
Richardson, M. G., 680
Richardson, R. J., 587
Richartz, Leon E., 438
Riez, Peter C., 404
Ring, L. Winston, 209, 462, 661
Rink, David R., 609
Rippe, Richard D., 346, 347
Robertson, A. B., 358, 705
Robinson, Bruce, 181, 419, 420, 715

Robinson, Patrick J., 262, 530, 738
Robinson, T. S., 204
Rogers, E. M., 703, 704
Rohloff, A. C., 245, 531, 534, 537–541, 543, 552, 779
Rokus, J. W., 563
Roscoe, A. Marvin, Jr., 300–302, 305
Roshwalb, Irving, 503
Rossiter, John R., 483
Rossow, G. L., 139, 330
Rothchild, Michael L., 203
Rothwell, R., 358
Rubinson, Joel R., 314
Rumelt, Richard P., 631
Russ, Frederick A., 433
Ruzdic, A. Api, 493, 496, 676, 677, 679
Ryans, A. B., 576
Ryde, D., 93

S

Saaty, Thomas, 640, 641, 643, 644, 646
Sabavala, Darius J., 692
Sackman, Harold, 330
Sahal, D., 719
Salamon, Gerald, 113
Saleh, F., 264
Samuels, S. A., 584, 585, 587, 597
Sanchez, C., 777
Sapra, Rakesh, 503
Sasieni, Maurice W., 31, 172, 303, 463, 500, 661
Sawyer, A., 291
Schainblatt, Alt, 34, 785
Scherer, F., 664
Schlaifer, Robert, 141, 179
Schmalensee, Richard, 172, 493, 500, 523
Schoeffler, Sidney, 626–628
Schoemaker, Paul H. J., 60
Schoeman, Milton, E. F., 714
Schonberger, Richard J., 766
Schroder, H. M., 787
Schultz, Randall L., 82, 83, 667, 773–777, 779, 787, 789, 790
Scott, Jerome E., 270, 277, 286
Scott Morton, Michael S., 747, 752, 760, 766, 767
Seaks, T. G., 348, 349

Sebastian, Karl-Heinz, 715
Segal, M., 587
Seipel, Carl-Magnus, 533
Seligman, Daniel, 490
Seligman, E. J., 708, 710
Semlow, W. J., 565, 566
Sen, Subrata K., 163, 231, 314, 377, 552, 738
Sengupta, J. K., 182
Sentell, Gerald, 462
Sethi, Suresh P., 172
Sewall, Murphy A., 458, 460
Sexton, Donald E., Jr., 660
Shakun, Melvin F., 408, 414, 415, 417, 423, 428
Shanker, R. J., 587, 588, 594, 598
Shapeneso, A., 622
Shapiro, Arlene, 345
Shapiro, Arthur, 15
Shapiro, Benson P., 403
Sharif, M. N., 715, 718
Shea, J. M., 261
Sheth, Jagdish N., 200, 204, 210, 222, 262, 268–271, 276, 285
Shiskin, J. A., 341
Shocker, Allan D., 163, 364, 368, 370, 374, 375, 377–382, 620–623
Shoemaker, Robert W., 533
Shubik, Martin, 426
Shugan, Steven M., 163, 215, 217, 219, 369, 377
Sicherman, Alan, 60
Silk, Alvin J., 286, 355, 374, 493, 503, 523, 572, 580, 705, 723, 728–730, 733, 735, 737, 739, 789
Simmonds, Kenneth, 426
Simmons, D. M., 170
Simmons, L. F., 423
Simon, Herbert A., 44
Simon, Hermann, 185, 396, 404, 408–414, 417, 501, 523, 613, 668, 715
Simon, J. L., 480
Simon, Leonard S., 444, 715, 718
Singer, E., 663
Sinha, Prabhakant, 165, 562, 576, 582, 587
Slevin, Dennis P., 773–776, 787, 789
Smith, Donald D., 327, 349

Smith, Harry, 116
Smith, Wendell R., 289
Sodaro, D., 427
Soden, J. V., 427, 750
Solgliero, G. C., 708, 710, 711
Solley, W., 261
Sonquist, John A., 299
Sorbom, D., 127, 217
Sorenson, Richard E., 788
Sowter, A. P., 401, 402
Speh, Thomas W., 439
Spekman, Robert E., 261, 277, 285, 559
Spivey, Allen W., 349
Sprague, Ralph H., Jr., 766
Srinivasan, V., 163, 364, 368, 370, 374, 375, 377–382, 593, 649–651, 653
Srivastava, Rajendra, 620–623
Staelin, Richard, 120, 129, 134, 227, 229, 330
Stamfield, J. D., 704
Stanley, T., 458, 460
Stapleton, E., 718
Starch, Daniel, 482
Starr, Martin K., 314, 517
Stasch, Stanley F., 755
Stefflre, Volney J., 374, 382
Stein, M. O., 622
Steiner, Gary A., 12, 717
Steiner, P. O., 152, 659, 693
Stern, Louis W., 261, 285, 439
Stern, Mark, 163
Sternthal, Brian, 534
Stever, Ralph, 171
Stewart, David N., 517
Stigler, George, 394, 407
Stobaugh, Robert, 128
Stoetzel, J., 401
Strang, Roger A., 533, 536
Summers, John O., 285
Swan, John E., 200, 609
Sweeney, Timothy W., 286
Swinyard, W. R., 481, 662
Swire, Donald J., 627, 640

T

Taha, H., 165
Talarzyk, W. Wayne, 220, 222
Talley, W. J., Jr., 563
Tangpanichdee, Vanchai, 217
Tapiero, C. S., 172
Tauber, Edward M., 359, 722

Taylor, Elmer D., 609, 612
Taylor, James R., 313
Taylor, James W., 200
Teach, Richard, 376, 731
Telser, Lester G., 242
Theil, Henri, 92, 116
Thiel, Michael, 523, 779
Thomas, Joseph, 422
Thomas, Robert, 260, 285
Thompson, G. C., 491
Thompson, Gerald L., 172
Thompson, W. W., 578
Thorelli, Hans B., 609, 631
Tiebout, Charles M., 346
Tigert, Douglas, 299, 376, 731
Tinter, G., 182
Tollefson, John O., 297, 307, 314
Torgerson, Warren S., 225, 731
Townsend, J., 358
Traver, Phillis A., 532
Treufort, S., 787
Trodahl, Verling C., 482
Tse, E., 477
Tull, Donald S., 29, 305, 367, 368
Turban, E., 789
Turner, Ronald E., 172, 330, 501, 587, 588, 594, 598
Turoff, Murray, 330
Twedt, Dik W., 293, 482, 503, 504
Twyman, Tony, 477, 478, 503
Tybout, Alice M., 534

U

Urban, Glen L., 12, 32–34, 60, 120, 163, 179, 211, 217, 218, 224, 225, 229, 355–357, 363, 366, 370–374, 382, 384, 385, 428, 523, 560, 564, 565, 622, 623, 723, 728–731, 733, 734, 737–739, 776, 782, 783, 789, 794, 796
Utterback, J. M., 366

V

Van Horne, J. C., 646
Van Rest, D. J., 267
Van Roy, J. J., 467
Vaughn, Charles L., 434
Venkatesan, M., 203, 285

Vidale, H. L., 84, 86, 93, 493, 718
Virts, John R., 621
Von Hippel, Eric A., 360–362

W

Wagner, Harvey M., 469
Wagner, Samuel, 382
Wahlbin, Clas, 714
Waid, C., 60, 567, 578
Wald, Herman, 128
Walker, Orville C., Jr., 588
Wallendorf, M., 204
Walters, C. G., 204
Warshaw, Martin R., 162, 517
Wasson, Chester R., 612
Webster, Frederick E., Jr., 44, 261, 264, 268, 271–273, 285
Weddle, David E., 222
Weinberg, Charles B., 566, 576, 582, 587, 593, 594
Weinberg, R. S., 675
Weinberger, D. B., 587
Weinstein, David, 561, 654, 670
Weiss, Doyle L., 95, 500, 660
Weitz, Barton A., 482, 504, 505
Welam, Ulf Peter, 693
Wellman, H. R., 578
Wells, William D., 314, 482
Wensley, Robin, 631, 640
Westfall, Ralph, 755
Weverbergh, M., 496
Wheelwright, Steven C., 327, 328, 336, 339

Whittaker, John D., 427
Wichern, D. W., 348, 349
Wierenga, B., 245
Wiersema, Frederik D., 630
Wiginton, J. C., 172, 501
Wildt, Albert R., 277, 286, 303, 481, 660, 661
Wilkie, William L., 220, 222, 364
Wilkinson, J. B., 534
Wilkinson, Maurice, 346, 347
Williams, A. C., 428
Wilson, Aubrey, 611
Wilson, David T., 221, 286
Wilson, R. Dale, 523, 553, 737–739, 798, 806
Wind, Yoram, 213, 258, 260, 261, 264, 266–268, 271–273, 285, 289–291, 294, 295, 297, 309, 310, 313, 314, 365, 368, 382, 606–608, 613, 632, 634, 637, 640, 641, 643, 644, 646, 648
Winer, R. L., 593
Winkler, R. L., 137–139
Wipple, Thomas W., 382
Wisniewski, Kenneth J., 251
Wittink, Dick R., 113, 369, 480, 661, 675
Wolfe, H. B., 84, 86, 93, 491, 493, 718
Wolinsky, Murray, 735
Wolverton, R. W., 750
Wong, M. Anthony, 262
Wonnacott, Ronald J., 125, 779

Wonnacott, Thomas H., 125, 779
Wood, Douglas, 327
Woodlock, Joseph W., 706, 707, 711, 718
Wootz, Bjorn, 286
Wright, Gordon, 232, 238
Wright, Peter, 270, 286
Wright, Roger L., 314
Wrobleski, William J., 349

Y

Yamanaka, Jiro, 482
Yelle, L. E., 614, 616
Yergin, Daniel, 128
Young, H., 341
Young, Shirley, 503
Yuspeh, Sonia, 613

Z

Zaltman, G., 204, 285, 777
Zand, Dale E., 788
Zangwill, Willard I., 170
Zaragoza, C. E., 572, 580, 789
Zellner, Arnold, 242, 303
Zentler, A. P., 93
Zielski, Hubert A., 483
Ziff, Ruth, 314, 503
Zionts, S., 493
Zoltners, Andris A., 165, 179, 429, 561, 562, 576, 582, 583, 587, 588, 594, 598
Zufryden, Fred S., 232, 250

Subject Index

A

Absolute profits (short run), 44
Acceptance operator, 243
Accounting models. *See* Models
Adaptive filtering, 336
ADBUDG
  curve, 79
  model. *See* Models
Additive independence, 56
Additive models, linear. *See* Models
Administered channels, 434
ADMOD, 523
Adoption
  process, 703
  research, 285
AD-TEL, 503
Advertising Age, 476
Advertising models. *See* Models
ADVISOR, 669, 784
Affordable method, 490
Agglomerative methods. *See* Cluster analysis
Aggregate response, 89
AHP. *See* Analytic hierarchy process
AID. *See* Automatic interaction detection
Allocation of selling effort. *See* Selling, effort allocation
American Builder, The, 503

American Iron and Steel Institute, 347
American Telephone & Telegraph, 4
Analogue method of site selection, 455
Analyst selected pooling methods, 138
Analytic hierarchy process (AHP), 640
"Annual Survey of Buying Power," 326
Approach, scientific, 26, 28
A priori models. *See* Models
AR. *See* Autoregressive
ARMA. *See* Autoregressive and moving average
ASI. *See* Audience Studies, Inc.
ASSESSOR, 722, 728
Assignment problem, 163
AT&T. *See* American Telephone & Telegraph
Attraction models. *See* Models
Attribute-based procedures. *See* Factor analysis
Attribute importance, 199
Attribute listing, 359
Audience Studies, Inc. (ASI), 502
Autocorrelation
  analysis, 104, 110
  function, 337
Autocracy model. *See* Models

Automatic interaction detection (AID), 299
Autoregressive (AR), 337
Autoregressive and moving average (ARMA), 332, 337, 339, 348
Autoregressive scheme, stepwise, 111, 348
Average linkage clustering. *See* Cluster analysis
Awareness model. *See* Models

B

BAN. *See* Best asymptotically normal
Bargain value model. *See* Models
Basis, 291
Batten, Barton, Durstine and Osborne, Inc. *See* (BBDO)
Bayesian estimation, 139
Bayesian regression analysis, multivariate, 142
Bayes rule, 235
(BBDO), 503
BCG. *See* Boston Consulting Group
Behavioral research, 285
Behavioral science models. *See* Models
Belief/importance model. *See* Models

Beliefs-only model. *See* Models

Benefit segmentation, 295, 369

Bernoulli model. *See also* Models
 heterogeneous, 90, 234
 homogeneous, 90

Best asymptotically normal (BAN), 106

Best theory, 38

Beta distribution, 136, 235
 shifted, 136

Binary dependent variables, parameter estimation, 119

Booz, Allen and Hamilton, 355, 358

Boston Consulting Group, 614, 615, 617–619, 634, 654

Brainstorming, 359

BRANDAID, 134, 549, 682, 692, 765

Brand-choice models. *See* Models

Brand-sales models. *See* Models

Brand switching, 621
 matrix, 233

Breakdown method, 563

Bureau of the Census, 321, 341

Burke, Inc., 503

Business Week, 331

Buying center, 261

Buying intentions, 330

Buy-response curve, 401

C

Calibration, 102

CALLPLAN, 190, 568

Cannibalization estimates. *See* Draw and cannibalization estimates

Capital asset pricing model. *See* Models

Cardinal utility, 50

Carryover effects, 6, 80

Cash balance, 639

Causal
 diagrams, 126
 methods, 341
 models. *See* Models

Census II method, 341

Center of gravity, 654

Central limit theorem, 107

Certainty monetary equivalent (CME), 51

Chain ratio method, 320

Chance-constrained programming. *See* Programming

Change process, 788

Checklist method of site selection, 455

Choffray and Lilien model. *See* Models

Choice models. *See* Models

Cluster analysis, 305
 agglomerative methods, 305
 average-linkage, 306
 complete-linkage, 306
 minimum-variance, 306
 single-linkage, 306

CME. *See* Certainty monetary equivalent

Cognitive dissonance theory, 201

Colonial Penn Insurance Company, 641

Commercial Credit Corporation, 331

Commissions, 588

Common factors, 214

Communality, 214, 215

Company demand, 318

Competition-oriented pricing. *See* Pricing

Competitive-advantage fee, 427

Competitive-bidding models. *See* Models

Competitive effects, 6

Competitive-parity method, 491

Competitive reactions/response, 36

Complete-linkage clustering. *See* Cluster analysis

Compositional methods. *See* Factor analysis

Computer-related decision support tools, 19

Computer simulation, 444

Concave
 envelope, 569
 function, 149, 150

Conceptual model. *See* Models

Conference Board, The, 331, 385

Confidence intervals, 141

Conflicting objectives. *See* Objectives

Conjoint analysis, 367, 640

Conjunctive model. *See* Models

Consistency, 106

Constant-elasticity demand-price function, 394

Constant-sum paired comparisons, 226, 369

Constant-utility model. *See* Models

Constraints, 42

Consumer behavior, rational, 390

Consumer buying behavior, 16, 18

Consumer-franchise building, 533

Consumer measurements, 356

Consumer models. *See* Models

Contractual channels, 434

Contrast theory, 201

Controlled experimentation, 31

Controlled test marketing. *See* Minimarket testing

Control theory, stochastic, 183

Convergent validity. *See* Validity

Convex function, 149, 150

Copy research, 482, 502

Copy testing. *See* Copy research

Corporate channels, 434

COSMOS, 692

Cost/benefit ratio, 12

Cost dynamics, 613

Cost-oriented pricing. *See* Pricing

Cost plus pricing. *See* Pricing

Costs, variable, 45

Couponing, 532

Covariance matrix, 109, 114

Coverage ratio, 322

CPM. *See* Critical path method

Critical path method (CPM), 163

Cross-classification analysis, 298

Cross elasticity of demand. *See* Elasticity

Current demand, 319
Current-revenue pricing. *See* Pricing
Customer decay rate, 80
Customer-holdover effect, 80
Customer judgments of substitutability, 622
Customer retention rate, 80

D

Data, 102
   primary, 9, 753, 756
   secondary, 753
Data-analysis systems, 750
Data-based management systems (DBMS), 749
DBMS. *See* Data-based management systems
Deciders. *See* Decision makers
Decision analysis, 173, 444
Decision calculus, 129, 134
Decision makers, 42, 43, 60, 261
Decision-making-unit (DMU), 310
Decision matrix, 138, 310, 311
Decision-sequence analysis, 622
Decision-support systems (DSS), 747, 749
Decision variables, 42
Decomposition methods, 211, 340, 467
Delayed response, 6, 80
Delphi method, 139, 330
Demand
   assessment, 318
   forecasting, 318, 319
Demand-price function, linear, 392
Descriptors, 291
DETAILER, 571
Development costs, 780
Diary Purchase Panel, 103
Diffusion
   of innovations, 703
   process, 703
Diffusion models. *See also* Models
   pure imitative, 706, 708
   pure innovative, 706
Discount rate, 49

Discriminant analysis, 307
Discriminant validity, 778
Discrimination tests, 779
Disjunctive model. *See* Models
Distribution
   location, 435, 445
   logistics, 435, 463
   management, 435, 469
   planning system, 464
   strategy, 435, 438
DMU. *See* Decision-making-unit
Dorfman-Steiner theorem, 152
Double exponential smoothing, 335
Double moving average, 334
   with trend adjustments, 334
Dow Chemical, 4
Draw and cannibalization estimates, 733
DSS. *See* Decision support systems
Dual variables, 162
Dun's Market Identifiers, 325
Dynamic programming. *See* Programming
DYNAMO, 519

E

Econometric models. *See* Models
Economies of scale, 613
EDP. *See* Electronic data processing
Efficiency, 106
Efficient portfolio, 646
Efficient set, 647
Eigenvalue, 214, 641
Elasticity, 390, 404
   cross, 620
   income, 391, 392
   long-run, 84
   sales, 668
Electronic data processing (EDP), 747
Electronic Design, 504
ENIAC, 769
Entropy, 121
Environmental variables, 657
Equiprobability model. *See* Models

Errors-in-variables, 123
Evaluative problems, 28
Expectancy-value models. *See* Models
Experience-curve, 418, 613, 614, 651
Experimentation, 31, 756
Exponential model. *See* Models
Exponential smoothing, 332, 335
EXPRESS, 760
Extended Fishbein model. *See* Models, Fishbein

F

Face validity. *See* Validity
Factor analysis, 211, 213, 363, 366
Factor naming, 217
Factor-score coefficients, 214
Feasibility model. *See* Models
File-drawer systems, 750
Financial models. *See* Models
Financial-portfolio analysis, 646
Fishbein model. *See* Models
Fixed-charge problem, 164
Fixed costs, 45
FORAN system, 341
Forced relationships, 359
Formulating problems, 31, 32
Fractile method, 134
Fractional-root model. *See* Models
Franchise organizations, 434
FRB-MIT-PENN model. *See* Models
Frequency, 512
Full information
   maximum likelihood, 124
   methods, 124
Functional, 172

G

Games, zero sum, 664
Game-theoretic approaches, 37, 664
Gamma distribution, 247
Gasoline games, 545
Gatekeeper, 261

Gauss-Markov theorem, 106, 109

General Electric Company, 666

Generalized least squares (GLS), 104, 109, 110, 112, 113, 142

Geographic segmentation, 291

GEOLINE model. *See Models*

Global maximum, minimum, 149, 150

GLS. *See Generalized least squares*

Goal programming. *See Programming*

Gompertz model. *See Models*

Graphical model. *See Models*

Gravitational models. *See Models*

GROOVY, 551, 687

Gross National Product (GNP), 343

Group
choice model. *See Models*
decision problem, 61

Growth
analysis, 608
model. *See Models*
patterns, 608

H

Happenings data, 753

Heinz, H. J., 15

Hendry Corporation, 238, 356

Hendry system, 121, 238, 356

Hessian matrix, 150

Heterogeneity, spurious effect of, 231

Heterogeneous Bernoulli model. *See Models*

Heteroscedasticity, 104, 110, 112

High-involvement choice models. *See Models*

Holt-Winter, 348

Homogeneity, 290

Homogeneous Bernoulli model. *See Models*

Homoscedasticity, 110

I

Ideal-point model. *See Models*

Idea sources, 359

Identification, 124

Identified
exactly, 124
just-, 124

Imitative pricing. *See Pricing*

Implementation, 19, 773
success, 784
successful, 773

Implementing and maintaining the solution, 32

IMS. *See Interactive Marketing Systems*

In- and on-pack premiums. *See Promotions*

Income elasticity of demand. *See Elasticity*

Incomplete habit extinction, 244

Incomplete habit formation, 244

Independence of irrelevant alternatives, 225, 229

Index-of-buying-power method, 325

Individual-choice models. *See Models*

Industry-coefficient index, 710

Industry-guidelines methods, 564

Influencers, 261

Information search, 198

Innovators, 704

Input-output analysis, 343

Inquiry, scientific, 25, 28

In-store displays, 532

Instrumental variables, 122

Integer programming. *See Programming*

Integrative models for sales-force decisions, 594

Interactions, 7, 72

Interactive Marketing Systems (IMS), 762

Intermarco, Ltd., 519

Internal accounting system, 753

Internal rate of return (IRR), 47

International Harvester, 640

IRR. *See Internal rate of return*

J

Jury of executive opinion, 329

K

Ken-L-Ration, 518

Koyck transformation, 82

L

Lagrange multiplier, 156

Lagrangian, 156

Lags, general, 83

Lanchester models. *See Models*

Large-system models. *See Models*

Latent variables, 214

Latin square, 369

Law of demand, 390, 392

Learning
constant, 614
curve, 614
models. *See Models*
rate, 614

Lexicographic model. *See Models*

Life, 503

Likelihood function, 107, 120, 140, 143

LIM. *See Limited information model*

Limit concept, 401

Limited information
maximum likelihood, 124
methods, 124
model (LIM), 630

Linearizeable models. *See Models*

Linear programming. *See Programming*

Linear programming, stochastic. *See Programming*

Linear programming under uncertainty. *See Programming*

LINMAP, 370, 374

LISREL, 127

Loadings, factor, 214

Logistic
curve, 708
equation, 77

Logit transformation, 77

Log-normal distribution, 137, 401

Long-run marketing-expenditure multiplier, 84

Loss leader pricing, 396
Low involvement choice models. *See* Models
Loyalty, spurious, 202
Luce's choice axiom. *See* Independence of irrelevant alternatives

M

MA. *See* Moving average method
McGraw-Hill, 331
Macrosegmentation, 296, 309
Maintenance costs, 780
Management information systems (MIS), 749
Management islands, 788
Management process, strategic, 606
Manufacturer price-off offer, 532
Marginal analysis, 517
Market-buildup method, 320
Market definition, 620
Market demand, 318
  assessing, 18
Marketing decision-support system (MDSS), 19, 747
Marketing-decision variables, 657
Marketing-mix interaction, 6, 657, 660
Marketing-mix models. *See* Models
Marketing process, strategic, 606
Market in transition, 676
Market planning, 605
  models. *See* Models
  and strategy, 605
Market potential, 319
Market-pricing models. *See* Models
Market profile, 323
Market Research Corporation of America (MRCA), 103, 755
Market segmentation, 289
  theory of, 18
Market-selection decision, 445
Market-share models. *See* Models

Market structure, 620, 623
Market tests, 331
Markov model. *See* Models
Markup pricing. *See* Pricing, cost plus
MARMA. *See* Multivariate ARMA
Maximum likelihood estimation, 107, 109
MDSS. *See* Marketing decision support system
Mean squared error, 106
Measure reliability. *See* Reliability
Measure validity. *See* Validity
MEDIAC, 514, 519
Media selection and scheduling, 511, 514
Microsegmentation, 274, 281, 282, 296, 309
Minimarket testing, 722
Minimum endorsement model. *See* Models
Minimum risk portfolio, 647
MIS. *See* Management information systems
Mixed autoregressive and moving average (ARMA), 337
Mixed-integer programming. *See* Programming
Mixed mode models. *See* Models
Mixing distribution, 230
  gamma, 247
Model
  costs and benefits, 780
  purpose, 10
  structure, 12, 778
  validity. *See* Validity
Model calibration
  multiple-assessor, 138
  single-assessor, 129
Models
  accounting, 751
  ADBUDG, 131, 133, 134
  advertising, 475
  a priori, 500
  attraction, 95
  autocracy, 280
  awareness, 274, 276
  bargain value, 553
  behavioral-science, 197
  belief/importance, 220
  beliefs-only, 222

Bernoulli, heterogeneous, 90, 234
Bernoulli, homogeneous, 90
brand-choice, 91, 232
brand-sales, 91, 93
capital-asset pricing, 52
causal, 125
Choffray/Lilien, 273
choice, 225, 363
compensatory, 220, 273
competitive-bidding, 424
conceptual, 12
conjunctive, 222, 273
constant-utility, 226
consumer, 356
customized, 626
decision, 11
descriptive, 10
diffusion, 706
diffusion, imitative, 706, 708
diffusion, innovative, 706
disjunctive, 223, 273
econometric, 17, 90, 128, 185, 500
equiprobability, 280
expectancy-value, 364
exponential, 75
extended Fishbein, 221
feasibility, 274, 276
financial, 626, 646
Fishbein, 220
fractional-root, 71
FRB-PENN-MIT, 348
GEOLINE, 584
Gompertz, 78, 719
graphical, 12
gravitational, 456
group choice, 274, 279
growth, 274, 281
high-involvement choice, 225
ideal-point, 222
individual-choice, 197, 274, 278
Lanchester, 493
large-system, 205, 268
learning, 233, 243
lexicographic, 223, 273
linear, 68
linearizable, 67
logit, 226
low-involvement choice, 229
marketing-mix, 675
marketing-planning, 18, 603

Models (*Continued*)
market-pricing, 422
market-share, 91, 94
Markov, 91, 233, 241, 371
minimum-endorsement, 279, 281
mixed, 500
modified exponential, 76
multinomial logit, 226
multinomial probit, 229
multiplicative, 73
NBD, 246
new products, sales, 699
noncompensatory, 220, 222
nonlinear, 75
nonlinear additive, 69
nonlinear in variables, linear in parameters, 67
normative, 11
portfolio, 626, 634
power-series, 69
preference/choice, 363
preference-perturbation, 279
pricing, 389
product-line-pricing, 428
product-class-sales, 91, 92
promotion, 529, 534, 537
purchase-timing, 91
regression, normal, 107
repeat-purchase, 720
representational, 752
saturation, 72
semilog, 71
shared-experience, 618, 626
Sheth, 268
square root, 71
S-shaped, 72
stochastic, 88, 90, 188
structural-equation, 125, 126
successful, 773
suggestion, 752
verbal, 12
Vidale-Wolfe, 84
voting, 279, 280
Webster and Wind, 271
weighted-probability, 279
Wharton econometric, 348
zero-order, 233, 234
Modified exponential model. *See* Models
Moment of inertia, 584
Monanova, 365, 367, 368
Monotone regression, 365

Monte Carlo simulation. *See* Simulation
Morphological analysis, 359
Moving average
method (MA), 332, 333, 337
simple, 334
with trend adjustment method, 332
MRCA. *See* Market Research Corporation of America
MUFCAP, 60
Multiattribute utility function. *See* Utility function
Multicollinearity, 81, 110, 114, 115
Multilinear form, 56
Multinomial logit model. *See* Models
Multinomial probit model. *See* Models
Multiple-equation modeling, 104, 121
Multiplicative model. *See* Models
Multivariate ARMA (MARMA), 339

N

Naive method, forecasting, 332
National Bureau of Economic Research, 332
Natural conjugate process, 141
Natural experiment, 676
NBD model. *See* Models
Need arousal, 198
Negative binomial distribution. *See* Models, NBD
New-product forecasting methods, 347
New products, sales models. *See* Models
Newton-Raphson method, 120
Nielsen, A. C., Company, 103, 755
NLP. *See* Programming, nonlinear
NMS. *See* Nonmetric multidimensional scaling
Noncompensatory models. *See* Models
Nonlinear additive models. *See* Models

Nonlinear in variables, linear in parameters models. *See* Models
Nonlinear models. *See* Models
Nonlinear programming (NLP). *See* Programming
Nonmetric multidimensional scaling (NMS), 211, 213
Nonoptimizing methods, 517
Normative models. *See* Models
Number of exposures, total, 513

O

Objective-and-task method, 491
Objectives, 43, 485
multiple, conflicting, 36
Ogilvy and Mather Research Department, 484, 485
OLS. *See* Ordinary least squares
Operational science, 25, 29
Opinion leaders, 703
Opportunity identification, 356
Optimal control, 171
Optimization methods, 147, 516, 752, 759
Optimum strategy reports, 630
Ordinary least squares (OLS), 109, 113, 339
Organizational buying behavior, 18
Overidentified, 124

P

Paired comparison. *See* Constant sum paired comparison
P&G. *See* Procter and Gamble
Parameter estimation
objective, 104
subjective, 128
Pareto optimum, 171
PAR model, 626, 627
Parsimony, 291
Partial least squares (PLS), 127
Part-worths, 368
Percentage-of-sales method, 490, 563
Perception, 358

PERCEPTOR, 370, 371
Perceptual mapping, 363, 622
Perceptual space, reduced, 372
PERT. *See* Program evaluation and review technique
PIMS, 25, 626, 669, 672, 784
Pi values. *See* Shadow prices
Place, 658
Planex, 519
PLS. *See* Partial least squares
Point estimate, 130
Poisson purchasing, 246
Policy-evaluation techniques, 148
Pooling methods, group-selected, 139
Positive definite, 151
Posterior distribution, 140, 235
Postpurchase feelings, 200
Potential, territorial, 320
Power-series model. *See* Models
Practice standards, 9
Preference, 200, 278
Preference/choice models. *See* Models
Preference-perturbation model. *See* Models
Preference regression, 365, 366
PREFMAP, 372
Present value, 47, 49
Pretest markets (purchase labs), 722
Price
  consciousness, 400
  discretion, 398
  elasticity, 390
  image, 400
  umbrella, 618
Pricing
  competition-oriented, 407
  cost-oriented, 405
  cost-plus, 396, 405
  current-revenue, 396
  demand-oriented, 407
  imitative, 407
  penetration, 420
  prestige, 396
  skimming, 396, 420
  target, 396, 407
Pricing models. *See* Models
  market. *See* Models
  product-line. *See* Models

Principal components, 115
Prior distribution, 140, 143
Priors, formulation of, 32
Proactive, 358
PROBE, 760
Problem
  analysis, 359
  finding, 32
  recognition, 17
Problems
  developmental, 28
  finding and formulating, 32
Process of inquiry, scientific, 26
Procter and Gamble (P&G), 4
Prodegy, 356, 622
Product attributes, 199
Product classification system, 321
Product-class-sales models. *See* Models
Product design techniques, 355, 363
Product life cycle, 608, 631
Product market, 620
Product-performance matrix, 640
Product-portfolio analysis, 608, 626, 634
PROFIT, 213
Profit impact of marketing strategy. *See* PIMS
Program evaluation and review technique (PERT), 136, 163
Programming
  chance-constrained, 181, 182
  dynamic, 179, 569
  goal, 55
  integer, 163
  linear, 121, 158, 181, 368, 374
  nonlinear, 165, 170
  quadratic, 169
  separable, 166
  stochastic, 181
Promotions
  effects, 532, 535
  in-pack, 532
  models. *See* Models
  objectives, 530
  on-pack, 532
  potential, 544
  pricing, 396

reach, 544
strength, 544
Pseudo sample size, 141
Psychographic variables, 293
Purchase frequency, 248
Purchase labs. *See* Pretest markets
Purchase timing models. *See* Models

Q

Q/A, 759

R

Rank orders, 369
Ratio-scale, 226, 369
Reaction function, 664
Reaction matrix, 666
Recall price, 400
Regression
  analysis, 301
  econometrics, 341
  model, normal. *See* Models
  multiple linear, 108, 301
Rejection operator, 243
Reliability
  measure, 507, 508, 778
  model, 778
Repeat purchase models. *See* Models
Representational models. *See* Models
Research process, 29
Reservation price, 401
Response function estimates, 131
Results data, 753
Retailer cooperatives, 434
Retail-store audit firms, 103
Return on investment (ROI), 46
RIDGE regression, 115, 116
Risk, 36
  analysis, 186
  averse, 52
  neutral, 52
  premium, 53
  prone, 52
Risk-return matrix, 653
ROI. *See* Return on investment

S

S-shaped model. *See* Models
Sales and Marketing Management, 326
Salesforce
  composite estimates, 329
  sizing, 562
Salesperson call-planning. *See* Selling, effort allocation
Sales-promotion models. *See* Models, promotion
Sales-response function, 6, 130
Sales-territory design, 577
Sales wave research, 722
Salience, 199
Sampling, 531
Satisficing, 55
Saturation model. *See* Models
Saturday Evening Post, 514
Scale and experience effects, 613
Scanner data, 755
Schwerin, 502
Science, 26, 28
Science, descriptive, 29
Scientific American, 285
Secondary source data. *See* Data
Second-order conditions, 151
Sectoral potential, 320
Securities and Exchange Commission, 331
Segmentation, 291
  normative theory of, 295
Selling, effort allocation, 567, 568
Semidefinite, 151
Semilog model. *See* Models
Sensitivity analysis, 183
Sequential unconstrained minimization technique (SUMT), 121
Shadow prices, 162
Shakeout period, 618
Shared-experience model. *See* Models
Sheth model. *See* Models
SIC. *See* Standard industrial classification
SIMAREX, 692
Similarities in usage behavior, 621

Similarity-based procedures (multidimensional scaling), 363
SIMULAMATICS, 519
Simulation, 518
  Monte Carlo, 185, 444
Simulmatics Corporation, 519
Sindlinger & Company, 331
Single decision maker, 44
Single linkage clustering. *See* Cluster analysis
Site selection, 454
Smoothing techniques, 333
Social-welfare function, 61
SOLEM, 523
Solution, evaluating, 31, 278
Source loyalty, 264
Specialization ratio, 322
Specification error analysis, 779
Square root model. *See* Models
Standard industrial classification (SIC), 321, 347
Standardized portfolio models. *See* Models, portfolio
Stepwise marginal analysis. *See* Marginal analysis
Stochastic choice models. *See* Models, stochastic
STRATPORT, 649
Structural-equation model. *See* Models
Subjective estimates, combining, 138
Suggestion model. *See* Models
SUMT. *See* Sequential unconstrained minimization technique
Survey Research Center, 331
Surveys, 757
Synectics, 359

T

Taylor series, 117
TBS. *See* Transaction-based systems
Technology substitution, 622
TELLUS (MSI Data Corporation), 756
Test markets, 722
Three-stage least squares, 124

Tracker, 726
Trade-off analysis, 369
Transaction-based systems (TBS), 749
Transportation problem, 163
Transshipment problem, 163
Triggering cue, 198
TSAM, 760
2SLS. *See* Two-stage least squares
Two-stage least squares (2SLS), 123, 125

U

Unbiased estimators, 106
Underidentified, 124
United Airlines, 570
U.S. Department of Commerce, 331
Universal Product Codes (UPCs), 755
UPC. *See* Universal Product Codes
Utility
  cardinal, 50
  independence, 56
  ordinal, 50
  random, 226
  theory, 224
Utility assessment
  direct, 444
  multiple objectives, 55
Utility function, 51
  multiattribute, 60

V

Validity
  convergent, 778
  face, 778
  measure, 507, 508, 778
  model, 777
  statistical, 779
Value (ordinal utility), 50
Variety seeking, 203
Vidale-Wolfe model. *See* Models
Voting model. *See* Models

W

Webster and Wind model. *See* Models

Weibull distribution, 137
Weighted-factor-score method, 444
Weighted least squares (WLS), 111
Weighted-probability model. *See* Models

Wharton econometric model. *See* Models
Wholesaler-sponsored voluntary chains, 434
Winner's curse, 428
WLS. *See* Weighted least squares

X
X-11 version (of Census II method), 341, 349
X/Markets (from Economic Information Systems, Inc.), 756
XSIM, 760

84 85 9 8 7 6 5 4 3 2